CLICK4™
What It Is and How to Use It

Unique to *Psychology in the New Millennium*, eighth edition, **CLICK4™** is designed to bring psychology to life by directly linking material in the main textbook to exciting, interactive information and activities on the accompanying book Web site and *Click4Psych!* CD-ROM.

Each **CLICK4™** item, placed by corresponding subject matter in the main text, is an active learning tool designed to enhance interest and improve understanding of primary psychological concepts. To begin, be sure to bookmark the *Psychology in the New Millennium*, eighth edition Web Resources Page at http://www.harcourtcollege.com/psych/PNM/siteresources.html. Or, depending on the browser used, make it a "favorite place." For CD-ROM activities, simply keep *Click4Psych!* handy.

CLICK4™ consists of 4 actions:

1. Open the *Psychology in the New Millennium*, eighth edition Web Resources Page OR insert and launch *Click4Psych!*
2. Click on a chapter number.
3. Click on an activity type.
4. Click on an activity number.

. . . and you're off! With **CLICK4™**, you're never more than four clicks away from where you want to be.

Psychology in the New Millennium offers 10 different Web and CD-ROM activity types:

Bulletin Board/Chat	denoted by	BBC
Primary Sources	denoted by	PS
Psychology and Modern Life	denoted by	PML
Essay Assignments	denoted by	E
WebSearch Activities	denoted by	WS
Weblinks	denoted by	L
Quizzes	denoted by	Q
Flash Cards	denoted by	FC
Videos and Animations	denoted by	V
Self-Assessments	denoted by	SA

In the margins of the main textbook, you'll see **CLICK4™** maps that look something like this:

www 12 BBC 4

CLICK4™ *a bulletin board discussion on free will: Is it merely an illusion?*

OR

CD 3 V 11

CLICK4™ *a video on the Moon Illusion.*

This translates as:
Web, Chapter 12, Bulletin Board/Chat Activity #4

This translates as:
CD-ROM, Chapter 3, Video #11

It's that simple!

PSYCHOLOGY

in the New Millennium

EIGHTH EDITION

PSYCHOLOGY
in the New Millennium

EIGHTH EDITION

SPENCER A. RATHUS

Montclair State University

THOMSON
™
WADSWORTH

Australia • Canada • Mexico • Singapore • Spain
United Kingdom • United States

THOMSON

WADSWORTH

Publisher	Earl McPeek	**Production Manager**	Cynthia Young
Acquisitions Editor	Brad Potthoff	**Cover Photo**	Spencer A. Rathus
Market Strategist	Katie Matthews	**Cover Printer**	Lehigh Press, Inc.
Developmental Editor	Michelle Vardeman	**Compositor**	Progressive Information Technologies
Project Editor	Michele Tomiak	**Printer**	R. R. Donnelley, Willard
Art Director	Burl Sloan		

Printed in the United States of America
3 4 5 6 7 05 04 03 02

For more information about our products, contact us at:
Thomson Learning Academic Resource Center
1-800-423-0563

For permission to use material from this text, contact us by:
Phone: 1-800-730-2214   **Fax:** 1-800-730-2215
Web: http://www.thomsonrights.com

Library of Congress Catalog Card Number: 2001089593
ISBN: 0-15-511282-1

Asia
Thomson Learning
60 Albert Street, #15-01
Albert Complex
Singapore 189969

Australia
Nelson Thomson Learning
102 Dodds Street
South Melbourne, Victoria 3205
Australia

Canada
Nelson Thomson Learning
1120 Birchmount Road
Toronto, Ontario M1K 5G4
Canada

Europe/Middle East/Africa
Thomson Learning
Berkshire House
168-173 High Holborn
London WC1 V7AA
United Kingdom

Latin America
Thomson Learning
Seneca, 53
Colonia Polanco
11560 Mexico D.F.
Mexico

Spain
Paraninfo Thomson Learning
Calle/Magallanes, 25
28015 Madrid, Spain

Dedicated with love to my wife,
Lois,
who has always been there to give me a lift

Preface

There is joy in psychology. I felt it as a student. I feel it when I teach and when I write. The joy in psychology is the joy of learning about ourselves, what makes us *tick*—and that joy is a constant in my life.

When I was an undergraduate student, my life was quite different. I was the first member of my family to go to college. College at first seemed strange and frightening, and I felt detached. Professors and textbooks seemed cold and aloof. I dropped out once, and I flunked out once. But I returned each time. All in all, it took me six years to earn my bachelor's degree.

I eventually realized that the problem did not lie in the subjects I studied, but in the way the subjects were presented, especially in the textbooks. When I eventually had the chance to write my own introductory psychology textbook, I vowed to avoid making psychology seem dry and remote—completely academic. Psychology is richer than that, fascinating and relevant to students' lives. I chose to communicate the fascination and the relevance. I chose to do the things in this book that I did to engage students in the classroom: to tell stories about psychologists and my own family, and to show how students could apply psychology to their own lives. I determined that this book would be warm, engaging, and relevant—not frightening, cool, and aloof. I believed that it was possible to write a textbook that presents psychology as the vigorous, enlightening science that it is, while at the same time motivating students and helping them understand and appreciate psychology. I attempted to somehow communicate through the written word the joy that psychology has added to my own life.

The eighth edition continues this tradition. It is also quite new. It reflects new developments in psychology, developments in science and society at large, and the views of many professors who had the opportunity to review the manuscript at every stage in its development.

PSYCHOLOGY IN THE NEW MILLENNIUM, EIGHTH EDITION

The eighth edition of *Psychology in the New Millennium* has been revised literally from cover to cover. It contains a new chapter, a new feature, a new pedagogical approach, new emphasis on the evolutionary perspective, and a new focus on interactive learning through the **CLICK4**™ method.[1]

The New Chapter: "Adolescent and Adult Development"

The eighth edition of *Psychology in the New Millennium* contains a *new* chapter, "Adolescent and Adult Development." While most professors want a textbook to be as succinct as possible, they do not want important topics in human growth and development to be given short shrift. The new chapter on adolescent and adult development allows us to cover many topics, some new, in greater depth. These include puberty, cognitive development in adolescence (including the imaginary audience and the personal fable), the year

---

[1] **CLICK4**™ is a trademark of text.com, Inc., which is also the holder of various intellectual property rights related thereto.

2000 CDC survey on youthful behavior, adolescent sexuality, physical development in late adulthood, sexual functioning in late adulthood, patterns of aging, crystallized versus fluid intelligence, postformal thought, the developmental "stage" of emerging adulthood, moratorium, lifestyles (being single, cohabitation, marriage and divorce), work, women in the workplace, emerging power among women in middle age, and retirement.

The New Feature: "CONTROVERSY IN PSYCHOLOGY"

The eighth edition of *Psychology in the new Millennium* includes a *new* feature: "Controversy in Psychology." Psychology is not a field that shies away from controversy, nor does *Psychology in the New Millennium*. We welcome controversies in psychology as vehicles for enhancing knowledge and stimulating critical thinking.

Some of the controversies exist between psychologists from various schools of psychology. For example, a controversy in the chapter on learning is titled "How Do We Define Learning?" We see at the outset of the chapter that behaviorists and cognitive psychologists define learning in different ways and that their definitions affect their entire view of the subject matter of learning. We continue the theme with another controversy in the same chapter: "What Really Happens During Classical Conditioning?" While some psychologists see conditioning as a "pure" behavioral phenomenon, others see conditioning as a cognitive event.

Other controversies address historic issues in psychology. For example, the chapter on psychological disorders contains the controversy "Is a Gay Male or Lesbian Sexual Orientation a Psychological Disorder?" We confront the issues involved in arriving at such a judgment. The key controversy we address in the chapter on methods of therapy is "Does Psychotherapy Work?" We refer to Eysenck's historic challenge to psychology and address the research evidence.

Still other controversies address the application of psychology in life. For example, in the chapter on motivation and emotion, we address the controversy "Is Aggression Natural?" We address political issues as well as psychological issues. In the chapter on learning, we ask the question, "Should Children Be Punished for Misbehavior?" We stimulate students to understand that many issues in psychology—and in society at large—are complex and require careful thought.

The New Pedagogical Approach: PQ4R

The eighth edition of *Psychology in the New Millennium* makes full use of the PQ4R pedagogical method. The PQ4R method promotes active learning; students are encouraged to become proactive rather than reactive. *PQ4R* stands for Preview, Question, Read, Reflect, Review, and Recite, a method that is based on the work of educational psychologist Francis P. Robinson.

Preview   Previewing the material fine-tunes students' expectations. It helps them create mental templates or "advance organizers" into which they fit the material. The eighth edition of *Psychology in the New Millen-nium* has two features at the beginning of each chapter that help students preview the material: a chapter Preview and Truth or Fiction? The *new* Preview feature does more than outline the sections in each chapter; it offers a series of challenging statements and questions that give students a sense of what each section covers, often in an entertaining manner. In this day of the "video byte," the Previews are visual as well as verbal—including interesting combinations of key visual elements within each chapter. The Truth or Fiction? items, found in previous editions, are intended to challenge common knowledge—which often has a way of be-ing common ignorance. They stimulate students to delve into the subject matter to see whether their preconceptions are supported by the evidence.

Question   Devising questions about the subject matter, before reading it in detail, is another feature of the PQ4R method. Writing questions gives students goals: They attend class or read the text *in order to answer the questions*. **New to this edition are questions in blue, situated in all primary sections of the text, which help students use the PQ4R method most effectively.** When they see a question, they have the opportunity to read the following material in order to answer it. If they wish, they can also write the questions and answers in their notebooks, as recommended by Robinson.

Read   Reading is the first *R* in the PQ4R method. Although students will have to read for themselves, they are not alone. The text helps them by providing lively Previews that help them organize the material, motivating them through Truth or Fiction? items, and presenting the subject matter in clear, stimulating prose. I may not always use the perfect word, but no word in the text is there by accident. Every sentence was written to be readable.

Reflect   Students learn more effectively when they *reflect* (the second *R* in PQ4R is for "Reflect") on what they are learning. As described in the chapter on memory, psychologists refer to reflection on subject matter as *elaborative rehearsal*. One way of reflecting on a subject is to relate it to things students already know about, whether it be academic material or events in their own lives (Willoughby et al., 1994[2]). Reflecting makes the material meaningful and easier to remember (Woloshyn et al., 1994[3]). It also makes it more likely that students will be able to *apply* the information to their own lives (Kintsch, 1994[4]). Through effective reflection, students can embed material firmly in their memory so that rote repetition is unnecessary.

> ▲ REFLECT
> When you are stressed out, do you seek out the company of others or do you tend to withdraw into yourself? Does research support the effectiveness of your social behavior under stress? Explain.

Because of the value of reflection, *new* Reflect features have been placed next to the running text. Some of them ask students to compare what they are reading with the ideas they had before they took the course.

REVIEW   The *new* Reviews follow major sections in the text. They include two types of items t(at foster active learning and retention. The first type of item is in a fill-in-the-blank format. Students are asked to *produce*, not simply *recognize*, the answer. For example, the first Review in the chapter on "Biology and Psychology" begins as follows: "(1) Neurons transmit messages to other neurons by means of chemical substances called _____. (2) Neurons have a cell body, or soma; _____, which receive "messages"; and an axon, which extends from the cell body." The second type of item, called *Pulling It Together*, includes questions that encourage students to think critically about the subject matter and relate it to the bigger picture. "Pulling It Together" items from the chapter on personality include "What would Freud have to say about the extent to which we can know our personal histories and our true feelings?" and "In what ways do behaviorism and social-cognitive theory differ in their views of people and personal freedom?"

Recite   The PQ4R method recommends that students regularly recite the answers to the questions aloud. Reciting answers aloud helps students remember them by means of repetition, by stimulating students to produce concepts and ideas they have learned, and by associating them with spoken words and gestures.

---

[2] Willoughby, T., Wood, E., & Khan, M. (1994). Isolating variables that impact on or detract from the effectiveness of elaboration strategies. *Journal of Educational Research, 86,* 279–289.

[3] Woloshyn, V. E., Paivio, A., & Pressley, M. (1994). Use of elaborative interrogation to help students acquire information consistent with prior knowledge and information inconsistent with prior knowledge. *Journal of Educational Psychology, 86,* 79–89.

[4] Kintsch, W. (1994). Text comprehension, memory, and learning. *American Psychologist, 49,* 294–303.

The *new* Recite sections are found at the end of each chapter. They help students summarize the material, but they are active summaries. They are written in question-and-answer format. To provide a sense of closure, the summaries repeat the questions found within the chapters and are again ***printed in blue***. The answers are concise but include most of the key terms found in the text.

The Recite sections are designed in two columns so that students can cover the second column (the answers) as they read the questions. A tear-off card to cover the second column is provided at the back of the text. They can recite the answers as they remember or reconstruct them, and then check what they have recited against the answers they had covered. Students should not feel that they are incorrect if they have not exactly produced the answer written in the second column; their individual approach might be slightly different, even more inclusive. The answers provided in the second column are meant as a guide, to provide a check on students' learning. They are not carved in stone.

New Emphasis on the Evolutionary Perspective

Psychology today recognizes the influence of evolution not only on physical traits, but also on behavior and mental processes. As humans and their ancestors evolved over millions of years, their fitness for survival gained prominence in terms of intelligence and the ability to acquire various skills, as well as in terms of traits such as sharpness of eye, fleetness of foot, and brawn. The eighth edition of *Psychology in the New Millennium* demonstrates its increased emphasis on the evolutionary perspective in a major new section in Chapter 2: "Evolution and Evolutionary Psychology." However, the overlaps between evolution and psychology are illustrated in nearly every chapter, as outlined below.

Chapter 2:   A major new section, "Evolution and Evolutionary Psychology."

Chapter 3:   The evolutionary perspective on how pain and the location of taste buds are adaptive and promote survival.

Chapter 5:   Discussion of the evolutionary value of taste aversions, spontaneous recovery, generalization and discrimination, and cognitive learning.

Chapter 9:   Discussion of evolution and instinct, stimulus motives, aggression, and universal recognition of facial expressions.

Chapter 12:   Discussion of the role of sports in our lives.

Chapter 13:   Discussion of the possible roles of evolution in gender typing, gender differences in mate selection, gender differences in pursuit of casual sexual relationships, and sexual aggression.

Chapter 14:   Discussion of gender differences in response to threats—such as the (predominantly male?) tendency for "fight or flight" as compared with the (predominantly female?) tendency to "tend and befriend."

Chapter 15:   Discussion of how evolutionary forces might have favored the survival of individuals who were predisposed toward acquiring fears of large animals, spiders, snakes, heights, entrapment, sharp objects, and strangers.

Chapter 17:   Discussion of the evolutionary benefits of altruism.

The Click4™ Method

At a time when the electronic revolution is shaping our lives and bringing with it the ability to provide interactive teaching and learning, the eighth edition of *Psychology in the New Millennium* is seamlessly connected to key Web sites and to the CD-ROM that accompanies the text through the **Click4**™ method. This means that activities—videos, demonstrations, interactive Self-Assessments, *Psychology and Modern Life* readings, primary sources in psychology, and important Web sites geared to further student knowledge and understanding—are no more than four clicks of the mouse away! Unique **Click4**™ maps in the margins of the text guide students through these clicks. The method is easy, informative, fast! There is no need to type in lengthy URLs to access the textbook's Web site or other Web sites. The **Click4**™ method provides students with less frustration and more learning. An explanation of the **Click4**™ method and how to use it appears at the front of the text.

Although the eighth edition is quite new, we did not "throw out the baby with the bath water." Much in your textbook is traditional and familiar. The text continues to recount psychology's rich tradition, the roots that can be traced beyond the sages of the ancient Greeks. A century ago, William James wrote "I wished, by treating Psychology like a natural science, to help her become one." Psychology, in the third millennium, is very much that science of which he spoke. Your textbook explores psychology's tradition as an empirical science. It also provides comprehensive coverage of the traditional areas of subject matter in psychology.

Reviewers of the text found many useful and enjoyable learning aids and features from earlier editions and asked us to keep them. These include:

▲ **Truth or Fiction?** items that stimulate students to delve into the subject matter by challenging folklore and common sense (which is often common *non*sense).

▲ **Running glossary** items that provide quick access to the meanings of key terms so that students can maintain their concentration on the flow of material in the chapter.

▲ **Coverage of human diversity.** This textbook is inclusive. It includes relevant information on the links between diversity—ethnicity, gender, sexual orientation, and so on—and psychology. This coverage helps students perceive why people of different backgrounds and genders behave and think in different ways, and how the science of psychology is enriched by addressing those differences.

▲ **Self-Assessments** that stimulate student interest by helping them satisfy their curiosities about themselves and enhance the relevance of the text to students' lives.

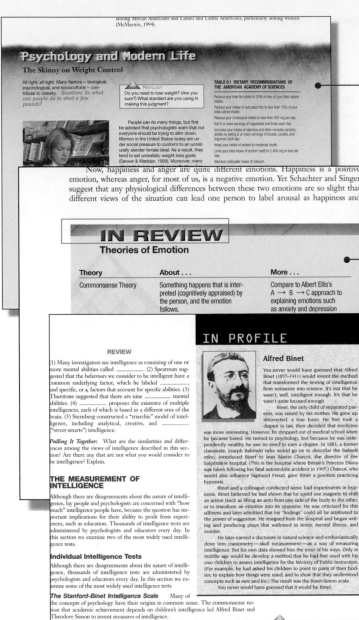

▲ **Psychology and Modern Life** features that demonstrate cutting-edge psychological theory and the ways psychology can help students cope with the everyday challenges of life.

▲ **In Review charts** provide concise, easy-to-follow summaries of many of the key concepts found within chapters.

▲ **In Profile** features firmly ground important psychologists and case studies in real, everyday life: Fascinating tidbits of information reveal the personal struggles, triumphs, and foibles of key figures and movements in psychology, deepening our understanding of the ever-evolving field of psychological theory and its application in society.

COVERAGE

The eighth edition of *Psychology in the New Millennium* covers the following:

"Becoming a Successful Student" now resides on the book Web site. Four chapter-length modules will help students be successful in psychology and their other college courses. The author's Click4™ method provides effortless access to Psychology and Modern Life readings: "Advice on Effective Studying," "Advice on Getting the Most from Classes," "Advice on Taking Tests" (including handling test anxiety), and "Advice on Managing Time."

Chapter 1: What Is Psychology? introduces psychology as a science. It discusses the specialties, history, and schools of psychology, critical thinking, and the ways in which psychologists expand and refine knowledge. There are several *new* Controversy in Psychology features, exploring the questions "What do psychologists mean by 'controlling' behavior and mental processes?", "Should we teach Freud's ideas?" (some professors believe that we should not), "Should psychologists ever break confidences?", "Is it ethical for psychologists to deceive research participants about the methods and objectives of their research?", and "Is it ethical to harm lower animals in conducting research when the results may be beneficial to humans?" There is a *new* Psychology and Modern Life feature on conducting "research online." *New* Click4™ features include "Thinking Critically About Astrology," "Thinking Critically About Self-Help Books," and "The Social-Desirability Scale" (an interactive Self-Assessment), as well as a host of Web sites, including those of APA journals, APA information about careers in psychology, and worldwide psychology links.

Chapter 2: Biology and Psychology addresses four areas of psychology that have important links with behavior and mental processes: the nervous system, the endocrine system, evolution, and heredity. The chapter contains a major *new* section on "Evolution and Evolutionary Psychology." There are *new* Controversy in Psychology features, exploring the questions "Are some people left-brained and others right-brained?", "Is being left-handed an asset or a liability?", and "Should athletes be permitted to use anabolic steroids?" *New* Click4™ items include access to journals such as *Neuron* and *NeuroReport*, primary sources including the classic writings of Charles Darwin and the Olds and Milner article on the pleasure center in the brain, the Visible Human Project and the Whole Brain Atlas, NASA's NeuronLab, and advice on coping with PMS.

Chapter 3: Sensation and Perception covers vision, visual perception, hearing, and the other senses. There is a *new* section, "Sensation and Perception on the Edge," which covers the topics of virtual reality and extrasensory perception. There is a *new* Psychology and Modern Life feature, describing how researchers are using microchips to help blind people see. There are *new* Controversy in Psychology features, exploring the questions "How many kinds of color receptors are there?" and "How do we explain pitch perception?" *New* Click4™ links include Web sites with online demonstrations such as those found at IllusionWorks and VisionScience, primary sources including the classic writings of Gibson and Walk on the visual cliff and Turnbull on the Pygmy Kenge, and articles on "smell-o-vision" and on HEAR (Hearing Education Awareness for Rockers).

Chapter 4: States of Consciousness covers sleep and dreams, hypnosis, meditation, biofeedback, and psychoactive drugs. There is a *new* questionnaire, "Sleep Quiz: Are You Getting Your Z's?", new reporting of gender differences in insomnia, and new coverage of human diversity and smoking. There are *new* Controversy in Psychology features, exploring the questions "Is consciousness a proper area for psychological study?", "How can psychologists explain hypnosis?", "Is a drink a day good for you?", and "Is marijuana harmful?" *New* Click4™ links include the Web site of the Center for Biological Timing (about circadian rhythms), Web sites on sleep disorders, the Web site of the National Institute on Alcohol Abuse and Alcoholism (NIAAA), an interactive Self-Assessment on smoking ("Why Do You Smoke?"), and the Monitoring the Future Web site at the University of Michigan, which continually surveys substance abuse in the United States.

Chapter 5: Learning addresses classical conditioning, operant conditioning, and cognitive factors in learning. There is a *new* profile on Roger Moore (not the actor, but the octopus). There are *new* Controversy in Psychology features examining the issues "How should we define learning?", "Why did Pavlov's dogs learn to salivate in response to the bell?", "Should children be punished for misbehavior?", "Contingency theory," and "Does violence in the media cause aggression?" *New* Click4™ links include primary sources such as the classic writings of Watson and Rayner on "Little Albert," Bandura and his colleagues on the effects of film-mediated aggressive behavior, Skinner on "Superstition in the Pigeon," and Tolman on "Cognitive Maps in Rats and Men"; the Web site of the B. F. Skinner Foundation; a profile of Edward L. Thorndike; and the behavioral journals *Journal of Applied Behavior Analysis* and *Journal of the Experimental Analysis of Behavior*.

Chapter 6: Memory covers the various kinds of memory, processes of memory, the stage model of memory, levels of processing, high-interest topics such as flashbulb memories and infantile amnesia, and the biology of memory. The discussion of kinds of memory is completely revised to include explicit memory (consisting of episodic and semantic memories) versus implicit memory and retrospective memory versus prospective memory. There is *new* coverage of *déjà vu*. There are *new* Controversy in Psychology features, including "Can we trust eyewitness testimony?" and "Do people really recover repressed memories of sexual abuse at an early age, or are these 'memories' implanted by interviewers?" *New* Click4™ links include a profile of George Miller, George Miller's classic article on "The Magical Number Seven, Plus or Minus Two," and the student-success module on "Effective Learning."

Chapter 7: Cognition and Language covers problem solving, creativity, reasoning, judgment and decision making, and language. There is a *new* diversity feature on "Cognitive Processes, East and West." The *new* Controversy in Psychology explores the issue, "Is bilingualism advantageous for cognitive and language development?" *New* Click4™ features include access to Web sites on linguistics, including the U.S. government's Office of Bilingual Education and Minority Language Affairs (OBLEMA) and the English Learners Web site of the California Department of Education, online experiments in cognitive psychology, and the Noam Chomsky archive.

Chapter 8: Intelligence covers theories, measurement, and determinants of intelligence. *New* Controversy in Psychology features explore the issues "Is 'emotional intelligence' a form of intelligence? Should it be taught in school?", "Just what do intelligence tests measure?", "The controversy over *The Bell Curve*," and "The Mozart effect." *New* Click4™ links feature several Web sites on artificial intelligence, including that of the *Journal of Artificial Intelligence Research*; online profiles of Charles Spearman, Lewis Terman, David Wechsler, and Robert Sternberg; the Web site of MENSA; sites related to mental retardation, such as the Special Olympics and the UN Declaration on the Rights of Mentally Retarded Persons; and information on facilitating the development of the gifted child.

Chapter 9: Motivation and Emotion addresses theories of motivation, hunger, stimulus motives, achievement motivation, affiliation, aggression, and emotion. There is a *new* diversity feature on "Heredity, Hormones, Aggression, and Sex." The *new* Controversy in Psychology features explore the issues "Do people respond instinctively to pheromones?", "Is aggression natural?", "The catharsis controversy," and "Just what do lie detectors detect?" *New* Click4™ features include Web sites concerning nutrition and obesity, online advice for those who eat on the run, calculation of calories they burn each hour, online advice on coping with anger, the journal *Aggressive Behavior*, and other primary sources—classic articles by Bexton, Heron, and Scott on sensory deprivation and by Festinger and Carlsmith on cognitive dissonance.

Chapter 10: Child Development covers human growth and development from conception through childhood. The chapter is completely reorganized to cover childhood in terms of physical development, cognitive development, and social and personality development. There is a *new* Psychology and Modern Life feature, "Child Sexual Abuse—What to Do, Where to Turn." Controversy in Psychology features address the questions "Is development influenced more by nature or by nurture?" and "Is development continuous or discontinuous?" *New* Click4™ features link students to numerous Web sites about pregnancy and childbirth, the Web site of the journal *Human Reproduction*, the site of the Society for Research in Child Development, the site of the Child Abuse and Prevention Network, advice on becoming an authoritative parent, and key classic primary sources: a chapter from Jean Piaget's *The Moral Judgment of the Child* and Harry Harlow's classic presidential address to the APA—"The Nature of Love."

New **Chapter 11: Adolescent and Adult Development** answers reviewers' requests for more comprehensive coverage of adolescence and adulthood. It is organized to cover physical, cognitive, and social personality development in adolescence and then repeats this presentation for adulthood. Controversy in Psychology features address the issues "Are there gender differences in moral development?", "Is there a *mano*pause?", and

"Do women experience an empty-nest syndrome when the youngest child leaves home?" A *new* Psychology and Modern Life feature points to a CDC study of risky behavior among youth in the United States today ("Youthful Behavior—Risky Stuff"). *New* Click4™ links permit students to readily access interactive Self-Assessments ("Do You Endorse a Traditional or Liberal Marital Role?," the "Attitudes Toward Aging Scale," and the "Death Concern Scale"), various Web sites with advice for and about adolescents (e.g., the National Campaign to Prevent Teen Pregnancy and "Talking with Kids"), on-line chapter-length advice on "Making the Transition from College to the Workplace," Web sites concerning forming and maintaining relationships (e.g., *Self-Help* magazine and "Smart Marriage"), and Web sites related to late adulthood (e.g., the National Institute on Aging and "Alzheimer's Gateway").

Chapter 12: Personality discusses five major perspectives in the study of personality—psychodynamic, trait, learning, humanistic-existential, and sociocultural—and personality measurement. There is a *new* Psychology and Modern Life feature on the value to the individual of "Identifying With the Team—More Than Just a Game." A *new* Controversy in Psychology addresses the question, "Just How Much Acculturation Is Enough" for one's self-esteem and adjustment to life in the United States? Chapter 12 includes *new* Click4™ access to classic primary sources by Sigmund Freud (a chapter from *Civilization and Its Discontents*) and Carl Rogers (a chapter from *On Becoming a Person*), an interactive Self-Assessment (the "Self-Acceptance Scale"), advice on "Finding a Career That Fits," a profile of Hermann Rorschach, and Web sites that contain information about various personality theorists (including the Adler Institute of San Francisco, the Horney Society, and the C. G. Jung Page).

Chapter 13: Gender and Sexuality covers gender-role stereotypes; gender differences and their development; attraction, love, and sexual orientation; sexual coercion; sexual response and sexual dysfunctions; and HIV/AIDS and other sexually transmitted infections. *New* Controversy in Psychology features address the issues "Are men really more aggressive than women?", "Why do men rape women?", "Are women to blame for whatever happens to them if they dress provocatively or use 'bad' language?", and "Where does normal male–female interaction end and sexual harassment begin?" *New* Click4™ features include Web sites of organizations with expertise in sexuality (e.g., AASECT, SSSS, Femina, and the Alan Guttmacher Institute), Web sites with information about sexual coercion (e.g., AMA Facts About Sexual Assault, RAINN, REACH [a Spanish-language Web site], and a CDC Fact Sheet About Rape), Web sites with information about HIV/AIDS and other STIs (UNAIDS, the CDC's *HIV/AIDS Surveillance Report*), information compiled by the American Psychological Association about sexual orientation and about sexual harassment, an interactive Self-Assessment (*The AIDS Awareness Inventory*), and the Web site of the APA Division of Lesbian, Gay, and Bisexual Issues.

Chapter 14: Stress and Health covers psychological and other factors in health and illness. The chapter contains Self-Assessments that permit students to assess the stress acting on them and whether they believe that they are in control of it, and important applications such as "Coping With Stress." There are *new* topics in human diversity: "Acculturative Stress" and "'Fight or Flight' or 'Tend and Befriend'? Gender Differences in Response to Stress." *New* Controversy in Psychology features address the questions "Just how are daily hassles and life changes connected with health problems?", "Can you maintain your health if your genes are 'against' you?", and "Does it matter whether your physician is a woman or a man?" *New* Click4™ features include access to Web sites such as those of the National Headache Foundation, the American Cancer Society, the American Heart Association (with links to journals such as *Circulation* and *Hypertension*), the American Institute of Stress, and the journals *Health Psychology, Psychosomatic Medicine*, and the *Journal of the American Medical Association*; online advice about Alleviating the Type A Behavior Pattern, Progressive Relaxation, High-Fat Versus Healthful Foods, Fitting in Fitness, Types of Exercise, and the Benefits of Walking; interactive Self-Assessments such as the "Irrational Beliefs Quiz," the "Optimism and Health" test, the "Activity and Heart Disease IQ," and the "Eating Smart Quiz"; and other Web sites that offer advice on stress management.

Chapter 15: Psychological Disorders covers diagnostic issues and a variety of psychological disorders. *New* Controversy in Psychology features address the issues "Is a gay male or lesbian sexual orientation a psychological disorder?", "Do dissociative disorders really exist?", "Are somatoform disorders the special province of women?", "Is there a thin line between genius and madness?", and "Should we ban the insanity plea?" The chapter contains *New* Click4™ links to journals concerning psychological disorders (including the *Journal of Abnormal Psychology*, *Archives of General Psychiatry*, and the *British Journal of Psychiatry*), Web sites of organizations connected with psychological disorders (including the American Psychiatric Association, the National Institute of Mental Health, the National Center for PTSD, and the International Association of Eating Disorders Professionals), an interactive Self-Assessment on depression, and additional information on psychological disorders (case studies on obsessive-compulsive disorder and PTSD, the Web site of Depression Central, information on schizophrenia from the American Psychiatric Association, and the issue of diagnosis by computer).

Chapter 16: Methods of Therapy explores psychological and biological methods of therapy. There are *new* case studies for psychoanalysis, Gestalt therapy, and Rogerian therapy (and, online, for behavior therapy). There is a *new* Psychology and Modern Life feature: "Virtual Reality Finds a Real Place as an Aid in Therapy." *New* Controversy in Psychology features address the questions "Does psychotherapy work?", "Is it ethical to try to change gay males' and lesbians' sexual orientations?", and "Should health professionals use electroconvulsive therapy?" *New* Click4™ links include ready access to Web sites of professional organizations (the Association for Advancement of Behavior Therapy, the Association for Advancement of Gestalt Therapy, the American Psychoanalytic Association, the American Association of Marriage and Family Therapists, the Albert Ellis Institute, and the Beck Institute), professional journals (including the *Journal of Consulting and Clinical Psychology* and *Cognitive Therapy and Research*), profiles on Albert Ellis and Fritz Perls, and advice on issues such as becoming more assertive and handling social provocations.

Chapter 17: Social Psychology discusses attitudes, social perception, social influence, group behavior, and environmental issues. The are *new* Click4™ links to classic primary sources (including Milgram's "Behavioral Study of Obedience," Asch's "Opinions and Social Pressure," and Darley and Latané's "Bystander Intervention in Emergencies: Diffusion of Responsibility"), and the Web sites of professional groups (the Social Psychology Network) and professional journals (including the *Journal of Environmental Psychology*).

Appendix A: Statistics in this eighth edition receives *new* complete "chapter" treatment. The appendix contains a chapter preview, Truth or Fiction items, questions to guide reading, "Reflect" items to help students relate what they are learning to things they already know, "Reviews" following each major section, and a "Recite" feature at the end of the appendix. Click4 items are also included.

THE PACKAGE

Integration is the core of the 8th edition ancillary package. All primary concepts in the main text are further explored through interactive media—videos, animations, and interactive Self-Assessments on the accompanying *Click4Psych!* CD-ROM, and a wealth of teaching and learning tools on the new book Web site accompanying *Psychology in the New Millennium*, 8th edition: www.harcourtcollege.com/psych/PNM/siteresources.html. Our print ancillaries, as well, have been reinvigorated: The *Instructor's Resources Manual* has been fully recreated to provide optimal flexibility in course structure and teaching style. The *Test Bank* has been revised and expanded and is now available as a downloadable supplement to keep it up to date and error-free. The student *Study Guide* is also completely new and is tied directly to the *Instructor's Resources Manual* through complementary learning objectives and activities, and to the main text through the PQ4R study method. Now, both students and teachers have everything they need to create an exciting and vibrant learning experience.

For Instructors

New! **Instructor's Resources Manual** by Dixon Bramblett is designed to fulfill the needs of both new and seasoned instructors of introductory psychology by providing a wide array of teaching tools, supplementary texts, media, and student activities that promote a maximum level of flexibility fitted to the way you teach your course. *Instructor's Resources* offers lecture topics and ideas, video supplements, and student and classroom activities with handouts to support all primary sections in each chapter of the main text. Each teaching objective is tied directly to a specific question in the *Test Bank* and to the learning objectives in the *Study Guide*. Detailed chapter outlines summarize the content of each chapter in a convenient, bulleted format for quick review and to serve as a template for structuring lectures and course content.

Revised and Expanded Test Bank by Anne Cooper offers 200 questions per chapter rated by cognitive type, difficulty level, and aligned to specific teaching and learning objectives. Page references to corresponding topics in the main text are also provided. The *Test Bank* is also available under Instructor Resources on the book Web site, downloadable on a chapter-by-chapter basis at www.harcourtcollege.com/psych/PNM/siteresources.html. Announcements about corrections or revisions to the *Test Bank* will also appear here so that instructors will always have the most current and accurate edition throughout the life of the main text.

Computerized Test Banks for Mac and Windows platforms are also available. The test bank software, *EXAMaster+*™, offers three unique features to the instructor. Easy Test creates a test from a single screen in just a few easy steps. FullTest offers a range of options that includes selecting, editing, adding, or linking questions or graphics; random selection of questions from a wide range of criteria; creating criteria; blocking questions; and printing up to 99 different versions of the same test and answer sheet. EXAMRecord™ records, curves, graphs, and prints out grades according to criteria the instructor selects. Grade distribution displays as a bar graph or plotted graph.

New! **PowerPoint Presentation** by Richard Davis brings psychology to life through this easy-to-use, fully customizable, overhead lecture software consisting of hundreds of slides conveniently organized according to the outline of the main text. Illustrations and video clips appear frequently, vividly depicting essential concepts found in the book.

Full-color Overhead Transparencies and accompanying guide provide more than 100 images for use in your introductory psychology course. Download them directly from Instructor's Resources on the book Web site at www.harcourtcollege.com/psych/PNM/siteresources.html.

Films for the Humanities and Sciences offers films in the areas of biopsychology, developmental psychology, abnormal psychology, social psychology, and more.

Qualifying criteria apply. Various selections from this library, along with ideas for integrating the material into lectures and classroom activities, appear throughout the *Instructor's Resources Manual*. A full library listing appears under Instructor Resources on the book Web site.

The Whole Psychology Catalog, fifth edition, prepared by Michael B. Reiner of Kennesaw State College, easily supplements your course with work and assignments. This ancillary has perforated pages containing experiential exercises, questionnaires, and visual aids. Each activity is classified by one of eight learning goals central to the teaching of psychology. Also included in the fifth edition is an informative section on using the World Wide Web. Various items from this catalog also appear in the *Instructor's Resources Manual*, paired with specific lecture topics and activities.

New! **WebCT General Psychology Course** includes all major topics covered in introductory psychology and is designed to help you to build a sophisticated Web-based learning environment for your students. Student features include:

▲ Course content aligned specifically to *Psychology in the New Millennium*, 8th edition, organized by chapter.
▲ Online self-quizzing and testing.
▲ Psychology glossary.
▲ Communications tools—mail, bulletin board, chat, and white board.
▲ Course management tools. You can build course calendars, provide online testing and grading, and track your students' progress—all available at the click of a button.

For Students

New! **Study Guide** by Lisa Valentino offers everything a student needs to get that desired "A" for the course. Aligned with the PQ4R learning model found in the main text, the *Study Guide* opens with a Preview section that encourages students to note initial impressions of chapter material—what surprised them, what they're curious about, and specific queries they have. The Question section poses the learning objectives in an outline format and serves as the foundation for the next sections, Reading for Understanding and Reflection Break. Reading for Understanding provides detailed fill-in-the-blank sections requiring students to actively produce key concepts from the main text. Reflection Breaks include cross-relational activities such as matching and critical thinking exercises, which build on material just covered. Review and Recite sections tie in directly with the main text and the book Web site, and Relate/Expand/Integrate pulls it all together in applied exercises such as research, writing, and Web activities.

New! ***Psychology in the New Millennium*** **Web Site,** with original content by Lisa Valentino, features a wide array of exciting, interactive learning tools, arranged by chapter. Visit www.harcourtcollege.com/psych/PNM/siteresources.html to see how technology can help your students learn more.

▲ **Bulletin Board/Chat** allows online class discussion about special topics found in the main text, especially *Psychology and Modern Life* and *Controversy in Psychology*.
▲ **Primary Sources** offers a library of key primary source readings in psychology.
▲ **Psychology and Modern Life** offers a wide array of readings geared to applying psychological theory to everyday life.
▲ **Essay Assignments** to help apply and cement student understanding of key concepts.
▲ **Web Search Activities** designed to further students' understanding of topics found in the main text.
▲ **Web Links** featuring some of the most interesting psychology sites on the Web.

▲ **Quizzing and Testing** offers two quizzes per chapter for student self-assessment.

▲ **Flash Cards** are a great way for students to quickly drill themselves on key terms and people in psychology.

▲ **Audio Glossary** for quick reference while online and audio pronunciations of difficult terms.

New Click4Psych! **CD-ROM** provides the following interactive features, which are tied directly to designated Click4 items in the margins of the main text:

▲ **Videos and animations** vividly illustrate some of the more difficult concepts in *Psychology in the New Millennium* and help bring psychological theory to life.

▲ **Interactive Self-Assessments,** including all those found in the main text, plus many more, process the information input by students, automatically tabulate scores, and provide interpretation of the results. A favorite of students!

To include *Click4Psych!* as a companion to the main text, be sure to order this Kit ISBN: 0-15-504257-2.

ACKNOWLEDGMENTS

Think about the development of psychology from the philosophical speculations of the ancients, to the firm grounding of the field as a scientific study in the 19th century, to the full-blown diverse theories and research of the beginning of a new millennium. Without the contributions of many individuals, psychology as a discipline would not and will not continue to progress. Those individuals, of course, include those who do the research in the laboratory or in the field, those who pass on the knowledge gained through the time devoted to students, and those who do both.

A textbook of psychology, any such textbook, relies upon all those contributions. While I, as author, am responsible for what appears in *Psychology in the new Millennium*, I could not have created this eighth edition and its earlier editions without the help of many of my colleagues in the discipline. My sincere thanks goes out to the following individuals who contributed to the development of the eighth edition: Holiday E. Adair, California University of Pennsylvania; Marilyn Andrews, Hartnell College; Alan Bates, Snead State Community College; Lucy Champion, Southern Union State Community College; Stephen Chew, Samford University; Steve Donohue, Grand Canyon University; Jose Feito, St. Mary's College, California; Colleen Gift, Highland Community College; Myra Harville, Holmes Community College; Alylene Hegar, Eastfield College; Shirin Khosropour, Austin Community College; Norman Kinney, Southeast Missouri State University; Jane Klingberg, Moraine Valley Community College; Marc Levy, Southern Oregon University; Erica Lilleleht, Seattle University; Barbara McFarland, Lehigh University; John Nichols, Tulsa Community College; Carol Pandey, L.A. Pierce College; Shane Pitts, Birmingham Southern College; Vicki Ritts, St. Louis Community College; Catherine Sanderson, Amherst College; Harvey R. Schiffman, Rutgers University; Joanne Stephenson, Union University; Lisa Valentino, Seminole Community College; and Mary P. Whitney, St. Joseph College.

My sincere thanks also to the reviewers of earlier editions: Ambrose Akinkunle, Olive Harvey College; Mark H. Ashcraft, Cleveland State University; Lynn Haller Augsbach, Morehead State University; Gladys J. Baez-Dickreiter, St. Phillip's College; Anne Barich, Lewis University; Patricia Barker, Schenectady County Community College; Barbara Basden, California State University; Melita Bauman, Glendale Community College; James Beaird, Western Oregon State University; Connie Beddingfield, Jefferson State Community College; William Bell, Olivet Nazarene University; Thomas L. Bennett, Colorado State University; John Benson, Texarkana College; Otto Berliner, SUNY-Alfred; Tom Billimek, San Antonio College; Joyce Bishop, Golden West College; Richard A. Block, Montana State University; C. Robert Boresen, Wichita State University; Theodore N. Bosack, Providence College; Charles M. Bourassa, University of Alberta; Betty Bowers, North Central Technical Institute; Peter J. Brady, Clark Technical

College; Jack Brennecke, Mount San Antonio College; Thomas Brothen, University of Minnesota; Evelyn Brown, Austin Community College; Conald Buckley, Cumberland Community College; Carol Burk-Braxton, Austin Community College; Robert Cameron, Fairmont State College; Lucy B. Champion, Southern Union State Community College; Garvin Chastain, Boise State University; John Childers, East Carolina University; John Clark, William Rainey Harper College; Samuel L. Clay II, Morehead State University; Michael Connor, Long Beach Community College; Lauren Coodley, Napa Valley College; Miki A. Cook, Gadsden State Community College; Terry Daniel, University of Arizona; Richard Day, Manchester Community College; Donald L. Daoust, Southern Oregon State College; Carl L. Denti, Dutchess County Community College; Robert DeStefano, Rockland Community College; Mary Dezindolet, Cameron University; Carol Doolin, Henderson County Junior College; Gene Douglas, Cameron University; Wendy L. Dunn, Coe College; Eve Efird, Johnston Community College; Jeanette Engles, Southeastern Oklahoma State University; Warren Fass, University of Pittsburgh at Bradford; Lawrence A. Fehr, Widener University; Gloria Foley, Austin Community College; John Foust, Parkland College; Bob Freudenthal, Moraine Valley Community College; Mary Rita Freudenthal, Moraine Valley Community College; Morton P. Friedman, University of California at Los Angeles; William Rick Fry, Youngstown State University; Michael Garza, Brookhaven College; David A. Gersh, Houston Community College; Marian Gibney, Phoenix College; Ron Gilkerson, Waubonsee Community College; Michael Goodstein, Moraine Valley Community College; Bernard Gorman, Nassau County Community College; Richard Gottwald, Indiana University at South Bend; Peter Gram, Pensacola Junior College; Nancy Grayson, McLennan Community College; Vincent J. Greco, Weschester Community College; Beverly Greene, St. John's University; John C. Greenwood, Lewis University; Gloria Griffith, Tennessee Technological University; Richard Griggs, University of Florida; Sandra L. Groeltz, DeVry Institute of Technology at Chicago; Lydia Guerra, Olive Harvey College; Arthur Gutman, Florida Institute of Technology; Jim Hail, McLennan Community College; Algea O. Harrison, Oakland University; Robert W. Hayes, Boston University; Alylene Hegar, Eastfield College; Lisa R. Hempel, Columbia Basin College; George Herrick, SUNY-Alfred; Sidney Hochman, Nassau Community College; Morton Hoffman, Metropolitan State College; Betsy Howton, Western Kentucky University; John H. Hummel, University of Houston; Sam L. Hutchinson, Radford University; Gayle Y. Iwamasa, Oklahoma State University; Jarvel Jackson, McClellan Community College; Ed James, Purdue University–Calumet; Rafael Art. Javier, St. John's University; Chwan-Shyang Jih, Lewis University; Robert L. Johnson, Umpqua Community College; Timothy Johnston, University of North Carolina at Greensboro; Eve Jones, Los Angeles City College; Karen Jones, University of the Ozarks; Kenneth Kallio, SUNY–Genesco; Charles Karis, Northwestern University; Ed Kearney, Lewis University; Kevin Keating, Broward Community College; Mary Louise Keen, University of California at Irvine; Judith Keith, Tarrant County Junior College; Richard Kellogg, SUNY–Alfred; Dan Kimble, University of Oregon; Gary King, Rose State College; Richard A. King, University of North Carolina at Chapel Hill; Dwight Kirkpatrick, Purdue University–Calumet; Mike Knight, Central State University; Wolanyo Kpo, Chicago State University; Velton Lacefield, Prairie State College; Alan Lanning, College of DuPage; Daniel Lapsley, University of Notre Dame; Mary Ann Larson, Fullerton College and Rancho Santiago College; Marliss Lauer, Moraine Part Technical College; John D. Lawry, Marymount College; Patsy Lawson, Volunteer State Community College; Charles A. Levin, Baldwin-Wallace College; Charles Levinthal, Hofstra University; William Levy, Manchester Community College; Robert G. Lowder, Bradley University; Robert MacAleese, Spring Hill College; Ricardo A. Machon, Loyola Marymount University; Daniel Madsen, University of Minnesota–Duluth; Adam Maher, Austin Community College; John Malone, University of North Carolina at Greensboro; George Martin, Mount San Antonio College; A. W. Massey, Eastfield College; S. R. Mathews, Converse College; Elaine Mawhinney, Horry-Georgetown Technical College; Michael M. Mayall, Tarrant County Junior College; James McCaleb, South Surburban College; Richard McCarbery, Lorain College; Joseph McNair, Miami–Dade Community College; Juan Mercado, McLennan Community College; Leroy Metze, Western Kentucky University; Joseph Miele, East Stroudsberg University; Richard E. Miller,

Navarro College; Thomas Minor, SUNY-Stony Brook; Thomas Moeschl, Broward Community College; Christopher F. Monte, Manhattanville College; Luis Montesinos, Montclair State University; Joel Morgovsky, Brookdale Community College; Walena C. Morse, Westchester University; Dave Murphy, Waubonsee Community College; Basil Najjar, College of DuPage; Robbye Nesmith, Navarro College; Jeffrey S. Nevid, St. John's University; John W. Nichols, Tulsa Junior College; Nora Noel, University of North Carolina at Wilmington; Joseph Paladino, Indiana State University at Evansville; Ursula Palmer, Eastfield College; Carol Pandey, L. A. Pierce College; Fred Patrizi, East Central University; John Pennachio, Adirondack Community College; Terry Pettijohn, Ohio State University–Marion; Gregory Pezzetti, Rancho Santiago College; Walter Pieper, Georgia State University; Carole Pierce, Austin Community College; Terrie Potts, Navarro College; Donis Price, Mesa Community College; Rosemary Price, Rancho Santiago College; Gerald Pudelko, Olympic College; Richard A. Rare, University of Maine; Rose Ray, Purdue University–Calumet; Bernard Rechlicz, Olive Harvey College; Victoria Reid, Olive Harvey College; Beth Rienzi, California State University, Bakersfield; Ross Robak, Pace University; Valda Robinson, Hillsborough Community College; James Roll, William Rainey Harper College; Laurie Rotando, Westchester Community College; George S. Rotter, Montclair State University; Patrick J. Ryan, Tompkins-Cortland Community College; H. R. Schiffman, Rutgers University; Sharon Sexton, McLennan Community College; Joseph Shaver, Fairmont State College; Larry J. Siegel, University of Lowell; Paul Silverstein, L. A. Pierce College; Pamela Simon, Baker College; Patricia J. Slocum, College of DuPage; Ron Smith, Navarro College; Susan Spooner, McLennan Community College; William Sproull, Texas Christian University South; Frank Stanicek, South Surburban College; Jacob Steinberg, Fairleigh Dickinson University; Doris Stevens, McLennan Community College; Valerie Stratton, Pennsylvania State University–Altoona; Elizabeth Street, Central Washington University; Adolph Streng, Eastfield College; Hugh Stroube, Navarro College; Ann Swint, North Harris County College; Sherrill Tabing, Los Angeles Harbor College; Robert S. Tacker, East Carolina University; Francis Terrell, North Texas State University; Harry A. Tiemann, Mesa State College; Larry M. Till, Fullerton College and Cerritos College; Linda Truesdale, Midland Technical College; Mary Vandendrope, Lewis University; Frank J. Vattano, Colorado State University; Benjamin Wallace, Cleveland State University; Douglas Wallen, Mankato State University; Cathrine Wambach, University of Minnesota; Glen Weaver, Calvin College; Charles Weichert, San Antonio College; Paul Wellman, Texas A & M University; Richard Whinery, Ohio University–Chillicothe; Kenneth Wildman, Ohio Northern University; Robert Williams, William Jewel College; Rob Winningham, McLennan Community College; Keith A. Wollen, Washington State University; and Walter Zimmerman, New Hampshire College.

This book could not have come into existence in its present form without the support, cooperation, and hard work of a great many Harcourt publishing professionals: Ted Buchholz, President, who is an old friend (no, he's not old; but the relationship spans two decades); Chris Klein, Senior Vice President, Editorial, who is a not-so-old friend, but a most reliable one; Brad Potthoff, Acquisitions Editor, a new friend and a valued one; Michelle Vardeman, Developmental Editor, who managed a vast load of information to get the book and all the electronic and print ancillaries into shape; Katie Matthews, Executive Market Strategist, who got the word out about the new edition to the sales force (why write a book without a Katie to market it?); Caroline Robbins, Picture and Rights Editor, who acquired the photos; Michele Tomiak, Senior Project Editor and goddess, who managed the transformation of my manuscript into the spendid book you are holding in your hands; Cindy Young, Senior Production Manager and saint, who bought and managed the composition and page makeup and provided extraordinary goodwill; Burl Sloan, Senior Art Director and Curmudgeon in Residence, who did a bang-up job of designing the text and the cover, but who more importantly is the proud new owner of a vintage leather Harley jacket; and Kimberly Dolejsi, Director of Manufacturing, who bought and managed the printing and binding for the book and the printed ancillaries.

Introduction— Your Online Guide to Success

(in Psychology and Your Other Courses)

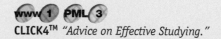

One of the wonderful things about psychology is that it is relevant to so many aspects of life. Psychology, for example, can help you become a successful student. This *Psychology in the New Millenium* feature—the few words here and the extensive online files—are intended to help you do well not only in psychology, but in all your college courses.

For many of you, this might be the first semester of college. We recognize that it is important that you do well in college and therefore begin with helpful information that can help you "burst out" of the starting gate. Psychologists are experts in the areas of learning and memory, and they have compiled hundreds of facts that can help you learn and remember the subject matter in your courses—all of your courses, not just psychology.

Advice on Effective Studying

Oh, how I wish I had had this information when I first went off to college! The truth is that I had little idea of what to expect. New faces, a new locale, responsibility for doing my own laundry (unbelievable!), new courses—it added up to an overwhelming assortment of changes. Perhaps the most stunning change of all was the new-found freedom. Nobody told me when to read or when to study.

Guess what. You have to be in charge of your learning. Your professors may give you assignments, but that doesn't mean that you can take a passive role in the learning process. You are the one who needs to advance your education. You are the one who needs a college degree. So accept your responsibility for what happens to you and take charge of your education. Psychological theory and research have taught us that an active approach to learning results in better grades than a passive approach. For example, it is better to look ahead and seek the answers to specific questions than to read page by page "like a good student." We tend to remember material better when we attend to it and when it is meaningful. Reading in order to answer questions boosts our attention to it and renders it meaningful. It is also helpful not to try to do it all in one sitting, as in cramming before tests. Learning takes time.

We have all that information laid out for you, as you can see by going to the text's Web site: **Click4**™ "Advice on Effective Studying."

Advice on Getting the Most From Classes

Another surprise when I arrived at college was that it was no longer enough to enroll in a course and sit in class. I had to come to grips with the fact that I was not a sponge and would not passively soak up knowledge. Active measures were required to take in the subject matter. As you will see on the text's Web site, one of the least understood but most effective ways of ingesting the subject matter is by going to class and participating. So **Click4**™ "Advice on Getting the Most From Classes." You will discover one of the great secrets of student success: Taking the time to attend classes saves you time.

www 1 PML 3
CLICK4™ *"Advice on Effective Studying."*

CLICK4™ *"Advice on Getting the Most From Classes."*

CLICK4™ *"Advice on Taking Tests."*

CLICK4™ *"Advice on Coping With Test Anxiety."*

Advice on Taking Tests

In college, each test struck me as something of a surprise. I did well on some tests and floundered on others. I will even confess that it took me six years and three colleges to earn my bachelor's degree. **Click4**™ "Advice on Taking Tests" to learn how to give your best performances on tests. Tests and grades are important, and we will give you hint upon hint about how to ace tests. Psychologists have studied the matter extensively, and you will find a flood of information that will help you, test after test! Tests will no longer be a mystery. You will learn how to prepare for them strategically.

Advice on Coping With Test Anxiety

Test anxiety can be an awful burden. When you have studied your heart out for a test, test anxiety seems to be a most cruel and unfair adversary. Test anxiety can confuse you and rob you of the very thought processes you need to focus on the test items and answer them correctly.

So **Click4**™ "Advice on Coping With Test Anxiety." The first thing you'll learn is what test anxiety *is*. Then you will be able to follow our step-by-step plan for putting test anxiety out of your mind and focusing on the test items, one by one.

CLICK4™ *"Advice on Managing Time."*

Advice on Managing Time

When I went off to college, I also discovered that it was up to me to plan ahead to do my course work but somehow manage to leave time for socializing and playing bridge. One of the problems in college—and throughout life, for that matter!—is that it might seem that there is never enough time to accomplish what you feel you need to do. Therefore, one of the online files will also help you fit classes, studying, meals, family life, a social life, work, extracurricular activities, recreational activities, and sleep into your schedule. **Click4**™ "Advice on Managing Time." The time you invest in checking out the advice will pay dividends by providing you with time to enjoy, and possibly time to spare.

There it is—your basic student survival kit. **Click4**™ the text's Web site for advice on studying, drinking in everything you can from your classes, acing tests, defeating test anxiety, and fitting it all into your schedule. These data files will help shepherd you a long way toward becoming a successful student—and also help you find the time to stop and smell the daisies (and other things in your environment).

Brief Contents

Contents

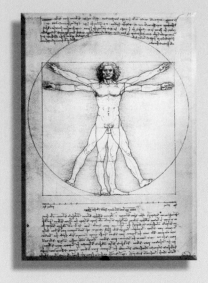

CHAPTER 4 Consciousness

CHAPTER 5 Learning

CHAPTER 7 Cognition and Language   228

CHAPTER 8 Intelligence

CHAPTER 9 Motivation and Emotion

CHAPTER 10 Child Development

CHAPTER 11   Adolescent and Adult Development   348

CHAPTER 14 Stress and Health

CHAPTER 16 Methods of Therapy

CHAPTER 17 Social Psychology

IN PROFILE

Features
Contents

IN REVIEW

Psychology and Modern Life

SELF-ASSESSMENT

PSYCHOLOGY

in the New Millennium

EIGHTH EDITION

PREVIEW

Psychology as a Science
▲ Psychology may not be what you think it is.
▲ "Controlling" what people do and think can be a good thing. (Really)

What Psychologists Do
▲ Psychologists do much more than you think they do.
▲ It is most excellent to be a critical person.

Where Psychology Comes From: A History
▲ As psychologist Wilhelm Wundt lay on his deathbed, his main concern was to analyze his experiences.
▲ Why did William James give Helen Keller an ostrich feather?
▲ John B. Watson was annoyed when he was asked to explain what a rat *thinks* while it is navigating a maze.
▲ Sometimes the whole equals *more* than the sum of its parts.

How Today's Psychologists View Behavior and Mental Processes
▲ Your thoughts, fantasies, and dreams are made possible by your nervous system.
▲ In the age-old struggle for survival, only the "fittest" (most adaptive) organisms manage to reach maturity and reproduce.
▲ Cognitive psychologists believe that you keep them "in mind."
▲ Have you ever felt that something within was trying to get the better of you? Sigmund Freud had ideas about what that something is.
▲ How much of human behavior is built in, and how much is learned?
▲ How have your cultural heritage, your church, your family, and your gender influenced you?

Gender, Ethnicity, and the Profession of Psychology
▲ A group that was once kept out of psychology now makes up the largest number of college graduates in psychology.

How Psychologists Study Behavior and Mental Processes
▲ Psychologists have many ways of observing you.
▲ How would you determine whether drinking makes people aggressive?

Ethical Issues in Psychological Research and Practice
▲ Is it right to harm animals for the benefit of people?

CHAPTER 1

What Is Psychology?

TRUTH 🔲 FICTION?

◪ A book on psychology, whose contents are similar to those of the book you are now holding, was written by Aristotle more than 2,000 years ago.

◪ The ancient Greek philosopher Socrates suggested a research method that is still used in psychology.

◪ Even though she had worked to complete all the degree requirements, the first female president of the American Psychological Association turned down the doctoral degree that was offered to her.

◪ Men receive the majority of doctoral degrees in psychology.

◪ You could survey 20 million voters and still not predict the outcome of a presidential election accurately.

◪ In many experiments, neither the participants nor the researchers know who is receiving the real treatment and who is not.

◪ Psychologists would not be able to carry out many kinds of studies without deceiving participants as to the purposes and methods of the studies.

"**W**hat a piece of work is man," wrote William Shakespeare. He was writing about you: "How noble in reason! How infinite in faculty! In form and moving how express and admirable! In action how like an angel! In apprehension how like a god! The beauty of the world! The paragon of animals!"

You probably had no trouble recognizing yourself in this portrait—"noble in reason," "admirable," godlike in understanding, head and shoulders above other animals. That's you to a *tee*, isn't it? Consider some of the noble and admirable features of human behavior:

▲ The human abilities to think and solve problems have allowed us to build cathedrals and computers and to scan the interior of the body without surgery. Yet just what is thinking? How do we solve problems?

▲ The human ability to create led to the writing of great works of literature and the composition of music from opera to rap. Yet what exactly is creativity?

▲ Human generosity and charity have encouraged us to care for older people, people who are ill, and people who are less advantaged than we are—even to sacrifice ourselves for those we love. Why do we care for others? What motivates us to care for our children and protect our families?

Some human behavior is not as noble or admirable as these examples suggest. In fact, human behavior varies greatly and some of it is downright puzzling. Consider some more examples:

▲ Although people can be generous, most adults on crowded city streets will not stop to help a person lying on the sidewalk. Why?

▲ Most people who overeat or smoke cigarettes know they are jeopardizing their health. Yet they continue their bad habits. Why?

▲ A person claims to have raped, killed, or mutilated a victim because of insanity. The person was overcome by an irresistible impulse, or by "another personality" that took control. What is insanity? What is an irresistible impulse?

Human behavior has always fascinated people. Sometimes we are even surprised at ourselves. We have thoughts or impulses that seem to be out of character, or we cannot recall something that seems to be hovering on the "tip of the tongue." Psychologists, like

"What a piece of work is man," wrote William Shakespeare. "How noble in reason! How infinite in faculty!" Chinese American artist Hung Liu, seen here with one of her paintings, illustrates the creativity that humans are capable of. Psychologists are interested in all aspects of human behavior and mental processes.

other people, are also intrigued by the mysteries of behavior, but for them the scientific study of behavior is their life's work.   *Question: What is psychology?*

PSYCHOLOGY AS A SCIENCE

Psychology is the scientific study of behavior and mental processes. Topics of interest to psychologists include the nervous system, sensation and perception, learning and memory, intelligence, language, thought, growth and development, personality, stress and health, psychological disorders, ways of treating those disorders, sexual behavior, and the behavior of people in social settings such as groups and organizations.

Sciences have certain goals.   *Question: What are the goals of psychology?* Psychology, like other sciences, seeks to describe, explain, predict, and control the events it studies. Psychology thus seeks to describe, explain, predict, and control behavior and mental processes.

When possible, descriptive terms and concepts are interwoven into **theories.** Theories are formulations of apparent relationships among observed events. They allow us to derive explanations and predictions. Many psychological theories combine statements about behavior (such as eating or aggression), mental processes (such as attitudes and mental images), and biological processes. For instance, many of our responses to drugs such as alcohol and marijuana can be measured as overt behavior, and they are presumed to reflect the biochemical actions of these drugs and our (mental) expectations about their effects.

A satisfactory psychological theory allows us to predict behavior. For instance, a theory of hunger should allow us to predict when people will or will not eat. If our observations cannot be adequately explained by, or predicted from, a given theory, we should consider revising or replacing it.

CLICK4™ *the Web sites of the American Psychological Association and the American Psychological Society.*

> **REFLECT**
> What are your theories as to why people act and think as they do? What is the evidence for your theories?

CONTROVERSY IN PSYCHOLOGY

What Do Psychologists Mean by "Controlling" Behavior and Mental Processes? "Controlling" behavior and mental processes doesn't mean what it sounds like to psychologists. Some people erroneously think that psychologists seek ways to make people do their bidding, like puppets on strings. This is not so. Psychologists are committed to a belief in the dignity of human beings, and human dignity demands that people be free to make their own decisions and choose their own behavior. Psychologists are learning more about the influences on human behavior all the time, but they implement this knowledge only on request and in order to help people clarify and meet their own goals.

The remainder of this chapter presents an overview of psychology as a science. You will see that psychologists have diverse interests and fields of specialization. We discuss the history of psychology and the major perspectives from which today's psychologists view behavior. Finally, we consider the research methods psychologists use to study behavior and mental processes.

REVIEW

(1) Psychology is defined as the study of _____ and mental processes. (2) Psychology seeks to describe, explain, _____, and control behavior. (3) Behavior is explained through psychological _____, which are sets of statements that involve assumptions about behavior.

Pulling It Together: Did you know that psychology is a science? How would you explain the characteristics of the science of psychology?

Psychology ▲ The science that studies behavior and mental processes.
Theory ▲ A formulation of relationships underlying observed events.

WHAT PSYCHOLOGISTS DO

Psychologists share a keen interest in behavior, but in other ways, they may differ markedly. ***Question: Just what do psychologists do?*** Psychologists engage in research, practice, and teaching. Some researchers engage primarily in basic, or **pure, research.** Pure research has no immediate application to personal or social problems and therefore has been characterized as research for its own sake. Others engage in **applied research,** which is designed to find solutions to specific personal or social problems. Although pure research is sparked by curiosity and the desire to know and understand, today's pure research frequently enhances tomorrow's way of life (Leibowitz, 1996; Miller, 1995). For example, pure research on learning and motivation in lower animals done early in the 20th century has found widespread applications in today's school systems. Pure research into the workings of the nervous system has enhanced knowledge of disorders such as epilepsy, Parkinson's disease, and Alzheimer's disease.

Many psychologists do not conduct research. Instead, they *practice* psychology by applying psychological knowledge to help people change their behavior so that they can meet their own goals more effectively. Still other psychologists engage primarily in teaching. They share psychological knowledge in classrooms, seminars, and workshops. Some psychologists engage in all three: research, practice, and teaching.

Let us describe the different fields of psychology and then bring psychologists back together again as we describe the approach to behavior and mental processes that is shared by all of them—critical thinking.

Fields of Psychology

Psychologists are found in a number of different specialties. Although some psychologists wear more than one hat, most of them carry out their functions in the following fields.

Clinical psychologists help people with psychological disorders adjust to the demands of life. People's problems may range from anxiety and depression to sexual dysfunctions to loss of goals. Clinical psychologists evaluate these problems through interviews and psychological tests. They help their clients resolve their problems and change self-defeating behavior. Clinical psychologists are the largest subgroup of psychologists (Kyle & Williams, 2000; see Figure 1.1). These psychologists differ from psychiatrists in that *psychiatrists* are *medical* doctors who specialize in the study and treatment of psychological disorders.

CLICK4™ *more information on careers in psychology.*

Pure research ▲ Research conducted without concern for immediate applications.

Applied research ▲ Research conducted in an effort to find solutions to particular problems.

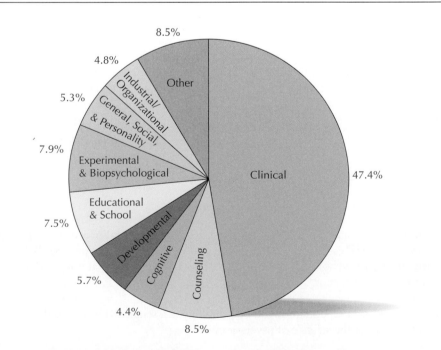

FIGURE 1.1   Students Enrolled in Doctoral Programs in Fields of Psychology.
Nearly half (47%) of the doctoral students who enrolled in doctoral programs in psychology in 1998–1999 enrolled in clinical programs. (Current enrollments were used because they are the best indicator of the current directions of psychology.) The next most popular field was counseling psychology. The figure combines students enrolled in public and private institutions.

SOURCE: Kyle, T. M., & Williams, S. (2000, May). Results of the 1998–1999 APA survey of graduate departments of psychology, Tables 13A & 13B. APA Research Office. Washington, D.C.: American Psychological Association.

Counseling psychologists, like clinical psychologists, use interviews and tests to define their clients' problems. Their clients typically have adjustment problems but not serious psychological disorders. Clients may have trouble making academic or vocational decisions, or making friends in college. They may experience marital or family conflicts, have physical disabilities, or have adjustment problems such as those encountered by people who lose their jobs because of mergers or downsizing. Counseling psychologists advise clients to help them clarify their goals and overcome obstacles. Counseling psychologists are often employed in college and university counseling and testing centers. As suggested by Figure 1.1, more than half of doctoral students in psychology are enrolled in clinical or counseling psychology programs.

School psychologists are employed by school systems to identify and assist students who have problems that interfere with learning. Such problems range from social and family problems to emotional disturbances and learning disorders. They help schools make decisions about the placement of students in special classes.

Educational psychologists, like school psychologists, attempt to facilitate learning. But they usually focus on course planning and instructional methods for a school system rather than on individual children. Educational psychologists research theoretical issues related to learning, measurement, and child development. For example, they study how learning is affected by psychological factors such as motivation and intelligence, sociocultural factors such as poverty and acculturation, and teacher behavior. Some educational psychologists prepare standardized tests such as the Scholastic Assessment Tests (SATs).

Developmental psychologists study the changes—physical, cognitive, social, and personality—that occur throughout the life span. They attempt to sort out the influences of heredity (nature) and the environment (nurture) on development. Developmental psychologists conduct research on issues such as the effects of maternal use of drugs on an embryo, the outcomes of various patterns of child rearing, children's concepts of space and time, conflicts during adolescence, and problems of adjustment among older people.

Personality psychologists attempt to define human traits; to determine influences on human thought processes, feelings, and behavior; and to explain psychological disorders. They are particularly concerned with issues such as anxiety, aggression, and gender roles.

Social psychologists are primarily concerned with the nature and causes of individuals' thoughts, feelings, and behavior in social situations. Whereas personality psychologists tend to look within the person for explanations of behavior, social psychologists tend to focus on external or social influences.

Psychologists in all specialties may conduct experiments. However, those called *experimental psychologists* specialize in basic processes such as the nervous system, sensation and perception, learning and memory, thought, motivation, and emotion.

Industrial psychology and organizational psychology are closely related fields. *Industrial psychologists* focus on the relationships between people and work. *Organizational psychologists* study the behavior of people in organizations such as businesses. *Human factors psychologists* make technical systems such as automobile dashboards and computer keyboards more user-friendly. *Consumer psychologists* study the behavior of shoppers in an effort to predict and influence their behavior. They advise store managers how to lay out the aisles of a supermarket in ways that boost impulse buying, how to arrange window displays to attract customers, and how to make newspaper ads and TV commercials more persuasive.

Health psychologists examine the ways in which behavior and mental processes such as attitudes are related to physical health. They study the effects of stress on health problems such as headaches, cardiovascular disease, and cancer. Health psychologists also guide clients toward healthier behavior patterns—such as exercising and quitting smoking—and diets.

Sport psychologists help people improve their performance in sports. Many teams have psychologists as well as coaches. Sports psychologists deal with issues such as the following:

Environmental Psychology.
Environmental psychologists focus on the ways in which people affect and are affected by their physical environment. How are city dwellers affected by crowding and "stimulus overload"?

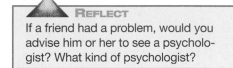

REFLECT
If a friend had a problem, would you advise him or her to see a psychologist? What kind of psychologist?

www 1 L 1

CLICK4™ *more information about specializations in psychology.*

www 1 L 7

CLICK4™ *more information about exercise and sport psychology.*

▲ **REFLECT**
Which fields of psychology are most in keeping with your own interests? Why?

Critical thinking ▲ An approach to thinking characterized by skepticism and thoughtful analysis of statements and arguments—for example, probing arguments' premises and the definitions of terms.

CLICK4™ *more information about thinking critically.*

CLICK4™ *advice on thinking critically about astrology.*

CLICK4™ *more information about astrology and modern life.*

▲ **REFLECT**
Do you think it is important to be a critical thinker? Are you a critical thinker? (Are you sure?)

▲ How athletes can concentrate on their performance and not on the crowd
▲ How athletes can use cognitive strategies such as positive visualization (imagining themselves making the right moves) to enhance performance
▲ The role of emotions in sports. For example, does it help or hurt performance to become angry with one's opponent?
▲ The relationships between sports and psychological well-being
▲ Handling choking up because of anxiety

Psychologists continue to apply their knowledge and skills in new areas.

Psychology and Critical Thinking

Regardless of their area of specialization, psychologists are scientists, and one hallmark of science is **critical thinking.** *Question: What is critical thinking?* Critical thinking has many meanings. On one level, it means taking nothing for granted. It means not believing things just because they are in print or because they were uttered by authority figures or celebrities. It means not necessarily believing that it is healthful to express all of your feelings just because a friend in "therapy" urges you to do so. On another level, critical thinking refers to a process of thoughtfully analyzing and probing the questions, statements, and arguments of others. It means examining definitions of terms, examining the premises or assumptions behind arguments, and then scrutinizing the logic with which arguments are developed.

A group of psychologists (McGovern, 1989) defined the goals of critical thinking as fostering the following thinking skills:

▲ Development of skepticism about explanations and conclusions
▲ The ability to inquire about causes and effects
▲ Increased curiosity about behavior
▲ Knowledge of research methods
▲ The ability to analyze arguments critically

Let us consider some principles of critical thinking that can be of help to you in college and beyond:

1. *Be skeptical.* Keep an open mind. Politicians and advertisers try to persuade you. Even research reported in the media or in textbooks may take a certain slant. Extend this principle to yourself. Are some of your own attitudes and beliefs superficial or unfounded? Accept nothing as truth until you have examined the evidence.

2. *Examine definitions of terms.* Some statements are true when a term is defined in one way but not when it is defined in another way. Consider the statement "Head Start programs have raised children's IQs." The correctness of the statement depends on the definition of "IQ." (You will see later in the text that *IQ* has a specific meaning and is not exactly the same as *intelligence*.)

3. *Examine the assumptions or premises of arguments.* Consider the statement that one cannot learn about human beings by engaging in research with animals. One premise in the statement seems to be that human beings are not animals. We are, of course. (Would you rather be a plant?)

4. *Be cautious in drawing conclusions from evidence.* For many years studies had shown that most clients who receive psychotherapy improve. It was therefore generally assumed that psychotherapy worked. Some 40 years ago, however, a psychologist named Hans Eysenck pointed out that most psychologically troubled people who did *not* receive psychotherapy also improved! The question thus becomes whether people receiving psychotherapy are *more* likely to improve than those who do not. Current research on the effectiveness of psychotherapy therefore carefully compares the benefits of therapy techniques to the benefits of other techniques or of no treatment at all. Be especially skeptical of anecdotes. When you hear "I know someone who—", ask yourself whether this one person's reported experience is satisfactory as evidence.

5. *Consider alternative interpretations of research evidence.* Does alcohol cause aggression? Is the assertion that it does so truth or fiction? Later in the chapter we see that evidence shows a clear *connection*, or "correlation," between alcohol and aggression. That is, many people who commit violent crimes have been drinking. But does the

evidence show that this connection is *causal?* Could other factors, such as gender, age, or willingness to take risks, account for both drinking and aggressive behavior?

6. *Do not oversimplify.* Most human behavior involves complex interactions of genetic and environmental influences. Also consider the issue of whether psychotherapy helps people with psychological problems. A broad answer to this question—a simple yes or no—might be oversimplifying. It is more worthwhile to ask, What *type* of psychotherapy, practiced by *whom*, is most helpful for *what kind of problem?*

7. *Do not overgeneralize.* Consider the statement that one cannot learn about human beings by engaging in research with animals. Is the truth of the matter an all-or-nothing issue? Are there certain kinds of information we can obtain about people from research with animals? What kinds of things are you likely to be able to learn only through research with people?

8. *Apply critical thinking to all areas of life.* A skeptical attitude and a demand for evidence are useful not only in college, but are of value in all areas of life. Be skeptical when you are bombarded by TV commercials, when political causes try to sweep you up, when you see the latest cover stories about Elvis and UFOs in supermarket tabloids. How many times have you heard the claim "Studies have shown that . . ."? Perhaps such claims sound convincing, but ask yourself: Who ran the studies? Were the researchers neutral scientists, or were they biased toward obtaining certain results?

These are the kinds of principles that guide psychologists' thinking as they observe behavior, engage in research, or advise clients as to how to improve the quality of their lives. Perhaps these principles will help you improve the quality of your own life.

CLICK4™ *advice on thinking critically about self-help books.*

▲ REFLECT
Why is learning to think critically a key part of higher education? How might critical thinking protect the individual from dictators, advertisers, and other tyrants of the mind?

REVIEW

(4) Some psychologists engage in basic, or _____, research, which has no immediate applications. (5) Other psychologists engage in _____ research, which seeks solutions to specific problems. (6) Clinical psychologists help people resolve problems through _____. (7) _____ psychologists work with individuals who have adjustment problems but do not show seriously abnormal behavior. (8) _____ psychologists assist students with problems that interfere with learning. (9) _____ psychologists are more concerned with theoretical issues concerning human learning. (10) _____ psychologists study the changes that occur throughout the life span. (11) _____ psychologists study the nature and causes of our thoughts, feelings, and behavior in social situations. (12) _____ psychologists conduct research into basic psychological processes, such as sensation and perception, learning and memory, and motivation and emotion. (13) _____ psychologists focus on the relationships between people and work. (14) As scientists, psychologists engage in _____ thinking, which is characterized by skepticism.

Pulling It Together: Can someone with a problem consult with any psychologist? Why or why not? How would you apply critical thinking in your own life?

WHERE PSYCHOLOGY COMES FROM: A HISTORY

> *Know then thyself, presume not God to scan,*
> *The proper study of mankind is man. . . .*
> *Created half to rise, and half to fall,*
> *Great lord of all things, and yet a prey to all;*
> *Sole judge of truth, in endless error hurled;*
> *The glory, jest, and riddle of the world!*
>
> From "An Essay on Man," Alexander Pope

The English poet Alexander Pope advised "Know then thyself" in the 1700s. He was not the first. The ancient Greek philosopher Socrates, writing more than 2,000 years earlier,

CLICK4™ *more information on psychology's theoretical roots.*

CLICK4™ *more information about the history of psychology.*

Aristotle

His father was physician to a king. He himself was trained as a physician and was a student of Plato. He tutored the child who would become Alexander the Great. He founded what has been considered the world's first university—the Lyceum. The Greek philosopher Aristotle (384–322 B.C.) is also the first philosopher to treat extensively topics that would later become part of the science of psychology.

How do we number Aristotle's contributions to psychology? He was a proponent of *empiricism*—the view that science could rationally treat only information gathered by the senses. He numbered the so-called five senses of vision, hearing, smell, taste, and touch. He explored the nature of cause and effect. He pointed out that people differ from other living things in their capacity for rational thought. He explained how the imagination and dreaming contained images that survived the stimulation that caused them. And he outlined laws of *associationism*, which have lain at the heart of learning theory for more than 2,000 years.

These are but a few of the topics Aristotle touched upon within the province of psychology. How daunting is it, then, to consider that he also made significant contributions to logic, physics, biology (he was the first to note that whales are mammals), politics, ethics, and rhetoric? But in one way, Aristotle would agree with some contemporary students: He did not believe that mathematics was all that important.

also advised "Know thyself." Psychology, which is in large part the endeavor to know ourselves, is as old as history and as modern as today. Knowledge of the history of psychology allows us to appreciate its theoretical conflicts, its place among the sciences, the evolution of its methods, and its social and political roles.

Question: Who were some of the ancient contributors to psychology? One of them is the ancient Greek philosopher Aristotle. In fact, the outline for this textbook could have been written by Aristotle. One of Aristotle's works, *Peri Psyches*, translates as "About the Psyche." Like this book, *Peri Psyches* begins with a history of psychological thought and historical perspectives on the nature of the mind and behavior. Aristotle argued that human behavior, like the movements of the stars and the seas, is subject to rules and laws. Then he delved into his subject matter topic by topic: personality, sensation and perception, thought, intelligence, needs and motives, feelings and emotion, and memory. This book presents these topics in a different order, but each is here.

Aristotle also declared that people are motivated to seek pleasure and avoid pain. This view remains as current today as it was in ancient Greece.

Other ancient Greek philosophers also contributed to psychology. Around 400 B.C., Democritus suggested that we could think of behavior in terms of a body and a mind. (Contemporary psychologists still talk about the interaction of biological and mental processes.) He pointed out that our behavior is influenced by external stimulation. Democritus was one of the first to raise the question of whether there is free will or choice. Putting it another way, where do the influences of others end and our "real selves" begin?

Plato (ca. 427–347 B.C.) was a disciple of the great philosopher Socrates. He recorded Socrates' advice to "Know thyself," which has remained a motto of psychology ever since. Socrates claimed that we could not attain reliable self-knowledge through our senses because the senses do not mirror reality exactly. Because the senses provide imperfect knowledge, Socrates suggested that we should rely on processes such as rational thought and **introspection**—careful examination of one's own thoughts and emotions—to achieve self-knowledge. He also pointed out that people are social creatures who influence one another.

Had we room enough and time, we could trace psychology's roots to thinkers even farther back in time than the ancient Greeks, and we could trace its development through the great thinkers of the Renaissance. As it is, we must move on to the development of psychology as a laboratory science during the second half of the 19th century. Some historians set the marker date at 1860. It was then that Gustav Theodor Fechner (1801–1887) published his landmark book *Elements of Psychophysics*, which showed how physical events (such as lights and sounds) are related to psychological sensation and perception. Fechner also showed how we can scientifically measure the effect of these events. Most historians set the debut of modern psychology as a laboratory science in the year 1879, when Wilhelm Wundt established the first psychological laboratory in Leipzig, Germany.

Structuralism: The Elements of Experience

Like Aristotle, Wilhelm Wundt saw the mind as a natural event that could be studied scientifically, like light, heat, and the flow of blood. Wundt used introspection to try to discover the basic elements of experience. When presented with various sights and sounds, he and his colleagues tried to look inward as objectively as possible to describe their sensations and feelings.

Wundt and his students founded the school of psychology called **structuralism.** *Question: What is structuralism?* Structuralism attempted to break conscious

▲ **REFLECT**

Do you think it is useful for this book to talk about topics like the history of psychology? Would you prefer it if the book just listed the 100 or 200 "facts" you need to know for the final exam? Why or why not?

Introspection ▲ Deliberate looking into one's own mind to examine one's own thoughts and feelings.

Structuralism ▲ The school of psychology that argues that the mind consists of three basic elements—sensations, feelings, and images—that combine to form experience.

experience down into *objective* sensations such as sight or taste, and *subjective* feelings such as emotional responses, will, and mental images like memories or dreams. Structuralists believed that the mind functions by combining objective and subjective elements of experience.

Functionalism: Making Psychology a Habit

I wished, by treating Psychology like a natural science, to help her become one.

William James

Toward the end of the 19th century, William James was a major figure in the development of psychology in the United States. James adopted a broad view of psychology that focused on the relation between conscious experience and behavior. He argued, for example, that the stream of consciousness is fluid and continuous. Introspection convinced him that experience cannot be broken down into objective sensations and subjective feelings as the structuralists maintained.

James was a founder of the school of **functionalism.** *Question: What is functionalism?* The school of functionalism dealt with behavior as well as consciousness. Functionalism addressed the ways in which experience permits us to function more adaptively in our environments—for example, how the development of habits allows us to cope with commonly occurring situations. It used behavioral observation in the laboratory to supplement introspection. The structuralists tended to ask, "What are the pieces that make up thinking and experience?" The functionalists tended to ask, "What are the *purposes* (functions) of behavior and mental processes? What difference do they make?"

James was influenced by Charles Darwin's theory of evolution. Earlier in the 19th century, Darwin had argued that organisms with adaptive features—that is, the "fittest"—survive and reproduce. Functionalists adapted Darwin's theory in the study of behavior and proposed that adaptive behavior patterns are learned and maintained. Maladaptive behavior patterns tend to drop out. They are discontinued, and the "fittest" behavior patterns survive. Adaptive actions tend to be repeated and become habits. James wrote that "habit is the enormous flywheel of society." Habit keeps civilization going from day to day.

The formation of habits is seen in acts such as lifting a fork to our mouth and turning a doorknob. At first, these acts require our full attention. If you are in doubt, stand by with paper towels and watch a baby's first efforts at self-feeding. Through repetition, the acts that make up self-feeding become automatic, or habitual. The multiple acts involved in learning to drive a car also become routine through repetition. We can then perform them without much attention, freeing ourselves to focus on other matters such as our clever conversation and the CD player. The idea of learning by repetition is also basic to the behavioral tradition in psychology.

Behaviorism: Practicing Psychology in Public

Imagine you have placed a hungry rat in a maze. It meanders down a pathway that ends in a T. It can then turn left or right. If you consistently reward the rat with food for turning right at this choice point, it will learn to turn right when it arrives there, at least when it is hungry. But what does the rat *think* when it is learning to turn right? "Hmm, last time I was in this situation and turned to the right, I was given some food. Think I'll try that again"?

Does it seem absurd to try to place yourself in the "mind" of a rat? So it seemed to John Broadus Watson (1878–1958), the founder of American behaviorism. *Question:*

▲ **REFLECT**

Why do behaviorists object to schools of psychology that use introspection? Do you agree with the behaviorist point of view? Why or why not?

Functionalism ▲ The school of psychology that emphasizes the uses or functions of the mind rather than the elements of experience.

William James

William James (1842–1910), brother of the novelist Henry James, has been called the first true American psychologist. He came from a wealthy family, and his home was visited regularly by the likes of Ralph Waldo Emerson, Henry David Thoreau, Nathaniel Hawthorne, Alfred Lord Tennyson, and John Stuart Mill. James received an M.D. degree from Harvard University but never practiced medicine. He made his career teaching at Harvard—first in physiology, then in philosophy, and finally in psychology. He described his views in the first modern psychology textbook, *The Principles of Psychology*, a huge two-volume work that was published in 1890. Two years later he came out with a brief edition, which students affectionately called the "Jimmy." He was often seen strolling across Harvard Yard, talking animatedly with students, in an era when most professors were more formal. James was also fascinated by religious experience and occult phenomena such as extrasensory perception. He once brought the young Helen Keller an ostrich feather—a gift he believed the blind and deaf girl could appreciate.

What is behaviorism? We will define behaviorism in a minute, but first let us note that Watson was asked to consider the same question as one of the requirements for his doctoral degree, which he received from the University of Chicago in 1903. Functionalism was the dominant view of psychology at the University of Chicago, and functionalists were concerned with the stream of consciousness as well as observable behavior. But Watson (1913) believed that if psychology was to be a natural science, like physics or chemistry, it must limit itself to observable, measurable events—that is, to behavior—hence, **behaviorism.** Observable behavior includes activities such as pressing a lever; turning left or right; eating and mating; even involuntary body functions such as heart rate, dilation of the pupils of the eyes, blood pressure, and emission of brain waves. These behaviors are *public.* They can be measured by simple observation or by laboratory instruments and different observers would readily agree about their existence and features. Behaviorists, by the way, define psychology as the scientific study of *behavior,* not of *behavior and mental processes.*

Harvard University psychologist B. F. Skinner (1904–1990) was another major contributor to behaviorism. Organisms, he believed, learn to behave in certain ways because they have been **reinforced** for doing so—that is, their behavior has had a positive outcome. He demonstrated that laboratory animals carry out behaviors, both simple and complex, because of reinforcement. They peck buttons, turn in circles, climb ladders, and push toys across the floor. Many psychologists adopted the view that, in principle, one could explain complex human behavior in terms of thousands of instances of learning through reinforcement.

Gestalt Psychology: Making Psychology Whole

In the 1920s, another school of psychology—**Gestalt psychology**—was prominent in Germany. In the 1930s, the three founders of the school—Max Wertheimer (1880–1943), Kurt Koffka (1886–1941), and Wolfgang Köhler (1887–1967)—left Europe to escape the Nazi threat. They carried on their work in the United States, giving further impetus to the growing American ascendance in psychology.

Question: What is Gestalt psychology? Wertheimer and other Gestalt psychologists focused on perception and on how perception influences thinking and problem

Behaviorism ▲ The school of psychology that defines psychology as the study of observable behavior and studies relationships between stimuli and responses.

Reinforcement ▲ A stimulus that follows a response and increases the frequency of the response.

Gestalt psychology ▲ The school of psychology that emphasizes the tendency to organize perceptions into wholes and to integrate separate stimuli into meaningful patterns.

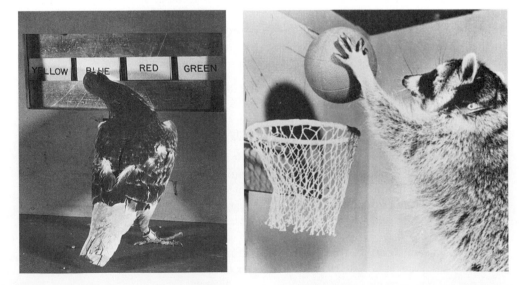

Examples of the Power of Reinforcement. In the photo on the left, we see how our feathered gift to city life has earned its keep in experiments on reinforcement. Here, the pigeon pecks the blue button because pecking it has been followed (reinforced) with food. In the photo on the right, "Air Racoon" shoots a basket. Behaviorists teach animals complex behavior such as shooting baskets by first reinforcing approximations to the goal (or target behavior). As time progresses, closer approximations are demanded before reinforcement is given.

solving. In contrast to the behaviorists, Gestalt psychologists argued that we cannot hope to understand human nature by focusing only on overt behavior. In contrast to the structuralists, they claimed that we cannot explain human perceptions, emotions, or thought processes in terms of basic units. Perceptions are *more* than the sums of their parts: Gestalt psychologists saw our perceptions as wholes that give meaning to parts.

Gestalt psychologists illustrated how we tend to perceive separate pieces of information as integrated wholes, including the contexts in which they occur. Consider Figure 1.2. The dots in the centers of the configurations at the left are the same size, yet we may perceive them as being of different sizes because of the contexts in which they appear. The inner squares in the central figure are equally bright, but they may look different because of their contrasting backgrounds. The second symbol in each line at the right is identical, but in the top row we may perceive it as a B and in the bottom row as the number 13. The symbol has not changed, only the context in which it appears. There are many examples of this in literature and everyday life. In *The Prince and the Pauper*, Mark Twain dressed a peasant boy as a prince, and the kingdom bowed to him. Do clothes sometimes make the man or woman? Try wearing cutoffs for a job interview!

Gestalt psychologists believed that learning could be active and purposeful, not merely responsive and mechanical as in Skinner's experiments. Wolfgang Köhler and the others demonstrated that much learning, especially in learning to solve problems, is accomplished by **insight,** not by mechanical repetition. Köhler was marooned during World War I on one of the Canary Islands, where the Prussian Academy of Science kept a colony of apes, and his research while there gave him, well, insight into the process of learning by insight.

Have you ever pondered a problem for quite a while and then, suddenly, seen the solution? Did the solution seem to come out of nowhere? In a "flash"? Consider the chimpanzee in Figure 1.3. At first, it is unsuccessful in reaching for bananas suspended from the ceiling. Then it suddenly stacks the boxes and climbs up to reach the bananas. It seems the chimp has experienced a sudden reorganization of the mental elements of the problem—that is, it has had a "flash of insight." Köhler's findings suggest that we often manipulate the elements of problems until we group them in such a way that we believe we will be able to reach a goal. The manipulations may take quite some time as mental

Insight ▲ In Gestalt psychology, the sudden reorganization of perceptions, allowing the sudden solution of a problem.

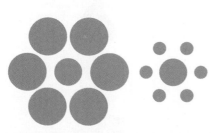

A. Are the dots in the center of the configurations the same size? Why not take a ruler and measure them?

B. Is the second symbol in each line the letter B or the number 13?

C. Which one of the gray squares is brighter?

FIGURE 1.2 The Importance of Context.
Gestalt psychologists have shown that our perceptions depend not only on our sensory impressions but also on the context of our impressions. You will interpret a man running toward you very differently depending on whether you are on a deserted street at night or at a track in the morning.

trial and error proceeds. Once the proper grouping has been found, however, we seem to perceive it all at once.

Psychoanalysis: Digging Beneath the Surface

Psychoanalysis, the school of psychology founded by Sigmund Freud, differs from the other schools in both background and approach. Freud's theory has invaded popular culture, and you may be familiar with a number of its concepts. For example, perhaps a friend has tried to "interpret" a slip of the tongue you made or has asked you what you thought might be the meaning of an especially vivid dream.

Question: What is psychoanalysis?   The notions that verbal errors and dreams represent unconscious wishes lie at the heart of the school of psychology known as psychoanalysis. These ideas largely reflect the influence of Freud (1856–1939), a Viennese physician who fled to England in the 1930s to escape the Nazi tyranny. While academic psychologists were conducting their research in the laboratory, Freud gained his understanding of people by working with patients. He was astounded at how little insight his patients seemed to have into their motives. Some patients justified, or rationalized, the most abominable behavior with absurd explanations. Others seized the opportunity to blame themselves for nearly every misfortune that had befallen the human species.

Freud came to believe that unconscious processes, especially sexual and aggressive impulses, are more influential than conscious thought in determining human behavior. He thought that most of the mind is unconscious—a seething cauldron of conflicting impulses, urges, and wishes. People are motivated to gratify these impulses, ugly as some of them are. But at the same time, people are motivated to see themselves as decent, and hence may delude themselves about their true motives. Because Freud proposed that the motion of underlying forces of personality determines our thoughts, feelings, and behavior, his theory is referred to as **psychodynamic.**

Freud devised a method of psychotherapy called psychoanalysis. Psychoanalysis aims to help patients gain insight into many of their deep-seated conflicts and find socially acceptable ways of expressing wishes and gratifying needs. It can extend for years.

Today we no longer find psychologists who describe themselves as structuralists or functionalists. Although the school of Gestalt psychology gave birth to current research approaches in perception and problem solving, few would consider themselves Gestalt psychologists. The numbers of orthodox behaviorists and psychoanalysts have also been declining (Robins et al., 1999). Many contemporary psychologists in the behaviorist

Psychoanalysis ▲ The school of psychology that emphasizes the importance of unconscious motives and conflicts as determinants of human behavior.
Psychodynamic ▲ Referring to Freud's theory, which proposes that the motion of underlying forces of personality determines our thoughts, feelings, and behavior.

FIGURE 1.3   Some Insight Into Insight.
At first, the chimpanzee cannot reach the bananas hanging from the ceiling. After some time has passed, it has an apparent "flash of insight" and piles the boxes on top of one another to reach the fruit.

tradition look on themselves as social-cognitive[1] theorists, and many psychoanalysts consider themselves neoanalysts rather than traditional Freudians. They have influenced or become part of contemporary perspectives in psychology.

REVIEW

(15) The Greek philosopher _____ was among the first to argue that human behavior is subject to rules and laws. (16) _____ proclaimed "Know thyself" and suggested the use of introspection to gain self-knowledge. (17) Wilhelm _____ founded the school of structuralism. (18) William James founded the school of _____, which dealt with behavior as well as conscious experience. (19) John B. Watson founded the school of _____, which argues that psychology must limit its subject matter to observable behavior. (20) _____ psychologists saw our perceptions as wholes that give meaning to parts. (21) Sigmund _____ founded the school of psychoanalysis.

Pulling It Together: How did the ancient Greeks influence the thinking of today? Which approaches to psychology seem most scientific to you? Why?

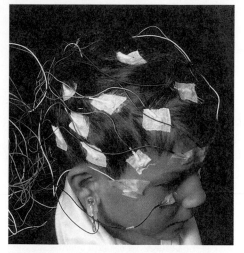

The Biological Perspective.
Psychologists with a biological perspective investigate the connections among biological processes, behavior, and mental processes. The electrodes taped to this girl's face and scalp measure the electrical activity in various parts of her brain.

HOW TODAY'S PSYCHOLOGISTS VIEW BEHAVIOR AND MENTAL PROCESSES

The history of psychological thought has taken many turns, and contemporary psychologists differ in their approaches. Today there are several broad, influential perspectives in psychology: the biological, cognitive, humanistic-existential, psychodynamic, learning, and sociocultural perspectives. Each emphasizes different topics of investigation. Each approaches its topics in its own ways.

The Biological Perspective

Psychologists assume that our thoughts, fantasies, and dreams are made possible by the nervous system and especially by the brain. ***Question: What is the biological perspective?*** Psychologists with a biological perspective seek the links between events in the brain—such as the activity of brain cells—and behavior and mental processes. They use techniques such as CAT scans and PET scans to show what parts of the brain are involved in activities like language, mathematical problem solving, and music. We have learned how natural chemical substances in the brain are involved in the formation of memories. Among some lower animals, electrical stimulation of parts of the brain prompts the expression of innate, or built-in, sexual and aggressive behaviors.

Biological psychologists are also concerned with the influences of hormones (naturally occurring chemicals that are released into the bloodstream and regulate behavior) and heredity. In people, for instance, the hormone prolactin stimulates production of milk. In rats, however, prolactin also gives rise to maternal behavior. In lower animals, sex hormones determine whether mating behavior will follow stereotypical masculine or feminine behavior patterns. In people, hormones play a subtler role.

Psychologists are interested in the role of heredity and evolution in behavior and mental processes such as psychological disorders, criminal behavior, and thinking. Generally speaking, our heredity provides a broad range of behavioral and mental possibilities. Environmental factors interact with inherited factors to determine specific behavior and mental processes.

Evolutionary psychologists focus on the evolution of behavior and mental processes. Charles Darwin argued that in the age-old struggle for survival, only the "fittest" (most

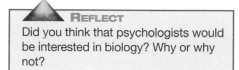

▲ **REFLECT**
Did you think that psychologists would be interested in biology? Why or why not?

---

[1]Formerly termed *social-learning theorists.*

▲ REFLECT

How would you define the *mind*? Why do some psychologists argue that it is fruitless to talk about people's minds?

Genes ▲ The basic building blocks of heredity.

Cognitive ▲ Having to do with mental processes such as sensation and perception, memory, intelligence, language, thought, and problem solving.

Humanism ▲ The philosophy and school of psychology that asserts that people are conscious, self-aware, and capable of free choice, self-fulfillment, and ethical behavior.

Existentialism ▲ The view that people are free and responsible for their own behavior.

adaptive) organisms manage to reach maturity and reproduce. For example, fish that swim faster or people who are naturally immune to certain diseases are more likely to survive and transmit their **genes** to future generations. Individuals die but species tend to evolve in adaptive directions. Evolutionary psychologists suggest that much human social behavior, such as aggressive behavior and mate selection, has a hereditary basis. People may be influenced by social rules, cultural factors, even personal choice, but evolutionary psychologists believe that inherited tendencies sort of whisper in people's ears and tend to move them in certain directions.

The biological perspective tends to focus on events that occur below the level of consciousness. The cognitive perspective is the essence of consciousness. *Question: What is the cognitive perspective?*

The Cognitive Perspective: Putting Psychology "In Mind"

Psychologists with a **cognitive** perspective venture into the realm of mental processes to understand human nature (Sperry, 1998). They investigate the ways in which we perceive and mentally represent the world, how we learn, remember the past, plan for the future, solve problems, form judgments, make decisions, and use language (Basic Behavioral Science Task Force, 1996a). Cognitive psychologists, in short, study those things we refer to as the *mind*.

The cognitive tradition has roots in Socrates' advice to "Know thyself" and in his suggested method of introspection. We also find cognitive psychology's roots in structuralism, functionalism, and Gestalt psychology, each of which, in its own way, addressed issues that are of interest to cognitive psychologists.

The Humanistic-Existential Perspective

The humanistic-existential perspective is related to Gestalt psychology and is cognitive in flavor. *Question: What is the humanistic-existential perspective?* Let us consider each of the parts of this perspective: *humanism* and *existentialism*. **Humanism** stresses the human capacity for self-fulfillment and the central roles of consciousness, self-awareness, and decision making. Humanistic psychology considers personal, or subjective experience to be the most important event in psychology. Humanists believe that self-awareness, experience, and choice permit us, to a large extent, to "invent ourselves" and our ways of relating to the world as we progress through life. Humanistic-existential psychologists stress the importance of subjective experience and assert that people have the freedom to make choices. Consciousness—our sense of being in the world—is seen as the force that unifies our personalities. **Existentialism** views people as free to choose and be responsible for choosing ethical conduct.

The Psychodynamic Perspective

In the 1940s and 1950s, Freud's psychodynamic theory dominated the practice of psychotherapy and was influential in scientific psychology and the arts. Most psychotherapists were psychodynamically oriented. Many renowned artists and writers consulted psychodynamic therapists as a way to liberate the expression of their unconscious ideas. Freud's influence continues to be felt, although it no longer dominates methods of psychotherapy.

Question: What is the role of psychoanalysis today? Contemporary psychologists who follow Freud are likely to call themselves *neoanalysts*. Neoanalysts such as Karen Horney and Erik Erikson focus less on unconscious processes and more on conscious choice and self-direction.

Many Freudian ideas are retained in some form by the population at large. For example, sometimes we have ideas or desires that seem unusual for us. We may say that it seems as if something is trying to get the better of us. In the Middle Ages, such thoughts and impulses were usually attributed to the devil or to demons. Dreams, likewise, were thought to enter us magically from the spirit world. Followers of Sigmund Freud tend to attribute dreams and unusual ideas or desires to unconscious processes within themselves.

Learning Perspectives

Many psychologists study the effects of experience on behavior. Learning, to them, is the essential factor in describing, explaining, predicting, and controlling behavior. The term *learning* has different meanings to psychologists of different persuasions, however. Some students of learning find roles for consciousness and insight. Others do not. This distinction is found among those who adhere to the behavioral and social-cognitive perspectives. *Question: What are the learning perspectives?*

For John B. Watson, behaviorism was an approach to life as well as a broad guideline for psychological research. Not only did Watson despair of measuring consciousness and mental processes in the laboratory, he also applied behavioral analysis to virtually all situations in his daily life. He viewed people as doing things because of their learning histories, their situations, and rewards rather than because of conscious choice.

Watson and other behaviorists emphasize environmental influences and the learning of habits through repetition and reinforcement. **Social-cognitive theorists** (previously termed *social-learning theorists*), in contrast, suggest that people can modify or even create their environments. They also grant cognition a key role. They note that people engage in intentional learning by observing others. Since the 1960s, social-cognitive theorists have gained influence in the areas of personality development, psychological disorders, and methods of therapy.

> ▲ **REFLECT**
> Do you learn by observing others? Is your learning intentional? How would you know?

The Sociocultural Perspective

The profession of psychology focuses mainly on the individual and is committed to the dignity of the individual. However, psychology students cannot understand people's behavior and mental processes without reference to their diversity (Basic Behavioral Science Task Force, 1996b). Studying perspectives other than their own helps students understand the role of a culture's beliefs, values, and attitudes in behavior and mental processes. It helps students perceive why people from diverse cultures behave and think in different ways, and how the science of psychology is enriched by addressing those differences (Denmark, 1998; Reid, 1994).

Question: What is the sociocultural perspective? The **sociocultural perspective** addresses many of the ways in which people differ from one another. It studies the influences of ethnicity, gender, culture, and socioeconomic status on behavior and mental processes (Allen, 1993; Lewis-Fernández & Kleinman, 1994). For example, what is often seen as healthful, self-assertive, outspoken behavior by most U.S. women may be interpreted as brazen behavior in Latino and Latina American or Asian American communities.

CLICK4™ *an essay assignment on psychology in the workplace.*

> ▲ **REFLECT**
> How does the sociocultural perspective help us understand behavior and mental processes? Why is knowledge of human diversity important to the dignity of the individual?

Ethnicity One kind of diversity involves people's ethnicity. Members of an **ethnic group** are united by their cultural heritage, race, language, and common history. The experiences of various ethnic groups in the United States highlight the impact of social, political, and economic factors on human behavior and development (Basic Behavioral Science Task Force, 1996b; Phinney, 1996).

The probing of human diversity enables students to appreciate the cultural heritages and historical problems of various ethnic groups. This textbook considers many psychological issues related to ethnicity, such as the representation of ethnic minority groups in psychological research studies, substance abuse among adolescents from various ethnic minority groups, bilingualism, ethnic differences in intelligence test scores, the prevalence of suicide among members of different ethnic groups, ethnic differences in vulnerability to physical problems and disorders ranging from obesity to hypertension and cancer, multicultural issues in the practice of psychotherapy, and prejudice.

Social-cognitive theory ▲ A school of psychology in the behaviorist tradition that includes cognitive factors in the explanation and prediction of behavior. Formerly termed *social-learning theory.*

Sociocultural perspective ▲ The view that focuses on the roles of ethnicity, gender, culture, and socioeconomic status in behavior and mental processes.

Ethnic group ▲ A group characterized by common features such as cultural heritage, history, race, and language.

The Sociocultural Perspective.

The United States is a mosaic of people from various ethnic backgrounds. The sociocultural perspective teaches that we cannot understand the hopes and problems of people from a particular ethnic group without understanding that group's history and cultural heritage. The sociocultural perspective helps us understand and appreciate the scope of behavior and mental processes.

Gender ▲ The state of being female or being male.

Gender   **Gender** is the state of being male or being female. Gender is not simply a matter of anatomic sex. It involves a complex web of cultural expectations and social roles that affect people's self-concepts and hopes and dreams as well as their behavior. How can sciences such as psychology and medicine hope to understand the particular viewpoints, qualities, and problems of women if most research is conducted with men and by men (Matthews et al., 1997)?

Just as members of ethnic minority groups have experienced prejudice, so too have women. Even much of the scientific research on gender roles and gender differences assumes that male behavior represents the norm (Ader & Johnson, 1994).

Our discussion of the sociocultural perspective naturally leads us to reflect on the roles of women and people from various racial and ethnic backgrounds in psychology.

REVIEW

(22) _____ -oriented psychologists study the links between behavior, the brain, hormones, and heredity. (23) _____ psychologists note that only the fittest organisms

reach maturity and reproduce, thereby transmitting their genes to future generations and causing species to evolve in adaptive directions. (24) _____ psychologists study the ways in which we perceive and mentally represent the world. (25) Humanistic-_____ psychologists stress the importance of self-awareness and people's freedom to make choices. Many contemporary psychoanalysts—neoanalysts—generally follow Freud but focus less on unconscious processes and more on people's capacity to make conscious choices. (26) _____-cognitive theorists are in the behaviorist tradition but also find roles for intentional learning and note that people can create or modify their environments. (27) The _____ perspective fosters the consideration of matters of ethnicity, gender, culture, and socioeconomic status in psychology.

Pulling It Together: How does the biological perspective differ from other perspectives in psychology? What is the value of the sociocultural perspective?

GENExITY GENDER, ETHNICITY, AND THE PROFESSION OF PSYCHOLOGY

Although the overwhelming majority of psychologists in the 1800s and early 1900s were European American males, women and people from various racial and ethnic backgrounds have made key contributions to the science of psychology in the past century. Let's consider some of the women.

Women in Psychology: Opening the Floodgates

Women have traditionally been channeled into domestic pursuits, regardless of their wishes as individuals. Not until relatively modern times were women generally considered suitable for higher education (and in many parts of the world women are still considered unsuited to education!). Women have attended college in the United States only since 1833, when Oberlin College opened its doors to women. Today, however, more than half of U.S. college students are women. Women today receive nearly three-quarters of the undergraduate degrees in psychology and two-thirds of the doctoral degrees (Kohout & Williams, 1999).

Question: What contributions have women made to psychology? There are interesting stories of particular women in psychology. Christine Ladd-Franklin (1847–1930) was born during an era in American history in which women were expected to remain at home and were excluded from careers in science (Minton, 2000). She nevertheless pursued a career in psychology, taught at Johns Hopkins and Columbia Universities, and formulated a theory of color vision. Margaret Floy Washburn (1871–1939) was the first woman to receive a Ph.D. in psychology. Washburn also wrote *The Animal Mind*, a work containing many ideas that would later become part of behaviorism.

Helen Bradford Thompson (1874–1947) was the first psychologist to study psychological gender differences. Her 1903 book *The Mental Traits of Sex* analyzed the performance of 25 women and 25 men on tests of intellect, emotional response, and sensation and perception (Milar, 2000). Thompson was ahead of her time in her conclusion that gender differences in these areas appeared to be strongly influenced by the social environment from early infancy through adulthood.

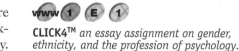

CLICK4™ *an essay assignment on gender, ethnicity, and the profession of psychology.*

CLICK4™ *a WebSearch activity on women and minorities in psychology.*

Kenneth B. Clark

Kenneth Bancroft Clark was born in the Panama Canal Zone in 1914, the son of West Indian parents. His mother brought her children to the United States for their education, and they settled in New York City's Harlem district. He earned his bachelor's degree from Howard University in Washington, DC, where he also met and married Mamie Phipps. The couple then earned their doctorates in psychology at Columbia University.

In the 1940s, the Clarks founded the Northside Center for Child Development and conducted research that showed the negative effects of school segregation on African American children. In one such study, African American children were shown white and brown dolls and asked to "Give me the pretty doll," or "Give me the doll that looks bad." Most children's choices showed that they preferred the white dolls over the brown ones. The Clarks concluded that the children had swallowed the larger society's preference for European Americans.

Kenneth Clark was an activist as well as a psychologist (Phillips, 2000). In the 1950s, he began working with the NAACP to end school segregation. Clark's research was cited by the Supreme Court when it overturned the "separate but equal" schools doctrine in 1954. Clark went on to study the quality of education and juvenile delinquency. He was among the first to recommend preschool classes, after-school programs, and community participation.

Ethnicity and Psychology

Question: What contributions to psychology have been made by people from various racial and ethnic groups? Numerous early psychologists came from different ethnic backgrounds. Back in 1901, Gilbert Haven Jones, an African American, received his Ph.D. in psychology in Germany. J. Henry Alston engaged in research on perception of heat and cold and was the first African American psychologist to be published in a major psychology journal (the year was 1920).

Today African Americans continue to have a powerful impact on the profession of psychology. For example, psychologist Robert Williams—sometimes referred to as the "father of Ebonics" (see profile in Chapter 10)—has offered us insight into language differences that are often found between European Americans and African Americans. Psychologist Claude Steele (profiled in Chapter 8) has shown that many African Americans self-destruct on intelligence tests because of *stereotype vulnerability*. That is, rather than focus on the test items, they worry about the stereotype, or widespread belief, that African Americans are not as bright as European Americans, and thereby hurt their own performance.

Latino and Latina American and Asian American psychologists have also made their mark. Jorge Sanchez, for example, was among the first to show how intelligence tests are culturally biased—to the disadvantage of Mexican American children. Asian American psychologist Stanley Sue has shown how discrimination may be connected with racial differences in intelligence and academic achievement.

Today two-thirds of the Ph.D.s in psychology are awarded to women (Kohout & Williams, 1999). African Americans make up 6% to 7% of first-year students in doctoral departments in psychology, and Latino and Latina Americans make up 5% of them (American Psychological Association Research Office, 2000). These percentages are far below their representation in the general population, unfortunately. About 1% of these students are Native American, and nearly 6% are Asian American. Psychology, like the societies in which it flourishes, is becoming increasingly diverse.

Put it another way: Psychology belongs to everyone.

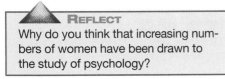

REFLECT

Why do you think that increasing numbers of women have been drawn to the study of psychology?

CLICK4™ *a quiz covering the first half of this chapter.*

REVIEW

Women and people from various ethnic groups have made key contributions to psychology. (28) Christine Ladd-_____ formulated a theory of color vision. (29) Mary Whiton _____ introduced the method of paired associates and discovered the primacy and recency effects. (30) Margaret Floy _____ wrote *The Animal Mind*. (31) Kenneth B. _____ influenced a key Supreme Court decision on desegregation. (32) Robert _____ is referred to as the father of Ebonics.

Pulling It Together: Summarize the history of women in psychology. Summarize the contributions of people from ethnic minority groups to psychology and society in general.

Psychology is the scientific study of behavior and mental processes. By now we have a sense of the various fields of psychology, the history of psychology, and the ways in which today's psychologists look at behavior and mental processes. Like other scientists, psychologists rely on research to seek answers to the questions that interest them. The next section follows through on some questions of interest to psychologists to demonstrate how research is conducted.

HOW PSYCHOLOGISTS STUDY BEHAVIOR AND MENTAL PROCESSES

CLICK4™ *journals published by the American Psychological Association.*

Consider some questions of interest to psychologists: Does alcohol cause aggression? Why do some people hardly ever think of food, whereas others are obsessed with it and snack all day long? Why do some unhappy people attempt suicide, whereas others seek ways of coping with their problems? Does having people of different ethnic backgrounds collaborate in their work serve to decrease or increase feelings of prejudice?

Many of us have expressed opinions on questions like these at one time or another. Different psychological theories also suggest a number of possible answers. Psychology is an *empirical* science, however. In an empirical science, assumptions about the behavior of cosmic rays, chemical compounds, cells, or people must be supported by evidence. Strong arguments, reference to authority figures, even tightly knit theories are not adequate as scientific evidence. Psychologists make it their business—literally and figuratively—to be skeptical.

Psychologists use research to study behavior and mental processes empirically. To undertake our study of research methods, let us recount some famous research undertaken at Yale University about four decades ago.

The Milgram Studies: Strange Happenings at Yale

CLICK4™ *Milgram's article, "A Study on Obedience."*

People are capable of boundless generosity and of hideous atrocities. Throughout history, people have sacrificed themselves for the welfare of their families, friends, and nations. Throughout history, people have maimed and destroyed other people to vent their rage or please their superiors.

Let us follow up on the negative side. Soldiers have killed civilians and raped women in occupied areas to obey the orders of their superiors or to win the approval of their comrades. Millions of Native Americans, Jews, Armenians, and Muslims have been slaughtered by people who were obeying the orders of officers.

How susceptible are people—how susceptible are you and I—to the demands of authority figures such as military officers? Is there something unusual or abnormal about people who follow orders and inflict pain and suffering on their fellow human beings? Are they very much unlike you and me? Or *are* they you and me?

It is easy to imagine that something must be terribly wrong with people who would hurt a stranger without provocation. There must be something abnormal about people who would slaughter innocents. But these are assumptions, and scientists are skeptical of assumptions. Psychologist Stanley Milgram wondered whether normal people would comply with authority figures who made immoral demands. But rather than speculate on the issue, he undertook a series of classic experiments at Yale University that have become known as the Milgram studies on obedience.

In an early phase of his work, Milgram (1963) placed ads in New Haven (Connecticut) newspapers for people who would be willing to participate in studies on learning and memory. He enlisted 40 people ranging in age from 20 to 50—teachers, engineers, laborers, salespeople, people who had not completed elementary school, people with graduate degrees.

Let's suppose that you have answered the ad. You show up at the university in exchange for a reasonable fee ($4.50, which in the early 1960s might easily fill your gas tank) and to satisfy your own curiosity. You may be impressed. After all, Yale is a venerable institution that dominates the city. You are no less impressed by the elegant labs, where you meet a distinguished behavioral scientist dressed in a white coat and another person who has responded to the ad. The scientist explains that the purpose of the experiment is to study the *effects of punishment on learning.* The experiment requires a "teacher" and a "learner." By chance, you are appointed the teacher and the other recruit the learner.

You, the scientist, and the learner enter a laboratory room containing a threatening chair with dangling straps. The scientist straps the learner in. The learner expresses some

FIGURE 1.4 The "Aggression Machine."
In the Milgram studies on obedience to authority, pressing levers on the "aggression machine" was the operational definition of aggression.

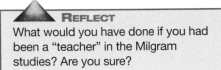

▲ REFLECT
What would you have done if you had been a "teacher" in the Milgram studies? Are you sure?

"Learner"

"Teacher"

FIGURE 1.5 The Experimental Set-Up in the Milgram Studies.
When the "learner" makes an error, the experimenter prods the "teacher" to deliver a painful electric shock.

concern, but this is, after all, for the sake of science. And this is Yale University, isn't it? What could happen to a person at Yale?

You follow the scientist to an adjacent room, from which you are to do your "teaching." This teaching promises to have an impact. You are to punish the learner's errors by pressing levers marked from 15 to 450 volts on a fearsome-looking console (see Figure 1.4). Labels describe 28 of the 30 levers as running the gamut from "Slight Shock" to "Danger: Severe Shock." The last two levers are simply labeled "XXX." Just in case you have no idea what electric shock feels like, the scientist gives you a sample 45-volt shock. It stings. You pity the person who might receive more.

Your learner is expected to learn pairs of words, which are to be read from a list. After hearing the list once, the learner is to produce the word that pairs with the stimulus word from a list of four alternatives. This is done by pressing a switch that lights one of four panels in your room. If it is the correct panel, you proceed to the next stimulus word. If not, you are to deliver an electric shock. With each error, you are to increase the voltage of the shock (Figure 1.5).

You probably have some misgivings. Electrodes have been strapped to the learner's wrists, and the scientist has applied electrode paste "to avoid blisters and burns." You have also been told that the shocks will cause "no permanent tissue damage," although they might be extremely painful. Still, the learner is going along. And after all, this is Yale.

The learner answers some items correctly and then makes some errors. With mild concern you press the levers up through 45 volts. You've tolerated that much yourself. Then a few more mistakes are made. You press the 60-volt lever, then 75. The learner makes another mistake. You pause and look at the scientist, who is reassuring: "Although the shocks may be painful, there is no permanent tissue damage, so please go on." The learner makes more errors, and soon you are up to a shock of 300 volts. But now the learner is pounding on the other side of the wall! Your chest tightens and you begin to perspire. "Damn science and the $4.50!" you think. You hesitate and the scientist says, "The experiment requires that you continue." After the delivery of the next stimulus word, the learner chooses no answer at all. What are you to do? "Wait for 5 to 10 seconds," the scientist instructs, "and then treat no answer as a wrong answer." But after the next shock the pounding on the wall resumes! Now your heart is racing, and you are convinced you are causing extreme pain and discomfort. Is it possible that no lasting damage is being done? Is the experiment that important, after all? What to

Experimenter

do? You hesitate again, and the scientist says, "It is absolutely essential that you continue." His voice is very convincing. "You have no other choice," he says, "you *must* go on." You can barely think straight, and for some unaccountable reason you feel laughter rising in your throat. Your finger shakes above the lever. *What are you to do?*

Milgram (1963, 1974) found out what most people in his sample would do. The sample was a cross-section of the male population of New Haven. Of the 40 men in this phase of his research, only 5 refused to go beyond the 300-volt level, the level at which the learner first pounded the wall. Nine other "teachers" defied the scientist within the 300-volt range. But 65% of the participants complied with the scientist throughout the series, believing they were delivering 450-volt, XXX-rated shocks.

Were these participants unfeeling? Not at all. Milgram was impressed by their signs of stress. They trembled, they stuttered, they bit their lips. They groaned, they sweated, they dug their fingernails into their flesh. Some had fits of laughter, although laughter was inappropriate. One salesperson's laughter was so convulsive that he could not continue with the experiment.

We return to the Milgram studies later in the chapter. They are a rich mine of information about human nature. They are also useful for our discussions of research issues such as replication, the experimental method, and ethics.

The Scientific Method: Putting Ideas to the Test

Question: What is the scientific method? The scientific method is an organized way of using experience and testing ideas in order to expand and refine knowledge. Psychologists do not necessarily follow the steps of the scientific method as we might follow a cookbook recipe. However, their research endeavors are guided by certain principles.

Psychologists usually begin by *formulating a research question.* Research questions can have many sources. Our daily experiences, psychological theory, even folklore all help generate questions for research. Consider some questions that may arise from daily experience. Daily experience in using day-care centers may motivate us to conduct research on whether day care affects the development of social skills or the bonds of attachment between children and mothers.

Or consider questions that might arise from psychological theory (see Figure 1.6). Social-cognitive principles of observational learning may prompt research on the effects of TV violence. Sigmund Freud's psychoanalytic theory may prompt research on whether the verbal expression of feelings of anger helps relieve feelings of depression.

Research questions may also arise from common knowledge. Consider familiar adages such as "Misery loves company," "Opposites attract," and "Seeing is believing." Psychologists may ask, *Does* misery love company? *Do* opposites attract? *Can* people believe what they see?

A research question may be studied as a question or reworded as a hypothesis (see Figure 1.6). A **hypothesis** is a specific statement about behavior or mental processes that is tested through research. One hypothesis about day care might be that preschoolers who are placed in day care will acquire greater social skills in relating to peers than preschoolers who are cared for in the home. A hypothesis about TV violence might be that elementary school children who watch more violent TV shows tend to behave more aggressively toward their peers. A hypothesis that addresses Freudian theory might be that verbally expressing feelings of anger will decrease feelings of depression.

Psychologists next examine the research question or *test the hypothesis* through controlled methods such as the experiment. For example, we could introduce children who are in day care and children who are not to a new child in a college child-research center and observe how children in each group interact with the new acquaintance.

Psychologists draw conclusions about their research questions or the accuracy of their hypotheses on the basis of their observations or findings. When their observations do not bear out their hypotheses, they may modify the theories from which the hypotheses were derived (see Figure 1.6). Research findings often suggest refinements to psychological theories and, consequently, new avenues of research.

In our research on day care, we would probably find that children in day care show greater social skills than children who are cared for in the home (Clarke-Stewart, 1991). We would probably also find that more aggressive children spend more time watching TV violence. Research on the effectiveness of psychoanalytic forms of therapy is usually based on case studies.

As psychologists draw conclusions from research evidence, they are guided by principles of critical thinking. For example, they try not to confuse correlations between findings with cause and effect. Although more aggressive children apparently spend more time watching violent TV shows, it may be erroneous to conclude from this kind of evidence that TV violence *causes* aggressive behavior. Perhaps a **selection factor** is at work—because the children studied choose (select) for themselves what they will watch. Perhaps more aggressive children are more likely than less aggressive children to tune in to violent TV shows.

To better understand the effects of the selection factor, consider a study on the relationship between exercise and health. Imagine that we were to compare a group of people who exercised regularly with a group of people who did not. We might find that the exercisers were physically healthier than the couch potatoes. But could we conclude that exercise is a causal factor in good health? Perhaps not. The selection factor—the fact that one group chose to exercise and the other did not—could also explain the results. Perhaps healthy people are more likely to *choose* to exercise.

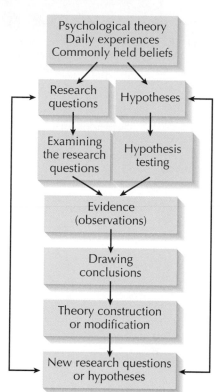

FIGURE 1.6 The Scientific Method.
The scientific method is a systematic way of organizing and expanding scientific knowledge. Daily experiences, common beliefs, and scientific observations all contribute to the development of theories. Psychological theories explain observations and lead to hypotheses about behavior and mental processes. Observations can confirm the theory or lead to its refinement or abandonment.

▲ REFLECT
Do you believe that it is possible to understand people from a scientific perspective? Why or why not?

Hypothesis ▲ In psychology, a specific statement about behavior or mental processes that is tested through research.
Selection factor ▲ A source of bias that may occur in research findings when participants are allowed to choose for themselves a certain treatment in a scientific study.

CLICK4™ *information about the scientific method from the perspective of physics and psychology professors.*

Some psychologists include publication of research reports in professional journals as a crucial part of the scientific method. Researchers are obligated to provide enough details of their work that others will be able to repeat or **replicate** it to see whether the findings hold up over time and with different participants. Publication of research also permits the scientific community at large to evaluate the methods and conclusions of other scientists.

Samples and Populations: Hitting the Target Population

Consider a piece of history that never quite happened: The Republican candidate Alf Landon defeated the incumbent president, Franklin D. Roosevelt, in 1936. Or at least Landon did so in a poll conducted by a popular magazine of the day, the *Literary Digest*. In the actual election, however, Roosevelt routed Landon by a landslide of 11 million votes. How, then, could the *Digest* predict a Landon victory? How was so great a discrepancy possible?

The *Digest*, you see, had surveyed voters by phone. Today telephone sampling is a widely practiced and reasonably legitimate polling technique. But the *Digest* poll was taken during the Great Depression, when people who had telephones were much wealthier than those who did not. People at higher income levels are also more likely to vote Republican. No surprise, then, that the overwhelming majority of those sampled said they would vote for Landon.

Question: How do psychologists use samples to represent populations? The *Digest* poll failed because of its method of sampling. Samples must be drawn so that they accurately *represent* the population they are intended to reflect. Only representative samples allow us to **generalize**—or *extend*—our findings from research samples to populations.

In surveys such as that conducted by the *Literary Digest*, and in other research methods, the individuals who are studied are referred to as a **sample.** A sample is a segment of a **population** (the group that is targeted for study). Psychologists and other scientists need to ensure that the people they observe *represent* their target population, such as U.S. voters, and not subgroups such as southern Californians or European American members of the middle class.

DIVERSITY　*Problems in Generalizing From Psychological Research*

> All *generalizations are dangerous, even this one*.
>
> *Alexandre Dumas*

Many factors must be considered in interpreting the accuracy of the results of scientific research. One is the nature of the research sample.

Milgram's initial research on obedience was limited to a sample of New Haven men. Could he generalize his findings to other men or to women? Would college students, who are considered to be independent thinkers, show more defiance? A replication of Milgram's study with a sample of Yale men yielded similar results. What about women, who are supposedly less aggressive than men? In subsequent research, women, too, administered shocks to the learners. All this took place in a nation that values independence and free will.

Later in the chapter we consider research in which the participants were drawn from a population of college men who were social drinkers. That is, they tended to drink at social gatherings but not when alone. Who do college men represent, other than themselves? To whom can we extend, or generalize, the results? For one thing, the results may not extend to women, not even to college women. In the chapter on consciousness, for example, we will learn that alcohol goes more quickly to women's heads than to men's.

College men also tend to be younger and more intelligent than the general adult population. We cannot be certain that the findings extend to older men of average intelligence, although it seems reasonable to assume they do. Social drinkers may also differ biologically and psychologically from alcoholics, who have difficulty controlling their

---

▲ **REFLECT**

Are you surprised that women in the Milgram study obeyed orders and shocked "learners" just as men did? Why or why not?

Replicate ▲ Repeat, reproduce, copy.
Generalize ▲ To extend from the particular to the general; to apply observations based on a sample to a population.
Sample ▲ Part of a population.
Population ▲ A complete group of organisms or events.

drinking. Nor can we be certain that college social drinkers represent people who do not drink at all.

By and large, we must also question whether findings of research with men can be generalized to women (Ader & Johnson, 1994), and whether research with European American men can be extended to members of ethnic minority groups. For example, personality tests completed by European Americans and by African Americans may need to be interpreted in diverse ways if accurate conclusions are to be drawn. The well-known Kinsey studies on sexual behavior (Kinsey et al., 1948, 1953) did not adequately represent African Americans, poor people, older people, and numerous other groups.

Random and Stratified Sampling

One way to achieve a representative sample is by means of **random sampling.** In a random sample, each member of a population has an equal chance of being selected to participate. Researchers can also use a **stratified sample,** which is selected so that identified subgroups in the population are represented proportionately in the sample. For instance, 13% of the American population is African American. A stratified sample would thus be 13% African American. As a practical matter, a large randomly selected sample will show reasonably accurate stratification. A random sample of 1,500 people will represent the general U.S. population reasonably well. A haphazardly drawn sample of 20 million, however, might not.

Large-scale magazine surveys of sexual behavior have asked readers to fill out and return questionnaires. Although many thousands of readers completed the questionnaires and sent them in, did they represent the general U.S. population? Probably not. These studies and similar ones may have been influenced by **volunteer bias.** People who offer or volunteer to participate in research studies differ systematically from people who do not. In the case of research on sexual behavior, volunteers may represent subgroups of the population—or of readers of the magazines in question—who are willing to disclose intimate information (Rathus et al., 2000). Volunteers may also be more interested in research than other people, as well as have more spare time. How might such volunteers differ from the population at large? How might such differences slant or bias the research outcomes?

Methods of Observation: The Better to See You With

Many people consider themselves experts on behavior and mental processes. How many times, for example, have grandparents told us what they have seen in their lives and what it means about human nature?

Indeed, we see much during our lifetimes. Our personal observations tend to be fleeting and uncontrolled, however. We sift through experience for the things that interest us. We often ignore the obvious because it does not fit our assumptions about the way things ought to be. Scientists, however, have devised more controlled ways of observing others. *Question: What methods of observation are used by psychologists?* In this section we consider three methods of observation widely used by psychologists and other behavioral scientists: the case study, survey, and naturalistic observation methods.

Case Study

We begin with the case study method because our own informal ideas about human nature tend to be based on **case studies,** or information we collect about individuals and small groups. But most of us gather our information haphazardly. We often see only what we want to see. Unscientific accounts of people's behavior are referred to as *anecdotes.* Psychologists attempt to gather information about individuals more carefully.

Sigmund Freud developed psychodynamic theory largely on the basis of case studies. He studied the people who sought his help in great depth, seeking the factors that seemed to contribute to certain patterns of behavior. He followed some people for many years, meeting with them several times a week.

Case studies are also often used to investigate rare occurrences, as in the case of "Eve." Eve was an example of a person with multiple personalities (technically termed *dissociative identity disorder*). "Eve White" was a mousy, well-intentioned woman who had

www 1 E 3
CLICK4™ *an opportunity to design an experiment to test the effectiveness of sex education.*

▲ **REFLECT**
Would a random sample of students from your own college or university represent the general U.S. population? Why or why not?

▲ **REFLECT**
What methods of observation do you use when you try to "figure out" other people? Are your methods scientific? Why or why not?

Random sample ▲ A sample drawn so that each member of a population has an equal chance of being selected to participate.

Stratified sample ▲ A sample drawn so that identified subgroups in the population are represented proportionately in the sample. How can stratified sampling be carried out to ensure that a sample represents the ethnic diversity we find in the population at large?

Volunteer bias ▲ A source of bias or error in research reflecting the prospect that people who offer to participate in research studies differ systematically from people who do not.

Case study ▲ A carefully drawn biography that may be obtained through interviews, questionnaires, and psychological tests.

CD 1 SA 1

CLICK4™ *a self-assessment: Do You Really Say What You Think?*

▲ REFLECT
Have you read the results of a survey or a poll in a popular magazine or on-line? Were they representative of the general population? Why or why not?

two other "personalities" living inside her. One of them was "Eve Black," a promiscuous personality who emerged now and then to take control of her behavior.

Case studies can provide compelling portraits of individuals, but they also have some sources of inaccuracy. For example, there are gaps and factual inaccuracies in people's memories (Azar, 1997; Brewin et al., 1993). People may also distort their pasts to please the interviewer or because they want to remember things in certain ways. Interviewers may also have certain expectations and may subtly encourage participants to fill in gaps in ways that are consistent with these expectations. Bandura (1986) notes, for example, that psychoanalysts have been criticized for guiding people who seek their help into viewing their own lives from the psychodynamic perspective. No wonder, then, that many people provide "evidence" that is consistent with psychodynamic theory. However, interviewers and other kinds of researchers who hold *any* theoretical viewpoint run the risk of indirectly prodding people into saying what they want to hear.

The Survey   In the good old days, we had to wait until the wee hours of the morning to learn the results of local and national elections. Throughout the evening and early morning hours, suspense would build as ballots from distant neighborhoods and states were tallied. Nowadays, we are barely settled with an after-dinner cup of coffee on election night when reporters announce that a computer has examined the ballots of a "scientifically selected sample" and predicted the next president of the United States. All of this may occur with less than 1% of the vote tallied.

Just as computers and pollsters predict election results and report national opinion on the basis of scientifically selected samples, psychologists conduct **surveys** to learn about behavior and mental processes that cannot be observed in the natural setting or studied experimentally. Psychologists conducting surveys may employ questionnaires and interviews or examine public records. One of the great advantages of the survey is that by distributing questionnaires and analyzing answers with a computer, psychologists can study many thousands of people at a time.

Alfred Kinsey of Indiana University and his colleagues published two surveys of sexual behavior, based on interviews, that shocked the nation. These were *Sexual Behavior in the Human Male* (1948) and *Sexual Behavior in the Human Female* (1953). Kinsey reported that masturbation was virtually universal in his sample of men at a time when masturbation was still widely thought to impair health. He also reported that about 1 woman in 3 who was still single at age 25 had engaged in premarital intercourse.

Surveys, like case studies, have various sources of inaccuracy. People may recall their behavior inaccurately or purposefully misrepresent it. Some people try to ingratiate themselves with their interviewers by answering in what they perceive to be the socially desirable direction. The Kinsey studies all relied on male interviewers, for example. It has been speculated that female interviewees might have been more open and honest with female interviewers. Similar problems may occur when interviewers and the people surveyed are from different ethnic or socioeconomic backgrounds. Other people may falsify their attitudes and exaggerate their problems in order to draw attention to themselves or intentionally foul up the results.

Consider some examples of survey measurement errors caused by inaccurate self-reports of behavior (Barringer, 1993). If people brushed their teeth as often as they claimed, and used the amount of toothpaste they indicated, three times as much toothpaste would be sold in the United States as is actually sold. People also appear to overreport church attendance and to underreport abortions (Barringer, 1993). Why do you think this is so?

Naturalistic Observation   You use **naturalistic observation**—that is, you observe people in their natural habitats—every day. So do psychologists. The next time you opt for a fast-food burger lunch, look around. Pick out slender people and overweight people and observe whether they eat their burgers and fries differently. Do the overweight people eat more rapidly? Chew less frequently? Leave less food on their plates? Psychologists have used this method to study the eating habits of normal weight and overweight people. In fact, while you're at McDonald's, if you notice people peering over

Survey ▲ A method of scientific investigation in which a large sample of people answer questions about their attitudes or behavior.

Naturalistic observation ▲ A scientific method in which organisms are observed in their natural environments.

sunglasses and occasionally tapping the head of a partly concealed microphone, perhaps they are recording their observations of other people's eating habits.

Naturalistic observation has the advantage of allowing psychologists and other scientists to observe behavior where it happens, or "in the field." In doing so, researchers use *unobtrusive* measures to avoid interfering with the behaviors they are observing. For example, Jane Goodall has observed the behavior of chimpanzees in their natural environment to learn about their social behavior, sexual behavior, use of tools, and other facts of chimp life. Her observations have shown us that (1) we were incorrect to think that only humans use tools; and (2) kissing, as a greeting, is apparently used by chimpanzees as well as by humans (Goodall & Peterson, 2000).

The Naturalistic-Observation Method.
Jane Goodall has observed the behavior of chimpanzees in the field, "where it happens." She has found that chimps use sticks to grub for food and that they apparently kiss each other as a social greeting. Scientists who use the naturalistic-observation method try not to interfere with the animals or people they observe, even though this sometimes means allowing an animal to be mistreated by other animals or to die from a curable illness.

Correlation: On How Things Go Together — Or Not

Are people with higher intelligence more likely to do well in school? Are people with a stronger need for achievement likely to climb higher up the corporate ladder? What is the relationship between stress and health?

Such questions are often answered by means of the correlational method. *Question: What is the correlational method?* Correlation follows observation. By using the correlational method, psychologists investigate whether observed behavior or a measured trait is related to, or correlated with, another. Consider the variables of intelligence and academic performance. These variables are assigned numbers such as intelligence test scores and academic averages. Then the numbers are mathematically related and expressed as a **correlation coefficient.** A correlation coefficient is a number that varies between $+1.00$ and -1.00.

Studies report **positive correlations** between intelligence test scores and academic achievement, as measured, for example, by grade point averages. Generally speaking, the higher people score on intelligence tests, the better their academic performance is likely to be. The scores attained on intelligence tests tend to be positively correlated (about $+0.60$ to $+0.70$) with academic achievement (see Figure 1.7). But factors *other* than performance on intelligence tests also contribute to academic success. These include achievement motivation, adjustment, and common sense (Collier, 1994; Sternberg et al., 1995).

There is a **negative correlation** between stress and health. As the amount of stress affecting us increases, the functioning of our immune system decreases. Under high levels of stress, many people show poorer health.

Correlational research may suggest but does not prove cause and effect. For instance, it may seem logical to assume that high intelligence makes it possible for children to profit from education. Research has also shown, however, that education contributes to higher scores on intelligence tests. Preschoolers who are placed in stimulating Head Start programs later attain higher scores on intelligence tests than age-mates who did not have this experience. The relationship between intelligence and academic performance may not be as simple as you might think. What of the link between stress and health? Does stress impair health, or is it possible that people in poorer health encounter more stress? Figure 1.8 considers the meaning of the correlation between academic grades and delinquency.

The Experimental Method: Trying Things Out

The people who signed up for the Milgram studies participated in an elaborate experiment. *Question: What is the experimental method?* In an experiment, the participants received a treatment. Milgram's participants received an intricate *treatment*—one that involved a well-equipped research laboratory. The experiment also involved deception. Milgram had even foreseen participants' objections to the procedure. He had

▲ REFLECT
What kinds of correlations (positive or negative) would you expect to find among behavior patterns such as the following: Churchgoing and crime? Language ability and musical ability? Level of education and incidence of teenage pregnancy? Grades in school and delinquency? Why?

CLICK4™ *a video on an experimental design to test whether marijuana causes memory loss.*

Correlation coefficient ▲ A number between $+1.00$ to -1.00 that expresses the strength and direction (positive or negative) of the relationship between two variables.
Positive correlation ▲ A relationship between variables in which one variable increases as the other also increases.
Negative correlation ▲ A relationship between two variables in which one variable increases as the other decreases.

FIGURE 1.7   Positive and Negative Correlations.

When there is a positive correlation between variables, as there is between intelligence and achievement, one increases as the other increases. By and large, the higher people score on intelligence tests, the better their academic performance is likely to be, as in the diagram to the left. (Each dot represents an individual's intelligence test score and grade point average.) But there is a negative correlation between stress and health. As the amount of stress we experience increases, the functioning of our immune system tends to decrease. Correlational research may suggest but does not demonstrate cause and effect.

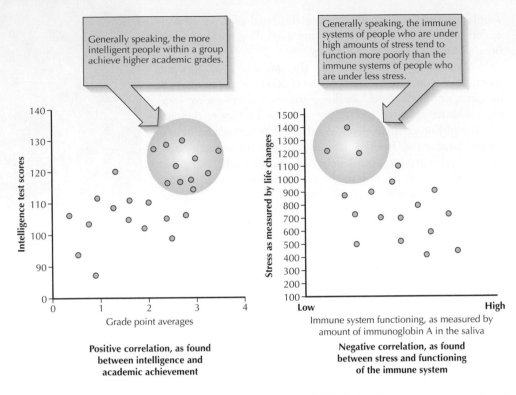

Generally speaking, the more intelligent people within a group achieve higher academic grades.

Generally speaking, the immune systems of people who are under high amounts of stress tend to function more poorly than the immune systems of people who are under less stress.

Positive correlation, as found between intelligence and academic achievement

Negative correlation, as found between stress and functioning of the immune system

therefore conceived standardized statements that his assistants would use when participants balked—for example: "Although the shocks may be painful, there is no permanent tissue damage, so please go on." "The experiment requires that you continue." "It is absolutely essential that you continue." "You have no other choice, you *must* go on." These statements, the bogus "aggression machine," the use of the "learner" (who was actually a confederate of the experimenter)—all these were part of the experimental treatment.

Although we can raise many questions about the Milgram studies, most psychologists agree that the preferred method for answering questions about cause and effect is the experiment. In an **experiment,** a group of participants obtains a **treatment,** such as a dose of alcohol, a change in room temperature, perhaps an injection of a drug. The participants are then observed carefully to determine whether the treatment makes a difference in their behavior. Does alcohol alter the ability to take tests, for example? What about differences in room temperatures and level of background noise?

Experiments are used whenever possible because they allow psychologists to control the experiences of participants and draw conclusions about cause and effect. A psychologist may theorize that alcohol leads to aggression because it reduces fear of consequences or because it energizes the activity levels of drinkers. She or he may then hypothesize that a treatment in which participants receive a specified dosage of alcohol will lead to increases in aggression. Let us follow the example of the effects of alcohol on aggression to further our understanding of the experimental method.

Independent and Dependent Variables   In an experiment to determine whether alcohol causes aggression, participants would be given an amount of alcohol and its effects would be measured. In this case, alcohol is an **independent variable.** The presence of an independent variable is manipulated by the experimenters so that its effects may be determined. The independent variable of alcohol may be administered at different levels, or doses, from none or very little to enough to cause intoxication or drunkenness.

The measured results, or outcomes, in an experiment are called **dependent variables.** The presence of dependent variables presumably depends on the independent variables. In an experiment to determine whether alcohol influences aggression, aggressive behavior would be a dependent variable. Other dependent variables of interest might

Experiment ▲ A scientific method that seeks to confirm cause-and-effect relationships by introducing independent variables and observing their effects on dependent variables.
Treatment ▲ In experiments, a condition received by participants so that its effects may be observed.
Independent variable ▲ A condition in a scientific study that is manipulated so that its effects may be observed.
Dependent variable ▲ A measure of an assumed effect of an independent variable.

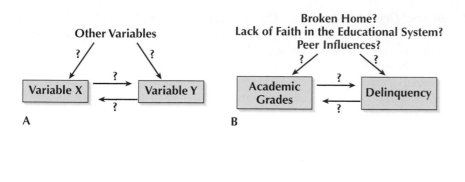

FIGURE 1.8 Correlational Relationships, Cause, and Effect.
Correlational relationships may suggest but do not demonstrate cause and effect. In part A, there is a correlation between variables X and Y. Does this mean that either variable X causes variable Y or that variable Y causes variable X? Not necessarily. Other factors could affect both variables X and Y. Consider the example of academic grades (variable X) and juvenile delinquency (variable Y) in part B. There is a negative correlation between the two. In what ways could we interpret the correlation?

include sexual arousal, visual–motor coordination, and performance on intellectual tasks such as defining words or doing numerical computations.

In an experiment on the relationships between temperature and aggression, temperature would be an independent variable and aggressive behavior would be a dependent variable. We could set temperatures from below freezing to blistering hot, and study their effects. We could also use a second independent variable such as social provocation. That is, we could insult some participants but not others. This method would allow us to study the ways in which two independent variables—temperature and social provocation—affect aggression, singly and together.

Experimental and Control Groups

Ideal experiments use experimental and control groups. Participants in **experimental groups** obtain the treatment. Members of **control groups** do not. Every effort is made to ensure that all other conditions are held constant for both groups. This method enhances the researchers' ability to draw conclusions about cause and effect. The researchers can be more confident that outcomes of the experiment are caused by the treatments and not by chance factors or chance fluctuations in behavior.

In an experiment on the effects of alcohol on aggression, members of the experimental group would ingest alcohol and members of the control group would not. In a complex experiment, different experimental groups might ingest different dosages of alcohol and be exposed to different types of social provocations.

Experimental groups ▲ In experiments, groups whose members obtain the treatment.
Control groups ▲ In experiments, groups whose members do not obtain the treatment, while other conditions are held constant.

What Are the Effects of Alcohol?

Psychologists have conducted numerous studies to determine the effects of alcohol. Questions have been raised about the soundness of research in which people know that they have drunk alcohol. Why is this research questioned?

Blinds and Double Blinds   One experiment on the effects of alcohol on aggression (Boyatzis, 1974) reported that men at parties where beer and liquor were served acted more aggressively than men at parties where only soft drinks were served. But participants in the experimental group *knew* they had drunk alcohol, and those in the control group *knew* they had not. Aggression that appeared to result from alcohol might not have reflected drinking per se. Instead, it might have reflected the participants' *expectations* about the effects of alcohol. People tend to act in stereotypical ways when they believe they have been drinking alcohol. For instance, men tend to become less anxious in social situations, more aggressive, and more sexually aroused.

A **placebo,** or "sugar pill," often results in the kind of behavior that people expect. Physicians sometimes give placebos to demanding, but healthy, people, many of whom then report that they feel better. When participants in psychological experiments are given placebos—such as tonic water—but think they have drunk alcohol, we can conclude that changes in their behavior stem from their beliefs about alcohol, not from the alcohol itself.

Well-designed experiments control for the effects of expectations by creating conditions under which participants are unaware of, or **blind** to, the treatment (Day & Altman, 2000). Yet researchers may also have expectations. They may, in effect, be "rooting for" a certain treatment. For instance, tobacco company executives may wish to show that cigarette smoking is harmless. In such cases, it is useful if the people measuring the experimental outcomes are unaware of which participants have received the treatment. Studies in which neither the participants nor the experimenters know who has obtained the treatment are called **double-blind studies.**

The Food and Drug Administration requires double-blind studies before it allows the marketing of new drugs. The drug and the placebo look and taste alike. Experimenters assign the drug or placebo to participants at random. Neither the participants nor the observers know who is taking the drug and who is taking the placebo. After the final measurements have been made, a neutral panel (a group of people who have no personal stake in the outcome of the study) judges whether the effects of the drug differed from those of the placebo.

In one double-blind study on the effects of alcohol, Alan Lang and his colleagues (1975) pretested a highball of vodka and tonic water to determine that it could not be discriminated by taste from tonic water alone. They recruited college men who described themselves as social drinkers to participate in the study. Some of the men drank vodka and tonic water. Others drank tonic water only. Of the men who drank vodka, half were misled into believing they had drunk tonic water only (Figure 1.9). Of those who drank tonic water only, half were misled into believing their drink contained vodka. Thus, half the participants were blind to their treatment. Experimenters who measured the men's aggressive responses were also blind concerning which particpants had drunk vodka.

The research team found that men who believed that they had drunk vodka responded more aggressively to a provocation than men who believed that they had drunk tonic water only. The actual content of the drink was immaterial. That is, men who had actually drunk alcohol acted no more aggressively than men who had drunk tonic water

▲ REFLECT

Can you devise a method in which researchers would use placebos and double blinds to investigate the effects of a new drug on the urge to smoke cigarettes?

Placebo ▲ A bogus treatment that has the appearance of being genuine.

Blind ▲ In experimental terminology, unaware of whether or not one has received a treatment.

Double-blind study ▲ A study in which neither the participants nor the observers know who has received the treatment.

FIGURE 1.9   The Experimental Conditions in the Lang Study.
The taste of vodka cannot be discerned when vodka is mixed with tonic water. For this reason, it was possible for participants in the Lang study on the effects of alcohol to be kept "blind" as to whether or not they had actually drunk alcohol. Blind studies allow psychologists to control for the effects of participants' expectations.

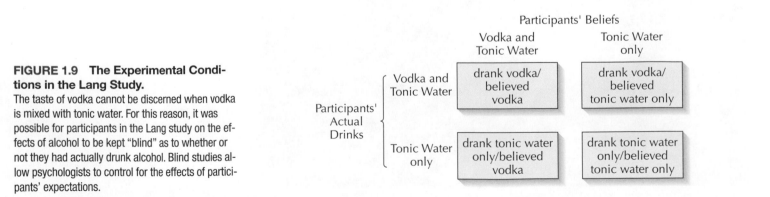

only. The results of the Lang study differ dramatically from those reported by Boyatzis, perhaps because the Boyatzis study did not control for the effects of expectations or beliefs about alcohol.

The nearby "Psychology and Modern Life" feature points out that not all psychology experiments are run in the laboratory. Today, in fact, a number of them are run online.

CLICK4™ *information about how to recognize psychological research.*

REVIEW

The scientific method is an organized way of expanding and refining knowledge. (33) Scientists often test a specific statement, or _____, about behavior or mental processes. (34) Samples must accurately represent the target _____. (35) In a _____ sample, each member of a population has an equal chance of being selected to participate. (36) A _____ sample is drawn so that identified subgroups in the population are represented proportionately in the sample. (37) A _____ study is a carefully drawn biography. (38) In the _____, a large sample of people answer questions about their attitudes or behavior. (39) The _____-observation method observes individuals in their natural habitats. (40) The _____ method reveals whether behaviors or traits are related to others. (41) Correlational research does not reveal _____ and effect. (42) An _____ is conducted in an effort to determine cause and effect. (43) The _____ variable is manipulated by the experimenters so that its effects may be determined. (44) Ideal experiments use experimental and _____ groups. (45) Well-designed experiments control for the effects of expectations by creating conditions under which participants are unaware of, or _____ to, the treatment they have received.

Pulling It Together: Explain the advantages and disadvantages of the various research methods presented in this section.

CLICK4™ *an opportunity to participate in an online research study.*

Psychology and Modern Life

Research Online

Once upon a time, Ken McGraw's University of Mississippi students had to wait their turn to use the psych lab's outdated computer. When their turn came, usually late on a Friday afternoon, they had to work in pairs because of lack of funds for equipment. The dinosaur computer would slowly chew the data and freeze from time to time.

But now, with their Internet site, PsychExps (**www.olemiss.edu/ psychexps/**), students can rapidly perform experiments on the World Wide Web—night or day, in the computer lab or in their dorm room (Azar, 2000; Murray, 1998). If the class is conducting an experiment on word recognition, the Web site efficiently records individual data and analyzes the results.

Using Web sites such as these, students and researchers anywhere can create and run their own online psychology experiments (Birnbaum, 2000). McGraw notes that "Data can be collected simultaneously

from as many people as choose to log on. This is a real benefit to students who are trying to cram an independent research project, like a senior thesis, into a single 15-week semester. Rather than spend the bulk of their time on data collection, they can spend it where it matters—on analysis and writing their report" (Murray, 1998).

The PsychExps Web site uses Macromedia's Authorware™ to develop and deliver programs on the Web. McGraw created and posted experiments for anybody to use. A Web site created by David Eckerman of the University of North Carolina and Dan Ariely of MIT also offers Authorware programs for psychology experiments (**web.mit.edu/ariely/www/psychlab/**). Gary Bradshaw of the University of Illinois created Internet Psychology Lab (**kahuna.psych.uiuc.edu/ipl**), which has online demonstrations in perception and cognition.

Users of PsychExps can use basic psychology experiments in areas such as facial recognition, mental rotation, judgment of the passage of time, and memory of musical pitches. The pitches experiment enables students to discern the similarity of various tones. University of Indiana psychologist David Huber had students try tasks with friends, including the Stroop Divided Field Experiment, which measures how long it takes people to name the color in which a word is printed, such as green, when the word labels another color, like "red." The students formed hypotheses and accumulated the data. Huber reports, "They felt ownership of the experiment because they did all the data gathering and analyses themselves, and they didn't know what the results would be" (Murray, 1998).

METHOD	WHAT HAPPENS	ABOUT . . .
Case Study	The researcher uses interviews and records to gather in-depth nformation about an individual or a small group.	The accuracy of case studies is compromised by gaps and mistakes in memory, and by participants' tendency to present themselves in a socially desirable manner.
The Survey	The researcher uses interviews, questionnaires, or public records to gather information about large numbers of people.	Surveys can include thousands of people but are subject to the same limitations as case studies. People who volunteer to participate in surveys may also differ from people who do not. There may thus be problems in generalization of results to people who do not participate.
Naturalistic Observation	The researcher observes behavior where it happens— "in the field."	Researchers try to avoid interfering with the behaviors they are observing by using *unobtrusive* measures.
Correlation	The researcher uses statistical (mathematical) methods to reveal positive and negative relationships between variables.	The correlational method does not show cause and effect. Correlation coefficients vary between $+1.00$ (a perfect positive correlation) and -1.00 (a perfect negative correlation).
Experiment	The researcher manipulates independent variables and observes their effects on dependent variables.	Experimental groups obtain the treatment; control groups do not. Researchers use *blinds* to control for the effect of expectations. With *double blinds*, neither the participants nor the observers know which participant has received which treatment. The experimental method allows researchers to draw conclusions about cause and effect.

ETHICAL ISSUES IN PSYCHOLOGICAL RESEARCH AND PRACTICE

It is in the area of ethics that we raise the most serious questions about the Milgram studies. The Milgram studies on obedience made key contributions to our understanding of the limits of human nature. In fact, it is difficult for professional psychologists to imagine a history of psychology without the knowledge provided by such studies. But the participants experienced severe psychological anguish. Were the Milgram studies **ethical?**

Question: What are the ethical issues that concern psychological research and practice with humans? Psychologists adhere to a number of ethical standards that are intended to promote individual dignity, human welfare, and scientific integrity (McGovern et al., 1991). The standards are also intended to ensure that psychologists do not undertake research methods or treatments that are harmful (American Psychological Association, 1992a).

Research With Humans

Recall the signs of stress shown by the participants in the Milgram studies on obedience. They trembled, stuttered, groaned, sweated, bit their lips, and dug their fingernails into their flesh. If Milgram had attempted to run his experiments today rather than in the 1960s, he might have been denied permission to do so by a university ethics review committee. In virtually all institutional settings, including colleges, hospitals, and research foundations, **ethics review committees** help researchers consider the potential harm of their methods and review proposed studies according to ethical guidelines. When such committees find that proposed research might be unacceptably harmful to participants, they may withhold approval until the proposal has been modified. Ethics review committees also weigh the potential benefits of research against the potential harm.

Today individuals must provide **informed consent** before they participate in research. Having a general overview of the research and the opportunity to choose not to participate apparently gives them a sense of control and decreases the stress of participating (Dill et al., 1982). Is there a way in which participants in the Milgram studies could have provided informed consent? What do you think?

Ethical ▲ Moral; referring to one's system of deriving standards for determining what is moral.

Ethics review committee ▲ A group found in an institutional setting that helps researchers consider the potential harm of their methods and reviews proposed studies according to ethical guidelines.

Informed consent ▲ The term used by psychologists to indicate that a person has agreed to participate in research after receiving information about the purposes of the study and the nature of the treatments.

Psychologists treat the records of research participants and clients as confidential. This is because they respect people's privacy and also because people are more likely to express their true thoughts and feelings when researchers or therapists keep their disclosures confidential. Sometimes conflicts of interest arise, however, for example, when a client threatens a third party and the psychologist feels an obligation to warn that person.

Ethics limit the types of research that psychologists may conduct. For example, how can we determine whether early separation from one's mother impairs social development? One way would be to observe the development of children who have been separated from their mothers at an early age. It is difficult to draw conclusions from such research, however, because of the selection factor. That is, the same factors that led to the separation—such as family tragedy or irresponsible parents—and *not* the separation, may have led to the outcome. Scientifically, it would be more sound to run experiments in which researchers separate children from their mothers at an early age and compare their development with that of other children. But psychologists would not undertake such research because of the ethical issues they pose. Yet, they run experiments with lower animals in which infants are separated from mothers.

Many psychological experiments cannot be run without deceiving the people who participate. However, the use of deception raises ethical issues. You are probably skeptical enough to wonder whether the "teachers" in the Milgram studies actually shocked the "learners" when the teachers pressed the levers on the console. They didn't. The only real shock in this experiment was the 45-volt sample given to the teachers. Its purpose was to make the procedure believable.

The learners in the experiment were actually confederates of the experimenter. They had not answered the newspaper ads but were in on the truth from the start. The "teachers" were the only real participants. They were led to believe they had been chosen at random for the teacher role, but the choosing was rigged so that newspaper recruits would always become teachers.

CLICK4™ *a bulletin board discussion on the ethics of deception in psychology.*

CONTROVERSY IN PSYCHOLOGY

Is It Ethical for Psychologists to Deceive Research Participants About the Methods and Objectives of Their Research?

Some studies could not be done if participants knew what the researchers were trying to find out, or which treatment they had received (e.g., a new medicine or a "sugar pill"). As you can imagine, psychologists have debated the ethics of deceiving participants in the Milgram studies. According to the American Psychological Association's (1992a) *Ethical Principles of Psychologists and Code of Conduct*, psychologists may use deception only when they believe the benefits of the research outweigh its potential harm, they believe the individuals might have been willing to participate if they had understood the benefits of the research, and participants are debriefed. **Debriefing** means that the purposes and methods of the research are explained afterward. Milgram provided participants with detailed explanations of his experiment after they participated. He emphasized the fact that they had not actually harmed anyone.

Return to the Lang (Lang et al., 1975) study on alcohol and aggression. In this study, the researchers (1) misinformed participants about the beverage they were drinking and (2) misled them into believing they were giving other participants electric shock when they, like the participants in the Milgram studies, were actually only pressing switches on a dead control board. (*Aggression* was defined as pressing these switches in the study.) In the Lang study, students who believed they had drunk vodka were "more aggressive"—that is, selected higher levels of shock—than students who believed they had not. The actual content of the beverages was immaterial.

Research With Animals

Psychologists and other scientists frequently use animals to conduct research that cannot be carried out with humans. For example, experiments on the effects of early separation from the mother have been done with monkeys and other animals. Such research has

Debrief ▲ To elicit information about a completed procedure.

CONTROVERSY IN PSYCHOLOGY

Is It Ethical to Harm Lower Animals in Conducting Research When the Results May Be Beneficial to Humans?

Researchers often use animals to conduct research that they could not carry out with people. Do you agree with the practice? Why or why not?

CLICK4™ *the Web site for the Animal Welfare Information Center (AWIC).*

CLICK4™ *a quiz on the second half of this chapter.*

CLICK4™ *electronic flash cards to review your knowledge of key terms and people in this chapter.*

Lesion ▲ An injury that results in impaired behavior or loss of a function.

Ethics and Animal Research.

Is it ethical for researchers to harm animals in order to obtain knowledge that may benefit humans?

helped psychologists investigate the formation of attachment bonds between parent and child.

Question: What are the ethical issues that concern research with animals? Experiments with infant monkeys highlight some of the ethical issues faced by psychologists and other scientists who contemplate potentially harmful research. Psychologists and biologists who study the workings of the brain destroy sections of the brains of laboratory animals to learn how they influence behavior. For instance, a **lesion** in one part of a brain structure causes a rat to overeat. A lesion elsewhere causes the rat to go on a crash diet. Psychologists generalize to humans from experiments such as these in the hope of finding solutions to problems such as eating disorders. Proponents of the use of animals in research argue that major advances in medicine and psychology could not have taken place without them (Fowler, 1992).

The majority of psychologists disapprove of research in which animals are exposed to pain or killed (Plous, 1996). According to the ethical guidelines of the American Psychological Association (1992b), animals may be harmed only when there is no alternative and when researchers believe that the benefits of the research justify the harm.

REVIEW

(46) Psychologists adhere to _____ standards that help promote the dignity of the individual, maintain scientific integrity, and protect participants or clients from harm. (47) In order to help avoid harm, human participants must provide _____ consent. Psychologists treat the records of research participants and clients as confidential. Many experiments, like the Lang and Milgram studies, cannot be run without deceiving people. (48) Ethics require that participants who are deceived be _____ afterward to help eliminate misconceptions and anxieties about the research. (49) Researchers use _____ to conduct research that cannot be carried out with humans. Psychologists follow the principle that animals should be harmed only when there is no alternative and the benefits of the research justify the harm.

Pulling It Together: Under what circumstances do researchers deceive participants? What does your own belief system say about the ethical treatment of animals?

TRUTH ▱ FICTION REVISITED

▱ It is true that a book on psychology, whose contents are similar to those of the book you are now holding, was written by Aristotle more than 2,000 years ago. *Its title is* Peri Psyches. *See page 8.*

▱ It is true that the ancient Greek philosopher Socrates suggested a research method that is still used in psychology. *That method is* introspection. *See page 8.*

▱ It is true that the first female president of the American Psychological Association turned down the doctoral degree that was offered to her. *She had earned it at Harvard, but the degree was offered from Radcliffe because Harvard was not yet accepting women students. See page 17.*

▱ It is not true that men receive the majority of degrees in psychology. *Women actually receive the majority of Ph.D.s in psychology today. See page 18.*

▱ It is true that you could survey 20 million voters and still not predict the outcome of a presidential election accurately. *Sample size alone does not guarantee that a sample will accurately represent the population from which it was drawn. See page 22.*

▱ It is true that in many experiments, neither the participants nor the researchers know who is receiving the real treatment and who is receiving a placebo ("sugar pill"). *Such* double-blind *studies control for the effects of participants' and researchers' expectations. See page 28.*

▱ It is true that psychologists would not be able to carry out certain kinds of research without deceiving participants as to the purposes and methods of the studies. *See page 31.*

1. What is psychology?

Psychology is the scientific study of behavior and mental processes.

2. What are the goals of psychology?

Psychology seeks to describe, explain, predict, and control behavior and mental processes. Behavior and mental processes are explained through psychological theories, which are sets of statements that involve assumptions about behavior. Explanations and predictions are derived from theories. Theories are revised, as needed, to accommodate new observations.

3. Just what do psychologists do?

Psychologists engage in research and practice. Research can be pure or applied. Basic or pure research has no immediate applications. Applied research seeks solutions to specific problems. Psychologists also specialize in various fields. Clinical psychologists help people with psychological disorders adjust to the demands of life. Counseling psychologists work with people with adjustment problems. School psychologists assist students with problems that interfere with learning. Developmental psychologists study the changes that occur throughout the life span. Personality psychologists study influences on our thought processes, feelings, and behavior. Social psychologists focus on the nature and causes of behavior in social situations. Experimental psychologists conduct research into basic psychological processes such as sensation and perception, learning and memory, and motivation and emotion. Industrial psychologists focus on the relationships between people and work. Health psychologists study the ways in which behavior and mental processes such as attitudes are related to physical health.

4. What is critical thinking?

Critical thinking is a hallmark of psychologists and of scientists in general. Critical thinking is associated with skepticism. It involves thoughtfully analyzing the questions, statements, and arguments of others. It means examining the definitions of terms, examining the premises or assumptions behind arguments, and scrutinizing the logic with which arguments are developed. Critical thinking also refers to the ability to inquire about causes and effects, as well as knowledge of research methods. Critical thinkers are cautious in drawing conclusions from evidence. They do not oversimplify or overgeneralize.

5. Who were some of the ancient contributors to psychology?

The ancient Greek philosopher Aristotle declared that people are motivated to seek pleasure and avoid pain. Another Greek, Democritus, suggested that we could think of behavior in terms of a body and a mind and raised the question of whether there is free will or choice. Plato recorded Socrates' advice to "Know thyself," primarily by means of introspection.

6. What is structuralism?

Structuralism, founded by Wilhelm Wundt, used introspection to study the objective and subjective elements of experience. Wundt also established the first psychological laboratory in Leipzig, Germany, in 1879.

7. What is functionalism?

Functionalism is the school founded by William James. It dealt with observable behavior as well as conscious experience and focused on the importance of habit.

8. What is behaviorism?

Behaviorism, founded by John B. Watson, argues that psychology must limit itself to observable behavior and not attempt to deal with subjective consciousness. Behaviorism focuses on learning by conditioning, and B. F. Skinner introduced the concept of reinforcement as an explanation of how learning occurs.

9. What is Gestalt psychology?

Gestalt psychology is the school of psychology founded by Wertheimer, Koffka, and Köhler. It is concerned with perception and argues that the wholeness of human experience is more than the sum of its parts.

10. What is psychoanalysis?

Psychoanalysis was founded by Sigmund Freud. The school asserts that people are driven by hidden impulses and that they distort reality to protect themselves from anxiety.

11. What is the biological perspective?

The biological perspective views the links between behavior and biological structures and events such as the brain, hormones, heredity, and evolution. Evolutionary psychology is based on the work of Charles Darwin, who argued that in the age-old struggle for survival, only the "fittest" organisms reach maturity and reproduce, thereby transmitting the traits that enable them to survive to their offspring.

12. What is the cognitive perspective?

The cognitive perspective is concerned with the ways in which we mentally represent the world and process information. Cognitive psychologists study how we learn, remember the past, plan for the future, solve problems, form judgments, make decisions, and use language.

13. What is the humanistic-existential perspective?

Humanistic-existential psychologists stress the importance of subjective experience and assert that people have the freedom to make choices.

14. What is the role of psychoanalysis today?

Contemporary psychoanalysts often call themselves *neoanalysts* because they focus less on unconscious processes and more on conscious choice and self-direction. Psychoanalysis remains popular in the culture at large.

15. What are the learning perspectives?

There are two learning perspectives: the behavioral perspective and the social-cognitive perspective. Behaviorism focuses on environmental influences on learning. Social-cognitive theory argues that psychologists can address thought processes, that people engage in intentional learning, and that people are free to modify and create environments.

16. What is the sociocultural perspective?

The sociocultural perspective focuses on the roles of ethnicity, gender, culture, and socioeconomic status in behavior and mental processes.

17. What contributions have women made to psychology?

Women have made major contributions to psychology in the United States for more than a century, despite the fact that many entered the field when it was still widely believed that "a woman's place" was in the home. Ladd-Franklin formulated a theory of color vision. Washburn's views presaged behaviorism. Calkins studied memory and heightened awareness of prejudice against women.

18. What contributions to psychology have been made by people from various racial and ethnic groups?

People from ethnic minority groups have contributed to all areas of psychology, but some, like Kenneth Clark and Robert Williams, have heightened awareness of issues concerning their groups, such as prejudice and Ebonics.

19. What is the scientific method?

The scientific method is an organized way of expanding and refining knowledge. Psychologists reach conclusions about their research questions or the accuracy of their hypotheses on the basis of their research observations or findings.

20. How do psychologists use samples to represent populations?

The individuals who participate in research are referred to as a sample. A sample is a segment of a population. Samples must accurately represent the population they are intended to reflect. In a *random sample*, each member of a population has an equal chance of being selected to participate. Researchers can also use a *stratified sample*, which is selected so that identified subgroups in the population are represented proportionately in the sample.

21. What methods of observation are used by psychologists?

The methods used include the case study, the survey, and naturalistic observation. Case studies gather information about the lives of individuals or small groups. The survey method uses interviews, questionnaires, or public records to gather information about behavior that cannot be observed directly. The naturalistic observation method observes behavior where it happens—"in the field."

22. **What is the correlational method?**

The correlational method reveals relationships between variables, but does not determine cause and effect. In a positive correlation, variables increase simultaneously. In a negative correlation, one variable increases while the other decreases.

23. **What is the experimental method?**

Experiments are used to discover cause and effect—that is, the effects of independent variables on dependent variables. Experimental groups receive a specific treatment, whereas control groups do not. Blinds and double blinds may be used to control for the effects of the expectations of the participants and the researchers. Results can be generalized only to populations that have been adequately represented in the research samples.

24. **What are the ethical issues that concern psychological research and practice with humans?**

The ethical standards of psychologists are intended to protect participants in research and clients in practice from harm. Records of human behavior are kept confidential. Ethics review committees judge the harmfulness of proposed research and help make it less harmful. Human participants are required to give informed consent prior to participating in research and are debriefed afterward.

25. **What are the ethical issues that concern research with animals?**

Some research can be conducted only with animals. Ethical standards require that animals may be harmed only if there is no alternative and the benefits justify the harm.

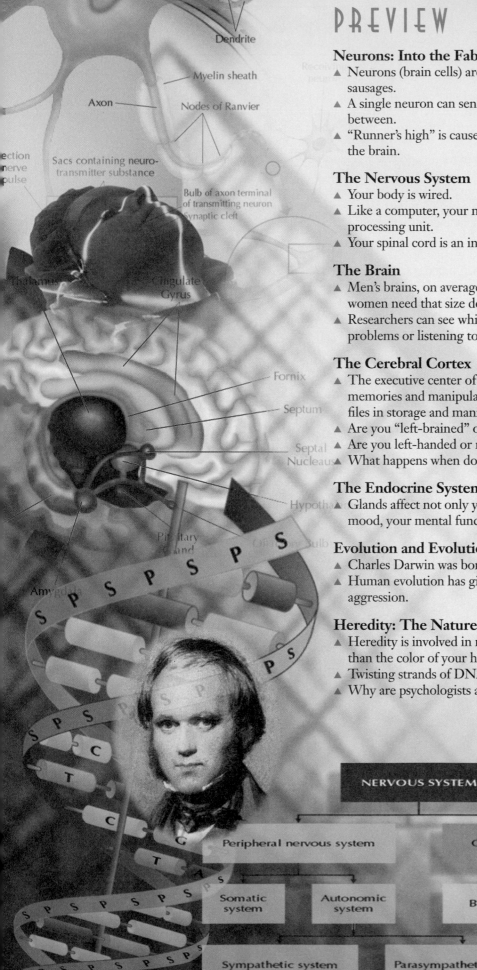

PREVIEW

Neurons: Into the Fabulous Forest
▲ Neurons (brain cells) are insulated with stuff that looks like little white sausages.
▲ A single neuron can send out hundreds of messages each second—and rest in between.
▲ "Runner's high" is caused by morphine-like chemicals that occur naturally in the brain.

The Nervous System
▲ Your body is wired.
▲ Like a computer, your nervous system has peripheral devices and a central processing unit.
▲ Your spinal cord is an information superhighway.

The Brain
▲ Men's brains, on average, are larger than women's, which is all the proof many women need that size doesn't matter.
▲ Researchers can see which parts of the brain are active when you're solving problems or listening to music.

The Cerebral Cortex
▲ The executive center of your brain retrieves images and other kinds of memories and manipulates them—as a computer retrieves information from files in storage and manipulates it in memory.
▲ Are you "left-brained" or "right-brained"? (Or *both?*)
▲ Are you left-handed or right-handed? Does it matter?
▲ What happens when doctors split the brain down the middle?

The Endocrine System
▲ Glands affect not only your anatomic sex and your growth rate, but also your mood, your mental functioning, even your self-confidence.

Evolution and Evolutionary Psychology
▲ Charles Darwin was born on the same day as Abraham Lincoln.
▲ Human evolution has given rise to language, art, committed relationships, and aggression.

Heredity: The Nature of Nature
▲ Heredity is involved in nearly all human traits and behavior—in much more than the color of your hair and the shape of your nose.
▲ Twisting strands of DNA are made up of genes.
▲ Why are psychologists and other researchers so interested in twins?

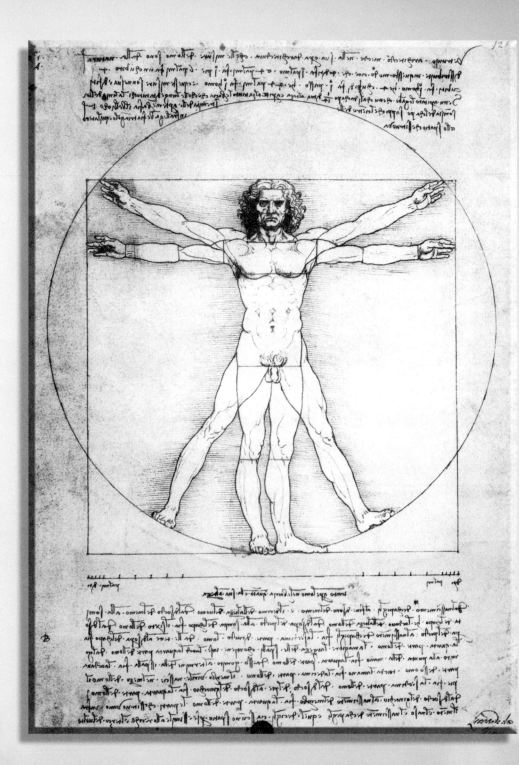

Biology and Psychology

TRUTH [or] FICTION?

- [ ] A single cell can stretch all the way down your leg.

- [ ] Messages travel in the brain by means of electricity.

- [ ] The human brain is larger than that of any other animal.

- [ ] Fear can give you indigestion.

- [ ] Men's brains are larger than women's brains.

- [ ] If a surgeon were to stimulate a certain part of your brain electrically, you might swear in court that someone had stroked your leg.

- [ ] A hormone turns a disinterested male rodent into a doting father.

- [ ] Women who are ovulating are less attracted to men with highly masculine facial features.

- [ ] A crocodile's sex is determined by the temperature at which the egg develops.

- [ ] You can't buy happiness.

Charles Darwin

In one of history's coincidences, Darwin was born on the same day as Abraham Lincoln (February 12, 1809). Darwin's father was a well-known physician and his mother was Susannah Wedgwood, of the chinaware family. His cousin was Sir Francis Galton, who made many innovations in psychological measurement. Darwin did so poorly in school that his father predicted that he would disgrace himself and the family. Nevertheless, Darwin went on to become a key figure in modern thought.

Darwin enjoyed collecting and classifying plants, minerals, and animals. He tried medical school, entered Cambridge University to become an Anglican priest, and eventually graduated with a degree in science. Independently wealthy, Darwin undertook the unpaid five-year position aboard the *Beagle*. The ship stopped at the Galápagos Islands where Darwin noticed how species of lizards, tortoises, and plants differed somewhat on different islands. Although Darwin undertook his voyage as a believer in the *Book of Genesis* account of creation, his observations convinced him that the organisms he observed shared common ancestors but had *evolved* in different directions.

In midlife Darwin almost missed the boat again. When he returned from his voyage, he initially did not want his theory of evolution to be published until after his death. He feared it would be immensely unpopular because it contradicted religious views, and that it would bring scorn on his family. He shared his ideas with a few fellow scientists, but he published them more broadly 20 years later because he learned that other scientists, including Alfred Russel Wallace, were about to present similar ideas on evolution. Needless to say, Darwin's views became better known. (Have you ever heard of Wallace's theory of evolution?)

He almost missed the boat. Literally. The British naturalist Charles Darwin had volunteered to serve as the scientist for an expedition by the HMS *Beagle*, but the captain, Robert Fitz-Roy, objected to Darwin because of the shape of his nose. Fitz-Roy believed that you could judge a person's character by the outline of his facial features, and Darwin's nose didn't fit the . . . bill. But Fitz-Roy relented, and in the 1830s, Darwin undertook the historic voyage that led to the development of his theory of evolution.

At the core of the theory of evolution is the concept of a *struggle for survival*. Since the beginning of time, the universe has been changing. For billions of years, microscopic particles have been forming immense gas clouds in space. Galaxies and solar systems have been condensing from the clouds, sparkling for some eons, then winking out.

Change has brought life and death and countless challenges to survival. As described by evolutionary theory, some creatures have adapted successfully to these challenges and their numbers have increased. Others have not met the challenges and have fallen back into the distant mists of time. The species that prosper and those that fade away are thus determined by *natural selection*.

When we humans first appeared on Earth, our survival required a different sort of struggle than it does today. We fought predators such as leopards. We foraged across parched lands for food. We might have warred with creatures very much like ourselves—creatures who have since become extinct. But because of the evolution of our intellect, not fangs or wings or claws, we prevailed. Our numbers have increased. We continue to transmit the traits that led to our selection down through the generations by means of genetic material whose chemical codes are only now being cracked.

Just what is handed down through the generations? The answer is biological, or physiological, structures and processes. Our biology serves as the material base for our behaviors, emotions, and cognitions (our thoughts, images, and plans). Biology somehow gives rise to specific behavioral tendencies in some organisms, such as the chick's instinctive fear of the shadow of the hawk. But the behavior of higher species, especially humans, is flexible and affected by learning and choice as well as by heredity.

Biological psychologists work at the interface of psychology and biology. They study the ways in which our mental processes and behaviors are linked to biological structures and processes. In recent years, biological psychologists have been exploring these links in several areas:

1. *Neurons.* Neurons are the building blocks of the nervous system. There are billions of neurons in the body—perhaps as many as the stars in the Milky Way galaxy. Biological psychologists are showing how neurons communicate with one another and how millions, perhaps billions, of such communications make up our mental images and thoughts.
2. *The nervous system.* Neurons combine to form the structures of the nervous system. The nervous system has branches that are responsible for muscle movement, perception, automatic functions such as breathing and the secretion of hormones, and psychological events such as thoughts and feelings.
3. *The cerebral cortex.* The cerebral cortex is the large, wrinkled mass inside your head that you think of as your brain. Actually, it is only one part of the brain— the part that is the most characteristically human.
4. *The endocrine system.* Through secretion of hormones, the endocrine system con-

▲ REFLECT

Psychology is the study of behavior and mental processes. Why, then, are psychologists interested in biological matters such as the nervous system, the endocrine system, and heredity?

trols functions ranging from growth in children to production of milk in nursing women.

5. *Evolution.* Evolutionary psychologists believe that many behavior patterns—such as aggression, preferences for mates, and self-sacrifice for the benefit of one's family—have evolved as adaptations to historic challenges to the human species.

6. *Heredity.* It is estimated that within every cell of your body, there are 30,000 to 40,000 genes (International Human Genome Sequencing Consortium, 2001). Genes are chemical substances that determine what type of creature you are, from the color of your hair to your body temperature to the fact that you have arms and legs rather than wings or fins.

NEURONS: INTO THE FABULOUS FOREST

Let us begin our journey in a fabulous forest of nerve cells, or **neurons.** *Question: What are neurons?* Neurons are cells that can be visualized as having branches, trunks, and roots—something like trees. As in other forests, many nerve cells lie alongside one another like a thicket of trees. Neurons can also lie end to end, however, with their "roots" intertwined with the "branches" of the neurons that lie below. Trees receive sunlight, water, and nutrients from the soil. Neurons receive "messages" from a number of sources such as light, other neurons, and pressure on the skin, and they can pass these messages along.

Neurons communicate by means of chemicals called **neurotransmitters.** They release neurotransmitters, which are taken up by other neurons, muscles, and glands. Neurotransmitters cause chemical changes in the receiving neuron so that the message can travel along its "trunk," be translated back into neurotransmitters in its "branches," and then travel through the small spaces between neurons to be received by the "roots" of yet other neurons. Each neuron transmits and coordinates messages in the form of neural impulses.

We are born with more than 100 billion neurons. Most of them are found in the brain. The nervous system also contains **glial cells.** Glial cells remove dead neurons and waste products from the nervous system, nourish and insulate neurons, and direct their growth. But neurons occupy center stage in the nervous system. The messages transmitted by neurons somehow account for phenomena ranging from the perception of an itch from a mosquito bite to the coordination of a skier's vision and muscles to the composition of a concerto to the solution of an algebraic equation.

The Makeup of Neurons

Neurons vary according to their functions and their location. Some neurons in the brain are only a fraction of an inch in length, whereas others in the legs are several feet long. Every neuron is a single nerve cell with a cell body, dendrites, and an axon (see Figure 2.1). The cell body contains the core or *nucleus* of the cell. The nucleus uses oxygen and nutrients to generate the energy needed to carry out the work of the cell. Anywhere from a few to several hundred short fibers, or **dendrites,** extend like roots from the cell body to receive incoming messages from thousands of adjoining neurons. Each neuron has one **axon** that extends like a trunk from the cell body. Axons are very thin, but those that carry messages from the toes to the spinal cord extend for several feet.

Like tree trunks, axons can divide and extend in different directions. Axons end in small bulb-shaped structures, aptly named *terminals.* Neurons carry messages in one direction only: from the dendrites or cell body through the axon to the axon terminals. The messages are then transmitted from the terminals to the dendrites or cell bodies of other neurons.

As a child matures, the axons of neurons become longer and the dendrites and terminals proliferate, creating vast interconnected networks for the transmission of complex messages. The number of glial cells also increases as the nervous system develops, contributing to its dense appearance.

www (2) (L) (6)

CLICK4™ *computer simulations of neurons, hosted by Duke University.*

▲ **REFLECT**
What does it mean to say that a cell "communicates" or "sends a message"? Is it the same thing as people communicating or sending messages to one another? Explain.

www (2) (WS) (1)

CLICK4™ *an opportunity to view and manipulate neurons online.*

Neuron ▲ A nerve cell.

Neurotransmitters ▲ Chemical substances involved in the transmission of neural impulses from one neuron to another.

Glial cells ▲ Cells that nourish and insulate neurons, direct their growth, and remove waste products from the nervous system.

Dendrites ▲ Rootlike structures, attached to the cell body of a neuron, that receive impulses from other neurons.

Axon ▲ A long, thin part of a neuron that transmits impulses to other neurons from branching structures called *terminals.*

CD 2 V 2
CLICK4™ *a virtual tour of the neuron.*

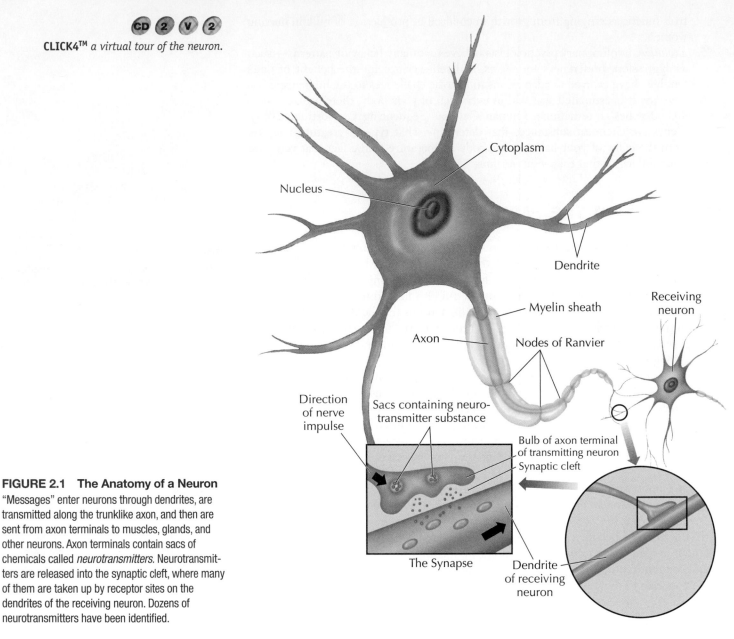

FIGURE 2.1   The Anatomy of a Neuron
"Messages" enter neurons through dendrites, are transmitted along the trunklike axon, and then are sent from axon terminals to muscles, glands, and other neurons. Axon terminals contain sacs of chemicals called *neurotransmitters.* Neurotransmitters are released into the synaptic cleft, where many of them are taken up by receptor sites on the dendrites of the receiving neuron. Dozens of neurotransmitters have been identified.

Myelin ▲ A fatty substance that encases and insulates axons, facilitating transmission of neural impulses.
Afferent neurons ▲ Neurons that transmit messages from sensory receptors to the spinal cord and brain. Also called *sensory neurons.*

Myelin   The axons of many neurons are wrapped tightly with white, fatty **myelin** that makes them look like strings of sausages under the microscope (bratwurst, actually). The fat insulates the axon from electrically charged atoms, or ions, found in the fluids that surround the nervous system. The myelin sheath minimizes leakage of the electrical current being carried along the axon, thereby allowing messages to be conducted more efficiently.

Myelination is part of the maturation process that leads to the child's ability to crawl and walk during the first year. Infants are not physiologically "ready" to engage in visual-motor coordination and other activities until the coating process reaches certain levels. In people with the disease multiple sclerosis, myelin is replaced with a hard fibrous tissue that throws off the timing of nerve impulses and disrupts muscular control. Affliction of the neurons that control breathing can result in suffocation.

Afferent and Efferent Neurons   If someone steps on your toes, the sensation is registered by receptors or sensory neurons near the surface of your skin. Then it is transmitted to the spinal cord and brain through **afferent neurons,** which are perhaps 2 to 3 feet long. In the brain, subsequent messages might be buffeted by associative neurons that are only a few thousandths of an inch long. You experience the pain through this process and perhaps entertain some rather nasty thoughts about the perpetrator, who is now apologizing and begging for understanding. Long before you arrive at any logical conclusions, however, motor neurons (**efferent neurons**) send messages to your foot so that you withdraw it and begin an impressive hopping routine. Other efferent neurons stimulate glands so that your heart is beating more rapidly, you are sweating, and the hair on the back of your arms has become erect! Being a good sport, you say, "Oh, it's nothing." But considering all the neurons involved, it really is something, isn't it?

In case you think that afferent and efferent neurons will be hard to distinguish because they sound pretty much the SAME to you, remember that they *are* the "SAME." That is, *Sensory = Afferent*, and *Motor = Efferent*. But don't tell your professor I let you in on this secret.

The Neural Impulse: Let Us "Sing the Body Electric"[1]

In the 18th century, the Italian physiologist Luigi Galvani (1737–1798) conducted a shocking experiment in a rainstorm. While his neighbors had the sense to remain indoors, Galvani and his wife were out on the porch connecting lightning rods to the heads of dissected frogs whose legs were connected by wires to a well of water. When lightning blazed above, the frogs' muscles contracted. This is not a recommended way to prepare frogs' legs. Galvani was demonstrating that the messages (**neural impulses**) that travel along neurons are electrochemical in nature.

Question: What are neural impulses? Neural impulses are messages that travel within neurons at somewhere between 2 (in nonmyelinated neurons) and 225 miles an hour (in myelinated neurons). This speed is not impressive when compared with that of an electrical current in a toaster oven or a lamp, which can travel at close to the speed of light—over 186,000 miles per second. Distances in the body are short, however, and a message will travel from a toe to the brain in perhaps 1/50th of a second.

An Electrochemical Process   The process by which neural impulses travel is electrochemical. Chemical changes take place within neurons that cause an electrical charge to be transmitted along their lengths. Neurons and body fluids contain ions—positively or negatively charged atoms. In a resting state—that is, when a neuron is not being stimulated by its neighbors—negatively charged chloride (Cl−) ions are plentiful within the neuron, giving it an overall negative charge in relation to the outside. The difference in electrical charge **polarizes** the neuron with a negative **resting potential** of about −70 millivolts in relation to the body fluid outside the cell membrane.

When an area on the surface of the resting neuron is adequately stimulated by other neurons, the cell membrane in the area changes its permeability to allow positively charged sodium ions to enter. Thus, the area of entry becomes positively charged, or **depolarized** with respect to the outside (Figure 2.2). The permeability of the cell membrane then changes again, allowing no more sodium ions to enter.

The inside of the cell at the disturbed area has an **action potential** of 110 millivolts. This action potential, added to the −70 millivolts that characterize the resting potential, brings the membrane voltage to a positive charge of about +40 millivolts. This inner change causes the next section of the cell to become permeable to sodium ions. At the same time, other positively charged (potassium) ions are being pumped out of the area of the cell that was previously affected, which returns the area to its resting potential. In this way, the neural impulse is transmitted continuously along an axon. Because the impulse is created anew as it progresses, its strength does not change.

Firing   The conduction of the neural impulse along the length of a neuron is what is meant by "firing." When a rifle fires, it sends a bullet speeding through its barrel and discharges it at more than 1,000 feet per second. *Question: What happens when a*

CLICK4™ *NASA's studies on the brain and nerves in space.*

CLICK4™ *a video on the action potential.*

> ▲ **REFLECT**
> Had you heard that the brain runs on electricity? If so, what did you imagine? How are messages actually transmitted in the nervous system?

Efferent neurons ▲ Neurons that transmit messages from the brain or spinal cord to muscles and glands. Also called *motor neurons*.

Neural impulse ▲ The electrochemical discharge of a nerve cell, or neuron.

Polarize ▲ To ready a neuron for firing by creating an internal negative charge in relation to the body fluid outside the cell membrane.

Resting potential ▲ The electrical potential across the neural membrane when it is not responding to other neurons.

Depolarize ▲ To reduce the resting potential of a cell membrane from about −70 millivolts toward zero.

Action potential ▲ The electrical impulse that provides the basis for the conduction of a neural impulse along an axon of a neuron.

---

[1]From a poem by Walt Whitman.

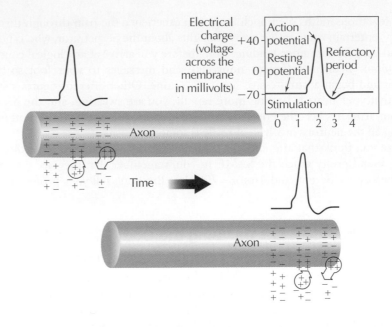

FIGURE 2.2 The Neural Impulse
When a section of a neuron is stimulated by other neurons, the cell membrane becomes permeable to sodium ions so that an action potential of about 40 millivolts is induced. This action potential is transmitted along the axon. The neuron fires according to the all-or-none principle.

CD 2 V 4

CLICK4™ *a video on what happens when drugs or toxins interfere with the action potential.*

neuron fires? Neurons also fire, but instead of a barrel, a neuron has an axon. Instead of discharging a bullet, it releases neurotransmitters.

Some neurons fire in less than 1/1,000th of a second. In firing, neurons attempt to transmit messages to other neurons, muscles, or glands. However, other neurons will not fire unless the incoming messages combine to reach an adequate *threshold.* A weak message may cause a temporary shift in electrical charge at some point along a neuron's cell membrane, but this charge will dissipate if the neuron is not stimulated to its threshold.

A neuron may transmit several hundred messages in a second. Yet, in accordance with the **all-or-none principle,** each time a neuron fires, it transmits an impulse of the same strength. Neurons fire more frequently when they have been stimulated by larger numbers of other neurons. Stronger stimuli cause more frequent firing.

For a few thousandths of a second after firing, a neuron is insensitive to messages from other neurons and will not fire. It is said to be in a **refractory period.** This period is a time of recovery during which sodium is prevented from passing through the neuronal membrane. When we realize that such periods of recovery might take place hundreds of times per second, it seems a rapid recovery and a short rest indeed.

The Synapse: On Being Well-Connected

CD 2 V 5

CLICK4™ *a video on synaptic transmission.*

A neuron relays its message to another neuron across a junction called a **synapse.** *Question: What is a synapse?* A synapse consists of a "branch," or an axon terminal from the transmitting neuron; a dendrite ("root"), or the body of a receiving neuron; and a fluid-filled gap between the two that is called the *synaptic cleft* (see Figure 2.1). Although the neural impulse is electrical, it does not jump across the synaptic cleft like a spark. Instead, when a nerve impulse reaches a synapse, axon terminals release chemicals into the synaptic cleft like myriad ships being cast into the sea.

Neurotransmitters: The Chemical Keys to Communication

All-or-none principle ▲ The fact that a neuron fires an impulse of the same strength whenever its action potential is triggered.
Refractory period ▲ A phase following firing during which a neuron is less sensitive to messages from other neurons and will not fire.
Synapse ▲ A junction between the axon terminals of one neuron and the dendrites or cell body of another neuron.
Receptor site ▲ A location on a dendrite of a receiving neuron tailored to receive a neurotransmitter.

Sacs called synaptic vesicles in the axon terminals contain neurotransmitters. When a neural impulse reaches the axon terminal, the vesicles release varying amounts of neurotransmitters—the chemical keys to communication—into the synaptic cleft. From there, they influence the receiving neuron. *Questions: Which neurotransmitters are of interest to psychologists? What do they do?*

Dozens of neurotransmitters have been identified. Each has its own chemical structure, and each can fit into a specifically tailored harbor, or **receptor site,** on the receiving cell. The analogy of a key fitting into a lock is often used to describe this process. Once released, not all molecules of a neurotransmitter find their way into receptor sites of other neurons. "Loose" neurotransmitters are usually either broken down or reabsorbed by the axon terminal (a process called *reuptake*).

Some neurotransmitters act to *excite* other neurons—that is, to cause other neurons to fire. Other neurotransmitters act to *inhibit* receiving neurons. That is, they prevent them from firing. The sum of the stimulation—excitatory and inhibitory—determines whether a neuron will fire and, if so, which neurotransmitters will be released.

Some Key Chemical Keys

Neurotransmitters are involved in physical processes such as muscle contraction and psychological processes such as thoughts and emotions. Excesses or deficiencies of neurotransmitters have been linked to psychological disorders such as depression and schizophrenia. Let us consider the effects of some neurotransmitters of interest to psychologists: acetylcholine (ACh), dopamine, noradrenaline, serotonin, and endorphins.

Acetylcholine (ACh) controls muscle contractions. It is excitatory at synapses between nerves and muscles that involve voluntary movement but inhibitory at the heart and some other locations. The effects of curare highlight the functioning of ACh. Curare is a poison that is extracted from plants by South American Indians and used in hunting. If an arrow tipped with curare pierces the skin and the poison enters the body, it prevents ACh from lodging within receptor sites in neurons. Because ACh helps muscles move, curare causes paralysis. The victim is prevented from contracting the muscles used in breathing and therefore dies from suffocation. Botulism, a disease that stems from food poisoning, prevents the release of ACh and has the same effect as curare.

ACh is also normally prevalent in a part of the brain called the **hippocampus,** a structure involved in the formation of memories. When the amount of ACh available to the brain decreases, memory formation is impaired, as in Alzheimer's disease (de Toledo-Morrell, 2000).

Dopamine is primarily an inhibitory neurotransmitter. It is involved in voluntary movements, learning and memory, and emotional arousal. Deficiencies of dopamine are linked to Parkinson's disease, in which people progressively lose control over their muscles (Olanow, 2000). They develop muscle tremors and jerky, uncoordinated movements. The drug L-dopa, a substance that stimulates the brain to produce dopamine, helps slow the progress of Parkinson's disease.

The psychological disorder *schizophrenia* is characterized by confusion and false perceptions, and it has been linked to dopamine. People with schizophrenia may have more receptor sites for dopamine in an area of the brain that is involved in emotional responding. For this reason, they may *overutilize* the dopamine available in the brain (Butcher, 2000). This leads to hallucinations and disturbances of thought and emotion. The phenothiazines, a group of drugs used in the treatment of schizophrenia, block the action of dopamine by locking some dopamine out of these receptor sites. Because of their action, phenothiazines may have Parkinson-like side effects, which are usually treated by lowering the dose, prescribing additional drugs, or switching to another drug.

Noradrenaline is produced largely by neurons in the brain stem. It acts both as a neurotransmitter and as a hormone. It is an excitatory neurotransmitter that speeds up the heartbeat and other body processes and is involved in general arousal, learning and memory, and eating. Excesses and deficiencies of noradrenaline have been linked to mood disorders.

The stimulants cocaine and amphetamines ("speed") facilitate the release of noradrenaline and also prevent its reabsorption by the releasing synaptic vesicles—that is, its reuptake. As a result, there are excesses of noradrenaline in the nervous system, increasing the firing of neurons and leading to persistent arousal.

Also primarily an inhibitory transmitter, **serotonin** is involved in emotional arousal and sleep. Deficiencies of serotonin have been linked to eating disorders, alcoholism, depression, aggression, and insomnia (Azar, 1997b; Leyton et al., 2000). The drug LSD decreases the action of serotonin and may also influence the utilization of dopamine. With LSD, "two no's make a yes." By inhibiting an inhibitor, it increases brain activity, in this case frequently producing hallucinations.

CLICK4™ *a video on what happens when drugs or toxins interfere with normal synaptic transmission.*

CLICK4™ *tutorials on neurons and synapses.*

CLICK4™ *a neuroscience treasure hunt!*

Acetylcholine ▲ A neurotransmitter that controls muscle contractions. Abbreviated *ACh*.

Hippocampus ▲ A part of the limbic system of the brain that is involved in memory formation.

Dopamine ▲ A neurotransmitter that is involved in Parkinson's disease and that appears to play a role in schizophrenia.

Noradrenaline ▲ A neurotransmitter whose action is similar to that of the hormone adrenaline and that may play a role in depression.

Serotonin ▲ A neurotransmitter, deficiencies of which have been linked to affective disorders, anxiety, and insomnia.

IN REVIEW
Key Neurotransmitters and Their Functions

Neurotransmitter	Functions	About . . .
Acetylcholine (ACh)	Causes muscle contractions and is involved in formation of memories	Found at synapses between motor neurons and muscles. Deficiencies are linked with paralysis and Alzheimer's disease.
Dopamine	Is involved in muscle contraction, learning and memory, and emotional response	Tremors of Parkinson's disease are linked with low levels of dopamine. People with schizophrenia may *overutilize* dopamine.
Noradrenaline	Accelerates the heart rate, affects eating, and is linked with activity levels, learning, and remembering	Imbalances are linked with mood disorders such as depression and bipolar disorder.
Serotonin	Is involved in behavior patterns and psychological problems, including obesity, depression, and insomnia, alcoholism, and aggression	Drugs that block the reuptake of serotonin are helpful in the treatment of depression.
Endorphins	Inhibit pain by locking pain-causing chemicals out of their receptor sites	Endorphins may be connected with some people's indifference to pain, the pain-killing effects of acupuncture, and the "runner's high" experienced by many long-distance runners.

Runner's High?
Why have thousands of people taken up long-distance running? Running promotes cardiovascular conditioning, muscle strength, and weight control. But many long-distance runners also experience a "runner's high" that appears to be connected with the release of endorphins. Endorphins are naturally occurring substances that are similar in function to the narcotic morphine.

CLICK4™ *a view of what happens when you stimulate the motor cortex.*

Endorphins ▲ Neurotransmitters that are composed of amino acids and that are functionally similar to morphine.

Endorphins are inhibitory neurotransmitters. The word *endorphin* is the contraction of *endogenous morphine. Endogenous* means "developing from within." Endorphins occur naturally in the brain and in the bloodstream and are similar to the narcotic morphine in their functions and effects. They lock into receptor sites for chemicals that transmit pain messages to the brain. Once the endorphin "key" is in the "lock," the pain-causing chemicals are locked out. Endorphins may also increase our sense of competence, enhance the functioning of the immune system, and be connected with the pleasurable "runner's high" reported by many long-distance runners (Jonsdottir et al., 2000).

There you have it—a fabulous forest of neurons in which billions upon billions of vesicles are pouring neurotransmitters into synaptic clefts at any given time: when you are involved in strenuous activity, now as you are reading this page, even as you are passively watching television. This microscopic picture is repeated several hundred times every second. The combined activity of all these neurotransmitters determines which messages will be transmitted and which ones will not. You experience your sensations, your thoughts, and your control over your body as psychological events, but the psychological events somehow result from many billions of electrochemical events.

REVIEW

(1) Neurons transmit messages to other neurons by means of chemical substances called _____. (2) Neurons have a cell body, or soma; _____, which receive "messages"; and an axon, which extends from the cell body. (3) The axons of many neurons have a fatty sheath made of a fatty substance called _____. (4) Myelin insulates the axon from chemically charged atoms called _____, allowing messages to be conducted more efficiently. Afferent neurons transmit sensory messages to the central nervous system. (5) _____ neurons conduct messages from the central nervous system that stimulate glands or cause muscles to contract. (6) The neuron has a _____

potential of -70 millivolts in relation to the body fluid outside the cell membrane and an action potential of $+110$ millivolts. (7) The conduction of the neural impulse along the length of the neuron is what is called _____. (8) A _____ consists of an axon terminal, a dendrite, and a fluid-filled gap between them. (9) _____ is the neurotransmitter that controls muscle contractions. (10) ACh is normally prevalent in a brain structure essential to the formation of memories: the _____. (11) It is theorized that people with _____ overutilize dopamine. (12) Deficiencies of _____ are linked to anxiety, depression, and insomnia. (13) "Runner's high" may be caused by the release of _____.

Pulling It Together: How can the structure of neurons be compared with trees? How can neurotransmitters be compared with ships sent into the sea?

THE NERVOUS SYSTEM

As a child, I did not think it was a good thing to have a "nervous" system. After all, if your system were not so nervous, you might be less likely to jump at strange noises.

Question: Just what is the nervous system? Later I learned that a nervous system is not a system that is nervous. It is a system of nerves involved in thought processes, heartbeat, visual-motor coordination, and so on. (A **nerve** is a bundle of axons and dendrites.) I also learned that the human nervous system is more complex than that of any other animal and that our brains are larger than those of any other animal. Now, this last piece of business is not quite true. A human brain weighs about 3 pounds, but the brains of elephants and whales may be four times as heavy. Still, our brains account for a greater part of our body weight than do those of elephants or whales. Our brains weigh about 1/60th of our body weight. Elephant brains weigh about 1/1,000th of their total weight, and whale brains are a paltry 1/10,000th of their weight. So, humans win the brain-as-a-percentage-of-body-weight contest.

The brain is only one part of the nervous system. The nervous system consists of the brain, the spinal cord, and the nerves linking them to the sensory organs, muscles, and glands. As shown in Figure 2.3, the brain and spinal cord make up the **central nervous system.** If you compare your nervous system to a computer, your central nervous system would be your central processing unit (CPU).

The sensory (afferent) neurons, which receive and transmit messages to the brain and spinal cord, and the motor (efferent) neurons, which transmit messages from the

Nerve ▲ A bundle of axons and dendrites from many neurons.
Central nervous system ▲ The brain and spinal cord.

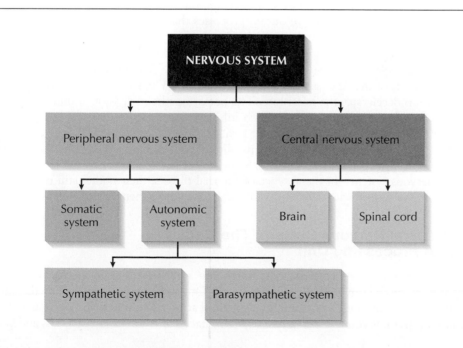

FIGURE 2.3   The Divisions of the Nervous System
The nervous system contains two main divisions: the central nervous system and the peripheral nervous system. The central nervous system consists of the brain and spinal cord. The peripheral nervous system contains the somatic and autonomic systems. In turn, the autonomic nervous system has sympathetic and parasympathetic divisions.

brain or spinal cord to the muscles and glands, make up the **peripheral nervous system.** In the comparison of the nervous system to a computer, the peripheral nervous system makes up the nervous system's peripheral devices—keyboard, mouse, diskettes, and so on. You would not be able to feed information to your computer's central processing unit without these *peripheral* devices. Other peripheral devices, such as your monitor and printer, allow you to follow what is happening inside your CPU and to see what it has accomplished.

The Peripheral Nervous System: The Body's Peripheral Devices

Question: What are the divisions and functions of the peripheral nervous system? The peripheral nervous system consists of sensory and motor neurons that transmit messages to and from the central nervous system. Without the peripheral nervous system, our brains would be like isolated CPUs. There would be no keyboards, mouses, diskettes, or other ways of inputting information. There would be no monitors, printers, modems, or other ways of displaying or transmitting information. We would be detached from the world: We would not be able to perceive it; we would not be able to act on it. The two main divisions of the peripheral nervous system are the *somatic nervous system* and the *autonomic nervous system.*

The **somatic nervous system** contains sensory (afferent) and motor (efferent) neurons. It transmits messages about sights, sounds, smells, temperature, body positions, and so on, to the central nervous system. As a result, we can experience the beauties and the horrors of the world, its physical ecstasies and agonies. Messages transmitted from the brain and spinal cord to the somatic nervous system control purposeful body movements such as raising a hand, winking, or running, as well as the tiny, almost imperceptible movements that maintain our balance and posture.

Autonomic means "automatic." The **autonomic nervous system** (ANS) regulates the glands and the muscles of internal organs. Thus, the ANS controls activities such as heartbeat, respiration, digestion, and dilation of the pupils of the eyes. These activities can occur automatically, while we are asleep. But some of them can be overridden by conscious control. You can breathe at a purposeful pace, for example. Methods like biofeedback and yoga also help people gain voluntary control of functions such as heart rate and blood pressure.

The ANS also has two branches, or divisions: **sympathetic** and **parasympathetic.** These branches have largely opposing effects. Many organs and glands are stimulated by both branches of the ANS (Figure 2.4). When organs and glands are simultaneously stimulated by both divisions, their effects can average out to some degree. In general, the sympathetic division is most active during processes that involve spending body energy from stored reserves, such as a fight-or-flight response to a predator or when you find out that your rent is going to be raised. The parasympathetic division is most active during processes that replenish reserves of energy, such as eating. When we are afraid, the sympathetic division of the ANS accelerates the heart rate. When we relax, the parasympathetic division decelerates the heart rate. The parasympathetic division stimulates digestive processes, but the sympathetic branch inhibits digestion. Because the sympathetic division predominates when we feel fear or anxiety, these feelings can cause indigestion.

The ANS is of particular interest to psychologists because its activities are linked to various emotions such as anxiety and love. Some people seem to have overly reactive sympathetic nervous systems. In the absence of external threats, their bodies still respond as though they were faced with danger. Psychologists often help them learn to relax.

The Central Nervous System: The Body's Central Processing Unit

It is your central nervous system that makes you so special. Other species see more sharply, smell more keenly, and hear more acutely. Other species run faster, or fly through the air or swim underwater—without the benefit of artificial devices such as airplanes and submarines. But it is your central nervous system that enables you to use symbols and lan-

---

▲ **REFLECT**
Is breathing voluntary or involuntary (autonomic, automatic)? Could it be both? Explain.

▲ **REFLECT**
Have you ever lost your appetite or thrown up because of anxiety or fear? What biological processes caused fear to produce indigestion?

Peripheral nervous system ▲ The part of the nervous system consisting of the somatic nervous system and the autonomic nervous system.

Somatic nervous system ▲ The division of the peripheral nervous system that connects the central nervous system with sensory receptors, skeletal muscles, and the surface of the body.

Autonomic nervous system (ANS) ▲ The division of the peripheral nervous system that regulates glands and activities such as heartbeat, respiration, digestion, and dilation of the pupils.

Sympathetic ▲ The branch of the ANS that is most active during emotional responses such as fear and anxiety that spend the body's reserves of energy.

Parasympathetic ▲ The branch of the ANS that is most active during processes such as digestion that restore the body's reserves of energy.

PARASYMPATHETIC BRANCH   SYMPATHETIC BRANCH

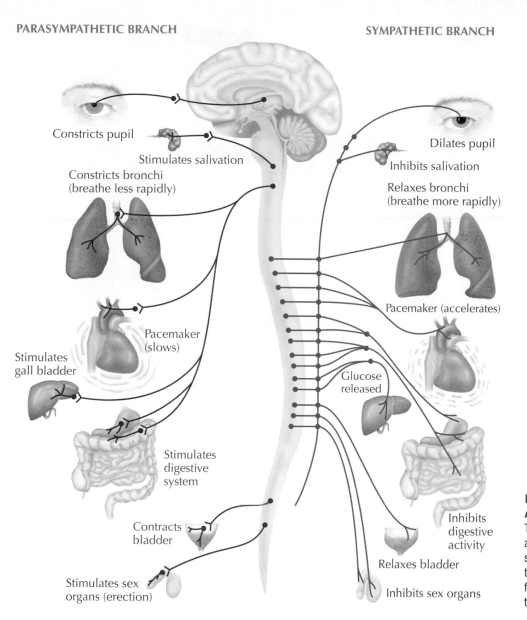

Constricts pupil

Stimulates salivation

Constricts bronchi
(breathe less rapidly)

Stimulates
gall bladder

Pacemaker
(slows)

Stimulates
digestive
system

Contracts
bladder

Stimulates sex
organs (erection)

Dilates pupil

Inhibits salivation

Relaxes bronchi
(breathe more rapidly)

Pacemaker (accelerates)

Glucose
released

Inhibits
digestive
activity

Relaxes bladder

Inhibits sex organs

FIGURE 2.4   The Branches of the Autonomic Nervous System (ANS)
The parasympathetic branch of the ANS generally acts to replenish stores of energy in the body. The sympathetic branch is most active during activities that expend energy. The two branches of the ANS frequently have antagonistic effects on the organs they service.

guage, the abilities that allow people not only to adapt to their environment but to create new environments and give them names (Bandura, 1999). *Question: What are the divisions and functions of the central nervous system?*   The central nervous system consists of the spinal cord and the brain.

The Spinal Cord

The **spinal cord** is a true "information superhighway"—a column of nerves about as thick as a thumb. It transmits messages from sensory receptors to the brain, and from the brain to muscles and glands throughout the body. The spinal cord is also capable of some "local government." That is, it controls some responses to external stimulation through **spinal reflexes.** A spinal reflex is an unlearned response to a stimulus that may involve only two neurons—a sensory (afferent) neuron and a motor (efferent) neuron (Figure 2.5). In some reflexes, a third neuron, called an **interneuron,** transmits the neural impulse from the sensory neuron through the spinal cord to the motor neuron.

We have many reflexes. We blink in response to a puff of air in our faces. We swallow when food accumulates in the mouth. A physician may tap the leg below the knee to elicit the knee-jerk reflex, a sign that the nervous system is operating adequately. Urinating and defecating are reflexes that occur in response to pressure in the bladder and the rectum. Parents typically spend weeks or months toilet-training infants—in other words,

Spinal cord ▲ A column of nerves within the spine that transmits messages from sensory receptors to the brain and from the brain to muscles and glands throughout the body.
Spinal reflex ▲ A simple, unlearned response to a stimulus that may involve only two neurons.
Interneuron ▲ A neuron that transmits a neural impulse from a sensory neuron to a motor neuron.

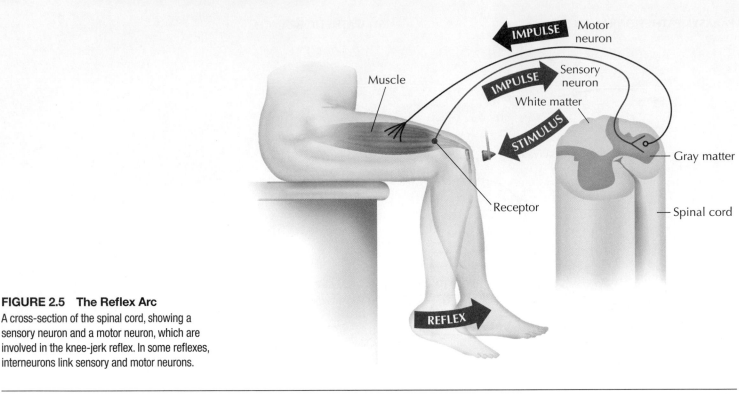

FIGURE 2.5   The Reflex Arc
A cross-section of the spinal cord, showing a sensory neuron and a motor neuron, which are involved in the knee-jerk reflex. In some reflexes, interneurons link sensory and motor neurons.

▲ REFLECT
Does it seem possible that sexual responses like erection and orgasm are reflexive? Why or why not?

CLICK4™ *an essay assignment comparing the nervous system to a computer.*

Gray matter ▲ In the spinal cord, the grayish neurons and neural segments that are involved in spinal reflexes.
White matter ▲ In the spinal cord, axon bundles that carry messages from and to the brain.

teaching them to involve their brains in the process of elimination. Learning to inhibit these reflexes makes civilization possible.

Sexual response also involves many reflexes. Stimulation of the genital organs leads to erection in the male, vaginal lubrication in the female (both are reflexes that make sexual intercourse possible), and the involuntary muscle contractions of orgasm. As reflexes, these processes need not involve the brain, but most often they do. Feelings of passion, memories of an enjoyable sexual encounter, and sexual fantasies usually contribute to sexual response by transmitting messages from the brain to the genitals through the spinal cord.

The spinal cord (and the brain) consists of gray matter and white matter. The **gray matter** is composed of nonmyelinated neurons. Some of these are involved in spinal reflexes. Others send their axons to the brain. The **white matter** is composed of bundles of longer, myelinated (and thus whitish) axons that carry messages to and from the brain. As you can see in Figure 2.5, a cross-section of the spinal cord shows that the gray matter, which includes cell bodies, is distributed in a butterfly pattern.

REVIEW

(14) A _____ is composed of a bundle of axons of neurons. (15) The nervous system is made up of the _____ and central nervous systems. (16) The peripheral nervous system is divided into the _____ and autonomic nervous systems. (17) The somatic nervous system transmits sensory information to the _____ nervous system. Messages from the central nervous system to the somatic nervous system control voluntary movements. (18) The _____ nervous system (ANS) regulates the glands and involuntary activities such as heartbeat and digestion. (19) The _____ division of the ANS dominates in responses that spend bodily resources, such as feeling anxious or fleeing a predator. (20) A spinal _____ may involve as few as two neurons: a sensory and a motor neuron.

Pulling It Together: How are the peripheral and central nervous systems like the peripheral devices and central processing unit of a computer?

THE BRAIN

Every show has a star, and the brain is the undisputed star of the human nervous system. The size and shape of your brain are responsible for your large, delightfully rounded head. In all the animal kingdom, you (and about 6 billion other people) are unique because of the capacities for learning and thinking residing in the human brain.

DIVERSITY The brains of men are about 15% larger than those of women on average (Blum, 1997), which, feminists might argue, proves that bigger is not necessarily better. In the human brain it may be that how well-connected one is (in terms of synapses) is more important than size. (After all, Albert Einstein's brain was only average in size [Witelson et al., 1999].) Moreover, women's brains "run hotter" than men's. Women metabolize more glucose and appear to use more of their brains on a given task (Blum, 1997). In fact, columnist Maureen Dowd (1997) suggests that men squander many of their neurons in preoccupation with things like seduction techniques, sexual fantasies, thinning hair, stock tips, Web sites, and better gear (like cross-training socks).

In any event, let us now turn to a larger issue. *Question: How do researchers learn about the functions of the brain?*

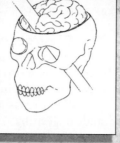
Looking Into the Brain

People have noted the effects of various kinds of damage to the brain throughout history. It has been known for about two centuries that damage to the left side of the brain is connected with loss of sensation or movement on the right side of the body, and vice versa. Thus it has been assumed that the brain's control mechanisms must cross over from right to left, and vice versa, as they descend into the body.

Accidents Many accidents have taught us about the brain. From injuries to the head—some of them minimal, some horrendous—we have learned that brain damage can impair consciousness and awareness. Brain damage can result in loss of vision and hearing, confusion, or loss of memory. In some cases, the loss of large portions of the brain may result in little loss of function. Ironically, the loss of smaller portions in particularly sensitive locations can result in language problems, memory loss, or death.

Accidents provide unplanned and uncontrolled opportunities of studying the brain. Scientists have learned more about the brain, however, through methods like experimentation, use of the electroencephalograph, and brain scans.

Experimenting With the Brain The results of disease (as in the case of Leborgne) and accidents (as in the case of Phineas Gage) have shown us how injury to some parts of the brain is connected with changes in behavior and mental processes. Scientists have also purposefully experimented with the brain to observe the results. For example, damaging—creating a **lesion** in—one part of the brain's limbic system causes monkeys to exhibit a so-called rage response at the slightest provocation. Damaging another area of this system causes rats and monkeys to behave gently. Damaging part of the brain region called the hypothalamus causes rats to overeat. Damaging another part of the hypothalamus causes them to stop eating. It is as if parts of the brain contain on–off switches for certain kinds of behavior, at least in lower animals.

Surgeon Wilder Penfield (1969) stimulated parts of the brain with electrical probes, and as a result his patients reported the occurrence of certain kinds of memories. Similar

> ▲ **REFLECT**
> Do you know of anyone who has had a "brain scan"? What kind of scan? For what purpose? What was the outcome?

Lesion (LEE-shun) ▲ An injury that results in impaired behavior or loss of a function.

49

The Computerized Axial Tomograph (CAT) Scan. In the CAT scan, an X-ray is passed through the head and the amount of radiation that passes through is measured from various angles. The computer integrates the measurements into a view of the brain.

CLICK4™ *an opportunity to design research studies using the MRI, PET, and CAT scans.*

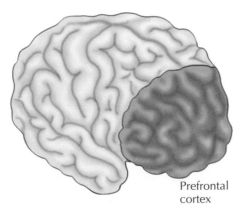

Prefrontal cortex

FIGURE 2.6 The Prefrontal Cortex of the Brain

The prefrontal cortex comes in pairs. One is found in each hemisphere, a bit above the outer edge of the eyebrow. The prefrontal cortex is highly active during visual and spatial problem solving. Some researchers claim that your sense of self also resides largely in the prefrontal cortex.

experiments in electrical stimulation of the brain have found that parts of the brain are connected with specific kinds of sensations (as of light or sound) or motor activities (such as movement of an arm or leg).

The Electroencephalograph   Penfield stimulated parts of the brain with an electrical current and asked people to report what they experienced as a result. Researchers have also used the electroencephalograph (EEG) to record the natural electrical activity of the brain.

When I was an undergraduate psychology student, I first heard that psychologists studied sleep by "connecting" people to the EEG. I had a gruesome image of people somehow being plugged in. Not so. Electrodes are simply attached to the scalp with tape or paste. Once the brain activity under study has been recorded, the electrodes are removed. A bit of soap and water and you're as good as new.

The EEG detects minute amounts of electrical activity—called brain waves—that pass between the electrodes. Certain brain waves are associated with feelings of relaxation and with various stages of sleep. Researchers and physicians use the EEG to locate the areas of the brain that respond to certain stimuli, such as lights or sounds, and to diagnose some kinds of abnormal behavior. The EEG also helps locate tumors.

Brain-Imaging Techniques   At the time when Phineas Gage had his fabled accident, the only ways to look into the brain were to drill holes or crack it open, neither of which would have contributed to the well-being of the subject. But in the latter years of the 20th century, researchers tapped the computer's capacity to generate images of the parts of the brain from sources of radiation to develop imaging techniques that have been useful to researchers and physicians.

The CAT (computerized axial tomograph) scan passes a narrow X-ray beam through the head and measures the structures that reflect the X-rays from various angles, generating a three-dimensional image of the brain. The CAT scan reveals deformities in shape and structure that are connected with blood clots, tumors, and other health problems.

A second method, positron emission tomography (PET scan), forms a computer-generated image of the activity of parts of the brain by tracing the amount of glucose used (or metabolized) by these parts. More glucose is metabolized in more active parts of the brain. To trace the metabolism of glucose, a harmless amount of a radioactive compound, called a *tracer*, is mixed with glucose and injected into the bloodstream. When the glucose reaches the brain, the patterns of activity are revealed by measurement of the positrons—positively charged particles—that are given off by the tracer. The PET scan has been used by researchers to see which parts of the brain are most active when we are, for example, listening to music, working out a math problem, using language, or playing chess. Research with the PET scan suggests that the prefrontal cortex of the brain may be where we process much of the information involved in verbal and spatial problem solving (Duncan et al., 2000). Figure 2.6 shows the prefrontal cortex. One prefrontal region is found in each hemisphere, a bit above the outer edge of the eyebrow.

A third imaging technique is magnetic resonance imaging (MRI). In MRI, the person lies in a powerful magnetic field and is exposed to radio waves that cause parts of the brain to emit signals, which are measured from multiple angles. MRI relies on subtle shifts in blood flow. (More blood flows to more active parts of the brain, supplying them with oxygen.) MRI can also be used to show which parts of the brain are active when we, say, are solving math problems (Rickard et al., 2000). MRI studies have shown that people with schizophrenia have smaller prefrontal regions of the cortex than other people (Flashman et al., 2000) but larger ventricles (hollow spaces) in the brain (Wright et al., 2000).

A Tour of the Brain

Your brain is a fascinating archaeological site. It reveals much of what is so special about you. It also holds a record of your connectedness with other animals that have walked, swum, and flown the Earth for hundreds of millions of years. In fact, some parts of your brain—those that we meet first on our tour—are not all that different from the

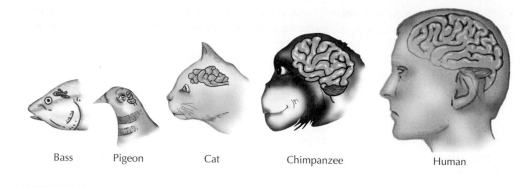

FIGURE 2.7   Comparison of the Human Brain to the Brains of Other Species
Some parts of the human brain, especially the older parts, are quite similar to the corresponding parts of the brains of other mammals. They are even somewhat similar to those of birds and fish, and are involved in survival functions such as breathing, feeding, and the regulation of the sleeping–waking cycle. However, the cerebrums, which are involved in cognitive processes, are quite different.

Bass   Pigeon   Cat   Chimpanzee   Human

corresponding parts of the brains of rats, cats, and monkeys. They even bear some resemblance to the brains of birds and fish (Figure 2.7). The "older" parts of your brain, evolutionarily speaking—those that are found beneath your rounded skull—also have functions very similar to those of these other species. They are involved in basic survival functions such as breathing, feeding, and the regulation of cycles of sleeping and waking. *Question: What are the structures and functions of the brain?*

Let us now begin our tour of the brain (Figure 2.8). We begin with the oldest part of our "archaeological dig"—the hindbrain, where the spinal cord rises to meet the brain. The hindbrain consists of three major structures: the medulla, the pons, and the cerebellum. Many pathways that connect the spinal cord to higher levels of the brain pass through the **medulla.** The medulla regulates vital functions such as heart rate, blood pressure, and respiration. It also plays a role in sleeping, sneezing, and coughing. The **pons** is a bulge in the hindbrain that lies forward of the medulla. *Pons* is the Latin word

Medulla ▲ An oblong area of the hindbrain involved in regulation of heartbeat and respiration.
Pons ▲ A structure of the hindbrain involved in respiration, attention, and sleep and dreaming.

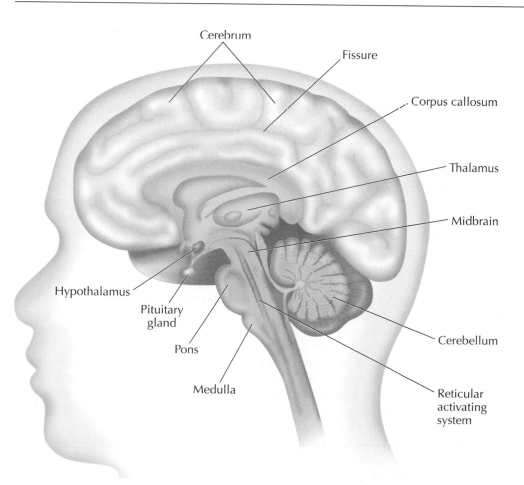

Cerebrum

Fissure

Corpus callosum

Thalamus

Midbrain

Cerebellum

Reticular activating system

Hypothalamus

Pituitary gland

Pons

Medulla

FIGURE 2.8   The Parts of the Human Brain
This view of the brain, split top to bottom, shows some of the most important structures.

www 2 L 8

CLICK4™ *the Web site of the* Whole Brain Atlas—Views of the Brain, *hosted by Harvard University.*

for "bridge." The pons is so named because of the bundles of nerves that pass through it. The pons transmits information about body movement and is involved in functions related to attention, sleep and alertness, and respiration.

Behind the pons lies the **cerebellum** ("little brain" in Latin). The cerebellum has two hemispheres that are involved in maintaining balance and in controlling motor (muscle) behavior. Injury to the cerebellum may lead to lack of motor coordination, stumbling, and loss of muscle tone.

The **reticular activating system** (RAS) begins in the hindbrain and ascends through the midbrain into the lower part of the forebrain. It is vital in the functions of attention, sleep, and arousal. Injury to the RAS may result in a coma. Stimulation of the RAS causes it to send messages to the cerebral cortex (the large wrinkled mass that you think of as your brain), making us more alert to sensory information. In classic neurological research, Giuseppe Moruzzi and Horace Magoun (1949) discovered that electrical stimulation of the reticular formation of a sleeping cat caused it to awaken at once. But when the reticular formation was severed from higher parts of the brain, the animal fell into a coma from which it would not awaken. Drugs known as central nervous system depressants, such as alcohol, are thought to work, in part, by lowering RAS activity.

Sudden loud noises stimulate the RAS and awaken a sleeping animal or person. But the RAS may become selective through learning. That is, it comes to play a filtering role. It may allow some messages to filter through to higher brain levels and awareness while screening others out. For example, the parent who has primary responsibility for child care may be awakened by the stirring sounds of an infant, while the sounds of traffic or street noise are filtered out, even though they are louder. The other parent, in contrast, may sleep through loud crying by the infant. If the first parent must be away for several days, however, the second parent's RAS may quickly become sensitive to noises produced by the child. This sensitivity may rapidly fade again when the first parent returns.

Also located in the midbrain are areas involved in vision and hearing. These include the area that controls eye reflexes such as dilation of the pupils and eye movements.

Key areas of the forward-most part of the brain, or forebrain, are the thalamus, the hypothalamus, the limbic system, and the cerebrum (see Figure 2.8). The **thalamus** is located near the center of the brain. It consists of two joined egg- or football-shaped structures. The thalamus serves as a relay station for sensory stimulation. Nerve fibers from the sensory systems enter from below; the information carried by them is then transmitted to the cerebral cortex by way of fibers that exit from above. For instance, the thalamus relays sensory input from the eyes to the visual areas of the cerebral cortex. The thalamus is also involved in controlling sleep and attention in coordination with other brain structures, including the RAS.

The **hypothalamus** lies beneath the thalamus and above the pituitary gland. It weighs only 4 grams, yet it is vital in the regulation of body temperature, concentration of fluids, storage of nutrients, and various aspects of motivation and emotion. Experimenters learn many of the functions of the hypothalamus by implanting electrodes in parts of it and observing the effects of an electrical current. They have found that the hypothalamus is involved in hunger, thirst, sexual behavior, caring for offspring, and aggression. Among lower animals, stimulation of various areas of the hypothalamus can trigger instinctual behaviors such as fighting, mating, or even nest building.

Canadian psychologists James Olds and Peter Milner (1954) made a wonderful mistake in the 1950s. They were attempting to implant an electrode in a rat's reticular formation to see how stimulation of the area might affect learning. Olds, however, was primarily a social psychologist and not a biological psychologist. He missed his target and found a part of the animal's hypothalamus instead. Olds and Milner dubbed this area the "pleasure center" because the animal would repeat whatever it was doing when it was stimulated. The term *pleasure center* is not used too frequently, because it appears to attribute human emotions to rats. Yet the "pleasure centers" must be doing something right, because rats stimulate themselves in these centers by pressing a pedal several thousand times an hour, until they are exhausted (Olds, 1969).

The hypothalamus is just as important to humans as it is to lower animals. Unfortunately (or fortunately), our "pleasure centers" are not as clearly defined as those of the rat. Then, too, our responses to messages from the hypothalamus are less automatic and rela-

▲ **REFLECT**

If your brain had a pleasure center, would you like to have your finger on the switch that turns it on or off? Might religious leaders be concerned? Why or why not?

CLICK4™ *Old's & Milner's classic article, "Positive Reinforcement Produced by Electrical Stimulation of the Septal Area and Other Regions of Rat Brain."*

Cerebellum ▲ A part of the hindbrain involved in muscle coordination and balance.

Reticular activating system ▲ A part of the brain involved in attention, sleep, and arousal.

Thalamus ▲ An area near the center of the brain involved in the relay of sensory information to the cortex and in the functions of sleep and attention.

Hypothalamus ▲ A bundle of nuclei below the thalamus involved in body temperature, motivation, and emotion.

tively more influenced by higher brain functions—that is, cognitive factors such as thought, choice, and value systems. It is all a part of being human.

The **limbic system** is made up of several structures, including the amygdala, hippocampus, and parts of the hypothalamus (Figure 2.9). The limbic system lies along the inner edge of the cerebrum and is fully evolved only in mammals. It is involved in memory and emotion, and in the drives of hunger, sex, and aggression. People in whom operations have damaged the hippocampus can retrieve old memories but cannot permanently store new information. As a result, they may reread the same newspaper day in and day out without recalling that they read it before. Or they may have to be perpetually reintroduced to people they have met just hours earlier (Squire, 1993, 1996).

The **amygdala** looks like two little almonds. Studies using lesioning and electrical stimulation show that the amygdala is connected with aggressive behavior in monkeys, cats, and other animals. Early in the 20th century Heinrich Klüver and Paul Bucy (1939) lesioned part of the amygdala of a rhesus monkey. Rhesus monkeys are normally a scrappy lot and try to bite or grab at intruders, but destruction of this animal's amygdala made it docile. No longer did it react aggressively to people. It even allowed people to poke and pinch it. Electrical stimulation of the part of the amygdala that Klüver and Bucy had destroyed, however, triggers a "rage response." For example, it causes a cat to hiss and arch its back in preparation to attack. The amygdala is also connected with a fear response (LeDoux, 1998). If you electrically stimulate another part of the amygdala, the cat cringes in fear when you cage it with a mouse. Not very tigerlike.

DIVERSITY The amygdala is also connected with vigilance. It is involved in emotions, learning, and memory, and it sort of behaves like a spotlight, focusing attention on matters that are novel and important to know more about. In studies reported in 2000, researchers used MRI to scan the amygdala while participants were shown faces of European Americans and African Americans. One study flashed the photos by four men and four women, half European American and half African American (Hart et al., 2000). The participants showed less activity in the amygdala when they viewed faces belonging to people of their own ethnic group, suggesting that they were more comfortable with "familiar" faces.

Other studies attempted to connect the "lighting up" of the amygdala with other racially oriented responses. In one, European American participants were shown photos of young European Americans and African Americans (Phelps et al., 2000). Days later, the participants were given tests to measure their responses to African Americans. For example, one test involved sitting at a computer and classifying the photos by race at the

Limbic system ▲ A group of structures involved in memory, motivation, and emotion that forms a fringe along the inner edge of the cerebrum.

Amygdala ▲ A part of the limbic system that apparently facilitates stereotypical aggressive responses.

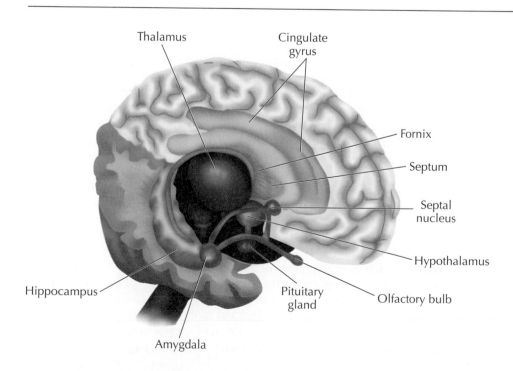

Thalamus

Cingulate gyrus

Fornix

Septum

Septal nucleus

Hypothalamus

Olfactory bulb

Hippocampus

Pituitary gland

Amygdala

FIGURE 2.9 The Limbic System
The limbic system is made up of structures that include the amygdala, the hippocampus, and parts of the hypothalamus. It is evolved fully only in mammals and forms a fringe along the inner edge of the cerebrum. The limbic system is involved in memory and emotion and in the drives of hunger, sex, and aggression.

CLICK4™ *views of the brain that you can spin!*

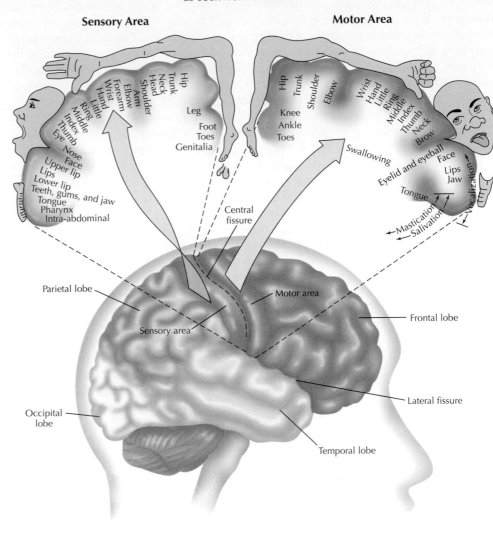

Cross-sections of motor and sensory areas of the cerebral cortex, as seen from the front

FIGURE 2.10 The Geography of the Cerebral Cortex

The cortex is divided into four lobes: frontal, parietal, temporal, and occipital. The visual area of the cortex is located in the occipital lobe. The hearing or auditory cortex lies in the temporal lobe. The sensory and motor areas face each other across the central fissure. What happens when a surgeon stimulates areas of the sensory or motor cortex during an operation?

same time they were classifying words flashing on the screen as "good" or "bad." Most participants tend to associate positive words like joy, love, and peace with European Americans and negative words like cancer, bomb, and devil with African Americans. It turned out that participants who were more likely to associate African Americans with negative words also showed greater activity in the amygdala when presented with faces of African Americans. The researchers do not suggest that the amygdala activity—or even the word-association test—is a sign of conscious prejudice. They offer the alternative hypothesis that European Americans may simply be less familiar with faces of African Americans, and that the relative lack of familiarity could trigger activity in the amygdala and negative feelings (fear of the unknown). The researchers find evidence for this interpretation in the fact that European Americans did *not* show the heightened activity of the amygdala when photos of familiar African Americans—Michael Jordan and Denzel Washington—flashed by.

The **cerebrum** is the crowning glory of the brain. Only in human beings does the cerebrum account for such a large proportion of the brain (Figure 2.10). The cerebrum is responsible for the cognitive abilities of thinking and language. The surface of the cerebrum is wrinkled, or convoluted, with ridges and valleys. This surface is termed the **cerebral cortex.** The convolutions allow a great deal of surface area to be packed into the brain—and surface area is apparently connected with human cognitive ability.

Cerebrum ▲ The large mass of the forebrain, which consists of two hemispheres.
Cerebral cortex ▲ The wrinkled surface area (gray matter) of the cerebrum.

Valleys in the cortex are called *fissures*. A key fissure almost divides the cerebrum in half, creating two hemispheres with something of the shape of a walnut. The hemispheres are connected by the **corpus callosum** (Latin for "thick body" or "hard body"), a bundle of some 200 million nerve fibers.

REVIEW

(21) Most historic discoveries about the brain were made by accident, as in the case of Phineas _____. (22) The _____ records the electrical activity of the brain. (23) Computerized axial _____ passes X-ray beams through the head and measures the structures that reflect them. (24) Positron _____ _____ forms an image of brain activity based on the amount of glucose metabolized by parts of the brain. (25) In magnetic _____ imaging, radio waves cause parts of the brain to emit signals.

(26) The _____ is involved in balance and coordination. (27) The _____ activating system is vital in attention, sleep, and arousal. (28) The _____ serves as a relay station for sensory stimulation. (29) The _____ is involved in body temperature, motivation, and emotion. (30) The _____ system is involved in memory and in the drives of hunger, sex, and aggression. (31) The hemispheres of the cerebrum are connected by the corpus _____.

Pulling It Together: How do researchers observe the inner workings of the brain? Since all parts of your brain developed after you were conceived, why do we speak of your hindbrain as the oldest part of your brain? Are the "older" parts of the brain more "primitive"? Explain.

THE CEREBRAL CORTEX

The cerebral cortex is the part of the brain that you usually think of as your brain. *Cortex* is a Latin word meaning "bark," as in the bark of a tree. Just as the bark is the outer coating of a tree, the cerebral cortex is the outer coating of the cerebrum. It is only about one-eighth of an inch thick.

The cerebral cortex is involved in almost every bodily activity, including most sensations and most responses. It is also the part of the brain that frees people from the tyranny of genetic dictates and instinct. It is the seat of thinking and language, and it enables humans to think deeply about the world outside and to make decisions. Other organisms run faster than we do, are stronger, or bite more sharply. Yet humans think faster, are intellectually "stronger," and, we might add, have a "biting" wit—all of which is made possible by the cerebral cortex. ***Question: What are the parts of the cerebral cortex?***

The cerebral cortex has two hemispheres, left and right. Each of the hemispheres is divided into four lobes, as shown in Figure 2.10. The **frontal lobe** lies in front of the central fissure and the **parietal lobe** behind it. The **temporal lobe** lies below the side, or lateral, fissure—across from the frontal and parietal lobes. The **occipital lobe** lies behind the temporal lobe and behind and below the parietal lobe.

When light strikes the eyes, neurons in the occipital lobe fire, and as a result, we "see" (that is, the image is projected in the brain). Direct artificial stimulation of the occipital lobe also produces visual sensations. If neurons in the occipital region of the cortex were stimulated with electricity, you would "see" flashes of light even if it were pitch black or your eyes were covered. The hearing or auditory area of the cortex lies in the temporal lobe along the lateral fissure. Sounds cause structures in the ear to vibrate. Messages are relayed from those structures to the auditory area of the cortex, and when you hear a noise, neurons in this area are firing.

Just behind the central fissure in the parietal lobe lies an area called the **somatosensory cortex,** which receives messages from skin senses all over the body. These sensations include warmth and cold, touch, pain, and movement. Neurons in different parts of the sensory cortex fire, depending on whether you wiggle your finger or raise your leg. If a brain surgeon were to stimulate the proper area of your somatosensory cortex with an electrical probe, it might seem as if someone were touching your arm or leg. A Swedish

CLICK4™ *a quiz covering the first half of this chapter.*

CLICK4™ *a WebSearch activity probing the motor cortex online.*

CLICK4™ *an interactive illustration of the parts of the cerebral cortex.*

CLICK4™ *a New York Times article: "Brain Signals Shown to Move a Robot's Arm."*

Corpus callosum ▲ A thick fiber bundle that connects the hemispheres of the cortex.

Frontal lobe ▲ The lobe of the cerebral cortex that lies to the front of the central fissure.

Parietal lobe ▲ The lobe that lies just behind the central fissure.

Temporal lobe ▲ The lobe that lies below the lateral fissure, near the temples of the head.

Occipital lobe ▲ The lobe that lies behind and below the parietal lobe and behind the temporal lobe.

Somatosensory cortex ▲ The section of cortex in which sensory stimulation is projected. It lies just behind the central fissure in the parietal lobe.

MRI study found that just the expectation of being tickled in a certain part of the body activates the corresponding area of the somatosensory cortex (Carlsson et al., 2000).

Figure 2.10 suggests that our face and head are overrepresented (too big) on the cortex compared with, say, our trunk and legs. This overrepresentation is one of the reasons that our face and head are more sensitive to touch than other parts of the body.

Many years ago it was discovered that patients with injuries to one hemisphere of the brain would show sensory or motor deficits on the opposite side of the body below the head. This led to the recognition that sensory and motor nerves cross in the brain and elsewhere. The left hemisphere controls acts on, and receives inputs from, the right side of the body. The right hemisphere controls acts on, and receives inputs from, the left side of the body.

How do you make a monkey smile? One way is by inserting an electrical probe in its motor cortex and giving it a burst of electricity. Let us see what we mean by this.

The **motor cortex** lies in the frontal lobe, just across the valley of the central fissure from the somatosensory cortex. Neurons firing in the motor cortex cause parts of our body to move. More than 100 years ago, German scientists electrically stimulated the motor cortex in dogs and observed that muscles contracted in response (Fritsch & Hitzig, 1870/1960). Since then, neuroscientists have mapped the motor cortex in people and lower animals by inserting electrical probes and seeing which muscles contract. For example, José Delgado (1969) caused one patient to make a fist even though he tried to prevent his hand from closing. The patient said, "I guess, doctor, that your electricity is stronger than my will" (Delgado, 1969, p. 114). Delgado also made a monkey smile in this manner, many thousands of times in a row. If a surgeon were to stimulate a certain area of the right hemisphere of the motor cortex with an electrical probe, you would raise your left leg. This action would be sensed in the somatosensory cortex, and you might have a devil of a time trying to figure out whether you had intended to raise that leg!

Thinking, Language, and the Cortex

Areas of the cerebral cortex that are not primarily involved in sensation or motor activity are called *association areas*. They make possible the breadth and depth of human learning, thought, memory, and language. *Question: What parts of the cerebral cortex are involved in thinking and language?* The association areas in the *prefrontal* region of the brain—that is, in the frontal lobes, near the forehead—could be called the brain's executive center. It appears to be where we solve problems and make plans and decisions (Chafee & Goldman-Rakic, 2000; Duncan et al., 2000; Levy & Goldman-Rakic, 1999).

Executive functions like problem solving also require memory, like the memory in your computer. These areas also provide the core of your working memory (Chafee & Goldman-Rakic, 2000; Levy & Goldman-Rakic, 1999). They are connected with various sensory areas in the brain and can tap whatever kind of sensory information is needed or desired. The prefrontal region of the brain thus retrieves visual, auditory, and other kinds of memories and manipulates them—similar to the way in which a computer retrieves information from files in storage and manipulates it in working memory.

Certain neurons in the visual area of the occipital lobe fire in response to the visual presentation of vertical lines. Others fire in response to presentation of horizontal lines. Although one group of cells may respond to one aspect of the visual field and another group of cells may respond to another, association areas put it all together. As a result, we see a box or an automobile or a road map and not a confusing array of verticals and horizontals.

Language Functions
In some ways, the left and right hemispheres of the brain duplicate each other's functions. In other ways, they differ. The left hemisphere contains language functions for nearly all right-handed people and for 2 out of 3 left-handed people (Pinker, 1994). However, the brain remains "plastic," or changeable, through about the age of 13. As a result, children who lose the left hemisphere of the brain because of surgery to control **epilepsy** usually transfer speech functions to the right hemisphere (Zuger, 1997).

▲ **REFLECT**
Do you believe that something happens in the brain every time you have a thought or an experience? Do you find this idea logical or unsettling? Explain.

Motor cortex ▲ The section of cortex that lies in the frontal lobe, just across the central fissure from the sensory cortex. Neural impulses in the motor cortex are linked to muscular responses throughout the body.

Epilepsy ▲ Temporary disturbances of brain functions that involve sudden neural discharges.

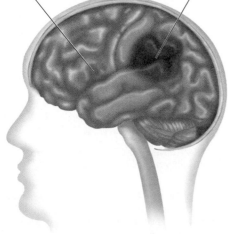

Broca's area   Wernicke's area

FIGURE 2.11 Broca's and Wernicke's Areas of the Cerebral Cortex
The areas that are most involved in speech are Broca's area and Wernicke's area. Damage to either area can produce an *aphasia*—a disruption of the ability to understand or produce language.

Two key language areas lie within the hemisphere of the cortex that contains language functions (usually the left hemisphere): Broca's area and Wernicke's area (see Figure 2.11). Damage to either area is likely to cause an **aphasia**—that is, a disruption of the ability to understand or produce language.

Wernicke's area lies in the temporal lobe near the auditory cortex. It responds mainly to auditory information. As you are reading this page, however, the visual information is registered in the visual cortex of your occipital lobe. It is then recoded as auditory information as it travels to Wernicke's area. Broca's area is located in the frontal lobe, near the section of the motor cortex that controls the muscles of the tongue, throat, and other areas of the face used when speaking (Pinker, 1994; Raichle, 1994). Broca's area processes the information and relays it to the motor cortex. The motor cortex sends the signals that cause muscles in your throat and mouth to contract. If you are "subvocalizing"—saying what you are reading "under your breath"—that is because Wernicke's area transmits information to Broca's area via nerve fibers.

People with damage to Wernicke's area may show **Wernicke's aphasia,** which impairs their abilities to comprehend speech and to think of the proper words to express their own thoughts. Ironically, they usually speak freely and with proper syntax. Wernicke's area is essential to understanding the relationships between words and their meanings. When Broca's area is damaged, people usually understand language well enough but speak slowly and laboriously, in simple sentences. This pattern is termed **Broca's aphasia.**

A part of the brain called the *angular gyrus* lies between the visual cortex and Wernicke's area. The angular gyrus "translates" visual information, as in perceiving written words, into auditory information (sounds) and sends it on to Wernicke's area. It appears that problems in the angular gyrus can give rise to *dyslexia*, or serious impairment in reading, because it becomes difficult for the reader to segment words into sounds (Pugh et al., 2000).

Paul Broca

One of French Surgeon Paul Broca's (1824–1880) hobbies was *craniometry*, or measurement of the skull. He believed that the size of the brain was related to intelligence. (Generally speaking, it isn't.) He argued that the brains of mature people were larger than those of older people, in "superior" races than in "inferior" ones, in men than in women, and in accomplished men than in run-of-the-mill men. Broca was well aware of evidence that contradicted his views. He knew that the brains of Asians were generally smaller than those of Europeans, although Asians were at least as bright. He knew of extremely intelligent women and of criminals with large brains. Nevertheless, he and his fellow craniometrists touted their views. Upon his death, it was discovered that Broca's own brain was but a bit above average in size—nothing to brag of.

Despite his only slightly-above-average-sized brain, Broca was the first to observe a behavior problem and then locate the area of the brain that caused it. In 1861, Leborgne, a 51-year-old patient at La Bicêtre, the Paris asylum, came down with gangrene in the leg and was admitted to the surgical ward. Leborgne could understand what was said to him but could only utter the meaningless sound "tan" and sometimes blurt out "Sacred name of God!" in frustration. Leborgne had entered the asylum 21 years earlier, when he had lost the ability to speak.

Leborgne died six days later and Broca performed an autopsy. He discovered that an egg-sized area on the left side of the brain, which we now call *Broca's area*, had deteriorated. Broca concluded that this part of the brain was the seat of speech.

CLICK4™ *an essay assignment on brain injuries and their effects.*

Left Brain, Right Brain?

We often hear of being "left-brained" or "right-brained." *Question: What would it mean to be "left-brained" or "right-brained"?* The notion is that the hemispheres of the brain are involved in very different kinds of intellectual and emotional functions and responses. According to this view, left-brained people would be primarily logical and intellectual. Right-brained people would be intuitive, creative, and emotional. Those of us who are fortunate enough to have our brains "in balance" would presumably have the best of it—the capacity for logic combined with emotional richness.

Like so many other popular ideas, the left-brain–right-brain notion is at best exaggerated. Research does suggest that in right-handed individuals, the left hemisphere is relatively more involved in intellectual undertakings that require logical analysis and problem solving, language, and mathematical computation (Gazzaniga, 1995). The other hemisphere (usually the right hemisphere) is usually superior in visual–spatial functions (it's better at putting puzzles together), recognition of faces, discrimination of colors, aesthetic and emotional responses, understanding metaphors, and creative mathematical reasoning.

Despite these differences, it would be erroneous to think that the hemispheres of the brain act independently—that some people are truly left-brained and others right-brained (Gazzaniga, 1995). The functions of the left and right hemispheres overlap to

▲ **REFLECT**

As you read the words on this page, neurons in your brain are firing. Where are the neurons whose firing results in your seeing the words? If you "hear" the words inside your head, what neurons are making that possible?

Aphasia ▲ A disruption in the ability to understand or produce language.

Wernicke's aphasia ▲ A language disorder characterized by difficulty comprehending the meaning of spoken language.

Broca's aphasia ▲ A language disorder characterized by slow, laborious speech.

CONTROVERSY IN PSYCHOLOGY

Are Some People Left-Brained and Others Right-Brained?

What aspects of behavior and mental processes are considered left-brained? Which are considered right-brained? Does research evidence support a sharp distinction between left-brain and right-brain functions?

CLICK4™ *a bulletin board discussion on being right-brained or left-brained.*

▲ REFLECT

Do you know anyone who was "changed" from a lefty to a righty? Why was the change made? How was it done? Was it successful? Explain.

CLICK4™ *an opportunity to participate online in a hand-preference study.*

some degree, and the hemispheres tend to respond simultaneously as we focus our attention on one thing or another. The hemispheres are aided in their "cooperation" by the corpus callosum, the bundle of 200 million axons that connects them.

Now let us consider another issue involving sidedness: left-handedness. People who are left-handed are different from people who are right-handed in terms of the way they write, throw a ball, and so on. But there are interesting questions as to whether people who are left-handed are psychologically different from "righties."

Handedness: Is It Gauche or Sinister to Be Left-Handed?

What do Michelangelo, Leonardo da Vinci, Pablo Picasso, and Steve Young all have in common? No, they are not all artists. Only one is a football player. But they are all left-handed. Some other well-known lefties are shown in Figure 2.12. *Questions: Does it matter whether one is left-handed? Why are people right-handed or left-handed?*

Being a "lefty" is often regarded as a deficiency. The language swarms with slurs on lefties. We speak of "left-handed compliments," of having "two left feet," of strange events as "coming out of left field." The word *sinister* means "left-hand or unlucky side" in Latin. *Gauche* is a French word that literally means "left," though in English it is used to mean awkward or ill-mannered. The English word *adroit*, meaning "skillful," derives from the French *à droit*, literally translated as "to the right." Also consider positive usages such as "being righteous" or "being on one's right side."

Yet, 8% to 10% of us are lefties. Left-handedness is more common in boys than girls (Rosenbaum, 2000). We are usually labeled right-handed or left-handed on the basis of our handwriting preferences, yet some people write with one hand and pass a football with the other. Some people even swing a tennis racket and pitch a baseball with different hands. President Ronald Reagan wrote and ate with his right hand, but shot pistols and waved with his left hand (Rosenbaum, 2000).

Being left-handed may not be gauche or sinister, but it may matter in that it appears to be connected with language problems such as dyslexia and stuttering and health prob-

---

FIGURE 2.12 Some Well-Known Left-Handed People

Being left-handed is connected with language problems such as dyslexia and stuttering, physical health problems such as migraine headaches and allergies, and psychological disorders like schizophrenia. However, left-handed people are also twice as likely as right-handed people to be artists, musicians, and mathematicians.

Source: Rosenbaum, D. E. (2000, May 16). On left-handedness, its causes and costs. *The New York Times*, p. F6.

FROM NAPOLEON TO OPRAH—FAMOUS LEFTIES

Historical Figures: Alexander the Great, Charlemagne, Julius Caesar, Napoleon Bonaparte, Dr. Albert Schweitzer

Napoleon Bonaparte— Soldier, Emperor, and Leftie

Entertainers (present): Oprah Winfrey, Whoopi Goldberg, Jay Leno, Jerry Seinfeld, Robert Redford

Oprah Winfrey—Talk Show Host, Actor, Author, and Leftie

People in the News: Gen. Colin L. Powell, Gen. H. Norman Schwarzkopf, Fidel Castro, Steve Forbes, Ross Perot

Entertainers (past): Marilyn Monroe, Greta Garbo, Judy Garland, W. C. Fields, Charlie Chaplin

Authors: Mark Twain, Lewis Carroll, Eudora Welty, James Baldwin, Peter Benchley

Athletes: Ben Hogan (golf), Mark Spitz (swimming), Pelé (soccer), Bill Russell (basketball), Bruce Jenner (track)

Artists: Leonardo da Vinci, Michelangelo, Pablo Picasso, Raphael, Albrecht Dürer

Music: Ludwig van Beethoven, Ringo Starr, Paul McCartney, Cole Porter, Jimi Hendrix

Law: Justice Ruth Bader Ginsberg, Justice Anthony M. Kennedy, Marcia Clark, Clarence Darrow, F. Lee Bailey

Criminals: John Dillinger, Billy the Kid, Boston Strangler, Jack-the-Ripper, John Wesley Hardin

lems such as migraine headaches and allergies (Geschwind & Galaburda, 1987). Left-handedness is also apparently connected with psychological disorders like schizophrenia (Rosenbaum, 2000). On the other hand, there may be advantages to being left-handed. According to a British study, left-handed people are twice as likely as right-handed people to be numbered among the ranks of artists, musicians, and mathematicians (Kilshaw & Annett, 1983). Figure 2.12 shows that some of the greatest artists were lefties.

Handedness is also apparently connected—although weakly—with sexual orientation. A meta-analysis of 20 studies found that gay males and lesbians are 39% more likely than people with a heterosexual orientation to be left-handed (Lalumière et al., 2000). Even so, we should note that the majority of gay males and lesbians are right-handed.

The origins of handedness are likely to have a genetic component. Left-handedness runs in families. In the English royal family, the Queen Mother, Queen Elizabeth II, and Princes Charles and William are all left-handed (Rosenbaum, 2000). If both of your parents are right-handed, your chances of being right-handed are about 92%. If one of your parents is left-handed, your chances of being right-handed drop to about 80%. And if both of your parents are left-handed, your chances of also being left-handed are about 1 in 2 (Rosenbaum, 2000). In any event, handedness comes early. A study employing ultrasound found that about 95% of fetuses suck their right thumbs rather than their left (Hepper et al., 1990). Geneticist Amar J. S. Klar believes that about 80% of people have a dominant gene that makes them right-handed. The other 20% lack this gene and have a 50-50 chance of becoming right-handed or left-handed. This view explains why about 10% of us are left-handed, and why about 18% of identical twins have different handedness (Rosenbaum, 2000). UCLA neurologist Daniel H. Geschwind (2000) agrees that handedness involves genetics, but he doubts that a single gene is responsible and finds a role for developmental factors.

Whether we are talking about language functions, being "left-brained" or "right-brained," or handedness, we are talking about people whose hemispheres of the cerebral cortex communicate back and forth. Now let us see what happens when the major avenue of communication between the hemispheres shuts down.

Split-Brain Experiments: When Hemispheres Go Their Own Way

A number of people with severe cases of epilepsy have split-brain operations in which much of the corpus callosum is severed (Engel, 1996). The purpose of the operation is to confine seizures to one hemisphere of the cerebral cortex rather than allowing a neural tempest to reverberate. Split-brain operations do seem to help people with epilepsy. *Question: What happens when the brain is split in two?*

People who have undergone split-brain operations can be thought of as winding up with two brains, yet under most circumstances their behavior remains ordinary enough. Still, some aspects of hemispheres that have stopped talking to each other are intriguing.

As reported by pioneering brain surgeon Joseph Bogen (1969), each hemisphere may have a "mind of its own." One split-brain patient reported that her hemispheres frequently disagreed on what she should be wearing. What she meant was that one hand might undo her blouse as rapidly as the other was buttoning it. A man reported that one hemisphere (the left hemisphere, which contained language functions) liked reading but the other one did not. If he shifted a book from his right hand to his left hand, his left hand would put it down. The left hand is connected with the right hemisphere of the cerebral cortex, which in most people—including this patient—does not contain language functions.

Michael Gazzaniga (1995) showed that people with split brains whose eyes are closed may be able to verbally describe an object such as a key when they hold it in one hand, but not when they hold it in the other hand. As shown in Figure 2.13, if a person with a split brain handles a key with his left hand behind a screen, tactile impressions of the key are projected into the right hemisphere, which has little or no language ability. Thus, he will not be able to describe the key. If he holds it in his right hand, he will have no trouble describing it because sensory impressions are projected into the left hemisphere of the cortex, which contains language functions. To further confound matters, if

CONTROVERSY IN PSYCHOLOGY

Is Being Left-Handed an Asset or a Liability?

Why are people left-handed (or right-handed)? How do we explain differences in behavior and mental processes between left-handed and right-handed people?

CLICK4™ *a bulletin board discussion on being left-handed. Is it an asset or liability?*

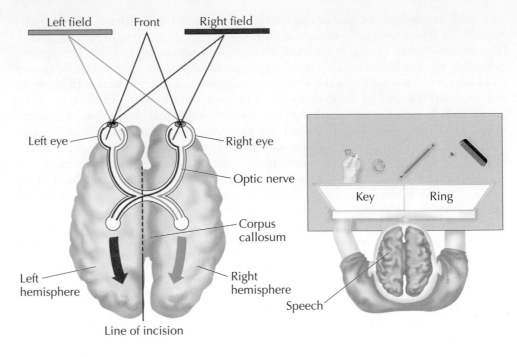

FIGURE 2.13 A Divided-Brain Experiment
In the drawing on the left, we see that visual sensations in the left visual field are projected in the occipital cortex of the right hemisphere. Visual sensations from the right visual field are projected in the occipital cortex in the left hemisphere. In the divided-brain experiment diagramed on the right, a person with a severed corpus callosum handles a key with his left hand and perceives the written word *key* in his left visual field. The word *key* is projected in the right hemisphere. Speech, however, is usually a function of the left hemisphere. The written word *ring*, perceived by the right visual field, is projected in the left hemisphere. So, when asked what he is handling, the divided-brain subject reports "ring," not "key."

the word *ring* is projected into the left hemisphere while the person is asked what he is handling, he will say "ring," not "key."

However, this discrepancy between what is felt and what is said occurs only in people with split brains. Most of the time the two hemispheres work together, even when we are playing the piano or solving math problems.

REVIEW

(32) The visual cortex is found in the _____ lobe of the cortex. (33) The auditory cortex is in the _____ lobe. (34) The sensory cortex lies behind the central fissure in the _____ lobe. (35) The motor cortex lies in the _____ lobe. (36) The executive center of the brain is found in the _____ lobe. (37) Language areas are usually found in the (left or right?) hemisphere. (38) Although the hemispheres of the brain tend to work together, the _____ hemisphere is relatively more involved in logic and problem solving. The right hemisphere is usually more involved in visual–spatial functions, face recognition, color discrimination, and aesthetic and emotional responses. (39) Being _____-handed appears to be connected with learning disabilities and some health problems. (40) Left-handed people are (more or less?) likely than right-handed people to be artists, musicians, and mathematicians. (41) Split-brain operations sever much of the corpus callosum in order to control _____. (42) People with split brains whose eyes are covered are usually able to verbally describe an object such as a key when it is held in (only one or either?) hand.

Pulling It Together: Where do we find brain activity when you think about raising your arm? Why do different aphasias reflect damage in different parts of the brain? So, what happens when doctors split the brain down the middle?

THE ENDOCRINE SYSTEM

The body contains two types of **glands:** glands with ducts and glands without ducts. A *duct* is a passageway that carries substances to specific locations. Saliva, sweat, tears, and breast milk all reach their destinations through ducts. Psychologists are interested in the substances secreted by ductless glands because of their behavioral effects. ***Question: What is the endocrine system?*** The ductless glands constitute the **endocrine sys-**

Gland ▲ An organ that secretes one or more chemical substances such as hormones, saliva, or milk.
Endocrine system ▲ The body's system of ductless glands that secrete hormones and release them directly into the bloodstream.

tem, and they secrete **hormones** (from the Greek *horman*, meaning "to stimulate" or "to excite").

Hormones are released into the bloodstream and circulate through the body. Like neurotransmitters, hormones have specific receptor sites. That is, they act only on receptors in certain locations. Some hormones that are released by the hypothalamus influence only the **pituitary gland.** Other hormones released by the pituitary influence the adrenal cortex; still others influence the testes and ovaries, and so on.

Question: What functions of hormones are of interest to psychologists? Much hormonal action helps the body maintain steady states, as in fluid levels, blood sugar levels, and so on. Bodily mechanisms measure current levels, and when these levels deviate from optimal, they signal glands to release hormones. The maintenance of steady states requires feedback of bodily information to glands. This type of system is referred to as a *negative feedback loop.* That is, when enough of a hormone has been secreted, the gland is signaled to stop.

REFLECT

Have you heard that adolescents are "hormonal" or affected by "glands"? If so, which glands would they be?

The Hypothalamus: Master of the Master Gland

The hypothalamus secretes a number of releasing hormones, or factors, that influence the pituitary gland—also called the master gland—to secrete related hormones. For example, growth hormone-releasing factor (hGRF) causes the pituitary to produce growth hormone. A dense network of blood vessels between the hypothalamus and the pituitary gland provides a direct route of influence for these factors.

The Pituitary Gland: The Pea-Sized Governor

The pituitary gland lies below the hypothalamus (see Figure 2.14). Although it is only about the size of a pea, it is so central to the body's functioning that it has been referred to as the "master gland." Despite this designation, today we know that the hypothalamus regulates much pituitary activity. The anterior (front) and posterior (back) lobes of the pituitary gland secrete many hormones. **Growth hormone** regulates the growth of muscles, bones, and glands. Children whose growth patterns are abnormally slow may catch up to their age-mates when they obtain growth hormone. **Prolactin** largely regulates

Hormone ▲ A substance secreted by an endocrine gland that regulates various body functions.
Pituitary gland ▲ The gland that secretes growth hormone, prolactin, antidiuretic hormone, and other hormones.
Growth hormone ▲ A pituitary hormone that regulates growth.
Prolactin ▲ A pituitary hormone that regulates production of milk and, in lower animals, maternal behavior.

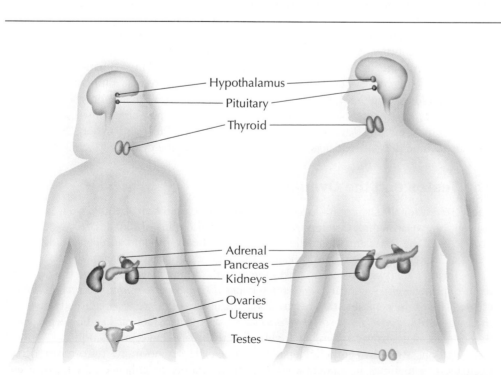

Hypothalamus
Pituitary
Thyroid

Adrenal
Pancreas
Kidneys

Ovaries
Uterus

Testes

FIGURE 2.14   Major Glands of the Endocrine System

The endocrine system consists of ductless glands that release hormones directly into the bloodstream. But hormones are only taken up by parts of the body that have appropriate receptor sites.

maternal behavior in lower mammals such as rats and stimulates production of milk in women. As a water conservation measure, **antidiuretic hormone** (ADH) inhibits production of urine when fluid levels in the body are low. ADH is also connected with stereotypical paternal behavior patterns in some mammals. For example, it transforms an unconcerned male prairie vole (a mouselike rodent) into an affectionate and protective mate and father.

Oxytocin stimulates labor in pregnant women and is connected with maternal behavior (cuddling and caring for young) in some mammals (Insel, 2000; Taylor et al., 2000). Obstetricians may induce labor by injecting pregnant women with oxytocin. During nursing, stimulation of nerve endings in and around the nipples sends messages to the brain that cause oxytocin to be secreted. Oxytocin then causes the breasts to eject milk.

The Pineal Gland

The pineal gland secretes the hormone **melatonin** which helps regulate the sleep–wake cycle and may affect the onset of puberty. Some researchers speculate that melatonin is also connected with aging. However, it appears that melatonin fosters sleep, and some people use it as a "sleeping pill" (Arendt, 2000; Nagtegaal et al., 2000).

The Thyroid Gland: The Body's Accelerator

Thyroxin is produced by the thyroid gland. It affects the body's *metabolism*—that is, the rate at which the body uses oxygen and produces energy. Some people are overweight because of *hypothyroidism*, a condition that results from too little thyroxin. Thyroxin deficiency in children can lead to *cretinism*, a condition characterized by stunted growth and mental retardation. Adults who secrete too little thyroxin may feel tired and sluggish and may put on weight. People who produce too much thyroxin may develop *hyperthyroidism*, which is characterized by excitability, insomnia, and weight loss.

The Adrenal Glands: Coping With Stress

The adrenal glands, located above the kidneys, have an outer layer, or cortex, and an inner core, or medulla. The adrenal cortex is regulated by pituitary ACTH. It secretes hormones known as **corticosteroids,** or cortical steroids. These hormones increase resistance to stress; promote muscle development; and cause the liver to release stored sugar, making more energy available in emergencies, as when you see another car veering toward your own.

Adrenaline and noradrenaline are secreted by the adrenal medulla. **Adrenaline,** also known as epinephrine, is manufactured exclusively by the adrenal glands, but noradrenaline (norepinephrine) is also produced elsewhere in the body. The sympathetic branch of the autonomic nervous system causes the adrenal medulla to release a mixture of adrenaline and noradrenaline that helps arouse the body to cope with threats and stress. Adrenaline is of interest to psychologists because it has emotional as well as physical effects. It intensifies most emotions and is crucial to the experience of fear and anxiety. Noradrenaline raises blood pressure and acts as a neurotransmitter in the nervous system.

The Testes and the Ovaries

If it were not for the secretion of the male sex hormone **testosterone** about 6 weeks after conception, we would all develop the external genital organs of females. Testosterone is produced by the testes and, in smaller amounts, by the ovaries and adrenal glands. A few weeks after conception, testosterone causes the male sex organs to develop.

During puberty, testosterone stokes the growth of muscle and bone and the development of primary and secondary sex characteristics. *Primary sex characteristics* such as the increased size of the penis and the sperm-producing ability of the testes are directly involved in reproduction. *Secondary sex characteristics* such as presence of a beard and a deeper voice differentiate males from females but are not directly involved in reproduction.

Anabolic steroids (synthetic versions of the male sex hormone testosterone) have been used, sometimes in tandem with growth hormone, to enhance athletic prowess.

▲ **REFLECT**

What hormones are involved in reproductive behavior? Has anyone you know been given any of these hormones by a physician? For what reason? Does it disturb you or anyone you know when scientists "interfere with nature"? Why?

Antidiuretic hormone ▲ A pituitary hormone that conserves body fluids by increasing reabsorption of urine and is connected with paternal behavior in some mammals. Also called *vasopressin*.

Oxytocin ▲ A pituitary hormone that stimulates labor and lactation.

Melatonin ▲ A pineal hormone which helps regulate the sleep–wake cycle and may affect the onset of puberty.

Thyroxin ▲ The thyroid hormone that increases metabolic rate.

Corticosteroids ▲ Steroids produced by the adrenal cortex that regulate carbohydrate metabolism and increase resistance to stress by fighting inflammation and allergic reactions. Also called *cortical steroids*.

Adrenaline ▲ A hormone produced by the adrenal medulla that stimulates sympathetic ANS activity. Also called *epinephrine*.

Testosterone ▲ A male sex hormone produced by the testes that promotes growth of male sexual characteristics and sperm.

Steroids increase muscle mass, heighten resistance to stress, and increase the body's energy supply by signaling the liver to release sugar into the bloodstream. Steroids may also spur the sex drive and self-confidence. Steroids are generally outlawed in amateur and professional sports. The lure of steroids is understandable. Sometimes the difference between an acceptable athletic performance and a great one is rather small. Thousands of athletes try to make it in the big leagues, and the "edge" offered by steroids—even if minor—can spell the difference between a fumbling attempt and a smashing success. If steroids help, why the fuss? Some of it is related to the ethics of competition—the idea that athletes should "play fair." But steroid use is also linked to liver damage and other health problems.

The ovaries produce **estrogen** and **progesterone**. Estrogen is also produced in smaller amounts by the testes. Estrogen fosters female reproductive capacity and secondary sex characteristics such as accumulation of fat in the breasts and hips. Progesterone stimulates growth of the female reproductive organs and prepares the uterus to maintain pregnancy.

Steroids and Mental Processes

Estrogen has psychological effects as well as biological effects. For one thing, higher levels of estrogen seem to be connected with optimal cognitive functioning and feelings of well-being among women (Ross et al., 2000; Yaffe et al., 2000). For example, older women placed on estrogen replacement showed improved memory functioning and visual–spatial abilities (Duka et al., 2000). Trials are even underway to determine whether estrogen replacement can help menopausal women with Alzheimer's disease fight to cognitive effects (memory impairment, etc.) of the disorder (Kawas, 2000; Sano, 2000). However, results to date are not very encouraging (Henderson et al., 2000; Mulnard et al., 2000; Shaywitz & Shaywitz, 2000). Women are also more interested in sexual activity when estrogen levels are high—particularly during ovulation, when they are fertile.

Estrogen even affects women's perceptions of who is attractive. Research shows that women in Britain and Japan prefer feminized male faces, as shown in Figure 2.15(b), during most phases of the menstrual cycle (Penton-Voak, 1999). Women apparently associate such facial features with personality traits like warmth and honesty. However, they prefer the masculinized faces, as shown in Figure 2.15(a), when they are ovulating. Perhaps they interpret such features as indicative of reproductive capacity—that is, they see these men as likely to father children but more "feminine" men as likely to be nurturant and friendly.

CONTROVERSY IN PSYCHOLOGY

Should Athletes Be Permitted to Use Anabolic Steroids?

Why do athletes turn to steroids? What are their side effects? What are the dangers in using them?

Estrogen ▲ A generic term for several female sex hormones that promote growth of female sex characteristics and regulate the menstrual cycle.

Progesterone ▲ A female sex hormone that promotes growth of the sex organs and helps maintain pregnancy.

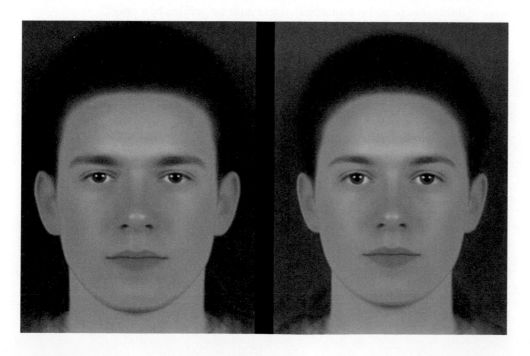

FIGURE 2.15 Which One Is Mr. Right?
The answer may depend on the phase of the woman's menstrual cycle. Women are apparently more attracted to men with masculinized features when they are capable of conceiving (part A), and men with more feminized features (part B) when they are not.

TABLE 2.1 SYMPTOMS OF PMS*

Depression

Anxiety

Mood swings

Anger and irritability

Loss of interest in usual activities

Difficulty concentrating

Lack of energy

Overeating or cravings for certain foods

Insomnia or too much sleeping

Feelings of being out of control or overwhelmed

Physical problems such as headaches, tenderness in the breasts, joint or muscle pain, weight gain or feeling bloated

*Most women experience only a few of these symptoms, if any at all.

▲ REFLECT

Were people with your cultural background reared with any negative attitudes toward menstruation? What were they? Do you personally believe in them? Explain.

CLICK4™ *a bulletin board discussion on cultural attitudes toward PMS.*

CLICK4™ *advice on coping with PMS.*

Testosterone is connected with the sex drive in both males and females (females secrete some testosterone in the adrenal glands). Testosterone is also connected with self-confidence, aggressiveness, even memory functioning in males (Janowsky et al., 2000).

The Menstrual Cycle   Whereas testosterone levels remain fairly stable, estrogen and progesterone levels vary markedly and regulate the woman's menstrual cycle. Following menstruation—the monthly sloughing off of the inner lining of the uterus—estrogen levels increase, leading to the ripening of an ovum (egg cell) and the growth of the lining of the uterus. Ovulation (release of the ovum by an ovary) occurs when estrogens reach peak blood levels. Then the lining of the uterus thickens in response to the secretion of progesterone, gaining the capacity to support an embryo if fertilization should occur. If the ovum is not fertilized, estrogen and progesterone levels drop suddenly, triggering menstruation once more.

DIVERSITY   **Cross-Cultural Perspectives on Menstruation**   In Peru, they speak of a "visit from Uncle Pepé." In Samoa, menstruation is referred to as "the boogie man." One of the more common epithets given to the menstrual period throughout history is "the curse." The Fulani of Burkina Faso in Africa use a term for it that translates as "to see dirt." Some nations even blame "the curse" on their historic enemies. The French once referred to menstruation as "the English" and to its onset as "the English are coming." Iranians used to say "The Indians have attacked" to announce menstrual bleeding. *Question: What prejudices do we find against menstruating women throughout the world?*

A common folk belief in preliterate societies is that menstrual blood is tainted. Men avoid contact with menstruating women for fear of their lives. To avoid contamination, menstruating women are sent to special huts on the fringe of the village. In the traditional Navajo culture, for instance, menstruating women would be consigned to huts that were set apart from other living quarters.

The Old Testament (Leviticus 15:19) warns against physical contact with a menstruating woman—including of course, sexual contact: "And if a woman have an issue, and her issue in her flesh be blood, she shall be put apart seven days; and whosoever toucheth her shall be unclean." Orthodox Jews still abstain from sex during menstruation and the week afterward. Prior to resuming sexual relations, the woman must attend a *mikvah*—a ritual cleansing.

Fears of contamination by menstruating women are nearly universal and persist today. As late as the 1950s, women were not allowed in some European breweries for fear that the beer would turn sour. Some Indian castes still teach that a man who touches a woman during her period is contaminated and must be purified by a priest.

We might laugh off these misconceptions as folly were it not for their effect on women. Women who suffer from premenstrual syndrome may be responding to negative cultural attitudes toward menstruation as well as to menstrual symptoms. The traditional view of menstruation as a time of pollution may make women highly sensitive to internal sensations at certain times of the month.

Premenstrual Syndrome (PMS)   Psychologists study the effects of menstruation because of stereotypes about menstruating women and because of the discomfort many of them experience. For several days prior to and during menstruation, according to the stereotype, "raging hormones" doom women to irritability and poor judgment—two facets of the condition known as *premenstrual syndrome* (PMS).

Women have historically been assumed to be more likely to commit suicide or crimes, call in sick at work, or develop physical and emotional problems during the eight-day period prior to and during menstruation. Moreover, the ability of college women to focus on academic tasks during this period has been called into question. Three out of four women report *some* psychological and physical problems, such as depression, anxiety, and headaches, during the four to six days that precede menstruation (Brody, 1996a). However, fewer than one woman in 10 has symptoms severe enough to impair her academic, occupational, or social functioning (Brody, 1996a). Symptoms of PMS are shown in Table 2.1.

IN REVIEW
The Endocrine System

Gland	Hormone	Functions
Hypothalamus	Releasing hormones, or factors (e.g., growth-hormone releasing factor, corticotrophin-releasing hormone)	Influences the pituitary gland to secrete corresponding hormones (e.g., growth hormone, adrenocorticotrophic hormone)
Pituitary		
Anterior Lobe	Growth hormone	Causes growth of muscles, bones, and glands
	Adrenocorticotrophic hormone (ACTH)	Regulates adrenal cortex
	Thyrotrophin	Causes thyroid gland to secrete thyroxin
	Follicle-stimulating hormone	Causes formation of sperm and egg cells
	Luteinizing hormone	Causes ovulation, maturation of sperm and egg cells
	Prolactin	Stimulates production of milk
Posterior Lobe	Antidiuretic hormone (ADH)	Inhibits production of urine
	Oxytocin	Stimulates uterine contractions during delivery and ejection of milk during nursing
Pineal	Melatonin	Involved in regulation of sleep–wake cycle; possibly connected with aging
Pancreas	Insulin	Enables body to metabolize sugar; regulates storage of fats
Thyroid	Thyroxin	Increases metabolic rate
Adrenal		
Cortex	Corticosteroids	Increase resistance to stress; regulate carbohydrate metabolism
Medulla	Adrenaline (epinephrine)	Increases metabolic activity (heart and respiration rates, blood sugar level, etc.)
	Noradrenaline (norepinephrine)	Raises blood pressure; acts as neurotransmitter
Testes	Testosterone	Promotes development of male sex characteristics
Ovaries	Estrogen	Regulates menstrual cycle; promotes development of female sex characteristics
	Progesterone	Promotes development of the uterine lining to maintain pregnancy

The symptoms of PMS appear to be linked to levels of hormones and serotonin (Mortola, 1998). For instance, prostaglandins cause many women to experience strong, unrelieved uterine contractions.

REVIEW

(43) The _____ secretes hormones that regulate the pituitary gland. (44) The pituitary hormone _____ regulates maternal behavior in lower animals and stimulates production of milk in women. (45) ADH increases the reabsorption of _____ to conserve fluid. (46) _____ stimulates labor in pregnant women. (47) _____ is secreted by the pineal gland and helps regulate the sleep–wake cycle. (48) The thyroid hormone _____ affects the metabolism. (49) Corticosteroids are secreted by the adrenal _____ and promote development of muscle mass and increase resistance to stress. (50) Adrenaline is secreted by the adrenal _____ and is involved in emotional arousal. Sex hormones foster prenatal sexual differentiation and are connected with psychological well-being. (51) Female sex hormones regulate the _____ cycle.

Pulling It Together: How do "negative feedback loops" govern the endocrine system? What kinds of behaviors and mental processes are affected by "glands"?

EVOLUTION AND EVOLUTIONARY PSYCHOLOGY

www 2 PS 4

CLICK4™ *landmark essays on evolution by Charles Darwin and Alfred Russel Wallace.*

Charles Darwin watched the unfolding of a huge game of "Survivor." But the game was real, and it involved every form of life on the planet. . . .

Let us return to Darwin's voyage on the *Beagle*. From his observations of sea lions and tortoises and insects and plants, he was ready to formulate his theory of evolution upon his return. Reading Thomas Malthus's *Essay of the Principle of Population*, which had been written back in 1798, also helped. Malthus pointed out that the Earth's food supply was increasing mathematically (1, 2, 3, 4, 5, 6, etc.) while population was increasing geometrically (1, 2, 4, 8, 16, 32, etc.). Therefore, the world's population would outstrip the world's ability to feed it, except for tragic events such as war, famine, and plague. Darwin applied Malthus's ideas to all species:

> In October 1838 . . . I happened to read for amusement Malthus on *Population*, and being well prepared to appreciate the struggle for existence which everywhere goes on from long-continued observation of the habits of animals and plants, it at once struck me that under these circumstances favourable variations would tend to be preserved and unfavourable ones to be destroyed. The result of this would be the formation of new species. Here, then, I had at last got a theory by which to work; but I was so anxious to avoid prejudice, that I determined not for some time to write even the briefest sketch of it. (F. Darwin, 1892/1958, pp. 42–43.)

Question: What are the basics of the theory of evolution? According to the theory of evolution, there is a struggle for survival as various species and individuals compete for the same territories. Organisms who are better adapted to their environments are more likely to survive (that is, to be "naturally selected"), to reproduce, and to transmit their features or traits to the next generation. Organisms evolve into more adaptive and complex creatures over time as those that are better adapted are selected and pool their genes. *Adaptation* and *natural selection* are key concepts in **evolutionary psychology.** *Question: What is evolutionary psychology?* This field of psychology studies the ways in which adaptation and natural selection—the core concepts in evolutionary theory—are connected with mental processes and behavior (Buss, 2000; Buss et al., 1998). Human evolution has given rise to such diverse activities as language, art, committed relationships, and warfare.

But for fear of "prejudice," Darwin delayed publication of his theory by more than 20 years. In fact, he might not have permitted it to be published until after his death except that he learned that a scientist who had worked in the Amazon, Alfred Russel Wallace, was about to publish his own views, which were very similar to Darwin's. Papers by both theorists were read at the Linnaean Society, and Darwin's *On the Origin of Species by Natural Selection* (1859) was published shortly thereafter. The public's interest in evolutionary theory had been aroused and the first printing sold out on the first day.

In 1871 Darwin published *The Descent of Man*, which made the case that humans, like other species, were a product of evolution. He argued that the great apes (chimpanzees, gorillas, and so on) and humans shared a common primate ancestor. Many ridiculed Darwin's views because they were displeased with the notion that they might have much in common with apes. Darwin's theory also contradicted the Book of Genesis, which stated that humans had been created in one day in the image of God.

One of the fascinating concepts of today's evolutionary psychologists is that not only physical traits but also social behavior evolves and is transmitted from generation to generation. In other words, some of the behavior patterns that help an organism to survive and reproduce are transmitted to the next generation (Fisher, 2000). Such behaviors are believed to include aggression, strategies of mate selection, even altruism (that is, self-sacrifice of the individual to help the perpetuation of the family grouping) (Archer, 1996). The behavior patterns are termed *instinctive* or *species-specific* because they evolved within certain species.

▲ REFLECT

Why was Darwin reluctant to publish his theory of evolution? Do you believe that this textbook, and other textbooks, should present the theory of evolution? Why or why not?

Evolutionary psychology ▲ The field of psychology that studies the ways in which adaptation and natural selection are connected with behavior and mental processes.

Consider some examples of instinctive behavior. If you place an egg from the nest of a goose a few inches in front of her, she will roll it back to the nest with her beak. If you raise a white-crowned sparrow in isolation from other sparrows, it will still sing a recognizable species-specific song when it matures. The male stickleback fish instinctively attacks fish (or pieces of painted wood) with the kinds of red bellies that are characteristic of other male sticklebacks. Linguist Steven Pinker (1994) and a number of psychologists characterize language as an instinct among humans. Psychologists are trying to determine what kinds of behavior in humans may be instinctive. However, even instinctive behavior can be modified by learning, and most psychologists agree that human behavior owes its complexity to learning ability.

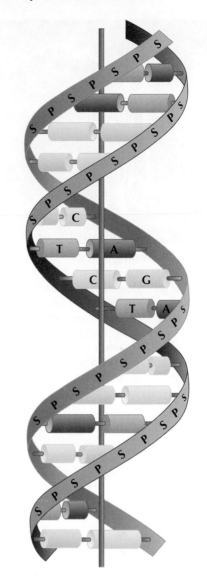

REVIEW

(52) According to the theory of evolution, there is a struggle for _____ as various species compete for resources. (53) Evolutionary _____ studies the ways in which adaptation and natural selection are connected with behavior and mental processes. (54) In his 1871 book, *The _____ of Man*, Darwin argued that humans are a product of evolution.

Pulling It Together: On which behaviors and mental processes do evolutionary psychologists focus? Why?

HEREDITY: THE NATURE OF NATURE

Consider some facts of life:

▲ People cannot breathe underwater (without special equipment).
▲ People cannot fly (again, without rather special equipment).
▲ Fish cannot learn to speak French or do an Irish jig even if you rear them in enriched environments and send them to finishing school.
▲ Chimpanzees and gorillas can use sign language but cannot speak.

People cannot breathe underwater or fly (without oxygen tanks, airplanes, or other devices) because of their **heredity**. *Question: What is meant by heredity?* Heredity defines one's nature—which is based on one's biological structures and processes. Heredity transmits traits that have evolved from generation to generation. Fish are limited in other ways by their natural traits. Chimpanzees and gorillas can understand many spoken words and express some concepts through nonverbal symbol systems such as American Sign Language. However, apes cannot speak. They have probably failed to inherit the humanlike speech areas of the cerebral cortex. Their nature differs from ours. Our speech mechanisms have evolved differently.

Heredity is basic to the transmission of physical traits such as height, hair texture, and eye color. Animals can be selectively bred to enhance desired physical and psychological traits. We breed cattle and chickens to be bigger and fatter so that they provide more food calories for less feed. We breed animals to enhance psychological traits such as aggressiveness and intelligence. For example, poodles are relatively intelligent. Golden retrievers are gentle and patient with children. Border collies show a strong herding instinct. Even as puppies, Border collies attempt to corral people who are out for a stroll.

Heredity both makes behaviors possible and places limits on them. The subfield of biology that studies heredity is called **genetics. Behavioral genetics** bridges the sciences of psychology and biology. It is concerned with the genetic transmission of traits that give rise to patterns of behavior.

Heredity is involved in almost all human traits and behavior (Rutter, 1997). Examples include sociability, shyness, social dominance, aggressiveness, leadership, thrill seeking, effectiveness as a parent or a therapist, even interest in arts and crafts (Carey & DiLalla, 1994; Lykken et al., 1992). Genetic influences are also involved in most behavioral problems, including anxiety and depression, schizophrenia, bipolar disorder,

FIGURE 2.16   The Double Helix of DNA
Segments of DNA are made up of genes that determine physical traits such as height, eye color, and whether pigs have wings (no, because of their genetic makeup, they don't). Psychologists debate the extent to which genes influence psychological traits such as intelligence, aggressiveness, and happiness and the appearance of psychological disorders such as schizophrenia.

Heredity ▲ The transmission of traits from one generation to another through genes.
Genetics ▲ The branch of biology that studies heredity.
Behavioral genetics ▲ The study of the genetic transmission of structures and traits that give rise to behavior.

A Person With Down Syndrome.
Down syndrome is caused by an extra chromosome on the 21st pair and becomes more likely to occur as the mother's age at the time of pregnancy increases. Persons with Down syndrome have characteristic facial features including downward-sloping folds of skin at the inner corners of the eyes, are mentally retarded, and usually have health problems that lead to death by middle age.

CLICK4™ *more information about the Human Genome Project.*

CLICK4™ *the Web site of the National Down Syndrome Society.*

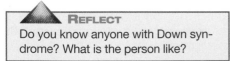

▲ REFLECT
Do you know anyone with Down syndrome? What is the person like?

Genes ▲ The basic building blocks of heredity, which consist of DNA.
Chromosomes ▲ Structures consisting of genes that are found in the nuclei of the body's cells.
Sex chromosomes ▲ The 23rd pair of chromosomes, which determine whether the child will be male or female.
Nature ▲ In behavior genetics, heredity.
Nurture ▲ In behavior genetics, environmental influences on behavior, such as nutrition, culture, socioeconomic status, and learning.

alcoholism, even criminal behavior (Kendler et al., 2000a, 2000b; Plomin, 2000; Sullivan et al., 2000). However, most behavior patterns also reflect life experiences and personal choice (Sullivan et al., 2000).

Heredity occurs by means of genes and chromosomes. *Question: What are the roles of genes and chromosomes in heredity?*

Genes and Chromosomes

Genes are the building blocks of heredity. They are the biochemical materials that regulate the development of specific traits. Some traits, such as blood type, are controlled by a single pair of genes. (One gene is derived from each parent.) Other traits are determined by combinations of genes. The inherited component of complex psychological traits, such as intelligence, is believed to be determined by combinations of genes. We have thousands of genes in every cell in our bodies.

Genes are segments of **chromosomes,** each of which consists of more than 1,000 genes. Each cell in the body contains 46 chromosomes arranged in 23 pairs. Chromosomes are large complex molecules of deoxyribonucleic acid, which has several chemical components. (You can breathe a sigh of relief, for this acid is usually referred to simply as DNA.) The tightly wound structure of DNA was first demonstrated in the 1950s by James Watson and Francis Crick. It takes the form of a double helix—a twisting ladder (see Figure 2.16). In all living things, the sides of the ladder consist of alternating segments of phosphate (P) and a kind of sugar (S). The "rungs" of the ladder are attached to the sugars and consist of one of two pairs of bases, either *adenine* with *thymine* (A with T) or *cytosine* with *guanine* (C with G). A single gene can contain hundreds of thousands of base pairs. The sequence of the rungs is the *genetic code* that will cause the unfolding organism to grow arms or wings, skin or scales.

We normally receive 23 chromosomes from our father's sperm cell and 23 chromosomes from our mother's egg cell (ovum). When a sperm cell fertilizes an ovum, the chromosomes form 23 pairs (Figure 2.17). The 23rd pair consists of **sex chromosomes,** which determine whether we are female or male. We all receive an X sex chromosome (so called because of the X shape) from our mother. If we also receive an X sex chromosome from our father, we develop into a female. If we receive a Y sex chromosome (named after the Y shape) from our father, we develop into a male.

Gender is not determined by sex chromosomes throughout the animal kingdom. Reptiles such as crocodiles, for example, do not have sex chromosomes. The crocodile's sex is determined by the temperature at which the egg develops (Crews, 1994). Some like it hot. That is, hatchlings are usually male when the eggs develop at temperatures in the mid-90s Fahrenheit or above. Some like it . . . well not cold perhaps, but certainly cooler. When crocodile eggs develop at temperatures below the mid-80s Fahrenheit, the hatchlings are usually female.[2]

When people do not have 46 chromosomes, physical and behavioral abnormalities may result. The risk of these abnormalities rises with the age of the parents. Most persons with Down syndrome, for example, have an extra, or third, chromosome on the 21st pair. The extra chromosome is usually contributed by the mother, and the condition becomes increasingly likely as the mother's age at the time of pregnancy increases. Persons with Down syndrome have a downward-sloping fold of skin at the inner corners of the eyes, a round face, a protruding tongue, and a broad, flat nose. They are mentally retarded and usually have physical problems that cause death by middle age (Schupf, 2000).

Behavior geneticists are attempting to sort out the relative importance of **nature** (heredity) and **nurture** (environmental influences) in the origins of behavior. Psychologists are especially interested in the roles of nature and nurture in intelligence and psychological disorders. Organisms inherit physical features that set the stage for certain behaviors. But none of us is the result of heredity alone. Environmental factors such as nutrition, learning opportunities, cultural influences, exercise, and (unfortunately) accident and illness also determine whether genetically possible behaviors will be displayed.

---

[2]This does not mean that male crocodiles are hot-blooded. Reptiles are cold-blooded animals.

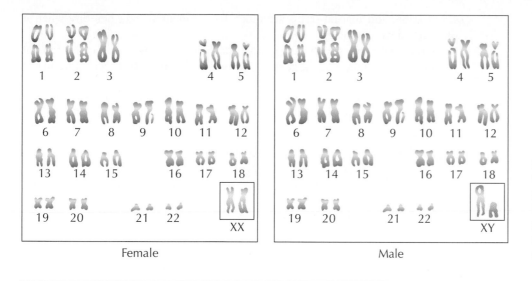

FIGURE 2.17   The 23 Pairs of Human Chromosomes
People normally have 23 pairs of chromosomes. Whether one is female or male is determined by the 23rd pair of chromosomes. Females have two X sex chromosomes (part A), whereas males have an X and a Y sex chromosome (part B).

Behavior thus represents the interaction of nature and nurture. A potential Shakespeare who is reared in poverty and never taught to read or write will not create a *Hamlet*.

Kinship Studies

The more *closely* people are related, the more *genes* they have in common. Parents and children have a 50% overlap in their genetic endowments, and so do siblings (brothers and sisters). Aunts and uncles related by blood have a 25% overlap with nieces and nephews. First cousins share 12.5% of their genetic endowment. If genes are involved in a trait or behavior pattern, people who are more closely related should be more likely to show similar traits or behavior.

Question: What are kinship studies?   **Kinship studies** are ways in which psychologists compare the presence of traits and behavior patterns in people who are biologically related or unrelated to help determine the role of genetic factors in their occurrence. Psychologists are especially interested in running kinship studies with twins and adopted individuals.

Twin Studies
The fertilized egg cell (ovum) that carries genetic messages from both parents is called a *zygote*. Now and then, a zygote divides into two cells that separate, so that instead of developing into a single person, it develops into two people with the same genetic makeup. Such people are identical, or **monozygotic (MZ), twins.** If the woman releases two ova in the same month and they are both fertilized, they develop into fraternal, or **dizygotic (DZ), twins.** DZ twins, like other siblings, share 50% of their genes. MZ twins are important in the study of the relative influences of nature (heredity) and nurture (the environment) because differences between MZ twins are the result of nurture. (They do not differ in heredity or nature because their genetic makeup is the same.)

Twin studies compare the presence of traits and behavior patterns in MZ twins, DZ twins, and other people to help determine the role of genetic factors in their occurrence. For example, twin studies show that genetic factors have a strong influence on physical features. MZ twins are more likely to look alike and to be similar in height, even to have more similar cholesterol levels than DZ twins (Heller et al., 1993). Psychologically speaking, MZ twins resemble one another more strongly than DZ twins and other siblings in the following ways:

1. Personality traits—for example, shyness, activity levels, irritability, sociability, authoritarianism, even happiness (McCourt et al., 1999; McCrae & Costa, 2000). Twin studies carried out by psychologist David Lykken and Auke Tellegen (1996) suggest that people inherit a tendency toward a certain level of happiness. Despite the ups and downs of experience, people tend to drift back to their usual levels of cheerfulness or grumpiness. Factors such as availability of money, level

> **REFLECT**
> Do you know sets of twins? Monozygotic or dizygotic? How are they alike? How do they differ?

Kinship studies ▲ Studies that compare the presence of traits and behavior patterns in people who are biologically related or unrelated in order to help determine the role of genetic factors in their occurrence.
Monozygotic (MZ) twins ▲ Identical twins. Twins who develop from a single zygote, thus carrying the same genetic instructions.
Dizygotic (DZ) twins ▲ Fraternal twins. Twins who develop from separate zygotes.

of education, and marital status are much less influential than heredity when it comes to human happiness.

2. Developmental factors such as cognitive functioning, autism, and early signs of attachment—smiling, cuddling, and expression of fear of strangers (DiLalla et al., 1996; Scarr & Kidd, 1983).

3. Presence of psychological disorders such as anxiety, substance dependence, and schizophrenia (DiLalla et al., 1996).

Adoptee Studies   The interpretation of kinship studies can be confused when relatives share similar environments as well as genes. This is especially true of identical twins, who may be dressed identically and encouraged to follow similar interests. Adoptee studies that compare children who have been separated from their parents at an early age (or in which identical twins are separated at an early age) and reared in different environments provide special opportunities for sorting out nature and nurture. Psychologists look for similarities between children and their adoptive and natural parents. When children reared by adoptive parents are more similar to their natural parents in a particular trait, strong evidence exists for a genetic role in the appearance of that trait.

REVIEW

(55) Genes consist of _____ acid (DNA). (56) Thousands of genes make up each _____. (57) People normally have (How many?) _____ chromosomes. (58) Identical twins are formed from (one or two?) zygote(s) and are termed monozygotic. (59) Fraternal twins are formed from two zygotes and are termed _____.

CLICK4™ *a quiz covering the second half of this chapter.*

Pulling It Together: What kinds of research do psychologists use to help sort out the effects of nature and nurture? What kinds of behaviors and mental processes seem to be affected strongly by heredity?

CLICK4™ *electronic flash cards to review your knowledge of key terms and people in this chapter.*

There are thus important connections between biological factors and psychological events. Thoughts and mental images may seem like intangible pictures that float in our heads, but they have substance. They involve billions of brain cells (neurons) and the transmission of thousands of chemicals from one brain cell to another—repeated perhaps many times per second. These countless bits and pieces of microscopic activity give rise to feelings, plans, computation, art and music, and all the cognitive activities that characterize being human. We pour chemicals called hormones into our own bloodstreams, and they affect our activity levels, our anxiety levels, even our sex drives. We inherit traits that make us human, that enable us to think more deeply and act more cleverly than any other organism (after all, we write the textbooks). We also inherit unique dispositions as individuals—dispositions that affect our personalities, our patterns of development, and our psychological stability. An understanding of biology helps us grasp many psychological events that might otherwise seem elusive and without substance.

TRUTH ▱ FICTION
REVISITED

▱ It is true that a single cell can stretch all the way down your leg. *These cells are neurons. How do you think it is possible that cells this long are "microscopic"? See page 39.*

▱ It is true that messages travel in the brain by means of electricity. *However, this is not the whole story. Messages also travel from neurons to other neurons, muscles, or glands via chemical messengers termed* neurotransmitters. *See page 41.*

▱ It is not true that the human brain is larger than that of any other animal. *Elephants and whales have larger brains. See page 45.*

▱ It is true that fear can give you indigestion. *Fear predominantly involves sympathetic ANS activity, whereas digestive processes involve parasympathetic activity. Because sympathetic activity can inhibit parasympathetic activity, fear can prevent digestion. See page 46.*

▱ It is true that men's brains, on average, are larger than women's brains. *However, as with the brains of whales and elephants, it seems that size doesn't matter here either. (Your author's wife could have told you that all along.) See page 49.*

▱ It is true that if a surgeon were to stimulate a certain part of your brain electrically, you might swear in court that someone had stroked your leg. *See page 56.*

▱ It is true that a hormone — ADH — turns a disinterested male rodent into a doting father. *(The hormone is not known to have such a powerful effect with humans, however.) See page 62.*

▱ Women are actually more attracted to men with highly masculine facial features when they are ovulating. *Estrogen peaks during the menstrual phase when women ovulate and are fertile, perhaps increasing their interest in men who seem more capable of impregnating them. See page 63.*

▱ It is true that a crocodile's sex is determined by the temperature at which the egg develops. *This is an intriguing departure from chromosomal determination of sex. See page 68.*

▱ It is apparently true that you can't buy happiness. *Heredity is a more important determinant of happiness than money and other social factors. See page 69.*

1. What are neurons?

The nervous system consists of neurons, which are cells that transmit information through neural impulses, and glial cells, which mainly serve support functions. Neurons have a cell body; dendrites, which receive messages; and trunklike axons, which conduct and then transmit messages to other cells by means of chemicals called neurotransmitters. Many neurons have a myelin coating that insulates their axons, allowing for more efficient conduction of messages. Afferent neurons transmit sensory messages to the central nervous system. Efferent neurons conduct messages from the central nervous system that stimulate glands or cause muscles to contract.

2. What are neural impulses?

Neural transmission is electrochemical. An electrical charge is conducted along an axon through a process that allows sodium ions to enter the cell and then pumps them out. The neuron has a resting potential of -70 millivolts and an action potential of about $+40$ millivolts.

3. What happens when a neuron fires?

Neurons fire by releasing neurotransmitters. They fire according to an all-or-none principle, up to hundreds of times per second. Each firing is followed by a refractory period, during which neurons are insensitive to messages from other neurons.

4. What is a synapse?

Neurons fire across synapses, which consist of an axon terminal from the transmitting neuron, a dendrite or the body of a receiving neuron, and a fluid-filled synaptic cleft between the two.

5. Which neurotransmitters are of interest to psychologists? What do they do?

These include acetylcholine, which is involved in muscle contractions and memory; dopamine, imbalances of which have been linked to Parkinson's disease and schizophrenia; noradrenaline, which accelerates the heartbeat and other body processes; serotonin, which is involved in eating, sleep, and emotional arousal; and endorphins, which are naturally occurring painkillers.

6. Just what is the nervous system?

A nerve is a bundle of axons and dendrites. The nervous system is one of the systems that regulates the body. It is involved in thought processes, emotional responses, heartbeat, motor activity, and so on.

7. What are the divisions and functions of the peripheral nervous system?

The peripheral nervous system has two main divisions: somatic and autonomic. The somatic nervous system transmits sensory information about skeletal muscles, skin, and joints to the central nervous system. It also controls skeletal muscular activity. The autonomic nervous system (ANS) regulates the glands and activities such as heartbeat, digestion, and dilation of the pupils. The sympathetic division of the ANS helps expend the body's resources, such as when fleeing from a predator, and the parasympathetic division helps build the body's reserves.

8. What are the divisions and functions of the central nervous system?

The central nervous system consists of the brain and spinal cord. Reflexes involve the spinal cord but not the brain. The central nervous system has gray matter, which is composed of nonmyelinated neurons, and white matter, which is composed of bundles of myelinated (and thus whitish) axons.

9. How do researchers learn about the functions of the brain?

Researchers historically learned about the brain by studying the effects of accidents. They have also studied the effects of purposeful damage to the brain, made by lesions. They have seen how animals and people respond to electrical stimulations of certain parts of the brain. They have studied the waves emitted by the brain with the electroencephalograph. Contemporary brains scans such as the CAT scan, the PET scan, and MRI are made possible by computer-generated images that are generally made possible by passing radiation of some sort through the brain.

10. What are the structures and functions of the brain?

The hindbrain includes the medulla, which regulates the heart rate, blood pressure, and respiration; the pons, which is involved in movement, attention, and respiration; and the cerebellum, which is involved in balance and coordination. The reticular activating system, which is involved in wakefulness and sleep, begins in the hindbrain and continues through the midbrain into the forebrain. Important structures of the forebrain include the thalamus, which serves as a relay station for sensory stimulation; the hypothalamus, which regulates body temperature and various aspects of motivation and emotion, such as eating and sexual behavior; the limbic system, which is involved in memory, emotion, and motivation; and the cerebrum, which is the brain's center of thinking and language.

11. What are the parts of the cerebral cortex?

The outer fringe of the cerebrum is the cerebral cortex, which is divided into two hemispheres and four lobes: frontal, parietal, temporal, and occipital. The visual cortex is in the occipital lobe, and the auditory cortex is in the temporal lobe. The somatosensory cortex lies behind the central fissure in the parietal lobe, and the motor cortex lies in the frontal lobe, across the central fissure from the somatosensory cortex. The prefrontal cortex may be the executive center of the brain—making plans, solving problems, and drawing upon sensory information from other areas of the cortex as needed.

12. What parts of the cerebral cortex are involved in thinking and language?

Language areas of the cortex usually lie in the left hemisphere, near the intersection of the frontal, temporal, and parietal lobes. Wernicke's area in the temporal lobe responds mainly to auditory information. Broca's area is located in the frontal lobe and is mainly responsible for speech. Damage to either area can result in an aphasia—a problem in understanding (Wernicke's aphasia) or producing (Broca's aphasia) language.

13. What would it mean to be "left-brained" or "right-brained"?

The left hemisphere is usually relatively more involved in cognitive functions involving logical analysis and problem solving, whereas the right hemisphere is usually superior in visual–spatial functions, aesthetic and emotional responses, and creative mathematical reasoning. But the notion that some people are "left-brained" (that is, only logical and lacking completely in functions involving visual–spatial responses, etc.) and others are "right-brained" is exaggerated.

14. Does it matter whether one is left-handed? Why are people right-handed or left-handed?

About 1 person in 10 is left-handed. Learning disabilities are somewhat more common among left-handed people, but so is creativity, as shown in the arts. Handedness appears to have a genetic component.

15. What happens when the brain is split in two?

For the most part, the behavior of people who have had split-brain operations (which sever most of the corpus callosum) is perfectly normal. However, although they may verbally be able to describe a screened-off object such as a pencil held in the hand connected to the hemisphere that contains language functions, they cannot do so when the object is held in the other hand.

16. What is the endocrine system?

The endocrine system consists of ductless glands that secrete hormones.

17. What functions of hormones are of interest to psychologists?

The pituitary gland secretes growth hormone; prolactin, which regulates maternal behavior in lower animals and stimulates production of milk in women; and oxytocin, which stimulates labor in pregnant women. The pineal hormone melatonin is connected with the sleep–wake cycle and the onset of puberty. Thyroxin affects the body's metabolism, and deficiency in childhood is connected with mental retardation. The adrenal cortex produces steroids, which promote the development of muscle mass and increase activity level. The adrenal medulla secretes adrenaline (epinephrine), which increases the metabolic rate and is involved in general emotional arousal. The sex hormones are responsible for prenatal sexual differentiation. Female sex hormones regulate the menstrual cycle; they are also connected with cognitive functioning and psychological well-being in women.

18. What prejudices do we find against menstruating women throughout the world?

Despite the fact that the menstrual flow is harmless, most cultures have viewed menstruation as a time of pollution.

19. What are the basics of the theory of evolution?

In nature there is a struggle for survival. Species that are adaptive manage to survive (they are said to be naturally selected); their numbers increase and they transmit their traits to future generations. Species that do not adapt dwindle in numbers and may become extinct.

20. What is evolutionary psychology?

Evolutionary psychology is the field of psychology that studies the ways in which adaptation and natural selection are connected with mental processes and behavior.

21. What is meant by heredity?

Heredity is the transmission of traits from generation to generation by means of genes and chromosomes ("nature," not nurture).

22. What are the roles of genes and chromosomes in heredity?

Genes, which consist of DNA, are the basic building blocks of heredity. A thousand or more genes make up each chromosome. People normally have 46 chromosomes arranged in 23 pairs in each cell in the body. They receive 23 chromosomes from the father and 23 from the mother.

23. What are kinship studies?

These are studies of the distribution of traits or behavior patterns among related people. When certain behaviors are shared by close relatives, such as identical twins, they may have a genetic component. This is especially so when the behaviors are shared by close blood relatives (parents and children, or identical twins) who have been separated early and thus influenced by different environments.

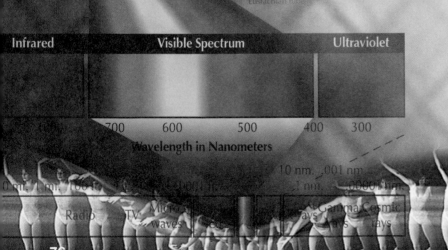

PREVIEW

Sensation and Perception: Your Tickets of Admission to the World Outside
▲ How do you know when something is there? How do you know when it has changed?
▲ We sometimes hear what we want to hear.
▲ A movie theater is dark when you enter, but after a while you can look around and see well enough. Why?

Vision: Letting the Sun Shine In
▲ Visible light is a form of electromagnetic energy, like radio waves and cosmic rays.
▲ Your eyes are your living cameras.
▲ A partly color-blind person might put on one red sock and one green sock, but would not mix red and blue socks.

Visual Perception: How Perceptive!
▲ You are an expert at organizing pieces of information into meaningful wholes.
▲ How do you judge the distance of a car heading in your direction? How do you know it's heading in your direction?
▲ You perceive a door to be a rectangle even when it is a trapezoid (when seen ajar) or a thick line (when seen on end).
▲ Visual illusions trick the eye—even your sophisticated eye.

Hearing: Making Sense of Sound
▲ Why is it that "In space, no one can hear you scream"?
▲ Like your stereo, your ears have amplifiers.
▲ How do you tell where a noise comes from?

The Chemical Senses: Smell and Taste
▲ You are a natural chemist: Your senses of smell and taste sample molecules.

The Skin Senses (Yes, It Does)
▲ Your skin is the largest sensory organ of your body.
▲ Rubbing or scratching a sore toe often relieves pain.

Kinesthesis and the Vestibular Sense
▲ You can touch your finger to your nose with your eyes closed. How do you do it?
▲ Which sense keeps you an upright person?

Sensation and Perception on the Edge: Virtual Reality and ESP
▲ What would life be like if you could not tell the difference between virtual reality and "real reality"?
▲ Do you believe that some people are "psychic"? What does the evidence say?

CHAPTER 3

Sensation and Perception

TRUTH *or* FICTION?

- People have five senses.
- On a clear, dark night you could probably see the light from a candle burning 30 miles away.
- If we could see waves of light with slightly longer wavelengths, warm-blooded animals would glow in the dark.
- "White" sunlight is actually composed of all the colors of the rainbow.
- When we mix blue and yellow light, we attain green light.
- Catfish have taste buds all over their bodies.
- The skin is a sensory organ as well as a protective coating for the body.
- Although people can have fierce headaches, there are no nerve endings for pain in the brain.
- People can experience pain in limbs that have been amputated.
- Some people can read other people's minds.

Five thousand years ago in China, give or take a day or two, an arrow was shot into the air. Where did it land? Ancient records tell us precisely where: in the hand of a fierce warrior and master of the martial arts. As the story was told to me, the warrior had grown so fierce because of a chronic toothache. Incessant pain had ruined his disposition.

One fateful day, our hero watched as invading hordes assembled on surrounding hills. His troops were trembling in the face of the enemy's great numbers, and he raised his arms to boost their morale. A slender wooden shaft lifted into the air from a nearby rise, arced, and then descended—right into the warrior's palm. His troops cringed and muttered among themselves, but our hero said nothing. Although he saw the arrow pass through his palm, he did not scream. He did not run. He did not even complain. He was astounded. His toothache had vanished. In fact, his whole jaw was numb.

Meanwhile the invaders looked on, horrified. They, too, muttered among themselves. What sort of warrior could watch an arrow pierce his hand with such indifference? Even with a smile? If this was the caliber of the local warriors, the invaders would be better off traveling west and looking for a brawl in Sumer or in Egypt. They sounded the retreat and withdrew.

Back in town, our warrior received a hero's welcome. A physician offered to remove the arrow without a fee—a tribute to bravery. But the warrior would have none of it. The arrow had worked wonders for his toothache, and he would brook no meddling. He had already discovered that if the pain threatened to return, he need only twirl the arrow and it would recede once more.

But all was not well on the home front. His wife was thrilled to find him jovial once more, but the arrow put a crimp in their romance. When he put his arm around her, she was in danger of being stabbed. Finally, she gave him an ultimatum: The arrow must go, or she would.

Placed in deep conflict, our warrior consulted a psychologist, who then huddled with the physician and the village elders. After much to-do, they asked the warrior to participate in an experiment. They would remove the arrow and replace it with a pin that the warrior could twirl as needed.

To the warrior's wife's relief, the pin worked. And here, in ancient China, lay the origins of the art of **acupuncture**—the use of needles to relieve pain and treat assorted ills.

I confess that this tale is not entirely accurate. To my knowledge, there were no psychologists in ancient China (their loss). Moreover, the part about the warrior's wife is fictitious. It is claimed, however, that acupuncture as a means of dealing with pain originated in ancient China when a soldier was, in fact, wounded in the hand by an arrow and discovered that a chronic toothache had disappeared. Historians say the Chinese then set out to map the body by sticking pins into various parts of it to learn how the pins would influence the perception of pain.

Control of pain is just one of the many issues that interest psychologists who study the closely related concepts of sensation and perception. *Question: What are sensation and perception?*   **Sensation** is the stimulation of sensory receptors and the transmission of sensory information to the central nervous system (the spinal cord or brain). Sensory receptors are located in sensory organs such as the eyes and ears, the skin, and elsewhere in the body. Stimulation of the senses is an automatic process. It results from sources of energy like light and sound or from the presence of chemicals, as in smell and taste.

Perception is not automatic. Perception is an active process in which sensations are organized and interpreted to form an inner representation of the world. Perception may begin with sensation, but it also reflects our experiences and expectations as it makes sense of sensory stimuli. A human shape and a 12-inch ruler may look to be equally tall; whether we interpret the shape to be a foot-long doll or a full-grown person 15 feet away is a matter of perception that depends on our experience with dolls and people.

In this chapter you will see that your personal map of reality—your ticket of admission to a world of changing sights, sounds, and other sources of sensory input—depends largely on the so-called five senses: vision, hearing, smell, taste, and touch. We will see, however, that touch is just one of several "skin senses," which also include pressure, warmth, cold, and pain. There are also senses that alert you to your own body position without your having to watch every step you take. As we explore the nature of each of

www ③ Ⓔ ①

CLICK4™ *an essay assignment on the difference between sensing and perceiving.*

www ③ Ⓛ ⑤

CLICK4™ *demonstrations of sensation and perception.*

Acupuncture ▲ The ancient Chinese practice of piercing parts of the body with needles to deaden pain and treat illness.

Sensation ▲ The stimulation of sensory receptors and the transmission of sensory information to the central nervous system.

Perception ▲ The process by which sensations are organized into an inner representation of the world.

these senses, we will find that similar sensations may lead to different perceptions in different people—or within the same person in different situations.

Gustav Theodor Fechner

He was interested in parapsychology and reported attending seances in which a bed, a table, and he himself moved in response to strange forces. He was interested in spiritual phenomena and wrote to a bereaved friend that death is but a transition to another state of existence, in which one's soul merges with others to join the Supreme Spirit. Under the pen name of "Dr. Mises," he argued (satirically) that angels must have no legs. Insects have six legs, mammals four, and birds, who ascend closest to heaven, only two. Angels, higher yet, must have none.

The son and grandson of German village pastors, Gustav Theodor Fechner (1801–1887), like his father, combined religious faith with a hardheaded scientific outlook. His father scandalously installed a lightning rod on the local church at a time when it was assumed that God would take care of heavenly threats to faithful parishes. His father also went against the fashion and preached without a wig, arguing that Jesus had done the same.

Young Fechner obtained a degree in medicine at the University of Leipzig, but his interests turned to physics and math. He founded the discipline known as *psychophysics*, which deals with the ways in which physical events such as lights and sounds are related to sensation and perception. Some historians believe that psychology as a science began in 1860 with Fechner's publication of *Elements of Psychophysics*.

Many of Fechner's laboratory methods remain in use today. Fechner also devoted his energies to aesthetics—attempting to learn why some works of art are more pleasing than others.

SENSATION AND PERCEPTION: YOUR TICKETS OF ADMISSION TO THE WORLD OUTSIDE

Before we begin our journey through the senses, let us consider a number of concepts that apply to all of them: absolute threshold, difference threshold, signal-detection theory, and sensory adaptation. In doing so, we will learn why we might be able to dim the lights gradually to near darkness without other people becoming aware that we are doing so. We will also learn why we might grow unaware of the savory aromas of delightful dinners. *Questions: How do we know when something is there? How do we know when it has changed?*

Absolute Threshold: Is It There or Isn't It?

Gustav Fechner used the term **absolute threshold** to refer to the weakest amount of a stimulus that can be distinguished from no stimulus at all. For example, the amount of physical energy required to activate the visual sensory system is the absolute threshold for light.

Psychophysicists determine the absolute thresholds of the senses by exposing participants to progressively stronger stimuli. In the **method of constant stimuli,** researchers present sets of stimuli with magnitudes close to the expected threshold. Participants say yes if they detect a stimulus and no if they do not. The stimuli are presented repeatedly in random order. An individual's absolute threshold for a stimulus is the lowest magnitude of the stimulus that he or she reports detecting 50% of the time. Weaker stimuli are detected less than 50% of the time, and stronger stimuli more than 50% of the time.

The relationship between the intensity of a stimulus (a physical event) and its perception (a psychological event) is labeled **psychophysical.** It bridges psychological and physical events.

Here are measures of the absolute thresholds for the senses of vision, hearing, taste, smell, and touch:

- ▲ For vision, the equivalent of a candle flame viewed from a distance of about 30 miles on a clear, dark night
- ▲ For hearing, the equivalent of the ticking of a watch from about 20 feet away in a quiet room
- ▲ For taste, the equivalent of about 1 teaspoon of sugar dissolved in 2 gallons of water
- ▲ For smell, the equivalent of about one drop of perfume diffused throughout a small house (1 part in 500 million)
- ▲ For touch, the equivalent of the pressure of the wing of a fly falling on a cheek from a distance of about 0.4 inch

There are individual differences in absolute thresholds. That is, some people are more sensitive than others. The same person may also differ somewhat in sensitivity from one day to the next or from one occasion to another.

If the absolute thresholds for the human senses differed substantially, our daily experiences would be unrecognizable. Our ears are particularly sensitive, especially to sounds that are low in **pitch.** If they were any more sensitive, we might hear the collisions among

REFLECT
What is the dimmest light you can see? The softest sound you can hear? How do psychophysicists answer such questions?

Absolute threshold ▲ The minimal amount of energy that can produce a sensation.

Psychophysicist ▲ A person who studies the relationships between physical stimuli (such as light or sound) and their perception.

Method of constant stimuli ▲ A psychophysical method for determining thresholds in which the researcher presents stimuli of various magnitudes and asks the person to report detection.

Psychophysical ▲ Bridging the gap between the physical and psychological worlds.

Pitch ▲ The highness or lowness of a sound, as determined by the frequency of the sound waves.

Ernst Heinrich Weber

His research tools included knitting needles, lamps, and the little weights druggists use to measure powders and potions. He showed that the sense of touch actually consists of several senses: pressure, temperature, and pain. He also showed that there is a "muscle sense" (*kinesthesis*) that people use to sense the movements of their arms, legs, and so on even when their eyes are closed.

Born in Wittenberg, Germany, Ernst Heinrich Weber (1795–1878) was the third of thirteen children and one of three sons who became distinguished scientists. (If the times had been different, one wonders what the sisters would have accomplished.) He obtained his doctorate in physiology at the University of Leipzig and taught there until his retirement. He devoted himself to the study of sensation and perception.

The knitting needles were used to touch people's backs. Weber would ask them to place a finger where the needle had been as a way of assessing their sensitivity to touch. Using a series of weights, he assessed the smallest difference—the *just noticeable difference*—that people could perceive. He found that the *jnd* differs for each sense.

molecules of air. Light consists of waves of energy, and if our eyes were sensitive to light with slightly longer wavelengths, we would see infrared light waves. Heat generates infrared light. Thus animals that are warm-blooded and give off heat—including our mates—would glow in the dark.

Difference Threshold: Is It the Same or Is It Different?

How much of a difference in intensity between two lights is required before you will detect one as being brighter than the other? The minimum difference in magnitude of two stimuli required to tell them apart is their **difference threshold**. As with the absolute threshold, psychologists have agreed to the criterion of a difference in magnitudes that can be detected 50% of the time.

Psychophysicist Ernst Weber discovered through laboratory research that the threshold for perceiving differences in the intensity of light is about 2% (actually closer to 1/60th) of their intensity. This fraction, 1/60th, is known as **Weber's constant** for light. A closely related concept is the **just noticeable difference** (jnd), the minimal amount by which a source of energy must be increased or decreased so that a difference in intensity will be perceived. In the case of light, people can perceive a difference in intensity 50% of the time when the brightness of a light is increased or decreased by 1/60th. Weber's constant for light holds whether we are comparing two quite bright lights or two rather dull lights. However, it becomes inaccurate when we compare extremely bright or extremely dull lights.

Weber's constant for noticing differences in lifted weight is 1/53rd. (Round it off to 1/50th.) That means that one would probably have to increase the weight on a 100-pound barbell by about 2 pounds before the lifter would notice the difference. Now think of the 1-pound dumbbells used by many runners. Increasing the weight of each dumbbell by 2 pounds would be readily apparent to almost anyone because the increase would be threefold, not a small fraction. Yet the increase is still "only" 2 pounds. Return to our power lifter. When he is pressing 400 pounds, a 2-pound difference is less likely to be noticeable than when he is pressing 100 pounds. This is because 2 pounds is only 1/200th of 400 pounds.

People are most sensitive to changes in the pitch (frequency) of sounds. The constant for pitch is 1/333, meaning that on average, people can tell when a tone rises or falls in pitch by one-third of 1%. (Singers have to be right on pitch. The smallest error makes them sound sharp or flat.) The sense of taste is much less sensitive. On average, people cannot detect differences in saltiness of less than 20%.

Signal-Detection Theory: Is Being Bright Enough?

Does our discussion so far strike you as "inhuman"? We have written about perception of sensory stimuli as if people are simply switched on by certain amounts of stimulation. This is not quite so. People are influenced by psychological factors as well as by external changes. **Signal-detection theory** considers the human aspects of sensation and perception. *Question: What is signal-detection theory?*

According to signal-detection theory, the intensity of the signal is just one factor that determines whether people will perceive sensory stimuli (signals) or a difference between signals. Another is the degree to which the signal can be distinguished from background noise. It is easier to hear a friend in a quiet room than in a room in which people are talking loudly and clinking glasses. The sharpness or acuteness of a person's biological sensory system is still another factor. Is sensory capacity fully developed? Is it diminished by advanced age?

Difference threshold ▲ The minimal difference in intensity required between two sources of energy so that they will be perceived as being different.

Weber's constant ▲ The fraction of the intensity by which a source of physical energy must be increased or decreased so that a difference in intensity will be perceived.

Just noticeable difference ▲ The minimal amount by which a source of energy must be increased or decreased so that a difference in intensity will be perceived.

Signal-detection theory ▲ The view that the perception of sensory stimuli involves the interaction of physical, biological, and psychological factors.

Signal-detection theory also considers psychological factors such as motivation, expectations, and learning. For example, the place in which you are reading this book may be abuzz with signals. If you are outside, perhaps a breeze is blowing against your face. Perhaps the shadows of passing clouds darken the scene now and then. If you are inside, perhaps there are the occasional clanks and hums emitted by a heating system. Perhaps the aromas of dinner are hanging in the air, or the voices from a TV set suggest a crowd in another room. Yet, you are focusing your attention on this page (I hope). Thus, the other signals recede into the background of your consciousness. One psychological factor in signal detection is the focusing or narrowing of attention to signals that the person deems important.

Consider some examples. One parent may sleep through a baby's crying while the other parent is awakened. This is not necessarily because one parent is innately more sensitive to the sounds of crying (although some fathers may conveniently assume that mothers are). Instead, it may be because one parent has been assigned the task of caring for the baby through the night and is therefore more motivated to attend to the sounds. Because of training, an artist might notice the use of line or subtle colors that would go undetected by another person looking at the same painting.

The relationship between a physical stimulus and a sensory response is more than mechanical or mathematical. People's ability to detect stimuli such as meaningful blips on a radar screen depends not only on the intensity of the blips themselves but also on the people's training (learning), motivation (desire to perceive meaningful blips), and psychological states such as fatigue or alertness.

Feature Detectors: Firing on Cue

Imagine that you are standing by the curb of a busy street as a bus approaches. When neurons in your sensory organs—in this case, your eyes—are stimulated by the approach of the bus, they relay information to the sensory cortex in the brain. Nobel prize winners David Hubel and Torsten Wiesel (1979) discovered that various neurons in the visual cortex fire in response to particular features of the visual input. ***Question: What are feature detectors?*** Many cells, for example, detect (fire in response to) lines presented at various angles—vertical, horizontal, and in between. Other cells fire in response to specific colors.

Because they respond to different aspects or features of a scene, these cells are termed **feature detectors.** In the example of the bus, visual feature detectors respond to the bus's edges, depth, contours, textures, shadows, speed, and kinds of motion (up, down, forward, and back). There are also feature detectors for other senses. Auditory feature detectors, for example, respond to the pitch, loudness, and other aspects of the sounds of the bus.

Sensory Adaptation: Where Did It Go?

Our sensory systems are admirably suited to a changing environment. ***Question: How do our sensory systems adapt to a changing environment?*** We become more sensitive to stimuli of low magnitude and less sensitive to stimuli that remain the same (such as the background noises outside the window). **Sensory adaptation** refers to these processes of adjustment.

Consider how the visual sense adapts to lower intensities of light. When we first walk into a darkened movie theater, we see little but the images on the screen. As time goes by, however, we become increasingly sensitive to the faces of those around us and to the features of the theater. The process of becoming more sensitive to stimulation is referred to as **sensitization,** or positive adaptation.

But we become less sensitive to constant stimulation. Sources of light appear to grow dimmer as we adapt to them. In fact, if you could keep an image completely stable on the retinas of your eyes—which is virtually impossible to accomplish without a motionless image and stabilizing equipment—the image would fade within a few seconds and be very difficult to see. Similarly, at the beach we soon become less aware of the lapping of the waves. When we live in a city, we become desensitized to traffic sounds except for the occasional backfire or siren. And as you may have noticed from experiences with

Signal Detection.
The detection of signals is determined not only by the physical characteristics of the signals but also by psychological factors such as motivation and attention. The people in this photo are tuned into their newspapers for the moment, and not to each other.

> ▲ **REFLECT**
> Have you ever been so involved in something that you didn't notice the heat or the cold? Have you gotten so used to sounds like those made by crickets or trains at night that you fall asleep without hearing them? How do these experiences relate to signal-detection theory?

Feature detectors ▲ Neurons in the sensory cortex that fire in response to specific features of sensory information such as lines or edges of objects.

Sensory adaptation ▲ The processes by which organisms become more sensitive to stimuli that are low in magnitude and less sensitive to stimuli that are constant or ongoing in magnitude.

Sensitization ▲ The type of sensory adaptation in which we become more sensitive to stimuli that are low in magnitude. Also called *positive adaptation.*

freshly painted rooms, sensitivity to disagreeable odors fades quite rapidly. The process of becoming less sensitive to stimulation is referred to as **desensitization,** or negative adaptation.

REVIEW

(1) _____ is a mechanical process that involves the stimulation of sensory receptors and the transmission of sensory information to the central nervous system. (2) _____ is the organization of sensations into an inner representation of the world and reflects learning and expectations, as well as sensations. (3) The _____ threshold for a stimulus, such as light, is the lowest intensity at which it can be detected. (4) The minimum difference in intensity that can be discriminated is the _____ threshold. (5) According to _____-detection theory, many factors determine perception of a stimulus: the sensory stimuli, the biological sensory system of the person, and psychological factors, such as motivation and attention.

Pulling It Together: What are the differences between sensation and perception? How do feature detectors and sensory adaptation help us adapt to the environment? Can you apply signal-detection theory to focusing on assignments?

VISION: LETTING THE SUN SHINE IN

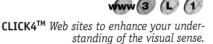

CLICK4™ *Web sites to enhance your understanding of the visual sense.*

Our eyes are our "windows on the world." More than half of the cerebral cortex is devoted to visual functions (Basic Behavioral Science Task Force, 1996b). Because vision is our dominant sense, blindness is the most debilitating type of sensory loss (Moore, 1995). To understand vision, let us consider the nature of light.

Light: What Is This Stuff?

Light is fascinating stuff. It radiates. It illuminates. It dazzles. It glows. It beckons like a beacon. We speak of the "light of reason." We speak of genius as "brilliance." In almost all cultures, light is a symbol of goodness and knowledge. People who aren't in the know are said to be "in the dark." *Question: Just what is this stuff called light?*

Visible light is the stuff that triggers visual sensations. It is just one small part of a spectrum of electromagnetic energy (see Figure 3.1). All forms of electromagnetic energy move in waves. Different kinds of electromagnetic energy have different wavelengths. Cosmic rays have extremely short wavelengths, only a few trillionths of an inch long. But some radio waves extend for miles. Although visible light seems to move in a steady stream, it also consists of waves of energy. Different colors have different wavelengths, with violet the shortest and red the longest. Radar, microwaves, and X-rays are also forms of electromagnetic energy.

You have probably seen rainbows or light that has been broken down into several colors as it filtered through your windows. Sir Isaac Newton, the British scientist, discovered that sunlight could be broken down into different colors by means of a triangular solid of glass called a *prism* (Figure 3.1). When I took introductory psychology, I was taught to remember the colors of the spectrum, from longest to shortest wavelengths, by using the mnemonic device *Roy G. Biv* (red, orange, yellow, green, blue, indigo, violet). I must have been a backward student because I found it easier to recall them in reverse order, using the meaningless acronym *vibgyor*.

The wavelength of visible light determines its color, or **hue.** The wavelength for red is longer than the wavelength for orange, and so on through the spectrum.

▲ **REFLECT**
Have you ever seen a rainbow? How do you account for the colors in it?

The Eye: The Better to See You With

Consider that magnificent invention called the camera, which records visual experiences. In traditional cameras, light enters an opening and is focused onto a sensitive surface, or film. Chemicals on film create a lasting impression of the image that entered the camera.

Desensitization ▲ The type of sensory adaptation in which we become less sensitive to constant stimuli. Also called *negative adaptation.*
Visible light ▲ The part of the electromagnetic spectrum that stimulates the eye and produces visual sensations.
Hue ▲ The color of light, as determined by its wavelength.

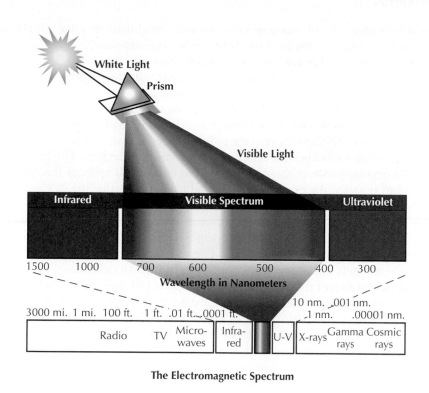

Infrared | Visible Spectrum | Ultraviolet

1500   1000   700   600   500   400   300
Wavelength in Nanometers

3000 mi. 1 mi. 100 ft. 1 ft. .01 ft. .0001 ft.   10 nm. .001 nm.   .1 nm.   .00001 nm.

Radio TV Micro-waves Infra-red U-V X-rays Gamma rays Cosmic rays

The Electromagnetic Spectrum

FIGURE 3.1 The Visible Spectrum.
By passing a source of white light, such as sunlight, through a prism, we break it down into the colors of the visible spectrum. The visible spectrum is just a narrow segment of the electromagnetic spectrum. The electromagnetic spectrum also includes radio waves, microwaves, X-rays, cosmic rays, and many others. Different forms of electromagnetic energy have wavelengths that vary from a few trillionths of a meter to thousands of miles. Visible light varies in wavelength from about 400 to 700 *billionths* of a meter. (A meter = 39.37 inches.)

Question: How does the eye work?   The eye—our living camera—is no less remarkable. Look at its major parts, as shown in Figure 3.2. As with a film or TV camera, light enters through a narrow opening and is projected onto a sensitive surface. Light first passes through the transparent **cornea,** which covers the front of the eye's surface. (The "white" of the eye, or *sclera*, is composed of hard protective tissue.) The amount of light that passes through the cornea is determined by the size of the opening of the muscle called the **iris,** which is the colored part of the eye. The opening in the iris is the **pupil.** The size of the pupil adjusts automatically to the amount of light present. You do not have to try purposefully to open your eyes further to see better in low lighting conditions. The more intense the light, the smaller the opening. In a similar fashion, we adjust the

CLICK4™ *an interactive illustration of the parts of the eye, including distal and proximal stimuli.*

Cornea ▲ Transparent tissue forming the outer surface of the eyeball.
Iris ▲ A muscular membrane whose dilation regulates the amount of light that enters the eye.
Pupil ▲ The apparently black opening in the center of the iris, through which light enters the eye.

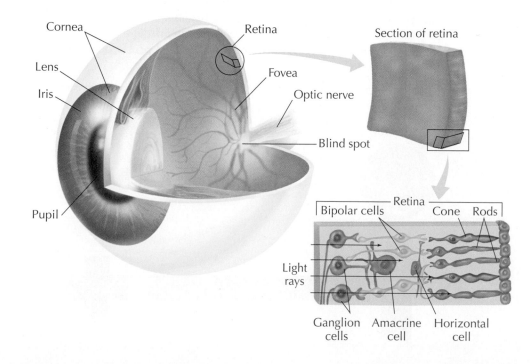

FIGURE 3.2 The Human Eye.
In both the eye and a camera, light enters through a narrow opening and is projected onto a sensitive surface. In the eye, the photosensitive surface is called the retina, and information concerning the changing images on the retina is transmitted to the brain. The retina contains photoreceptors called rods and cones. Rods and cones transmit sensory input back through the bipolar neurons to the ganglion neurons. The axons of the ganglion neurons form the optic nerve, which transmits sensory stimulation through the brain to the visual cortex of the occipital lobe.

CLICK4™ *a video on the transmission of light through the eye and into the brain.*

CLICK4™ *a video on the way the brain processes inverted visual stimuli.*

Lens ▲ A transparent body behind the iris that focuses an image on the retina.

Retina ▲ The area of the inner surface of the eye that contains rods and cones.

Photoreceptors ▲ Cells that respond to light.

Bipolar cells ▲ Neurons that conduct neural impulses from rods and cones to ganglion cells.

Ganglion cells ▲ Neurons whose axons form the optic nerve.

Optic nerve ▲ The nerve that transmits sensory information from the eye to the brain.

Fovea ▲ An area near the center of the retina that is dense with cones and where vision is consequently most acute.

Blind spot ▲ The area of the retina where axons from ganglion cells meet to form the optic nerve.

Visual acuity ▲ Sharpness of vision.

Nearsighted ▲ Capable of seeing nearby objects with greater acuity than distant objects.

Farsighted ▲ Capable of seeing distant objects with greater acuity than nearby objects.

Presbyopia ▲ A condition characterized by brittleness of the lens.

amount of light allowed into a camera according to its brightness. Pupil size is also sensitive to emotional response: We can literally be "wide-eyed with fear."

Once light passes through the iris, it encounters the **lens.** The lens adjusts or accommodates to the image by changing its thickness. Changes in thickness permit a clear image of the object to be projected onto the retina. These changes focus the light according to the distance of the object from the viewer. If you hold a finger at arm's length and slowly bring it toward your nose, you will feel tension in the eye as the thickness of the lens accommodates to keep the retinal image in focus. When people squint to bring an object into focus, they are adjusting the thickness of the lens. The lens in a camera does not accommodate to the distance of objects. Instead, to focus the light that is projected onto the film, the camera lens is moved farther from the film or closer to it, as in a zoom lens.

The **retina** is like the film or image surface of the camera. However, the retina consists of cells called **photoreceptors** that are sensitive to light (photosensitive). There are two types of photoreceptors: *rods* and *cones.* The retina (see Figure 3.2) contains several layers of cells: the rods and cones, **bipolar cells,** and **ganglion cells.** All of these cells are neurons. Light travels past the ganglion cells and bipolar cells and stimulates the rods and cones. The rods and cones then send neural messages through the bipolar cells to the ganglion cells. The axons of the million or so ganglion cells in our retinas form the **optic nerve.** The optic nerve conducts sensory input to the brain, where it is relayed to the visual area of the occipital lobe. Other neurons in the retina—amacrine cells and horizontal cells—make sideways connections at a level near the receptor cells and at another level near the ganglion cells. As a result of these lateral connections, many rods and cones funnel visual information into one bipolar cell, and many bipolar cells funnel information to one ganglion cell. Receptors outnumber ganglion cells by more than 100 to 1.

The **fovea** is the most sensitive area of the retina (see Figure 3.2). Receptors there are more densely packed. The **blind spot,** in contrast, is insensitive to visual stimulation. It is the part of the retina where the axons of the ganglion cells collect to form the optic nerve (Figure 3.3).

Visual acuity (sharpness of vision) is connected with the shape of the eye. People who have to be unusually close to an object to discriminate its details are **nearsighted.** People who see distant objects unusually clearly but have difficulty focusing on nearby objects are **farsighted.** Nearsightedness can result when the eyeball is elongated so that the images of distant objects are focused in front of the retina. When the eyeball is too short, the images of nearby objects are focused behind the retina, causing farsightedness. Eyeglasses or contact lenses can be used to help nearsighted people focus distant objects on their retinas. Farsighted people usually see well enough without eyeglasses until they reach their middle years, when they may need glasses for reading.

Beginning in the late 30s to the mid 40s, the lenses grow brittle, making it difficult to accommodate to, or focus on, objects. This condition is called **presbyopia,** from the

FIGURE 3.3 Locating the Blind Spots in Your Eyes.

To try a "disappearing act," first look at drawing 1. Close your right eye. Then move the book back and forth about 1 foot from your left eye while you stare at the plus sign. You will notice the circle disappear. When the circle disappears it is being projected onto the blind spot of your retina, the point at which the axons of ganglion neurons collect to form the optic nerve. Now look at drawing 2. You can make this figure disappear and "see" the black line continue through the spot where it was by closing your right eye and staring at the plus sign with your left. When this figure is projected onto your blind spot, your brain "fills in" the line, which is one reason that you're not usually aware that you have blind spots.

Greek words for "old man" and "eyes," but presbyopia occurs by middle adulthood, not late adulthood. Presbyopia makes it difficult to perceive nearby visual stimuli. People who had normal visual acuity in their youth often require corrective lenses to read in middle adulthood and beyond.

Rods and Cones

Rods and **cones** are the photoreceptors in the retina (see Figure 3.4). About 125 million rods and 6.5 million cones are distributed across the retina. The fovea is composed almost exclusively of cones. Cones become more sparsely distributed as you work forward from the fovea toward the lens. Rods, in contrast, are nearly absent at the fovea but are distributed more densely as you approach the lens.

Rods are sensitive only to the intensity of light. They allow us to see in black and white. Cones provide color vision. In low lighting, it is possible to photograph a clearer image with black-and-white film than with color film. Similarly, rods are more sensitive to light than cones. Therefore, as the illumination grows dim, as during the evening and nighttime hours, objects appear to lose their color well before their outlines fade from view.

Light Adaptation

Immediately after we enter it, a movie theater may seem too dark to allow us to find seats readily. But as time goes on we begin to see the seats and other people clearly. The process of adjusting to lower lighting conditions is called **dark adaptation.**

Figure 3.5 shows the amount of light needed for detection as a function of the amount of time spent in the dark. The cones and rods adapt at different rates. The cones, which permit perception of color, reach their maximum adaptation to darkness in about 10 minutes. The rods, which allow perception of light and dark only, are more sensitive and continue to adapt to darkness for up to about 45 minutes.

Adaptation to brighter lighting conditions takes place much more rapidly. When you emerge from the theater into the brilliance of the afternoon, you may at first be painfully surprised by the featureless blaze around you. The visual experience is not unlike turning the brightness of the TV set to its maximum setting, at which the edges of objects seem to dissolve into light. Within a minute or so of entering the street, however, the brightness of the scene dims and objects regain their edges.

The "Psychology and Modern Life" feature on page 86 speaks of even more fascinating examples of adaptation—how researchers are developing ways of seeing when cells in the retina, even the optic nerve itself, fail to function.

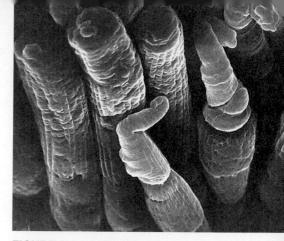

FIGURE 3.4   A Much Enlarged Photograph of Rods and a Cone.
Cones are usually upright fellows. However, the cone at the bottom right of this photo has been bent by the photographic process. You have about 125 million rods and 6.5 million cones distributed across the retina of each eye. Only cones provide sensations of color. The fovea of the eye is almost exclusively populated by cones, which are then distributed more sparsely as you work forward toward the lens.

Rods ▲ Rod-shaped photoreceptors that are sensitive only to the intensity of light.

Cones ▲ Cone-shaped photoreceptors that transmit sensations of color.

Dark adaptation ▲ The process of adjusting to conditions of lower lighting by increasing the sensitivity of rods and cones.

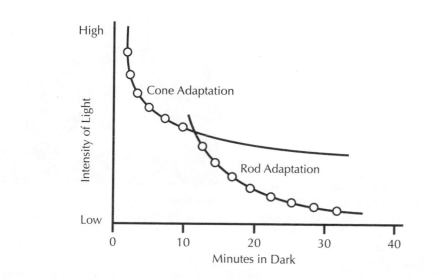

FIGURE 3.5   Dark Adaptation.
This illustration shows the amount of light necessary for detection as a function of the amount of time spent in the dark. Cones and rods adapt at different rates. Cones, which permit perception of color, reach maximum dark adaptation in about 10 minutes. Rods, which permit perception of dark and light only, are more sensitive than cones. Rods continue to adapt for up to about 45 minutes.

Color Vision: Creating an Inner World of Color

For most of us, the world is a place of brilliant colors—the blue-greens of the ocean, the red-oranges of the setting sun, the deepened greens of June, the glories of rhododendron and hibiscus. Color is an emotional and aesthetic part of our everyday lives. In this section we explore some of the psychological dimensions of color and then examine theories about how we manage to convert different wavelengths of light into perceptions of color. *Question: What are some psychological dimensions of color?* These include hue, brightness, and warmth.

The wavelength of light determines its color, or *hue*. The brightness (or *value*) of a color is its degree of lightness or darkness. The brighter the color, the lighter it is.

If we bend the colors of the spectrum into a circle, we create a color wheel, as shown in Figure 3.6. Yellow is the lightest color on the color wheel. As we work our way around the wheel from yellow to violet-blue, we encounter darker colors.

Psychology and Modern Life

Blind People Use Microchips to See the Light

On the TV "Star Trek: The Next Generation" series, the blind Geordi was given a sense of vision by bionic eyes. Are such eyes the stuff of science fiction or right around the corner? The answer seems to be that they are somewhere in between.

Millions of people around the world suffer from diseases of the retina that cause blindness: macular degeneration and retinitis pigmentosa. In both diseases, the rods and cones in the retina die. Yet much of the other retinal circuitry remain relatively intact. For example, when the ganglion cells are electrically stimulated, they can often generate signals to the visual cortex in the occipital lobe via the optic nerve. A team of researchers led by Dr. John Wyatt, an electrical engineer at MIT and Dr. Joseph Rizzo, a neuro-ophthalmologist at Harvard Medical School, are working on a retinal implant to stimulate the ganglion cells (Eisenberg, 1999).

As silicon chips grow more powerful, researchers are developing microscopic light-sensitive transistors that can be placed on chips and embedded in the retina. The Harvard–MIT group plans a slightly different approach. They intend to use two microchips. They will mount one along with a camera on a pair of glasses. Images will be transmitted wirelessly to the chip embedded in the eye. The chip in the eye will stimulate the functional cells in the retina.

In one experiment, blind patients' retinas were stimulated by handheld electrodes similar to the tiny chips that will be implanted. Patients reported seeing points of light, dim outlines, and the shapes of letters. This is not the brilliant technicolor display we have in normal vision, but the capacity to see changes in traffic light and the dim outlines of cars and people will create a brilliant enough visual world for people who would otherwise see nothing.

And what are scientists working on for people whose optic nerves are not intact, but who have functional visual cortex remaining in the occipital lobe of the brain? Bypassing the eye and optic nerve altogether seems to be one answer.

Dr. William Dobelle wired a tiny camera directly into the brain of a blind volunteer, enabling him to see scattered specks of light and a limited ability to perceive objects, such as a 2-inch-high letter from a distance of a few feet ("Brain-link camera," 2000). The volunteer also found a mannequin in a room, retrieved a black stocking cap hanging on a white wall, and placed it on the mannequin's head.

The volunteer wore sunglasses. A small pinhole camera was mounted on one lens, and an ultrasonic range finder was mounted on the other. The devices signaled a light-weight computer carried on the hip, which highlighted the edges of the shapes captured by the camera. The computer then instructed a second computer to transmit signals to tiny electrodes implanted on the visual cortex in the volunteer's brain.

With exposure to various arrays of light and dark, and practice, the individual begins to organize the specks of light into meaningful displays. This is not full-blown cinematography either, but it's a start.

Bionic Eyes.
The blind Geordi, a character in *Star Trek: The Next Generation*, was enabled to see by means of bionic eyes. Are such eyes the stuff of science fiction or right around the corner?

Warm and Cool Colors   Psychologically, the colors on the green-blue side of the color wheel are considered to be cool in temperature. Those colors on the yellow-orange-red side are considered to be warm. Perhaps greens and blues suggest the coolness of the ocean and the sky, whereas things that are burning tend to be red or orange. A room decorated in green or blue may seem more appealing on a hot July day than a room decorated in red or orange.

Complementary Colors   The colors across from one another on the color wheel are labeled **complementary**. Red-green and blue-yellow are the major complementary pairs. If we mix complementary colors together, they dissolve into gray.

"But wait!" you say. "Blue and yellow cannot be complementary because by mixing pigments of blue and yellow we create green, not gray." True enough, but we have been talking about mixing *lights*, not *pigments*. Light is the source of all color. Pigments reflect and absorb different wavelengths of light selectively. The mixture of lights is an *additive* process. The mixture of pigments is *subtractive*. Figure 3.7 shows mixtures of lights and pigments of various colors.

Pigments gain their colors by absorbing light from certain segments of the spectrum and reflecting the rest. For example, we see most plant life as green because the pigment in chlorophyll absorbs most of the red, blue, and violet wavelengths of light. The remaining green is reflected. A red pigment absorbs most of the spectrum but reflects red. White pigments reflect all colors equally. Black pigments reflect very little light.

Complementary ▲ Descriptive of colors of the spectrum that when combined produce white or nearly white light.

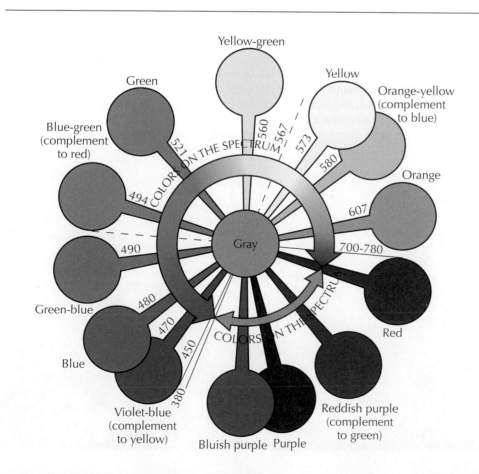

Yellow-green
Green
Blue-green (complement to red)
560
567
521
573
494
COLORS ON THE SPECTRUM
580
Yellow
Orange-yellow (complement to blue)
490
607
Gray
Orange
480
700–780
Green-blue
470
Red
450
COLORS ON THE SPECTRUM
380
Blue
Violet-blue (complement to yellow)
Bluish purple **Purple**
Reddish purple (complement to green)

FIGURE 3.6   The Color Wheel.
A color wheel can be formed by bending the colors of the spectrum into a circle and placing complementary colors across from one another. (A few colors between violet and red are not found in the spectrum and must be added to complete the circle.) When lights of complementary colors such as yellow and violet-blue are mixed, they dissolve into neutral gray. The afterimage of a color is its complement.

FIGURE 3.7 Additive and Subtractive Color Mixtures Produced by Lights and Pigments.
Thomas Young discovered that white light and all the colors of the spectrum could be produced by adding combinations of lights of red, green, and violet-blue and varying their intensities (see part A). Part B shows subtractive color mixtures, which are formed by mixing pigments, not light.

In *Sunday Afternoon on the Island of La Grande Jatte* (Figure 3.8), French painter Georges Seurat molded his figures and forms from dabs of color. Instead of mixing his pigments, he placed points of pure color next to one another. When the painting is viewed from very close, the sensations are of pure color (see detail, Figure 3.8). But from a distance the juxtaposition of pure colors creates the impression of mixtures of color.

Afterimages Before reading on, why don't you try a brief experiment? Look at the strangely colored American flag in Figure 3.9 for at least half a minute. Then look at a sheet of white or gray paper. What has happened to the flag? If your color vision is working properly, and if you looked at the miscolored flag long enough, you should see a flag composed of the familiar red, white, and blue. The flag you perceive on the white sheet of paper is an **afterimage** of the first. (If you didn't look at the green, black, and yellow flag long enough the first time, try it again. It will work any number of times.) In afterimages, persistent sensations of color are followed by perception of the complementary color when the first color is removed. The same holds true for black and white. Staring at one

Afterimage ▲ The lingering visual impression made by a stimulus that has been removed.

FIGURE 3.8 Sunday Afternoon on the Island of La Grande Jatte.
The French painter Seurat molded his figures and forms from dabs of color. Up close (see the detail), the dabs of pure color are visible. From afar, they create the impression of color mixtures.

FIGURE 3.9   Three Cheers for the . . . Green, Black, and Yellow?
Don't be concerned. We can readily restore Old Glory to its familiar hues. Place a sheet of white paper beneath the book, and stare at the center of the flag for 30 seconds. Then remove the book. The afterimage on the paper beneath will look familiar.

will create an afterimage of the other. The phenomenon of afterimages has contributed to one of the theories of color vision, as we will see.

Theories of Color Vision

Adults with normal color vision can discriminate many thousands of colors across the visible spectrum. Different colors have different wavelengths. Although we can vary the physical wavelengths of light in a continuous manner from shorter to longer, many changes in color are discontinuous. For example, our perception of a color shifts suddenly from blue to green, even though the change in wavelength may be smaller than that between two blues.

Question: How do we perceive color?   Our ability to perceive color depends on the eye's transmission of different messages to the brain when lights with different wavelengths stimulate the cones in the retina.

CONTROVERSY IN PSYCHOLOGY

What happens in the eye and in the brain when lights with different wavelengths stimulate the retina? How many kinds of color receptors are there?

In this section we explore this controversy by discussing two theories of color vision: the *trichromatic theory* and the *opponent-process theory*.

Trichromatic theory is based on an experiment conducted by the British scientist Thomas Young in the early 1800s. As in Figure 3.7, Young projected three lights of different colors onto a screen so that they partly overlapped. He found that he could create any color from the visible spectrum by simply varying the intensities of the lights. When all three lights fell on the same spot, they created white light, or the appearance of no color at all. The three lights manipulated by Young were red, green, and blue-violet.

The German physiologist Hermann von Helmholtz saw in Young's discovery an explanation of color vision. Von Helmholtz suggested that the eye must have three different types of photoreceptors or cones. Some must be sensitive to red light, some to green, and some to blue. We see other colors when two different types of color receptors are stimulated. The perception of yellow, for example, would result from the simultaneous stimulation of receptors for red and green. The trichromatic theory is also known as the Young-Helmholtz theory.

In 1870, Ewald Hering proposed the **opponent-process theory** of color vision: There are three types of color receptors; however, they are not sensitive to the simple

CLICK4™ *an essay assignment on theories of color vision.*

Trichromatic theory ▲ The theory that color vision is made possible by three types of cones, some of which respond to red light, some to green, and some to blue. (From the Greek roots *treis*, meaning "three," and *chroma*, meaning "color.")
Opponent-process theory ▲ The theory that color vision is made possible by three types of cones, some of which respond to red or green light, some to blue or yellow, and some only to the intensity of light.

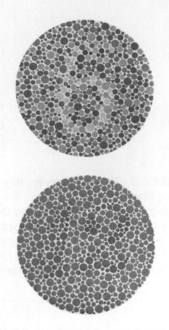

FIGURE 3.10   Plates From a Test for Color Blindness.
Can you see the numbers in these plates from a test for color blindness? A person with red-green color blindness would not be able to see the 6, and a person with blue-yellow color blindness would probably not discern the 12. (Caution: These reproductions cannot be used for actual testing of color blindness.)

▲ REFLECT
How do you imagine that color-blind people know when to stop at a traffic light and when to proceed?

hues of red, green, and blue. Hering suggested instead that afterimages (such as that of the American flag shown in Figure 3.9) are made possible by three types of color receptors: red-green, blue-yellow, and a type that perceives differences in brightness. A red-green cone could not transmit messages for red and green at the same time. According to Hering, staring at the green, black, and yellow flag for 30 seconds would disturb the balance of neural activity. The afterimage of red, white, and blue would represent the eye's attempt to reestablish a balance.

Research suggests that each theory of color vision is partially correct. For example, it shows that some cones are sensitive to blue, some to green, and some to red parts of the spectrum (Solomon et al., 1993). But studies of the bipolar and ganglion neurons suggest that messages from cones are transmitted to the brain and relayed by the thalamus to the occipital lobe in an opponent-process fashion (DeValois & Jacobs, 1984). Some opponent-process cells that transmit messages to the visual centers in the brain are excited ("turned on") by green light but inhibited ("turned off") by red light. Others can be excited by red light but are inhibited by green light. A second set of opponent-process cells responds in an opposite manner to blue and yellow. A third set responds in an opposite manner to light and dark.

A neural rebound effect apparently helps explain the occurrence of afterimages. That is, a green-sensitive ganglion that had been excited by green light for half a minute or so might switch briefly to inhibitory activity when the light is shut off. The effect would be to perceive red even though no red light is present.

These theoretical updates allow for the afterimage effects with the green, black, and yellow flag and are also consistent with Young's experiments in mixing lights of different colors.

Color Blindness: What Kind of "Chromat" Are You?

If you can discriminate among the colors of the visible spectrum, you have normal color vision and are labeled a **trichromat.** This means that you are sensitive to red-green, blue-yellow, and light-dark. *Questions: What is color blindness? Why are some people color blind?* People who are totally color blind, called **monochromats,** are sensitive only to lightness and darkness. Total color blindness is rare. Fully color-blind individuals see the world as trichromats would on a black-and-white TV set or in a black-and-white movie.

Partial color blindness is more common than total color blindness. Partial color blindness is a sex-linked trait that affects mostly males. Partially color-blind people are called **dichromats.** They can discriminate only among two colors—red and green, or blue and yellow—and the colors that are derived from mixing these colors. Figure 3.10 shows the types of tests that are used to diagnose color blindness.

A dichromat might put on one red sock and one green sock, but would not mix red and blue socks. Monochromats might put on socks of any color. They would not notice a difference as long as the socks' colors did not differ in intensity—that is, brightness.

Trichromat ▲ A person with normal color vision.
Monochromat ▲ A person who is sensitive to black and white only and hence color blind.
Dichromat ▲ A person who is sensitive to black-white and either red-green or blue-yellow and hence partially color blind.

REVIEW

(6) Visible light is part of a spectrum of _____ energy. (7) The color of visible light is determined by its _____. (8) Light enters the eye through the _____. (9) The muscle called the _____ determines the amount of light that is let in. (10) The _____ accommodates to an image by changing thickness and focusing light onto the retina. (11) The retina is made up of photoreceptors called rods and _____. (12) The axons of ganglion cells make up the _____ nerve, which conducts visual information to the brain. (13) Rods transmit sensations of light and dark, and cones permit perception of _____.

Pulling it Together: Describe evidence concerning the kinds of photoreceptors in the retina. Why do dichromats usually find it difficult to tell red and green apart? How would you bypass the eye to feed light into the brain?

VISUAL PERCEPTION: HOW PERCEPTIVE!

Perception is the process by which we organize or make sense of our sensory impressions. Although visual sensations are caused by electromagnetic energy, visual perception also relies on our knowledge, expectations, and motivations. Whereas sensation may be thought of as a mechanical process, perception is an active process through which we interpret the world around us.

For example, just what do you see in Figure 3.11? Do you see random splotches of ink or a rider on horseback? If you perceive a horse and rider, it is not just because of the visual sensations provided by the drawing. Each of the blobs is meaningless in and of itself, and the pattern they form is also less than clear. Despite the lack of clarity, however, you may still perceive a horse and rider. *Question: How do we organize bits of information like perceptions into meaningful wholes?* The answer has something to do with your general knowledge and your desire to fit incoming bits and pieces of information into familiar patterns.

In the case of the horse and rider, your integration of disconnected pieces of information into a meaningful whole also reflects what Gestalt psychologists refer to as the principle of **closure,** or the tendency to perceive a complete or whole figure even when there are gaps in the sensory input. Put another way, in perception the whole can be very much more than the mere sum of the parts. A collection of parts can be meaningless. It is their configuration that matters.

FIGURE 3.11 Closure.
Meaningless splotches of ink or a horse and rider? This figure illustrates the Gestalt principle of closure.

Closure ▲ The tendency to perceive a broken figure as being complete or whole.
Perceptual organization ▲ The tendency to integrate perceptual elements into meaningful patterns.
Ambiguous ▲ Having two or more possible meanings.

Perceptual Organization: Getting It Together

Early in the 20th century, Gestalt psychologists noted certain consistencies in the way we integrate bits and pieces of sensory stimulation into meaningful wholes. They attempted to identify the rules that govern these processes. Max Wertheimer, in particular, discovered many such rules. As a group, these rules are referred to as the laws of **perceptual organization.** We examine several of them, beginning with those concerning figure-ground perception. Then we consider top-down and bottom-up processing.

Figure-Ground Perception If you look out your window, you may see people, buildings, cars, and streets, or perhaps grass, trees, birds, and clouds. All these objects tend to be perceived as figures against backgrounds. Cars seen against the background of the street are easier to pick out than cars seen piled on top of one another in a junkyard. Birds seen against the sky are more likely to be perceived than birds seen "in the bush."

When figure-ground relationships are **ambiguous,** or capable of being interpreted in various ways, our perceptions tend to be unstable, shifting back and forth. As an example, look for a while at Figure 3.12. How many people, objects, and animals can you find? If your eye is drawn back and forth, so that sometimes you are perceiving light figures on a dark background and at other times dark figures on a light background, you are experiencing figure-ground reversal. In other words, a shift is occurring in your perception of what is figure and what is ground, or background. The artist was able to have some fun with us because of our tendency

FIGURE 3.12 Figure and Ground.
How many animals and demons can you find in this Escher print? Do we have white figures on a black background or black figures on a white background? Figure-ground perception is the tendency to perceive geometric forms against a background.

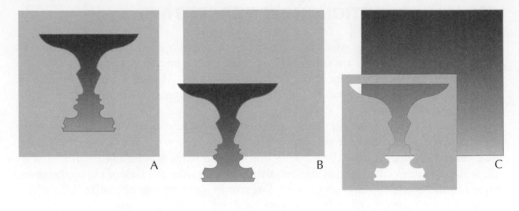

FIGURE 3.13 The Rubin Vase.
A favorite drawing used by psychologists to demonstrate figure-ground perception. Part A is ambiguous, with neither the vase nor the profiles clearly the figure or the ground. In part B, the vase is the figure; in part C, the profiles are.

▲ REFLECT

Why is it easier to spot a friend walking alone than in a crowd?

Proximity ▲ Nearness. The perceptual tendency to group together objects that are near one another.
Similarity ▲ The perceptual tendency to group together objects that are similar in appearance.
Continuity ▲ The tendency to perceive a series of points or lines as having unity.
Common fate ▲ The tendency to perceive elements that move together as belonging together.

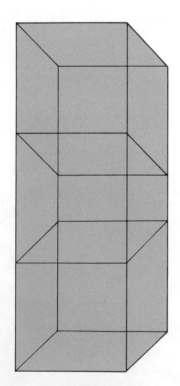

FIGURE 3.14 Necker Cubes.
Ambiguity in the drawing of the cubes makes perceptual shifts possible.

to try to isolate geometric patterns or figures from a background. However, in this case the "background" is as meaningful and detailed as the "figure." Therefore, our perceptions shift back and forth.

Figure 3.13 shows a Rubin vase, one of psychologists' favorite illustrations of figure-ground relationships. The figure-ground relationship in part A of the figure is ambiguous. There are no cues that suggest which area must be the figure. For this reason, our perception may shift from seeing the vase as the figure to seeing two profiles as the figure. There is no such problem in part B. Since it seems that a white vase has been brought forward against a colored ground, we are more likely to perceive the vase than the profiles. In part C, we are more likely to perceive the profiles than the vase because the profiles are whole and the vase is broken against the background. Of course, if we wish to, we can still perceive the vase in part C, because experience has shown us where it is. Why not have some fun with friends by covering up parts B and C and asking them what they see? (They'll catch on quickly if they can see all three drawings at once.)

The Necker cube (Figure 3.14) is another ambiguous drawing that can lead to perceptual shifts. Hold this page at arm's length and stare at the center of the figure for 30 seconds or so. Try to allow your eye muscles to relax. (The feeling is of your eyes "glazing over.") After a while you will notice a dramatic shift in your perception of these "stacked boxes." What was once a front edge is now a back edge, and vice versa. The perceptual shift is made possible by the fact that the outline of the drawing permits two interpretations.

Other Gestalt Rules for Organization   In addition to the law of closure, Gestalt psychologists have noted that our perceptions are guided by rules or laws of *proximity*, *similarity*, *continuity*, and *common fate*.

Without reading further, describe part A of Figure 3.15. Did you say it consists of six lines or of three groups of two parallel lines? If you said three sets of lines, you were influenced by the **proximity**, or nearness, of some of the lines. There is no other reason for perceiving them in pairs or subgroups: All of the lines are parallel and of equal length.

Now describe part B of the figure. Did you perceive the figure as a 6 × 6 grid, or as three columns of *x*'s and three columns of *o*'s? According to the law of **similarity**, we perceive similar objects as belonging together. For this reason, you may have been more likely to describe part B in terms of columns than in terms of rows or a grid.

What about part C? Is it a circle with two lines stemming from it, or is it a (broken) line that goes through a circle? If you saw it as a single (broken) line, you were probably organizing your perceptions according to the rule of **continuity**. That is, we perceive a series of points or a broken line as having unity.

According to the law of **common fate**, elements seen moving together are perceived as belonging together. A group of people running in the same direction appears unified in purpose. Birds that flock together seem to be of a feather. (Did I get that right?) Part D of Figure 3.15 provides another example of the law of closure. The arcs tend to be perceived as a circle (or circle with gaps) rather than as just a series of arcs.

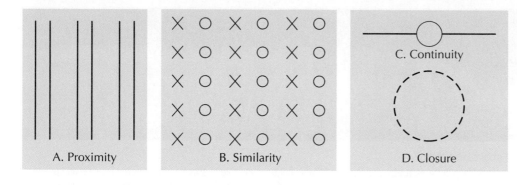

FIGURE 3.15 Some Gestalt Laws of Perceptual Organization.
These drawings illustrate the Gestalt laws of proximity, similarity, continuity, and closure.

Top-Down Versus Bottom-Up Processing   Imagine that you are trying to put together a thousand-piece puzzle—a task I usually avoid, despite the cajoling of my children. Now imagine that you are trying to accomplish it after someone has walked off with the box showing the picture formed by the completed puzzle.

When you have the box—when you know what the "big picture" or pattern looks like—cognitive psychologists refer to the task of assembling the pieces as **top-down processing.** The "top" of the visual system refers to the image of the pattern in the brain, and the top-down strategy for putting the puzzle together implies that you use the pattern to guide subordinate perceptual motor tasks such as hunting for particular pieces. Without knowledge of the pattern, the assembly process is referred to as **bottom-up processing.** You begin with bits and pieces of information and become aware of the pattern formed by the assembled pieces only after you have worked at it for a while.

Life in Motown — Perception of Movement

We all live in "motown." Moving objects—whether they are other people, animals, cars, or boulders plummeting down a hillside—are vital sources of sensory information. Moving objects even capture the attention of newborn infants. *Question: How do we perceive movement?*

To understand how we perceive movement, recall what it is like to be on a train that has begun to pull out of the station while the train on the adjacent track remains stationary. If your own train does not lurch as it accelerates, you might think at first that the other train is moving. Or you might not be certain whether your train is moving forward or the other train is moving backward.

The visual perception of movement is based on change of position relative to other objects. To early scientists, whose only tool for visual observation was the naked eye, it seemed logical that the sun circled the earth. You have to be able to imagine the movement of the earth around the sun as seen from a theoretical point in outer space—you cannot observe it directly.

How, then, do you determine which train is moving when your train is pulling out of the station (or the other train is pulling in)? One way is to look for objects that you know are stable, such as platform columns, houses, signs, or trees. If you are stationary in relation to them, your train is not moving. Observing people walking on the station platform may not provide the answer, however, because they are also changing their position relative to stationary objects. You might also try to sense the motion of the train in your body. You know from experience how to do these things quite well, although it may be difficult to phrase explanations for them.

We have been considering the perception of real movement. Psychologists have also studied several types of apparent movement, or **illusions** of movement. These include the *autokinetic effect, stroboscopic motion,* and the *phi phenomenon.*

The Autokinetic Effect   If you were to sit quietly in a dark room and stare at a point of light projected onto the far wall, after a while it might appear that the light had begun to move, even if it actually remained quite still. The tendency to perceive a stationary point of light as moving in a dark room is called the **autokinetic effect.**

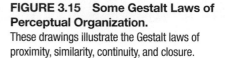

REFLECT
Have you had the experience of being in a train and not knowing whether your train or one on the next track was moving? How do you explain your confusion? How did you figure out which one was really moving?

Top-down processing ▲ The use of contextual information or knowledge of a pattern in order to organize parts of the pattern.

Bottom-up processing ▲ The organization of the parts of a pattern to recognize, or form an image of, the pattern they compose.

Ilusions ▲ Sensations that give rise to misperceptions.

Autokinetic effect ▲ The tendency to perceive a stationary point of light in a dark room as moving.

Stroboscopic Motion.
In a motion picture, viewing a series of stationary images at the rate of about 16 to 22 frames per second provides an illusion of movement termed *stroboscopic motion.* The actual movement that is occurring is the rapid switching of stationary images.

Over the years, psychologists have conducted interesting experiments in which they have asked people, for example, what the light is "spelling out." The light has spelled out nothing, of course, and the words perceived by participants reflect their own cognitive processes, not external sensations.

Stroboscopic Motion

Stroboscopic motion makes motion pictures possible. In **stroboscopic motion,** the illusion of movement is provided by the presentation of a rapid progression of images of stationary objects. So-called motion pictures do not really consist of images that move. Rather, the audience is shown 16 to 22 pictures, or *frames,* per second. Each frame differs slightly from that preceding it. Showing the frames in rapid succession provides the illusion of movement.

At the rate of at least 16 frames per second, the "motion" in a film seems smooth and natural. With fewer than 16 or so frames per second, the movement looks jumpy and unnatural. That is why slow motion is achieved by filming perhaps 100 or more frames per second. When they are played back at about 22 frames per second, the movement seems slowed down, yet still smooth and natural.

www ③ PS ⑤
CLICK4™ *Gibson & Walk's classic article, "The Visual Cliff."*

IStroboscopic motion ▲ A visual illusion in which the perception of motion is generated by a series of stationary images that are presented in rapid succession.
Phi phenomenon ▲ The perception of movement as a result of sequential presentation of visual stimuli.

The Phi Phenomenon

Have you seen news headlines spelled out in lights that rapidly wrap around a building? Have you seen an electronic scoreboard in a baseball or football stadium? When the home team scores, some scoreboards suggest explosions of fireworks. What actually happens is that a row of lights is switched on and then off. As the first row is switched off, a second row is switched on, and so on for dozens, perhaps hundreds of rows. When the switching occurs rapidly, the **phi phenomenon** occurs: the on–off process is perceived as movement.

Like stroboscopic motion, the phi phenomenon is an example of apparent motion. Both appear to occur because of the law of continuity. We tend to perceive a series of points as having unity, so each series of lights (points) is perceived as a moving line.

Depth Perception

Think of the problems you might have if you could not judge depth or distance. You might bump into other people, believing them to be farther away. An outfielder might not be able to judge whether to run toward the infield or the fence to catch a fly ball. You might give your front bumper a workout in stop-and-go traffic. *Question: How do we perceive depth?* It happens that *monocular and binocular cues* both help us perceive the depth of objects—that is, their distance from us.

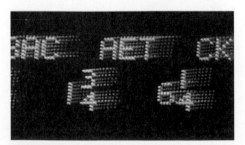

The Phi Phenomenon.
The phi phenomenon is an illusion of movement that is produced by lights blinking on and off in sequence, as with this New York Stock Exchange electronic "ticker" and various electronic scoreboards.

Monocular Cues

Now that you have considered how difficult it would be to navigate through life without depth perception, ponder the problems of the artist who attempts to portray three-dimensional objects on a two-dimensional surface. Artists use **monocular cues**—also termed pictorial cues—to create an illusion of depth. These are cues that can be perceived by one eye (*mono-* means "one"). They include perspective, relative size, clearness, interposition, shadows, and texture gradient, and they cause certain objects to appear more distant from the viewer than others.

Distant objects stimulate smaller areas on the retina than nearby ones. The amount of sensory input from them is smaller, even though they may be the same size. The distances between far-off objects also appear to be smaller than equivalent distances between nearby objects. For this reason, the phenomenon known as **perspective** occurs. That is, we tend to perceive parallel lines as coming closer together, or converging, as they recede from us. However, as we will see when we discuss *size constancy*, experience teaches us that distant objects that look small are larger when they are close. In this way, their relative size also becomes a cue to their distance.

The two engravings in Figure 3.16 represent impossible scenes in which the artists use principles of perspective to fool the viewer. In the one on the left, *Waterfall*, note that the water appears to be flowing away from the viewer in a zigzag because the stream gradually becomes narrower (that is, lines we assume to be parallel are shown to be converging) and the stone sides of the aqueduct appear to be stepping down. However, given that the water arrives at the top of the fall, it must actually be flowing upward somehow. However, the spot from which it falls is no farther from the viewer than the collection point from which it appears to (but does not) begin its flow backward.

Monocular cues ▲ Stimuli suggestive of depth that can be perceived with only one eye.

Perspective ▲ A monocular cue for depth based on the convergence (coming together) of parallel lines as they recede into the distance.

FIGURE 3.16 What Is Wrong With These Pictures?
In *Waterfall*, to the left, how does Dutch artist M. C. Escher suggest that fallen water flows back upward, only to fall again? In *False Perspective*, to the right, how does English artist William Hogarth use monocular cues for depth perception to deceive the viewer?

FRONTISPIECE TO KERBY.

FIGURE 3.17　The Effects of Interposition.
The four circles are all the same size. Which circles seem closer? The complete circles or the circles with chunks bitten out of them?

Artists normally use *relative size*—the fact that distant objects look smaller than nearby objects of the same size—to suggest depth in their works. The paradoxes in the engraving on the right, *False Perspective*, are made possible because more distant objects are *not* necessarily depicted as smaller than nearby objects. Thus, what at first seems to be background suddenly becomes foreground, and vice versa.

The *clearness* of an object also suggests its distance. Experience teaches us that we sense more details of nearby objects. For this reason, artists can suggest that objects are closer to the viewer by depicting them in greater detail. Note that the "distant" hill in the Hogarth engraving (Figure 3.16) is given less detail than the nearby plants at the bottom of the picture. Our perceptions are mocked when a man "on" the distant hill in the background is shown conversing with a woman leaning out a window in the middle ground.

We also learn that nearby objects can block our view of more distant objects. Overlapping, or **interposition,** is the placing of one object in front of another. Experience teaches us that partly covered objects are farther away than the objects that obscure them (Figure 3.17). In the Hogarth engraving (Figure 3.16), which looks closer: the trees in the background (background?) or the moon sign hanging from the building (or is it buildings?) to the right? How does the artist use interposition to confuse the viewer?

Additional information about depth is provided by **shadowing** and is based on the fact that opaque objects block light and produce shadows. Shadows and highlights give us information about an object's three-dimensional shape and its relationship to the source of light. For example, the left part of Figure 3.18 is perceived as a two-dimensional circle, but the right part tends to be perceived as a three-dimensional sphere because of the highlight on its surface and the shadow underneath. In the "sphere," the highlighted central area is perceived as closest to us, with the surface receding to the edges.

FIGURE 3.18　Shadowing as a Cue for Depth.
Shadowing makes the circle on the right look three-dimensional.

Another monocular cue is **texture gradient.** (A gradient is a progressive change.) Closer objects are perceived as having rougher textures. In the Hogarth engraving (Figure 3.16), the building just behind the large fisherman's head has a rougher texture and therefore seems to be closer than the building with the window from which the woman is

Interposition ▲ A monocular cue for depth based on the fact that a nearby object obscures a more distant object behind it.

Shadowing ▲ A monocular cue for depth based on the fact that opaque objects block light and produce shadows.

Texture gradient ▲ A monocular cue for depth based on the perception that closer objects appear to have rougher (more detailed) surfaces.

IN REVIEW

Cues for Depth Perception

MONOCULAR CUES		
Pictorial Cues*	Perspective	Perceiving parallel lines as coming closer together, or converging, as they recede from us
	Relative Size	Perceiving larger objects as being closer to us
	Clearness	Perceiving objects with greater detail as being closer to us
	Interposition	Perceiving objects that block our view of other objects as being closer to us (also called *overlapping*)
	Shadowing	Perceiving shadows and highlights as giving depth to two-dimensional objects
	Texture Gradient	Perceiving objects with rougher textures as being closer
Motion Cues	Motion Parallax	Perceiving objects that seem to move forward with us as distant and objects that seem to move backward as nearby
BINOCULAR CUES		
Retinal Disparity		Perceiving objects that cast more greatly differing images on the retinas of the eyes as being closer
Convergence		Perceiving objects for whom focusing requires greater inward movement of the eyes (and therefore greater feelings of tension in the eyes) as being closer

*These cues are commonly used by artists to create the impression of depth (a third dimension) in two-dimensional works such as drawings and paintings.

leaning. Our surprise is heightened when the moon sign is seen as hanging from both buildings.

Motion Cues   Motion cues are another kind of monocular cue. If you have ever driven in the country, you have probably noticed that distant objects such as mountains and stars appear to move along with you. Objects at an intermediate distance seem to be stationary, but nearby objects such as roadside markers, rocks, and trees seem to go by quite rapidly. The tendency of objects to seem to move backward or forward as a function of their distance is known as **motion parallax.** We learn to perceive objects that appear to move with us as being at greater distances.

Earlier we noted that nearby objects cause the lens of the eye to accommodate or bend more in order to bring them into focus. The sensations of tension in the eye muscles also provide a monocular cue to depth, especially when we are within about 4 feet of the objects.

Binocular Cues   **Binocular cues,** or cues that involve both eyes, also help us perceive depth. Two binocular cues are *retinal disparity* and *convergence*.

Try an experiment. Hold your index finger at arm's length. Now, gradually bring it closer until it almost touches your nose. If you keep your eyes relaxed as you do so, you will see two fingers. An image of the finger will be projected onto the retina of each eye, and each image will be slightly different because the finger will be seen from different angles. The difference between the projected images is referred to as **retinal disparity** and serves as a binocular cue for depth perception. Note that the closer your finger comes, the farther apart the "two fingers" appear to be. Closer objects have greater retinal disparity.

If we try to maintain a single image of the nearing finger, our eyes must turn inward, or converge on it, making us cross-eyed. **Convergence** causes feelings of tension in the eye muscles and provides another binocular cue for depth. (After convergence occurs, try looking at the finger first with one eye closed, then the other. You will readily see how different the images are in each eye.) The binocular cues of retinal disparity and convergence are strongest when objects are close.

Perceptual Constancies

The world is a constantly shifting display of visual sensations. Think how confusing it would be if you believed that a door was a trapezoid and not a rectangle because it is ajar. Or what if we perceived a doorway to be a different doorway when seen from 6 feet away as compared to 4 feet. As we neared it, we might think it was larger than the door we were seeking and become lost. Or consider the problems of the pet owner who recognizes his dog from the side but not from above because its shape is different when seen from above. Fortunately, these problems tend not to occur—at least with familiar objects—because perceptual constancies enable us to recognize objects even when their apparent shape or size differs. *Questions: What are perceptual constancies? Why do we perceive a door to be a rectangle even when it is ajar?*

There are a number of perceptual constancies, including that of **size constancy.** We may say that people "look like ants" when viewed from the top of a tall building, but because of size constancy, we know they remain people even if the details of their forms are lost in the distance. We can thus say that we *perceive* people to be the same size, even when viewed from different distances.

The image of a dog seen from 20 feet away occupies about the same amount of space on your retina as an inch-long insect crawling on your hand. Yet you do not perceive the dog to be as small as the insect. Through your visual experiences you have acquired size constancy—that is, the tendency to perceive an object as the same size even though the size of its image on your retina varies as a function of its distance. Experience teaches us about perspective—that the same object seen at a distance appears to be smaller than when it is nearby.

Color constancy is the tendency to perceive objects as retaining their color even though lighting conditions may alter their appearance. Your bright yellow car may edge

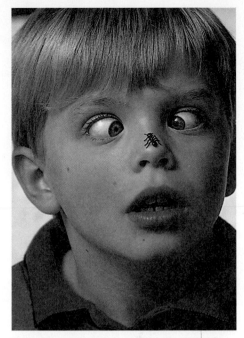

Retinal Disparity and Convergence as Cues for Depth.
As an object nears your eyes, you begin to see two images of it because of retinal disparity. To maintain perception of a single image, your eyes must converge on the object.

REFLECT
Have you ever driven in the country and perceived the stars or distant hills to be moving along with you? How do you explain the phenomenon?

CLICK4™ the classic article by Turnbull, "Some Observations Regarding the Experiences and Behavior of the BaMbuti Pygmies."

CLICK4™ a video on size constancy and visual illusions.

Motion parallax ▲ A monocular cue for depth based on the perception that nearby objects appear to move more rapidly in relation to our own motion.

Binocular cues ▲ Stimuli suggestive of depth that involve simultaneous perception by both eyes.

Retinal disparity ▲ A binocular cue for depth based on the difference in the image cast by an object on the retinas of the eyes as the object moves closer or farther away.

Convergence ▲ A binocular cue for depth based on the inward movement of the eyes as they attempt to focus on an object that is drawing nearer.

Size constancy ▲ The tendency to perceive an object as being the same size even as the size of its retinal image changes according to the object's distance.

Color constancy ▲ The tendency to perceive an object as being the same color even though lighting conditions change its appearance.

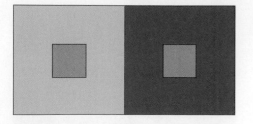

FIGURE 3.19 Brightness Constancy.
The orange squares within the blue squares are the same hue, yet the orange within the dark blue square is perceived as brighter. Why?

Brightness constancy ▲ The tendency to perceive an object as being just as bright even though lighting conditions change its intensity.

Shape constancy ▲ The tendency to perceive an object as being the same shape although the retinal image varies in shape as it rotates.

CLICK4™ *a video on the Ames Room.*

CLICK4™ *a video on the Moon illusion.*

CLICK4™ *a demonstration of visual illusions on the Web.*

FIGURE 3.20 Shape Constancy.
When closed, this door is a rectangle. When open, the retinal image is trapezoidal. But because of shape constancy, we still perceive it as rectangular.

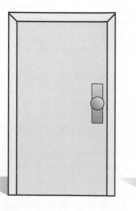
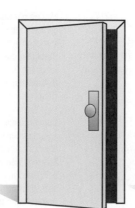
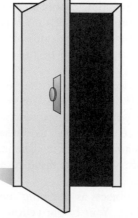

toward gray as the hours wend their way through twilight to nighttime. But when you finally locate the car in the parking lot, you may still think of it as yellow. You expect to find a yellow car and still judge it to be "more yellow" than the (faded) red and green cars on either side of it.

Brightness constancy is similar to color constancy. Consider Figure 3.19. The orange squares within the blue squares are equally bright, yet the one within the dark blue square is perceived as brighter. Why? Again, consider the role of experience. If it were nighttime, we would expect orange to fade to gray. The fact that the orange within the dark square stimulates the eye with equal intensity suggests that it must be much brighter than the orange within the lighter square.

Shape constancy is the tendency to perceive objects as maintaining their shape, even if we look at them from different angles so that the shape of their image on the retina changes dramatically. You perceive the top of a coffee cup or a glass to be a circle even though it is a circle only when seen from above. When seen from an angle, it is an ellipse. When the cup or glass is seen on edge, its retinal image is the same as that of a straight line. So why do you still describe the rim of the cup or glass as a circle? Perhaps for two reasons: First, experience has taught you that the cup will look circular when seen from above. Second, you may have labeled the cup as circular or round. Experience and labels help make the world a stable place. Can you imagine the chaos that would prevail if we described objects as they appear as they stimulate our sensory organs with each changing moment?

Let us return to the door that "changes shape" when it is ajar. The door is a rectangle only when viewed straight on (Figure 3.20). When we move to the side or open it, the left or right edge comes closer and appears to be larger, changing the retinal image to a trapezoid. Yet we continue to think of doors as rectangles.

Visual Illusions: How Our Eyes Play Tricks on Us

The principles of perceptual organization make it possible for our eyes to "play tricks on us." Psychologists, like magicians, enjoy pulling a rabbit out of a hat now and then. Let me demonstrate how the perceptual constancies trick the eye through *visual illusions.*

The Hering-Helmholtz and Müller-Lyer illusions (Figure 3.21, part A) are named after the people who devised them. In the Hering-Helmholtz illusion, the horizontal lines are straight and parallel. However, the radiating lines cause them to appear to be bent outward near the center. The two lines in the Müller-Lyer illusion are the same length, but the line on the left, with its reversed arrowheads, looks longer. *Question: How can principles of visual perception be used to trick the eye?*

Let us try to explain these illusions. Because of our experience and lifelong use of perceptual cues, we tend to perceive the Hering-Helmholtz drawing as three-dimensional. Because of our tendency to perceive bits of sensory information as figures against grounds, we perceive the white area in the center as a circle in front of a series of radiating lines, all of which lie in front of a white ground. Next, because of our experience with perspective, we perceive the radiating lines as parallel. We perceive the two horizontal lines as intersecting the "receding" lines, and we know that they would have to appear bent out at the center if they were to be equidistant at all points from the center of the circle.

Experience probably compels us to perceive the vertical lines in the Müller-Lyer illusion as the corners of a room as seen from inside a house, at left, and from outside a house, at right (see Figure 3.21, part B). In such an example, the reverse arrowheads to the left are lines where the walls meet the ceiling and the floor. We perceive such lines as extending toward us. They push the corner away from us. The arrowheads to the right are lines where exterior walls meet the roof and foundation.

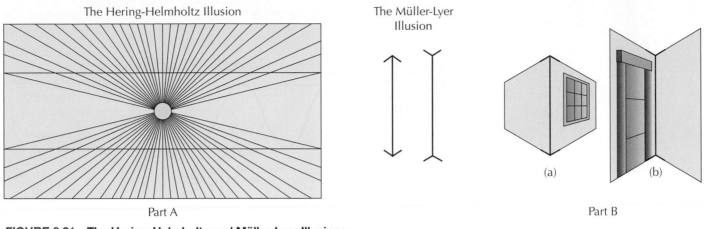

The Hering-Helmholtz Illusion

The Müller-Lyer Illusion

Part A

Part B

FIGURE 3.21   The Hering-Helmholtz and Müller-Lyer Illusions.
In the Hering-Helmholtz illusion, are the horizontal lines straight or curved? In the Müller-Lyer illusion, are the vertical lines equal in length?

We perceive them as receding from us. They push the corner toward us. The vertical line to the left therefore is perceived as being farther away. Because both vertical lines stimulate equal expanses across the retina, the principle of size constancy encourages us to perceive the line to the left as longer.

Figure 3.22 is known as the Ponzo illusion. In this illusion, the two horizontal lines are the same length. However, do you perceive the top line as longer? The rule of size constancy may give us some insight into this illusion as well. Perhaps the converging lines again strike us as being lines receding into the distance, like train tracks. If so, we assume from experience that the horizontal line at the top is farther down the track—that is, farther away from us. And again, the rule of size constancy tells us that if two objects appear to be the same size and one is farther away, the farther object must be larger. So we perceive the top line as larger.

REVIEW

(14) Perceptual organization concerns the grouping of bits of sensory stimulation into a meaningful _____. (15) Gestalt rules of perceptual organization refer to _____-ground relationships, proximity, similarity, continuity, common fate, and closure. (16) When we are putting puzzle pieces together, a picture of the result enables us to engage in _____-_____ processing; otherwise we must solve the puzzle by bottom-up processing. (17) We perceive movement by sensing motion across the _____ and change of position in relation to other objects. (18) _____ motion, used in films, is an illusion of motion caused by the rapid presentation of a series of still images.

Pulling It Together: How do visual illusions trick the eye? What monocular and binocular cues allow us to perceive depth? How do constancies for shape, color, and size reveal the importance of perception as opposed to simple sensation?

HEARING: MAKING SENSE OF SOUND

Consider the advertising slogan for the science-fiction film *Alien:* "In space, no one can hear you scream." It's true. Space is an almost perfect vacuum. Hearing requires a medium through which sound can travel, such as air or water. *Question: What is sound?*

Sound, or **auditory** stimulation, travels through the air like waves. Sound is caused by changes in air pressure that result from vibrations. These vibrations, in turn, can be

REFLECT
Are you familiar with the violin, viola, cello, and bass fiddle? How do their sounds differ? How do you account for the differences?

www 3 Q 1
CLICK4™ *a quiz covering the first half of this chapter.*

Auditory ▲ Having to do with hearing.

FIGURE 3.22   The Ponzo Illusion.
The horizontal lines in this drawing are equal in length, but the top line is perceived as being longer. Can you use the principle of size constancy to explain why?

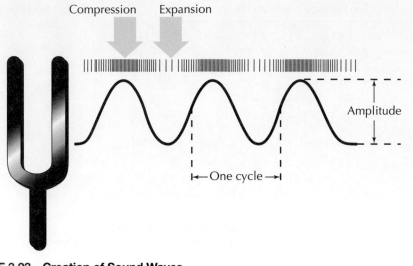
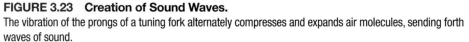

FIGURE 3.23   Creation of Sound Waves.
The vibration of the prongs of a tuning fork alternately compresses and expands air molecules, sending forth waves of sound.

created by a tuning fork, your vocal cords, guitar strings, or the slam of a book thrown down on a desk.

Figure 3.23 shows how a tuning fork creates sound waves. During a vibration back and forth, the right prong of the tuning fork moves to the right. In doing so, it pushes together, or compresses, the molecules of air immediately to the right. Then the prong moves back to the left, and the air molecules to the right expand. By vibrating back and forth, the tuning fork actually sends air waves in many directions. A cycle of compression and expansion is one wave of sound. Sound waves can occur many times in 1 second. The human ear is sensitive to sound waves with frequencies of from 20 to 20,000 cycles per second.

FIGURE 3.24   Sound Waves of Various Frequencies and Amplitudes.
Which sounds have the highest pitch? Which are loudest?

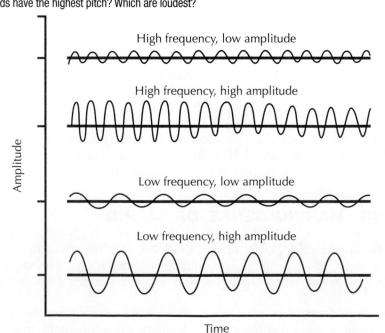

Pitch and Loudness — All Sorts of Vibes

Pitch and loudness are two psychological dimensions of sound. The pitch of a sound is determined by its frequency, or the number of cycles per second as expressed in the unit **hertz** (Hz). One cycle per second is 1 Hz. The greater the number of cycles per second (Hz), the higher the pitch of the sound. The pitch of women's voices is usually higher than that of men's voices because women's vocal cords are usually shorter and therefore vibrate at a greater frequency. The strings of a violin are shorter than those of a viola or bass viol. They vibrate at greater frequencies, and we perceive them as higher in pitch. Pitch detectors in the brain allow us to tell the difference.

The loudness of a sound is determined by the height, or **amplitude,** of sound waves. Figure 3.24 shows records of sound waves that vary in frequency and amplitude. Frequency and amplitude are independent. Both high- and low-pitched sounds can be either high or low in loudness.

The loudness of a sound is expressed in **decibels** (dB). Zero dB is equivalent to the threshold of hearing—the lowest sound that the typical person can hear. How loud is that? It's about as loud as the ticking of a watch 20 feet away in a very quiet room.

The decibel equivalents of many familiar sounds are shown in Figure 3.25. Twenty dB is equivalent in loudness to a whisper at 5 feet. Thirty dB is roughly the limit of loudness at which your librarian would like to keep your college library. You may suffer hearing damage if you are exposed to sounds of 85 to 90 dB for very long periods.

Now let us turn our attention to the human ear—the marvelous instrument that senses all these different "vibes."

The Ear: The Better to Hear You With

The human ear is good for lots of things—including catching dust, combing your hair around, hanging jewelry from, and nibbling. It is also admirably suited for sensing sounds. ***Question: How does the ear work?*** The ear is shaped and structured so as to capture sound waves, vibrate in sympathy with them, and transmit them to centers in the brain. In this way, you not only hear something, you can also figure out what it is. The ear has three parts: the outer ear, middle ear, and inner ear (see Figure 3.26).

Hertz ▲ A unit expressing the frequency of sound waves. One Hertz, or *1 Hz*, equals one cycle per second.
Amplitude ▲ Height.
Decibel ▲ A unit expressing the loudness of a sound. Abbreviated *dB*.

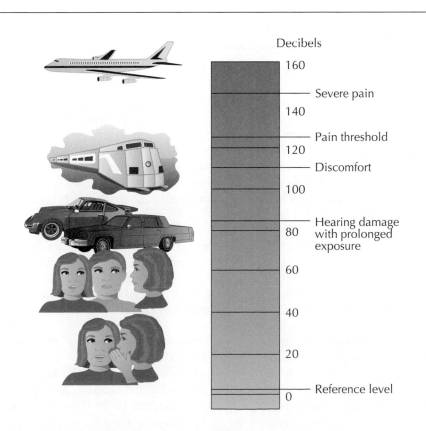

Decibels

160

— Severe pain

140

— Pain threshold

120

— Discomfort

100

— Hearing damage with prolonged exposure

80

60

40

20

— Reference level

0

FIGURE 3.25 Decibel Ratings of Familiar Sounds.
Zero dB is the threshold of hearing. You may suffer hearing loss if you incur prolonged exposure to sounds of 85–90 dB.

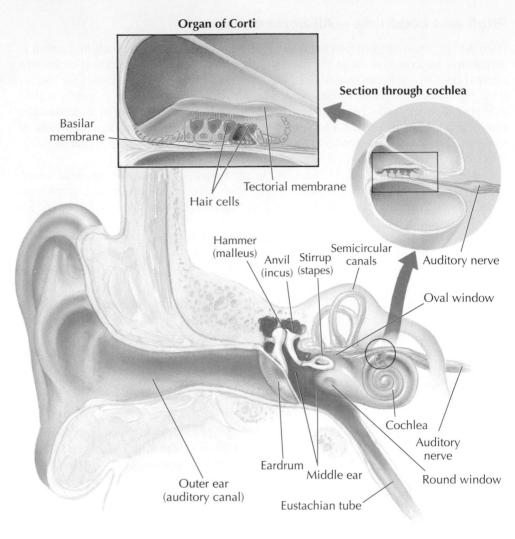

Organ of Corti

Basilar membrane

Section through cochlea

Tectorial membrane

Hair cells

Hammer (malleus)

Anvil (incus)

Stirrup (stapes)

Semicircular canals

Auditory nerve

Oval window

Cochlea

Auditory nerve

Eardrum

Middle ear

Round window

Outer ear (auditory canal)

Eustachian tube

FIGURE 3.26   The Human Ear.
The outer ear funnels sound to the eardrum. Inside the eardrum, vibrations of the hammer, anvil, and stirrup transmit sound to the inner ear. Vibrations in the cochlea transmit the sound to the auditory nerve by way of the basilar membrane and the organ of Corti.

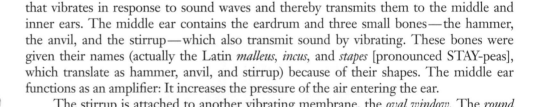

CLICK4™ *more information about making sense of sound.*

Eardrum ▲ A thin membrane that vibrates in response to sound waves, transmitting the waves to the middle and inner ears.

Cochlea ▲ The inner ear; the bony tube that contains the basilar membrane and the organ of Corti.

Basilar membrane ▲ A membrane that lies coiled within the cochlea.

Organ of Corti ▲ The receptor for hearing that lies on the basilar membrane in the cochlea.

Auditory nerve ▲ The axon bundle that transmits neural impulses from the organ of Corti to the brain.

The outer ear is shaped to funnel sound waves to the **eardrum,** a thin membrane that vibrates in response to sound waves and thereby transmits them to the middle and inner ears. The middle ear contains the eardrum and three small bones—the hammer, the anvil, and the stirrup—which also transmit sound by vibrating. These bones were given their names (actually the Latin *malleus, incus,* and *stapes* [pronounced STAY-peas], which translate as hammer, anvil, and stirrup) because of their shapes. The middle ear functions as an amplifier: It increases the pressure of the air entering the ear.

The stirrup is attached to another vibrating membrane, the *oval window.* The *round window* shown in Figure 3.26 balances the pressure in the inner ear. It pushes outward when the oval window pushes in, and it is pulled inward when the oval window vibrates outward.

The oval window transmits vibrations into the inner ear, the bony tube called the **cochlea** (from the Greek word for "snail"). The cochlea, which is shaped like a snail shell, contains two longitudinal membranes that divide it into three fluid-filled chambers. One of the membranes that lies coiled within the cochlea is called the **basilar membrane.** Vibrations in the fluids within the chambers of the inner ear press against the basilar membrane.

The **organ of Corti,** sometimes referred to as the "command post" of hearing, is attached to the basilar membrane. There are some 16,000 receptor cells—called hair cells because they project like hair from the organ of Corti—in each ear (Larkin, 2000). Hair cells "dance" in response to the vibrations of the basilar membrane. Their up-and-down movements generate neural impulses, which are transmitted to the brain via the **auditory**

nerve. Auditory input is then projected onto the hearing areas of the temporal lobes of the cerebral cortex.

Locating Sounds—Up, Down, and Around

How do you balance the loudness of a stereo set? You sit between the speakers and adjust the volume until the sound seems to be equally loud in each ear. If the sound to the right is louder, the musical instruments are perceived as being toward the right rather than straight ahead.

Question: How do we locate sounds? There is a resemblance between balancing a stereo set and locating sounds. A sound that is louder in the right ear is perceived as coming from the right. A sound coming from the right also reaches the right ear first. Both loudness and the sequence in which the sounds reach the ears provide directional cues.

But it may not be easy to locate a sound coming from directly in front or in back of you or overhead. Such sounds are equally distant from each ear and equally loud. So what do we do? Simple—usually we turn our head slightly to determine in which ear the sound increases. If you turn your head a few degrees to the right and the loudness increases in your left ear, the sound must be coming from in front of you. Of course, we also use vision and general knowledge in locating the source of sounds. If you hear the roar of jet engines, most of the time you can bet that the airplane is overhead.

Perception of Loudness and Pitch

Sounds are heard because they cause vibration in parts of the ear and information about these vibrations is transmitted to the brain. *Question: How do we perceive loudness and pitch?*

The loudness and pitch of sounds appear to be related to the number of receptor neurons on the organ of Corti that fire and how often they fire. Psychologists generally agree that sounds are perceived as louder when more of these sensory neurons fire.

CONTROVERSY IN PSYCHOLOGY

How do we explain pitch perception? What happens when the basilar membrane runs out of places to vibrate? What happens when it cannot vibrate fast enough?

It takes two processes to explain perception of color: *trichromatic theory* and *opponent-process theory*. Similarly, it takes at least two processes to explain pitch perception—that is, perception of sound waves with frequencies that vary from 20 to 20,000 cycles per second: *place theory* and *frequency theory*.

Hermann von Helmholtz helped develop the place theory of pitch discrimination as well as the Young-Helmholtz (trichromatic) theory of color vision. **Place theory** holds that the pitch of a sound is sensed according to the place along the basilar membrane that vibrates in response to it. In classic research with guinea pigs and cadavers that led to the award of a Nobel prize, Georg von Békésy (1957) found evidence for place theory. He determined that receptors at different sites along the membrane fire in response to tones of differing frequencies. Receptor neurons appear to be lined up along the basilar membrane like piano keys. The higher the pitch of a sound, the closer the responsive neurons lie to the oval window (Larkin, 2000). However, place theory appears to apply only to pitches greater than 4,000 Hz, and people sense pitches as low as 20 Hz.

Frequency theory accounts for pitches at the lower end of the range. **Frequency theory** notes that pitch perception depends on the stimulation of neural impulses that match the frequency of the sound waves. That is, in response to low pitches—pitches of about 20 to 1,000 cycles per second—hair cells on the basilar membrane fire at the same frequencies as the sound waves. However, neurons cannot fire more than 1,000 times per second. Therefore, frequency theory can account only for perception of pitches between 20 and 1,000 cycles per second. In actuality, frequency theory appears to account only for pitch perception between 20 and a few hundred cycles per second.

REFLECT
Have you ever been unsure where a sound was coming from? How did you locate the source of the sound?

CLICK4™ *an essay assignment on pitch perception.*

CLICK4™ *an exploration of subliminal perception.*

Place theory ▲ The theory that the pitch of a sound is determined by the section of the basilar membrane that vibrates in response to the sound.

Frequency theory ▲ The theory that the pitch of a sound is reflected in the frequency of the neural impulses that are generated in response to the sound.

I noted that it takes *at least two processes* to explain how people perceive pitch. The *volley principle* is the third, and it accounts for pitch discrimination between a few hundred and 4,000 cycles per second (Matlin & Foley, 1995). In response to sound waves of these frequencies, groups of neurons take turns firing, in the way that one row of soldiers used to fire rifles while another row knelt to reload. Alternating firing—that is, volleying—appears to transmit sensory information about pitches in the intermediate range.

Pitch and rhythm are the two basic dimensions of the perception of music (Krumhansl, 2000). Some of us are "tone deaf," meaning that we are insensitive to changes of pitch in music. But others of us are much more than tone deaf: Many of us do not perceive sounds of certain frequencies, and some of us do not perceive sound at all. Let us now consider deafness.

Deafness

CLICK4™ *information about Hearing Education and Awareness for Rockers.*

REFLECT
Do you know anyone with hearing problems? What is the source of the impairment? How does the person cope with the impairment?

CLICK4™ *an opportunity to design a public service advertisement on the dangers of exposure to loud noise.*

More than 1 in 10 Americans has a hearing impairment, and 1 in 100 cannot hear at all (Canalis & Lambert, 2000). Deaf people are deprived of a key source of information about the world around them. In recent years, however, society has made greater efforts to bring them into the mainstream of sensory experience. People are usually on hand to convert political and other speeches into hand signs (such as those of American Sign Language) for hearing-impaired members of the audience. Many TV shows are "closed captioned" so that they can be understood by people with hearing problems. Special decoders render the captions visible. ***Questions: What is deafness? What can we do about it?***

There are two major types of deafness: conductive deafness and sensorineural deafness. **Conductive deafness** is a result of damage to the structures of the middle ear—either to the eardrum or to the three bones that conduct (and amplify) sound waves from the outer ear to the inner ear (Canalis & Lambert, 2000). This is the type of hearing impairment often found among older people. People with conductive deafness often profit from hearing aids, which provide the amplification that the middle ear does not.

Sensorineural deafness usually stems from damage to the structures of the inner ear, most often the loss of hair cells, which normally do not regenerate. (However, researchers are attempting to stimulate production of new hair cells by means of gene therapy and other measures [Larkin, 2000].) Sensorineural deafness can also stem from damage to the auditory nerve, for example, because of disease or because of acoustic trauma (prolonged exposure to very loud sounds). In sensorineural deafness, people tend to be more sensitive to some pitches than to others. In Hunter's notch, hearing impairment is limited to particular frequencies—in this case, the frequencies of the sound waves generated by a gun firing. Prolonged exposure to 85 dB can cause hearing loss. People who attend rock concerts, where sounds may reach 140 dB, risk damaging their ears, as do workers who run pneumatic drills or drive noisy vehicles. The ringing sensation that often follows exposure to loud sounds probably means that hair cells in the inner ear have been damaged. If you find yourself suddenly exposed to loud sounds, remember that your fingertips serve as good emergency ear protectors.

Cochlear implants, or "artificial ears," contain microphones that sense sounds and electronic equipment that transmits sounds past damaged hair cells to stimulate the auditory nerve directly. Such implants have helped many people with sensorineural deafness. However, they cannot assume the functions of damaged auditory nerves.

REVIEW

CLICK4™ *information about careers in communication disorders.*

Conductive deafness ▲ The forms of deafness in which there is loss of conduction of sound through the middle ear.
Sensorineural deafness ▲ The forms of deafness that result from damage to hair cells or the auditory nerve.

(19) Sound waves alternately _____ and expand molecules of a medium such as air or water. (20) The human ear can hear sounds varying in frequency from 20 to _____ cycles per second (Hz). (21) The frequency of sound waves determines their _____. (22) Loudness is measured in _____ (dB). (23) The middle ear contains three bones—the "hammer," "_____," and "stirrup"—which amplify and transmit sound waves to the inner ear. (24) The cochlea contains fluids that vibrate against the _____ membrane. (25) The "command post" of hearing—called the or-

gan of _____—is attached to the basilar membrane. (26) Sound waves travel from the organ of Corti to the brain by the _____ nerve.

Pulling It Together: How does the ear transform sound waves into auditory information? How does the ear respond to pitches of various frequencies? How do hearing aids amplify or bypass the functions of the ear?

THE CHEMICAL SENSES: SMELL AND TASTE

Smell and taste are the chemical senses. In the cases of vision and hearing, physical energy strikes our sensory receptors. With smell and taste, we sample molecules of the substances being sensed.

Smell

You could say that we are underprivileged when it comes to the sense of smell. Dogs, for instance, devote about seven times as much of the cerebral cortex as we do to the sense of smell. Male dogs sniff in order to determine where the boundaries of other dogs' territories leave off and whether female dogs are sexually receptive. Some dogs even make a living sniffing out illegal drugs in closed packages and suitcases for law enforcement agencies.

Still, smell has an important role in human behavior. It makes a crucial contribution to the flavor of foods, for example. If you did not have a sense of smell, an onion and an apple would taste the same to you! People's sense of smell may be deficient when we compare them to those of a dog, but we can detect the odor of 1 one-millionth of a milligram of vanilla in a liter of air.

Question: How does the sense of smell work? Smell is the sense that senses odors. An odor is a sample of the substance being sensed. Odors are detected by sites on receptor neurons in the **olfactory** membrane high in each nostril. Receptor neurons fire when a few molecules of the substance in gaseous form come into contact with them. Their firing transmits information about odors to the brain via the **olfactory nerve.** That is how the substance is smelled.

It is unclear how many basic kinds of odors there are. In any event, olfactory receptors may respond to more than one kind of odor. Mixtures of smell sensations also help produce the broad range of odors that we can perceive.

The sense of smell adapts rapidly to odors, such that you lose awareness of them, even obnoxious ones. This might be fortunate if you are in a locker room or an outhouse. It might not be so fortunate if you are exposed to paint fumes or secondhand smoke, because you may lose awareness of them while danger remains. One odor can mask another, which is how air fresheners work.

Soon we may be wondering about masking odors that come from the TV set. The Click4 feature on "smell-o-vision" speaks of the transmission of odors over vast distances—just as TV transmits sights and sounds. Or put it this way: If you think that much of TV programming "stinks" right now, just wait a few years.

Taste

Your cocker spaniel may jump at the chance to finish off your ice cream cone, but your Siamese cat may turn up her nose at the opportunity. Why? Dogs can perceive the taste quality of sweetness, as can pigs, but cats cannot.

Question: How does the sense of taste work? There are four primary taste qualities: sweet, sour, salty, and bitter. The *flavor* of a food involves its taste but is more complex. Although apples and onions are similar in taste, their flavors differ greatly. After all, you wouldn't chomp into a nice cold onion on a warm day, would you? The flavor of a food depends on its odor, texture, and temperature as well as on its taste. If it were not for odor, heated tenderized shoe leather might pass for steak.

REFLECT

Has food ever seemed to lose its flavor when you had a cold or an allergy attack? Why?

www 3 PML 9

CLICK4™ *Smell-o-Vision!*

Olfactory ▲ Having to do with the sense of smell.
Olfactory nerve ▲ The nerve that transmits information concerning odors from olfactory receptors to the brain.

Sensational?
The flavors of foods are determined not only by their taste, but also by their odor, texture, and temperature.

Taste is sensed through **taste cells**—receptor neurons located on **taste buds.** You have about 10,000 taste buds, most of which are located near the edges and back of your tongue. Taste buds tend to specialize a bit. Some, for example, are more responsive to sweetness, whereas others react to several tastes. Other taste receptors are found in the roof, sides, and back of the mouth, and in the throat. Some taste buds are even found in the stomach, although we only perceive tastes in the mouth and top of the throat. Buds deep in the mouth are evolutionarily adaptive because they can warn of poisonous food as it is about to be swallowed (Brand, 2000).

According to Joseph Brand (2000) of the Monell Chemical Senses Center in Philadelphia, catfish are "swimming tongues." They can detect food through murky water and across long distances because their bodies are studded with nearly 150,000 taste buds.

People live in different taste worlds. Those of us with low sensitivity for the sweet taste may require twice the sugar to sweeten our food as others who are more sensitive to sweetness. Those of us who claim to enjoy very bitter foods may actually be taste blind to them. Sensitivities to different tastes apparently have a strong genetic component (Bartoshuk, 2000).

By eating hot foods and scraping your tongue, you regularly kill off many taste cells. But you need not be alarmed at this inadvertent oral aggression. Taste cells are the rabbits of the sense receptors. They reproduce rapidly enough to completely renew themselves about once a week.

Although older people often complain that their food has little or no "taste," they are more likely to experience a decline in the sense of smell. Because the flavor of a food represents both its tastes and its odors or aromas, older people experience loss in the *flavor* of their food. Older people often spice their food heavily to enhance its flavor.

REVIEW

An odor is a sample of molecules of the substance being smelled. (27) Odors are detected by the _____ membrane in each nostril. (28) There are four primary taste qualities: sweet, sour, salty, and _____. (29) The receptor neurons for taste are called _____ cells, which are located in taste buds on the tongue.

Pulling It Together: What is the difference between the taste and the flavor of food? Why do older people often heavily spice their food?

THE SKIN SENSES (YES, IT DOES)

The skin is much more than a protective coating for your body. As you may know from lying on the sand beneath a broiling sun, and perhaps from touching the person lying next to you, the skin also discriminates among many kinds of sensations. *Questions: What are the skin senses? How do they work?* The skin senses include touch, pressure, warmth, cold, and pain (see Figure 3.27). We have distinct sensory receptors for pressure, temperature, and pain, but some nerve endings may receive more than one type of sensory input.

Touch and Pressure

Sensory receptors located around the roots of hair cells appear to fire when the surface of the skin is touched. You may have noticed that if you are trying to "get the feel of" a fabric or the texture of a friend's hair, you must move your hand over it. Otherwise the sensations quickly fade. If you pass your hand over the fabric or hair and then hold it still, again the sensations of touching will fade. This sort of "active touching" involves reception of information concerning not only touch per se but also pressure, temperature, and feedback from the muscles involved in movements of our hands.

Other structures beneath the skin are sensitive to pressure. Different parts of the body are more sensitive to touch and pressure than others. Psychophysicists use methods such as the **two-point threshold** to assess sensitivity to pressure. This method deter-

CLICK4™ *more information about the chemical senses.*

▲ REFLECT
Why do older people tend to spice their food heavily?

▲ REFLECT
Can you think of instances of active touching in your own life?

Taste cells ▲ Receptor cells that are sensitive to taste.
Taste buds ▲ The sensory organs for taste. They contain taste cells and are located on the tongue.
Two-point threshold ▲ The least distance by which two rods touching the skin must be separated before the person will report that there are two rods, not one, on 50% of occasions.

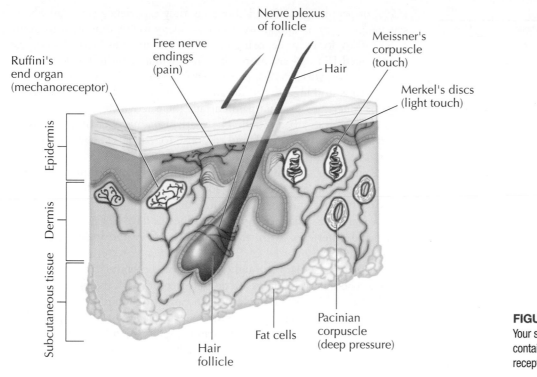

FIGURE 3.27   Skin—A Complex Organ. Your skin may be more complex than you think. It contains several layers and various kinds of sensory receptors.

mines the smallest distance by which two rods touching the skin must be separated before the (blindfolded) individual reports that there are two rods rather than one. With this method, psychophysicists have found that our fingertips, lips, noses, and cheeks are more sensitive than our shoulders, thighs, and calves. That is, the rods can be closer together but perceived as distinct when they touch the lips more than when they touch the shoulders. Why the difference in sensitivity? First, nerve endings are more densely packed in the fingertips and face than in other locations. Second, more sensory cortex is devoted to the perception of sensations in the fingertips and face.

The sense of pressure, like the sense of touch, undergoes rapid adaptation. For example, you may have undertaken several minutes of strategic movements to wind up with your hand on the arm or leg of your date, only to discover that adaptation to this delightful source of pressure reduces the sensation.

Temperature

The receptors for temperature are neurons located just beneath the skin. When skin temperature increases, the receptors for warmth fire. Decreases in skin temperature cause receptors for cold to fire.

Sensations of temperature are relative. When we are at normal body temperature, we might perceive another person's skin as warm. When we are feverish, though, the other person's skin might seem cool. We also adapt to differences in temperature. When we walk out of an air-conditioned house into the July sun, we feel intense heat at first. Then the sensations of heat tend to fade (although we may still be uncomfortable because of high humidity). Similarly, when we first enter a swimming pool, the water may seem cool or cold because it is below our body temperature. Yet after a few moments an 80°F pool may seem quite warm. In fact, we may chide a newcomer for not diving right in.

Pain: The Often Unwanted Message

For most people in the United States, pain is a frequent visitor. Headaches, backaches, toothaches—these are only a few of the types of pain that most of us encounter from time to time. According to a national Gallup survey of 2,002 adults in the United States (Arthritis Foundation, 2000), 89% experience pain at least once a month. More than half

REFLECT Why do you think that women are more likely than men to experience pain? What is the gender difference in willingness to see the doctor about pain? How would you explain the gender difference in willingness to see the doctor?

TABLE 3.1: GENDER DIFFERENCES IN EXPERIENCING AND RESPONDING TO PAIN

Percent Who Report . . .	Women	Men
Experiencing daily pain	46	37
Feeling they have a great deal of control over their pain	39	48
Feeling that tension and stress are their leading causes of pain	72	56
Going to see the doctor about pain only when other people urge them to do it	27	38
Balancing the demands of work and family life to be the key cause of their pain	35	24
Frequent headaches	17	8
Frequent backaches	24	19
Arthritis	20	15
Sore feet	25	17

SOURCE OF DATA: Arthritis Foundation (2000, April 6). Pain in America: Highlights from a Gallup survey. *http://www.arthritis.org*

Analgesic ▲ Giving rise to a state of not feeling pain though fully conscious.

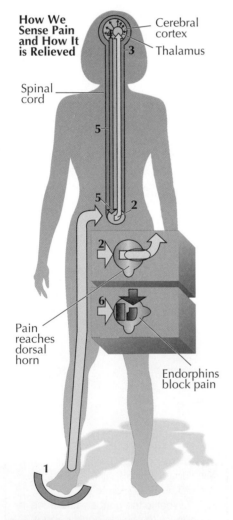

FIGURE 3.28 Perception of Pain.
Pain originates at the point of contact, and the pain message to the brain is initiated by the release of prostaglandins, bradykinin, and substance *P*.

(55%) of people aged 65 and above say they experience pain daily. Sad to say, people aged 65 and above are most likely to attribute pain to getting older (88%), for example, being more likely to incur arthritis. By contrast, people aged 18 to 34 are more likely to attribute pain to tension or stress (73%), to overwork, (64%), or to their lifestyle (51%). When we assume that there is nothing we can do about pain, we are less likely to try. Yet 43% of Americans say that pain curtails their activities, and 50% say that pain puts them in a bad mood. There are also a number of gender differences in the experiencing of, and response to, pain, as shown in Table 3.1.
Questions: What is pain? What can we do about it?

Pain means something is wrong in the body. Evolutionary psychologists would point out that pain is adaptive, if unpleasant, because it motivates us to do something about it. For some of us, however, chronic pain—pain that lasts once injuries or illnesses have cleared—saps our vitality and interferes with the pleasures of everyday life (Karoly & Ruehlman, 1996).

We can sense pain throughout most of the body, but pain is usually sharpest where nerve endings are densely packed, as in the fingers and face. Pain can also be felt deep within the body, as in the cases of abdominal pain and back pain. Even though headaches may seem to originate deep inside the head, there are no nerve endings for pain in the brain. Brain surgery can be done with a local anesthetic that prevents the patient from feeling the drilling of a small hole through the skull. Can it be that the lack of nerve endings in the brain is evolution's way of saying that normally speaking, when someone has a reason to experience pain deep inside the brain, it might be too late to do anything about it?

Pain usually originates at the point of contact, as with a stubbed toe (see Figure 3.28). But its reverberations throughout the nervous system are extensive. The pain message to the brain is initiated by the release of chemicals, including prostaglandins, bradykinin, and a chemical called *P* (yes, *P* stands for "pain"). Prostaglandins facilitate transmission of the pain message to the brain and heighten circulation to the injured area, causing the redness and swelling that we call inflammation. Inflammation serves the biological function of attracting infection-fighting blood cells to the affected area to protect it against invading germs. **Analgesic** drugs such as aspirin and ibuprofen work by inhibiting the production of prostaglandins.

The pain message is relayed from the spinal cord to the thalamus and then projected to the cerebral cortex, making us aware of the location and intensity of the damage. Ronald Melzack (1999) speaks of a "neuromatrix" that includes these chemical reactions but involves other aspects of our physiology and psychology in our reaction to pain. For example, visual and other sensory inputs tell us what is happening and influence the cognitive interpretation of the situation. Our emotional response affects the degree of pain, and so do the ways in which we respond to stress. For example, if the pain derives from an object we fear, perhaps a knife or needle, we may experience more pain. If we perceive that there is nothing we can do to change the situation, perception of pain may increase. If we have self-confidence and a history of successful responding to stress, the perception of pain may diminish. It all fits rather well with signal-detection theory.

Phantom Limb Pain One of the more fascinating phenomena of psychology is the fact that many people experience pain in limbs that are no longer there (Sherman, 1997; Kooijman et al., 2000). About two out of three combat veterans with amputated limbs report feeling pain in missing, or "phantom," limbs (Sherman, 1997; Kooijman et al., 2000). In such cases, the pain occurs in the absence of (present) tissue damage, but the pain itself is real enough. It sometimes involves activation of nerves in the stump of the missing limb, but local anesthesia does not always eliminate the pain. Therefore, the pain must also reflect activation of neural circuits that have stored memories connected with the missing limb (Melzack, 1997).

Gate Theory Simple remedies like rubbing and scratching an injured toe frequently help relieve pain. Why? One possible answer lies in the *gate theory* of pain originated by Melzack (1999). From this perspective, the nervous system can process only a limited amount of stimulation at a time. Rubbing or scratching the toe transmits sensations to the brain that, in a sense, compete for the attention of neurons. Many nerves are thus prevented from transmitting pain messages to the brain. The mechanism is analogous to shutting down a "gate" in the spinal cord. It is like a switchboard being flooded with calls. The flooding prevents any of the calls from getting through.

www ③ **BBC** ②

CLICK4™ *a bulletin board discussion on gender differences in pain.*

Psychology and Modern Life

Coping With Pain

Coping with that age-old enemy—pain—has traditionally been a medical issue. The primary treatment has been chemical, as in the use of pain-killing drugs. However, psychology has dramatically expanded our arsenal of weapons for fighting pain.

Accurate Information　　One irony of pain management is that giving people accurate and thorough information about their condition often helps them manage pain (Jacox et al., 1994; Ross & Berger, 1996). Most people in pain try *not* to think about why things hurt during the early phases of an illness (Moyers, 1993). Physicians, too, often neglect the human aspects of relating to their patients. That is, they focus on diagnosing and treating the causes of pain, but they often fail to discuss with patients the meaning of the pain and what the patient can expect.

Yet when uncomfortable treatment methods are used, such as cardiac catheterization or chemotherapy for cancer, knowledge of the details of the treatment, including how long it will last and how much pain there will be, can help people cope with the pain (Ludwick–Rosenthal & Neufeld, 1993). Knowledge of medical procedures reduces stress by helping people maintain control over their situation. Some people, on the other hand, do not *want* information about painful medical procedures. Their attitude is "Do what you have to do and get it over with." It may be most helpful to match the amount of information provided with the amount desired (Ludwick-Rosenthal & Neufeld, 1993).

Distraction and Fantasy: The Nintendo Approach to Coping With Pain?　　Diverting attention from pain helps many people cope with it (Jensen & Karoly, 1991; Keefe et al., 1992). Psychologists frequently recommend that people use distraction or fantasy as ways of coping with pain. For example, imagine that you've injured your

leg and you're waiting to see the doctor in an emergency room. You can distract yourself by focusing on details of your environment. You can count ceiling tiles or the hairs on the back of a finger. You can describe (or criticize!) the clothes of medical personnel or passers-by. For children, playing video games diminishes the pain and discomfort of the side effects of chemotherapy (Kolko & Rickard-Figueroa, 1985; Redd et al., 1987). While the children are receiving injections of nausea-producing chemicals, they are embroiled in battles on the video screen. Other distraction methods that help children deal with pain include combing one's hair and blowing on a noisemaker (Adler, 1990).

Hypnosis　　In 1842 London physician W. S. Ward amputated a man's leg after using a rather strange anesthetic: hypnosis. According to reports, the man experienced no discomfort. Several years later, operations were being performed routinely under hypnosis at his infirmary. Today hypnosis is often used to reduce chronic pain (Patterson & Ptacek, 1997) and as an anesthetic in dentistry, childbirth, even in some forms of surgery (Montgomery et al., 2000).

In using hypnosis to manage pain, the hypnotist usually instructs the person that he or she feels nothing or that the pain is distant and slight. Hypnosis can also aid in the use of distraction and fantasy. For example, the hypnotist can instruct the person to imagine that he or she is relaxing on a warm, exotic shore.

Relaxation Training and Biofeedback
When we are in pain, we often tense up. Tensing muscles is uncomfortable in itself, arouses the sympathetic nervous system, and focuses our attention on the pain. Relaxation counteracts these self-defeating behavior patterns (Ross & Berger, 1996). Some psychological methods of relaxation focus on relaxing muscle groups. Some in-

volve breathing exercises. Others use relaxing imagery: The imagery distracts the person and deepens feelings of relaxation. Biofeedback is also used to help people relax targeted muscle groups. Relaxation training with biofeedback seems to be at least as effective as most medications for chronic pain in the lower back and jaw (Flor & Birbaumer, 1993).

Coping With Irrational Beliefs　　Irrational beliefs can heighten pain (Ukestad & Wittrock, 1996). For example, telling oneself that the pain is unbearable and that it will never cease increases discomfort (Keefe et al., 1992). Some people seem to feel obligated to focus on things that distress them. They may be unwilling to allow themselves to be distracted from pain and discomfort. Thus, cognitive methods aimed at changing irrational beliefs hold some promise (Jensen et al., 1994; Stroud et al., 2000).

Other Methods　　Pain is a source of stress, and psychologists have uncovered many factors that seem to moderate the effects of stress. One is a sense of commitment. For example, if we are undergoing a painful medical procedure to diagnose or treat an illness, it might help if we recall that we *chose* to participate, rather than see ourselves as helpless victims. Thus, we are in control of the situation, and a sense of control enhances the ability to cope with pain (Jensen & Karoly, 1991).

Supportive social networks help as well. The benefits of having friends visit us—or visiting friends who are unwell—are as consistent with psychological findings as they are with folklore.

And don't forget gate theory. When you feel pain in a toe, squeeze all your toes. When you feel pain in your calf, rub your thighs. People around you may wonder what you're doing, but you're entitled to try to "flood the switchboard" so that some pain messages don't get through.

Kinesthesis.
This young acrobat receives information about the position and movement of the parts of his body through the sense of kinesthesis. Information is fed to his brain from sensory organs in the joints, tendons, and muscles. This allows him to follow his own movements without looking at himself.

www 3 E 4

CLICK4™ *an essay assignment on coping with pain.*

REFLECT
Can you touch your nose with your finger when you close your eyes? How do you manage to find your nose?

Kinesthesis ▲ The sense that informs us about the positions and motion of parts of our bodies.

Acupuncture   Thousands of years ago, the Chinese began mapping the body to learn where pins might be placed to deaden pain. Acupuncture remained largely unknown in the West, even though Western powers occupied much of China during the 1800s. But in the 1970s *New York Times* columnist James Reston underwent an appendectomy in China, with acupuncture his primary anesthetic. He reported no discomfort. More recently, TV journalist Bill Moyers (1993) reported on current usage of acupuncture in China. For example, one woman underwent brain surgery to remove a tumor after receiving anesthesia that consisted of a mild sedative, a small dose of narcotics, and six needles placed in her forehead, calves, and ankles. The surgery itself and the use of a guiding CAT scan were consistent with contemporary U.S. practices.

Traditional acupuncturists believe that the practice balances the body's flow of energy, but science reveals that it stimulates nerves that reach the hypothalamus and may also result in the release of *endorphins* (Reaney, 1998). Endorphins are naturally occurring chemical messengers that are similar to the narcotic morphine in their chemical structure and effects. The drug *naloxone* blocks both the painkilling effects of morphine and of acupuncture. Therefore, the analgesic effects of acupuncture may be due to the morphinelike endorphins.

REVIEW

(30) The _____ - _____ threshold method allows psychophysicists to assess sensitivity to pressure by determining the distance by which two rods touching the skin must be separated before a person will report that there are two rods, not one. (31) When the skin is touched, sensory receptors around the _____ of hair cells fire. Pain is transmitted to the brain by chemicals including prostaglandins, bradykinin, and substance P. (32) Amputees can experience _____ -limb pain.

Pulling It Together: How do methods for coping with pain focus on either sensations of pain or on the perception of pain?

KINESTHESIS AND THE VESTIBULAR SENSE

Try this experiment. Close your eyes, and then touch your nose with your finger. If you weren't right on target, I'm sure you came close. But how? You didn't see your hand moving, and you didn't hear your arm swishing through the air.

Kinesthesis: How Moving

Question: What is kinesthesis?   **Kinesthesis** is the sense that informs you about the position and motion of parts of the body. The term is derived from the ancient Greek words for "motion" *(kinesis)* and "perception" *(aisthesis)*. In kinesthesis, sensory information is fed back to the brain from sensory organs in the joints, tendons, and muscles. You were able to bring your finger to your nose by employing your kinesthetic sense. When you make a muscle in your arm, the sensations of tightness and hardness are also provided by kinesthesis.

Imagine going for a walk without kinesthesis. You would have to watch the forward motion of each leg to be certain you had raised it high enough to clear the curb. And if you had tried our brief experiment without the kinesthetic sense, you would have had no sensory feedback until you felt the pressure of your finger against your nose (or cheek, or eye, or forehead), and you probably would have missed dozens of times.

Are you in the mood for another experiment? Close your eyes again. Then "make a muscle" in your right arm. Could you sense the muscle without looking at it or feeling it with your left hand? Of course you could. Kinesthesis also provides information about muscle contractions.

IN REVIEW
The Senses

Sense	What We Sense	Receptor Organs	Nature of Sensory Receptors
Vision	Visible light (part of the spectrum of electro-magnetic energy; different colors have different wavelengths)	Eyes	Photoreceptors in the retinas (*rods*, which are sensitive to the intensity of light; and *cones*, which are sensitive to color)
Hearing	Changes in air pressure (or in another medium, such as water) that result from vibrations called *sound waves*	Ears	"Hair cells" in the organ of Corti, which is attached to a membrane (the *basilar membrane*) within the inner ear (the *cochlea*)
Smell	Molecules of the substance	Nose	Receptor neurons in the olfactory membrane high in each nostril
Taste	Molecules of the substance	Tongue	Taste cells located on taste buds on the tongue
Touch, Pressure	Pushing or pulling of the surface of the body	Skin	Nerve endings in the skin, some of which are located around the hair follicles
Kinesthesis	Muscle contractions	Sensory organs in joints, tendons, and muscles	Receptor cells in joints, tendons, and muscles
The Vestibular Sense	Movement and position in relation to gravity	Sensory organs in the ears (e.g., in the *semicircular canals*)	Receptor cells in the ears

The Vestibular Sense: On Being Upright

Your **vestibular sense** tells you whether you are upright (physically, not morally). *Question: How does the vestibular sense work?* Sensory organs located in the **semicircular canals** and elsewhere in the ears monitor your body's motion and position in relation to gravity. They tell you whether you are falling and provide cues to whether your body is changing speed, such as when you are in an accelerating airplane or automobile.

It is thus the vestibular sense that keeps us physically upright. It apparently takes more than the vestibular sense to keep us morally upright.

REVIEW

(33) Kinesthesis is the sensing of bodily _____ and movement. (34) Kinesthesis relies on sensory organs in the joints, tendons, and _____. (35) The vestibular sense informs us as to whether we are in an _____ position or changing speeds. (36) The vestibular sense is housed mainly in the _____ _____ of the ears.

Pulling It Together: Lie down with your eyes closed. Keeping them closed, touch your nose with a finger and then stand. How did you manage to do these things?

Vestibular sense ▲ The sense of equilibrium that informs us about our bodies' positions relative to gravity.
Semicircular canals ▲ Structures of the inner ear that monitor body movement and position.

SENSATION AND PERCEPTION ON THE EDGE: VIRTUAL REALITY AND ESP

CLICK4™ *an exploration of parapsychology on the Web.*

Sensation is the peripheral device that feeds information into our central processing unit—the brain. A number of fascinating topics on the edge of psychology explore the types of things that might happen if the sensations we perceive do not represent reality, or if sensation were bypassed altogether and we directly perceived things in the world outside. Make no mistake: These topics are indeed on the edge. For the time being there is little chance of mistaking virtual reality and, well, real reality. Also, the hard research evidence comes down pretty hard against perception in the absence of sensation. Nevertheless, these topics have captured the imagination of the public and are worth at least a sideways glance.

Sensation, Perception, and Virtual Reality

"Seeing is believing," or so goes the saying. But can we always believe what we see—or smell or hear or taste or feel? Not necessarily.

In the science-fiction film *The Matrix*, we envision a world in which all of us are deceived into believing the world we sense every day is real, when it is actually a vanished dream. The Matrix is science fiction on the theme of virtual reality. But virtual reality is in use today, employing computer-generated imagery. Although few would be fooled into believing a virtual visual world is real, psychologists are now using computer-generated images to help people overcome phobias such as fear of heights (Azar, 1996e). When they view the images, people perceive themselves as gradually rising to greater heights, even though they are actually remaining still. Because the images are computer generated rather than real, they are referred to as *virtual reality*. Children also use virtual reality—often in the form of virtual reality goggles or helmets—to feel that they are participating more fully in computer games.

Virtual Rooms   Virtual reality may also radically transform the ways in which people get together. For example, Jim Blascovich and his colleagues at the University of California at Santa Barbara Research Center for Virtual Environments and Behavior are working on an "immersive virtual environment" that will permit people to "be" in the same room no matter where they're located in the real world and represent their images in three dimensions. The technology has tremendous implications for online relationships, Blascovich says. Instead of just talking by phone, it will enable people to congregate in a "virtual room" and observe each other's body language.

"I can only speculate at this point, but this technology will have a major impact," says Blascovich (2000), adding that these environments are right around the corner. "Whatever you can do on the Internet, for good or for bad, will be magnified a thousandfold by immersive virtual environments."

Cybersex   Also consider what some futurists refer to as *cybersex* or *virtual sex* (DeAngelis, 2000). You don headphones, 3-D glasses, and a light bodysuit with miniature detectors that follow your movements, as well as tiny stimulators for your skin. The detectors and stimulators are connected to computers that record your responses and create the impression of being touched by textures such as virtual satin, virtual wool, or virtual skin. The information superhighway allows you either to interact with another online person who is outfitted with similar gear or to be connected with a "canned" program.

What are some of the psychological implications of virtual sex? If we could electronically dress up as movie stars, would our sense of self and our dignity as individuals suffer? If we could at a moment's notice access a satisfying virtual sexual encounter with an appealing person (or program) who was concerned only with meeting our needs, would we become less sensitive to the needs of our real-life romantic partners? Would virtual sex provide additional outlets for people whose needs were not being fully met by others? Or would they become the preferred sexual outlets? What would be the implications for the family? For children?

Will the courts consider a virtual sex interaction to be adultery? What will the future bring? Your guess is as good as mine.

CONTROVERSY IN PSYCHOLOGY

Is perception possible without sensation? Does ESP exist?

Imagine the wealth you could amass if you had *precognition*, that is, if you were able to perceive future events in advance. Perhaps you would check the next week's stock market reports and know what to buy or sell. Or you could bet with confidence on who would win the next Super Bowl or World Series. Or think of the power you would have if you were capable of *psychokinesis*, that is, of mentally manipulating or moving objects. You may have gotten a glimpse of the possibilities in films like *Carrie*, *The Sixth Sense*, and *Star Wars*. Precognition and psychokinesis are two concepts associated with *extrasensory perception* (ESP) or psi communication. Two other theoretical forms of ESP are *telepathy*, or direct transmission of thoughts or ideas from one person to another, and *clairvoyance*, or the perception of objects that do not stimulate the sensory organs. An example of clairvoyance is "seeing" what card will be dealt next, even though it is still in the deck and unseen even by the dealer.

Research on ESP is discussed in this section. It's meaning is very clear, but will all readers be convinced? Why or why not?

Extrasensory perception (ESP)—also referred to as psi communication—refers to the perception of objects or events through means other than sensory organs. Psi communication refers to the transfer of information through an irregular or unusual process—not through the usual senses. Many psychologists do not believe that ESP is an appropriate area for scientific inquiry. Scientists study natural events, but ESP smacks of the supernatural, even the occult. ESP also has the flavor of a nightclub act in which a blindfolded "clairvoyant" calls out the contents of an audience member's pocketbook. Other psychologists, however, believe that there is nothing wrong with investigating ESP. The issue for them is not whether ESP is sensationalistic but whether its existence can be demonstrated in the laboratory. *Question: Is there really such a thing as extrasensory perception (ESP)?*

Perhaps the best known of the respected ESP researchers was the late Joseph Banks Rhine of Duke University. Rhine studied ESP for several decades, beginning in the late 1920s. In a typical experiment in clairvoyance, Rhine would use a pack of 25 Zener cards, which contained 5 sets of the 5 cards shown in Figure 3.29. Pigeons pecking patterns at random to indicate which one was about to be turned up would select the correct one 20% of the time. Rhine found that some people guessed correctly significantly more often than the 20% chance rate. He concluded that these individuals may have had some degree of ESP.

A preferred contemporary method for studying telepathy is the *ganzfeld procedure* (Parker, 2000). In this method, one person acts as a "sender" and the other as a "receiver." The sender views randomly selected visual stimuli such as photographs of videotapes, while the receiver, who is in another room and whose eyes and ears are covered, tries to mentally tune in to the sender. After a session, the receiver is shown four visual stimuli and asked to select the one that was transmitted by the sender. A person guessing which stimulus was "transmitted" would be correct 25% of the time (1 time in 4) by chance alone. An analysis of 28 experiments using the ganzfeld procedure, however, found that receivers correctly identified the visual stimulus 38% of the time (Honorton, 1985), a percentage highly unlikely to be due to chance. A series of 11 more studies by Honorton and his colleagues using the ganzfeld procedure obtained comparable results (Bem & Honorton, 1994; Honorton et al., 1990).

Overall, however, there are many reasons for skepticism of ESP. One is the *file-drawer problem*. Buyers of supermarket magazines tend to forget "psychics predictions when they fail to come true (they "file" them away) (Tavris, 1998). Similarly, ESP researchers are less likely to report research results that show failure. Therefore, we would expect unusual findings (for example, a participant with a high success rate at psi-communication tasks over a period of several days) to appear in the research literature. In

> ▲ **REFLECT**
> Do you believe in ESP? Why or why not?

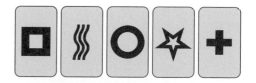

FIGURE 3.29 Zener Cards.
Zener cards have been used in research on clairvoyance. Participants are asked to predict which card will be turned up.

other words, if you flip a coin indefinitely, eventually you will flip 10 heads in a row. The odds against this are high, but if you report your eventual success and do not report the weeks of failure, you give the impression that you have unique coin-flipping ability. (You may even fool yourself.)

Then, too, it has not been easy to replicate experiments in ESP. People who have "demonstrated" ESP with one researcher have failed to do so with another researcher or have refused to participate in other studies. Also, the findings in one study are usually noticeably absent in follow-ups or under careful analysis. For example, Julie Milton and Richard Wiseman (1999) reviewed the research reported by Bem and Honorton (1994). They used meta-analysis to weigh the results of 30 ganzfeld ESP studies from 7 laboratories. They found no evidence—zero—that participants in these studies scored above chance levels on the ESP task.

Let's make this point a bit more strongly: From all of these studies, *not one person has emerged who can reliably show psi communication from one occasion to another and from one researcher to another.* Science, in other words, has not identified a single indisputable telepath or clairvoyant.

In any event, most psychologists do not grant ESP research much credibility. They prefer to study perception that involves sensation. After all, what is life without sensation?

CLICK4™ *a bulletin board discussion: Which sense is most essential?*

CLICK4™ *a quiz covering the second half of this chapter.*

CLICK4™ *electronic flash cards to review your knowledge of key terms and people in this chapter.*

REVIEW

(37) _____ reality uses electronic media to feed in false information about the world outside through the senses. (38) _____ is a controversial issue that refers to perception of objects or events through means other than sensory organs. (39) Joseph Banks Rhine used _____ cards to study clairvoyance. The ganzfeld procedure is currently used to study telepathy. (40) One reason for skepticism about ESP is the _____ - drawer problem; that is, ESP researchers are less likely to report research results that show failure. (41) It has also been difficult to _____ "positive" results.

Pulling It Together: Why do you think so many people are fascinated by virtual reality and ESP? Why do you think many people will persist in believing in ESP despite lack of evidence that it exists?

TRUTH [img] FICTION
REVISITED

◪ It is not true that people have five senses. *People have more, as we have seen. See page 78.*

◪ It is true that on a clear, dark night you could probably see the light from a candle burning 30 miles away. *This figure is in keeping with the absolute threshold for light. It is also true that if we could see light with slightly longer wavelengths, warm-blooded animals would glow in the dark. See page 80.*

◪ It is true that white sunlight is actually composed of all the colors of the rainbow. *See page 82.*

◪ It is not true that we obtain green light by mixing blue light and yellow light. *We obtain a green pigment when we mix blue and yellow pigments. See page 86.*

◪ It is true that catfish have 150,000 taste buds all over their bodies. *Therefore, they taste well. (Whether they taste good is another issue.) See page 106.*

◪ It is true that the skin is a sensory organ as well as a protective coating for the body. *The skin senses touch, pressure, temperature, and pain. See page 106.*

◪ It is true that there are no nerve endings for pain in the brain, even though people can have fierce headaches. *The pain actually originates elsewhere in the head. See page 108.*

◪ It is true that many amputees experience pain in limbs that have been removed. *The pain apparently reflects activation of neural circuits that have stored memories connected with the missing limbs. See page 108.*

◪ It is not true that some people can read other people's minds. *Of course, we can make educated guesses about the feelings of people whom we know well. We may also be able to interpret other people's smiles and frowns. But it has not been shown that we can directly read other people's minds. See page 114.*

1. What are sensation and perception?

Sensation is a mechanical process that involves the stimulation of sensory receptors (neurons) and the transmission of sensory information to the central nervous system. Perception is not mechanical. Perception is the active organization of sensations into a representation of the outside world, and it reflects learning and expectations.

2. How do we know when something is there? How do we know when it has changed?

We know something is there when the intensity of the stimulus, such as a light, exceeds the absolute threshold for that stimulus. The absolute threshold is the lowest intensity at which the stimulus can be detected. We know that something has changed when the change in intensity exceeds the difference threshold. The difference threshold is the minimum difference in intensity that can be discriminated. Difference thresholds are expressed in Weber's constants.

3. What is signal-detection theory?

Signal-detection theory explains the ways in which stimulus characteristics and psychological factors—for example, motivation, familiarity with a stimulus, and attention—interact to influence whether a stimulus will be detected.

4. What are feature detectors?

Feature detectors are neurons that fire in response to specific features of sensed stimuli. For example, detectors in the visual cortex fire in response to particular features of visual input, such as lines sensed at various angles or specific colors.

5. How do our sensory systems adapt to a changing environment?

We become more sensitive to stimuli of low magnitude and less sensitive to stimuli that remain the same (such as the background noises outside the window). Growing more sensitive to stimulation is termed sensitization, or positive adaptation. Growing less sensitive to continuous stimulation is called desensitization, or negative adaptation.

6. Just what is this stuff called light?

Visible light triggers visual sensations and is part of the spectrum of electromagnetic energy. Light is made up of waves of energy; the color violet has the shortest wavelength, and red has the longest. White sunlight can be broken down into the colors of the rainbow by means of a prism.

7. How does the eye work?

The eye senses and transmits visual stimulation to the occipital lobe of the cerebral cortex. After light passes through the cornea, the size of the pupil determines the amount that can pass through the lens. The lens focuses light onto the retina, which is composed of photoreceptors (neurons) called rods and cones. Cones permit perception of color. Rods transmit sensations of light and dark only. Light is transmitted from the retina to the brain via the optic nerve, which is made up of the axons of retinal ganglion cells. Visual acuity is connected with the shape of the eye and age. As we age, the lenses grow brittle, making it difficult to focus; the condition is called presbyopia. Rods are more sensitive than cones to lowered lighting and continue to adapt to darkness once cones have reached their peak adaptation.

8. What are some psychological dimensions of color?

These include hue, brightness, and warmth. The wavelength of light determines its hue. Yellow-orange-red colors are considered to be warm. Greens and blues are considered to be cool. Colors across from each other on the color wheel are complementary. In after-images, persistent sensations of color are followed by perception of the complementary color when the first color is removed.

9. How do we perceive color?

There are two theories as to how we perceive color. According to the trichromatic theory, there are three types of cones—some sensitive to red, others to green, and still others to blue-violet. The opponent-process theory proposes three types of color receptors: red-green, blue-yellow, and light-dark. Opponent-process theory is supported by the appearance of afterimages.

10. What is color blindness? Why are some people color blind?

People with normal color vision are called trichromats. Monochromats see no color, and dichromats are blind to some parts of the spectrum. Partial color blindness is a sex-linked trait that impairs the working of cones sensitive to red-green.

11. How do we organize bits of information like perceptions into meaningful wholes?

Perceptual organization involves recognizing patterns and processing information about relationships between parts and the whole. Gestalt rules of perceptual organization involve figure-ground relationships, proximity, similarity, continuity, common fate, and closure. Perception of a whole followed by perception of parts is termed top-down processing. Perception of the parts that leads to perception of a whole is termed bottom-up processing.

12. How do we perceive movement?

We visually perceive movement when the light reflected by moving objects moves across the retina, and also when objects shift in relation to one another. Distant objects appear to move more slowly than nearby objects, and objects in the middle ground may give the illusion of moving backward. Stroboscopic motion, responsible for the illusion of motion pictures, occurs through the presentation of a rapid progression of images of stationary objects (frames).

13. How do we perceive depth?

Depth perception involves monocular and binocular cues. Monocular cues include perspective, clearness, interposition, shadows, texture gradient, motion parallax, and accommodation. Binocular cues include retinal disparity and convergence.

14. What are perceptual constancies? Why do we perceive a door to be a rectangle even when it is ajar?

Perceptual constancies are acquired through experience and make the world a stable place. For example, we learn to assume that objects retain their size, shape, brightness, and color despite their distance from us, their position, or changes in lighting conditions.

15. How can principles of visual perception be used to trick the eye?

Visual illusions such as the Hering-Helmholtz and Müller-Lyer illusions tend to trick the eye because they play with perceptual constancies.

16. What is sound?

Sound waves, also called auditory stimulation, require a medium such as air or water in order to be transmitted. Sound waves alternately compress and expand molecules of the medium, creating vibrations. The human ear can hear sounds varying in frequency from 20 to 20,000 cycles per second (Hz). The greater the frequency, the higher the sound's pitch. The loudness of a sound corresponds to the amplitude of sound waves as measured in decibels (dB). We can experience hearing loss if we are exposed to protracted sounds of 85 to 90 dB or more.

17. How does the ear work?

The ear captures sound waves, vibrates in sympathy with them, and transmits auditory information to the brain. The outer ear funnels sound waves to the eardrum, which vibrates in sympathy with them and transmits the auditory information through the bones of the middle ear to the cochlea of the inner ear. The basilar membrane of the cochlea transmits those stimuli to the organ of Corti. From there, sound travels to the brain via the auditory nerve.

18. How do we locate sounds?

We locate sounds by determining in which ear they are louder. We may turn our heads to pin down that information.

19. How do we perceive loudness and pitch?

Sounds are perceived as louder when more sensory neurons fire. The place theory of pitch perception holds that the pitch of a sound is sensed according to the place along the basilar membrane that vibrates in response to it; it accounts for sounds whose frequencies exceed 4,000 Hz. Frequency theory states that pitch perception depends on the stimulation of neural impulses that match the frequency of the sound waves and accounts for frequencies of 20 to 1,000 Hz. The volley principle accounts for pitch discrimination between a few hundred and 4,000 cycles per second.

20. What is deafness? What can we do about it?

Conductive deafness—common among older people—is caused by damage to the middle ear and is often ameliorated by hearing aids, which amplify sounds. Sensorineural deafness is usually caused by damage to neurons in the inner ear, and can sometimes be corrected by cochlear implants.

21. How does the sense of smell work?

The sense of smell is chemical. It samples molecules of substances called odors through the olfactory membrane in each nostril. Smell makes a key contribution to the flavor of foods.

22. How does the sense of taste work?

There are four primary taste qualities: sweet, sour, salty, and bitter. Flavor involves the odor, texture, and temperature of food, as well as its taste. Taste is sensed through taste cells, which are located in taste buds on the tongue.

23. What are the skin senses? How do they work?

The skin senses include touch, pressure, warmth, cold, and pain. Touches and pressure are sensed by receptors located around the roots of hair cells below the surface of the skin. We have separate receptors for warmth and cold beneath the skin.

24. What is pain? What can we do about it?

Pain originates at the point of contact and is transmitted to the brain by various chemicals, including prostaglandins, bradykinin, and *P*. Melzack's theory of the "neuro-matrix" suggests that perception of pain also reflects our cognitive interpretation of the situation, our emotional response, and the ways in which we respond to stress. Amputees often experience pain in "phantom" limbs. Rubbing or scratching painful areas can decrease perception of pain by transmitting additional messages that have the effect of shutting down a "gate" in the spinal cord. Acupuncture may decrease pain by causing release of endorphins.

25. What is kinesthesis?

Kinesthesis is the sensation of body position and movement. It relies on sensory organs in the joints, tendons, and muscles.

26. How does the vestibular sense work?

The vestibular sense is housed primarily in the semicircular canals of the ears and tells us whether we are in an upright position.

27. Is there really such a thing as extrasensory perception (ESP)?

ESP, or psi communication, refers to the perception of objects or events through means other than sensory organs. Many psychologists do not believe that ESP is an appropriate area for scientific inquiry. The ganzfeld procedure studies telepathy by having one person (the sender) try to mentally transmit visual information to a receiver in another room. Because of the file-drawer problem and lack of replication of positive results, there is no reliable evidence for the existence of ESP.

PREVIEW

Just What *Is* Consciousness?
▲ Are you conscious? (How do you know?)

Sleep and Dreams
▲ If there were no clocks and you did not see the sun rise and set, would you awaken at the same time each day?
▲ Researchers are not certain as to why we sleep.
▲ Do dreams have meanings?
▲ Can you force yourself to get to sleep at night?

Hypnosis: On Being Entranced
▲ Can anybody be hypnotized?
▲ What is a "trance"?
▲ You must know what is expected of you in order to be hypnotized.

Meditation: Letting the World Fade Away
▲ Is meditation a spiritual or psychological event?
▲ Meditation can be good for your blood pressure.

Biofeedback: Getting in Touch With the Untouchable
▲ You can learn how to emit a specific brain wave.

Altering Consciousness Through Drugs
▲ Substance abuse and dependence usually begin with experimental use.
▲ Why can some people try drugs and walk away from them, while other people become dependent on them?

Depressants
▲ People self-medicate themselves with alcohol to relieve anxiety, depression, even social shyness.
▲ About 4 college students in 10 have bouts of binge drinking.
▲ Heroin was so named because it made people feel "heroic."

Stimulants
▲ The most harmful substance in the United States is legal.
▲ Cocaine boosts your self-confidence but also the burden on your heart.

Hallucinogenics
▲ Marijuana could once be bought without prescription in any drugstore.
▲ The controversies over the effects and uses of marijuana have become highly politicized.

CHAPTER 4

Consciousness

- ◤ We act out our forbidden fantasies in our dreams.

- ◤ Many people have insomnia because they try too hard to fall asleep at night.

- ◤ It is dangerous to awaken a sleepwalker.

- ◤ People can be hypnotized against their will.

- ◤ Some people have managed to control high blood pressure through meditation.

- ◤ Rats will learn to do whatever they can, such as pressing a lever, to obtain a burst of electricity in the brain.

- ◤ You can learn to change your heart rate just by thinking about it.

- ◤ Alcohol "goes to women's heads" more quickly than men's.

- ◤ Heroin was once used as a cure for addiction to morphine.

- ◤ A stimulant is commonly used to treat children who are hyperactive.

- ◤ At one time Coca-Cola "added life" through a powerful but now illegal stimulant.

W hen you talk to yourself, who talks, and who listens? This is the type of question posed by philosophers and scientists who study consciousness. *Question: What is consciousness?*

JUST WHAT *IS* CONSCIOUSNESS?

CLICK4™ *an essay assignment on the nature of consciousness.*

Consciousness cannot be directly seen or touched, yet it is real enough to most people. Consciousness, like anxiety or aggressiveness, is a psychological **construct** (pronounced CON-struct)—that is, a concept that is devised to help us understand our observations of behavior. The construct of consciousness has several meanings.

Consciousness as Sensory Awareness
One meaning of consciousness is *sensory awareness* of the environment. The sense of vision enables us to see, or be *conscious* of, the sun gleaming on the snow. The sense of hearing allows us to hear, or be conscious of, a concert.

Consciousness as the Selective Aspect of Attention
Sometimes we are not aware of sensory stimulation. We may be unaware, or unconscious, of sensory stimulation when we do not pay attention to it. The world is abuzz with signals, yet you are conscious of, or focusing on, only the words on this page (I hope).

Focusing one's consciousness on a particular stimulus is referred to as **selective attention.** The concept of selective attention is important to self-control. To pay attention in class, you must screen out the pleasant aroma of the cologne or perfume wafting toward you from the person in the next seat. To keep your car on the road, you must pay more attention to driving conditions than to your hunger pangs or your feelings about an argument with a friend. If you are out in the woods at night, attending to rustling sounds in the brush nearby may be crucial to your survival.

Adaptation to our environment involves learning which stimuli must be attended to and which ones can be safely ignored. Selective attention makes our senses keener (Basic Behavioral Science Task Force, 1996b). This is why we can pick out the speech of a single person across a room at a cocktail party, a phenomenon suitably termed the *cocktail party effect.*

Although we can decide where and when we will focus our attention, various kinds of stimuli also tend to capture attention. Among them are these:

▲ Sudden changes, as when a cool breeze enters a sweltering room or we receive a particularly high or low grade on an exam,

▲ Novel stimuli, as when a dog enters the classroom or a person shows up with an unusual hairdo,

▲ Intense stimuli, such as bright colors, loud noises, or sharp pain,

▲ Repetitive stimuli, as when the same TV commercial is played a dozen times throughout the course of a football game.

How do advertisers of Nike, Microsoft, or cologne use these facts to get "into" our consciousness and, they hope, into our pocketbooks?

Consciousness as Direct Inner Awareness
Close your eyes and imagine spilling a can of bright red paint across a black tabletop. Watch it spread across the black, shiny surface and then spill onto the floor. Although this image may be vivid, you did not "see" it literally. Neither your eyes nor any other sensory organs were involved. You were *conscious* of the image through **direct inner awareness.**

We are conscious of—or have direct inner awareness of—thoughts, images, emotions, and memories. We may not be able to measure direct inner awareness scientifically. Nevertheless, many psychologists argue "It is detectable to anyone that has it" (Miller, 1992, p. 180). These psychological processes are connected with the firings of myriads of neurons. We do not consciously experience the firing of individual neurons, but consciousness reflects the total of these millions or billions of neural events.

▲ REFLECT

Are *you* conscious, or aware, of yourself and the world around you? How do you know whether you are?

Construct ▲ As a noun, a concept or a theory that is devised in order to help make sense of, or integrate, our observations of a phenomenon. Consciousness, anxiety, and achievement motivation are examples of constructs of interest to psychologists.

Selective attention ▲ The focus of one's consciousness on a particular stimulus.

Direct inner awareness ▲ Knowledge of one's own thoughts, feelings, and memories without use of sensory organs.

Sigmund Freud, the founder of psychoanalysis, differentiated between the thoughts and feelings we are conscious, or aware, of and those that are preconscious and unconscious. **Preconscious** material is not currently in awareness but is readily available. For example, if you answer the following questions, you will summon up "preconscious" information: What did you eat for dinner yesterday? About what time did you wake up this morning? What is your phone number? You can make these preconscious bits of information conscious by directing your inner awareness, or attention, to them.

According to Freud, still other mental events are **unconscious.** This means that they are unavailable to awareness under most circumstances. Freud believed that some painful memories and sexual and aggressive impulses are unacceptable to us, so we *automatically* (unconsciously) eject them from our awareness. In other words, we *repress* them. **Repression** of these memories and impulses allows us to avoid feelings of anxiety, guilt, or shame.

People can also *choose* to stop thinking about unacceptable ideas or distractions. When we consciously eject unwanted mental events from awareness, we are engaging in **suppression.** We may, for example, suppress thoughts of a date when we need to study for a test. We may also try to suppress thoughts of a test while we are on a date!

Some bodily processes, such as the firings of neurons, are **nonconscious.** They cannot be experienced through sensory awareness or direct inner awareness. The growing of hair and the carrying of oxygen in the blood are nonconscious. We can see that our hair has grown, but we have no sense receptors that give us sensations of growing. We can feel the need to breathe but do not directly experience the exchange of carbon dioxide and oxygen.

Consciousness as Personal Unity: The Sense of Self

As we develop, we differentiate ourselves from that which is not us. We develop a sense of being persons, individuals. There is a totality to our impressions, thoughts, and feelings that makes up our conscious existence—our continuing sense of self in a changing world. That self forms intentions and guides its own behavior. In this usage of the word, consciousness *is* self.

Consciousness as the Waking State

The word *conscious* also refers to the waking state as opposed, for example, to sleep. From this perspective, sleep, meditation, the hypnotic "trance," and the distorted perceptions that can accompany use of consciousness-altering drugs are considered *altered states of consciousness.*

CONTROVERSY IN PSYCHOLOGY

Is Consciousness a Proper Area for Psychological Study?

Although it might seem that psychologists, who study the brain and mental processes, are also well-equipped to look into consciousness, consciousness has not always been an acceptable topic in psychology (Crick & Koch, 1997). In 1904, for example, William James wrote an article with the intriguing title "Does Consciousness Exist?" James did not think that consciousness was a proper area of study for psychologists because no scientific method could directly observe or measure another person's consciousness.

John Watson, the "father of modern behaviorism," agreed. Watson insisted that only observable, measurable behavior is the province of psychology: "The time seems to have come when psychology must discard all references to consciousness" (1913, p. 163). In 1914, Watson was elected president of the American Psychological Association. This honor further cemented his ideas in the minds of many psychologists.

Today, however, many psychologists believe that we cannot capture the richness of the human experience without referring to consciousness. Psychological constructs like consciousness acquire scientific status from being tied to behavior (Kimble, 1994), and studies connecting consciousness with behavior have turned from a stream into a flood. Psychologists, neuroscientists, philosophers, physicists, even computer scientists are searching for the elusive marvel of consciousness. Most assume that consciousness dwells within the brain. And some (e.g., Chafee & Goldman-Rakic, 2000; Duncan et al., 2000) suggest that the biological basis for consciousness can be found in specific sites in the brain.

▲ **REFLECT**

Do you think people have an "unconscious" mind? If so, what do you think happens within it?

CLICK4™ *a bulletin board discussion on the study of consciousness in psychology.*

Preconscious ▲ In psychodynamic theory, descriptive of material that is not in awareness but can be brought into awareness by focusing one's attention.

Unconscious ▲ In psychodynamic theory, descriptive of ideas and feelings that are not available to awareness.

Repression ▲ In psychodynamic theory, the automatic (unconscious) ejection of anxiety-evoking ideas, impulses, or images from awareness.

Suppression ▲ The deliberate, or conscious, placing of certain ideas, impulses, or images out of awareness.

Nonconscious ▲ Descriptive of bodily processes such as the growing of hair, of which we cannot become conscious. We may "recognize" that our hair is growing but cannot directly experience the biological process.

In the remainder of this chapter, we explore various types of altered states of consciousness. They include sleep and dreams, hypnosis, meditation, biofeedback, and finally, the effects of psychoactive drugs.

REVIEW

(1) John B. Watson argued that only observable _____ should be studied by psychologists. (2) However, _____ psychologists believe that we cannot discuss meaningful human behavior without referring to consciousness. (3) *Consciousness* has several meanings, including sensory awareness, the selective aspect of attention, direct inner _____, personal unity, and the waking state. (4) Sigmund _____ differentiated among ideas that are conscious, preconscious, and unconscious.

Pulling It Together: Can you use each meaning of *consciousness* in a sentence? Distinguish between conscious, preconscious, and unconscious ideas.

SLEEP AND DREAMS

Sleep is a fascinating topic. After all, we spend about one third of our adult lives asleep. Sleep experts recommend that adults get 8 hours of sleep a night, but according to the National Sleep Foundation (2000b), adults in the United States typically get a bit less than 7. About one-third get 6 hours or less of sleep a night during the workweek. One-third admits that lack of sleep impairs their ability to function during the day, and nearly 1 in 5 admits to falling asleep at the wheel at some time within the past year.

Our alternating periods of wakefulness and sleep provide an example of an internally generated **circadian rhythm.** *Question: What is a circadian rhythm?* A circadian rhythm is a cycle that is connected with the 24-hour period of the earth's rotation. A cycle of wakefulness and sleep is normally 24 hours long. However, when people are removed from cues that signal day or night, a cycle tends to become extended to about 25 hours, and people sleep nearly 10 of them (National Sleep Foundation, 2000b). Why? We do not know.

Why do we sleep? Why do we dream? Next we explore the nature of sleep, dreams, and sleep disorders.

The Stages of Sleep

A major tool of sleep researchers is the electroencephalograph, or EEG. The EEG measures the electrical activity of the brain, or brain waves. Figure 4.1 shows EEG patterns that reflect the frequency and strength of brain waves that occur during the waking state, when we are relaxed, and when we are in the various stages of sleep. *Question: What occurs during sleep?*

Brain waves, like other waves, are cyclical. During the various stages of sleep, the brain emits waves with different *frequencies* (numbers of waves per second) and *amplitudes* (heights—an index of strength). The printouts in Figure 4.1 show what happens during a period of 15 seconds or so. Brain waves that are high in frequency are associated with wakefulness. The amplitude of brain waves reflects their strength. The strength or energy of brain waves is expressed in volts (an electrical unit).

Figure 4.1 shows five stages of sleep: four stages of **non-rapid-eye-movement (NREM) sleep** and one stage of **rapid-eye-movement (REM) sleep.** When we close our eyes and begin to relax before going to sleep, our brains emit many **alpha waves.** Alpha waves are low-amplitude brain waves of about 8 to 13 cycles per second.

As we enter stage 1 sleep, our brain waves slow down from the alpha rhythm and enter a pattern of **theta waves.** Theta waves, with a frequency of about 6 to 8 cycles per second, are accompanied by slow, rolling eye movements. The transition from alpha waves to theta waves may be accompanied by a **hypnagogic state** during which we may experience brief dreamlike images that resemble vivid photographs. Stage 1 sleep is the lightest stage of sleep. If we are awakened from stage 1 sleep, we may feel that we have not slept at all.

CLICK4™ *an essay assignment on circadian rhythms and their impact on behavior.*

CLICK4™ *an interactive questionnaire on circadian rhythms: Are You an Owl or a Lark?*

CLICK4™ *Web-O-Rhythm to chart your own circadian cycle.*

Circadian rhythm ▲ Referring to cycles that are connected with the 24-hour period of the earth's rotation.
Non-rapid-eye-movement sleep ▲ Stages of sleep 1 through 4. Abbreviated *NREM* sleep.
Rapid-eye-movement sleep ▲ A stage of sleep characterized by rapid eye movements, which have been linked to dreaming. Abbreviated *REM* sleep.
Alpha waves ▲ Rapid low-amplitude brain waves that have been linked to feelings of relaxation.
Theta waves ▲ Slow brain waves produced during the hypnagogic state.
Hypnagogic state ▲ The drowsy interval between waking and sleeping, characterized by brief, hallucinatory, dreamlike experiences.

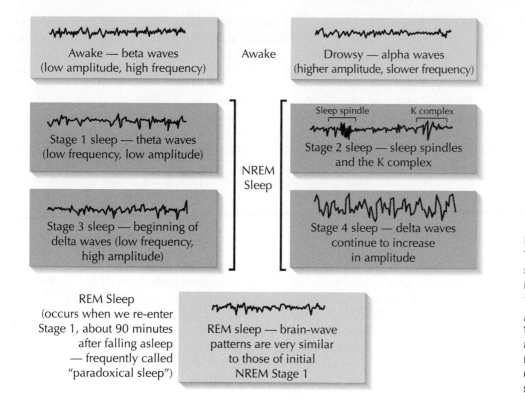

FIGURE 4.1   The Stages of Sleep.
This figure illustrates typical EEG patterns for the stages of sleep. During REM sleep, EEG patterns resemble those of the lightest stage of sleep, stage 1 sleep. For this reason, REM sleep is often termed *paradoxical* sleep. As sleep progresses from stage 1 to stage 4, brain waves become slower and their amplitude increases. Dreams, including normal nightmares, are most vivid during REM sleep. More disturbing sleep terrors tend to occur during deep stage 4 sleep.

After 30 to 40 minutes of stage 1 sleep, we undergo a rather steep descent into stages 2, 3, and 4 (see Figure 4.2). During stage 2, brain waves are medium in amplitude with a frequency of about 4 to 7 cycles per second, but these are punctuated by *sleep spindles.* Sleep spindles have a frequency of 12 to 16 cycles per second and represent brief bursts of rapid brain activity.

During deep sleep stages 3 and 4, our brains produce slower **delta waves.** During stage 3, the delta waves have a frequency of 1 to 3 cycles per second. Delta waves reach relatively great amplitude compared with other brain waves. Stage 4 is the deepest stage of sleep, from which it is the most difficult to be awakened. During stage 4 sleep, the delta waves slow to about 0.5 to 2 cycles per second, and their amplitude is greatest.

After perhaps half an hour of deep stage 4 sleep, we begin a relatively rapid journey back upward through the stages until we enter REM sleep (Figure 4.2). REM sleep derives its name from the *rapid eye movements*, observable beneath the closed eyelids, that characterize this stage. During REM sleep we produce relatively rapid, low-amplitude brain waves that resemble those of light stage 1 sleep. REM sleep is also called *paradoxical sleep* because the EEG patterns observed suggest a level of arousal similar to that of the

CLICK4™ *"Chrono Links" at the Center for Biological Timing.*

CLICK4™ *a video on brain wave patterns during the stages of sleep.*

Delta waves ▲ Strong, slow brain waves usually emitted during stage 4 sleep.

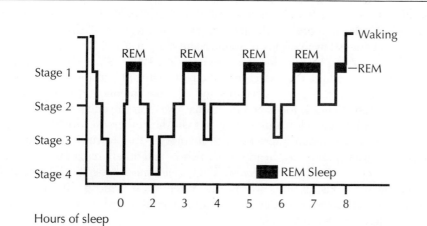

Hours of sleep

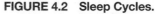

FIGURE 4.2   Sleep Cycles.
This figure illustrates the alternation of REM and non-REM sleep for the typical sleeper. There are about five periods of REM sleep during an 8-hour night. Sleep is deeper earlier in the night, and REM sleep tends to become prolonged toward morning.

waking state (Figure 4.1). However, it is difficult to awaken a person during REM sleep. When people are awakened during REM sleep, as is the practice in sleep research, about 80% of the time they report that they have been dreaming. (We also dream during NREM sleep, but less frequently. People report dreaming only about 20% of the time when awakened during NREM sleep.)

Each night we tend to undergo five trips through the stages of sleep (see Figure 4.2). These trips include about five periods of REM sleep. Our first journey through stage 4 sleep is usually longest. Sleep tends to become lighter as the night wears on. Our periods of REM sleep tend to become longer, and toward morning our last period of REM sleep may last close to half an hour.

Now that we have some idea of what sleep is like, let us consider *why* we sleep.

Functions of Sleep

CLICK4™ *Web sites on sleep and dreaming.*

> ▲ **REFLECT**
> How much sleep do you need? (How do you know?) Did you ever "pull an all-nighter"? What were the effects?

Question: Why do we sleep? Researchers do not have all the answers as to why we sleep. One hypothesis is that sleep helps rejuvenate a tired body. Most of us have had the experience of going without sleep for a night and feeling "wrecked" or "out of it" the following day. Perhaps the next evening we went to bed early in order to "catch up on our sleep." What happens to you if you do not sleep for one night? For several nights?

Compare people who are highly sleep deprived with people who have been drinking heavily. Sleepless people's abilities to concentrate and perform may be seriously impaired, but they may be the last ones to recognize their limitations (Adler, 1993).

Most students can pull successful "all-nighters" (Webb, 1993). They can cram for a test through the night and then perform reasonably well the following day. When we are deprived of sleep for several nights, however, aspects of psychological functioning such as attention, learning, and memory deteriorate notably (Maas, 1998). The National Sleep Foundation (2000b) estimates that sleep deprivation is connected with 100,000 crashes and 1,500 vehicular deaths each year. Many people sleep late or nap on their days off (National Sleep Foundation, 2000b). Perhaps they suffer from mild sleep deprivation during the week and catch up on the weekend.

The amount of sleep we need seems to be in part genetically determined (Webb, 1993). People also tend to need more sleep during periods of stress, such as a change of job, an increase in workload, or an episode of depression (Maas, 1998). Sleep seems to help us recover from stress.

Newborn babies may sleep 16 hours a day, and teenagers often sleep around the clock. It is widely believed that older people need less sleep than younger adults do. However, sleep in older people is often interrupted by physical discomfort or the need to go to the bathroom. Older people often sleep more during the day to make up for sleep lost at night.

CLICK4™ *the* New York Times *article, "Experts Explore Deep Sleep and the Making of Memories."*

Sleep, Learning, and Memory REM sleep and deep sleep are both connected with the consolidation of learning and memory (Adler, 1993; Blakeslee, 2000). In some studies, animals or people have been deprived of REM sleep. Under these conditions animals and people learn more slowly and forget what they have learned more rapidly (Adler, 1993). Fetuses have periods of waking and sleeping, and REM sleep may foster the development of the brain before birth (McCarley, 1992). REM sleep may also help maintain neurons in adults by "exercising" them at night. Deprivation of REM sleep is accomplished by monitoring EEG records and eye movements and waking the person during REM sleep. There is too much individual variation to conclude that people who are deprived of REM sleep learn more poorly than they otherwise would. It does seem, though, that such deprivation interferes with memory—that is, retrieval of information that has been learned previously. In any event, people and other animals that are deprived of REM sleep tend to show *REM rebound*. They spend more time in REM sleep during subsequent sleep periods. In other words, they catch up. It is mostly during REM sleep that we dream. Let us now consider dreams, a mystery about which philosophers, poets, and scientists have theorized for centuries.

Dreams

To quote from Shakespeare's *The Tempest*, Just what is the "stuff"[1] of dreams? What are they "made on"? ***Question: What are dreams and why do we dream what we dream?*** Like memories and fantasies, dreams involve imagery in the absence of external stimulation. Some dreams seem very real. In college I often had "anxiety dreams" the night before a test. I dreamed repeatedly that I had taken the test and it was all over. (Imagine the disappointment when I awakened and realized that the test still lay before me!)

Dreams are most likely to have vivid imagery during REM sleep. Images are vaguer and more fleeting during NREM sleep. You may dream every time you are in REM sleep. So if you sleep for 8 hours and undergo five sleep cycles, you may have five dreams. Upon waking, you may think that time seemed to expand or contract during your dream, so that during 10 or 15 minutes of actual time, the content of your dream ranged over days or weeks. But dreams actually tend to take place in "real time." Fifteen minutes of events fills about 15 minutes of dreaming. Your dream theater is quite flexible. You can dream in black and white or in full color.

Theories of the Content of Dreams You may recall dreams involving fantastic adventures, but most dreams involve memories of the activities and problems of the day (Wade, 1998). If we are preoccupied with illness or death, sexual or aggressive urges, or moral dilemmas, we are likely to dream about them. The characters in our dreams are more likely to be friends and neighbors than spies, monsters, and princes.

"A dream is a wish your heart makes," is a song lyric from the Disney film *Cinderella*. Freud theorized that dreams reflect unconscious wishes and urges. He argued that through dreams we can express impulses we would censor during the day. Moreover, he said that the content of dreams is symbolic of unconscious fantasized objects such as the genitals (see Table 4.1). A key part of Freud's method of psychoanalysis involved interpretation of his clients' dreams. Freud also believed that dreams "protect sleep" by providing imagery that helps keep disturbing, repressed thoughts out of awareness.

TABLE 4.1 DREAM SYMBOLS IN PSYCHODYNAMIC THEORY

SYMBOLS FOR THE MALE GENITAL ORGANS				
airplanes	fish	neckties	tools	weapons
bullets	hands	poles	trains	
feet	hoses	snakes	trees	
fire	knives	sticks	umbrellas	

SYMBOLS FOR THE FEMALE SEXUAL ORGANS				
bottles	caves	doors	ovens	ships
boxes	chests	hats	pockets	tunnels
cases	closets	jars	pots	

SYMBOLS FOR SEXUAL INTERCOURSE	
climbing a ladder	entering a room
climbing a staircase	flying in an airplane
crossing a bridge	riding a horse
driving an automobile	riding a roller coaster
riding an elevator	walking into a tunnel or down a hall

SYMBOLS FOR THE BREASTS	
apples	peaches

NOTE: Freud theorized that the content of dreams symbolizes urges, wishes, and objects of fantasy that we would censor if we were awake.

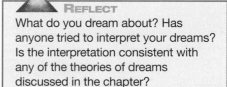

REFLECT

What do you dream about? Has anyone tried to interpret your dreams? Is the interpretation consistent with any of the theories of dreams discussed in the chapter?

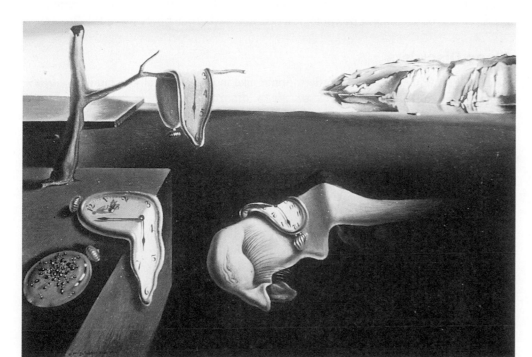

Dream Images?

In *The Persistence of Memory*, Salvador Dali seems to depict images born in dreams.

CLICK4™ *an essay assignment on dream interpretation.*

---

[1] The phrase "such stuff as dreams are made on" comes from Shakespeare's *The Tempest*.

Activation-synthesis model ▲ The view that dreams reflect activation of cognitive activity by the reticular activating system and synthesis of this activity into a pattern by the cerebral cortex.

CLICK4™ *more information on sleep disorders.*

CLICK4™ *a WebSearch activity: Is melatonin a safe sleep aid?*

▲ REFLECT
How would you explain the gender differences in factors that disrupt sleep that we find in Table 4.2?

DIVERSITY **TABLE 4.2 GENDER DIFFERENCES IN FACTORS REPORTED AS DISRUPTING SLEEP**

Factor	Percent of women reporting factor	Percent of men reporting factor
Stress: 22% of adults overall	26	20
Pain: 20% of adults overall	25	13
Children: 17% of adults overall	21	12
Partner's snoring: 16% of adults overall	22	7
Pauses in partner's breathing: 8% of adults overall	11	2

Based on data reported by the National Sleep Foundation, 2000b.

The theory that dreams protect sleep has been challenged by the observation that disturbing events tend to be followed by disturbing dreams on the same theme—not by protective imagery (Reiser, 1992). Our behavior in dreams is also generally consistent with our waking behavior. Most dreams, then, are unlikely candidates for the expression of repressed urges (even disguised). A person who leads a moral life tends to dream moral dreams.

There are also biological views of the "meanings" of dreams. According to the **activation-synthesis model,** acetylcholine (a neurotransmitter) and the pons (a structure in the lower part of the brain) stimulate responses that lead to dreaming (Hobson & McCarley, 1977). One is *activation* of the reticular activating system (RAS), which arouses us, but not to waking. During the waking state, firing of these cells in the reticular formation is linked to movement, particularly the movements involved in walking, running, and other physical acts. During REM sleep, however, neurotransmitters generally inhibit activity so we usually do not thrash about as we dream (Bassetti et al., 2000). In this way, we save ourselves (and our bed partners) some wear and tear. The eye muscles are stimulated and thus show the rapid eye movement associated with dreaming. The RAS also stimulates neural activity in the parts of the cortex involved in memory. The cortex then *synthesizes*, or puts together, these sources of stimulation to some degree to yield the stuff of dreams. Yet research with the PET scan shows that the frontal lobes of the brain, which seem to be where we make sense of experience, are pretty much shut down during sleep (Wade, 1998). Dreams are therefore more likely to be emotionally gripping than coherent in plot.

Another view of dreams is that with the brain cut off from the world outside, memories are replayed and consolidated during sleep (Wade, 1998). Still another possibility is that REM activity is a way of testing whether the individual has benefited from the restorative functions of sleep (Wade, 1998). When restoration is adequate, the brain awakens. According to this view, dreams are just the by-products of the testing.

Nightmares   Have you ever dreamed that something heavy was sitting on your chest and watching you as you breathed? Or that you were trying to run away from a terrible threat but couldn't gain your footing or coordinate your leg muscles?

Nightmares, like most pleasant dreams, are generally products of REM sleep. College students report an average of two nightmares a month in dream logs (Wood & Bootzin, 1990). Traumatic events can spawn nightmares, as reported in a study of survivors of the San Francisco earthquake of 1989 (Wood et al., 1992). People who suffer frequent nightmares are more likely than other people to also suffer from anxieties, depression, and other kinds of psychological discomfort (Berquier & Ashton, 1992).

Sleep Disorders

There are a number of sleep disorders. Some, like insomnia, are all too familiar. *Question: What types of problems or sleep disorders can we encounter as we sleep?* In this section we discuss insomnia, narcolepsy, apnea, and the deep-sleep disorders—sleep terrors, bed-wetting, and sleepwalking.

Insomnia   According to the National Sleep Foundation (2000b), more than half of American adults (58%) are affected by insomnia in any given year. Women complain of insomnia more often than men do, by 61% to 53% (National Sleep Foundation, 2000b). People who experience insomnia show greater restlessness and muscle tension than those who do not (Lacks & Morin, 1992). People with insomnia are also more likely to worry and report "racing thoughts" at bedtime (White & Nicassio, 1990). Factors contributing to insomnia include stress (22% of adults), pain (20%), children (17%), environmental factors such as noise, light, and temperature (16%), one's partner's snoring (16%), the bedding (14%), nasal congestion (12%), allergies (11%), indigestion (8%), and pauses in one's partner's breathing (8%) (National Sleep Foundation, 2000b). Insomnia comes and goes with many people, increasing during periods of stress. Table 4.2 shows some gender differences in reporting of factors that disturb sleep.

People with insomnia tend to compound their sleep problems when they try to force themselves to fall asleep. Their concern heightens autonomic activity and muscle tension (Bootzin et al., 1991). You cannot force or will yourself to go to sleep. You can only set

CLICK4™ *an interactive version of this Self-Assessment.*

Sleep Quiz: Are You Getting Your Z's?

This questionnaire can help you learn whether you are getting enough sleep. Simply respond to the following items by circling the *T* if an item is true or mostly true for you, or the *F* if an item is false or mostly false for you. Try to work rapidly. Then check the meaning of your answers in Appendix B.

1. T F I need an alarm clock in order to wake up at the appropriate time.

2. T F It's a struggle for me to get out of bed in the morning.

3. T F Weekday mornings I hit the snooze button several times to get more sleep.

4. T F I feel tired, irritable, and stressed out during the week.

5. T F I have trouble concentrating and remembering.

6. T F I feel slow with critical thinking, problem solving, and being creative.

7. T F I often fall asleep watching television.

8. T F I often fall asleep after heavy meals or after a low dose of alcohol.

9. T F I often fall asleep while relaxing after dinner.

10. T F I often fall asleep within 5 minutes of getting into bed.

11. T F I often feel drowsy while driving.

12. T F I often sleep extra hours on weekend mornings.

13. T F I often need a nap to get through the day.

14. T F I have dark circles around my eyes.

SOURCE: James Maas (1999). *Power Sleep*. New York: HarperCollins.

---

the stage for sleep by lying down and relaxing when you are tired. If you focus on sleep too closely, it will elude you.

Narcolepsy **Narcolepsy** is, in a sense, the mirror image of insomnia. A person with narcolepsy falls asleep suddenly and irresistibly. Narcolepsy afflicts as many as 100,000 people in the United States and seems to run in families. The "sleep attack" may last about 15 minutes, after which the person awakens feeling refreshed. Nevertheless, these sleep episodes are dangerous and frightening. They can occur while a person is driving or working with sharp tools. They also may be accompanied by the sudden collapse of muscle groups or even of the entire body—a condition called *sleep paralysis*. In sleep paralysis, the person cannot move during the transition from the waking state to sleep, and hallucinations (such as of a person or object sitting on the chest) occur.

Narcolepsy ▲ A "sleep attack" in which a person falls asleep suddenly and irresistibly.

Insomnia.
"You know I can't sleep at night" goes the 1960s song by the Mamas and the Papas. Why are women more likely than men to have insomnia? What can people do about insomnia?

Although the causes are unknown, narcolepsy is thought to be a disorder of REM-sleep functioning. Stimulants and antidepressant drugs have helped many people with narcolepsy.

Apnea   **Apnea** is a dangerous sleep disorder in which the air passages are obstructed. People with apnea stop breathing periodically, upwards of 10 times an hour (National Sleep Foundation, 2000b). Obstruction may cause the sleeper to suddenly sit up and gasp for air, before falling back asleep. People with apnea are stimulated nearly, but not quite, to waking by the buildup of carbon dioxide. Some 10 million Americans have apnea, and it is associated with obesity and chronic loud snoring. Apnea is more than a sleep problem. It can lead to high blood pressure, heart attacks, and strokes (Lave et al., 2000; Papered et al., 2000).

Causes of apnea include anatomical deformities that clog the air passageways, such as a thick palate, and problems in the breathing centers in the brain. Apnea is treated by

Apnea ▲ Temporary absence or cessation of breathing. (From Greek and Latin roots meaning "without" and "breathing.")

Psychology and Modern Life

Coping With Insomnia

No question about it: The most common medical method for fighting insomnia in the United States is taking pills (Murtaugh & Greenwood, 1995). Sleeping pills may work — for a while. So may tranquilizers. They generally work by reducing arousal. At first, lowered arousal may be effective in itself. Focusing on changes in arousal may also distract you from trying to *get* to sleep. Expectations of success may also help.

But there are problems with sleeping pills. First, you attribute your success to the pill and not to yourself. You thus depend on the pill rather than become self-reliant. Second, you develop a tolerance for many kinds of sleeping pills. With regular use, you come to need higher doses to achieve the same effects. Third, high doses of these chemicals can be dangerous, especially if mixed with alcohol. Both sleeping pills and alcohol depress the central nervous system, and their effects are additive. Fourth, sleeping pills do not enhance your skills at handling insomnia. Thus, when you stop taking the pills, your sleep problems are likely to return (Morin et al., 1999).

There are also psychological methods for coping with insomnia (Mimeault & Morin, 1999). Some methods like muscle relaxation exercises reduce tension directly. Psychological methods also divert us from the "task" of trying somehow to *get* to sleep, which, of course, is one of the ways in which we keep ourselves awake. Instead, we need only recline when we are tired and allow sleep to happen.

Relax. Take a hot bath at bedtime or try meditating. Releasing muscle tension has

been shown to reduce the amount of time needed to fall asleep and the incidence of waking up during the night. It increases the number of hours slept and leaves us feeling more rested in the morning (Murtagh & Greenwood, 1995). Biofeedback training (BFT) for insomnia usually focuses on reducing muscle tension in the forehead or in the arms. BFT has also been used to teach people to produce the kinds of brain waves that are associated with relaxation and sleep.

Challenge exaggerated fears. You need not be a sleep expert to realize that convincing yourself that the day will be ruined unless you get to sleep *right now* may increase, rather than decrease, bedtime tension. Sleep seems to restore us, especially after physical exertion. However, we often exaggerate the problems that will befall us if we do not sleep (Morin et al., 1999). Table 4.3 shows some beliefs that increase bedtime tension and some alternatives.

Don't ruminate in bed. Don't plan or worry about tomorrow while in bed (National Sleep Foundation, 2000a). When you lie down for sleep, you may organize your thoughts for the day for a few minutes, but then allow yourself to relax or engage in fantasy. If an important idea comes to you, jot it down on a handy pad so that you won't lose it. If thoughts persist, however, get up and follow them elsewhere. Let your bed be a place for relaxation and sleep — not your second office. A bed — even a waterbed — is not a think tank.

Establish a regular routine. Sleeping late can encourage sleep-onset insomnia.

TABLE 4.3 BELIEFS THAT INCREASE TENSION AND ALTERNATIVES

Beliefs that increase tension	Alternatives
If I don't get to sleep, I'll feel wrecked tomorrow.	Not necessarily. If I'm tired, I can go to bed early tomorrow night.
It's unhealthy for me not to get more sleep.	Not necessarily. Some people do very well on only a few hours of sleep.
I'll wreck my sleeping schedule for the whole week if I don't get to sleep very soon.	Not at all. If I'm tired, I'll just go to bed a bit earlier. I'll get up about the same time with no problem.
If I don't get to sleep, I won't be able to concentrate on that big test/conference tomorrow.	Possibly, but my fears may be exaggerated. I may just as well relax or get up and do something enjoyable for a while.

Set your alarm for the same time each morning and get up, regardless of how many hours you have slept (Mimeault & Morin, 1999; National Sleep Foundation, 2000a). By rising at a regular time, you'll encourage yourself to go to sleep at a regular time as well.

Try fantasy. Fantasies or daydreams are almost universal and may occur naturally as we fall asleep. You can allow yourself to "go with" fantasies that occur at bedtime, or purposefully use fantasies to get to sleep. You may be able to ease yourself to sleep by focusing on a sun-drenched beach with waves lapping on the shore or on a walk through a mountain meadow on a summer day. You can construct your own "mind trips" and paint in the details. With mind trips, you conserve fuel and avoid delays at airports.

such measures as weight loss, surgery, and *continuous positive airway pressure*. Airway pressure through the nose keeps the airway open during sleep.

Deep-Sleep Disorders: Sleep Terrors, Bed-Wetting, and Sleepwalking

Sleep terrors, bed-wetting, and sleepwalking all occur during deep (stage 3 or 4) sleep, are more common among children, and may reflect immaturity of the nervous system.

Sleep terrors are similar to, but more severe than, nightmares. They usually occur during deep sleep, whereas nightmares take place during REM sleep. Sleep terrors occur during the first couple of sleep cycles; nightmares are more likely to occur later on. Experiencing a surge in the heart and respiration rates, the dreamer may suddenly sit up, talk incoherently, and move about wildly. The dreamer is never fully awake, returns to sleep, and may recall a vague image as of someone pressing on his or her chest. (Memories of nightmares tend to be more vivid.) Sleep terrors are often decreased by taking a minor tranquilizer at bedtime. The drug reduces the amount of time spent in stage 4 sleep.

Bed-wetting is often seen as a stigma that reflects parental harshness or the child's attempt to punish the parents, but this disorder, too, may stem from immaturity of the nervous system. In most cases it resolves itself before adolescence, often by age 8. Behavior-therapy methods that condition children to awaken when they are about to urinate have been helpful. The drug imipramine often helps, although the reason is not fully known. Sometimes all that is needed is reassurance that no one is to blame for bed-wetting and that most children "outgrow" it.

Perhaps half of all children occasionally talk in their sleep. Nearly 15% walk in their sleep (Mindelo, 1993). Sleepwalkers may roam about almost nightly while their parents fret about the accidents that could befall them. Sleepwalkers typically do not remember their excursions, although they may respond to questions while they are up and about. Contrary to myth, there is no evidence that sleepwalkers become violent if they are awakened, although they may be confused and upset. Mild tranquilizers and maturity typically put an end to sleepwalking.

The Greek word for "sleep" is *hypnos*, which raises the question as to whether there are connections between the state of consciousness we call sleep and another one we call hypnosis. Although many people are hypnotized by being told that they are "going to sleep," we now see many differences between sleep and hypnosis.

REVIEW

(5) EEG research shows that different stages of sleep are characterized by different _____ waves. (6) There are four stages of _____ (NREM) sleep. (7) After a half hour or so of stage _____ sleep, we journey upward through the stages until we enter REM sleep. (8) Because EEG patterns during REM sleep resemble those of the waking state, REM sleep is also called _____ sleep. (9) During a typical 8-hour night, we undergo about _____ trips through the different stages of sleep. (10) Dreams are most vivid during (REM or NREM?) sleep. (11) According to the _____-synthesis model, dreams reflect neural activity. (12) Sleep terrors, bed-wetting, and sleepwalking all occur during _____ sleep.

Pulling It Together: What are the stages of sleep? How do we "descend" and "ascend" through these stages. When do we dream? What is known about why we sleep? What is known about why we dream?

HYPNOSIS: ON BEING ENTRANCED

Perhaps you have seen films in which Count Dracula hypnotized resistant victims into a stupor. Then he could give them a bite in the neck with no further nonsense. Perhaps you have watched a fellow student try to place a friend in a "trance" after reading a book on hypnosis. Or perhaps you have seen an audience member hypnotized in a nightclub act. If so, chances are the person acted as if he or she had returned to childhood, imagined that a snake was about to have a nip, or lay rigid between two chairs for a while. *Question: What is hypnosis?*

Hypnosis, a term derived from the Greek word for sleep, is an altered state of consciousness in which people appear to be highly suggestible and behave as though they are

CLICK4™ *questionnaires about sleep on the Web.*

Sleep terrors ▲ Frightening dreamlike experiences that occur during the deepest stage of NREM sleep. Nightmares, in contrast, occur during REM sleep.

Hypnosis ▲ A condition in which people appear to be highly suggestible and behave as though they are in a trance.

Franz Anton Mesmer

He was the rage of Paris and Vienna. His clients paid a fortune to be "mesmerized." Imagine him dressed in a flowing purple robe, grandly entering mirrored rooms in palaces while music was played by an instrument called a glass harmonica. He commands one man *"Dormez"* ("Sleep"), and the man's head drops to his chest while others gasp. He points an iron rod at a woman, and she shrieks that she feels tingling sensations running through her body. Thus did the Austrian Franz Anton Mesmer (1734–1815) use his theory of animal magnetism to "cure" afflictions ranging from paralysis to "vapors."

Mesmer was trained as a physician, and his marriage to an older, wealthy woman gained him entrance to Viennese society. A music lover, he became skillful with the glass harmonica, which had been invented by Benjamin Franklin. Wolfgang Amadeus Mozart's first opera, *Bastien und Bastienne*, debuted in Mesmer's home when Mozart was 12 years old.

Mesmer's theory held that illnesses could be cured through realignment of the magnetic forces in the body. Although his theory is nonsense, he seems to have sincerely believed in it. Mesmer's life work has contributed to our knowledge of the power of suggestion, to modern hypnotism, and, of course, to dramatic nightclub acts.

in a trance. Hypnosis has only recently become a respectable subject for psychological inquiry. Modern hypnosis seems to have begun with the ideas of Franz Mesmer in the 18th century. Mesmer asserted that everything in the universe was connected by forms of magnetism—which actually may not be far from the mark. He claimed that people, too, could be drawn to one another by "animal magnetism." (No bull's-eye here.) Mesmer used bizarre props to bring people under his "spell." He did manage a respectable cure rate for minor ailments. However, scientists attribute his successes to the placebo effect, not to animal magnetism.

Today hypnotism retains its popularity in nightclubs, but it is also used as an anesthetic in dentistry, childbirth, even surgery (Montgomery et al., 2000). Some psychologists use hypnosis to teach clients how to reduce anxiety or overcome fears (Pinnell & Covino, 2000). A study with 241 surgery patients in a Boston hospital shows how hypnosis can help people deal with pain and anxiety. The patients underwent procedures in which only local anesthetics were used (Lang et al., 2000). They could use as much pain medication as they desired by means of an intravenous tube. Patients who were hypnotized during these procedures needed less additional medication for pain and experienced less anxiety as measured by blood pressure and heart rate. The hypnotized patients focused on pleasant imagery rather than the details of the surgery. Research shows that hypnosis is a useful supplement to other forms of therapy, especially in helping obese people lose weight (Kirsch et al., 1995). Police also use hypnosis to prompt the memories of witnesses.

The state of consciousness called the *hypnotic trance* has traditionally been induced by asking people to narrow their attention to a small light, a spot on the wall, an object held by the hypnotist, or the hypnotist's voice. The hypnotist usually suggests that the person's limbs are becoming warm, heavy, and relaxed. People may also be told that they are becoming sleepy or falling asleep. Hypnosis is *not* sleep, however. This is shown by differences between EEG recordings for the hypnotic trance and the stages of sleep. But the word *sleep* is understood by participants to suggest a hypnotic trance.

It is also possible to induce hypnosis through instructions that direct participants to remain active and alert (Miller et al., 1991). So the effects of hypnosis probably cannot be attributed to relaxation.

People who are readily hypnotized are said to have *hypnotic suggestibility*. Part of "suggestibility" is knowledge of what is expected during the "trance state." Generally speaking, suggestible people are prone to fantasy, can compartmentalize unwanted memories, and want to cooperate with the hypnotist (Barber, 2000). As a result, they pay close attention to the hypnotist's instructions. It is therefore extremely unlikely that someone could be hypnotized against his or her will.

Changes in Consciousness Brought About by Hypnosis

Question: What changes in consciousness are induced by hypnosis? Hypnotists and people who have been hypnotized report that hypnosis can bring about the following changes in consciousness. As you read about them, bear in mind that changes in "consciousness" are inferred from changes in observable behavior and self-reports.

- ▲ *Passivity.* When being hypnotized or in a trance, people await instructions and appear to suspend planning.
- ▲ *Narrowed attention.* People focus on the hypnotist's voice or on a spot of light and avoid attending to background noise or intruding thoughts.
- ▲ *Pseudomemories and hypermnesia.* People may be instructed to report pseudomemories (false memories), or **hypermnesia.** In police investigations, for example, hypnotists attempt to heighten witnesses' memories by instructing them to focus

Hypermnesia ▲ Greatly enhanced or heightened memory.

on details of a crime and then reconstruct the scene. Studies suggest, however, that although people may report recalling more information when they are hypnotized, such information is often incorrect (Weekes et al., 1992).

▲ *Suggestibility.* People may respond to suggestions that an arm is becoming lighter and will rise or that the eyelids are becoming heavier and must close. They may act as though they cannot unlock hands clasped by the hypnotist or bend an arm "made rigid" by the hypnotist. Hypnotized individuals serving as witnesses may incorporate ideas presented by interviewers into their "memories" and report them as facts (Loftus, 1994).

▲ *Playing unusual roles.* Most people expect to play sleepy, relaxed roles, but they may also be able to play roles calling for increased strength or alertness, such as riding a bicycle with less fatigue than usual. In **age regression,** people may play themselves as infants or children. Research shows that many supposed childhood memories and characteristics are played inaccurately. Nonetheless, some people show excellent recall of such details as hairstyle or speech pattern. A person may speak a language forgotten since childhood.

▲ *Perceptual distortions.* Hypnotized people may act as though hypnotically induced **hallucinations** and delusions are real. In the "thirst hallucination," for example, people act as if they are parched, even if they have just had a drink. Psychologists are looking into explanations for such hallucinations. For example, it may be that the hypnotist's command to perceive something that is not there persuades the individual to develop a mental image that is erroneously attributed to the world outside (Woody & Szechtman, 2000). People may also behave as though they cannot hear loud noises, smell odors, or feel pain (Miller & Bowers, 1993).

▲ *Posthypnotic amnesia.* Many people apparently cannot recall events that take place under hypnosis (Barber, 2000; Bowers & Woody, 1996) or, if so directed, that they were hypnotized at all. However, if they are hypnotized again, they can usually recall what occurred when instructed by the hypnotist to do so.

▲ *Posthypnotic suggestion.* For instance, during hypnosis a person may be directed to fall into a deep trance when awake again when given the simple command, "Sleep!" Smokers frequently seek the help of hypnotists to break their habit, and they may be given the suggestion that upon "waking" they will find cigarette smoke aversive (Green & Lynn, 2000). But the effectiveness of hypnosis for helping people quit smoking is uncertain (Lancaster et al., 2000).

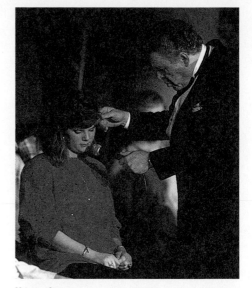

Hypnosis.
Hypnotized people become passive and follow the suggestions of the hypnotist. Only recently has hypnosis become a respectable subject for psychological inquiry.

CONTROVERSY IN PSYCHOLOGY

How Can Psychologists Explain Hypnosis?

Hypnotism is no longer explained in terms of animal magnetism, but psychodynamic and learning theorists have offered explanations. According to Freud, hypnotized adults permit themselves to return to childish modes of responding that emphasize fantasy and impulse rather than fact and logic. Modern views of hypnosis are quite different. *Question: How do modern psychologists explain the effects of hypnosis?*

Role Theory   Theodore Sarbin offers a **role theory** view of hypnosis (Sarbin & Coe, 1972). He points out that the changes in behavior attributed to the hypnotic trance can be successfully imitated when people are instructed to behave *as though* they were hypnotized. For example, people can lie rigid between two chairs whether they are hypnotized or not. Also, people cannot be hypnotized unless they are familiar with the hypnotic "role"—the behavior that constitutes the trance. Sarbin is not saying that participants *fake* the hypnotic role. Research evidence suggests that most people who are hypnotized are not faking (Kinnunen et al., 1994). Instead, Sarbin is suggesting that people *allow* themselves to enact this role under the hypnotist's directions.

Response Set Theory   The **response set theory** of hypnosis is closely related to role theory. It suggests that response expectancies (the things we know we are expected to do) play a key role in the production of personal experiences, and also in experiences suggested by the hypnotist (Kirsch, 2000).

Age regression ▲ In hypnosis, taking on the role of childhood, commonly accompanied by vivid recollections of one's past.

Hallucinations ▲ Perceptions in the absence of sensation.

Role theory ▲ A theory that explains hypnotic events in terms of the person's ability to *act as though* he or she were hypnotized. Role theory differs from faking in that participants cooperate and focus on hypnotic suggestions instead of pretending to be hypnotized.

Response set theory ▲ The view that response expectancies play a key role in the production of the experiences suggested by the hypnotist.

Role theory and response set theory appear to be supported by research evidence that "suggestible" people want to be hypnotized, are good role players, have vivid and absorbing imaginations, and also know what is expected of them (Barber, 2000; Kirsch, 2000). The fact that the behaviors shown by hypnotized people can be mimicked by people who know what is expected of them means that we need not resort to the concept of the "hypnotic trance"—an unusual and mystifying altered state of awareness—to explain hypnotic events.

Neodissociation Theory   Runners frequently get through the pain and tedium of long-distance races by *dissociating*—by imagining themselves elsewhere, doing other things. (My students inform me that they manage the pain and tedium of *other* instructors' classes in the same way.) Ernest Hilgard (1994) similarly explains hypnotic phenomena through **neodissociation theory.** This is the view that we can selectively focus our attention on one thing (like hypnotic suggestions) and dissociate ourselves from the things going on around us—just as the surgery patients in the Boston study focused on pleasant thoughts and not on the surgery itself (Lang et al., 2000).

Participants in one experiment related to neodissociation theory were hypnotized and instructed to submerge their arms in ice water—causing "cold pressor pain" (Miller et al., 1991). Participants were given suggestions to the effect that they were not in pain, however. Highly hypnotizable people reported dissociative experiences that allowed them to avoid the perception of pain, such as imagining that they were at the beach or that their limbs were floating in air above the ice water.

Although hypnotized people may be focusing on the hypnotist's suggestions and perhaps imagining themselves to be somewhere else, they still tend to perceive their actual surroundings peripherally. In a sense, we do this all the time. We are not fully conscious, or aware, of everything going on about us. Rather, at any given moment we selectively focus on events such as tests, dates, or television shows that seem important or relevant. Yet, while taking a test we may be peripherally aware of the color of the wall or the sound of rain.

Role theory and neodissociation theory do not suggest that the phenomena of hypnosis are phony. Instead, they suggest that we do not need to explain these events through an altered state of awareness called a trance. Hypnosis may not be special at all. Rather, it is *we* who are special—through our imagination, our role-playing ability, and our capacity to divide our consciousness—concentrating now on one event that we deem important, and concentrating on another event later.

Let us now consider two other states of consciousness that involve different ways of focusing our attention: meditation and biofeedback.

REVIEW

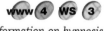

CLICK4™ *more information on hypnosis and its representation in society.*

CLICK4™ *FAQs on Hypnosis.com.*

(13) Franz Mesmer explained the hypnotic "trance" through his concept of animal _____. (14) Hypnosis typically brings about the following changes in consciousness: passivity, narrowed attention, _____ (heightened memory), suggestibility, assumption of unusual roles, perceptual distortions, posthypnotic amnesia, and posthypnotic suggestion. (15) According to Freud, the hypnotic trance represents _____. (16) According to role theory, hypnotized people enact the _____ of being in a trance. (17) According to _____ set theory, knowledge of what one is expected to do is a key component of being hypnotized.

Pulling It Together: Hypnotists often induce a "trance" by instructing people to "sleep." Is hypnosis sleep? Why does the command "Sleep" induce a trance?

MEDITATION: LETTING THE WORLD FADE AWAY

Question: What is meditation? The dictionary defines *meditation* as the act or process of thinking. But the concept usually suggests thinking deeply about the universe or about one's place in the world, often within a spiritual context. As the term is com-

Neodissociation theory ▲ A theory of hypnotic events as the splitting of consciousness.

monly used by psychologists, however, meditation refers to various ways of focusing one's consciousness to alter one's relationship to the world. As used by psychologists, ironically, *meditation* can also refer to a process in which people seem to suspend thinking and allow the world to fade away.

The kinds of meditation that psychologists and other kinds of helping professionals speak of are *not* the first definition you find in the dictionary. Rather, they tend to refer to rituals, exercises, and even passive observation—activities that alter the normal relationship between the person and her or his environment. They are various methods of suspending problem solving, planning, worries, and awareness of the events of the day. These methods alter consciousness—that is, the normal focus of attention—and help people cope with stress by inducing feelings of relaxation.

Let us consider one common form of meditation in more detail. **Transcendental meditation (TM)** is a simplified form of Far Eastern meditation that was brought to the United States by the Maharishi Mahesh Yogi in 1959. Hundreds of thousands of Americans practice TM by repeating and concentrating on *mantras*—words or sounds that are claimed to help the person achieve an altered state of consciousness. TM has a number of spiritual goals, such as expanding consciousness so that it encompasses spiritual kinds of experiences, but there are also more worldly goals, such as reducing anxiety and normalizing blood pressure.

Question: What are the effects of meditation? In early research, Herbert Benson (1975) found no scientific evidence that TM expands consciousness (how do you measure spiritual experience with earthly instruments?), despite the claims of many of its practitioners. However, TM lowered the heart and respiration rates—changes that can be measured through commonly used medical instruments—and also produced what Benson labeled a *relaxation response*. The blood pressure of people with hypertension—a risk factor in cardiovascular disease—decreased. In fact, people who meditated twice daily tended to show more normal blood pressure through the day. Meditators produced more frequent alpha waves—brain waves associated with feelings of relaxation. Meditation also increases night-time concentrations of the hormone melatonin, which is relaxing and helps people get to sleep (Tooley et al., 2000).

In more recent years, an apparently careful research program has been conducted at the College of Maharishi Vedic Medicine in Fairfield, Iowa (Ready, 2000). It has focused on older African Americans because African Americans are more prone to hypertension than European Americans. Two studies compared the effects of TM, progressive relaxation (a muscle relaxation technique), and a "health education" placebo on high blood pressure (Alexander et al., 1996; Schneider et al., 1995). They both found that TM was significantly more effective at reducing high blood pressure than progressive relaxation or the placebo. A third study reported that African Americans aged 20 and above who practiced TM for 6 to 9 months were significantly more likely than the health education placebo to reduce the progression of atherosclerosis (hardening of the arteries) (Castillo-Richmond et al., 2000).

Meditation.
People use many forms of meditation to try to expand their inner awareness and experience inner harmony. Although practitioners of some forms of meditation claim that it has spiritual effects, research does suggest that meditation can have healthful effects on the blood pressure and other health-related bodily functions.

 **REFLECT**
Do you know anyone who has tried meditation? What was the purpose? Were the effects consistent with what is reported in this text? Why or why not?

REVIEW

(18) In meditation, one focuses "passively" on a _____ in order to alter the normal person–environment relationship. (19) Investigators have shown that meditation can reduce high _____ pressure.

Pulling It Together: What are the similarities and differences between sleep, hypnosis, and meditation?

BIOFEEDBACK: GETTING IN TOUCH WITH THE UNTOUCHABLE

Let us begin our discussion of biofeedback by recounting some remarkable experiments in which psychologist Neal E. Miller (1969) trained laboratory rats to increase or decrease their heart rates. His procedure was simple but ingenious. As discovered by psychologists James Olds and Peter Milner, there is a "pleasure center" in the rat's hypo-

CLICK4™ *an essay assignment on transcendental meditation.*

Transcendental meditation (TM) ▲ The simplified form of meditation brought to the United States by the Maharishi Mahesh Yogi and used as a method for coping with stress.

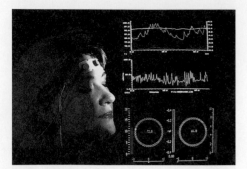

Biofeedback.
Biofeedback is a system that provides, or "feeds back," information about a bodily function to an organism. Through biofeedback training, people have learned to gain voluntary control over a number of functions that are normally automatic, such as heart rate and blood pressure.

▲ **REFLECT**
How do you think that a rat manages to elevate or decrease its heart rate? Does it seem pointless to speculate on an answer? Why or why not?

CLICK4™ *a quiz covering the first half of this chapter.*

Biofeedback training (BFT) ▲ The systematic feeding back to an organism information about a bodily function so that the organism can gain control of that function.
Electromyograph (EMG) ▲ An instrument that measures muscle tension.
Psychoactive substances ▲ Drugs that have psychological effects such as stimulation or distortion of perceptions.

thalamus. A small burst of electricity in this center is strongly reinforcing: Rats learn to do what they can, such as pressing a lever, to obtain this shock.

Miller implanted electrodes in the rats' pleasure centers. Then some rats were given an electric shock whenever their heart rate happened to increase. Other rats received a shock when their heart rate went lower. In other words, one group of rats was consistently "rewarded" (that is, shocked) when their heart rate showed an increase. The other group was consistently rewarded for a decrease in heart rate. After a single 90-minute training session, the rats learned to alter their heart rates by as much as 20% in the direction for which they had been rewarded.

Miller's research was an early example of **biofeedback training (BFT).** *Question: What is biofeedback training?* Biofeedback is a system that provides, or "feeds back," information about a bodily function. Miller used electrical stimulation of the brain to feed back information to rats when they had engaged in a targeted bodily response (in this case, raised or lowered their heart rates). Somehow the rats then used this information to raise or lower their heart rates voluntarily.

Similarly, people have learned to change various bodily functions voluntarily, including heart rate, that were once considered to be beyond their control.

However, electrodes are not implanted in people's brains. Rather, people hear a "blip" or observe some other signal that informs them when the targeted response is being displayed.

Question: How is biofeedback training used? BFT has been used in many ways, including helping people combat stress, tension, and anxiety. For example, people can learn to emit alpha waves (and feel somewhat more relaxed) through feedback from an EEG. A blip may increase in frequency whenever alpha waves are being emitted. The psychologist's instructions are simply to "make the blip go faster." An **electromyograph (EMG),** which monitors muscle tension, is commonly used to help people become more aware of muscle tension in the forehead and elsewhere and to learn to lower the tension. Through the use of other instruments, people have learned to lower their heart rate, their blood pressure, and the amount of sweat in the palm of the hand. All of these changes are relaxing. Biofeedback is widely used by sports psychologists to teach athletes how to relax muscle groups that are unessential to the task at hand so that they can control anxiety and tension.

People have also learned to elevate the temperature of a finger. Why bother, you ask? It happens that limbs become subjectively warmer when more blood flows into them. Increasing the temperature of a finger—that is, altering patterns of blood flow in the body—helps some people control migraine headaches, which may be caused by dysfunctional circulatory patterns.

Sleep, hypnosis, meditation, and biofeedback training all involve "natural" ways of deploying our attention or consciousness. Some altered states depend on the ingestion of psychoactive chemical substances we call "drugs." Let us now deploy our attention to the effects of alcohol and other drugs.

REVIEW

(20) Neal Miller taught rats to increase or decrease their _____ rates by giving them an electric shock in their "pleasure centers" when they performed the targeted response. (21) Through biofeedback training, people and lower animals have learned to control _____ functions like the heart rate.

Pulling It Together: Why does the method of biofeedback blur the lines between voluntary behavior (such as moving an arm) and involuntary behavior (such as changing one's heart rate)?

ALTERING CONSCIOUSNESS THROUGH DRUGS

The world is a supermarket of **psychoactive substances,** or drugs. The United States is flooded with drugs that distort perceptions and change mood—drugs that take you up, let you down, and move you across town. Some people use drugs because their friends do or because their parents tell them not to. Some are seeking pleasure; others are seeking inner truth or escape.

For better or worse, drugs are part of American life. Young people often become involved with drugs that impair their ability to learn at school and are connected with reckless behavior (Basen-Engquist et al., 1996). Alcohol is the most popular drug on high school and college campuses (Johnston et al., 2000). More than 40% of college students have tried marijuana, and 1 in 6 or 7 smokes it regularly. Many Americans take **depressants** to get to sleep at night and **stimulants** to get going in the morning. Karl Marx charged that "religion . . . is the opium of the people," but heroin is the real "opium of the people." Cocaine was, until recently, a toy of the well-to-do, but price breaks have brought it into the lockers of high-school students.

Substance Abuse and Dependence: Crossing the Line

Where does drug use end and abuse begin? *Question: What are substance abuse and dependence?* The American Psychiatric Association (2000) defines **substance abuse** as repeated use of a substance despite the fact that it is causing or compounding social, occupational, psychological, or physical problems. If you are missing school or work because you are drunk or "sleeping it off," you are abusing alcohol. The amount you drink is not as crucial as the fact that your pattern of use disrupts your life.

Dependence is more severe than abuse. Dependence has both behavioral and biological aspects (American Psychiatric Association, 2000). Behaviorally, dependence is often characterized by loss of control over one's use of the substance. Dependent people may organize their lives around getting and using a substance. Biological or physiological dependence is typified by tolerance, withdrawal symptoms, or both. **Tolerance** is the body's habituation to a substance so that with regular usage, higher doses are required to achieve similar effects. There are characteristic withdrawal symptoms, or an **abstinence syndrome,** when the level of usage suddenly drops off. The abstinence syndrome for alcohol includes anxiety, tremors, restlessness, weakness, rapid pulse, and high blood pressure.

When doing without a drug, people who are *psychologically* dependent show signs of anxiety (such as shakiness, rapid pulse, and sweating) that may be similar to abstinence syndromes. Because of these signs, they may believe that they are physiologically dependent on—or addicted to—a drug when they are actually psychologically dependent. But symptoms of abstinence from some drugs are unmistakably physiological. One is **delirium tremens** ("the DTs"), experienced by some chronic alcoholics when they suddenly lower their intake of alcohol. The DTs are characterized by heavy sweating, restlessness, general disorientation, and terrifying hallucinations—often of crawling animals.

CLICK4™ *the Web site of "Monitoring the Future," the University of Michigan group that surveys student drug use.*

> ▲ **REFLECT**
> Do you know anyone who has a problem with substance abuse or dependence? Does he or she admit to the problem or deny it? What can be done about the problem?

Causal Factors in Substance Abuse and Dependence

Question: What are the causes of substance abuse and dependence? Substance abuse and dependence usually begin with experimental use in adolescence (Chassin et al., 2000). Why do people experiment with drugs? Reasons include curiosity, conformity to peer pressure, parental use, rebelliousness, escape from boredom or pressure, and the seeking of excitement or pleasure (Chassin et al., 2000; Finn et al., 2000; Wills et al., 2000; Unger et al., 2000). There are even some parents who introduce their children to illicit drugs (Leinwand, 2000).

A CDC survey of more than 15,000 teenagers across the United States found that use of drugs and cigarettes has increased over the past decade, despite public-education campaigns about the risks (Centers for Disease Control, 2000b). Cigarette smoking was up slightly, with 35% of teenagers reporting lighting up in the previous month. The number of teens who reported smoking marijuana in the previous month nearly doubled from about 15% in 1991 to 27% at the turn of the millennium. Self-reported cocaine use also doubled in the same period, from about 2% to 4%. Alcohol use (within the past month) remained steady at about 50%. However, drinking in early adolescence is a risk factor for alcohol abuse later on (De Wit et al., 2000). Let us have a look at some theories of substance abuse.

Depressant ▲ A drug that lowers the rate of activity of the nervous system.

Stimulant ▲ A drug that increases activity of the nervous system.

Substance abuse ▲ Persistent use of a substance even though it is causing or compounding problems in meeting the demands of life.

Tolerance ▲ Habituation to a drug, with the result that increasingly higher doses of the drug are needed to achieve similar effects.

Abstinence syndrome ▲ A characteristic cluster of symptoms that results from sudden decrease in an addictive drug's level of usage.

Delirium tremens ▲ A condition characterized by sweating, restlessness, disorientation, and hallucinations. The DTs occurs in some chronic alcohol users when there is a sudden decrease in usage.

Psychological Views   Social-cognitive theorists suggest that people commonly try tranquilizing agents such as Valium (the generic name is diazepam) and alcohol on the basis of a recommendation or observation of others. Expectations about the effects of a substance are powerful predictors of its use (Cumsille et al., 2000). In one study, researchers studied a diary of stress, expectations about alcohol, and drinking (Armeli et al., 2000). They found that men who expected that alcohol would lessen feelings of stress were more likely to drink on stressful days. But men who expected that alcohol would impair their coping ability drank *less* on stressful days.

Use of a substance may be reinforced by peers or by the drug's positive effects on mood and its reduction of unpleasant sensations such as anxiety, fear, and tension (Unger et al., 2000). For people who are physiologically dependent, avoidance of withdrawal symptoms is also reinforcing. Carrying a supply of the substance is reinforcing because one need not worry about doing without it. Some people, for example, do not leave home without it—Valium, that is.

Parents who use drugs may increase their children's knowledge of drugs. They also, in effect, show their children when to use them—for example, when drinking alcohol to reduce tension or to "lubricate" social interactions (Stacy & Newcomb, 1999).

Biological Views   Certain people may have a genetic predisposition toward physiological dependence on various substances, including alcohol, opioids, cocaine, and nicotine (Ellenbroek et al., 2000; Finn et al., 2000; Kendler et al., 2000a, 2000d). For example, the biological children of alcoholics who are reared by adoptive parents seem more likely to develop alcohol-related problems than the natural children of the adoptive parents. An inherited tendency toward alcoholism may involve greater sensitivity to alcohol (that is, greater enjoyment of it) and greater tolerance of it (Pihl et al., 1990). College students with alcoholic parents exhibit better muscular control and visual-motor coordination when they drink than do college students whose parents are not alcoholics. They also feel less intoxicated when they drink (Pihl et al., 1990).

There are many kinds of psychoactive drugs. Some are depressants, others stimulants, and still others hallucinogenics. Let us consider the effects of these drugs on consciousness.

REVIEW

(22) Substance use is considered _____ when it causes or worsens social, occupational, psychological, or physical problems. (23) Substance dependence is characterized by loss of _____ over the substance. (24) Physiological dependence is evidenced by tolerance or by an _____ syndrome when one discontinues use of the substance. (25) Some people have genetic predispositions to become _____ dependent on certain substances.

Pulling It Together: Why do people experiment with various substances? What factors contribute to continuing use of them?

DEPRESSANTS

Depressant drugs generally act by slowing the activity of the central nervous system. There are also effects that are specific to each depressant drug. In this section we consider the effects of alcohol, opiates, barbiturates, and methaqualone.

Alcohol — The Swiss Army Knife of Psychoactive Substances

No drug has meant so much to so many as alcohol. Alcohol is our dinnertime relaxant, our bedtime sedative, our cocktail-party social facilitator. We use alcohol to celebrate holy days, applaud our accomplishments, and express joyous wishes. The young assert their maturity with alcohol. Alcohol is used at least occasionally by the majority of high-school and college students (Johnston et al., 2000; Wilgoren, 2000). Older people use alcohol to stimulate circulation in peripheral areas of the body. Alcohol even kills germs on surface wounds.

People use alcohol like a Swiss Army knife. It does it all. Alcohol is the all-purpose medicine you can buy without prescription. It is the relief from anxiety, depression, or loneliness that you can swallow in public without criticism or stigma (Bonin et al., 2000; Swendsen et al., 2000). A man who takes a Valium tablet may look weak. A man who downs a bottle of beer may be perceived as "macho."

But the army knife also has a sharp blade. It is also true that no drug has been so abused as alcohol. Ten million to 20 million Americans are alcoholics. In contrast, 750,000 to 1 million use heroin regularly and about 800,000 use cocaine regularly (O'Brien, 1996). Excessive drinking has been linked to lower productivity, loss of employment, and downward movement in social status. Yet, half of all Americans use alcohol regularly. Experiments with rats (Feola et al., 2000) and humans (De Wit et al., 2000) show that alcohol lowers inhibitions. Binge drinking (having five or more drinks in a row) is connected with aggressive behavior, poor grades, sexual promiscuity, and serious accidents (Vik et al., 2000). Nevertheless, 44% of college students binge at least twice a month, and half this number binge three or more times every two weeks (Wilgoren, 2000). Despite widespread marijuana use, alcohol is the drug of choice among adolescents. The nearby Self-Assessment offers insight on reasons for drinking.

Effects of Alcohol
Question: What are the effects of alcohol? The effects of alcohol vary with the dose and the duration of use. Low doses of alcohol may be stimulating. Higher doses of alcohol have a sedative effect, which is why alcohol is classified as a depressant. Alcohol relaxes people and deadens minor aches and pains. Alcohol also intoxicates: It impairs cognitive functioning, slurs the speech, and reduces motor coordination. Alcohol is involved in about half of the fatal automobile accidents in the United States.

Alcohol consumption is connected with a drop-off in sexual activity (Leigh, 1993). Yet, because alcohol lessens inhibitions, drinkers may do things they would not do if they were sober, such as engage in sexual activity on the first date or engage in unprotected sex (MacDonald et al., 2000; Vik et al., 2000). Why? Perhaps alcohol impairs the thought processes needed to inhibit impulses (Steele & Josephs, 1990). When drunk, people may be less able to foresee the consequences of their behavior. They may also be less likely to summon up their moral beliefs. Then, too, alcohol induces feelings of elation and euphoria that may wash away doubts. Alcohol is also associated with a liberated social role in our culture. Drinkers may place the blame on alcohol ("It's the alcohol, not me"), even though they choose to drink.

Adolescent involvement with alcohol has repeatedly been linked to poor school grades and other stressors (Wills et al., 2000). Drinking can, of course, contribute to poor grades and other problems, but adolescents may drink to reduce academic and other stresses.

Regardless of how or why one starts drinking, regular drinking can lead to physiological dependence. People are then motivated to drink to avoid withdrawal symptoms. Still, even when alcoholics have "dried out"—withdrawn from alcohol—many return to drinking (Schuckit, 1996). Perhaps they still want to use alcohol as a way of coping with stress or as an excuse for failure.

REFLECT
Do you believe that people can be held responsible for their behavior when they have been drinking? Why or why not?

www 4 L 8
CLICK4™ *the Web site of the National Institute on Alcohol Abuse and Alcoholism.*

CONTROVERSY IN PSYCHOLOGY

Is a Drink a Day Good for You?

What are the physical and cognitive effects of drinking? The effects of alcohol on health are complex. Light drinking can be beneficial. One effect of having a drink or two a day is to increase levels of high-density lipoprotein (HDL, or "good" cholesterol) in the bloodstream and thus decreases the risk of cardiovascular disorders (Gaziano et al., 1993). Another positive effect is cognitive: A study of 400 older adults by researchers at the Institute of Psychiatry in London found that those who had been having a drink a day from before the age of 60 were less likely to see their cognitive abilities decline with age (Cervilla et al., 2000). A drink or two a day may even cut the risk of Alzheimer's disease (Norton, 2000). According to the London researchers (Cervilla et al., 2000), the path to

SELF-ASSESSMENT

Why Do You Drink?

Do you drink? If so, why? To enhance your pleasure? To cope with your problems? To help you in your social encounters? Half of all Americans use alcohol for a variety of reasons. Perhaps as many as 1 user in 10 is an alcoholic.

To gain insight into your reasons for using alcohol, respond to the following items by circling the *T* if an item is true or mostly true for you, or the *F* if an item is false or mostly false for you. Then turn to the answer key in Appendix B.

1. T F I find it very unpleasant to do without alcohol for some time.

2. T F Alcohol makes it easier for me to talk to other people.

3. T F I drink to appear more grown-up and more sophisticated.

4. T F When I drink, the future looks brighter to me.

5. T F I like the taste of what I drink.

6. T F If I go without a drink for some time, I am not bothered or uncomfortable.

7. T F I feel more relaxed and less tense about things when I drink.

8. T F I drink so that I will fit in better with the crowd.

9. T F I worry less about things when I drink.

10. T F I have a drink when I get together with the family.

11. T F I have a drink as part of my religious ceremonies.

12. T F I have a drink when a toothache or some other pain is disturbing me.

13. T F I feel much more powerful when I have a drink.

14. T F You really can't blame me for the things I do when I have been drinking.

15. T F I have a drink before a big test, date, or interview when I'm afraid of how well I'll do.

16. T F I find I have a drink for the taste alone.

17. T F I've found a drink in my hand when I can't remember putting it there.

18. T F I'll have a drink when I feel "blue" or want to take my mind off my cares and worries.

19. T F I can do better socially and sexually after having a drink or two.

20. T F Drinking makes me do stupid things.

21. T F Sometimes when I have a few drinks, I can't get to work.

22. T F I feel more caring and giving after having a drink or two.

23. T F I drink because I like the look of a drinker.

24. T F I like to drink more on festive occasions.

25. T F When a friend or I have done something well, we're likely to have a drink or two.

26. T F I have a drink when some problem is nagging away at me.

27. T F I find drinking pleasurable.

28. T F I like the "high" of drinking.

29. T F Sometimes I pour a drink without realizing I still have one that is unfinished.

30. T F I feel I can better get others to do what I want when I've had a drink or two.

31. T F Having a drink keeps my mind off my problems at home, at school, or at work.

32. T F I get a real gnawing hunger for a drink when I haven't had one for a while.

33. T F A drink or two relaxes me.

34. T F Things look better when I've had a drink or two.

35. T F My mood is much better after I've been drinking.

36. T F I see things more clearly when I've been drinking.

37. T F A drink or two enhances the pleasure of sex and food.

38. T F When I'm out of alcohol, I immediately buy more.

39. T F I would have done much better on some things if it weren't for alcohol.

40. T F When I have run out of alcohol, I find it almost unbearable until I can get some more.

CLICK4™ *an interactive version of this Self-Assessment.*

positive cognitive results from alcohol may be through the heart: Small doses of alcohol may help maintain a healthful flow of oxygen-laden blood to the brain. On the other hand, the positive effects of alcohol tend to disappear among people who drink heavily (Cervilla et al., 2000). Also, there is the danger that people who drink lightly to achieve positive effects may run into problems with self-control.

Now, for the negative. As a food, alcohol is fattening. Even so, chronic drinkers may be malnourished. Although it is high in calories, alcohol does not contain nutrients such as vitamins and proteins. Moreover, it can interfere with the body's absorption of vitamins, particularly thiamine, a B vitamin. Thus chronic drinking can lead to a number of disorders such as **cirrhosis of the liver,** which has been linked to protein deficiency, and **Wernicke-Korsakoff syndrome,** which has been linked to vitamin B deficiency. Chronic heavy drinking has been linked to cardiovascular disorders and cancer. In particular, heavy drinking places women at risk for breast cancer (McTiernan, 1997). Drinking by a pregnant woman may also harm the embryo.

So, is a drink a day good for you? Apparently, yes. However, most health professionals are reluctant to advise that people drink regularly, though lightly. One cause for concern is that regular drinkers may lose control of the quantity of alcohol they ingest, become physiologically dependent and then suffer the effects of heavy drinking.

DIVERSITY *Alcoholism, Gender, and Ethnicity* Men are more likely than women to become alcoholics. Why? A cultural explanation is that tighter social constraints are usually placed on women. A biological explanation is that alcohol hits women harder. If, for example, you have the impression that alcohol "goes to women's heads" more quickly than to men's, you are probably correct. Women seem to be more affected by alcohol because they metabolize very little of it in the stomach. Women have less of an enzyme that metabolizes alcohol in the stomach than men do (Lieber, 1990). Thus alcohol reaches women's bloodstream and brain relatively intact. Women metabolize alcohol mainly in the liver. According to one health professional, for women "drinking alcohol has the same effect as injecting it intravenously" (Lieber, 1990). Strong stuff indeed.

Ethnicity is connected with alcohol abuse. Native Americans and Irish Americans have the highest rates of alcoholism in the United States. Jewish Americans have relatively low rates of alcoholism, a fact for which a cultural explanation is usually offered. Jewish Americans tend to expose children to alcohol (wine) early in life, but they do so within a strong family or religious context. Wine is offered in small quantities, with consequent low blood alcohol levels. Alcohol therefore is not connected with rebellion, aggression, or failure in Jewish culture.

There are also biological explanations for low levels of drinking among some ethnic groups (e.g., Asian Americans). Asians are more likely than Europeans and European Americans to show a "flushing response" to alcohol, as evidenced by redness of the face, rapid heart rate, dizziness, and headaches (Ellickson et al., 1992). Such sensitivity to alcohol may inhibit immoderate drinking among Asian Americans as it may among women.

Treating Alcoholism Alcoholics Anonymous (AA) is the most widely used program to treat alcoholism, yet research suggests that other approaches work as well for most people (Ouimette et al., 1997; "Tailoring treatments," 1997). The National Institute on Alcohol Abuse and Alcoholism funded an 8-year study in which more than 1,700 problem drinkers were randomly assigned to AA's 12-step program, cognitive-behavioral therapy, or "motivational-enhancement therapy." The cognitive-behavioral treatment taught problem drinkers how to cope with temptations and how to refuse offers of drinks. Motivational enhancement was designed to enhance drinkers' desires to help themselves. The treatments worked equally well for most people with some exceptions. For example, people with psychological problems fared somewhat better with cognitive-behavioral therapy.

Research is also under way on the use of medicines in treating problem drinking. Disulfiram (Antabuse), for example, cannot be mixed with alcohol. People who take disulfiram experience symptoms such as nausea and vomiting if they drink (Schuckit, 1996).

Opiates

Opiates are a group of **narcotics** that are derived from the opium poppy, from which they obtain their name. **Opioids** are similar in chemical structure but are synthesized in a laboratory. The ancient Sumerians gave the opium poppy its name: It means "plant of joy." Opiates include morphine, heroin, codeine, Demerol, and similar drugs. *Question: What are the effects of opiates?* The major medical application of this group of drugs is relief from pain.

Morphine was introduced in the United States in the 1860s, at about the time of the Civil War, and in Europe during the Franco-Prussian War. It was used liberally to deaden

Why Does Alcohol Affect Women More Quickly Than Men?
Alcohol "goes to women's heads" more quickly, even when we control for body weight.

CLICK4™ *an exploration of the different approaches of Moderation Management and Alcoholics Anonymous.*

Cirrhosis of the liver ▲ A disease caused by protein deficiency in which connective fibers replace active liver cells, impeding circulation of the blood. Alcohol does not contain protein; therefore, persons who drink excessively may be prone to this disease.

Wernicke-Korsakoff syndrome ▲ A cluster of symptoms associated with chronic alcohol abuse and characterized by confusion, memory impairment, and filling in gaps in memory with false information (confabulation).

Opiates ▲ A group of narcotics derived from the opium poppy that provide a euphoric rush and depress the nervous system.

Narcotics ▲ Drugs used to relieve pain and induce sleep. The term is usually reserved for opiates.

Opioids ▲ Chemicals that act on opiate receptors but are not derived from the opium poppy.

CLICK4™ *a video on opiates and their interaction with endorphins.*

▲ REFLECT

Do you think that cocaine and narcotics such as heroin are the most dangerous psychoactive drugs? Why or why not?

pain from wounds. Physiological dependence on morphine therefore became known as the "soldier's disease." Little stigma was attached to dependence before morphine became a legally restricted substance. Even so, 70% of people in the United States believe that drugs such as morphine—even in high doses—should be available to people who are suffering severe pain ("Painkillers are fine," 1998).

Heroin was so named because it made people feel "heroic." It was also hailed as the "hero" that would cure physiological dependence on morphine.

Heroin can provide a strong euphoric "rush." Users claim that it is so pleasurable it can eradicate any thought of food or sex. Although regular users develop tolerance for heroin, high doses can cause drowsiness and stupor, alter time perception, and impair judgment.

Heroin is illegal. Because the penalties for possession or sale are high, it is also expensive. For this reason, many physiologically dependent people support their habit through dealing (selling heroin), prostitution, or selling stolen goods.

Methadone is a synthetic opioid. It has been used to treat physiological dependence on heroin in the same way that heroin was once used to treat physiological dependence on morphine. Methadone is slower acting than heroin and does not provide the thrilling rush. Some people must be maintained on methadone for many years before they can be gradually withdrawn from it (O'Brien, 1996). Some must be maintained on methadone indefinitely because they are unwilling to undergo any withdrawal symptoms.

Narcotics can have distressing withdrawal syndromes, especially when used in high doses. Such syndromes may begin with flu-like symptoms and progress through tremors, cramps, chills alternating with sweating, rapid pulse, high blood pressure, insomnia, vomiting, and diarrhea. However, these syndromes are variable from one person to another.

Many people who obtain prescriptions for opiates for pain relief neither experience a euphoric rush nor become psychologically dependent on them (Joranson et al., 2000). If they no longer need opiates for pain but have become physiologically dependent on them, they can usually quit with few, if any, side effects by gradually decreasing their dosage (Joranson et al., 2000). Thus difficulty or ease of withdrawal may be connected with one's motives for using psychoactive drugs. Those who are seeking habitual relief from psychological pain seem to become more dependent on them than people who are seeking time-limited relief from physical pain.

Barbiturates and Methaqualone

Question: What are the effects of barbiturates and methaqualone? **Barbiturates** are depressants with several medical uses, including relief of anxiety and tension, relief from pain, and treatment of epilepsy, high blood pressure, and insomnia. Barbiturates lead rapidly to physiological and psychological dependence. The effects of the depressant **methaqualone** are similar to those of barbiturates. Methaqualone also leads to physiological dependence.

Barbiturates and methaqualone are popular as street drugs because they are relaxing and produce mild euphoria. High doses of barbiturates result in drowsiness, motor impairment, slurred speech, irritability, and poor judgment. A physiologically dependent person who is withdrawn abruptly from barbiturates may experience severe convulsions and die. Because of additive effects, it is dangerous to mix alcohol and other depressants.

REVIEW

(26) Alcohol is an intoxicating depressant that (does or does not?) lead to physiological dependence. (27) Women seem to be (more or less?) affected by alcohol than men. (28) Opiates are depressants that are used in medicine to reduce _____, but they are bought "on the street" because of the euphoric rush they provide. (29) The synthetic narcotic _____ has been used to treat heroin dependence. (30) Barbiturates are used medically to treat _____.

Barbiturate ▲ An addictive depressant used to relieve anxiety or induce sleep.

Methaqualone ▲ An addictive depressant. Often called "ludes."

Pulling It Together: If depressants have medical uses, why are health professionals reluctant to prescribe them?

STIMULANTS

All stimulants increase the activity of the nervous system. Their other effects vary somewhat, and some contribute to feelings of euphoria and self-confidence.

Amphetamines

Question: What are the effects of amphetamines?   **Amphetamines** are a group of stimulants that were first used by soldiers during World War II to help them remain alert through the night. Truck drivers have used them to stay awake all night. Amphetamines have become perhaps more widely known through students, who have used them for all-night cram sessions, and through dieters, who use them because they reduce hunger. Because amphetamines stimulate cognitive activity, they apparently help rats (Feola et al., 2000) and humans (De Wit et al., 2000) control impulses.

Called speed, uppers, bennies (for Benzedrine), and dexies (for Dexedrine), these drugs are often abused for the euphoric rush they can produce in high doses. Some people swallow amphetamines in pill form or inject liquid methedrine, the strongest form, into their veins. They may stay awake and high for days on end. Such highs must end. People who have been on prolonged highs sometimes "crash," or fall into a deep sleep or depression. Some people commit suicide when crashing.

A related stimulant, methylphenidate (Ritalin), is widely used to treat **attention-deficit hyperactivity disorder** in children. Although critics believe that Ritalin is prescribed too freely (Pear, 2000), Ritalin has been shown to increase attention span, decrease aggressive and disruptive behavior, and lead to academic gains (Klorman et al., 1994). Why should Ritalin, a stimulant, calm children? Hyperactivity may be connected with immaturity of the cerebral cortex, and Ritalin may stimulate the cortex to exercise control over more primitive centers in the brain.

High doses of amphetamines may cause restlessness, insomnia, loss of appetite, hallucinations, paranoid delusions (e.g., false ideas that others are eavesdropping or intend to harm them), and irritability.

Cocaine

Do you recall the commercials claiming that "Coke adds life"? Given its caffeine and sugar content, "Coke"—Coca-Cola, that is—should provide quite a lift. But Coca-Cola hasn't been "the real thing" since 1906, when the company discontinued the use of cocaine in its formula. Cocaine is derived from coca leaves—the plant from which the soft drink took its name.

Question: What are the effects of cocaine?   Cocaine is a stimulant that produces euphoria, reduces hunger, deadens pain, and bolsters self-confidence. Only about 4% of adolescents aged 15 to 19 have used cocaine within the past month (Centers for Disease Control, 2000b). Most high school students believe that use of cocaine is harmful (Johnston et al., 2000).

Cocaine may be brewed from coca leaves as a "tea," "snorted" in powder form, or injected in liquid form. Repeated snorting constricts blood vessels in the nose, drying the skin and sometimes exposing cartilage and perforating the nasal septum. These problems require cosmetic surgery. The potent cocaine derivatives known as "crack" and "bazooka" are inexpensive because they are unrefined.

Biologically speaking, cocaine stimulates sudden rises in blood pressure, constricts the coronary arteries and thickens the blood (both of which decrease the oxygen supply to the heart), and quickens the heart rate (Kaufman et al., 1998). These events occasionally result in respiratory and cardiovascular collapse (Moliterno et al., 1994; Tang, 1999). The sudden deaths of a number of athletes have been caused in this way. Overdoses can lead to restlessness and insomnia, tremors, headaches, nausea, convulsions, hallucinations, and delusions. Use of crack has been connected with strokes.

Cocaine—also called *snow* and *coke*, like the slang term for the soft drink—has been used as a local anesthetic since the early 1800s. In 1884 it came to the attention of a young Viennese neurologist named Sigmund Freud, who used it to fight his own

CLICK4™ *a video on the neurotransmitter dopamine and its synaptic transmission.*

CLICK4™ *a video on amphetamines and their interaction with dopamine.*

CLICK4™ *a video on cocaine and its interaction with dopamine.*

Amphetamines ▲ Stimulants derived from *alpha-*methyl-beta-*phenyl-*ethyl-*amine*, a colorless liquid consisting of carbon, hydrogen, and nitrogen.
Attention-deficit/hyperactivity disorder ▲ A disorder that begins in childhood and is characterized by a persistent pattern of lack of attention, with or without hyperactivity and impulsive behavior.

Snorting Cocaine.
Cocaine is a powerful stimulant that boosts self-confidence. However, health professionals have become concerned about its physical effects, including sudden rises in blood pressure, constriction of blood vessels, and acceleration of heart rate. Several athletes have died from cocaine overdoses.

TABLE 4.4 SNAPSHOT, U.S.A.: HUMAN DIVERSITY AND SMOKING

Factor	Group	Percent Who Smoke
Gender	Women	22
	Men	27
Ethnic Group	African American	
	Women	22
	Men	32
	Asian American/Pacific Islander	
	Women	12
	Men	20
	Latina and Latino American	
	Latina American	14
	Latino American	25
	Native American/Alaskan Native	
	Women	30
	Men	41
	European American	
	Women	24
	Men	27
Level of Education	Fewer than 12 years	38
	16 years and above	14

NOTE: From American Heart Association (2000) 2000 Heart and Stroke Statistical Update, _http://www.americanheart.org_; American Lung Association (2000). Smoking Fact Sheet, _http://www.lungusa.org_.

Cigarettes: Smoking Guns?

The perils of cigarette smoking are widely known today. One Surgeon General declared that cigarette smoking is the chief preventable cause of death in the United States. The numbers of Americans who die from smoking are comparable to the number of lives that would be lost if two jumbo jets crashed _every day_. If flying were that unsafe, would the government ground all flights? Would the public continue to make airline reservations?

depression and published an article about it titled "Song of Praise." Freud's early ardor was tempered when he learned that cocaine is habit-forming and can cause hallucinations and delusions. Cocaine causes physiological as well as psychological dependence (Tang, 1999).

Nicotine

Smoking: a "custome lothesome to the Eye, hatefull to the Nose, harmefull to the Braine, dangerous to the Lungs."

King James I, 1604

Nicotine is the stimulant found in cigarettes and cigars. **_Question: What are the effects of nicotine?_** Nicotine stimulates discharge of the hormone adrenaline and the release of many neurotransmitters, including dopamine and acetylcholine. Adrenaline creates a burst of autonomic activity that disrupts normal heart rhythms (Wang et al., 2000), accelerates the heart rate, and pours sugar into the blood. Acetylcholine is vital in memory formation, and nicotine appears to enhance memory and attention, improve performance on simple, repetitive tasks (Kinnunen et al., 1996; O'Brien, 1996), and enhance the mood. Despite its stimulative properties, it also appears to relax people and reduce stress (O'Brien, 1996).

Nicotine depresses the appetite and raises the metabolic rate. Thus some people smoke cigarettes in order to control their weight (Jeffery et al., 2000b). People also tend to eat more when they stop smoking (Jeffery et al., 2000b), causing some to return to the habit.

Nicotine is the agent that creates physiological dependence on tobacco products (Baker et al., 2000; American Lung Association, 2000). Nicotine may be as addictive as heroin or cocaine (MacKenzie et al., 1994). Regular smokers adjust their smoking to maintain fairly even levels of nicotine in their bloodstream (Shiffman et al., 1997). Symptoms of withdrawal from nicotine include nervousness, drowsiness, loss of energy, headaches, irregular bowel movements, lightheadedness, insomnia, dizziness, cramps, palpitations, tremors, and sweating. Because many of these symptoms resemble those of anxiety, it was once thought that they might reflect the anxiety of attempting to quit smoking, rather than addiction.

The Perils of Smoking It's no secret. Cigarette packs sold in the United States carry messages like "Warning: The Surgeon General Has Determined That Cigarette Smoking Is Dangerous to Your Health." Cigarette advertising has been banned on radio and television. Nearly 430,000 Americans die from smoking-related illnesses each year (American Lung Association, 2000). This is the equivalent of two jumbo jets colliding in midair each day with all passengers lost. It is higher than the number of people who die from motor vehicle accidents, alcohol and drug abuse, suicide, homicide, and AIDS _combined_.

The percentage of American adults who smoke cigarettes declined from more than 40% in the mid-1960s to about 25% in recent years, but there have been increases among women, African Americans, and 8th to 12th graders (American Lung Association, 2000). The incidence of smoking is connected with gender, ethnicity, and level of education (see Table 4.4) (American Lung Association, 2000). Better-educated people are less likely to smoke (Cavelaars et al., 2000). They are also more likely to quit smoking (Rose et al., 1996).

A survey of college students in the United States reveals a somewhat different picture. Nancy Rigotti and her colleagues (2000) polled more than 14,000 students from 119 nationally representative 4-year colleges and universities. Sixty percent of students polled responded to the survey. As you can see in Table 4.5, among college students, European Americans were most likely to smoke cigarettes and African Americans were least likely to smoke. In addition to smoking cigarettes, many men reported using cigars, pipes, and smokeless tobacco, all of which are also associated with health risks. Athletes and more achievement-oriented students were less likely to smoke than students whose priorities were more social. Thus many students experiment with tobacco in college, and many become dependent on nicotine—a dependence that threatens to haunt them for a lifetime.

Every cigarette smoked steals about 7 minutes of a person's life. The carbon monoxide in cigarette smoke impairs the blood's ability to carry oxygen, causing shortness of breath. It is apparently the **hydrocarbons** ("tars") in cigarette and cigar smoke that lead to lung cancer (American Lung Association, 2000). Smoking is responsible for about 87% of cases of lung cancer (American Lung Association, 2000). Cigarette smoking is also linked to death from heart disease, chronic lung and respiratory diseases, and other health problems. Women who smoke show reduced bone density, increasing the risk of fracture of the hip and back (Brody, 1996b; Hopper & Seeman, 1994). Pregnant women who smoke have a higher risk of miscarriage, preterm births, low birth-weight babies, and stillborn babies (American Lung Association, 2000).

Cigar smokers are less likely to inhale than cigarette smokers, so it had been assumed that cigar smoking was relatively safe. However, researchers at the American

DIVERSITY   **TABLE 4.5: PERCENT OF COLLEGE STUDENTS WHO SMOKE**

	European American (n = 10,545)	Latino and Latina American (n = 1,018)	Asian American (n = 1,117)	African American (n = 788)
Men	30.4	22.5	25.3	12.1
Women	31.9	21.5	19.5	10.7
Men & women combined	31.3	21.9	21.7	11.2

SOURCE OF DATA: Nancy A. Rigotti, Jae Eun Lee, & Henry Wechsler (2000). U.S. College Students' Use of Tobacco Products: Results of a National Survey. *Journal of the American Medical Association*, 284(6), 699–705.

Hydrocarbons ▲ Chemical compounds consisting of hydrogen and carbon.

Psychology and Modern Life

Quitting Smoking

Is being a quitter a good thing? When it comes to smoking, the answer is yes. More than 40 million Americans have successfully quit smoking (American Lung Association, 2000). Former smokers have mortality rates similar to those of people who have never smoked. So, rather than focusing on the damage already done, people who quit smoking can look forward to a reasonably normal life expectancy.

About two out of three smokers report that they would like to quit smoking completely (American Lung Association, 2000). For those who have decided to quit smoking, the following suggestions may be of help:

- Tell your family and friends that you're quitting — make a public commitment.
- Pick a time to quit when you are likely to be under less stress than usual or away from your usual surroundings. For example, go on a smoke-ending vacation to get away from places and situations in which you're used to smoking.
- Start when you wake up, at which time you've already gone 8 hours without nicotine.
- Think of specific things to tell yourself when you feel the urge to

smoke: how you'll be stronger, free from fear of cancer, ready for the marathon, and so on.
- Tell yourself that the first few days are the hardest — after that, withdrawal symptoms decrease dramatically.
- Throw out ashtrays and don't allow smokers to visit you at home for a while.
- Don't carry matches or light other people's cigarettes.
- Sit in nonsmokers' sections of restaurants and trains.
- Fill your days with novel activities — things that won't remind you of smoking.
- Use sugar-free mints, cinnamon sticks (don't light them up!), nonprescription gum (regular or containing nicotine), or nicotine skin patches as substitutes for cigarettes. Nicotine substitutes reduce the craving for nicotine (Tiffany et al., 2000). Prescription nicotine sprays and inhalers as well as a prescription non-nicotine pill (Zyban) may also be of help.
- Buy yourself presents with all the cash you're not spending on cigarettes.

- Imagine living a prolonged, non-coughing life. Ah, freedom!

Nicotine gums and skin patches help many people (Lancaster et al., 2000). Some, however, find it difficult to wean themselves from these nicotine replacement methods. Nicotine gum also appears to help many people avoid gaining weight after they quit smoking (Doherty et al., 1996). A combination of cognitive behavior therapy and nicotine replacement as by nicotine gum and patches looks promising: People experience less discomfort from withdrawal than they do from cognitive behavior therapy alone (Cinciripini et al., 1996).

There is also a high relapse rate for people who quit smoking. Be on guard: We are most likely to relapse — that is, return to drugs such as alcohol and nicotine — when we feel highly anxious, angry, or depressed (Cooney et al., 1997; Kinnunen et al., 1996). If you are tempted, you can reduce the risk of relapse by using almost any of the strategies described here, such as reminding yourself of reasons for quitting, having a mint, or going for a walk.

▲ REFLECT

Do you think that researchers have exaggerated the dangers of smoking? Why or why not?

Cancer Society and the Centers for Disease Control and Prevention have found that cigar smokers are five times as likely as nonsmokers to develop lung cancer, even when they do not inhale ("Cigars increase lung cancer risk," 2000). When they do inhale, cigar smokers run eleven times the risk of lung cancer as nonsmokers. Cigar smokers also run increased risks of cancers of the mouth, throat, and esophagus (Baker et al., 2000).

Passive smoking is also connected with respiratory illnesses, asthma, and other health problems. Prolonged exposure to household tobacco smoke during childhood is a risk factor for lung cancer (Janerich et al., 1990). Because of the noxious effects of secondhand smoke, smoking has been banished from many public places such as airplanes, restaurants, and elevators.

Why, then, do people smoke? For many reasons—such as the desire to look sophisticated (although these days smokers may be more likely to be judged foolish than sophisticated), to have something to do with their hands, and—of course—to take in nicotine.

REVIEW

CD 4 SA 4

CLICK4™ *a self-assessment on why you smoke—if you do.*

(31) Stimulants (increase or decrease?) the activity of the nervous system. (32) Amphetamines produce euphoria in high doses, but high doses may also cause restlessness, insomnia, psychotic symptoms, and a "crash" upon withdrawal. (33) Ritalin is widely used to treat _____-deficit hyperactivity disorder in children. (34) _____ is a stimulant that boosts self-confidence, but high doses can lead to restlessness, insomnia, and psychotic reactions. (35) Cocaine also triggers rises in blood pressure and constricts the coronary _____, which may lead to cardiovascular collapse. (36) Tobacco contains the stimulant _____tine. (37) People with more education and higher income are (more or less?) likely to smoke.

Pulling It Together: Since the hazards of using stimulants are no secret, why do many people use them, especially cigarettes? What are the similarities and differences in the effects of depressants and stimulants?

HALLUCINOGENICS

Hallucinogenic drugs are so named because they produce hallucinations—that is, sensations and perceptions in the absence of external stimulation. But hallucinogenic drugs may also have additional effects such as relaxation, euphoria, or, in some cases, panic.

Marijuana

CLICK4™ *a video on THC and its interaction with the neurotransmitter anandamide.*

Marijuana is a substance that is produced from the *Cannabis sativa* plant, which grows wild in many parts of the world. *Question: What are the effects of marijuana?* Marijuana helps some people relax and can elevate their mood. It also sometimes produces mild hallucinations, which is why we discuss it in the section on **psychedelic**, or hallucinogenic, drugs. The major psychedelic substance in marijuana is delta-9-tetrahydrocannabinol, or THC. THC is found in the branches and leaves of the plant, but it is highly concentrated in the sticky resin. **Hashish**, or "hash," is derived from the resin. Hashish is more potent than marijuana.

In the 19th century, marijuana was used much as aspirin is used today for headaches and minor aches and pains. It could be bought without a prescription in any drugstore. Today marijuana use and possession are illegal in most states. Marijuana also carries a number of health risks. For example, it impairs the perceptual-motor coordination used in driving and operating machines. It impairs short-term memory and slows learning (Ashton, 2001). Although it causes positive mood changes in many people, there are also disturbing instances of anxiety and confusion and occasional reports of psychotic reactions (Johns, 2001).

Some people report that marijuana helps them socialize at parties. Moderate to strong intoxication is linked to reports of heightened perceptions and increases in self-insight, creative thinking, and empathy for the feelings of others. Time seems to pass

Passive smoking ▲ Inhaling of smoke from the tobacco products and exhalations of other people; also called *secondhand smoking.*

Hallucinogenic ▲ Giving rise to hallucinations.

Marijuana ▲ The dried vegetable matter of the *Cannabis sativa* plant.

Psychedelic ▲ Causing hallucinations, delusions, or heightened perceptions.

Hashish ▲ A drug derived from the resin of *Cannabis sativa.* Often called "hash."

more slowly for people who are strongly intoxicated. A song might seem to last an hour rather than a few minutes. There is increased awareness of bodily sensations such as heartbeat. Marijuana smokers also report that strong intoxication heightens sexual sensations. Visual hallucinations are not uncommon. Strong intoxication may cause smokers to experience disorientation. If the smoker's mood is euphoric, loss of a sense of personal identity may be interpreted as being in harmony with the universe.

Some marijuana smokers have negative experiences. An accelerated heart rate and heightened awareness of bodily sensations leads some smokers to fear that their heart will "run away" with them. Some smokers find disorientation threatening and are afraid that they will not regain their identity. Strong intoxication sometimes causes nausea and vomiting.

People can become psychologically dependent on marijuana, but use of marijuana had not been thought to lead to physiological dependence. Recent research, however, suggests that regular users of marijuana may experience tolerance and withdrawal symptoms (American Psychiatric Association, 2000; Johns, 2001).

CONTROVERSY IN PSYCHOLOGY

Is Marijuana Harmful? Should It Be Available as a Medicine?

There are many controversies concerning marijuana. One is the issue as to whether marijuana should be made available as a medicine to those who could benefit from it. Marijuana has been used to treat health problems, including glaucoma and the nausea experienced by cancer patients undergoing chemotherapy (Robson, 2001). Psychiatrist Lester Grinspoon (2000), a long-time supporter of marijuana for medical uses, refers to it as an inexpensive, versatile, and reasonably safe medicine. Other medical researchers agree that marijuana has some positive effects, but the action of THC also has its negatives (Nahas et al., 2000). THC binds to a membrane receptor, 7TM, which is found in every cell. THC displaces the natural substance that would bind with the receptor and disrupts the receptor's signaling. As a result, the functioning of the brain, the immune system, and the cardiovascular and reproductive systems (e.g., it interferes with development of sperm and conception) is all impaired. Moreover, in some cases, alternate drugs achieve similar benefits (Watson et al., 2000).

Marijuana smoke also contains more hydrocarbons than tobacco smoke—a risk factor in cancer. Smokers of marijuana often admit that they know that marijuana smoke can be harmful, but they counter that compared with cigarette smokers, they smoke very few "joints" per day. Yet, as noted, marijuana elevates the heart rate and, in some people, the blood pressure. This higher demand on the heart and circulation poses a threat to people with hypertension and cardiovascular disorders. One study found that middle-aged men were five times more likely to have a heart attack within an hour of smoking marijuana (Middleman, 2000).

Another issue is whether researchers and public figures exaggerate the dangers of marijuana to discourage people from using it. Does the information about marijuana in this textbook seem to be biased? Why or why not? What can you do to sort out "truth" from "fiction" in the case of marijuana?

Marijuana has been with us for decades, but new research on its effects continues—with more sophisticated methods. For example, it has been known that marijuana usage impairs learning and memory, but it was assumed by many that marijuana distracted people from learning tasks. Now, however, laboratory research suggests that marijuana also reduces the release of neurotransmitters involved in the consolidation of learning (Sullivan, 2000). MRI and PET scan studies suggest that marijuana may have little or no effect on the size or makeup of the brain of adults (Block et al., 2000). However, males who began using marijuana before the age of 17 may have smaller brains and less gray matter than other males (Wilson et al., 2000). Both males and females who started using marijuana early may be generally smaller in height and weight than other people. William Wilson and his colleagues (2000) suggest that these differences may reflect the effect of marijuana on pituitary and sex hormones.

CLICK4™ *more information about marijuana and its impact on health and society.*

An LSD Trip?
This hallucinogenic drug can give rise to a vivid parade of colors and visual distortions. Some users claim to have achieved great insights while "tripping," but typically they have been unable to recall or apply them afterward.

More research is needed on the effects of marijuana. While some of the horror stories of the 1960s and 1970s may have been exaggerated, marijuana could be quite harmful in a number of ways, especially when used by adolescents. More evidence—not more speculation—is needed.

LSD and Other Hallucinogenics

LSD is the abbreviation for lysergic acid diethylamide, a synthetic hallucinogenic drug. *Question: What are the effects of LSD and other kinds of hallucinogenic drugs?* Users of "acid" claim that it "expands consciousness" and opens up new worlds to them. Sometimes people believe they have achieved great insights while using LSD, but when it wears off they often cannot apply or recall these discoveries. As a powerful hallucinogenic, LSD produces vivid and colorful hallucinations.

Some LSD users have **flashbacks**—distorted perceptions or hallucinations that mimic the LSD "trip" but occur days, weeks, or longer after usage. Some researchers have speculated that flashbacks stem from chemical changes in the brain produced by LSD. Others suggest psychological explanations for flashbacks. Matefy (1980) found that LSD users who have flashbacks can become engrossed in role-playing. Perhaps flashbacks involve enacting the role of being on a trip. This does not mean that people who claim to have flashbacks are lying. They may be more willing to surrender personal control in their quest for psychedelic experiences. Users who do not have flashbacks prefer to be more in charge of their thought processes and choose to focus on the demands of daily life.

Other hallucinogenic drugs include **mescaline** (derived from the peyote cactus) and **phencyclidine** (PCP). Regular use of hallucinogenics may lead to tolerance and psychological dependence. But hallucinogenics are not known to lead to physiological dependence. High doses may induce frightening hallucinations, impaired coordination, poor judgment, mood changes, and paranoid delusions.

REVIEW

CLICK4™ *Web sites that explore drugs and their impact on individuals and society.*

CLICK4™ *a quiz covering the second half of this chapter.*

CLICK4™ *electronic flash cards to review your knowledge of key terms and people in this chapter.*

LSD ▲ Lysergic acid diethylamide. A hallucinogenic drug.
Flashbacks ▲ Distorted perceptions or hallucinations that occur days or weeks after LSD usage but mimic the LSD experience.
Mescaline ▲ A hallucinogenic drug derived from the mescal (peyote) cactus.
Phencyclidine ▲ Another hallucinogenic drug whose name is an acronym for its chemical structure. Abbreviated *PCP.*

(38) _____ substances distort perceptions. (39) _____ often produces feelings of relaxation and empathy, the feeling that time is slowing down, and reports of new insights. (40) However, it raises the _____ rate, and the smoke can be harmful. (41) LSD produces vivid _____. (41) The causes of LSD flashbacks are (known or unknown?).

Pulling It Together: What does the research evidence show about the effects of marijuana? How do hallucinogenics differ from depressants and stimulants?

Consciousness is that precious thing that enables us to observe and make sense of our environment and to act on our environment. Most conscious activity occurs in what we call the "normal" waking state, but we apparently need rest from this state through sleep. Being creative, humans have also experimented with many ways of altering consciousness, often as a way of enhancing the nature of everyday experience or gaining special insight. The widespread use of alcohol indicates that some methods of altering consciousness have become an integral part of our culture. However, as noted in this chapter, many ways of altering consciousness—including the use of alcohol—carry certain risks. Rather than focusing on ways of altering consciousness, most of us can probably do a great deal more to appreciate the normal waking state—perhaps by listening to music, exploring hobbies, getting involved in exercise, visiting museums, and thinking about our philosophies of life. It's a big universe out there, filled with endless potential, and our consciousness is our way of connecting to it.

IN REVIEW

Psychoactive Drugs and Their Effects

Drug	Type	How Taken	Desired Effects	Tolerance	Abstinence Syndrome	Side Effects
Alcohol	Depressant	By mouth	Relaxation, euphoria, lowered inhibitions	Yes	Yes	Impaired coordination, poor judgment, hangover
Opiates	Depressants	Injected, smoked, by mouth	Relaxation, euphoria, relief from anxiety and pain	Yes	Yes	Impaired coordination and mental functioning, drowsiness, lethargy
Barbiturates and Methaqualone	Depressants	By mouth, injected	Relaxation, sleep, euphoria, lowered inhibitions	Yes	Yes	Impaired coordination and mental functioning, drowsiness, lethargy
Amphetamines	Stimulants	By mouth, injected	Alertness, euphoria	Yes	?	Restlessness, loss of appetite, psychotic symptoms
Cocaine	Stimulant	By mouth, snorted, injected	Euphoria, self-confidence	Yes	Yes	Restlessness, loss of appetite, convulsions, strokes, psychotic symptoms
Nicotine	Stimulant	By tobacco (smoked, chewed, or sniffed)	Relaxation, stimulation, weight control	Yes	Yes	Cancer, heart disease, lung and respiratory diseases
Marijuana	Hallucinogenic	Smoked, by mouth	Relaxation, perceptual distortions, enhancement of experience	?	?	Impaired coordination, learning, respiratory problems, panic
LSD, Mescaline, PCP	Hallucinogenics	By mouth	Perceptual distortions, vivid hallucinations	Yes	No	Impaired coordination, psychotic symptoms, panic

TRUTH ⊘ FICTION
REVISITED

- It is not true that we act out our forbidden fantasies in our dreams. *Most dreams are humdrum. See page 128.*

- It is true that many people have insomnia because they try too hard to fall asleep at night. *Trying to go to sleep heightens tension and anxiety, both of which counter the feelings of relaxation that help induce sleep. See page 128.*

- It is not true that it is dangerous to awaken a sleepwalker. *Sleepwalkers may be confused and startled when awakened but not usually violent. See page 131.*

- There is no evidence that people can be hypnotized against their will. *People who are readily hypnotized desire the experience and cooperate with the hypnotist. See page 132.*

- It is true that people have managed to bring high blood pressure under control through meditation. *See page 135.*

- It is true that rats will learn to do what they can to obtain a burst of electricity in the brain—*when the electricity stimulates the so-called pleasure centers of their brains. See page 136.*

- It is true that you can learn to change your heart rate just by thinking about it—*particularly when "thinking about it" involves biofeedback training. See page 136.*

- It is true that alcohol goes to women's heads more quickly than to men's. *Women metabolize alcohol less rapidly. See page 141.*

- It is true that heroin was once used as a cure for addiction to morphine. *Today an opioid, methadone, is used to help addicts avert the symptoms caused by withdrawal from heroin. See page 142.*

- It is true that a stimulant is commonly used to treat children who are hyperactive. *That stimulant is methylphenidate, or Ritalin. See page 143.*

- It is true that Coca-Cola once "added life" through a powerful but now illegal stimulant. *That stimulant is cocaine. See page 143.*

1. What is consciousness?

The term *consciousness* has several meanings, including (1) sensory awareness, (2) direct inner awareness of cognitive processes, (3) personal unity or the sense of self, and (4) the waking state.

2. What is a circadian rhythm?

A circadian rhythm is a cycle that is connected with the 24-hour period of the earth's rotation, such as the sleep-wake cycle.

3. What occurs during sleep?

We undergo several stages of sleep. According to electroencephalograph (EEG) records, each stage of sleep is characterized by a different type of brain wave. There are four stages of non-rapid-eye-movement (NREM) sleep and one stage of REM sleep. Stage 1 sleep is the lightest, and stage 4 is the deepest.

4. Why do we sleep?

Sleep apparently serves a restorative function, but we do not know exactly how sleep restores us or how much sleep we need. Animals and people who have been deprived of REM sleep learn more slowly and forget what they have learned more rapidly.

5. What are dreams and why do we dream what we dream?

Dreams are a form of cognitive activity that occurs mostly while we are sleeping. Most dreaming occurs during REM sleep. Freud believed that dreams reflected unconscious wishes and "protected sleep" by keeping unacceptable ideas out of awareness. The activation-synthesis hypothesis suggests that dreams largely reflect automatic biological activity by the pons and the synthesis of subsequent sensory stimulation by the frontal part of the brain. The content of most dreams is an extension of the events of the previous day. Nightmares are also dreams that occur during REM sleep.

6. What types of problems or sleep disorders can we encounter as we sleep?

A common sleep disorder is insomnia, which is most often encountered by people who are anxious and tense. Deep sleep disorders include sleep terrors, bed-wetting, and sleepwalking.

7. What is hypnosis?

Hypnosis is an altered state of consciousness in which people are suggestible and behave as though they are in a trance.

8. What changes in consciousness are induced by hypnosis?

People who are hypnotized may show passivity, narrowed attention, hypermnesia (heightened memory), suggestibility, assumption of unusual roles, perceptual distortions, posthypnotic amnesia, and posthypnotic suggestion.

9. How do modern psychologists explain the effects of hypnosis?

Current theories of hypnosis deny the existence of a special trance state. Rather, they emphasize people's ability to role-play the "trance" (role theory), to do what is expected of them (response set theory), and to divide their consciousness (neodissociation theory) as directed by the hypnotist.

10. What is meditation?

In meditation, one focuses "passively" on an object or a mantra in order to alter the normal relationship between oneself and the environment. In this way, consciousness (that is, the normal focuses of attention) is altered.

11. What are the effects of meditation?

Meditation often has the effect of inducing relaxation. TM appears to reduce the blood pressure of hypertensive individuals.

12. What is biofeedback training?

Biofeedback is a method for increasing consciousness of bodily functions. In biofeedback, the organism is continuously provided with information about a targeted biological response such as heart rate or emission of alpha waves.

13. How is biofeedback training used?

People and lower animals can learn to control involuntary functions such as heart rate, blood pressure, even the emission of certain brain waves through biofeedback training.

14. What are substance abuse and dependence?

Substance abuse is use of a substance that persists even though it impairs one's functioning. Dependence has behavioral and physiological aspects. It may be haracterized by organizing one's life around getting and using the substance and by the development of tolerance, withdrawal symptoms, or both.

15. What are the causes of substance abuse and dependence?

People usually try drugs out of curiosity, but usage can be reinforced by anxiety reduction, feelings of euphoria, and other positive sensations. People are also motivated to avoid withdrawal symptoms once they become physiologically dependent on a drug. People may have genetic predispositions to become physiologically dependent on certain substances.

16. What are the effects of alcohol?

Alcohol, the most widely used drug, is a depressant. It belongs to the group of substances that act by slowing the activity of the central nervous system. Alcohol is also intoxicating and can lead to physiological dependence. It provides an excuse for failure or for antisocial behavior, but it has not been shown to induce such behavior directly.

17. What are the effects of opiates?

The opiates morphine and heroin are depressants that reduce pain, but they are also bought on the street because of the euphoric "rush" they provide. Opiate use can lead to physiological dependence.

18. What are the effects of barbiturates and methaqualone?

Barbiturates and a similar drug, methaqualone, are depressants. Barbiturates have medical uses, including relaxation, pain management, and treatment of epilepsy, high blood pressure, and insomnia. Barbiturates lead rapidly to physiological and psychological dependence.

19. What are the effects of amphetamines?

Stimulants are substances that act by increasing the activity of the nervous system. Amphetamines are stimulants that produce feelings of euphoria when taken in high doses. But high doses may also cause restlessness, insomnia, psychotic symptoms, and a "crash" upon withdrawal. Amphetamines and a related stimulant, Ritalin, are commonly used to treat hyperactive children.

20. What are the effects of cocaine?

Psychologically speaking, the stimulant cocaine provides feelings of euphoria and bolsters self-confidence. Physically, it causes sudden rises in blood pressure and constricts blood vessels. Overdoses can lead to restlessness, insomnia, psychotic reactions, and cardiorespiratory collapse.

21. What are the effects of nicotine?

Nicotine is an addictive stimulant that can paradoxically help people relax. Nicotine is the drug found in cigarette smoke, but cigarette smoke also contains carbon monoxide and hydrocarbons. Cigarette smoking has been linked to death from heart disease and cancer, and to other health problems.

22. What are the effects of marijuana?

Hallucinogenic substances produce distorted sensations and perceptions. Marijuana is a hallucinogenic substance whose active ingredients, including THC, often produce relaxation, heightened and distorted perceptions, feelings of empathy, and reports of new insights. Hallucinations may occur. Marijuana elevates the heart rate and the smoke is likely to be harmful. Although it has some medical uses, it impairs learning and memory and may affect the growth of adolescents.

23. What are the effects of LSD and other kinds of hallucinogenic drugs?

LSD is a hallucinogenic drug that produces vivid hallucinations. Some LSD users have "flashbacks" to earlier experiences.

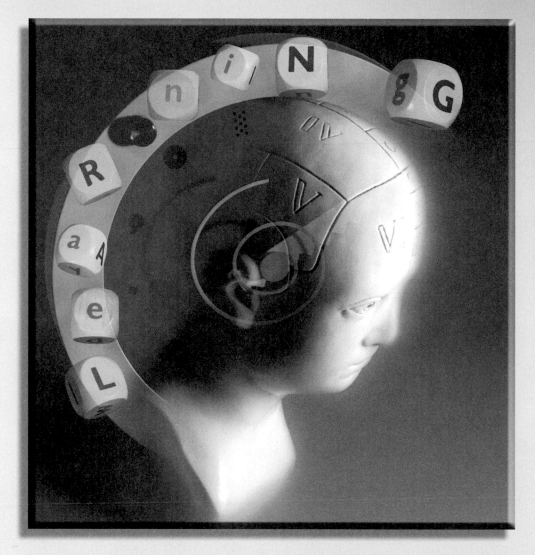

CHAPTER 5

Learning

TRUTH ⚫ FICTION?

☐ Dogs can be trained to salivate when a bell is sounded.

☐ One nauseating meal can give rise to a food aversion that persists for years.

☐ Psychologists helped a young boy overcome his fear of rabbits by having him eat cookies while a rabbit was brought progressively nearer to him.

☐ During World War II, a psychologist devised a plan for training pigeons to guide missiles to their targets.

☐ Punishment does not work.

☐ Rats can be trained to climb a ramp, cross a bridge, climb a ladder, pedal a toy car, and do several other tasks—all in proper sequence.

☐ Psychologists fashioned a method to teach an emaciated 9-month-old infant to stop throwing up.

☐ We must make mistakes if we are to learn.

☐ Despite all the media hoopla, no scientific connection has been established between violence viewed on TV and aggressive behavior in real life.

I was teaching my new dog, Phoebe, to fetch. I bought a soft yellow ball for her that squeaked when she bit into it. She enjoyed playing with it, and I assumed she would want to run after it. (Wrong!) I waved it under her nose. She sniffed at it, barked, and wagged her tail excitedly.

Then, as Phoebe watched, I tossed the ball about 20 feet away. "Fetch!" I said as the ball bounced invitingly in the grass.

"People say, 'Take it!'" my teenage daughter Allyn said.

Perhaps Allyn was right. Phoebe watched the ball but didn't run after it. Instead, she barked at me and snapped softly at my legs.

"Okay," I said (to both of them). I ran after the ball, picked it up, and waved it under Phoebe's nose again. She barked and wagged her tail rapidly like a reed in a brisk wind.

"Take it!" I said and tossed the ball into the air again.

Again Phoebe refused to run after it. She barked and snapped at my legs again. "This is ridiculous," I muttered, and I went to get the ball. As I brought it back to Phoebe, Allyn said, "Don't you see what's happening?"

"What?"

"Phoebe's teaching you to fetch," Allyn laughed.

"Don't you mean to 'take it'?" I said.

LEARNING

Yes, Phoebe was teaching me to fetch. Somehow she got me to run after the ball. When I brought it back to her, she responded to my behavior with a show of excitement and (apparent) glee. One could say that Phoebe was teaching me what to do by showing excitement when I did the "right" thing. I was learning. Learning is a key area in psychology.

Question: What is learning?

From the behaviorist perspective, **learning** is defined as a relatively permanent change in behavior that arises from experience. But changes in behavior also arise from maturation and physical changes; such changes do not reflect learning. For example, frogs hatch as tadpoles that swim. After they develop legs, they hop on land. The behaviorist defines learning in terms of the changes in behavior by which it is known. From the behaviorist perspective, I learned to fetch the ball (a change in behavior) because Phoebe reinforced me for doing so.

From the cognitive perspective, learning is a mental change that may or may not be evident in terms of behavior. Cognitive psychologists see learning in terms of experience changing the way that organisms mentally represent the environment. Changes in mental representation may affect, but do not directly cause, changes in behavior. Learning is *demonstrated* by changes in behavior, but learning itself is a mental process. From the cognitive perspective, Phoebe's reinforcement of my fetching of the ball did not make me fetch. Rather, it gave me information. It showed me that Phoebe wanted me to repeat the act. But my continued fetching was not mechanical or automatic. (At least I don't think it was.)

In lower organisms, much behavior is unlearned. It is labeled instinctive, or inborn. Fish (and tadpoles) are born "knowing" how to swim. Salmon instinctively use the sense of smell to find and return to spawn in the stream where they were hatched after they have spent years roaming the seas. Robins instinctively know how to sing the song of their species and to build nests. Rats instinctively mate and rear their young. Among humans, however, the variety and complexity of behavior patterns are largely products of experience. Experience is essential to learning to walk and acquiring the language of our parents and community. We learn to read, to compute numbers, and to surf the Net. We learn to seek out the foods that are valued in our culture when we are hungry. We get into the habit of starting our day with coffee, tea, or other beverages. We learn which behavior patterns are deemed socially acceptable and which are considered wrong. And, of course, our families and communities use verbal guidance, set examples, and apply rewards and punishments to teach us to stick to the straight and narrow.

Sometimes our learning experiences are direct, like Phoebe's reinforcement of my fetching the ball. But we can also learn from the experiences of others. For example, I warn my children against the perils of jumping from high places and running wild in the

▲ **REFLECT**
What is the difference between instinctive behavior and learned behavior? What does it mean to say that fish "know" how to swim when they are born?

CLICK4™ *a bulletin board discussion on the nature of learning.*

CLICK4™ *an interesting approach to learning at epsych, a Web psychology book.*

Learning ▲ (1) According to behaviorists, a relatively permanent change in behavior that results from experience. (2) According to cognitive theorists, the process by which organisms make relatively permanent changes in the way they represent the environment because of experience. These changes influence the organism's behavior but do not fully determine it.

CONTROVERSY IN PSYCHOLOGY

How Should We Define Learning?

Psychologists disagree on the definition of learning. Behaviorists define learning as a relatively permanent change in behavior that arises from experience. Cognitive psychologists define learning as a matter of experience changing the way in which an organism represents the environment. Why do they have these different approaches?

house. (Now and then they heed me.) From books and visual media, we learn about the past, about other peoples, and about how to put things together. And we learn as we invent ways of doing things that have never been done before.

In this chapter we will consider various kinds of learning. These include the simple forms of learning called classical and operant conditioning, and kinds of learning in which cognition plays a more central role. We will see that learning is crucial to the adaptation and survival of organisms, and that we humans engage in many different kinds of learning, which makes us the most adaptive organisms on planet Earth.

REVIEW

(1) Behaviorists define learning in terms of a change in _____. (2) Cognitive psychologists define learning in terms of a change in the way organisms mentally _____ the environment.

Pulling It Together: How do you know when you have learned something?

CLASSICAL CONDITIONING

Classical conditioning involves some of the ways in which we learn to associate events with other events. Consider this: We have a distinct preference for a grade of A rather than F. We are also (usually) more likely to stop for a red light than for a green light. Why? We are not born with instinctive attitudes toward the letters *A* and *F*. Nor are we born knowing that red means stop and green means go. We learn the meanings of these symbols because they are associated with other events. A's are associated with instructor approval and the likelihood of getting into graduate school. Stopping at red lights is associated with avoiding accidents and traffic citations.

On the next day, I showed Phoebe the ball again. She became excited and barked at the door of the family room, apparently because she had learned to associate the ball with the fun we had the day before. Such learning by association is an example of classical conditioning.

Question: What is classical conditioning? **Classical conditioning** is a simple form of associative learning that enables organisms to anticipate events.

Ivan Pavlov Rings a Bell

Lower animals also learn relationships among events, as the Russian physiologist Ivan Pavlov (1927) discovered in research with dogs. *Question: What is the contribution of Ivan Pavlov to the psychology of learning?* Ivan Pavlov made his contribution to the psychology of learning by accident. Pavlov was actually attempting to identify neural receptors in the mouth that triggered a response from the salivary glands. But his efforts were hampered by the dogs' salivating at undesired times, such as when a laboratory assistant inadvertently clanged a food tray.

Because of its biological makeup, a dog salivates if meat powder is placed on its tongue. Salivation in response to meat powder is a **reflex**. Reflexes are simple unlearned responses to stimuli. Reflexes are evoked by stimuli. A **stimulus** is an environmental condition that evokes a response from an organism, such as meat on the tongue or tapping the leg just below the knee. Ivan Pavlov discovered that reflexes (involuntary responses) can also be learned, or *conditioned*, through association. His dogs began salivating in response to clinking food trays because in the past this noise had repeatedly been paired

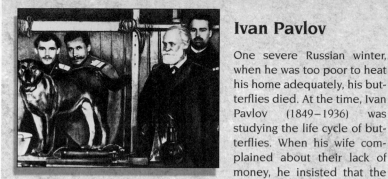
Classical conditioning ▲ A simple form of learning in which an organism comes to associate or anticipate events. A neutral stimulus comes to evoke the response usually evoked by another stimulus by being paired repeatedly with the other stimulus. (Cognitive theorists view classical conditioning as the learning of relationships among events so as to allow an organism to represent its environment.) Also referred to as *respondent conditioning* or *Pavlovian conditioning*.

Reflex ▲ A simple unlearned response to a stimulus.

Stimulus ▲ An environmental condition that elicits a response.

with the arrival of food. The dogs would also salivate when an assistant entered the laboratory. Why? In the past, the assistant had brought food.

When we are faced with novel events, we sometimes have no immediate way of knowing whether they are important. When we are striving for concrete goals, for example, we often ignore the unexpected, even when the unexpected is just as important, or more important, than the goal. So it was that Pavlov at first viewed the uncalled-for canine salivation as an annoyance, a hindrance to his research. But in 1901 he decided that his "problem" was worth looking into. He set about to show that he could train, or condition, his dogs to salivate when he wished and in response to any stimulus he chose.

Pavlov termed these trained salivary responses "conditional reflexes." They were *conditional* upon the repeated pairing of a previously neutral stimulus (such as the clinking of a food tray) and a stimulus (in this case, food) that predictably elicited the target response (in this case, salivation). Today, conditional reflexes are more generally referred to as **conditioned responses** (CRs). They are responses to previously neutral stimuli that have been learned, or conditioned.

Pavlov demonstrated conditioned responses by strapping a dog into a harness like the one shown in Figure 5.1. When meat powder was placed on the dog's tongue, the dog salivated. Pavlov repeated the process several times, with one difference. He preceded the meat powder by half a second or so with the sounding of a bell on each occasion. After several pairings of meat powder and bell, Pavlov sounded the bell but did *not* follow the bell with the meat powder. Still the dog salivated. It had learned to salivate in response to the bell.

REFLECT

Had you heard the expression "That rings a bell"? If so, did you know what it referred to?

CONTROVERSY ✕ IN PSYCHOLOGY

Why Did Pavlov's Dogs Learn to Salivate in Response to the Bell?

Behaviorists and cognitive psychologists explain the learning process in very different ways. Put on your critical thinking cap: Would behaviorists say that after a few pairings of bell and food a dog "knows" that the bell "means" food is on its way? Why or why not?

Behaviorists explain the outcome of this process, termed *classical conditioning*, in terms of the publicly observable conditions of learning. They define classical conditioning as a simple form of learning in which one stimulus comes to evoke the response usually evoked by a second stimulus by being paired repeatedly with the second stimulus. In Pavlov's demonstration, the dog learned to salivate in response to the bell *because* the sounding of the bell had been paired with meat powder. That is, in classical conditioning, the organism forms associations between stimuli because the stimuli are *contiguous*—that is, they occur at about the same time. Behaviorists do *not* say that the dog "knew" food was on the way. They argue that we cannot speak meaningfully about what a dog "knows." We can only outline the conditions under which targeted behaviors reliably occur.

Conditioned response (CR) ▲ In classical conditioning, a learned response to a conditioned stimulus.

FIGURE 5.1 Pavlov's Demonstration of Conditioned Reflexes in Laboratory Dogs.
From behind the two-way mirror at the left, a laboratory assistant rings a bell and then places meat on the dog's tongue. After several pairings, the dog salivates in response to the bell alone. A tube collects saliva and passes it to a vial. The quantity of saliva is taken as a measure of the strength of the animal's response.

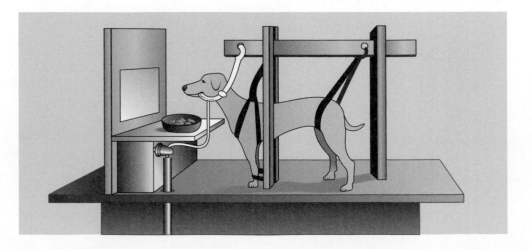

Cognitive psychologists view classical conditioning as the learning of relationships among events. The relationships allow organisms to mentally represent their environments and make predictions (Rescorla, 1988). In Pavlov's demonstration, the dog salivated in response to the bell because the bell—from the cognitive perspective—became mentally connected with the meat. The cognitive focus is on *the information gained by the organism*. Organisms are seen as seekers of information that generate and test rules about relationships among events (Weiner, 1991).

Stimuli and Responses in Classical Conditioning

In the demonstration just described, the meat powder is an unlearned or **unconditioned stimulus (US).** Salivation in response to the meat powder is an unlearned or **unconditioned response (UR).** The bell was at first a meaningless or neutral stimulus. It might have produced an *orienting reflex* in the dog because of its distinctness. That is, the animal might have oriented itself toward the bell by turning toward it. But the bell was not yet associated with food. Then, through repeated association with the meat powder, the bell became a learned, or **conditioned stimulus (CS)** for the salivation response. Salivation in response to the bell (or CS) is a learned or conditioned response (CR). A conditioned response is a response similar to an unconditioned response, but the response evoked by the conditioned stimulus is defined as a conditioned response, not an unconditioned response (see Figure 5.2).

Types of Classical Conditioning

The Pavlovian experiments we have described so far involve one kind of classical conditioning. ***Question: What are the various types of classical conditioning?*** We have described the most efficient type of classical conditioning, which tends to occur when the conditioned stimulus (CS) is presented about 0.5 second before the unconditioned stimulus (US) and is continued until the learner responds to the US. This is an example of **delayed conditioning,** in which the conditioned stimulus (for example, a light) can be presented anywhere from a fraction of a second to several seconds before the unconditioned stimulus (in this case, meat powder) and is left on until the response (salivation) is shown (see Figure 5.3).

Conditioning can also take place via **simultaneous conditioning.** In simultaneous conditioning, a conditioned stimulus, such as a light, is presented along with an unconditioned stimulus, such as meat powder. In **trace conditioning,** the conditioned stimulus (for example, a light) is presented and then removed (or turned off) prior to presentation of the unconditioned stimulus (meat powder). Therefore, only the memory trace of the conditioned stimulus (light) remains to be conditioned to the unconditioned stimulus.

CD **5** **V** **20**
CLICK4™ *a video on the basics of classical conditioning.*

Unconditioned stimulus (US) ▲ A stimulus that elicits a response from an organism prior to conditioning.
Unconditioned response (UR) ▲ An unlearned response to an unconditioned stimulus.
Conditioned stimulus (CS) ▲ A previously neutral stimulus that elicits a conditioned response because it has been paired repeatedly with a stimulus that already elicited that response.
Delayed conditioning ▲ A classical conditioning procedure in which the CS is presented before the US and remains in place until the response occurs.
Simultaneous conditioning ▲ A classical conditioning procedure in which the CS and US are presented at the same time.
Trace conditioning ▲ A classical conditioning procedure in which the CS is presented and then removed before the US is presented.

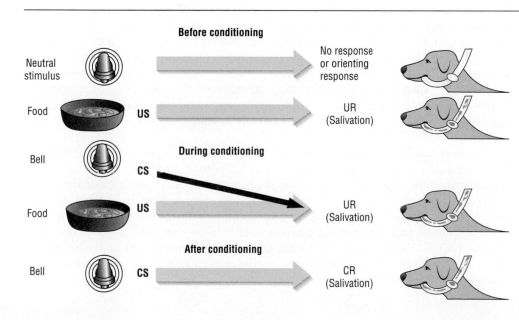

FIGURE 5.2   A Schematic Representation of Classical Conditioning.
Prior to conditioning, food elicits salivation. The bell, a neutral stimulus, elicits either no response or an orienting response. During conditioning, the bell is rung just before meat is placed on the dog's tongue. After several repetitions, the bell, now a CS, elicits salivation, the CR.

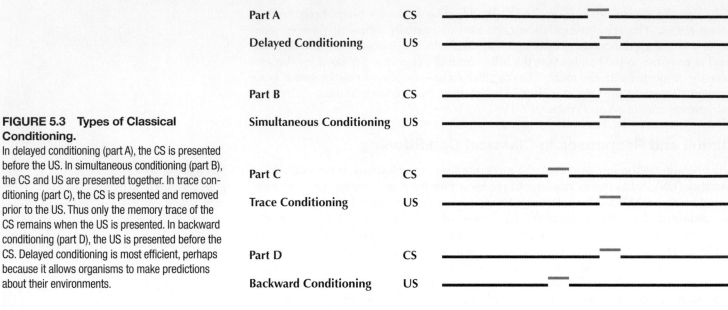

FIGURE 5.3   Types of Classical Conditioning.
In delayed conditioning (part A), the CS is presented before the US. In simultaneous conditioning (part B), the CS and US are presented together. In trace conditioning (part C), the CS is presented and removed prior to the US. Thus only the memory trace of the CS remains when the US is presented. In backward conditioning (part D), the US is presented before the CS. Delayed conditioning is most efficient, perhaps because it allows organisms to make predictions about their environments.

Conditioning may occur most effectively in delayed conditioning because it is most adaptive. That is, in delayed conditioning, the occurrence of the conditioned stimulus signals the consequent appearance of the unconditioned stimulus. As a result, organisms can learn to make predictions about their environment. Predictability is adaptive because it allows the organism to prepare for future events. Learning is inefficient and may not take place at all when the unconditioned stimulus is presented before the conditioned stimulus—a sequence referred to as **backward conditioning.** Why? Perhaps because backward conditioning may not permit an organism to make predictions about its environment.

Taste Aversion: All Stimuli Are Not Created Equal

When I was a child in The Bronx, my friends and I would go to the movies on Saturday mornings. There would be a serial followed by a feature film, and the price of admission was a quarter. We would also eat candy (I loved Nonpareils and Raisinets) and popcorn. One morning my friends dared me to eat two huge containers of buttered popcorn by myself. I rose to the challenge: Down went an enormous container of buttered popcorn. More slowly—much more slowly—I stuffed down the second container. Predictably, I felt bloated and nauseated. The taste of the butter, corn, and salt lingered in my mouth and nose, and my head spun. It was obvious to me that I would have no more popcorn that day. But I was surprised that I couldn't face buttered popcorn again for a year.

Years later I learned that psychologists refer to my response to buttered popcorn as a *taste aversion.*   **Questions: What are taste aversions? Why are they of special interest to psychologists?**   Many decades have now passed (how many is my business), and the odor of buttered popcorn still turns my stomach. Such is the power of taste aversions.

Taste aversions are fascinating examples of classical conditioning. Taste aversions are adaptive because they motivate organisms to avoid potentially harmful foods. Although taste aversions are acquired by association, they are of special interest because they differ from other kinds of classical conditioning in a couple of ways. First, only one association may be required. I did not have to go back for seconds at the movies to develop my aversion for buttered popcorn! Second, whereas most kinds of classical conditioning require that the unconditioned stimulus (US) and conditioned stimulus (CS) be contiguous, in taste aversion the unconditioned stimulus (in this case, nausea) can occur hours after the conditioned stimulus (in this case, the flavor of food).

▲ **REFLECT**
Do you have any taste aversions? If so, do you know how you acquired them?

CLICK4™ *an essay assignment on taste aversions.*

Backward conditioning ▲ A classical conditioning procedure in which the unconditioned stimulus is presented prior to the conditioned stimulus.

Taste Aversion and the Evolutionary Perspective   Research on taste aversion also challenges the behaviorist view that organisms learn to associate any stimuli that are contiguous. In reality, not all stimuli are created equal. The evolutionary perspective suggests that organisms would be biologically predisposed to develop aversions that are adaptive in their environmental settings (Garcia et al., 1989). That is, animals that develop taste aversions quickly are less likely to feast on poisonous food, more likely to survive, and thus more likely to contribute their genes to future generations.

In a classic study, Garcia and Koelling (1966) conditioned two groups of rats. Each group was exposed to the same three-part conditioned stimulus (CS): a taste of sweetened water, a light, and a clicker. Afterward, one group was presented with an unconditioned stimulus (US) of nausea (induced by poison or radiation), and the other group was presented with an unconditioned stimulus (US) of electric shock.

After conditioning, the rats who had been nauseated showed an aversion for sweetened water but not to the light or clicker. Although all three stimuli had been presented at the same time, *the rats had acquired only the taste aversion.* After conditioning, the rats that had been shocked avoided both the light and the clicker, *but they did not show a taste aversion to the sweetened water.* For each group of rats, the conditioning that took place was adaptive. In the natural scheme of things, nausea is more likely to stem from poisoned food than from lights or sounds. So, for nauseated rats, acquiring the taste aversion was appropriate. Sharp pain, in contrast, is more likely to stem from natural events involving lights (fire, lightning) and sharp sounds (twigs snapping, things falling). Therefore, it was more appropriate for the shocked animals to develop an aversion to the light and the clicker than to the sweetened water.

This finding fits my experience as well. My nausea led to a taste aversion to buttered popcorn—but not to an aversion to the serials I watched (which, in retrospect, were more deserving of nausea) or the movie theater. I returned every Saturday morning to see what would happen next. Yet, the serial and the theater, as much as the buttered popcorn, had been associated with my nausea. That is, the stimuli had been contiguous.

Let us now consider various factors in classical conditioning.

Formation of a Taste Aversion?
Taste aversions may be acquired as a result of only one association of the US and the CS. Most kinds of classical conditioning require that the US and CS be contiguous, but in a taste aversion the US (nausea) can occur hours after the CS (flavor of food).

REVIEW

(3) Classical conditioning is a simple form of learning in which an originally _____ stimulus comes to elicit the response usually brought forth by another stimulus by being paired repeatedly with that stimulus. (4) A _____ is an environmental condition that evokes a response from an organism. (5) A response to an unconditioned stimulus (US) is called an _____ response (UR). (6) A response to a conditioned stimulus (CS) is termed a _____ response (CR). (7) In _____ conditioning, the CS is presented before the US. (8) In _____ conditioning, the US is presented prior to the CS. (9) In conditioning a taste aversion, (only one or several?) association(s) is/are usually required.

Pulling It Together: Agree or disagree with the following statement and support your answer: The existence of taste aversions provides support for the evolutionary perspective.

CLICK4™ *more information about classical conditioning on the Web.*

FACTORS IN CLASSICAL CONDITIONING

In classical conditioning organisms learn to connect stimuli, such as a bell, with food. In the following section we consider various factors in classical conditioning, beginning with what happens when the connection between stimuli is severed.

Extinction and Spontaneous Recovery

Question: What are the roles of extinction and spontaneous recovery in classical conditioning? Extinction and spontaneous recovery are aspects of conditioning that help organisms adapt by updating their expectations or revising their representations of the changing environment. For example, a dog may learn to associate a new scent (a conditioned stimulus, or CS) with the appearance of a dangerous animal. It can then take evasive action when it catches a whiff of that scent. A child may learn to connect hearing a car pull into the driveway (a conditioned stimulus, or CS) with the arrival of his or her parents (an unconditioned stimulus, or US). Thus, the child may begin to squeal with delight (squealing is a conditioned response, or CR) when the car is heard.

But times can change. The once dangerous animal may no longer be a threat. (What a puppy perceives to be a threat may lose its fearsomeness once the dog matures.) After moving to a new house, the child's parents may commute by means of public transportation. The sound of a car in a nearby driveway may signal a neighbor's, not a parent's, homecoming. When conditioned stimuli (such as the scent of a dog or the sound of a car) are no longer followed by unconditioned stimuli (a dangerous animal, a parent's homecoming), they lose their ability to elicit conditioned responses. In this way the organism adapts to a changing environment.

Extinction

In classical conditioning, **extinction** is the process by which conditioned stimuli (CSs) lose the ability to elicit conditioned responses (CRs) because the conditioned stimuli (CSs) are no longer associated with unconditioned stimuli (USs). From the cognitive perspective, extinction teaches the organism to change its representation of the environment because the learned or conditioned stimulus (CS) no longer allows it to make predictions.

In experiments on the extinction of conditioned responses (CRs), Pavlov found that repeated presentations of the conditioned stimulus (in this case, the bell) without the unconditioned stimulus (in this case, meat powder) led to extinction of the conditioned response (salivation in response to the bell). Figure 5.4 shows that a dog that had been conditioned began to salivate (show a conditioned response) in response to a bell (the conditioned stimulus) after only a couple of pairings—referred to as *acquisition trials*—of the bell with meat powder. Continued pairings of the stimuli led to increased salivation (measured in number of drops of saliva). After seven or eight trials, salivation leveled off at 11 to 12 drops.

In the next series of experiments, salivation in response to the bell was extinguished through several trials—referred to as *extinction trials*—in which the bell was presented without the meat powder. After about 10 extinction trials, the animal no longer salivated, that is, it no longer showed the learned or conditioned response (salivation in response to the bell) when the bell was rung (the bell is the learned or conditioned stimulus).

Spontaneous Recovery

What would happen if we were to allow a day or two to pass after we had extinguished salivation (the CR) in a dog and then again rang the bell (the CS)? Where would you place your bet? Would the dog salivate or not?

If you bet that the dog would again show the conditioned response (in this case, salivation in response to the bell), you were correct. Organisms tend to show **spontaneous recovery** of extinguished conditioned responses (CRs) merely as a function of the passage

▲ **REFLECT**
What is the difference between extinction and forgetting?

CLICK4™ *an essay assignment on extinction and forgetting.*

Extinction ▲ An experimental procedure in which stimuli lose their ability to evoke learned responses because the events that had followed the stimuli no longer occur. (The learned responses are said to be *extinguished*.)

Spontaneous recovery ▲ The recurrence of an extinguished response as a function of the passage of time.

FIGURE 5.4 Learning and Extinction Curves.

Actual data from Pavlov (1927) compose the jagged line, and the curved lines are idealized. In the acquisition phase, a dog salivates (shows a CR) in response to a bell (the CS) after a few trials in which the bell is paired with meat powder (the US). Afterward, the CR is extinguished in about 10 trials during which the CS is not followed by the US. After a rest period, the CR recovers spontaneously. A second series of extinction trials leads to more rapid extinction of the CR.

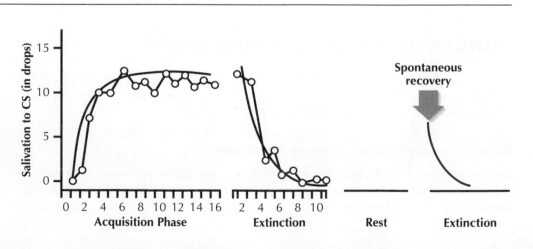

of time. For this reason, the term *extinction* may be a bit misleading. When a species of animal becomes extinct, all the members of that species capable of reproducing have died. The species vanishes. But the experimental extinction of conditioned responses (CRs) does not lead to their permanent eradication. Rather, it seems that they *inhibit* the response. The response remains available for future performance under the "right" conditions.

Consider Figure 5.4 again. When spontaneous recovery of the conditioned response (salivation in response to the bell) does occur, its strength as measured by the number of drops of saliva is weaker than it was at the end of the series of acquisition trials. A second set of extinction trials also extinguishes the conditioned response (salivation) more rapidly than the first series of trials. Although the second time around the conditioned response (salivation) is weaker at first, pairing the conditioned stimulus (the bell) with the unconditioned stimulus (meat powder) again builds response strength rapidly. That is, the animal will make the connection between the bell and the meat powder more easily the second time around.

Evolutionary psychologists note that spontaneous recovery, like extinction, is adaptive. What would happen if the child heard no car in the driveway for several months? It could be that the next time a car entered the driveway, the child would associate the sounds with a parent's homecoming (rather than with the arrival of a neighbor). This expectation could be appropriate. After all, *something* had changed when no car entered the nearby driveway for so long. In the wild, a waterhole may contain water for only a couple of months during the year. But evolution would favor the survival of animals that associate the waterhole with the thirst drive from time to time so that they will return to it when it again holds water.

As time passes and the seasons change, things sometimes follow circular paths and arrive where they were before. Spontaneous recovery seems to function as a mechanism whereby organisms can adapt successfully to situations that recur from time to time.

Generalization at the Crossroads.
Chances are that you have never seen these particular traffic lights in this particular setting. Because of generalization, however, we can safely bet that you would know what to do if you were to drive up to them.

CLICK4™ *a video on the features and phases of classical conditioning.*

Generalization and Discrimination

No two things are exactly alike. Traffic lights are hung at slightly different heights, and shades of red and green differ a little. The barking of two dogs differs, and the sound of the same animal differs slightly from one bark to the next. Rustling sounds in the undergrowth differ, but evolution would favor the survival of rabbits and deer that flee when they perceive any one of many possible rustling sounds. Adaptation requires us to respond similarly (or *generalize*) to stimuli that are equivalent in function and to respond differently to (or *discriminate* between) stimuli that are not. *Question: What are the roles of generalization and discrimination in classical conditioning?*

Generalization   Pavlov noted that responding to different stimuli as though they are functionally equivalent—*generalizing*—is adaptive for animals. **Generalization** is the tendency for a conditioned response to be evoked by stimuli that are similar to the stimulus to which the response was conditioned. In a demonstration of generalization, Pavlov first conditioned a dog to salivate when a circle was presented. During each acquisition trial, the dog was shown a circle (a learned or conditioned stimulus—CS) and then given meat powder (an unlearned or unconditioned stimulus—US). After several trials the dog salivated when presented with the circle alone. Pavlov demonstrated that the dog also displayed the learned or conditioned response (in this case, salivation) in response to closed geometric figures such as ellipses, pentagons, and even squares. The more closely the figure resembled a circle, the greater the *strength* of the response (as measured by drops of saliva).

Discrimination   Organisms must also learn that (1) many stimuli perceived as being similar are functionally different and (2) they must respond adaptively to each. During the first couple of months of life, babies can discriminate their mother's voice from those of other women. They often stop crying when they hear their mother but not when they hear a stranger.

Generalization ▲ In conditioning, the tendency for a conditioned response to be evoked by stimuli that are similar to the stimulus to which the response was conditioned.

Pavlov showed that a dog conditioned to salivate in response to circles could be trained *not* to salivate in response to ellipses. The type of conditioning that trains an organism to respond to a narrow range of stimuli (in this case, circular rather than elliptical geometric figures) is termed **discrimination training.** Pavlov trained the dog by presenting it with circles and ellipses but associating the meat powder with circles only. After a while, the dog no longer salivated in response to the ellipses. Instead, it showed **discrimination:** It salivated only in response to circles.

Pavlov found that increasing the difficulty of the discrimination task apparently tormented the dog. After the dog was trained to salivate in response to circles but not ellipses, Pavlov showed it a series of progressively rounder ellipses. Eventually the dog could no longer discriminate the ellipses from circles. The animal then put on an infantile show. It urinated, defecated, barked profusely, and snapped at laboratory personnel.

How do we explain the dog's belligerent behavior? In a classic work written more than half a century ago, titled *Frustration and Aggression, a* group of behaviorally oriented psychologists suggested that frustration induces aggression (Dollard et al., 1939). Why is failure to discriminate circles from ellipses frustrating? For one thing, in such experiments, rewards—such as food—are usually contingent on correct discrimination. That is, if the dog errs, it doesn't get fed. Cognitive theorists, however, propose that organisms are motivated to construct realistic mental maps of the world. They fine-tune these maps as needed so that they fit a changing environment (Rescorla, 1988). In Pavlov's experiment, the dog lost the ability to adjust its mental map of the environment as the ellipses grew more circular. Thus it was frustrated.

Daily living requires appropriate generalization and discrimination. No two hotels are alike, but when we travel from one city to another it is adaptive to expect to stay in a hotel. It is encouraging that a green light in Washington has the same meaning as a green light in Paris. But returning home in the evening requires the ability to discriminate between our home and those of others. And if we could not readily discriminate our spouse from others, we might land in divorce court.

Higher-Order Conditioning

Consider children who learn that when they hear a car in the driveway their parents are about to arrive. It may be the case that a certain TV cartoon show starts a few minutes before the car enters the driveway. The TV show can come to evoke the expectation that the parents are arriving by being paired repeatedly with the car's entering the driveway. This is an example of higher-order conditioning. *Question: What is higher-order conditioning?*

In **higher-order conditioning,** a previously neutral stimulus comes to serve as a learned or conditioned stimulus (CS) after being paired repeatedly with a stimulus that has already become a learned or conditioned stimulus (CS). Pavlov demonstrated higher-order conditioning by first conditioning a dog to salivate in response to a bell (a CS). He then repeatedly paired the shining of a light with the sounding of a bell. After several pairings, shining the light (the higher-order conditioned stimulus) came to evoke the response (salivation) that had been elicited by the bell (the first-order conditioned stimulus).

In another example of higher-order conditioning, a boy may burn himself by touching a hot stove. After this experience, the sight of the stove may evoke fear (or, more technically, serve as a CS for eliciting a fear response). And because hearing the word *stove* may evoke a mental image of the stove, just hearing the word may evoke fear.

CLICK4™ *an essay assignment on generalization and discrimination.*

CLICK4™ *more information about classical conditioning as applied to the training of dogs.*

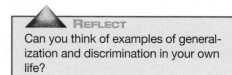

▲ **REFLECT**
Can you think of examples of generalization and discrimination in your own life?

CLICK4™ *a video on classical conditioning and emotional responses.*

Discrimination training ▲ Teaching an organism to show a learned response in the presence of only one of a series of similar stimuli, accomplished by alternating the stimuli but following only the one stimulus with the unconditioned stimulus.

Discrimination ▲ In conditioning, the tendency for an organism to distinguish between a conditioned stimulus and similar stimuli that do not forecast an unconditioned stimulus.

Higher-order conditioning ▲ (1) According to behaviorists, a classical conditioning procedure in which a previously neutral stimulus comes to elicit the response brought forth by a *conditioned* stimulus by being paired repeatedly with that conditioned stimulus. (2) According to cognitive psychologists, the learning of relationships among events, none of which evokes an unlearned response.

REVIEW

(10) Repeated presentation of a CS (e.g., a bell) without the US (e.g., meat) will _____ the CR (salivation). (11) Extinguished responses often show _____ recovery as a function of the passage of time. (12) In stimulus_____, organisms show a CR in response to a range of stimuli similar to the CS. (13) In stimulus _____, organisms learn to show a CR in response to a more limited range of stimuli. (14) In _____-order conditioning, a previously neutral stimulus comes to serve as a CS after being paired repeatedly with another CS.

Pulling It Together: Think as an evolutionary psychologist for a moment: Why are organisms who are capable of extinction and spontaneous recovery of conditioned responses more likely to survive and transmit their genes to subsequent generations?

APPLICATIONS OF CLASSICAL CONDITIONING

Classical conditioning is a major means by which we learn. It is how stimuli come to serve as signals for other stimuli. It is why, for example, we come to expect that someone will be waiting outside when the doorbell is rung or why we expect a certain friend to appear when we hear a characteristic knock at the door. *Question: What are some applications of classical conditioning?*

The Bell-and-Pad Treatment for Bed-Wetting

By the age of 5 or 6, children normally awaken in response to the sensation of a full bladder. They inhibit the urge to urinate, which is an automatic or reflexive response to bladder tension, and instead go to the bathroom. But bed-wetters tend not to respond to bladder tension while asleep. They remain asleep and frequently wet their beds.

By means of the bell-and-pad method, children are taught to wake up in response to bladder tension. They sleep on a special sheet or pad that has been placed on the bed. When the child starts to urinate, the water content of the urine causes an electrical circuit in the pad to close. The closing of the circuit triggers a bell or buzzer, and the child is awakened. (Similar buzzer circuits have been built into training pants as an aid to toilet training.) In terms of classical conditioning, the bell is a US that wakes the child (waking up is the UR). By means of repeated pairings, a stimulus that precedes the bell becomes associated with the bell and also gains the capacity to awaken the child. What is that stimulus? The sensation of a full bladder. In this way, bladder tension (the CS) gains the capacity to awaken the child *even though the child is asleep during the classical conditioning procedure.*

The bell-and-pad method is a superb example of why behaviorists prefer to explain the effects of classical conditioning in terms of the pairing of stimuli and not in terms of what the learner knows. The behaviorist may argue that we cannot assume a sleeping child "knows" that wetting the bed will cause the bell to ring. We can only note that by repeatedly pairing bladder tension with the bell, the child eventually *learns* to wake up in response to bladder tension alone. *Learning* is demonstrated by the change in the child's behavior. One can only speculate on what the child *knows* about the learning process.

In any event, it appears that humans are capable of learning by means of simple association as well as cognitive means, which are explored later in the chapter. In terms of the evolutionary perspective, it would appear that organisms that can learn by means of several routes—including conditioning and conscious reflection—would have a greater chance of survival than organisms whose learning is limited to a single route.

Flooding and Systematic Desensitization

Two behavior therapy methods for reducing specific fears—flooding and systematic desensitization—are based on the classical conditioning principle of extinction (Wolpe & Plaud, 1997). In one, called **flooding,** the client is exposed to the fear-evoking stimulus until the fear response is extinguished. Little Albert, for example, might have been placed in close contact with a rat until his fear had become fully extinguished. In extinction, the

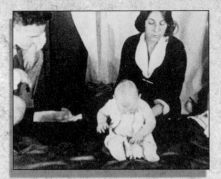
> ▲ **REFLECT**
> Do you find it easier to explain the effects of the bell-and-pad method in terms of conditioning or in terms of what the learner "knows"? Explain.

CLICK4™ *"Advice on Effective Studying," an application of the psychology of learning.*

Flooding ▲ A behavioral fear-reduction technique based on principles of classical conditioning. Fear-evoking stimuli (CSs) are presented continuously in the absence of actual harm so that fear responses (CRs) are extinguished.

Can Chocolate Chip Cookies Countercondition Fears?

In the 1920s Mary Cover Jones helped a boy overcome his fear of rabbits by having him munch on cookies as the animal was brought closer.

CLICK4™ *the classic article by Watson and Rayner, "Conditioned Emotional Reactions."*

CLICK4™ *more about applications of Pavlovian conditioning.*

CLICK4™ *a quiz covering the first half of this chapter.*

▲ **REFLECT**
Were you ever taught to overcome a fear? If so, how?

Systematic desensitization ▲ A behavioral fear-reduction technique in which a hierarchy of fear-evoking stimuli is presented while the person remains relaxed.

Counterconditioning ▲ A fear-reduction technique in which pleasant stimuli are associated with fear-evoking stimuli so that the fear-evoking stimuli lose their aversive qualities.

CS (in this case, the rat) is presented repeatedly in the absence of the US (the clanging of the steel bars) until the CR (fear) is no longer evoked.

Although flooding is usually effective, it is unpleasant. (When you are fearful of rats, being placed in a small room with one is no picnic.) For this reason, behavior therapists frequently prefer to use **systematic desensitization** (see Chapter 16), in which the client is gradually exposed to fear-evoking stimuli under circumstances in which he or she remains relaxed. For example, while feeling relaxed, Little Albert might have been given an opportunity to look at photos of rats or to see live rats from a distance before they were brought closer to him. Systematic desensitization takes longer than flooding but is not as unpleasant.

Counterconditioning: Are Cookies Psychological Health Food?

Early in the 20th century, John Watson's protégé Mary Cover Jones (1924) reasoned that if fears could be conditioned by painful experiences, she could *countercondition* them by substituting pleasant experiences. In **counterconditioning**, a pleasant stimulus is repeatedly paired with a fear-evoking object, thereby counteracting the fear response.

Two-year-old Peter had an intense fear of rabbits. Jones arranged for a rabbit to be gradually brought closer to Peter while he engaged in some of his favorite activities, such as munching on candy and cookies. They did not simply plop the rabbit in Peter's lap, as in flooding. Had she done so, the cookies on the plate, not to mention those already eaten, might have decorated the walls. Instead, she first placed the rabbit in a far corner of the room while Peter munched and crunched. Peter, to be sure, cast a wary eye, but he continued to consume the treat. Gradually the animal was brought closer until eventually, Peter ate treats and touched the rabbit at the same time. Jones theorized that the joy of eating was incompatible with fear and thus counterconditioned it.

REVIEW

(15) The bell-and-_____ method teaches children to wake up when they experience sensations of a full bladder. (16) John Watson and Rosalie Rayner conditioned "Little _____" to fear rats by clanging steel bars behind his head when he played with a rat. (17) In the fear-reduction method of _____, the client is exposed to the fear-evoking stimulus until fear is extinguished. (18) In _____, a pleasant stimulus is paired repeatedly with a fear-evoking object to counteract the fear response.

Pulling It Together: Can you explain how each of the applications discussed in this section applies principles of classical conditioning?

OPERANT CONDITIONING

Through classical conditioning, we learn to associate stimuli so that a simple, usually passive, response made to one stimulus is then made in response to the other. In the case of Little Albert, clanging noises were associated with a rat, so the rat came to elicit the fear response brought forth by the noise. However, classical conditioning is only one kind of learning that occurs in these situations. After Little Albert acquired his fear of the rat, his voluntary behavior changed. He avoided the rat as a way of reducing his fear. Thus, Little Albert engaged in another kind of learning—*operant conditioning*.

After I had acquired my taste aversion, I stayed away from buttered popcorn. My avoidance can also be explained in terms of operant conditioning. In *operant conditioning*, organisms learn to do things—or *not* to do things—because of the consequences of their behavior. I avoided buttered popcorn in order to prevent nausea. But we also seek fluids when we are thirsty, sex when we are aroused, and an ambient temperature of 68° to 70°F when we feel too hot or too cold. *Classical conditioning focuses on how organisms form anticipations about their environments. Operant conditioning focuses on what they* do *about them.*

We begin this section with the historic work of psychologist Edward L. Thorndike. Then we examine the more recent work of B. F. Skinner.

Edward L. Thorndike and the Law of Effect

In the 1890s stray cats were mysteriously disappearing from the streets and alleyways of Harlem. Some of them, it turned out, were being brought to the quarters of Columbia University doctoral student Edward Thorndike. Thorndike was using the cats as subjects in experiments on the effects of rewards and punishments on learning.

Thorndike placed the cats in so-called puzzle boxes. If the animal managed to pull a dangling string, a latch would be released, allowing it to jump out and reach a bowl of food.

When first placed in a puzzle box, a cat would try to squeeze through any opening and would claw and bite at the confining bars and wire. It would claw at anything it could reach. Through such random behavior, it might take 3 to 4 minutes for the cat to chance upon the response of pulling the string. Pulling the string would open the cage and allow the cat to reach the food. When placed back in the cage, it might again take several minutes for the animal to pull the string. But with repetition, it took progressively less time for the cat to pull the string. After seven or eight repetitions, the cat might pull the string immediately when placed back in the box.

The Law of Effect Thorndike explained the cat's learning to pull the string in terms of his **law of effect**. According to this law, a response (such as string pulling) is "stamped in" or strengthened in a particular situation (such as being inside a puzzle box) by a reward (escaping from the box and eating). Rewards, that is, stamp in S-R (stimulus-response) connections. Punishments, in contrast, "stamp out" stimulus-response connections. Organisms would learn *not* to engage in punished responses. Later we shall see that the effects of punishment on learning are not so certain.

B. F. Skinner and Reinforcement

"What did you do in the war, Daddy?" is a question familiar to many who served during America's conflicts. Some stories involve heroism, others involve the unusual. When it comes to unusual war stories, few will top that of Harvard University psychologist B. F. Skinner. One of Skinner's wartime efforts was "Project Pigeon." *Question: What is the contribution of B. F. Skinner to the psychology of learning?*

During World War II Skinner proposed that pigeons be trained to guide missiles to their targets. In their training, the pigeons would be **reinforced** with food pellets for pecking at targets projected onto a screen (see Figure 5.5). Once trained, the pigeons would be placed in missiles. Their pecking at similar targets displayed on a screen would correct the missile's flight path, resulting in a "hit" and a sacrificed pigeon. However, plans for building the necessary missile—for some reason called the *Pelican* and not the *Pigeon*—were scrapped. The pigeon equipment was too bulky and, Skinner lamented, his

www **5** **L** **5**

CLICK4™ *more about E. L. Thorndike and B. F. Skinner.*

Law of effect ▲ Thorndike's principle that responses are "stamped in" by rewards and "stamped out" by punishments.
Reinforce ▲ To follow a response with a stimulus that increases the frequency of the response.

FIGURE 5.5 Project Pigeon.
During World War II, B. F. Skinner suggested using operant conditioning to train pigeons to guide missiles to their targets. The pigeons would first be reinforced for pecking targets projected on a screen. Afterward, in combat, pecking the on-screen target would keep the missile on course.

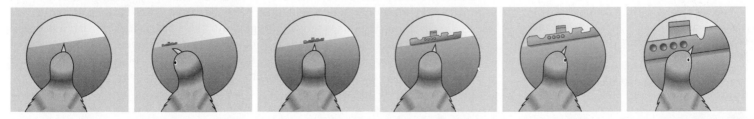

Burrhus Frederic Skinner

During his first TV appearance he was asked, "Would you, if you had to choose, burn your children or your books?" He said he would choose to burn his children, since his contribution to the future lay more in his writings than in his genes. B. F. Skinner (1904–1990) delighted in controversy, and his response earned him many TV appearances.

Skinner was born into a middle-class Pennsylvania family. As a youth he was always building things—scooters, sleds, wagons, rafts, slides, and merry-go-rounds. Later he would build the so-called Skinner box, which improved on Thorndike's puzzle box, as a way of studying operant behavior. He earned an undergraduate degree in English and turned to psychology only after failing to make his mark as a writer in New York's Greenwich Village.

A great popularizer of his own views, Skinner used reinforcement to teach pigeons to play basketball and the piano—sort of. On a visit to his daughter's grammar school class, it occurred to him that similar techniques might work with children. Thus he developed *programmed learning*. Although he had earlier failed at writing, he gathered a cultish following when he published *Walden II*, a novel in which children are socialized to *want* to behave prosocially.

Skinner and his followers have applied his principles not only to programmed learning but also to behavior modification programs for helping people with disorders ranging from substance abuse to phobias to sexual dysfunctions. He died eight days after receiving an unprecedented Lifetime Contribution to Psychology award from the American Psychological Association.

suggestion was not taken seriously. Apparently the Defense Department concluded that Project Pigeon was for the birds.

Project Pigeon may have been scrapped, but the principles of learning that Skinner applied to the project have found wide application. Project Pigeon also affords insight into the inventiveness of B. F. Skinner. Not only did Skinner make contributions to the understanding of learning, we will see that he also made technological innovations such as the "Skinner box" and the cumulative recorder. In operant conditioning, an organism learns to *do* something because of the effects or consequences of that behavior.

Skinner taught pigeons and other animals to engage in **operant behavior,** behavior that operates on, or manipulates, the environment. In classical conditioning, involuntary responses such as salivation or eyeblinks are often conditioned. In operant conditioning, *voluntary* responses such as pecking at a target, pressing a lever, or many of the skills required for playing tennis are acquired, or conditioned.
Question: What is operant conditioning?

Operant conditioning is defined as a simple form of learning in which an organism learns to engage in certain behavior because of the effects of that behavior. Phoebe taught me that fetching the ball would be followed by pleasant events, leading me to repeat the behavior.

In operant conditioning, organisms (such as your author!) learn to engage in operant behaviors, also known simply as **operants,** that result in presumably desirable consequences such as food, a hug, an A on a test, attention, or social approval. Some children learn to conform their behavior to social rules to earn the attention and approval of their parents and teachers. Other children, ironically, may learn to "misbehave," since misbehavior also gets attention from other people. In particular, children may learn to be "bad" when their "good" behavior is routinely ignored.

Methods of Operant Conditioning

In his most influential work, *The Behavior of Organisms*, Skinner (1938) made many theoretical and technological innovations. Among them was his focus on discrete behaviors such as lever pressing as the *unit*, or type, of behavior to be studied (Glenn et al., 1992). Other psychologists might focus on how organisms think or "feel." Skinner focused on measurable things that they do. Many psychologists have found these kinds of behavior inconsequential, especially when it comes to explaining and predicting human behavior. But Skinner's supporters point out that focusing on discrete behavior creates the potential for helpful changes. For example, in helping people combat depression, one psychologist might focus on their "feelings." A Skinnerian psychologist would focus on cataloguing (and modifying) the types of things that depressed people actually *do*. Directly modifying depressive behavior might also brighten clients' self-reports about their "feelings of depression."

To study operant behavior efficiently, Skinner devised an animal cage (or "operant chamber") that was dubbed the *Skinner box* by psychologist Clark Hull, whose theory of drive reductionism is discussed in Chapter 9. (Skinner himself repeatedly requested that his operant chamber *not* be called a Skinner box. History has thus far failed to honor his wishes, however.) Such a box is shown in Figure 5.6. The cage is ideal for laboratory experimentation because experimental conditions (treatments) can be carefully introduced and removed, and the effects on laboratory animals (defined as changes in rates of lever pressing) can be carefully observed. The operant chamber (or Skinner box) is also energy-efficient—in terms of the energy of the experimenter. In contrast to Thorndike's puzzle box, a "correct" response does not allow the animal to escape and have to be recaptured

Operant behavior ▲ Voluntary responses that are reinforced.
Operant conditioning ▲ A simple form of learning in which an organism learns to engage in behavior because it is reinforced.
Operant ▲ The same as an operant behavior.

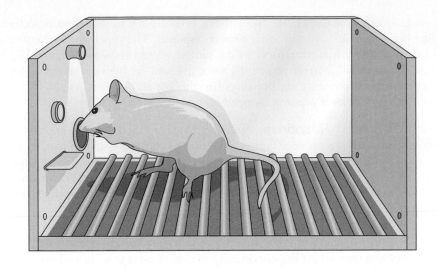

FIGURE 5.6 The Effects of Reinforcement.
One of the celebrities of modern psychology, an albino laboratory rat, earns its keep in a Skinner box. The animal presses a lever because of reinforcement—in the form of food pellets—delivered through the feeder. The habit strength of this operant is the frequency of lever pressing.

and placed back in the box. According to psychologist John Garcia, Skinner's "great contribution to the study of behavior was the marvelously efficient operant methodology" (1993, p. 1158).

The rat in Figure 5.6 was deprived of food and placed in a Skinner box with a lever at one end. At first it sniffed its way around the cage and engaged in random behavior. When organisms are behaving in a random manner, responses that have favorable consequences tend to occur more frequently. Responses that do not have favorable consequences are performed less frequently.

The rat's first pressing of the lever was inadvertent. However, because of this action, a food pellet dropped into the cage. The arrival of the food pellet increased the probability that the rat would press the lever again. The pellet is thus said to have *reinforced* lever pressing.

Skinner further mechanized his laboratory procedure by making use of a turning drum, or cumulative recorder, a tool that had previously been used by physiologists (see Figure 5.7). The cumulative recorder provides a precise measure of operant behavior. The experimenter need not even be present to record the number of correct responses.

www 5 PS 9

CLICK4™ *Skinner's classic article, "Superstition in the Pigeon."*

Total number of responses 26

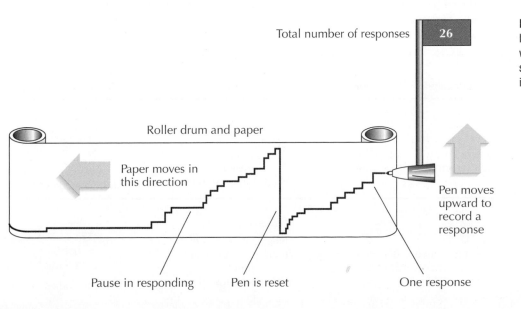

Roller drum and paper

Paper moves in this direction

Pen moves upward to record a response

Pause in responding   Pen is reset   One response

FIGURE 5.7 The Cumulative Recorder.
In the cumulative recorder, paper moves to the left while a pen jerks up to record each targeted response. When the pen reaches the top of the paper, it is automatically reset to the bottom.

In the example used, the lever in the Skinner box is connected to the recorder so that the recording pen moves upward with each correct response. The paper moves continuously to the left at a slow but regular pace. In the sample record shown in Figure 5.7, lever pressings (which record correct responses) were few and far between at first. But after several reinforced responses, lever pressings became fast and furious. When the rat was no longer hungry, the lever pressing dropped off and then stopped.

The First "Correct" Response

In operant conditioning, it matters little how the first response that is reinforced comes to be made. The organism can happen on it by chance, as in random learning. The organism can also be physically guided to make the response. You may command your dog to "Sit!" and then press its backside down until it is in a sitting position. Finally you reinforce sitting with food or a pat on the head and a kind word.

Animal trainers use physical guiding or coaxing to bring about the first "correct" response. Can you imagine how long it would take to train your dog if you waited for it to sit or roll over and then seized the opportunity to command it to sit or roll over? Both of you would age significantly in the process.

People, of course, can be verbally guided into desired responses when they are learning tasks such as spelling, adding numbers, or operating a machine. But they need to be informed when they have made the correct response. Knowledge of results often is all the reinforcement people need to learn new skills.

Types of Reinforcers

Any stimulus which increases the probability that responses preceding it will be repeated serves as a reinforcer. **Question: What are the various kinds of reinforcers?** Reinforcers include food pellets when an organism has been deprived of food, water when it has been deprived of liquid, the opportunity to mate, and the sound of a bell that has previously been associated with eating. Skinner distinguished between positive and negative reinforcers.

Positive and Negative Reinforcers

Positive reinforcers increase the probability that an operant will occur when they are applied. Food and approval usually serve as positive reinforcers. **Negative reinforcers** increase the probability that an operant will occur when they are *removed* (see Figure 5.8). People often learn to plan ahead so that they need not fear that things will go wrong. In such cases fear acts as a negative reinforcer, because *removal* of fear increases the probability that the behaviors preceding it (such as planning ahead or fleeing a predator) will be repeated.

Greater reinforcers prompt more rapid learning than do lesser reinforcers. Organisms typically choose larger reinforcers as well. For example, pigeons who learn that one food well has more food than another choose the well with more food (Olthof & Roberts, 2000). (Size matters.) Similarly, you would probably choose a job that paid $1,000 over a

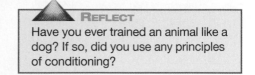

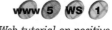

www **5** WS **1**

CLICK4™ *a Web tutorial on positive reinforcement.*

Positive reinforcer ▲ A reinforcer that when *presented* increases the frequency of an operant.

Negative reinforcer ▲ A reinforcer that when *removed* increases the frequency of an operant.

FIGURE 5.8 Positive Versus Negative Reinforcers.
All reinforcers *increase* the frequency of behavior. However, negative reinforcers are aversive stimuli that increase the frequency of behavior when they are *removed*. In these examples, teacher approval functions as a positive reinforcer when students study harder because of it. Teacher *disapproval* functions as a negative reinforcer when its *removal* increases the frequency of studying. Can you think of situations in which teacher approval might function as a negative reinforcer?

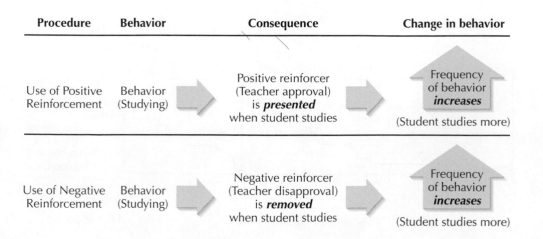

Procedure	Behavior	Consequence	Change in behavior
Use of Positive Reinforcement	Behavior (Studying)	Positive reinforcer (Teacher approval) **is presented** when student studies	Frequency of behavior **increases** (Student studies more)
Use of Negative Reinforcement	Behavior (Studying)	Negative reinforcer (Teacher disapproval) **is removed** when student studies	Frequency of behavior **increases** (Student studies more)

similar job that paid $10. (If not, get in touch with me—I have some chores for you.) With sufficient reinforcement, operants become *habits*. They have a high probability of recurrence in certain situations.

Immediate Versus Delayed Reinforcers   Immediate reinforcers are more effective than delayed reinforcers. Therefore, the short-term consequences of behavior often provide more of an incentive than the long-term consequences. Some students socialize when they should be studying because the pleasure of socializing is immediate. Studying may not pay off until the final exam or graduation. (This is why younger students do better with frequent tests.) It is difficult to quit smoking cigarettes because the reinforcement of nicotine is immediate and the health hazards of smoking more distant. Focusing on short-term reinforcement is also connected with careless sexual behavior.

Primary and Secondary Reinforcers   We can also distinguish between primary and secondary, or conditioned, reinforcers. **Primary reinforcers** are effective because of an organism's biological makeup. Food, water, adequate warmth (positive reinforcers), and pain (a negative reinforcer) all serve as primary reinforcers. **Secondary reinforcers** acquire their value through being associated with established reinforcers. For this reason they are also termed **conditioned reinforcers.** We may seek money because we have learned that it may be exchanged for primary reinforcers. Money, attention, social approval—all are conditioned reinforcers in our culture. We may be suspicious of, or not "understand," people who are not interested in money or the approval of others. Part of understanding others lies in being able to predict what they will find reinforcing.

Reinforcers are a key factor in operant conditioning. Let us consider others.

REVIEW

(19) Thorndike originated the law of _____ in learning. (20) He believed that _____ stamp in behavior and punishments stamp it out. (21) Skinner developed the concept of _____ as an alternative to those of reward and punishment. (22) _____ reinforcers increase the probability that operants will occur when they are applied. (23) _____ reinforcers increase the probability that operants will occur when they are removed. (24) _____ reinforcers such as food have their value because of the biological makeup of the organism. (25) _____ reinforcers, such as money, acquire their value through association with established reinforcers.

Pulling It Together: What kind of gadgetry did Skinner innovate to study operant conditioning? How do Skinner's views differ from those of Thorndike?

FACTORS IN OPERANT CONDITIONING

Reinforcers are used to strengthen responses. What happens, then, when reinforcement stops? ***Question: What are the roles of extinction and spontaneous recovery in operant conditioning?***   In the following sections we consider this question and others.

Extinction and Spontaneous Recovery in Operant Conditioning

In operant conditioning as in classical conditioning, extinction is a process in which stimuli lose the ability to evoke learned responses because the events that followed the stimuli no longer occur. In classical conditioning, however, the "events" that normally follow and confirm the appropriateness of the learned response (that is, the conditioned response) are the unconditioned stimuli. In Pavlov's experiment, for example, the meat powder was the event that followed and confirmed the appropriateness of salivation. In operant conditioning, in contrast, the ensuing events are reinforcers. Thus, in operant conditioning the extinction of learned responses (that is, operants) results from the repeated performance of operant behavior without reinforcement. After a number of trials, the operant

> ◢◣ **REFLECT**
>
> Is extinction within classical conditioning the same as extinction within operant conditioning? Explain.

Primary reinforcer ▲ An unlearned reinforcer.
Secondary reinforcer ▲ A stimulus that gains reinforcement value through association with established reinforcers.
Conditioned reinforcer ▲ Another term for a secondary reinforcer.

CLICK4™ *more information on negative reinforcement at Negative Reinforcement University.*

Punishment ▲ An unpleasant stimulus that suppresses the behavior it follows.

behavior is no longer displayed. If you go for a month without mail, you may stop checking the mailbox.

When some time is allowed to pass after the extinction process, an organism will usually perform the operant again when placed in a situation in which the operant had been reinforced previously. Such spontaneous recovery of learned responses occurs in operant conditioning as well as in classical conditioning. If the operant is reinforced at this time, it quickly regains its former strength. (Finding a few letters in the mailbox one week may again encourage you to check the mailbox daily.) Spontaneous recovery of extinguished operants suggests that they are inhibited or suppressed by the extinction process and not lost permanently.

Reinforcers Versus Rewards and Punishments

Reinforcers are defined as stimuli that increase the frequency of behavior. *Question: Why did Skinner make a point of distinguishing between reinforcers on the one hand and rewards and punishments on the other?* Reinforcers are known by their effects, whereas rewards and punishments are known by how they feel. It may be that most reinforcers—food, hugs, having the other person admit to starting the argument, and so on—feel good, or are pleasant events. Yet things that we might assume would feel bad, such as a slap on the hand or disapproval from a teacher, may be reinforcing to some—perhaps because such experiences confirm negative feelings toward teachers.

Rewards, like reinforcers, tend to increase the frequency of behavior, but rewards are defined as pleasant events, things that tend to feel good. Skinner preferred the concept of reinforcement to that of reward because reinforcement does not suggest trying to "get inside the head" of an organism (whether a human or lower animal) to guess what it would find pleasant or unpleasant. A list of reinforcers is arrived at scientifically, *empirically*— that is, by observing what sorts of stimuli increase the frequency of the behavior. However, we should note that some psychologists use the term *reward* synonymously with *positive reinforcement*.

Punishments are defined as aversive events that suppress or decrease the frequency of the behavior they follow (see Figure 5.9). Punishment can rapidly suppress undesirable behavior and may be warranted in "emergencies," such as when a child tries to run into the street.

Question: Why do many psychologists disapprove of punishment? Despite the fact that punishment usually works, many learning theorists agree that punishment often fails to achieve the goals of parents, teachers, and others (Collins, 1995). Consider the following reasons for avoiding the use of punishment:

1. It hurts.
2. Punishment does not in itself suggest an alternative acceptable form of behavior.

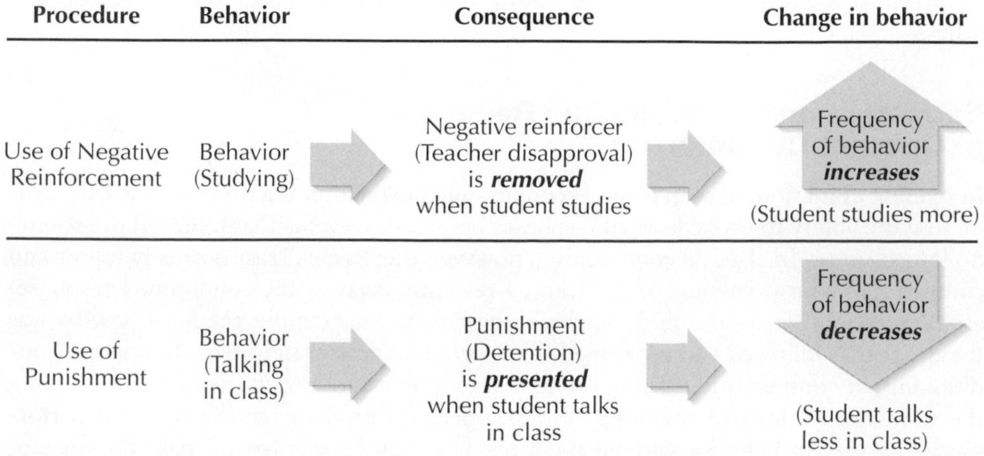

FIGURE 5.9   Negative Reinforcers Versus Punishments.
Negative reinforcers and punishments both tend to be aversive stimuli. However, reinforcers *increase* the frequency of behavior. Punishments *decrease* the frequency of behavior. Negative reinforcers increase the frequency of behavior when they are *removed*. Punishments decrease or suppress the frequency of behavior when they are *applied*. Can you think of situations in which punishing students might have effects other than those desired by the teacher?

Procedure	Behavior	Consequence	Change in behavior
Use of Negative Reinforcement	Behavior (Studying)	Negative reinforcer (Teacher disapproval) is **removed** when student studies	Frequency of behavior **increases** (Student studies more)
Use of Punishment	Behavior (Talking in class)	Punishment (Detention) is **presented** when student talks in class	Frequency of behavior **decreases** (Student talks less in class)

3. Punishment tends to suppress undesirable behavior only under circumstances in which its delivery is guaranteed. It does not take children long to learn that they can "get away with murder" with one parent or teacher but not with another.

4. Punished organisms may withdraw from the situation. Severely punished children may run away, cut class, or drop out of school.

5. Punishment can create anger and hostility. Adequate punishment almost always suppresses unwanted behavior—but at what cost? The child may express accumulated feelings of hostility against other children.

6. Punishment may generalize too far. A child who is punished severely for bad table manners may stop eating altogether. Overgeneralization is more likely to occur when children do not know exactly why they are being punished and when they have not been shown alternative acceptable behaviors.

7. Punishment may be modeled as a way of solving problems or coping with stress (Straus, 1994). We will see that one way children learn is by observing others. Even though children may not immediately perform the behavior they observe, they may perform it later on, even as adults, when their circumstances are similar to those of the model.

8. Finally, children learn responses that are punished. Whether or not children choose to perform punished responses, punishment draws their attention to these responses.

It is usually preferable to focus on rewarding children for desirable behavior than on punishing them for unwanted behavior. By ignoring their misbehavior, or by using **time out** from positive reinforcement, we can consistently avoid reinforcing children for misbehavior.

To reward or positively reinforce children for desired behavior takes time and care. Avoiding the use of punishment is not enough. First, we must pay attention to children when they are behaving well. If we take their desirable behavior for granted and respond to them only when they misbehave, we may be encouraging misbehavior. Second, we must be certain that children are aware of, and capable of performing, desired behavior. It is harmful and fruitless merely to punish children for unwanted behavior. We must also carefully guide them, either physically or verbally, into making the desired responses, and then reward them. We cannot teach children table manners by waiting for them to exhibit proper responses at random and then reinforcing them for their responses. Try holding a reward of ice cream behind your back and waiting for a child to exhibit proper manners. You will have a slippery dining room floor long before the child develops good table manners.

Discriminative Stimuli

B. F. Skinner might not have been able to get his pigeons into the drivers' seats of missiles, but he had no problem training them to respond to traffic lights. Try the following experiment for yourself.

Find a pigeon. Or sit on a park bench, close your eyes, and one will find you. Place it in a Skinner box with a button on the wall. Drop a food pellet into the cage whenever the pigeon pecks the button. (Soon it will learn to peck the button whenever it has not eaten for a while.) Now place a small green light in the cage. Turn it on and off intermittently throughout the day. Reinforce button pecking with food whenever the green light is on, but not when the light is off. It will not take long for this clever city pigeon to learn that it will gain as much by grooming itself or cooing and flapping around as it will by pecking the button when the light is off.

The green light will have become a discriminative stimulus. ***Question: What are discriminative stimuli?*** **Discriminative stimuli** such as green or red lights act as cues. They provide information about when an operant (in the case of the pigeon, pecking a button) will be reinforced (by a food pellet being dropped into the cage).

Operants that are not reinforced tend to be extinguished. For the pigeon in our experiment, the behavior of pecking the button *when the light is off* is extinguished.

A moment's reflection will suggest many ways in which discriminative stimuli influence our behavior. Isn't it more efficient to answer the telephone when it is ringing? Do

A Discriminative Stimulus.
You might not think that pigeons are very discriminating, yet they readily learn that pecking will not bring food in the presence of a discriminative stimulus such as a red light.

▲ **REFLECT**
Can you think of instances in which you have been — or are — affected by rewards and punishments?

Time out ▲ Removal of an organism from a situation in which reinforcement is available when unwanted behavior is shown.

Discriminative stimulus ▲ In operant conditioning, a stimulus that indicates that reinforcement is available.

you think it is wise to try to get smoochy when your date is blowing smoke in your face or downing a bottle of antacid tablets?

We noted that a pigeon learns to peck a button if food drops into its cage when it does so. What if you want the pigeon to continue to peck the button but you're running out of food? Do not despair. (Worse things have happened.) As we see in the following section, you can keep that bird pecking away indefinitely, even as you hold up on most of the food.

Schedules of Reinforcement

In operant conditioning, some responses are maintained by means of **continuous reinforcement.** You probably become warmer every time you put on heavy clothing. You probably become less thirsty every time you drink water. Yet if you have ever watched people tossing away money down the maws of slot machines, you know that behavior can also be maintained by means of **partial reinforcement.** *Questions: What are the various schedules of reinforcement? How do they affect behavior?*

Folklore about gambling is based on solid learning theory. You can get a person "hooked" on gambling by fixing the game so as to allow heavy winnings at first. Then you gradually space out the winnings (reinforcements) until gambling is maintained by infrequent winning—or even no winning at all. Partial reinforcement schedules can maintain gambling behavior, like other behavior, for a great deal of time, even though it goes unreinforced (Pulley, 1998).

New operants or behaviors are acquired most rapidly through continuous reinforcement or, in some cases, through "one-trial learning" that meets with great reinforcement. People who cannot control their gambling often had big wins at the racetrack or casino or in the lottery in their late teens or early twenties (Greene, 1982). But once the operant has been acquired, it can be maintained by tapering off to a schedule of partial reinforcement.

Responses that have been maintained by partial reinforcement are more resistant to extinction than responses that have been maintained by continuous reinforcement (Rescorla, 1999). From the cognitive perspective, we could suggest that organisms that have experienced partial reinforcement do not expect reinforcement every time they engage in a response. Therefore, they are more likely to persist in the absence of reinforcement.

There are four basic types of reinforcement schedules. They are determined by changing either the *interval* of time that must elapse between correct responses before reinforcement occurs or the *ratio* (number) of responses that must occur before reinforcement is provided. If reinforcement of responses is immediate (zero seconds), the reinforcement schedule is continuous. A larger interval of time, such as 1 or 30 seconds, is one kind of partial-reinforcement schedule. A one-to-one (1:1) ratio of correct responses to reinforcements is also a continuous-reinforcement schedule. A higher ratio such as 2:1 or 5:1 creates another kind of partial-reinforcement schedule.

More specifically, the four basic reinforcement schedules are *fixed-interval, variable-interval, fixed-ratio,* and *variable-ratio* schedules (see Figure 5.10).

Interval Schedules   In a **fixed-interval schedule,** a fixed amount of time—say, a minute—must elapse between the previous and subsequent times when reinforcement for correct responses occurs. With a fixed-interval schedule, an organism's response rate falls off after each reinforcement and then picks up again as the time when reinforcement will occur approaches. For example, in a 1-minute fixed-interval schedule, a rat is reinforced with, say, a food pellet for the first operant—for example, the first pressing of a lever—that occurs after a minute has elapsed. After each reinforcement, the rat's rate of lever pressing slows down, but as the end of the 1-minute interval draws near, lever pressing increases in frequency, as suggested in Figure 5.10. It is as if the rat has learned that it must wait a while before it is reinforced. The resultant record on the cumulative recorder shows a series of characteristic upward-moving waves, or scallops, which are referred to as a *fixed-interval scallop.*

Car dealers use fixed-interval reinforcement schedules when they offer incentives for buying up the remainder of the year's line every summer and fall. In a sense, they are sup-

Continuous reinforcement ▲ A schedule of reinforcement in which every correct response is reinforced.
Partial reinforcement ▲ One of several reinforcement schedules in which not every correct response is reinforced.
Fixed-interval schedule ▲ A schedule in which a fixed amount of time must elapse between the previous and subsequent times that reinforcement is available.

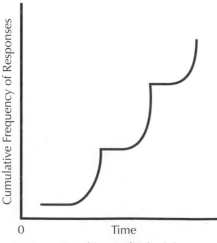

FIGURE 5.10   The "Fixed-Interval Scallop."
Organisms who are reinforced on a fixed-interval schedule tend to slack off responding after each reinforcement. The rate of response picks up as they near the time when reinforcement will become available. The results on the cumulative recorder look like upward-moving waves, or scallops.

pressing buying at other times, except for consumers whose current cars are in their death throes or those with little self-control. Similarly, you learn to check your e-mail only at a certain time of day if your correspondent writes at that time each day.

Reinforcement is more unpredictable in a **variable-interval schedule.** Therefore, the response rate is steadier but lower. If the boss calls us in for a weekly report, we probably work hard to pull things together just before the report is to be given, just as we might cram the night before a weekly quiz. But if we know that the boss might call us in for a report on the progress of a certain project at any time (variable-interval schedule), we are likely to keep things in a state of reasonable readiness at all times. However, our efforts are unlikely to have the intensity they would in a fixed-interval schedule (for example, a weekly report). Similarly, we are less likely to cram for unpredictable pop quizzes than we are to study for regularly scheduled quizzes. But we are likely to do at least some studying on a regular basis. If you receive e-mail from your correspondent at irregular intervals, you are likely to check your e-mail regularly, but with somewhat less eagerness.

Ratio Schedules   In a **fixed-ratio schedule,** reinforcement is provided after a fixed number of correct responses have been made. In a **variable-ratio schedule,** reinforcement is provided after a variable number of correct responses have been made. In a 10:1 variable-ratio schedule, the mean number of correct responses that would have to be made before a subsequent correct response would be reinforced is 10, but the ratio of correct responses to reinforcements might be allowed to vary from, say, 1:1 to 20:1 on a random basis.

Fixed- and variable-ratio schedules maintain a high response rate. With a fixed-ratio schedule, it is as if the organism learns that it must make several responses before being reinforced. It then "gets them out of the way" as rapidly as possible. Consider the example of piecework. If a worker must sew five shirts to receive $10, he or she is on a fixed-ratio (5:1) schedule and is likely to sew at a uniformly high rate, although there might be a brief pause after each reinforcement. With a variable-ratio schedule, reinforcement can come at any time. This unpredictability also maintains a high response rate. Slot machines tend to pay off on variable-ratio schedules, and players can be seen popping coins into them and yanking their "arms" with barely a pause. I have seen players who do not even stop to pick up their winnings. Instead, they continue to pop in the coins, whether from their original stack or from the winnings tray.

Shaping   If you are teaching the macarena to people who have never danced, do not wait until they have performed it precisely before telling them they're on the right track. The foxtrot will be back in style before they have learned a thing.

We can teach complex behaviors by **shaping.**   *Question: How can we use shaping to teach complex behavior patterns?*   Shaping reinforces progressive steps toward the behavioral goal. At first, for example, it may be wise to smile and say, "Good" when a reluctant newcomer gathers the courage to get out on the dance floor, even if your feet are flattened by his initial clumsiness. If you are teaching someone to drive a car with a standard shift, at first generously reinforce the learner simply for shifting gears without stalling.

But as training proceeds, we come to expect more before we are willing to provide reinforcement. We reinforce **successive approximations** of the goal. If you want to train a rat to climb a ladder, first reinforce it with a food pellet when it turns toward the ladder. Then wait until it approaches the ladder before giving it a pellet. Then do not drop a pellet into the cage until the rat touches the ladder. In this way, the rat will reach the top of the ladder more quickly than if you had waited for the target behavior to occur at random.

Learning to drive a new standard-shift automobile to a new job also involves a complex sequence of operant behaviors. At first we actively seek out all the discriminative stimuli or landmarks that give us cues for when to turn—signs, buildings, hills, valleys. We also focus on shifting to a lower gear as we slow down so that the car won't stall. After many repetitions, these responses, or chains of behavior, become "habitual" and we need to pay very little attention to them.

Have you ever driven home from school or work and suddenly realized as you got out of your car that you couldn't recall exactly how you had returned home? Your entire

CLICK4™ *an essay assignment on schedules of reinforcement.*

▲ **REFLECT**
A pianist's fingers fly over the keys faster than the player can read notes or even think notes. What kinds of learning are at work in learning to play the piano?

▲ **REFLECT**
What role does habit play in your life? Do you have "good habits" and "bad habits"? How did they develop?

Variable-interval schedule ▲ A schedule in which a variable amount of time must elapse between the previous and subsequent times that reinforcement is available.
Fixed-ratio schedule ▲ A schedule in which reinforcement is provided after a fixed number of correct responses.
Variable-ratio schedule ▲ A schedule in which reinforcement is provided after a variable number of correct responses.
Shaping ▲ A procedure for teaching complex behaviors that at first reinforces approximations of the target behavior.
Successive approximations ▲ Behaviors that are progressively closer to a target behavior.

Reciting the Pledge.
Operant conditioning plays a role in the socialization of children. Parents and teachers usually reward children for expressing attitudes that coincide with their own and punish or ignore them when they express "deviant" attitudes.

trip may seem "lost." Were you in great danger? How could you allow such a thing to happen? Actually, it may be that your responses to the demands of the route and to driving your car had become so habitual that you did not have to focus on them. As you drove, you were able to think about dinner, a problem at work, or the weekend. But if something unusual had occurred on the way, such as hesitation in your engine or a severe rainstorm, you would have devoted as much attention to your driving as was needed to arrive home. Your trip was probably quite safe after all.

REVIEW

(26) In operant conditioning, repeated performance of a learned response in the absence of reinforcement leads to _____ of that response. (27) _____ are aversive stimuli that suppress the frequency of behavior. (28) A _____ stimulus indicates when an operant will be reinforced. (29) In a _____-_____ schedule, a specific amount of time must elapse since a previous correct response before reinforcement again becomes available. (30) In a _____-_____ schedule, the number of correct responses that must be performed before reinforcement becomes available is allowed to vary. (31) In shaping, we reinforce _____ approximations to the goal.

Pulling It Together: How can you use reinforcement schedules to maintain behavior indefinitely? Agree or disagree with the following statement and support your answer: We should not punish children.

APPLICATIONS OF OPERANT CONDITIONING

Operant conditioning, like classical conditioning, is not just an exotic laboratory procedure. We use it every day in our efforts to influence other people. ***Question: What are some applications of operant conditioning?*** Parents and peers induce children to acquire so-called gender-appropriate behavior patterns through rewards and punishments. Parents also tend to praise their children for sharing their toys and to punish them for being too aggressive. Peers participate in this **socialization** process by playing with children who are generous and nonaggressive and, often, by avoiding those who are not (Warman & Cohen, 2000).

Operant conditioning also plays a role in attitude formation. Adults often reward children for expressing attitudes that coincide with their own and punish or ignore them for expressing contradictory attitudes. Let us now consider some specific applications of operant conditioning.

Biofeedback Training: Gaining "Bleep" Control?

Biofeedback training (BFT) is based on principles of operant conditioning. BFT has enabled people and lower animals to learn to control autonomic responses in order to attain reinforcement (Miller, 1969). BFT has been an important innovation in the treatment of health-related problems during the past few decades.

Through BFT, organisms can gain control of autonomic functions such as the flow of blood in a finger. They can also learn to improve their control over functions that can be manipulated voluntarily, such as muscle tension. When people receive BFT, reinforcement is given in the form of *information*. Perhaps a sound changes in pitch or frequency of occurrence to signal that they have modified the autonomic function in the desired direction. For example, we can learn to emit alpha waves—the kind of brain wave associated with feelings of relaxation—through feedback from an electroencephalograph (an instrument that measures brain waves). Through the use of other instruments, people have learned to lower their muscle tension, their heart rates, and even their blood pressure.

BFT is also used with people who have lost neuromuscular control of parts of their body as a result of an accident. A "bleep" sound informs them when they have contracted a muscle or sent an impulse down a neural pathway. By concentrating on changing the bleeps, they also gradually regain voluntary control over the damaged function.

▲ REFLECT
Does it seem possible that people can learn to emit particular brain waves? How do learning theorists explain this outcome of learning?

Socialization ▲ Guidance of people into socially desirable behavior by means of verbal messages, the systematic use of rewards and punishments, and other methods of teaching.

Token Economies: Fishing for Chips

Behavior therapists apply operant conditioning in mental hospitals to foster desired responses such as social skills and to extinguish unwanted behaviors such as social withdrawal. In a **token economy,** psychologists give hospital residents or prison inmates tokens such as poker chips as reinforcements for desired behavior. The tokens reinforce the desired behavior because they can be exchanged for time watching television, desserts, and other commodities.

Principles of operant conditioning have also enabled psychologists and educators to develop many beneficial innovations, such as behavior modification in the classroom and programmed learning.

Case Study: Using Avoidance Learning to Save a Baby's Life

Operant conditioning techniques are sometimes used with children who are too young or distressed to respond to verbal forms of therapy. In one example, reported by Lang and Melamed (1969), a 9-month-old infant vomited regularly within 10 to 15 minutes after eating. Physicians could find no medical basis for the problem, and medical treatments were of no avail. When the case was brought to the attention of Lang and Melamed, the infant weighed only 9 pounds and was in critical condition, being fed by means of a pump.

The psychologists monitored the infant for the first physical indications (local muscle tension) that vomiting was to occur. When the child tensed prior to vomiting, a tone was sounded. The tone was followed by a painful but (presumably) harmless electric shock. After two 1-hour treatment sessions, the infant's muscle tensions ceased in response to the sounding of the tone in the absence of the shock, and vomiting soon ceased altogether. At a 1-year follow-up, the infant was still not vomiting and had gained a reasonable amount of weight.

How do we use principles of conditioning to explain this remarkable procedure? The psychologists first used classical conditioning. Through repeated pairings, the tone (CS) came to elicit the expectation of electric shock (US). Therefore, the psychologists could use the painful shock sparingly.

Use of punishment explains the infant's halting of vomiting. The electric shock and the tone (which became associated with the shock through classical conditioning) suppressed the local muscle tensions that led to vomiting and, of course, vomiting itself.

This learning occurred at an age long before any sort of verbal intervention could have been understood, and it apparently saved the infant's life. Similar procedures have been used to teach autistic children not to mutilate themselves.

Behavior Modification in the Classroom: Accentuating the Positive

Remember that reinforcers are defined as stimuli that increase the frequency of behavior—not as pleasant events. Ironically, adults frequently reinforce undesirable behavior in children by paying attention to them, or punishing them, when they misbehave but ignoring them when they behave in desirable ways. Similarly, teachers who raise their voices when children misbehave may be unintentionally conferring hero status on those pupils in the eyes of their peers (Wentzel, 1994). To the teacher's surprise, some children may go out of their way to earn disapproval.

Teacher preparation and in-service programs show teachers how to use behavior modification to reverse these response patterns. Teachers are taught to pay attention to children when they are behaving appropriately and, when possible, to ignore (that is, avoid reinforcing) misbehavior (Abramowitz & O'Leary, 1991). The younger the child, the more powerful the teacher's attention and approval seem to be.

Among older children and adolescents, peer approval is often a more powerful reinforcer than teacher approval. Peer approval may maintain misbehavior, and ignoring misbehavior may only allow peers to become more disruptive. In such cases it may be necessary to separate troublesome children from less-disruptive peers.

Praise.
Praise from the teacher reinforces desirable behavior in most children. Behavior modification in the classroom applies principles of operant conditioning.

www **5** **WS** **3**

CLICK4™ *Fuzz, a virtual animal, and train him with conditioning techniques!*

▲ **REFLECT**
Had you heard of behavior modification? Is it what you thought it was?

Token economy ▲ An environmental setting that fosters desired behavior by reinforcing it with tokens (secondary reinforcers) that can be exchanged for other reinforcers.

Teachers also frequently use time out from positive reinforcement to discourage misbehavior. In this method, children are placed in a drab, restrictive environment for a specified period, usually about 10 minutes, when they behave disruptively. While they are isolated, they cannot earn the attention of peers or teachers, and no reinforcers are present.

Programmed Learning: Step By Step

B. F. Skinner developed an educational method called **programmed learning** that is based on operant conditioning. This method assumes that any complex task involving conceptual learning as well as motor skills can be broken down into a number of small steps. These steps can be shaped individually and then combined in sequence to form the correct behavioral chain.

Programmed learning does not punish errors. Instead, correct responses are reinforced. Every child earns "100," but at her or his own pace. Programmed learning also assumes it is the task of the teacher (or program) to structure the learning experience in such a way that errors will not be made.

Some argue that behaviorism is too mechanical to be applied to humans. But the bell-and-pad method, behaviorist methods of fear reduction, use of avoidance learning to prevent the baby from vomiting, and other methods suggest that some useful methods would not have been derived from any other psychological theory. Because of applications like these, some psychologists argue that the full promise of behaviorism has not yet been realized (DeGrandpre, 2000).

Using Counterconditioning to Help Children Overcome Fears

Imagine that you want to encourage a child to try a new food—perhaps restaurant chicken as opposed to Daddy or Mommy chicken. You may be concerned that forcing the child to eat the new food could lead to hatred of that food. So you may wind up softly urging, "Just take one little bite." In your most encouraging voice, with your broadest smile, and nodding your head, you repeat, "Just one." If the child still refuses, perhaps you say, "Then just smell it!" You may use a little *modeling*, too. You may take a bite and say, "Mmmm, this is delicious!" and then encourage the child once more. If the child tries the chicken, you show great approval, including ample hugs and kisses *(reinforcements)*. Another reinforcer, we might hope, would be the taste of the food itself. (If not, find another restaurant.)

The method is *counterconditioning*. In counterconditioning, a pleasing stimulus is paired repeatedly with a fear-evoking object or situation. In this way, it comes to counteract the fear response.

How about encouraging a hesitant child to walk into the surf? Perhaps you cajole the child into putting in one foot at a time to avoid severe anxiety. Then you show approval with each additional step. Once in the water, fear may be further counterconditioned by the fun of splashing around. Counterconditioning is a gradual process that requires some patience.

Some parents, of course, toss a resistant child into the water. This method could be called *flooding* or sink-or-swim. The assumption is that the child will learn that the water is fun and see that hesitating was silly. But the method could backfire; the child could continue to fuss and develop a lasting aversion to swimming. By the way, cognitive therapist Aaron Beck overcame his own fear of blood by forcing himself to watch surgical operations.

REVIEW

(32) _____ training enables organisms to gain control of autonomic responses in order to attain reinforcement. (33) Lang and Melamed used _____ learning to save the life of a baby that repeatedly vomited after eating. (34) In using behavior _____, teachers reinforce desired behavior and extinguish undesired behavior by ignoring it. (35) _____ learning breaks down learning tasks into small steps and reinforces correct performance of each step.

▲ REFLECT
Have you learned from your mistakes? Why or why not?

www 5 L 7

CLICK4™ *Web sites exploring the many applications of operant conditioning, from biofeedback to animal training, at Sea World.*

Programmed learning ▲ A method of learning in which complex tasks are broken down into simple steps, each of which is reinforced. Errors are not reinforced.

Pulling It Together: How do the topics discussed in this section apply principles of operant conditioning?

COGNITIVE FACTORS IN LEARNING

Classical and operant conditioning were originally conceived of as relatively simple forms of learning. Much of conditioning's appeal is that it can be said to meet the behaviorist objective of explaining behavior in terms of observable events—in this case, laboratory conditions. Building on this theoretical base, some psychologists have suggested that the most complex human behavior involves the summation of a series of instances of conditioning. However, many psychologists believe that conditioning is too mechanical a process to explain all instances of learned behavior, even in laboratory rats (Weiner, 1991). They turn to cognitive factors to describe and explain additional findings in the psychology of learning.   *Question: How do we explain what happens during classical conditioning from a cognitive perspective?*

In addition to concepts such as *association* and *reinforcement*, cognitive psychologists use concepts such as *mental structures, schemas, templates,* and *information processing.* Cognitive psychologists see people as searching for information, weighing evidence, and making decisions. Let us consider some classic research that points to cognitive factors in learning, as opposed to mechanical associations. These cognitive factors are not necessarily limited to humans—although, of course, people are the only species that can talk about them.

www 5 L 6

CLICK4™ *Dr. P's virtual library on the training and behavior of dogs.*

CONTROVERSY IN PSYCHOLOGY

Contingency Theory

We have noted that behaviorists and cognitive psychologists interpret the conditioning process in different ways. Behaviorists explain it in terms of the pairing of stimuli. Cognitive psychologists explain classical conditioning in terms of the ways in which stimuli provide information that allows organisms to form and revise mental representations of their environment (Basic Behavioral Science Task Force, 1996b). Robert Rescorla conducted research in an effort to demonstrate which view is more accurate. His *contingency theory* suggests that learning occurs only when the conditioned stimulus provides *information* about the unconditioned stimulus.

In classical conditioning experiments with dogs, Rescorla (1967) obtained some results that are difficult to explain without reference to cognitive concepts. Each phase of his work paired a tone (a learned or conditioned stimulus, or CS) with an electric shock (an unlearned or unconditioned stimulus, or US), but in different ways. With one group of animals, the shock was consistently presented after the tone. That is, the unconditioned stimulus followed on the heels of the conditioned stimulus, as in Pavlov's studies. The dogs in this group learned to show a fear response when the tone was presented.

A second group of dogs heard an equal number of tones and received an equal number of electric shocks, but the shock never immediately followed the tone. In other words, the tone and the shock were not paired. Now, from the behaviorist perspective, the dogs should not have learned to associate the tone and the shock because one did not predict the other. Actually, the dogs learned quite a lot: They learned that they had nothing to fear when the tone was sounded! They showed vigilance and fear when the laboratory was quiet—for the shock could apparently come at any time—but they were calm in the presence of the tone.

The third group of dogs also received equal numbers of tones and shocks, but the stimuli were presented at purely random intervals. Occasionally they were paired, but most often they were not. According to Rescorla, behaviorists might argue that intermittent pairing of the tones and shocks should have brought about some learning. Yet it did not. The animals showed no fear in response to the tone. Rescorla suggests that the animals in this group learned nothing because the tones did not allow them to make predictions about electric shock.

Rescorla concluded that contiguity—that is, the co-appearance of two events (the unconditioned stimulus and the conditioned stimulus)—cannot in itself explain classical conditioning. Instead, learning occurs only when the conditioned stimulus (in this case, the tone) provides information about the unconditioned stimulus (in this case, the shock). According to **contingency theory,** learning occurs because a conditioned stimulus indicates that the unconditioned stimulus is likely to follow.

Behaviorists might counter, of course, that for the second group of dogs the *absence* of the tone became the signal for the shock. Shock may be a powerful enough event that the fear response becomes conditioned to the laboratory environment. For the third group of dogs, the shock was as likely to occur in the presence of the neutral stimulus as in its absence. Therefore, many behaviorists would expect no learning to occur.

Latent Learning: Forming Cognitive Maps

I'm all grown up. I know the whole mall.

The author's daughter Jordan at age 7

Many behaviorists argue that organisms acquire only responses, or operants, for which they are reinforced. E. C. Tolman, however, showed that rats also learn about their environment in the absence of reinforcement. In doing so, he demonstrated that rats must form cognitive maps of their surroundings. *Question: What is the evidence that people and lower organisms form cognitive maps of their environments?*

Tolman trained some rats to run through mazes for standard food goals. Other rats were permitted to explore the same mazes for several days without food goals or other rewards. After the unrewarded rats had been allowed to explore the mazes for 10 days, food rewards were placed in a box at the far end of the maze. The previously unrewarded rats reached the food box as quickly as the rewarded rats after only one or two reinforced trials (Tolman & Honzik, 1930).

Tolman concluded that rats learned about mazes in which they roamed even when they were unrewarded for doing so. He distinguished between *learning* and *performance.* Rats would acquire a cognitive map of a maze, and even though they would not be motivated to follow an efficient route to the far end, they would learn rapid routes from one end to the other just by roaming about within the maze. Yet this learning might remain hidden, or **latent,** until they were motivated to follow the rapid routes to obtain food goals.

Observational Learning: Monkey See, Monkey *May* Choose to Do

How many things have you learned from watching other people in real life, in films, and on television? From films and television, you may have gathered vague ideas about how to sky-dive, ride a surfboard, climb sheer cliffs, run a pattern to catch a touchdown pass in the Super Bowl, and dust for fingerprints, even if you have never tried these activities yourself. *Question: How do people learn by observing others?*

In their studies of social learning, Albert Bandura and his colleagues conducted experiments (e.g., Bandura et al., 1963) that show that we can acquire operants by observing the behavior of others. We may need some practice to refine the operants, but we can learn them through observation alone. We may also allow these operants or skills to remain latent. For example, we may not imitate aggressive behavior unless we are provoked and believe that we are more likely to be rewarded than punished for it.

Observational learning may account for most human learning. It occurs when, as children, we watch our parents cook, clean, or repair a broken appliance. Observational learning takes place when we watch teachers solve problems on the blackboard or hear them speak in a foreign language. Observational learning is not mechanically acquired through reinforcement. We can learn through observation without engaging in overt responses at all. It appears sufficient to pay attention to the behavior of others.

In the terminology of observational learning, a person who engages in a response to be imitated is a **model.** When observers see a model being reinforced for displaying an

How Do We Learn to Play a Musical Instrument? Can we explain playing the flute as the summation of myriad instances of conditioning, or must we explain it in terms of mental representations and cognitive maps? What developments in the nervous system make us "ready" to learn to play an instrument? What biological changes register the memories of the skills involved?

www 5 PS 10

CLICK4™ *Tolman's classic article, "Cognitive Maps in Rats and Men."*

▲ REFLECT
Have you ever studied an atlas, a road map, a cookbook, or a computer manual for the pleasure of doing so? What kind of learning were you engaging in?

Contingency theory ▲ The view that learning occurs when stimuli provide information about the likelihood of the occurrence of other stimuli.

Latent ▲ Hidden or concealed.

Observational learning ▲ The acquisition of knowledge and skills through the observation of others (who are called *models*) rather than by means of direct experience.

Model ▲ An organism that engages in a response that is then imitated by another organism.

operant, the observers are said to be *vicariously* reinforced. Display of the operant thus becomes more likely for the observer as well as for the model. What happens when the model is *violent?*

The Effects of Media Violence

Much human learning occurs through observation. We learn by observing parents and peers, attending school, reading books, and—in one of the more controversial aspects of modern life—watching media such as television and films. Nearly all of us have been exposed to television, videotapes, and films in the classroom. Children in day care centers often watch *Sesame Street*. There are filmed and videotaped versions of great works of literature such as Orson Welles' *Macbeth* or Laurence Olivier's *Hamlet*. Nearly every school shows films of laboratory experiments. Sometimes we view "canned lectures" by master teachers.

But what about our viewing *outside* the classroom? Television is one of our major sources of informal observational learning. Children are routinely exposed to scenes of murder, beating, and sexual assault—just by turning on the TV set (Huesmann & Miller, 1994; Wilson, 1997). If a child watches 2 to 4 hours of TV a day, she or he will have seen 8,000 murders and another 100,000 acts of violence *by the time she or he has finished elementary school* (Eron, 1993). Are kids less likely to be exposed to violence by going to the movies? No. One study found that virtually all G-rated animated films have scenes of violence, with a mean duration of 9 to 10 minutes per film (Yokota & Thompson, 2000).

Moreover, violence tends to be glamorized on TV. For example, in one cartoon show, superheroes battle villains who are trying to destroy or take over the world. Violence is often shown to have only temporary or minimal effects. (How often has Wile E. Coyote fallen from a cliff and been pounded into the ground by a boulder, only to bounce back and pursue the Road Runner once more?) In the great majority of violent TV shows, there is no remorse, criticism, or penalty for violent behavior (Cantor, 1997; Wilson, 1997). Few TV programs show harmful long-term consequences of aggressive behavior.

Why all this violence? Simple: Violence sells. But does violence do more than sell? **Question: What do we know about the effects of media violence?** Does media violence *cause* real violence? If so, what can parents and educators do to prevent the fictional from spilling over into the real world?

In any event, most organizations of health professionals agree that media violence does contribute to aggression (Holland, 2000). Consider a number of ways in which depictions of violence make such a contribution:

WWW 5 PS 11

CLICK4™ *the classic Bandura, Ross, and Ross article, "Transmission of Aggression Through Imitation of Aggressive Models."*

FIGURE 5.11 Classic Research on the Imitation of Aggressive Models.
Albert Bandura and his colleagues showed that children frequently imitate aggressive behavior that they observe. In the top row, an adult model strikes a clown doll. The lower rows show a boy and a girl imitating the aggressive behavior.

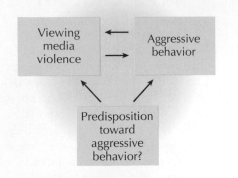

FIGURE 5.12   What Are the Connections Between Media Violence and Aggressive Behavior?
Does media violence lead to aggression? Does aggressive behavior lead to a preference for viewing violence? Or does a third factor, such as a predisposition toward aggressive behavior, contribute to both? Might such a predisposition be in part genetic?

▲ *Observational Learning.* Children learn from observation (Holland, 2000). TV violence supplies *models* of aggressive "skills," which children may acquire. In fact, children are more likely to imitate what their parents do than to heed what they say. If adults say that they disapprove of aggression but smash furniture or slap each other when frustrated, children are likely to develop the notion that aggression is the way to handle frustration. Classic experiments show that children tend to imitate the aggressive behavior they see on the media (Bandura et al., 1963) (see Figure 5.11). Media violence also provides viewers with aggressive *scripts*— that is, ideas about how to behave in situations like those they have observed (Huesmann & Miller, 1994).

▲ *Disinhibition.* Punishment inhibits behavior. Conversely, media violence may disinhibit aggressive behavior, especially when media characters "get away" with violence or are rewarded for it.

▲ *Increased Arousal.* Media violence and aggressive video games increase viewers' level of arousal. That is, television "works them up." We are more likely to be aggressive under high levels of arousal.

▲ *Priming of Aggressive Thoughts and Memories.* Media violence "primes" or arouses aggressive ideas and memories (Berkowitz, 1988).

▲ *Habituation.* We become "habituated to," or used to, repeated stimuli. Repeated exposure to TV violence may decrease viewers' sensitivity to real violence. If children come to perceive violence as the norm, they may become more tolerant of it and place less value on restraining aggressive urges (Holland, 2000).

A joint statement issued by the American Medical Association, the American Academy of Pediatrics, the American Psychological Association, and the American Academy of Child and Adolescent Psychiatry (Holland, 2000) made some additional points:

▲ Children who see a lot of violence are more likely to view violence as an effective way of settling conflicts. Children exposed to violence are more likely to assume that violence is acceptable.

▲ Viewing violence can decrease the likelihood that one will take action on behalf of a victim when violence occurs.

▲ Viewing violence may lead to real-life violence. Children exposed to violent programming at a young age are more likely to be violent themselves later on in life.

Violent video games are also connected with aggressive behavior. Craig Anderson and Karen Dill (2000) found that playing violent video games increases aggressive

Psychology and Modern Life

Teaching Children *Not* to Imitate Media Violence

Our children are going to be exposed to media violence—if not in Saturday morning cartoon shows, then in evening dramas and in the news. Or they'll hear about violence from friends, watch other children get into fights, or read about violence in the newspapers. If all those sources of violence were somehow hidden from view, they would learn about violence in *Hamlet, Macbeth,* even the Bible. The notion of preventing children from being exposed to violent models may be impractical.

What, then, should be done? Parents and educators can do many things to tone down the impact of media violence (Broder, 2000; Huesmann et al., 1983). Children who watch violent shows act less aggressively when they are informed that:

1. The violent behavior they observe in the media does *not* represent the behavior of most people.

2. The apparently aggressive behaviors they watch are *not* real. They reflect camera tricks, special effects, and stunts.

3. Most people resolve conflicts by nonviolent means.

4. The real-life consequences of violence are harmful to the victim and, often, the aggressor.

In observational learning, the emphasis is on the cognitive. If children consider violence to be inappropriate for them, they will probably not act aggressively even if they have acquired aggressive skills.

IN REVIEW
Kinds of Learning

Kind of Learning	What Is Learned	How It Is Learned
Classical Conditioning	Association of events; anticipations, signs, expectations; automatic responses to new stimuli	A neutral stimulus (CS) is repeatedly paired with a stimulus (US) that elicits a response (UR) until the neutral stimulus produces a response (CR) that anticipates and prepares for the US.
Operant Conditioning	Behavior that operates on, or affects, the environment to produce consequences	A response is rewarded or reinforced so that it occurs with greater frequency in similar situations.
Observational Learning	Expectations (if-then relationships), knowledge, and skills	A person observes the behavior of another person (live or through media such as films, television, or books) and its effects.

thoughts and behavior in the laboratory. It is also connected with a history of juvenile delinquency. However, males are relatively more likely than females to act aggressively after playing violent video games, and are more likely to see the world as a hostile place. Students who obtain higher grades are also less likely to behave aggressively following exposure to violent media games. Thus cultural stereotyping of males and females, possible biological gender differences, and moderating variables like academic achievement also come into play when we are talking about the effects of media violence. As in so many other areas of psychology and life, there is no simple one-to-one connection between media violence and violence in real life.

There seems to be a circular relationship between exposure to media violence and aggressive behavior (Craig & Dill, 2000; Eron, 1982; Funk et al., 2000). Yes, TV violence and violent video games contribute to aggressive behavior, but aggressive youngsters are also more likely to seek out this kind of "entertainment."

Aggressive children are frequently rejected by their nonaggressive peers—at least in middle-class culture (Eron, 1982; Warman & Cohen, 2000). Aggressive children may watch more television because their peer relationships are less fulfilling and because the high incidence of TV violence tends to confirm their view that aggressive behavior is normal (Eron, 1982). Media violence also interacts with other contributors to violence. For example, parental rejection and use of physical punishment further increase the likelihood of aggression in children (Eron, 1982). A harsh home life may further confirm the TV viewer's vision of the world as a violent place and further encourage reliance on television for companionship.

REVIEW

(36) According to _____ theory, learning occurs when the CS provides information about the US. (37) Tolman's work with rats suggests that they develop _____ maps of the environment. (38) Tolman refers to learning without performing as _____ learning. Media violence contributes to violent behavior by supplying models for aggressive skills, disinhibiting aggressive impulses, priming aggressive thoughts, increasing arousal, and habituating observers to violence.

Pulling It Together: How do the results of research into cognitive factors in learning challenge behaviorist principles? Refer to contingency theory, latent learning, and observational learning in your answer.

www 5 Q 2
CLICK4™ *a quiz covering the second half of this chapter.*

www 5 FC 1
CLICK4™ *electronic flash cards to review your knowledge of key terms and people in this chapter.*

What Are the Effects of Media Violence?
Preschool children in the United States watch TV an average of four hours a day. Schoolchildren spend more hours at the TV set than in the classroom. Is it any wonder that psychologists, educators, and parents express concern about the effects of media violence?

It would be of little use to discuss how we learn if we were not capable of remembering what we learn from second to second, from day to day, or in many cases for a lifetime. In the next chapter we turn our attention to the subject of memory. In Chapters 7 and 8 we will see how learning is intertwined with cognition, language, and intelligence.

TRUTH ▨ FICTION
REVISITED

▱ **It is true that dogs can be trained to salivate when a bell is sounded.** *The training is accomplished by means of the classical conditioning method of pairing the sound of the bell with the delivery of food. See page 156.*

▱ **It is true that one nauseating meal can give rise to a food aversion that persists for years.** *See page 158.*

▱ **It is true that psychologists helped a young boy overcome fear of rabbits by having him eat cookies while a rabbit was brought progressively nearer to him.** *The method was pioneered by John B. Watson and Mary Cover Jones. See page 164.*

▱ **It is true that during World War II a psychologist devised a plan for training pigeons to guide missiles to their targets.** *That psychologist was B. F. Skinner, and his plan employed principles of operant conditioning. See page 166.*

▱ **Actually, punishment does work.** *Strong punishment generally suppresses the behavior it follows. The issues pertaining to punishment concern its limitations and side effects. See page 171.*

▱ **It is true that rats can be trained to climb a ramp, cross a bridge, climb a ladder, pedal a toy car, and do several other tasks—all in sequence.** *The procedure used to do so is called* shaping. *See page 173.*

▱ **It is true that psychologists fashioned a method to teach an emaciated 9-month-old infant to stop throwing up.** *They derived the method from principles of conditioning. Conditioning allowed the psychologists to focus on what the child actually* did *and not on what the child might know or understand. See page 175.*

▱ **It is not true that we must make mistakes if we are to learn.** *The idea that we must make mistakes derives from folklore to the effect that we learn from (bad) experience. However, we also learn from good (positively reinforced) experiences and from the experiences of others. See page 176.*

▱ **Actually, a scientific connection has been established between TV violence and aggression in real life.** *But does media violence* cause *aggression? What are the possible relationships between media violence and aggression? (See Figure 5.12.) See page 180.*

1. What is learning?

Learning is the process by which experience leads to modified representations of the environment (the cognitive perspective) and relatively permanent changes in behavior (the behavioral perspective).

2. What is classical conditioning?

Classical conditioning is a simple form of associative learning in which a previously neutral stimulus (the conditioned stimulus, or CS) comes to elicit the response evoked by a second stimulus (the unconditioned stimulus, or US) as a result of repeatedly being paired with the second stimulus.

3. What is the contribution of Ivan Pavlov to the psychology of learning?

The Russian physiologist Ivan Pavlov happened upon conditioning by chance, as he was studying salivation in laboratory dogs. Pavlov discovered that reflexes can be learned, or *conditioned*, through association.

4. What are the various types of classical conditioning?`

In delayed conditioning, the CS is presented before the US. In the most efficient delayed conditioning procedure, the CS is presented about 0.5 second before the US. Other classical conditioning procedures include trace conditioning, simultaneous conditioning, and backward conditioning, in which the US is presented first.

5. What are taste aversions? Why are they of special interest to psychologists?

Taste aversions are examples of classical conditioning in which organisms learn that a food is noxious on the basis of nauseating experience. Taste aversions are of special interest because learning may occur on the basis of a single association and because the unconditioned stimulus (in this case, nausea) can occur hours after the conditioned stimulus (in this case, the flavor of food). Taste aversions apparently provide organisms with an evolutionary advantage.

6. What are the roles of extinction and spontaneous recovery in classical conditioning?

Extinction and spontaneous recovery help organisms adapt to environmental changes. After a US-CS association has been learned, for example, repeated presentation of the CS (for example, a bell) without the US (meat powder) extinguishes the CR (salivation). Extinguished responses may show spontaneous recovery as a function of the time that has elapsed since extinction occurred.

7. What are the roles of generalization and discrimination in classical conditioning?

Generalization and discrimination are also adaptive. Generalization helps organisms adapt to new events by responding to a range of stimuli similar to the CS. In discrimination, organisms learn to show a CR in response to a more limited range of stimuli by pairing only the limited stimulus with the US.

8. What is higher-order conditioning?

In higher-order conditioning, a previously neutral stimulus comes to serve as a CS after being paired repeatedly with a stimulus that has already become a CS.

9. What are some applications of classical conditioning?

Some applications of classical conditioning include the bell-and-pad method for treating bed-wetting, the conditioning of emotional responses (as in the case of "Little Albert"), extinction of fears through methods such as flooding or systematic desensitization, and counterconditioning of fears.

10. What is the contribution of B. F. Skinner to the psychology of learning?

Skinner developed the concept of reinforcement, encouraged the study of discrete behaviors such as lever pressing by rats, and innovated many techniques for studying operant conditioning such as the "Skinner box" and the cumulative recorder. He was also involved in the development of behavior modification and programmed learning.

11. What is operant conditioning?

Operant conditioning is a simple form of learning in which organisms learn to engage in behavior that is reinforced. Reinforced responses occur with greater frequency.

12. What are the various kinds of reinforcers?

These include positive, negative, primary, and secondary reinforcers. Positive reinforcers increase the probability that operants will occur when they are applied. Negative reinforcers increase the probability that operants will occur when they are removed. Primary reinforcers have their value because of the organism's biological makeup. Secondary reinforcers such as money and approval acquire their value through association with established reinforcers.

13. What are the roles of extinction and spontaneous recovery in operant conditioning?

Extinction and spontaneous recovery are also adaptive in operant conditioning. In operant conditioning, learned responses are extinguished as a result of repeated performance in the absence of reinforcement. (Why continue to engage in a response that goes unreinforced?) And as in classical conditioning, spontaneous recovery occurs as a function of the passage of time, which is adaptive because things may return to the way they were.

14. Why did Skinner make a point of distinguishing between reinforcers on the one hand, and rewards and punishments on the other?

Rewards and punishments are defined, respectively, as pleasant and aversive events that affect behavior. Skinner preferred the concept of *reinforcement* because its definition does not rely on getting inside the head of the organism. Instead, lists of reinforcers are obtained empirically, by observing their effects on behavior.

15. Why do many psychologists disapprove of punishment?

Many psychologists recommend not using punishment because it hurts, it does not suggest acceptable behavior, it may create feelings of hostility, it may only suppress behavior in the specific situation in which it is used, it may generalize to the suppression of wide varieties of behavior, and it may suggest that recipients punish others as a way of coping with stress.

16. **What are discriminative stimuli?**

Discriminative stimuli (such as a green light) indicate when operants (such as pecking a button) will be reinforced (as with food).

17. **What are the various schedules of reinforcement? How do they affect behavior?**

Continuous reinforcement leads to the most rapid acquisition of new responses, but operants are maintained most economically through partial reinforcement. There are four basic schedules of reinforcement. In a fixed-interval schedule, a specific amount of time must elapse after a previous correct response before reinforcement again becomes available. In a variable-interval schedule, the amount of time is allowed to vary. In a fixed-ratio schedule, a fixed number of correct responses must be performed before one is reinforced. In a variable-ratio schedule, this number is allowed to vary. Ratio schedules maintain high response rates.

18. **How can we use shaping to teach complex behavior patterns?**

In shaping, successive approximations of the target response are reinforced, leading to the performance of a complex sequence of behaviors.

19. **What are some applications of operant conditioning?**

Applications of operant conditioning include socialization, biofeedback training, the token economy, avoidance learning, behavior modification, and programmed learning.

20. **How do we explain what happens during classical conditioning from a cognitive perspective?**

According to contingency theory, organisms learn associations between stimuli only when stimuli provide new information about each other. From this perspective, classical conditioning occurs not mechanically but because it provides information.

21. **What is the evidence that people and lower organisms form cognitive maps of their environments?**

Some evidence is derived from Tolman's research on latent learning. He demonstrated that rats can learn—that is, they can modify their cognitive map of the environment—in the absence of reinforcement.

22. **How do people learn by observing others?**

Bandura has shown that people can learn to do things simply by observing others; it is not necessary that they emit responses that are reinforced in order to learn. Learners may then choose to perform the behaviors they have observed "when the time is ripe"—that is, when they believe that the learned behavior is appropriate or is likely to be rewarded.

23. **What do we know about the effects of media violence?**

Media violence can contribute to violent behavior by providing violent models, disinhibiting aggressive impulses, increasing the viewer's level of arousal, priming aggressive thoughts and memories, and habituating the viewer to violence.

PREVIEW

Kinds of Memory: Looking Back, Looking Ahead
▲ Some memories contain concrete information—"Just the facts, Ma'am."
▲ Other memories involve *doing* things rather than knowing about them.
▲ Do you have trouble remembering to get to work on that term paper?

Processes of Memory: Processing Information in Our Most Personal Computers
▲ Your memory is the mind's "Save" function.
▲ Your memory also has a "Find" function.
▲ As with a computer, you usually need to know the names of the files in your memory if you expect to find them.

Stages of Memory: Making *Sense* of the *Short* and the *Long* of It
▲ How do you try to juggle a telephone number inside your head before you get a chance to jot it down?
▲ Like a computer, you have a working memory.
▲ You are most likely to remember to bring home the first and last items on your mental shopping list.
▲ Seven is a "magic number"—sort of.
▲ You have a biochemical hard drive with no known limits on the gigabytes of information it can store.
▲ Yes, doing all those problems in the math book helps you remember the formulas.
▲ Some events, like the deaths of Princess Diana or JFK Jr., can be etched in memory for a lifetime.
▲ It may be better to study in the room in which you will be tested.

Forgetting
▲ Learning Spanish can make it harder to remember French—and vice versa.
▲ Freud believed that we toss unpleasant thoughts out of consciousness (without knowing we're doing it!).
▲ Can children remember the things that happen to them during the first couple of years of life?
▲ Why can't the quarterback remember the play in which he was knocked unconscious?

Using the Psychology of Memory to Improve Your Memory
▲ Here's how you can do better at remembering the names of people you meet at a party and the material that's going to be on the test.

The Biology of Memory: From Engrams to Adrenaline
▲ Your memory uses "better living through chemistry"—chemicals in the brain are connected with memory.
▲ The brain works like a time machine.

CHAPTER 6

Memory

TRUTH [ ] FICTION?

- A woman who had no memory of who she was automatically dialed her mother's phone number when the police gave her a telephone.

- Everyone who can see has a photographic memory.

- It may be easier for you to recall the name of your first-grade teacher than the name of someone you just met at a party.

- All of our experiences are permanently imprinted on the brain so the proper stimulus can cause us to remember them exactly.

- Learning must be meaningful if we are to remember it.

- If you study with the stereo on, you would probably do better to take the test with the stereo on.

- You can use tricks to improve your memory.

My oldest daughter Jill was talking about how she had run into a friend from elementary school and they had had a splendid time recalling the goofy things they did during their school years. Her sister Allyn, age 6 at the time, was not to be outdone. "I can remember when I was born," she put in.

The family's ears perked up. Being a psychologist, I knew exactly what to say. "You can remember when you were born?" I said.

"Oh, yes," she insisted. "Mommy was there."

So far she could not be faulted. I cheered her on, and she related a remarkably detailed account of how it had been snowing in the wee hours of a bitter December morning when Mommy had to go to the hospital. You see, she said, her memory was so good that she could also summon up what it had been like *before* she was born. She wove a wonderful patchwork quilt, integrating details we had given her with her own recollections of the events surrounding the delivery of her younger sister, Jordan. All in all, she seemed quite satisfied that she had pieced together a faithful portrait of her arrival on the world stage.

Later in the chapter, we will see that children usually do not recall events that occurred in their first two years, much less those of their first hours. But Allyn's tale dramatized the way we "remember" many of the things that have happened to us. When it comes to long-term memories, truth can take a back seat to drama and embellishment. Very often, our memories are like the bride's apparel—there's something old, something new, something borrowed, and from time to time something blue.

Memory is what this chapter is about. Without memory, there is no past. Without memory, experience is trivial and learning is lost. Shortly we will see what psychologists have learned about the ways in which we remember things. First, try to meet the following challenges to your memory.

FIVE CHALLENGES TO MEMORY

Before we go any further, let's test your memory. If you want to participate, find four sheets of blank paper and number them 1 through 4. Then follow these directions:

1.   Following are 10 letters. Look at them for 15 seconds. Later in the chapter, I will ask you if you can write them on sheet number 1. (No cheating! Don't do it now.)

THUNSTOFAM

2.   Look at these nine figures for 30 seconds. Then try to draw them in the proper sequence on sheet number 2. (Yes, right after you've finished looking at them. We'll talk about your drawings later.)

3.   Okay, here's another list of letters, 17 this time. Look at the list for 60 seconds and then see whether you can reproduce it on sheet number 3. (I'm being generous this time—a full minute.)

GMC-BSI-BMA-TTC-IAF-BI

4.   Which of these pennies is an accurate reproduction of the Lincoln penny you see every day? This time there's nothing to draw on another sheet; just circle or put a checkmark by the penny that you think resembles the ones you throw in the back of the drawer.

5. Examine the following drawings for 1 minute. Then copy the names of the figures on sheet number 4. When you're finished, just keep reading. Soon I'll be asking you to draw those figures.

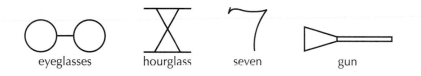

KINDS OF MEMORY: LOOKING BACK, LOOKING AHEAD

There are various kinds of memories. Allyn remembered some things she had personally done, for example, such as what she had for breakfast on the morning of Jill's visit. Remembering what you had for breakfast is an example of an *episodic memory*—an episode in your life. But Allyn claimed to remember when she was born, which was clearly an invented memory based on her general knowledge of the process, not of that particular episode in her life. While she was talking about all this, she was "remembering" how to talk and prance about the room. And while all this was happening, I was trying to remind myself over and over again not to forget to jot down notes about it and write it up as soon as I could. All of these are different kinds of memories, and psychologists debate whether they represent different systems of memory or are just different examples of the same system of memory (Schacter, 1992). Let us consider each type of memory identified by psychologists today.

Explicit Versus Implicit Memories

Question: What is meant by explicit memory?   **Explicit memory**—also referred to as *declarative memory*—is memory for specific information. Things that are *explicit* are clear, or clearly stated or explained. The use of the term *declarative* indicates that these memories state or reveal (i.e., *declare*) specific information. The information may be autobiographical or refer to general knowledge. ("Well, I declare!")

Implicit memory—also referred to as *nondeclarative memory*—is memory of how to perform a task, how to do something (Schacter et al., 1993). First let us talk more about two kinds of explicit memories described by psychologist Endel Tulving (1985; Tulving & Markowitsch, 1998): episodic and semantic. They are identified according to the type of information they hold.

Episodic Memory   *Question: What is meant by episodic memory?* **Episodic memories** are kinds of explicit memories. They are memories of the things that happen to us or take place in our presence (Wheeler et al., 1997). Episodic memory is also referred to as *autobiographical memory*. Your memories of what you ate for breakfast and of what your professor said in class this afternoon are examples of episodic memory.

Return to Allyn's "recollection." Of course Allyn could not really remember her own birth. That is, she could not recall the particular event or *episode* in which she had participated. What Allyn did recount is more accurately characterized as generalized knowledge

> **▲ REFLECT**
> What are the earliest episodes you can remember? Is your memory for them accurate? Can you be sure?

Explicit memory ▲ Memory that clearly and distinctly expresses (explicates) specific information.
Implicit memory ▲ Memory that is suggested (implied) but not plainly expressed, as illustrated in the things that people *do* but do not state clearly.
Episodic memory ▲ Memories of events experienced by a person or that take place in the person's presence.

than as an episodic or autobiographical memory of her birth. From listening to her parents and from her experience with the events of her sister Jordan's birth, she had learned much about what happens during childbirth. She erroneously thought that this knowledge represented her own birth.

It is common for us to build or "reconstruct" inaccurate memories that have a bit of this and that—something that might reflect autobiographical experience, things we hear about from family members and others, the stuff we read about or see in the media, and even things that other people suggest might have happened to us. These memories are fiction, as we see in novels, but we may believe that they are truly autobiographical (Clancy et al., 2000).

Semantic Memory: On Not Getting Personal

Question: What is meant by semantic memory? General knowledge is referred to as **semantic memory.** *Semantics* concerns meanings. Allyn was reporting her understanding of the meaning of childbirth rather than an episode in her own life. You can "remember" that the United States has 50 states without visiting them and personally adding them up. You "remember" who authored *Hamlet*, although you were not looking over Shakespeare's shoulder as he did so. These, too, are examples of semantic memory.

Your future recollection that there are several kinds of memory is more likely to be semantic than episodic. In other words, you are more likely to "know" that there are several types of memory than to recall the date on which you learned about them, where you were and how you were sitting, and whether you were also thinking about dinner at the time. We tend to use the phrase "I remember . . . " when we are referring to episodic memories, as in "I *remember* the blizzard of 1998." But we are more likely to say "I know . . . " in reference to semantic memories, as in "I *know* about—" (or, "I heard about—") "—the blizzard of 1898." Put it another way: You may *remember* that you wrote your mother, but you *know* that Shakespeare wrote *Hamlet*.

Implicit Memory: When Remembering Is Doing

Now let us think more about *implicit* memory. *Question: What is meant by implicit memory?* As the term *implicit* implies (should I start this sentence again?), implicit memories are suggested (or implied) but not plainly stated or expressed (not declared). Implicit memories are illustrated by the things that people *do* but not by the things they state clearly. Implicit memories involve skills, both cognitive and physical; they reveal habits; and they involve the effects of conditioning. My taste aversion to buttered popcorn is an implicit memory. Because I was once nauseated by buttered popcorn, I feel queasy when I smell it. It's a conditioned response. I don't have to think about it. (And I don't want to think about it, to tell you the truth. I wrote about it here because of my deep commitment to you.)

Here are some other examples of implicit memories: you have learned and now remember how to speak at least one language, how to ride a bicycle, how to swim or swing a bat, how to type, how to turn on the lights, and how to drive a car. It is said that you never "forget" how to ride a bicycle. This is because implicit memories can persist even when we have not used them for many years. Getting to class "by habit"—without paying attention to landmarks or directions—is another instance of implicit memory. If someone asked you what 2 times 2 is, the number 4 would probably "jump" into your mind without much thinking about it or conscious calculation. After going over the alphabet or multiplication tables hundreds of times, our memory of them becomes automatic or implicit. We don't have to pay conscious attention to them in order to remember them.

Your memory of the alphabet or the multiplication tables is the result of a great deal of repetition that makes associations relatively automatic, a phenomenon which psychologists also refer to as *priming*. Daniel Schacter and his colleagues (1993) note that priming is the most frequently studied issue in implicit memory. Years of priming helps people make complete words out of the word fragments (Roediger et al., 1992; Schacter et al., 1999). Even though the perceptual cues in the following word fragments are limited, you may very well make a variety of associations to them:

> ▲ **REFLECT**
> You remember that classes have professors, and you remember your professor's name (I hope). Which of these is an episodic memory? Which is a semantic memory? Can you explain the difference between the two?

> ▲ **REFLECT**
> You remember how to walk or use a pen, but do you remember *how* or *when* you learned these things? Will you ever forget how to walk, ride a bicycle, or use a pen or pencil? What kinds of "memories" are these?

Semantic memory ▲ General knowledge as opposed to episodic memory.

PYGY   NVSY   MRCA   TXT   BUFL

By the way, let us jump ahead to the next chapter ("Cognition and Language") to mention a couple of factors that will be involved in how many words you can make out of these fragments. One is your expertise with the English language. If it is a second language, you will probably make fewer associations to these fragments than if it is your first language. In fact, you might not perceive any complete words. Another factor could be creativity. Can you think of any other factors?

Daniel Schacter (1992) also illustrates implicit memory with the story of the woman with amnesia who was wandering the streets. The police picked her up and discovered that she could not remember who she was, or any other fact about her life, and that she had no identification. After extensive fruitless interviewing, the police hit on the idea of asking her to dial phone numbers—just any number at all. Even though the woman did not "know" what she was doing, she dialed her mother's number. When asked for the phone numbers of people she knew, she had no answer. She could not *declare* her mother's phone number. She could not make the number *explicit*. She could not even remember her mother's name, or whether she had a mother. All this explicit information was gone. But dialing her mother's phone number was apparently a habit, and she did it "on automatic pilot." We can assume that she had been *primed* for this task by dialing the number hundreds of times, perhaps many thousands of times. Implicit memory reveals the effects of experience when we are not specifically trying to recall information.

An Example of an Implicit Memory.
Memories of how to ride a bicycle, how to type, how to turn the lights on and off, and how to drive a car are implicit memories. Implicit memories tend to persist even when we do not use them for many years. Here Jean Piaget, the cognitive-developmental theorist discussed in Chapter 10, demonstrates that we may never forget how to ride a bicycle.

Retrospective Memory Versus Prospective Memory

Retrospective memory is the recalling of information that has been previously learned. *Episodic*, *semantic*, and *implicit memories* all involve remembering things that have been previously learned. *Question: What is the difference between retrospective memory and prospective memory?*

Prospective memory involves remembering to do things in the future. Tasks that depend on prospective memory include remembering to brush your teeth before going out, to pay your bills (yuck), to take out some cash, and to make the list of things to do so that you won't forget what to do! And if one does make a list of things to do, one must remember to use it. Most of us have had failures of prospective memory in which we have the feeling that we were supposed to do something, but we can't remember what. Prospective memory tends to fail when we are preoccupied (caught up in surfing the Net or fantasizing about you-know-who), distracted (we get a phone call just as we are about to get going on something), or feeling the stress of time pressure (Schacter, 1999).

There are various kinds of prospective memory tasks. For example *habitual tasks* such as getting to class on time are easier to remember than occasional tasks such as meeting someone for coffee at an arbitrary time (d'Ydewalle et al., 1999). But motivation also plays a role. You are more likely to remember the coffee date if the person you are meeting is the local Justin Timberlake or Christina Aguilera lookalike. Psychologists also distinguish between event-based and time-based prospective memory tasks (McDonald-Miszczak et al., 1999). *Event-based tasks* are triggered by events, such as remembering to take one's medicine at breakfast or to brush one's teeth after eating. *Time-based tasks* are to be performed at a certain time or after a certain amount of time has elapsed between occurrences, such as tuning in to a favorite news program at 7:30 P.M. or taking a pill every 4 hours (d'Ydewalle et al., 1999).

There is an age-related decline in both retrospective and prospective memory (Einstein et al., 1998; West & Craik, 1999). In the case of prospective memory, older adults appear to be about as aware of specific cues or reminders as young adults; however, it takes them longer to respond to the cues or reminders (West & Craik, 1999). That is, if they meet with a friend, they are likely to remember that they were supposed to ask something, but it may take longer for them to remember the particular question. Divided attention (distraction) plays a role and older people are especially vulnerable (Einstein et al., 1998). However, older adults with greater verbal ability and occupational status are better able to keep their intentions in mind (Cherry & LeCompte, 1999).

Retrospective memory ▲ Memory for past events, activities, and learning experiences, as shown by explicit (episodic and semantic) and implicit memories.

Prospective memory ▲ Memory to perform an act in the future, as at a certain time or when a certain event occurs.

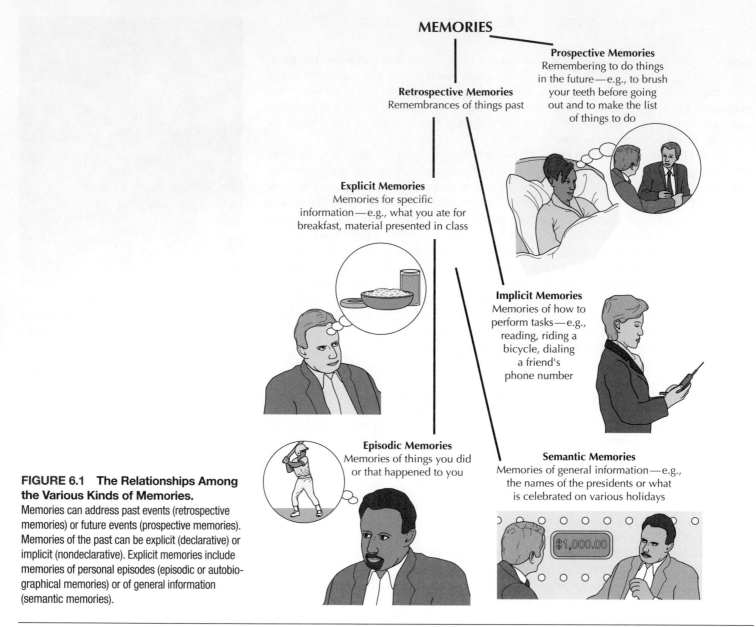

FIGURE 6.1   The Relationships Among the Various Kinds of Memories.
Memories can address past events (retrospective memories) or future events (prospective memories). Memories of the past can be explicit (declarative) or implicit (nondeclarative). Explicit memories include memories of personal episodes (episodic or autobiographical memories) or of general information (semantic memories).

Moods and attitudes have an effect on prospective memory (Villa & Abeles, 2000). For example, negative emotional states such as depression also impair prospective memory. Depressed people are less likely to push to remind themselves to do what they intend to do (Rude et al., 1999). On the other hand, older people who are confident in their ability to remember to carry out tasks are more likely to actually remember to do them (McDonald-Miszczak et al., 1999). Yet the same confidence in one's memory does not appear to be associated with better performance at *retrospective* memory tasks (recalling the past) (McDonald-Miszczak et al., 1999). The various kinds of memory are summarized in Figure 6.1.

Before proceeding to the next section, why don't you turn to the piece of paper on which you wrote the names of the four figures—that is, sheet number 4—and draw them from memory as exactly as you can. Hold on to the drawings. We'll talk about them a bit later.

REVIEW

(1) _____ memories are memories of specific information. (2) Memories of the events that happen to a person are _____ memories. (3) _____ memories concern generalized knowledge.

Pulling It Together: Can you think of some implicit memories you have? What do you need to do after finishing this section? How do you remember?

PROCESSES OF MEMORY: PROCESSING INFORMATION IN OUR MOST PERSONAL COMPUTERS

Both psychologists and computer scientists speak of processing information. Think of using a computer to write a term paper. Once the system is up and operating, you begin to enter information. You can enter information into the computer's memory by, for example, typing letters on a keyboard or—in the case of voice recognition technology—speaking. If you were to do some major surgery on your computer (which I am often tempted to do) and open up its memory, however, you wouldn't find these letters or sounds inside it. This is because the computer is programmed to change the letters or sounds—that is, the information you have entered—into a form that can be placed in its electronic memory. Similarly, when we perceive information, we must convert it into a form that can be remembered if we are to place it in our memory.

CLICK4™ *"Advice on Effective Studying," an application of the psychology of memory.*

Encoding: The Memory's "Transformer"

Information about the outside world reaches our senses in the form of physical and chemical stimuli. The first stage of information processing is changing information so that we can place it in memory: **encoding.** *Question: What is the role of encoding in memory?* When we encode information, we transform it into psychological formats that can be represented mentally. To do so, we commonly use visual, auditory, and semantic codes.

Let us illustrate the uses of coding by referring to the list of letters you first saw in the section on challenges to memory. Try to write the letters on sheet number 1. Go on, take a minute and then come back.

Okay, now: if you had used a **visual code** to try to remember the list, you would have mentally represented it as a picture. That is, you would have maintained—or attempted to maintain—a mental image of the letters. Some artists and art historians seem to maintain marvelous visual mental representations of works of art. This enables them to quickly recognize whether a work is authentic.

You may also have decided to read the list of letters to yourself—that is, to silently say them in sequence: "t," "h," "u," and so on. By so doing, you would have been using an **acoustic code,** or representing the stimuli as a sequence of sounds. You may also have read the list as a three-syllable word, "thun-sto-fam." This is an acoustic code, but it also involves the "meaning" of the letters, in the sense that you are interpreting the list as a word. This approach has elements of a semantic code.

Semantic codes represent stimuli in terms of their meaning. Our 10 letters were meaningless in and of themselves. However, they can also serve as an acronym—a term made up of the first letters of a phrase—for the familiar phrase "THe UNited STates OF AMerica." This observation lends them meaning.

Storage: The Memory's "Save" Function

The second memory process is **storage.** *Question: What is the role of storage in memory?* Storage means maintaining information over time. If you were given the task of storing the list of letters—that is, told to remember it—how would you attempt to place it in storage? One way would be by **maintenance rehearsal**—by mentally repeating the list, or saying it to yourself. Our awareness of the functioning of our memory, referred to by psychologists as **metamemory,** becomes more sophisticated as we develop.

Encoding ▲ Modifying information so that it can be placed in memory. The first stage of information processing.

Visual code ▲ Mental representation of information as a picture.

Acoustic code ▲ Mental representation of information as a sequence of sounds.

Semantic code ▲ Mental representation of information according to its meaning.

Storage ▲ The maintenance of information over time. The second stage of information processing.

Maintenance rehearsal ▲ Mental repetition of information in order to keep it in memory.

Metamemory ▲ Self-awareness of the ways in which memory functions, allowing the person to encode, store, and retrieve information effectively.

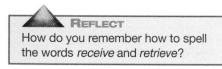

REFLECT

Consider this list of letters: THUNSTOFAM. Can you think of various strategies for entering the list into the storage bins of your mind? Which strategy might make it easiest to retrieve the list? Why?

You could also have condensed the amount of information you were rehearsing by reading the list as a three-syllable word; that is, you could have rehearsed three syllables (said "thun-sto-fam" over and over again) rather than 10 letters. In either case, repetition would have been the key to memory. (We talk more about such condensing, or "chunking," very soon.)

However, you could also encode the list of letters by relating it to something that you already know. This kind of coding is referred to as **elaborative rehearsal.** That is, you are elaborating or extending the semantic meaning of the letters you are trying to remember. For example, did you recognize that the list of 10 letters is an acronym for "The United States of America"? (That is, you take the first two letters of each of the words in the phrase and string them together to make up the 10 letters of THUNSTOFAM.) If you had recognized this, storage of the list of letters might have been almost instantaneous, and it would probably have been permanent.

Retrieval: The Memory's "Find" Function

The third memory process is **retrieval.** *Question: What is the role of retrieval in memory?* The retrieval of stored information means locating it and returning it to consciousness. With well-known information such as our names and occupations, retrieval is effortless and, for all practical purposes, immediate. But when we are trying to remember massive quantities of information, or information that is not perfectly understood, retrieval can be tedious and not always successful. It is easiest to retrieve information stored in a computer by using the name of the file. Similarly, retrieval of information from our memories requires knowledge of the proper cues.

If you had encoded THUNSTOFAM as a three-syllable word, your retrieval strategy would involve recollection of the word and rules for decoding. In other words, you would say the "word" *thun-sto-fam* and then decode it by spelling it out. You might err in that "thun" sounds like "thumb" and "sto" could also be spelled "stow." However, using the semantic code, or recognition of the acronym for "The United States of America," could lead to flawless recollection.

REFLECT

How do you remember how to spell the words *receive* and *retrieve*?

I stuck my neck out by predicting that you would immediately and permanently store the list if you recognized it as an acronym. Here, too, there would be recollection (of the name of our country) and rules for decoding. That is, to "remember" the 10 letters, you would have to envision the phrase ("The United States of America") and read off the first two letters of each word. Since using this semantic code is more complex than simply seeing the entire list (using a visual code), it may take a while to recall (actually, to reconstruct) the list of 10 letters. But by using the phrase, you are likely to remember the list of letters permanently.

Now, what if you were not able to remember the list of 10 letters? What would have gone wrong? In terms of the three processes of memory, it could be that you had (1) not encoded the list in a useful way, (2) not entered the encoded information into storage, or (3) stored the information but lacked the proper cues for remembering it—such as the phrase "The United States of America" or the rule for decoding the phrase.

By now you may have noticed that I have discussed three kinds of memory and three processes of memory, but I have not yet *defined* memory. No apologies—we weren't ready for a definition yet. Now that we have explored some basic concepts, let us give it a try: **Memory** is the processes by which information is encoded, stored, and retrieved.

REVIEW

(4) _____ is the transforming of information so that we can remember it. (5) One way of storing information is by _____ rehearsal, or by mentally repeating it. (6) Another is by _____ rehearsal, in which we relate new information to things we already know. (7) _____ of information from storage requires knowledge of the proper cues.

Pulling It Together: How are you encoding the information on this page? What kind of rehearsal will you use to remember it?

Elaborative rehearsal ▲ The kind of coding in which new information is related to information that is already known.
Retrieval ▲ The location of stored information and its return to consciousness. The third stage of information processing.
Memory ▲ The processes by which information is encoded, stored, and retrieved.

STAGES OF MEMORY: MAKING *SENSE* OF THE *SHORT* AND THE *LONG* OF IT

William James (1890) was intrigued by the fact that some memories are unreliable, "going in one ear and out the other," while others could be recalled for a lifetime. He wrote:

> The stream of thought flows on, but most of its elements fall into the bottomless pit of oblivion. Of some, no element survives the instant of their passage. Of others, it is confined to a few moments, hours, or days. Others, again, leave vestiges which are indestructible, and by means of which they may be recalled as long as life endures.

Yes, the world is a constant display of sights and sounds and other sources of sensory stimulation, but only some of these things are remembered. James was correct in observing that we remember various "elements" of thought for different lengths of time, and many we do not remember at all. Psychologists Richard Atkinson and Richard Shiffrin (1968) suggested a model for how some stimuli are lost immediately, others held briefly, and still others for a lifetime. ***Question: What is the Atkinson-Shiffrin model of memory?*** Atkinson and Shiffrin proposed that there are three stages of memory and suggested that the progress of information through these stages determines whether (and how long) it is retained (see Figure 6.2). These stages are *sensory memory*, *short-term memory (STM)*, and *long-term memory (LTM)*.

There is a saying that when you cover a topic completely, you are talking about "the long and short of it." In the case of the stages of memory, we could say that we are trying to "make *sense* of the *short* and the *long* of it."

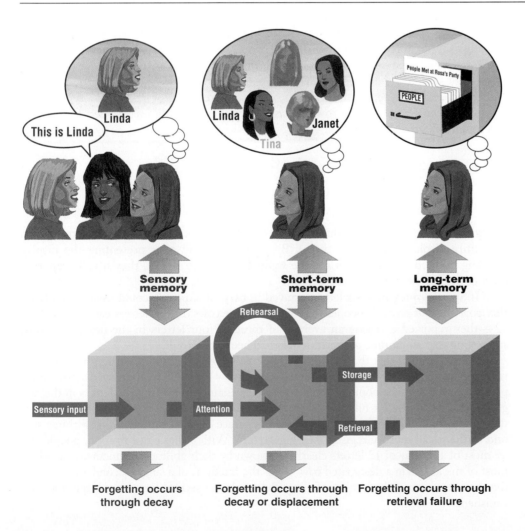

FIGURE 6.2   Three Stages of Memory.
The Atkinson-Shiffrin model proposes that there are three distinct stages of memory. Sensory information impacts upon the registers of sensory memory, where memory traces are held briefly before decaying. If we attend to the information, much of it is transferred to short-term memory (STM). Information in STM may decay or be displaced if it is not transferred to long-term memory (LTM). We can use rehearsal or elaborative strategies to transfer memories to LTM. If information in LTM is organized poorly, or if we cannot find cues to retrieve it, it may be lost.

Sensory Memory: Flashes on the Mental Monitor

William James also wrote about the stream of thought, or consciousness:

> Consciousness . . . does not appear to itself chopped up in bits. A "river" or a "stream" are the metaphors by which it is most naturally described. In talking of it hereafter, let us call it the stream of thought, of consciousness, or of subjective life.

When we look at a visual stimulus, our impressions may seem fluid enough. Actually, however, they consist of a series of eye fixations referred to as **saccadic eye movements.** These movements jump from one point to another about four times each second. Yet the visual sensations seem continuous, or streamlike, because of **sensory memory.** Sensory memory is the type or stage of memory that is first encountered by a stimulus. Although sensory memory holds impressions briefly, it is long enough so that a series of perceptions seem to be connected.   *Question: How does sensory memory function?*

To explain the functioning of sensory memory, let us return to our list of letters: THUNSTOFAM. If the list were flashed on a screen for a fraction of a second, the visual impression, or **memory trace,** of the stimulus would also last for only a fraction of a second afterward. Psychologists speak of the memory trace of the list as being held in a visual **sensory register.**

www 6 L 1

CLICK4™ *online exhibits, memory games, and articles at The Exploratorum.*

If the letters had been flashed on a screen for, say, 1/10 of a second, your ability to remember them on the basis of sensory memory alone would be limited. Your memory would be based on a single eye fixation, and the trace of the image would vanish before a single second had passed. At the turn of the century, psychologist William McDougall (1904) engaged in research in which he showed people 1 to 12 letters arranged in rows—just long enough to allow a single eye fixation. Under these conditions, people could typically remember only 4 or 5 letters. Thus recollection of THUNSTOFAM, a list of 10 letters arranged in a single row, would probably depend on whether one had encoded it so that it could be processed further.

George Sperling (1960) modified McDougall's experimental method and showed that there is a difference between what people can see and what they can report. McDougall had used a *whole-report procedure,* in which people were asked to report every letter they saw in the array. Sperling used a modified *partial-report procedure,* in which people were asked to report the contents of one of three rows of letters. In a typical procedure, Sperling flashed three rows of letters like the following on a screen for 50 milliseconds (1/20 of a second):

A G R E

V L S B

N K B T

Using the whole-report procedure, people could report an average of four letters from the entire display (one out of three). But if immediately after presenting the display Sperling pointed an arrow at a row he wanted viewers to report, they usually reported most of the letters in the row successfully.

If Sperling presented six letters arrayed in two rows, people could usually report either row without error. If people were flashed three rows of four letters each—a total of 12—they reported correctly an average of three of four letters in the designated row, suggesting that about nine of the 12 letters had been perceived.

Sperling found that the amount of time that elapsed before indicating the row to be reported was crucial. If he delayed pointing the arrow for a few fractions of a second after presenting the letters, people were much less successful in reporting the letters in the target row. If he allowed a full second to elapse, the arrow did not aid recall at all. From these data, Sperling concluded that the memory trace of visual stimuli *decays* within a second in the visual sensory register (see Figure 6.2). With a single eye fixation, people can *see* most of a display of 12 letters clearly, as shown by their ability to immediately read off most of the letters in a designated row. Yet as the fractions of a single second are elapsing, the memory trace of the letters is fading. By the time a second has elapsed, the trace has vanished.

Saccadic eye movement ▲ The rapid jumps made by a person's eyes as they fixate on different points.

Sensory memory ▲ The type or stage of memory first encountered by a stimulus. Sensory memory holds impressions briefly, but long enough so that series of perceptions are psychologically continuous.

Memory trace ▲ An assumed change in the nervous system that reflects the impression made by a stimulus. Memory traces are said to be "held" in sensory registers.

Sensory register ▲ A system of memory that holds information briefly, but long enough so that it can be processed further. There may be a sensory register for every sense.

Iconic Memory   Psychologists believe we possess a sensory register for each one of our senses. The mental representations of visual stimuli are referred to as **icons.** The sensory register that holds icons is labeled **iconic memory.** Iconic memory is one kind of sensory memory. Iconic memories are accurate, photographic memories. So those of us who mentally represent visual stimuli have "photographic memories." However, iconic memories are very brief. What most of us normally think of as a photographic memory—the ability to retain exact mental representations of visual stimuli over long periods of time—is technically referred to as *eidetic imagery.*

Eidetic Imagery   A few individuals retain visual stimuli, or icons, in their sensory memories for remarkably long periods of time. About 5% of children can look at a detailed picture, turn away, and several minutes later recall the particulars of the picture with exceptional clarity—as if they were still seeing it. This extraordinary visual sensory memory is referred to as **eidetic imagery** (Haber, 1980). This ability declines with age, however, all but disappearing by adolescence.

Figure 6.3 provides an example of a test of eidetic imagery. Children are asked to look at the first drawing in the series for 20 to 30 seconds, after which it is removed. The children then continue to gaze at a neutral background. Several minutes later the drawing in the center is placed on the backdrop. When asked what they see, many report "a face." A face would be seen only if the children had retained a clear image of the first picture and fused it with the second so that they are, in effect, perceiving the third picture in Figure 6.3 (Haber, 1980).

Eidetic imagery appears remarkably clear and detailed. It seems to be essentially a perceptual phenomenon in which encoding or rehearsal is not necessary to continue to "see" a visual stimulus. Although eidetic imagery is rare, iconic memory, as we see in the following section, universally transforms visual perceptions into smoothly unfolding impressions of the world.

Iconic Memory and Saccadic Eye Movements   Iconic memory smooths out the bumps in the visual ride. Saccadic eye movements occur about four times every second. Iconic memory, however, holds icons for up to a second. As a consequence, the flow of visual information seems smooth and continuous. Your impression that the words you are reading flow across the page, rather than jumping across in spurts, is a product of your iconic memory. Similarly, motion pictures present 16 to 22 separate frames, or still images, each second. Iconic memory allows you to perceive the imagery in the film as being seamless (G. R. Loftus, 1983).

Echoic Memory   Mental representations of sounds, or auditory stimuli, are called **echoes.** The sensory register that holds echoes is referred to as **echoic memory.**

The memory traces of auditory stimuli (that is, echoes) can last for several seconds, many times longer than the traces of visual stimuli (icons). The difference in the duration of traces is probably based on biological differences between the eye and the ear. This difference is one of the reasons that acoustic codes aid in the retention of information that

CLICK4™ *an essay assignment on stages of memory.*

CLICK4™ *a WebSearch activity on gender differences in memory.*

Icon ▲ A mental representation of a visual stimulus that is held briefly in sensory memory.

Iconic memory ▲ The sensory register that briefly holds mental representations of visual stimuli.

Eidetic imagery ▲ The maintenance of detailed visual memories over several minutes.

Echo ▲ A mental representation of an auditory stimulus (sound) that is held briefly in sensory memory.

Echoic memory ▲ The sensory register that briefly holds mental representations of auditory stimuli.

FIGURE 6.3   A Research Strategy for Assessing Eidetic Imagery.
Children look at the first drawing for 20 to 30 seconds, after which it is removed. Next, the children look at a neutral background for several minutes. They are then shown the second drawing. When asked what they see, children with the capacity for eidetic imagery report a face. The face is seen only by children who retain the first image and fuse it with the second, thus perceiving the third image.

Echoic Memory.
The mental representations of auditory stimuli are called echoes, and the sensory register that holds echoes is referred to as echoic memory. By encoding visual information as echoes and rehearsing the echoes, we commit them to memory.

▲ REFLECT
Why are girls more likely than boys to remember the dolls and teddy bears they see in a picture?

▲ REFLECT
What do you do to try to remember names and telephone numbers? What could you do to improve your memory of them?

CLICK4™ *an essay assignment on short-term memory.*

Short-term memory ▲ The type or stage of memory that can hold information for up to a minute or so after the trace of the stimulus decays. Also called *working memory.*
Working memory ▲ Same as *short-term memory.*

has been presented visually—or why saying the letters or syllables of THUNSTOFAM makes the list easier to remember.

Yet echoes, like icons, fade with time. If they are to be retained, we must pay attention to them. By selectively attending to certain stimuli, we sort them out from the background noise. For example, in studies on the development of patterns of processing information, young children have been shown photographs of rooms full of toys and then been asked to recall as many of the toys as they can. One such study found that 2-year-old boys are more likely to attend to and remember toys such as cars, puzzles, and trains. Two-year-old girls are more likely to attend to and remember dolls, dishes, and teddy bears (Renninger & Wozniak, 1985). Even by this early age, the things that children attend to frequently fall into stereotypical patterns.

Short-Term Memory: Keeping Things "In Mind"

Imagine that you are completing a writing assignment and you keyboard or speak words and phrases into your word-processing program. They appear on your monitor as a sign that your computer has them in *memory.* Your word-processing program allows you to add words, delete words, see if they are spelled correctly, add images, and move whole paragraphs from place to place. So you can manipulate the information in your computer's memory, but it isn't saved. It hasn't been entered into storage. If the program or the computer crashes, the information is gone. The computer's memory is a short-term affair. To maintain a long-term connection with the information, you have to save it. Saving it means giving it a name—hopefully a name that you will remember so that you can later find and retrieve the information—and instructing your computer to save it (keep it in storage until told otherwise).

If you focus on a stimulus in the sensory register, you will tend to retain it in your own **short-term memory**—also referred to as **working memory**—for a minute or so after the trace of the stimulus decays. ***Question: How does short-term memory function?*** As one researcher describes it, "Working memory is the mental glue that links a thought through time from its beginning to its end" (Goldman-Rakic, 1995). When you are given a phone number by the information operator and write it down or immediately dial the number, you are retaining the number in your short-term memory. When you are told the name of someone at a party and then use that name immediately in addressing that person, you are retaining the name in short-term memory. In short-term memory, the image tends to fade significantly after 10 to 12 seconds if it is not repeated or rehearsed. It is possible to focus on maintaining a visual image in the short-term memory, but it is more common to encode visual stimuli as sounds, or auditory stimuli. Then the sounds can be rehearsed, or repeated.

Most of us know that one way of retaining information in short-term memory—and possibly storing it permanently—is to rehearse it. When an information operator tells me a phone number, I usually rehearse it continuously while I am dialing it or running around frantically searching for a pencil and a scrap of paper so that I can "save" it. The more times we rehearse information, the more likely we are to remember it. We have the capacity (if not the will or the time) to rehearse information and thereby keep it in short-term memory indefinitely.

Once information is in our short-term memories, we can work on it. Like the information in the word-processing program, we can manipulate it. But it isn't necessarily saved. If we don't do something to save it (like write down that telephone number on a scrap of paper or in a personal digital assistant), it can be gone forever. We can try to reconstruct it, but it may never be the same. Getting most of the digits in someone's phone number right doesn't get you a date for the weekend—at least not with the person you were thinking of!

Keeping THUNSTOFAM in Short-Term Memory   Let us now return to the task of remembering the first list of letters in the challenges to memory at the beginning of the chapter. If you had encoded the letters as the three-syllable word THUN-STO-FAM, you would probably have recalled them by mentally rehearsing (saying to yourself) the three-syllable "word" and then spelling it out from the sounds. A few minutes later, if someone asked whether the letters had been uppercase (THUNSTOFAM) or lowercase (thunstofam), you might not have been able to answer with confidence. You used an acoustic code to help recall the list, and uppercase and lowercase letters sound alike.

Because it can be pronounced, THUNSTOFAM is not too difficult to retain in short-term memory. But what if the list of letters had been TBXLFNTSDK? This list of letters cannot be pronounced as it is. You would have to find a complex acronym to code these letters, and do so within a fraction of a second—most likely an impossible task. To aid recall, you would probably choose to try to repeat the letters rapidly—to read each one as many times as possible before the memory trace fades. You might visualize each letter as you say it and try to get back to it (that is, to run through the entire list) before it decays.

Let us assume that you encoded the letters as sounds and then rehearsed the sounds. When asked to report the list, you might mistakenly say T-V-X-L-F-N-T-S-T-K. This would be an understandable error because the incorrect *V* and *T* sounds are similar, respectively, to the correct *B* and *D* sounds.

George Miller

The Serial-Position Effect

If asked to recall the list of letters TBXLFNTSDK, you would also be likely to recall the first and last letters in the series, *T* and *K*, more accurately than the others. ***Question: Why are we most likely to remember the first and last items in a list?*** The tendency to recall the first and last items in a series is known as the **serial-position effect.** This effect may occur because we pay more attention to the first and last stimuli in a series. They serve as the visual or auditory boundaries for the other stimuli. It may also be that the first items are likely to be rehearsed more frequently (repeated more times) than other items. The last items are likely to have been rehearsed most recently and hence are most likely to be retained in short-term memory.

According to cognitive psychologists, the tendency to recall the initial items in a list is referred to as the **primacy effect.** Social psychologists have also noted a powerful primacy effect in our formation of impressions of other people. In other words, first impressions tend to last. The tendency to recall the last items in a list is referred to as the **recency effect.** If we are asked to recall the last items in a list soon after we have been shown the list, they may still be in short-term memory. As a result, they can be "read off." Earlier items, in contrast, may have to be retrieved from long-term memory.

CLICK4™ *a profile of George Miller.*

CLICK4™ *George Miller's classic article, "The Magical Number Seven, Plus or Minus Two."*

Chunking

Rapidly rehearsing 10 meaningless letters is not an easy task. With TBXLFNTSDK there are 10 discrete elements, or **chunks,** of information that must be kept in short-term memory. When we encode THUNSTOFAM as three syllables, there are only three chunks to swallow at once—a memory task that is much easier on the digestion.

George Miller (1956) wryly noted that the average person is comfortable with digesting about seven integers at a time, the number of integers in a telephone number: "My problem is that I have been persecuted by an integer [the number *seven*]. For seven years this number has followed me around, has intruded in my most private data, and has assaulted me from the pages of our most public journals" (1956). ***Question: Is seven a magic number, or did the phone company get lucky?***

It may sound as if Miller was being paranoid or magical, but he was actually talking about research findings. Research shows that most people have little trouble recalling five chunks of information, as in a zip code. Some can remember nine, which is, for all but a few, an upper limit. So seven chunks, plus or minus one or two, is a "magic" number in the sense that the typical person can manage to remember that many chunks of information and not a great deal more.

So how, you ask, do we manage to include area codes in our recollections of telephone numbers, hence making them 10 digits long? The truth of the matter is that we usually don't. We tend to recall the area code as a single chunk of information derived from our general knowledge of where a person lives. So we are more likely to remember (or "know") the 10-digit numbers of acquaintances who reside in locales with area codes that we use frequently.

Serial-position effect ▲ The tendency to recall more accurately the first and last items in a series.
Primacy effect ▲ The tendency to recall the initial items in a series of items.
Recency effect ▲ The tendency to recall the last items in a series of items.
Chunk ▲ A stimulus or group of stimuli that are perceived as a discrete piece of information.

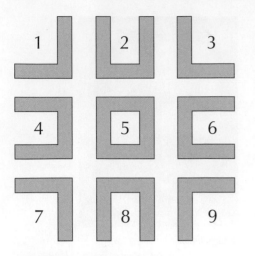

FIGURE 6.4   A Familiar Grid.
The nine drawings in the second challenge to memory form this familiar tic-tac-toe grid when the numbers are placed inside them and they are arranged in order. This method for recalling the shapes collapses nine chunks of information into two. One is the tic-tac-toe grid. The second is the rule for decoding the drawings from the grid.

▲ REFLECT
Are you trying to learn anything by rote in the courses you are taking now? Would another strategy also be of help?

CLICK4™ *an online experiment about short-term memory from the University of Indiana.*

CLICK4™ *a bulletin board discussion on using the psychology of memory to improve your memory.*

Businesses pay the phone company hefty premiums so that they can attain numbers with two or three zeroes—for example, 592-2000 or 614-3300. These numbers include fewer chunks of information and hence are easier to remember. Customer recollection of business phone numbers increases sales. One financial services company uses the toll-free number CALL-IRA, which reduces the task to two chunks of information that also happen to be meaningfully related (semantically coded) to the nature of the business. Similarly, a clinic that helps people quit smoking arranged for a telephone number that can be reached by dialing the letters NO SMOKE.

Return to the third challenge to memory presented earlier. Were you able to remember the six groups of letters? Would your task have been simpler if you had grouped them differently? How about moving the dashes forward by a letter, so that they read GM-CBS-IBM-ATT-CIA-FBI? If we do this, we have the same list of letters, but we also have six chunks of information that can be coded semantically (according to what they mean). You may have also been able to generate the list by remembering a rule, such as "big corporations and government agencies."

If we can recall seven or perhaps nine chunks of information, how do children remember the alphabet? The alphabet contains 26 discrete pieces of information. How do children learn to encode the letters of the alphabet, which are visual symbols, as spoken sounds? There is nothing about the shape of an *A* that suggests its sound. Nor does the visual stimulus *B* sound "B-ish." Children learn to associate letters with their spoken names by **rote**. It is mechanical associative learning that takes time and repetition. If you think that learning the alphabet by rote is a simple task, try learning the Russian alphabet.

If you had recognized THUNSTOFAM as an acronym for the first two letters of each word in the phrase "THe UNited STates OF AMerica," you would also have reduced the number of chunks of information that had to be recalled. You could have considered the phrase to be a single chunk of information. The rule that you must use the first two letters of each word of the phrase would be another chunk.

Reconsider the second challenge to memory presented earlier. You were asked to remember nine chunks of visual information. Perhaps you could have used the acoustic codes "L" and "Square" for chunks 3 and 5, but no obvious codes are available for the seven other chunks. Now look at Figure 6.4. If you had recognized that the elements in the challenge could be arranged as the familiar tic-tac-toe grid, remembering the nine elements might have required two chunks of information. The first would have been the mental image of the grid, and the second would have been the rule for decoding: Each element corresponds to the shape of a section of the grid if read like words on a page (from upper left to lower right). The number sequence 1 through 9 would not in itself present a problem, because you learned this series by rote many years ago and have rehearsed it in countless calculations since then.

Interference in Short-Term Memory   I mentioned that I often find myself running around looking for a pencil and a scrap of paper[1] to write down a telephone number that has been given to me. If I keep on rehearsing the number while I'm looking, I'm okay. But I have also often cursed myself for failing to keep a pad and pencil by the telephone, and sometimes this has interfered with my recollection of the number. (The moral of the story? Avoid self-reproach.) It has also happened that I have actually looked up a phone number and been about to dial it when someone has asked me for the time or where I said we were going to dinner. Unless I say, "Hold on a minute!" and manage to jot down the number on something, it's back to the phone book. Attending to distracting information, even briefly, prevents me from rehearsing the number, so it falls through the cracks of my short-term memory.

In an experiment with college students, Lloyd and Margaret Peterson (1959) demonstrated how prevention of rehearsal can wreak havoc with short-term memory.

Rote ▲ Mechanical associative learning that is based on repetition.

---
[1]Yes, I also mentioned a personal digital assistant. I'm cool; I'm up to date.

They asked students to remember three-letter combinations such as HGB—normally, three easy chunks of information. They then had the students count backward from an arbitrary number, such as 181, by threes (that is, 181, 178, 175, 172, and so on). The students were told to stop counting and to report the letter sequence after the intervals of time shown in Figure 6.5. The percentage of letter combinations that were recalled correctly fell precipitously within seconds. After 18 seconds of interference, counting had dislodged the letter sequences in almost all of these bright young students' memories.

Psychologists say that the appearance of new information in short-term memory **displaces** the old information. Remember: Only a few bits of information can be retained in short-term memory at the same time. (Unfortunately we cannot upgrade our human memories from, say, 64 megabytes to 128 or 256 megabytes.) Think of short-term memory as a shelf or workbench. Once it is full, some things fall off it when new items are shoved onto it. Here we have another possible explanation for the recency effect: The most recently learned bit of information is least likely to be displaced by additional information.

Displacement occurs at cocktail parties, and I'm not referring to jostling by the crowd. The point is this: When you meet Linda or Latrell at the party, you should have little trouble remembering the name. But then you may meet Tamara or Timothy and, still later, Keith or LaToya. By that time you may have a hard time dredging up Jennifer or Jonathan's name—unless, of course, you were very, very attracted to one of them. A passionate response would set a person apart and inspire a good deal of selective attention. According to signal-detection theory, if you were enamored enough, we may predict that you would "detect" the person's name (sensory signals) with a vengeance, and the other names would dissolve into background noise.

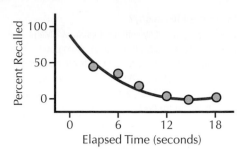

FIGURE 6.5   The Effect of Interference on Short-Term Memory.
In this experiment, college students were asked to remember a series of three letters while they counted backward by threes. After just 3 seconds, retention was cut by half. Ability to recall the words was almost completely lost by 15 seconds.

Displace ▲ In memory theory, to cause information to be lost from short-term memory by adding new information.
Long-term memory ▲ The type or stage of memory capable of relatively permanent storage.
Repression ▲ In Freud's psychodynamic theory, the ejection of anxiety-evoking ideas from conscious awareness.
Schema ▲ A way of mentally representing the world, such as a belief or an expectation, that can influence perception of persons, objects, and situations.

Long-Term Memory: Your Memory's "Hard Drive"

Long-term memory is the third stage of information processing. Think of your long-term memory as a vast storehouse of information containing names, dates, places, what Johnny did to you in second grade, and what Susan said about you when you were 12. *Question: How does long-term memory function?*

Some psychologists (Freud was one) used to believe that nearly all of our perceptions and ideas are stored permanently. We might not be able to retrieve all of them, but some memories might be "lost" because of lack of proper cues, or they might be kept unconscious by the forces of **repression.** Adherents to this view often pointed to the work of neurosurgeon Wilder Penfield (1969). When parts of their brains were electrically stimulated, many of Penfield's patients reported the appearance of images that had something of the feel of memories.

Today most psychologists view this notion as exaggerated. Memory researcher Elizabeth Loftus, for example, notes that the "memories" stimulated by Penfield's probes lacked detail and were sometimes incorrect (Loftus & Loftus, 1980; Loftus, 1983). Now let us consider some other questions about long-term memory.

How Accurate Are Long-Term Memories?   Psychologist Elizabeth Loftus notes that memories are distorted by our biases and needs—by the ways in which we conceptualize our worlds. We represent much of our world in the form of **schemas.**

To understand what is meant by the term *schema,* consider the problems of travelers who met up with Procrustes, the legendary highwayman of ancient Greece. Procrustes had a quirk. He was interested not only in travelers' pocketbooks but also in their height. He had a concept—a schema—of how tall people should be, and when people did not fit his schema, they were in trouble. You see, Procrustes also had a bed, the famous "Procrustean bed." He made his victims lie down in the bed, and if they were too short for it, he stretched them to make them fit. If they were too long for the bed, he practiced surgery on their legs.

Displacement.
Information can be lost to short-term memory through displacement. We may have little trouble remembering the names of the first or second person we meet at a gathering. But as introductions continue, new names may displace the old ones and we may forget the names of people we met only a few minutes earlier.

Eyewitness Testimony?

How trustworthy is eyewitness testimony? Memories are reconstructive rather than photographic. The wording of questions also influences the content of the memory. Attorneys therefore are sometimes instructed not to phrase questions in such a way that they "lead" the witness.

▲ REFLECT
Were you ever convinced that you were remembering something accurately, only to discover, later, that your memory was incorrect? How do you account for the distorted memory? Why were you convinced it was accurate at the time?

How Fast Were These Cars Going When They Collided?

Our schemas influence our processing of information. When shown pictures such as these, people who were asked how fast the cars were going when they *smashed* into each other offer higher estimates than people who were told that the cars *hit* each other.

Although the myth of Procrustes may sound absurd, it reflects a quirky truth about each of us. We all carry our cognitive Procrustean beds around with us—our unique ways of perceiving the world—and we try to make things and people fit them.

Let me give you an example. "Retrieve" the fourth sheet of paper you prepared according to the instructions for the challenges to memory. The labels you wrote on the sheet will remind you of the figures. Take a minute or two to draw them now. Then continue reading.

Now that you have made your drawings, turn to Figure 6.6. Are your drawings closer in form to those in group 1 or to those in group 2? I wouldn't be surprised if they were more like those in group 1—if, for example, your first drawing looked more like eyeglasses than a dumbbell. After all, they were labeled like the drawings in group 1. The labels serve as *schemas* for the drawings—ways of organizing your knowledge of them— and these schemas may have influenced your recollections.

Consider another example of the power of schemas in processing information. Loftus and Palmer (1974) showed people a film of a car crash and then asked them to fill out questionnaires that included a question about how fast the cars were going at the time. The language of the question varied in subtle ways, however. Some people were asked to estimate how fast the cars were going when they "hit" each other. Others were asked to estimate the cars' speed when they "smashed into" each other. On average, people who reconstructed the scene on the basis of the cue "hit" estimated a speed of 34 mph. People who watched the same film but reconstructed the scene on the basis of the cue "smashed" estimated a speed of 41 mph! In other words, the use of the word *hit* or *smashed* caused people to organize their knowledge about the crash in different ways. That is, the words served as diverse schemas that fostered the development of very different ways of processing information about the crash.

Participants in the same study were questioned again a week later: "Did you see any broken glass?" Since there was no broken glass shown in the film, an answer of "yes" would be wrong. Of those who had earlier been encouraged to process information about the accident in terms of one car "hitting" the other, 14% incorrectly answered yes. But 32% of the participants who had processed information about the crash in terms of one car "smashing into" the other reported, incorrectly, that they had seen broken glass.

DIVERSITY An experiment reported by Elizabeth Loftus (1979) shows that people may reconstruct their experiences according to their prejudices. Participants in the study were shown a picture that contained an African American man who was holding a hat and a European American man who was holding a razor. Later, when they were asked what they had seen, many participants erroneously recalled the razor as being in the hands of the African American. The participants recalled information that was consistent with their schemas, but it was wrong.

CONTROVERSY IN PSYCHOLOGY

Can We Trust Eyewitness Testimony?

Jean Piaget, the investigator of children's cognitive development, distinctly remembered an attempt to kidnap him from his baby carriage as he was being wheeled along the Champs Élysées. He recalled the excited throng, the abrasions on the face of the nurse who rescued him, the police officer's white baton, and the flight of the assailant. Although they were graphic, Piaget's memories were false. Years later, the nurse admitted that she had made up the tale.

Can eyewitness testimony be trusted? Is there reason to believe that the statements of eyewitnesses are any more factual than Piaget's? Legal professionals are concerned about the accuracy of our long-term memories as reflected in eyewitness testimony (Wells et al., 2000). Misidentifications of suspects "create a double horror: The wrong person is devastated by this personal tragedy, and the real criminal is still out on the streets" (Loftus, 1993, p. 550). Let us consider what can go wrong—and what can go right—with eyewitness testimony.

One problem with eyewitness testimony is that the words chosen by an experimenter—and those chosen by a lawyer interrogating a witness—have been shown to influence the reconstruction of memories (Wells et al., 2000). For example, as in the experiment described earlier, an attorney for the plaintiff might ask the witness, "How fast was the defendant's car going when it *smashed into* the plaintiff's car?" In such a case, the car might be reported as going faster than if the question had been: "How fast was the defendant's car going when the accident occurred?" (Loftus & Palmer, 1974). Could the attorney for the defendant claim that use of the word *smashed* biased the witness? What about jurors who heard the word *smashed?* Would they be biased toward assuming that the driver had been reckless?

Children tend to be more suggestible witnesses than adults, and preschoolers are more suggestible than older children (Ceci & Bruck, 1993). But when questioned properly, even young children may be able to provide accurate and useful testimony (Ceci & Bruck, 1993).

There are cases in which the memories of eyewitnesses have been "refreshed" by hypnosis. Sad to say, hypnosis does more than amplify memories; it can also distort them (Loftus, 1994). One problem is that witnesses may accept and embellish suggestions made by the hypnotist. Another is that hypnotized people may report fantasized occurrences as compellingly as if they were real (Loftus, 1994).

There are also problems in the identification of criminals by eyewitnesses. For one thing, witnesses may pay more attention to the suspect's clothing than to more meaningful characteristics such as facial features, height, and weight. In one experiment, viewers of a videotaped crime incorrectly identified a man as the criminal because he wore the eyeglasses and T-shirt that had been worn by the perpetrator on the tape. The man who had actually committed the crime was identified less often (Sanders, 1984).

Other problems with eyewitness testimony include the following:

▲ Identification is less accurate when suspects belong to ethnic or racial groups that differ from that of the witness (Egeth, 1993).
▲ Identification of suspects is confused when interrogators make misleading suggestions (Loftus, 1997).
▲ Witnesses are seen as more credible when they claim to be certain in their testimony, but there is little evidence that claims of certainty are accurate (Wells et al., 2000).

There are thus many problems with eyewitness testimony. Yet even Elizabeth Loftus (1993), who has extensively studied the accuracy of eyewitness testimony, agrees that it is a valuable tool in the courtroom. After all, identifications made by eyewitnesses are

www 6 E 4

CLICK4™ *an essay assignment on memory and eyewitness testimony.*

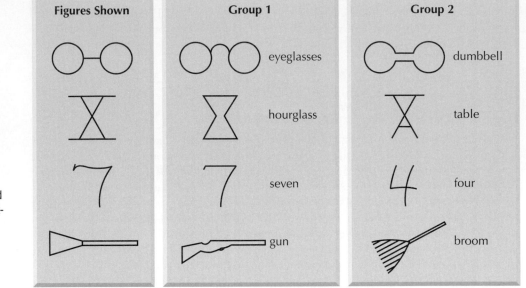

FIGURE 6.6 Memory as Reconstructive.

In their classic experiment, Carmichael, Hogan, and Walter (1932) showed people the figures in the left-hand box and made remarks as suggested in the other boxes. For example, the experimenter might say, "This drawing looks like eyeglasses [or a dumbbell]." When people later reconstructed the drawings, they were influenced by the labels.

frequently correct, and what, Loftus asks, would be the alternative to the use of eyewitnesses? If we were to prevent eyewitnesses from testifying, how many criminals would go free?

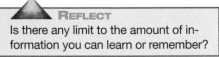

REFLECT

Is there any limit to the amount of information you can learn or remember?

How Much Information Can Be Stored in Long-Term Memory?

How many gigabytes of storage are there in your most personal computer—your brain? Unlike a computer, the human ability to store information is, for all practical purposes, unlimited (Goldman-Rakic, 1995). Even the largest hard drives fill up quickly when we save Web pages from the Internet, pictures, or movies. Yet how many "movies" of the past have you saved in your own long-term memory? How many thousands of scenes and stories can you rerun at will? And assuming that you have an intact sensory system, the movies in your personal storage bins not only have color and sound, but also aromas, tactile sensations, and much more. *Your long-term memory is a biochemical "hard drive" with no known limits on the gigabytes of information it can store.*

Yes, new information may replace older information in short-term memory, but there is no evidence that long-term memories—those in "storage"—are lost by displacement. Long-term memories may endure for a lifetime. Now and then it may seem that we have forgotten, or "lost," a long-term memory such as the names of our elementary- or high-school classmates. Yet it may be that we cannot find the proper cues to help us retrieve them. It is like forgetting a file name when working with a computer. If long-term memories are lost, they may be lost in the same way that a misplaced object or computer file is lost. It is "lost," but we sense that it is still somewhere in the room or on the hard drive. In other words, it is lost but not destroyed or deleted.

Transferring Information From Short-Term to Long-Term Memory: Using the "Save" Function

How can you transfer information from short-term to long-term memory? By and large, the more often chunks of information are rehearsed, the more likely they are to be transferred to long-term memory. Repeating information over and over to prevent it from decaying or being displaced is termed *maintenance rehearsal*. But maintenance rehearsal does not give meaning to information by linking it to past learning. Thus it is not considered the best way to permanently store information (Simpson et al., 1994).

A more effective method is to make information more meaningful—to purposefully relate new information to things that are already well known (Woloshyn et al., 1994). For example, to better remember the components of levers, physics students might use see-saws, wheelbarrows, and oars as examples (Scruggs & Mastropieri, 1992). The nine chunks of information in our second challenge to memory were made easier to reconstruct once they were associated with the familiar tic-tac-toe grid in Figure 6.4. Relating new material to well-known material is known as **elaborative rehearsal.** For example, have you seen this word before?

FUNTHOSTAM

Say it aloud. Do you know it? If you had used an acoustic code alone to memorize THUNSTOFAM, the list of letters you first saw on page 188, it might not have been easy to recognize FUNTHOSTAM as an incorrect spelling. Let us assume, however, that by now you have used elaborative rehearsal and encoded THUNSTOFAM semantically (according to its "meaning") as an acronym for "The United States of America." Then you would have been able to scan the spelling of the words in the phrase "The United States of America" to determine that FUNTHOSTAM is an incorrect spelling.

Rote repetition of a meaningless group of syllables, such as *thun-sto-fam*, relies on maintenance rehearsal for permanent storage. The process might be tedious (continued rehearsal) and unreliable. Elaborative rehearsal—tying THUNSTOFAM to the name of a country—might make storage instantaneous and retrieval foolproof.

Levels of Processing Information   People who use elaborative rehearsal to remember things are *processing information at a deeper level* than people who use maintenance rehearsal. ***Question: What is the levels-of-processing model of memory?*** Fergus Craik and Robert Lockhart (1972) pioneered the levels-of-processing model of memory, which holds that memories tend to endure when information is processed *deeply*—attended to, encoded carefully, pondered, and related to things we already know. Remembering relies on how *deeply* people process information, not on whether memories are transferred from one *stage* of memory to another.

Evidence for the importance of levels of processing information is found in an experiment with three groups of college students, all of whom were asked to study a picture of a living room for 1 minute (Bransford et al., 1977). The groups' examination of the picture entailed different approaches. Two groups were informed that small *x*'s were imbedded in the picture. The first of these groups was asked to find the *x*'s by scanning the picture horizontally and vertically. The second group was informed that the *x*'s could be found in the edges of the objects in the room and was asked to look for them there. The third group was asked, instead, to think about how it would use the objects pictured in the room. As a result of the divergent sets of instructions, the first two groups (the *x* hunters) processed information about the objects in the picture superficially. But the third group rehearsed the objects elaboratively—that is, members of this group thought about the objects in terms of their meanings and uses. It should not be surprising that the third group remembered many times more objects than the first two groups.

In another experiment, researchers asked participants to indicate whether they recognized photos of faces they had been shown under one of three conditions: (1) being asked to recall the gender of the person in the photo, (2) being asked to recall the width of the person's nose, or (3) being asked to judge whether the person is honest (Bloom & Mudd, 1991). Participants who were asked to form judgments about the persons' honesty recognized more faces. Asking people to judge other people's honesty may stimulate deeper processing of the facial features. That is, participants may study each face in detail to see if they can relate what they see to their ideas about human nature.

Language arts teachers encourage students to use new vocabulary words in sentences to process them more deeply. Each new usage is an instance of elaborative rehearsal. Usage helps build semantic codes that make it easier to retrieve the meanings of words in the future. When I was in high school, teachers of foreign languages told us that learning classical languages "exercises the mind" so that we would understand English better. Not exactly. The mind is not analogous to a muscle that responds to

Elaborative rehearsal ▲ A method for increasing retention of new information by relating it to information that is well known.

Flashbulb Memories.

Where were you and what were you doing on the morning of September 11, 2001? Many older Americans never forgot where they were and what they were doing when they learned about the attack on Pearl Harbor on December 7, 1941. Major events can illuminate everything about them so that we recall everything that was happening at the time.

exercise. However, the meanings of many English words are based on foreign ones. A person who recognizes that *retrieve* stems from roots meaning "again" (*re-*) and "find" (*trouver* in French) is less likely to forget that *retrieval* means "finding again" or "bringing back."

Think, too, of all the algebra and geometry problems we were asked to solve in high school. Each problem is an application of a procedure and, perhaps, of certain formulas and theorems. By repeatedly applying the procedures, formulas, and theorems in different contexts, we rehearse them elaboratively. As a consequence, we are more likely to remember them. Knowledge of the ways in which a formula or an equation is used helps us remember the formula. Also, by building one geometry theorem on another, we relate new theorems to ones that we already understand. As a result, we process information about them more deeply and remember them better.

There is also a good deal of biologically oriented research that connects deep processing with activity in certain parts of the brain, notably the prefrontal area of the cerebral cortex (Grady et al., 1999). Fergus Craik and his colleagues (e.g., Grady et al., 1999) are discovering that one reason that older adults show memory loss is that they tend not to process information quite as deeply as younger people do. Deep processing requires sustained attention, and older adults, along with people who have suffered brain injuries and strokes, are apparently not capable of focusing their attention as well as they had previously (Iidaka et al., 2000; Winocur et al., 2000).

Before proceeding to the next section, cover the preceding paragraph with your hand. Which of the following words is spelled correctly: *retrieval* or *retreival?* The spellings sound alike, so an acoustic code for reconstructing the correct spelling would fail. Yet a semantic code, such as the spelling rule "*i* before *e* except after *c*," would allow you to reconstruct the correct spelling: retr*ie*val.

Flashbulb Memories: "To Leave a Scar Upon the Cerebral Tissues"

The attention which we lend to an experience is proportional to its vivid or interesting character; and it is a notorious fact that what interests us most vividly at the time is, other things equal, what we remember best. An impression may be so exciting emotionally as almost to leave a scar upon the cerebral tissues.

William James

Many of us will never forget where we were or what we were doing when we learned of the attacks on the World Trade Center and the Pentagon on September 11, 2001. Some of us will similarly recall where we were and what we were doing when we learned that John F. Kennedy Jr.'s airplane had crashed into the ocean in 1999— or that his father had been assassinated in 1963. Others will recall the day in 1997 when Britain's Princess Diana died in an automobile accident. We may also have a detailed memory of what we were doing when we learned of a relative's death. An older generation of Americans recalled where they were and what they were doing when they learned of the attack on Pearl Harbor on December 7, 1941.

Question: Why is it that some events, like the attack of September 11, 2001, can be etched in memory for a lifetime? It appears that we tend to remember events that are surprising, important, and emotionally stirring more clearly. Such events can create "flashbulb memories," which preserve experiences in detail (Conway et al., 1994; Finkenauer et al., 1998). Why is the memory etched when the "flashbulb" goes off? One factor is the

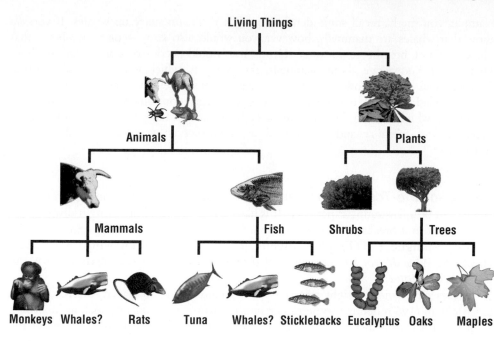

FIGURE 6.7   The Hierarchical Structure of Long-Term Memory.

Where are whales filed in the hierarchical cabinets of your memory? Your classification of whales may influence your answers to these questions: Do whales breathe underwater? Are they warm-blooded? Do they nurse their young?

distinctness of the memory. It is easier to discriminate stimuli that stand out. Such events are striking in themselves. The feelings caused by them are also special. It is thus relatively easy to pick them out from the storehouse of memories. Major events such as the assassination of a president or the loss of a close relative also tend to have important effects on our lives. We are likely to dwell on them and form networks of associations. That is, we are likely to rehearse them elaboratively. Our rehearsal may include great expectations, or deep fears, for the future.

Biology is intimately connected with psychology. Strong feelings are connected with the secretion of stress hormones, and stress hormones help etch events into our memory—"as almost to leave a scar upon the cerebral tissues," poetically speaking.

Organization in Long-Term Memory

The storehouse of long-term memory is usually well organized. Items are not just piled on the floor or thrown into closets. *Question: How is knowledge organized in long-term memory?* We tend to gather information about rats and cats into a certain section of the storehouse, perhaps the animal or mammal section. We put information about oaks, maples, and eucalyptus into the tree section. Such categorization of stimuli is a basic cognitive function. It allows us to make predictions about specific instances and to store information efficiently.

We tend to organize information according to a *hierarchical structure*, as shown in Figure 6.7. A *hierarchy* is an arrangement of items (or chunks of information) into groups or classes according to common or distinct features. As we work our way up the hierarchy shown in Figure 6.7, we find more encompassing, or *superordinate*, classes to which the items below them belong. For example, all mammals are animals, but there are many types of animals other than mammals.[2]

When items are correctly organized in long-term memory, you are more likely to recall—or know—accurate information about them. For instance, do you "remember" whether whales breathe underwater? If you did not know that whales are mammals (or, in Figure 6.7, *subordinate* to mammals), or if you knew nothing about mammals, a correct answer might depend on some remote instance of rote learning. That is, you might be depending on chancy episodic memory rather than on reliable semantic memory. For

---

[2]A note to biological purists: Figure 6.7 is not intended to represent phyla, classes, orders, and so on accurately. Rather, it shows how an individual's classification scheme might be organized.

example, you might recall some details from a TV documentary on whales. If you *did* know that whales are mammals, however, you would also know—or remember—that whales do not breathe underwater. How? You would reconstruct information about whales from knowledge about mammals, the group to which whales are subordinate. Similarly, you would know, or remember, that because they are mammals, whales are warm-blooded, nurse their young, and are a good deal more intelligent than, say, tunas and sharks, which are fish. Had you incorrectly classified whales as fish, you might have searched your memory and constructed the incorrect answer that they do breathe underwater.

The Tip-of-the-Tongue Phenomenon

Having something on the tip of your tongue can be a frustrating experience. It is like reeling in a fish but having it drop off the line just before it breaks the surface of the water. Psychologists term this experience the **tip-of-the-tongue (TOT) phenomenon,** or the **feeling-of-knowing experience.** *Question: Why do we sometimes feel that the answer to a question is on the tip of our tongue?*

Research provides insight into the TOT phenomenon. In classic research, Brown and McNeill (1966) defined some rather unusual words for students, such as *sampan,* a small riverboat used in China and Japan. The students were then asked to recall the words they had learned. Some of the students often had the right word "on the tip of their tongue" but reported words with similar meanings such as *junk, barge,* or *houseboat.* Still other students reported words that sounded similar, such as *Saipan, Siam, sarong,* and *sanching.* Why?

To begin with, the words were unfamiliar, so elaborative rehearsal did not take place. The students, that is, did not have an opportunity to relate the words to other things they knew. Brown and McNeill also suggested that our storage systems are indexed according to cues that include both the sounds and the meanings of words—that is, according to both acoustic and semantic codes. By scanning words similar in sound and meaning to the word on the tip of the tongue, we sometimes find a useful cue and retrieve the word for which we are searching.

The feeling-of-knowing experience also seems to reflect incomplete or imperfect learning. In such cases, our answers may be "in the ballpark" if not on the mark. In some feeling-of-knowing experiments, people are often asked trivia questions. When they do not recall an answer, they are then asked to guess how likely it is that they will recognize the right answer if it is among a group of possibilities. People turn out to be very accurate in their estimations about whether or not they will recognize the answer. Similarly, Brown and McNeill found that the students in their TOT experiment proved to be very good at estimating the number of syllables in words that they could not recall. The students often correctly guessed the initial sounds of the words. They sometimes recognized words that rhymed with them.

Sometimes an answer seems to be on the tip of our tongue because our knowledge of the topic is incomplete. We may not know the exact answer, but we know something. (As a matter of fact, if we have good writing skills, we may present our incomplete knowledge so forcefully that we earn a good grade on an essay question on the topic!) At such times, the problem lies not in retrieval but in the original encoding and storage.

Context-Dependent Memory: Been There, Done That?

> *It's* déjà vu *all over again.*
>
> Yogi Berra

The context in which we acquire information can also play a role in retrieval. I remember walking down the halls of the apartment building where I had lived as a child. Cooking odors triggered a sudden assault of images of playing under the staircase, of falling against a radiator, of the shrill voice of a former neighbor calling for her child at

---

▲ **REFLECT**

Have you ever been so close to retrieving information that it seemed to be on "the tip of your tongue," yet you could not quite remember it? Were you eventually able to retrieve it? How?

▲ **REFLECT**

Did you ever have a *déjà vu* experience? For example, did you ever walk through your old neighborhood and recall people's faces or aromas of cooking that were so real that you actually salivated? How do you explain such experiences?

Tip-of-the-tongue (TOT) phenomenon ▲ The feeling that information is stored in memory although it cannot be readily retrieved. Also called the *feeling-of-knowing experience.*
Feeling-of-knowing experience ▲ Same as *tip-of-the-tongue phenomenon.*

dinnertime. Have you ever walked the halls of an old school building and been assaulted by memories of faces and names that you had thought would be lost forever? Odors, it turns out, are particularly likely to trigger related memories (Pointer & Bond, 1998).

My experience was an example of a **context-dependent memory.** My memories were particularly clear in the context in which they were formed. ***Question: Why may it be useful to study in the room in which we will be tested?*** One answer is that being in the proper context—for example, studying in the exam room or under the same conditions—can dramatically enhance recall (Isarida & Isarida, 1999). One fascinating experiment in context-dependent memory included a number of people who were "all wet." Members of a university swimming club were asked to learn lists of words either while they were submerged or while they were literally high and dry (Godden & Baddeley, 1975). Students who learned the list underwater showed superior recall of the list when immersed. Similarly, those who had rehearsed the list ashore showed better retrieval on terra firma.

Other studies have found that students do better on tests when they study under the same conditions—either in silence or with the stereo on (Grant et al., 1998). When police are interviewing witnesses to crimes, they ask the witnesses to paint the scene verbally as vividly as possible, or they visit the scene of the crime with the witnesses. People who mentally place themselves in the context in which they encoded and stored information frequently retrieve it more accurately.

One of the more eerie psychological experiences is *déjà vu* (French for "already seen"). Sometimes we meet someone new or find ourselves in a strange place, yet we have the feeling that we know this person or have been there before. The *déjà vu* experience seems to occur when we are in a context similar to one we have been in before—or when we meet someone who has a way of talking or moving similar to that of someone we know or once knew. Familiarity with the context leads us to think, "I've been here before." Some people might even wonder whether they had experienced the situation in a former life, or whether their experience is something supernatural. Although your feelings and ideas are flooding in because of the similarity of the context, the sense that you have been there before, or done this thing before, can be so strong that you just stand back and wonder.

State-Dependent Memory

State-dependent memory is an extension of context-dependent memory. It sometimes happens that we retrieve information better when we are in a physiological or emotional state that is similar to the one in which we encoded and stored the information. Feeling the rush of love may trigger images of other times when we fell in love. The grip of anger may prompt memories of incidents of frustration and rage. The research in this area even extends to states in which we are sober or inebriated!

Gordon Bower (1981) ran experiments in which happy or sad moods were induced by hypnotic suggestion. The participants then learned lists of words. People who learned a list while in a happy mood showed better recall when a happy state was induced again. But people who had learned the list while in a sad mood showed superior recall when they were saddened again.

Studies of this kind are usually run with normal participants. However, one study was carried out with people with bipolar disorder (also known as manic-depressive disorder). In this psychological disorder, moods swing from the heights of elation to the depths of depression and back, with no apparent external cause. The researchers found that the participants in the study had better recall of events that occurred when they were "up" or "down" when they were in the same mood (Eich et al., 1997).

Psychologists suggest that in day-to-day life a happy mood influences us to focus on positive events (Eich, 1995; Matt et al., 1992). As a result, we have better recall of these events in the future. A sad mood, unfortunately, leads us to focus on and recall the negative. Happiness may feed on happiness, but under extreme circumstances, sadness can develop into a vicious cycle and lead to depression.

www 6 WS 3

CLICK4™ *demonstrations and tutorials about memory and cognition from Southwest Missouri State University.*

Context-dependent memory ▲ Information that is better retrieved in the context in which it was encoded and stored, or learned.

State-dependent memory ▲ Information that is better retrieved in the physiological or emotional state in which it was encoded and stored, or learned.

IN REVIEW
Processes and Stages of Memory

Concept	What It Means	Example
PROCESSES OF MEMORY		
Encoding	Modifying information so that it can be placed in memory, sometimes from one sensory modality (e.g., vision) to another (hearing)	Mental representation of the words in this table as a sequence of sounds (an acoustic code)
Storage	Maintenance of information over time	Mental repetition (maintenance rehearsal) of the information in this chart in order to keep it in memory
Retrieval	Finding of stored information and bringing it into conscious awareness	Recall of the information in this chart; using a mnemonic device such as Roy G. Biv to recall the colors of the visible spectrum
STAGES OF MEMORY		
Sensory Memory	Type or stage of memory that is first encountered by a stimulus and briefly holds impressions of it	Continuing briefly to "see" a visual stimulus after it has been removed
Short-Term Memory	Type or stage of memory that can hold information for up to a minute or so after the trace of the stimulus decays; also termed *working memory*	Repeating someone's name in order to remember it, or relating something new to things that are already known
Long-Term Memory	Type or stage of memory that is capable of relatively permanent storage	The "file cabinets" of memory, where you store items like the names of your primary school teachers and your memories of holidays when you were little

REVIEW

CLICK4™ *an essay assignment on methods of improving your memory.*

CLICK4™ *a quiz covering the first half of this chapter.*

(8) The Atkinson and Shiffrin model hypothesizes three stages of memory: sensory memory, _____-term memory, and long-term memory. (9) The mental representations of visual stimuli are referred to as _____. (10) The ability to retain exact mental representations of visual stimuli over long amounts of time is termed _____ imagery. (11) The mental representations of _____ stimuli are called *echoes*. (12) According to the _____-position effect, we are most likely to recall the first and last items in a series. (13) The Petersons showed that information can be displaced from short-term memory by means of_____. (14) Elizabeth Loftus and other psychologists have shown that we _____ our memories according to our schemas. (15) We need the proper _____ to retrieve information in long-term memory. (16) Detailed memories of surprising, important, and emotional events are termed "_____ memories." (17) Information in long-term memory is organized in a _____ structure. (18) The _____-of-the-tongue phenomenon reflects incomplete learning. (19) _____-dependent memory refers to information that is better retrieved under the circumstances in which it was encoded and stored.

Pulling It Together: How is information lost in each stage of memory? How will you avoid losing the information in this section?

FORGETTING

What do DAL, RIK, BOF, and ZEX have in common? They are all **nonsense syllables.** Nonsense syllables are meaningless sets of two consonants with a vowel sandwiched in between. They were first used by Hermann Ebbinghaus to study memory and forgetting. Because nonsense syllables are intended to be meaningless, remembering them should depend on simple acoustic coding and maintenance rehearsal rather than on elaborative rehearsal, semantic coding, or other ways of making learning meaningful. They are thus well suited for use in the measurement of forgetting. *Question: What types of memory tasks are used in measuring forgetting?*

Memory Tasks Used in Measuring Forgetting

Three basic memory tasks have been used by psychologists to measure forgetting: recognition, recall, and relearning. Nonsense syllables have been used in studying each of them. The study of these memory tasks has led to several conclusions about the nature of forgetting.

Recognition   One aspect of forgetting is failure to recognize something we have experienced. There are many ways of measuring **recognition.** In many studies, psychologists ask participants to read a list of nonsense syllables. The participants then read a second list of nonsense syllables and indicate whether they recognize any of the syllables as having appeared on the first list. Forgetting is defined as failure to recognize a syllable that has been read before.

In another kind of recognition study, Harry Bahrick and his colleagues (1975) studied high-school graduates who had been out of school for various lengths of time. They interspersed photos of the graduates' classmates with four times as many photos of strangers. Recent graduates correctly recognized former classmates 90% of the time. Those who had been out of school for 40 years recognized former classmates 75% of the time. A chance level of recognition would have been only 20% (1 photo in 5 was of an actual classmate). Thus even older people showed rather solid long-term recognition ability.

Recognition is the easiest type of memory task. This is why multiple-choice tests are easier than fill-in-the-blank or essay tests. We can recognize correct answers more easily than we can recall them unaided.

Recall   In his own studies of **recall,** another kind of memory task, Ebbinghaus would read lists of nonsense syllables aloud to the beat of a metronome and then see how many he could produce from memory. After reading through a list once, he usually would be able to recall seven syllables—the typical limit for short-term memory.

Psychologists also often use lists of pairs of nonsense syllables, called **paired associates,** to measure recall. A list of paired associates is shown in Figure 6.8. Participants read through the lists pair by pair. Later they are shown the first member of each pair and asked to recall the second. Recall is more difficult than recognition. In a recognition task, one simply indicates whether an item has been seen before or which of a number of items is paired with a stimulus (as in a multiple-choice test). In a recall task, the person must retrieve a syllable, with another syllable serving as a cue.

Retrieval is made easier if the two syllables can be meaningfully linked—that is, encoded semantically—even if the "meaning" is stretched a bit. Consider the first pair of

Nonsense syllables ▲ Meaningless sets of two consonants, with a vowel sandwiched in between, that are used to study memory.

Recognition ▲ In information processing, the easiest memory task, involving identification of objects or events encountered before.

Recall ▲ Retrieval or reconstruction of learned material.

Paired associates ▲ Nonsense syllables presented in pairs in experiments that measure recall.

211

FIGURE 6.8 Paired Associates.
Psychologists often use paired associates to measure recall. Retrieving CEG in response to the cue WOM is made easier by an image of a WOMan smoking a "CEG-arette."

nonsense syllables in Figure 6.8. The image of a WOMan smoking a CEG-arette may make CEG easier to retrieve when the person is presented with the cue WOM.

It is easier to recall vocabulary words from foreign languages if you can construct a meaningful link between the foreign and English words (Atkinson, 1975). The *peso*, pronounced *pay-so*, is a unit of Mexican money. A link can be formed by finding a part of the foreign word, such as the *pe-* (pronounced *pay*) in *peso*, and constructing a phrase such as "You pay with money." When you read or hear the word *peso* in the future, you recognize the *pe-* and retrieve the link or phrase. From the phrase, you then reconstruct the translation, "a unit of money."

Relearning: Is Learning Easier the Second Time Around? Relearning is a third method of measuring retention. Do you remember having to learn all of the state capitals in grade school? What were the capitals of Wyoming and Delaware? Even when we cannot recall or recognize material that had once been learned, such as Cheyenne for Wyoming and Dover for Delaware, we can relearn it more rapidly the second time. Similarly, as we go through our thirties and forties we may forget a good deal of our high-school French or geometry. Yet the second time around we could learn what previously took months or years much more rapidly.

To study the efficiency of relearning, Ebbinghaus (1885/1913) devised the **method of savings.** First he recorded the number of repetitions required to learn a list of nonsense syllables or words. Then he recorded the number of repetitions required to relearn the list after a certain amount of time had elapsed. Next he computed the difference in the number of repetitions to determine the **savings.** If a list had to be repeated 20 times before it was learned, and 20 times again after a year had passed, there were no savings. Relearning, that is, was as tedious as the initial learning. However, if the list could be learned with only 10 repetitions after a year had elapsed, half the number of repetitions required for learning had been saved.

Figure 6.9 shows Ebbinghaus's classic curve of forgetting. As you can see, there was no loss of memory as measured by savings immediately after a list had been learned. However, recollection dropped quite a bit, by half, during the first hour after learning a list. Losses of learning then became more gradual. It took a month (31 days) for retention to be cut in half again. In other words, forgetting occurred most rapidly right after material was learned. We continue to forget material as time elapses, but at a slower pace.

Before leaving this section, I have one question for you: What are the capitals of Wyoming and Delaware?

Interference Theory

When we do not attend to, encode, and rehearse sensory input, we may forget it through decay of the trace of the image. Material in short-term memory, like material in sensory memory, can be lost through decay. It can also be lost through displacement, as may happen when we try to remember several new names at a party.

Question: Why can learning Spanish make it harder to remember French? The answer may be found in **interference theory.** According to this view, we also forget material in short-term and long-term memory because newly learned material interferes with it. The two basic types of interference are retroactive interference (also called *retroactive inhibition*) and proactive interference (also called *proactive inhibition*).

Retroactive Interference In **retroactive interference,** new learning interferes with the retrieval of old learning. For example, a medical student may memorize the names of the bones in the leg through rote repetition. Later he or she may find that learning the names of the bones in the arm makes it more difficult to retrieve the names of the leg bones, especially if the names are similar in sound or in relative location on each limb.

Proactive Interference In **proactive interference,** older learning interferes with the capacity to retrieve more recently learned material. High-school Spanish may pop in when you are trying to retrieve college French or Italian words. All three are

Relearning ▲ A measure of retention. Material is usually relearned more quickly than it is learned initially.
Method of savings ▲ A measure of retention in which the difference between the number of repetitions originally required to learn a list and the number of repetitions required to relearn the list after a certain amount of time has elapsed is calculated.
Savings ▲ The difference between the number of repetitions originally required to learn a list and the number of repetitions required to relearn the list after a certain amount of time has elapsed.
Interference theory ▲ The view that we may forget stored material because other learning interferes with it.
Retroactive interference ▲ The interference of new learning with the ability to retrieve material learned previously.
Proactive interference ▲ The interference by old learning with the ability to retrieve material learned recently.

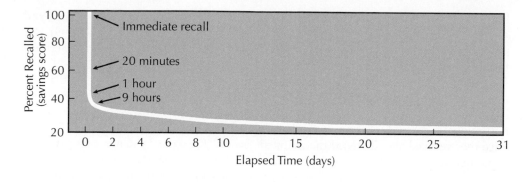

FIGURE 6.9 **Ebbinghaus's Classic Curve of Forgetting.**
Recollection of lists of words drops sharply during the first hour after learning. Losses of learning then become more gradual. Retention drops by half within the first hour. However, it takes a month (31 days) for retention to be cut in half again.

Romance languages, with similar roots and spellings. Previously learned Japanese words probably would not interfere with your ability to retrieve more recently learned French or Italian, because the roots and sounds of Japanese differ considerably from those of the Romance languages.

Consider motor skills. You may learn to drive a standard shift on a car with three forward speeds and a clutch that must be let up slowly after shifting. Later you may learn to drive a car with five forward speeds and a clutch that must be released rapidly. For a while, you may make errors on the five-speed car because of proactive interference. (Old learning interferes with new learning.) If you return to the three-speed car after driving the five-speed car has become natural, you may stall it a few times. This is because of retroactive interference (new learning interfering with the old).

Repression: Ejecting the Unwanted From Consciousness

According to Sigmund Freud, we are motivated to forget painful memories and unacceptable ideas because they produce anxiety, guilt, and shame. *Question: What is the Freudian concept of repression?* Repression, according to Freud, is the automatic ejection of painful memories and unacceptable urges from conscious awareness. It is motivated by the desire to avoid facing painful memories and emotions. Psychoanalysts believe that repression is at the heart of disorders such as **dissociative amnesia** (see Chapter 15). There is a current controversy in psychology as to whether repression (motivated forgetting) exists and, if it does, how it works. One interesting finding is that stress

Dissociative amnesia ▲ Amnesia thought to stem from psychological conflict or trauma.

Interference.
In retroactive interference, new learning interferes with the retrieval of old learning. In proactive interference, older learning interferes with the capacity to retrieve material learned more recently. For example, high-school French vocabulary may "pop in" when you are trying to retrieve words you have learned for a Spanish test in college.

CLICK4™ *an essay assignment on interference theory.*

hormones—the kind we secrete when we experience extremes of anxiety, guilt, and shame—*heighten* memory formation (Clayton & Williams, 2000; Ferry et al., 1999). But supporters of the concept of repression do not claim that repressed memories were ill-formed; they say, rather, that we do not focus on them.

There is much research on repression, often in the form of case studies that are found in psychoanalytic journals (e.g., Eagle, 2000). Much has been made of case studies in which veterans have supposedly forgotten traumatic battlefield experiences, developed posttraumatic stress disorder (once called "battlefield neurosis"), and then "felt better" once they recalled and discussed the traumatic events (Karon & Widener, 1998). Critics argue that the evidence for such repression and recovery of memories is weak, and that this kind of "memory" can be implanted by the suggestions of interviewers (Lilienfeld & Loftus, 1998; Loftus & Polage, 1999). The issue remains controversial, as highlighted in the following pages.

CONTROVERSY IN PSYCHOLOGY

Do People Really Recover Repressed Memories of Sexual Abuse at an Early Age, or Are These "Memories" Implanted by Interviewers?

CLICK4™ *more information about false memories at the False Memory Syndrome Foundation.*

There is apparently little doubt that the memory of traumatic events can be repressed. But as we see in this section, there is also little doubt that many so-called recovered memories, particularly memories of childhood sexual abuse, are sometimes induced by a therapist.[3]

A young woman in psychotherapy recovered the memory that at age 13 she was raped by her teacher, became pregnant, and underwent an abortion. No corroborating evidence for this event existed. In fact, the woman had not reached menarche until 15, so the pregnancy was medically impossible. Still, she filed criminal charges against the teacher, who had to spend his life savings to defend himself against the false accusation. Eventually, the court ruled that recovery of a repressed memory lacked sufficient scientific foundation to be admissible evidence.

There is apparently little question that the memory of traumatic events is sometimes repressed. For example, an otherwise law-abiding man who in a fit of rage committed a heinous crime might report it to police as if someone else had done it and make no attempt to escape or to defend himself when he is accused of the crime. Or a woman who was violently raped may afterward be unable to explain her bruises or shock until perhaps she returns to the crime scene.

CLICK4™ *a bulletin board discussion on repressed memories.*

CLICK4™ *more information about recovered memories of childhood abuse and the recovered memory debate.*

Truth or Fiction? But there is also little question that many so-called recovered memories, particularly those involving allegations of childhood sexual abuse by a parent or other close relative, teacher, or friend, are sometimes fictions induced by the concerted efforts of a therapist who fosters a belief that becomes so deeply held it seems like a real memory. This "false memory syndrome" has resulted in many family tragedies: alienation of children from their parents, loss of jobs, ostracism, and divorces.

"We don't know what percent of these recovered memories are real and what percent are pseudomemories," said psychiatrist Harold Lief, who was one of the first to question these induced memories. "But we do know there are hundreds, maybe thousands of cases of pseudomemories and that many families have been destroyed by them. We also know that many therapists who track down these memories and focus on them fail to deal with the patient's real problems." Indeed, many adults who had in treatment recovered a memory of childhood sexual abuse and accused the supposed perpetrator later retracted the claim.

"Making of an Illness" For example, Gail Macdonald, the author of *Making of an Illness,* had seen a social worker who used hypnosis and guided imagery to convince her that prior sexual abuse by her father was the cause of her current emotional problems.

---

[3]Adapted from Jane E. Brody. (2000, April 25). Memories of things that never were. *The New York Times,* p. F8.

The social worker said she had dissociative identity disorder, a diagnosis he inflicted, she said, on "120 people in my little community."

As a result of the false memory, Ms. Macdonald said she divorced herself from her family, suffered horrible nightmares, wrote compulsively in journals about the abuses her father had supposedly committed and lost so much weight she was described as corpse-like until she sought the help of a psychiatrist who said she had developed "post-traumatic stress disorder as a direct result of therapy" and helped her realize that her recovered memory was false.

How can someone tell if a recovered memory is false? Serious questions should be raised when corroborating evidence is lacking, when the so-called memory occurs before a child is able to remember and when details of the memory are preposterous (like a rape by aliens), said psychiatrist Paul McHugh. McHugh also questioned the reliability of methods typically used to elicit these "memories." Among the most common are hypnosis and guided imagery, during which a therapist may introduce the notion that sexual abuse had occurred and ask the patient to try to remember the circumstances and who the perpetrator might have been. Sometimes patients participate in a recovered memory group where other members pressure the newcomer to recall prior sexual abuse and even suggest how it may have occurred.

Psychologist Elizabeth Loftus cited numerous studies that demonstrated how easy it was to implant a false memory. By asking a series of leading questions and by having a supposed "witness" talk about the made-up experience, it is often possible to convince someone that the event actually happened. In one study, researchers easily convinced half the adult participants that they had been hospitalized in severe pain as children or that they had been lost in a shopping mall at age 5. Several people with these false memories provided detailed embellishments.

This is especially true for young children. In a study conducted by psychologist Stephen J. Ceci, preschool children were asked weekly about whether a fictitious event had ever happened to them. By the 10th week, more than half reported that it had happened and provided cogent details about it.

In one experiment, interviewers told the children: "Think real hard. Did you get your hand caught in a mousetrap and go to the hospital to get it off?" Ceci reported: "So compelling did the children's narrative appear that we suspected that some of the children had come to truly believe they had experienced the fictitious events. Neither parents nor researchers were able to convince 27% of the children that the events never happened."

Based on his research, Ceci concluded, "It is exceedingly, devilishly difficult for professionals to tell fact from fiction when a child has been repeatedly suggestively interviewed over a long period of time. They look and act the way children do when they are trying to be accurate and honest."

CLICK4™ *the Recovered Memory Projects Archives, hosted by Brown University.*

CLICK4™ *a WebSearch activity on false memory.*

Infantile Amnesia: Why Can't Johnny Remember?

Question: Can children remember events from the first couple of years of life? When he interviewed people about their early experiences, Freud discovered that they could not recall episodes that had happened prior to the age of 3 or so, and that recall was cloudy through the age of 5. This phenomenon is referred to as **infantile amnesia.**

Infantile amnesia has little to do with the fact that the episodes occurred in the distant past. Middle-aged and older people have vivid memories from the ages of 6 and 10, yet the events happened many decades ago. But 18-year-olds show steep declines in memory when they try to recall episodes that occurred earlier than the age of 6, even though they happened less than 18 years earlier (Wetzler & Sweeney, 1986).

Freud believed that young children have aggressive impulses and perverse lusts toward their parents. He attributed infantile amnesia to repression of these impulses. However, the episodes lost to infantile amnesia are not weighted in the direction of such "primitive" impulses.

Infantile amnesia probably reflects the interaction of physiological and cognitive factors. For example, a structure of the limbic system (the **hippocampus**) that is involved in the storage of memories does not become mature until we are about 2 years old (Squire,

REFLECT

Do children really remember little or nothing from the first two years of life? Don't they remember (recognize) their caregivers? Don't they remember language? Don't they remember how to crawl and sit up and walk? To what kinds of memories, then, does the concept of infantile amnesia apply?

Infantile amnesia ▲ Inability to recall events that occur prior to the age of 2 or 3. Also termed *childhood amnesia.*
Hippocampus ▲ A structure in the limbic system that plays an important role in the formation of new memories.

1993, 1996). Also, myelination of brain pathways is incomplete for the first few years, contributing to the inefficiency of information processing and memory formation.

There are also cognitive explanations for infantile amnesia:

1. Infants are not particularly interested in remembering the past (Neisser, 1993).
2. Infants, in contrast to older children, tend not to weave episodes together into meaningful stories of their own lives. Information about specific episodes thus tends to be lost. Research shows that when parents reminisce about the past with children, infants' memories are strengthened (Harley & Reese, 1999; Pillemer, 1998). (Of course, one could question the accuracy of some of these reminiscences.)
3. Infants do not make reliable use of language to symbolize or classify events. Their ability to *encode* sensory input—that is, to apply the auditory and semantic codes that facilitate memory formation—is therefore limited. Yet research shows that young infants can recall events throughout the period when infantile amnesia is presumed to occur if they are now and then exposed to nonverbal reminders (Rovee-Collier, 1999).

CLICK4™ *a WebSearch activity on infantile amnesia.*

In any event, we are unlikely to remember episodes from the first two years of life unless we are reminded of them from time to time as we develop. (Really, Allyn, believe me.) Many of the early childhood memories that seem clear today are likely to be reconstructed, and they may hold many inaccuracies. They might also be memories of events that occurred later than the period to which we attribute them. Yet there is no evidence that such early memories are systematically repressed.

Anterograde and Retrograde Amnesia

Question: Why do people frequently have trouble recalling being in accidents? In so-called **anterograde amnesia,** there are memory lapses for the period following a trauma such as a blow to the head, an electric shock, or an operation. In some cases the trauma seems to interfere with all the processes of memory. The ability to pay attention, the encoding of sensory input, and rehearsal are all impaired. A number of investigators have linked certain kinds of brain damage—such as damage to the hippocampus—to amnesia (Henke et al., 1999; Reed & Squire, 1997; Squire, 1996).

Consider the classic case of a man with the initials H. M. Parts of the brain are sometimes lesioned to help people with epilepsy. In H. M.'s case, a section of the hippocampus was removed (Milner, 1966). Right after the operation, H. M.'s mental functioning appeared normal. As time went on, however, it became clear that he had problems processing new information. For example, two years after the operation, H. M. believed he was 27—his age at the time of the operation. When his family moved to a new address, H. M. could not find his new home or remember the new address. He responded with appropriate grief to the death of his uncle, yet he then began to ask about his uncle and why he did not visit. Each time he was informed of his uncle's passing, he grieved as he had when he first heard of it. All in all, it seems that H. M.'s operation prevented him from transferring information from short-term to long-term memory.

In **retrograde amnesia,** the source of trauma prevents people from remembering events that took place before the accident. A football player who is knocked unconscious or a person in an auto accident may be unable to recall events that occurred for several minutes prior to the trauma. The football player may not recall taking the field. The person in the accident may not recall entering the car. It also sometimes happens that the individual cannot remember events that occurred for several years prior to the traumatic incident.

In one well-known case of retrograde amnesia, a man received a head injury in a motorcycle accident (Baddeley, 1982). When he regained consciousness, he had lost memory for all events that had occurred after the age of 11. In fact, he appeared to believe that he was still 11 years old. During the next few months he gradually recovered more knowledge of his past. He moved toward the present year by year, up until the critical motorcycle ride. But he never did recover the events just prior to the accident. The accident had apparently prevented the information that was rapidly unfolding before him

Anterograde amnesia ▲ Failure to remember events that occur after physical trauma because of the effects of the trauma.

Retrograde amnesia ▲ Failure to remember events that occur prior to physical trauma because of the effects of the trauma.

from being transferred to long-term memory. In terms of stages of memory, it may be that our perceptions and ideas need to consolidate, or rest undisturbed for a while, if they are to be transferred to long-term memory (Nader et al., 2000).

REVIEW

(20) The German psychologist Hermann _____ originated the use of nonsense syllables in the study of memory and forgetting. (21) According to Ebbinghaus's classic curve of forgetting, recollection drops (gradually or sharply?) during the first hour after learning a list. (22) In _____ interference, new learning interferes with the retrieval of old learning. (23) In _____ interference, older learning interferes with the capacity to retrieve more recently learned material. (24) Infantile amnesia probably reflects immaturity of the brain structure called the _____ and lack of language. (25) In _____ amnesia there are memory lapses for the period following a traumatic event. (26) In _____ amnesia the source of trauma prevents people from remembering events that took place beforehand.

Pulling It Together: In your educational experience, what types of assessment situations measure recognition, recall, and savings? What kinds of interference have you experienced in learning and memory?

USING THE PSYCHOLOGY OF MEMORY TO IMPROVE YOUR MEMORY

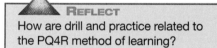

CLICK4™ *Mind Tools Memory Techniques to improve the power of your memory.*

Humans have survived the Ice Age, the Stone Age, the Iron Age, and, a bit more recently, the Industrial Revolution. Now we are trying to cope with the so-called Age of Information, in which there has been an explosion of information. Computers have been developed to process it. Humans, too, process information, and there is more of it to process than ever before. We can always add more memory to our computers, but— ***Question: How can people improve their memory?*** Fortunately, psychologists have helped devise methods for improving memory. Let us consider some of them.

Drill and Practice: "A, B, C, D, . . ."

Repetition (rote maintenance rehearsal) helps transfer information from short-term to long-term memory. Does maintenance rehearsal seem too mechanical for you as a college student? If so, don't forget that this is how you learned the alphabet and how to count! Schoolchildren write spelling words over and over to remember them. Athletes repeat motions so that they will become an implicit memory. When you have memorized formulas, during a test you can use your time to think about when to apply them, rather than using up valuable time trying to recall them.

Some students use flash cards to help them remember facts. For example, they might write "The originator of modern behaviorism is _____" on one side of the card and "John Broadus Watson" on the flip side.

In his book *Super Memory*, Douglas Herrmann (1991) recommends the following methods for remembering a person's name:

1. Say the name out loud.
2. Ask the person a question, using her or his name.
3. Use the person's name as many times as you can during your conversation.
4. Write down the name when the conversation has ended.

Relate New Information to What Is Already Known

Relating new information to what is already known is a form of elaborative rehearsal that helps us to remember it (Willoughby et al., 1994). Herrmann (1991) also suggests that you can better remember the name of a new acquaintance by thinking of a rhyme for it. Now you have done some active thinking about the name, and you also have two tags for

▲ **REFLECT**
How are drill and practice related to the PQ4R method of learning?

the person, not one. If you are trying to retrieve the spelling of the word *retrieve*, do so by retrieving the rule "*i* before *e* except after *c*." There are exceptions, of course: Remember that "weird" doesn't follow the rule because it's a "weird" word.

REFLECT

Can you explain how various "Reflect" items throughout the text, including this one, help you relate new information to things you already know?

We normally expand our knowledge base by relating new items to things already known. Children learn that a cello is like a violin, only bigger. A bass fiddle is also like a violin, but bigger yet. We remember information about whales by relating whales to other mammals. Similarly, we are better able to recall information about porpoises and dolphins if we think of them as small whales (not as bright fish).

The media are filled with stories about people who exhibit psychological disorders of one kind or another. To help remember the disorders discussed in Chapter 15, think of film or TV characters with those disorders. How were the characters' behaviors consistent (or inconsistent) with the descriptions in the text (and those offered by your professor)? You will remember the subject matter better *and* become a good critic of media portrayals of psychological problems if you use this technique.

Form Unusual, Exaggerated Associations

Psychologist Charles L. Brewer uses an interesting method to teach psychology students the fundamentals of shaping:

> In a recent class, Dr. Brewer first danced on his desk, then bleated like a sheep and finally got down on "all fours and oinked like a pig," he said. His antics were in response to a session he teaches on "successive approximation"—shaping behavior into a desired response.
>
> To get students to "shape" him, he told them he would try to figure out what they wanted him to do. If he guessed wrong, they'd "boo and hiss," while if he did what they wanted, they'd applaud him—which is why he eventually acted like a pig. "I'll do anything to get them to learn," he said (DeAngelis, 1994, p. 40).

It is easier to recall stimuli that stand out from the crowd. We pay more attention to them. Sometimes, therefore, we are better able to remember information when we create unusual, exaggerated associations.

Assume that you are trying to remember the geography of the cerebral cortex, as shown in Figure 2.10 on page 54. Why not think of what you look like in right profile? (Use your left profile if it is better.) Then imagine a new imaging technique in which we can see through your skull and find four brightly colored lobes in the right hemisphere of your cerebral cortex. Not only that, but there are little people (let's call them "homunculi") who are flapping about in the sensory and motor areas (see Figure 2.13 again). In fact, imagine that you're in a crowded line and someone steps on your toe. As a result, the homunculus[4] (a "homunculus" is a single member of the homunculi clan) in the sensory cortex has a throbbing toe. This is communicated to the association areas of the cortex, where you decide that you are annoyed. The language areas of the cortex think up some choice words that are relayed to the throat and mouth of the homunculus in the motor cortex. Then they are sent into your throat and mouth. You also send some messages through the motor cortex that ready your muscles to attack.

Then you see that the perpetrator of the crime is a very attractive and apologetic stranger! What part of the occipital lobe is flashing the wonderful images?

Use the Method of Loci: Meatloaf in the Navel

REFLECT

Can you remember what to buy at the supermarket without a list? How do you do so?

Another way to form unusual associations is the *method of loci* (pronounced LOW-sigh). Select a series of related images such as the parts of your body or the furniture in your home. Then imagine an item from your shopping list, or another list you want to remember, as being attached to each image. Consider this meaty application: Remember your shopping list by imagining meatloaf in your navel and a strip of bacon draped over your nose.

---

[4]I will give extra credit to students who research (and find) the meaning and origin of the word *homunculus*. My generosity does not obligate your professor, of course.

By placing meatloaf or a favorite complete dinner in your navel, rather than a single item such as ground beef, you can combine several items into one chunk of information. At the supermarket, you recall the ingredients for meatloaf and consider whether you need each one.

Use Mediation: Find a Conceptual Bridge

The method of mediation also relies on forming associations: You link two items with a third one that ties them together.

What if you are having difficulty remembering that John's wife's name is Tillie? You can mediate between John and Tillie as follows. Reflect that *john* is a slang term for bathroom. Bathrooms often have ceramic *tiles*. *Tiles*, of course, sounds like *Tillie*. So it goes: John → bathroom tiles → Tillie.

I used a combination of mediation and formation of unusual associations to help me remember foreign vocabulary words in high school. For example, the Spanish word *mujer* (pronounced moo-hair [almost]), means "woman" in English. Women have mo' hair than I do. Woman → mo' hair → mujer. This particular example would no longer work for me because now most men also have more hair than I, but the association was so outlandish that it stuck with me.

Use Mnemonic Devices: "Soak Her Toe"

Broadly speaking, methods for jogging memory can all be termed *mnemonics*, or systems for remembering information. But so-called **mnemonic devices** usually combine chunks of information into a format such as an acronym, jingle, or phrase.[5] For example, recalling the phrase "Every Good Boy Does Fine" has helped many people remember the treble staff E, G, B, D, F. In Chapter 2, we saw that the acronym *SAME* serves as a mnemonic device for distinguishing between afferent and efferent neurons. In Chapter 3, we noted that most psychology students use the acronym *Roy G. Biv* to remember the colors of the rainbow, even though your "backward" author chose to use the "word" *vibgyor*:

Acronyms have found applications in many disciplines. Consider geography. The acronym *HOMES* stands for the Great Lakes: *H*uron, *O*ntario, *M*ichigan, *E*rie, and Superior. In astronomy, the phrase "*M*ercury's *v*ery *e*ager *m*other *j*ust *s*erved *us* *n*ine *p*otatoes" helps students recall the order of the planets Mercury, Venus, Earth, Mars, Jupiter, Saturn, Uranus, Neptune, and Pluto. Table 6.1 lists some of my favorite mnemonic devices.

What about biology? You can remember that Dromedary camels have one hump while Bactrian camels have two by turning the letters *D* and *B* on their sides.

And how can you math students ever be expected to remember the reciprocal of pi (that is, 1 divided by 3.14)? Simple: Just remember the question "Can I remember the reciprocal?" and count the number of letters in each word. The reciprocal of pi, it turns out, is 0.318310. (Remember the last two digits as 10, not as 1 and 0.)

Finally, how can you remember how to spell *mnemonics*? Easy—be willing to grant "a*MN*esty" to those who cannot.

TABLE 6.1 MNEMONIC DEVICES

Mnemonic Device	Encoded Information
HOMES	The names of the Great Lakes: Huron, Ontario, Michigan, Erie, and Superior
No Plan Like Yours to Study History Wisely.	The royal houses of England: Norman, Plantagenet, Lancaster, York, Tudor, Stuart, Hanover, Windsor.
X shall stand for playmates Ten.	The value of the Roman numerals. "D for Five" means D = 500.
V for Five stalwart men.	
I for One, D for Five.	
M for a Thousand soldiers true.	
And L for Fifty, I'll tell you.	
Mary Eats Peanut Butter.	The first four hydrocarbons of the Alkane class: Methane, Ethane, Propane, and Butane, in ascending order of the number of carbon atoms in their chains.
These Ten Valuable Amino Acids Have Long Preserved Life in Man.	Ten vital amino acids: Threonine, Tryptophan, Valine, Arginine, Histidine, Lysine, Phenylalanine, Leucine, Isoleucine, Methionine.
All Hairy Men Will Buy Razors.	Constituents of soil: Air, Humus, Mineral salts, Water, Bacteria, Rock particles.
Soak Her Toe.	Translates into SOHCAHTOA, or: Sine = Opposite/Hypotenuse Cosine = Adjacent/Hypotenuse Tangent = Opposite/Adjacent
Krakatoa Positively Casts Off Fumes; Generally Sulfurous Vapors.	Biological classifications in descending order: Kingdom, Phylum, Class, Order, Family, Genus, Species, Variety.
Never Lower Tillie's Pants; Mother Might Come Home.	The eight bones of the wrist: Navicular, Lunate, Triangular, Pisiform, Multangular greater, Multangular lesser, Capitate, Hamate.
Roy G. Biv	The colors of the spectrum: red, orange, yellow, green, blue, indigo, violet
Lazy French Tarts Sit Naked In Anticipation.	The nerves that pass through the superior orbital fissure of the skull: Lachrymal, Frontal, Trochlear, Superior, Nasal, Inferior, Abducent.

CD 6 V 23
CLICK4™ *a video on using mnemonics.*

▲ **REFLECT**
Do you use any mnemonic devices? What are they? How do they help you?

---

[5]By the way, the word *mnemonic* is derived from Mnemosyne, the Greek goddess of memory. Her name is pronounced *Nee-MOS-uh-nee*. How can you remember the pronunciation? Why not think of the goddess getting down on her two knees (*nee-nee*) to worship? (End of commercial for mnemonic devices.)

Mnemonic devices ▲ Systems for remembering in which items are related to easily recalled sets of symbols such as acronyms, phrases, or jingles.

THE BIOLOGY OF MEMORY: FROM ENGRAMS TO ADRENALINE

Psychologists assume that mental processes such as the encoding, storage, and retrieval of information—that is, memory—are accompanied by changes in the brain. Early in the century, many psychologists used the concept of the **engram** in their study of memory. Engrams were viewed as electrical circuits in the brain that corresponded to memory traces—neurological processes that paralleled experiences. Yet biological psychologists such as Karl Lashley (1950) spent many fruitless years searching for such circuits or for the structures of the brain in which they might be housed. Much contemporary research on the biology of memory focuses on the roles of neurons, neurotransmitters, hormones, and structures in the brain.

Neural Activity and Memory: "Better Living Through Chemistry"

Question: What neural events are connected with memory?   Rats who are reared in richly stimulating environments provide some answers. The animals develop more dendrites and synapses in the cerebral cortex than rats reared in relatively impoverished environments (Neisser, 1997). It also has been shown that the level of visual stimulation rats receive is associated with the number of synapses they develop in the visual cortex (Turner & Greenough, 1985). In sum, there is reason to believe that the storage of experience requires the number of avenues of communication among brain cells to be increased.

Thus, changes occur in the visual cortex as a result of visual experience. Changes are also likely to occur in the auditory cortex as a result of heard experiences. Information received through the other senses is just as likely to lead to corresponding changes in the cortical regions that represent them. Experiences that are perceived by several senses are also stored in numerous areas of the brain. The recollection of experiences, as in the production of visual images, apparently involves neural activity in the appropriate regions of the brain (Kosslyn, 1994).

Research with sea snails such as *Aplysia* and *Hermissenda* has offered insight into the events that take place at existing synapses when learning occurs. *Aplysia*, for example, has only about 20,000 neurons compared with humans' *billions*. As a result, researchers have actually been able to study how experience is reflected at the synapses of specific neurons. The sea snail will reflexively withdraw its gills when it receives electric shock, in the same way that a person will reflexively withdraw a hand from a hot stove or a thorn. In one kind of experiment, researchers have preceded the shock with a squirt of water and noted that after a few repetitions the sea snail becomes conditioned to withdraw its gills when squirted with the water. They have been able to determine that when sea snails are conditioned, they release more of the neurotransmitter serotonin at certain synapses. As a consequence, transmission at these synapses becomes more efficient as trials (learning) progress (Kandel & Hawkins, 1992). This greater efficiency is termed **long-term potentiation** (LTP). There is a great deal of research on serotonin and LTP. It has also been shown, for example, that rats who are given substances that enhance LTP learn mazes with fewer errors; that is, they are less likely to turn down the wrong alley (Service, 1994).

Serotonin and many other naturally occurring chemical substances, including adrenaline, noradrenaline, acetylcholine, glutamate, antidiuretic hormone, even estrogen have also been shown to play roles in memory. Consider the following examples:

▲ Serotonin. This neurotransmitter increases the efficiency of conditioning in sea snails (Kandel & Hawkins, 1992). It is released when stimuli are paired repeatedly, increasing the efficiency of neural transmission (LTP) at certain synapses. As a result, it appears that neural circuits are sort of carved out to represent or contain the relevant information.

▲ Acetylcholine (ACh). This neurotransmitter is vital in memory formation; low levels of ACh are connected with Alzheimer's disease. Increased levels of ACh promote conditioning in mice (Farr et al., 2000a).

Engram ▲ (1) An assumed electrical circuit in the brain that corresponds to a memory trace. (2) An assumed chemical change in the brain that accompanies learning. (From the Greek *en-*, meaning "in," and *gramma*, meaning "something that is written or recorded.")

Long-term potentiation ▲ Enhanced efficiency in synaptic transmission that follows brief, rapid stimulation.

▲ Glutamate. Agents that increase the action of glutamate in the brain promote conditioning in mice (Farr et al., 2000a, 2000b).

▲ Adrenaline and noradrenaline (also called *epinephrine* and *norepinephrine)*. The hormone adrenaline and the related hormone and neurotransmitter noradrenaline both strengthen memory when they are released into the bloodstream following learning. Stressful events stimulate release of stress hormones from the adrenal glands—adrenaline and steroids—which, in turn, stimulate a structure in the limbic system (the amygdala—see Figure 6.10) to release noradrenaline. These hormones and neurotransmitter, acting together, heighten memory for stressful events (Clayton & Williams, 2000; Ferry et al., 1999; Nader et al., 2000).

▲ Vasopressin. Also known as *antidiuretic hormone*, vasopressin affects fluid retention in the body. But like so many other chemical substances in the body, it has multiple chores, one of which is facilitating memory functioning, particularly working memory (de Wied, 1997; Dietrich & Allen, 1997). Sniffing vasopressin in the form of a nasal spray has complex but generally beneficial effects on memory (Perras et al., 1997).

▲ Estrogen and testosterone. The sex steroids, estrogen and testosterone, facilitate the functioning of working memory in, respectively, females and males (Janowsky et al., 2000). Estrogen replacement helps older, postmenopausal women retain cognitive functioning.

Other research has focused on the potential of the stimulant nicotine to aid in the formation of memories, even to delay the progression of Alzheimer's disease.

Brain Structures and Memory: The Brain as a Time Machine

Question: What structures in the brain are connected with memory?   Memory does not reside at a single point in the brain, or in a single structure of the brain. The ability to recall one's past relies on large-scale neural networks that draw on the functions of various parts of the brain (Nyberg et al., 2000).

Yet various parts of the brain appear to play more or less specific roles in memory. Consider the problems that beset H. M. after his operation. Certain parts of the brain such as the hippocampus also appear to be involved in the formation of new memories— or the transfer of information from short-term to long-term memory. The hippocampus, a part of the limbic system, does not comprise the "storage bins" for memories themselves, because H. M.'s memories prior to the operation were not destroyed. For example, memory for places learned long ago remains intact after damage to the hippocampus (Teng & Squire, 1999). Rather, it is involved in relaying incoming sensory information to parts of the cortex. Research shows that alcohol interferes with learning and memory by changing cellular activity in the hippocampus and related structures (White et al., 2000). Therefore, the hippocampus is vital to the storage of new information even if old information can be retrieved without it (Reed & Squire, 1997; Squire, 1996).

Where are the storage bins? Figure 6.10 shows that the brain stores parts of memories in the appropriate areas of the sensory cortex. Sights are stored in the visual cortex, sounds in the auditory cortex, and so on. The limbic system is largely responsible for integrating these pieces of information when we recall an event. However, research with animals and people suggests that an area in the frontal lobe (labeled "Place and Time") stores information about where and when an event occurred (Chafee & Goldman-Rakic, 2000; Goldman-Rakic et al., 2000).

But what of the decision to try to recall something? What of the spark of consciousness that drives us to move backward in time or to strive to remember to perform an action in the future? The prefrontal cortex acts apparently as the executive center in memory. It appears to empower people with consciousness—the ability to mentally represent and become aware of experiences that occur in the past, present, and future. It enables people to mentally travel back in subjective time to reexperience the personal, autobiographical past (Wheeler et al., 1997). It also enables people to focus on the things they intend to do in the future, such as mail a letter on the way to class or brush their

▲ **REFLECT**
Can you think of any uses of knowledge about how various neurotransmitters and other substances affect memory formation?

www 6 L 8

CLICK4™ *more information about Alzheimer's disease at the Alzheimer's Association homepage.*

CLICK4™ *a bulletin board discussion on "smart drugs."*

FIGURE 6.10   Where Memories Are Stored.
The brain apparently stores parts of memories in various sections of the sensory cortex. Memories of sights and sounds are kept in separate bins and pieced back together when we recall an event. An area in the frontal lobe (labeled "Place and Time") apparently stores much information as to the sources of memories.

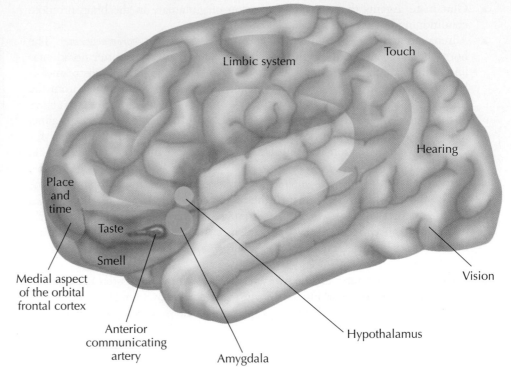

teeth before going to bed (Fuster, 2000; McDaniel et al., 1999). People in whom the prefrontal cortex is damaged frequently try to fill in the memory gaps by making up stories about when and where certain events took place.

The hippocampus is much involved in the where and when of things. The hippocampus does not become mature until we are about 2 years old. Immaturity may be connected with infantile amnesia. Adults with hippocampal damage may be able to form new procedural memories, even though they cannot form new episodic ("where and when") memories. For example, they can acquire the skill of reading words backwards even though they cannot recall individual practice sessions (Reed & Squire, 1997; Squire, 1996).

The thalamus is involved in verbal memories. Part of the thalamus of an Air Force cadet known as N. A. was damaged in a freak fencing accident. After the episode, N. A. could no longer form verbal memories. However, his ability to form visual memories was not impaired (Squire, 1996).

The encoding, storage, and retrieval of information thus involve biological activity on several levels. As we learn, new synapses are developed, and changes occur at existing synapses. Various parts and structures of the brain are also involved in the formation of different kinds of memories. In the next chapter, we see how people manipulate the information they have stored to adapt to the environment or create new environments.

REVIEW

CLICK4™ *a quiz covering the second half of this chapter.*

CLICK4™ *electronic flash cards to review your knowledge of key terms and people in this chapter.*

(27) Experience enhances the avenues of communication among brain cells by development of dendrites and _____ . (28) Conditioning of sea snails causes more of the neurotransmitter _____ to be released at certain synapses, making transmission at these synapses more efficient. (29) The hippocampus appears vital to the storage of (new or old?) information. (30) The _____ seems to be involved in the formation of verbal memories.

Pulling It Together: Why are we more likely to remember stressful experiences?

TRUTH ▰ FICTION
REVISITED

▱ It is true that a woman who had no memory of who she was automatically dialed her mother's phone number when the police gave her a telephone. *She made use of implicit memory when explicit memory failed her. See page 191.*

▱ It is true that everyone who can see has a photographic memory. *People who can see have an* iconic *memory, which is what is meant technically by a photographic memory. However, only a few people have* eidetic imagery, *which refers to the ability to continue to "see" the memory trace of a visual stimulus in the visual sensory register long after the trace would have decayed in most people. See page 197.*

▱ It is true that it may be easier for you to recall the name of your first-grade teacher than of someone you just met at a party. *Your first-grade teacher's name is stored in long-term memory. However, you may be juggling a new acquaintance's name with many others in short-term memory. See page 201.*

▱ It is not true that all of our experiences are permanently imprinted on the brain so that proper stimulation can cause us to remember them exactly. *We appear to be more likely to store incidents that have a greater impact on us—events that have more personal meaning. See page 201.*

▱ It is not true that learning must be meaningful if we are to remember it. *Nevertheless,* elaborative rehearsal, *which is based on the meanings of events or subject matter, is more efficient than* maintenance rehearsal, *which is based on rote repetition (Simpson et al., 1994). See page 205.*

▱ It is true that you would probably do better to take the test with the stereo on if you study with the stereo on. *What you learned is likely to be at least partly dependent on the context in which you learned it. See page 209.*

▱ It is true that you can use tricks to improve your memory. *The "tricks" all involve ways of forming associations. See page 219.*

Recite Recite Recite

1. What is meant by explicit memory?

Explicit memories contain specific information—information that can be clearly stated or declared. The information can be autobiographical or general.

2. What is meant by episodic memory?

An episodic memory is a memory of a specific event that one has observed or participated in.

3. What is meant by semantic memory?

Semantic memory is general knowledge, as in remembering that the United States has 50 states or that Shakespeare wrote *Hamlet*.

4. What is meant by implicit memory?

Procedural memory means knowing how to do things like write with a pencil or ride a bicycle. It is also called *skill memory*.

5. What is the difference between retrospective memory and prospective memory?

Retrospective memories concern events in the past that can be explicit or implicit. Prospective memories involve remembering to do things in the future. Prospective memory is affected by factors such as distraction, mood, and age.

6. What is the role of encoding in memory?

Encoding information means transforming it so that we can place it in memory. We commonly use visual, auditory, and semantic codes to convert physical and chemical stimulation into psychological formats that can be remembered.

7. What is the role of storage in memory?

Storage means the maintenance of information over time. The main methods of storing information are maintenance rehearsal (rote repetition) and elaborative rehearsal (relating it to things we already know).

8. What is the role of retrieval in memory?

Retrieval means locating stored information and bringing it back into consciousness. Retrieval requires use of the proper cues (just as to retrieve information stored on a hard drive, we need to know the filename). Memory is defined as the processes by which information is encoded, stored, and retrieved.

9. What is the Atkinson-Shiffrin model of memory?

Atkinson and Shiffrin propose that there are three stages of memory—sensory memory, short-term memory, and long-term memory—and that the progress of information through these stages determines whether and how long it is remembered.

10. How does sensory memory function?

Each sense is believed to have a sensory register that briefly holds the *memory traces* of stimuli in sensory memory. The traces then *decay*. Visual sensory memory makes discrete visual sensations—produced by saccadic eye movements—seem continuous.

McDougall used the whole-report procedure to demonstrate that visual stimuli are maintained in sensory memory for only a fraction of a second. Sperling used the partial-report procedure to show that we can see more objects than we can report afterward. Icons are mental representations of visual stimuli. Some people, usually children, can maintain icons over long periods of time and are said to have eidetic imagery. Echoes are representations of auditory stimuli (sounds). Echoes can be held in sensory memory for several seconds.

11. How does short-term memory function?

Focusing on a stimulus allows us to maintain it in short-term memory—also called *working memory*—for a minute or so after the trace decays. Rehearsal allows us to maintain information indefinitely. Miller showed that we can hold seven chunks of information (plus or minus two) in short-term memory. The appearance of new information in short-term memory *displaces* the old information.

12. Why are we most likely to remember the first and last items in a list?

This phenomenon is referred to as the serial-position effect. We tend to remember the initial items in a list because they are rehearsed most often (the primacy effect). We tend to remember the final items in a list because they are least likely to have been displaced by new information (the recency effect).

13. Is seven a magic number, or did the phone company get lucky?

Seven may not be a magic number, but it seems that the typical person can remember about seven chunks of information (juggle that many pieces of information in short-term memory).

14. How does long-term memory function?

There is no known limit to the amount of information that can be stored in long-term memory, and memories can be stored for a lifetime. However, long-term memories have not been shown to be perfectly accurate. They are frequently biased because they are reconstructed according to our schemas—that is, our ways of mentally organizing our experiences. The memories of eyewitnesses can also be distorted by leading questions. Information is usually transferred from short-term to long-term memory by one of two paths: maintenance rehearsal (rote repetition) and elaborative rehearsal (relating information to things that are already known).

15. What is the levels-of-processing model of memory?

This model views memory in terms of a single dimension—not three stages. It is hypothesized that we encode, store, and retrieve information more efficiently when we have processed it more deeply.

16. Why is it that some events, like the death of JFK Jr., can be etched in memory for a lifetime?

So-called *flashbulb memories*, as of the death of a public figure like Princess Diana or JFK Jr., tend to occur within a web of unusual and emotionally arousing circumstances. We may elaborate them extensively—that is, relate them to many things.

17. **How is knowledge organized in long-term memory?**

We tend to organize information according to a hierarchical structure. That is, we classify or arrange chunks of information into groups or classes according to common features.

18. **Why do we sometimes feel that the answer to a question is on the tip of our tongue?**

Research suggests that the tip-of-the-tongue phenomenon often reflects incomplete learning.

19. **Why may it be useful to study in the room in which we will be tested?**

This is because memories are frequently dependent on the context in which they were formed. That is, context dependence refers to the finding that we often retrieve information more efficiently when we are in the same context we were in when we acquired it. State dependence refers to the finding that we often retrieve information better when we are in the same state of consciousness or mood we were in when we learned it.

20. **What types of memory tasks are used in measuring forgetting?**

Nonsense syllables were developed by Ebbinghaus in the 19th century as a way of measuring the functions of memory. (How he would use them.) Retention is often tested through three types of memory tasks: recognition, recall, and relearning.

21. **Why can learning Spanish make it harder to remember French?**

This is an example of retroactive interference, in which new learning interferes with old learning. In proactive interference, on the other hand, old learning interferes with new learning. According to interference theory, people can forget because learning can cause cues (such as English words) to be connected with the wrong information (perhaps a Spanish word when a French word is sought).

22. **What is the Freudian concept of repression?**

Repression refers to Freud's concept of motivated forgetting. Freud suggested that we are motivated to forget threatening or unacceptable material. Research on the recovery of repressed memories is quite controversial.

23. **Can children remember events from the first couple of years of life?**

Probably not. This phenomenon is referred to as infantile amnesia. Freud believed that infantile amnesia is due to repression, but modern psychologists believe that infantile amnesia reflects factors such as immaturity of the hippocampus and failure to use acoustic and semantic codes to help remember information.

24. *Why do people frequently have trouble recalling being in accidents?*

This is because the physical trauma can interfere with memory formation. Two kinds of amnesia are caused by physical trauma. In anterograde amnesia, a traumatic event such as damage to the hippocampus prevents the formation of new memories. In retrograde amnesia, shock or other trauma prevents previously known information from being retrieved.

25. *How can people improve their memory?*

People can improve their memory through use of maintenance rehearsal, as in drill and practice, or elaborative rehearsal, as in relating new information to what is already known, forming unusual and exaggerated associations, using the method of loci, using mediation, or using mnemonic devices.

26. *What neural events are connected with memory?*

Learning is apparently connected with the proliferation of dendrites and synapses in the brain. Learning and memory are also connected with the release of the neurotransmitters serotonin and acetylcholine and the hormones adrenaline and vasopressin.

27. *What structures in the brain are connected with memory?*

The hippocampus relays sensory information to the cortex and is therefore vital in formation of new memories. Visual memories appear to be stored in the visual cortex, auditory memories in the auditory cortex, and so on. The thalamus is connected with the formation of visual memories.

PREVIEW

Cognition
▲ Cognition is the mental activity involved in processing and communicating information.

Concepts: Building Blocks of Cognition
▲ Concepts provide mental categories that allow you to group objects (dogs and cats belong to categories such as *mammals*, *pets*, and—in my case—*animals that mess up homes*).

Problem Solving
▲ It helps to understand a problem before solving it. (Surprise?)
▲ Sometimes our familiarity with the elements of a problem interferes with solving it.

Creativity
▲ Do people have to be smart to be creative?
▲ Do people sabotage your creative efforts when they promise you rewards?

Reasoning
▲ Illogical conclusions let us get on with our daily lives.

Judgment and Decision Making
▲ People sometimes arrive at conclusions by weighing the pluses and minuses, and sometimes by, well, jumping to conclusions.
▲ People frame information in order to persuade other people.
▲ You are probably convinced that you are right, even when you are dead wrong.

Language: "Of Shoes and Ships and Sealing Wax, . . . and Whether Pigs Have Wings"
▲ The definition of a "true" language places us ahead of the birds and the bees in the use of language (end even the walruses).
▲ What are languages made of?
▲ Is it good for children to learn one language at home and another in the culture in which they live?

Language and Cognition
▲ Do you need words to think?

CHAPTER 7

Cognition and Language

TRUTH *or* FICTION?

- Using a "tried and true" formula is the most efficient way to solve a problem.
- Only humans can solve problems by means of insight.
- The best way to solve a frustrating problem is to keep plugging away at it.
- People with great academic ability are also creative.
- A conclusion can be logical but wrong.
- If a couple has five sons, the sixth child is likely to be a daughter.
- People change their opinions when they are shown to be wrong.
- The majority of people around the world speak at least two languages.

When she was 9, my daughter Jordan stumped me with a problem about a bus driver that she had heard in school. Because I firmly believe in exposing students to the kinds of torture I have undergone, see what you can do with her problem:

> You're driving a bus that's leaving from Pennsylvania. To start off with, there were 32 people on the bus. At the next bus stop, 11 people got off and 9 people got on. At the next bus stop, 2 people got off and 2 people got on. At the next bus stop, 12 people got on and 16 people got off. At the next bus stop, 5 people got on and 3 people got off. What color are the bus driver's eyes?

I was not about to be fooled when I was listening to this problem. Although it seemed clear that I should be keeping track of how many people were on the bus, I had an inkling that a trick was involved. Therefore, I told myself to remember that the bus was leaving from Pennsylvania. Being clever, I also kept track of the number of stops rather than the number of people getting on and off the bus. When I was finally hit with the question about the bus driver's eyes, I was at a loss. I protested that Jordan had said nothing about the bus driver's eyes, but she insisted that she had given me enough information to answer the question.

One of the requirements of problem solving is paying attention to relevant information (de Jong & Das-Smaal, 1995). To do that, you need some familiarity with the type of problem you are dealing with. I immediately classified the bus driver problem as a trick question and paid attention to information that apparently was superfluous. But I wasn't good enough.

COGNITION

CLICK4™ *an opportunity to participate in cognitive psychology experiments online at Purdue University and The Experimental Psych Lab.*

CLICK4™ *the University of Alberta's Cognitive Science Dictionary.*

The Greek philosopher Aristotle pointed out that people differ from lower organisms in their capacity for rational thinking. Thinking enables us to build skyscrapers, create computers, and scan the interior of the body without surgery. Some people even manage to keep track of their children and balance their checkbooks.

Question: What is cognition? **Cognition** may be defined as the mental activity involved in understanding, processing, and communicating information. Cognition—also referred to as *thinking*—entails attending to information, representing it mentally, reasoning about it, and making judgments and decisions about it. The term *thinking* generally refers to conscious, planned attempts to make sense of our world. Other aspects of cognition—for example, dreaming and day-dreaming—may be unplanned and seem to proceed more or less on their own.

In this chapter we explore cognition and the related topic of language. We begin with concepts, which provide building blocks for cognition. But before we proceed, I have one question for you: What color were the bus driver's eyes?

CONCEPTS: BUILDING BLOCKS OF COGNITION

I began the chapter with Jordan's problem. Let me proceed with an oral riddle from my own childhood: "What's black and white and read all over?" Because this riddle was spoken, not written, and involved the colors black and white, you would probably assume that "read" meant "red." Thus, in seeking an answer, you might scan your memory for an object that was red although it also somehow managed to be black and white. The answer to the riddle, "newspaper," was usually met with a groan.

The word *newspaper* is a **concept.** *Red*, *black*, and *white* are also concepts—color concepts. Concepts are mental categories used to group together objects, relations, events, abstractions, or qualities that have common properties.

Question: How do concepts function as building blocks of cognition? Concepts are crucial to cognition. Concepts can represent objects, events, and activities—and visions of things that never were. Much thinking has to do with categorizing new concepts and manipulating relationships among concepts.

Cognition ▲ Mental activity that is involved in understanding, manipulating, and communicating about information. Cognition entails paying attention to information, mentally representing it, reasoning about it, and making decisions about it.

Concept ▲ A mental category that is used to class together objects, relations, events, abstractions, or qualities that have common properties.

We tend to organize concepts in *hierarchies*. The newspaper category includes objects such as your school paper and the *Los Angeles Times*. Newspapers, college textbooks, novels, and merchandise catalogs can be combined into higher-order categories such as *printed matter* or *printed devices that store information*. If you add floppy disks and DVDs, you can create a still higher category, *objects that store information*. Now consider a question that requires categorical thinking: How are a newspaper and a DVD alike? Answers to such questions entail supplying the category that includes both objects. In this case, we can say that both objects store information. That is, their functions are similar, even if their technology differs.

Prototypes are examples that best match the essential features of categories. In less technical terms, prototypes are good examples. When new stimuli closely match people's prototypes of concepts, they are readily recognized as examples (Sloman, 1996). Which animal seems more birdlike to you, a robin or an ostrich? Why? Which of the following better fits the prototype of a fish, a sea horse or a shark? Both self-love and maternal love may be forms of love, but more people readily agree that maternal love is a kind of love. Apparently maternal love better fits their prototype of love (Fehr & Russell, 1991).

Many simple prototypes, such as *dog* and *red*, are taught by means of **exemplars.** We point to a dog and say "dog" or "This is a dog" to a child. Dogs represent *positive instances* of the dog concept. *Negative instances*—that is, things that are not dogs—are then shown to the child while we say, "This is *not* a dog." Negative instances of one concept may be positive instances of another. So in teaching a child we may be more likely to say, "This is not a dog—it's a cat" than simply, "This is not a dog."

Children may at first include horses and other four-legged animals within the dog schema or concept until the differences between dogs and horses are pointed out. (To them, the initial category could be more appropriately labeled "fuzzy-wuzzies.") In language development, such overinclusion of instances in a category (reference to horses as dogs) is labeled *overextension*. Children's prototypes become refined after children are shown positive and negative instances and given explanations. Abstract concepts such as *bachelor* or *square root* tend to be formed through verbal explanations that involve more basic concepts.

A Goat or a Dog?
Yes, yes, you know the answer, but little children may at first include goats, horses, and other four-legged animals within the dog concept until they understand the differences among the animals.

▲ **REFLECT**
When you were a child, some people were probably introduced to you as Aunt Bea or Uncle Harry. Do you remember when you first understood the concept of aunt or uncle? Can you think of ways of teaching these concepts to small children without using verbal explanation?

REVIEW

(1) _____ is defined as mental activity involved in understanding, processing, and communicating information. (2) _____ are mental categories used to class objects, relations, or events with common properties. (3) Examples of concepts that best match the key features of categories are termed _____.

Pulling It Together: Can you think of examples that make the best prototypes of the city and automobile concepts? Why did you select them? Can you teach their meanings by using exemplars?

www **7** **L** **2**

CLICK4™ 100 of the Most Influential Works in Cognitive Sciene from the 20th Century, *compiled by the University of Minnesota.*

PROBLEM SOLVING

Now I would like to share something personal with you. One of the pleasures I derived from my own introductory psychology course lay in showing friends the textbook and getting them involved in the problems in the section on problem solving. First, of course, I struggled with them myself. Now it's your turn. Get some scrap paper, take a breath, and have a go at them. The answers will be discussed in the following pages, but don't peek. *Try* the problems first.

    1. Provide the next two letters in the series for each of the following:

        a. ABABABAB??
        b. ABDEBCEF??
        c. OTTFFSSE??

Prototype ▲ A concept of a category of objects or events that serves as a good example of the category.
Exemplar ▲ A specific example.

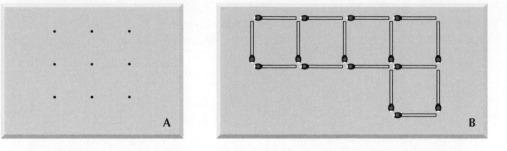

FIGURE 7.1 Two Problems.
Draw straight lines through all the points in part A, using only four lines. Do not lift your pencil or retrace your steps. Move three matches in part B to make four squares equal in size. Use all the matches.

2. Draw straight lines through all the points in part A of Figure 7.1, using only *four* lines. Do not lift your pencil from the paper or retrace your steps. (See Figure 7.4 for answer.)

3. Move three matches in part B of Figure 7.1 to make four squares of the same size. You must use *all* the matches. (See Figure 7.4 for answer.)

4. You have three jars—A, B, and C—which hold the amounts of water, in ounces, shown in Table 7.1. For each of the seven problems in Table 7.1, use the jars in any way you wish in order to arrive at the indicated amount of water. Fill or empty any jar as often as you wish. How do you obtain the desired amount of water in each problem? (The solutions are discussed on p. 236.)

Approaches to Problem Solving: Getting From Here to There

Question: How do people go about solving problems? To answer this question, begin by considering the steps you used to try to solve parts a and b of problem 1. Did you first make sure you understood the problem by rereading the instructions? Or did you dive right in as soon as you saw them on the page? Perhaps the solutions to 1a and 1b came easily, but I'm sure you studied 1c very carefully.

After you believed you understood what was required in each problem, you probably tried to discover the structure of the cycles in each series. Series 1a has repeated cycles of two letters: *AB*, *AB*, and so on. Series 1b may be seen as having four cycles of two consecutive letters: *AB*, *DE*, *BC*, and so on.

Again, did you solve 1a and 1b in a flash of insight, or did you try to find rules that govern each series? In series 1a, the rule is simply to repeat the cycle. Series 1b is more complicated, and different sets of rules can be used to describe it. One correct set of rules is that odd-numbered cycles (*1* and *3*, or *AB* and *BC*) simply repeat the last letter of the previous cycle (in this case *B*) and then advance by one letter in the alphabet. The same rule applies to even-numbered cycles (*2* and *4*, or *DE* and *EF*).

If you found rules for problems 1a and 1b, you used them to produce the next letters in the series: *AB* in series 1a and *CD* in series 1b. Perhaps you then evaluated the effectiveness of your rules by checking your answers against the solutions in the preceding paragraphs.

Understanding the Problem   Let us begin our discussion of understanding problems by considering a bus driver problem very similar to the one Jordan gave me. This one, however, appeared in the psychological literature:

> Suppose you are a bus driver. On the first stop, you pick up 6 men and 2 women. At the second stop, 2 men leave and 1 woman boards the bus. At the third stop, 1 man leaves and 2 women enter the bus. At the fourth stop, 3 men get on and 3 women get off. At the fifth stop, 2 men get off, 3 men get on, 1 woman gets off and 2 women get on. What is the bus driver's name? (Halpern, 1989, p. 392)

Both versions of the bus driver problem demonstrate that a key to understanding a problem is focusing on the right information. If we assume it is crucial to keep track of the numbers of people getting on and off the bus, we focus on information that turns out to be unessential. In fact, it distracts us from the important information.

When we are faced with a novel problem, how can we know which information is relevant and which is not? Background knowledge helps. If you are given a chemistry

CLICK4™ *The Big6 approach to problem solving.*

CLICK4™ *a bulletin board discussion on the ability to improve one's problem solving skills.*

▲ **REFLECT**
How did you go about solving (or trying to solve) the problems presented at the beginning of the section? Why?

TABLE 7.1 WATER-JAR PROBLEMS
For each problem, how can you use some combination of the three jars given, and a tap, to obtain precisely the amount of water shown?

THREE JARS ARE PRESENT WITH THE LISTED CAPACITY (IN OUNCES)

Problem	Jar A	Jar B	Jar C	Goal
1	21	127	3	100
2	14	163	25	99
3	18	43	10	5
4	9	42	6	21
5	20	59	4	31
6	23	49	3	20
7	10	36	7	3

SOURCE: Adapted from *Rigidity of Behavior* (p. 109), by Abraham S. Luchins and Edith H. Luchins, 1959, Eugene: University of Oregon Press.

problem, it helps if you have taken courses in chemistry. If Jordan gives you a problem, it is helpful to expect the unexpected. (In case you still haven't gotten it, the critical information you need to solve both bus driver problems is provided in the first sentence.)

Successful understanding of a problem generally requires three features:

1. *The parts or elements of our mental representation of the problem relate to one another in a meaningful way.* If we are trying to solve a problem in geometry, our mental triangles should have angles that total 180 degrees, not 360 degrees.
2. *The elements of our mental representation of the problem correspond to the elements of the problem in the outer world.* If we are neutralizing an acid in order to produce water and a salt, our mental representation of water should be H_2O, not OH. The elements of our mental representations must include the key elements for solving the problem, such as the information in the first sentence of the bus driver problem. We prepare ourselves to solve a problem by familiarizing ourselves with its elements and defining our goals.
3. *We have a storehouse of background knowledge that we can apply to the problem.* We have taken the necessary courses to solve problems in algebra and chemistry. When given a geometry problem involving a triangle, for example, we may think, "Is this problem similar to problems I've solved by using the quadratic equation?"

Algorithms

An **algorithm** is a specific procedure for solving a type of problem. An algorithm invariably leads to the solution—if it is used properly, that is. Mathematical formulas like the Pythagorean theorem are examples of algorithms. They yield correct answers to problems *as long as the right formula is used*. Finding the right formula to solve a problem may require scanning one's memory for all formulas that contain variables that represent one or more of the elements in the problem. The Pythagorean theorem, for example, concerns triangles with right angles. Therefore, it is appropriate to consider using this formula for problems concerning right angles, but not for others.

Consider anagram problems, in which we try to reorganize groups of letters into words. Some anagram problems require us to use every letter from the pool of letters; others allow us to use only some of the letters. How many words can you make from the pool of letters *DWARG*? If you were to use the **systematic random search** algorithm, you would list every possible letter combination, using from one to all five letters. You could use a dictionary or a spell-checking program to see whether each result is, in fact, a word. Such a method might be time-consuming, but it would work.

Heuristics

Question: Is it best to use a tried and true formula to solve a problem? Not necessarily. Sometimes people use shortcuts that enable them to jump to conclusions—including the correct conclusion. Such shortcuts are called heuristics, or heuristic devices. **Heuristics** are rules of thumb that help us simplify and solve problems. In contrast to algorithms, heuristics do not guarantee a correct solution to a problem. But when they work, they permit more rapid solutions. A heuristic device for solving the anagram problem would be to look for familiar letter combinations and then check the remaining letters for words that include these combinations. In *DWARG*, for example, we can find the familiar combinations *dr* and *gr*. We may then quickly find *draw*, *drag*, and *grad*. The drawback to this method, however, is that we might miss some words.

One type of heuristic device is the **means-end analysis.** In using this heuristic device, we assess the difference between our current situation and our goals and then do what we can to reduce this discrepancy. Let's say that you are out in your car and have gotten lost. One heuristic device based on analysis of what you need to do to get to where you want to go might be to ask for directions. This approach requires no "sense of direction." An algorithm might be more complicated and require some geographical knowledge. Let us say that you know your destination is west of your current location and on the other side of the railroad tracks. You might therefore drive toward the setting sun (west) and, at the same time, watch for railroad tracks. If the road comes to an end and you must turn left or right, you can scan in both directions for tracks. If you don't see any, turn right or left, but at the next major intersection turn toward the setting sun. Eventually you may get there. If not, you can always ask for directions.

CLICK4™ *a WebSearch activity exploring heuristic devices and judgments applied to information in self-help books.*

CLICK4™ *advice on thinking critically about self-help books.*

▲ **REFLECT**

Have you ever gotten lost and asked for directions? Is asking for directions an algorithm or a heuristic device? (And why are so many men reluctant to ask for directions?!)

Algorithm ▲ A systematic procedure for solving a problem that works invariably when it is correctly applied.

Systematic random search ▲ An algorithm for solving problems in which each possible solution is tested according to a particular set of rules.

Heuristics ▲ Rules of thumb that help us simplify and solve problems.

Means-end analysis ▲ A heuristic device in which we try to solve a problem by evaluating the difference between the current situation and the goal.

Analogies   An *analogy* is a partial similarity among things that are different in other ways. During the Cold War, some people in the United States believed in the so-called domino theory. Seeing the nations of Southeast Asia as analogous to dominoes, they argued that if one nation were allowed to fall to communism, its neighbor would be likely to follow. In the late 1980s, a sort of reverse domino effect actually occurred as communism collapsed in the nations of Eastern Europe. When communism collapsed in one nation, it became more likely to collapse in neighboring nations as well.

The analogy heuristic applies the solution of an earlier problem to the solution of a new one. We use the analogy heuristic whenever we try to solve a new problem by referring to a previous problem (Halpern et al., 1990). Consider the water jar problems in Table 7.1. Problem 2 is analogous to problem 1. Therefore, the approach to solving problem 1 works with problem 2. (Later we consider what happens when the analogy heuristic fails.)

Let us see whether you can use the analogy heuristic to your advantage in the following number series problem: To solve problems 1a, 1b, and 1c on page 231, you had to figure out the rules that govern the order of the letters. Scan the following series of numbers and find the rule that governs their order:

$$8, 5, 4, 9, 1, 7, 6, 3, 2, 0$$

Hint: The problem is somewhat analogous to problem 1c.[1]

Factors That Affect Problem Solving

The way you approach a problem is central to how effective you are at solving it. Other factors also influence your effectiveness at problem solving. *Question: What factors make it easier or harder to solve problems?*   Three such factors—your level of expertise, whether you fall prey to a mental set, and whether you develop insight into the problem—reside within you. A couple of characteristics of problems also affect your ability to solve them effectively: the extent to which the elements of the problem are fixed in function, and the way the problem is defined.

Expertise   To appreciate the role of expertise in problem solving, unscramble the following anagrams, taken from Novick and Coté (1992). In each case use all of the letters to form an actual English word:

DNSUO

RCWDO

IASYD

How long did it take you to unscramble each anagram? Would a person whose native language is English—that is, an "expert"—unscramble each anagram more efficiently than a bilingual person who spoke another language in the home? Why or why not?

Experts solve problems more efficiently and rapidly than novices do. Generally speaking, people who are experts at solving a certain kind of problem share the following characteristics:

- ▲ They know the particular area well,
- ▲ They have a good memory for the elements in the problems,
- ▲ They form mental images or representations that facilitate problem solving (Clement, 1991),
- ▲ They relate the problem to similar problems, and
- ▲ They have efficient methods for problem solving (Hershey et al., 1990).

These factors are interrelated. Art historians, for example, acquire a database that permits them to understand the intricacies of paintings. As a result, their memory for paintings—and who painted them—expands vastly.

▲ **REFLECT**
Why do math textbooks have all those problems at the end of each chapter? How is solving them of help to you?

CLICK4™ *puzzle and game links to challenge your problem-solving abilities.*

CLICK4™ *a WebSearch activity on problem solving and expertise.*

▲ **REFLECT**
Are you an expert at solving math problems? Social problems? Automobile problems? Musical problems? How did you get to be an expert?

---

[1]The analogous element is that there is a correspondence between these numbers and the first letter in the English word that spells them out.

Novick and Coté (1992) found that the solutions to the anagram problems seemed to "pop out" in under 2 seconds among experts. The experts apparently used more efficient methods than the novices. Experts seemed to use *parallel processing*. That is, they dealt simultaneously with two or more elements of the problems. In the case of DNSUO, for example, they may have played with the order of the vowels (*UO* or *OU*) at the same time that they tested which consonant (D, N, or S) was likely to precede them, arriving quickly at *sou* and *sound*. Novices were more likely to engage in *serial processing*—that is, to handle one element of the problem at a time.

Mental Sets   Jordan hit me with another question: "A farmer had 17 sheep. All but 9 died. How many sheep did he have left?" Being a victim of a mental set, I assumed that this was a subtraction problem and gave the answer 8. She gleefully informed me that she hadn't said "9 died." She had said "*all but* 9 died." Therefore, the correct answer was 9. (Get it?) Put it another way: I had not *understood* the problem. My mental representation of the problem did not correspond to the actual elements of the problem.

Return to problem 1, part c (page 231). To try to solve this problem, did you seek a pattern of letters that involved cycles and the alphabet? If so, it may be because this approach worked in solving parts a and b.

The tendency to respond to a new problem with the same approach that helped solve similar problems is termed a **mental set.** Mental sets usually make our work easier, but they can mislead us when the similarity between problems is illusory, as in part c of problem 1. Here is a clue: Part c is not an alphabet series. Each of the letters in the series *stands for* something. If you can discover what they stand for (that is, if you can discover the rule), you will be able to generate the 9th and 10th letters. (See Figure 7.4 for the answer.)

Insight: Aha!   To gain insight into the role of insight in problem solving, consider the following problem, posed by Janet Metcalfe (1986):

> A stranger approached a museum curator and offered him an ancient bronze coin. The coin had an authentic appearance and was marked with the date 544 B.C. The curator had happily made acquisitions from suspicious sources before, but this time he promptly called the police and had the stranger arrested. Why? (p. 624)

I'm not going to give you the answer to this problem. Instead, I'll make a guarantee. When you arrive at the solution, it will hit you all at once. You'll think "Aha!" or "Of course!" (or something less polite). It will seem as though the pieces of information in the problem have suddenly been reorganized so that the solution leaps out at you—in a flash.

Bismarck, one of University of Michigan psychologist N. R. F. Maier's rats, provided evidence of insight in laboratory rats (Maier & Schneirla, 1935). Bismarck had been trained to climb a ladder to a tabletop where food was placed. On one occasion Maier used a mesh barrier to prevent the rat from reaching his goal. But, as shown in Figure 7.2, a second ladder was provided and was clearly visible to the animal. At first Bismarck sniffed and scratched and made every effort to find a path through the mesh barrier. Then he spent some time washing his face, an activity that apparently signals frustration in rats. Suddenly he jumped into the air, turned, ran down the familiar ladder and around to the new ladder, ran up the new ladder, and claimed his just desserts. It seems that Bismarck suddenly perceived the relationships between the elements of his problem so that the solution occurred by insight. He seems to have had what Gestalt psychologists have termed an "Aha! experience."

Incubation   Let us return to the problems at the beginning of the section. How did you do with problem 1, part c, and problems 2 and 3? Students tend to fiddle around with them for a while. The solutions, when they come, appear to arrive in a flash. Students set the stage for the flash of insight by studying the elements in the problems carefully, repeating the rules to themselves, and trying to imagine what a solution might look like. If you tried out solutions that did not meet the goals, you may have become frustrated and thought, "The heck with it! I'll come back to it later." Standing back from the problem may allow for the **incubation** of insight. An incubator warms chicken eggs for a while so

Jordan.
The author's daughter, Jordan, posed the problem, "A farmer had 17 sheep. All but 9 died. How many sheep were left?" What is the answer?

> ▲ **REFLECT**
> Have you ever thought about a problem for a while and then had the solution come to you "in a flash"? Why do you think it happened like that? What was the experience like?

Mental set ▲ The tendency to respond to a new problem with an approach that was successfully used with similar problems.

Insight ▲ In Gestalt psychology, a sudden perception of relationships among elements of the "perceptual field," permitting the solution of a problem.

Incubation ▲ In problem solving, a hypothetical process that sometimes occurs when we stand back from a frustrating problem for a while and the solution "suddenly" appears.

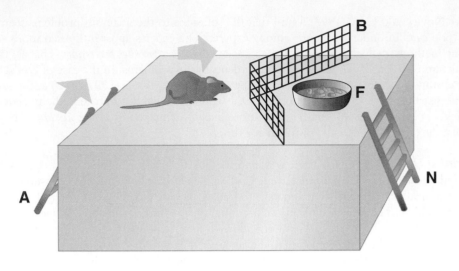

FIGURE 7.2   Bismarck Uses a Cognitive Map to Claim His Just Desserts.
Bismarck has learned to reach dinner by climbing ladder *A*. But now the food goal *(F)* is blocked by a wire mesh barrier *B*. Bismarck washes his face for a while, but then, in an apparent flash of insight, he runs back down ladder *A* and up new ladder *N* to reach the goal.

CLICK4™ *an essay assignment on incubation and problem solving.*

CLICK4™ *a video on hindrances to problem solving caused by the mental set and functional fixedness: the Elevator Riddle.*

CLICK4™ *a video on the match problem and its solution.*

CLICK4™ *the solution to the Elevator Riddle.*

Functional fixedness ▲ The tendency to view an object in terms of its name or familiar usage.

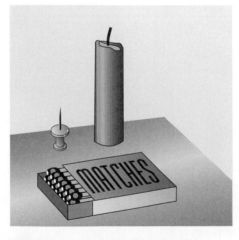

FIGURE 7.3   The Duncker Candle Problem.
Can you use the objects shown on the table to attach the candle to the wall of the room so that it will burn properly?

that they will hatch. Incubation in problem solving refers to standing back from the problem for a while as some mysterious process within us continues to work on it. Later, the answer may occur to us in a flash of insight. When standing back from the problem is helpful, it may be because it distances us from unprofitable but persistent mental sets (Azar, 1995).

Have another look at the role of incubation in helping us overcome mental sets. Consider the seventh water jar problem in Table 7.1. What if we had tried several solutions involving the three water jars and none had worked? We could distance ourselves from the problem for a day or two. At some point we might recall a 10, a 7, and a 3—three elements of the problem—and suddenly realize that we can arrive at the correct answer by using only two water jars!

Functional Fixedness   **Functional fixedness** may also hinder problem solving. For example, first ask yourself what a pair of pliers is. Is it a tool for grasping, a paperweight, or a weapon? A pair of pliers could function as any of these, but your tendency to think of it as a grasping tool is fostered by your experience with it. You have probably used pliers only for grasping things. Functional fixedness is the tendency to think of an object in terms of its name or its familiar function. It can be similar to a mental set in that it makes it difficult to use familiar objects to solve problems in novel ways.

Now that you know what functional fixedness is, let's see if you can overcome it by solving the Duncker candle problem. You enter a room that has the following objects on a table: a candle, a box of matches, and some thumbtacks (see Figure 7.3). Your task is to use the objects on the table to attach the candle to the wall of the room so that it will burn properly. (See Figure 7.4 on page 238 for the answer.)

REVIEW

(4) Problem solving begins with trying to _____ the problem. (5) An _____ is a specific procedure for solving a type of problem. (6) _____ devices are rules of thumb that serve as shortcuts to rapid solutions. (7) We use the _____ heuristic when we solve a new problem by referring to a previous problem. (8) A _____ set is the tendency to respond to a new problem with the same approach that helped solve similar problems. (9) Some problems are solved by rapid "perception of relationships" among the elements of the problem, which is called _____. (10) _____ fixedness is the tendency to think of an object in terms of its name or its familiar usage.

Pulling It Together: What do you think happens within us when we stand back from a problem and allow insight to "incubate"? How would you solve the problem of being lost while driving?

Pablo Picasso at Work.
We know that the great artist was creative, but what about his academic ability? Academic ability and creativity often go hand in hand, but academic ability is no guarantee of imagination or of specific talents.

CLICK4™ *a bulletin board discussion on creativity.*

CREATIVITY

CLICK4™ *a WebSearch activity on creativity.*

Creativity is the ability to do things that are novel and useful (Sternberg & Lubart, 1996). Creative people can solve problems to which there are no preexisting solutions, no tried and tested formulas (Simonton, 2000). Creative people share several characteristics (Sternberg & Lubart, 1995, 1996):

- ▲ They take chances.
- ▲ They refuse to accept limitations and try to do the impossible.
- ▲ They appreciate art and music.
- ▲ They use the materials around them to make unique things.
- ▲ They challenge social norms.
- ▲ They take unpopular stands.
- ▲ They examine ideas that other people accept at face value.

A professor of mine once remarked that there is nothing new under the sun, only new combinations of existing elements. Many psychologists agree. They see creativity as the ability to make unusual, sometimes remote, associations to the elements of a problem to generate new combinations. An essential aspect of a creative response is the leap from the elements of the problem to the novel solution. A predictable solution is not creative, even if it is hard to reach.

> ***Question: What are the relationships among creativity, problem solving, and intelligence?*** Creative problem solving demands divergent rather than convergent thinking. In **convergent thinking,** thought is limited to present facts; the problem solver narrows his or her thinking to find the best solution. (You use convergent thinking to arrive at the right answer to a multiple-choice question.) In **divergent thinking,** the problem solver associates freely to the elements of the problem, allowing "leads" to run a

Creativity ▲ The ability to generate novel and useful solutions to problems.
Convergent thinking ▲ A thought process that attempts to narrow in on the single best solution to a problem.
Divergent thinking ▲ A thought process that attempts to generate multiple solutions to problems.

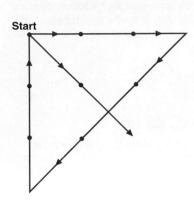

Start

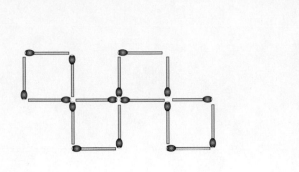

FIGURE 7.4   Answers to Problems on Pages 231, 232, and 236.
For problem 1C, note that each of the letters is the first letter of the numbers one through eight. Therefore, the two missing letters are *NT*, for *n*ine and *t*en. The solutions to problems 2 and 3 are shown in this illustration. To solve the Duncker candle problem, use the thumbtack to pin the matchbox to the wall. Then set the candle on top of the box. Functional fixedness prevents many people from conceptualizing the matchbox as anything more than a device to hold matches. Commonly given *wrong* answers include trying to affix the bottom of the candle to the wall with melted wax or trying to tack the candle to the wall.

nearly limitless course. (You may use divergent thinking when you are trying to generate ideas to answer an essay question on a test.) Problem solving can involve both kinds of thinking. At first divergent thinking helps generate many possible solutions. Convergent thinking is then used to select likely solutions and reject others.

Creativity and Academic Ability

It might seem that a creative person would also have high academic ability of the sort measured on intelligence tests. However, the relationship between intelligence test scores and creativity is only moderate (Simonton, 2000; Sternberg & Williams, 1997a). Intelligence test questions usually require analytical, convergent thinking to focus in on the one right answer. Tests of creativity determine how flexible a person's thinking is (Simonton, 2000). Here, for example, is an item from a test used by Getzels and Jackson (1962) to measure associative ability, a factor in creativity: "Write as many meanings as you can for each of the following words: (a) duck; (b) sack; (c) pitch; (d) fair." Those who write several meanings for each word, rather than only one, are rated as potentially more creative.

Another measure of creativity might ask people to produce as many words as possible that begin with T and end with N within a minute. Still another item might give people a minute to classify a list of names in as many ways as possible. How many ways can you classify the following group of names?

MARTHA   PAUL   JEFFRY   SALLY   PABLO   JOAN

Factors That Affect Creativity

There is only a modest connection between creativity and other aspects of intelligence. *Question: What factors other than intelligence are connected with creativity?* Some factors reside within the person and some involve the social setting.

Personal Factors   Creative people show flexibility, fluency (in generating words and ideas), and originality (Simonton, 2000). They spend time alone, thinking about who they are and exploring new ideas (McIntosh, 1996). Getzels and Jackson (1962) found

▲ REFLECT
Do you know some brilliant people who aren't very creative? Do you know some creative people who are not necessarily brilliant? What is the connection between intelligence and creativity?

CD 7 SA 5

CLICK4™ *the interactive version of this self-assessment.*

The Remote Associates Test

One aspect of creativity is the ability to associate freely to all aspects of a problem. Creative people take far-flung ideas and piece them together in novel combinations. Following are items from the Remote Associates Test, which measures the ability to find words that are distantly related to stimulus words. For each set of three words, try to think of a fourth word that is related to all three words. For example, the words *rough, resistance,* and *beer* suggest the word *draft,* as in the phrases *rough draft, draft resistance,* and *draft beer.* The answers are given in Appendix B.

1.	charming	student	valiant
2.	food	catcher	hot

3.	hearted	feet	bitter
4.	dark	shot	sun
5.	Canadian	golf	sandwich
6.	tug	gravy	show
7.	attorney	self	spending
8.	magic	pitch	power
9.	arm	coal	peach
10.	type	ghost	story

that creative schoolchildren tend to express, rather than inhibit, their feelings and to be playful and independent. Creative children are often at odds with their teachers because of their independence. Faced with managing large classes, teachers may label quiet and submissive children as "good" and less-inhibited children as "bad."

www 7 E 2

CLICK4™ *an essay assignment on creativity and intelligence.*

Social Evaluation
Research evidence shows that concern about evaluation by other people reduces creativity. In one experiment, college students were asked to write poems under two very different sets of expectations (Amabile, 1990). Half the students were informed that the experimenter only intended to examine their handwriting—not the aesthetic value of the poetry. The remaining students were informed that judges, who were poets, would supply them with written evaluations of their poetry's content and form. The students who expected to be evaluated according to the form and content of their work turned in significantly less creative poems.

The literature is mixed as to whether people are more creative when they are rewarded for being creative. It has been argued that rewards reduce inner interest in problem solving and thereby undermine creativity. Yet the research shows that rewarding people for being creative on one task can actually enhance creativity on other tasks (Eisenberger & Cameron, 1996).

Brainstorming
Brainstorming is a group process that is intended to encourage creativity. The group leader stimulates group members to generate a great number of ideas—even wild ideas. In order to avoid inhibiting group members, judgment is suspended until a great many ideas are on the table. Psychologists have become somewhat skeptical of the brainstorming concept, however (Matlin, 1997). For one thing, research evidence suggests that people working alone are often more creative than people working in groups. (Consider the saying, "A camel is a horse made by a committee.") Moreover, the ideas produced by brainstorming are often lower in quality than those produced by people working alone.

> ▲ **REFLECT**
> Can you force creativity? You have probably felt pressured to arrive at creative solutions to problems on tests. How did the pressure (for example, the amount of time left) affect you? Did it stimulate you to be more creative, or did it add to the difficulty? Why?

REVIEW

(11) Creativity demands _____ thinking rather than convergent thinking. (12) High intelligence (is or is not?) a guarantee of creativity.

Pulling It Together: Can creativity help you do well in college? Is creativity irrelevant to performance in your courses? Explain.

Brainstorming ▲ A group process that encourages creativity by stimulating a large number of ideas and suspending judgment until the process is completed.

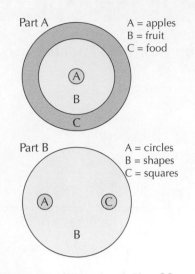

FIGURE 7.5 When Are A Also C?
In part A of this figure, A (apples) are also C (food) because food represents a higher-order category that contains all apples. In part B, however, C (squares) is not higher order than A (circles). Therefore, C does not contain A. B (shapes), however, is higher order than both A and C and contains both.

CLICK4™ *a quiz covering the first half of this chapter.*

▲ **REFLECT**
Can you provide examples of deductive reasoning and inductive reasoning that are connected with your own life?

Reasoning ▲ The transforming of information to reach conclusions.

Deductive reasoning ▲ A form of reasoning about arguments in which conclusions are deduced from premises. The conclusions are true if the premises are true.

Inductive reasoning ▲ A form of reasoning in which we reason from individual cases or particular facts to a general conclusion.

REASONING

We are not finished. I have more puzzles to solve, more weighty things to consider. Ponder this proposition:

> If some A are B, and some B are C, then some A are C.

Is it true or false? What say you?

I confess that on first seeing this proposition, I believed it was true. It seemed that we were logically progressing to higher-order categories at each step along the way (see Figure 7.5, part A). For example, if apples (A) are fruit (B), and fruit (B) are food (C), then apples (A) are food (C). But I was bamboozled by the "some." My example with the apples omitted the word. Consider another example of this proposition, one that uses "some": If *some* circles (A) are shapes (B), and *some* shapes (B) are squares (C), then *some* circles (A) are squares (C). Not so! By using the qualifying term "some," we can move both up, to a higher-order category (from circles to shapes), and back down, to a lower-order category (from shapes to squares) (see Figure 7.5, part B).

Types of Reasoning

We have been toying with an example of reasoning. **Reasoning** is the transformation of information in order to reach conclusions. *Question: How do people reason?* Let us consider two kinds of reasoning: deductive and inductive.

Deductive reasoning is a form of reasoning in which the conclusion must be true if the premises are true. Consider this classic three-sentence argument:

1. All persons are mortal.
2. Socrates is a person.
3. Therefore, Socrates is mortal.

Sentences 1 and 2 in this argument are the *premises*. Premises provide the assumptions or basic information that allow people to draw conclusions. Sentence 3 is the conclusion. In this example, sentence 1 makes a statement about a category (persons). Sentence 2 assigns an individual (Socrates) to the category (persons). Sentence 3 concludes that what is true of the category (persons) is true for the member of the category (Socrates). The conclusion, sentence 3, is said to be *deduced* from the premises. The conclusion about Socrates is true if the premises are true.

In **inductive reasoning,** we reason from individual cases or particular facts to a general conclusion. Consider this transformation of the previous example:

1. Socrates is a person.
2. Socrates is mortal.
3. Therefore, persons are mortal.

The conclusion happens to be correct, but it is illogical. The fact that one person is mortal does not guarantee that all people are mortal.

Inductive reasoning, then, does not permit us to draw absolute conclusions (Sloman, 1996). Yet inductive reasoning is used all the time. We conclude that a certain type of food will or will not make us feel sick because of our experiences on earlier occasions. ("Buttered popcorn made me nauseous. This is buttered popcorn. Therefore, this will make me nauseous.") We assume that a cheerful smile and "Hello!" will break the ice with a new acquaintance because it has worked before. Although none of these conclusions is as logical as a deductive conclusion, inductive conclusions are correct often enough so that we can get on with our daily lives with some degree of confidence.

Cognitive Processes, East and West: Shall the Twain Meet?

Most psychologists have assumed that all humans engage in the same basic cognitive processes, whether they are goat-herders in Tibet or systems analysts in California. Cultural differences might provide different substance for thought—kinds of snow for adolescent Eskimoes and kinds of cars for adolescent Californians—but the ways in which people processed information about these cultural objects would be the same, and be exemplified by logical reasoning, categorization, and an urge to understand events in terms of cause and effect (Choi et al., 1999).

However, recent work by University of Michigan psychologist Richard Nisbett and his colleagues challenges this view. In studies comparing European Americans to East Asians, Nisbett and his colleagues have found that people reared in different cultures do not just think about different things: they think differently. "We used to think that everybody uses categories in the same way, that logic plays the same kind of role for everyone in the understanding of everyday life, that memory, perception, rule application and so on are the same," Nisbett (2000) explains. "But we're now arguing that cognitive processes themselves are just far more malleable than mainstream psychology assumed."

Something Fishy

The studies—carried out in the United States, Japan, China, and Korea—find that Easterners seem to think more "holistically"; that is, they pay more attention to context and relationship. They also rely more on experience than logic and show more tolerance for contradiction than Westerners do (Ji et al., 2000; Peng & Nisbett, 1999). Westerners are more "analytic." Westerners tend to think more abstractly, avoid contradictions, and rely on logic. In one study, Nisbett and a graduate student, Takahiko Masuda, showed students from Japan and the United States an animated aquatic underwater scene, in which a large fish swam among smaller fishes and other underwater life. When asked to describe what they saw, the Japanese participants were more likely to first set the scene, saying for example, "There was a lake or pond" or "The bottom was rocky," or "The water was green." But Americans usually began their narratives with the large fish, saying, for example, "There was what looked like a trout swimming to the right." The Japanese students made 70% more statements about the background environment than Americans, and twice as many about the relationships between the fish and the background. "Americans were much more likely to zero in on the biggest fish, the brightest object, the fish moving the fastest," noted Nisbett (2000). "That's where the money is as far as they're concerned."

The greater attention East Asians paid to context and relationship also made it more difficult for them to recognize the large fish when it was shown swimming against another background. That is, the Japanese students' perception of the fish was bound up with their perception of the fish in a certain environment. Similarly, perhaps because they were reared in a more collectivist society, Asians were more likely to attribute people's behavior to situational pressures rather than individual choice.

Living With Shades of Gray

East Asians are also apparently more capable than European Americans of living with "shades of gray." That is, they respond differently when they are presented with arguments that contradict their opinions. Presenting Americans with weak arguments that run contrary to their opinions seems to solidify their opinions, according to Nisbett (2000), resolving the potential contradiction in their own minds. When Asians are presented with weak arguments that contradict their views, however, they are more likely to modify their own positions, acknowledging that the weaker arguments might have some merit. In one study, East Asian and European American participants were presented with strong arguments in favor of funding research on adoption. Another group received strong arguments favoring the project and weaker arguments against it. Both Asian and American participants in the first group voiced support for the project. But Asian participants in the second group lessened their support for the project when presented with the weaker opposing arguments, while American participants actually increased their support for the research when they were presented with weak opposing arguments. Americans preferred the black-or-white resolution of contradictory views—support or no support. The Asians were more comfortable maintaining the shades of gray.

Nisbett and Kaiping Peng, a colleague at the University of California at Berkeley, found that Chinese participants were more comfortable than American participants in letting contradictions go unresolved in evaluating social conflict as well. When participants from both groups were asked to analyze a conflict between mothers and daughters,

CLICK4™ *an essay assignment on inductive and deductive reasoning.*

the Americans quickly sided with one group or the other. But the Chinese participants were more likely to see value in the views of both mothers and daughters.

Do Rabbits Hibernate? (Yes or No!)   Nisbett and Ara Norenzayan of the University of Illinois have also found that Americans are more likely to rely on logic than experience when faced with contradictions, in keeping with a tradition of logic that we trace to the syllogistic thinking of the Ancient Greeks. Consider this syllogism: "All animals with fur hibernate. Rabbits have fur. Therefore rabbits hibernate." Americans were more likely to accept the "truth" of the argument, which flowed logically from its premises. But Asians were more skeptical because of experience with the fact that not all animals with fur do in fact hibernate. (Don't misunderstand: The conclusion that rabbits hibernate is logical but wrong because the premise that "all animals with fur hibernate" is wrong.)

The East–West differences in thinking are connected with a host of differences in philosophy, religion, and social behavior. East-West language traditions and even geography are quite different. According to Nisbett (2000), each style of thinking has its pluses and its minuses, but neither seems to be genetically based. The thinking of Asian Americans who are born in the United States is like the thought of European Americans, not like that of their cousins who dwell in the East.

REVIEW

(13) A _____ of an argument is an assumption that allows people to draw conclusions. (14) In _____ reasoning, the conclusion is true if the premises are true. (15) In _____ reasoning, we reason from individual cases to a general conclusion.

Pulling It Together: Can you think of an example of holistic reasoning? Of analytic reasoning?

JUDGMENT AND DECISION MAKING

> ▲ REFLECT
> Do you have trouble making decisions? What kinds of decisions? What is the difficulty?

Decisions, decisions. Should you go to breakfast before classes begin or catch a few extra winks? Should you get married or remain single? Should you take a job or go on for advanced training when you complete your college program? If you opt for the job, cash will soon be jingling in your pockets. Yet later you may wonder if you have enough education to reach your full potential. By furthering your education, you may have to delay independence and gratification, but you may find a more fulfilling position later on. Ah, decisions, decisions.

Other kinds of decisions are judgments about the nature of the world. We make judgments about which route to school or work will be the least crowded. We make judgments about where it will be safe and convenient to live. We make judgments about what political candidates to vote for and which brand of ice cream to buy.

> ▲ REFLECT
> Do you sometimes make decisions without all the information you need? Why?

Question: How do people go about making judgments and decisions? You might like to think that people are so rational that they carefully weigh all the pros and cons when they make judgments or decisions. Or you might think that they insist on finding and examining all the relevant information. Actually, people make most of their decisions on the basis of limited information. They take shortcuts. They use heuristic devices—rules of thumb—in their judgments and decision making, just as they do in problem solving. For example, they may let a financial adviser select stocks for them rather than research the companies themselves. Or they may see a doctor recommended by a friend rather than examine the doctor's credentials. In this section we consider various factors in judgment and decision making.

Heuristics in Decision Making: If It Works, Must It Be Logical?

Let us begin by asking you to imagine that you flip a coin six times. In the following three possible outcomes, H stands for head and T for tail. Circle the most likely sequence:

H H H H H H

H H H T T T

T H H T H T

Did you select T H H T H T as the most likely sequence of events? Most people do. Why? There are two reasons. First, people recognize that the sequence of six heads in a row is unlikely. (The probability of achieving it is 1/2 × 1/2 × 1/2 × 1/2 × 1/2 × 1/2, or 1/64.) Three heads and three tails are more likely than six heads (or six tails). Second, people recognize that the sequence of heads and tails ought to appear random. T H H T H T has a random look to it, whereas H H H T T T does not.

People tend to select T H H T H T because of the **representativeness heuristic.** According to this decision-making heuristic, people make judgments about events (samples) according to the populations of events that they appear to represent (Kosonen & Winne, 1995). In this case, the sample of events is six coin tosses. The "population" is an infinite number of random coin tosses. But guess what? *Each* of the sequences is equally likely (or unlikely). If the question had been whether six heads or three heads and three tails had been more likely, the correct answer would have been three and three. If the question had been whether heads and tails would be more likely to be consecutive or in random order, the correct answer would have been random order.

But each of the three sequences shown is a *specific* sequence. What is the probability of attaining the specific sequence T H H T H T? The probability that the first coin toss will result in a tail is 1/2. The probability that the second will result in a head is 1/2, and so on. Thus, the probability of attaining the exact sequence T H H T H T is identical to that of achieving any other specific sequence: 1/2 × 1/2 × 1/2 × 1/2 × 1/2 × 1/2 × 1/64th. (Don't just sit there. Try this out on a friend.)

Or consider this question: If a couple has five children, all of whom are boys, is their sixth child more likely to be a boy or a girl? Use of the representativeness heuristic might lead us to imagine that the couple is due for a girl. That is, five boys and one girl is closer to the assumed random distribution that accounts for roughly equal numbers of boys and girls in the world. But people with some knowledge of reproductive biology might predict that another boy is actually more likely because five boys in a row may be too many to be a random biological event. If the couple's conception of a boy or girl were truly random, however, what would be the probability of conceiving another boy? Answer: 1/2.

Another heuristic device used in decision making is the **availability heuristic.** According to this heuristic, our estimates of frequency or probability are based on how easy it is to find examples of relevant events. Let me ask you whether there are more art majors or sociology majors at your college. Unless you are familiar with the enrollment statistics, you will probably answer on the basis of the numbers of art majors and sociology majors that you know personally.

The **anchoring and adjustment heuristic** suggests that there can be a good deal of inertia in our judgments. In forming opinions or making estimates, we have an initial view, or presumption. This is the anchor. As we receive additional information, we make adjustments, sometimes grudgingly. That is, if you grow up believing that one religion or one political party is the "right" one, that belief serves as a cognitive anchor. When inconsistencies show up in your religion or political party, you may adjust your views of them, but perhaps not very willingly.

Let us illustrate further by means of a math problem. Write each of the following multiplication problems on a separate piece of paper:

A. 8 × 7 × 6 × 5 × 4 × 3 × 2 × 1
B. 1 × 2 × 3 × 4 × 5 × 6 × 7 × 8

Show problem A to a few friends. Give them each 5 seconds to estimate the answer. Show problem B to some other friends and give them 5 seconds to estimate the answer.

The answers to the multiplication problems are the same because the order of the quantities being multiplied does not change the outcome. However, when Tversky and Kahneman (1982) showed these problems to high-school students, the average estimate given by students who were shown version A was significantly higher than that given by

Representativeness heuristic ▲ A decision-making heuristic in which people make judgments about samples according to the populations they appear to represent.

Availability heuristic ▲ A decision-making heuristic in which our estimates of frequency or probability of events are based on how easy it is to find examples.

Anchoring and adjustment heuristic ▲ A decision-making heuristic in which a presumption or first estimate serves as a cognitive anchor. As we receive additional information, we make adjustments, but tend to remain in the proximity of the anchor.

students who were shown version B. Students who saw 8 in the first position offered an average estimate of 2,250. Students who saw 1 in the first position gave an average estimate of 512. That is, the estimate was larger when 8 served as the anchor. By the way, what is the correct answer to the multiplication problems? Can you use the anchoring and adjustment heuristic to explain why both groups of students were so far off?

The Framing Effect: Say That Again?

If you were on a low-fat diet, would you be more likely to choose an ice cream that is 97% fat free or one whose fat content makes up 10% of its calorie content? On one shopping excursion I was impressed with an ice cream package's claims that the product was 97% fat free. Yet when I read the label closely, I noticed that a 4-ounce serving had 160 calories, 27 of which were contributed by fat. Fat, then, accounted for 27/160ths, or about 17%, of the ice cream's calorie content. But fat accounted only for 3% of the ice cream's *weight*. The packagers of the ice cream knew all about the *framing effect*. They understood that labeling the ice cream as "97% fat free" would make it sound more healthful than "Only 17% of calories from fat."

Question: How do people frame information in order to persuade others? The **framing effect** refers to the way in which wording, or the context in which information is presented, can influence decision making. Political groups are as aware as advertisers of the role of the framing effect and choose their words accordingly. For example, proponents of legalized abortion refer to themselves as "pro-choice" and opponents refer to themselves as "pro-life." Thus each group frames itself in a way that is positive ("pro" something) and refers to a value (freedom, life) with which it would be difficult to argue.

Parents are also aware of the framing effect. My 3-year-old, Taylor, was invited to a play date at Abigail's house. I asked Taylor, "Would you like to play with Abigail at her house?" The question met with a resounding no. I thought things over and reframed the question: "Would you like to play at Abigail's house and have a real fun time? She has lots of toys and games, and I'll pick you up real soon." This time Taylor's decision was yes.

Overconfidence: Is Your Hindsight 20–20?

Whether our decisions are correct or incorrect, most of us tend to be overconfident about them (Lundeberg et al., 1994). Overconfidence applies to judgments as wide ranging as whether one will be infected by the virus that causes AIDS (Goldman & Harlow, 1993), predicting the outcome of elections (Hawkins & Hastie, 1990), asserting that one's answers to test items are correct (Lundeberg et al., 1994), and selecting stocks. Many people refuse to alter their judgments even in the face of statistical evidence that shows them to be flawed. (Have you ever known someone to maintain unrealistic confidence in a candidate who was far behind in the polls?)

We also tend to view our situations with 20–20 hindsight. When we are proven wrong, we frequently find a way to show that we "knew it all along." We also become overconfident that we would have known the actual outcome if we had had access to the information that became available after the event (Hawkins & Hastie, 1990). For example, if we had known that a key player would pull a hamstring muscle, we would have predicted a different outcome for the football game. If we had known that it would be blustery on Election Day, we would have predicted a smaller voter turnout and a different outcome.

Question: Why do people tend to be convinced that they are right, even when they are dead wrong? There are several reasons for overconfidence, even when our judgments are wrong. Here are some of them:

▲ We tend to be unaware of how flimsy our assumptions may be.
▲ We tend to focus on examples that confirm our judgments and ignore those that do not.
▲ Because our working memories have limited space, we tend to forget information that runs counter to our judgments.
▲ We work to bring about the events we believe in, so they sometimes become self-fulfilling prophecies.

▲ REFLECT
Did you ever use the framing effect to try to persuade someone? What did you say?

▲ REFLECT
Do you know people who refuse to change their minds even when they are shown to be wrong? How do you explain their reluctance to change?

Framing effect ▲ The influence of wording, or the context in which information is presented, on decision making.

▲ Even when people are told that they tend to be overconfident in their decisions, they usually ignore this information (Gigerenzer et al., 1991).

REVIEW

(16) People use rules of thumb called _____ devices in making judgments and decisions, just as they do in problem solving. (17) According to the _____ heuristic, people make judgments about events according to the populations of events that they appear to represent. (18) According to the _____ heuristic, people's estimates of frequency or probability are based on how easy it is to find examples of relevant events. (19) In forming opinions or making estimates, our initial view serves as a _____ anchor. (20) The _____ effect refers to the fact that wording, or the context in which information is presented, can influence decision making. (21) People tend (to be or not to be?[2]) confident in their decisions.

Pulling It Together: What kinds of heuristic devices do most people use when they make judgments as to the reliability of the information found in self-help books?

LANGUAGE: "OF SHOES AND SHIPS AND SEALING WAX, . . . AND WHETHER PIGS HAVE WINGS"

> *"The time has come," the Walrus said,*
> *"To talk of many things*
> *Of shoes—and ships—and sealing wax—*
> *Of cabbages—and kings—*
> *And why the sea is boiling hot—*
> *And whether pigs have wings."*
>
> Lewis Carroll, *Through the Looking-Glass*

Lewis Carroll wasn't quite telling the truth. The sea is not boiling hot—in most places and at most times. Nor do Walruses speak. At the risk of alienating walrus fans across the land, let me assert, most boldly, that walruses neither speak nor use other forms of language to communicate.

On the other hand, the time has come indeed to talk of how talking—of how language—permits us to communicate about shoes and ships and . . . you get the idea. When I was in high school, I was taught that humans differ from other creatures that run, swim, or fly because only we can use tools and language. Then I learned that lower animals also use tools. Otters use rocks to open clam shells. Chimpanzees toss rocks as weapons and use sticks to dig out grubs for food.

In recent years our exclusive claim to language has also been questioned because apes have been taught to use symbols to communicate. (*Symbols* such as words stand for or represent other objects, events, or ideas.) Some communicate by making signs with their hands. Others use plastic symbols or press keys on a computer keyboard. (Walruses do neither.) Scientists debate how well chimpanzees and gorillas understand and produce language, but there is no doubt that they have learned to use symbols to communicate (Hixon, 1998; Savage-Rumbaugh & Fields, 2000). *Question: How do we define language?*

Language is the communication of thoughts and feelings by means of symbols that are arranged according to rules of grammar. Language makes it possible for one person to communicate knowledge to another and for one generation to communicate to another. It creates a vehicle for recording experiences. It allows us to put ourselves in the shoes of other people, to learn more than we could ever learn from direct experience. Language also provides many of the basic units of cognition.

---

[2]Sound familiar?

Language ▲ The communication of information by means of symbols arranged according to rules of grammar.

An Ape Uses Signs to Communicate.
Apes at Emory University's Yerkes Primate Center have been taught to express concepts by pressing keys on a computer-controlled keyboard.

CLICK4™ *a WebSearch activity on the nature of language.*

> ▲ **REFLECT**
>
> Have you ever known someone to claim that a pet could "speak" or understand English or another language? *Did* the pet really "speak"? *Did* the pet "understand" language? What was the nature of the evidence? What is your conclusion?

Language is one of our great strengths. Other species may be stronger, run faster, smell more keenly, even live longer, but only humans have produced literature, music, mathematics, and science. Language ability has made all this possible.

Many species have systems of communication. Birds warn other birds of predators. Through particular types of chirps and shrieks, they communicate that they have taken possession of a certain tree or bush. The "dances" of bees inform other bees of the location of a food source or a predator. Vervet monkeys make sounds that signal the distance and species of predators. But these are all inborn communication patterns. Swamp sparrows that have been reared in isolation, for example, produce songs that are very similar to those produced by birds that have been reared naturally in the wild. But we humans are ahead of the birds and the bees in communicating, and even vervet monkeys and walruses. Let us see how.

Question: What are the properties of a "true" language as opposed to an inborn communication system? True language is distinguished from the communication systems of lower animals by properties such as semanticity, infinite creativity, and displacement (Ratner & Gleason, 1993).

Semanticity refers to the fact that the sounds (or signs) of a language have meaning. Words serve as symbols for actions, objects, relational concepts (*over, in, more,* and so on), and other ideas. The communications systems of the birds and the bees lack semanticity. Specific sounds and—in the case of bees—specific waggles do *not* serve as symbols.

Infinite creativity refers to the capacity to combine words into original sentences. An "original" sentence is *not* one that has never been spoken before. Rather, it is a sentence that is produced by the individual instead of imitated. To produce original sentences, children must have a basic understanding of *syntax,* or the structure of grammar. Two-year-old children string signs (words) together in novel combinations.

Displacement is the capacity to communicate information about events and objects in another time or place.[3] Language makes possible the efficient transmission of complex knowledge from one person to another and from one generation to another. Displacement permits parents to warn children about the mistakes they made as children. Displacement allows children to tell their parents what they did in school (or to distort the truth).

Semanticity ▲ Meaning. The quality of language in which words are used as symbols for objects, events, or ideas.

Infinite creativity ▲ The capacity to combine words into original sentences.

Displacement ▲ The quality of language that permits one to communicate information about objects and events in another time and place.

---

[3]The word *displacement* has a different meaning in Sigmund Freud's psychodynamic theory, as we will see in Chapter 12.

Basic Concepts of Language: The Language of Language

Question: What basic concepts are used to discuss language?   The basic concepts of language include *phonology* (sounds[4]), *morphology* (units of meaning), *syntax* (word order), and *semantics* (the meanings of words and groups of words).

CLICK4™ *the American Association for Applied Linguistics, concerned with language education, language loss, bilingualism, and literacy.*

CLICK4™ *Language Links, which provides a listing of sites offering everything from Akkadian and Yoruba to Klingon and Esperanto.*

Phonology   **Phonology** is the study of the basic sounds in a language. There are 26 letters in the English alphabet but a greater number of **phonemes,** or basic sounds. These include the *t* and *p* in *tip*, which a psycholinguist would designate as the /t/ and /p/ phonemes. The *o* in *go* and the *o* in *gone* are different phonemes. They are spelled with the same letter, but they sound different. English speakers who learn French may be confused because /o/, as in the word *go*, has various spellings in French, including *o, au, eau,* even *eaux*.

Morphology   **Morphemes** are the smallest units of meaning in a language. A morpheme consists of one or more phonemes in a certain order. Some morphemes, such as *dog* and *cat*, function as words, but others must be used in combination. The words *dogs* and *cats* each consist of two morphemes. Adding /z/ to *dog* makes the word plural. Adding /s/ to *cat* serves the same function.

An *ed* morpheme at the end of a regular verb places it in the past tense, as with *add* and *added* and *subtract* and *subtracted*. A *ly* morpheme at the end of an adjective often makes the word an adverb, as with *strong* and *strongly* and *weak* and *weakly*.

Morphemes such as *s* and *ed* tacked onto the ends of nouns and verbs are referred to as grammatical "markers," or **inflections.** Inflections change the form of words to indicate grammatical relationships such as number (singular or plural) and tense (for example, present or past). Languages have grammatical rules for the formation of plurals, tenses, and other inflections.

Syntax

> *since feeling is first*
> *who pays any attention*
> *to the syntax of things*
> *will never wholly kiss you* . . .
>
>   *e. e. cummings*

The lines from the e. e. cummings poem are intriguing because their syntax permits various interpretations. Syntax deals with the ways words are strung together, or ordered, to create phrases and sentences. The rules for word order are the *grammar* of a language.

In English, statements usually follow the pattern *subject, verb,* and *object of the verb*. Note this example:

The young boy (subject) → has brought (verb) → the book (object).

The sentence would be confusing if it were written "The young boy *has* the book *brought*." But this is how the words would be ordered in German. German syntax differs from that of English. In German, a past participle *(brought)* is placed at the end of the sentence, whereas the helping verb *(has)* follows the subject. Although the syntax of German differs from that of English, children reared in German-speaking homes[5] acquire German syntax readily.

Phonology ▲ (foe-NOLL-oh-gee). The study of the basic sounds in a language.

Phoneme ▲ (FOE-neem). A basic sound in a language.

Morpheme ▲ (MORE-feem). The smallest unit of meaning in a language.

Inflections ▲ Grammatical markers that change the forms of words to indicate grammatical relationships such as number and tense.

---

[4]American Sign Language and Signed English, which are languages used by people whose hearing is impaired, are exceptions.

[5]No, homes do not speak German or any other language. This is an example of idiomatic English. Idioms like these are readily acquired by children.

Semantics **Semantics** is the study of meaning. It involves the relationship between language and the objects or events that language depicts. Words that sound (and are spelled) alike can have different meanings, depending on their usage. Compare these sentences:

A rock sank the boat.

Don't rock the boat.

CLICK4™ *the Human Languages Page, a catalog of language-related Internet resources.*

In the first sentence, *rock* is a noun and is the subject of the verb *sank*. The sentence probably means that the hull of a boat was ripped open by an underwater rock, causing the boat to sink. In the second sentence, *rock* is a verb. The second sentence is usually used as a figure of speech in which a person is being warned not to change things—not to "make waves" or "upset the apple cart."

Compare these sentences:

The chicken is ready for dinner.

The lion is ready for dinner.

The shark is ready for dinner.

The first sentence probably means that a chicken has been cooked and is ready to be eaten. The second sentence probably means that a lion is hungry or about to devour its prey. Our interpretation of the phrase "is ready for dinner" reflects our knowledge about chickens and lions. Whether we expect a shark to be eaten or to do some eating might reflect our seafood preferences or whether we saw the movies *Jaws* or *Blue Sea*.

▲ REFLECT

Did you grow up speaking a language other than English in the home? If so, what special opportunities and problems were connected with the experience?

Bilingualism: Linguistic Perspectives on the World

Most people throughout the world speak two or more languages. Most countries have minority populations whose languages differ from the national tongue. Nearly all Europeans are taught English and the languages of neighboring nations. Consider the Netherlands. Dutch is the native tongue, but all children are also taught French, German, and English and are expected to become fluent in each of them.

Bilingualism.

Throughout the world most people speak two or more languages, and most countries have minority populations whose languages differ from that of the dominant population. It was once thought that children reared in bilingual homes were retarded in their cognitive and language development, but today most linguists consider it advantageous for children to be bilingual. Knowledge of more than one language certainly expands people's awareness of diverse cultures and broadens their perspectives.

For more than 30 million people in the United States, English is a second language (Barringer, 1993). Spanish, French, Chinese, Russian, or Arabic is spoken in the home and, perhaps, the neighborhood. *Question: What does research reveal about the advantages and disadvantages of bilingualism?*

Semantics ▲ The study of the meanings of a language—the relationships between language and objects and events.

CONTROVERSY ✖ IN PSYCHOLOGY

Is Bilingualism Advantageous for Cognitive and Language Development?

A century ago it was widely believed that children reared in bilingual homes were retarded in their cognitive and language development. The theory was that cognitive capacity is limited, so people who store two linguistic systems are crowding their mental abilities (Lambert, 1990). However, the U.S. Bureau of the Census reports that more than 75% of Americans who first spoke another language in the home also speak English "well" or "very well" (Barringer, 1993). Moreover, a careful analysis of older studies in bilingualism shows that the bilingual children observed often lived in families with low socioeconomic status and little education. Yet these bilingual children were compared to middle-class monolingual children. In addition, achievement and intelligence tests were conducted in the monolingual child's language, which was the second language of the bilingual child (Reynolds, 1991). Lack of education and inadequate testing methods, rather than bilingualism per se, accounted for the apparent differences in achievement and intelligence.

Today most linguists consider it advantageous for children to be bilingual. For one thing, knowledge of more than one language expands children's awareness of different cultures and broadens their perspectives (Cavaliere, 1996). For example, bilingual children are more likely to understand that the symbols used in language are arbitrary. Monolingual children are more likely to think erroneously that the word *dog* is somehow intertwined with the nature of the beast. Bilingual children therefore have somewhat more cognitive flexibility. Second, learning a second language does not crowd children's available "cognitive space." Instead, learning a second language has been shown to increase children's expertise in their first (native) language. Research evidence reveals that learning French enhances knowledge of the structure of English among Canadian children whose native language is English (Lambert et al., 1991).

CLICK4™ the English Learners Web site at the California Department of Education.

CLICK4™ resources on bilingual education, hosted by the University of Texas at Austin.

CLICK4™ language resources hosted by the University of Memphis.

Language and Diversity: Bilingual Education

DIVERSITY Many U.S. children who speak a different language in the home experience difficulty when learning English in school. Early in the century the educational approach to teaching English to non-English-speaking children was simple: sink or swim. Children were taught in English from the outset. They had to catch on as best they could. Most children swam. Some sank.

The sink-or-swim method is also called *total immersion*. Total immersion has a checkered history. There are many successes but there are also more failures than most educators are willing to tolerate. For this reason, bilingual education has been adopted in many school systems.

Bilingual education legislation requires that non-English-speaking children be given the chance to study in their own language to smooth the transition into life in the United States. The official purpose of federal bilingual programs is to help children who speak foreign languages use their native tongue to learn English rapidly, then switch to a regular school program. Yet the degree of emphasis on English differs from one program to another.

So-called *transitional programs* shoot students into regular English-speaking classrooms as quickly as possible. In a second technique, called the *maintenance method*, rapid mastery of English is still the goal. But students continue to study their own culture and language. A third approach is *two-way immersion*. Two-way immersion encourages native-

▲ **REFLECT**
Should children who do not speak English in the home be taught in their native language in U.S. schools? Why or why not?

born U.S. children to achieve fluency in a foreign language at the same time that immigrant children are learning English (Cavaliere, 1996). Students in these programs study half a day in Spanish and half a day in English. Research shows that English-speaking children who are placed in Spanish immersion programs develop vocabularies—English vocabularies, that is—that are superior to children who are not placed in such programs (Cunningham & Graham, 2000). The benefits appear to be largely derived from learning Spanish words that have English *cognates*—that is, words that are similar in both languages and have the same meaning.

Critics of bilingual education contend that it is often more political than educational. For example, children with Spanish surnames may remain segregated long after they have shown that they can handle lessons in English. Also, some children never "graduate" from bilingual classes or high school either (Steinberg, 2000). These critics recognize the benefits of cultural pluralism but believe that the key to success in the United States is the ability to communicate in English.

In recent years there has been a backlash against bilingual education, largely because of concern that many children do not seem to profit from it. The research evidence on the issue leaves much to be desired. For example, the state of California assessed children for whom English was a second language two years after they ended bilingual education and returned to the sink-or-swim method. The state found that second graders increased from the 19th percentile in national rankings for reading to the 28th percentile during that period (Steinberg, 2000). It might sound wonderful, but there are limitations, such as the fact that California did not provide for experimental and control groups. It turns out that California reduced the average class size in the elementary grades from in excess of 30 students per class to 20 students per class during the same period. In addition, assessment revealed a great deal of variation in reading scores among school districts: Some gained by double digits and others gained not at all. All in all, it seems clear that the gains were not made just *because* California dropped bilingual education. On the other hand, it makes sense to reduce class sizes where possible and to find out why some school districts do a better job than others. In any event, we do not yet have clear-cut experimental evidence as to the benefits or disadvantages of bilingual education.

www 7 L 13

CLICK4™ *the U.S. Office of Bilingual Education and Minority Languages Affairs.*

www 7 BBC 3

CLICK4™ *a bulletin board discussion on the advantages and disadvantages of being bilingual.*

REVIEW

(22) Apes (have or have not?) been taught to use symbols to communicate. (23) Language is the communication of thoughts and feelings by means of symbols that are arranged according to rules of _____. The basic concepts of language include phonology, morphology, syntax, and semantics. (24) Most psychologists today consider it (advantageous or disadvantageous?) for children to be bilingual.

Pulling It Together: How do psychologists distinguish true language from the communication systems of lower animals?

LANGUAGE AND COGNITION

Let us bring the chapter full circle by returning to matters of cognition. *Question: What are the relationships between language and cognition?* The relationships between language and cognition are complex and not always obvious. For example, can you think *without* using language? (The answer seems to be yes, but of course you would not be able to use thoughts that entail symbols that are arranged according to rules of grammar.) Would you be able to solve problems without using words or sentences? (That depends on the problem.)

Jean Piaget believed that language reflects knowledge of the world but that much knowledge can be acquired without language. For example, it is possible to understand

Inuit Eskimos in an Igloo.
The Inuit of Alaska and the Canadian Northwestern Territories have many more words for snow than most of us. They spend most of their lives in snow, and the subtle differences among various kinds of snow are meaningful to them.

the concepts of roundness or redness even when we do not know or use the words *round* or *red*.   *Question: Is it possible for English speakers to share the thoughts experienced by people who speak other languages?*

The Linguistic-Relativity Hypothesis

DIVERSITY   Different languages have different words for the same concepts, and concepts do not necessarily fully overlap. Can we be certain that English speakers can truly share or understand the ideas of people who speak other languages? This question brings us to the linguistic-relativity hypothesis.

The **linguistic-relativity hypothesis** was proposed by Benjamin Whorf (1956). Whorf believed that language structures the way we perceive the world. That is, the categories and relationships we use to understand the world are derived from our language. Therefore, speakers of various languages conceptualize the world in different ways.

Thus most English speakers' ability to think about snow may be limited compared with that of the Inuit (Eskimos). We have only a few words for snow. The Inuit have many words. They differ according to whether the snow is hard-packed, falling, melting, covered by ice, and so on. When we think about snow, we have fewer words to choose from and have to search for descriptive adjectives. The Inuit, however, can readily find a single word that describes a complex weather condition. It might therefore be easier for them to think about this variety of snow in relation to other aspects of their world. Similarly, the Hanunoo people of the Philippines use 92 words for rice, depending on whether the rice is husked or unhusked and on how it is prepared. And whereas we have one word for camel, Arabs have more than 250.

In English, we have hundreds of words to describe different colors, but people who speak Shona use only three words for colors. People who speak Bassa use only two words for colors; these correspond to light and dark. It may be that there are no universal basic color categories and that our tendency to separate, says, blues from greens as we do is learned within a cultural setting (Wierzbicka, 1999).

CLICK4™ *an essay assignment on language and cognition in various cultures.*

CLICK4™ *links on linguistics hosted by the University of Rochester.*

▲ **REFLECT**
Is it possible that we see a sharp distinction between green and blue because our culture separates greens from blues in certain ways? If we were reared in another culture, might there be more overlap between these colors, or might we see three or four families of colors rather than two?

Linguistic-relativity hypothesis ▲ The view that language structures the way in which we view the world.

The Hopi Indians had two words for flying objects, one for birds and an all-inclusive word for anything else that might be found traveling through the air. Does this mean that the Hopi were limited in their ability to think about bumblebees and airplanes? Are English speakers limited in their ability to think about skiing conditions? Are people who speak Shona and Bassa "color-blind" for practical purposes? Probably not. People who use only a few words to distinguish among colors seem to perceive the same color variations as people with dozens of words. For example, the Dani of New Guinea, like the Bassa, have just two words for colors: one that refers to yellows and reds, and one that refers to greens and blues. Yet performance on matching and memory tasks shows that the Dani can discriminate the many colors of the spectrum when they are motivated to do so. English-speaking skiers who are concerned about different skiing conditions have developed a comprehensive vocabulary about snow, including the terms *powder, slush, ice, hard packed,* and *corn snow,* that allows them to communicate and think about snow with the facility of the Inuit. When a need to expand a language's vocabulary arises, the speakers of that language apparently have little difficulty meeting the need.

Modern cognitive scientists generally do not accept the linguistic-relativity hypothesis (Pinker, 1990). For one thing, adults use images and abstract logical propositions, as well as words, as units of thought. Infants, moreover, display considerable intelligence before they have learned to speak. Another criticism is that a language's vocabulary suggests the range of concepts that the speakers of the language have traditionally found important, not their cognitive limits. For example, people who were magically lifted from the 19th century and placed inside an airplane probably would not think they were flying inside a bird or a large insect, even if their language lacked a word for airplane.

Before leaving the section on thinking, I have a final problem for you:

> You're driving a bus that's leaving from Pennsylvania. To start off with, there were 32 people on the bus. At the next bus stop, 11 people got off and 9 people got on. At the next bus stop, 2 people got off and 2 people got on. At the next bus stop, 12 people got on and 16 people got off. At the next bus stop, 5 people got on and 3 people got off. How many people are now on the bus?

REVIEW

CLICK4™ *a quiz covering the last half of this chapter.*

CLICK4™ *electronic flash cards to review your knowledge of key terms and people in this chapter.*

(25) According to the _____-relativity hypothesis, language structures (and limits) the way in which we perceive the world. (26) Critics of the linguistic-relativity hypothesis argue that the _____ of a language may suggest the concepts deemed important by its users, but does not necessarily prevent thinking about concepts for which there are no words.

Pulling It Together: Think of fields such as computer science, mathematics, psychology, economics, art, and music. What special vocabularies are used in fields like these.

TRUTH ☑ FICTION
REVISITED

- It is not true that using a "tried and true" formula is the most efficient way to solve a problem. *Using a tried and true formula—that is, an algorithm—may be less efficient than using a heuristic device. See page 233.*

- It is not true that only humans can solve problems by means of insight. *Classic research evidence shows that lower animals, even rats, are also capable of insight (a sudden reorganization of the perceptual field). See page 235.*

- It is not true that the best way to solve a frustrating problem is to keep plugging away at it. *It may be better to distance oneself from the problem for a while and allow it to "incubate." Eventually you may solve the problem in what seems to be a flash of insight. See page 236.*

- It is not necessarily true that people with academic ability are creative. *Bright people are more likely to be creative than duller people, but many bright people are uncreative. See page 238.*

- It is true that a conclusion can be logical but wrong. *The conclusion would be incorrect if a premise is incorrect. See page 242.*

- It is not true that if a couple has five sons, the sixth child is likely to be a daughter. *See page 243.*

- It is not necessarily true that people change their opinions when they are shown to be wrong. *In some cases they may, but the statement is too general to be true. See page 244.*

- It is true that the majority of people around the world speak at least two languages. *Bilingualism thus is the normal state of affairs, not merely an issue of concern to immigrants. See page 248.*

1. What is cognition?

Cognition is mental activity that is involved in the understanding, processing, and communicating of information. It refers to conscious, planned attempts to make sense of the world.

2. How do concepts function as building blocks of cognition?

Concepts provide mental categories that allow for the grouping together of objects, events, or ideas with common properties. We tend to organize concepts in hierarchies. Prototypes are good examples of particular concepts. Simple prototypes are usually taught by means of exemplars, or positive and negative instances of the concept. Abstract concepts are usually formed through explanations involving more basic concepts.

3. How do people go about solving problems?

People first attempt to understand the problem. Then they use various strategies for attacking the problem, including algorithms, heuristic devices, and analogies. Algorithms are specific procedures for solving problems (such as formulas) that invariably work as long as they are applied correctly.

4. Is it best to use a tried and true formula to solve a problem?

Not necessarily. Heuristic devices often help us "jump" to correct conclusions. Heuristics are rules of thumb that help us simplify and solve problems. Heuristics are less reliable than algorithms, but when they are effective, they allow us to solve problems more rapidly. One commonly used heuristic device is means-end analysis, in which we assess the difference between our current situation and our goals and do what we can to reduce the discrepancy. The analogy heuristic applies the solution of an earlier problem to the solution of a new, similar problem.

5. What factors make it easier or harder to solve problems?

Key factors include one's level of expertise, whether one falls prey to a mental set, whether one develops insight into a problem, incubation, and functional fixedness.

6. What are the relationships among creativity, problem solving, and intelligence?

Creativity is the ability to make unusual and sometimes remote associations to or among the elements of a problem in order to generate new combinations.
There is only a moderate relationship between creativity and academic ability.

7. What factors other than intelligence are connected with creativity?

Creativity is characterized by divergent thinking. Creative people show traits such as flexibility, fluency, and independence. The pressure of social evaluation appears to reduce creativity, rewards may foster creativity, and the effects of brainstorming on creativity are debatable.

8. How do people reason?

Two types of reasoning used by people are deductive and inductive reasoning. In deductive reasoning, one reaches conclusions about premises that are true so long as the premises are true. In inductive reasoning, we reason from individual cases or particular facts to a general conclusion that is not necessarily true.

9. How do people go about making judgments and decisions?

People sometimes make decisions by carefully weighing the pluses and minuses, but most make decisions on the basis of limited information. Decision makers frequently use rules of thumb or heuristics, which are shortcuts that are correct (or correct enough) most of the time. According to the representativeness heuristic, people make judgments about events according to the populations of events that they appear to represent. According to the availability heuristic, people's estimates of frequency or probability are based on how easy it is to find examples of relevant events. According to the anchoring and adjustment heuristic, we adjust our initial estimates as we receive additional information—but we often do so unwillingly.

10. **How do people frame information in order to persuade others?**

People frequently phrase or frame arguments in ways to persuade others. For example, people on both sides of the abortion issue present themselves as being in favor of an important value—either pro-life or pro-choice.

11. **Why do people tend to be convinced that they are right, even when they are dead wrong?**

People tend to retain their convictions, even when proven false, because they are unaware of the flimsiness of their assumptions, focus on events that confirm their judgments, and work to bring about results consistent with their judgments.

12. **How do we define language?**

Language is the communication of thoughts and feelings by means of symbols that are arranged according to rules of grammar.

13. **What are the properties of a "true" language as opposed to an inborn communication system?**

True language is distinguished from the communication systems of lower animals by properties such as semanticity, infinite creativity, and displacement. Semanticity means that the symbols of a language have meaning. Infinite creativity is the capacity to combine words into original sentences. Displacement is the ability to communicate information about events and objects from another time or place.

14. **What basic concepts are used to discuss language?**

The basic concepts of language include phonology (sounds), morphology (units of meaning), syntax (word order), and semantics (the meanings of words and groups of words). Phonemes are the smallest units of sound in a language, and morphemes, the smallest units of meaning.

15. **What does research reveal about the advantages and disadvantages of bilingualism?**

Most people throughout the world are bilingual. Contemporary research reveals that bilingualism broadens people's perspectives and often helps them better learn their first language.

16. **What are the relationships between language and cognition?**

Language is not necessary for cognition, but language makes possible cognitive activity that involves use of symbols arranged according to rules of grammar.

17. **Is it possible for English speakers to share the thoughts experienced by people who speak other languages?**

Perhaps it is. According to the linguistic-relativity hypothesis, the concepts we use to understand the world are derived from our language. Therefore, speakers of various languages would think about the world in different ways. However, modern cognitive scientists suggest that the vocabulary of a language suggests the range of concepts that the users have traditionally found to be useful, not their cognitive limits.

PREVIEW

What Is Intelligence?
▲ Intelligence enables you to understand the world and cope with its challenges.
▲ Can we break intelligence up into pieces? How many?
▲ Are musical talent and sensitivity to people's feelings kinds of intelligence?

The Measurement of Intelligence
▲ Alfred Binet, the originator of a widely used intelligence test, once tried to use magnets to shift an action (such as lifting an arm) from one side of the body to the other.
▲ Your vocabulary and math ability are signs of your intelligence.

Socioeconomic and Ethnic Differences in Intelligence
▲ Do rich people obtain higher intelligence test scores than poor people?
▲ Ethnic differences in IQ are a source of great controversy.

Extremes of Intelligence
▲ What does it mean to be mentally retarded?
▲ What does it mean to be gifted?

The Testing Controversy
▲ Do intelligence tests really measure intelligence?

Determinants of Intelligence: Where Does Intelligence Come From?
▲ How much of your intellectual functioning can we attribute to your genetic heritage?
▲ How much of your intellectual functioning can we attribute to your early learning experiences and other environmental factors?

Intelligence

W hat form of life is so adaptive that it can survive in desert temperatures of 120°F or Arctic climes of −40°F? What form of life can run, walk, climb, swim, live underwater for months on end, and fly to the moon and back?

I won't keep you in suspense any longer. We are that form of life. Yet our unclad bodies do not allow us to adapt to these extremes of temperature. Brute strength does not allow us to live underwater or travel to the moon. Rather, it is our **intelligence** that permits us to adapt to these conditions and to challenge our physical limitations.

WHAT IS INTELLIGENCE?

CLICK4™ *an essay assignment on defining intelligence.*

Question: Just what is intelligence? The concept of intelligence is closely related to the concept of cognition. Whereas cognition involves the understanding and manipulating of information, *intelligence* is somewhat more broadly thought of as the underlying ability to understand the world and cope with its challenges. In other words, intelligence is seen as making cognition possible.

Although these concepts overlap, psychologists tend to be concerned with *how* we think, but laypeople and psychologists are often concerned with *how much* intelligence we have. At an early age, we gain impressions of how intelligent or bright we are compared to other people.

Intelligence provides the cognitive basis for academic achievements. It allows us to profit from experiences such as educational experiences. Intelligence allows people to think—to understand complex ideas, reason, and solve problems—and to learn from experience and adapt effectively to the environment (Neisser et al., 1996). As we see in architecture, in the creation of mechanisms for heating and cooling, and in travel through space and under water, intelligence even permits people to create new environments. Although intelligence, like thinking, cannot be directly seen or touched, psychologists tie the concept to predictors such as school performance and occupational status (Wagner, 1997).

We now discuss theories about the nature of intelligence. We see how intelligence is measured and discuss group differences in intelligence. Finally, we examine the determinants of intelligence: heredity and the environment.

▲ REFLECT
When did you form an impression of how intelligent you are? Has this impression helped you or hurt you? Explain.

CLICK4™ *a profile of Charles Spearman.*

Factor Theories of Intelligence

Many investigators have viewed intelligence as consisting of one or more *factors*. *Question: What are factor theories of intelligence?* Factor theories argue that intelligence is made up of a number of mental abilities, ranging from one to hundreds.

In 1904, British psychologist Charles Spearman suggested that the behaviors we consider intelligent have a common underlying factor. He labeled this factor **g,** for "general intelligence" or broad reasoning and problem-solving abilities. Spearman supported his view by noting that people rarely score very high in one area (such as knowledge of the meaning of words) and very low in another (such as the ability to compute numbers). People who excel in one area are also likely to excel in others. But he also noted that even the most capable people are relatively superior in some areas—such as music or business or poetry. For this reason, he suggested that specific, or **s,** factors account for specific abilities.

To test his views, Spearman developed **factor analysis.** Factor analysis is a statistical technique that allows researchers to determine which items on tests seem to be measuring the same things. In his research on relationships among scores on tests of verbal, mathematical, and spatial reasoning, Spearman repeatedly found evidence supporting the existence of *s* factors. The evidence for *g* was more limited.

The U.S. psychologist Louis Thurstone (1938) used factor analysis with various tests of specific abilities and also found only limited evidence for the existence of *g.* Thurstone concluded that Spearman had oversimplified the concept of intelligence. Thurstone's data suggested the presence of nine specific factors, which he labeled **primary mental abilities** (see Table 8.1). Thurstone suggested, for example, that we might have high word fluency, enabling us to rapidly develop lists of words that rhyme but not enabling us to solve math problems efficiently.

▲ REFLECT
From your own experiences, what seem to be the relationships between general intelligence *(g)* and special talents, such as musical or artistic ability? Do you know people who are "good at everything"? Do you know people who are talented in some areas but not in others? In what areas are they talented?

Intelligence ▲ A complex and controversial concept. According to David Wechsler (1975), the "capacity . . . to understand the world [and] resourcefulness to cope with its challenges."

g ▲ Spearman's symbol for general intelligence, which he believed underlay more specific abilities.

s ▲ Spearman's symbol for *specific* factors, or *s factors,* which he believed accounted for individual abilities.

Factor analysis ▲ A statistical technique that allows researchers to determine the relationships among large numbers of items such as test items.

Primary mental abilities ▲ According to Thurstone, the basic abilities that make up intelligence.

TABLE 8.1   PRIMARY MENTAL ABILITIES, ACCORDING TO THURSTONE

Ability	About . . .
Visual and spatial abilities	Visualizing forms and spatial relationships
Perceptual speed	Grasping perceptual details rapidly, perceiving similarities and differences between stimuli
Numerical ability	Computing numbers
Verbal meaning	Knowing the meanings of words
Memory	Recalling information (words, sentences, etc.)
Word fluency	Thinking of words quickly (rhyming, doing crossword puzzles, etc.)
Deductive reasoning	Deriving examples from general rules
Inductive reasoning	Deriving general rules from examples

Over the years, psychologist J. P. Guilford (1988) expanded the numbers of factors found in intellectual functioning to hundreds. The problem with this approach seems to be that the more factors we generate, the more overlap we find among them. For example, several of his "factors" deal with solving math problems and computing numbers.

The Theory of Multiple Intelligences

Howard Gardner (1983/1993) proposes the existence of several kinds of intelligence. ***Question: What is meant by multiple intelligences?*** Gardner refers to each kind of intelligence in his theory as "an intelligence" because they can be so different from one another (see Figure 8.1). He also believes that each kind of intelligence has its neurological base in a different area of the brain. Two of these "intelligences" are familiar ones: language ability and logical-mathematical ability. However, Gardner also refers to bodily-kinesthetic talents (of the sort shown by dancers, mimes, and athletes), musical talent, spatial-relations skills, and two kinds of personal intelligence: awareness of one's own inner feelings and sensitivity to other people's feelings. Gardner (2001) has recently added "naturalist intelligence," which refers to the type of scientific insight of a Charles Darwin, and is also considering adding "existential intelligence," which refers to dealing with the larger philosophical issues of life. According to Gardner, one can compose symphonies or advance mathematical theory yet be average in, say, language and personal skills. (Are not some academic "geniuses" foolish in their personal lives?)

Critics of Gardner's view agree that people function more intelligently in some aspects of life than in others. They also agree that many people have special talents, such as bodily-kinesthetic talents, even if their overall intelligence is average. But they question whether such special talents are really "intelligences" or . . . special talents (Neisser et al., 1996). Language skills, reasoning ability, and ability to solve math problems seem to be more closely related than musical or gymnastic talent to what most people mean by intelligence. If people have no musical ability, do we really think of them as *unintelligent*?

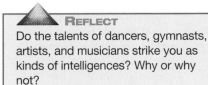

REFLECT
Do the talents of dancers, gymnasts, artists, and musicians strike you as kinds of intelligences? Why or why not?

CLICK4™ *a bulletin board discussion on types of intelligence.*

Musical

Logical-mathematical

Language

Intrapersonal skills

Spatial-relations skills

Interpersonal skills

Bodily-kinesthetic talent

FIGURE 8.1   Types of Multiple Intelligences According to Gardner's Theory.
According to Gardner, there are several *intelligences*, not one, each based in a different area of the brain. Language ability and logic are familiar aspects of intelligence. But Gardner also refers to bodily talents, musical ability, spatial-relations skills, and two kinds of personal intelligence—sensitivity to one's own feelings (intrapersonal sensitivity) and sensitivity to the feelings of others (interpersonal sensitivity) as *intelligences*. Gardner's critics question whether such special talents are truly "intelligences" or specific talents.

CLICK4™ *Web sites on multiple intelligences.*

Analytical Intelligence
(Academic Ability)
Abilities to solve problems,
compare and contrast, judge,
evaluate, and criticize

Creative Intelligence
(Creativity and Insight)
Abilities to invent, discover,
suppose, or theorize

Practical Intelligence
("Street Smarts")
Abilities to adapt to the demands
of one's environment, apply
knowledge in practical situations

FIGURE 8.2   Sternberg's Theory of Intelligence.
According to Robert Sternberg, there are three types of intelligence: analytical (academic ability), creative, and practical ("street smarts").

The Triarchic Theory of Intelligence

Psychologist Robert Sternberg (2000) has constructed a three-pronged, or *triarchic*, theory of intelligence, which is reminiscent of a view proposed by the Greek philosopher Aristotle (Tigner & Tigner, 2000).   *Question: What is Sternberg's triarchic model of intelligence?*   The three types are *analytical*, *creative*, and *practical* (see Figure 8.2).

Analytical Intelligence   Analytical intelligence is similar to Aristotle's "theoretical intelligence" and may be defined as what we generally think of as academic ability. It enables us to solve problems and to acquire new knowledge. Problem-solving skills include encoding information, combining and comparing pieces of information, and generating a solution. Consider Sternberg's analogy problem:

CLICK4™ *a profile of Robert Sternberg.*

> *Washington* is to *1* as *Lincoln* is to (a) 5, (b) 10, (c) 15, (d) 50?

To solve the analogy, we must first correctly *encode* the elements—*Washington*, *1*, and *Lincoln*—by identifying them and comparing them to other information. We must first encode *Washington* and *Lincoln* as the names of presidents[1] and then try to combine *Washington* and *1* in a meaningful manner. Two possibilities quickly come to mind. Washington was the first president, and his picture is on the $1 bill. We can then generate two possible solutions and try them out. First, was Lincoln the 5th, 10th, 15th, or 50th president? Second, on what bill is Lincoln's picture found? (Do you need to consult a history book or peek into your wallet at this point?)

Sternberg illustrates academic intelligence through the example of a Yale graduate student. Let's call her Ashley. Ashley scored high on standardized tests such as the Graduate Record Exam (GRE) and had a nearly perfect undergraduate record. But the GRE does not always predict success (Sternberg & Williams, 1997). Ashley did well her first year of graduate school but then dropped in academic standing because of difficulty generating ideas for research.

---

[1]There are other possibilities. Both are the names of memorials and cities, for example.

Creative Intelligence   Creative intelligence is similar to Aristotle's "productive intelligence" and defined by the abilities to cope with novel situations and to profit from experience. The ability to quickly relate novel situations to familiar situations (that is, to perceive similarities and differences) fosters adaptation. Moreover, as a result of experience, we also become able to solve problems more rapidly.

"Beth," another of Sternberg's students, had obtained excellent letters of recommendation from undergraduate instructors who found her to be highly creative. However, her undergraduate average and her standardized test scores were relatively low when compared to those of other students applying to Yale. Nevertheless, Beth's analytical skills were adequate and because of her imagination, she surpassed Ashley in performance.

Practical Intelligence   Aristotle and Sternberg both speak of practical intelligence, or "street smarts." Practical intelligence enables people to adapt to the demands of their environment. For example, keeping a job by adapting one's behavior to the employer's requirements is adaptive. But if the employer is making unreasonable demands, reshaping the environment (by changing the employer's attitudes) or selecting an alternate environment (by finding a more suitable job) is also adaptive (Sternberg, 1997b).

A third graduate student of Sternberg's—"Cheryl"—had the greatest practical intelligence of the three. Cheryl's test scores and letters of recommendation fell between those of Ashley and Beth. Cheryl did average-quality graduate work but landed the best job of the three upon graduation—apparently because of her practical intelligence.

> **▲ REFLECT**
> Do you know people with "street smarts"? Do street smarts strike you as a kind or form of intelligence? Why or why not?

CONTROVERSY ✦ IN PSYCHOLOGY

Is "Emotional Intelligence" a Form of Intelligence? Should It Be Taught in School?

Psychologists Peter Salovey and John Mayer developed the theory of emotional intelligence, which was popularized by the *New York Times* writer Daniel Goleman (1995). The theory holds that social and emotional skills are a form of intelligence, just as academic skills are. ***Question: Just what is "emotional intelligence"?***   Emotional intelligence bears more than a little resemblance to two of Gardner's "intelligences"—intrapersonal skills and interpersonal skills.

The theory suggests that self-awareness and social awareness are best learned during childhood. Failure to develop emotional intelligence is connected with childhood depression and aggression. Moreover, childhood experiences may even mold the brain's emotional responses to life's challenges. Therefore, it is useful for schools to teach skills related to emotional intelligence as well as academic ability. "I can foresee a day," wrote Goleman (1995), "when education will routinely include [teaching] essential human competencies such as self-awareness, self-control and empathy, and the arts of listening, resolving conflicts and cooperation."

No one argues that self-awareness, self-control, empathy, and cooperation are unimportant. But critics of the theory of emotional intelligence argue that schools may not have the time (or the competence) to teach these skills, and that emotional intelligence may not really be a kind of intelligence at all.

Should emotional intelligence be taught in the schools? Some psychologists believe that "emotional literacy" is as important as literacy (in reading). However, psychologist Robert McCall (1997) echoes the views of other psychologists when he says that "There are so many hours in a day, and one of the characteristics of American schools is we've saddled them with teaching driver's education, sex education, drug education and other skills, to the point that we don't spend as much time on academics as other countries do. There may be consequences for that."

Is emotional intelligence a form of intelligence? Psychologist Ulric Neisser (1997b) says that "The skills that Goleman describes . . . are certainly important for determining life outcomes, but nothing is to be gained by calling them forms of intelligence."

If there is controversy over whether emotional intelligence is a form of intelligence, what of artificial intelligence? Just how bright are computers?

CLICK4™ *links to information and articles about artificial intelligence.*

CLICK4™ *an opportunity to interact online with artificial intelligence "bots" like Brian, a computer that thinks it's an 18-year-old college student.*

CLICK4™ *Web sites concerned with artificial intelligence.*

There are thus many views of intelligence—what intelligence is and how many types or kinds of intelligence there may be. We do not yet have the final word on the nature of intelligence, but I would like to share with you David Wechsler's definition of intelligence. Wechsler is the originator of the most widely used series of contemporary intelligence tests, and he defined intelligence as the "capacity of an individual to understand the world [and the] resourcefulness to cope with its challenges" (1975, p. 139). To Wechsler, intelligence involves accurate representation of the world and effective problem solving (adapting to one's environment, profiting from experience, selecting the appropriate formulas and strategies, and so on). His definition leaves room for others to continue to consider the kinds of resourcefulness—academic, practical, emotional, even perhaps bodily—that are considered intelligent.

Psychology and Modern Life

Wired—The Awesome Future of Artificial Intelligence

> **Saying that Deep Blue (an IBM computer) doesn't really think is like saying an airplane doesn't really fly because it doesn't flap its wings.**
>
> **Drew McDermott**

Science has brought us a number of artificial objects — artificial sweeteners, designer drugs, and artificial limbs, to name a few. But one of the major scientific developments is in the realm of artificial intelligence. Artificial intelligence, or A.I., is the duplication of human intellectual functioning in computers.

The concept of A.I. has a long history both in science fiction and in practice. Think of HAL, the computer in the film *2001*. Not only could HAL coordinate the monitors and controls of a spaceship; it could also engage in such human activities as committing murder, lying with a straight . . . monitor, and striving to save its own . . . memory chips. The robot C3PO in *Star Wars* not only mimicked human intelligence but also displayed remarkably human anxieties and self-doubts. What about the *Terminator* films? The programming in the artificial combination of flesh and metal portrayed by Arnold Schwarzenegger presented him with options that enabled him to size up any situation and efficiently curse, kill, or utter notable Arnoldisms like "I'll be back."

So much for Hollywood. The idea that human intelligence could be copied in computer form originated in the 1950s. It was predicted that machines with A.I. would "one day" be able to understand spoken language, decipher bad handwriting, search

their memories for relevant information, reason, solve problems, make decisions, write books, and explain themselves out loud. At the time, these predictions were visionary. No longer. "One day" is today. Within certain limits, today's computers are very, very good at encoding, storing, retrieving, and manipulating information to solve problems and make decisions. And to some degree, they can even learn from experience (Fogel, 2000).

In some ways, A.I. goes beyond human intelligence. "Deep Blue," the IBM computer that defeated grandmaster Garry Kasparov in a 1997 chess match, examined 200 million possible chess moves *each second* (McDermott, 1997). A.I. can solve problems that would take people years to solve, if they could solve them at all. Given clear direction and the right formulas, computers can carry out complex intellectual functions in a flash. "Who," asks University of Illinois professor Patrick Hayes (1993), "can keep track of 10,000 topics like a computer?"

But Deep Blue was baby steps. Despite its skill at chess, in nearly every other way it was much less than human. Deep Blue did not have the insights, intuitions, and creativity found in people. The sparks of brilliance we find in the best of today's computers turn into dense wood when we ask them to write prose or compose music. (I hope my computer's not reading this.)

However, we are likely to approach human processing power in most areas within a decade or two (Kurzweil, 2000). At that point we may have moved beyond silicon — the substance of the microchip — to "nanotubes," which are arrays of carbon

atoms that would permit 1 million times the processing power of the human brain to be packed into a cubic inch of circuitry (Kurzweil, 2000). Computing power has been doubling every 12 to 18 months. Therefore, once we reach the human level of information processing, we (or the computers themselves!) will probably quickly push beyond. Moreover, when you learn Spanish or calculus, other people cannot easily "download" the information from you. If they could (as in the science fiction film, *The Matrix*), education as we know it would vanish. Also, one computer that learned something could rapidly share the information with all the other computers on the planet (and elsewhere).

Some futurists speak of the merging of human and computer intelligence. They speak of things like "chipping" the human brain (installing microchips that would boost our knowledge and processing power) or of microscopic robots ("nanobots") that could set up shop at synapses and boost neuronal communication or supplant it with virtual realities that would have all the immediacy of true experience (again, as in the film *The Matrix?*).

It's all stimulating and somewhat scary. We're making computers that think more like people, and we may use computers (or they may use us?) to boost our own intellectual powers. What the worlds of natural and artificial intelligence will look like a century from now is anybody's guess. But for the moment at least, the qualities that make our psychological processes fully human have not been captured by computer science. That thought doesn't bother me a byte.

REVIEW

(1) Many investigators see intelligence as consisting of one or more mental abilities called _____. (2) Spearman suggested that the behaviors we consider to be intelligent have a common underlying factor, which he labeled _____, and specific, or *s,* factors that account for specific abilities. (3) Thurstone suggested that there are nine _____ mental abilities. (4) _____ proposes the existence of multiple intelligences, each of which is based in a different area of the brain. (5) Sternberg constructed a "triarchic" model of intelligence, including analytical, creative, and _____ ("street smarts") intelligence.

Pulling It Together: What are the similarities and differences among the views of intelligence described in this section? Are there any that are not what you would consider to be intelligence? Explain.

THE MEASUREMENT OF INTELLIGENCE

Although there are disagreements about the nature of intelligence, lay people and psychologists are concerned with "how much" intelligence people have, because the question has important implications for their ability to profit from experiences, such as education. Thousands of intelligence tests are administered by psychologists and educators every day. In this section we examine two of the most widely used intelligence tests.

Individual Intelligence Tests

Although there are disagreements about the nature of intelligence, thousands of intelligence tests are administered by psychologists and educators every day. In this section we examine some of the most widely used intelligence tests.

The Stanford-Binet Intelligence Scale Many of the concepts of psychology have their origins in common sense. The commonsense notion that academic achievement depends on children's intelligence led Alfred Binet and Theodore Simon to invent measures of intelligence.

Question: What is the Stanford-Binet Intelligence Scale? Early in the 20th century, the French public school system was looking for a test that could identify children who were unlikely to benefit from regular classroom instruction. If these children were identified, they could be given special attention. The first version of such a test, the Binet-Simon scale, came into use in 1905. Since that time it has undergone much revision and refinement. The current version is the Stanford-Binet Intelligence Scale (SBIS).

Binet assumed that intelligence increases with age, so older children should get more items right than younger children. Binet therefore included a series of age-graded questions, as in Table 8.2, arranged in order of difficulty.

The Binet-Simon scale yielded a score called a **mental age,** or MA. The MA shows the intellectual level at which a child is functioning. For example, a child with an MA of 6 is functioning intellectually like the average 6-year-old. In taking the test, children earned "months" of credit for each correct answer. Their MA was determined by adding up the years and months of credit they attained.

Louis Terman adapted the Binet-Simon scale for use with children in the United States. The first version of the *Stanford*-Binet Intelligence Scale (SBIS) was published in 1916. (The test is so named because Terman carried out his work at Stanford University.) The SBIS included more items than the original test and was used with children aged 2 to

Mental age ▲ The accumulated months of credit that a person earns on the Stanford-Binet Intelligence Scale. Abbreviated *MA.*

TABLE 8.2   ITEMS SIMILAR TO THOSE ON THE STANFORD-BINET INTELLIGENCE SCALE

Level (Years)	Item	
2	1.	Children show knowledge of basic vocabulary words by identifying parts of a doll, such as the mouth, ears, and hair.
	2.	Children show counting and spatial skills along with visual-motor coordination by building a tower of four blocks to match a model.
4	1.	Children show word fluency and categorical thinking by filling in the missing words when they are asked questions such as:
		"Father is a man; mother is a _____?"
		"Hamburgers are hot; ice cream is _____?"
	2.	Children show comprehension by answering correctly when they are asked questions such as:
		"Why do people have automobiles?"
		"Why do people have medicine?"
9	1.	Children can point out verbal absurdities, as in this question: "In an old cemetery, scientists unearthed a skull which they think was that of George Washington when he was only 5 years of age. What is silly about that?"
	2.	Children display fluency with words, as shown by answering these questions:
		"Can you tell me a number that rhymes with snore?"
		"Can you tell me a color that rhymes with glue?"
Adult	1.	Adults show knowledge of the meanings of words and conceptual thinking by correctly explaining the differences between word pairs like "sickness and misery," "house and home," and "integrity and prestige."
	2.	Adults show spatial skills by correctly answering questions like: "If a car turned to the right to head north, in what direction was it heading before it turned?"

Intelligence quotient (IQ) ▲ (1) Originally, a ratio obtained by dividing a child's score (or mental age) on an intelligence test by chronological age. (2) Generally, a score on an intelligence test.

Taking the Wechsler.
The Wechsler intelligence scales consist of verbal and performance subtests such as the one shown in this photograph.

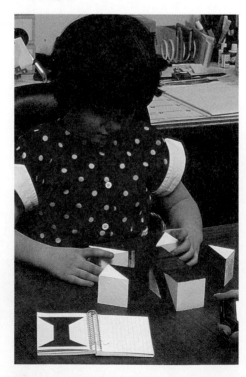

16. The SBIS also yielded an **intelligence quotient (IQ)** rather than an MA. As a result, American educators developed interest in learning the IQs of their pupils. The SBIS is used today with children from the age of 2 upward and with adults.

The IQ reflects the relationship between a child's mental age and his or her actual or chronological age (CA). Use of this ratio reflects the fact that the same MA score has different implications for children of different ages. That is, an MA of 8 is an above-average score for a 6-year-old but below average for a 10-year-old. In 1912, the German psychologist Wilhelm Stern suggested the IQ as a way to deal with this problem. Stern computed IQ using the formula

$$IQ = \frac{\text{Mental Age (MA)}}{\text{Chronological Age (CA)}} \times 100$$

According to this formula, a child with an MA of 6 and a CA of 6 would have an IQ of 100. Children who can handle intellectual problems as well as older children do have IQs above 100. For instance, an 8-year-old who does as well on the SBIS as the average 10-year-old would attain an IQ of 125. Children who do not answer as many items correctly as other children of the same age attain MAs lower than their CAs. Thus, their IQ scores are below 100.

IQ scores on the SBIS today are derived by comparing their results to those of other people of the same age. People who answer more items correctly than the average for people of the same age attain IQ scores above 100. People who answer fewer items correctly than the average for their age attain scores below 100.

The Wechsler Scales   David Wechsler developed a series of scales for use with children and adults. ***Question: What is different about the Wechsler scales of intelligence?***   The Wechsler scales group test questions into a number of separate subtests such as those shown in Table 8.3. Each subtest measures a different type of intellectual task. For this reason, the test shows how well a person does on one type of task (such as defining words) as compared with another (such as using blocks to construct geometric designs). In this way, the Wechsler scales highlight children's relative strengths and weaknesses, as well as measure overall intellectual functioning.

As you can see in Table 8.3, Wechsler described some of his scales as measuring *verbal* tasks and others as assessing *performance* tasks. In general, verbal subtests require knowledge of verbal concepts, whereas performance subtests require familiarity with spatial-relations concepts. (Figure 8.3 shows items similar to those found on the performance scales of the Wechsler tests.) But it is not that easy to distinguish between the two groupings. For example, associating to the name of the object being pieced together in subtest 11—a sign of word fluency and general knowledge as well as of spatial-relations ability—helps the person construct it more rapidly. In any event, Wechsler's scales permit the computation of verbal and performance IQs. It is not unusual for nontechnically oriented college students to attain higher verbal than performance IQs.

Wechsler also introduced the concept of the deviation IQ. Instead of dividing mental by chronological age to compute an IQ, he based IQ scores on how a person's answers compared with those attained by people in the same age group. The average test result at any age level is defined as an IQ score of 100. Wechsler distributed IQ scores so that the middle 50% of them were defined as the "broad average range" of 90 to 110.

As you can see in Figure 8.4, most IQ scores cluster around the average. Only 4% of the population have IQ scores of above 130 or below 70. Table 8.4 indicates the labels that Wechsler assigned to various IQ scores and the approximate percentages of the population who attain IQ scores at those levels.

Group Tests

The SBIS and Wechsler scales are administered to one person at a time. This one-to-one ratio is considered optimal. It allows the examiner to facilitate performance (within the limits of the standardized directions) and to observe the test taker closely. Examiners thus are alerted to factors that impair performance, such as language difficulties, illness, or a noisy or poorly lit room. But large institutions with few trained examiners, such as the public schools and armed forces, require tests that can be administered simultaneously to large groups of people.

Group tests for children, first developed during World War I, were administered to 4 million children by 1921, a couple of years after the war had ended. At first these tests were heralded as remarkable instruments because they helped school administrators place children. However, as the years passed, group tests came under increasing attack, because

TABLE 8.3   SUBTESTS FROM THE WECHSLER ADULT INTELLIGENCE SCALE

Verbal Subtests	Performance Subtests
1. *Information:* "What is the capital of the United States?" "Who was Shakespeare?"	7. *Digit Symbol:* Learning and drawing meaningless figures that are associated with numbers.
2. *Comprehension:* "Why do we have ZIP codes?" "What does 'A stitch in time saves 9' mean?"	8. *Picture Completion:* Pointing to the missing part of a picture.
3. *Arithmetic:* "If 3 candy bars cost 25 cents, how much will 18 candy bars cost?"	9. *Block Design:* Copying pictures of geometric designs using multicolored blocks.
4. *Similarities:* "How are good and bad alike?" "How are peanut butter and jelly alike?"	10. *Picture Arrangement:* Arranging cartoon pictures in sequence so that they tell a meaningful story.
5. *Digit Span:* Repeating a series of numbers forwards and backwards.	11. *Object Assembly:* Putting pieces of a puzzle together so that they form a meaningful object.
6. *Vocabulary:* "What does *canal* mean?"	

NOTE: Items for verbal subtests 1, 2, 3, 4, and 6 are similar, but not identical, to actual test items on the Wechsler Adult Intelligence Scale.

▲ REFLECT

What types of items do you believe ought to be on intelligence tests? Do the tests discussed in this section include the types of things that you consider important?

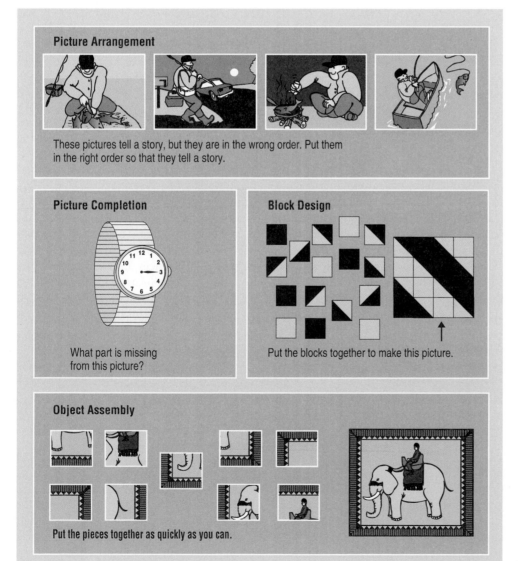

Picture Arrangement

These pictures tell a story, but they are in the wrong order. Put them in the right order so that they tell a story.

Picture Completion

What part is missing from this picture?

Block Design

Put the blocks together to make this picture.

Object Assembly

Put the pieces together as quickly as you can.

FIGURE 8.3   Performance Items of an Intelligence Test.
These tasks resemble those in the performance subtests of the Wechsler Adult Intelligence Scale.

FIGURE 8.4   Approximate Distribution of IQ Scores.
Wechsler defined the deviation IQ so that 50% of scores fall within the broad average range of 90–110. This bell-shaped curve is referred to as a *normal curve* by psychologists. It describes the distribution of many traits, including height.

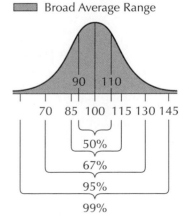

■ Broad Average Range

90 110
70 85 100 115 130 145
50%
67%
95%
99%

TABLE 8.4 VARIATIONS IN IQ SCORES

Range of Scores	Percentage of Population	Interpretation
130 and above	2	Very superior
120–129	7	Superior
110–119	16	Above average
100–109	25	High average
90–99	25	Low average
80–89	16	Slow learner
70–79	7	Borderline
Below 70	2	Intellectually Deficient

CLICK4™ *Click4™ Testing Materials Resource Book Online, a one-stop source of information on standardized tests.*

www 8 WS 2

CLICK4™ *online IQ tests.*

www 8 BBC 2

CLICK4™ *a bulletin board discussion on the measurement of intelligence.*

www 8 L 11

CLICK4™ *a profile of David Wechsler.*

▲ **REFLECT**

What is your own ethnic background? Are there any stereotypes as to how people from your ethnic background perform in school or on intelligence tests? If so, what is your reaction to these stereotypes? Why?

CLICK4™ *a video on intelligence testing in different cultures.*

many administrators relied on them exclusively and did not seek other sources of information about children's abilities and achievements.

At their best, intelligence tests provide just one source of information about individual children. Numbers alone, and especially IQ scores, cannot adequately reflect children's special abilities and talents.

REVIEW

(6) Alfred _____ devised a scale for measuring intelligence to help the French school system identify children who were likely to need special attention. (7) Louis _____ adapted the scale for use in the United States, and it is called the Stanford-Binet Intelligence Scale (SBIS). (8) The SBIS yields a score called an _____ _____ (IQ), which reflects the relationship between mental age and chronological age. (9) The _____ scales have verbal and performance subtests. (10) The average test result is defined as an IQ score of _____.

Pulling It Together: Agree or disagree with the following statement and support your answer: The items on the SBIS and Wechsler scales actually measure achievements rather than intelligence per se.

DIVERSITY SOCIOECONOMIC AND ETHNIC DIFFERENCES IN INTELLIGENCE

There is a body of research suggestive of differences in intelligence between socioeconomic and ethnic groups. ***Question: What are the socioeconomic and ethnic differences in intelligence?*** Lower-class U.S. children obtain IQ scores some 10 to 15 points lower than those obtained by middle- and upper-class children. African American children tend to obtain IQ scores some 15 points lower than those obtained by their European American age-mates (Neisser et al., 1996). Latino and Latina American and Native American children also tend to score below the norms for European American children (Neisser et al., 1996).

Several studies of IQ have confused the factors of social class and ethnicity because disproportionate numbers of African Americans, Latino and Latina Americans, and Native Americans are found among the lower socioeconomic classes (Neisser et al., 1996). When we limit our observations to particular ethnic groups, however, we still find an effect for social class. That is, middle-class European Americans outscore lower-class European Americans. Middle-class African Americans, Latino and Latina Americans, and Native Americans also outscore lower-class members of their own ethnic groups.

Research has also suggested possible cognitive differences between Asians and Caucasians. Asian Americans, for example, frequently outscore European Americans on the math portion of the Scholastic Aptitude Test. Students in China (Taiwan) and Japan also outscore European Americans on standardized achievement tests in math and science (Stevenson et al., 1986). In the United States, moreover, people of Asian Indian, Korean, Japanese, Filipino, and Chinese descent are more likely to graduate from high school and complete four years of college than European Americans, African Americans, and Latino and Latina Americans (Sue & Okazaki, 1990). Asian Americans are vastly overrepresented in competitive colleges and universities in the United States.

There are differences in mathematics ability between high-school students in Germany and Japan. Japanese students, who are Asian, outscore their German counterparts, who are Caucasian (Randel et al., 2000). Most psychologists believe that ethnic differences such as these reflect cultural attitudes toward education rather than inborn racial differences in cognitive ability per se (Neisser et al., 1996). That is, the Asian children may be more motivated to work hard in school. Research shows that Chinese and Japanese students and their mothers tend to attribute academic successes to hard work (Randel et al., 2000). American mothers, in contrast, are more likely to attribute their children's academic successes to "natural" ability (Basic Behavioral Science Task Force, 1996b). That is, Asians are more likely to believe that they can work to make good scores happen, and then they do that work.

Sue and Okazaki (1990) agree. They note that the achievements of Asian and Asian American students reflect their values in the home, the school, or the culture at large. They note that Asian Americans have been discriminated against in blue-collar careers. Therefore, they have come to emphasize the importance of education. Looking to other environmental factors, Steinberg and his colleagues (1996) claim that parental encouragement and supervision in combination with peer support for academic achievement partially explain the superior performances of European Americans and Asian Americans as compared with African Americans and Latino and Latina Americans. Later we will see that other environmental factors, such as stereotype vulnerability, also contribute to these differences.

REVIEW

(11) Lower-class U.S. children attain IQ scores some 10 to 15 points (higher or lower?) than those of middle- and upper-class children. (12) African American, Latino and Latina American, and Native American children score (above or below?) the norms of European American children. (13) Students in China and Japan obtain (higher or lower?) scores than Americans on standardized achievement tests in math and science.

Pulling It Together: What evidence suggests that ethnic differences in IQ reflect socioeconomic differences rather than racial differences per se? How can we explain the differences in IQ between Asians and Caucasians?

EXTREMES OF INTELLIGENCE

The average IQ score in the United States is very close to 100. About 50% of U.S. children obtain IQ scores in the broad average range from 90 to 110. Nearly 95% obtain scores between 70 and 130. But what about the other 5%? Children who obtain IQ scores below 70 are generally labeled as intellectually deficient or mentally retarded. Children who obtain scores of 130 or above are usually labeled as gifted. Both of these labels create certain expectations. Both can place heavy burdens on children and their parents.

CLICK4™ *a quiz covering the first half of this chapter.*

CLICK4™ *a bulletin board discussion on extremes of intelligence.*

CLICK4™ *Web sites devoted to extremes of intelligence, such as ARC, Special Olympics, and MENSA.*

Who's Smart?
Asian children and Asian American children frequently outperform European American children on tests of cognitive skills. Sue and Okazaki suggest that Asian Americans place great value on education because they have been discriminated against in careers that do not require advanced education.

TABLE 8.5 ITEMS FROM THE VINELAND ADAPTIVE BEHAVIOR SCALES

Age Level	Item
1 year, 8 months	Removes front-opening coat, sweater, or shirt without assistance.
1 year, 10 months	Says at least 50 recognizable words.
3 years, 7 months	Tells popular story, fairy tale, lengthy joke, or plot of television program.
4 years, 9 months	Ties shoelaces into a bow without assistance.
5 years, 2 months	Keeps secrets or confidences for more than one day.
7 years, 7 months	Watches television or listens to radio for information about a particular area of interest.
8 years, 8 months	Uses the telephone for all kinds of calls without assistance.
10 years, 2 months	Responds to hints or indirect cues in conversation.
12 years, 2 months	Looks after own health.

SOURCE: Adapted from *Vineland Adaptive Behavior Scales*, by S. S. Sparrow, D. A. Ballo, and D. V. Cicchetti, 1984, Circle Pines, MN: American Guidance Service.

▲ REFLECT

Do you know someone who is mentally retarded? What is known about the causes of the retardation? Does he or she have social and other adjustment problems? What kind of educational or training experiences is he or she receiving? Do they seem to be appropriate? Why or why not?

CLICK4™ *an essay assignment on how society responds to those with exceptional intelligence.*

CLICK4™ *online information resources for gifted and talented students, their parents, and educators.*

CLICK4™ *a profile of Lewis Terman.*

▲ REFLECT

Do you know someone who is gifted? Does he or she have special talents as in math, music, or art? Does the giftedness seem to be connected with social advantages or social problems? How so? What kinds of educational experiences is he or she receiving? Do they seem to be appropriate? Why or why not?

Mental Retardation

Question: What is mental retardation? According to the American Association on Mental Retardation, mental retardation "refers to substantial limitations in present functioning [as] characterized by significantly sub-average intellectual functioning [including an IQ score of no more than 70 to 75], existing concurrently with related limitations in two or more of the following applicable adaptive skill areas: communication, self-care, home living, social skills, community use, self-direction, health and safety, functional academics, leisure and work" (Michaelson, 1993). Mental retardation is typically assessed through a combination of children's IQ scores and behavioral observations. A number of scales have been developed to assess adaptive behavior. Items from the Vineland Adaptive Behavior Scales are shown in Table 8.5.

Table 8.6 describes several levels of retardation. Most of the children who are retarded (about 80%) are mildly retarded. They are capable of adjusting to the demands of educational institutions and, eventually, to society at large. Mildly retarded children are also likely to be taught in regular classrooms, as opposed to being placed in special needs classes. This approach is intended to give mildly retarded children the best possible education and encourage socialization with children at all intellectual levels. Unfortunately, some mildly retarded children are overwhelmed by regular classrooms and avoided by their classmates.

Children with Down syndrome are most likely to fall within the moderately retarded range. As suggested in Table 8.6, moderately retarded children can learn to speak; to dress, feed, and clean themselves; and eventually to engage in work under supportive conditions, as in sheltered workshops. However, they usually do not learn how to read or compute numbers. Severely and profoundly retarded children may not acquire speech and self-help skills and are likely to remain highly dependent on others throughout their lives.

Causes of Retardation
Some of the causes of mental retardation are biological. Retardation, for example, can stem from chromosomal abnormalities such as Down syndrome, from genetic disorders such as phenylketonuria, or from brain damage. Brain damage may have many origins, including accidents during childhood and problems during pregnancy. Maternal alcohol abuse, malnutrition, or diseases during pregnancy can all lead to retardation in the infant.

Giftedness

Question: What does it mean to be gifted? Giftedness involves more than excellence in the tasks provided by standard intelligence tests. Most educators include children who have outstanding abilities, are capable of high performance in a specific academic area such as language arts or mathematics, or who show creativity or leadership, distinction in the visual or performing arts, or talent in physical activities such as gymnastics and dancing. This view of giftedness exceeds the realm of intellectual ability alone and is consistent with Gardner's view that there are multiple intelligences, not just one.

The Terman Studies of Genius
Much of our knowledge of the progress of children who are gifted in overall intellectual functioning stems from Louis Terman's classic longitudinal studies of genius (Janos, 1987). In 1921, Terman began to track the progress of some 1,500 California schoolchildren who had attained IQ scores of 135 or above. The average score was 150, which places these children in a very superior group.

As adults, the group was extremely successful, compared with the general population, in terms of level of education (nearly 10% had earned doctoral degrees), socioeconomic status, and creativity (the group had published more than 90 books and many more shorter pieces). Boys were much more likely than girls to climb the corporate ladder or distinguish themselves in science, literature, or the arts. But we must keep in mind that the Terman study began in the 1920s, when it was generally agreed that a woman's place was in the home. As a result, more than two-thirds of the girls became full-time homemakers or office workers (Lips, 1993). Some of the women later expressed regret that they had not fulfilled their potential. But both the women and men in the study were well-adjusted, with rates of psychological disorders and suicide below the national average.

REVIEW

(14) Children who obtain IQ scores below _____ are labeled intellectually deficient. (15) Children who obtain scores of _____ or above are usually labeled gifted. (16) Biological causes of mental retardation include _____ abnormalities, as in Down syndrome, genetic disorders, and brain damage. Gifted children usually have outstanding abilities in specific academic or artistic areas. (17) Much of our knowledge of the progress of gifted children comes from _____ man's studies of genius.

Pulling It Together: What do we know of the origins of extremes in intelligence? How should society respond to people with "exceptional" intelligence?

TABLE 8.6 LEVELS OF RETARDATION, TYPICAL RANGES OF IQ SCORES, AND TYPES OF ADAPTIVE BEHAVIORS

Approximate IQ Score Range	Preschool Age (0–5): Maturation and Development	School Age (6–21): Training and Education	21 and Over: Social and Vocational Adequacy
Mild (50–70)	Often not noticed as retarded by casual observer but is slower than most children to walk, feed self, and talk.	Can acquire practical skills and useful reading and arithmetic to a 3rd- to 6th-grade level with special education. Can be guided toward social conformity.	Can usually achieve social and vocational skills adequate to self-maintenance; may need occasional guidance and support when under unusual social or economic stress.
Moderate (35–49)	Noticeable delays in motor development, especially in speech; responds to training in various self-help activities.	Can learn simple communication, elementary health and safety habits, and simple manual skills; does not progress in functional reading or arithmetic.	Can perform simple tasks under sheltered conditions; participates in simple recreation; travels alone in familiar places; usually incapable of self-maintenance.
Severe (20–34)	Marked delay in motor development; little or no communication skill; may respond to training in elementary self-help —e.g., self-feeding.	Usually walks, barring specific disability; has some understanding of speech and some response; can profit from systematic habit training.	Can conform to daily routines and repetitive activities; needs continuing direction and supervision in protective environment.
Profound (Below 20)	Gross retardation; minimal capacity for functioning in sensorimotor areas; needs nursing care.	Obvious delays in all areas of development; shows basic emotional responses; may respond to skillful training in use of legs, hands, and jaws; needs close supervision.	May walk, need nursing care, have primitive speech; will usually benefit from regular physical activity; incapable of self-maintenance.

CLICK4™ *advice on facilitating the development of the gifted child.*

THE TESTING CONTROVERSY

It is no secret that during the 1920s intelligence tests were used to prevent many Europeans and others from immigrating to the United States. For example, testing pioneer H. H. Goddard assessed 178 newly arrived immigrants at Ellis Island and claimed that the great majority of Hungarians, Italians, and Russians were "feeble-minded." Apparently it was of little concern to Goddard that these immigrants, by and large, did not understand English—the language in which the tests were administered!

It is now recognized that intelligence tests cannot be considered valid when they are used with people who do not understand the language. But what of cultural differences? *Question: Do intelligence tests contain cultural biases against ethnic minority groups and immigrants?* Are the tests valid when used with ethnic minority groups or people who are poorly educated? A survey of psychologists and educational specialists by Mark Snyderman and Stanley Rothman (1987) found that most consider intelligence tests to be *culturally biased* against African Americans and members of the lower classes. Elementary and secondary schools may also place too much emphasis on them in making educational placements.

Intelligence tests measure traits that are required in developed, high-tech societies. The vocabulary and arithmetic subtests on the Wechsler scales, for example, reflect achievements in language skills and computational ability. The broad achievements measured by these tests reflect intelligence, but they also reflect familiarity with the cultural concepts required to answer test questions correctly. In particular, the tests seem to reflect middle-class European American culture.

CONTROVERSY IN PSYCHOLOGY

Just What Do Intelligence Tests Measure?

As we see in this section, some psychologists and social critics claim that intelligence tests measure many things other than intelligence—including familiarity with the dominant middle-class culture in the United States and motivation to perform well. Is it possible to construct intelligence tests that provide a fair estimate of the intellectual capacity of those who are less familiar with middle-class culture?

269

(18) A survey found that most psychologists and educational specialists (do or do not?) consider intelligence tests to be biased against African Americans and members of the lower classes. During the 1920s, intelligence tests were misused to prevent the immigration of many people into the United States.

Pulling It Together: What is meant by a culturally biased intelligence test? Do the SBIS and Wechsler types of items we presented in this chapter seem to be culturally biased? Explain.

DETERMINANTS OF INTELLIGENCE: WHERE DOES INTELLIGENCE COME FROM?

Let us now discuss the roles of nature (heredity) and nurture (environmental influences) in intellectual functioning. If different ethnic groups tend to score differently on intelligence tests, psychologists—like educators and other people involved in public life—want to know why. We will see that this is one debate that can make use of key empirical findings. Psychologists can point with pride to a rich mine of contemporary research on the roles of nature (genetic influences) and nurture (environmental influences) in the development of intelligence. But first we tackle a controversy in psychology—one that has poured hot oil onto the red-hot issues involving sociocultural factors in intelligence.

CLICK4™ *a bulletin board discussion on what intelligence tests actually measure.*

CLICK4™ *an essay assignment on culturally based intelligence tests.*

CLICK4™ *the "Chitling" Test, an interactive, culture-specific intelligence test.*

CONTROVERSY ✸ IN PSYCHOLOGY

The Controversy Over *The Bell Curve*

When I was in graduate school, a professor remarked that many people think of intelligence as "a knob in the head. Some people have a bigger knob and some people have a smaller one." That is, many people see intelligence as a fixed commodity. From this perspective, some people have more intelligence, some people less, and nothing much can be done about it. The view of intelligence as a knob in the head was expressed forcefully by psychologist Richard Herrnstein and political theorist Charles Murray (1994) in their book *The Bell Curve*. *The Bell Curve* poured oil onto the fires of controversy over social class, race, and intelligence by making the following assertions:

1.   Intelligence tests are valid indicators of intelligence (that is, *IQ* is an accurate measure of intelligence).
2.   A person's intelligence is mainly due to heredity.
3.   People with less intelligence (smaller "knobs in the head") are having more children than people with more intelligence ("bigger knobs"), so that the overall intelligence of the population of the United States is declining.
4.   The United States is becoming divided in two, with a large lower class of people with low intelligence and a smaller class of wealthier people who are higher in intelligence.
5.   Education can do little to affect intelligence (the size of the "knob").

CLICK4™ *a WebSearch activity on The Bell Curve controversy.*

However, intelligence is *not* a knob in the head. Nor is intelligence mainly heritable. Critics argue that IQ is affected by early learning experiences, academic and vocational motivation, and formal education (Kamin, 1995; Steele, 1994).

In this section we will see that the argument of *The Bell Curve* that intelligence tests are valid indicators of intelligence begins to fall apart with the nature of the testing situation. By doing nothing more than make testing conditions more optimal for all children, we may narrow the IQ gap between European American and African American children. We will see that research findings on the roles of the home environment and educational experiences on intelligence contradict *The Bell Curve's* argument that little or nothing can be done to enhance intellectual functioning in children. Finally, we will see that intellectual functioning appears to reflect the interaction of a complex web of genetic, physical, personal, and sociocultural factors. The views of *The Bell Curve*—that intelligence is

CLICK4™ *an essay assignment exploring where intelligence comes from.*

largely heritable and that little can be done to affect intellectual functioning—are contradicted by evidence that clearly supports a more balanced view.

Genetic Influences on Intelligence

Question: What are the genetic influences on intelligence? Research on the genetic influences on human intelligence has employed several basic strategies. These include kinship studies, twin studies, and adoptee studies (Neisser et al., 1996). Let us consider each of them to see how genes may affect intellectual functioning.

Kinship Studies

We can examine the IQ scores of closely and distantly related people who have been reared together or apart. If heredity is involved in human intelligence, closely related people ought to have more similar IQs than distantly related or unrelated people, even when they are reared separately.

Figure 8.5 is a composite of the results of more than 100 studies of IQ and heredity in human beings (Bouchard et al., 1990). The IQ scores of identical (monozygotic, or MZ) twins are more alike than scores for any other pairs, even when the twins have been reared apart. There are moderate correlations between the IQ scores of fraternal (dizygotic, or DZ) twins, between those of siblings, and between those of parents and their children. Correlations between the scores of children and their foster parents and between those of cousins are weak.

Twin Studies

The results of large-scale twin studies are consistent with the data in Figure 8.5. For instance, a study of 500 pairs of MZ and DZ twins in Louisville, Kentucky (Wilson, 1983), found that the correlations in intelligence between MZ twins were about the same as that for MZ twins in Figure 8.5. The correlations in intelligence between DZ twin pairs was the same as that between other siblings. Research at the University of Minnesota with sets of twins who were reared together and others who were reunited in adulthood has obtained essentially similar results (Bouchard et al., 1990). In the MacArthur Longitudinal Twin Study, Robert Emde (1993) and his colleagues examined the intellectual abilities of 200 primarily European American, healthy 14-month-old pairs

> **REFLECT**
>
> Does your own family seem to be generally similar in overall intellectual functioning? Are there one or more family members who appear to stand out from the others because of intelligence? If so, in what ways? Where do you seem to stand in your family in terms of intellectual functioning?

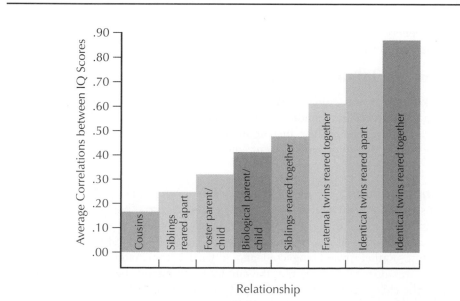

FIGURE 8.5   Findings of Studies of the Relationship Between IQ Scores and Heredity.
The data are a composite of studies summarized in *Science* magazine (Bouchard et al., 1990). By and large, correlations are greater between pairs of people who are more closely related. Yet people who are reared together also have more similar IQ scores than people who are reared apart. Such findings suggest that both genetic and environmental factors contribute to IQ scores.

Claude Steele

"His research may shed fresh light on why many [African Americans] do poorly on standardized tests," writes Ethan Watters (1995), but "It has done little to improve his standing with one leading [African American] intellectual—his twin brother, Shelby." Claude, a Stanford University psychologist, and Shelby Steele are the sons of a social worker (their mother) and a truck driver (their father) who met while taking part in the civil rights movement. Shelby, a conservative essayist, is probably the better known of the brothers outside the field of psychology.

Claude has noted that African Americans experience a feeling of *racial vulnerability* when, for example, they see Band-Aids tinted to match pink skin. His concept of *stereotype vulnerability* describes what African Americans feel when they see standardized tests that seem to be designed to match pink skin. Shelby has argued that African Americans need willpower to achieve despite the odds, not affirmative action. Claude argues that the sense of vulnerability is hard to overcome, and that society as well as individuals must change.

Claude Steele began developing his ideas in the 1980s when he took a teaching position at the University of Michigan and became aware of the greater dropout rate of African American students. He helped create the 21st Century Program, which maintains racially integrated dormitories and requires that dorm members take some classes with other dorm members. This program has reduced the grade gap between African and European American students. It remains to be seen whether the future will reduce the gap between Claude and Shelby Steele.

CLICK4™ *a bulletin board discussion of socioeconomic and ethnic differences in intelligence.*

of twins. They found that identical (MZ) twins were more similar than fraternal (DZ) twins in spatial memory, ability to categorize things, and word comprehension. Emde and his colleagues concluded that genes tend to account for about 40% to 50% of differences in children's cognitive skills.

All in all, studies generally suggest that the **heritability** of intelligence is between 40% and 60% (Bouchard et al., 1990; Neisser et al., 1996). In other words, about half of the variations (the technical term is *variance*) in IQ scores can be accounted for by heredity. This is *not* the same as saying that you inherited about half of your intelligence. The implication of such a statement would be that you "got" the other half of your intelligence somewhere else. It means, rather, that about half of the difference between your IQ score and the IQ scores of other people can be explained in terms of genetic factors.

Note, too, that genetic pairs (such as MZ twins) who were reared together show higher correlations in their IQ scores than similar genetic pairs (such as other MZ twins) who were reared apart. This finding holds for DZ twins, siblings, parents and their children, and unrelated people. Being reared together is therefore related with similarities in IQ. *For this reason, the same group of studies used to demonstrate a role for the heritability of IQ scores also suggests that the environment plays a role in determining IQ scores.*

Adoptee Studies

Another strategy for exploring genetic influences on intelligence is to compare the correlations between the IQ scores of adopted children and those of their biological and adoptive parents. When children are separated from their biological parents at an early age, one can argue that strong relationships between their IQs and those of their natural parents reflect genetic influences. Strong relationships between their IQs and those of their adoptive parents might reflect environmental influences.

Several studies with 1- and 2-year-old children in Colorado (Baker et al., 1983), Texas (Horn, 1983), and Minnesota (Scarr & Weinberg, 1983) have found a stronger relationship between the IQ scores of adopted children and those of their biological parents than between the children's scores and those of their adoptive parents. The Scarr and Weinberg report concerns African American children reared by European American adoptive parents. We return to its findings in the section on environmental influences on intelligence.

In sum, genetic factors may account for about half of the variation in intelligence test scores among individuals. Environmental factors also affect scores on intelligence tests.

Environmental Influences on Intelligence

Question: What are the environmental influences on intelligence? To answer this question we must consider studies of environmental influences, which also employ a variety of research strategies. These include manipulation of the testing situation, observation of the role of the home environment, and evaluation of the effects of educational programs.

The Testing Situation

One approach focuses on the situational factors that determine IQ scores. Remember that an IQ is a score on a test. Thus, in some cases the testing situation itself can explain part of the social-class difference in IQ. In one study the experimenters (Zigler et al., 1982) simply made children as comfortable as possible during the test. Rather than being cold and impartial, the examiner was warm and friendly. Care was also taken to see that the children understood the directions. One result was that the children's test anxiety was markedly reduced. Another was that their IQ

Heritability ▲ The degree to which the variations in a trait from one person to another can be attributed to, or explained by, genetic factors.

scores were 6 points higher than those for a control group of children who were treated in a more indifferent manner. Disadvantaged children made relatively greater gains from the modified testing procedure.

DIVERSITY *Intelligence Testing and Diversity: Stereotype Vulnerability and Intelligence Test Scores*   **Stereotype vulnerability** is another aspect of the testing situation, and it also affects test scores. Psychologist Claude Steele (1996, 1997) suggests that African American students carry an extra burden in performing scholastic tasks: They believe that they risk confirming their group's negative stereotype by doing poorly on such tasks. This concern creates performance anxiety. Performance anxiety distracts them from the tasks, and as a result they perform more poorly than European American students.

In an experiment designed to test this view, Steele and Aronson (1995) gave two groups of African American and European American Stanford undergraduates the most difficult verbal skills test questions from the GRE. One group was told that the researchers were attempting to learn about the "psychological factors involved in solving verbal problems." The other group was told that the items were "a genuine test of your verbal abilities and limitations." African American students who were given the first message performed as well as European American students. African American students who were given the second message—that proof of their abilities was on the line—performed significantly more poorly than the European American students. Apparently the second message triggered their stereotype vulnerability, which led them to self-destruct on the test. Steele's findings are further evidence of the limits of intelligence tests as valid indicators of intelligence.

CLICK4™ *an essay assignment on socioeconomic and ethnic differences in intelligence.*

> ▲ **REFLECT**
> Does performance anxiety affect you on tests? What kinds of thoughts make you anxious? What can you do about it?

Home Environment and Styles of Parenting   The home environment and styles of parenting also appear to have an effect on IQ scores (Olson et al., 1992; Steinberg et al., 1996; Suzuki & Valencia, 1997). Children of mothers who are emotionally and verbally responsive, furnish appropriate play materials, are involved with their children, encourage independence, and provide varied daily experiences during the early years obtain higher IQ scores later on (Gottfried et al., 1994; Molfese et al., 1997). Organization and safety in the home have also been linked to higher IQs at later ages and to higher achievement test scores during the first grade (Bradley et al., 1989).

Dozens of other studies support the view that children's early environment is linked to IQ scores and academic achievement. For example, Victoria Molfese and her colleagues (1997) found that the home environment was the single most important predictor of scores on IQ tests among children aged 3 to 8.

CLICK4™ *Web sites dedicated to intelligence testing and evaluation.*

> ▲ **REFLECT**
> As you look back on your own childhood, can you point to any kinds of family or educational experiences that seem to have had an impact on your intellectual development? Would you say that your background, overall, was deprived or enriched? In what ways?

CONTROVERSY ✕ IN PSYCHOLOGY

The Mozart Effect: Will Music Provide Children With the Sweet Sounds of Success? Technological innovations are overleaping themselves in the new millennium. Parents are concerned about what they can do to help their children grasp the new technologies. Whatever environmental factors are found to enhance children's intellectual functioning may well be music to parents' ears. But it may also turn out that music will be spatial reasoning to children's ears.

Research suggests that listening to and studying music may enhance at least one aspect of intellectual functioning—spatial reasoning. In 1993, the research team of Frances Rauscher, Gordon Shaw, and Katherine Ky published an intriguing article in *Nature* on the effects of exposure to Mozart's music. They claimed that listening to 10 minutes of Mozart's Piano Sonata K 448 enhanced college students' scores on spatial reasoning tasks. For example, they were better able to perceive the design of a "snowflake," after mentally cutting and folding a piece of paper, and they were better able to rotate and compare objects in space (Hershenson, 2000).

At the 1994 meeting of the American Psychological Association, a research team headed by Rauscher reported the results of a follow-up study with preschoolers in a paper titled "Music and spatial task performance: A causal relationship." They recruited 19

CLICK4™ *a WebSearch activity on the Mozart Effect.*

Stereotype vulnerability ▲ The tendency to focus on a conventional, negative belief about one's group, such that the individual risks behaving in a way that confirms that belief.

The Sweet Sounds of Success?
Some research suggests that training in music enhances children's intellectual functioning, particularly in visual-spatial areas. Perhaps perception of music and spatial relations occupy overlapping neural pathways. However, it should be noted that this field of research is in its infancy and that psychologists disagree as to its implications.

preschool children aged from 3 years to 4 years 9 months and gave them 8 months of music lessons, including singing and use of a keyboard. After the lessons the children's scores on an object assembly task significantly exceeded those of 15 preschoolers who did not receive the musical training.

Cognitive psychologist Lois Hetland (2000) reports that children given keyboard lessons perform better on spatial reasoning tests. She also analyzed research with college students and concluded that they scored higher on spatial-reasoning tests after hearing the music of Mozart, Schubert, and Mendelssohn but not the music of Philip Glass (a contemporary composer of classical-style music) or of Pearl Jam and other rock groups. That is, music with complex structure and rhythm apparently had more beneficial cognitive benefits.

How might listening to music or training in music affect spatial reasoning? It may be that neural pathways involved in processing music overlap those involved in other cognitive functions—such as spatial reasoning (Rauscher, 1998). Musical training thus develops the neural firing patterns used in spatial reasoning, which may eventually help children solve geometry problems, design skyscrapers, navigate ships, perhaps even fit suitcases into the trunk of a car.

The researchers caution that their findings should be considered preliminary. Attempts to replicate the Rauscher studies have met with mixed success (Rauscher & Shaw, 1998). Moreover, it is unclear exactly what aspects of the "treatment" may have influenced students (Nantais & Schellenberg, 1999). Is it the music itself, or could it be related factors like the spatial patterns made by the black and white keys on the keyboard, or even a mood change caused by the music (Hershenson, 2000)? We do not have the answers (Schellenberg, 2000).

But perhaps the findings are enticing enough to encourage school administrators to maintain music programs, which are often among the first to go when school districts tighten the purse strings. Music, after all, may contribute to the sweet sounds of success.

Education Although intelligence is viewed as permitting people to profit from education, education also apparently contributes to intelligence. For example, government-funded efforts to provide preschoolers with enriched early environments have led to measurable intellectual gains. Head Start programs, for example, enhance the IQ scores, achievement test scores, and academic skills of disadvantaged children (Barnett & Escobar, 1990; Zigler, 1999) by exposing them to materials and activities that middle-class children take for granted. These include letters and words, numbers, books, exercises in drawing, pegs and pegboards, puzzles, toy animals, and dolls. Head Start also helps poor

Head Start.
Preschoolers who are placed in Head Start programs have shown dramatic improvements in readiness for elementary school and in IQ scores.

children get medical and dental care, serves nutritious meals, and helps children develop the social skills necessary to succeed in school (Zigler, 1999).

Preschool intervention programs can have long-term positive effects on children. During the elementary- and high-school years, graduates of preschool programs are less likely to be left back or placed in classes for slow learners. They are more likely to graduate from high school, go on to college, and earn higher incomes.

Schooling at later ages also contributes to intelligence test scores. When children of about the same age start school a year apart because of admissions standards related to their date of birth, children who have been in school longer obtain higher IQ scores (Neisser et al., 1996). Moreover, IQ test scores tend to decrease during the summer vacation (Neisser et al., 1996).

The findings on intelligence, the home environment, and educational experiences show that much indeed can be done to enhance intellectual functioning in children.

www 8 PML 13

CLICK4™ *advice on enhancing intellectual functioning.*

Adoptee Studies   The Minnesota adoption studies reported by Scarr and Weinberg suggest a genetic influence on intelligence. But the same studies (Scarr & Weinberg, 1976, 1977) also suggest a role for environmental influences. African American children who were adopted during their first year by European American parents with above-average income and education obtained IQ scores some 15 to 25 points higher than those obtained by African American children reared by their natural parents (Scarr & Weinberg, 1976). There are two cautions regarding these findings. One is that the adoptees' average IQ score, about 106, remained below those of their adoptive parents' natural children— 117 (Scarr & Weinberg, 1977). The second is that follow-up studies of the adopted children at the age of 17 found that the mean IQ score of the adopted African American children had decreased by 9 points, to 97 (Weinberg et al., 1992). The meaning of the change remains to be unraveled (Neisser, 1997a).

As suggested by Figure 8.6, intellectual functioning would appear to reflect the interaction of genetic, physical, personal, and sociocultural factors. We can put to rest the assertions of *The Bell Curve*—that intelligence is inherited and little can be done to affect it. An impartial reading of the evidence demands a more balanced view.

DIVERSITY   Ethnicity and Intelligence: A Concluding Note

Many psychologists believe that heredity and environment interact to influence intellectual functioning (Lubinski & Benbow, 2000; Winner, 2000). Forty-five percent of Snyderman and Rothman's (1987, 1990) sample of 1,020 psychologists and educational specialists believe that differences in IQ between African Americans and European Americans are a "product of both genetic and environmental variation, compared to only 15% who feel the difference is entirely due to environmental variation

Genetic Factors

Health

Socioeconomic status
Stimulating home environment
Possession of academic basics
Flexible personality
Achievement motivation
Academic/educational adjustment
Belief that intellectual functioning
   is a key to fulfillment

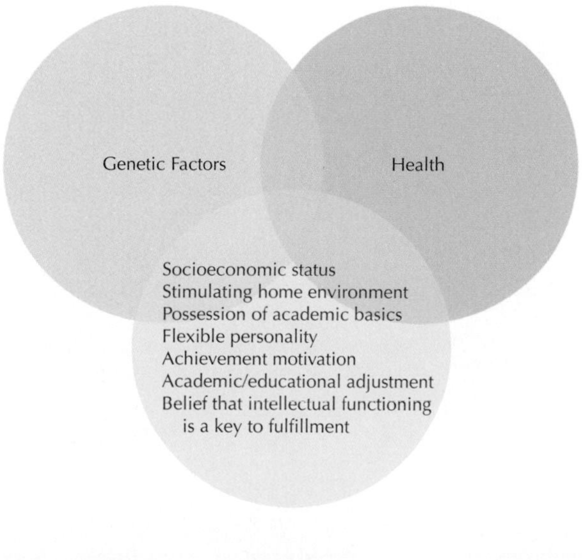

FIGURE 8.6 The Complex Web of Factors That Appears to Affect Intellectual Functioning in Children and Adults.

Intellectual functioning appears to be influenced by the interaction of genetic factors, health, personality, and sociocultural factors.

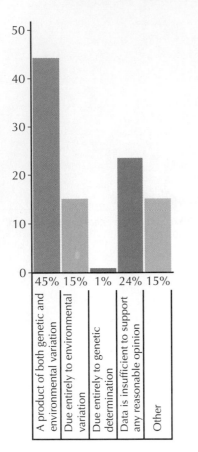

FIGURE 8.7   Beliefs of Psychologists and Educational Specialists Concerning Reasons for Racial Differences in IQ.

The largest group of psychologists and educational specialists views racial differences in IQ as reflecting the interaction of genetic and environmental factors.

SOURCE: Snyderman and Rothman (1987, 1990).

CLICK4™ *a quiz covering the second half of this chapter.*

CLICK4™ *Click4™ electronic flash cards to review your knowledge of key terms and people in this chapter.*

[see Figure 8.7]. Twenty-four percent of experts do not believe there are sufficient data to support any reasonable opinion, [and 1%] indicate a belief in an entirely genetic determination" (1987, p. 141).

Diana Baumrind (1993) and Jacquelyne Jackson (1993) of the Institute of Human Development at the University of California argue that belief in the predominance of genetic factors can undermine parental and educational efforts to enhance children's intellectual development. Such a view can be particularly harmful to African American children. Parents are most effective when they *believe* that their efforts will improve their children's functioning. Since parents cannot change their children's genetic codes, it is better for parents to assume that good parenting can make a difference.

Perhaps we need not be so concerned with whether we can sort out exactly how much of a person's IQ is due to heredity and how much is due to environmental influences. A majority of psychologists and educators believe that IQ reflects the complex interaction of heredity, early childhood experiences, sociocultural factors and expectations, and even the atmosphere in which intelligence tests are conducted. Psychology has traditionally supported the dignity of the individual. It might be more appropriate for us to try to identify children *of all ethnic groups* whose environments place them at risk for failure and do what we can to enrich their environments. As noted by Paul Ehrlich (2000), professor of biology and population studies at Stanford University:

> There is no such thing as a fixed human nature, but rather an interaction between our genotypes—the genetic information we have—and the different environments we live in, with the result that all our natures are unique.

REVIEW

(19) Research on the _____ influences on intelligence focuses on kinship studies, twin studies, and adoptee studies. (20) When children are separated from their biological parents early, strong relationships between their IQs and those of their biological parents probably reflect (genetic or environmental?) influences. (21) Estimates place the _____ of intelligence at about 40% to 60%. (22) Steele showed that many African Americans perform poorly on intelligence tests due to _____ vulnerability. (23) _____ Start programs enhance IQ scores by exposing poor children to materials and activities that middle-class children take for granted. (24) The largest number of psychologists and educators believe that intellectual functioning reflects the interaction of genetic and _____ factors.

Pulling It Together: Give examples of the kinds of studies that are used to determine the role of heredity in IQ. Give examples of the kinds of studies that are used to determine the role of the environment.

◪ According to Sternberg, "street smarts" are a type of intelligence—practical intelligence. *See page 261.*

◪ The terms *intelligence* and *IQ* do not mean the same thing. Intelligence *is a hypothetical concept on whose meanings psychologists do not agree. An* IQ *is a score on an intelligence test. Can you see any danger in using the terms as if they meant the same thing? See page 264.*

◪ It is true that two children can answer exactly the same items on an intelligence test correctly, yet one can be above average and the other below average in IQ. *This is because the ages of the children may differ. The more intelligent child would be the younger of the two. See page 264.*

◪ It is true that early users of IQ tests administered them in English to immigrants who did not understand the language. *See page 269.*

◪ It is true that Head Start programs have raised children's IQs. *See page 274.*

Recite Recite Recite

1. Just what is intelligence?

Intelligence underlies (provides the cognitive basis for) thinking and academic achievement. Wechsler defined it as the "capacity . . . to understand the world . . . and . . . resourcefulness to cope with its challenges."

2. What are factor theories of intelligence?

Spearman and Thurstone believed that intelligence is composed of a number of factors. Spearman believed that a common factor, *g*, underlies all intelligent behavior but that people also have specific abilities, or *s* factors. Thurstone suggested that there are several primary mental abilities, including word fluency and numerical ability.

3. What is meant by multiple intelligences?

Gardner believes that people have several intelligences, not one, and that each is based in a different area of the brain. Two such "intelligences" are language ability and logical-mathematical ability, but Gardner also includes bodily-kinesthetic intelligence and others.

4. What is Sternberg's triarchic model of intelligence?

Sternberg's triarchic theory proposes three kinds of intelligence: analytical (academic ability), creative, and practical ("street smarts"). Analytical intelligence is not necessarily the best predictor of success.

5. Just what is "emotional intelligence"?

The theory of emotional intelligence holds that social and emotional skills are a form of intelligence that helps children avert violence and depression. The theory suggests that emotional skills are best learned during childhood.

6. What is the Stanford-Binet Intelligence Scale?

This is the test originated by Alfred Binet in France and developed by Louis Terman at Stanford University. It includes a series of age-graded questions. The SBIS derives an IQ score by dividing a child's mental age score by the child's chronological age and then multiplying by 100.

7. What is different about the Wechsler scales of intelligence?

The Wechsler scales use deviation IQs, which are derived by comparing a person's performance with that of age-mates. The Wechsler scales contain verbal and performance subtests that measure general information, comprehension, similarities (conceptual thinking), vocabulary, mathematics, block design (copying designs), and object assembly (piecing puzzles together).

8. What are the socioeconomic and ethnic differences in intelligence?

Lower-class U.S. children obtain IQ scores some 10 to 15 points lower than those of middle- and upper-class children. African American children tend to obtain IQ scores some 15 to 20 points lower than those of their European American age-mates. Asians and Asian Americans usually obtain higher IQ scores than Britishers or European Americans.

9. What is mental retardation?

Mental retardation is defined as substantial limitation in functioning that is characterized by an IQ score of not more than 70 to 75 and problems in adaptive skills. Most people who are retarded are mildly retarded. Children with Down syndrome are most likely to be moderately retarded.

10. What does it mean to be gifted?

Giftedness involves high scores on intelligence tests along with high performance in a specific academic area, creativity, leadership, or talent in physical activities. Terman's longitudinal studies of genius found that gifted children generally turned out to be successful as adults.

11. Do intelligence tests contain cultural biases against ethnic minority groups and immigrants?

Intelligence tests were used historically to prevent many Europeans and others from immigrating to the United States. They were administered in English to people who did not know English. Most psychologists and educators believe that intelligence tests are biased against African Americans and people in the lower classes in that they require familiarity with cultural concepts, particularly those that reflect middle-class European American culture.

12. What are the genetic influences on intelligence?

Research on the genetic influences on human intelligence is generally based on kinship studies, twin studies, and adoptee studies. There appears to be a stronger relationship between the IQ scores of adopted children and those of their biological parents than between the children's scores and those of their adoptive parents. Studies generally suggest that the heritability of intelligence is between 40% and 60%.

13. What are the environmental influences on intelligence?

Research on environmental influences on intelligence considers factors such as stereotype vulnerability, which leads many African American test-takers to self-destruct; the effects of the home environment, including styles of parenting; the effects of education, including Head Start programs; and, among adults, links to lifestyle, such as engaging in cultural activities; and even exercise. The majority of psychologists and educators believe that intelligence reflects a complex interaction of genetic factors, childhood experiences, and sociocultural factors and expectations.

PREVIEW

The Psychology of Motivation: The *Whys* of Why
▲ What does it mean to be motivated? To be driven? To need something?

Theories of Motivation: Which Why Is Which?
▲ Are we prewired to experience certain motives?
▲ Some functions of your body work like heating systems on thermostats.
▲ If your basic needs are met, will you just go to sleep?
▲ Do you have a need to understand the world around you?

Hunger: Do You Go by "Tummy-Time"?
▲ Why do you feel hungry?
▲ Why do people eat too much when they know it's no good for them?
▲ Here's the skinny on weight control.

Stimulus Motives
▲ Some motives aim to increase the tension you experience.
▲ You might find it difficult to "work" by doing nothing at all—even for $100 a day.
▲ Puppies and kittens explore their environments when they are brought into new homes.

Cognitive-Dissonance Theory: Making Things Fit
▲ People who go unrewarded for a task are more likely than those who are rewarded to think or say that what they are doing is worthwhile for its own sake.

The Three A's of Motivation: Achievement, Affiliation, and Aggression
▲ Some people strive to get ahead.
▲ Sometimes people just need people.
▲ Why do people kill, maim, and injure one another?

Emotion: Adding Color to Life
▲ Can you read the facial expressions of people in foreign cultures to tell whether they are happy or sad?
▲ Smiling can make you feel better.
▲ How do you *feel*?
▲ Do you know what lie detectors detect?

Foods That
Cause
You
To Lose
Weight

The
Negative
Calorie
Effect

Self-
Actualization

Esteem
Achievement, competence,
approval, recognition,
prestige, status

Love and Belongingness
Intimate relationships,
social groups,
friends

Safety
Protection from environment, housing,
clothing, crime security

Physiological
Hunger, thirst, elimination, warmth, fatigue,
pain avoidance, sexual release

External stimulus

External
stimulus

Physiological
arousal

Interpretation of arousal
according to situation

Processing by brain

Experiencing the emotion

Cannon–Bard

CHAPTER 9

Motivation and Emotion

TRUTH ❑ FICTION?

◢ Birds who have been reared without ever seeing another bird or a nest will still build nests during the mating season.

◢ More than half of adult Americans are overweight.

◢ Americans overeat by enough to feed the nation of Germany.

◢ Getting away from it all by going on a vacation from all sensory input for a few hours is relaxing.

◢ We appreciate things more when we have to work for them.

◢ Efficient, skillful employees are evaluated more highly than hard-working employees who must struggle to get the job done.

◢ Misery loves company.

◢ A good way to prevent harmful aggression is to encourage the venting of aggressive impulses through activities such as cheering on a football team or attending a prize fight.

◢ Smiling can produce pleasant feelings.

◢ You may be able to fool a lie detector by wiggling your toes.

The Seekers were quite a group. Their brave leader, Marian Keech, dutifully recorded the messages that she believed were sent to her by the Guardians from outer space. One particular message was somewhat disturbing. It specified that the world would come to an end on December 21. A great flood would engulf Lake City, the home of Ms. Keech and many of her faithful followers.

A second message brought good news, however. Ms. Keech received word that the Seekers would be rescued from the flood. You see, Ms. Keech reported that she received messages through "automatic writing." The messengers would communicate through her: She would write down their words, supposedly without awareness. This bit of writing was perfectly clear: The Seekers would be saved by flying saucers at the stroke of midnight on the 21st.

In their classic observational study, Leon Festinger and his colleagues (1956) described how they managed to be present in Ms. Keech's household at the fateful hour by pretending to belong to the group. Their purpose was to observe the behavior of the Seekers during and following (what they assumed would be) the prophecy's failure.

Let us return to the moment of truth. Many Seekers had quit their jobs and gone on spending sprees before the anticipated end. Now they were all gathered together. As midnight approached they fidgeted, awaiting the flying saucers. Midnight came, but no saucers. Anxious glances were exchanged. Silence. Coughs. A few minutes passed, tortuously slowly. Watches were checked, more glances exchanged. At 4:00 A.M. a bitter and frantic Ms. Keech complained that she sensed that members of the group were doubting her. At 4:45 A.M., however, she seemed suddenly relieved. A third message was arriving, and Ms. Keech was spelling it out through automatic writing! The Seekers, it turned out, had managed to save the world through their faith. The universal powers had decided to let the world travel on along its sinful way for a while longer. Why? Because of the faith of the Seekers, there was hope!

You guessed it. The faith of most of those present was renewed. They called wire services and newspapers to spread the word. All but three psychologists from the University of Minnesota. They went home, weary but enlightened, and wrote a book entitled *When Prophecy Fails*, which serves as one of the key documents of cognitive-motivational theory.

What about Mr. Keech? He was a tolerant sort. He slept through it all.

▲ **REFLECT**
Are you surprised at the reactions of the Seekers to their leader's failure at prophecy? Why or why not?

THE PSYCHOLOGY OF MOTIVATION: THE *WHYS* OF WHY

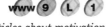

CLICK4™ *online articles about motivation theory and practice.*

Festinger was working on a cognitive theory of motivation called **cognitive-dissonance theory.** The theory suggested that when the prophecy failed, the Seekers would be caught between two key conflicting cognitions: (1) Ms. Keech is a prophet, and (2) Ms. Keech is wrong. Ms. Keech, as it happened, was shown to be wrong. How did the seekers resolve the conflict? One way would have been for the Seekers to lose faith in Ms. Keech—and in their own judgment in following her. But the researchers argued that such a course might be humiliating. (Who likes to admit that he or she has been a fool?) Still, according to cognitive-dissonance theory, the Seekers needed some way to resolve the conflict. Thus they apparently jumped at the "solution" of accepting the "truthfulness" of Ms. Keech's third message—the message that their faith had saved the world. It is good for the self-esteem to save the world now and then. The Seekers went out to spread the word and find additional converts.

The Seekers were *motivated* to resolve the conflict. They *needed* to maintain their self-esteem. They were *driven* to find a way out. They could not ignore the *incentive* provided by accepting Ms. Keech's third message: it erased the conflict and showed that they, the Seekers, retained the special status.

Questions: What is the psychology of motivation? What are motives, needs, drives, and incentives? The psychology of motivation concerns the *whys* of behavior. Why do people do this or that? Let us begin our journey with some definitions. **Motives** are hypothetical states within an organism that activate behavior and propel the organism toward goals. Why do we say "hypothetical states"? Because motives are not

Cognitive-dissonance theory ▲ The view that we are motivated to make our cognitions or beliefs consistent.

Motive ▲ A hypothetical state within an organism that propels the organism toward a goal. (From the Latin *movere*, meaning "to move.")

seen and measured directly. Like many other psychological concepts, they are inferred from behavior. Psychologists assume that motives give rise to behavior. Motives may take the form of *needs*, *drives*, and *incentives*.

Psychologists speak of physiological and psychological **needs.** We must meet physiological needs to survive. Examples include the needs for oxygen, food, drink, pain avoidance, proper temperature, and elimination of waste products. Some physiological needs, such as hunger and thirst, are states of physical deprivation. When we have not eaten or drunk for a while, we develop needs for food and water. The body also has needs for oxygen, vitamins, minerals, and so on.

Examples of psychological needs are the needs for achievement, power, self-esteem, social approval, and belonging. Psychological needs differ from physiological needs in two ways. First, psychological needs are not necessarily based on states of deprivation. A person with a need for achievement may already have a history of successful achievements. Second, psychological needs may be acquired through experience, or learned. By contrast, physiological needs reside in the physical makeup of the organism. Because our biological makeups are similar, we all share similar physiological needs. However, we are influenced by our sociocultural milieu, and our needs may be expressed in diverse ways. All people need food, for example, but some prefer a vegetarian diet whereas others prefer meat. Because learning enters into psychological needs, these needs can differ markedly from one person to the next.

Needs give rise to **drives.** Depletion of food gives rise to the hunger drive, and depletion of liquids gives rise to the thirst drive. **Physiological drives** are the psychological counterparts of physiological needs. When we have gone without food and water, our body may *need* these substances. However, our *experience* of the drives of hunger and thirst is psychological. Drives arouse us to action. Our drive levels tend to be greater the longer we have been deprived. Thus, we are usually more highly aroused by the hunger drive when we have not eaten for several hours than when we have not eaten for, say, 5 minutes.

Psychological needs for approval, achievement, and belonging also give rise to drives. We can be driven to get ahead in the business world just as surely as we can be driven to eat. The drives for achievement and power consume the daily lives of many people.

An **incentive** is an object, person, or situation that is perceived as being capable of satisfying a need or as desirable for its own sake. Money, food, a sexually attractive person, social approval, and attention can all act as incentives that motivate behavior.

In the following section, we explore theories of motivation. We ask: Just what is so motivating about motives?

Leon Festinger

Stanley Schachter

Leon Festinger and Stanley Schachter

For seven weeks, Festinger and two colleagues, Henry Riecken and Stanley Schachter, were undercover agents pretending to be true followers of Marian Keech, the leader of the Seekers. When Ms. Keech asked for their names, Schachter—with what Hunt (1993) calls an "irrepressible sense of humor"—said "Leon Festinger." Stunned, Festinger took the name of Stanley Schachter. The twosome had to maintain each others' names throughout their relationship with Ms. Keech and the Seekers.

Hunt characterizes Festinger as "a peppery fellow, . . . a lover of cribbage and chess, both of which he played with fierce competitiveness. Festinger had the tough, brash, aggressive spirit so often found in men who grew up between the world wars on the tempestuous Lower East Side of New York" (p. 406). He describes Schachter as a "bluff, craggy-faced man with a zany sense of humor and . . . a taste for daring and deceptive experimentation" (p. 497).

Festinger is best known for his research on cognitive dissonance. We will see more of Schachter's "daring and deceptive experimentation" later in the chapter, where we discuss the role of cognitive appraisal in emotional states.

CLICK4™ *the classic article by L. Festinger and J. M. Carlsmith, "Cognitive Consequences of Forced Compliance."*

THEORIES OF MOTIVATION: WHICH WHY IS WHICH?

Although psychologists agree that it is important to understand why humans and lower animals do things, they do not agree about the precise nature of motivation. Let us consider four theoretical perspectives on motivation.

The Biological Perspective: "Doing What Comes Naturally"

The biological perspective considers the roles of the nervous system, the endocrine system (hormones), and evolution and heredity in behavior and mental processes. For example, animals tend to be neurally "prewired"—that is, born with preprogrammed

Need ▲ A state of deprivation.
Drive ▲ A condition of arousal in an organism that is associated with a need.
Physiological drives ▲ Unlearned drives with a biological basis, such as hunger, thirst, and avoidance of pain.
Incentive ▲ An object, person, or situation perceived as being capable of satisfying a need.

A Fixed-Action Pattern (FAP).
In the presence of another male, Siamese fighting fish assume threatening stances in which they extend their fins and gills and circle each other. If neither male retreats, there will be a conflict. FAPs are considered to be inborn, or instinctive. Do humans have instincts? If so, what are they?

CLICK4™ *a WebSearch activity on instinctual response to pheromones.*

Instinct ▲ An inherited disposition to activate specific behavior patterns that are designed to reach certain goals.
Pheromones ▲ Chemical secretions detected by other members of the same species that stimulate stereotypical behaviors.

tendencies—to respond to certain situations in certain ways. Birds reared in isolation from other birds build nests during the mating season even though they have never observed another bird building a nest or, for that matter, seen a nest. Siamese fighting fish reared in isolation from other fish assume stereotypical threatening stances and attack other males when they are introduced into their tank.

These behaviors are found in particular species. They are *species-specific*. **Question: What is meant by species-specific behaviors?** Species-specific behaviors do not rely on learning. They are also called **instincts,** or *fixed-action patterns* (FAPs). FAPs occur in response to stimuli called *releasers*. Spiders spin webs instinctively. Bees "dance" instinctively to communicate the location of food to other bees. All of this activity is inborn. It is genetically transmitted from generation to generation.

CONTROVERSY ✦ IN PSYCHOLOGY

Do People Respond Instinctively to Pheromones?

For centuries people have searched for a love potion—a magical formula that could make other people fall in love with them or be strongly attracted to them. Some scientists suggest that such potions may already exist in the form of chemical secretions known as **pheromones.** Responses to pheromones would be instinctive. That is, pheromones would release certain fixed action patterns. Do pheromones release instinctive sexual responses in humans? Let us consider the research evidence.

Pheromones are odorless chemicals that are detected through a "sixth sense"—the *vomeronasal organ (VNO)*. People possess such an organ, located in the mucous lining of the nose (Rodriguez et al., 2000). During the embryonic period, the VNO acts as a pathway for sex hormones into the brain, aiding in sexual differentiation (Rodriguez et al., 2000). But prior to birth, the VNO in humans shrinks and there is debate about whether it stops working. If it does continue to work, it might detect pheromones and communicate information about them to the hypothalamus, where certain pheromones might affect sexual response (Cutler, 1999). People might also use pheromones in many ways. Infants might use them to recognize their mothers, and adults might respond to them in seeking a mate. Research clearly shows that lower animals use pheromones to stimulate sexual response, organize food gathering, maintain pecking orders, sound alarms, and mark territories (Cutler, 1999). Pheromones induce mating behavior in insects. Male rodents such as mice are extremely sensitive to several kinds of pheromones (Leinders-Zufall et al., 2000). Male rodents show less sexual arousal when their sense of smell is blocked, but the role of pheromones in sexual behavior becomes less vital as one moves upward through the ranks of the animal kingdom.

So what about humans? In a typical study, Winnifred Cutler and her colleagues (1998) had men wear a suspected male pheromone, whereas a control group wore a placebo. The men using the pheromone increased their frequency of sexual intercourse with their female partners but did not increase the frequency of masturbation. The researchers conclude that the substance increased the sexual attractiveness of the men to their partners, although they do not claim that it directly stimulated sexual behavior. In fact, it has not been conclusively shown that pheromones—or suspected pheromones—directly affect the behavior of people at all (Wysocki & Preti, 1998).

Even so, some other studies are also of interest. Consider a couple of double-blind studies that exposed men and women to certain steroids (androstadienone produced by males and estratetraenol produced by females) suspected of being pheromones. They found that both steroids enhanced the moods of women but not of men; the substances also apparently reduced feelings of nervousness and tension in women, but again, not in men (Grosser et al., 2000; Jacob & McClintock, 2000). The findings about estratetraenol are not terribly surprising. This substance is related to estrogen, and women tend to function best during the time of the month when estrogen levels are highest (Ross et al., 2000). The fact that the women responded positively to the androstadienone is of somewhat greater interest. It suggests that women may generally feel somewhat better when they are around men (although my wife believes this is nonsense), even if the chemical substances that may be connected with their moods do not have direct sexual effects. Of course, being in a good (or better) mood could indirectly contribute to a woman's interest in sex. By the way, androstadienone is found on underarm skin and hair in men, so we appreciate the dedication of the humans who have participated in these studies. (Actually, I jest. The steroid itself is odorless.)

If the current studies stand up to the scrutiny of replication and time, we may conclude that certain substances might enhance the moods of women and thus make them more receptive to sexual advances. Still, the substances do not "release" sexual fixed-action patterns. They do not directly stimulate behavior, as pheromones do with lower animals. If pheromones with such effects on humans exist, they have not yet been isolated. And they may not exist, because the higher we go up the evolutionary ladder, the less important is the role of prewired (instinctive) behavior.

The question generally arises whether humans have instincts, and if so, how many. A century ago, psychologists William James (1890) and William McDougall (1908) argued that humans have instincts that foster self-survival and social behavior. James asserted that we have social instincts such as love, sympathy, and modesty. McDougall compiled 12 "basic" instincts, including hunger, sex, and self-assertion. Other psychologists have made longer lists, and still others deny that people have any instincts. The question remains unresolved.

Sigmund Freud also used the term *instincts* to refer to physiological needs in humans. He believed that the instincts of sex and aggression give rise to *psychic energy*, which is perceived as a feeling of tension. Tension motivates us to restore ourselves to a calmer, resting state. The specific behavior patterns we use to reduce the tension—for example, using a weapon or a push when acting aggressively—are largely learned.

DIVERSITY ***Heredity, Hormones, Aggression, and Sex*** During prenatal development, genes and sex hormones are responsible for the physical development of female and male sex organs. Sex hormones may also "masculinize" or "feminize" the embryonic brain by creating tendencies to behave in some stereotypical ways (Bailey et al., 2000). For example, testosterone, the male sex hormone, is apparently connected with feelings of self-confidence, high activity levels, and—the negative side—aggressiveness (Pope et al., 2000; Sullivan, 2000). It also appears that deficiencies in testosterone, as found among many older men and men with health problems such as infection with the AIDS virus, are connected with feelings of depression (Barrett-Connor et al., 1999; Sullivan, 2000). Moreover, hormone replacement therapy (that is, injections of testosterone) is often helpful in treating depression among these groups (Sullivan, 2000; Yates, 2000). Similarly, low levels of estrogen, as experienced prior to and during menstruation, are frequently connected with depression and low activity levels among women (Friedrich, 2000; McGrath et al., 1990).

Sex hormones are also known to affect the sex drive. Research with men who produce little testosterone—due either to age or to health problems—show increased sex drive when they receive testosterone (Sullivan, 2000; Yates, 2000). The most common sexual problem among women is lack of sexual desire or interest. Although men produce 10 to 20 times the testosterone produced by women, women produce androgens ("male" sex hormones) in the adrenal glands, and the sex drive in women is also connected with testosterone levels (Friedrich, 2000). Research also shows that the administration of testosterone can heighten the sex drive in women who do not produce enough of the hormone themselves (Tuiten et al., 2000). Therefore, sex hormones have been shown to be connected with sexual motivation and with mood (emotional response) in both women and men.

Drive-Reductionism and Homeostasis: "Steady, Steady . . ."

Freud asserted that tension motivates us to behave in ways that restore ourselves to a resting state. His views are similar to those of the **drive-reduction theory** of learning, as set forth by psychologist Clark Hull in the 1930s. ***Questions: What is drive-reduction theory? How is it related to homeostasis?***

According to Hull, **primary drives** such as hunger, thirst, and pain trigger arousal (tension) and activate behavior. We learn to engage in behaviors that reduce the drives.

www 9 L 7
CLICK4™ *a profile of William McDougall.*

▲ **REFLECT**
Do you know people who cannot accumulate enough money? What do you think motivates them?

Drive-reduction theory ▲ The view that organisms learn to engage in behaviors that have the effect of reducing drives.
Primary drives ▲ Unlearned, or physiological, drives.

Through association, we also learn **acquired drives.** We may acquire a drive for money because money enables us to obtain food, drink, and homes, which protect us from predators and extremes of temperature. We might acquire drives for social approval and affiliation because other people, and their good will, help us reduce primary drives, especially when we are infants. In all cases, reduction of tension is the goal. Yet some people appear to acquire what could be considered excessive drives for money or affiliation. They gather money apparently for its own sake, long after they have obtained the things that money can buy, and some people find it difficult to be alone, even briefly.

Primary drives like hunger are triggered when we are in a state of deprivation. Sensations of hunger motivate us to act in ways that will restore the bodily balance. This tendency to maintain a steady state is called **homeostasis.** Homeostasis works much like a thermostat. When the temperature in a room drops below the set point, the heating system is triggered. The heat stays on until the set point is reached. Similarly, most animals eat until they are no longer hungry. (The fact that many people eat "recreationally"—for example, when they are presented with an appealing dessert—suggests that there is more to eating than drive reduction.)

Humanistic Theory: "I've Got to Be Me"

CLICK4™ *an essay assignment on the humanistic theory of motivation.*

Humanistic psychologists, particularly Abraham Maslow, note that the instinct and drive-reduction theories of motivation are defensive. These theories suggest that human behavior is rather mechanical and aimed toward survival and reduction of tension. *Question: How does humanistic theory differ from the instinct and drive-reduction theories of motivation?*

As a humanist, Maslow believed that people are also motivated by the conscious desire for personal growth. Humanists note that people tolerate pain, hunger, and many other sources of tension to obtain personal fulfillment.

Maslow believed that we are separated from lower animals by our capacity for **self-actualization,** or self-initiated striving to become whatever we believe we are capable of being. Maslow considered self-actualization to be as important a need in humans as hunger. The need for self-actualization pushes people to strive to become concert pianists, chief executive officers, or best-selling authors.

Maslow (1970) organized human needs into a hierarchy. *Question: What is Maslow's hierarchy of needs?* Maslow's hierarchy ranges from physiological needs such as hunger and thirst, through self-actualization (see Figure 9.1). He believed that we naturally strive to travel up through this hierarchy. Maslow's hierarchy consists of the following sets of needs:

> ▲ **REFLECT**
> College students frequently *like* humanistic theory more than they like instinct theory or drive-reductionism. Why do you think this is so?

1. *Physiological needs:* hunger, thirst, elimination, warmth, fatigue, pain avoidance, sexual release.
2. *Safety needs:* protection from the environment through housing and clothing; security from crime and financial hardship.
3. *Love and belongingness needs:* love and acceptance through intimate relationships, social groups, and friends. Maslow believed that in a generally well-fed society such as ours, much frustration stems from failure to meet needs at this level.
4. *Esteem needs:* achievement, competence, approval, recognition, prestige, status.
5. *Self-actualization:* fulfillment of our unique potentials. For many individuals, self-actualization involves needs for cognitive understanding (novelty, exploration, knowledge) and aesthetic needs (music, art, poetry, beauty, order).

> ▲ **REFLECT**
> Where would you place yourself in Maslow's hierarchy? Where do you see yourself as being headed? Why?

Cognitive Theory: "I Think, Therefore I Am Consistent"

> *The brain within its groove*
> *Runs evenly and true . . .*
>
> —*Emily Dickinson*

"I think, therefore I am," said the French philosopher René Descartes. If he had been a cognitive psychologist, he might have said, "I think, therefore I am *consistent."*

Acquired drives ▲ Drives acquired through experience, or learned.
Homeostasis ▲ The tendency of the body to maintain a steady state.
Self-actualization ▲ According to Maslow and other humanistic psychologists, self-initiated striving to become what one is capable of being. The motive for reaching one's full potential, for expressing one's unique capabilities.

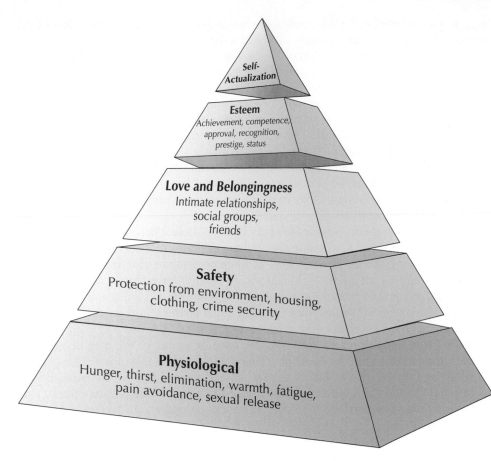

FIGURE 9.1   Maslow's Hierarchy of Needs.
Maslow believed we progress toward higher psychological needs once basic survival needs have been met. Where do you fit in this picture?

Cognitive theorists note that people represent their worlds mentally. They hypothesize that people are born scientists who strive to understand the world so that they can predict and control events. *Question: Why are people motivated to eliminate inconsistencies in their worldviews?* The answer seems to be that people must represent the world accurately in order to predict and control events.

For example, Albert Bandura (Bussey & Bandura, 1999) and Sandra Bem (1993) suggest that children try to create consistency between their own gender and what experience teaches them that boys and girls are expected to do. As soon as children know whether they are male or female, they imitate the behavior of adults of the same gender. Leon Festinger (1957) believed that people are generally motivated to hold consistent beliefs and to justify their behavior. That is why we are more likely to appreciate what we must work to obtain.

Evaluation of Theories of Motivation

There are thus various perspectives on motivation. *Question: How do we make sense of all these different views of motivation?* Let us evaluate these views to see which one or ones seem to be most logical and most consistent with the research evidence.

There is no question that motivation and emotion are connected with organisms' biology. Many animals are born with preprogrammed tendencies to respond to certain situations in certain ways. Yet instinct theory has been criticized for providing circular explanations of human behavior. In a circular explanation, we say that one thing (A) causes another (B); then, when we see B, we say it is occurring because of A. For example, we might argue a maternal instinct (A) causes mothers to care for their children (B); then we observe a mother caring for her child (B) and accept her behavior as proof of the existence of the maternal instinct (A). We have really just come full circle and explained nothing. As another example, consider William James's notion that sympathy is an instinct.

Many people are cruel and cold-hearted; are we to assume that they possess less of this "instinct"? Such an explanation would also be circular.

Then, too, there is the question of how important preprogrammed tendencies are in human beings. Some behaviors, including reflexes and the development of attachment in infants, may be considered instinctive (Ainsworth & Bowlby, 1991). It also appears that sex hormones are connected with the development of behavior patterns and mental processes. They may influence most males and most females in the direction of stereotypical "masculine" or "feminine" behavior patterns. On the other hand, there is so much variation in human behavior and mental processes that it would also appear to be learned, planned, or influenced by cultural values. Still, we should not neglect the roles of sex hormones in problems such as low sex drive (a motivational issue) and feelings of depression (an emotional issue). Ignoring biology in such instances may prevent individuals from obtaining effective treatment.

Drive-reduction theory appears to apply in physiological drives such as hunger and thirst. However, we often eat when we are not hungry! Drive reduction also runs aground when we consider evidence showing that we often act in ways that *increase*, rather than decrease, the tensions acting on us. When we are hungry, for example, we may take the time to prepare a gourmet meal instead of a snack, even though the snack would satisfy the hunger drive sooner. We drive fast cars, ride roller coasters, and sky dive for sport—all activities that heighten rather than decrease arousal.

People and many lower animals also seek novel stimulation. We may be willing to try a new dish ("just a taste") even when we feel full. We often seek novel ways of doing things—shunning the tried and the true—because of the novelty. Yet the familiar tried-and-true ways would reduce tension more reliably. In view of examples like these, some psychologists have theorized the existence of stimulus motives that outweigh the motivation to reduce drives.

Critics of Maslow's theory argue that there is too much individual variation for the hierarchy of motives to apply to everyone. Some people whose physiological, safety, and love needs are met show little interest in achievement and recognition. Some artists, musicians, and writers devote themselves fully to their art, even if they have to live in an attic or basement to do so. However, people do appear to seek distant, self-actualizing goals, even while exposing themselves to great danger. This behavior is certainly more consistent with a humanistic than a drive-reductionist explanation of human behavior.

Some psychologists criticize cognitive theory for its reliance on unobservable concepts such as mental representations rather than observable behavior. However, cognitive psychologists tie their concepts to observable behavior, whenever possible. It also appears to be difficult to explain a child's active efforts to experiment with and understand other people and the world without resorting to cognitive concepts (Meltzoff & Gopnik, 1997).

Each theory of motivation may have something to offer. Each might apply to certain aspects of behavior. As the chapter progresses, we will describe research that lends support to each theory. Let us first describe research on the hunger drive. Hunger is based on physiological needs, and drive reduction would appear to explain some—although not all—eating behavior.

REVIEW

(1) _____ are hypothetical states that activate behavior and direct organisms toward goals. (2) Physiological needs generally reflect states of physical _____. (3) An _____ is an object, person, or situation that is perceived as being capable of satisfying a need. (4) According to the _____ theory of motivation, animals are born with preprogrammed tendencies to behave in certain ways. (5) According to Hull's theory, rewards are pleasant because they reduce _____. (6) Drives help the body maintain a steady state, a tendency that is called _____. (7) Humanistic psychologist Maslow argued that people have a hierarchy of needs, the highest of which is the need for _____. (8) _____ psychologists suggest that people strive to predict and control events.

Pulling It Together: Does the research evidence show that people have instincts? Explain.

HUNGER: DO YOU GO BY "TUMMY-TIME"?

I go by tummy-time and I want my dinner.

—*Sir Winston Churchill*

We need food to survive, but to many of us food means more than survival. Food is a symbol of family togetherness and caring. We associate food with the nurturance of the parent–child relationship, with visits home during holidays. Friends and relatives offer us food when we enter their homes, and saying no may be viewed as a personal rejection. Bacon and eggs, coffee with cream and sugar, meat and mashed potatoes—all seem to be part of sharing U.S. values and agricultural abundance. *Questions: What bodily mechanisms regulate the hunger drive? What psychological processes are at work?*

Biological Influences on Hunger

In considering the bodily mechanisms that regulate hunger, let us begin with the mouth. This is an appropriate choice because we are discussing eating. Chewing and swallowing provide some sensations of **satiety,** or satisfaction with the amount eaten. If they did not, we might eat for a long time after we had taken in enough food. It takes the digestive tract time to metabolize food and provide signals of satiety to the brain by way of the bloodstream.

In classic "sham feeding" experiments with dogs, researchers implanted a tube in the animals' throats so that any food swallowed fell out of the dog's body. Even though no food arrived at the stomach, the animals stopped feeding after a brief period (Janowitz & Grossman, 1949). Thus the sensations of chewing and swallowing must provide some feelings of satiety. However, the dogs in the study resumed feeding sooner than animals whose food did reach the stomach. Let us proceed to the stomach, too, as we seek further regulatory factors in hunger.

The Stomach   An empty stomach leads to stomach contractions, which we call *hunger pangs.* Classic research suggested that stomach contractions are crucial to hunger. A man (A. L. Washburn) swallowed a balloon that was inflated in his stomach. His stomach contractions squeezed the balloon, so the contractions could be recorded by observers. Washburn also pressed a key when he felt hungry, and the researchers found a correspondence between his stomach contractions and his feelings of hunger (Cannon & Washburn, 1912).

But stomach contractions are not as influential as formerly thought. (We apparently go by more than "tummy-time.") Medical observations and classic research also find that people and animals whose stomachs have been removed still regulate food intake so as to maintain their normal weight (Tsang, 1938). (Food is absorbed through their intestines.) This finding led to the discovery of many other mechanisms that regulate hunger, including the hypothalamus, blood sugar level, and even receptors in the liver. When we are deprived of food, the level of sugar in the blood drops. The drop in blood sugar is communicated to the hypothalamus and apparently indicates that we have been burning energy and need to replenish it by eating.

The Hypothalamus   If you were just reviving from a surgical operation, fighting your way through the fog of the anesthesia, food would probably be the last thing on your mind. But when a researcher uses a probe to destroy the **ventromedial nucleus** (VMN) of a rat's hypothalamus, the rat will grope toward food as soon as its eyes open. Then it eats vast quantities of Purina Rat Chow or whatever.

The VMN seems to be able to function like a "stop-eating center" in the rat's brain. If the VMN is electrically stimulated—that is, "switched on"—the rat stops eating until the current is turned off. When the VMN is destroyed, the rat becomes **hyperphagic.** It continues to eat until it has about doubled its normal weight. Then it will level off its eating rate and maintain the higher weight. It is as if the set point of the stop-eating center

Hunger.
How do *you* feel while waiting for someone to carve the meat? Hunger is a physiological drive that motivates us to eat. Why do we feel hungry? Why do we feel satiated? Why do many people continue to eat when they have already supplied their bodies with the needed nutrients?

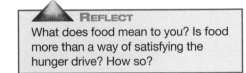

REFLECT
What does food mean to you? Is food more than a way of satisfying the hunger drive? How so?

REFLECT
How do you know when you are hungry? What do you experience?

CLICK4™ *Web sites on obesity, health, and weight management.*

Satiety ▲ The state of being satisfied; fullness.
Ventromedial nucleus ▲ A central area on the underside of the hypothalamus that appears to function as a stop-eating center.
Hyperphagic ▲ Characterized by excessive eating.

A Hyperphagic Rat.
This rodent winner of the basketball look-alike contest went on a binge after it received a lesion in the ventromedial nucleus (VMN) of the hypothalamus. It is as if the lesion pushed the "set point" for body weight up several notches; the rat's weight is now about five times normal. But now it eats only enough to maintain its pleasantly plump stature, so you need not be concerned that it will eventually burst. If the lesion had been made in the lateral hypothalamus, the animal might have become the "Twiggy" of the rat world.

www 9 L 8

CLICK4™ *an online calculator that will help you determine your Body Mass Index (BMI).*

has been raised to a higher level, like turning up the thermostat in a house from 65°F degrees to 70°F. Hyperphagic rats are also more finicky. They eat more fats or sweet-tasting food, but if their food is salty or bitter they actually eat less. Some people develop tumors near the base of the brain, damaging the VMN and apparently causing them to overeat and grow obese (Miller, 1995).

The **lateral hypothalamus** may function like a "start-eating center." If you electrically stimulate the lateral hypothalamus, the rat starts to eat (Miller, 1995). If you destroy the lateral hypothalamus, the rat may stop eating altogether—that is, become **aphagic.** If you force-feed an aphagic rat for a while, however, it begins to eat on its own and levels off at a relatively low body weight. It is as if you have lowered the rat's set point. It is like turning down the thermostat from, say, 70°F to 40°F.

Psychological Influences on Hunger

Although many areas of the body work in concert to regulate the hunger drive, this is only part of the story. In human beings, the hunger drive is more complex. Psychological as well as physiological factors play an important role. How many times have you been made hungry by the sight or aroma of food? How many times have you eaten not because you were hungry but because you were at a relative's home or hanging around in a cafeteria? Or because you felt anxious or depressed? Or simply because you were bored? The next section further explores psychological factors that affect eating.

Obesity — A Serious and Pervasive Problem

There is no sincerer love than the love of food.

—*George Bernard Shaw*

The two biggest sellers in any bookstore are the cookbooks and the diet books. The cookbooks tell you how to prepare the food and the diet books tell you how not to eat any of it.

—*Andy Rooney*

Consider some facts about obesity:

▲ More than half of adult Americans are overweight according to the National Body Mass Index (BMI[1]) guidelines, and 18% are obese—that is, more than 30% above their BMI ideal (Mokdad et al., 2000).

▲ Flab is on the upswing in the United States; for example, 38% of Californians were overweight in 1984, as compared with 45% in 1990 and 53% in 1999 (Californians losing fight, 2000).

▲ Nearly half of African American women are obese, possibly because they have lower metabolic rates than European American women (Brody, 1997).

▲ Americans eat more than a total of 800 billion calories of food each day (200 billion calories more than they need to maintain their weights). The extra calories could feed a nation of 80 million people.

▲ About 300,000 Americans die each year because of excess weight (Pinel et al., 2000).

▲ Weight control is elusive for most people, who regain most of the weight they have lost, even when they have dieted "successfully" (Jeffery et al., 2000a).

American culture idealizes slender heroes and heroines. For those who "more than measure up" to TV and film idols, food may have replaced sex as the central source of guilt. Obese people encounter more than their fair share of illnesses, including heart disease,

Lateral hypothalamus ▲ An area at the side of the hypothalamus that appears to function as a start-eating center.
Aphagic ▲ Characterized by undereating.

[1]You can calculate your Body Mass Index as follows: Write down your weight in pounds. Multiply it by 703. Divide the product by your height in inches squared. For example, if you weigh 160 lbs and are 5′8″ tall, your BMI is $(160 \times 703)/68^2$, or 24.33. A BMI of more than 25 is defined as overweight.

stroke, diabetes, gall bladder disease, gout, respiratory problems, even certain kinds of cancer (Pinel et al., 2000). *Question: If obesity is connected with health problems and unhappiness with the image in the mirror, why are so many people overweight?* Research has contributed to our understanding of obesity and what can be done about it.

Biological Factors in Obesity

Numerous biological factors are involved in obesity, including heredity, adipose tissue (body fat), and the metabolism (the rate at which the individual converts calories to energy).

Obesity runs in families. It was once assumed that obese parents encouraged their children to be overweight by serving fattening foods and setting poor examples. However, a study of Scandinavian adoptees by Stunkard and his colleagues (1990) found that children bear a closer resemblance in weight to their biological parents than to their adoptive parents. Today it is widely accepted that heredity plays a role in obesity (Devlin et al., 2000).

The efforts of obese people to maintain a slender profile may also be sabotaged by microscopic units of life within their own bodies: fat cells. No, fat cells are not overweight cells. They are adipose tissue, or cells that store fat. Hunger might be related to the amount of fat stored in these cells. As time passes after a meal, the blood sugar level drops. Fat is then drawn from these cells to provide further nourishment. At some point, referred to as the *set point*, fat deficiency in these cells is communicated to the hypothalamus, triggering the hunger drive.

People with more adipose tissue than others feel food-deprived earlier, even though they may be equal in weight. This might occur because more signals are being sent to the brain. Obese and *formerly* obese people tend to have more adipose tissue than people of normal weight. Thus many people who have lost weight complain that they are always hungry when they try to maintain normal weight levels.

Fatty tissue also metabolizes (burns) food more slowly than muscle does. For this reason, a person with a high fat-to-muscle ratio metabolizes food more slowly than a person of the same weight with a lower fat-to-muscle ratio. That is, two people who are identical in weight metabolize food at different rates, depending on the distribution of muscle and fat in their bodies. Obese people therefore are doubly handicapped in their efforts to lose weight—not only by their extra weight but by the fact that much of their body is composed of adipose tissue.

In a sense, the normal distribution of fat cells could be considered "sexist." The average man is 40% muscle and 15% fat. The average woman is 23% muscle and 25% fat. If a man and a woman with typical distributions of muscle and fat are of equal weight, therefore, the woman—who has more fat cells—has to eat less to maintain that weight.

Ironically, the very act of dieting can make it progressively more difficult to lose additional weight. This is because people on diets and those who have lost substantial amounts of weight burn fewer calories. That is, their metabolic rates slow down (Schwartz & Seeley, 1997; Wadden et al., 1997). This appears to be a built-in mechanism that helps preserve life in times of famine. However, it also makes it more difficult for dieters to continue to lose weight. The pounds seem to come off more and more reluctantly.

Psychological Factors in Obesity

> We are in real trouble. Having a culture bombarded with rushed lifestyles, fast foods, and physical inactivity has caught up with us.
> —*Carmen Nevarez, vice president of the Berkeley, California, Public Health Institute (Californians losing fight, 2000)*

Psychological factors, such as observational learning, stress, and emotional states, also "bombard" us and play a role in obesity (Greeno & Wing, 1994). Children in the United States are exposed to an average of 10,000 food commercials a year. More than 9 of 10 of these commercials are for fast foods (like McDonald's fries), sugared cereals, candy, and soft drinks (Brownell, 1997). Situations also play a role. Family celebrations, watching

REFLECT

Is your weight similar to that of other family members? If so, why?

CLICK4™ *a WebSearch activity on weight control programs.*

REFLECT

If you have difficulty controlling your weight, which of the behavior patterns discussed in the text seem to be contributing to the problem? What can you do about it?

TV, arguments, and tension at work can all lead to overeating or going off a diet (Drapkin et al., 1995). Efforts to diet may be also impeded by negative emotions like depression and anxiety, which can lead to binge eating (Cools et al., 1992; Stice et al., 2000).

CLICK4™ *"Tips for Students Who Eat on the Run."*

DIVERSITY   *Sociocultural Factors in Obesity*   Rates of obesity differ between ethnic groups in our society. Obesity is more prevalent among people of color, especially African Americans, Latino and Latina Americans, and Native Americans than it is among European Americans. Racial and ethnic differences are most pronounced among women (see Figure 9.2). The question is, why? Many of the answers might be found in socioeconomic factors and acculturation.

Socioeconomic status (SES) plays a role in obesity. Obesity is more prevalent among poorer people (Ernst & Harlan, 1991; Stunkard & Sørensen, 1993). People of color are typically of lower SES than European Americans, so rates of obesity tend to be higher among African Americans and Latino and Latina Americans, particularly among women (McMurtrie, 1994).

Psychology and Modern Life

The Skinny on Weight Control

All right, all right. Many factors — biological, psychological, and sociocultural — contribute to obesity. *Question: So what can people do to shed a few pounds?*

A Sampler of Dietary Methods.
At any given time nearly half of the adult American population is on a diet. Dieting has become the "normal" pattern of eating for women. Dozens of diets vie for attention on bookstore shelves. How can we know which ones contain truth and which ones contain fiction? Why do you think this woman (this quite slender woman!) is "surfing" books on losing weight?

REFLECT
Do you need to lose weight? (Are you sure?) What standard are you using in making this judgment?

People can do many things, but first be advised that psychologists warn that not everyone should be trying to slim down. Women in the United States today are under social pressure to conform to an unnaturally slender female ideal. As a result, they tend to set unrealistic weight loss goals (Sarwer & Wadden, 1999). Moreover, many attempts to lose weight are ineffective. For many obese people, however, especially those who are severely obese, shedding excess pounds lowers the risks of health problems such as diabetes and heart disease.

Research on motivation and on methods of therapy has enhanced our knowledge of healthful ways to lose weight. Sound weight control programs do not involve fad diets such as fasting, eliminating carbohydrates, or eating excessive amounts of one particular food (Kolata, 2000a). Instead, they involve changes in lifestyle that include improving nutritional knowledge, decreasing calorie intake, exercising, and changing eating habits (see Table 9.1).

Most people in the United States eat too much fat and not enough fruits and vegetables (Stampfer et al., 2000). Eating

TABLE 9.1 DIETARY RECOMMENDATIONS OF THE AMERICAN ACADEMY OF SCIENCES

Reduce your total fat intake to 30% or less of your total calorie intake.

Reduce your intake of saturated fats to less than 10% of your total calorie intake.

Reduce your cholesterol intake to less than 300 mg per day.

Eat 5 or more servings of vegetables and fruits each day.

Increase your intake of starches and other complex carbohydrates by eating 6 or more servings of breads, cereals, and legumes each day.

Keep your intake of protein to moderate levels.

Limit your total intake of sodium (salt) to 2,400 mg or less per day.

Maintain adequate intake of calcium.

foods low in saturated fats and cholesterol not only is good for the heart but also can contribute to weight loss. Because dietary fat is converted into bodily fat more efficiently than carbohydrates are, a low-fat diet also leads to weight loss. Nutritional knowledge leads to suggestions for taking in fewer calories, which results in lower weight. Taking in fewer calories does not just mean eating smaller portions. It means switching to some lower-calorie foods — relying more on fresh, unsweetened fruits and vegetables (eating apples rather than apple pie), fish and poultry, and skim milk and cheese. It means cutting down on — or eliminating — butter, margarine, oils, and sugar.

The same foods that help control weight also tend to be high in vitamins and fiber and low in fats. Such foods therefore

People on the lower rungs of the socioeconomic ladder appear to have a greater risk of obesity for several reasons. One is that more affluent people have greater access to information about nutrition and health. They have greater access to health care providers. The fitness boom has been largely limited to more affluent people, so that poorer people are more likely to remain sedentary. Wealthier people also have the time and income to participate in organized fitness programs. Many poor people in the inner city also turn to food as a way of coping with the stresses of poverty, discrimination, crowding, and crime.

Results from a study in San Antonio, Texas, provide clear evidence of the link between SES and obesity (Hazuda et al., 1991). Obesity is less prevalent among both Mexican Americans and European Americans who live in higher-income neighborhoods than among those living in poorer neighborhoods. In other words, the link between SES and obesity holds across ethnic groups.

Acculturation is the process by which immigrant or native groups adopt the cultural values, attitudes, and behaviors of the host or dominant society. Acculturation may help immigrant people to adapt more successfully to their new culture, but it can become a

www 9 E 2

CLICK4™ an essay assignment on eating patterns and their effect on your health.

CD 9 PML 15

CLICK4™ information on calories you burn in 1 hour.

CD 9 V 29

CLICK4™ a video on hunger and its relationship to external cues.

---

may also reduce the risk of heart disease, cancer, and other illnesses.

Dieting plus exercise is more effective than dieting alone for shedding pounds and keeping them off. When we restrict our intake of calories, our metabolic rate compensates by slowing down (Wadden et al., 1997). Exercise burns calories and builds muscle tissue, which metabolizes more calories than fatty tissue does.

Cognitive and behavioral methods have also provided many strategies for losing weight. Among them are the following:

- Establish calorie-intake goals and keep track of whether you are meeting them. Get a book that shows how many calories are found in foods. Keep a diary of your calorie intake.
- Substitute low-calorie, low-fat foods for high-calorie, high-fat foods. Fill your stomach with celery rather than cheesecake and enchiladas. Eat pre-planned low-calorie snacks instead of binge eating peanuts or ice cream.
- Take a 5-minute break between helpings. Ask yourself whether you're still hungry. If not, stop eating.
- Avoid temptations that have side-tracked you in the past. Shop at the mall with the Alfalfa Sprout Café, not the Cheesecake Factory. Plan your meal before entering a restaurant. (Avoid ogling that tempting full-color

menu.) Attend to your own plate, not to the sumptuous dish at the next table. (Your salad probably looks greener to them, anyhow.) Shop from a list. Walk briskly through the supermarket, preferably after dinner when you're no longer hungry. Don't be sidetracked by pretty packages (fattening things may come in them). Don't linger in the kitchen. Study, watch TV, or write letters elsewhere. Don't bring fattening foods into the house. Prepare only enough food to keep within your calorie goals.

- Exercise to burn more calories and increase your metabolic rate. Reach for your mate, not your plate (to coin a phrase). Take a brisk walk instead of eating an unplanned snack. Build exercise routines by adding a few minutes each week.
- Reward yourself for meeting calorie goals (but not with food). Imagine how great you'll look in that new swimsuit next summer. Do not go to the latest movie unless you have met your weekly calorie goal. When you meet your weekly calorie goal, put cash in the bank toward a vacation or a new camera.
- Use imagery to help yourself lose weight. Tempted by a fattening dish? Imagine that it's rotten, that you would be nauseated by it and have a sick taste in your mouth for the rest of the day.

- Mentally walk through solutions to problem situations. Consider what you will do when cake is handed out at the office party. Rehearse your next visit to relatives who tell you how painfully thin you look and try to stuff you with food (Drapkin et al., 1995). Imagine how you will politely (but firmly) refuse seconds and thirds, despite their objections.
- Above all, if you slip from your plan for a day, don't blow things out of proportion. Dieters are often tempted to binge, especially when they rigidly see themselves either as perfect successes or as complete failures or when they experience powerful emotions — either positive or negative (Cools et al., 1992). Consider the weekly or monthly trend, not just a single day. Credit yourself for the long-term trend. If you do binge, resume dieting the next day.

Losing weight — and keeping it off — is not easy, but it can be done. Making a commitment to losing weight and establishing a workable plan for doing so are two of the keys.

▲ REFLECT

If you need to shed some pounds, which of the strategies mentioned here are likely to work for you? Why?

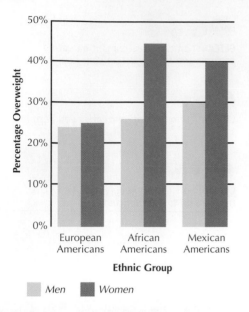

FIGURE 9.2 Prevalence of Overweight Individuals Among European Americans, African Americans, and Mexican Americans.
What factors contribute to ethnic differences in obesity?

▲ REFLECT

Do you have ways of trying to increase the stimulation impacting on you? What are they? (Hints: How about going to the movies or an amusement park?)

Stimulus motives ▲ Motives to increase the stimulation impinging upon an organism.

double-edged sword in terms of health if it involves adoption of unhealthful dietary practices of the host culture. For example, Japanese American men living in California and Hawaii eat a higher-fat diet than Japanese men living in Japan do. Not surprisingly, *the prevalence of obesity is two to three times higher among the Japanese American men than among men living in Japan* (Curb & Marcus, 1991).

Acculturation may also contribute to high rates of obesity among Native Americans, who are more likely than European Americans to have diseases linked to obesity, such as cardiovascular disease and diabetes (Broussard et al., 1991; Young & Sevenhuysen, 1989). A study of several hundred Cree and Ojibwa Indians in Canada found that nearly 90% of the women in the 45 to 54 age group were obese. The adoption of a high-fat Western-style diet, the destruction of physically demanding native industries, and chronic unemployment combined with low levels of physical activity are cited as factors contributing to obesity among Native Americans in the United States and Canada.

REVIEW

(9) Biological factors in hunger include stomach contractions, the blood _____ level, and the hypothalamus. (10) The _____ nucleus (VMN) of the hypothalamus functions as a stop-eating center. (11) The _____ hypothalamus functions as a start-eating center. (12) A study of Scandinavian adoptees found that children are closer in weight to their (biological or adoptive?) parents. (13) As time passes after a meal, the _____ sugar level drops and fat is drawn from fat cells to provide nourishment. (14) When the _____ point is reached, loss of fat is communicated to the hypothalamus, triggering hunger.

Pulling It Together: How do healthy weight control programs make use of knowledge of the hunger drive?

STIMULUS MOTIVES

One day when my daughter Taylor was 5 months old, I was batting her feet. (Why not?) She was sitting back in her mother's lap, and I repeatedly batted her feet up toward her middle with the palms of my hands. After a while, she began to laugh. When I stopped, she pushed a foot toward me, churned her arms back and forth, and blew bubbles as forcefully as she could. So I batted her feet again. She laughed and pushed them toward me again. This went on for a while, and it dawned on me that Taylor was doing what she could to make the stimulation last.

Physical needs give rise to drives like hunger and thirst. In such cases, organisms are motivated to *reduce* the tension or stimulation that impinges on them. **Question: Are all motives aimed at the reduction of tension?** No, in the case of **stimulus motives,** organisms seek to *increase* stimulation, as Taylor did when she sought to have me bat her feet. Stimulus motives include sensory stimulation, activity, exploration, and manipulation of the environment.

Some stimulus motives provide a clear evolutionary advantage. Humans and lower animals that are motivated to learn about and manipulate their environment are more likely to survive. Learning about the environment increases awareness of resources and of potential dangers, and manipulation permits one to change the environment in beneficial ways. Exploring the environment helps animals locate sources of food and places to hide from predators. Learning and manipulation thus increase the animal's chances of survival until sexual maturity and of transmitting whatever genetic codes may underlie these motives to future generations.

Sensory Stimulation and Activity

When I was a teenager during the 1950s, I was unaware that some lucky students at McGill University in Montreal were being paid $20 a day (which, with inflation, would now be well above $100) for doing absolutely nothing. Would you like to "work" by doing nothing for $100 a day? Don't answer too quickly. According to the results of classic research on sensory deprivation, you might not like it at all.   *Questions: Do we need to be active? Do we need to stimulate our senses?*

In that experiment, student volunteers in the study were placed in quiet cubicles and blindfolded (Bexton et al., 1954). Their arms were bandaged, and they could hear nothing but the dull, continuous hum of air conditioning. With nothing to do, many slept for a while. After a few hours of sensory-deprived wakefulness, most felt bored and irritable. As time went on, many grew more uncomfortable, and some reported hallucinations of images of dots and geometric shapes.

Many students quit the experiment during the first day despite the financial incentive. Many of those who remained for a few days found it hard to concentrate on simple problems for a few days afterward. For many, the experiment did not provide a relaxing vacation. Instead, it produced boredom and disorientation.

Exploration and Manipulation

Have you ever brought a dog or cat into a new home? At first, it may show excitement. New kittens are also known to hide under a couch or bed for a few hours. But then they begin to explore every corner of their new environment. When placed in novel environments, many animals appear to possess an innate motive to engage in exploratory behavior.

Question: Why do puppies and kittens explore their environments when they are brought into new homes?   Both lower animals and humans appear to be motivated to seek novel stimulation. For example, when they have not been deprived of food for a great deal of time, rats often explore unfamiliar arms of mazes rather than head straight for the section of the maze in which they have learned to expect food. Animals that have just copulated and thereby reduced their sex drives often show renewed interest in sexual behavior when presented with a novel sex partner. Monkeys learn how to manipulate gadgets for the incentive of being able to observe novel stimulation through a window. Children spend hour after hour manipulating the controls of video games for the pleasure of zapping video monsters.

CLICK4™ *the classic article by Bexton, Heron, and Scott, "Effects of Decreased Variation in Sensory Environment."*

REFLECT
Can you lie contentedly on the beach for hours, or do you get restless rather soon? What do you think your answer might mean?

CLICK4™ *a WebSearch activity on sensation seeking: What motivates you?*

REFLECT
Do you like going out for drives or walks and exploring new neighborhoods or countries? What motivates you?

The Allure of Novel Stimulation.
People and many lower animals are motivated to explore the environment and to seek novel stimulation. This monkey has learned to unlock a door for the privilege of viewing a model train.

The Sensation-Seeking Scale

Some people seek higher levels of stimulation and activity than others. John is a couch potato, content to sit by the TV set all evening. Marsha doesn't feel right unless she's out on the tennis court or jogging. Cliff isn't content unless he has ridden his motorcycle over back trails at breakneck speeds, and Janet feels exuberant when she's catching the big wave or free-fall diving from an airplane.

What about you? Are you content to read or watch television all day? Or must you catch the big wave or bounce the bike across the dunes of the Mojave Desert? Sensation-seeking scales measure the level of stimulation or arousal a person will seek.

Marvin Zuckerman and his colleagues have identified four factors that are involved in sensation seeking: (1) seeking thrill and adventure, (2) disinhibition (that is, tendency to express impulses), (3) seeking experience, and (4) susceptibility to boredom. People who are high in sensation seeking are also less tolerant of sensory deprivation. They are more likely to use drugs and become involved in sexual experiences, to be drunk in public, and to volunteer for high-risk activities and unusual experiments (Pihl & Peterson, 1992).

A shortened version of one of Zuckerman's scales follows. To gain insight into your own sensation-seeking tendencies, circle the choice, A or B, that best describes you. Then compare your answers to those in the answer key in Appendix B.

1. A. I would like a job that requires a lot of traveling.
   B. I would prefer a job in one location.

2. A. I am invigorated by a brisk, cold day.
   B. I can't wait to get indoors on a cold day.

3. A. I get bored seeing the same old faces.
   B. I like the comfortable familiarity of everyday friends.

4. A. I would prefer living in an ideal society in which everyone is safe, secure, and happy.
   B. I would have preferred living in the unsettled days of our history.

5. A. I sometimes like to do things that are a little frightening.
   B. A sensible person avoids activities that are dangerous.

6. A. I would not like to be hypnotized.
   B. I would like to have the experience of being hypnotized.

7. A. The most important goal in life is to live it to the fullest and experience as much as possible.
   B. The most important goal in life is to find peace and happiness.

8. A. I would like to try parachute jumping.
   B. I would never want to try jumping out of a plane, with or without a parachute.

9. A. I enter cold water gradually, giving myself time to get used to it.
   B. I like to dive or jump right into the ocean or a cold pool.

10. A. When I go on a vacation, I prefer the change of camping out.
    B. When I go on a vacation, I prefer the comfort of a good room and bed.

11. A. I prefer people who are emotionally expressive even if they are a bit unstable.
    B. I prefer people who are calm and even tempered.

12. A. A good painting should shock or jolt the senses.
    B. A good painting should give one a feeling of peace and security.

13. A. People who ride motorcycles must have some kind of unconscious need to hurt themselves.
    B. I would like to drive or ride a motorcycle.

www 9 SA 6

CLICK4™ *the interactive version of this Self-Assessment.*

CLICK4™ *more information about sensation seeking: Do you carry the "extreme gene"?*

CLICK4™ *a quiz covering the first half of this chapter.*

The question has arisen of whether people and animals seek to explore and manipulate their environment *because* these activities help them reduce primary drives such as hunger and thirst or whether they engage in these activities for their own sake. Many psychologists believe that such stimulating activities are reinforcing in and of themselves. Monkeys do seem to get a kick out of "monkeying around" with gadgets. They learn how to manipulate hooks and eyes and other mechanical devices without any external incentive whatsoever (Harlow et al., 1950). Young children prolong their play with "busy boxes"—boxes filled with objects that honk, squeak, rattle, and buzz when manipulated in certain ways. They seem to find discovery of the cause-and-effect relationships in these gadgets pleasurable even though they are not rewarded with food, ice cream, or even hugs from their parents.

REVIEW

(15) Stimulus motives motivate us to (increase or decrease?) the stimulation impinging upon us. (16) Studies in sensory _____ show that lack of stimulation is aversive and irritating.

Pulling It Together: How would inborn drives for exploration and manipulation provide organisms with an evolutionary advantage?

COGNITIVE-DISSONANCE THEORY: MAKING THINGS FIT

> Do I *contradict myself?*
> Very well then I *contradict myself,*
> (I *am large,* I *contain multitudes.*)
>
> —*Walt Whitman,* Song of Myself

Most of us are unlike Walt Whitman, according to cognitive-dissonance theory (Festinger, 1957; Festinger & Carlsmith, 1959). Whitman may not have minded contradicting himself, but most people do not like their attitudes (cognitions) to be inconsistent. Cognitive theorists propose that organisms are motivated to create realistic mental maps of the world. Organisms adjust their representations of the world, as needed, to make things fit. Awareness that two cognitions are dissonant, or that our attitudes are incompatible with our behavior, is unpleasant and motivates us to reduce the discrepancy.

Effort Justification: "If I Did It, It Must Be Important"?

In the first and still one of the best-known studies on cognitive dissonance, one group of participants received $1 (worth $5–$10 today) for telling someone else that a boring task was interesting (Festinger & Carlsmith, 1959). Members of a second group received $20 (worth $100–$200 today) to describe the chore positively. Both groups were paid to engage in **attitude-discrepant behavior**—that is, behavior that ran counter to their cognitions. After "selling" the job to others, the participants were asked to rate their own liking for it. Ironically, those who were paid *less* rated the task as more interesting. *Question: Why are people who go unrewarded more likely than those who are rewarded to think or say that what they are doing is worthwhile for its own sake?*

According to learning theory, this result would be confusing. Learning theory would say that the more we are reinforced for doing something, the more we should like it. But that is not what happened here. In contrast, cognitive-dissonance theory would predict this "less-leads-to-more effect" for the following reason: The cognitions "I was paid very little" and "I told someone that this assignment was interesting" are dissonant. People tend to engage in **effort justification.** The discomfort of cognitive dissonance motivates them to explain their behavior to themselves in such a way that unpleasant undertakings seem worth it. Participants who were paid only $1 may have justified their lie by concluding that they may not have been lying in the first place. Similarly, we appreciate things more when they are more difficult to obtain.

Consider another situation. Many people have very strong political beliefs and fear what might happen if the "wrong" candidate is elected to public office. They tend to see their own candidates as better for their town or state or country, and some even believe that their candidate must win to save the nation from harmful forces. They are therefore strongly motivated to believe that their candidate will be elected. They pin their hopes as well as their ideology on their candidate. Cognitive dissonance would then be created if they were to believe that their candidates were likely to lose and not to win. Research shows that in presidential elections from 1952 to 1980, 4 out of 5 people reduced such dissonance by expressing the belief that their candidate would win (Granberg & Brent, 1983). Nearly half of them were wrong, of course. Yet they often clung to their prediction

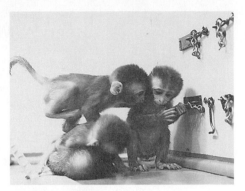

Monkeying Around.
Is there such a thing as a manipulation drive? These young rhesus monkeys appear to monkey around with gadgets just for the fun of it. No external incentives are needed. Children similarly enjoy manipulating gadgets that honk, squeak, rattle, and buzz, even though the resultant honks and squeaks do not satisfy physiological drives such as hunger or thirst.

CLICK4™ *readings on cognitive dissonance and its relationship to social psychology and propaganda.*

> ▲ **REFLECT**
> Were you ever subjected to difficult hazing upon joining a sorority, fraternity, or other kind of club? Did the experience affect your feelings about being a member of the group? How? Can you connect your experience to the concept of *effort justification?*

CLICK4™ *an essay assignment on effort justification.*

Attitude-discrepant behavior ▲ Behavior inconsistent with an attitude that may have the effect of modifying an attitude.

Effort justification ▲ In cognitive-dissonance theory, the tendency to seek justification (acceptable reasons) for strenuous efforts.

Henry A. Murray

His psychoanalysis with Carl Jung was an "explosive experience" from which he emerged "a reborn man." Henry Murray (1893–1988) had taken many years to find himself. In his youth he stuttered. At college he began as a history major. Then he completed medical school and specialized in surgery. After that he was a chemist. Still dissatisfied with life, he spent three weeks with Jung in Zürich, Switzerland. He had daily therapy sessions during the week and marathon sessions on the weekends. Having left his stuttering behind, Murray dedicated himself to the scientific study of psychoanalytic psychology at Harvard University. Whereas William James had been warm and friendly with Harvard students, Murray was cooler, more aristocratic.

The Thematic Apperception Test was created by Murray and a research assistant, Christiana Morgan. Murray and Morgan based the test on the assumption that people expose their personalities when they are placed in—and must interpret—unclear social situations. People are unaware that they may be revealing their inmost ideas and fantasies when they are reporting what they perceive others to be doing—as on the TAT cards. As a result, they are less defensive and more willing to open up.

despite lopsided polls to the contrary. It is the triumph of dissonance reduction, and perhaps of hope, over judgment.

As thinking creatures, people tend to seek consistency in their behaviors and their attitudes (Albarracin & Wyer, 2000). It helps make the world a predictable place. But the fact that thoughts are private does not make them free. By manipulating people's behavior it is sometimes possible to control their thoughts.

REVIEW

(17) Awareness that our cognitions are _____ is unpleasant and motivates us to reduce the discrepancy. (18) Engaging in _____-discrepant behavior may lead us to seek cognitive consistency by changing our attitudes.

Pulling It Together: Why would we appreciate things more if we have to work for them?

THE THREE A'S OF MOTIVATION: ACHIEVEMENT, AFFILIATION, AND AGGRESSION

Let us consider some of the powerful motives that bind us together or tear us asunder: achievement, affiliation, and aggression. The Harvard psychologist Henry Murray (1938) hypothesized that each of these "A's" reflects a psychological need. He also referred to them as *social motives*, which he believed differ from primary motives such as hunger in that they are acquired through social learning. However, contemporary researchers believe that hereditary predispositions may also play a role in these behavior patterns. Evolutionary psychologists believe that "genetic whisperings" influence tendencies toward achievement, affiliation, aggression, and many other aspects of personality and social behavior, even if we can also often point to environmental influences (Buss et al., 1998; Plomin et al., 1997; Rose, 1995).

Achievement: "Just Do It"

CLICK4™ *an essay assignment on achievement.*

CLICK4™ *more information about the need for achievement and its relationship to success.*

Many students persist in studying despite being surrounded by distractions. Many people strive relentlessly to get ahead, to "make it," to earn large sums of money, to invent, to accomplish the impossible. *Question: Why do some people strive to get ahead?* These people are said to have strong achievement motivation.

Psychologist David McClelland (1958) helped pioneer the assessment of achievement motivation through evaluation of fantasies. One method involves the Thematic Apperception Test (TAT), developed by Henry Murray. The TAT contains cards with pictures and drawings that are subject to various interpretations. Individuals are shown one or more TAT cards and asked to construct stories about the pictured theme: to indicate what led up to it, what the characters are thinking and feeling, and what is likely to happen.

One TAT card is similar to that in Figure 9.3. The meaning of the card is ambiguous—unclear. Is the girl sleeping, thinking about the book, wishing she were out with friends? Consider two stories that could be told about this card:

Story 1: "She's upset that she's got to read the book because she's behind in her assignments and doesn't particularly like to work. She'd much rather be out with her friends, and she may very well sneak out to do just that."

Story 2: "She's thinking, 'Someday I'll be a great scholar. I'll write books like this, and everybody will be proud of me.' She reads all the time."

FIGURE 9.3   Tapping Fantasies in Personality Research.
This picture is similar to a Thematic Apperception Test card used to measure the need for achievement. What is happening in this picture? What is the person thinking and feeling? What is going to happen? Your answers to these questions reflect your own needs as well as the content of the picture itself.

The second story suggests the presence of more achievement motivation than the first. Classic studies find that people with high achievement motivation earn higher grades than people with comparable learning ability but lower achievement motivation. They are more likely to earn high salaries and be promoted than less motivated people with similar opportunities. They perform better at math problems and at unscrambling anagrams, such as decoding RSTA into STAR, TARS, ARTS, or RATS.

McClelland (1965) used the TAT to sort college students into groups—students with high achievement motivation and students with low achievement motivation. He found that 83% of college graduates with high achievement motivation found jobs in occupations characterized by risk, decision making, and the chance for great success, such as business management, sales, or self-employment. Most (70%) of the graduates who chose nonentrepreneurial positions showed low achievement motivation. People with high achievement motivation seem to prefer challenges and are willing to take moderate risks to achieve their goals.

What Flavor Is Your Achievement Motivation?

Do you want to do well in this course? If you do, why? Carol Dweck (1997) finds that achievement motivation can be driven by different forces. Are you motivated mainly by performance goals? That is, is your grade in the course of most importance? If it is, it may be in part because your motives concern tangible rewards such as getting into graduate school, landing a good job, reaping approval from parents or your instructor, or avoiding criticism. Performance goals are usually met through extrinsic rewards such as prestige and income. Parents of children who develop performance goals are likely to respond to good grades with tangible rewards such as toys or money and to respond to poor grades with anger and removal of privileges.

> ▲ **REFLECT**
> Why do some people seem satisfied to just get by, whereas other people are driven to work and improve despite their achievements?

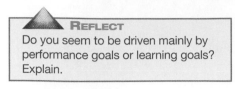

REFLECT
Do you seem to be driven mainly by performance goals or learning goals? Explain.

www 9 BBC 1

CLICK4™ *a bulletin board discussion on the psychology of motivation.*

REFLECT
Do you feel a strong need to make friends, join groups, and do things with other people? Why or why not?

Or do learning goals mainly motivate you to do well? That is, is your central motive the enhancing of your knowledge and skills—your ability to understand and master the subject matter? Learning goals usually lead to intrinsic rewards, such as satisfaction with oneself. Students who develop learning goals often have parents with strong achievement motivation, parents who encourage their children to think and act independently from an early age. They help their children develop learning goals by showing warmth and praising them for their efforts to learn, exposing them to novel and stimulating experiences, and encouraging persistence (Dweck, 1997; Ginsburg & Bronstein, 1993; Gottfried et al., 1994). Children of such parents frequently set high standards for themselves, associate their achievements with self-worth, and attribute their achievements to their own efforts rather than to chance or to the intervention of others.

Of course, many of us strive to meet both performance and learning goals in many subjects, as well as in other areas of life. Grades are important because they are connected with (very) tangible benefits, but learning for its own sake is also of value.

Achievement motivation resides within the individual. However, as noted in the nearby "Psychology and Modern Life" feature, psychologists have done much to enhance achievement motivation—and productivity—on the job.

Affiliation: "People Who Need People"

The motive for **affiliation** prompts us to make friends, join groups, and prefer to do things with others rather than alone. Affiliation motivation is part of the social glue that holds families and other groups together. In this sense, it is certainly a positive trait. Yet some people have such a strong need to affiliate that they find it painful to make their own decisions or to be alone.

Psychology and Modern Life

Enhancing Productivity and Job Satisfaction

Achievement motivation, productivity, and job satisfaction go hand in hand. Enhancing workers' satisfaction on the job motivates them to be more productive (Katzell & Thompson, 1990). That is why businesses and organizations employ industrial/organizational (I/O) psychologists to help them enhance worker satisfaction.

Many I/O psychologists apply behavioral principles to train workers in a step-by-step fashion, to modify problem behaviors at work, and to make sure workers are rewarded for targeted behaviors. When required behaviors are made clear and the rewards (raises, bonuses, promotions, time off) for completing tasks are spelled out, workers' morale rises and complaints about favoritism decrease.

Consider some of the functions of I/O psychologists in recruitment, training, and evaluation.

Recruitment and Placement   Worker motivation is enhanced right at the begin-

ning when the right person for the job is hired. When the company's needs mesh with the worker's, both profit. Unfortunately, people sometimes get hired for reasons that are irrelevant to their potential to perform well in the job. Sometimes people are hired because they are physically attractive (Mack & Rainey, 1990). On other occasions relatives or friends of friends are chosen. By and large, however, businesses seek employees who can do the job and are likely to be reasonably satisfied with it. Employees who are satisfied with their jobs are less likely to be absent or quit. I/O psychologists facilitate recruitment procedures by analyzing jobs, specifying the skills and personal attributes that are needed, and constructing tests and interviews to determine whether candidates have those skills and attributes. These procedures can enhance job satisfaction and productivity.

Psychologists help improve methods of selecting, training, and evaluating managers for sensitive positions (Hogan et al., 1994). As we reach the new millennium,

only 15% of new workers will be European American males, as compared with more than 40% during the 1980s. As the workforce becomes more diverse — including more minority and female employees — we should be increasing the numbers of minority group members and women in management (Hogan and others, 1994). This can be accomplished with the assistance of psychologists who develop appropriate testing and selection procedures.

Training and Instruction   I/O psychologists are versed in principles of learning, and worker training and instruction is the most common way of enhancing productivity (Katzell & Thompson, 1990). Training gives workers the appropriate skills, knowledge, and attitudes. Equipping them to solve problems on the job also reduces the stress they will encounter and enhances their feelings of self-worth. Why do psychologists address workers' attitudes? Consider just one example: A factory worker might resist wearing protective de-

Question: Why do people need people? There are many reasons. Sometimes we learn that we can accomplish more by doing things with others than we can alone. Certainly infants cannot survive without the support of other people. But the need to affiliate with others may also be instinctive—an inborn aspect of our makeup as social beings. Research by Stanley Schachter suggests that a particularly high need to affiliate may also indicate anxiety, such as when people "huddle together" in fear of an outside force.

In a classic experiment on the effects of anxiety on affiliation, Schachter (1959) manipulated participants' anxiety levels by leading them to believe that they would receive either painful electric shocks (the high-anxiety condition) or mild electric shocks (the low-anxiety condition). Participants were then asked to wait while the shock apparatus was supposedly being set up. They could choose to wait alone or in a room with others. The majority (63%) of those who expected a painful shock chose to wait in a room with other people. Only one third (33%) of those who expected a mild shock chose to wait with others.

Highly anxious participants were placed in two social conditions. In the first, they could choose either to wait alone or with others who would also receive painful shocks. Sixty percent of these people chose to affiliate—that is, to wait with others. In the second condition, highly anxious participants could choose to wait alone or with people they believed were not involved with the study. In this second condition, no one chose to affiliate.

Why did participants in Schachter's study wish to affiliate only with people who shared their misery? Schachter explained their choice with his **theory of social comparison.** This theory holds that in an ambiguous situation—that is, a situation in which we are not certain about what we should do or how we should feel—we affiliate with people with whom we can compare feelings and behaviors. Schachter's anxious recruits could

CLICK4™ *a bulletin board discussion on your motivation for going to college.*

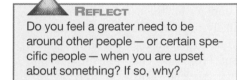

REFLECT

Do you feel a greater need to be around other people — or certain specific people — when you are upset about something? If so, why?

Affiliation ▲ Association or connection with a group.
Theory of social comparison ▲ The view that people look to others for cues about how to behave when they are in confusing or unfamiliar situations.

---

vices, even when taught how to do so, if he has the attitude that safety devices are for sissies.

Appraisal of Workers' Performance
Workers are more highly motivated when they receive individualized guidance and re-inforcers are based on accurate appraisals of their performance. Criticism of workers' performance is necessary if workers are to improve, but it is important that criticism be delivered in a constructive way (Weisinger, 1990; see Table 9.2). Destructive criticism saps workers' motivation and belief in their ability to perform. Constructive criticism helps workers feel that they are being shown how to improve their performance (Baron, 1990).

In an ideal world, appraisal of workers' performances would be based solely on how well they do their jobs. But cognitive biases play a role in worker appraisal. Sometimes managers focus on the *worker* rather than on the performance. A supervisor is more likely to positively appraise the

TABLE 9.2 CRITICISM: THE GOOD, THE BAD, AND THE UGLY

Constructive Criticism (Good)	Destructive Criticism (Bad and Ugly)
Specific: The supervisor is specific about what the employee is doing wrong. For example, she or he says "This is what you did that caused the problem, and this is why it caused the problem."	**Vague:** The supervisor makes a blanket condemnation, such as, "That was an awful thing to do," or "That was a lousy job." No specifics are given.
Supportive: The supervisor gives the employee the feeling that the criticism is meant to help him or her perform better on the job.	**Condemnatory of the employee:** The supervisor attributes the problem to an unchangeable cause such as the employee's personality.
Helpful in problem solving: The supervisor helps employees improve things or solve their problems on the job.	**Threatening:** The supervisor attacks the employee, as by saying, "If you do this again, you'll be docked," or "Next time, you're fired."
Timely: The supervisor offers the criticism as soon as possible after the problem occurs.	**Pessimistic:** The supervisor seems doubtful that the employee will be able to improve.

work of a subordinate who is also a friend. There is also a tendency — called the *halo effect* — to rate workers according to general impressions (for example, liking or disliking).

Another bias in appraisal is the tendency to evaluate workers according to how much effort they put into their work.

Many managers evaluate "hard workers" more positively than other workers, even if they accomplish less (Dugan, 1989; Tsui & O'Reilly, 1989). Hard work is not necessarily good work, however. (Should students who work harder than you do be given higher grades on tests, even when you get the answers right and they make errors?)

CLICK4™ *a bulletin board discussion on aggression—is it natural?*

CLICK4™ *more information about aggression and health.*

compare their reactions with those of other "victims," but not with people who had no reason to feel anxious. Anxious participants may also have resented uninvolved people for "getting away free."

Aggression: Some Facts of Life and Death

Consider the following facts:

▲ After the end of the Cold War, you might have expected the world to become more peaceful. Yet civil wars and other conflicts rage on every continent.

▲ In the United States, violence is the leading cause of death among young people. Homicide is the second leading cause of death among 15- to 24-year-olds (CDC, 2000b). (Accidents are the leading cause.)

▲ Aggression is not limited to foreign battlefields or dark streets and alleyways. Each year more than a million U.S. children are brought to the attention of authorities as victims of child abuse.

▲ About 2,000 women die each year from domestic violence (CDC, 2000b). Women are more likely to be raped, injured, or killed by intimate partners than by other types of assailants (CDC, 2000b).

▲ Domestic violence is a greater threat to pregnant women than high blood pressure, diabetes, or any other complication of pregnancy (CDC, 2000b).

Question: Why do people kill, maim, and injure one another? Let us consider some theories of aggression.

The Biological Perspective Numerous biological structures and chemicals appear to be involved in aggression. In response to certain stimuli, many lower animals show instinctive aggressive reactions. For example, the male robin responds aggressively to the red breast of another robin. The hypothalamus appears to be involved in this inborn reaction pattern: Electrical stimulation of part of the hypothalamus triggers stereotypical aggressive behaviors in many lower animals. However, in humans, whose brains are more complex, other brain structures apparently moderate possible aggressive instincts.

Chemistry is also involved in aggression, especially in the form of the male sex hormone testosterone. Testosterone appears to affect the tendencies to dominate and control other people. Men have higher testosterone levels than women do and are also (usually) more aggressive than women, especially in contacts with male strangers (Pope et al., 2000). Studies show, for example, that 9- to 11-year-old boys with conduct disorders are likely to have higher testosterone levels than their less aggressive peers (Chance et al., 2000), and that members of so-called "rambunctious" fraternities have higher testosterone levels, on average, than members of more "well-behaved" fraternities (Dabbs et al., 1996). Testosterone levels also vary with the occasion: Men's testosterone levels tend to be higher when they are "winning"—whether in athletic competitions such as football or even in chess (Bernhardt et al., 1998). It could be that one reason men are more sexually aggressive than women is because of their general tendency to attempt to dominate others.

Even if aggression is "natural," intelligence is also a key to survival in the case of humans. The capacity to outwit other species may be more important to human survival than aggressiveness. Now that humans have organized themselves into societies in which aggression is either outlawed or confined to athletic contests, it could be that factors such as intelligence and organizational skills are more important than aggressiveness in having one's genes transmitted to future generations.

The Psychodynamic Perspective Sigmund Freud believed that aggressive impulses are inevitable reactions to the frustrations of daily life. Children (and adults) normally desire to vent aggressive impulses on other people, including parents, because even the most attentive parents cannot gratify all of their demands immediately. Yet children also fear punishment and loss of love, so they repress most aggressive impulses and store them in the unconscious recesses of the mind. The Freudian perspective, in a sense, sees humans as "steam engines." By holding in steam rather than venting it, we set the stage for future explosions. Pent-up aggressive impulses demand an outlet. They may be expressed toward parents in roundabout ways, such as destroying furniture; later in life they may be expressed toward strangers.

CONTROVERSY IN PSYCHOLOGY

The Catharsis Controversy

Does watching violent sports such as football, boxing, and pro wrestling make viewers more or less likely to engage in violent behavior themselves?

According to psychodynamic theory, the best way to prevent harmful aggression may be to encourage less harmful aggression. In the steam engine analogy, verbal aggression (through wit, sarcasm, or expression of negative feelings) may vent some of the aggressive steam in a person's unconscious mind. So might cheering on a football team or attending a prize fight. Psychoanalysts refer to the venting of aggressive impulses as **catharsis.** Thus, catharsis is viewed as a safety valve. But research findings on the usefulness of catharsis are mixed. Some studies suggest that catharsis leads to pleasant reductions in tension and reduced likelihood of future aggression (e.g., Doob & Wood, 1972). Other studies, however, suggest that "venting" some steam actually encourages more aggression later on (e.g., Bushman et al., 1999). Research evidence has been hard on the psychodynamic perspective, yielding partial support for Freud's views at best.

The Cognitive Perspective
Cognitive psychologists assert that our behavior is influenced by our values, by how we interpret situations, and by choice. From the cognitive perspective, for example, people who believe that aggression is necessary and justified—as during wartime—are likely to act aggressively. People who believe that a particular war or act of aggression is unjust, or who oppose aggression regardless of the circumstances, are less likely to behave aggressively (Huesmann & Guerra, 1997).

One cognitive theory suggests that frustration and discomfort trigger unpleasant feelings (Rule et al., 1987). These feelings, in turn, prompt aggression. Aggression is *not* automatic, however. Cognitive factors intervene (Berkowitz, 1994). People *decide*—sometimes making "split-second decisions"—whether they will strike out or not on the basis of factors such as their previous experiences with aggression and their interpretation of the other person's motives.

Researchers find that many aggressive people distort other people's motives. For example, they assume that other people wish them harm when they actually do not (Akhtar & Bradley, 1991; Crick & Dodge, 1994). Cognitive therapists note that we are more likely to respond aggressively to a provocation when we magnify the importance of the insult or otherwise stir up feelings of anger (e.g., Lochman & Dodge, 1994). How do you respond when someone bumps into you? If you view it as an intentional insult to your honor, you may respond with aggression. If you view it as an accident, or as a social problem in need of a solution, you are less likely to act aggressively.

Learning Perspectives
Two types of learning perspectives are the behavioral perspective and the social-cognitive perspective. From the behavioral perspective, learning is acquired through reinforcement. Organisms reinforced for aggressive behavior are more likely to behave aggressively in similar situations. Environmental consequences make it more likely that strong, agile organisms will be reinforced for aggressive behavior. Research shows that children are less likely to behave aggressively when teachers and fellow students communicate strong disapproval of aggressive behavior (Henry et al., 2000).

From the social-cognitive perspective, aggressive skills are mainly acquired by observation. Social-cognitive theorists do believe that consciousness and choice may play a role, however. In this view, we are not likely to act aggressively unless we believe that aggression is appropriate under the circumstances.

DIVERSITY The Sociocultural Perspective on Aggression
The sociocultural perspective focuses on ways in which ethnicity, gender, and cultural factors may be related to aggression.

Catharsis?
Are these football fans harmlessly venting aggressive impulses, or are they building the likelihood of behaving aggressively themselves? What does Freudian theory say about "catharsis"? Does the research support Freud's theory?

www 9 WS 5

CLICK4™ *a WebSearch activity on the catharsis controversy.*

▲ **REFLECT**
Consider people whom you would label as "violent." Do you believe that they simply explode or that they decide to behave violently? Explain.

www 9 WS 4

CLICK4™ *a WebSearch activity on aggression and gender, ethnicity, and culture.*

Catharsis ▲ In psychodynamic theory, the purging of strong emotions or the relieving of tensions.

▲ **REFLECT**

What are your feelings about the "lessons" males learn in competitive sports? Explain.

The experiences of anthropologist Margaret Mead (1935) on the South Pacific island of New Guinea showed how the sociocultural milieu influences motives such as aggressiveness and nurturance. Among the Mundugumor, a tribe of headhunters and cannibals, both women and men were warlike and aggressive. The women felt that motherhood sidetracked them from more important activities, such as butchering inhabitants of neighboring villages. In contrast, both women and men of the Arapesh tribe were gentle and nurturant of children. Then there were the Tchambuli. In that tribe the women earned a living while the men spent most of their time nurturing the children, primping, and gossiping.

Psychologists have observed that U.S. culture has a way of breeding violence. Adolescents born in the United States tend to be more accepting of aggression than adolescents born elsewhere, as in the Middle East (Souweidane & Huesmann, 1999). In Thailand and Jamaica, for example, aggression in children is discouraged and politeness and deference are encouraged (Tharp, 1991). Children in the United States are more likely to be argumentative, disobedient, and belligerent (Tharp, 1991). Competitiveness and independence are encouraged in the United States, especially among males. The lessons learned in competitive sports may particularly dispose males to violence (Levy, 1991). Coaches often urge boys to win at all costs. Boys are encouraged to dominate and vanquish their opponents, even if winning requires injuring or "taking out" the opposition. This philosophy may be carried from the playing field into social relationships. Some athletes distinguish between sports and social relationships, but others do not.

REVIEW

www ⑨ PML ⑯

CLICK4™ *advice on coping with anger.*

(19) Students with _____ goals are mainly motivated by factors such as good grades, rewards from parents, and the prospect of landing a good job. (20) Students with _____ goals are usually more motivated by intrinsic rewards like self-satisfaction. (21) Schachter found that anxiety tends to (increase or decrease?) the need for affiliation. (22) Schachter's theory of social _____ holds that when we are in ambiguous situations, we seek to affiliate with people with whom we can compare feelings and behaviors. (23) The hormone _____ seems to be connected with social dominance and aggression in humans. (24) Psychodynamic theorists view _____ as a safety valve for venting aggressive impulses, but research does not support this theory. (25) The _____ perspective focuses on ways in which ethnicity, gender, and culture are related to aggression.

Pulling It Together: How do psychologists use fantasy to assess people's motives? Agree or disagree with the following statement and support your answer: Aggression is natural.

EMOTION: ADDING COLOR TO LIFE

▲ **REFLECT**

Do you consider yourself to be an "emotional person"? Why or why not? Do you see "being emotional" in a positive or negative light? Explain.

Emotions color our lives. We are green with envy, red with anger, blue with sorrow. Poets paint a thoughtful mood as a "brown study." Positive emotions such as love and desire can fill our days with pleasure. Negative emotions such as fear, depression, and anger can fill us with dread and make each day a chore. ***Question: Just what is an emotion?***

An emotion can be a response to a situation, in the way that fear is a response to a threat. An emotion can motivate behavior (e.g., anger can motivate us to act aggressively). An emotion can also be a goal in itself. We may behave in ways that will lead us to experience joy or feelings of love.

Emotions are feeling states with physiological, cognitive, and behavioral components (Carlson & Hatfield, 1992). In terms of physiology, strong emotions arouse the autonomic nervous system (LeDoux, 1997). The greater the arousal, the more intense the emotion. It also appears that the type of arousal affects the emotion being experienced. Although the word *emotion* might seem to be about feeling and not about thinking, cognitions—particularly interpretations of the meanings of events—are important aspects of emotions. *Fear*, which usually occurs in response to a threat, involves cognitions that one is in danger as well as arousal of the **sympathetic nervous system** (rapid heartbeat and

Emotion ▲ A state of feeling that has cognitive, physiological, and behavioral components.

Sympathetic nervous system ▲ The branch of the autonomic nervous system that is most active during processes that spend body energy from stored reserves, such as in a fight-or-flight reaction to a predator or when you are anxious about a big test. When people experience fear, the sympathetic nervous system accelerates the heart rate, raises the blood pressure, tenses muscles, and so on.

breathing, sweating, muscle tension). Emotions also involve behavioral tendencies. The emotion of fear is connected with behavioral tendencies to avoid or escape from the situation (see Table 9.3). As a response to a social provocation, *anger* involves cognitions that the provocateur should be paid back, arousal of both the sympathetic and **parasympathetic nervous systems,** and tendencies to attack.

Depression usually involves cognitions of helplessness and hopelessness, parasympathetic arousal, and tendencies toward inactivity—or, some-times—self-destruction. *Joy, grief, jealousy, disgust, embarrassment, liking*—all have cognitive, physiological, and behavioral components.

Just how many emotions are there and what are they? The ancient Chinese believed in four basic or instinctive emotions—happiness, anger, sorrow, and fear. They arise, respectively, in the heart, liver, lungs, and kidneys (Carlson & Hatfield, 1992). (No, there is no evidence for this view.) The behaviorist psychologist John B. Watson (1924) believed that there are three basic or inborn emotions: fear, rage, and love. Others, such as Paul Ekman (1980) and Robert Plutchik (2001), argue for larger numbers of basic emotions. The question remains unresolved.

TABLE 9.3 COMPONENTS OF EMOTIONS

Emotion	Physiological	Cognitive	Behavioral
Fear	Sympathetic arousal	Belief that one is in danger	Avoidance tendencies
Anger	Sympathetic and parasympathetic arousal	Frustration or belief that one is being mistreated	Attack tendencies
Depression	Parasympathetic arousal	Thoughts of helplessness, hopelessness, worthlessness	Inactivity, possible self-destructive tendencies

Parasympathetic nervous system ▲ The branch of the autonomic nervous system that is most active during processes that restore reserves of energy to the body, such as relaxing and eating. When people relax, the parasympathetic nervous system decelerates the heart rate, normalizes the blood pressure, relaxes muscles, and so on. The parasympathetic division also stimulates digestion.

The Expression of Emotions

Joy and sadness are found in all cultures, but, *Question: How can we tell when other people are happy or despondent?* It turns out that the expression of many emotions may be universal (Rinn, 1991). Smiling is apparently a universal sign of friendliness and approval. Baring the teeth, as noted by Charles Darwin (1872) in the 19th century, may be a universal sign of anger. As the originator of the theory of evolution, Darwin believed that the universal recognition of facial expressions would have survival value. For example, in the absence of language, facial expressions could signal the approach of enemies (or friends).

Most investigators (e.g., Buss, 1992; Izard, 1994) concur that certain facial expressions suggest the same emotions in all people. Moreover, people in diverse cultures recognize the emotions manifested by certain facial expressions. In a classic study, Paul Ekman (1980) took photographs of people exhibiting anger, disgust, fear, happiness, sadness, and surprise (see Figure 9.4). He then asked people around the world to indicate what emotions were being depicted. Those queried ranged from European college students to members of the Fore, a tribe that dwells in the New Guinea highlands. All groups, including the Fore, who had almost no contact with Western culture, agreed on

FIGURE 9.4 Photographs Used in Research by Paul Ekman.
Ekman's research suggests that the facial expressions connected with several important emotions such as happiness, anger, surprise, and fear are universally recognized.

 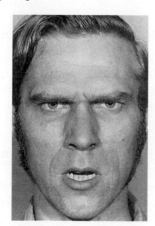 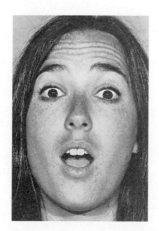 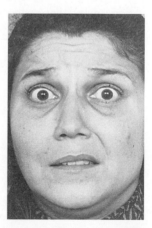

the emotions being portrayed. The Fore also displayed familiar facial expressions when asked how they would respond if they were the characters in stories that called for basic emotional responses. Ekman and his colleagues (1987) obtained similar results in a study of 10 cultures. In that study, participants were allowed to identify more than one emotion in facial expressions. The participants generally agreed on which two emotions were being shown and which emotion was more intense.

On the other hand, there is no perfect one-to-one relationship between facial expressions and emotions. Facial expressions sometimes occur in the absence of the emotion they are thought to accompany (Camras, 2000). As noted by psychologist Joseph Campos (2000), the voice, posture, and gestures also provide clues as to what people are feeling and about to do.

The Facial-Feedback Hypothesis

www 9 E 5

CLICK4™ *an essay assignment on the facial-feedback hypothesis.*

The face has a special place among visual stimuli. Social animals like humans need to be able to differentiate and recognize members of their group and, in people, the face is the most distinctive key to identity (Parr et al., 2000). Faces are also a key to social communication. Facial expressions reflect emotional states, and our ability to "read" these expressions enables us to interact appropriately with other people.

It is known that various emotional states give rise to certain patterns of electrical activity in the facial muscles and in the brain (Cacioppo et al., 1988). But can it work the other way around? The **facial-feedback hypothesis** argues that facial expressions can also affect our emotional state, that the causal relationship between emotions and facial expressions can work in the opposite direction. *Questions: Can smiling give rise to feelings of good will? Can frowning produce anger?* Perhaps they can.

Psychological research has yielded some interesting findings concerning the facial-feedback hypothesis (Ekman, 1993a). Inducing people to smile, for example, leads them to report more positive feelings (Basic Behavioral Science Task Force, 1996b) and to rate cartoons as more humorous. When induced to frown, they rate cartoons as more aggressive. When they exhibit pain through facial expressions, they rate electric shocks as more painful.

What are the possible links between facial feedback and emotion? One link is arousal. Intense contraction of facial muscles such as those used in signifying fear heightens arousal, which, in turn, boosts emotional response. Feedback from the contraction of facial muscles may also induce feeling states. Ekman (1993b) has found that engaging in the so-called Duchenne smile, characterized by "crow's feet wrinkles around the eyes and a subtle drop in the eye cover fold so that the skin above the eye moves down slightly toward the eyeball," can induce pleasant feelings.

You may have heard the British expression "Keep a stiff upper lip" as a recommendation for handling stress. It might be that a "stiff" lip suppresses emotional response—as long as the lip is relaxed rather than quivering with fear or tension. But when the lip is stiffened through strong muscle tension, facial feedback may heighten emotional response.

▲ REFLECT
Have you tried to "keep a stiff upper lip" when you were under stress, or have you preferred to "let it all hang out"? What do the facial-feedback hypothesis and various theories of emotional expression suggest about the effects of one approach or the other?

Theories of Emotion: *"How* Do You Feel?"

David, 32, is not sleeping well. He wakes before dawn and cannot get back to sleep. His appetite is off, his energy level is low, he has started smoking again. He has a couple of drinks at lunch and muses that it's lucky that any more alcohol makes him sick to his stomach—otherwise, he'd probably be drinking too much, too. Then he thinks, "So what difference would it make?" Sometimes he is sexually frustrated; at other times he wonders whether he has any sex drive left. Although he's awake, each day it's getting harder to drag himself out of bed in the morning. This week he missed one day of work and was late twice. His supervisor has suggested in a nonthreatening way that he "do something about it." David knows that her next warning will not be unthreatening. It's been going downhill since Sue walked out. Suicide has even crossed David's mind. He wonders if he's going crazy.

Facial-feedback hypothesis ▲ The view that stereotypical facial expressions can contribute to stereotypical emotions.

David is experiencing the emotion of depression, seriously so. Depression is to be expected following a loss, such as the end of a relationship, but David's feelings have lingered. His friends tell him that he should get out and do things, but David is so down that he hasn't the motivation to do much of anything at all. After much prompting by family and friends, David consults a psychologist who, ironically, also pushes him to get out and do things—the things he used to enjoy. The psychologist also shows David that part of his problem is that sees himself as a failure who cannot make meaningful changes.

Question: How do the physiological, situational, and cognitive components of emotions interact to produce feelings and behavior?   Some psychologists argue that physiological arousal is a more basic component of emotional response than cognition and that the type of arousal we experience strongly influences our cognitive appraisal and our labeling of the emotion (e.g., Izard, 1984). For these psychologists, the body takes precedence over the mind. Do David's bodily reactions—for example, his loss of appetite and energy—take precedence over his cognitions? Other psychologists argue that cognitive appraisal and physiological arousal are so strongly intertwined that cognitive processes may determine the emotional response. Are David's ideas that he is helpless to make meaningful changes more at the heart of his feelings of depression?

The "commonsense theory" of emotions is that something happens (a situation) that is cognitively appraised (interpreted) by the person, and the feeling state (a combination of arousal and thoughts) follows. For example, you meet someone new, appraise that person as delightful, and feelings of attraction follow. Or, as in the case of David, a social relationship comes to an end, you recognize your loss, feel powerless to change it, and feel down in the dumps.

However, both historic and contemporary theories of how the components of emotions interact are at variance with this commonsense view. Let us consider a number of theories and see whether we can arrive at some useful conclusions.

The James-Lange Theory   A century ago, William James suggested that our emotions follow, rather than cause, our behavioral responses to events. At about the same time this view was also proposed by the Danish physiologist Karl G. Lange. It is therefore termed the James-Lange theory of emotion.

According to James and Lange, certain external stimuli instinctively trigger specific patterns of arousal and action, such as fighting or fleeing (see Figure 9.5, part A). We then become angry *because* we are acting aggressively or become afraid *because* we are running away. Emotions are simply the cognitive representations (or by-products) of automatic physiological and behavioral responses.

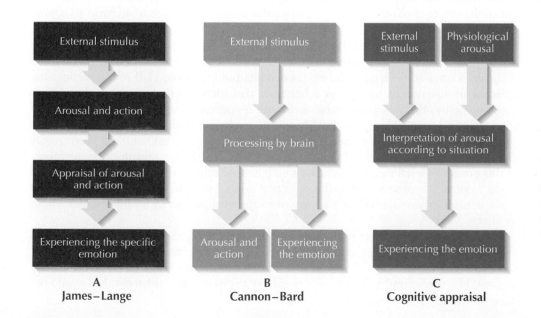

A
James–Lange

B
Cannon–Bard

C
Cognitive appraisal

FIGURE 9.5   Three Theories of Emotion.
Several theories of emotion have been advanced, each of which proposes a different role for the components of emotional response. According to the James-Lange theory (part A), events trigger specific arousal patterns and actions. Emotions result from our appraisal of our body responses. According to the Cannon-Bard theory (part B), events are first processed by the brain. Body patterns of arousal, action, and our emotional responses are then triggered simultaneously. According to the theory of cognitive appraisal (part C), events and arousal are appraised by the individual. The emotional response stems from the person's appraisal of the situation and his or her level of arousal.

▲ REFLECT
Have you ever been able to change the way you feel by *doing* something? (Have you ever purposefully worked yourself up into a rage? Have you ever done something enjoyable to elevate your mood?)

The James-Lange theory is consistent with the facial-feedback hypothesis. That is, smiling apparently can induce pleasant feelings, even if the effect may not be strong enough to overcome feelings of sadness (Ekman, 1993b). The theory also suggests that we may be able to change our feelings by changing our behavior. Changing one's behavior to change one's feelings is one aspect of behavior therapy. When David's psychologist urges him to get out and do things, she is assuming that by changing his behavior, David can have a positive effect on the way he feels.

Walter Cannon (1927) criticized the James-Lange assertion that each emotion has distinct physiological correlates. He argued that the physiological arousal associated with emotion A is not as distinct from the arousal associated with emotion B as the theory asserts. Note that the James-Lange view downplays the importance of human cognition; it denies the roles of cognitive appraisal, personal values, and personal choice in our behavioral and emotional responses to events.

The Cannon-Bard Theory

Cannon (1927) was not content to criticize the James-Lange theory. Along with Philip Bard (1934), he suggested that an event might *simultaneously* trigger bodily responses (arousal and action) and the experience of an emotion. As shown in Figure 9.5 (part B), when an event is perceived (processed by the brain), the brain stimulates autonomic and muscular activity (arousal and action) *and* cognitive activity (experience of the emotion). Thus, according to the Cannon-Bard theory, emotions *accompany* bodily responses. They are not *produced by* bodily changes, as in the James-Lange theory.

The central criticism of the Cannon-Bard theory focuses on whether bodily responses (arousal and action) and emotions are actually stimulated simultaneously. For example, pain or the perception of danger may trigger arousal before we begin to feel distress or fear. Also, many of us have had the experience of having a "narrow escape" and becoming aroused and shaky afterward, when we have had time to consider the damage that might have occurred. What is needed is a theory that allows for an ongoing interaction of external events, physiological changes (such as autonomic arousal and muscular activity), and cognitive activities.

CLICK4™ *more information about research on emotion.*

The Theory of Cognitive Appraisal

More recent theoretical approaches to emotion have stressed cognitive factors. Among those who argue that thinking comes first are Gordon Bower, Richard Lazarus, Stanley Schachter, and Robert Zajonc.

Stanley Schachter asserts that emotions are associated with similar patterns of bodily arousal that may be weaker or stronger, depending on the level of arousal. The label we give to an emotion depends largely on our cognitive appraisal of the situation. Cognitive appraisal is based on many factors, including our perception of external events and the ways in which other people seem to respond to those events (see Figure 9.5, part C). Given the presence of other people, we engage in social comparison to arrive at an appropriate response.

▲ REFLECT
Were you ever emotionally aroused but uncertain as to exactly what you were feeling? How does such an experience relate to the Schachter-Singer theory of emotional response? And did you eventually decide what you were feeling? How?

In a classic experiment, Schachter and Singer (1962) showed that arousal can be labeled quite differently, depending on the situation. The investigators told participants that they wanted to determine the effects of a vitamin on vision. Half of the participants received an injection of adrenaline, a hormone that increases the arousal of the sympathetic branch of the autonomic nervous system. A control group received an injection of an inactive solution. Those who had been given adrenaline then received one of three "cognitive manipulations," as shown in Table 9.4. Group 1 was told nothing about possible emotional effects of the "vitamin." Group 2 was deliberately misinformed; members of this group were led to expect itching, numbness, or other irrelevant symptoms. Group 3 was informed accurately about the increased arousal they would experience. Group 4 was a control group injected with an inactive substance and given no information about its effects.

After receiving injections and cognitive manipulations, the participants were asked to wait in pairs while the experimental apparatus was being set up. The participants did not know that the person with whom they were waiting was a confederate of the experimenter. The confederate's purpose was to exhibit a response that the individual would believe was caused by the injection.

TABLE 9.4 INJECTED SUBSTANCES AND COGNITIVE MANIPULATIONS IN THE SCHACHTER-SINGER STUDY

Group	Substance	Cognitive Manipulation
1	Adrenaline	No information given about effects
2	Adrenaline	Misinformation given: itching, numbness, etc.
3	Adrenaline	Accurate information given: physiological arousal
4	Inactive	None

SOURCE: Schachter & Singer (1962).

Some of those who took part in the experiment waited with a confederate who acted in a happy-go-lucky manner. He flew paper airplanes about the room and tossed paper balls into a wastebasket. Other participants waited with a confederate who acted angry. He complained about the experiment, tore up a questionnaire, and left the waiting room in a huff. As the confederates worked for their Oscar® awards, the real participants were observed through a one-way mirror.

The people in groups 1 and 2 were likely to imitate the behavior of the confederate. Those who were exposed to the happy-go-lucky confederate acted jovial and content. Those who were exposed to the angry confederate imitated that person's complaining, aggressive behavior. But those in groups 3 and 4 were less influenced by the confederate's behavior.

Schachter and Singer concluded that participants in groups 1 and 2 were in an ambiguous situation. Members of these groups felt arousal from the adrenaline injection but couldn't label their arousal as any specific emotion. Social comparison with a confederate led them to attribute their arousal either to happiness or to anger. Members of group 3 expected arousal from the injection, with no particular emotional consequences. These participants did not imitate the confederate's display of happiness or anger because they were not in an ambiguous situation; they knew they felt arousal because of the shot of adrenaline. Members of group 4 had no physiological arousal for which they needed an attribution, except perhaps for some arousal induced by observing the confederate. They also did not imitate the behavior of the confederate.

Now, happiness and anger are quite different emotions. Happiness is a positive emotion, whereas anger, for most of us, is a negative emotion. Yet Schachter and Singer suggest that any physiological differences between these two emotions are so slight that different views of the situation can lead one person to label arousal as happiness and

IN REVIEW

Theories of Emotion

Theory	About . . .	More . . .
Commonsense Theory	Something happens that is interpreted (cognitively appraised) by the person, and the emotion follows.	Compare to Albert Ellis's A → B → C approach to explaining emotions such as anxiety and depression (in Chapter 14).
The James-Lange Theory	Emotions follow, rather than cause, our behavioral responses to events. Certain stimuli trigger specific instinctive patterns of arousal and action.	Research does not show that each emotion has distinct biological correlates.
The Cannon-Bard Theory	Events simultaneously trigger bodily responses (arousal and action) and the experience of an emotion. Emotions *accompany* bodily responses but are not *produced by* them.	Research does not show that bodily responses (arousal and action) and emotions are stimulated simultaneously.
Theory of Cognitive Appraisal	The label we give to an emotion depends largely on our cognitive appraisal of the situation. Emotions are associated with similar patterns of bodily arousal. When we are uncertain about what we feel, we engage in social comparison to arrive at an appropriate emotional response.	Research suggests that the patterns of arousal associated with different emotions are more specific than suggested by Schachter and Singer.

another person to label it as anger. The Schachter-Singer view could not be further removed from the James-Lange theory, which holds that each emotion is associated with specific and readily recognized body sensations.

The truth, it happens, may lie somewhere in between.

In science, it must be possible to replicate experiments and attain identical or similar results; otherwise, a theory cannot be considered valid. The Schachter and Singer study has been replicated, but with *different* results. For instance, a number of studies found that participants were less likely to imitate the behavior of the confederate and were likely to perceive unexplained arousal in negative terms, attributing it to nervousness, anger, even jealousy (Zimbardo et al., 1993).

Evaluation   What can we make of all this? Research by Paul Ekman and his colleagues (1987) suggests that the patterns of arousal connected with various emotions are more specific than suggested by Schachter and Singer—although less so than suggested by James and Lange. Research with the PET scan suggests that different emotions, such as happiness and sadness, involve different structures within the brain (Goleman, 1995a). Moreover, lack of control over our emotions and lack of understanding of what is happening to us are disturbing experiences (Zimbardo et al., 1993). Thus our cognitive appraisals of situations apparently do affect our emotional responses, even if not quite in the way envisioned by Schachter.

The fact that emotions are accompanied by bodily arousal has led to the development of so-called lie detectors, as we see next.

CLICK4™ *a video on genuine and false smiles.*

CONTROVERSY ✕ IN PSYCHOLOGY

Just What Do Lie Detectors Detect?

The connection between autonomic arousal and emotions has led to the development of many kinds of lie detectors. Such instruments detect something, but do they detect specific emotional responses that signify lies? Let us take a closer look at the problem of lying.

Lying—for better or worse—is a part of life. A *New York Times* poll found that 60% of U.S. adults believe that it is sometimes necessary to lie, especially to protect people's feelings (Smiley, 2000). Political leaders lie to get elected. Some students lie about why they have not completed assignments (Saxe, 1991). ('Fess up!) The great majority of people lie to their lovers—most often about other relationships (Rowatt et al., 1999; Saxe, 1991). (Is it really true that you never kissed anyone before?) People also lie about their qualifications to obtain jobs, and, of course, some people lie in denying guilt for crimes. Although we are unlikely to subject political leaders, students, and lovers to lie detector tests, such tests are frequently used in hiring and in police investigations.

Facial expressions often offer clues to deceit, but some people can lie with a straight face—or a smile. As Shakespeare pointed out in *Hamlet,* "One may smile, and smile, and be a villain." The use of devices to detect lies has a long, if not laudable, history:

> The Bedouins of Arabia . . . until quite recently required conflicting witnesses to lick a hot iron; the one whose tongue was burned was thought to be lying. The Chinese, it is said, had a similar method for detecting lying: Suspects were forced to chew rice powder and spit it out; if the powder was dry, the suspect was guilty. A variation of this test was used during the Inquisition. The suspect had to swallow a "trial slice" of bread and cheese; if it stuck to the suspect's palate or throat he or she was not telling the truth. (Kleinmuntz & Szucko, 1984, pp. 766–767)

These methods may sound primitive, even bizarre, but they are broadly consistent with modern psychological knowledge. Anxiety about being caught in a lie is linked to arousal of the sympathetic division of the autonomic nervous system. One sign of sympathetic arousal is lack of saliva, or dryness in the mouth. The emotions of fear and guilt are also linked to sympathetic arousal and, hence, to dryness in the mouth.

▲ **REFLECT**

Can you tell when people are lying to you? What cues or clues do you focus on?

CLICK4™ *a bulletin board discussion on the efficacy of lie detectors.*

CLICK4™ *information about lie detectors from the APA.*

Questions: How do lie detectors work? How reliable are they? Modern lie detectors, or polygraphs, monitor indicators of sympathetic arousal while a witness or suspect is being examined. These indicators include heart rate, blood pressure, respiration rate, and electrodermal response (sweating). Questions have been raised about the validity of assessing truth or fiction in this way, however (Saxe & Ben-Shakhar, 1999).

The American Polygraph Association claims that use of the polygraph is 85% to 95% accurate. Critics find polygraph testing to be less accurate and claim that it is sensitive to more than lies (Saxe & Ben-Shakhar, 1999). Factors such as tense muscles, drugs, and previous experience with polygraph tests can significantly reduce their accuracy rate. In one experiment, people were able to reduce the accuracy of polygraph-based judgments to about 50% by biting their tongue (to produce pain) or by pressing their toes against the floor (to tense muscles) while being interviewed (Honts et al., 1985).

Iacono and Lykken (1997) conducted a mail survey of members of the Society for Psychophysiological Research and the General Psychology division of the American Psychological Association. Response rates were high—91% and 74%, respectively. Most respondents replied that polygraph lie detection was not theoretically sound, that claims for its validity were overstated, that people can easily learn to beat the test, and that polygraph results should not be admitted as evidence in courts of law.

It appears that no identifiable pattern of bodily responses pinpoints lying (Iacono & Lykken, 1997; Saxe & Ben-Shakhar, 1999). Because of validity problems, results of polygraph examinations are no longer admitted as evidence in many courts.

In sum, various components of an experience—cognitive, physiological, and behavioral—contribute to our emotional responses. Physiological arousal is a part of emotional response, but people appraise their situations when they feel aroused such that arousal does not appear to directly cause one emotion or another. Humans are thinking beings who gather information from all three sources in determining their behavioral responses and labeling their emotional responses. The fact that none of the theories of emotion we have discussed applies to all people in all situations is comforting. Apparently our emotions are not quite as easily understood, manipulated, or—as in the case of the polygraph—even detected as some theorists have suggested.

What Do "Lie Detectors" Detect?
The polygraph monitors heart rate, blood pressure, respiration rate, and sweat in the palms of the hands. Is the polygraph sensitive to lying only? Is it foolproof? Because of the controversy surrounding these questions, many courts no longer admit polygraph evidence.

REVIEW

(26) An emotion is a _____ state. (27) The emotion of anxiety mainly involves arousal of the _____ division of the autonomic nervous system (ANS). (28) _____ involves arousal of the parasympathetic division of the ANS and cognitions of hopelessness. (29) The expression of emotions such as anger, fear, happiness, and surprise appears to be (culture-specific or universal?). (30) According to the James-Lange theory, emotions have specific patterns of arousal and _____. (31) The Cannon-Bard theory proposes that processing of events by the brain gives rise simultaneously to _____ activity (arousal) and the experiencing of the emotion. (32) According to the theory of _____ appraisal, the emotion a person will experience reflects his or her appraisal of the situation. (33) Lie detectors assess heart rate, blood _____, respiration rate, and electrodermal response (sweating).

Pulling It Together: What are emotions? Does "being emotional" provide people with an evolutionary advantage? Explain.

CLICK4™ *a quiz covering the second half of this chapter.*

CLICK4™ *electronic flash cards to review your knowledge of key terms and people in this chapter.*

TRUTH ☒ FICTION
REVISITED

◩ It is true that birds who have never seen another bird or a nest will still build nests during the mating season. *Nest-building is an example of instinctive behavior. See page 284.*

◩ It is true that more than half of adult Americans are overweight. *See page 290.*

◩ Yes, Americans do overeat by an amount great enough to feed the entire nation of Germany. *The excess calories would feed another 80 million people! See page 290.*

◩ It is not true that getting away from it all by going on a vacation from all sensory input for a few hours is relaxing. *If it is carried out like the experiment at McGill University, such a "vacation" may be highly stressful. See page 295.*

◩ It is true that we appreciate things more when we have to work for them. *This is an example of the principle of effort justification. See page 297.*

◩ It is not true that efficient, skillful employees are evaluated more highly than hard-working employees who must struggle to get the job done. *Supervisors often focus on employees' efforts, sometimes more so than on their performance. See page 300.*

◩ Schachter found that misery does love company—but only company of a special sort. *That is, anxious people preferred to affiliate with other people who were anxious, not with people who seemed to be relaxed. See page 301.*

◩ Research does not support the value of catharsis as a way to prevent harmful aggression. *Research evidence suggests that expressing ("venting") aggressive impulses may encourage additional aggressive behavior. See page 303.*

◩ It is true that smiling can produce pleasant feelings. *Research has shown that the Duchenne smile can indeed give rise to pleasant feelings. See page 306.*

◩ It is true that you may be able to fool a lie detector by wiggling your toes. *This creates patterns of autonomic arousal that may be misread in interpreting the polygraph. See page 311.*

1. **What is the psychology of motivation? What are motives, needs, drives, and incentives?**

The psychology of motivation concerns why people do certain things. *Motives* are hypothetical states within an organism that activate behavior and propel the organism toward goals. Psychologists also speak of physiological *needs*, such as those for oxygen and food, and of psychological needs, such as those for achievement and self-esteem. Needs give rise to *drives*; for example, depletion of food gives rise to the hunger drive. An *incentive* is an object, person, or situation that can satisfy a need or is desirable for its own sake.

2. **What is meant by species-specific behaviors?**

According to instinct theory, organisms are born with preprogrammed tendencies—called *instincts* or *species-specific behaviors* or *fixed-action patterns* (FAPs)—to behave in certain ways in certain situations. FAPs occur in the presence of stimuli called *releasers*. Male members of many species are sexually aroused by pheromones secreted by females. Psychologists debate whether humans have instincts, and if so, what they are.

3. **What is drive-reduction theory? How is it related to homeostasis?**

According to drive-reduction theory, we are motivated to engage in behavior that reduces drives. *Primary drives* such as hunger and pain are based on the biological makeup of the organism. *Acquired drives* such as the drive for money are learned. Drives trigger arousal and activate behavior. We learn to do what reduces drives. The body has a tendency called *homeostasis* to maintain a steady state; therefore, food deprivation leads to the hunger drive and eating, which reduces the hunger drive.

4. **How does humanistic theory differ from the instinct and drive-reduction theories of motivation?**

Whereas instincts and drives are mainly defensive, aimed at survival and reproduction, humanistic psychologists argue that people are self-aware and that behavior can be growth oriented; people are motivated to strive for self-actualization.

5. **What is Maslow's hierarchy of needs?**

Maslow hypothesized that people have a hierarchy of needs. Once lower-level needs such as physiological and safety needs are satisfied, people strive to meet higher-level needs such as those for love, esteem, and self-actualization.

6. **Why are people motivated to eliminate inconsistencies in their worldviews?**

According to cognitive theory, people are motivated to understand and predict events. People must represent the world accurately in order to accomplish these goals, and therefore their cognitions need to be harmonious or consistent with one another.

7. **How do we make sense of all these different views of motivation?**

There is no question that many animals are born with instincts; the question remains as to what instincts people have and how compelling they are. Drive-reduction theory appears to apply to physiological drives such as hunger and thirst, but people often act to increase rather than decrease the tension they experience. Although humanistic theory has been criticized as unscientific, many psychologists make room for conscious striving in their views of humans. Cognition appears to be a fact of human life, although psychologists debate ways of directly assessing it.

8. **What bodily mechanisms regulate the hunger drive? What psychological processes are at work?**

Hunger is regulated by several internal mechanisms, including stomach contractions, blood sugar level, receptors in the mouth and liver, and the responses of the hypothalamus. Stomach contractions correspond with hunger but do not fully regulate it. The *ventromedial nucleus* (VMN) of the hypothalamus functions as a stop-eating center. Damage to this area leads to *hyperphagia* in rats; that is, the animals grow to several times their normal body weight. The *lateral hypothalamus* may function as a start-eating center. External stimuli such as the aroma of food can also trigger hunger. Chewing and swallowing provide some satiety.

9. *If obesity is connected with health problems and unhappiness with the image in the mirror, why are so many people overweight?*

Biological factors in obesity include heredity, adipose tissue (body fat), and the metabolic rate (the rate at which the individual converts calories to energy). Psychological factors such as stress can also contribute to overeating. Obesity is more prevalent among poorer people. Since people of color are typically of lower socioeconomic status than European Americans, rates of obesity tend to be higher among African and Latino and Latina Americans.

10. *So what can people do to shed a few pounds?*

Sound weight control programs involve improving nutritional knowledge (e.g., eating more fruits and vegetables and fewer fatty foods), decreasing calorie intake, exercising, and changing eating habits. Behavior modification helps people construct healthful diets and cope with temptations.

11. *Are all motives aimed at the reduction of tension?*

Apparently not. Stimulus motives, like physiological motives, are innate, but they involve motives to increase rather than decrease "tension" or the amount of stimulation acting on the organism.

12. *Do we need to be active? Do we need to stimulate our senses?*

Sensory-deprivation studies suggest that inactivity and lack of stimulation are aversive in humans. People and many lower animals have needs for stimulation and activity.

13. *Why do puppies and kittens explore their environments when they are brought into new homes?*

People and many lower animals have needs for exploration and manipulation. Many psychologists believe that exploration is reinforcing in and of itself.

14. *Why are people who go unrewarded more likely than those who are rewarded to think or say that what they are doing is worthwhile for its own sake?*

Cognitive-dissonance theory hypothesizes that people dislike situations in which their attitudes and behavior are inconsistent. Such situations apparently induce cognitive dissonance, which people can reduce by changing their attitudes. For example, people engage in effort justification; that is, they tend to justify boring or fruitless behavior to themselves by concluding that their efforts are worthwhile, even when they go unrewarded.

15. *Why do some people strive to get ahead?*

One reason may be that they have more achievement motivation than other people. Achievement motivation is the need to accomplish things. McClelland studied achievement motivation by means of people's responses to TAT cards. People with high achievement motivation attain higher grades and earn more money than people of comparable ability with lower achievement motivation. People may be motivated to achieve in school by performance or learning goals. Performance goals are tangible rewards, such as money or getting into graduate school. Learning goals involve the enhancement of knowledge or skills.

16. *Why do people need people?*

People may have an inborn (instinctive) need to affiliate with other people. Anxiety tends to increase the need for affiliation, especially with people who share one's predicament.

17. Why do people kill, maim, and injure one another?

Certainly people engage in warfare and other kinds of combat as members of groups. However, psychological theories also address the problem of aggression. Biological theory views aggression as instinctive and linked to brain structures, hormone levels, and the Darwinian concept of the "survival of the fittest." Psychodynamic theory views aggression as stemming from inevitable frustrations. Cognitive perspectives predict that people may be aggressive when they see aggression as being appropriate for them, or when they interpret other people's behavior as insults to their honor. Learning theories view aggression as stemming from experience and reinforcement of aggressive skills. The sociocultural perspective examines the effects of culture—such as the culture of athletic competition—on aggression.

18. Just what is an emotion?

An emotion is a state of feeling with physiological, cognitive, and behavioral components. Emotions motivate behavior and also serve as goals. Fear, for example, is connected with arousal of the sympathetic division of the autonomic nervous system, cognitions that one is in danger, and behavioral tendencies to escape.

19. How can we tell when other people are happy or despondent?

Facial expressions are one factor in the expression of emotion. According to Ekman, there are several basic emotions whose expression is recognized in cultures around the world. Darwin believed that the universal recognition of facial expressions had survival value.

20. Can smiling give rise to feelings of good will? Can frowning produce anger?

It does appear that facial expressions can influence one's experience of emotion. The contraction of facial muscles may be influential.

21. How do the physiological, situational, and cognitive components of emotions interact to produce feelings and behavior?

According to the James-Lange theory, emotions are associated with specific patterns of arousal and action that are triggered by certain external events. The emotion follows the behavioral response. The Cannon-Bard theory proposes that processing of events by the brain gives rise simultaneously to feelings and bodily responses. According to this view, feelings accompany bodily responses. According to Schachter and Singer's theory of cognitive appraisal, emotions are associated with similar patterns of arousal, but the level of arousal can differ. The emotion a person experiences in response to an external stimulus reflects that person's appraisal of the stimulus. Research evidence suggests that patterns of arousal are more specific than suggested by the theory of cognitive appraisal, but that cognitive appraisal also plays a role in determining our responses to events.

22. How do lie detectors work? How reliable are they?

Lie detectors—also called polygraphs—monitor indicators of sympathetic arousal, including heart rate, blood pressure, respiration rate, and electrodermal response (sweating) while a witness or suspect in a crime is being examined. These responses are presumed to indicate the presence of emotions—anxiety and/or guilt—that might be induced by lying. Critics find polygraph testing to be unreliable and argue that it is sensitive to more emotions than those that might be connected with lying.

PREVIEW

Prenatal Development: The Beginning of Our Life Story
▲ The most dramatic changes in development occur prior to birth.

Childhood: Physical Development
▲ Within a few months you develop from a helpless baby that lies around into a being that runs around to get what it needs and wants.

Childhood: Cognitive Development
▲ Prior to 6 months or so of age, "out of sight" is literally "out of mind."
▲ Language develops from mindless crying to sophisticated use of grammar—all within a couple of years.
▲ Which is more important: *what* children think is right and wrong, or *how* they arrive at that conclusion?

Childhood: Social and Personality Development
▲ During the first year, we come to trust that our needs will be met. (Or not.)
▲ Why do children become attached to their parents? (Or not?)
▲ Parenting styles are connected with the development of self-esteem, achievement motivation, and independence in children.

Controversies in Developmental Psychology
▲ Which has the greater influence on development: nature or nurture?
▲ Don't bother making threats; house plants won't talk.
▲ Which aspects of development occur gradually? Which take place more abruptly?

CHAPTER 10

Child Development

TRUTH [☑] FICTION?

▰ Fertilization takes place in the uterus.

▰ Your heart started beating when you were only one fifth of an inch long and weighed a fraction of an ounce.

▰ The way to a baby's heart is through its stomach — that is, babies become emotionally attached to those who feed them.

▰ Children with strict parents are most likely to be successful.

▰ Children placed in day care are more aggressive than children cared for in the home.

▰ Child abusers frequently were abused themselves as children.

There is no cure for birth or death save to enjoy the interval.

—George Santayana

We have a story to tell. An important story. A fascinating story. It is your story. It is about the remarkable journey you have already taken through childhood and adolescence. It is about the unfolding of your adult life. Billions have made this journey before. You have much in common with them. Yet you are unique and things will happen to you, and because of you, that have never happened before.

Let us watch as Ling and Patrick Chang begin such a story by conceiving a child. On a summerlike day in October, Ling and Patrick rush to their jobs as usual. While Ling, a trial attorney, is preparing a case to present in court, a very different drama is unfolding in her body. Hormones are causing a follicle (egg container) in one of her ovaries to ovulate—that is, to rupture and release an egg cell, or ovum. Ling, like other women, possessed from birth all the egg cells she will ever have. How this particular ovum was selected to ripen and be released this month is unknown. But in any case, Ling will be capable of becoming pregnant for only a couple of days following ovulation.

When it is released, the ovum begins a slow journey down a 4-inch-long fallopian tube to the uterus. It is within this tube that one of Patrick's sperm cells will unite with the egg. The fertilized ovum, or zygote, is 1/175th of an inch across—a tiny stage for the drama that is about to unfold.

Developmental psychologists are interested in studying the development of Patrick and Ling's new child from the time of conception until death for several reasons. The discovery of early influences and developmental sequences helps psychologists understand adults. Psychologists are also interested in the effects of genetic factors, early interactions with parents and siblings (brothers and sisters), and the school and community on traits such as aggressiveness and intelligence.

Developmental psychologists seek to learn the causes of developmental abnormalities. For instance, should pregnant women abstain from smoking and drinking? (Yes.) Is it safe for a pregnant woman to take aspirin for a headache or tetracycline to ward off a bacterial invasion? (Perhaps not. Ask your obstetrician.) What factors contribute to child abuse? Some developmental psychologists focus on adult development. For example, what conflicts and disillusionments can we expect as we journey through our 30s, 40s, and 50s? The information acquired by developmental psychologists can help us make decisions about how we rear our children and lead our own lives.

Let us now turn to prenatal developments—the changes that occur between conception and birth. Although they may be literally "out of sight," the most dramatic biological changes occur within the short span of 9 months.

PRENATAL DEVELOPMENT: THE BEGINNING OF OUR LIFE STORY

www 10 L 1

CLICK4™ *Web sites on prenatal development and birth psychology.*

The most dramatic gains in height and weight occur during prenatal development. *Question: What developments occur from conception through birth?* Within 9 months a child develops from a nearly microscopic cell to a **neonate** (newborn) about 20 inches long. Its weight increases a billionfold.

During the months following conception, the single cell formed by the union of sperm and egg—the **zygote**—multiplies, becoming two, then four, then eight, and so on. By the time the infant is ready to be born, it contains trillions of cells.

The zygote divides repeatedly as it proceeds on its 3- to 4-day journey to the uterus. The ball-like mass of multiplying cells wanders about the uterus for another 3 to 4 days before beginning to implant in the uterine wall. Implantation takes another week or so. The period from conception to implantation is called the **germinal stage,** or the **period of the ovum.**

The **embryonic stage** lasts from implantation until about the eighth week of development. During this stage, the major body organ systems take form. As you can see from

Neonate ▲ A newly born child.

Zygote ▲ A fertilized ovum (egg cell).

Germinal stage ▲ The first stage of prenatal development during which the dividing mass of cells has not become implanted in the uterine wall.

Period of the ovum ▲ Another term for the *germinal stage.*

Embryonic stage ▲ The baby from the third through the eighth weeks following conception, during which time the major organ systems undergo rapid differentiation.

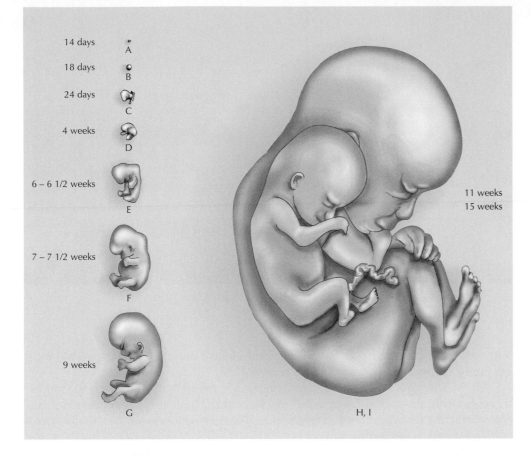

14 days — A
18 days — B
24 days — C
4 weeks — D
6 – 6 1/2 weeks — E
7 – 7 1/2 weeks — F
9 weeks — G
11 weeks / 15 weeks
H, I

FIGURE 10.1   Embryos and Fetuses at Various Intervals of Prenatal Development.
Development of the head (and brain) precedes that of other parts of the body. The development of the organs—
heart, lungs, and so on—also precedes the development of the limbs. The relatively early maturation of the brain
and the organ systems allows them to participate in the nourishment and further development of the embryo.

the relatively large heads of embryos (see Figure 10.1), the growth of the head precedes that of other parts of the body. The growth of the organs—heart, lungs, and so on—also precedes the growth of the extremities. The relatively early maturation of the brain and the organ systems allows them to participate in the nourishment and further development of the embryo. During the fourth week, a primitive heart begins to beat and pump blood—in an organism that is one fifth of an inch long. The heart will continue to beat without rest every minute of every day for perhaps 80 or 90 years.

By the end of the second month, the head has become rounded and the facial features distinct—all in an embryo that is about 1 inch long and weighs 1/30th of an ounce. During the second month, the nervous system begins to transmit messages. By 5 to 6 weeks, the embryo is only a quarter to half an inch long, yet nondescript sex organs have formed. By about the seventh week, the genetic code (XY or XX) begins to assert itself, causing the sex organs to differentiate. If a Y sex chromosome is present, testes form and begin to produce **androgens** (male sex hormones), which further masculinize the sex organs. In the absence of these hormones, the embryo develops female sex organs.

As it develops, the embryo is suspended within a protective **amniotic sac** in the mother's uterus. The sac is surrounded by a clear membrane and contains amniotic fluid.

www **10**   WS **1**

CLICK4™ *a WebSearch activity on embryology and observe the changes that occur in prenatal development.*

Androgens ▲ Male sex hormones.
Amniotic sac ▲ A sac within the uterus that contains the embryo or fetus.

An Exercise Class for Pregnant Women.
Years ago pregnant women were not expected to exert themselves. Today, it is recognized that exercise is healthful for pregnant women because it promotes fitness, which is beneficial during childbirth—and in general.

www 10 E 1

CLICK4™ *an essay assignment on prenatal screening.*

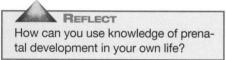

▲ **REFLECT**
How can you use knowledge of prenatal development in your own life?

Placenta ▲ A membrane that permits the exchange of nutrients and waste products between the mother and her developing child but does not allow the maternal and fetal bloodstreams to mix.

Umbilical cord ▲ A tube between the mother and her developing child through which nutrients and waste products are conducted.

Fetus ▲ The baby from the third month following conception through childbirth, during which time there is maturation of organ systems and dramatic gains in length and weight.

The fluid is a sort of natural air bag, allowing the child to move or even jerk around without injury. It also helps maintain an even temperature.

From now until birth, the embryo exchanges nutrients and wastes with the mother through a pancake-shaped organ called the **placenta.** The embryo is connected to the placenta by the **umbilical cord.** The placenta is connected to the mother by the system of blood vessels in the uterine wall.

The circulatory systems of the mother and baby do not mix. A membrane in the placenta permits only certain substances to pass through. Oxygen and nutrients are passed from the mother to the embryo. Carbon dioxide and other wastes are passed from the child to the mother, where they are removed by the mother's lungs and kidneys. Unfortunately, a number of other substances can pass through the placenta. They include some microscopic disease organisms—such as those that cause syphilis and German measles—and some chemical agents, including acne drugs, aspirin, narcotics, alcohol, and tranquilizers. Because these and other agents may be harmful to the baby, pregnant women are advised to consult their physicians before using any drugs, even those sold over the counter.

The fetal stage lasts from the beginning of the third month until birth. By the end of the third month, the major organ systems and the fingers and toes have formed. In the middle of the fourth month, the mother usually detects the first fetal movements. By the end of the sixth month, the **fetus** moves its limbs so vigorously that mothers often feel that they are being kicked. The fetus opens and shuts its eyes, sucks its thumb, alternates between periods of being awake and sleeping, and perceives light. It also turns somersaults, which can be perceived clearly by the mother. The umbilical cord is composed so that it will not break or become dangerously wrapped around the fetus, no matter how many acrobatic feats the fetus performs.

During the last 3 months, the organ systems of the fetus continue to mature. The heart and lungs become increasingly capable of sustaining independent life. The fetus gains about $5\frac{1}{2}$ pounds and doubles in length. Newborn boys average about $7\frac{1}{2}$ pounds and newborn girls about 7 pounds.

REVIEW

(1) It is possible to become pregnant for a day or so after _____. (2) A sperm cell combines with an ovum to form a _____. (3) The zygote implants in the wall of the _____. (4) Prenatal development is divided into three stages: the germinal stage, the _____ stage (which lasts from 2 weeks to about 2 months after conception), and the fetal stage.

Pulling It Together: Provide examples of how key developments occur most rapidly during prenatal development.

CHILDHOOD: PHYSICAL DEVELOPMENT

Childhood begins with birth. When my children are enjoying themselves, I kid them and say "Stop having fun. You're a child and childhood is the worst time of life." I get a laugh because they know that childhood is supposed to be the best time of life—a time for play and learning and endless possibilities. For many children it is that, but other children suffer from problems such as malnutrition, low self-esteem, and child abuse.

Let us chronicle the events of childhood. The most obvious aspects of child development are physical. Let us therefore begin with physical development. However, we will see that cognitive developments and social and personality developments are also essential.

Physical development includes gains in height and weight; maturation of the nervous system; and development of bones, muscles, and organs. *Question: What physical developments occur during childhood?*

During infancy—the first two years of childhood—dramatic gains in height and weight continue. Babies usually double their birth weight in about 5 months and triple it by their first birthday. Their height increases by about 10 inches in the first year. Children grow another 4 to 6 inches during the second year and gain some 4 to 7 pounds. After that, they gain about 2 to 3 inches a year until they reach the adolescent growth spurt. Weight gains also remain fairly even at about 4 to 6 pounds per year until the spurt begins.

Let us now consider other aspects of physical development in childhood: reflexes, perceptual development, and motor development.

Reflexes — Entering the World Prewired

Soon after you were born, a doctor or nurse probably pressed her fingers against the palms of your hands. Although you would have had no idea what to do in response, most likely you grasped the fingers firmly—so firmly that you could have been lifted from your cradle! Grasping at birth is inborn. It is one of the neonate's many **reflexes**—simple, unlearned, stereotypical responses elicited by specific stimuli. Reflexes are essential to survival and do not involve higher brain functions. They occur automatically—that is, without thinking about them.

Newborn children do not know that it is necessary to eat to survive. Fortunately, they have rooting and sucking reflexes that cause them to eat. They turn their head toward stimuli that prod or stroke the cheek, chin, or corner of the mouth. This is termed **rooting.** They suck objects that touch their lips.

Neonates have numerous other reflexes that aid in survival. They withdraw from painful stimuli. This is known as the withdrawal reflex. They draw up their legs and arch their backs in response to sudden noises, bumps, or loss of support while being held. This is the startle, or Moro, reflex. They grasp objects that press against the palms of their hands (the grasp, or palmar, reflex). They fan their toes when the soles of their feet are stimulated (the Babinski reflex). Pediatricians assess babies' neural functioning by testing these reflexes.

Babies also breathe, sneeze, cough, yawn, and blink reflexively. And it is guaranteed that you will learn about the sphincter (anal muscle) reflex if you put on your best clothes and hold an undiapered neonate on your lap for a while.

Perceptual Development: On *Not* Going Off the Deep End

Newborn children spend about 16 hours a day sleeping and do not have much opportunity to learn about the world. Yet they are capable of perceiving the world reasonably well soon after birth.

Within a couple of days, infants can follow, or track, a moving light with their eyes (Kellman & von Hofsten, 1992). By the age of 3 months, they can discriminate most

▲ **REFLECT**
Why do you think that babies are born with reflexes?

www 10 E 2

CLICK4™ *an essay assignment on infant reflexes.*

Reflex ▲ A simple unlearned response to a stimulus.
Rooting ▲ The turning of an infant's head toward a touch, such as by the mother's nipple.

▲ REFLECT
Why do you think developmental psychologists are interested in when and how babies develop an interest in human faces?

CLICK4™ *more information from the Child Development Institute about physical, mental, and emotional growth in children.*

Fixation time ▲ The amount of time spent looking at a visual stimulus.

colors (Banks & Shannon, 1993; Teller, 1998). Neonates are nearsighted but by about the age of 4 months, infants seem able to focus on distant objects about as well as adults can.

The visual preferences of infants are measured by the amount of time, termed **fixation time,** they spend looking at one stimulus instead of another. In classic research by Robert Fantz (1961), 2-month-old infants preferred visual stimuli that resembled the human face to newsprint, a bull's-eye, and featureless red, white, and yellow disks. At this age the complexity of facelike patterns may be more important than their content. For example, babies have been shown facelike patterns that differ either in the number of elements they contain or the degree to which they are organized to match the human face. Five- to 10-week-old babies fixate longer on patterns with high numbers of elements. The organization of the elements—that is, the degree to which they resemble the face— is less important. By 15 to 20 weeks, the organization of the pattern also matters. At that age babies dwell longer on facelike patterns (e.g., Haaf et al., 1983).

Infants thus seem to have an inborn preference for complex visual stimuli. However, preference for faces as opposed to other equally complex stimuli may not emerge until infants have had experience with people.

Classic research has shown that infants tend to respond to cues for depth by the time they are able to crawl (at about 6 to 8 months). Most also have the good sense to avoid crawling off ledges and table tops into open space (Campos et al., 1978). Note the setup (Figure 10.2) in the classic "visual cliff" experiment run by Walk and Gibson (1961). An 8-month-old infant crawls freely above the portion of the glass with a checkerboard pattern immediately beneath it, but hesitates to crawl over the portion of the glass beneath which the checkerboard has been dropped a few feet. Because the glass would support the infant, this is a "visual cliff," not an actual cliff.

Normal neonates hear well unless their middle ears are clogged with amniotic fluid. In such cases, hearing improves rapidly after the ears are opened up. Most neonates reflexively turn their heads toward unusual sounds, suspending other activities as they do so. This finding, along with findings about visual tracking, suggests that infants are preprogrammed to survey their environments. Speaking or singing softly in a low-pitched tone soothes infants. This is why some parents use lullabies to get infants to fall asleep.

Three-day-old babies prefer their mother's voice to those of other women, but they do not show a similar preference for their father's voice (DeCasper & Prescott, 1984; Freeman et al., 1993). By birth, of course, babies have had many months of "experience" in the uterus. For at least 2 or 3 months before birth, babies have been capable of hearing sounds. Because they are predominantly exposed to sounds produced by their mother, learning may contribute to neonatal preferences.

FIGURE 10.2   The Classic Visual Cliff Experiment.
This young explorer has the good sense not to crawl out onto an apparently unsupported surface, even when Mother beckons from the other side. Rats, pups, kittens, and chicks also will not try to walk across to the other side. (So don't bother asking why the chicken crossed the visual cliff.)

The nasal preferences of babies are similar to those of adults. Newborn infants spit, stick out their tongue, and literally wrinkle their nose at the odor of rotten eggs. They smile and make licking motions in response to chocolate, strawberry, vanilla, and honey. The sense of smell, like the sense of hearing, may provide a vehicle for mother-infant recognition. Within the first week, nursing infants prefer to turn to look at their mother's nursing pads (which can be discriminated only by smell) rather than those of strange women (Macfarlane, 1975). By 15 days, nursing infants prefer their mother's underarm odor to those of other women (Porter et al., 1992). Bottle-fed babies do not show this preference.

Shortly after birth, infants can discriminate tastes. They suck liquid solutions of sugar and milk but grimace and refuse to suck salty or bitter solutions.

Newborn babies are sensitive to touch. Many reflexes (including rooting and sucking) are activated by pressure against the skin. Newborns are relatively insensitive to pain, however. This may be adaptive, considering the squeezing that occurs during the birth process. Sensitivity to pain increases within a few days.

The sense of touch is an extremely important avenue of learning and communication for babies. Sensations of skin against skin appear to provide feelings of comfort and security that may contribute to the formation of affectionate bonds between infants and their caregivers.

Motor Development — Getting a Move On

Motor development provides some of the most fascinating changes in infants, in part because so much seems to happen so quickly—and so much of it during the first year. Children gain the capacity to move about through a sequence of activities that includes rolling over, sitting up, crawling, creeping, walking, and running. There is a great deal of variation in the ages at which infants first engage in these activities, but the sequence generally remains the same (see Figure 10.3). A number of children will skip a step, however. For example, an infant may creep without ever having crawled.

Let us now consider cognitive developments during childhood. Physical development is not possible without the participation of the brain, and the brain is also the seat of cognition.

REVIEW

(5) Infants double their birth weight in about (how many?) _____ months and triple it by the first birthday. (6) Infants are generally capable of depth perception by the time they are able to _____. (7) The taste and nasal preferences of babies (are or are not?) similar to those of adults. (8) Although newborns are sensitive to touch, they are relatively insensitive to _____.

Pulling It Together: Explain how reflexes enable the survival of the infant. Why do you think that newborns prefer their mothers' voices to those of other women?

CHILDHOOD: COGNITIVE DEVELOPMENT

The ways in which children mentally represent and think about the world—that is, their *cognitive development*—are explored in this section. Because cognitive functioning

www 10 BBC 1

CLICK4™ *a bulletin board discussion on physical development in childhood.*

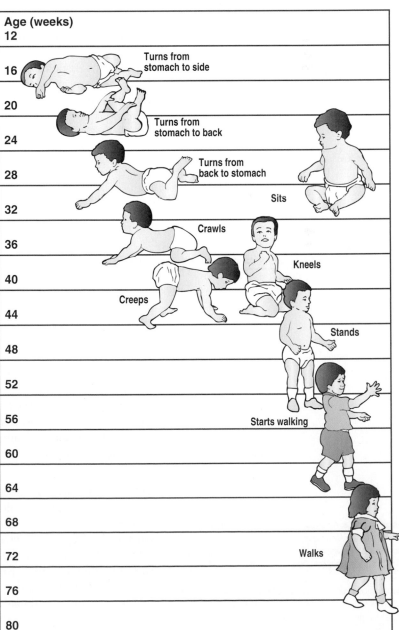

FIGURE 10.3   Motor Development.
At birth, infants appear to be bundles of aimless "nervous energy." They have reflexes but also engage in random movements that are replaced by purposeful activity as they mature. Motor development proceeds in an orderly sequence. Practice prompts sensorimotor coordination, but maturation is essential. The times in the figure are approximate: An infant who is a bit behind may develop with no problems at all, and a precocious infant will not necessarily become a rocket scientist (or gymnast).

Age (weeks)
12
16   Turns from stomach to side
20   Turns from stomach to back
24
28   Turns from back to stomach
     Sits
32   Crawls
36   Kneels
40   Creeps
44   Stands
48
52
56   Starts walking
60
64
68
72   Walks
76
80

TABLE 10.1 PIAGET'S STAGES OF COGNITIVE DEVELOPMENT

Stage	Approximate Age	About ...
Sensorimotor	Birth–2 years	At first, the child lacks language and does not use symbols or mental representations of objects. In time, reflexive responding ends and intentional behavior begins. The child develops the object concept and acquires the basics of language.
Preoperational	2–7 years	The child begins to represent the world mentally, but thought is egocentric. The child does not focus on two aspects of a situation at once and therefore lacks conservation. The child shows animism, artificialism, and objective responsibility for wrongdoing.
Concrete operational	7–12 years	The child develops conservation concepts, can adopt the viewpoint of others, can classify objects in series, and shows comprehension of basic relational concepts (such as one object being larger or heavier than another).
Formal operational	12 years and above	Mature, adult thought emerges. Thinking is characterized by deductive logic, consideration of various possibilities (mental trial and error), abstract thought, and the formation and testing of hypotheses.

CLICK4™ *an essay assignment on Piaget's theory of cognitive development.*

▲ REFLECT

Can you provide some examples of assimilation and accommodation in learning about psychology?

Assimilation ▲ According to Piaget, the inclusion of a new event into an existing scheme.

Scheme ▲ According to Piaget, a hypothetical mental structure that permits the classification and organization of new information.

Accommodation ▲ According to Piaget, the modification of schemes so that information inconsistent with existing schemes can be integrated or understood.

develops over many years, young children have ideas about the world that differ considerably from those of adults. Many of these ideas are charming but illogical—at least to adults. *Question: What are Jean Piaget's views of cognitive development?*

Jean Piaget's Cognitive-Developmental Theory

The Swiss biologist and psychologist Jean Piaget contributed significantly to our understanding of children's cognitive development. He hypothesized that children's cognitive processes develop in an orderly sequence of stages. Although some children may be more advanced than others at particular ages, the developmental sequence remains the same. Piaget (1963) identified four major stages of cognitive development: sensorimotor, preoperational, concrete operational, and formal operational (see Table 10.1).

Assimilation and Accommodation Piaget described human thought, or intelligence, in terms of two basic concepts: assimilation and accommodation. **Assimilation** means responding to a new stimulus through a reflex or existing habit. Infants, for example, usually try to place new objects in their mouth to suck, feel, or explore. Piaget would say that the child is assimilating a new toy to the sucking scheme. A **scheme** is a pattern of action or a mental structure involved in acquiring or organizing knowledge.

Piaget regarded children as natural physicists who seek to learn about and control their world. In the Piagetian view, children who squish their food and laugh enthusiastically are often acting as budding scientists. In addition to enjoying the responses of their parents, they are studying the texture and consistency of their food. (Parents, of course, often wish their children would practice these experiments in the laboratory, not the dining room.)

Accommodation is the creation of new ways of responding to objects or looking at the world. In accommodation, children transform existing schemes—action patterns or ways of organizing knowledge—to incorporate new events. Children (and adults) accommodate to objects and situations that cannot be integrated into existing schemes. (For example, children who study biology learn that whales cannot be assimilated into the "fish" scheme. They accommodate by constructing new schemes, such as "mammals without legs that live in the sea.") The ability to accommodate to novel stimuli advances as a result of maturation and experience.

Most of the time, newborn children assimilate environmental stimuli according to reflexive schemes, although adjusting the mouth to contain the nipple is a primitive kind of accommodation. Reflexive behavior, to Piaget, is not "true" intelligence. True intelligence involves adapting to the world through a smooth, fluid balancing of the processes of assimilation and accommodation. Let us now apply these concepts to the stages of cognitive development.

The Sensorimotor Stage The newborn infant is capable of assimilating novel stimuli only to existing reflexes (or ready-made schemes) such as the rooting and sucking reflexes. But by the time an infant reaches the age of 1 month, it already shows purposeful behavior by repeating behavior patterns that are pleasurable, such as sucking its hand. During the first month or so, an infant apparently does not connect stimuli perceived through different senses. Reflexive turning toward sources of auditory and olfactory stimulation cannot be considered purposeful searching. But within the first few months the infant begins to coordinate vision with grasping so that it looks at what it is holding or touching.

A 3- or 4-month-old infant may be fascinated by its own hands and legs. It may become absorbed in watching itself open and close its fists. The infant becomes increasingly interested in acting on the environment to make interesting results (such as the sound of a rattle) last longer or occur again. Behavior becomes increasingly intentional and purposeful. Between 4 and 8 months of age, the infant explores cause-and-effect relationships such as the thump that can be made by tossing an object or the way kicking can cause a hanging toy to bounce.

Prior to the age of 6 months or so, out of sight is literally out of mind. Objects are not yet represented mentally. For this reason, as you can see in Figure 10.4, a child makes no effort to search for an object that has been removed or placed behind a screen. By the age of 8 to 12 months, however, infants realize that objects removed from sight still exist and attempt to find them. In this way, they show what is known as **object permanence,** thereby making it possible to play peek-a-boo.

By the way, comparative psychologists have also studied the development of object permanence in nonhuman species, including dogs and cats . . . and magpies. Magpies are notorious thieves in the bird world, and they also hide their food to keep it safe from other animals—especially other magpies. Bettina Pollock and her colleagues (2000) found that magpies develop object permanence before they begin to hide food. Magpies would not profit from secreting away their food if out of sight meant the same thing as "out of existence."

Between 1 and 2 years of age, children begin to show interest in how things are constructed. It may be for this reason that they persistently touch and finger their parents' faces and their own. Toward the end of the second year, children begin to engage in mental trial and error before they try out overt behaviors. For instance, when they look for an object you have removed, they will no longer begin their search in the last place they saw it. Rather, they may follow you, assuming you are carrying the object even though it is not visible. It is as though they are anticipating failure in searching for the object in the place where they last saw it.

Because the first stage of development is dominated by learning to coordinate perception of the self and of the environment with motor (muscular) activity, Piaget termed it the **sensorimotor stage.** This stage comes to a close with the acquisition of the basics of language at about age 2.

The Preoperational Stage

The **preoperational stage** is characterized by the use of words and symbols to represent objects and relationships among them. But be warned—any resemblance between the logic of children between the ages of 2 and 7 and your own logic very often is purely coincidental. Children may use the same words that adults do, but this does not mean their views of the world are similar to adults'. A major limit on preoperational children's thinking is that it tends to be one-dimensional—to focus on one aspect of a problem or situation at a time.

One consequence of one-dimensional thinking is **egocentrism.** Preoperational children cannot understand that other people do not see things the same way they do. When Allyn was 2½, I asked her to tell me about a trip to the store with her mother. "You tell me," she replied. Upon questioning, it seemed she did not understand that I could not see the world through her eyes.

To egocentric preoperational children, all the world's a stage that has been erected to meet their needs and amuse them. When asked, "Why does the sun shine?" they may say,

CLICK4™ *a video on the absence of object permanence during the sensorimotor stage.*

CLICK4™ *a video on the presence of object permanence.*

CLICK4™ *a WebSearch activity on recent research in cognitive development—does it support Piaget's view?*

Object permanence ▲ Recognition that objects removed from sight still exist, as demonstrated in young children by continued pursuit.

Sensorimotor stage ▲ The first of Piaget's stages of cognitive development, characterized by coordination of sensory information and motor activity, early exploration of the environment, and lack of language.

Preoperational stage ▲ The second of Piaget's stages, characterized by illogical use of words and symbols, spotty logic, and egocentrism.

Egocentric ▲ According to Piaget, assuming that others view the world as one does oneself.

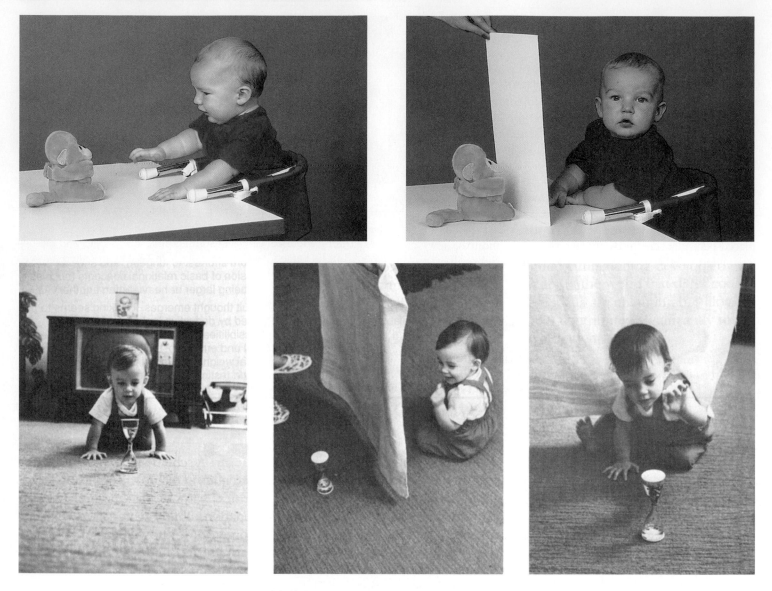

FIGURE 10.4 Object Permanence.
To the infant at the top, who is in the early part of the sensorimotor stage, out of sight is truly out of mind. Once a sheet of paper is placed between the infant and the toy elephant, the infant loses all interest in it. The toy is apparently not yet mentally represented. The photos on the bottom show a child later in the sensorimotor stage. This child does mentally represent objects and pushes through a towel to reach one that has been screened from sight.

▲ REFLECT

Can you think of examples of adults using egocentrism, animism, or artificialism in their own thinking? Why do you imagine that they do?

Animism ▲ The belief that inanimate objects move because of will or spirit.
Artificialism ▲ The belief that natural objects have been created by human beings.

"To keep me warm." If asked, "Why is the sky blue?" they may respond, "'Cause blue's my favorite color." Preoperational children also show **animism.** They attribute life and consciousness to physical objects like the sun and the moon. They also show **artificialism.** They believe that environmental events like rain and thunder are human inventions. Asked why the sky is blue, 4-year-olds may answer, "'Cause Mommy painted it." Examples of egocentrism, animism, and artificialism are shown in Table 10.2.

To gain further insight into preoperational thinking, consider these problems:

1. Imagine that you pour water from a tall, thin glass into a low, wide glass. Now, does the low, wide glass contain more, less, or the same amount of water that was in the tall, thin glass? I won't keep you in suspense. If you said the same amount of water (with possible minor exceptions for spillage and evaporation), you were correct. Now that you're on a roll, go on to the next problem.

2. If you flatten a ball of clay into a pancake, do you wind up with more, less, or the same amount of clay? If you said the same amount of clay, you are correct once more.

To arrive at the correct answers to these questions, you must understand the law of **conservation.** This law holds that basic properties of substances such as mass, weight, and volume remain the same— that is, are *conserved*—when you change superficial properties such as their shape or arrangement.

Conservation requires the ability to think about, or **center** on, two aspects of a situation at once, such as height and width. Conserving the mass, weight, or volume of a substance requires the recognition that a change in one dimension can compensate for a change in another. But the preoperational boy in Figure 10.5 focuses on only one dimension at a time. First he is shown two tall, thin glasses of juice and agrees that they contain the same amount of juice. Then, while he watches, juice is poured from a tall glass into a squat glass. Now he is asked which glass contains more juice. After mulling over the problem, he points to the tall glass. Why? Because when he looks at the glasses he is "overwhelmed" by the fact that the thinner glass is taller. The preoperational child focuses on the most apparent dimension of the situation—in this case, the greater height of the thinner glass. He does not realize that the increased width of the squat glass compensates for the decreased height. By the way, if you ask him whether any juice has been added or taken away in the pouring process, he readily says no. But if you then repeat the question about which glass contains *more* juice, he again points to the taller glass.

If all this sounds rather illogical, that is because it is illogical—or, in Piaget's terms, preoperational.

After you have tried the experiment with the juice, try the following. Make two rows of five pennies each. In the first row, place the pennies about half an inch apart. In the second row, place the pennies 2 to 3 inches apart. Ask a 4- to 5-year-old child which row has more pennies. What do you think the child will say? Why?

TABLE 10.2 EXAMPLES OF PREOPERATIONAL THOUGHT

Type of Thought	Sample Questions	Typical Answers
Egocentrism	Why does it get dark out? Why does the sun shine? Why is there snow? Why is grass green? What are TV sets for?	So I can go to sleep. To keep me warm. For me to play in. Because that's my favorite color. To watch my favorite shows and cartoons.
Animism (attributing life and consciousness to physical objects)	Why do trees have leaves? Why do stars twinkle? Why does the sun move in the sky? Where do boats go at night?	To keep them warm. Because they're happy and cheerful. To follow children and hear what they say. They sleep like we do.
Artificialism (assuming that environmental events are human inventions)	What makes it rain? Why is the sky blue? What is the wind? What causes thunder? How does a baby get in Mommy's tummy?	Someone emptying a watering can. Somebody painted it. A man blowing. A man grumbling. Just make it first. (How?) You put some eyes on it, then put on the head.

CD 10 V 33

CLICK4™ *a video on conservation of quantity during the preoperational stage.*

Conservation ▲ According to Piaget, recognition that basic properties of substances such as weight and mass remain the same when superficial features change.
Center ▲ According to Piaget, to focus one's attention.

FIGURE 10.5 Conservation.
The boy in drawing A agreed that the amount of juice in two identical containers was equal. He then (drawing B) watched as juice from one container was poured into a tall, thin container. In drawing C, he is examining one of the original containers and the new container. When asked whether he thinks the amounts of juice in the two containers are now the same, he says no. Apparently, he is impressed by the height of the new container, and, prior to the development of conservation, he focuses on only one dimension of the situation at a time—in this case, the height of the new container.

A   B   C

Piaget (1997) found that the moral judgment of preoperational children is also one-dimensional. Five-year-olds are slaves to rules and authority. When you ask them why something should be done in a certain way, they may insist "Because that's the way to do it!" or "Because my Mommy says so!" Right is right and wrong is wrong. Why? "Because!"—that's why.

According to most older children and adults, an act is a crime only when there is criminal intent. Accidents may be hurtful, but the perpetrators are usually seen as blameless. But in the court of the one-dimensional, preoperational child, there is **objective responsibility.** People are sentenced (and harshly!) on the basis of the amount of damage they have done, not their motives or intentions.

To demonstrate objective responsibility, Piaget would tell children stories and ask them which character was naughtier and why. John, for instance, accidentally breaks 15 cups when he opens a door. Henry breaks 1 cup when he sneaks into a kitchen cabinet to find forbidden jam. The preoperational child usually judges John to be naughtier. Why? Because he broke more cups.

The Concrete-Operational Stage

By about age 7, the typical child is entering the stage of **concrete operations.** In this stage, which lasts until about age 12, children show the beginnings of the capacity for adult logic. However, their logical thoughts, or *operations*, generally involve tangible objects rather than abstract ideas. Concrete operational children are capable of **decentration;** they can center on two dimensions of a problem at once. This attainment has implications for moral judgments, conservation, and other intellectual undertakings.

Children now become **subjective** in their moral judgments. When assigning guilt, they center on the motives of wrongdoers as well as on the amount of damage done. Concrete-operational children judge Henry more harshly than John because John's misdeed was an accident.

Concrete-operational children understand the laws of conservation. The boy in Figure 10.5, now a few years older, would say that the squat glass still contains the same amount of juice. If asked why, he might reply, "Because you can pour it back into the other one." Such an answer also suggests awareness of the concept of **reversibility**—the recognition that many processes can be reversed or undone so that things are restored to their previous condition. Centering simultaneously on the height and the width of the glasses, the boy recognizes that the loss in height compensates for the gain in width.

Concrete-operational children can conserve *number* as well as weight and mass. They recognize that the number of pennies in each of the rows described earlier is the same, even though one row may be spread out to look longer than the other.

Children in this stage are less egocentric. They are able to take on the roles of others and to view the world, and themselves, from other people's perspectives. They recognize that people see things in different ways because of different situations and different sets of values.

During the concrete-operational stage, children's own sets of values begin to emerge and acquire stability. Children come to understand that feelings of love between them and their parents can endure even when someone feels angry or disappointed at a particular moment.

We discuss the formal-operational stage and evaluate Piaget's theory in the section on adolescence.

CLICK4™ *a video on conservation of quantity during the concrete operational stage.*

CLICK4™ *a video on the concrete operational stage and its relation to abstract reasoning.*

▲ REFLECT
Is reliance on objective responsibility limited to children? Can you think of situations in which adults you know have shown objective responsibility in their thinking?

Objective responsibility ▲ According to Piaget, the assignment of blame according to the amount of damage done rather than the motives of the actor.

Concrete-operational stage ▲ Piaget's third stage, characterized by logical thought concerning tangible objects, conservation, and subjective morality.

Decentration ▲ Simultaneous focusing on more than one dimension of a problem, so that flexible, reversible thought becomes possible.

Subjective moral judgment ▲ According to Piaget, moral judgments that are based on the motives of the perpetrator.

Reversibility ▲ According to Piaget, recognition that processes can be undone, that things can be made as they were.

DIVERSITY   Cognitive Development and Concepts of Ethnicity and Race

What is the connection between cognitive development and the development of concepts about people from different ethnic and racial backgrounds? When is it most useful to intervene to help children develop open attitudes toward people from different backgrounds?

From interviews of 500 African American, Asian American, Latino and Latina American, and Native American children, psychologist Stephen Quintana (1998; Rabasca, 2000) concluded that children undergo four levels of understanding of ethnicity and race.

Between the ages of 3 and 6, children generally think about racial differences in physical terms. They do not necessarily see race as a fixed or stable attribute. They may think that a person could change his or her race by means of surgery or tanning in the sun.

From the ages of 6 to 10, children generally understand that race is a matter of ancestry that affects not only physical appearance but also one's language, diet, and leisure activities. But understanding at this stage is literal or concrete. For example, children believe that being Mexican American means that one speaks Spanish and eats Mexican-style food. Interethnic friendships are likely to develop among children of this age group.

From the age of about 10 to 14, children tend to link ethnicity with social class. They become aware of connections between race and income, race and neighborhood, and race and affirmative action.

During adolescence, many individuals begin to take pride in their ethnic heritage and experience a sense of belonging to their ethnic group. They are less open to intergroup relationships than younger children are.

Quintana's research tells him that middle childhood and early adolescence (the ages 6 to 14) are probably the best times to fend off the development of prejudice by teaching children about peoples from different cultural backgrounds. "That's when [children are] able to go beyond the literal meaning of the words and address their own observations about race and ethnicity," he notes (cited in Rabasca, 2000). Children at these ages also tend to be more open to forming relationships with children from different backgrounds than they are during adolescence.

Friends.
According to psychologist Stephen Quintana, children develop through four levels of understanding of ethnicity and race. Between the ages of 6 and 10, children are most likely to form friendships with children from other ethnic groups. It is also during these years that children come to understand that ethnicity affects not only physical appearance but also one's language, diet, and leisure activities.

Language Development: The Two-Year Explosion

Language is the communication of thoughts and feelings through symbols that are arranged according to rules of grammar. Language makes it possible for one person to communicate knowledge to another and for one generation to record information for another. Language allows people to learn more than they could from direct experience. It enables parents to give children advice, which now and then they heed. Language also provides many of the basic units of thinking, which is at the core of cognition. *Question: How does language develop?*

Piaget theorized that children's cognitive development follows a specific sequence of steps. Such sequencing also applies to language development, beginning with the *prelinguistic* vocalizations of crying, cooing, and babbling. These sounds are not symbols. That is, they do not represent objects or events. Therefore, they are *pre*linguistic, not linguistic.

As parents are well aware, newborn children have one inborn, highly effective form of verbal expression: crying—and more crying. During the second month, babies begin *cooing*. Babies use their tongues when they coo, so coos are more articulated than cries. Coos are often vowel-like and resemble "oohs" and "ahs." Cooing appears to be linked to feelings of pleasure. Babies do not coo when they are hungry, tired, or in pain. Parents soon learn that different cries and coos can indicate different things: hunger, gas pains, or pleasure at being held or rocked.

By the fifth or sixth month, children begin to *babble*. Babbling sort of sounds like speech. Children babble sounds that occur in many languages, including the throaty German *ch*, the clicks of certain African languages, and rolling *r*'s. In babbling, babies frequently combine consonants and vowels, as in "ba," "ga," and, sometimes, the much-valued "dada." "Dada" at first is purely coincidental (sorry, dads), despite the family's delight over its appearance.

Babbling, like crying and cooing, is inborn. Children from cultures whose languages sound very different all seem to babble the same sounds, including many they could not have heard (Gleason & Ratner, 1993). But children single out the sounds used in the

REFLECT
Some people have pets, like dogs, who communicate very clearly what they want at times. How do they do so without language?

CLICK4™ *"Classic Theories of Child Development."*

home within a few months. By the age of 9 or 10 months they repeat them regularly and foreign sounds begin to drop out.

Babbling, like crying and cooing, is prelinguistic. Yet infants usually understand much of what others are saying well before they utter their first words. Understanding precedes the production of language, and infants show what they understand by their actions.

Development of Vocabulary

Ah, that long-awaited first word! What a thrill! What a milestone! Children tend to utter their first word at about 1 year of age, but many parents miss it, often because it is not pronounced clearly or because pronunciation varies from one usage to the next. *Ball* may be pronounced "ba," "bee," or even "pah." The majority of an infant's early words are names of things (Nelson et al., 1993).

The growth of vocabulary is slow at first. It may take children 3 to 4 months to achieve a 10-word vocabulary after they have spoken their first word (Nelson, 1973). By about 18 months, children are producing nearly two dozen words. Reading to children increases their vocabulary, so parents do well to stock up on story books (Arnold et al., 1994; Robbins & Ehri, 1994).

Children try to talk about more objects than they have words for. As a result they often extend use of a word to refer to other things and actions for which they do not yet have words. This phenomenon is termed **overextension.** At some point, for example, many children refer to horses as *doggies*. At age 6, my daughter Allyn counted by tens as follows: sixty, seventy, eighty, ninety, tenty.

Development of Grammar

Children's first linguistic utterances are single words, but they may express complex meanings. When they do, they are called **holophrases.** For example, *mama* may be used by the child to signify meanings as varied as "There goes Mama," "Come here, Mama," and "You are my Mama." Similarly, *poo-cat* can signify "There is a pussycat," "That stuffed animal looks just like my pussycat," or "I want you to give me my pussycat right now!" Most children readily teach their parents what they intend by augmenting their holophrases with gestures, intonations, and reinforcers. That is, they act delighted when parents do as requested and howl when they do not.

Toward the end of the second year, children begin to speak two-word sentences. These sentences are termed *telegraphic speech* because they resemble telegrams. Telegrams cut out the "unnecessary" words. "Home Tuesday" might stand for "I expect to be home on Tuesday." Similarly, only essential words are used in children's telegraphic speech—in particular, nouns, verbs, and some modifiers. When a child says "That ball," the words *is* and *a* are implied.

Two-word utterances seem to appear at about the same time in the development of all languages (Slobin, 1983). Although two-word utterances are brief, they show understanding of grammar. The child says, "Sit chair" to tell a parent to sit in a chair, not "Chair sit." The child says, "My shoe," not "Shoe my," to show possession. "Mommy go" means Mommy is leaving. "Go Mommy" expresses the wish for Mommy to go away. (For this reason, "Go Mommy" is not heard often.)

There are different kinds of two-word utterances. Some, for example, contain nouns or pronouns and verbs ("Daddy sit"). Others contain verbs and objects ("Hit ball"). The sequence of emergence of the various kinds of two-word utterances is apparently the same in all languages—languages diverse as English, Luo (an African tongue), German, Russian, and Turkish (Slobin, 1983). The invariance of this sequence has implications for theories of language development, as we see later in the chapter.

Between the ages of 2 and 3, children's sentence structure usually expands to include the missing words in telegraphic speech. Children add articles (*a, an, the*), conjunctions (*and, but, or*), possessive and demonstrative adjectives (*your, her, that*), pronouns (*she, him, one*), and prepositions (*in, on, over, around, under,* and *through*) to their utterances. Their grasp of grammar is shown in linguistic oddities such as *your one* instead of simply *yours,* and *his one* instead of *his.*

REFLECT
Why are parents concerned with exactly when their children learn to talk? Did you know that Einstein did not talk until the age of 3?

www 10 L 3

CLICK4™ *more information about intellectual development in infants and children, including the latest in research on language development.*

Overextension ▲ Overgeneralizing the use of words to objects and situations to which they do not apply—a normal characteristic of the speech of young children.

Holophrase ▲ A single word used to express complex meanings.

Overregularization   One intriguing language development is **overregulariza-tion.** To understand children's use of overregularization, consider the formation of the past tense and of plurals in English. We add *d* or *ed* to make the past tense of regular verbs and *s* or *z* sounds to make regular nouns plural. Thus, *walk* becomes *walked* and *look* becomes *looked*. *Pussycat* becomes *pussycats* and *doggy* becomes *doggies*. There are also irregular verbs and nouns. For example, *see* becomes *saw*, *sit* becomes *sat*, and *go* becomes *went*. *Sheep* remains *sheep* (plural) and *child* becomes *children*.

At first children learn a small number of these irregular verbs by imitating their parents. Two-year-olds tend to form them correctly—at first! Then they become aware of the grammatical rules for forming the past tense and plurals. As a result, they tend to make charming errors (Pinker, 1997). Some 3- to 5-year-olds, for example, are more likely to say "I seed it" than "I saw it" and to say "Mommy sitted down" than "Mommy sat down." They are likely to talk about the "gooses" and "sheeps" they "seed" on the farm and about all the "childs" they ran into at the playground. This tendency to regularize the irregular is what is meant by overregularization.

Some parents recognize that at one point their children were forming the past tense of irregular verbs correctly and that they later began to make errors. The thing to remember is that overregularization reflects knowledge of grammar, not faulty language development. In another year or two, *mouses* will be boringly transformed into *mice*, and Mommy will no longer have *sitted* down. Parents might as well enjoy overregularization while they can.

Toward More Complex Language   As language develops beyond the third year, children show increasing facility in their use of pronouns (such as *it* and *she*) and prepositions (such as *in*, *before*, or *on*), which represent physical or temporal relationships among objects and events. Children's first questions are telegraphic and characterized by a rising pitch (which signifies a question mark) at the end. "More milky?" for example, can be translated into "May I have more milk?" or "Would you like more milk?" or "Is there more milk?"—depending on the context.

Wh questions usually appear after age 2. Consistent with the child's general cognitive development, certain *wh* questions *(what, who,* and *where)* appear earlier than others *(why, when, which,* and *how)* (Bloom et al., 1982). *Why* is usually too philosophical for the 2-year-old, and *how* is too involved. Two-year-olds are also likely to be now-oriented, so *when* is of less than immediate concern. By the fourth year, however, most children are asking *why, when,* and *how* questions—and frequently their parents despair as to how to answer them.

By the fourth year, children are also taking turns talking and engaging in lengthy conversations. By the age of 6, their vocabularies have expanded to 10,000 words, give or take a few thousand. By age 7 to 9, most children realize that words can have more than one meaning, and they are entertained by riddles and jokes that require some sophistication with language ("What's black and white, but read all over?").

Between the elementary school and high school years, language becomes still more complex and vocabulary continues to grow rapidly. Vocabulary, in fact, can grow for a lifetime, especially in one's fields of specialization and interest.

Languages have vocabularies and rules of grammar. As we see in the following section, millions of children in the United States speak a language that is like standard English but with some quite different rules of grammar.

DIVERSITY   ***Ebonics***   The term *Ebonics* is derived from the words *ebony* and *phonics*. It was coined by the African American psychologist Robert Williams (Burnette, 1997). Ebonics was previously called Black English or Black Dialect (Pinker, 1994a). Williams explains that a group of African American scholars convened "to name our language, which had always been named by White scholars in the past" (Burnette, 1997, p. 12).

According to linguists, Ebonics is rooted in the remnants of the West African dialects used by slaves. It reflects attempts by the slaves, who were denied formal education,

www **10** **L** **9**
CLICK4™ *the Web site of Kaufman Children's Center for Speech and Language Disorder.*

Overregularization ▲ The application of regular grammatical rules for forming inflections (e.g., past tense and plurals) to irregular verbs and nouns.

Robert Williams

He wasn't supposed to become a psychologist. He wasn't even supposed to go to college. His guidance counselor told him he had obtained a score of 82 on an IQ test (a score of 100 is considered average), and that perhaps he might be better off as a manual laborer.

So after he graduated from high school Robert Williams obtained work as a waiter in his hometown of Little Rock, Arkansas. But when he helped a friend solve an algebra problem, the friend encouraged him to go back to school. Williams followed the advice, enrolling in a local junior college and eventually receiving his doctorate in clinical psychology from St. Louis's Washington University.

Williams's own experience with intelligence tests led him to wonder whether they are culturally biased. He hypothesized that African American children would fare better on them if they were sensitive to African American culture. To demonstrate his point, Williams devised the BITCH—the Black Intelligence Test of Cultural Homogeneity. One question asked children to select a synonym for *blood* from the following choices: (a) a vampire, (b) a dependent individual, (c) an injured person, (d) a brother of color. The correct choice is *d*, and African American students proved to be more "intelligent" than European American students, according to the BITCH.

Williams is retired, but he has remained an active voice in the Ebonics debate and on the issue of cultural bias in intelligence testing.

to imitate the speech of the dominant White culture. Some observers believe that Ebonics uses verbs haphazardly, downgrading standard English. As a result, some school systems react to the concept of Ebonics with contempt—which is hurtful to the child who speaks Ebonics. Other observers say that Ebonics has different grammatical rules than standard English, but that the rules are consistent and allow for complex thought (Pinker, 1994a). In 1996, the Oakland, California, school board recognized Ebonics as the primary language of African American students, just as Spanish had been recognized as the primary language of Latino and Latina American students. "I was honored," said Williams. "And truthfully, I was shocked. It was like the truth that had been covered up in the ground for so long just exploded one day" (Burnette, 1997, p. 12).

"To Be or Not to Be": Use of Verbs in Ebonics. There are differences between Ebonics and standard English in the use of verbs. For example, the Ebonics usage "She-ah touch us" corresponds to the standard English "She will touch us." The Ebonics "He be gone" is the equivalent of the standard English "He has been gone for a long while." "He gone" is the same as "He is not here right now" in standard English.

Consider the rules in Ebonics that govern the use of the verb *to be*. In standard English, *be* is part of the infinitive form of the verb and is used to form the future tense, as in "I'll be angry tomorrow." Thus, "I *be* angry" is incorrect. But in Ebonics *be* refers to a continuing state of being. The Ebonics sentence "I be angry" is the same as the standard English "I have been angry for a while" and is grammatically correct.

Ebonics leaves out *to be* in cases in which standard English would use a contraction. For example, the standard "She's the one I'm talking about" could be "*She* the one *I* talking about" in Ebonics. Ebonics also often drops *ed* from the past tense and lacks the possessive *'s*.

"Not to Be or Not to Be Nothing": Negation in Ebonics. Consider the sentence "I don't want no trouble," which is, of course, commendable. Middle-class White children would be corrected for using double negation (do*n't* along with *no*) and would be encouraged to say "I don't want *any* trouble." Yet double negation is acceptable in Ebonics (Pinker, 1994). Nevertheless, many teachers who use standard English have demeaned African American children who speak this way.

Some African American children are bicultural and bilingual. They function competently within the dominant culture in the United States and among groups of people from their own ethnic background. They use standard English in a conference with their teacher or in a job interview, but switch to Ebonics among their friends. Other children cannot switch back and forth. The decision by the Oakland school board was intended in part to help children maintain their self-esteem and stay in school (Seymour et al., 1999).

▲ **REFLECT**
How do you feel when people correct your English? Why?

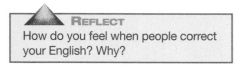

CLICK4™ *a bulletin board discussion on Ebonics: Do you think it should be recognized as a language?*

CLICK4™ *a quiz covering the first half of this chapter.*

Lawrence Kohlberg's Theory of Moral Development

Another aspect of cognitive development has to do with the ways in which people arrive at judgments of right or wrong. ***Question: How do children reason about what is right and wrong?*** Cognitive-developmental theorist Lawrence Kohlberg (1981) used the following tale in his research into children's moral reasoning. Before going on, why not read the tale yourself?

> In Europe a woman was near death from a special kind of cancer. There was one drug that the doctors thought might save her. It was a form of radium that a druggist in the same town had recently discovered. The drug was expensive to make, but the druggist was charging ten times what the drug cost him to make. He paid $200 for the radium and charged $2,000 for a small dose of the drug. The sick woman's husband, Heinz, went to everyone he knew to borrow the money, but he could only get together about $1,000, which was half of what it cost. He told the druggist that his wife was dying and asked him to sell it cheaper or let him pay later. But the druggist said: "No, I discovered the drug and I'm going to make money from it." So Heinz got desperate and broke into the man's store to steal the drug for his wife. (Kohlberg, 1969)

Heinz is caught in a moral dilemma in which a legal or social rule (in this case, the law forbidding stealing) is pitted against a strong human need (his desire to save his wife). According to Kohlberg's theory, children and adults arrive at yes or no answers for different reasons. These reasons can be classified according to the level of moral development they reflect.

As a stage theorist, Kohlberg argues that the stages of moral reasoning follow a specific sequence (see Table 10.3). Children progress at different rates, and not all children (or adults) reach the highest stage. But the sequence is always the same: Children must go through stage 1 before they enter stage 2, and so on. According to Kohlberg, there are three levels of moral development and two stages within each level.

When it comes to the dilemma of Heinz, Kohlberg believed that people could justify Heinz's stealing of the drug or his decision not to steal it by the reasoning of any level or stage of moral development. In other words, Kohlberg was not as interested in the eventual "yes" or "no" as he was in *how a person reasoned* to arrive at a yes or no answer.

The Preconventional Level

The **preconventional level** applies to most children through about the age of 9. Children at this level base their moral judgments on the consequences of behavior. For instance, stage 1 is oriented toward obedience and punishment. Good behavior is obedient and allows one to avoid punishment. However, a child in stage 1 can decide that Heinz should or should not steal the drug, as shown in Table 10.3.

In stage 2, good behavior allows people to satisfy their needs and those of others. (Heinz's wife needs the drug; therefore, stealing the drug—the only way of obtaining it—is not wrong.)

The Conventional Level

In the **conventional level** of moral reasoning, right and wrong are judged by conformity to conventional (familial, religious, societal) standards of right and wrong. According to the stage 3, "good-boy orientation," moral behavior is that which meets the needs and expectations of others. Moral behavior is what is "normal"—what the majority does. (Heinz should steal the drug because that is what a "good husband" would do. It is "natural" or "normal" to try to help one's wife. Or, Heinz should *not* steal the drug because "good people do not steal.")

In stage 4, moral judgments are based on rules that maintain the social order. Showing respect for authority and doing one's duty are valued highly. (Heinz *must* steal the

Lawrence Kohlberg

His car was found parked beside Boston Harbor. Three months later his body washed up onto the shore. He had discussed the moral dilemma posed by suicide with a friend, and perhaps Lawrence Kohlberg (1927–1987) had taken his own life. He was suffering from a painful parasitic intestinal disease that he had acquired 40 years earlier while smuggling Jewish refugees from Europe past the British blockade into Palestine (now Israel). There had also been recent disappointments in his work. Nevertheless, Carol Gilligan wrote that he had "almost singlehanded established moral development as a central concern of developmental psychology" (Hunt, 1993, p. 381).

Kohlberg was born into a wealthy family in suburban New York. He graduated from Phillips Academy as World War II came to an end. Rather than go on immediately to college, he became a merchant mariner and helped save people who had been displaced by the war. He was captured and imprisoned on the Mediterranean island of Cyprus. He soon escaped, but not before acquiring the disease that would bring him a lifetime of pain. Between high school and college, Kohlberg had already decided that one must attend more to one's own conscience than to law and authority figures in determining what was right and wrong.

▲ **REFLECT**
What do you think? Should Heinz have tried to steal the drug? Was he right or wrong? Is the answer more complicated than a simple yes or no?

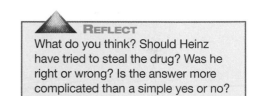

CLICK4™ *a chapter from Jean Piaget's classic book,* The Moral Judgment of the Child: *"Objective Responsibility: Clumsiness and Stealing."*

Preconventional level ▲ According to Kohlberg, a period during which moral judgments are based largely on expectation of rewards or punishments.

Conventional level ▲ According to Kohlberg, a period during which moral judgments largely reflect social conventions. A "law-and-order" approach to morality.

TABLE 10.3   KOHLBERG'S LEVELS AND STAGES OF MORAL DEVELOPMENT

Stage of Development	Examples of Moral Reasoning That Support Heinz's Stealing the Drug	Examples of Moral Reasoning That Oppose Heinz's Stealing the Drug
LEVEL I: PRECONVENTIONAL		
STAGE 1: Judgments guided by obedience and the prospect of punishment (the consequences of the behavior)	It isn't wrong to take the drug. Heinz did try to pay the druggist for it, and it's only worth $200, not $2,000.	Taking things without paying is wrong because it's against the law. Heinz will get caught and go to jail.
STAGE 2: Naively egoistic, instrumental orientation (Things are right when they satisfy people's needs.)	Heinz ought to take the drug because his wife really needs it. He can always pay the druggist back.	Heinz shouldn't take the drug. If he gets caught and winds up in jail, it won't do his wife any good.
LEVEL II: CONVENTIONAL		
STAGE 3: Good-boy orientation (Moral behavior helps others and is socially approved.)	Stealing is a crime, so it's bad, but Heinz should take the drug to save his wife or else people would blame him for letting her die.	Stealing is a crime. Heinz shouldn't just take the drug because his family will be dishonored and they will blame him.
STAGE 4: Law-and-order orientation (Moral behavior is doing one's duty and showing respect for authority.)	Heinz must take the drug to do his duty to save his wife. Eventually, he has to pay the druggist for it, however.	If everyone took the law into their own hands, civilization would fall apart, so Heinz shouldn't steal the drug.
LEVEL III: POSTCONVENTIONAL		
STAGE 5: Contractual, legalistic orientation (One must weigh pressing human needs against society's need to maintain social order.)	This thing is complicated because society has a right to maintain law and order, but Heinz has to take the drug to save his wife.	I can see why Heinz feels he has to take the drug, but laws exist for the benefit of society as a whole and can't simply be cast aside.
STAGE 6: Universal ethical principles orientation (People must follow universal ethical principles and their own conscience, even if it means breaking the law.)	In this case, the law comes into conflict with the principle of the sanctity of human life. Heinz must take the drug because his wife's life is more important than the law.	If Heinz truly believes that stealing the drug is worse than letting his wife die, he should not take it. People have to make sacrifices to do what they think is right.

drug; it would be his fault if he let his wife die. He would pay the druggist later, when he had the money.) Many people do not mature beyond the conventional level.

The Postconventional Level
Postconventional moral reasoning is more complex and focuses on dilemmas in which individual needs are pitted against the need to maintain the social order and on personal conscience. We discuss the postconventional level of moral reasoning in the section on adolescence.

REVIEW

(9) Piaget defined _____ as action patterns and mental structures that are involved in acquiring or organizing knowledge. (10) Piaget saw intelligence as including _____ (responding to events according to existing schemes) and accommodation. (11) Object permanence develops during the _____ period of cognitive development. (12) The _____ period is characterized by egocentrism, animism, artificialism, and inability to center on more than one aspect of a problem at a time. (13) The _____-operational period is characterized by conservation and reversibility. (14) Crying, cooing, and babbling are (prelinguistic or linguistic?) events. (15) _____ are one-word utterances that have the meanings of sentences. (16) Children use _____, as in "I seed it" and "Mommy sitted down." (17) Kohlberg hypothesizes that moral reasoning develops through (how many?) _____ "levels" and two stages within each level. (18) In the _____ level, moral judgments are based on expectation of rewards or punishments.

Pulling It Together: Does research in cognitive development support Piaget's view that children are budding scientists? Why can we consider language development to be "explosive"? Are the ways in which children reach conclusions about what is right and wrong more important than the conclusions themselves?

CLICK4™ *an opportunity to develop a temperament profile of yourself or your child.*

CHILDHOOD: SOCIAL AND PERSONALITY DEVELOPMENT

Social relationships are crucial to us as children. When we are infants, our very survival depends on them. Later in life, they contribute to our feelings of happiness and satisfaction. In this section we discuss many aspects of social development, including Erikson's theory of psychosocial development, attachment, styles of parenting, and the effects of day care and child abuse.

Erik Erikson's Stages of Psychosocial Development

According to Erik Erikson, we undergo several stages of psychosocial development (see Table 10.4).   *Question: What are Erikson's stages of psychosocial development?*

TABLE 10.4 ERIKSON'S STAGES OF PSYCHOSOCIAL DEVELOPMENT

Time Period	Life Crisis	The Developmental Task
Infancy (0–1)	Trust versus mistrust	Coming to trust the mother and the environment—to associate surroundings with feelings of inner goodness
Early childhood (1–3)	Autonomy versus shame and doubt	Developing the wish to make choices and the self-control to exercise choice
Preschool years (4–5)	Initiative versus guilt	Adding planning and "attacking" to choice, becoming active and on the move
Elementary school years (6–12)	Industry versus inferiority	Becoming eagerly absorbed in skills, tasks, and productivity; mastering the fundamentals of technology
Adolescence	Identity versus role diffusion	Connecting skills and social roles to formation of career objectives; developing a sense of who one is and what one stands for
Young adulthood	Intimacy versus isolation	Committing the self to another; engaging in sexual love
Middle adulthood	Generativity versus stagnation	Needing to be needed; guiding and encouraging the younger generation; being creative
Late adulthood	Integrity versus despair	Accepting the time and place of one's life cycle; achieving wisdom and dignity

SOURCE: From Erikson, 1963, pp. 247–269.

During Erikson's first stage, **trust versus mistrust,** we depend on our primary caregivers (usually our parents) and come to expect that our environments will—or will not—meet our needs. During early childhood and the preschool years, we begin to explore the environment more actively and try new things. At this time, our relationships with our parents and friends can encourage us to develop **autonomy** (self-direction) and initiative, or feelings of shame and guilt. During the elementary school years, friends and teachers take on more importance, encouraging us to become industrious or to develop feelings of inferiority.

Attachment: Ties That Bind

At the age of 2, my daughter Allyn almost succeeded in preventing me from finishing a book. When I locked myself into my study, she positioned herself outside the door and called, "Daddy, oh Daddy." At other times, she would bang on the door or cry outside. When I would give in (several times a day) and open the door, she would run in and say, "I want you to pick up me" and hold out her arms or climb into my lap. Although we were separate human beings, it was as though she were very much *attached* to me. *Questions: How do feelings of attachment develop? What kinds of experiences affect attachment?*

Psychologist Mary D. Salter Ainsworth (1913–1999) defined **attachment** as an emotional tie that is formed between one animal or person and another specific individual. Attachment keeps organisms together—it is vital to the survival of the infant—and it tends to endure.

The behaviors that define attachment include (1) attempts to maintain contact or nearness and (2) shows of anxiety when separated. Babies and children try to maintain contact with caregivers to whom they are attached. They engage in eye contact, pull and tug at them, ask to be picked up, and may even jump in front of them in such a way that they will be "run over" if they are not picked up!

The Strange Situation and Patterns of Attachment   The ways in which infants behave in strange situations are connected with their bonds of attachment with their caregivers. Given this fact, Ainsworth and her colleagues (1978) innovated the *strange situation method* to measure attachment in infants. The method involves a series of separations and reunions with a caregiver (usually the mother) and a stranger. Infants are led through episodes involving the mother and a stranger in a laboratory room. For example, the mother carries the infant into the room and puts him or her down. A stranger enters and talks with the mother. The stranger then approaches the infant with a toy and the mother leaves the room. The mother and stranger take turns interacting with the infant in the room, and the infant's behavior is observed in each case.

Using the strange situation, Ainsworth and her colleagues (1978) identified three major types of attachment: secure attachment and two types of insecure attachment:

1. *Secure attachment.* Securely attached infants mildly protest their mother's departure, seek interaction upon reunion, and are readily comforted by her.
2. *Avoidant attachment.* Infants who show avoidant attachment are least distressed by their mother's departure. They play by themselves without fuss and ignore their mothers when they return.

Trust versus mistrust ▲ Erikson's first stage of psychosexual development, during which children do—or do not—come to trust that primary caregivers and the environment will meet their needs.
Autonomy ▲ Self-direction.
Attachment ▲ The enduring affectional tie that binds one person to another.

Allyn.
At the age of 2 the author's daughter Allyn nearly succeeded in preventing the publication of a book by continually pulling him away from the computer when he was at work. Because of their mutual attachment, separation was painful.

3. *Ambivalent/resistant attachment.* Infants with ambivalent/resistant attachment are the most emotional. They show severe signs of distress when their mother leaves and show ambivalence upon reunion by alternately clinging to and pushing their mother away when she returns.

Attachment is connected with the quality of care that infants receive. The parents of securely attached children are more likely to be affectionate and reliable caregivers (Cox et al., 1992; Isabella, 1998). A wealth of research literature speaks of the benefits of secure attachment. For example, securely attached children are happier, more sociable, and more cooperative than insecurely attached children (Belsky et al., 1991; Thompson, 1991a). Securely attached preschoolers have longer attention spans, are less impulsive, and are better at solving problems (Frankel & Bates, 1990; Lederberg & Mobley, 1990). At ages 5 and 6, securely attached children are liked better by their peers and teachers, are more competent, and have fewer behavior problems than insecurely attached children (Young-blade & Belsky, 1992). In this vein, we can also note that having mother present during stressful situations, such as pediatric exams, helps children cope with these situations (Ybarra et al., 2000).

Not all psychologists agree that infant attachment as measured by means of the strange situation predicts adjustment later on. For example, Michael Lewis (1997) located 84 high school seniors who had been evaluated by the strange situation method at age 1. Extensive interviews showed that of the 49 who had been considered securely attached at age 1, 43% were currently maladjusted. Of the 35 who had been considered insecurely attached in infancy, only 26% were rated as currently maladjusted. Lewis (1998) suggests that childhood events such as accidents, parental divorce, and illness can be more powerful influences on adolescents' security than the quality of parenting during the first year. But most developmental psychologists continue to endorse the strange situation as a predictor of adjustment later in life (Blakeslee, 1998). For example, Alan Sroufe (1998) found that insecure attachment at the age of 1 year predicted psychological disorders at the age of 17.

Stages of Attachment

Ainsworth also studied phases in the development of attachment. She and her colleagues observed infants in many societies, including the African country of Uganda. She noted the efforts of infants to maintain contact with the mother, their protests when separated from her, and their use of her as a base for exploring their environment. At first, infants show **indiscriminate attachment.** That is, they prefer being held or being with someone to being alone, but they show no preferences for particular people. Specific attachment to the mother begins to develop at about 4 months of age and becomes intense by about 7 months of age. Fear of strangers, which develops in some but not all children, follows 1 or 2 months later.

From studies such as these, Ainsworth identified three stages of attachment:

1. The **initial-preattachment phase,** which lasts from birth to about 3 months and is characterized by indiscriminate attachment.
2. The **attachment-in-the-making phase,** which occurs at about 3 or 4 months and is characterized by preference for familiar figures.
3. The **clear-cut-attachment phase,** which occurs at about 6 or 7 months and is characterized by intensified dependence on the primary caregiver.

John Bowlby (1988), a colleague of Mary Ainsworth, believed that attachment is also characterized by fear of strangers ("stranger anxiety"). That is, at about 8 to 10 months of age, children may cry and cling to their parents when strangers try to befriend them. But not all children develop fear of strangers. It therefore does not seem necessary to include fear of strangers as an essential part of the process of attachment.

Theoretical Views of Attachment

Early in the century, behaviorists argued that attachment behaviors are learned through experience. Caregivers feed their infants and tend to their other physiological needs. Thus, infants associate their caregivers with gratification of needs and learn to approach them to meet their needs. The feelings of

▲ **REFLECT**

Do you know children (or adults) who seem to be quite independent of their parents? Do you know others who find it difficult to separate from their parents? Can you account for the difference?

CLICK4™ *the classic article on attachment by H. F. Harlow, "The Nature of Love."*

CLICK4™ *more information about social and emotional growth in middle childhood.*

▲ **REFLECT**

Have you had experience with a child who showed fear of strangers? How did he or she act in their presence?

Indiscriminate attachment ▲ Showing attachment behaviors toward any person.

Initial-preattachment phase ▲ The first phase in forming bonds of attachment, characterized by indiscriminate attachment.

Attachment-in-the-making phase ▲ The second phase in forming bonds of attachment, characterized by preference for familiar figures.

Clear-cut-attachment phase ▲ The third phase in forming bonds of attachment, characterized by intensified dependence on the primary caregiver.

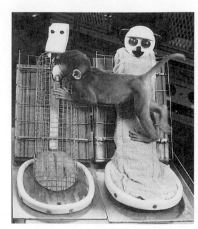  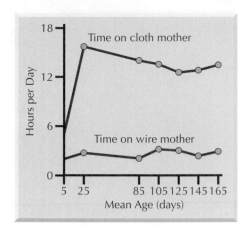

FIGURE 10.6 Attachment in Infant Monkeys.
Although this rhesus monkey infant is fed by the wire "mother," it spends most of its time clinging to the soft, cuddly terry cloth "mother." It knows where to get a meal, but contact comfort is apparently more important than food in the development of attachment in infant monkeys (and infant humans?).

gratification associated with the meeting of basic needs generalize into feelings of security when the caregiver is present.

Classic research by psychologist Harry F. Harlow suggests that skin contact may be more important than learning experiences. Harlow noted that infant rhesus monkeys reared without mothers or companions became attached to pieces of cloth in their cages. They maintained contact with them and showed distress when separated from them. Harlow conducted a series of experiments to find out why (Harlow, 1959).

In one study, Harlow placed infant rhesus monkeys in cages with two surrogate mothers, as shown in Figure 10.6. One "mother" was made of wire mesh from which a baby bottle was extended. The other surrogate mother was made of soft, cuddly terrycloth. The infant monkeys spent most of their time clinging to the cloth mother, even though "she" did not gratify their need for food. Harlow concluded that monkeys—and perhaps humans—have an inborn need for **contact comfort** that is as basic as the need for food. Gratification of the need for contact comfort, rather than food, might be why infant monkeys (and humans) cling to their mothers.

Harlow and Zimmerman (1959) found that a surrogate mother made of terrycloth could also serve as a comforting base from which an infant monkey could explore its environment. Toys such as stuffed bears and oversized wooden insects were placed in cages with infant rhesus monkeys and their surrogate mothers. When the infants were alone or had wire surrogate mothers for companions, they cowered in fear as long as the "bear monster" or "insect monster" was present. But when the terrycloth mothers were present, the infants clung to them for a while and then explored the intruding "monster." With human infants, too, the bonds of mother-infant attachment appear to provide a secure base from which infants feel encouraged to express their curiosity.

Other researchers, such as ethologist Konrad Lorenz, note that for many animals, attachment is an instinct—inborn. Attachment, like other instincts, is theorized to occur in the presence of a specific stimulus and during a **critical period** of life—that is, a period during which the animal is sensitive to the stimulus.

Some animals become attached to the first moving object they encounter. The unwritten rule seems to be, "If it moves, it must be Mother." It is as if the image of the moving object becomes "imprinted" on the young animal. The formation of an attachment in this manner is therefore called **imprinting.**

Lorenz (1981) became well known when pictures of his "family" of goslings were made public. How did Lorenz acquire his following? He was present when the goslings hatched and during their critical period, and he allowed them to follow him. The critical period for geese and some other animals is bounded, at the younger end, by the age at which they first walk and, at the older end, by the age at which they develop fear of

Contact comfort ▲ A hypothesized primary drive to seek physical comfort through contact with another.
Critical period ▲ A period of time when an instinctive response can be elicited by a particular stimulus.
Imprinting ▲ A process occurring during a critical period in the development of an organism, in which that organism responds to a stimulus in a manner that will afterward be difficult to modify.

Security.
With its terry-cloth surrogate mother nearby, this infant rhesus monkey apparently feels secure enough to explore the "bear monster" placed in its cage. But infants with wire surrogate mothers or no mothers at all cower in a corner when such "monsters" are introduced.

Imprinting.
Quite a following? Konrad Lorenz may not look like Mommy to you, but these goslings became attached to him because he was the first moving object they perceived and followed. This type of attachment process is referred to as *imprinting*.

CLICK4™ *advice on becoming an authoritative parent.*

CLICK4™ *an essay assignment on parenting styles.*

▲ **ʀᴇꜰʟᴇᴄᴛ**
Would you characterize your parents as having been warm or cold, restrictive or permissive? In what ways? How did the parenting style you experienced affect your feelings and behavior?

Instrumental competence ▲ Ability to manipulate one's environment to achieve one's goals.
Authoritative parents ▲ Parents who are strict and warm. Authoritative parents demand mature behavior but use reason rather than force in discipline.
Authoritarian parents ▲ Parents who are rigid in their rules and who demand obedience for the sake of obedience.
Permissive parents ▲ Parents who impose few, if any, rules and who do not supervise their children closely.

strangers. The goslings followed Lorenz persistently, ran to him when they were frightened, honked with distress at his departure, and tried to overcome barriers between them. If you substitute crying for honking, it all sounds rather human.

Ainsworth and Bowlby (1991) consider attachment to be instinctive in humans. However, the process would not be quite the same as with ducks and geese. The upper limit for waterbirds is the age at which they develop fear of strangers, but not all children develop this fear. When children do develop fear of strangers, they do so at about 6 to 8 months of age—*prior to* independent locomotion, or crawling, which usually occurs 1 or 2 months later. Moreover, the critical period with humans would be quite extended.

Another issue in social and personality development is parenting styles. Parental behavior not only contributes to the development of attachment, but also to the development of self-esteem, self-reliance, achievement motivation, and competence.

Parenting Styles

Many psychologists have been concerned about the relationships between parenting styles and the personality development of the child. *Question: What types of parental behavior are connected with variables such as self-esteem, achievement motivation, and independence in children?* Diana Baumrind (1973) and her colleagues (Lamb & Baumrind, 1978) have been particularly interested in the connections between parental behavior and the development of **instrumental competence** in their children. (*Instrumental competence* refers to the ability to manipulate the environment to achieve one's goals.) Baumrind has largely focused on four aspects of parental behavior: (1) strictness; (2) demands for the child to achieve intellectual, emotional, and social maturity; (3) communication ability; and (4) warmth and involvement. She labeled the three most important parenting styles the *authoritative*, *authoritarian*, and *permissive* styles.

1. *Authoritative parents.* The parents of the most competent children rate high in all four areas of behavior (see Table 10.5). They are strict (restrictive) and demand mature behavior. However, they temper their strictness and demands with willingness to reason with their children, and with love and support. They expect a lot, but they explain why and offer help. Baumrind labeled these parents **authoritative parents** to suggest that they know what they want but are also loving and respectful of their children.

2. *Authoritarian parents.* **Authoritarian parents** view obedience as a virtue to be pursued for its own sake. They have strict guidelines about what is right and wrong, and they demand that their children adhere to those guidelines. Both authoritative and authoritarian parents adhere to strict standards of conduct. However, authoritative parents explain their demands and are supportive, whereas authoritarian parents rely on force and communicate poorly with their children. Authoritarian parents do not respect their children's points of view, and they may be cold and rejecting. When their children ask them why they should behave in a certain way, authoritarian parents often answer, "Because I say so!"

3. *Permissive parents.* **Permissive parents** are generally easygoing with their children. As a result, the children do pretty much whatever they wish. Permissive parents are warm and supportive, but poor at communicating.

Research evidence shows that warmth is superior to coldness in rearing children. Children of warm parents are more likely to be socially and emotionally well-adjusted and to internalize moral standards—that is, to develop a conscience (MacDonald, 1992; Miller et al., 1993).

Strictness also appears to pay off, provided it is tempered with reason and warmth. Children of authoritative parents have greater self-reliance, self-esteem, social competence, and achievement motivation than other children (Baumrind, 1991b; Putallaz & Hefflin, 1990). Children of authori*tarian* parents are often withdrawn or aggressive, and they usually do not do as well in school as children of authoritative parents (Olson et al., 1992; Westerman, 1990). Children of permissive parents seem to be the least mature.

They are frequently impulsive, moody, and aggressive. In adolescence, lack of parental monitoring is often linked to delinquency and poor academic performance.

Day Care

In the new millennium, only a small percentage of U.S. families fit the traditional model in which the husband is the breadwinner and the wife is a full-time homemaker. Most mothers, including more than half of mothers of children younger than 1 year of age, work outside the home (Erel et al., 2000; U.S. Bureau of the Census, 1998). As a consequence, millions of American preschoolers are placed in day care. Parents and psychologists are concerned about what happens to children in day care. What, for example, are the effects of day care on cognitive development and social development?

In part, the answer depends on the quality of the day care center. A large-scale study funded by the National Institute on Child Health and Human Development found that children in high-quality day care—for example, children who have learning resources, a low children-to-caregiver ratio, and individual attention—did as well on cognitive and language tests as children who remained in the home with their mother (Azar, 1997d). Children whose day care providers spent time talking to them and asking them questions also achieved the highest scores on tests of cognitive and language ability. A Swedish study found that children in high-quality day care outperformed children who remained in the home on tests of math and language skills (Broberg et al., 1997).

TABLE 10.5 PARENTING STYLES

| | | PARENTAL BEHAVIOR | | |
Style of Parenting	Restrictiveness	Demands for Mature Behavior	Communication Ability	Warmth and Support
Authoritative	High (use of reasoning)	High	High	High
Authoritarian	High (use of force)	Moderate	Low	Low
Permissive	Low (easygoing)	Low	Low	High

NOTE: According to Baumrind, the children of authoritative parents are the most competent. The children of permissive parents are the least mature.

▲ REFLECT

Have you or your parents made use of day care services? How did the experience work out? Why?

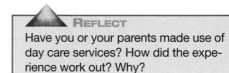

CLICK4™ *a bulletin board discussion on day care and its effects on social and emotional development.*

Day Care.

Because most parents in the United States are in the work force, day care is a major influence on the lives of millions of children.

Studies of the effects of day care on parent–child attachment yield mixed results. Children in full-time day care show less distress when their mothers leave them and are less likely to seek out their mother when they return. Some psychologists suggest that this distancing from the mother could signify insecure (avoidant) attachment (Belsky, 1990). Others suggest, however, that the children are adapting to repeated separations from, and reunions with, their mother (Field, 1991; Lamb et al., 1992; Thompson, 1991b).

Day care seems to have both positive and negative influences on children's social development. First, the positive: Children in day care are more likely to share their toys and be independent, self-confident, and outgoing (Clarke-Stewart, 1991; Field, 1991). However, some studies have found that children in day care are less compliant and more aggressive than are other children (Belsky et al., 2001). Perhaps some children in day care do not receive the individual attention or resources they need. When placed in a competitive situation, they become more aggressive in an attempt to meet their needs. Clarke-Stewart (1990), however, interprets the greater noncompliance and aggressiveness of children placed in day care as signs of greater independence rather than social maladjustment.

All in all, it would appear that nonmaternal care per se does not affect child development (Erel et al., 2000). Day care itself has not been found to affect children's attachment to their parents or their general adjustment. The quality of care is more important than who does it.

▲ REFLECT

Do you know anyone who was abused as a child? Do you think that the person has been affected by the experience? How?

Child Abuse

Although the incidence of child abuse is seriously underreported, it is estimated that nearly 3 million children in the United States are neglected or abused by their parents or other caregivers each year (Herman-Giddens et al., 1999). More than half a million of these suffer serious injuries, and thousands die.

Psychology and Modern Life

Selecting a Day-Care Center

Because it is economically, vocationally, and socially unrealistic for most parents to spend the day at home, most parents strive to secure day care that will foster the social and emotional development of their children.

Selecting a day-care center can be an overwhelming task. Standards for day-care centers vary from locale to locale, so licensing is no guarantee of adequate care. To help make a successful choice, parents can weigh factors such as the following:

1. Is the center licensed? By what agency? What standards must be met to acquire a license?

2. What is the ratio of children to caregivers? Everything else being equal, caregivers can do a better job when there are fewer children in their charge.

3. What are the qualifications of the center's caregivers? How well aware are they of children's needs and patterns of de-

velopment? Day-care workers are typically poorly paid, and financial frustrations lead many of the best to seek work in other fields. Children apparently fare better when their caregivers have specific training in child development. If the administrators of a day-care center are reluctant to discuss the training and experience of their caregivers, consider another center.

4. How safe is the environment? Do toys and swings seem to be in good condition? Are dangerous objects out of reach? Would strangers have a difficult time breaking in? Ask something like, "Have children been injured in this center?" Administrators should report previous injuries without hesitation.

5. What is served at mealtime? Is it nutritious and appetizing? Will *your child* eat it?

6. Which caregivers will be responsible for your child? What are their back-

grounds? How do they seem to relate to children? To *your* child?

7. What toys, games, books, and other educational materials are provided?

8. What facilities are provided to promote the motor development of your child? How well supervised are children when they use things like swings and tricycles?

9. Are the hours offered by the center convenient for your schedule?

10. Is the location of the center convenient?

As you can see, the considerations can be overwhelming. Perhaps no day-care center within reach will score perfectly on every factor. Some factors are more important than others, however. Perhaps this list of considerations will help you focus your primary concerns.

Many factors contribute to child abuse: stress, a history of child abuse in at least one of the parents' families of origin, acceptance of violence as a way of coping with stress, failure to become attached to the children, substance abuse, and rigid attitudes toward child rearing (Belsky, 1993; Kaplan, 1991). Unemployment and low socioeconomic status are common stressors that lead to abuse (Lewin, 1995; Trickett et al., 1991).

Children who are abused are quite likely to develop personal and social problems and psychological disorders. They are less likely than other children to venture out to explore the world (Aber & Allen, 1987). They are more likely to have psychological problems such as anxiety, depression, and low self-esteem (Wagner, 1997). They are less likely to be intimate with their peers and more likely to be aggressive (DeAngelis, 1997; Parker & Herrera, 1996; Rothbart & Ahadi, 1994). As adults, they are more likely to be violent toward their dates and spouses (Malinosky-Rummell & Hansen, 1993).

Many children are also victims of sexual abuse. Child sexual abuse is sometimes hard to define (Haugaard, 2000), because adults often interact with children in ambiguous ways. However, some adults have sexual intercourse with children or fondle their sexual organs, and these acts are clearly abusive. Acts such as touching children's sexual organs while changing or bathing them, sleeping with children, or appearing nude before them are open to interpretation and often innocent.

The effects of child sexual abuse are variable, and it does not appear that there is a single, identifiable syndrome that results from such abuse (Saywitz et al., 2000). Nevertheless, the research literature shows that sexually abused children are more likely to develop physical and psychological health problems than unabused children (Saywitz et al., 2000). Child sexual abuse can also have lasting effects on children's relationships once they become adults.

One way in which child abuse may set the stage for psychological disorders in adulthood is by increasing people's bodily responses to stress. Responses to stress are typically measured in terms of the reactivity of the endocrine system (particularly stress hormones such as ACTH and cortisol) and the autonomic nervous system (e.g., heart rate). A study by Christine Heim and her colleagues (2000) recruited 49 generally healthy women with an average age of 35. Twenty-seven of the women reported childhood physical and/or sexual abuse in interviews; 22 did not. Twenty-three of the women were currently diagnosed with major depression; 26 were not. All 49 women were exposed to a stressor that has been shown to induce endocrine and autonomic reactions in a number of studies: The women anticipated and presented a public speech that included some mental arithmetic. Meanwhile, their levels of stress hormones and heart rates were being assessed. As shown in Table 10.6, the presence of depression alone did not distinguish women who were depressed (group B) from women who were not (group A). However, women who reported a history of child abuse (groups C and D) were significantly more likely to show higher blood levels of ACTH and cortisol in response to the stressor than women who did not report a history of child abuse (groups A and B). Group D, consisting of women who reported a history of abuse and who were also diagnosed with major depression showed significantly higher levels of stress hormones and heart rate than all other groups. Therefore, the combination of early abuse and current depression apparently makes the body most sensitive to stress. But even among women who were not depressed, the history of abuse was connected with greater reactivity of the endocrine system and autonomic nervous system.

The Heim study has its shortcomings: For example, it categorized women according to self-reported history of child abuse. Not all women in the study could provide independent confirmation of abuse, such as court records. Also, it is unclear how well the stressor used in the experiment represents the types of stress people are actually exposed to in their lives. Nevertheless, the experiment suggests that

www 10 L 6

CLICK4™ *the Web site of the Child Abuse Prevention Network.*

TABLE 10.6   RESPONSES OF WOMEN TO STRESSOR, AS MEASURED BY LEVELS OF STRESS HORMONES AND HEART RATE

	Without Major Depression	With Major Depression
Without History of Child Abuse	**Group A:** $n = 12$ ACTH peak: 4.7 parts/liter Cortisol peak: 339 parts/liter Heart rate: 78.4/minute	**Group B:** $n = 10$ ACTH peak: 5.3 parts/liter Cortisol peak: 337 parts/liter Heart rate: 83.8/minute
With History of Child Abuse	**Group C:** $n = 14$ ACTH peak: 9.3 parts/liter Cortisol peak: 359 parts/liter Heart rate: 82.2/minute	**Group D:** $n = 13$ ACTH peak: 12.1 parts/liter Cortisol peak: 527 parts/liter Heart rate: 87.7/minute

child abuse may well affect bodily reactivity to stress that endures well into adulthood, and further research along these lines is certainly warranted.

Child abuse runs in families to some degree (Ertem et al., 2000). That is, child abusers are more likely to have been abused than is true for the general population. Even so, *the majority of children who are abused do* not *abuse their own children as adults* (Kaufman & Zigler, 1989).

Why does abuse run in families? There are several hypotheses (Belsky, 1993). One is that parents serve as role models. According to Murray Strauss (1995), "Spanking teaches kids that when someone is doing something you don't like and they won't stop doing it, you hit them." Another is that children adopt parents' strict philosophies about discipline. Exposure to violence in their own home leads some children to view abuse as normal. A third is that being abused can create feelings of hostility that are then expressed against others, including one's own children.

The years of childhood may seem to pass rapidly, but a great deal occurs during them in terms of physical, cognitive, and social and personality development. Following childhood is the period of adolescence, which is for many a period of passage to adulthood. For many adolescents, and for their parents, the goals of adolescence and the behaviors deemed acceptable loom as huge question marks. Because of these questions, psychologists have focused a great deal of attention on adolescence, as we see in the following chapter.

Psychology and Modern Life

Child Sexual Abuse—What To Do, Where To Turn

Child sexual abuse is a difficult matter to handle, difficult for the child, and difficult for adults who try to help. The American Psychological Association offers these guidelines*:

- Give the child a safe environment in which to talk to you or another trusted adult. Encourage the child to talk about what he or she has experienced, but be careful to not suggest events to him or her that may not have happened. Guard against displaying emotions that would influence the child's telling of the information.
- Reassure the child that he or she did nothing wrong.
- Seek mental-health assistance for the child.
- Arrange for a medical examination for the child. Select a medical provider who has experience in examining children and identifying sexual and physical trauma. It may be necessary to explain to the child the difference between a medical examination and the abuse incident.
- Be aware that many states have laws requiring that persons who know or have a reason to suspect

that a child has been sexually abused must report that abuse to either local law enforcement officials or child protection officials. In all 50 states, medical personnel, mental health professionals, teachers, and law enforcement personnel are required by law to report suspected abuse.

The APA also lists the following resources as places to go to for help:

American Professional Society on the Abuse of Children
407 South Dearborn
Suite 1300
Chicago, IL 60605
(312) 554-0166
http://www.apsac.org/

National Center for Missing and Exploited Children
Charles B. Wang International Children's Building
699 Prince Street
Alexandria, VA 22314-3175
24-hour hotline: 1-800-THE-LOST
http://www.missingkids.com/

Child Help USA
15757 North 78th Street
Scottsdale, AZ 85260
(800) 4-A-CHILD
http://www.childhelpusa.org/

National Clearinghouse on Child Abuse and Neglect Information
U.S. Department of Health and Human Services
P.O. Box 1182
Washington, DC 20013
(800) FYI-3366
http://www.calib.com/nccanch/

Prevent Child Abuse America
332 S. Michigan Ave
Suite 1600
Chicago, IL 60604-4357
(800) CHILDREN
http://www.childabuse.org/

* The Office of Public Communications, The American Psychological Association, 750 First Street, NE, Washington, DC 20002-4242. (202) 336-5700.
http://www.apa.org/releases/sexabuse

REVIEW

(19) Erikson presents a theory of _____ development. (20) During the first stage, trust versus _____, infants depend on primary caregivers and come to expect that the environment will—or will not—meet their needs. (21) Ainsworth defines _____ as an affectional tie that binds organisms together. (22) She proposed three major types of attachment: _____, avoidant, and ambivalent/resistant. (23) She also identified three stages of attachment: The _____-_____ phase, which is characterized by indiscriminate attachment, the attachment-in-the-making phase, and the clear-cut-attachment phase. (24) Behaviorists argue that children become attached to mothers through _____, because their mothers feed them and attend to other basic needs. (25) The Harlow studies with monkeys suggest that _____ comfort is more important than conditioning in the development of attachment. (26) Ethologists argue that attachment is an _____ that occurs during a critical period. (27) In her studies of the connections between parental behavior and competence in children, Baumrind has focused on four aspects of parental behavior: _____, demands for maturity, communication ability, and warmth and involvement. (28) She labeled the three most important parenting styles _____, authoritarian, and permissive.

Pulling It Together: Apply what you have learned about social and personality development to discuss the effects of day care and child abuse on children.

CONTROVERSIES IN DEVELOPMENTAL PSYCHOLOGY

Now that we have traced development from conception through childhood, we are ready to consider some controversies in developmental psychology. These have to do with the relative importance of nature and nurture in development, and with whether development is continuous or occurs in stages (that is, is discontinuous).

CONTROVERSY ✕ IN PSYCHOLOGY

Is Development Influenced More by Nature or by Nurture?

Question: What is the nature-nurture controversy about?   The nature-nurture controversy reflects the effort to sort out the relative influences of nature and nurture on development.

Psychologists seek to understand the influences of nature in our genetic heritage, in the functioning of the nervous system, and in the process of **maturation** (that is, the unfolding of traits, as determined by the genetic code). Psychologists look for the influences of nurture in our nutrition, cultural and family backgrounds, and opportunities for learning, including early mental stimulation and formal education. The American psychologist Arnold Gesell (1880-1961) leaned heavily toward natural explanations of development. He argued that all areas of development are self-regulated by the unfolding of natural plans and processes. John Watson and other behaviorists, in contrast, leaned heavily toward environmental explanations. Let us consider the relative influences of nature and nurture in language development.

Nature and Nurture in Language Development

> Since all normal humans talk but no house pets or house plants do, no matter how pampered, heredity must be involved in language. But since a child growing up in Japan speaks Japanese whereas the same child brought up in California would speak English, the environment is also crucial. Thus, there is no question about whether heredity or environment is involved in language, or even whether one or the other is "more important." Instead, . . . our best hope [might be] finding out how they interact.
>
> —Steven Pinker

CLICK4™ *a bulletin board discussion on the nature versus nurture debate.*

CLICK4™ *a WebSearch activity examining research methods and the developmental theories of nature/nurture and continuity/discontinuity: What is your view?*

Maturation ▲ The orderly unfolding of traits, as regulated by the genetic code.

Noam Chomsky

If you were casting a film about an intellectual, you might choose Noam Chomsky for the role. He is your stereotypical "shaggy-haired, bespectacled, rumpled genius" (Hunt, 1993). Chomsky grew up in New York during the Great Depression and was influenced by liberal politics. He planned to leave the University of Pennsylvania after two years of undergraduate study to join a leftist group in the newly born nation of Israel when a professor—Zellig Harris—got him more excited about linguistics.

If you think about it, the liberal view of language would be that environmental factors have the greatest influence on language learning. (Similarly, the liberal view of the determinants of intelligence would be that early exposure to a rich learning environment is more important than genetic factors.) Chomsky worked diligently, in fact, trying to find evidence for precisely this point of view. But he could not satisfy himself. Instead, he came to believe that the key to language ability is inborn—an innate language acquisition device. This device allows children to perceive deep grammatical relationships in sentences and to produce original sentences as a result.

Chomsky illustrates his idea, tongue in cheek, by noting that the following sentence makes sense (sort of): "Colorless green ideas sleep furiously." It is surely nonsensical but seems much more correct to an English speaker than, say, "Sleep green colorless furiously ideas." Why is the first sentence more familiar and comfortable?

CLICK4™ *the Noam Chomsky Archive.*

Billions of children have acquired the languages spoken by their parents and passed them down, with minor changes, from generation to generation. Language development, like many other areas of development, apparently reflects the interactions between the influences of heredity (nature) and the environment (nurture). ***Question: How is the nature-nurture controversy applied to language development?***

Learning theorists see language as developing according to laws of learning (Gleason & Ratner, 1993). They usually refer to the concepts of imitation and reinforcement. From a social-cognitive perspective, parents serve as *models*. Children learn language, at least in part, through observation and imitation. It seems likely that many words, especially nouns and verbs (including irregular verbs), are learned by imitation.

At first children accurately repeat the irregular verb forms they observe. This repetition can probably be explained in terms of modeling, but modeling does not explain all the events involved in learning. Children later begin to overregularize irregular verb forms *because of* their knowledge of rules of grammar, not through imitation. Nor does imitative learning explain how children come to utter phrases and sentences that they have *not* observed. Parents, for example, are unlikely to model utterances such as "bye-bye sock" and "allgone Daddy," but children do say them.

Learning theory cannot account for the unchanging sequence of language development and the spurts in children's language acquisition. Even the types of two-word utterances emerge in a consistent pattern in diverse cultures. Although timing differs from one child to another, the types of questions used, passive versus active sentences, and so on, all emerge in the same order.

The nativist theory of language development holds that innate or inborn factors—which make up children's *nature*—cause children to attend to and acquire language in certain ways. From this perspective, children bring a certain neurological "prewiring" to language learning (Newport, 1998; Pinker, 1994a).

According to **psycholinguistic theory,** language acquisition involves the interaction of environmental influences—such as exposure to parental speech and reinforcement—and an inborn tendency to acquire language. Noam Chomsky (1980, 1991) refers to the inborn tendency as a **language acquisition device** (LAD). Evidence for an LAD is found in the universality of human language abilities and in the specific sequence of language development.

The LAD prepares the nervous system to learn grammar. On the surface, languages differ a great deal. However, the LAD serves children all over the world because languages share what Chomsky refers to as a "universal grammar"—an underlying set of rules for turning ideas into sentences (Pinker, 1994a). Consider an analogy with computers: According to psycholinguistic theory, the universal grammar that resides in the LAD is the same as a computer's basic operating system. The particular language that a child learns to use is the same as a word-processing program.

Today, most researchers would agree that both nature and nurture affect most areas of development. We can argue as to which is more prominent in a given area of development, but as in the case of language development, they are both essential.

Psycholinguistic theory ▲ The view that language learning involves an interaction between environmental factors and an inborn tendency to acquire language.

Language acquisition device (LAD) ▲ In psycholinguistic theory, neural "prewiring" that facilitates the child's learning of grammar.

CONTROVERSY ✕ IN PSYCHOLOGY

Is Development Continuous or Discontinuous?

Do developmental changes tend to occur gradually (continuously)? Or do they tend to occur in major leaps (discontinuously) that dramatically alter our bodies and behavior? ***Question: Does development occur gradually or in stages?***

Watson and other behaviorists viewed development as a mainly continuous process in which the effects of learning mount gradually, with no major sudden changes. Maturational theorists, however, argue that people are prewired or preset to change dramatically at certain times of life. Rapid qualitative changes can be ushered in during new stages of development. They point out that the environment, even when enriched, profits us little until we are ready, or mature enough, to develop in a certain direction. For example, newborn babies do not imitate their parents' speech, even when the parents speak clearly and deliberately. Nor does aided practice in "walking" during the first few months after birth significantly accelerate the date at which the child can walk on her own.

Stage theorists, such as Sigmund Freud and Jean Piaget, saw development as discontinuous. Both theorists saw biological changes as providing the potential for psychological changes. Freud focused on the ways in which sexual development might provide the basis for personality development. Piaget's research centered on the ways in which maturation of the nervous system permits cognitive advances.

Certain aspects of physical development do occur in stages. For example, from the age of 2 to the onset of puberty (the period of development during which reproduction becomes possible), children gradually grow larger. Then, as we see in the next chapter, the adolescent growth spurt occurs. It is ushered in by hormones and characterized by rapid changes in structure and function (as in the development of the sex organs) as well as in size. Thus a new stage of life has begun. Psychologists disagree more strongly on whether aspects of development such as cognitive development, attachment, and gender typing occur in stages.

The next chapter begins with the adolescent growth spurt and follows development throughout the remainder of the life span.

REVIEW

(29) The nature-_____ controversy reflects the effort to sort out the relative influences of heredity and the environment on development. (30) Gesell leaned toward _____ explanations of development. (31) Behaviorists lean toward _____ explanations. (32) Watson and other behaviorists viewed development as mainly (continuous or discontinuous?). (33) Stage theorists, such as Freud and Piaget, saw development as mainly (continuous or discontinuous?).

Pulling It Together: What is the evidence for roles for nature and nurture in language development? Which aspects of language development are continuous? Which are discontinuous?

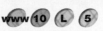

CLICK4™ *more information about developmental psychology from* Development Psychology Journal, *Child Study Net, and the Society for Research in Child Development.*

CLICK4™ *a quiz covering the second half of this chapter.*

CLICK4™ *electronic flash cards to review your knowledge of key terms and people in this chapter.*

TRUTH ▨ FICTION
REVISITED

◤ **It is not true that fertilization takes place in the uterus.** *Fertilization normally occurs in a fallopian tube. See page 318.*

◤ **It is true that your heart started beating when you were only one fifth of an inch long and weighed a fraction of an ounce.** *It started about 3 weeks after conception. See page 319.*

◤ **It is not true that the way to a baby's heart is through its stomach. Babies do not necessarily become attached to the people who feed them.** *Contact comfort may be a stronger wellspring of attachment. The path to a baby's heart may lie through its skin, not its stomach. See page 337.*

◤ **It is true that children with strict parents are most likely to be successful.** *This is especially so when the parents also reason with their children and are loving and supportive. See page 338.*

◤ **It is true that children placed in day care are more aggressive than children cared for in the home.** *Perhaps they are so because they have become more independent. See page 340.*

◤ **It is true that child abusers have frequently been abused as children.** *However, the majority of victims of abuse do not abuse their own children. See page 341.*

1. What developments occur from conception through birth?

Prenatal development occurs in stages: the germinal, embryonic, and fetal stages. During the germinal stage, the zygote divides as it travels through the fallopian tube and becomes implanted in the uterine wall. The major organ systems are formed during the embryonic stage, and the fetal stage is characterized by maturation and gains in size.

2. What physical developments occur during childhood?

Early physical development—prenatal and infant—occurs the most rapidly. Reflexes are inborn responses to stimuli that in many cases are essential to the survival of the infant. Examples include sucking and swallowing. Newborn babies can see quite well and show greater interest in complex visual stimuli than in simple ones. Infants are capable of depth perception by the time they can crawl. Newborns can normally hear and show a preference for their mother's voice. Newborns show preferences for pleasant odors and sweet foods. Motor development usually proceeds in a particular sequence in which infants roll over and sit before they stand and walk.

3. What are Jean Piaget's views of cognitive development?

Piaget saw children as budding scientists who actively strive to make sense of the perceptual world. He defined intelligence as involving the processes of assimilation (responding to events according to existing schemes) and accommodation (changing schemes to permit effective responses to new events). Piaget's view of cognitive development includes four stages: sensorimotor (prior to the use of symbols and language); preoperational (characterized by egocentric thought, animism, artificialism, and inability to center on more than one aspect of a situation); concrete operational (characterized by conservation, less egocentrism, reversibility, and subjective moral judgments); and formal operational (characterized by abstract logic).

4. How does language develop?

Children make the prelinguistic sounds of crying, cooing, and babbling before true language develops. Single-word utterances occur at about 1 year of age; two-word utterances by the age of 2. Early language is characterized by overextension of familiar words and concepts to unfamiliar objects (calling horses *doggies*), and by overregularization of verbs ("She *sitted* down"). As time passes, vocabulary grows larger, and sentence structure grows more complex.

5. How do children reason about what is right and wrong?

Lawrence Kohlberg hypothesized that children's moral reasoning develops through three levels, each of which consists of two stages. Moral decisions develop from being based on pain and pleasure ("preconventional"), through necessity to maintain the social order ("conventional"), to reliance on one's own conscience ("postconventional"). Not all individuals reach the postconventional level.

6. What are Erikson's stages of psychosocial development?

Erikson hypothesizes that there are eight stages of psychosocial development. Each represents a life crisis. The first of these is "trust versus mistrust," during which the crisis centers on the child's learning that the world is a good place that can meet its needs.

7. **How do feelings of attachment develop? What kinds of experiences affect attachment?**

Mary Ainsworth developed the strange situation method to study attachment. According to Ainsworth, there are three stages of attachment: the initial-preattachment phase, which is characterized by indiscriminate attachment; the attachment-in-the-making phase, which is characterized by preference for familiar figures; and the clear-cut-attachment phase, which is characterized by intensified dependence on the primary caregiver. Bowlby adds fear of strangers as a factor in attachment. Behaviorists have argued that children become attached to their mothers through conditioning because their mothers feed them and attend to their other needs. Harlow's studies with rhesus monkeys suggest that an innate motive, contact comfort, may be more important than conditioning in the development of attachment. There are critical developmental periods during which animals such as geese and ducks will become attached instinctively to (or imprinted on) an object that they follow.

8. **What types of parental behavior are connected with variables such as self-esteem, achievement motivation, and independence in children?**

Styles of parental behavior include the authoritative, authoritarian, and permissive styles. The children of authoritative parents are the most achievement-oriented and well-adjusted.

9. **What is the nature-nurture controversy about?**

The nature-nurture controversy concerns the relative influences of heredity (nature) and nurture (environmental influences) on development. Development appears to reflect an interaction between nature (genetic factors) and nurture (environmental influences). Maturational theorists focus on the influences of nature, whereas learning theorists focus on environmental influences.

10. **How is the nature-nurture controversy applied to language development?**

The two main theories of language development are learning theories and nativist theories. Learning theories focus on the roles of reinforcement and imitation. Nativist theories assume that innate factors cause children to attend to and perceive language in certain ways.

11. **Does development occur gradually or in stages?**

Stage theorists like Freud and Piaget view development as discontinuous. According to them, people go through distinct periods of development that differ in quality and follow an orderly sequence. Learning theorists, in contrast, tend to view psychological development as a more continuous process. Some aspects of development, such as the adolescent growth spurt, are discontinuous. There is controversy as to whether cognitive development is continuous or discontinuous.

PREVIEW

Adolescence: Physical Development

▲ Adolescents are neither fish nor fowl—like adults physically but often treated like children.

Adolescence: Cognitive Development

▲ Adolescents often see themselves as invulnerable and as the center of attention.

Adolescence: Social and Personality Development

▲ Adolescents strive for independence, yet their views of the world are much like their parents'.

Adulthood: Physical Development

▲ Women outlive men and European Americans outlive African Americans. Why?

▲ Why do we age? Can we do anything to delay it?

Adulthood: Cognitive Development

▲ We usually stay on top of the things we know about even if it becomes more difficult to learn "new tricks."

▲ The mental abilities of older people do not usually decline as much as is assumed.

Adulthood: Social and Personality Development

▲ Some psychologists speak of a stage between adolescence and young adulthood—emerging adulthood—which occurs only in wealthy societies like our own.

▲ There is no single "singles scene."

▲ People expect as much from marriage as ever—maybe more.

▲ Half of the marriages in the United States end in divorce.

▲ Many, perhaps most, people would work even if they did not have to.

▲ Middle adulthood is a vital productive period of life.

▲ Many stereotypes of late adulthood are out of date.

On Death and Dying

▲ What does psychology teach us about death and dying?

CHAPTER 11

Adolescent and Adult Development

TRUTH [OR] FICTION?

▨ A girl can become pregnant when she has her first menstrual period.

▨ Adolescents see themselves as being on stage.

▨ Most Americans would continue to work even if they did not need the money.

▨ Menopause signals the end of a woman's sexual interest.

▨ Frank Lloyd Wright created the innovative design for New York's Guggenheim Museum at the age of 65.

▨ Alzheimer's disease is a normal part of growing old.

▨ Single people are swingers.

▨ About half the marriages that took place during the past decade were preceded by cohabitation.

▨ Mothers suffer from the "empty-nest syndrome" when their youngest child leaves home.

▨ The secret to successful aging is taking a rest from the challenges of life.

Development continues for a lifetime. If we include the formation of the genetic codes and the sperm and ova that gave rise to us and that give rise to our children, development becomes a continuous process that chronicles the existence of humans on planet earth and possibly, as we move further into the new millennium, our existence on other orbs. Development stems from the interaction of the unfolding of genetically directed processes and the effects of the environments into which we are plunged. But then we grow aware of those environments and learn how to change them to better meet our needs. Learning and wisdom are as much a part of development as prenatal differentiation and the exciting changes of puberty.

This chapter begins the further chronicle of human development with the physical changes of adolescence, including those of puberty. It then follows development throughout adulthood and in many cases, as we will see, second adulthood.

ADOLESCENCE: PHYSICAL DEVELOPMENT

CLICK4™ *an essay assignment on rates of development during puberty.*

CLICK4™ *Web sites on physical development during adolescence.*

Adolescence is a time of transition from childhood to adulthood. In our society, adolescents often feel that they are "neither fish nor fowl," as the saying goes—neither children nor adults. Although adolescents may be old enough to have children and are as large as their parents, they are often treated quite differently than adults. They may not be eligible for a driver's license until they are 16 or 17. They cannot attend R-rated films unless they are accompanied by an adult. They are prevented from working long hours. They are usually required to remain in school through age 16 and may not marry until they reach the "age of consent." Adolescence entails physical, cognitive, and social and personal changes. In this section, we focus on the physical changes of adolescence.

Following infancy, children grow about 2 to 3 inches a year. Weight gains also remain fairly even at about 4 to 6 pounds per year. *Question: What physical developments occur during adolescence?* One of the most noticeable physical developments of adolescence is a growth spurt. The adolescent growth spurt lasts for 2 to 3 years and ends the stable patterns of growth in height and weight that characterize most of childhood. Within this short span of years, adolescents grow some 8 to 12 inches. Most boys wind up taller and heavier than most girls.

In boys, the weight of the muscle mass increases notably. The width of the shoulders and circumference of the chest also increase. Adolescents may eat enormous quantities of food to fuel their growth spurt. Adults fighting the "battle of the bulge" stare at them in wonder as they wolf down french fries and shakes at the fast-food counter and later go out for pizza.

> **▲ REFLECT**
> Did you undergo puberty early or late as compared to your peers? How did your experience with puberty affect your popularity and your self-esteem?

Adolescents.

In our culture adolescents are "neither fish nor fowl." Although they may be old enough to reproduce and may be as large as their parents, they are often treated like children.

Adolescence ▲ The period of life bounded by puberty and the assumption of adult responsibilities.

Puberty

Puberty is the period during which the body becomes sexually mature. It heralds the onset of adolescence. Puberty begins with the appearance of **secondary sex characteristics** such as body hair, deepening of the voice in males, and rounding of the breasts and hips in females (see Table 11.1). In boys, pituitary hormones stimulate the testes to increase the output of testosterone, which in turn causes enlargement of the penis and testes and the appearance of bodily hair. By the early teens, erections become common, and boys may ejaculate. Ejaculatory ability usually precedes the presence of mature sperm by at least a year. Ejaculation thus is not evidence of reproductive capacity.

In girls, a critical body weight in the neighborhood of 100 pounds is thought to trigger a cascade of hormonal secretions in the brain that cause the ovaries to secrete higher levels of the female sex hormone, estrogen (Frisch, 1997). Estrogen stimulates the growth of breast tissue and fatty and supportive tissue in the hips and buttocks. Thus the pelvis widens, rounding the hips. Small amounts of androgens produced by the adrenal glands, along with estrogen, spur the growth of pubic and underarm hair. Estrogen and androgens together stimulate the development of female sex organs. Estrogen production becomes cyclical during puberty and regulates the menstrual cycle. The beginning of menstruation, or **menarche,** usually occurs between the ages of 11 and 14. Girls cannot become pregnant until they begin to ovulate, however, and this may occur as much as two years after menarche.

REVIEW

(1) Puberty begins with the appearance of _____ sex characteristics, such as the growth of bodily hair, deepening of the voice in males, and rounding of the breasts and hips in females. (2) The changes of puberty are stimulated by _____ in the male and by estrogen and androgens in the female. (3) _____ regulates the menstrual cycle.

Pulling It Together: How do the physical changes of adolescence represent *discontinuity* in development?

ADOLESCENCE: COGNITIVE DEVELOPMENT

I am a college student of extremely modest means. Some crazy psychologist interested in something called "formal operational thought" has just promised to pay me $20 if I can make a coherent logical argument for the proposition that the federal government should under no circumstances ever give or lend more to needy college students. Now what could people who believe *that* possibly say by way of supporting argument? Well, I suppose they *could* offer this line of reasoning . . .

Adapted from Flavell et al., 1993, p. 140

The adolescent thinker approaches problems very differently from the elementary school child. *Question: What cognitive developments occur during adolescence?* Let

TABLE 11.1 STAGES OF PUBERTAL DEVELOPMENT

IN FEMALES	
Beginning sometime between ages 8 and 11	Pituitary hormones stimulate ovaries to increase production of estrogen. Internal reproductive organs begin to grow.
Beginning sometime between ages 9 and 15	First the areola (the darker area around the nipple) and then the breasts increase in size and become more rounded. Pubic hair becomes darker and coarser. Growth in height continues. Body fat continues to round body contours. A normal vaginal discharge becomes noticeable. Sweat and oil glands increase in activity, and acne may appear. Internal and external reproductive organs and genitals grow, making the vagina longer and the labia more pronounced.
Beginning sometime between ages 10 and 16	Areola and nipples grow, often forming a second mound sticking out from the rounded breast mound. Pubic hair begins to grow in a triangular shape and to cover the center of the mons. Underarm hair appears. Menarche occurs. Internal reproductive organs continue to develop. Ovaries may begin to release mature eggs capable of being fertilized. Growth in height slows.
Beginning sometime between ages 12 and 19	Breasts near adult size and shape. Pubic hair fully covers the mons and spreads to the top of the thighs. The voice may deepen slightly (but not as much as in males). Menstrual cycles gradually become more regular. Some further changes in body shape may occur into the young woman's early 20s.

IN MALES	
Beginning sometime between ages 9 and 15	The testicles begin to grow. The skin of the scrotum becomes redder and coarser. A few straight pubic hairs appear at the base of the penis. Muscle mass develops, and the boy begins to grow taller. The areola grows larger and darker.
Beginning sometime between ages 11 and 16	The penis begins to grow longer. The testicles and scrotum continue to grow. Pubic hair becomes coarser and more curled and spreads to cover the area between the legs. The body gains in height. The shoulders broaden. The hips narrow. The larynx enlarges, resulting in a deepening of the voice. Sparse facial and underarm hair appears.
Beginning sometime between ages 11 and 17	The penis begins to increase in circumference as well as in length (though more slowly). The testicles continue to increase in size. The texture of the pubic hair is more like an adult's. Growth of facial and underarm hair increases. Shaving may begin. First ejaculation occurs. In nearly half of all boys, gynecomastia (breast enlargement) occurs, which then decreases in a year or two. Increased skin oils may produce acne.
Beginning sometime between ages 14 and 18	The body nears final adult height, and the genitals achieve adult shape and size, with pubic hair spreading to the thighs and slightly upward toward the belly. Chest hair appears. Facial hair reaches full growth. Shaving becomes more frequent. For some young men, further increases in height, body hair, and muscle growth and strength continue into their early 20s.

This table is a general guideline. Changes may appear sooner or later than shown and do not always appear in the indicated sequence.

SOURCE: Copyright © 1990 by the Kinsey Institute for Research in Sex, Gender, and Reproduction. From *The Kinsey Institute New Report on Sex*.

Puberty ▲ The period of physical development during which sexual reproduction first becomes possible.

Secondary sex characteristics ▲ Characteristics that distinguish the sexes, such as distribution of body hair and depth of voice, but that are not directly involved in reproduction.

Menarche ▲ The beginning of menstruation.

us begin to answer this question by comparing the child's thought processes to that of the adolescent. The child sticks to the facts, to concrete reality. Speculating about abstract possibilities and what might be, is very difficult. The adolescent, on the other hand, is able to deal with the abstract and the hypothetical. As shown in the above example, adolescents realize that one does not have to believe in the truth or justice of something in order to argue for it (Flavell et al., 1993). In this section we explore some of the cognitive developments of adolescence by referring to the theories of Jean Piaget and Lawrence Kohlberg.

The Formal Operational Stage

CD 11 V 36

CLICK4™ *a video on abstract reasoning at the formal operational stage.*

According to Piaget, children typically undergo three stages of cognitive development prior to adolescence: sensorimotor, preoperational, and concrete operational. They develop from infants who respond automatically to their environment to older children who can focus on various aspects of a situation at once and solve complex problems. The stage of **formal operations** is the final stage in Jean Piaget's theory of cognitive development, and it represents cognitive maturity. For many children in Western societies, formal operational thought begins at about the beginning of adolescence—the age of 11 or 12. However, not all individuals enter this stage at this time, and some individuals never reach it.

The major achievements of the stage of formal operations involve classification, logical thought, and the ability to hypothesize. Central features are the ability to think about ideas as well as objects and to group and classify ideas—symbols, statements, entire theories. The flexibility and reversibility of operations, when applied to statements and theories, allow adolescents to follow arguments from premises to conclusions and back again.

▲ **REFLECT**
Did you go through a phase of adolescence during which you thought you "knew it all"? Why do you think that happened?

Several features of formal operational thought give the adolescent a generally greater capacity to manipulate and appreciate the outer environment and the world of the imagination: hypothetical thinking, the ability to use symbols to stand for symbols, and deductive reasoning.

Formal-operational adolescents (and adults) think abstractly. They become capable of solving geometric problems about circles and squares without reference to what the circles and squares may represent in the real world. Adolescents in this stage derive rules for behavior from general principles and can focus, or center, on many aspects of a situation at once in arriving at judgments and solving problems.

In a sense, it is during the stage of formal operations that adolescents tend to emerge as theoretical scientists—even though they may see themselves as having little or no interest in science. They become capable of dealing with hypothetical situations. They realize that situations can have different outcomes, and they think ahead, experimenting with different possibilities. Adolescents also conduct experiments to determine whether their hypotheses are correct. These experiments are not conducted in the laboratory. Rather, adolescents may try out different tones of voice, ways of carrying themselves and of treating others to see what works best for them.

Adolescent Egocentrism: "You Just Don't Understand!" Adolescents in the formal operational stage can reason deductively, or draw conclusions about specific objects or people once they have been classified accurately. Adolescents can be somewhat proud of their new logical abilities, and so a new sort of egocentrism can develop in which adolescents emotionally press for acceptance of their logic without recognizing the exceptions or practical problems that are often considered by adults. Consider this example: "It is wrong to hurt people. Company A occasionally hurts people" (perhaps through pollution or economic pressures). "Therefore, Company A must be severely punished or shut down." This thinking is logical. By impatiently pressing for immediate major changes or severe penalties, however, one may not fully consider various practical problems such as the thousands of workers who would be laid off if the company were shut down. Adults frequently have undergone life experiences that lead them to see shades of gray in situations, rather than just black or white.

▲ **REFLECT**
Did you have an intense need for privacy as an adolescent? How do you explain that need in terms of Piaget's theory?

The thought of preschoolers is characterized by egocentrism in which they cannot take another's point of view. Adolescent thought is marked by another sort of egocentrism, in which they can understand the thoughts of others but still have trouble separating things that are of concern to others and those that are of concern only to themselves

Formal-operational stage ▲ Piaget's fourth stage, characterized by abstract logical thought; deduction from principles.

(Elkind, 1985). Adolescent egocentrism gives rise to two interesting cognitive developments: *the imaginary audience* and the *personal fable*.

The concept of the **imaginary audience** refers to the belief that other people are as concerned with our thoughts and behavior as we are. As a result, adolescents see themselves as the center of attention and assume that other people are about as preoccupied with their appearance and behavior as they are (Frankenberger, 2000; Milstead et al., 1993). Adolescents may feel they are on stage and all eyes are focused on them.

The concept of the imaginary audience may fuel the intense adolescent desire for privacy. It helps explain why adolescents are so self-conscious about their appearance, why they worry about every facial blemish and spend long hours grooming. Self-consciousness seems to peak at about the age of 13 and then decline. Girls tend to be more self-conscious than boys (Elkind & Bowen, 1979).

The **personal fable** is the belief that our feelings and ideas are special, even unique, and that we are invulnerable. The personal fable seems to underlie adolescent behavior patterns such as showing off and taking risks (Cohn et al., 1995; Milstead et al., 1993). Some adolescents adopt an "It can't happen to me" attitude; they assume they can smoke without risk of cancer or engage in sexual activity without risk of sexually transmitted infections (STIs) or pregnancy. "All youth—rich, poor, black, white—have this sense of invincibility, invulnerability," says Ronald King (2000) of the HIV Community Coalition of Washington, D.C., explaining why many teens who apparently know the risks still expose themselves to HIV. Another aspect of the personal fable is the idea that no one else has experienced or can understand one's "unique" feelings such as needing independence or being in love. The personal fable may underlie the common teenage lament, "You just don't understand me!"

Evaluation of Piaget's Theory

A number of questions have been raised concerning the accuracy of Piaget's views. Among them are these:

1. *Was Piaget's timing accurate?* Some critics argue that Piaget's methods led him to underestimate children's abilities (Bjorklund, 1995; Meltzoff & Gopnik, 1997). Other researchers using different methods have found, for example, that preschoolers are less egocentric and that children are capable of conservation at earlier ages than Piaget thought.

2. *Does cognitive development occur in stages?* Cognitive events such as egocentrism and conservation appear to develop more continuously than Piaget thought—that is, they may not occur in stages (Bjorklund, 1995; Flavell, 2000). Although cognitive developments appear to build on previous cognitive developments, the process may be more gradual than stagelike.

3. *Are developmental sequences always the same?* Here, Piaget's views have fared better. It seems there is no variation in the sequence in which cognitive developments occur.

In sum, Piaget's theoretical edifice has been rocked, but it has not been reduced to rubble. Psychologist Andrew Meltzoff believes that "Piaget's theories were critical for getting the field of [cognitive development] off the ground, . . . but it's time to move on" (1997, p. 9). Some psychologists are moving on to *information processing*. That is, they view children (and adults) as akin to computer systems. Children, like computers, obtain information (receive "input") from their environment, store it, retrieve, manipulate it (think about it), and then respond to it overtly in terms of their behavior (produce "output"). One goal of the information-processing approach is to learn just how children do these things, how their "mental programs" develop. Critical issues involve children's capacity for memory and their use of cognitive strategies, such as the ways in which they focus their attention (Bjorklund, 1995; Case, 1992; Kail, 2000). The future of cognitive development remains to be written.

The Postconventional Level of Moral Reasoning

Lawrence Kohlberg's theory of moral reasoning involves three levels: preconventional, conventional, and postconventional. Individuals can arrive at the same decision—for example, as to whether or not Heinz should save his wife by taking the drug without paying

Adolescent Self-Consciousness.
The concept of the imaginary audience may help explain why adolescents are self-conscious about their appearance, why they worry about minor facial imperfections, and why they devote so much time to grooming.

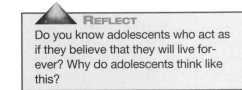

REFLECT
Do you know adolescents who act as if they believe that they will live forever? Why do adolescents think like this?

REFLECT
Can you think of situations — historic or current — in which people have had to break the law in order to do the right thing? Can you think of situations in which people have done the wrong thing by following the law?

Imaginary audience ▲ An aspect of adolescent egocentrism: The belief that other people are as concerned with our thoughts and behaviors as we are.
Personal fable ▲ Another aspect of adolescent egocentrism: The belief that our feelings and ideas are special and unique and that we are invulnerable.

for it—but they would be doing so for a different kind of reason. (Deciding not to take the drug for fear of punishment is cognitively less complex than not taking the drug because of the belief that doing so could have negative consequences for the social order.)

None of Kohlberg's levels is tied precisely to a person's age. Although postconventional reasoning is the highest level, for example, most adolescents and adults reason conventionally. However, when postconventional reasoning does emerge, it usually does so in adolescence. Kohlberg's (1969) research showed that postconventional moral judgments were clearly absent among the 7- to 10-year-olds. But by age 16, stage 5 reasoning is shown by about 20% of adolescents, and stage 6 reasoning is shown by about 5% of adolescents.

At the **postconventional level,** moral reasoning is based on the person's own moral standards. In each instance, moral judgments are derived from personal values, not from conventional standards or authority figures. In the contractual, legalistic orientation characteristic of stage 5, it is recognized that laws stem from agreed-upon procedures and that the rule of law is in general good for society; therefore, laws should not be violated. But under exceptional circumstances laws cannot bind the individual. (Although it is illegal for Heinz to steal the drug, in this case it is the right thing to do.)

Stage 6 moral reasoning demands adherence to supposed universal ethical principles such as the sanctity of human life, individual dignity, justice, and the Golden Rule ("Do unto others as you would have them do unto you"). If a law is unjust or contradicts the rights of the individual, it is wrong to obey it.

People at the postconventional level look to their conscience as the highest moral authority. This point has created confusion. To some it suggests that it is right to break the law when it is convenient. But this interpretation is incorrect. Kohlberg means that people at this level of moral reasoning must do what they believe is right even if this action runs counter to social rules or laws or requires personal sacrifice.

Evaluation of Kohlberg's Theory

Consistent with Kohlberg's theory, research suggests that moral reasoning does follow a developmental sequence (Snarey, 1985), even though most people do not reach the level of postconventional thought. Postconventional thought, when found, first occurs during adolescence. It also seems that Piaget's stage of formal operations is a prerequisite for postconventional reasoning, which requires the capacities to understand abstract moral principles and to empathize with the attitudes and emotional responses of other people (Flavell et al., 1993).

Also consistent with Kohlberg's theory, children do not appear to skip stages as they progress (Flavell et al., 1993). Classic research shows that when children are exposed to adult models who exhibit a lower stage of moral reasoning, they can be enticed to follow along (Bandura & McDonald, 1963). Children who are exposed to examples of moral reasoning above and below their own stage generally prefer the higher stage, however (Rest, 1983). The thrust of moral development would therefore appear to be from lower to higher in terms of Kohlberg's levels and stages, even if children can be influenced by the opinions of others.

CONTROVERSY ✕ IN PSYCHOLOGY

Are There Gender Differences in Moral Development?

CLICK4™ *a bulletin board discussion on gender differences in moral development.*

A number of studies using Heinz's dilemma have found that boys show higher levels of moral reasoning than girls. But Carol Gilligan (1982; Gilligan et al., 1989) argues that this gender difference reflects different patterns of socialization for boys and girls—not differences in morality. Gilligan points to 11-year-old Jake. Jake weighs the scales of justice like a math problem. He shows that life is worth more than property and concludes that it is Heinz's duty to steal the drug (stage 4 reasoning). Gilligan also points to 11-year-old Amy. Amy vacillates. Amy says that stealing the drug and letting Heinz's wife die are both wrong. So Amy looks for alternatives, such as getting a loan, because it wouldn't help Heinz's wife if he went to jail.

Gilligan finds Amy's reasoning to be as sophisticated as Jake's, yet Amy would be rated as showing a lower level of moral development in Kohlberg's scheme. Gilligan

Postconventional level ▲ According to Kohlberg, a period during which moral judgments are derived from moral principles and people look to themselves to set moral standards.

asserts that Amy and other girls are socialized to focus on the needs of others and forgo simplistic judgments of right and wrong. Amy is therefore more likely to show stage 3 reasoning, which focuses in part on empathy—on caring for others. Jake has been socialized to make judgments based on logic. To him, clear-cut conclusions are derived from premises.

We could argue endlessly about which form of moral reasoning—Jake's or Amy's—is "higher." Instead, let us point to a meta-analysis of the research in the area that shows that there is only a slight tendency for boys to favor Jake's "justice" approach, and a slight tendency for girls to favor Amy's "caring" approach (Jaffee & Hyde, 2000). We cannot say that the justice orientation is used predominantly by boys, or the care orientation predominantly by girls.

REVIEW

(4) _____ operational thought is characterized by hypothetical thinking and deductive logic. (5) Adolescent egocentrism gives rise to the _____ audience and the personal fable. (6) Adolescents in Kohlberg's stage 5 _____, legalistic orientation believe that laws stem from agreed-upon procedures and that laws cannot bind the individual's behavior in unusual circumstances. (7) In stage 6 moral reasoning, people consider behavior that is consistent with _____ ethical standards as right.

Pulling It Together: How do cognitive developments of adolescence contribute to the desire for privacy and to risk-taking?

ADOLESCENCE: SOCIAL AND PERSONALITY DEVELOPMENT

Adolescents also differ markedly from children in their social and personality development. *Question: What social and personality developments occur during adolescence?* In terms of social and personality development, adolescence has been associated with turbulence. In the 19th century, psychologist G. Stanley Hall described adolescence as a time of *Sturm und Drang*—storm and stress. Certainly, many American teenagers abuse drugs, get pregnant, contract STIs, become involved in violence, fail in school, even attempt suicide (CDC, 2000b). Each year nearly 1 in 10 adolescent girls becomes pregnant. Nearly 10% of teenage boys and 20% of teenage girls attempt suicide. Motor vehicle crashes are the leading cause of death among adolescents in the United States, and many of these involve alcohol or distraction of the driver by passengers (Chen et al., 2000). Other common causes of death are injuries other than auto accidents, homicide, and suicide.

Hall attributed the conflicts and distress of adolescence to biological changes. Research evidence suggests that hormonal changes affect the activity levels, mood swings, and aggressive tendencies of many adolescents, but that sociocultural influences have a relatively greater impact (Buchanan et al., 1992).

Striving for Independence

Adolescents do try to become more independent from their parents, which often leads to some bickering (Smetana & Gaines, 1999). They usually bicker about issues such as homework, chores, money, appearance, curfews, and dating (Galambos & Turner, 1999). Arguments are common when adolescents want to make their own choices about matters such as clothes and friends.

The striving for independence is also characterized by withdrawal from family life, at least relative to prior involvement. In one study, children ranging in age from 9 to 15 carried electronic pagers for a week so that they could report what they were doing and whom they were with when signaled (Larson & Richards, 1991). The amount of time spent with family members decreased dramatically with greater age. The 15-year-olds spent only half as much time with their families as the 9-year-olds. Yet this change does not mean that most adolescents spend their time on the streets. For 15-year-old boys in

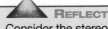

CLICK4™ *more information about adolescent development from the* Piaget Archives *and the* Journal of Adolescence.

CLICK4™ *a WebSearch activity on stereotypes: Does psychological research support the idea of adolescence as a time of "storm and stress"?*

▲ REFLECT

Consider the stereotype of adolescence as a time of "storm and stress." Does this stereotype fit your own experiences as an adolescent? How or how not?

TABLE 11.2   MEAN RATINGS OF PERCEIVED HARMFULNESS OF VARIOUS ACTIVITIES

Activity	EXPERIMENTAL INVOLVEMENT (DOING ACTIVITY ONCE OR TWICE TO SEE WHAT IT IS LIKE)		FREQUENT INVOLVEMENT	
	Teenager	Teenager's Parents	Teenager	Teenager's Parents
Drinking alcohol	2.6	3.5	4.4	4.8
Smoking cigarettes	3.0	3.6	4.4	4.8
Using diet pills	2.8	3.8	4.1	4.7
Not using seat belts	3.0	4.3	4.0	4.8
Getting drunk	3.2	4.2	4.4	4.8
Sniffing glue	3.6	4.6	4.6	4.9
Driving home after drinking a few beers	3.8	4.5	4.6	4.8
Drag racing	3.8	4.6	4.5	4.8
Using steroids	3.8	4.4	4.7	4.9

▲ **REFLECT**

Have you yet formed your own ego identity? If so, what was the process like? If not, are you concerned? Why or why not?

Ego identity ▲ Erikson's term for a firm sense of who one is and what one stands for.

Role diffusion ▲ Erikson's term for lack of clarity in one's life roles (due to failure to develop ego identity).

Adolescent Relationships With Parents.
Adolescents strive for some independence from their parents, including some distancing. But most adolescents continue to feel love, respect, and loyalty toward their parents. Adolescents and parents also tend to share social, political, religious, and economic views.

the study, time with the family tended to be replaced by time spent alone. For older girls, this time was divided between friends and solitude.

Adolescents and parents are often in conflict because adolescents experiment with many things that can be harmful to their health. Yet—apparently because of the personal fable—adolescents often do not perceive such activities to be as risky as their parents see them as being. Lawrence Cohn and his colleagues (1995) found, for example, that parents perceived drinking, smoking, failure to use seat belts, drag racing, and a number of other activities to be riskier than did their teenagers (see Table 11.2).

Some distancing from parents is beneficial for adolescents (Galambos & Turner, 1999). After all, they do have to form relationships outside the family. But greater independence does not necessarily mean that adolescents become emotionally detached from their parents or fall completely under the influence of their peers. Most adolescents continue to feel love, respect, and loyalty toward their parents (Eberly & Montemayor, 1999). Adolescents who feel close to their parents actually show greater self-reliance and independence than do those who are distant from their parents. Adolescents who retain close ties with their parents also fare better in school and have fewer adjustment problems (Davey, 1993; Steinberg, 1996).

Despite parent–adolescent conflict over issues of control, parents and adolescents tend to share social, political, religious, and economic views (Sagrestano et al., 1999). In sum, there are frequent differences between parents and adolescents on issues of personal control. However, there apparently is no "generation gap" on broader matters.

The nearby "Psychology and Modern Life" feature offers additional insight into risk-taking behavior among adolescents in the United States.

Ego Identity Versus Role Diffusion

According to Erik Erikson, individuals undergo eight stages of psychosocial development, each of which is characterized by a certain kind of "crisis." Four of these stages, beginning with the stage of trust versus mistrust, occur during the years of childhood. The fifth stage, that of *ego identity versus role diffusion*, occurs during adolescence. The major challenge of adolescence is the creation of an adult identity. Identity is achieved mainly by committing oneself to a particular occupation or a role in life. But identity also extends to sexual, political, and religious beliefs and commitments.

Erikson (1963) theorized that adolescents experience a life crisis of *ego identity versus role diffusion*. **Ego identity** is a firm sense of who one is and what one stands for. It can carry one through difficult times and give meaning to one's achievements. Adolescents who do not develop ego identity may experience **role diffusion**. They spread themselves too thin, running down one blind alley after another and placing themselves at the mercy of leaders who promise to give them the sense of identity that they cannot find for themselves.

DIVERSITY   Identity Formation, Gender, and Ethnicity

Don Terry (2000) used to do anything he could to put off going to bed. One of his favorite delaying tactics was to engage his mother in a discussion about the important questions of the day, questions he and his friends had debated in the backyards of their neighborhood that afternoon—like Who did God root for, the Cubs or the White Sox? (The correct answer was, and still is, the White Sox.)

Then one night he remembers asking his mother something he had been wondering for a long time. "Mom," he asked, "What am I?"

"You're my darling Donny," she said.

"I know. But what else am I?"

"You're a precious little boy who someday will grow up to be a wonderful, handsome man."

"What I mean is, you're white and Dad's black, so what does that make me?"

"Oh, I see," she said. "Well, you're half-black and you're half-white, so you're the best of both worlds."

The next day, he told his friends that he was neither "black" nor "white." "I'm the best of both worlds," he announced proudly.

"Man, you're crazy," one of the backyard boys said. "You're not even the best of your family. Your sister is. That girl is fine."

For much of his life, he has tried to believe his mother. Having grown up in a family of blacks and whites, he had long thought he saw race more clearly than most people. He appreciated being able to get close to both worlds, something few ever do. It was like having a secret knowledge.

And yet he has also known from an early age that things were more complicated than his mother made them out to be. Our country, from its very beginnings, has been obsessed with determining people's race.

Being European American or African American, or both, is part of one's identity. So is being male or female, Christian, Muslim, or Jew.

Erik Erikson's views of the development of identity were intended to apply primarily to males (Archer, 1992). In Erikson's theory, the stage of identity development includes embracing a philosophy of life and commitment to a career. It is in the next stage that people develop the capacity to form intimate relationships. Erikson believed that the development of interpersonal relationships was more important to women's identity than occupational and ideological issues because women's identities were intimately connected with women's roles as wives and mothers. Men's identities did not depend on their roles as husbands and fathers.

But research shows that in the United States, young women's identities are also strongly connected with occupational issues (Archer, 1992). The economic realities of life in the United States call for full participation of women in the workplace. Thus, adolescent girls today voice their occupational plans with about as equal concern as boys. But girls also express concern about how to balance the needs of a career and a family in their daily lives (Archer, 1992). Although most women will be full-time workers, they still usually bear the primary responsibility for rearing the children and maintaining the home. (When is the last time you heard a man wonder how he will balance the demands of a career and a family?)

Identity formation is more complicated for adolescents from ethnic minority groups (Collins, 2000; Phinney, 2000). These adolescents may be faced with two sets of cultural

CLICK4™ *a bulletin board discussion on adolescent development and ego identity.*

CLICK4™ *an essay assignment on adolescent behaviors such as risk taking and the need for privacy.*

www 11 L 3

CLICK4™ *more information about social and personality development in adolescence, including peer pressure and the effects of race on identity.*

Psychology and Modern Life

Youthful Behavior—Risky Stuff

The U. S. Centers for Disease Control and Prevention regularly survey the behavior of young people in an effort to uncover risks to health. The CDC (2000b) recently reported that 72% of all deaths among people aged 10 to 24 years result from only four causes: motor-vehicle crashes (31%), other unintentional injuries (11%), homicide (18%), and suicide (12%). Numerous high school students engage in behaviors that increase their likelihood of death from these four causes:

- 16% rarely or never wear seat belts.
- 33% ride with drivers who have been drinking alcohol.

- 17% carry weapons.
- 50% drank alcohol during the 30 days preceding the survey.
- 27% used marijuana during the 30 days preceding the survey.
- 8% attempted suicide during the 12 months preceding the survey.

Statistics collected on the behavior of high school students revealed that:

- 50% had engaged in sexual intercourse.
- 42% of the sexually active students did not use a condom during their last sexual encounter.

- 2% had injected an illegal drug.

Two thirds of all deaths among people aged 25 and above result from two causes: cardiovascular disease and cancer. The majority of risk behaviors associated with these two causes of death are initiated during adolescence. For example, 35% of high school students had smoked cigarettes within the past 30 days; 76% did not eat enough fruits and vegetables; 16% were at risk for becoming overweight; and 71% did not exercise regularly.

Adolescent Sexuality.
The changes of puberty ready adolescents' bodies for sexual activity, and surging hormone levels increase sexual desire. Many adolescents therefore struggle to find ways of expressing—or suppressing—their awakening sexuality. In the United States, they also dwell within a culture that sends them mixed messages about sex. Although teenagers may be advised to wait until they have married, TV and radio commercials, print advertising, and virtually every other medium may give them the (exaggerated) impression that everyone is sexually active.

▲ **REFLECT**
How important a part of your adolescence (or that of your peers) was sexuality? Did any of your peers experience problems related to their sexuality during adolescence? Did they resolve these problems? If so, how?

CLICK4™ *a WebSearch activity on adolescent sex and sexuality.*

CLICK4™ *"Talking with Kids," a Web site devoted to issues such as sex, drugs, alcohol, AIDS, and violence.*

www 11 BBC 1

CLICK4™ *a bulletin board discussion on different rates of physical and emotional development during adolescence.*

values: those of their ethnic group and those of the dominant culture (Phinney, 2000; Phinney & Devich-Navarro, 1997). When these values are in conflict, minority adolescents need to reconcile the differences and, frequently, decide where they stand. A Muslim American adolescent explains why she skipped the prom: "At the time of the prom, I was sad, but just about everyone I knew had sex that night, which I think was immoral. Now, I like saying that I didn't go. I didn't go there just because it was a cool thing to do" ("Muslim Women," 1993, p. B9).

Biracial adolescents whose parents are of different religions wrestle with yet another issue as to what constitutes their own dominant cultural heritage (Collins, 2000; Phinney, 2000). Parents from different ethnic groups may decide to spend their lives together, but their values sometimes do not dwell contentedly side by side in the minds of their children.

A key aspect of identity is sexual identity—how the adolescent perceives himself or herself as a sexual being. The sex organs of adolescents undergo rapid maturation, and adolescents develop the capacity for reproduction. As we see next, many of them do reproduce before they are socially, emotionally, and financially ready to do so.

Adolescent Sexuality

My first sexual experience occurred in a car after the high school junior prom. We were both virgins, very uncertain but very much in love. We had been going together since eighth grade. The experience was somewhat painful. I remember wondering if I would look different to my mother the next day. I guess I didn't because nothing was said. (Adapted from Morrison et al., 1980, p. 108)

Although adolescents may not form enduring romantic relationships or be able to support themselves, the changes of puberty ready their bodies for sexual activity. High hormone levels also stir interest in sex. Adolescents therefore wrestle with issues of how and when to express their awakening sexuality. To complicate matters, Western culture sends mixed messages about sex. Teenagers may be advised to wait until they have married or at least entered into meaningful relationships, but they are also bombarded by sexual messages in films, TV and radio commercials, print advertising, and virtually every other medium. All in all, about half of U.S. high school students have engaged in sexual intercourse (CDC, 2000b).

Adolescent girls by and large obtain little advice at home or in school about how to resist sexual advances. Nor do most of them have ready access to effective contraception. Fewer than half of the adolescents who are sexually active report using contraceptives consistently (CDC, 2000b). As a result, about 800,000 teenage girls get pregnant each year, resulting in 500,000 births (CDC, 2000d). Nearly 3 million teenagers in the United States contract an STI each year (CDC, 2000b).

Why is teenage pregnancy so common? Some teenage girls become pregnant as a way of eliciting a commitment from their partner or rebelling against their parents. But most become pregnant because they misunderstand reproduction and contraception or miscalculate the odds of conception. Even those who are well-informed about contraception often do not use it consistently. Peers also play an important role in determining the sexual behavior of adolescents. When teenagers are asked why they do not wait to have sexual intercourse until they are older, the top reason cited is usually peer pressure (Dickson et al., 1998).

The medical, social, and economic costs of unplanned teenage pregnancies are enormous to teenage mothers and their children. Teenage mothers are more likely to have medical complications during pregnancy and to have prolonged labor. Their babies are more likely to be born prematurely and to have low birth weight. It appears that these medical problems are largely due not to the young age of the mother, but to the inadequate prenatal care and poor nutrition obtained by teenage mothers living in poverty (Fraser et al., 1995).

Teenage mothers are also less likely to graduate from high school or attend college (CDC, 2000b). Their lack of educational achievement leads to a lower standard of living and a greater need for public assistance. Few receive consistent financial or emotional help from the babies' fathers, who generally are unable to support themselves, let alone a family.

Still, there is some encouraging news. The final decade of the 20th century saw a decline in the teenage pregnancy rate because of increased use of contraception as well as the leveling off of sexual activity among teenagers (CDC, 2000b). The teenage pregnancy rate was falling (CDC, 2000b). CDC researchers attribute the decrease in risky sexual behavior to educational campaigns in the schools, the media, churches, and communities.

REVIEW

(8) Psychologist G. Stanley Hall described adolescence as a time of *Sturm und Drang*— storm and _____. (9) The leading cause of death among adolescents is _____. (10) Adolescents tend to see experimentation with cars, drugs, and sex as (more or less?) risky than their parents do. (11) Parents and adolescents tend to (agree or disagree?) on social, political, religious, and economic issues. (12) Erik Erikson considers the life crisis of adolescence to be ego identity versus role _____.

Pulling It Together: How do the physical, cognitive, and social/personal aspects of adolescent development contribute to ego identity?

ADULTHOOD: PHYSICAL DEVELOPMENT

Development continues throughout the lifespan. Many theorists believe that adult concerns and involvements follow observable patterns, so that we can speak of "stages" of adult development. Others argue that there may no longer be a standard life cycle with predictable stages or phases (Sheehy, 1995). Age now has an "elastic quality" (Butler, 1998). People are living longer than ever before and are freer than ever to choose their own destiny.

The most obvious aspects of development during adulthood are physical. *Question: What physical developments occur during adulthood?* In the following section we consider the physical developments that take place in young, or early, adulthood, which covers the period between the ages of 20 and 40; middle adulthood, which spans the ages of about 45 to 65; and late adulthood, which begins at 65. When we explore social and personality development, we will see that some theorists have added a period that spans the years from 18 to 25 and is labeled *emerging adulthood*.

Young Adulthood

Physical development peaks in young adulthood. Most people are at their height of sensory sharpness, strength, reaction time, and cardiovascular fitness. Women gymnasts find themselves going downhill in their early 20s because they accumulate body fat and lose suppleness and flexibility. Other athletes are more likely to experience a decline in their 30s. Most athletes retire before they reach 40.

Sexually speaking, most people in early adulthood become readily aroused. They tend to attain and maintain erections as desired, and to lubricate readily. A man in his 20s is more likely to be concerned about ejaculating too quickly than about whether or not he will be able to obtain an erection.

Middle Adulthood

As we enter our middle years, we are unlikely to possess the strength, coordination, and stamina that we had during our 20s and 30s. The decline is most obvious in the professional sports ranks, where peak performance is at a premium. Gordie Howe still played hockey at 50 and George Blanda was still kicking field goals at that age, but most professionals at those ages can no longer keep up with the "kids."

But the years between 40 and 60 are reasonably stable. There is gradual physical decline, but it is minor and only likely to be of concern if we insist on competing with young adults—or with idealized memories of ourselves (Morley & van den Berg, 2000).

CLICK4™ the Web site of the National Campaign to Prevent Teen Pregnancy, with tips for teens and parents.

CLICK4™ "ScarleTeen," a sex-education Web site for teenagers.

And many of us first make time to develop our physical potentials during middle adulthood. The 20-year-old couch potato occasionally becomes the 50-year-old marathoner. By any reasonable standard, we can maintain excellent cardiorespiratory condition throughout middle adulthood.

Because the physical decline in middle adulthood is gradual, people who begin to eat more nutritious diets (e.g., decrease intake of fats and increase intake of fruits and vegetables) and to exercise during this stage of life may find themselves looking and feeling better than they did in young adulthood. Sedentary people in young adulthood may gasp for air if they rush half a block to catch a bus, whereas fit people in middle adulthood—even in late adulthood—may run for miles before they feel fatigued.

▲ REFLECT

Do you know anyone who has undergone menopause? What was the experience like?

Menopause Menopause, or cessation of menstruation, usually occurs during the late 40s or early 50s, although there are wide variations in the age at which it occurs. Menopause is the final stage of a broader female experience, the *climacteric*, which is caused by a falling off in the secretion of the hormones estrogen and progesterone, and during which many changes occur that are related to the gradual loss of reproductive ability (Morley & van den Berg, 2000). At this time ovulation also draws to an end. There is some loss of breast tissue and of elasticity in the skin. There can also be a loss of bone density that leads to osteoporosis (a condition in which the bones break easily) in late adulthood.

During the climacteric, many women encounter symptoms such as hot flashes (uncomfortable sensations characterized by heat and perspiration) and loss of sleep. Loss of estrogen can be accompanied by feelings of anxiety and depression, but women appear to be more likely to experience serious depression *prior* to menopause, when they may feel overwhelmed by the combined demands of the workplace, child rearing, and homemaking (Depression research, 2000). Most women get through the mood changes that can accompany menopause without great difficulty. According to psychologist Karen Matthews, who followed a sample of hundreds of women through menopause, "The vast majority [of women] have no problem at all getting through the menopausal transition" (Matthews, 1994, p. 25).

Myths About Menopause We are better able to adjust to life's changes when we have accurate information about them. Menopause is a major life change for most women, and many of us harbor false beliefs about it. Consider the following myths and realities about menopause:

Myth 1. *Menopause is abnormal.* No, menopause is a normal development in women's lives.

Myth 2. *The medical establishment defines menopause as a disease.* No longer. Today menopause is conceptualized as a "deficiency syndrome," in recognition of the drop-off in secretion of estrogen and progesterone. Sad to say, the term *deficiency* also has negative connotations.

Myth 3. *After menopause, women need complete replacement of estrogen.* Not necessarily. Some estrogen is still produced by the adrenal glands, fatty tissue, and the brain. The pros and cons of estrogen-replacement therapy are still being debated.

Myth 4. *Menopause is accompanied by depression and anxiety.* Not necessarily. Much of the emotional response to menopause reflects its meaning to the individual rather than physiological changes.

Myth 5. *At menopause, women suffer debilitating hot flashes.* Many women do not have them at all. Those who do usually find them mild.

Myth 6. *Menopause signals an end to women's sexual interests.* Not so. Many women find the separation of sex from reproduction to be sexually liberating. Some of the physical problems that may stem from the fall-off in hormone production may be alleviated by hormone replacement therapy (Grodstein et al., 1997). A more important issue may be what menopause means to the individual. Women who equate menopause with loss of femininity are likely to encounter more distress than those who do not (Sheehy, 1995).

Menopause ▲ The cessation of menstruation.

Myth 7. *Menopause brings an end to a woman's child-bearing years.* Not necessarily! After menopause, women no longer produce ova. However, ova from donors have been fertilized in laboratory dishes, and the developing embryos have been successfully implanted in the uteruses of post-menopausal women.

Myth 8. *A woman's general level of activity is lower after menopause.* Research shows that many postmenopausal women become peppier and more assertive.

CONTROVERSY IN PSYCHOLOGY

Is There a *Man*opause?

Men cannot experience menopause, of course. Yet now and then we hear the term *male menopause*, or "manopause." Middle-aged or older men may be loosely alluded to as menopausal. This epithet is doubly offensive: It reinforces the negative, harmful stereotypes of aging people, especially aging women, as crotchety and irritable. Nor is the label consistent with the biology or psychology of aging. Alternate terms are *andropause* (referring to a drop-off in androgens, or male sex hormones) and *viropause* (referring to the end of virility).

For women, menopause is a time of relatively acute age-related declines in sex hormones and fertility. In men, however, the decline in the production of male sex hormones and fertility is more gradual (Morley & van den Berg, 2000). It therefore is not surprising to find a man in his 70s or older fathering a child. Moreover, some viable sperm are produced even in late adulthood. However, many men in their 50s and 60s experience intermittent problems in achieving and maintaining erections (Laumann et al., 1994), which may reflect circulatory problems and may or may not have to do with hormone production.

Sexual performance is only one part of the story, however. Between the ages of 40 and 70, the typical American male loses 12 to 20 pounds of muscle, about 2 inches in height, and 15% of his bone mass. (Men as well as women are at risk for osteoporosis.) The amount of fat in the body nearly doubles. The eardrums thicken, as do the lenses of the eyes, resulting in some loss of hearing and vision. There is also loss of endurance as the cardiovascular system and lungs become less capable of responding effectively to exertion.

Some of these changes can be slowed or even reversed. Exercise helps maintain muscle tone and keep the growth of fatty tissue in check. A diet rich in calcium and vitamin D can help ward off bone loss in men as well as in women. Hormone replacement may also help, but is controversial. Although testosterone replacement appears to boost strength, energy, and the sex drive, it is connected with increased risks of prostate cancer and cardiovascular disease (Morley & van den Berg, 2000). Erection is made possible by the flow of blood into the caverns within the penis (vasocongestion), which then stiffens as does a balloon when air or water is pumped in. The drug Viagra facilitates erection by relaxing the muscles that surround the caverns, enabling blood vessels in the region to dilate.

Even though sexual interest and performance decline, men can remain sexually active and father children at advanced ages (Morley & van den Berg, 2000). For both genders, attitudes toward the biological changes of aging—along with general happiness—may affect sexual behavior as much as biological changes do.

Late Adulthood

Did you know that an *agequake* is coming? With improved health care and knowledge of the importance of diet and exercise, more Americans than ever before are 65 or older (Abeles, 1997). In 1900, only 1 American in 30 was over 65, compared with 1 in 9 in 1970. By 2030, 1 American in 5 will be 65 or older ("Longer, healthier, better," 1997; see Figure 11.1).

Various changes—some of them troublesome—do occur during the later years (Figure 11.2). Changes in calcium metabolism lead to increased brittleness in the bones

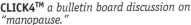

CLICK4™ *a bulletin board discussion on "manopause."*

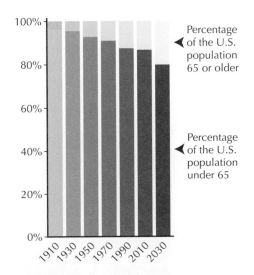

FIGURE 11.1 Living Longer.
In the third millennium, more people than ever in the United States are living to be age 65 or above. The increased effects of the presence of older people on financial and cultural institutions have been referred to as an "agequake."

and heightened risk of breaks due to accidents such as falls. The skin becomes less elastic and subject to wrinkles and folds.

The senses are also affected. Older people see and hear less acutely. Because of a decline in the sense of smell, they may use more spice to flavor their food. Older people need more time (called **reaction time**) to respond to stimuli. Older drivers, for example, need more time to respond to traffic lights, other vehicles, and changing road conditions. As we grow older, our immune system also functions less effectively, leaving us more vulnerable to disease. These changes ultimately result in death.

Cosmetic Changes

People develop wrinkles and gray hair if they live long enough. The hair grows gray as the production of *melanin*, the pigment responsible for hair color, declines. Hair loss also accelerates as people age, especially in men.

The aging body produces less *collagen* and *elastin*, proteins that make the skin elastic, soft, and supple. The body also produces fewer of the kinds of cells found in the outer layer of skin, so the skin becomes drier, more brittle, and prone to wrinkles. The tendency to wrinkling reflects one's heredity as well as hormonal balances and environmental influences such as diet and exposure to the sun. Exposure to ultraviolet (UV) rays accelerates the aging of the skin. People—including older people—who lie on the beach, especially at midday, are not only aging their skin; they are also heightening their risk of skin cancer.

Sensory Changes

Age-related changes in vision usually begin in the mid-30s. The lenses of the eyes become brittle so they are less capable of focusing on fine print (which is why people tend to need reading glasses as they age) or nearby objects. Other changes of aging can lead to eye problems such as *cataracts* and *glaucoma*. Cataracts cloud the lens, impairing the focusing of light on the retina, resulting in blurred vision and possible blindness. Glaucoma is caused by increased pressure in the eyeball, causing hardening of the eyeball, tunnel vision (loss of peripheral vision), and possible blindness. These conditions are treated with medication or surgery.

The sense of hearing also declines with age, more quickly in men than women. Many older people secrete more ear wax, which can impair hearing. But hearing loss in late adulthood frequently results from loss of flexibility in the bones and membranes of the middle and inner ears, and decreased circulation in the inner ear. Hearing aids amplify sounds and often compensate for hearing loss.

Smell and taste lose their sharpness as people age, so food loses much of its flavor. The sense of smell declines more sharply. Older people often spice their food heavily to obtain flavor.

Reaction Time

Age-related changes in the nervous system increase reaction time—the amount of time it takes to respond to a stimulus. Older people cannot catch rapidly moving baseballs or footballs or dodge other cars as easily when driving.

Changes in Lung Capacity, Muscle Mass, and Metabolism

The walls of the lungs stiffen as people age, no longer expanding as readily as when people were younger. Between the ages of 20 and 70, lung capacity may decline by 40% or so. Regular exercise can prevent much of this decline, however.

The very composition of the body changes. Muscle cells are lost with age, especially after the age of 45 (Morley & van den Berg, 2000). Fat replaces muscle. There is a consequent reshaping of the body and loss of muscle strength. However, exercise can compensate for much of the loss by increasing the size of the muscle cells that remain.

The metabolic rate declines as we age, largely because of the loss of muscle tissue and the corresponding increase in body fat. Muscle burns more calories—has a faster metabolic rate—than fat. People also require fewer calorics to maintain their weight as they age, and extra calories are deposited as fat. Older people are thus likely to gain weight if they eat as much as they did when they were younger. Regular exercise helps older people maintain a healthful weight just as it does with younger people. Not only does exercising burn calories; it also builds the muscle mass, and muscle burns calories more efficiently than fat.

Reaction time ▲ The amount of time required to respond to a stimulus.

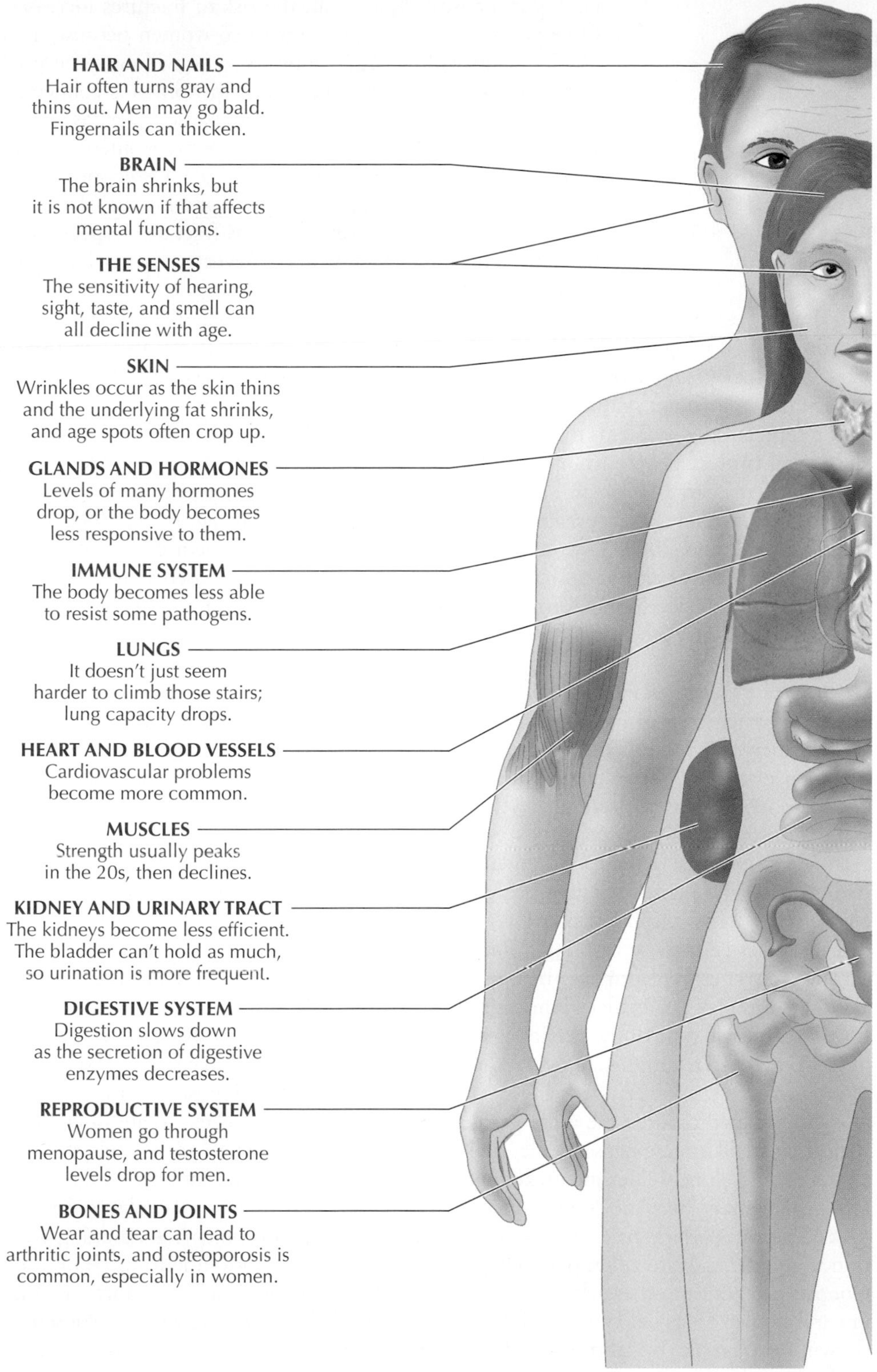

HAIR AND NAILS
Hair often turns gray and
thins out. Men may go bald.
Fingernails can thicken.

BRAIN
The brain shrinks, but
it is not known if that affects
mental functions.

THE SENSES
The sensitivity of hearing,
sight, taste, and smell can
all decline with age.

SKIN
Wrinkles occur as the skin thins
and the underlying fat shrinks,
and age spots often crop up.

GLANDS AND HORMONES
Levels of many hormones
drop, or the body becomes
less responsive to them.

IMMUNE SYSTEM
The body becomes less able
to resist some pathogens.

LUNGS
It doesn't just seem
harder to climb those stairs;
lung capacity drops.

HEART AND BLOOD VESSELS
Cardiovascular problems
become more common.

MUSCLES
Strength usually peaks
in the 20s, then declines.

KIDNEY AND URINARY TRACT
The kidneys become less efficient.
The bladder can't hold as much,
so urination is more frequent.

DIGESTIVE SYSTEM
Digestion slows down
as the secretion of digestive
enzymes decreases.

REPRODUCTIVE SYSTEM
Women go through
menopause, and testosterone
levels drop for men.

BONES AND JOINTS
Wear and tear can lead to
arthritic joints, and osteoporosis is
common, especially in women.

FIGURE 11.2 The Relentless March of Time.
A number of physical changes occur during the later years. However, the reasons for aging are not yet completely understood. People can also affect the pace of their aging by eating properly, exercising, maintaining a positive outlook, and finding and meeting challenges that are consistent with their abilities.

The cardiovascular system becomes less efficient with age. The heart pumps less blood and the blood vessels carry less blood, which has implications for sexual functioning, as we see later.

Changes in Bone Density

Bones consist mainly of calcium, and they begin to lose density in early middle age, frequently leading to osteoporosis. *Osteoporosis* literally translates as "porous bone," meaning that the bone becomes porous rather than main-

TABLE 11.3 CHANGES IN SEXUAL RESPONSE CONNECTED WITH AGING

Changes That Occur in Women	Changes That Occur in Men
Less interest in sex	Less interest in sex
Less blood flow to the genitals	Less blood flow to the genitals
Less vaginal lubrication	More time needed to attain erection and reach orgasm
Less elasticity in vaginal walls	More need for direct stimulation (touch) to attain erection
Smaller increases in breast size	Less firm erections
Less intense orgasms	Less ejaculate
	Less intense orgasms
	More time needed to become aroused (erect) again

taining its density. As a result, the risk of fractures increases. Osteoporosis poses a greater threat to women because men usually begin with a larger bone mass, providing some protection against the disease. Bone loss in women is connected with low levels of estrogen at menopause (Delmas et al., 1997). Bones break more readily, and some women develop curvature of the spine ("dowager's hump"). Osteoporosis can be severely handicapping, even life threatening. Brittleness of the bones increases the risk of serious fractures, especially of the hip, and many older women never recover from these fractures (Marwick, 2000).

Loss of estrogen can also have psychological effects (Yaffe et al., 2000). It can impair cognitive functioning—making it more difficult to solve problems. It can also give rise to feelings of anxiety and depression, which further impair the ability to cope with stress.

Some women use synthetic estrogen and progesterone (hormone-replacement therapy) to prevent the problems that can attend menopause. Estrogen has the added benefits of helping protect people from heart disease, which is why women are less likely than men to suffer heart attacks until after menopause. Estrogen replacement also lowers the risks of colon cancer and, perhaps, of Alzheimer's disease (Grodstein et al., 1996, 1997; Kawas, 2000; Sano, 2000; Yaffe et al., 2000). But estrogen replacement can heighten the risk of breast cancer and some other health problems, so it is not used universally. Researchers are now developing forms of estrogen replacement that do not increase the risk of breast cancer and other disorders.

Changes in Sexual Functioning   Age-related changes affect sexual functioning as well as other areas of functioning (see Table 11.3). Yet people are capable of enjoying sexual experience for a lifetime if they make some adjustments, including adjustments to their expectations. Older men and women may both experience less interest in sex, which is apparently related to lowered levels of testosterone (yes, women naturally produce some testosterone) in both genders.

Many physical changes in older women reflect the lower estrogen levels of menopause. The vaginal opening becomes constricted and the vaginal walls become less elastic. The vagina shrinks in size. Less vaginal lubrication is produced. All these changes can make sexual activity irritating. Some of these changes may be arrested or reversed through estrogen-replacement therapy. Natural lubrication may be increased through elaborate foreplay. An artificial lubricant can also be of help.

The muscle tone of the pelvic region decreases so that orgasms become less intense. Still, women can retain the ability to reach orgasm into advanced old age. The experience of orgasm can remain very satisfying, regardless of the intensity of muscle contractions.

Age-related changes are more gradual in men and not connected to any single biological event like menopause. Male adolescents can attain erection in seconds through sexual fantasy alone. Older men take more time to attain erections, and the erections are less firm. Fantasy may no longer do it; extensive direct stimulation (stroking) may be needed. Many, perhaps half, of men have at least intermittent problems in attaining erection in middle and late adulthood. They also usually require more time to reach orgasm. Couples can adjust to these changes by extending the length and variety of foreplay. Viagra and similar drugs help men attain erections (and also help women become aroused, as shown, for example, by lubrication of the vaginal barrel) by increasing the flow of blood to the genitals when sexual stimulation alone does not do it.

The testes may decrease slightly in size and produce less testosterone with age. Testosterone production usually declines gradually through middle adulthood and begins to level off in late adulthood. An adolescent may require but a few minutes to regain erection and ejaculate again after a first orgasm, whereas older men may require hours. Older men produce less ejaculate, and it may seep out rather than gush out. Orgasms become weaker as measured by the physical aspects of orgasm—that is, the strength and number of muscle contractions at the base of the penis. But physical measures do not translate exactly into pleasure. An older man may enjoy orgasms as much as he did when younger. Again, attitudes and expectations are crucial to the continued enjoyment of sexual activity.

In sum, late adulthood need not bring one's sex life to a halt. Expectations and the willingness of partners to adjust are crucial factors in sexual fulfillment.

DIVERSITY *Aging, Gender, and Ethnicity: Different Patterns of Aging*   Although Americans in general are living longer, there are gender and ethnic differences in life expectancy. **Question: What are the gender and ethnic differences in life expectancy?**   For example, women in our society tend to live longer, but older men tend to live *better* ("Longer, healthier, better," 1997). European Americans live longer on the average than do Latino and Latina Americans, African Americans, and Native Americans (CDC, 2000e). Life expectancy for Latino and Latina Americans falls somewhere between the figures for African Americans and European Americans. The longevity of Asian Americans falls closer to that of European Americans than to that of African Americans. Native Americans have the lowest average longevity of the major racial/ethnic groups in the United States.

Women in the United States outlive men by six to seven years. Why? For one thing, heart disease, the nation's leading killer, typically develops later in women than in men. Men are also more likely to die because of accidents, cirrhosis of the liver, strokes, suicide, homicide, AIDS, and cancer (CDC, 2000e). Many deaths from these causes are the result of unhealthy habits more typical of men, such as excessive drinking and reckless behavior.

Many men are also reluctant to have regular physical exams or to talk to their doctors about their health problems. "In their 20's, [men are] too strong to need a doctor; in their 30's, they're too busy, and in their 40's, too scared" (Courtenay, 2000). Women are much more likely to examine themselves for signs of breast cancer than men are even to recognize the early signs of prostate cancer.

Although women tend to outlive men, their prospects for a happy and healthy old age are dimmer. Men who beat the statistical odds by living beyond their 70s are far less likely than their female counterparts to live alone, suffer from disabling conditions, or be poor. Older women are more likely than men to live alone largely because they are more likely to be widowed. One reason that older women are more likely to be poor is that women who are now age 65 or older were less likely to hold jobs. If they had jobs, they were paid far less than men and received smaller pensions and other retirement benefits.

Socioeconomic differences play a role in ethnic differences in life expectancy. Members of ethnic minority groups in our society are more likely to be poor, and poor people tend to eat less nutritious diets, encounter more stress, and have less access to health care. There is a seven-year difference in life expectancy between people in the highest income brackets and those in the lowest. Yet other factors, such as cultural differences in diet and lifestyle, the stress of coping with discrimination, and genetic differences, may partly account for ethnic group differences in life expectancy.

Theories of Aging

Although it may be hard to believe it will happen to us, every person who has walked the Earth so far has aged—which may not be a bad fate, considering the alternative. **Question: Why do we age?**   Various factors, some of which are theoretical, apparently contribute to aging.

The theory of **programmed senescence** sees aging as determined by a biological clock that ticks at a rate governed by instructions in the genes. Just as genes program children to grow and reach sexual maturation, they program people to deteriorate and die. There is evidence to support a role for genes in aging. Longevity runs in families. People whose parents and grandparents lived into their 80s and 90s have a better chance of reaching these ages themselves.

Breaks in the strands of genetic material—DNA—that guide our development and help maintain our well-being are common enough throughout our lifetime, but they are repaired better when we are young (Roth & Gellert, 2000). As we age, our genetic codes tend to stray from their original design, permitting the development of cancer and other health problems.

The **wear-and-tear theory** does not suggest that people are programmed to self-destruct. Instead, environmental factors such as pollution, disease, and ultraviolet light are

CLICK4™ *a bulletin board discussion on patterns of aging.*

▲ **REFLECT**
How do older people you know cope with the physical changes that occur in late adulthood?

Programmed senescence ▲ The view that aging is determined by a biological clock that ticks at a rate governed by genes.

Wear-and-tear theory ▲ The view that factors such as pollution, disease, and ultraviolet light contribute to wear and tear on the body, so that the body loses the ability to repair itself.

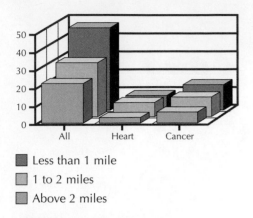

■ Less than 1 mile

□ 1 to 2 miles

■ Above 2 miles

FIGURE 11.3   Causes of Death and Distance Walked in Miles Per Day Among Participants in the Honolulu Heart Program.

Men who walked more than 2 miles a day had a lower mortality rate than men who walked between 1 and 2 miles a day and men who walked less than a mile a day. Men who took long walks were less likely to die from cancer and heart disease (Hakim et al., 1998).

assumed to contribute to wear and tear of the body over time. The body is like a machine whose parts wear out through use. Wear and tear saps cells of the ability to regenerate themselves, and vital organs are worn down.

Research with roundworms can be said to support both the programmed senescence and wear-and-tear theories (Wolkow, et al., 2000). Genetically determined messages from the brain may determine the timing of growth and development. However, the brain cells become damaged in part because of damaging effects of by-products of metabolism ("free radicals"). Then the body begins to decay.

Our behavior also influences our aging. Cigarette smoking, overeating, stress, and risky behavior can contribute to an early death. Fortunately, we can exert control over some of these factors.

Americans are living longer than ever, and part of the reason is that many of them are taking charge of their own lives, influencing not only how long they live, but how well they live (Clay, 2000). Regular medical evaluations, proper diet (for example, consuming less fat), and exercise all help people live longer.

Exercise helps older people maintain flexibility and cardiovascular condition. The exercise need not be of the type that pounds the body and produces rivers of sweat. Because older people tend to have more brittle bones and more rigid joints, fast or prolonged walking are excellent aerobic choices.

Amy Hakim of the University of Virginia School of Medicine and her colleagues (1998) provided dramatic evidence of the value of exercise—in this case, walking—for older people. They reviewed 12 years of data on 707 retired men from the Honolulu Heart Program and found that 43.1% of the men who walked less than a mile per day died during that period, as compared with 27.7% of those who walked from 1 to 2 miles a day and 21.5% of those who walked at least 2 miles daily. Additional findings: 6.6% of the men who walked less than a mile a day died from coronary heart disease or strokes, as compared with only 2.1% of those who walked upwards of 2 miles (see Figure 11.3). Moreover, 13.4% of the men who walked less than a mile died from cancer, as compared with 5.3% of men who walked more than 2 miles a day. Because the study was not experimental, one can ask whether those who walked less died sooner because they were hobbled by health problems that made them less able or willing to walk. Hakim and her colleagues recognized this problem and got around it partly by using data only on nonsmokers who were physically able to walk a few miles. Older people can also continue to fight heart disease and cancer by eating diets low in cholesterol and saturated fats.

REVIEW

▓▓▓ 11 Q 1

CLICK4™ *a quiz covering the first half of this chapter.*

(13) In _____ adulthood, most people are at their height in sensory acuteness, reaction time, and cardiovascular fitness. (14) Cessation of menstruation, termed _____, usually occurs during the late 40s or early 50s. (15) Loss of the hormone _____ can be accompanied by hot flashes and feelings of anxiety and depression. (16) In late adulthood, changes in _____ metabolism lead to brittleness in the bones. (17) The time required to respond to stimuli—called _____ time—increases. (18) According to the _____-_____ theory of aging, aging is determined by a genetic biological clock. (19) According to _____-and-tear theory, cells lose the ability to regenerate because of environmental factors such as pollution, disease, and ultraviolet light.

Pulling It Together: Do the changes of aging in adults appear to be continuous or discontinuous? What factors may contribute to differences in health and longevity among people of different genders and ethnic groups?

ADULTHOOD: COGNITIVE DEVELOPMENT

Question: What cognitive developments occur during adulthood?   As is the case with physical development, people are also at the height of their cognitive powers during early adulthood. Many professionals show the broadest knowledge of their fields at about the time they are graduating from college or graduate school. At this time their course

How Long Will You Live? The Life-Expectancy Scale

The life-expectancy scale is one of several used by physicians and insurance companies to estimate how long people will live. Scales such as these are far from precise—which is a good thing, if you think about it. But they make reasonable "guesstimates" based on our heredity, medical histories, and life-styles.

Directions: To complete the scale, begin with the age of 72. Then add or subtract years according to the following directions:

RUNNING TOTAL **PERSONAL FACTS:**

_____ 1. If you are male, **subtract 3.**

_____ 2. If female, **add 4.**

_____ 3. If you live in an urban area with a population over 2 million, **subtract 2.**

_____ 4. If you live in a town with under 10,000 people or on a farm, **add 2.**

_____ 5. If any grandparent lived to 85, **add 2.**

_____ 6. If all four grandparents lived to 80, **add 6.**

_____ 7. If either parent died of a stroke or heart attack before the age of 50, **subtract 4.**

_____ 8. If any parent, brother, or sister under 50 has (or had) cancer or a heart condition, or has had diabetes since childhood, **subtract 3.**

_____ 9. Do you earn over $75,000* a year? If so, **subtract 2.**

_____ 10. If you finished college, **add 1.** If you have a graduate or professional degree, **add 2 more.**

_____ 11. If you are 65 or over and still working, **add 3.**

_____ 12. If you live with a spouse or friend, **add 5.** If not, **subtract 1** for every 10 years alone since age 25.

LIFESTYLE STATUS:

_____ 13. If you work behind a desk, **subtract 3.**

_____ 14. If your work requires regular, heavy physical labor, **add 3.**

_____ 15. If you exercise strenuously (tennis, running, swimming, etc.) five times a week for at least a half-hour, **add 4.** If two or three times a week, **add 2.**

_____ 16. Do you sleep more than 10 hours each night? **Subtract 4.**

_____ 17. Are you intense, aggressive, easily angered? **Subtract 3.**

_____ 18. Are you easygoing and relaxed? **Add 3.**

_____ 19. Are you happy? **Add 1.** Unhappy? **Subtract 2.**

_____ 20. Have you had a speeding ticket in the last year? **Subtract 1.**

_____ 21. Do you smoke more than two packs a day? **Subtract 8.** One or two packs? **Subtract 6.** One-half to one? **Subtract 3.**

_____ 22. Do you drink the equivalent of 1 oz. of liquor a day? **Subtract 1.**

_____ 23. Are you overweight by 50 lbs. or more? **Subtract 8.** By 30 to 50 lbs? **Subtract 4.** By 10 to 30 lbs? **Subtract 2.**

_____ 24. If you are a man over 40 and have annual check-ups, **add 2.**

_____ 25. If you are a woman and see a gynecologist once a year, **add 2.**

AGE ADJUSTMENT:

_____ 26. If you are between 30 and 40, **add 2.**

_____ 27. If you are between 40 and 50, **add 3.**

_____ 28. If you are between 50 and 70, **add 4.**

_____ 29. If you are over 70, **add 5.**

_____ **YOUR LIFE EXPECTANCY**

SOURCE: From Robert F. Allen with Shirley Linde (1986). *Lifegain*. Human Resources Institute Press, Tempe Wick Road, Morristown, NJ.

*This figure is an inflation-adjusted estimate.

CD **11** **SA** **7**

CLICK4™ *the interactive version of this Self-Assessment.*

work is freshest. They may have just recently studied for comprehensive examinations. Once they enter their fields, they often specialize. As a result, knowledge deepens in certain areas, but understanding of related areas may grow relatively superficial.

Cognitive development in adulthood has many aspects—creativity, memory functioning, and intelligence. People can be creative for a lifetime. At the age of 80, Merce Cunningham choreographed a dance that made use of computer-generated digital images (Teachout, 2000). Hans Hofmann created some of his most vibrant paintings at 85, and Pablo Picasso was painting in his 90s. Grandma Moses did not even begin painting until

CLICK4™ *NorthWestern Mutual's longevity game.*

she was 78 years old. Giuseppe Verdi wrote his joyous opera *Falstaff* at the age of 79. The architect Frank Lloyd Wright designed New York's innovative spiral-shaped Guggenheim Museum when he was 89 years old.

Memory functioning declines with age. It is common enough for older people to have trouble recalling the names of common objects or people they know. Memory lapses can be embarrassing, and older people sometimes lose confidence in their memories, which then lowers their motivation to remember things (Cavanaugh & Green, 1990). But declines in memory are not usually as large as people assume, and are often reversible (Villa & Abeles, 2000). Memory tests usually measure ability to recall meaningless information. Older people show better memory functioning in areas in which they can apply their experience, especially their specialties, to new challenges (Graf, 1990). For example, who would do a better job of learning and remembering how to solve problems in chemistry—a college history major or a retired professor of chemistry?

People also obtain the highest intelligence test scores in young adulthood (Baltes, 1997). Yet people tend to retain their verbal skills, as demonstrated by their vocabularies and general knowledge, into advanced old age. It is their performance on tasks that require speed and visual-spatial skills, such as putting puzzles together, that tends to fall off (Schaie, 1994).

Crystallized Versus Fluid Intelligence

Consider the difference between *crystallized intelligence* and *fluid intelligence*. **Crystallized intelligence** represents one's lifetime of intellectual attainments, as shown by vocabulary and accumulated facts about world affairs. Therefore, crystallized intelligence generally increases over the decades. **Fluid intelligence** is defined as mental flexibility, demonstrated by the ability to process information rapidly, as in learning and solving problems in new areas of endeavor.

In terms of people's worth to their employers, familiarity in solving the kinds of problems found on the job (their crystallized intelligence) may be more important than their fluid intelligence. Experience on the job enhances people's specialized vocabularies and their knowledge of the area. People draw on fluid intelligence when the usual solutions no longer work, but experience is often more valuable than fluid intelligence.

The role of experience brings us to what some developmental theorists refer to as **postformal thought** (Labouvie-Vief & Diehl, 2000), which is shown by some adults, including some in late adulthood. *Formal* operational thought is the highest stage of intellectual development within Jean Piaget's theory. It is characterized by deductive logic, consideration of various ways of solving problems (mental trial and error), abstract thought, and the formation and testing of hypotheses. *Post*formal thought is characterized by creative thinking, the ability to solve complex problems, and the posing of new questions. People usually show postformal thinking in their areas of expertise or specialization, providing one more suggestion that experience often compensates for age-related losses in intellectual functioning.

The Seattle Longitudinal Study

Psychologist Walter Schaie and his colleagues (Schaie, 1994) have been studying the cognitive development of adults for four decades and discovered factors that contribute to intellectual functioning across the life-span:

1. *General health*. People in good health tend to retain higher levels of intellectual functioning into late adulthood. Therefore, paying attention to one's diet, exercising, and having regular medical checkups contribute to intellectual functioning as well as physical health.
2. *Socioeconomic status (SES)*. People with high SES tend to maintain intellectual functioning more adequately than people with low SES. High SES is also connected with above-average income and levels of education, a history of stimulating occupational pursuits, maintenance of intact families, and better health.
3. *Stimulating activities*. Cultural events, travel, participation in professional organizations, and extensive reading contribute to intellectual functioning.
4. *Marriage to a spouse with a high level of intellectual functioning*. The spouse whose level of intellectual functioning is lower at the beginning of a marriage tends to in-

▲ **REFLECT**
Can you apply the concepts of crystallized intelligence and fluid intelligence to older people in your own life?

CLICK4™ *an essay assignment on crystallized and fluid intelligence.*

Crystallized intelligence ▲ One's lifetime of intellectual achievement, as shown largely through vocabulary and knowledge of world affairs.

Fluid intelligence ▲ Mental flexibility as shown in learning rapidly to solve new kinds of problems.

Postformal thought ▲ An hypothesized stage of cognitive development that follows formal operational thought and is characterized by creative thinking, the ability to solve complex problems, and the posing of new questions.

crease in intellectual functioning as time goes by. Perhaps that partner is continually challenged by the other.

5. *Openness to new experience.* Being open to new challenges of life apparently helps keep us young—at any age.

Alzheimer's Disease   *Questions: What is Alzheimer's disease? What are its origins?*   **Alzheimer's disease** is a progressive form of mental deterioration that affects about 10% of people over the age of 65 and nearly half of those over the age of 85 (Katzman, 2000). Although Alzheimer's is connected with aging, it is a disease and not a normal part of aging (Haan, 2000).

We consider Alzheimer's disease within the section on cognitive development because it is characterized by general, gradual deterioration in mental processes such as memory, language, and problem solving. As the disease progresses, people may fail to recognize familiar faces or forget their names. At the most severe stage, people with Alzheimer's disease become helpless. They become unable to communicate or walk and require help in toileting and feeding. More isolated memory losses (for example, forgetting where one put one's glasses) may be a normal feature of aging (Abeles, 1997). Alzheimer's, in contrast, seriously impairs vocational and social functioning.

Alzheimer's disease is characterized by reduced levels of the neurotransmitter acetylcholine (ACh) and by the build-up of a sticky plaque in the brain. One form of drug therapy has aimed at boosting ACh levels by slowing its breakdown. This approach achieves modest benefits with many people. The plaque is formed from fragments of a body protein (beta amyloid) (Cotman, 2000; Frangione, 2000). Normally, the immune system prevents the build-up of plaque, but not effectively in the case of people with Alzheimer's disease. Thus another approach to the treatment of Alzheimer's is the development of a vaccine made from beta amyloid that will stimulate the immune system to recognize and attack the plaque more vigorously (Janus et al., 2000; Morgan et al., 2000; Schenk, 2000).

Alzheimer's, as noted, is a disease and does not reflect the normal aging process. However, there are normal, more gradual declines in intellectual functioning and memory among older people (Villa & Abeles, 2000; Butler, 1998). But we understand very little about *why* these declines occur. Depression and losses of sensory acuity and motivation may contribute to lower cognitive test scores. B. F. Skinner (1983) argued that much of the fall-off is due to an "aging environment" rather than an aging person. That is, the behavior of older people often goes unreinforced. This idea is substantiated by a classic study of nursing home residents who were rewarded for remembering recent events and showed improved scores on tests of memory (Langer et al., 1979).

CLICK4™ *Web sites devoted to education about and awareness of Alzheimer's disease.*

REVIEW

(20) People tend to retain (verbal skills or performance on tasks that require speed and visual-spatial skills?) into advanced old age. (21) _____ intelligence refers to one's lifetime of intellectual achievement, as shown by vocabulary and general knowledge. (22) _____ intelligence is mental flexibility, as shown by the ability to solve new kinds of problems. (23) Alzheimer's disease (is or is not?) a normal feature of the aging process. (24) People with Alzheimer's disease show reduced levels of the neurotransmitter _____ (ACh) in the brain. (25) They also have a build-up of plaque in the brain formed from fragments of beta _____.

Pulling It Together: What can we look forward to in terms of cognitive development as we age?

ADULTHOOD: SOCIAL AND PERSONALITY DEVELOPMENT

Changes in social and personality development during adulthood are probably the most "elastic" or fluid. These changes are clearly affected by cultural expectations and individual behavior patterns. As a result, there is so much variety that it can be misleading to expect that any individual will follow a particular pattern. Nevertheless,

Alzheimer's disease (AHLTS-high-mers) ▲ A progressive form of mental deterioration characterized by loss of memory, language, problem solving, and other cognitive functions.

many developmental theorists suggest that there are enough commonalities that we can speak of trends. One trend that will become obvious, however, is that the outlook for older people has become much more optimistic over the past generation—not only because of medical advances but also because the behavior and mental processes of many older people are remaining younger than at any other time in history.

There is more good news. Research evidence suggests that people tend to grow psychologically healthier as they advance from adolescence through middle adulthood. Psychologists Constance Jones and William Meredith (2000) studied information on 236 participants in California growth studies who had been followed from early adolescence for about 50 years and found that they generally became more productive and had better interpersonal relationships as the years went on. Certainly there are individual differences, but many individuals, even some with a turbulent adolescence, showed dramatically better psychological health at age 62 than they had half a century earlier.

Young Adulthood

Question: What social and personality developments occur during young adulthood? Many theorists suggest that young adulthood is the period of life during which people tend to establish themselves as independent members of society. However, Jeffrey Arnett (2000) suggests that in the United States we have a period that bridges adolescence and independence: *emerging adulthood.* *Question: Just what is meant by "emerging adulthood"?*

Emerging Adulthood

> When our mothers were our age, they were engaged. . . . They at least had some idea what they were going to do with their lives . . . I, on the other hand, will have a dual degree in majors that are ambiguous at best and impractical at worst (English and political science), no ring on my finger and no idea who I am, much less what I want to do. . . . Under duress, I will admit that this is a pretty exciting time. Sometimes, when I look out across the wide expanse that is my future, I can see beyond the void. I realize that having nothing ahead to count on means I now have to count on myself; that having no direction means forging one of my own.
>
> Kristen, Age 22 (Page, 1999, pp. 18, 20)

▲ **REFLECT**

Would you characterize yourself as being in emerging adulthood? Why or why not?

According to psychologist Jeffrey Arnett (2000), Kristen is in a period of life that we can label emerging adulthood. **Emerging adulthood** is a hypothesized period of development that spans the ages of 18 through 25 and exists only in societies that permit young people extended periods of independent role exploration. These are rich societies, such as our own. These societies that have the ability to grant young people the luxury of developing their unique identities and their individual life plans through parental help, government-funded student loans, and the like. This is not to say that people undergoing emerging adulthood are spoiled. After all, they are dealing with their own reality as it is. But we should also note that even in wealthy societies, many individuals do not have the resources to linger in emerging adulthood.

Erik Erikson (1968) had earlier noted that industrialized societies tend to prolong the period of adolescence. He wrote that there is commonly a **moratorium** in the extended adolescence during which the individual engages in a deep search for personal identity. Although some people in such societies get a job right out of high school, or get married or bear children early, many others—perhaps most—tend to further their education and to delay marriage into their mid to late 20s, or their 30s. Women in such societies frequently find themselves racing against the "biological clock" to bear children once they do settle down.

Arnett (2000) notes that when people in their late teens and early 20s are asked whether they think they have reached adulthood, nearly 60% say something to the effect, "in some respects yes and in other respects no." They seem to feel that they are beyond the conflicts and types of exploration they underwent in adolescence, but they are not yet ready to assume the responsibilities they equate with being adults.

Emerging adulthood ▲ A hypothesized period of development found in industrialized societies that spans the ages of 18 to 25 and is characterized by prolonged role exploration.

Moratorium ▲ Erik Erikson's term for the examination of alternative values and life possibilities while in the throes of an identity crisis.

The Trying 20s   At some point during the 20s, many people become fueled by ambition. Journalist Gail Sheehy (1976) labeled the 20s the **Trying 20s**—a period during which people basically strive to advance their careers. When she was theorizing a quarter of a century ago, fewer people were attending graduate school, and they were marrying somewhat earlier than today. But whether the 20s become "trying" in the early, mid, or late 20s, many or most people become concerned about establishing their pathway in life sometime during this decade. They either skip emerging adulthood or else they, well, emerge from it. Then they become generally responsible for their own support, make their own choices, and are largely free from parental influences. Many young adults adopt what theorist Daniel Levinson and his colleagues (1978) call the **dream**—the drive to "become" someone, to leave their mark on history—which serves as a tentative blueprint for their life. The "Kristens" of our society now tend to have inner direction.

Intimacy Versus Isolation

Intimacy Versus Isolation   During young adulthood, people tend to leave their families of origin and to create families of their own. Erik Erikson (1963) characterized young adulthood as the stage of **intimacy versus isolation.** Erikson saw the establishment of intimate relationships as central to young adulthood. Young adults who have evolved a firm sense of identity during adolescence are ready to "fuse" their identities with those of other people through marriage and abiding friendships. People who do not reach out to develop intimate relationships risk retreating into isolation and loneliness.

Erikson warned that we may not be able to commit ourselves to others until we have achieved ego identity—that is, established stable life roles. Achieving ego identity is the central task of adolescence. Lack of personal stability is connected with the high divorce rate for teenage marriages.

DIVERSITY   ***Personality Development and Gender***   Most Western men consider separation and individuation to be key goals of personality development during young adulthood (Guisinger & Blatt, 1994). For women, however, the establishment and maintenance of social relationships are also of primary importance (Gilligan et al., 1990, 1991). Women, as Gilligan (1982) has pointed out, are likely to undergo a transition from being cared for by others to caring for others. In becoming adults, men are more likely to undergo a transition from being restricted by others to autonomy and perhaps control of other people.

Although there are differences in the development of women and men, between the ages of 21 and 27 college women also develop in terms of individuation and autonomy

> **▲ REFLECT**
> Where do you fit into the chronicle of the adult years? Do events in your own life fit with any of the research findings or theories presented in this chapter?

Establishing Intimate Relationships.
According to Erik Erikson, establishing intimate relationships is a central task of young adulthood.

Trying 20s ▲ Sheehy's term for the third decade of life, when people are frequently occupied with advancement in the career world.

Dream ▲ In this usage, Levinson's term for the overriding drive of youth to become someone important, to leave one's mark on history.

Intimacy versus isolation ▲ Erikson's life crisis of young adulthood, which is characterized by the task of developing abiding intimate relationships.

(Helson, 1993). Women, like men, assert increasing control over their own lives. College women, on average, are relatively liberated and career oriented compared with their less-well-educated peers.

The Thirties

Levinson labeled the ages of 28 to 33 the **age-30 transition.** For men and women, the late 20s and early 30s are commonly characterized by reassessment: "Where is my life going?" "Why am I doing this?" Sheehy (1976) labeled this period the **Catch 30s** because of this tendency toward reassessment. During our 30s, we often find that the lifestyles we adopted during our 20s do not fit as comfortably as we had expected. One response to the disillusionments of the 30s, according to Sheehy,

> is the tearing up of the life we have spent most of our 20s putting together. It may mean striking out on a secondary road toward a new vision or converting a dream of "running for president" into a more realistic goal. The single person feels a push to find a partner. The woman who was previously content at home with children chafes to venture into the world. The childless couple reconsiders children. And almost everybody who is married . . . feels a discontent. (1976, p. 34)

Many psychologists find that the later 30s are characterized by settling down or planting roots. Many young adults feel a need to make a financial and emotional investment in their home. Their concerns become more focused on promotion or tenure, career advancement, and long-term mortgages.

Lifestyles of the Rich and Famous — And of the Rest of Us

Part of social and personality development involves cultivating intimate relationships with other people. Erikson, for example, believed that a key issue of young adulthood is intimacy versus isolation—that is, whether we would join our life with that of another person through an abiding relationship or remain alone. Developmental psychologist Robert Havighurst (1972) believed that each stage of development involved certain "tasks." His developmental tasks for young adulthood include the following:

1. Getting started in an occupation
2. Selecting and courting a mate
3. Learning to live contentedly with one's partner
4. Starting a family and becoming a parent
5. Assuming the responsibilities of managing a home
6. Assuming civic responsibilities
7. Finding a congenial social group

Erikson and Havighurst were theorizing 30 or 40 years ago, when it was widely assumed that young adults would want to get married and start families. Many young adults in the United States, perhaps most, still have these goals. But there are many different lifestyles today. Some people, for example, choose to remain single. Others choose to live together without getting married.

The Singles Scene: Swinging, Lonely, or All of the Above?

At the turn of the millennium, there is a dramatic increase in the numbers of young adults who remain single. Being single is the nation's most common lifestyle for people in their early 20s. Young adults are delaying marriage for a variety of reasons. More people are going for advanced education and many women are placing career objectives ahead of marriage and child-bearing. *Question: Just what is the "singles scene" like today?*

Yet many young adults do not view being single as a stage of life that precedes marriage. Because career women are no longer financially dependent on men, a number of them choose to remain single (Edwards, 2000). Many young adults are single by choice and see being single as an alternative, open-ended lifestyle. Although most single mothers in the United States are young and poorly educated, larger numbers of single, older, well-educated professional women chose to become mothers in recent years (Edwards, 2000).

▲ REFLECT

Have you made "false starts" in life? Have you reassessed your life's paths? Are your experiences of value to you? Explain.

CLICK4™ *the iVillage Web site, with quizzes, advice for singles, and information about topics such as domestic abuse.*

Age-30 transition ▲ Levinson's term for the ages from 28 to 33, which are characterized by reassessment of the goals and values of the 20s.

Catch 30s ▲ Sheehy's term for the fourth decade of life, when many people undergo major reassessments of their accomplishments and goals.

There is no single "singles scene." Being single is varied in intent and style of life. For some, it means singles bars and a string of one-night affairs. Some "swinging singles" do not want to be "trapped" with a single partner. They opt for many partners for the sake of novel sexual stimulation, the personal growth that can be attained through meeting many people, and the maintenance of independence. Yet many singles have become disillusioned with frequent casual sexual involvements. The singles bar provokes anxieties about physical and sexual abuse, fear of STIs, and feelings of alienation as well as opportunities for sexual experience.

Other single people limit sex to affectionate relationships only. Many singles are delaying marriage until they find Mr. or Ms. Right. Along the way many practice *serial monogamy*. That is, they become involved in one exclusive relationship after another, rather than having multiple sexual relationships at the same time. Many single people find that being single is not always as free as it seems. Some complain that employers and co-workers view them with skepticism and are reluctant to assign them responsibility. Their families may see them as selfish, as failures, or as sexually loose. Many single women complain that once they have entered their middle 20s, men are less willing to accept a "No" at the end of a date.

The goals and values that seem rock solid in the 20s may be shaken in the 30s. In their late 20s and 30s, many people who had chosen to remain single decide they would prefer to get married and have children. For women, of course, the "biological clock" may seem to be running out during the 30s. Yet some people choose to remain single for a lifetime.

Cohabitation: "There's Nothing That I Wouldn't Do If You Would Be My POSSLQ"

There's Nothing That I Wouldn't Do If You Would Be My POSSLQ is the name of a book by television commentator Charles Osgood. *POSSLQ?* That's the unromantic abbreviation for "Person of Opposite Sex Sharing Living Quarters"—the official term used for cohabitors by the U.S. Bureau of the Census. **Question: Who cohabits today, and why?**

Some social scientists believe that **cohabitation** has become accepted within the social mainstream (Steinhauer, 1995). Whether or not this is so, society in general has become more tolerant of it. We seldom hear cohabitation referred to as "living in sin" or "shacking up" as we once did. People today are more likely to refer to cohabitation with value-free expressions such as "living together."

Perhaps the current tolerance reflects societal adjustment to the increase in the numbers of cohabiting couples. Or perhaps the numbers of cohabiting couples have increased as a consequence of tolerance. The numbers of households consisting of unmarried adults of the other gender living together in the United States has more than tripled from 1.6 million couples in 1980 to nearly 5 million couples today (Smock, 2000).

Note some facts about cohabitation:

▲ Much of the attention on cohabitation has focused on college students living together, but cohabitation is more prevalent among the less-well-educated and less-affluent classes (Willis & Michael, 1994). The cohabitation rate is about twice as high among African American couples as European American couples.
▲ About 50% to 60% of the marriages that took place during the past decade were preceded by cohabitation (Smock, 2000).
▲ About 55% of couples who cohabit wind up marrying (each other), but 40% of them get divorced later on.
▲ Nearly half (48%) of women in their late 30s in the United States report having cohabited (Smock, 2000).
▲ Nearly half of the divorced people who cohabit (with new partners) have children living with them (Smock, 2000).
▲ About 35% of never-married cohabiting couples have children living in their household.

Divorced people are more likely than people who have never been married to cohabit (Smock, 2000). The experience of divorce may make some people more willing to

www 11 L 9

CLICK4™ Self-Help Magazine *online, featuring articles on relationships.*

CD 11 SA 8

CLICK4™ *an interactive Self-Assessment: Do You Endorse a Traditional or Liberal Marital Role?*

Cohabitation ▲ An intimate relationship in which—pardon me—POSSLQs (pronounced POSS-'l-cues?) live as though they are married, but without legal sanction.

share their lives than their bank accounts—the second or third time around (Steinhauer, 1995).

Willingness to cohabit is related to more liberal attitudes toward sexual behavior, less-traditional views of marriage, and less-traditional views of gender roles (Huffman et al., 1994). Cohabitors are less likely than married people to attend church regularly (Laumann et al., 1994).

Why do people cohabit? Cohabitation is an alternative to the loneliness that can accompany living alone. Cohabitation, like marriage, creates a home life. Romantic partners may have deep feelings for each other but not be ready to get married. Some couples prefer cohabitation because it provides a consistent relationship without the legal entanglements of marriage (Steinhauer, 1995). It is unclear whether cohabitation is replacing marriage or serves as a new phase of engagement (Smock, 2000).

Economic factors also come into play. Some couples decide to cohabit because of the economic advantages of sharing household expenses. Cohabiting individuals who receive public assistance (social security or welfare checks) risk losing support if they get married (Steinhauer, 1995). Some older people live together rather than marry because of resistance from adult children. Some children fear that a parent will be victimized by a needy senior citizen. Others may not want their inheritances jeopardized or may not want to have to decide where to bury the remaining parent.

Marriage

Marriage is a great institution, but I'm not ready for an institution, yet.

—Mae West

CLICK4™ *the Smart Marriage Web site, answering questions about marriage and divorce.*

Question: What is the role of marriage today? Despite increasing numbers of adults who remain single or cohabit, marriage remains our most popular lifestyle. In the United States 75% to 80% of people get married at least once. Despite our "liberated" times, a *New York Times* poll found that the great majority of people in the United States see marriage as permanent. When asked "If you got married today, would you expect to stay married for the rest of your life, or not?", 86% of respondents said "Yes" (only 11% said "No") (Eggers, 2000). Throughout Western history, marriage has helped people meet their personal and social needs. Marriage regulates and legitimizes sexual relations. Marriage creates a home life and provides an institution for the financial support and socialization of children. Marriage also permits the orderly transmission of wealth from one generation to another, and from one family to another.

Notions such as romantic love, equality, and the radical concept that men, like women, should be faithful are recent additions to the structure of marriage. Today many people believe that sex is acceptable within the bounds of an affectionate relationship, so the desire for a sexual relationship is less likely to motivate marriage. But marriage still offers a sense of emotional and psychological security—a partner with whom to share feelings, experiences, and goals. Among the highly educated, intimacy and companionship are central motives.

We tend to marry people to whom we are attracted. They are usually similar to us in physical attractiveness and hold similar attitudes on major issues. The concept of like marrying like is termed **homogamy.** In the United States, we only rarely marry people of different races or socioeconomic classes. According to the U.S. Bureau of the Census (USBC, 1998), only 2% of U.S. marriages are interracial. More than 90% of married couples are of the same religion.

We also follow *age homogamy*. Husbands tend to be 2 to 3 years older than their wives. Age homogamy reflects the tendencies to get married soon after achieving adulthood and to select partners, such as classmates, with whom we have been in close contact. People who are getting remarried, or marrying at later ages, are less likely to marry partners so close in age.

By and large, however, we seem to be attracted to and to get married to the boy or girl (almost) next door in a quite predictable manner. Marriages seem to be made in the neighborhood—not in heaven.

Homogamy ▲ The principle of like marrying like.

Divorce

> *Whenever I date a guy, I think, is this the man I want my children to spend their weekends with?*
>
> —Rita Rudner

> *My wife and I were considering a divorce, but after pricing lawyers we decided to buy a new car instead.*
>
> —Henny Youngman

Questions: How many marriages end in divorce? Why do people get divorced?
In 1920, about 1 marriage in 7 ended in divorce. By 1960 this figure had risen to 1 in 4. Today at least half of the marriages in the United States end in divorce (Carrère et al., 2000). More than one quarter (27%) of children under the age of 18 live in single-parent households (Edwards, 2000). Divorced women outnumber divorced men, in part because men are more likely to remarry (Edwards, 2000).

Why do so many people get divorced? One reason is the relaxation of legal restrictions on divorce, especially the introduction of the so-called no-fault divorce. Until the 1960s, adultery was the only legal grounds for divorce in New York State. Other states were equally strict. But no-fault divorce laws have since been enacted in nearly every state, allowing a divorce to be granted without a finding of marital misconduct. Another reason is the increased economic independence of women. Today a higher percentage of women in the United States have the financial means to break away from a troubled marriage. Today, more people regard marriage as an alterable condition than in prior generations.

It is ironic that another reason for the high divorce rate is that people today hold *higher* expectations of marriage than their parents or grandparents did. They expect marriage to be personally fulfilling as well as meet the traditional expectation of marriage as an institution for rearing children. Many demand the right to be happy in marriage. The most common reasons given for a divorce today are problems in communication and a lack of understanding. Key reasons for divorce today include a husband's criticism, contempt, and unwillingness to share the power in the relationship (Carrère et al., 2000; Gottman et al., 1998). Years ago it was more likely to be lack of financial support.

Divorce usually has financial and emotional repercussions. When a couple split, their resources may not be sufficient to maintain the former standard of living for both of them. A divorced woman's income drops by one quarter on the average, whereas a divorced man's income drops by less than 10% (Bianchi & Spain, 1997). The divorced woman who has not pursued a career may find herself competing for work with younger, more experienced people. Because women usually have custody of the children, they are also likely to bear—or to continue to bear—the main or sole responsibility for rearing the children as well as attempting to increase their income. The divorced man may not be able to manage alimony and child support and also establish a new home of his own.

People who are separated and divorced have the highest rates of physical illness and psychological disorders in the population (Carrére et al., 2000; Gottman et al., 1998). Divorced people are subject to greater stress and feel that they exert less control over their lives. Feelings of failure as a spouse and parent, loneliness, and uncertainty prompt feelings of depression. But divorce can enable an individual to become a whole, autonomous person once more—or for the first time. Some people find that despite the pain and aggravation, the experience of divorce provides opportunities for self-renewal.

Divorce has repercussions for the children (Ellis, 2000). Research shows that the children of divorced people are more likely to have behavioral problems, engage in substance abuse, and earn lower grades in school (O'Connor et al., 2000). The emergence of such problems does not mean that it is best for parents to stay together for the sake of the children, however. Marital conflicts make relationships between parents and children more difficult and are also connected with eventual marital conflict in the children (Ellis, 2000; Erel & Burman, 1995; Harold et al., 1997).

It also seems that it is not so much parental separation that affects the children, but the breakdown in the quality of parenting that often follows separation (Erel & Burman,

1995; Harold et al., 1997). Clarke-Stewart and her colleagues (2000) analyzed data from the National Institute of Child Health and Human Development Study of Early Child Care to examine the effects of marital separation on children during the first 3 years of life. The families studied included nearly 100 separated or divorced mothers and a comparison group of 170 two-parent families. All in all, the children in two-parent families obtained higher scores on tests of cognitive ability, showed more social skills, fewer problem behaviors, and were more securely attached to their mothers. However, when the researchers considered the mothers' level of education and socioeconomic status, the differences between the children in one-parent versus two-parent families became nonsignificant. Thus, the psychological development of the children in this study was not affected by parental separation or divorce per se. Instead, it was related to the mother's income, level of education, behavior, and psychological problems, such as depression. The results of this study suggest that children may fare better in homes with capable and well-adjusted mothers than in homes with constantly bickering parents. In order to protect the children, psychologists usually advise parents who are getting divorced to try to agree on how they will treat the children (e.g., children often ask a parent for something after the other parent has said no), help each other maintain a good parent–child relationship, and not criticize each other to or in front of the children.

The World of Work

Work is the refuge of people who have nothing better to do.

—Oscar Wilde

CLICK4™ *an interactive Self-Assessment: The Job Satisfaction Index.*

CLICK4™ *advice on making the transition from college to the workplace.*

CLICK4™ *a WebSearch activity on gender equity in the workplace.*

A century ago, the British playwright George Bernard Shaw pronounced, "Drink is the greatest evil of the working class." Upon sober reflection, he added, "Work is the greatest evil of the drinking class."

Humor aside, work in Shaw's day for most people involved back-breaking labor or mind-numbing factory work, sunrise to sunset, 6 days a week. Although most of today's workers put in fewer hours and are as likely to exercise their brains as their arms and backs, work is still at the core of the lives of many adults.

Extrinsic Versus Intrinsic Motives for Working   Question: Why do people work?   One of the major reasons for working, if not *the* major reason, is economic. Work provides us with the means to pay our bills. The paycheck, fringe benefits, security in old age—all these are external or extrinsic motives for working. But work also satisfies many internal or intrinsic motives, including the opportunity to engage in stimulating and satisfying activities (Katzell & Thompson, 1990). Three Americans in four say they would work even if they did not have to, and half would stay in their present jobs (Hugick & Leonard, 1991).

Intrinsic reasons for working include the work ethic, self-identity, self-fulfillment, self-worth, and the social values of work. Occupational identity becomes intertwined with self-identity so that we are likely to think, "I *am* a nurse" or "I *am* a lawyer" rather than "I work as a nurse" or "as an attorney." We often express our personal needs, interests, and values through our work. The self-fulfilling values of the work of the astronaut, scientist, and athlete may seem obvious. But factory workers, plumbers, police officers, and firefighters can also find self-enrichment as well as cash rewards for their work. Recognition and respect for a job well done contribute to self-esteem. The workplace also extends our social contacts. It introduces us to friends, lovers, challenging adversaries. At work, we may meet others who share our interests. We may form social networks that in our highly mobile society sometimes substitute for family.

Middle Adulthood

There are also a number of key changes in social and personality development that tend to occur during middle adulthood. *Question: What social and personality developments occur during middle adulthood?* Consider Erikson's views on the middle years.

Generativity Versus Stagnation   Erikson (1963) labeled the life crisis of the middle years **generativity versus stagnation.** Generativity involves doing things that we believe are worthwhile, such as rearing children or producing on the job. Generativity enhances and maintains self-esteem. Generativity also involves helping to shape the new generation. This shaping may involve rearing our own children or making the world a better place, for example, through joining church or civic groups. Stagnation means treading water, as in keeping the same job at the same pay for 30 years, or even moving backward, as in moving into a less responsible and poorer paying job or removing oneself from rearing one's children. Stagnation has powerful destructive effects on self-esteem.

Midlife Transition   According to Levinson and his colleagues (1978), whose research involved case studies of 40 men, there is a **midlife transition** at about age 40 to 45 characterized by a shift in psychological perspective. Previously, men had thought of their age in terms of the number of years that had elapsed since birth. Now they begin to think of their age in terms of the number of years they have left. Men in their 30s still think of themselves as older brothers to "kids" in their 20s. At about age 40 to 45, however, some marker event—illness, a change of job, the death of a friend or parent, or being beaten at tennis by their son—leads men to realize that they are a full generation older. Suddenly there seems to be more to look back on than forward to. It dawns on men that they will never be president or chairperson of the board. They will never play shortstop for the Dodgers. They mourn the passing of their own youth and begin to adjust to the specter of old age and the finality of death.

There are gender differences. Research suggests that women may undergo a midlife transition a number of years earlier than men do (Stewart & Ostrove, 1998). Sheehy (1976) writes that women enter midlife about 5 years earlier than men, at about age 35 instead of 40. Why? Much of it has to do with the winding down of the "biological clock"—that is, the abilities to conceive and bear children. For example, once they turn 35, women are usually advised to have their fetuses routinely tested for Down syndrome and other chromosomal disorders. At age 35, women also enter higher risk categories for side effects from birth control pills. Yet many women today are having children in their 40s and, now and then, beyond.

The Midlife Crisis   According to Levinson, the midlife transition may trigger a crisis—the **midlife crisis.** The middle-level, middle-aged businessperson looking ahead to another 10 to 20 years of grinding out accounts in a Wall Street cubbyhole may encounter severe depression. The housewife with two teenagers, an empty house from 8:00 A.M. to 4:00 P.M., and a 40th birthday on the way may feel that she is coming apart at the seams. Both feel a sense of entrapment and loss of purpose. Some people are propelled into extramarital affairs by the desire to prove to themselves that they are still attractive.

Mastery   Sheehy (1995) is much more optimistic than Levinson. She terms the years from 45 to 65 the "Age of Mastery." Rather than viewing them as years of decline, her interviews suggest that many Americans find that these years present opportunities for new direction and fulfillment. Many people are at the height of their productive powers during this period. Sheehy believes that the key task for people aged 45 to 55 is to decide what they will do with their "second adulthoods"—the 30 to 40 healthy years that may be left for them once they reach 50. She believes that both men and women can experience great success and joy if they identify meaningful goals and pursue them wholeheartedly.

▲ **REFLECT**
Do you see your future as open-ended or as quite limited? Why?

Generativity versus stagnation ▲ Erikson's term for the crisis of middle adulthood, characterized by the task of being productive and contributing to younger generations.
Midlife transition ▲ Levinson's term for the ages from 40 to 45, which are characterized by a shift in psychological perspective from viewing ourselves in terms of years lived to viewing ourselves in terms of the years we have left.
Midlife crisis ▲ A crisis experienced by many people during the midlife transition when they realize that life may be more than halfway over and reassess their achievements in terms of their dreams.

Mid-Life Crisis or "Middlescence?"
According to Gail Sheehy, many middle-aged people undergo a second quest for identity (the first occurs during adolescence). They are trying to decide what they will do with their "second adulthoods"—the three to four healthy decades they may have left.

CLICK4™ *a WebSearch activity on the "empty nest syndrome."*

Middlescence ▲ Sheehy's term for a stage of life, from 45 to 55, when people seek new identity and are frequently "lost in a buzz of confusion."

Empty-nest syndrome ▲ A sense of depression and loss of purpose felt by some parents when the youngest child leaves home.

Identity certainty ▲ A strong and clear sense of who one is and what one stands for.

Confident power ▲ Feelings of self-confidence, self-efficacy.

Ego integrity versus despair ▲ Erikson's term for the crisis of late adulthood, characterized by the task of maintaining one's sense of identity despite physical deterioration.

"Middlescence"   Yet people need to define themselves and their goals. Sheehy coined the term **middlescence** to describe a period of searching that is in some ways similar to adolescence or to emerging adulthood. Both are times of transition or of what Stewart and Ostrove (1998) refer to as midcourse corrections. Middlescence involves a search for a new identity: "Turning backward, going around in circles, feeling lost in a buzz of confusion and unable to make decisions—all this is predictable and, for many people, a necessary precursor to making the passage into midlife" (Sheehy, 1995).

Women frequently experience a renewed sense of self in their 40s and 50s as they emerge from "middlescence" (Sheehy, 1995). Many women in their early 40s are already emerging from some of the fears and uncertainties that are first confronting men. For example, women in their early 40s are more likely than women in their early 30s to feel confident; to exert an influence on their community; to feel secure and committed; to feel productive, effective, and powerful; and to extend their interests beyond their family (Helson et al., 1995; Stewart & Ostrove, 1998).

CONTROVERSY IN PSYCHOLOGY

Do Women Experience an "Empty-Nest Syndrome" When the Youngest Child Leaves Home?

In earlier decades, psychologists placed great emphasis on a concept referred to as the **empty-nest syndrome.** This concept was applied most often to women. It was assumed that women experience a profound sense of loss when their youngest child goes off to college, gets married, or moves out of the home. The sense of loss was assumed to be greatest among women who had remained in the home (Stewart & Ostrove, 1998).

Research findings paint a more optimistic picture, however. Certainly there can be a sense of loss when the children have left home, and the loss applies to both parents. Parents may find it difficult to let go of the children after so many years of mutual dependence. However, many mothers report increased marital satisfaction and personal changes such as greater mellowness, self-confidence, and stability once the children have left home (Stewart & Ostrove, 1998).

Stewart and her colleagues (1998) developed scales to assess four personality variables in women of various ages: identity certainty, generativity, confident power, and awareness of aging. **Identity certainty** is the feeling of having a strong and clear identity. *Generativity* is Erikson's sense of an enlarged vision of one's role in the world and increased feelings of responsibility and commitment to society. **Confident power** is the same as feelings of self-efficacy. Awareness of aging is self-explanatory (and all too familiar to your author!). The researchers assessed these variables among college women in their 40s and 50s, and retrospectively for the 30s. The evidence revealed that all of these variables grew to be more prominent in the 40s than in the 30s, and then again in the 50s than in the 40s. Yes, the older women were more aware of their aging, both because of physical changes (e.g., menopause) and psychosocial markers (e.g., the maturation of the children). However, they were also more certain as to who they were and what they stood for. They had assumed more responsibility for society at large (e.g., occupational, civic, and political activities), and were more achievement oriented, self-confident, dominant, and self-assertive. It is as if middle age frees many women—at least educated women—from traditional gender-related shackles.

Late Adulthood

It's never too late to be what you might have been.

—*George Eliot*

Question: What social and personality developments occur during late adulthood?   According to Erikson, late adulthood is the stage of **ego integrity versus despair.** The basic challenge is to maintain the belief that life is meaningful and worthwhile

in the face of the inevitability of death. Ego integrity derives from **wisdom,** which can be defined as expert knowledge about the meaning of life, balancing one's own needs and those of others, and pushing toward excellence in one's behavior and achievements (Baltes & Staudinger, 2000; Sternberg, 2000). Erikson also believed that wisdom enabled people to accept their lifespan as occurring at a certain point in the sweep of history and as being limited. We spend most of our lives accumulating objects and relationships. Erikson also argues that adjustment in the later years requires the ability to let go. Other views of late adulthood stress the importance of creating new challenges; however, biological and social realities may require older people to become more selective in their pursuits.

Successful Aging

The later years were once seen mainly as a prelude to dying. Older people were viewed as crotchety and irritable. It was assumed that they reaped little pleasure from life. *No more.* Many stereotypes about aging are becoming less prevalent. *Question: How do people in the United States age today?* Despite the changes that accompany aging, most people in their 70s report being generally satisfied with their lives (Volz, 2000). Americans are eating more wisely and exercising at later ages, so many older people are robust. According to a national poll of nearly 1,600 adults by the *Los Angeles Times*, 75% of older people feel younger than their age—19 years on average (Stewart & Armet, 2000). People in their 70s and 80s felt as though they were in their 60s. People in their 60s reported feeling as though they were in their early 50s.

One aspect of successful aging is subjective well-being. A sense of well-being in late adulthood is linked to more than physical health and feeling younger than one's years. A meta-analysis of 286 studies noted three factors that are connected with subjective well-being: socioeconomic status, social network, and competence (Pinquart & Sörensen, 2000). One's level of income is more important to subjective well-being than is his or her level of education. Having social contacts with friends and one's own adult children are both related to subjective well-being. Competence enables one to take charge of one's life to fill one's days with meaningful activities and handle the problems that can arise at any age.

Sheehy (1995) coined the term *middlescence* to highlight her finding that people whom she interviewed in their 50s were thinking about what they would do with their *second adulthood*—the 30 to 40 healthy years they had left! Developmental psychologists are using another new term: *successful aging* (Volz, 2000). The term is not just meant to put a

CLICK4™ *more information about aging from the National Institute on Aging and Duke's Center for the Study of Aging and Human Development.*

Wisdom ▲ Expert knowledge concerning the meaning of life, concern for people's welfare, and a push toward excellence.

positive spin on the inevitable. "Successful agers" have a number of characteristics that can inspire all of us to lead more enjoyable and productive lives. There are three components of successful aging:

1. *Reshaping one's life to concentrate on what one finds to be important and meaningful.* Laura Carstensen's (1997) research on people aged 70 and above reveals that successful agers form emotional goals that bring them satisfaction. For example, rather than cast about in multiple directions, they may focus on their family and friends. Successful agers may have less time left than younger people, but they tend to spend it more wisely (Garfinkel, 1995).

Researchers (Baltes, 1997; Schulz & Heckhausen, 1996) use terms such as "selective optimization and compensation" to describe the manner in which successful agers lead their lives. That is, successful agers no longer seek to compete in arenas best left to younger people—such as certain kinds of athletic or business activities. Rather, they focus on matters that allow them to maintain a sense of control over their own actions. Moreover, they use available resources to make up for losses. If their memory is not quite what it once was, they make notes or other reminders. For example, if their senses are no longer as acute, they use devices such as hearing aids or allow themselves more time to take in information. There are also some ingenious individual strategies. The great pianist Arthur Rubinstein performed into his 80s, even after he had lost much of his pianistic speed. In his later years, he would slow down before playing faster passages in order to enhance the impression of speed during those passages.

2. *A positive outlook.* For example, some older people attribute occasional health problems such as aches and pains to *specific* and *unstable* factors like a cold or jogging too long. Others attribute aches and pains to *global* and *stable* factors such as aging itself. Not surprisingly, those who attribute these problems to specific, unstable factors are more optimistic about surmounting them. They thus have a more positive outlook or attitude. Of particular interest here is research conducted by William Rakowski (1995). Rakowski followed 1,400 people aged 70 or older with nonlethal health problems such as aches and pains. He found that those who blamed the problems on aging itself were significantly more likely to die in the near future than those who blamed the problems on specific, unstable factors.

3. *Self-challenge.* Many people look forward to late adulthood as a time when they can rest from life's challenges. But sitting back and allowing the world to pass by is a prescription for vegetating, not for living life to its fullest. Consider an experiment conducted by Curt Sandman and Francis Crinella (1995) with 175 people whose average age was 72. They randomly assigned participants either to a foster grandparent program with neurologically impaired children or to a control group, and followed both groups for 10 years. The foster grandparents carried out various physical challenges, such as walking a few miles each day, and also engaged in new kinds of social interactions. Those in the control group did not engage in these activities. When they were assessed by the experimenters, the foster grandparents showed improved overall cognitive functioning, including memory functioning, and better sleep patterns. Moreover, the foster grandparents showed superior functioning in these areas compared with people assigned to the control group.

The *Los Angeles Times* poll found that 25% of people who had retired believed that they had done so too soon (Stewart & Armet, 2000). Many older adults today are in what they call their "third age" (following their second or middle age). They are returning to school in record numbers, becoming entrepreneurs, volunteering, and, in many cases, continuing to work. According to retirement specialist Helen Dennis (2000),

> Work is a tremendous social environment. Generally, people spend more time at work with colleagues and friends than they do with their families. Those people who are currently retiring have had long-term experiences with an employer. They've lived through marriages, births, deaths, Christmases and Thanksgivings.

Nearly half (45%) of those polled by the *Los Angeles Times* agreed with the statement, "When you give up your job, you give up a large part of who you are" (Stewart & Armet, 2000).

▲ **REFLECT**
Some people age faster than others, physically, cognitively, and socially. Considering the older people in your own experience, how do you account for the differences?

CD **11** **SA** **10**

CLICK4™ *an interactive Self-Assessment: What Are Your Attitudes Toward Aging?*

www **11** **E** **4**

CLICK4™ *an essay assignment on ethnic and gender differences in health and longevity.*

www **11** **L** **5**

CLICK4™ *the home page of the American Association of Retired Persons.*

REVIEW

(26) Erikson noted that there is commonly a _____ in extended adolescence during which the individual engages in a deep search for personal identity. (27) Many young adults adopt what Levinson calls the _____, that is, the drive to leave one's mark on history. (28) The most common lifestyle for people in their early 20s in the United States is being (married or single?). (29) About 50% to 60% of the marriages that took place during the past decade were preceded by living together, or _____. (30) Most people in the United States see marriage as (temporary or permanent?). (31) The most common reason given for divorce today is problems in _____. (32) Erikson labeled the life crisis of the middle years _____ versus stagnation. (33) According to Levinson, the midlife transition may trigger a midlife _____, which is characterized by a sense of entrapment and loss of purpose. (34) Research shows that most middle-aged U.S. women (do or do not?) suffer from the empty-nest syndrome. (35) Erikson labeled late adulthood the stage of ego _____ versus despair. (36) Research shows that older people in the United States report feeling (younger or older?) than their years.

Pulling It Together: Are you undergoing, or did you undergo, a period of "emerging adulthood"? Explain. What factors contribute to successful aging—at any age?

ON DEATH AND DYING

Death is the last great taboo. Psychiatrist Elisabeth Kübler-Ross commented on our denial of death in her landmark book *On Death and Dying:* "We use euphemisms, we make the dead look as if they were asleep, we ship the children off to protect them from the anxiety and turmoil around the house if the [person] is fortunate enough to die at home, [and] we don't allow children to visit their dying parents in the hospital" (1969, p. 8).

Question: What are psychological perspectives on death and dying?

In her work with terminally ill patients, Kübler-Ross found some common responses to news of impending death. She identified five stages of dying through which many patients pass, and she suggested that older people who suspect that death is approaching may undergo similar stages:

1. *Denial.* In the denial stage, people feel that "It can't be happening to me. The diagnosis must be wrong."
2. *Anger.* Denial usually gives way to anger and resentment toward the young and healthy and, sometimes, toward the medical establishment—"It's unfair. Why me?"
3. *Bargaining.* Next, people may try to bargain with God to postpone their death, promising, for example, to do good deeds if they are given another six months, another year to live.
4. *Depression.* With depression come feelings of loss and hopelessness—grief at the inevitability of leaving loved ones and life itself.
5. *Final acceptance.* Ultimately, an inner peace may come, a quiet acceptance of the inevitable. Such "peace" does not resemble contentment. It is nearly devoid of feeling.

Psychologist Edwin Shneidman, who has specialized in the concerns of suicidal and dying individuals, acknowledges the presence of feelings such as those identified by Kübler-Ross, but he does not perceive them to be linked in a sequence like the one just described. Instead, he suggests that dying people show a variety of emotional and cognitive responses that tend to be fleeting or relatively stable, to ebb and flow, and to reflect pain and bewilderment. He also points out that the kinds of responses shown by individuals reflect their personality traits and their philosophies of life.

▲ **REFLECT**
Erik Erikson wrote that one aspect of wisdom is the ability to visualize one's role in the march of history and to accept one's own death. Do you believe that acceptance of death is a sign of wisdom? Why or why not?

CLICK4™ *an interactive Self-Assessment: How Concerned Are You About Death?*

CLICK4™ *a bulletin board discussion on death: Is accepting it a sign of wisdom?*

"Lying Down to Pleasant Dreams . . ."

The American poet William Cullen Bryant is best known for his poem "Thanatopsis," which he composed at the age of 18. "Thanatopsis" expresses Erik Erikson's goal of ego integrity—optimism that we can maintain a sense of trust through life. By meeting squarely the challenges of our adult lives, perhaps we can take our leave with dignity. When our time comes to "join the innumerable caravan"—the billions who have died before us—perhaps we can depart life with integrity.

Live, wrote the poet, so that

> . . . when thy summons comes to join
> The innumerable caravan that moves
> To that mysterious realm, where each shall take
> His chamber in the silent halls of death,
> Thou go not, like the quarry-slave at night,
> Scourged to his dungeon, but, sustained and soothed
> By an unfaltering trust, approach thy grave
> Like one that wraps the drapery of his couch
> About him, and lies down to pleasant dreams.

Bryant, of course, wrote "Thanatopsis" at age 18, not at 85, the age at which he died. At that advanced age, his feelings—and his verse—might have differed. But literature and poetry, unlike science, need not reflect reality. They can serve to inspire and warm us.

REVIEW

CLICK4™ *a quiz covering the second half of this chapter.*

CLICK4™ *electronic flash cards to review your knowledge of key terms and people in this chapter.*

(37) Kübler-Ross identifies five stages of dying among the terminally ill: _____, anger, bargaining, depression, and final acceptance. (38) Research by other investigators finds that psychological reactions to approaching death are (more or less?) varied than Kübler-Ross suggests.

Pulling It Together: When, and under what kinds of circumstances, do people become concerned about their own mortality?

TRUTH ▨ FICTION
REVISITED

▰ It is not usually true that girls are capable of becoming pregnant when they have their first menstrual period. *Menarche can precede ovulation by a year or more. See page 351.*

▰ It is true that adolescents tend to see themselves as being on stage. *This is a manifestation of adolescent egocentrism and fuels the adolescent desires for privacy and physical perfection. See page 353.*

▰ It is not true that menopause signals the end of a woman's sexual interests. *Some women, in fact, feel sexually liberated because of the separation of sexual expression and reproduction. See page 360.*

▰ It is not true that Frank Lloyd Wright created the innovative design for the Guggenheim Museum at the age of 65. *But the reason is that he created the New York City museum at the age of 89! See page 368.*

▰ Alzheimer's disease is *not* a normal part of growing old. *See page 369.*

▰ It is not true that single people are swingers. *The statement is too general to be accurate. Single people follow a number of different kinds of styles of life. See page 373.*

▰ It is true that about half—in fact, at least half—of the marriages that took place during the last decade were preceded by cohabitation. *See page 373.*

▰ It is true that most Americans would continue to work even if they did not need the money. *We work not only for extrinsic rewards such as the paycheck and financial security, but also for intrinsic rewards, such as the opportunity to engage in challenging activities and broaden social contacts. See page 376.*

▰ It is not true that mothers in general suffer from the "empty-nest syndrome" when their youngest child leaves home. *Most mothers (and fathers) do* not *suffer when their youngest child leaves home. See page 379.*

▰ *Actually, one of the "secrets" to successful aging is taking on new challenges, not avoiding challenge. See page 381.*

1. What physical developments occur during adolescence?

Adolescence is a period of life that begins at puberty and ends with assumption of adult responsibilities. Changes that lead to reproductive capacity and secondary sex characteristics are stimulated by increased levels of testosterone in the male and of estrogen and androgens in the female. During the adolescent growth spurt, young people may grow 6 or more inches in a year.

2. What cognitive developments occur during adolescence?

Formal operational thinking appears in adolescence, but not everyone reaches this stage. Two consequences of adolescent egocentrism are the imaginary audience and the personal fable. The imaginary audience refers to the adolescent beliefs that they are the center of attention and that other people are as concerned with their appearance and behavior as they are. The personal fable refers to the adolescent belief that one's feelings and ideas are special, even unique, and that one is invulnerable.

3. What social and personality developments occur during adolescence?

Adolescents and parents are often in conflict because adolescents desire more independence and may experiment with things that can jeopardize their health. Despite bickering, most adolescents continue to love and respect their parents. According to Erikson, adolescents strive to forge an ego identity—a sense of who they are and what they stand for. The changes of puberty prepare the body for sexual activity, and high hormone levels also stir interest in sex. But most sexually active adolescents do not use contraceptives reliably. Thus about 1 teenage girl in 10 gets pregnant each year.

4. What physical developments occur during adulthood?

People are usually at the height of their physical powers during young adulthood. Middle adulthood is characterized by a gradual decline in strength. Menopause has been thought to depress many women, but research suggests that most women go through this passage without great difficulty. Older people show less sensory acuity, and their reaction time lengthens. The immune system weakens and changes occur that eventually result in death.

5. What are the gender and ethnic differences in life expectancy?

Women outlive men by nearly 7 years, and European and Asian Americans tend to outlive other ethnic groups in the United States. By and large, the groups who live longer are more likely to seek and make use of health care.

6. Why do we age?

Heredity plays a role in longevity. One theory (programmed senescence) suggests that aging and death are determined by our genes. Another theory (wear-and-tear theory) holds that factors such as pollution, disease, and ultraviolet light weaken the body so that it loses the ability to repair itself. Lifestyle factors such as exercise, proper nutrition, and *not* smoking also contribute to longevity.

7. What cognitive developments occur during adulthood?

People are usually at the height of their cognitive powers during early adulthood, but people can be creative for a lifetime. Memory functioning declines with age, but are not usually as large as people assume. People tend to retain verbal ability, as shown by vocabulary and general knowledge, into advanced old age. Crystallized intelligence—one's vocabulary and accumulated knowledge—generally increases with age. Fluid intelligence—the ability to process information rapidly—declines more rapidly but workers' familiarity with solving specific kinds of problems is often more important than their fluid intelligence.

8. What is Alzheimer's disease? What are its origins?

Alzheimer's disease is characterized by cognitive deterioration in memory, language, and problem solving. On a biological level, it is connected with reduced levels of acetylcholine in the brain and with the build-up of plaque in the brain.

9. What social and personality developments occur during young adulthood?

Young adulthood is generally characterized by efforts to advance in the business world and the development of intimate ties. Many young adults reassess the directions of their lives during the "age-30 transition."

10. Just what is meant by "emerging adulthood"?

Emerging adulthood is a hypothesized period that exists in wealthy societies. It roughly spans the ages of 18 through 25 and affords young people extended periods of role exploration. The concept dovetails with Erikson's concept of a prolonged adolescence we find in industrialized societies, one that permits a period of moratorium during which the individual searches for personal identity

11. Just what is the "singles scene" like today?

Being single has become the nation's most common lifestyle for people in their early 20s as they delay marriage to pursue education and careers. For some being single is a stage that precedes marriage; for others, it is an open-ended lifestyle. For some, being single means a string of affairs. Some engage in serial monogamy, in which they have a series of exclusive sexual relationships.

12. Who cohabits today, and why?

Cohabitation has become so common in the United States that about 5 million couples cohabit today and at least half of couples who got married during the past decade had cohabited first. Liberal, well-educated, and divorced people are somewhat more likely to cohabit than are other people.

13. What is the role of marriage today?

Marriage remains the most popular lifestyle in the United States, and people still think of marriage as permanent. Marriage legitimizes sexual relations, creates a home life, and provides an institution for the rearing of children. People continue to have high expectations of marriage, including feelings of romantic love.

14. How many marriages end in divorce? Why do people get divorced?

At least half of today's marriages end in divorce, mainly because of problems in communication. But relaxed legal restrictions and women's greater economic independence have also contributed to the divorce rate.

15. Why do people work?

People work for extrinsic (e.g., money, financial security) and intrinsic reasons (self-identity, the social values of work, a way of structuring one's time).

16. What social and personality developments occur during middle adulthood?

Many theorists view middle adulthood as a time of crisis (the "midlife crisis") and further reassessment. Many adults try to come to terms with the discrepancies between their achievements and the dreams of their youth during middle adulthood. Some middle-aged adults become depressed when their youngest child leaves home (the so-called empty-nest syndrome), but many report increased satisfaction, stability, and self-confidence. On a more positive note, many people in middle adulthood experience "middlescence"—a phase during which they redefine themselves and their goals for the 30 to 40 healthy years they expect lie ahead of them.

17. What social and personality developments occur during late adulthood?

Erikson characterizes late adulthood as the stage of ego integrity versus despair. He saw the basic challenge as maintaining the belief that life is worthwhile in the face of physical deterioration.

18. How do people in the United States age today?

Many stereotypes about aging are growing less prevalent. Most older Americans report being generally satisfied with their lives. Those who experience "successful aging" reshape their lives to focus on what they find to be important, maintain a positive outlook, and find new challenges.

19. What are psychological perspectives on death and dying?

Kübler-Ross has identified five stages of dying among people who are terminally ill: denial, anger, bargaining, depression, and final acceptance. However, other investigators find that psychological reactions to approaching death are more varied than Kübler-Ross suggests.

PREVIEW

Introduction to Personality: "Why Are They Sad and Glad and Bad?"
▲ You've got personality. So what does that mean?

The Psychodynamic Perspective
▲ Is your behavior controlled by conscious choice or by forces deep within? How would you know the difference?

The Trait Perspective
▲ The ancient Greek physician Hippocrates devised a way of looking at personality that—with a little "tweaking"—remains in use today.
▲ You may have heard of the Big Ten athletic conference. Your personality may be made up of the Big Five.

Learning-Theory Perspectives
▲ John Watson believed he could select any infant at random and train him or her to become a doctor, lawyer, or merchant-chief—even a "beggar-man" or thief.
▲ B. F. Skinner argued that society conditions us to "want" what is good for society.
▲ Social-cognitive theorists admit that the environment influences you, but they also believe that you influence the environment—in fact, that you can create environments.

The Humanistic-Existential Perspective
▲ Abraham Maslow believed that you keep on wanting to go higher . . . and higher and higher.
▲ Carl Rogers believed that if people around you are supportive, you will strive to become everything you are capable of being.

Personality and Diversity: The Sociocultural Perspective
▲ How would you complete this statement: "I am . . ."
▲ How have you been influenced by your gender? By your cultural background?

Measurement of Personality
▲ Are there right and wrong answers on a personality test?

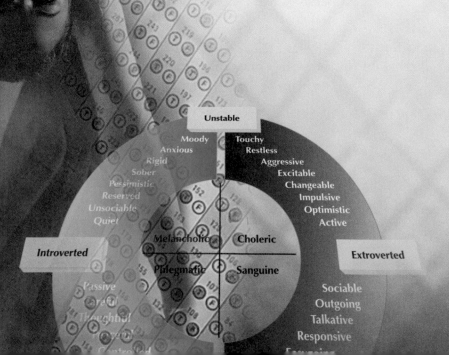

CHAPTER 12

Personality

TRUTH ██ FICTION?

◣ According to Sigmund Freud, the human mind is like a vast submerged iceberg. Only its tip rises above the surface into conscious awareness.

◣ According to Freud, biting one's fingernails or smoking cigarettes as an adult is a sign of conflict experienced during very early childhood.

◣ Bloodletting and vomiting were once recommended ways of coping with depression.

◣ By controlling a child's environment, any child can be reared to become a "doctor, lawyer, merchant-chief," or even a beggar or a thief.

◣ We are more likely to persist at difficult tasks when we believe we will succeed.

◣ We can build our self-esteem by becoming good at something.

◣ The best-adjusted immigrants are those who abandon the language and customs of their country of origin and become like members of the dominant culture in the new host country.

◣ Psychologists can determine whether a person has told the truth on a personality test.

◣ There are no right or wrong answers on some psychological tests.

◣ There is a psychological test made up of inkblots, and test-takers are asked to say what the blots look like to them.

I was reading Dr. Seuss's *One Fish, Two Fish, Red Fish, Blue Fish* to my daughter Taylor when she was 2 years old. The sneaky author had set up a trap for fathers. A part of the book reads that "Some [fish] are sad. And some are glad. And some are very, very bad. Why are they sad and glad and bad? I do not know. Go ask your dad."

Thanks, Dr. Seuss.

For many months I had just recited this section and then moved on. One day, however, Taylor's cognitive development had apparently flowered, and she would not let me get away with glossing over this. Why, indeed, she wanted to know, were some fish sad whereas others were glad and bad? I paused and then, being a typical American dad, I gave the answer I'm sure has been given by thousands of other fathers:

"Uh, some fish are sad and others are glad or bad because of, uh, the interaction of nature and nurture—I mean, you know, heredity and environmental factors."

At which Taylor laughed and replied, "Not!"

INTRODUCTION TO PERSONALITY: "WHY ARE THEY SAD AND GLAD AND BAD?"

I'm still not certain whether Taylor thought my words came out silly or that my psychological theorizing was simplistic or off base. When applied to people—that is, why are people sad or glad or bad—this is the kind of question that is of interest to psychologists who study personality.

Question: Just what is personality?   People do not necessarily agree on what the word **personality** means. Many equate personality with liveliness, as in "She's got a lot of personality." Others characterize a person's personality as consisting of his or her most striking traits, as in a "shy personality" or a "happy-go-lucky personality." Psychologists define personality as the reasonably stable patterns of emotions, motives, and behavior that distinguish one person from another.

Psychologists also seek to explain how personality develops—that is, why some (people) are sad or glad or bad—and to predict how people with certain personality traits respond to life's demands. In this chapter we explore five perspectives on personality: the psychodynamic, trait, learning, humanistic-existential, and sociocultural perspectives. Then we discuss personality tests—the methods used to measure whether people are sad, glad, bad, and lots of other things.

THE PSYCHODYNAMIC PERSPECTIVE

There are several **psychodynamic theories** of personality, each of which owes its origin to the thinking of Sigmund Freud. These theories have a number of features in common. Each teaches that personality is characterized by conflict—by a dynamic struggle. At first the conflict is external: Drives like sex, aggression, and the need for superiority come into conflict with laws, social rules, and moral codes. But at some point laws and social rules are brought inward, or *internalized*. After that the conflict is between opposing *inner* forces. At any given moment our behavior, thoughts, and emotions represent the outcome of these inner contests.   *Question: What is Freud's theory of psychosexual development?*

Sigmund Freud's Theory of Psychosexual Development

Sigmund Freud was trained as a physician. Early in his practice he was astounded to find that some people apparently experience loss of feeling in a hand or paralysis of the legs in the absence of any medical disorder. These odd symptoms often disappear once the person has recalled and discussed stressful events and feelings of guilt or anxiety that seem to be related to the symptoms. For a long time, these events and feelings have lain hidden beneath the surface of awareness. Even so, they have the capacity to influence behavior.

From this sort of clinical evidence, Freud concluded that the human mind is like an iceberg. Only the tip of an iceberg rises above the surface of the water; the great mass of

---

▲ **REFLECT**

Think of a friend who is single. If you were trying to fix him or her up on a date and you were asked what kind of "personality" he or she had, what would you answer? As you read through the chapter, ask yourself whether your description would change.

CLICK4™ *more information about Freud and the psychodynamic perspective.*

CLICK4™ *a bulletin board discussion on the unconscious: Does it really exist?*

Personality ▲ The distinct patterns of behavior, thoughts, and feelings that characterize a person's adaptation to life.

Psychodynamic theory ▲ Sigmund Freud's perspective, which emphasizes the importance of unconscious motives and conflicts as forces that determine behavior. *Dynamic* refers to the concept of (psychological) forces being in motion.

it is hidden in the depths (see Figure 12.1). Freud came to believe that people, similarly, are aware of only a small portion of the ideas and impulses that dwell within their minds. He argued that a much greater portion of the mind—our deepest images, thoughts, fears, and urges—remains beneath the surface of conscious awareness, where little light illumines them.

Freud labeled the region that pokes through into the light of awareness the **conscious** part of the mind. He called the regions below the surface the *preconscious* and the *unconscious.* The **preconscious** mind contains elements of experience that are out of awareness but can be made conscious simply by focusing on them. The **unconscious** mind is shrouded in mystery. It contains biological instincts such as sex and aggression. Some unconscious urges cannot be experienced consciously because mental images and words could not portray them in all their color and fury. Other unconscious urges may be kept below the surface through repression.

Repression is the automatic ejection of anxiety-evoking ideas from awareness. Research evidence suggests that many people repress bad childhood experiences (Myers & Brewin, 1994). Perhaps "something shocking happens, and the mind pushes it into some inaccessible corner of the unconscious" (Loftus, 1993). Repression may also protect us from perceiving morally unacceptable impulses.

In the unconscious mind, primitive drives seek expression, while internalized values try to keep them in check. The conflict can arouse emotional outbursts and psychological problems.

To explore the unconscious mind, Freud engaged in a form of mental detective work called **psychoanalysis.** For this reason, his theory of personality is also referred to as *psychoanalytic theory*. In psychoanalysis, people are prodded to talk about anything that pops into their mind while they remain comfortable and relaxed. They may gain self-insight by pursuing some of the thoughts that pop into awareness. But they are also motivated to evade threatening subjects. The same repression that ejects unacceptable thoughts from awareness prompts **resistance,** or the desire to avoid thinking about or discussing those thoughts. Repression and resistance can make psychoanalysis a tedious process that lasts for years, or even decades.

The Structure of Personality Freud spoke of mental or **psychic structures** to describe the clashing forces of personality. Psychic structures cannot be seen or measured directly, but their presence is suggested by behavior, expressed thoughts, and emotions. Freud believed that there are three psychic structures: the id, the ego, and the superego.

The **id** is present at birth. It represents physiological drives and is entirely unconscious. Freud described the id as "a chaos, a cauldron of seething excitations" (1927/1964, p. 73). The conscious mind might find it inconsistent to love and hate the same person, but Freud believed that conflicting emotions could dwell side by side in the id. In the id, one can feel hatred for one's mother for failing to gratify immediately all of one's needs, while also feeling love for her.

The id follows what Freud termed the **pleasure principle.** It demands instant gratification of instincts without consideration of law, social custom, or the needs of others.

The **ego** begins to develop during the first year of life, largely because a child's demands for gratification cannot all be met immediately. The ego stands for reason and good sense, for rational ways of coping with frustration. It curbs the appetites of the id and makes plans that fit social conventions. Thus, a person can find gratification yet avoid social disapproval. The id informs you that you are hungry, but the ego decides to microwave enchiladas.

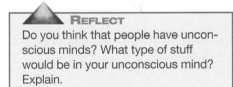

REFLECT
Do you think that people have unconscious minds? What type of stuff would be in your unconscious mind? Explain.

Conscious ▲ Self-aware.

Preconscious ▲ Capable of being brought into awareness by the focusing of attention.

Unconscious ▲ In psychodynamic theory, not available to awareness by simple focusing of attention.

Repression ▲ A defense mechanism that protects the person from anxiety by ejecting anxiety-evoking ideas and impulses from awareness.

Psychoanalysis ▲ In this usage, Freud's method of exploring human personality.

Resistance ▲ A blocking of thoughts whose awareness could cause anxiety.

Psychic structure ▲ In psychodynamic theory, a hypothesized mental structure that helps explain different aspects of behavior.

Id ▲ The psychic structure, present at birth, that represents physiological drives and is fully unconscious.

Pleasure principle ▲ The governing principle of the id—the seeking of immediate gratification of instinctive needs.

Ego ▲ The second psychic structure to develop, characterized by self-awareness, planning, and delay of gratification.

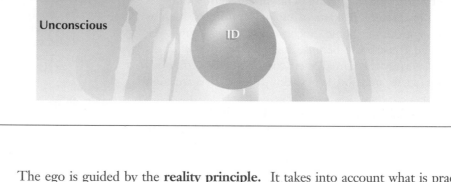

FIGURE 12.1   The Human Iceberg According to Freud.
According to psychodynamic theory, only the tip of human personality rises above the surface of the mind into conscious awareness. Material in the preconscious can become conscious if we direct our attention to it. Unconscious material tends to remain shrouded in mystery.

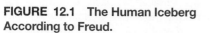

REFLECT
Freud chose the term *Id* because *id* is the Latin word meaning "it." Would it make a difference if we referred to "the id" simply as "it"? Explain.

Reality principle ▲ Consideration of what is practical and possible in gratifying needs; the governing principle of the ego.

Defense mechanism ▲ In psychodynamic theory, an unconscious function of the ego that protects it from anxiety-evoking material by preventing accurate recognition of this material.

Supergo ▲ The third psychic structure, which functions as a moral guardian and sets forth high standards for behavior.

Identification ▲ In psychodynamic theory, the unconscious assumption of the behavior of another person.

Moral principle ▲ The governing principle of the superego, which sets moral standards and enforces adherence to them.

Eros ▲ In psychodynamic theory, the basic instinct to preserve and perpetuate life.

Libido ▲ (1) In psychodynamic theory, the energy of Eros; the sexual instinct. (2) Generally, sexual interest or drive.

The ego is guided by the **reality principle.** It takes into account what is practical along with what is urged by the id. The ego also provides the person's conscious sense of self.

Although most of the ego is conscious, some of its business is carried out unconsciously. For instance, the ego also acts as a censor that screens the impulses of the id. When the ego senses that improper impulses are rising into awareness, it may use psychological defenses to prevent them from surfacing. Repression is one such psychological defense, or **defense mechanism.** Several defense mechanisms are described in Table 12.1.

The **superego** develops throughout early childhood, usually incorporating the moral standards and values of parents and important members of the community through **identification.** The superego functions according to the **moral principle.** The superego holds forth shining examples of an ideal self and also acts like the conscience, an internal moral guardian. Throughout life, the superego monitors the intentions of the ego and hands out judgments of right and wrong. It floods the ego with feelings of guilt and shame when the verdict is negative.

The ego hasn't an easy time of it. It stands between the id and the superego, striving to satisfy the demands of the id and the moral sense of the superego. From the Freudian perspective, a healthy personality has found ways to gratify most of the id's demands without seriously offending the superego. Most of the id's remaining demands are contained or repressed. If the ego is not a good problem solver or if the superego is too stern, the ego will have a hard time of it.

According to psychodynamic theory, identification is a means by which people usually incorporate the moral standards and values of parents and important members of the community. As we see in the "Psychology and Modern Life" feature on page 392, "important members of the community" can have a way of including athletic teams.

Stages of Psychosexual Development
Freud stirred controversy by arguing that sexual impulses are a central factor in personality development, even among children. Freud believed that sexual feelings are closely linked to children's basic ways of relating to the world, such as sucking on their mother's breasts and moving their bowels.

Freud believed that a major instinct, which he termed **eros,** is aimed at preserving and perpetuating life. Eros is fueled by psychological, or psychic, energy, which Freud labeled **libido.** Libidinal energy involves sexual impulses, so Freud considered it to be *psychosexual*. As the child develops, libidinal energy is expressed through sexual feelings in different parts of the body, or **eroge- nous zones.** To Freud, human development involves the transfer of libidinal energy from one erogenous zone to another. He hypothesized five periods of **psychosexual development:** oral, anal, phallic, latency, and genital.

During the first year of life a child experiences much of its world through the mouth. If it fits, into the mouth it goes. This is the **oral stage.** Freud argued that oral activities such as sucking and biting give the child sexual gratification as well as nourishment.

Freud believed that children encounter conflict during each stage of psychosexual development. During the oral stage, conflict centers on the nature and extent of oral gratification. Early weaning (cessation of breast feeding) could lead to frustration. Excessive gratification, on the other hand, could lead an infant to expect that it will routinely be given anything it wants. Insufficient or excessive gratification in any stage could lead to **fixation** in that stage and to the development of traits that are characteristic of that stage. Oral traits include dependency, gullibility, and excessive optimism or pessimism (depending on the child's experiences with gratification).

Freud theorized that adults with an *oral fixation* could experience exaggerated desires for "oral activities," such as smoking, overeating, alcohol abuse, and nail biting. Like the infant whose very survival depends on the mercy of an adult, adults with oral fixations may be disposed toward clinging, dependent relationships.

During the **anal stage** sexual gratification is attained through contraction and relaxation of the muscles that control elimination of waste products from the body. Elimination, which was controlled reflexively during most of the first year of life, comes under voluntary muscular control, even if such control is not reliable at first. The anal stage is said to begin in the second year of life.

During the anal stage children learn to delay the gratification that comes from eliminating as soon as they feel the urge. The general issue of self-control may become a source of conflict between parent and child. *Anal fixations* may stem from this conflict and lead to two sets of traits in adulthood. So-called *anal-retentive* traits involve excessive use of self-control. They include perfectionism, a strong need for order, and exaggerated neatness and cleanliness. *Anal-expulsive* traits, on the other hand, "let it all hang out." They include carelessness, messiness, even sadism.

Children enter the **phallic stage** during the third year of life. During this stage the major erogenous zone is the phallic region (the penis in boys, and the clitoris in girls). Parent-child conflict is likely to develop over masturbation, to which parents may respond with threats or punishment. During the phallic stage children may develop strong sexual attachments to the parent of the other gender and begin to view the parent of the same gender as a rival for the other parent's affections. Thus boys may want to marry Mommy and girls may want to marry Daddy.

Children have difficulty dealing with feelings of lust and jealousy. Home life would be tense indeed if they were aware of them. These feelings, therefore, remain unconscious, but their influence is felt through fantasies about marriage with the parent of the other gender and hostility toward the parent of the same gender. In boys, this conflict is labeled the **Oedipus complex,** after the legendary Greek king who unwittingly killed his father and married his mother. Similar feelings in girls give rise to the **Electra complex.**

TABLE 12.1   DEFENSE MECHANISMS

Defense Mechanism	Definition	Examples
Repression	Ejection of anxiety-evoking ideas from awareness.	• A student forgets that a difficult term paper is due. • A person in therapy forgets an appointment when anxiety-evoking material is to be discussed.
Regression	The return, under stress, to a form of behavior characteristic of an earlier stage of development.	• An adolescent cries when forbidden to use the family car. • An adult becomes highly dependent on his parents after the breakup of his marriage.
Rationalization	The use of self-deceiving justifications for unacceptable behavior.	• A student blames her cheating on her teacher's leaving the room during a test. • A man explains his cheating on his income tax by saying "Everyone does it."
Displacement	The transfer of ideas and impulses from threatening or unsuitable objects to less threatening objects.	• A worker picks a fight with her spouse after being sharply criticized by her supervisor.
Projection	The thrusting of one's own unacceptable impulses onto others so that others are assumed to have those impulses.	• A hostile person perceives the world as a dangerous place. • A sexually frustrated person interprets innocent gestures as sexual advances.
Reaction formation	Engaging in behavior that opposes one's genuine impulses in order to keep those impulses repressed.	• A person who is angry with a relative behaves in a "sickly sweet" manner toward that relative. • A sadistic individual becomes a physician.
Denial	The refusal to face the true nature of a threat.	• Belief that one will not contract cancer or heart disease even though one smokes heavily. • "It can't happen to me."
Sublimation	The channeling of primitive impulses into positive, constructive efforts.	• A person paints nudes for the sake of "beauty" and "art." • A hostile person becomes a tennis star.

▲ **REFLECT**

If you were fixated in a stage of psychosocial development, which stage would it be? Explain.

Erogenous zone ▲ An area of the body that is sensitive to sexual sensations.

Psychosexual development ▲ In psychodynamic theory, the process by which libidinal energy is expressed through different erogenous zones during different stages of development.

Oral stage ▲ The first stage of psychosexual development, during which gratification is hypothesized to be attained primarily through oral activities.

Fixation ▲ In psychodynamic theory, arrested development. Attachment to objects of an earlier stage.

Anal stage ▲ The second stage of psychosexual development, when gratification is attained through anal activities.

Phallic stage ▲ The third stage of psychosexual development, characterized by a shift of libido to the phallic region. (From the Greek *phallos,* referring to an image of the penis. However, Freud used the term *phallic* to refer both to boys and girls.)

Oedipus complex ▲ A conflict of the phallic stage in which the boy wishes to possess his mother sexually and perceives his father as a rival in love.

Electra complex ▲ A conflict of the phallic stage in which the girl longs for her father and resents her mother.

The Oral Stage?

According to Sigmund Freud, during the first year the child is in the oral stage of development. If it fits, into the mouth it goes. What, according to Freud, are the effects of insufficient or excessive gratification during the oral stage? Is there evidence to support his views?

According to Greek legend, Electra was the daughter of the king Agamemnon. She longed for him after his death and sought revenge against his slayers—her mother and her mother's lover.

The Oedipus and Electra complexes are resolved by about the ages of 5 or 6. Children then repress their hostilities toward the parent of the same gender and begin to identify with her or him. Identification leads them to play the social and gender roles of that parent and to internalize his or her values. Sexual feelings toward the parent of the other gender are repressed for a number of years. When the feelings emerge again during adolescence, they are **displaced,** or transferred, to socially appropriate members of the other gender.

Freud believed that by the age of 5 or 6, children have been in conflict with their parents over sexual feelings for several years. The pressures of the Oedipus and Electra complexes cause them to repress all sexual urges. In so doing, they enter a period of **latency** during which their sexual feelings remain unconscious. During the latency phase it is not uncommon for children to prefer playmates of their own gender.

Freud believed that we enter the final stage of psychosexual development, the **genital stage,** at puberty. Adolescent males again experience sexual urges toward their mother and adolescent females experience such urges toward their father. However, the **incest taboo** causes them to repress these impulses and displace them onto other adults or adolescents of the other gender. Boys might seek girls "just like the girl that married dear old Dad." Girls might be attracted to boys who resemble their fathers.

People in the genital stage prefer, by definition, to find sexual gratification through intercourse with a member of the other gender. In Freud's view, oral or anal stimulation, masturbation, and sexual activity with people of the same gender all represent *pregenital* fixations and immature forms of sexual conduct. They are not consistent with the life instinct, eros.

Psychology and Modern Life

Identifying With the Team—More Than Just a Game

Has life got you down? Do you feel isolated? Is life humdrum? Are you lost and lonely? If so, then rise up and . . . identify with a sports team! (A winning team, that is.) At least that seems to be one of the messages to be derived from research by personality, social, and sport psychologists.

There seems to be little question that people form deep and enduring bonds of attachment with sports teams. Once they identify with a team, their self-esteem can rise and fall with the teams wins and losses (Wann et al., 2000). Wins are connected with surges of testosterone in males (Bernhardt et al., 1998). Testosterone is connected with aggressiveness and self-confidence in males. But wins increase the optimism of both males and females, so that they feel they will be more effective at things as varied as hitting the bull's-eye in darts and getting a date.

Psychodynamic theory suggests that children identify with parents and other "big" people in their lives because big peo-

ple seem to hold the keys to the resources they need for sustenance and stimulation or excitement. Entertainers — the rich and famous — have their fan clubs, filled with people who tie their own lights to the brilliant suns of their stars.

Teams and sports heroes provide both entertainment and the kind of gutsy competition that evolutionary psychologists believe still whisper to us from our genes, pushing us toward aggression and ascendance. If we can't do it on our own, we can do it *through* someone else. In some kind of psychological sense, we can *be* someone who is more effective at climbing the heap of humankind into the sun. Evolutionary psychologists also connect adoration of sports heroes to a time when humans lived in tribes and their warrior-protectors were their true genetic representatives. Today, college and professional athletes may be very different from fans in a genetic sense, but fans maintain the capacity to identify with and worship their heroes, even if on

some level they recognize that it's sort of silly. "Our sports heroes are our warriors," notes Arizona State psychologist Robert Cialdini (2000), who has deeply studied fans' identification with athletes. "This is not some light diversion to be enjoyed for its inherent grace and harmony. The self is centrally involved in the outcome of the event. Whoever you root for represents you."

Yet sports fans do not seem to be alienated, introspective loners — people who would prefer to spend time in the wanderings of their minds than with others. Fans seem to be people who are seeking a sense of community — the "home team" becomes something of their psychological home. Today's community is often an impersonal megalopolis. The extended family today is often extended from coast to coast, and even get-togethers on holidays are often too far a reach. People today switch allegiances from job to job, neighborhood to neighborhood, city to city, and — half the time — spouse to spouse,

Other Psychodynamic Theorists

Several personality theorists are among Freud's intellectual heirs. Their theories, like his, include dynamic movement of psychological forces, conflict, and defense mechanisms. In other respects, their theories differ considerably. *Questions: Who are some other psychodynamic theorists? What are their views on personality?*

Carl Jung   Carl Jung (1875–1961) was a Swiss psychiatrist who had been a member of Freud's inner circle. He fell into disfavor with Freud when he developed his own psychodynamic theory—**analytical psychology.** In contrast to Freud (for whom, he said, "the brain is viewed as an appendage of the genital organs"), Jung downplayed the importance of the sexual instinct. He saw it as just one of several important instincts.

Jung, like Freud, was intrigued by unconscious processes. He believed that we not only have a *personal* unconscious that contains repressed memories and impulses but also an inherited **collective unconscious.** The collective unconscious contains primitive images, or **archetypes,** that reflect the history of our species. Examples of archetypes are the all-powerful God, the young hero, the fertile and nurturing mother, the wise old man, the hostile brother—even fairy godmothers, wicked witches, and themes of rebirth or resurrection. Archetypes themselves remain unconscious, but Jung declared that they influence our thoughts and emotions and cause us to respond to cultural themes in stories and films.

Alfred Adler   Alfred Adler (1870–1937), another follower of Freud, also felt that Freud had placed too much emphasis on sexual impulses. Adler believed that people are basically motivated by an **inferiority complex.** In some people, feelings of inferiority may be based on physical problems and the need to compensate for them. Adler believed, however, that all of us encounter some feelings of inferiority because of our small size as children, and that these feelings give rise to a **drive for superiority.** For instance, the

▲ **REFLECT**
At what age do you believe children should be toilet-trained? Why?

CLICK4™ *the C. G. Jung Page, with links to archives, events, and Jungian therapists.*

Displaced ▲ Transferred.
Latency ▲ A phase of psychosexual development characterized by repression of sexual impulses.
Genital stage ▲ The mature stage of psychosexual development, characterized by preferred expression of libido through intercourse with an adult of the other gender.
Incest taboo ▲ The cultural prohibition against marrying or having sexual relations with a close blood relative.
Analytical psychology ▲ Jung's psychodynamic theory, which emphasizes the collective unconscious and archetypes.
Collective unconscious ▲ Jung's hypothesized store of vague racial memories.
Archetypes ▲ Basic, primitive images or concepts hypothesized by Jung to reside in the collective unconscious.
Inferiority complex ▲ Feelings of inferiority hypothesized by Adler to serve as a central motivating force.
Drive for superiority ▲ Adler's term for the desire to compensate for feelings of inferiority.

but allegiances to the teams of one's childhood often remain intact, even when players are traded from team to team (Witt et al., 1999).

Some fans identify so strongly with their teams, that their commitment remains even if they relocate far from home, and even if the team goes into the tank for decades — like the long suffering fans of the Chicago Cubs. "It's the highly identified fans who demonstrate this fierce connection and feel elation and dejection along with the team," notes Cialdini (2000). Cialdini conducted classic research on identification in sports fans back in the 1970s.

Every fall, along with the swirling leaves, football mania sweeps across the campuses. From the ivied halls of Michigan, Notre Dame, and Ohio State to the palm trees of Arizona State and USC, "fans of championship teams gloat over their team's accomplishments and proclaim their affiliation with buttons on their clothes, bumper stickers on their cars, and banners on their

public buildings. Despite the fact that they have never caught a ball or thrown a block in support of their team's success, the tendency of such fans is to claim for themselves part of their team's glory. It is perhaps informative that the shout is always "We're number one!" never, "They're number one!'" (Cialdini et al., 1976).

In Cialdini's research, psychologists on several prominent football campuses surreptitiously observed their students on the Mondays following football games. On Mondays following victories, significantly higher percentages of students wore clothing with school insignias or mascots as compared with the percentages of students doing so on the Mondays following defeats.

The psychologists determined that the choice of clothing did not simply reflect students' liking their schools more following a victory. They asked students to describe the outcome of the weekend game. Surely enough, when their team won, students were likely to write "We won." But when

their team lost, the students more often described what happened in terms of "they" — that is, "They lost."

The ability to identify with teams can create such loyalty that the team comes to take precedence over family and friends. A relative of mine went to a Super Bowl game with his favorite team rather than be with his wife when she was delivering a child. New Yorker Michelle Musler became an avid Knicks fan after "My ex-husband ran away with the lady next door and I didn't seem to fit into suburbia anymore. The Knicks gave me a purpose, something to do, a place to go" (McKinley, 2000). Musler is a season ticket-holder and has missed only a handful of games since 1974. She has lost friends because invitations to weddings and graduations have conflicted with playoff games. But her sense of community with other fans, season ticket-holders, and team officials compensates: "What has happened through the years is that the Knicks have become my social life."

Karen Horney

She was drummed out of the New York Psychoanalytic Institute because she took issue with the way in which psychoanalytic theory portrayed women. Early in the century, psychoanalytic theory taught that a woman's place was in the home. Women who sought to compete with men in the business world were assumed to be suffering from unconscious penis envy. Psychoanalytic theory taught that little girls feel inferior to boys when they learn that boys have a penis and they do not. Karen Horney (1885–1952) argued that little girls do *not* feel inferior to boys, and that these views were founded on Western cultural prejudice, not scientific evidence.

Horney was born in Germany and emigrated to the United States before the outbreak of World War II. Trained in psychoanalysis, she agreed with Freud that childhood experiences are important factors in the development of adult personality. Like other neoanalysts, however, she asserted that unconscious sexual and aggressive impulses are less important than social relationships in children's development. She also believed that genuine and consistent love can alleviate the effects of even the most traumatic childhood.

www 12 L 5

CLICK4™ *the Web site of the International Karen Horney Society.*

English poet Lord Byron, who had a crippled leg, became a champion swimmer. As a child Adler was crippled by rickets and suffered from pneumonia, and it may be that his theory developed in part from his own childhood striving to overcome repeated bouts of illness.

Adler believed that self-awareness plays a major role in the formation of personality. He spoke of a **creative self,** a self-aware aspect of personality that strives to overcome obstacles and develop the individual's potential. Because each person's potential is unique, Adler's views have been termed **individual psychology.**

Erik Erikson   Erik Erikson (1902–1994) also believed that Freud had placed undue emphasis on sexual instincts. He asserted that social relationships are more crucial determinants of personality than sexual urges. To Erikson, the nature of the mother-infant relationship is more important than the details of the feeding process or the sexual feelings that might be stirred by contact with the mother. Erikson also argued that to a large extent we are the conscious architects of our own personalities. His view grants more powers to the ego than Freud did. In Erikson's theory, it is possible for us to make real choices. In Freud's theory, we may think that we are making choices but may actually be merely rationalizing the compromises forced upon us by internal conflicts.

Erikson, like Freud, is known for devising a comprehensive theory of personality development. But whereas Freud proposed stages of psycho*sexual* development, Erikson proposed stages of psycho*social* development. Rather than label stages for various erogenous zones, Erikson labeled them for the traits that might be developed during them (see Table 10.4). Each stage is named according to its possible outcomes. For example, the first stage of **psychosocial development** is labeled the stage of trust versus mistrust because of its two possible outcomes: (1) A warm, loving relationship with the mother (and others) during infancy might lead to a sense of basic trust in people and the world. (2) On the other hand, a cold, ungratifying relationship might generate a pervasive sense of mistrust. Erikson believed that most people would wind up with some blend of trust and mistrust—hopefully more trust than mistrust. A basic sense of mistrust could interfere with the formation of relationships unless it was recognized and challenged.

For Erikson, the goal of adolescence is the attainment of **ego identity,** not genital sexuality. The focus is on who we see ourselves as being and what we stand for, not on sexual interests.

Evaluation of the Psychodynamic Perspective

Psychodynamic theories have tremendous appeal. They involve many concepts and explain many varieties of human behavior and traits. ***Question: What are the strengths and weaknesses of the psychodynamic perspective?***

Although today concepts such as "the id" and "libido" strike many psychologists as unscientific, Freud fought for the idea that human personality and behavior are subject to scientific analysis. He developed his theories at a time when many people still viewed psychological problems as signs of possession by the devil or evil spirits, as they had during the Middle Ages. Freud argued that psychological disorders stem from problems within the individual—not evil spirits. His thinking contributed to the development of compassion for people with psychological disorders and methods for helping them.

Psychodynamic theory has also focused attention on the far-reaching effects of childhood events. Freud and other psychodynamic theorists are to be credited for suggesting that personality and behavior *develop* and that it is important for parents to be aware of the emotional needs of their children.

Freud has helped us recognize that sexual and aggressive urges are commonplace and that there is a difference between acknowledging these urges and acting on them. As

Creative self ▲ According to Adler, the self-aware aspect of personality that strives to achieve its full potential.

Individual psychology ▲ Adler's psychodynamic theory, which emphasizes feelings of inferiority and the creative self.

Psychosocial development ▲ Erikson's theory of personality and development, which emphasizes social relationships and eight stages of growth.

Ego identity ▲ A firm sense of who one is and what one stands for.

W. Bertram Wolfe put it, "Freud found sex an outcast in the outhouse, and left it in the living room an honored guest."

Freud also noted that people have defensive ways of looking at the world. His list of defense mechanisms has become part of everyday speech. Whether or not we attribute these cognitive distortions to unconscious ego functioning, our thinking may be distorted by our efforts to avert anxiety and guilt. Because defense mechanisms are unconscious, they have been difficult to assess and were rejected by academic psychologists in the 1950s and 1960s. However, the cognitive revolution of more recent years has again made them the subject of scientific investigation, and cognitive, developmental, and personality psychologists have found some evidence for their existence (Cramer, 2000; Somerfield & McCrae, 2000). This debate remains unresolved.

A number of critics note that "psychic structures" such as the id, ego, and superego are too vague to measure scientifically (Hergenhahn, 2000). Nor can they be used to predict behavior with precision. They are little more than useful fictions—poetic ways to express inner conflict. Freud's critics thus have the right to use other descriptive terms.

Nor have the stages of psychosexual development escaped criticism. Children begin to masturbate as early as the first year, not in the phallic stage. As parents know from discovering their children play "doctor," the latency stage is not as sexually latent as Freud believed. Much of Freud's thinking about the Oedipus and Electra complexes remains little more than speculation. The evidence for some of Erikson's developmental views seems somewhat sturdier. For example, people who fail to develop ego identity in adolescence seem to encounter problems developing intimate relationships later on.

Freud's method of gathering evidence from clinical sessions is also suspect (Hergenhahn, 2000). In subtle ways, therapists may influence clients to produce memories and feelings they expect to find. Therapists may also fail to separate what they are told from their own interpretations. Also, Freud and many other psychodynamic theorists restricted their evidence gathering to case studies with individuals who sought help for psychological problems. Their clients were also mostly European and European American and from the middle and upper classes. People who seek therapy are likely to have more problems than the general population.

> ▲ **REFLECT**
> If Freud's theory has so many scientific problems, why do you think it remains popular in the general population?

REVIEW

(1) Psychodynamic theories of personality teach that personality is characterized by _____ between primitive drives and laws, social rules, and moral codes. (2) According to Freud, the unconscious psychic structure called the _____ is present at birth and operates according to the pleasure principle. (3) The _____ is the sense of self and operates according to the reality principle. (4) The ego uses _____ mechanisms such as repression to protect itself from anxiety. (5) The _____ is the moral sense and develops by internalizing the standards of parents and others. (6) The stages of psychosexual development include the oral, _____, phallic, latency, and genital stages. (7) _____ in a stage may lead to the development of traits associated with the stage. (8) In the Oedipus and Electra complexes, children long to possess the parent of the (same or other?) gender and resent the parent of the same gender. (9) Jung believed that in addition to a personal unconscious mind, people also have a _____ unconscious. (10) Adler believed that people are motivated by an _____ complex. (11) Karen _____, like Freud, saw parent–child relationships as paramount in importance. (12) Erikson extended Freud's five developmental stages to (how many?).

CLICK4™ *Chapter 7 from Sigmund Freud's classic work,* Civilization and Its Discontents.

CLICK4™ *an essay assignment on the superego.*

CLICK4™ *the Alfred Adler Institute of San Francisco, featuring distance training in Adlerian therapy.*

Pulling It Together: What would Freud have to say about the extent to which we can know our personal histories and our true feelings?

THE TRAIT PERSPECTIVE

In most of us by the age of thirty, the character has set like plaster, and will never soften again.

—William James

The notion of **traits** is very familiar. If I asked you to describe yourself, you would probably do so in terms of traits such as bright, sophisticated, and witty. (That is you, is it not?) We also describe other people in terms of traits. *Question: What are traits?*

Traits are reasonably stable elements of personality that are inferred from behavior. If you describe a friend as "shy," it may be because you have observed social anxiety or withdrawal in that person's encounters with others. Traits are assumed to account for consistent behavior in diverse situations. You probably expect your "shy" friend to be retiring in most social confrontations—"all across the board," as the saying goes. The concept of traits is also found in other approaches to personality. Freud linked the development of certain traits to children's experiences in each stage of psychosexual development.

From Hippocrates to the Present

Question: What is the history of the trait perspective? The trait perspective dates back to the Greek physician Hippocrates (ca. 460–377 B.C.) and could be even older (Maher & Maher, 1994). It has generally been assumed that traits are embedded in people's bodies, but *how?* Hippocrates believed that traits are embedded in bodily fluids, which give rise to certain types of personalities. In his view, an individual's personality depends on the balance of four basic fluids, or "humors," in the body. Yellow bile is associated with a choleric (quick-tempered) disposition; blood with a sanguine (warm, cheerful) one; phlegm with a phlegmatic (sluggish, calm, cool) disposition; and black bile with a melancholic (gloomy, pensive) temperament. Disease was believed to reflect an imbalance among the humors. Methods such as bloodletting and vomiting were recommended to restore the balance (Maher & Maher, 1994). Although Hippocrates' theory was pure speculation, the terms *choleric, sanguine,* and so on are still used in descriptions of personality.

More enduring trait theories assume that traits are heritable and are embedded in the nervous system. They rely on the mathematical technique of factor analysis in attempting to determine which traits are basic.

Sir Francis Galton was among the first scientists to suggest that many of the world's languages use single words to describe fundamental differences in personality. More than 50 years ago, Gordon Allport and a colleague (Allport & Oddbert, 1936) catalogued some 18,000 human traits from a search through word lists like dictionaries. Some were physical traits such as *short, black,* and *brunette*. Others were behavioral traits such as *shy* and *emotional*. Still others were moral traits such as *honest*. This exhaustive list has served as the basis for personality research by many other psychologists. *Question: How have contemporary researchers used factor analysis to reduce the universe of traits to smaller lists of traits that show common features?*

Hans Eysenck

Psychologist Hans J. Eysenck (1916–1997) was born in Berlin but moved to England in 1934 to escape the Nazi threat. Ironically, he was not allowed to enter the British military to fight the Nazis during World War II because he was still a German citizen (Farley, 2000).

Eysenck developed the first English training program for clinical psychologists and focused much of his research on the relationships between two personality traits: **introversion-extraversion** and emotional stability-instability (Eysenck & Eysenck, 1985). (Emotional *in*stability is also known as **neuroticism**). Carl Jung was first to distinguish between introverts and extraverts. Eysenck added the dimension of emotional stability-instability to introversion-extraversion. He catalogued various personality traits according

---

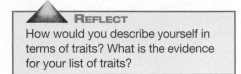

▲ REFLECT
How would you describe yourself in terms of traits? What is the evidence for your list of traits?

CLICK4™ *advice on finding a career that fits.*

CLICK4™ *an essay assignment on the trait perspective—how would you describe yourself?*

▲ REFLECT
Where would you place athletes and artists in terms of the dimensions of introversion-extraversion and emotional stability? Where would you place yourself?

Trait ▲ A relatively stable aspect of personality that is inferred from behavior and assumed to give rise to consistent behavior.
Introversion ▲ A trait characterized by intense imagination and the tendency to inhibit impulses.
Extraversion ▲ A trait characterized by tendencies to be socially outgoing and to express feelings and impulses freely.
Neuroticism ▲ Eysenck's term for emotional instability.

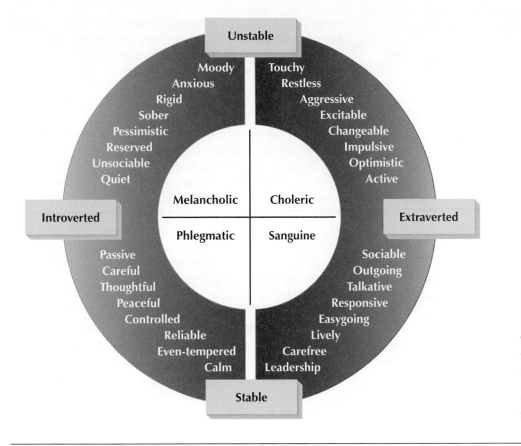

Unstable

Moody   Touchy
Anxious   Restless
Rigid   Aggressive
Sober   Excitable
Pessimistic   Changeable
Reserved   Impulsive
Unsociable   Optimistic
Quiet   Active

Melancholic | Choleric

Introverted   **Extraverted**

Phlegmatic | Sanguine

Passive   Sociable
Careful   Outgoing
Thoughtful   Talkative
Peaceful   Responsive
Controlled   Easygoing
Reliable   Lively
Even-tempered   Carefree
Calm   Leadership

Stable

FIGURE 12.2   Eysenck's Personality Dimensions and Hippocrates' Personality Types.
Various personality traits shown in the outer ring fall within the two major dimensions of personality suggested by Hans Eysenck. The inner circle shows how Hippocrates' four major personality types—choleric, sanguine, phlegmatic, and melancholic—fit within Eysenck's dimensions.

to where they are situated along these dimensions or factors (see Figure 12.2). For instance, an anxious person would be high in both introversion and neuroticism—that is, preoccupied with his or her own thoughts and emotionally unstable.

Eysenck noted that his scheme is reminiscent of that suggested by Hippocrates. According to Eysenck's dimensions, the choleric type would be extraverted and unstable; the sanguine type, extraverted and stable; the phlegmatic type, introverted and stable; and the melancholic type, introverted and unstable.

The Five-Factor Model

More recent research suggests that there may be five basic personality factors. These include the two found by Eysenck—extraversion and neuroticism—along with conscientiousness, agreeableness, and openness to experience (see Table 12.2). Many personality theorists, especially Robert McCrae and Paul T. Costa Jr., have played a role in the development of the five-factor model. Cross-cultural research has found that these five factors appear to define the personality structure of American, German, Portuguese, Hebrew, Chinese, Korean, and Japanese people (McCrae & Costa, 1997). A study of more than 5,000 German, British, Spanish, Czech, and Turkish people suggests that the factors are related to people's basic temperaments, which are considered to be largely inborn (McCrae et al., 2000). The researchers interpret the results to suggest that our personalities tend to mature rather than be shaped by environmental conditions, although the expression of personality traits is certainly affected by culture. (A person who is "basically" open to new experience is likely to behave less openly in a restrictive society than in an open society.)

The five-factor model—also known as the "Big Five" model—is hot right now. There are hundreds of studies correlating scores on the five factors, according to a psychological test constructed by Costa and McCrae (the *NEO Five-Factor Inventory*), with various behavior patterns, psychological disorders, and kinds of "personalities." Consider driving. Significant negative correlations have been found between the numbers of tickets people get and accidents people get into, on the one hand, and the factor of

REFLECT
Are you conscientious? Are you open to experience? Is there such as thing as being *too* conscientious? As being *too* open to experience? Explain.

CLICK4™ *a bulletin board discussion on the five-factor model of personality: Are five factors enough?*

TABLE 12.2 THE FIVE-FACTOR MODEL

Factor	Name	Traits
I	Extraversion	Contrasts talkativeness, assertiveness, and activity with silence, passivity, and reserve
II	Agreeableness	Contrasts kindness, trust, and warmth with hostility, selfishness, and distrust
III	Conscientiousness	Contrasts organization, thoroughness, and reliability with carelessness, negligence, and unreliability
IV	Neuroticism	Contrasts traits such as nervousness, moodiness, and sensitivity to negative stimuli with coping ability
V	Openness to Experience	Contrasts imagination, curiosity, and creativity with shallowness and lack of perceptiveness

www **12** **WS** **3**

CLICK4™ *a WebSearch activity on trait theory.*

Circular ▲ Descriptive of an explanation that restates its own concepts instead of offering additional information.

An Extraverted Individual.
Hans Eysenck based much of his research on the relationships between two personality traits: introversion–extraversion and emotional stability–instability. Extraversion is characterized by tendencies to be socially outgoing and to freely express feelings and impulses. Some people are mostly extraverted, others mostly introverted, and some are balanced—both outgoing (extraverted) and reflective (introverted).

Agreeableness on the other (Cellar et al., 2000). As we have long suspected, it's safer to share the freeway with agreeable people. People who are not judgmental—who will put up with your every whim, like puppy dogs—tend to score low on Conscientiousness (they don't examine you too closely) and high on Agreeableness (you can be yourself; that's cool) (Bernardin et al., 2000).

The five-factor model is being used in the realm of politics. For example, studies in the United States (Butler, 2000) and Belgium and Poland (van Hiel et al., 2000) show that people who are right-wing authoritarians ("Do it the way it's always been done! Why? Because I say so!") score low on Openness to experience ("Turn off that TV!" "Get off the Net now!" "There's no dancing in Beaumont!").

Researchers are also studying the way in which the five factors are connected with the ways in which people interact with their friends, lovers, and families (e.g., Wan et al., 2000; Wintre & Sugar, 2000). In the realm of psychological disorders, researchers are studying links between the factors and disorders such as anxiety disorders (Clark et al., 1994), hypochondriasis (Cox et al., 2000), depression and suicide attempts (Duberstein et al., 2000), schizophrenia (Gurrera et al., 2000), and personality disorders (Widiger & Costa, 1994). The five-factor model is apparently helping us describe these disorders. It remains to be seen how well the model will enable us to explain and predict them, and control them (that is, prevent them or come to the aid of people who develop them).

Evaluation of the Trait Perspective

Trait theories, like psychodynamic theories, have their pluses and minuses. **Question: What are the strengths and weaknesses of trait theory?** Trait theorists have focused much attention on the development of personality tests. They have also given rise to theories about the fit between personality and certain kinds of jobs (Holland, 1996). The qualities that suit a person for various kinds of work can be expressed in terms of abilities, personality traits, and interests. By using interviews and tests to learn about an individual's abilities and traits, testing and counseling centers can make valuable suggestions about that person's chances of success and fulfillment in various kinds of jobs.

One limitation of trait theory is that it has tended to be more descriptive than explanatory. It has historically focused on describing traits rather than on tracing their origins or finding out how they may be modified. Moreover, the "explanations" provided by trait theory are sometimes criticized as being **circular**. That is, they restate what is observed and do not explain it. Saying that John failed to ask Marsha on a date *because* of shyness is an example of a circular explanation: We have merely restated John's (shy) behavior as a trait (shyness). If asked to account for the shyness, it can be of little help to be told whether or not it is a "basic" trait, and suggesting that shyness is largely inborn does not quite explain *how* it is inborn or what we can do about it.

REVIEW

(13) _____ are personality elements that endure and account for behavioral consistency. (14) Eysenck used factor analysis to derive two basic traits: introversion–extraversion and emotional _____. (15) Five-factor theory suggests that there are five basic personality factors: introversion–extraversion, emotional stability, _____, agreeableness, and openness to experience.

Pulling It Together: How has trait theory changed since the time of Hippocrates?

LEARNING-THEORY PERSPECTIVES

Learning theory not only contributes to our understanding of the acquisition of behavior. It also contributes to our understanding of personality. ***Question: What does learning theory have to contribute to our understanding of personality?*** In this section we focus on the contributions of two learning-theory approaches to personality: behaviorism and social-cognitive theory.

Behaviorism

> *You have freedom when you're easy in your harness.*
>
> —*Robert Frost*

In 1924, at Johns Hopkins University, John B. Watson raised the battle cry of the behaviorist movement:

> Give me a dozen healthy infants, well-formed, and my own specified world to bring them up in and I'll guarantee to take any one at random and train him to become any type of specialist I might suggest—doctor, lawyer, merchant-chief and, yes, even beggar-man and thief, regardless of his talents, penchants, tendencies, abilities, vocations, and the race of his ancestors. (p. 82)

Question: What is Watson's contribution to personality theory? Watson's view is extreme and inconsistent with the thrust of evidence concerning the heritability of various personality traits. But his proclamation underscores the behaviorist view that personality is plastic—that situational variables or environmental influences, not internal, individual variables, are the key shapers of human preferences and behaviors. In contrast to the psychoanalysts and structuralists of his day, Watson argued that unseen, undetectable mental structures must be rejected in favor of that which can be seen and measured.

In the 1930s Watson's battle cry was taken up by B. F. Skinner, who agreed that psychologists should avoid trying to see into the "black box" of the organism and instead emphasized the effects that reinforcements have on behavior.

The views of Watson and Skinner largely ignored the notions of personal freedom, choice, and self-direction. Most of us assume that our wants originate within us. But Skinner suggested that environmental influences such as parental approval and social custom shape us into *wanting* certain things and *not wanting* others.

Question: How did Skinner develop Watson's views? In his novel *Walden Two*, Skinner (1948) described a Utopian society in which people are happy and content because they are allowed to do as they please. However, from early childhood, they have been trained or conditioned to be cooperative. Because of their reinforcement histories, they *want* to behave in decent, kind, and unselfish ways. They see themselves as free because society makes no effort to force them to behave in particular ways.

Some object to behaviorist notions because they play down the importance of consciousness and choice. Others argue that humans are not blindly ruled by pleasure and pain. In some circumstances people have rebelled against the so-called necessity of survival by choosing pain and hardship over pleasure, or death over life. Many people have sacrificed their own lives to save those of others.

The behaviorist defense might be that the apparent choice of pain or death is forced on altruistic individuals just as conformity to social custom is forced on others. The altruist is also shaped by external influences, even if those influences differ from those that affect many other people.

Social-Cognitive Theory

Social-cognitive theory[1] is a contemporary view of learning developed by Albert Bandura (1986, 1999) and other psychologists (e.g., Mischel & Shoda, 1995). It focuses on

---

[1] The name of this theory is in flux. It was formerly referred to as social-learning theory. Today it is also sometimes referred to as *cognitive social theory* (Miller et al., 1996).

www 12 WS 1
CLICK4™ *a WebSearch activity on personality—is it stable?*

> ▲ **REFLECT**
> Given cultural and social conditioning, is true freedom possible? To behaviorists, even our telling ourselves that we have free will is determined by the environment. Is free will merely an illusion? Explain your point of view.

Social-cognitive theory ▲ A cognitively oriented learning theory in which observational learning and person variables such as values and expectancies play major roles in individual differences.

the importance of learning by observation and on the cognitive processes that underlie individual differences. ***Question: How does social-cognitive theory differ from the behaviorist view?*** Social-cognitive theorists differ from behaviorists in that they see people as influencing their environment just as their environment influences them. Bandura terms this mutual pattern of influence **reciprocal determinism.** Social-cognitive theorists agree with behaviorists and other empirical psychologists that discussions of human nature should be tied to observable experiences and behaviors. They assert, however, that variables within people—which they call **person variables**—must also be considered if we are to understand them.

One goal of psychological theories is the prediction of behavior. We cannot predict behavior from situational variables alone. Whether a person will behave in a certain way also depends on the person's **expectancies** about the outcomes of that behavior and the perceived or **subjective values** of those outcomes.

To social-cognitive theorists, people are not simply at the mercy of the environment. Instead, they are self-aware and purposefully engage in learning. They seek to learn about their environment and to alter it in order to make reinforcers available.

Observational Learning

Observational learning (also termed **modeling** or *cognitive learning*) refers to acquiring knowledge by observing others. For operant conditioning to occur, an organism (1) must engage in a response, and (2) that response must be reinforced. But observational learning occurs even when the learner does not perform the observed behavior. Therefore, direct reinforcement is not required either. Observing others extends to reading about them or seeing what they do and what happens to them in books, TV, radio, and film.

Our expectations stem from our observations of what happens to ourselves and other people. For example, teachers are more likely to call on males and more accepting of "calling out" in class by males than by females (Sadker & Sadker, 1994). As a result, many males expect to be rewarded for calling out. Females, however, may learn that they will be reprimanded for behaving in what some might term an "unladylike" manner.

Social-cognitive theorists believe that behavior reflects person variables and situational variables. Person variables include competencies, encoding strategies, expectancies, emotions, and self-regulatory systems and plans (Mischel & Shoda, 1995; see Figure 12.3).

Competencies: What Can You Do?

Competencies include knowledge of rules that guide conduct, concepts about ourselves and other people, and skills. Our ability to use information to make plans depends on our competencies. Knowledge of the physical world and of cultural codes of conduct are important competencies. So are academic skills such as reading and writing, athletic skills such as swimming and tossing a football, social skills such as knowing how to ask someone out on a date, and many others. Individual differences in competencies reflect genetic variation, learning opportunities, and other environmental factors. People do not perform well at given tasks unless they have the competencies needed to do so.

Encoding Strategies: How Do You See It?

Different people **encode** (symbolize or represent) the same stimuli in different ways. Their encoding strategies are an important factor in their behavior. One person might encode a tennis game as a chance to bat the ball back and forth and have some fun. Another person might encode the game as a demand to perfect his or her serve. One person might encode a date that doesn't work out as a sign of her or his social incompetence. Another person might encode the date as reflecting the fact that people are not always "made for each other."

Some people make themselves miserable by encoding events in self-defeating ways. A linebacker may encode an average day on the field as a failure because he didn't make any sacks. Cognitive therapists foster adjustment by challenging people to view life in more optimistic ways.

Expectancies: What Will Happen?

There are various kinds of expectancies. Some are predictions about what will follow various stimuli or signs. For example, some

CLICK4™ *a bulletin board discussion on gender and ethnic differences in personality development.*

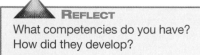
REFLECT
What competencies do you have? How did they develop?

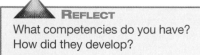
REFLECT
Do you expect that you will succeed? Do you believe in your abilities? How do your attitudes toward yourself affect your self-esteem and your behavior?

Reciprocal determinism ▲ Bandura's term for the social-cognitive view that people influence their environment just as their environment influences them.

Person variables ▲ Factors within the person, such as expectancies and competencies, that influence behavior.

Expectancies ▲ Personal predictions about the outcomes of potential behaviors.

Subjective value ▲ The desirability of an object or event.

Model ▲ In social-cognitive theory, an organism that exhibits behaviors that others will imitate or acquire through observational learning.

Competencies ▲ Knowledge and skills.

Encode ▲ Interpret; transform.

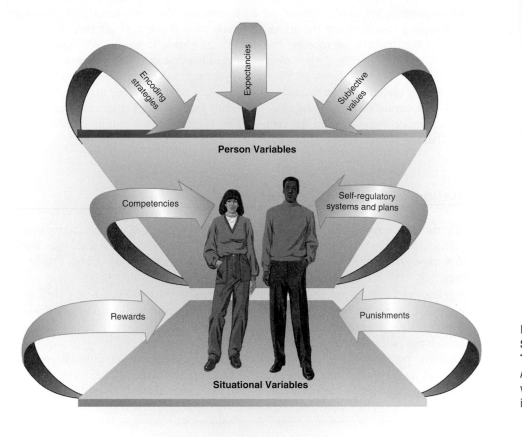

FIGURE 12.3 Person Variables and Situational Variables in Social-Cognitive Theory.
According to social-cognitive theory, person variables and situational variables interact to influence behavior.

people predict other people's behavior on the basis of signs such as "tight lips" or "shifty eyes" (Ross & Nisbett, 1991). Other expectancies involve what will happen if we engage in certain behaviors. **Self-efficacy expectations** are beliefs that we can accomplish certain things, such as speaking before a group, doing a backflip into a swimming pool, or solving math problems (Bandura, 1997).

Competencies influence expectancies. Expectancies, in turn, influence motivation to perform. People with positive self-efficacy expectations have higher self-esteem (Sanna & Meier, 2000) and are more likely to try difficult tasks than people who do not believe that they can master those tasks. Lack of belief in self-efficacy is often associated with depression and hopelessness (Bandura et al., 1999). One way that psychotherapy helps people is by changing their self-efficacy expectations from "I can't" to "I can" (Bandura, 1999). As a result, people are motivated to try new things.

Emotions: How Does It Feel?   Because of our different learning histories, similar situations can arouse different feelings in us—anxiety, depression, fear, hopelessness, and anger. What frightens one person may entice another. What bores one person may excite another. From the social-cognitive perspective, in contrast to the behaviorist perspective, we are not controlled by stimuli. Instead, stimuli arouse feelings in us, and feelings influence our behavior. Hearing Chopin may make one person weep and another person switch to a rock 'n' roll station.

Self-Regulatory Systems and Plans: How Can You Achieve It?   We tend to regulate our own behavior, even in the absence of observers and external constraints. We set our own goals and standards. We make plans to achieve them. We congratulate or criticize ourselves, depending on whether or not we achieve them (Bandura, 1999).

CLICK4™ *a WebSearch activity on the learning theory perspective: Do you expect to succeed?*

▲ **REFLECT**
How do you regulate your own behavior to help achieve your goals? Can you think of examples at home, at work, or in school?

Self-efficacy expectations ▲ Beliefs to the effect that one can handle a task.

How Do Competencies Contribute to Performance?

What factors contribute to this girl's performance? Individual differences in competencies stem from variations in genetic endowment, nutrition, and learning opportunities.

Self-regulation helps us influence our environments. We can select the situations to which we expose ourselves and the arenas in which we will compete. Depending on our expectancies, we may choose to enter the academic or athletic worlds. We may choose marriage or the single life. And when we cannot readily select our environment, we can to some degree select our responses within an environment—even an aversive one. For example, if we are undergoing an uncomfortable medical procedure, we may try to reduce the stress by focusing on something else—an inner fantasy or an environmental feature such as the cracks in the tiles on the ceiling. This is one of the techniques used in prepared or "natural" childbirth.

Evaluation of the Learning Perspective

Learning theorists have made monumental contributions to the scientific understanding of behavior, but they have left some psychologists dissatisfied. ***Question: What are the strengths and weaknesses of learning theories as they apply to personality?***

Psychodynamic theorists and trait theorists propose the existence of psychological structures that cannot be seen and measured directly. Learning theorists—particularly behaviorists—have dramatized the importance of referring to publicly observable variables, or behaviors, if psychology is to be accepted as a science.

Similarly, psychodynamic theorists and trait theorists focus on internal variables such as unconscious conflict and traits to explain and predict behavior. Learning theorists emphasize the importance of environmental conditions, or situational variables, as determinants of behavior. They have also elaborated on the conditions that foster learning—even automatic kinds of learning. They have shown that we can learn to do things because of reinforcements and that many behavior patterns are acquired by observing others.

On the other hand, behaviorism is limited in its ability to explain personality. Behaviorism does not describe, explain, or even suggest the richness of inner human experience. We experience thoughts and feelings and browse through our complex inner maps of the world, but behaviorism does not deal with these. To be fair, the so-called limitations of behaviorism are self-imposed. Personality theorists have traditionally dealt with thoughts, feelings, and behavior, whereas behaviorism, which insists on studying only that which is observable and measurable, deals with behavior alone.

Critics of social-cognitive theory cannot accuse its supporters of denying the importance of cognitive activity and feelings. But they often contend that social-cognitive theory has not come up with satisfying statements about the development of traits or accounted for self-awareness. Also, social-cognitive theory—like its intellectual forebear, behaviorism—may not pay enough attention to genetic variation in explaining individual differences in behavior. Learning theories have done very little to account for the development of traits or personality types.

REVIEW

CLICK4™ *a quiz covering the first half of this chapter.*

(16) The behaviorists John B. Watson and B. F. _____ argued that environmental contingencies shape people into wanting to do the things that are required of them. (17) _____-cognitive theory argues that people can shape the environment and learn by intention. (18) Social-cognitive theorists believe that we must consider situational and _____ variables to predict behavior. (19) _____ variables include competencies, which refer to knowledge and skills; encoding strategies; expectancies; emotions; and self-regulatory systems and plans.

Pulling It Together: In what ways do behaviorism and social-cognitive theory differ in their views of people and personal freedom?

Will You Be a Hit or a Miss? The Expectancy for Success Scale

Life is filled with opportunities and obstacles. What happens when you are faced with a difficult challenge? Do you rise to meet it, or do you back off? Social-cognitive theorists note that our self-efficacy expectancies influence our behavior. When we believe that we are capable of succeeding through our own efforts, we marshal our resources and apply ourselves.

The following scale, created by Fibel and Hale (1978), can give you insight as to whether you believe that your own efforts are likely to meet with success. You can compare your own expectancies for success with those of other undergraduates taking psychology courses by turning to the scoring key in the appendix.

Directions: Indicate the degree to which each item applies to you by circling the appropriate number, according to this key:

1 = highly improbable
2 = improbable
3 = equally improbable and probable, not sure
4 = probable
5 = highly probable

IN THE FUTURE I EXPECT THAT I WILL:

1. Find that people don't seem to understand what I'm trying to say   1 2 3 4 5

2. Be discouraged about my ability to gain the respect of others   1 2 3 4 5

3. Be a good parent   1 2 3 4 5

4. Be unable to accomplish my goals   1 2 3 4 5

5. Have a stressful marital relationship   1 2 3 4 5

6. Deal poorly with emergency situations   1 2 3 4 5

7. Find my efforts to change situations I don't like are ineffective   1 2 3 4 5

8. Not be very good at learning new skills   1 2 3 4 5

9. Carry through my responsibilities successfully   1 2 3 4 5

10. Discover that the good in life outweighs the bad   1 2 3 4 5

11. Handle unexpected problems successfully   1 2 3 4 5

12. Get the promotions I deserve   1 2 3 4 5

13. Succeed in the projects I undertake   1 2 3 4 5

14. Not make any significant contributions to society   1 2 3 4 5

15. Discover that my life is not getting much better   1 2 3 4 5

16. Be listened to when I speak   1 2 3 4 5

17. Discover that my plans don't work out too well   1 2 3 4 5

18. Find that no matter how hard I try, things just don't turn out the way I would like   1 2 3 4 5

19. Handle myself well in whatever situation I'm in   1 2 3 4 5

20. Be able to solve my own problems   1 2 3 4 5

21. Succeed at most things I try   1 2 3 4 5

22. Be successful in my endeavors in the long run   1 2 3 4 5

23. Be very successful working out my personal life   1 2 3 4 5

24. Experience many failures in my life   1 2 3 4 5

25. Make a good first impression on people I meet for the first time   1 2 3 4 5

26. Attain the career goals I have set for myself   1 2 3 4 5

27. Have difficulty dealing with my superiors   1 2 3 4 5

28. Have problems working with others   1 2 3 4 5

29. Be a good judge of what it takes to get ahead   1 2 3 4 5

30. Achieve recognition in my profession   1 2 3 4 5

NOTE: Reprinted with permission from Fibel and Hale, 1978, p. 931.

CLICK4™ *the interactive version of this Self-Assessment.*

THE HUMANISTIC-EXISTENTIAL PERSPECTIVE

You are unique, and if that is not fulfilled, then something has been lost.
—Martha Graham

Humanists and existentialists dwell on the meaning of life. Self-awareness is the hub of the humanistic-existential search for meaning. ***Questions: What is humanism? What is existentialism?***

The term **humanism** has a long history and many meanings. It became a third force in American psychology in the 1950s and 1960s, partly in response to the predominant psychodynamic and behavioral models. Humanism puts people and self-awareness at the

> ▲ **REFLECT**
> Do you know anyone who seems to be alienated? How is the person alienated? What do you think led to feelings of alienation?

Humanism ▲ The view that people are capable of free choice, self-fulfillment, and ethical behavior.

center of consideration and argues that they are capable of free choice, self-fulfillment, and ethical behavior. Humanism also represented a reaction to the "rat race" spawned by industrialization and automation. Humanists felt that work on assembly lines produced "alienation" from inner sources of meaning. The humanistic views of Abraham Maslow and Carl Rogers emerged from these concerns.

Existentialism in part reflects the horrors of mass destruction of human life through war and genocide, frequent events in the 20th century. The European existentialist philosophers Jean-Paul Sartre and Martin Heidegger saw human life as trivial in the grand scheme of things. But psychiatrists like Viktor Frankl, Ludwig Binswanger, and Medard Boss argued that seeing human existence as meaningless could give rise to withdrawal and apathy—even suicide. Psychological salvation therefore requires giving personal meaning to things and making personal choices. Yes, there is pain in life, and yes, sooner or later life ends, but people can see the world for what it is and make genuine choices.

Freud argued that defense mechanisms prevent us from seeing the world as it is. Therefore, the concept of free choice is meaningless. Behaviorists view freedom as an illusion determined by social forces. Social-cognitive theorists also speak of external or situational forces that influence us. To existentialists, we are really and painfully free to do what we choose with our lives. Moreover, the meaning of our lives is the meaning that we give to our lives.

Abraham Maslow and the Challenge of Self-Actualization

Humanists see Freud as preoccupied with the "basement" of the human condition. Freud wrote that people are basically motivated to gratify biological drives and that their perceptions are distorted by their psychological needs. *Question: How do humanistic psychologists differ from psychodynamic theorists?* The humanistic psychologist Abraham Maslow argued that people also have a conscious need for **self-actualization**— to become all that they can be—and that people can see the world as it is. Because people are unique, they must follow unique paths to self-actualization. People are not at the mercy of unconscious, primitive impulses. Rather, one of the main threats to individual personality development is control by other people. We must each be free to get in touch with and actualize our selves. But self-actualization requires taking risks. Many people prefer to adhere to the tried and . . . what may be untrue for them. But people who adhere to the "tried and true" may find their lives degenerating into monotony and predictability.

Let us learn more about the nature of the self by examining Carl Rogers's self theory. Rogers offers insights into the ways in which the self develops—or fails to develop— in the real social world.

Carl Rogers's Self Theory

The humanistic psychologist Carl Rogers (1902–1987) wrote that people shape themselves—their selves—through free choice and action. *Questions: Just what is your self? What is self theory?*

Rogers defined the *self* as the center of experience. Your self is your ongoing sense of who and what you are, your sense of how and why you react to the environment and how you choose to act on the environment. Your choices are made on the basis of your values, and your values are also part of your self. Rogers's self theory focuses on the nature of the self and the conditions that allow the self to develop freely. Two of his major concerns are the self-concept and self-esteem.

The Self-Concept and Frames of Reference
Our self-concepts consist of our impressions of ourselves and our evaluations of our adequacy. It may be helpful to think of us as rating ourselves according to various scales or dimensions such as good–bad, intelligent–unintelligent, strong–weak, and tall–short.

Rogers believed that we all have unique ways of looking at ourselves and the world—that is, unique **frames of reference.** It may be that we each use a different set of

www 12 BBC 4
CLICK4™ *a bulletin board discussion on free will: Is it merely an illusion?*

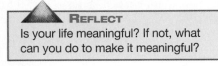
▲ **REFLECT**
Is your life meaningful? If not, what can you do to make it meaningful?

www 12 PS 15
CLICK4™ *the classic article by Carl Rogers, "A Therapist's View of the Good Life: The Fully Functioning Person."*

▲ **REFLECT**
How is your own frame of reference unique? Think of some things that are unique about you. (Yes — you can!)

Existentialism ▲ The view that people are completely free and responsible for their own behavior.
Self-actualization ▲ In humanistic theory, the innate tendency to strive to realize one's potential.
Frame of reference ▲ One's unique patterning of perceptions and attitudes according to which one evaluates events.

Do You Strive to Be All That You Can Be?

Are you a self-actualizer? Do you strive to be all that you can be? Psychologist Abraham Maslow attributed the following eight characteristics to the self-actualizing individual. How many of them describe you? Why not check them and undertake some self-evaluation? (There are no norms for this Self-Assessment. Just read the items and do some thinking.)

YES NO

____ ____ 1. *Do you fully experience life in the present—the here and now?* (Self-actualizers do not focus excessively on the lost past or wish their lives away as they stride toward distant goals.)

____ ____ 2. *Do you make growth choices rather than fear choices?* (Self-actualizers take reasonable risks to develop their unique potentials. They do not bask in the dull life of the status quo. They do not "settle.")

____ ____ 3. *Do you seek to acquire self-knowledge?* (Self-actualizers look inward. They search for values, talents, and meaningfulness. It might be enlightening to take an interest inventory—a test frequently used to help make career decisions—at your college testing and counseling center.)

____ ____ 4. *Do you strive toward honesty in interpersonal relationships?* (Self-actualizers strip away the social facades and games that stand in the way of self-disclosure and the formation of intimate relationships.)

____ ____ 5. *Do you behave self-assertively and express your own ideas and feelings, even at the risk of occasional social disapproval?* (Self-actualizers do not bottle up their feelings for the sake of avoiding social disapproval.)

____ ____ 6. *Do you strive toward new goals? Do you strive to be the best that you can be in a chosen life role?* (Self-actualizers do not live by the memory of past accomplishments. Nor do they present second-rate efforts.)

____ ____ 7. *Do you seek meaningful and rewarding life activities?* Do you experience moments of actualization that humanistic psychologists call *peak experiences?* (Peak experiences are brief moments of rapture filled with personal meaning. Examples might include completing a work of art, falling in love, redesigning a machine tool, suddenly solving a complex problem in math or physics, or having a baby. Note that we differ as individuals; one person's peak experience might bore another person silly.)

____ ____ 8. *Do you remain open to new experiences?* (Self-actualizers do not hold themselves back for fear that novel experiences might shake their views of the world, or of right and wrong. Self-actualizers are willing to revise their expectations, values, and opinions.)

dimensions in defining ourselves and that we judge ourselves according to different sets of values. To one person, achievement–failure may be the most important dimension. To another person, the most important dimension may be decency–indecency. A third person may not even think in terms of decency.

Self-Esteem and Positive Regard

Rogers assumed that we all develop a need for self-regard, or self-esteem, as we develop and become aware of ourselves. At first, self-esteem reflects the esteem in which others hold us. Parents help children develop self-esteem when they show them **unconditional positive regard**—that is, when they accept them as having intrinsic merit regardless of their behavior at the moment. But when parents show children **conditional positive regard**—that is, when they accept them only when they behave in a desired manner—children may develop **conditions of worth.** That is, they may come to think that they have merit only if they behave as their parents wish them to behave.

Because each individual is thought to have a unique potential, children who develop conditions of worth must be somewhat disappointed in themselves. We cannot fully live up to the wishes of others and remain true to ourselves. This does not mean that the expression of the self inevitably leads to conflict. Rogers was optimistic about human nature. He believed that we hurt others or act in antisocial ways only when we are frustrated

> **◢ REFLECT**
> Were you shown unconditional or conditional positive regard as a child? What were the effects on you?

Unconditional positive regard ▲ A persistent expression of esteem for the value of a person, but not necessarily an unqualified acceptance of all of the person's behaviors.

Conditional positive regard ▲ Judgment of another person's value on the basis of the acceptability of that person's behaviors.

Conditions of worth ▲ Standards by which the value of a person is judged.

Unique.
According to humanistic psychologists like Carl Rogers, each of us views the world from a unique frame of reference. What matters to one person may mean little to another.

in our efforts to develop our potential. But when parents and others are loving and tolerant of our differentness, we, too, are loving—even if some of our preferences, abilities, and values differ from those of our parents.

However, children in some families learn that it is bad to have ideas of their own, especially about sexual, political, or religious matters. When they perceive their caregivers' disapproval, they may come to see themselves as rebels and label their feelings as selfish, wrong, or evil. If they wish to retain a consistent self-concept and self-esteem, they may have to deny many of their feelings or disown aspects of themselves. In this way the self-concept becomes distorted. According to Rogers, anxiety often stems from recognition that people have feelings and desires that are inconsistent with their distorted self-concept. Since anxiety is unpleasant, people may deny the existence of their genuine feelings and desires.

According to Rogers, the path to self-actualization requires getting in touch with our genuine feelings, accepting them, and acting on them. This is the goal of Rogers's method of psychotherapy, *client-centered therapy*.

Rogers also believed that we have mental images of what we are capable of becoming. These are termed **self-ideals.** We are motivated to reduce the discrepancy between our self-concepts and our self-ideals.

According to humanistic-existential theory, self-esteem is central to our sense of well-being. Self-esteem helps us develop our potential as unique individuals. It may originate in childhood and reflect the esteem others have for us. Nevertheless, as we see in the nearby "Psychology and Modern Life" feature, there are many things you can do—here and now—to raise your own self-esteem.

Evaluation of the Humanistic-Existential Perspective

Question: What are the strengths and weaknesses of humanistic-existential theory?

Humanistic-existential theories have tremendous appeal for college students because of their focus on the importance of personal experience. We tend to treasure our conscious experiences (our "selves") and those of the people we care about. For lower organisms, to be alive is to move, to process food, to exchange oxygen and carbon dioxide, and to reproduce. But for human beings, an essential aspect of life is conscious experience—the sense of oneself as progressing through space and time.

Psychodynamic theories see individuals largely as victims of their childhood. Learning theories, to some degree, see people as "victims of circumstances"—or at least as victims of situational variables. But humanistic-existential theorists see humans as free to make choices. Psychodynamic theorists and learning theorists wonder whether our sense of freedom is merely an illusion. Humanistic-existential theorists, in contrast, begin by assuming personal freedom.

Ironically, the primary strength of the humanistic-existential approaches—their focus on conscious experience—is also their main weakness. Conscious experience is private and subjective. Therefore, the validity of formulating theories in terms of consciousness has been questioned. On the other hand, some psychologists (e.g., Bevan & Kessel, 1994) believe that the science of psychology can afford to loosen its methods somewhat if this will help it address the richness of human experience.

Self-actualization, like trait theory, yields circular explanations for behavior. When we see someone engaging in what seems to be positive striving, we gain little insight by attributing this behavior to a self-actualizing force. We have done nothing to account for the origins of the force. And when we observe someone who is not engaging in growth-oriented striving, it seems arbitrary to "explain" this outcome by suggesting that the self-actualizing tendency has been blocked or frustrated.

Humanistic-existential theories, like learning theories, have little to say about the development of traits and personality types. They assume that we are all unique, but they do not predict the sorts of traits, abilities, and interests we will develop.

CLICK4™ *more information about self-esteem and its relation to aggression.*

CLICK4™ *an interactive Self-Assessment, "Are You One of Your Favorite People?"*

Self-ideal ▲ A mental image of what we believe we ought to be.

REVIEW

(20) The humanistic view argues that people (are or are not?) capable of free choice and self-fulfillment. (21) _____ assert that our lives have the meaning we give to them. (22) Maslow argued that people have growth-oriented needs for self-_____. (23) Rogers's theory begins with the assumption of the existence of the _____. (24) We see the world through unique frames of _____.

Pulling It Together: Under what conditions does the self achieve optimal development?

DIVERSITY PERSONALITY AND DIVERSITY: THE SOCIOCULTURAL PERSPECTIVE

Thirteen-year-old Hannah brought her lunch tray to the table in the cafeteria. Her mother, Julie, eyed with horror the french fries, the plate of mashed potatoes in gravy, the bag of potato chips, and the large paper cup brimming with soda. "You can't eat that!" she said. "It's garbage!"

"Oh come on, Mom! Chill, okay?" Hannah rejoined before taking her tray to sit with some friends rather than with us.

I used to spend Saturdays with my children at the Manhattan School of Music. Not only did they study voice and piano, they—and I—widened our cultural perspective by relating to families and students from all parts of the world.

Julie and Hannah are Korean Americans. Flustered, Julie shook her head and said, "I've now been in the United States longer than I was in Korea, and I still can't get used to the way children act here." Dimitri, a Russian American parent, chimed in. "I never

www 12 E 3

CLICK4™ *an essay assignment on enhancing self-esteem.*

Psychology and Modern Life

Enhancing Self-Esteem

No one can make you feel inferior without your consent.

—**Eleanor Roosevelt**

There are many things you can do to enhance your self-esteem. Broadly speaking, they involve changing the things you can change and having the wisdom to accept those you cannot change.

Improve Yourself   For example, are you miserable because of excess dependence on another person? Perhaps you can enhance your social skills or your vocational skills in an effort to become more independent. Are you too heavy? Perhaps you can follow some of the suggestions for losing weight, presented in Chapter 9.

Challenge the Realism of Your Ideal Self Our internal list of "oughts" and "shoulds" can create perfectionistic standards. We constantly fall short of these standards and experience frustration. Challenge your perfectionistic demands on yourself and, when

appropriate, revise them. It may be harmful to abolish worthy and realistic goals, even if we do have trouble measuring up now and then. However, some of our goals or values may not stand up to scrutiny. It is useful to consider them objectively.

Substitute Realistic Goals for Unattainable Goals   Perhaps we will never be as artistic, as tall, or as graceful as we would like to be. We can work to enhance our drawing skills, but if it becomes clear that we will not become Michelangelos, perhaps we can enjoy our scribblings for what they are and also find satisfaction elsewhere. We cannot make ourselves taller (except by wearing elevator shoes or high heels), but we can take off five pounds and cut our time for running the mile by a few seconds. We can also learn to whip up a great fettuccine Alfredo.

Build Self-Efficacy Expectations   Our self-efficacy expectations define the degree to which we believe that our efforts will bring about a positive outcome. They affect

our willingness to take on challenges and persist in efforts to meet them. We can build self-efficacy expectations by selecting tasks that are consistent with our interests and abilities and then working at those tasks. Psychologists have devised many tests to help people focus in on their interests and abilities. They are probably available at your college testing and counseling center. But we can also build self-efficacy expectations by working at athletics or hobbies or charitable causes.

Realistic self-assessment, realistic goals, and a reasonable schedule for improvement are the keys to building self-efficacy expectations. Chances are that you will not be able to run a four-minute mile, but after a few months of reasonably taxing workouts under the advice of a skilled trainer, you might be able to put a few seven- or eight-minute miles back to back. (You might even enjoy them.)

would have spoken to my parents the way Michael speaks to me. I would have been . . . whipped or beaten."

"I try to tell Hannah she is part of the family," Julie continued. "She should think of other people. When she talks that way, it's embarrassing."

"Over here children are not part of the family," said Ken, an African American parent. "They are either part of their own crowd or they are 'individuals.'"

"Being an individual does not mean you have to talk back to your mother," Julie said. "What do you think, Spencer? You're the psychologist."

I think I made some unhelpful comments about the ketchup on the french fries having antioxidants and some slightly helpful comments about what is typical of teenagers in the United States. But I'm not sure, because I was thinking deeply about Hannah at the time. Not about her lunch, but about the formation of her personality and the influences on her behavior.

Question: Why is the sociocultural perspective important to the understanding of personality?   As I thought about Hannah, I realized that in our multicultural society, personality cannot be understood without reference to the **sociocultural perspective.** According to a *New York Times* poll, 91% of people in the United States agree that "being an American is a big part" of who they are (Powers, 2000). Seventy-nine percent say that their religion has played a big role or some role in making them who they are, and 54% say that their race has played a big role or some role (Powers, 2000). Moreover, trends in birth rates and immigration are making the population an even richer mix (Hollmann & Mulder, 2000; see Figures 12.4 and 12.5). Different cultural groups within the United States have different attitudes, beliefs, norms, self-definitions, and values (Basic Behavioral Science Task Force, 1996c; Phinney, 2000).

Back to Hannah. Perhaps there were some unconscious psychodynamic influences operating on her. Her traits included exceptional academic ability and musical talent, which were at least partly determined by her heredity. Clearly, she was consciously striving to become a great violinist. But one could not fully understand her personality without also considering the sociocultural influences acting on her.

> ▲ **REFLECT**
> How do people from your sociocultural background react when children "talk back" to parents? Why?

Sociocultural perspective ▲ The view that focuses on the roles of ethnicity, gender, culture, and socioeconomic status in personality formation, behavior, and mental processes.

FIGURE 12.4   Numbers of Various Racial and Ethnic Groups in the United States, Today Versus Year 2050 (in millions).
The numbers of each of the various racial and ethnic groups in the United States will grow over the next half century, with the numbers of Latino and Latina Americans and Asian Americans and Pacific Islanders growing most rapidly.

SOURCE: U.S. Census Bureau, 2000.

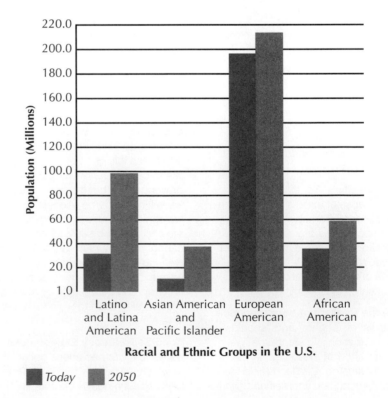

Racial and Ethnic Groups in the U.S.

■ *Today*   ■ *2050*

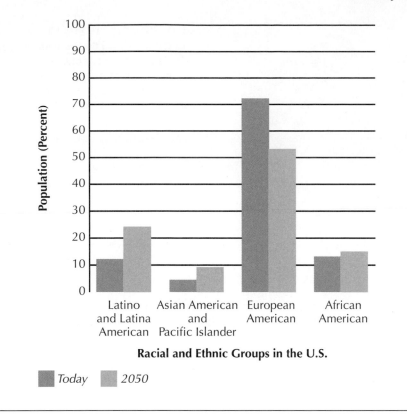

FIGURE 12.5 Percentages of Various Racial and Ethnic Groups in the United States, Today Versus Year 2050.

SOURCE: U.S. Census Bureau, 2000.

Here was a youngster who was strongly influenced by her peers—she was completely at home with blue jeans and french fries. She was also a daughter in an Asian American immigrant group that views education as the key to success in our culture (Gibson & Ogbu, 1991; Ogbu, 1993). Belonging to this ethnic group had certainly contributed to her ambition. But being a Korean American had not prevented her from becoming an outspoken American teenager. (Would she have been outspoken if she had been reared in Korea? I wondered. Of course, this question cannot be answered with certainty.) Her outspoken behavior had struck her mother as brazen and inappropriate. Julie was deeply offended by behavior that I consider acceptable in my own children. She reeled off the things that were "wrong" with Hannah from her Korean American perspective. I listed some things that were very right with Hannah and encouraged Julie to worry less.

Let us consider how sociocultural factors can affect one's sense of self.

Individualism Versus Collectivism

One could say that Julie's complaint was that Hannah saw herself as an individual and an artist to a greater extent than as a family member and a Korean girl. *Questions: What does it mean to be individualistic? What is meant by individualism and collectivism?* Cross-cultural research reveals that people in the United States and many northern European nations tend to be individualistic. **Individualists** tend to define themselves in terms of their personal identities and to give priority to their personal goals (Triandis, 1995). When asked to complete the statement "I am . . . ," they are likely to respond in terms of their personality traits ("I am outgoing," "I am artistic") or their occupations ("I am a nurse," "I am a systems analyst") (Triandis, 1990). In contrast, many people from cultures in Africa, Asia, and Central and South America tend to be collectivistic (Basic Behavioral Science Task Force, 1996c). **Collectivists** tend to define themselves in terms of the groups to which they belong and to give priority to the group's

REFLECT
Do you see yourself as individualistic or collectivistic? Has your view of yourself led to conflict with others? Explain.

Individualist ▲ A person who defines herself or himself in terms of personal traits and gives priority to her or his own goals.

Collectivist ▲ A person who defines herself or himself in terms of relationships to other people and groups and gives priority to group goals.

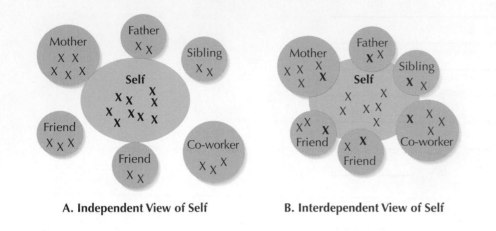

A. Independent View of Self   B. Interdependent View of Self

FIGURE 12.6 The Self in Relation to Others From the Individualist and Collectivist Perspectives.
To an individualist, the self is separate from other people (part A). To a collectivist, the self is complete only in terms of relationships to other people (part B).

SOURCE: Based on Markus & Kitayama (1991).

CLICK4™ *information about psychology and modern life: searching for the self online.*

CLICK4™ *a bulletin board discussion on creating alternate identities online: Why do we do this, and is it healthy?*

Personality and Acculturation.

This Latina American is highly acculturated to life in the United States. Some immigrants are completely assimilated by the dominant culture and abandon the language and customs of their country of origin. Others retain the language and customs of their country of origin and never become comfortable with those of their new country. Still others become bicultural. They become fluent in both languages and blend the customs and values of both cultures.

goals (Triandis, 1995). They feel complete in terms of their relationships with others (Markus & Kitayama, 1991; see Figure 12.6). They are more likely than individualists to conform to group norms and judgments (Bond & Smith, 1996; Okazaki, 1997). When asked to complete the statement "I am. . . ," they are more likely to respond in terms of their families, gender, or nation ("I am a father," "I am a Buddhist," "I am a Japanese") (Triandis, 1990, 1994).

The seeds of individualism and collectivism are found in the culture in which a person grows up. The capitalist system fosters individualism to some degree. It assumes that individuals are entitled to amass personal fortunes and that the process of doing so creates jobs and wealth for large numbers of people. The individualist perspective is found in the self-reliant heroes and antiheroes of Western literature and mass media—from Homer's Odysseus to Clint Eastwood's gritty cowboys and Walt Disney's Pocahontas. The traditional writings of the East have exalted people who resisted personal temptations in order to do their duty and promote the welfare of the group.

Sociocultural Factors and the Self

Carl Rogers noted that our self-concepts tend to reflect how other people see us. *Question: How do sociocultural factors affect the self-concept and self-esteem?* Members of the dominant culture in the United States are likely to have a positive sense of self because they share in the expectations of personal achievement and respect that are accorded to those who rise to power. Similarly, members of ethnic groups that have been subjected to discrimination and poverty may have poorer self-concepts and lower self-esteem than members of the dominant culture (Greene, 1993; Lewis-Fernández & Kleinman, 1994).

Despite the persistence of racial prejudices, a survey by the American Association of University Women (1992) found that African American girls are likely to be happier with their appearance than European American girls are. Sixty-five percent of African American elementary schoolgirls said that they were happy with the way they were, compared with 55% of European American girls. By high school age, 58% of African American girls remained happy with the way they were, compared with a surprisingly low 22% of European Americans. Why the discrepancy? It appears that the parents of African American girls teach them that there is nothing wrong with them if they do not match the ideals of the dominant culture. The world mistreats them because of prejudice, not because of who they are as individuals (Williams, 1992). The European American girls are more likely to blame themselves for not attaining the unreachable ideal.

Another issue from the sociocultural perspective is acculturation. Just how much acculturation is good for you? *Question: How does acculturation affect the psychological well-being of immigrants and their families?*

CONTROVERSY IN PSYCHOLOGY

Just How Much Acculturation Is Enough?

Should Hindu women who emigrate to the United States surrender the sari in favor of California Casuals? Should Russian immigrants try to teach their children English at home? Should African American children be acquainted with the music and art of African peoples or those of Europe? Such activities are examples of **acculturation,** in which immigrants become acclimated to the customs and behavior patterns of their new host culture.

How do various patterns of acculturation affect the individual? The answer to the question probably depends on the variables one chooses to measure. Consider that catch-all of psychological well-being: self-esteem. Self-esteem has been shown to be connected with patterns of acculturation among immigrants (Phinney et al., 1997). Those patterns take various forms. Some immigrants are completely assimilated by the dominant culture. They lose the language and customs of their country of origin and become like the domi-nant culture in the new host country. Others maintain almost complete separation. They retain the language and customs of their country of origin and never acclimate to those of the new country. Still others become bicultural (Ryder et al., 2000). For example, they re-main fluent in the language of their country of origin but also become conversant in the language of their new country. They also blend the customs and values of both cultures. They can switch "mental gears." That is they apply the values of one culture under some

www 12 BBC 6

CLICK4™ *a bulletin board discussion on acculturation: How much is too much?*

IN REVIEW

Perspectives on Personality

www 12 L 1

CLICK4™ *more information about the various personality theories and the issues involved.*

Perspective	Focus	About . . .
Psychodynamic	Unconscious conflict, in which drives such as sex, aggression, and the need for superiority come into conflict with laws, social rules, and moral codes	Freud hypothesized three structures of personality (id, ego, superego) and five stages of psychosexual development (oral, anal, phallic, latency, genital).
Trait	Use of mathematical techniques to catalogue and organize basic human personality traits	Hippocrates hypothesized the existence of four basic traits, which were, in effect, updated by Eysenck. Contemporary researchers find five (the five-factor model).
Learning	Factors that determine behavior	Behaviorists see personality as plastic and determined by external, situational variables. Social-cognitive theorists also look for variables within the person—person variables such as competencies, encoding strategies, expectancies, emotions, and self-regulatory systems—that affect behavior.
Humanistic-Existential	The experiences of being human and developing one's unique potential within an often hostile environment	People have inborn drives to become what they are capable of being. Uncondi-tional positive regard leads to self-esteem, which facilitates individual growth and development.
Sociocultural	The roles of ethnicity, gender, culture, and socioeconomic status in personality formation and behavior	Development differs in individualistic and collectivist societies. Discrimination, poverty, and acculturation affect the self-concept and self-esteem.

Acculturation ▲ The process of adaptation in which immi-grants and native groups identify with a new, dominant cul-ture by learning about that culture and making behavioral and attitudinal changes.

circumstances and apply the values of the other culture under others (Hong et al., 2000). Perhaps they relate to other people in one way at work or in school, and in another way at home or in the neighborhood.

Research evidence suggests that people who identify with the bicultural pattern have the highest self-esteem (Phinney et al., 1997; Phinney & Devich-Navarro, 1997). For example, Mexican Americans who are more proficient in English are less likely to be anxious and depressed than less-proficient Mexican Americans (Salgado de Snyder et al., 1990). The ability to adapt to the ways of the new society, combined with a supportive cultural tradition and a sense of ethnic identity, apparently helps people adjust.

Evaluation of the Sociocultural Perspective

The sociocultural perspective provides valuable insights into the roles of ethnicity, gender, culture, and socioeconomic status in personality formation. When we ignore sociocultural factors, we deal only with the core of the human being—the potentials that allow the person to adapt to external forces. Sociocultural factors are external forces that are internalized. They run through us deeply, touching many aspects of our cognitions, motives, emotions, and behavior. Without reference to sociocultural factors, we may be able to understand generalities about behavior and cognitive processes. However, we will not be able to understand how individuals think, behave, and feel about themselves within a given cultural setting. The sociocultural perspective enhances our sensitivity to cultural differences and expectations and allows us to appreciate the richness of human behavior and mental processes.

CLICK4™ *a WebSearch activity comparing the humanistic-existential and sociocultural perspectives.*

REVIEW

(25) The _____ perspective considers the influences of ethnicity, gender, and socioeconomic status on personality. (26) _____ define themselves in terms of their personal identities and give priority to their personal goals. (27) _____ define themselves in terms of the groups to which they belong and to give priority to group goals. (28) Members of minority ethnic groups who have been subjected to discrimination and poverty tend to have (higher or lower?) self-esteem than members of the dominant culture. (29) Immigrants who identify with the bicultural pattern of assimilation have the (highest or lowest?) self-esteem.

Behavior-rating scale ▲ A systematic means for recording the frequency with which target behaviors occur.
Aptitude ▲ A natural ability or talent.

Pulling It Together: Can one "believe in" more than one theory of personality? For example, could one accept the sociocultural perspective *along with* another perspective?

MEASUREMENT OF PERSONALITY

Methods of personality assessment take a sample of behavior to predict future behavior. Standardized interviews are often used. Some psychologists use computers to conduct routine interviews. **Behavior-rating scales** assess behavior in settings such as classrooms or mental hospitals. With behavior-rating scales, trained observers usually check off each occurrence of a specific behavior within a certain time frame—say, 15 minutes. As we enter the new millennium, behavior-rating scales are growing in popularity, especially for use with children (Kamphaus et al., 2000). However, standardized objective and projective tests are used more frequently, and we focus on them in this section.

Question: How are personality measures used? Measures of personality are used to make important decisions, such as whether a person is suited for a certain type of work, a particular class in school, or a drug to reduce agitation. As part of their admissions process, graduate schools often ask professors to rate prospective students on scales that assess traits such as intelligence, emotional stability, and cooperation. Students may take tests to measure their **aptitudes** and interests to gain insight into whether they are suited for certain occupations. It is assumed that students who share the aptitudes and interests of people who function well in certain positions are also likely to function well in those positions.

Let us now consider the two most widely used types of personality tests: objective tests and projective tests.

Is This Test-Taker Telling the Truth?
How can psychologists determine whether or not people answer test items honestly? What are the validity scales of the MMPI?

Objective Tests

Question: What are objective personality tests?
Objective tests present respondents with a **standardized** group of test items in the form of a questionnaire. Respondents are limited to a specific range of answers. One test might ask respondents to indicate whether items are true or false for them. (I have included questionnaires of this sort in several chapters of this book.) Another might ask respondents to select the preferred activity from groups of three.

Some tests have a **forced-choice format,** in which respondents are asked to indicate which of two statements is more true for them or which of several activities they prefer. The respondents are not usually given the option of answering "none of the above." Forced-choice formats are frequently used in interest inventories, which help predict whether the person would function well in a certain occupation. The following item is similar to those found in occupational interest inventories:

I would rather
a. be a forest ranger.
b. work in a busy office.
c. play a musical instrument.

The Minnesota Multiphasic Personality Inventory (MMPI) contains hundreds of items presented in a true–false format. The MMPI is designed to be used by clinical and counseling psychologists to help diagnose psychological disorders. Accurate measurement of an individual's problems should point to appropriate treatment. The MMPI is the most widely used psychological test in clinical work (Watkins et al., 1995). It is also the most widely used instrument for personality measurement in psychological research.

Psychologists can score tests by hand, send them to computerized scoring services, or have them scored by on-site computers. Computers generate reports by interpreting the test record according to certain rules or by comparing it with records in memory.

The MMPI is usually scored for the 4 **validity scales** and 10 **clinical scales** described in Table 12.3. The validity scales suggest whether answers actually represent the person's thoughts, emotions, and behaviors. However, they cannot guarantee that deception will be disclosed.

The validity scales in Table 12.3 assess different **response sets,** or biases, in answering the questions. People with high L scores, for example, may be attempting to present themselves as excessively moral and well-behaved individuals. People with high F scores may be trying to seem bizarre or are answering haphazardly. Many personality measures have some kind of validity scale. The clinical scales of the MMPI assess the problems shown in Table 12.3, as well as stereotypical masculine or feminine interests and introversion.

The MMPI scales were constructed *empirically*—that is, on the basis of actual clinical data rather than on the basis of psychological theory. A test-item bank of several hundred items was derived from questions that are often asked in clinical interviews. Here are some examples of the kinds of items that were used:

My father was a good man.	T	F
I am very seldom troubled by headaches.	T	F
My hands and feet are usually warm enough.	T	F
I have never done anything dangerous for the thrill of it.	T	F
I work under a great deal of tension.	T	F

TABLE 12.3 MINNESOTA MULTIPHASIC PERSONALITY INVENTORY (MMPI) SCALES

VALIDITY SCALES

Scale	Abbreviation	Possible Interpretations
Question	?	Corresponds to number of items left unanswered
Lie	L	Lies or is highly conventional
Frequency	F	Exaggerates complaints or answers items haphazardly; may have bizarre ideas
Correction	K	Denies problems

CLINICAL SCALES

Scale	Abbreviation	Possible Interpretations
Hypochondriasis	Hs	Has bodily concerns and complaints
Depression	D	Is depressed; has feelings of guilt and helplessness
Hysteria	Hy	Reacts to stress by developing physical symptoms; lacks insight
Psychopathic deviate	Pd	Is immoral, in conflict with the law; has stormy relationships
Masculinity/Femininity	Mf	High scores suggest interests and behavior considered stereotypical of the other gender
Paranoia	Pa	Is suspicious and resentful, highly cynical about human nature
Psychasthenia	Pt	Is anxious, worried, high-strung
Schizophrenia	Sc	Is confused, disorganized, disoriented; has bizarre ideas
Hypomania	Ma	Is energetic, restless, active, easily bored
Social introversion	Si	Is introverted, timid, shy; lacks self-confidence

CLICK4™ *an essay assignment on personality tests: Should they be used for prospective employee screening?*

CLICK4™ *a WebSearch activity on the Keirsey Temperament Sort compared with other personality tests: How do you score on each? What do your scores suggest?*

Objective tests ▲ Tests whose items must be answered in a specified, limited manner. Tests whose items have concrete answers that are considered correct.

Standardized test ▲ A test that is given to a large number of respondents so that data concerning the typical responses can be accumulated and analyzed.

Forced-choice format ▲ A method of presenting test questions that requires a respondent to select one of a number of possible answers.

Validity scales ▲ Groups of test items that indicate whether a person's responses accurately reflect that individual's traits.

Clinical scales ▲ Groups of test items that measure the presence of various abnormal behavior patterns.

Response set ▲ A tendency to answer test items according to a bias—for instance, to make oneself seem perfect or bizarre.

FIGURE 12.7   A Rorschach Inkblot.
The Rorschach is the most widely used projective
personality test. What does this inkblot look like to
you? What could it be?

▲ **REFLECT**

Before you read further, what does the
inkblot in Figure 12.7 look like to you?
What could it be? What do you think
your answers say about your personality? Explain.

CLICK4™ *a profile of Hermann Rorschach.*

CLICK4™ *a WebSearch activity on the Thematic
Apperception Test.*

www 12 L 4

CLICK4™ *more information on personality
tests, including the Myers-Briggs Profile.*

The items were administered to people with previously identified symptoms, such as depressive or schizophrenic symptoms. Items that successfully set these people apart were
included on scales named for these conditions. Confidence in the MMPI has developed
because of its extensive use.

Now that we have defined objective tests and surveyed the MMPI, we may ask—
***Questions: How do projective tests differ from objective tests? What are some
of the more widely used projective tests?***

Projective Tests

In **projective tests** there are no clear, specified answers. People are shown ambiguous
stimuli such as inkblots or ambiguous drawings and asked to say what they look like or to
tell stories about them. There is no one correct response. It is assumed that people *project*
their own personalities into their responses. The meanings they attribute to these stimuli
are assumed to reflect their personalities as well as the drawings or blots themselves.

The Rorschach Inkblot Test
You may have heard that there is a personality test
that asks people what a drawing or inkblot looks like and that people commonly answer
"a bat." There are a number of such tests, the best known of which is the Rorschach
inkblot test, named after its originator, Hermann Rorschach.

People are given the inkblots, one by one, and are asked what they look like or what
they could be. A response that reflects the shape of the blot is considered a sign of
adequate **reality testing**. A response that richly integrates several features of the blot is
considered a sign of high intellectual functioning. Supporters of the Rorschach believe that
it provides insight into a person's intelligence, interests, cultural background, personality
traits, psychological disorders, and many other variables. Critics argue that there is little
empirical evidence to support the test's validity (Goode, 2001; Hunsley & Bailey, 1999).

Although there is no single "correct" response to the Rorschach inkblot shown in
Figure 12.7, some responses are not in keeping with the features of the blot. Figure 12.7
could be a bat or a flying insect, the pointed face of an animal, the face of a jack o' lantern,
or many other things. But responses like "an ice cream cone," "diseased lungs," or "a
metal leaf in flames" are not suggested by the features of the blot and may indicate personality problems.

The Thematic Apperception Test
The Thematic Apperception Test (TAT)
was developed in the 1930s by Henry Murray and Christiana Morgan. It consists of
drawings, like the one shown in Figure 9.3 (see p. 299), that are open to a variety of interpretations. Individuals are given the cards one at a time and asked to make up stories
about them.

The TAT is widely used in research on motivation and in clinical practice (Watkins
et al., 1995). The notion is that we are likely to project own needs into our responses to
ambiguous situations, even if we are unaware of them or reluctant to talk about them.
The TAT is also widely used to assess attitudes toward other people, especially parents,
lovers, and spouses.

In this chapter, we have laid some broad foundations for the understanding of personality.
In Chapter 13 we consider aspects of personality related to gender roles and sexual
behavior. In Chapter 14 we examine the relationships between personality, stress, and
adjustment. And in Chapter 15 we consider connections between personality and psychological disorders.

REVIEW

(30) Personality tests sample _____ to predict future behavior. (31) _____ tests
present standardized sets of test items in the form of questionnaires. (32) Projective tests
present _____ stimuli and permit the respondent a broad range of answers. (33)
The MMPI is an objective test that uses a _____–false format to assess psychological disorders. (34) The foremost projective technique is the _____ inkblot test.

Pulling It Together: Do the measurement methods discussed in this section seem to be
associated with any particular theory or theories of personality? Explain.

Projective test ▲ A psychological test that presents
ambiguous stimuli onto which the test-taker projects his or
her own personality in making a response.
Reality testing ▲ The capacity to perceive one's environment and oneself according to accurate sensory impressions.

TRUTH ☞ FICTION
REVISITED

▧ According to Freud, it is true that the human mind is like a vast submerged iceberg. Only the top rises above the surface into conscious awareness. *Most personality theorists place more emphasis on conscious thought than Freud did. See page 389.*

▧ According to Freud, it is true that biting one's fingernails or smoking cigarettes as an adult is a sign of conflict during very early childhood. *Freud believed that adult problems tend to have their origins in childhood conflicts that have long been lost to conscious awareness. See page 391.*

▧ It is true that bloodletting and vomiting were once recommended ways of coping with depression. *Hippocrates and others believed that depression was caused by an excess of black bile, and bloodletting and vomiting were thought to be ways of restoring a proper balance of bodily fluids. See page 396.*

▧ Although the environment has effects, it is not true that by environmental control alone a child can be reared to be a "doctor, lawyer, merchant-chief," or a beggar or a thief. *Genetic factors are also involved in personality development, and it does not appear that everyone inherits traits that enable him or her to succeed in any and every walk of life. See page 399.*

▧ It is true that we are more likely to persist at difficult tasks when we believe we shall succeed. *Positive self-efficacy expectations motivate us to persevere. See page 401.*

▧ It is true that we can build our self-esteem by becoming good at something. *Competence boosts self-esteem. See page 405.*

▧ It is not true that the best-adjusted immigrants are those who abandon the language and customs of their country of origin and become like the dominant culture in the new host country. *Research shows that immigrants who identify with a bicultural pattern have the highest self-esteem. See page 411.*

▧ Psychologists cannot necessarily determine whether a person has told the truth on a personality test. *However, validity scales allow them to make educated guesses. See page 413.*

▧ It is true that there are no right or wrong answers on some psychological tests. *These are mainly personality tests. See page 413.*

▧ It is true that there is a psychological test made up of inkblots, and test-takers are asked to say what the blots look like to them. *It is the Rorschach inkblot test. See page 413.*

CLICK4™ *a quiz covering the second half of this chapter.*

CLICK4™ *electronic flash cards to review your knowledge of key terms and people in this chapter.*

1. Just what is personality?

Personality is defined as the reasonably stable patterns of behavior, including thoughts and emotions, that distinguish one person from another.

2. What is Freud's theory of psychosexual development?

Freud's theory is termed psycho*dynamic* because it assumes that we are driven largely by unconscious motives and by the movement of unconscious forces within our minds. People experience conflict as basic instincts of hunger, sex, and aggression come up against social pressures to follow laws, rules, and moral codes. At first this conflict is external, but as we develop, it is internalized. The unconscious id represents psychological drives and seeks instant gratification. The ego, or the sense of self or "I," develops through experience and takes into account what is practical and possible in gratifying the impulses of the id. Defense mechanisms such as repression protect the ego from anxiety by repressing unacceptable ideas or distorting reality. The superego is the conscience and develops largely through the Oedipus complex and identification with others. People undergo psychosexual development as psychosexual energy, or libido, is transferred from one erogenous zone to another during childhood. There are five stages of development: oral, anal, phallic, latency, and genital. Fixation in a stage leads to development of traits associated with the stage.

3. Who are some other psychodynamic theorists? What are their views on personality?

Carl Jung's theory, analytical psychology, features a collective unconscious and numerous archetypes, both of which reflect the history of our species. Alfred Adler's theory, individual psychology, features the inferiority complex and the compensating drive for superiority. Karen Horney's theory focuses on parent–child relationships and the possible development of feelings of anxiety and hostility. Erik Erikson's theory of psychosocial development highlights the importance of early social relationships rather than the gratification of childhood sexual impulses. Erikson extended Freud's five developmental stages to eight, including stages that occur in adulthood.

4. What are the strengths and weaknesses of the psychodynamic perspective?

Freud fought for the idea that personality is subject to scientific analysis at a time when many people still viewed psychological problems as signs of possession. He also focused attention on the importance of sexuality, the effects of child rearing, and the fact that people distort perceptions according to their needs. On the other hand, there is no evidence for the existence of psychic structures, and his theory is fraught with inaccuracies about child development.

5. What are traits?

Traits are personality elements that are inferred from behavior and that account for behavioral consistency. Trait theory adopts a descriptive approach to personality.

6. What is the history of the trait perspective?

Hippocrates, the ancient Greek physician, believed that personality reflects the balance of liquids ("humors") in the body. Galton in the 19th century and Allport in the 20th century surveyed traits by studying words that referred to them in dictionaries.

7. How have contemporary researchers used factor analysis to reduce the universe of traits to smaller lists of traits that show common features?

Hans Eysenck used factor analysis to arrive at two broad, independent personality dimensions: introversion–extraversion and emotional stability–instability (neuroticism). More recent mathematical analyses point to the existence of five key factors (five-factor theory): extraversion, agreeableness, conscientiousness, emotional stability, and openness to experience.

8. What are the strengths and weaknesses of trait theory?

Trait theorists have helped develop personality tests and used them to predict adjustment in various lines of work. Critics argue that trait theory is descriptive, not explanatory.

9. What does learning theory have to contribute to our understanding of personality?

Behaviorists believe that we should focus on observable behavior rather than hypothesized unconscious forces, and that we should emphasize the situational determinants of behavior.

10. What is Watson's contribution to personality theory?

John B. Watson, the "father" of modern behaviorism, rejected notions of mind and personality altogether. He also argued that he could train any child to develop into a professional or a criminal by controlling the child's environment.

11. How did Skinner develop Watson's views?

B. F. Skinner like Watson opposed the idea of personal freedom. In *Walden Two*, Skinner argued that environmental contingencies can shape people into wanting to do the things that are required of them.

12. How does social-cognitive theory differ from the behaviorist view?

Social-cognitive theory has a cognitive orientation and focuses on learning by observation. To predict behavior, social-cognitive theorists consider situational variables (rewards and punishments) and person variables (competencies, encoding strategies, expectancies, emotions, and self-regulatory systems and plans).

13. What are the strengths and weaknesses of learning theories as they apply to personality?

Learning theorists have highlighted the importance of referring to publicly observable behaviors in theorizing. However, behaviorism does not describe, explain, or suggest the richness of inner human experience. Critics of social-cognitive theory note that it does not address self-awareness or adequately account for the development of traits. It may also not pay enough attention to genetic variation in explaining individual differences in behavior.

14. What is humanism? What is existentialism?

Humanism argues that we are capable of free choice, self-fulfillment, and ethical behavior. Existentialists argue that our lives have meaning when we give them meaning.

15. How do humanistic psychologists differ from psychodynamic theorists?

Whereas Freud wrote that people are motivated to gratify unconscious drives, humanistic psychologists believe that people have a conscious need for self-actualization.

16. Just what is your self? What is self theory?

According to Rogers, the self is an organized and consistent way in which a person perceives his or her "I" in relation to others. Self theory begins by assuming the existence of the self and each person's unique frame of reference. The self attempts to actualize (develop its unique potential) and best does so when the person receives unconditional positive regard. Conditions of worth may lead to a distorted self-concept, to disowning of parts of the self, and to anxiety.

17. What are the strengths and weaknesses of humanistic-existential theory?

Humanistic-existential theory is appealing because of its focus on self-awareness and freedom of choice, but critics argue that concepts such as conscious experience and self-actualization are unscientific.

18. Why is the sociocultural perspective important to the understanding of personality?

One cannot fully understand the personality of an individual without understanding the cultural beliefs and socioeconomic conditions that have affected that individual. The sociocultural perspective encourages us to consider the roles of ethnicity, gender, culture, and socioeconomic status in personality formation, behavior, and mental processes.

19. What does it mean to be individualistic? What is meant by individualism and collectivism?

Individualists define themselves in terms of their personal identities and to give priority to their personal goals. Collectivists define themselves in terms of the groups to which they belong and to give priority to the group's goals. Many Western societies are individualistic and foster individualism in personality. Many Eastern societies are collectivist and foster collectivism in personality.

20. How do sociocultural factors affect the self-concept and self-esteem?

Members of the dominant culture in the United States are likely to have positive self-concepts because they share expectations of achievement and respect. Members of ethnic groups that have been subjected to discrimination and poverty tend to have poorer self-concepts and lower self-esteem.

21. How does acculturation affect the psychological well-being of immigrants and their families?

Immigrants who retain the customs and values of their country of origin but who also learn those of their new host country, and blend the two, tend to have higher self-esteem than immigrants who either become completely assimilated or who maintain complete separation from the new dominant culture.

22. How are personality measures used?

Personality measures are used in many ways, including assessing psychological disorders, predicting the likelihood of adjustment in various lines of work, measuring aptitudes, and determining academic placement.

23. What are objective personality tests?

Objective tests present test-takers with a standardized set of test items to which they must respond in specific, limited ways (as in multiple-choice or true–false tests). A forced-choice format asks respondents to indicate which of two or more statements is true for them or which of several activities they prefer. The Minnesota Multiphasic Personality Inventory (MMPI) is widely used in the assessment of psychological disorders.

24. How do projective tests differ from objective tests? What are some of the more widely used projective tests?

Projective tests do not have specific correct answers. They present ambiguous stimuli and allow the test-taker to give a range of responses that reflect individual differences. Examples include the Rorschach inkblot test and the Thematic Apperception Test.

PREVIEW

This chapter, "Gender and Sexuality," covers the following:

Gender Polarization: Gender Stereotypes and Their Costs
▲ What does it mean to be "masculine"? To be "feminine"?
▲ Gender-role stereotypes can be harmful to your health.

Psychological Gender Differences: Vive la Différence or Vive la Similarité?
▲ Are males and females more alike, or more different, in their cognitive abilities?
▲ Males and females differ in their nurturance and social dominance.

Gender-Typing: On Becoming a Woman or a Man
▲ Are gender differences hard-wired by our biology?
▲ Cultural influences affect gender-typing.

Attraction: On Liking, Loving, and Relationships
▲ Physical attractiveness is not the only factor in the psychology of attraction.
▲ After reading this section, you will be one of the enlightened who can explain what romantic love is!
▲ Some people are romantically attracted to people of their own gender.
▲ Gay males and lesbians do not choose their sexual orientation any more than other people do.

Sexual Response
▲ Surprise: Males and females are quite alike in their sexual responses.
▲ While younger people may wonder "Should I?", older people may wonder "Can I?"

Sexual Coercion
▲ Rape is common in the United States.
▲ A number of U.S. cultural beliefs have the effect of supporting rape.
▲ There is a big difference between a sexual invitation and sexual harassment.

AIDS and Other Sexually Transmitted Infections
▲ Everyone is concerned about HIV/AIDS, but there are many other STIs to think about—and do something about.

CHAPTER 13

Gender and Sexuality

TRUTH OR FICTION?

- While Christmas Eve is a time of religious devotion in most Western nations, it has become a time of sexual devotion in Japan.

- Men behave more aggressively than women do.

- Beauty is in the eye of the beholder.

- People are perceived as being more attractive when they are smiling.

- Opposites attract.

- Most Americans believe that some women like to be talked into sex.

- Women say no when they mean yes.

- The earlobes swell when people are sexually aroused.

- People who truly love each other enjoy the sexual aspects of their relationships.

- Only gay males and substance abusers are at serious risk for contracting AIDS.

Off the misty coast of Ireland lies the small island of Inis Beag. From the air it is a green jewel, warm and inviting. At ground level, things are somewhat cooler.

For example, the residents of Inis Beag do not believe that women experience orgasm. The woman who chances to find pleasure in sex is considered deviant. Premarital sex is all but unknown. Women engage in sexual relations to conceive children and to appease their husbands' carnal cravings. They need not worry about being called on for frequent performances, however, since the men of Inis Beag believe, erroneously, that sex saps their strength. Sex on Inis Beag is carried out in the dark—both literally and figuratively—and with nightclothes on. The man lies on top in the so-called missionary position. In accordance with local concepts of masculinity, he ejaculates as fast as he can. Then he rolls over and falls asleep.

If Inis Beag does not sound like your cup of tea, you may find the atmosphere of Mangaia more congenial. Mangaia is a Polynesian pearl of an island, lifting lazily from the blue waters of the Pacific. It is on the other side of the world from Inis Beag—in more ways than one.

From an early age, Mangaian children are encouraged to get in touch with their sexuality through masturbation. Mangaian adolescents are expected to engage in sexual intercourse. They may be found on secluded beaches or beneath the swaying fronds of palms, diligently practicing techniques learned from village elders.

Mangaian women are expected to reach orgasm several times before their partners do. Young men want their partners to reach orgasm, and they compete to see who is more effective at bringing young women to multiple orgasms.

On the island of Inis Beag, a woman who has an orgasm is considered deviant. On Mangaia, multiple orgasms are the norm (Rathus et al., 2000). If we take a quick tour of the world of sexual diversity, we also find that

- ▲ Nearly every society has an incest taboo, but some societies believe that a brother and sister who eat at the same table are engaging in a mildly sexual act and forbid it.
- ▲ What is considered sexually arousing varies enormously among different cultures. Women's breasts and armpits stimulate a sexual response in some cultures, but not in others.
- ▲ Kissing is nearly universal in the United States but unpopular in Japan and unknown in some cultures in Africa and South America. Upon seeing European visitors kissing, a member of an African tribe remarked, "Look at them—they eat each other's saliva and dirt."
- ▲ In Iran's conservative Islamic republic, flirting or holding hands in public can get one arrested or beaten (Riot, 2000; Sciolino, 2000). Nevertheless, many couples obtain officially sanctioned temporary marriages, called *sigheh*, that enable them to live together and engage in sexual relations without being disturbed by the state. A *sigheh* can last from a few minutes to 99 years.
- ▲ Sexual exclusiveness in marriage is valued highly in most parts of the United States, but among the people of Alaska's Aleutian Islands it is considered good manners for a man to offer his wife to a houseguest.
- ▲ The United States has its romantic Valentine's Day, but Japan has eroticized another day—Christmas Eve. (You read that right: Christmas Eve.) On Christmas Eve single people seek a date that includes an overnight visit (Reid, 1990). During the weeks prior to Christmas, the media brim with reports on hotels for overnight stays, the correct attire, and breakfast ideas for the morning after. Where do Tokyo singles like to go before their overnighter? Tokyo Disneyland.

The residents of Inis Beag and Mangaia have similar anatomical features but vastly different attitudes toward sex. Their sociocultural settings influence their patterns of sexual behavior and the pleasure they find—or do not find—in sex. Sex may be a natural function, but few natural functions have been influenced so strongly by religious and moral beliefs, cultural tradition, folklore, and superstition.

This chapter is about gender and sexuality. We begin by exploring gender polarization—the behaviors that make up the "masculine" and "feminine" stereotypes.

▲ REFLECT

In which society would you rather live? Inis Beag or Mangaia? In which society would you rather rear your children? Explain.

CLICK4™ *the SSSS—the Society for the Scientific Study of Sexuality, dedicated to the advancement of scientific knowledge about sex.*

We examine *actual* psychological gender differences and consider the origins of these differences. Next we turn our attention to attraction, love, and relationships. We ask why some people are attracted to people of their own gender while most are attracted to people of the other gender. We discuss important issues in sexual coercion, including rape and sexual harassment. We examine sexual response and see that women and men are probably more alike in their sexual response than you may have thought. We consider sexual dysfunctions and their treatment. Finally, we discuss HIV/AIDS[1] and other sexually transmitted infections (STIs). Although AIDS captures most of the headlines, other STIs can be quite serious and are more widespread.

GENDER POLARIZATION: GENDER STEREOTYPES AND THEIR COSTS

"Why Can't a Woman Be More Like a Man?" You may recognize this song title from the musical *My Fair Lady*. In the song, Henry Higgins laments that women are emotional and fickle whereas men are logical and dependable.

The excitable woman is a **stereotype.** *Question: What are gender-role stereotypes?* Stereotypes are fixed, conventional ideas about a group of people that can give rise to prejudice and discrimination. A gender stereotype is a fixed, conventional idea about how men and women ought to behave. The logical man is a **gender**-role stereotype. Higgins's stereotypes reflect cultural beliefs. Cultural beliefs about men and women involve clusters of stereotypes called **gender roles.** Gender-role stereotypes define the ways in which men and women are expected to behave within a given culture.

Sandra Lipsitz Bem (1993) writes that three beliefs about women and men have prevailed throughout the history of Western culture:

1. Women and men have basically different psychological and sexual natures.
2. Men are the superior, dominant gender.
3. Gender differences and male superiority are "natural."

These beliefs have tended to polarize our views of women and men. It is thought that gender differences in power and psychological traits are natural, but what does "natural" mean? Throughout most of history, people viewed naturalness in terms of religion, or God's scheme of things (Bem, 1993). For the past century or so, naturalness has been seen in biological, evolutionary terms—at least by most scientists. But these views ignore cultural influences.

What are perceived as the "natural" gender roles? Gender polarization in the United States is linked to the traditional view of men as breadwinners and women as homemakers (Eagly & Wood, 1999). In our society, people tend to see the feminine gender role as warm, emotional, dependent, gentle, helpful, mild, patient, submissive, and interested in the arts (Bem, 1993). The typical masculine gender role is perceived as independent, competitive, tough, protective, logical, and competent at business, math, and science. Women are typically expected to care for the kids and cook the meals. Cross-cultural studies confirm that these gender-role stereotypes are widespread (see Table 13.1).

www 13 BBC 3

CLICK4™ *a bulletin board discussion on differences in cognitive ability and its relation to beliefs of gender superiority.*

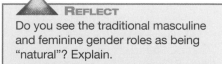

▲ **REFLECT**
Do you see the traditional masculine and feminine gender roles as being "natural"? Explain.

Stereotype ▲ A fixed, conventional idea about a group.
Gender ▲ The state of being male or female.
Gender role ▲ A cluster of behaviors that characterizes traditional female or male behaviors within a cultural setting.

---

[1]HIV stands for human immunodeficiency virus, the disease agent that causes AIDS.

TABLE 13.1   GENDER ROLE STEREOTYPES AROUND THE WORLD

Psychologists John Williams and Deborah Best (1994) found that people in 30 nations around the world tended to agree on the nature of masculine and feminine gender-role stereotypes. Men are largely seen as more adventurous and hardheaded than women. Women are generally seen as more emotional and dependent.

Stereotypes of Males		Stereotypes of Females	
Active	Opinionated	Affectionate	Nervous
Adventurous	Pleasure-seeking	Appreciative	Patient
Aggressive	Precise	Cautious	Pleasant
Arrogant	Quick	Changeable	Prudish
Autocratic	Rational	Charming	Self-pitying
Capable	Realistic	Complaining	Sensitive
Coarse	Reckless	Complicated	Sentimental
Conceited	Resourceful	Confused	Sexy
Confident	Rigid	Dependent	Shy
Courageous	Robust	Dreamy	Softhearted
Cruel	Sharp-witted	Emotional	Sophisticated
Determined	Show-off	Excitable	Submissive
Disorderly	Steady	Fault-finding	Suggestible
Enterprising	Stern	Fearful	Superstitious
Hardheaded	Stingy	Fickle	Talkative
Individualistic	Stolid	Foolish	Timid
Inventive	Tough	Forgiving	Touchy
Loud	Unscrupulous	Frivolous	Unambitious
Obnoxious		Fussy	Understanding
		Gentle	Unstable
		Imaginative	Warm
		Kind	Weak
		Mild	Worrying
		Modest	

SOURCE OF DATA: Williams & Best, 1994, p. 193, Table 1.

CLICK4™ *a bulletin board discussion on gender: Are males and females really opposite?*

▲ **REFLECT**
Gloria Steinem wrote, "I have yet to hear a man ask for advice on how to combine marriage and a career." Have you ever heard a man express such a concern? Why are women more likely to have this concern?

For example, in their survey of 30 countries, John Williams and Deborah Best (1994) found that men are more likely to be judged to be active, adventurous, aggressive, arrogant, and autocratic (and we have only gotten through the *a*'s.) Women are more likely to be seen as fearful, fickle, foolish, frivolous, and fussy (and these are only a handful of *f*'s.)

Even emotions are stereotyped. Participants in one study believed that women more often than men experienced the emotions of sadness, fear, and sympathy (Plant et al., 2000). But they thought that men were more likely to feel anger and pride.

Costs of Gender Polarization

Gender polarization is more than tradition, more than a cultural artifact. It can be extremely costly for both genders in terms of education, activities, careers, psychological well-being, and interpersonal relationships. *Question: What are the costs of gender polarization?*

Education   Polarization has historically worked to the disadvantage of women. In past centuries, girls were considered unable to learn. Even the great Swiss-French philosopher Jean-Jacques Rousseau, who was in the forefront of a movement toward a more open approach to education, believed that girls are basically irrational and naturally disposed to child rearing and homemaking—certainly not to commerce, science, and industry, pursuits for which education is required.

Intelligence tests show that boys and girls are about equal in overall learning ability. Nevertheless, girls are expected to excel in language arts, and boys in math and science. Girls, therefore, tend to have less confidence in their ability at math and to blame difficulties on their own lack of ability than on the nature of the task (Vermeer et al., 2000). These attitudes dissuade girls from taking advanced courses in the so-called male domain. Boys take more math courses in high school than girls do (AAUW, 1992). Math courses open doors for them in fields such as natural science, engineering, and economics. There are several reasons why boys are more likely than girls to feel at home with math (AAUW, 1992):

1. Fathers are more likely than mothers to help children with math homework.
2. Advanced math courses are more likely to be taught by men.
3. Teachers often show higher expectations for boys in math courses.
4. Math teachers spend more time working with boys than with girls.

Given these experiences, we should not be surprised that by junior high, boys view themselves as more competent in math than girls do, even when they receive the same grades (AAUW, 1992). Boys are more likely to have positive feelings about math. Girls are more likely to have math anxiety. Even girls who excel in math and science are less likely than boys to choose courses or careers in these fields (AAUW, 1992).

If women are to find their places in professions related to math, science, and engineering, we may need to provide more female role models in these professions. Role models will help shatter the stereotype that these are men's fields. We also need to encourage girls to take more courses in math and science.

Careers   Women are less likely than men to enter higher-paying careers in math, science, and engineering (Cejka & Eagly, 1999). Women account for perhaps 1 in 6 of the nation's scientists and engineers. Although women are awarded more than half of the bachelor's degrees in the United States, they receive fewer than one third of the degrees in science and engineering. Why? It is partly because math, science, and engineering are perceived as being inconsistent with the feminine gender role. Many little girls are dissuaded from thinking about professions such as engineering and architecture because they are given dolls, rather than trucks and blocks, as toys. Many boys are likewise deterred from entering child care and nursing professions because others scorn them when they play with dolls. Once women choose a career in science, they are frequently subject to discrimination in hiring, promotion, placement on committees, awards, the allocation of laboratory space and grants to conduct research, even in high-profile institutions such as Massachusetts Institute of Technology (Loder, 2000).

There are also inequalities in the workplace. For example, women's wages average only 76.5% of men's (Grimsley, 2000). Women physicians and college professors earn less than men in the same positions (Honan, 1996; "Study finds smaller pay gap," 1996). Women are less likely than men to be promoted into high-level managerial positions (Valian, 1998). Once in managerial positions, women often feel pressured to be "tougher" than men in order to seem just as tough. They feel pressured to be careful about their appearance because coworkers pay more attention to what they wear, how they style their hair, and so forth. If they don't look crisp and tailored every day, others may think they are not in command. But if they dress up too much, they may be denounced as fashion plates rather than serious workers! Female managers who are deliberate and take time making decisions may be seen as "wishy-washy." What happens when female managers change their minds? They run the risk of being labeled fickle and indecisive rather than flexible.

Women who work also usually have the responsibility of being the major caretaker for children in the home (Bianchi & Spain, 1997). Research shows that when young couples do not have children, moves to another city are usually planned to benefit both partners' careers (Nasser, 2000). But once children arrive on the scene, such moves usually mean a promotion for the man but set the woman's career back.

A Female Architectural Engineer.
Women remain underrepresented in many kinds of careers. Although women have made marked gains in medicine and law, their numbers remain relatively low in math and engineering. Why?

Psychological Well-Being and Relationships

Gender polarization also interferes with psychological well-being and relationships. Women who adhere to the traditional feminine gender role are likely to believe that women, like children, should be seen and not heard. They therefore are unlikely to assert themselves to make their needs and wants known. They are likely to feel frustrated as a result.

Men who accept the traditional masculine gender role are less likely to feel comfortable performing the activities involved in caring for children, such as bathing them, dressing them, and feeding them (Bem, 1993). Such men are less likely to ask for help—including medical help—when they need it (Courtenay, 2000). They are also less likely to be sympathetic and tender or express feelings of love in their marital relationships (Coleman & Ganong, 1985).

REFLECT
Have you experienced any inequalities for men and women in school or in the workplace? What did you experience? What did you do about it?

CLICK4™ *the Bem Sex Role Inventory: Are your sex role ratings masculine or feminine?*

CLICK4™ *an essay assignment on what it means to be masculine or feminine in the United States.*

REVIEW

(1) _____ are fixed, conventional ideas about a group of people. (2) _____-role stereotypes define behavioral expectations of men and women. (3) Throughout Western history, women and men have been seen as having (similar or different?) psychological and sexual natures. (4) Gender polarization has historically worked mostly to the disadvantage of (women or men?).

Pulling It Together: What does it mean to be "feminine" or "masculine" in the United States today?

PSYCHOLOGICAL GENDER DIFFERENCES: VIVE LA DIFFÉRENCE OR VIVE LA SIMILARITÉ?

The French have an expression "Vive la différence," which means "Long live the difference" (between men and women). Yet modern life has challenged our concepts of what it means to be a woman or a man. The anatomical differences between women and men are obvious and are connected with the biological aspects of reproduction. Biologists

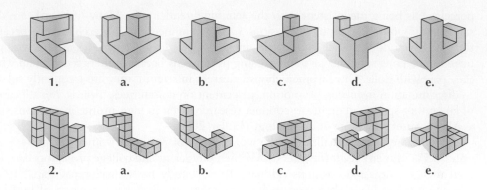

FIGURE 13.1 Rotating Figures in Space.
Males as a group outperform females on spatial relations tasks, such as rotating figures in space and picturing the results. However, females do as well as males when they receive training in the task.

www 13 WS 2

CLICK4™ *a WebSearch activity on cognition and gender stereotypes.*

www 13 L 1

CLICK4™ *more information about sex differences and gender stereotypes.*

▲ REFLECT

Do any of the gender differences discussed here fit with, or counter, your own observations over the years? Explain.

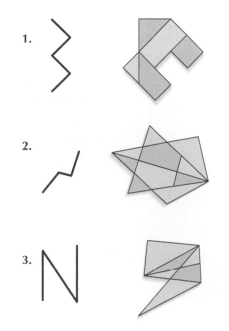

FIGURE 13.2 Items From an Embedded-Figures Test.

therefore have a relatively easy time of it describing and interpreting the gender differences they study. The task of psychology is more complex and is wrapped up with sociocultural and political issues. Psychological gender differences are not as obvious as biological gender differences. In fact, in many ways women and men are more similar than different.

Put it another way: To reproduce, women and men have to be biologically different. Throughout history, it has also been assumed that women and men must be psychologically different in order to fulfill different roles in the family and society (Bem, 1993). But what are the psychological differences between women and men? Let us begin by asking: *Question: What are the gender differences in cognitive abilities?*

Gender Differences in Cognitive Abilities

It was once believed that males were more intelligent than females because of their greater knowledge of world affairs and their skill in science and industry. We now know that greater male knowledge and skill did not reflect differences in intelligence. Rather, it reflected the systematic exclusion of females from world affairs, science, and industry. Assessments of intelligence do not show overall gender differences in cognitive abilities (Halpern & LaMay, 2000). However, reviews of the research suggest that girls are somewhat superior to boys in verbal abilities, such as verbal fluency, ability to generate words that are similar in meaning to other words, spelling, knowledge of foreign languages, and pronunciation (Halpern, 1997). Males seem to be somewhat superior in the ability to manipulate visual images in working memory.

Girls seem to acquire language somewhat faster than boys do. Also, in the United States far more boys than girls have reading problems, ranging from reading below grade level to severe disabilities (Halpern, 1997; Neisser et al., 1996). On the other hand, males headed for college seem to catch up in verbal skills.

Males apparently excel in visual-spatial abilities of the sort used in math, science, even map reading (Grön et al., 2000; Halpern & LaMay, 2000). One study compared the navigation strategies of 90 male and 104 female university students (Dabbs et al., 1998). In giving directions, men more often referred to miles and directional coordinates in terms of North, South, East, and West, whereas women were more likely to refer to landmarks and turns to the right or left. Psychological tests of spatial ability assess skills such as mentally rotating figures in space (see Figure 13.1) and finding figures embedded within larger designs (see Figure 13.2).

Studies in the United States and elsewhere find that males generally obtain higher scores on math tests than females (Beller & Gafni, 2000; Gallagher et al., 2000; Halpern & LaMay, 2000). Females excel in computational ability in elementary school, however. Males excel in mathematical problem solving in high school and college. Boys outperform girls on the math section of the Scholastic Assessment Test.

The gender differences thus appear to exist, at least for the time being. However, psychologists note that:

- In most cases, the differences are small (Hyde & Plant, 1995). Differences in verbal, math, and visual-spatial abilities also appear to be narrowing as more females pursue course work in fields that had been typically preserved for males.
- These gender differences are *group* differences. There is greater variation in these skills between individuals *within* the groups than between males and females (Maccoby, 1990). That is, there may be a greater difference in, say, verbal skills between two women than between a woman and a man. Millions of females outdistance the "average" male in math and spatial abilities. Men have produced their Shakespeares. Women have produced their Madame Curies.
- Some differences may largely reflect sociocultural influences. In our culture spatial and math abilities are stereotyped as masculine. Women who are given just a few hours of training in spatial skills—for example, rotating geometric figures or studying floor plans—perform at least as well men on tests of these skills (Baenninger & Elenteny, 1997; Lawton & Morrin, 1999).

Gender Differences in Social Behavior

There are many other psychological differences between males and females. For example, women exceed men in extraversion, anxiety, trust, and nurturance (Feingold, 1994). Men exceed women in assertiveness and tough-mindedness. *Question: What are the gender differences in social behavior?* In the arena of social behavior, women seem more likely than men to cooperate with other people and hold groups, such as families, together (Bjorklund & Kipp, 1996).

Men's friendships with other men tend to be shallower and less supportive than women's friendships with other women. Research with 565 college students suggests that emotional restraint and fear of gay males (homophobia) partly explain men's relative lack of intimacy with other men (Bank & Hansford, 2000). Competitive striving with other men played a lesser role.

Despite the stereotype of women as gossips and chatterboxes, research in communication styles suggests that in many situations men spend more time talking than women do. Men are more likely to introduce new topics and to interrupt (Hall, 1984). Women seem more willing to reveal their feelings and personal experiences (Dindia & Allen, 1992).

Women interact at closer distances than men do. They also seek to keep more space between themselves and strangers of the other gender than men do (Rüstemli, 1986). Men are made more uncomfortable by strangers who sit across from them, whereas women are more likely to feel "invaded" by strangers who sit next to them. In libraries, men tend to pile books protectively in front of them. Women place books and coats in adjacent seats to discourage others from taking them.

There are also gender differences in areas of social behavior such as sex and aggression. Women are more likely to want to combine sex with a romantic relationship (Fisher, 2000). Men are more interested than women in casual sex and in multiple sex partners. But in our society there are constraints on unbridled sexual behavior, so most men are not promiscuous (Archer, 1996).

In most cultures, it is the males who march off to war and battle for glory (and sneaker ads in TV commercials). Researchers find that male children and adults generally behave more aggressively than females do (Archer, 1996).

In a classic review of the research on gender differences in aggression, Ann Frodi and her colleagues (1977) found that females are more likely to act aggressively under some circumstances than others:

1. Females are more likely to feel anxious or guilty about aggression. Such feelings inhibit aggressive behavior.
2. Females behave as aggressively as males when they have the means to do so and believe that aggression is justified.
3. Females are more likely to empathize with the victim—to put themselves in the victim's place. Empathy encourages helping behavior, not aggression.
4. Gender differences in aggression decrease when the victim is anonymous. Anonymity may prevent females from empathizing with their victims.

CONTROVERSY IN PSYCHOLOGY

Are Men Really More Aggressive Than Women?

Despite the stereotype of male aggressiveness, a meta-analysis of the research reveals that women are actually slightly more likely to hit, kick, use a weapon, and so on against their spouses, cohabitants, or dating partners (Archer, 2000). Yet women in these relationships are more likely to be injured (Archer, 2000).

Let us be cautious about how we interpret this data. For one thing, the findings were limited to intimate partners. Men remain much more likely to act violently toward strangers and other people of the same gender (Frieze, 2000). You usually need not be concerned about running into a woman on a deserted street. The difference in injury rate is also instructive: Men on average are stronger than women, may choose more harmful weapons, and, when they attack, may be more likely to intend to cause injury. So even if women engage in aggressive acts more often with their intimate partners, men clearly remain more dangerous. It should also be noted that feminists are concerned by the reporting of research findings that women act violently with their intimate partners because the reports seem to suggest that we should focus on the frequency of aggressive acts rather than the incidence of injury. In so doing, we may undermine efforts to end the victimization of women (O'Leary, 2000; White et al., 2000). The findings also tend to divert attention from the fact that men still retain more power than women do in our society, as evidenced by their ascendance in various occupations.

But let's not toss out the findings because they stir controversy. They suggest that women as well as men can turn to violence when they are frustrated. To be human is . . . to be human.

www 13 BBC 2

CLICK4™ *a bulletin board discussion on gender and aggression.*

REVIEW

(5) (Girls or Boys?) are somewhat superior in verbal abilities. (6) (Girls or Boys?) are somewhat superior in visual-spatial abilities and math. (7) (Women or Men?) tend to be more assertive and tough-minded. (8) (Women or Men?) are more interested in casual sex.

Pulling It Together: How do actual gender differences fit—or fail to fit—gender-role stereotypes?

GENDER-TYPING: ON BECOMING A WOMAN OR A MAN

CLICK4™ *an essay assignment on social/ political issues and their relation to gender differences in brain structure and function.*

CLICK4™ *a WebSearch activity: Are masculinity and femininity inborn or learned?*

There are thus a number of psychological gender differences. They include minor differences in cognitive functioning and differences in personality and social behavior. The process by which these differences develop is termed **gender-typing.** In this section we explore several possible sources of gender-typing, both biological and psychological. *Question: What are some biological views of gender-typing?*

Biological Influences on Gender-Typing

According to evolutionary psychologists like David Buss (2000), gender differences were fashioned by natural selection in response to problems in adaptation that were repeatedly encountered by humans over thousands of generations. The evolutionary process is expressed through structural differences between males and females, as are found in the brain, and through differences in body chemistry, as are found in the endocrine system.

Brain Organization   Researchers have found gender differences in the functioning and organization of the brain. Males and females have the same structures in the brain, but they seem to use them somewhat differently. For example, Matthias Riepe and his colleagues (Grön et al., 2000) found that men use the hippocampus in both hemispheres when they are trying to navigate through mazes, whereas women use only the hippocampus in the right hemisphere along with the right prefrontal cortex. It has also been found that most women tend to rely on landmarks to navigate ("Turn right at the drugstore, then left at the grocery"), whereas men use geometry, as in deriving information from a map ("The museum should be over that way") (Ritter, 2000). Riepe (2000) speculates that the women's activity in the cortex might be due to the effort of keeping landmark cues in mind, whereas the hippocampal activity in men might reflect the more geometric approach. Riepe (2000) has found the same gender difference in brain functioning in rats that are navigating mazes.

Then too, some psychological activities, such as language, seem to be controlled largely by the left side of the brain. Other psychological activities, such as aesthetic and emotional responses, seem to be controlled largely by the right side. Brain-imaging research suggests that the brain hemispheres may be more specialized in males than in females (Shaywitz et al., 1995). For example, men with damage to the left hemisphere are more likely to experience difficulties in verbal functioning than women with similar damage. Men with damage to the right hemisphere are more likely to have problems with spatial relations than women with similar injuries.

Gender differences in brain organization might explain, in part, why women excel in verbal skills that require some spatial organization, such as reading, spelling, and crisp articulation of speech. Men, however, might be superior at more specialized spatial-relations tasks such as interpreting road maps and visualizing objects in space.

Sex Hormones   Sex hormones and other chemical substances, such as GABA, are responsible for the prenatal differentiation of sex organs (Davis et al., 2000). These substances may also "masculinize" or "feminize" the brain by creating predispositions consistent with some gender-role stereotypes (Collaer & Hines, 1995; Crews, 1994). Yet

▲ REFLECT

Are there possible social or political problems connected with attributing gender differences in cognitive abilities to organization of the brain? Does the belief that females and males might be different in cognitive abilities and behavior imply that one gender is superior or inferior to the other?

Gender-typing ▲ The process by which people acquire a sense of being female or male and acquire the traits considered typical of females or males within a cultural setting.

John Money (1987) argues that social learning plays a stronger role in the development of **gender identity,** personality traits, and preferences. Money claims that social learning is powerful enough to counteract many prenatal predispositions.

Some evidence for the possible role of hormonal influences have been obtained from animal studies (Collaer & Hines, 1995; Crews, 1994). For example, male rats are generally superior to females in maze-learning ability, a task that requires spatial skills. Female rats that are exposed to androgens in the uterus (e.g., because they have several male siblings in the uterus with them) or soon after birth learn maze routes as rapidly as males, however. They also roam larger distances and mark larger territories than most females do (Vandenbergh, 1993).

Men are more aggressive than women, and aggressiveness is connected with the male sex hormone **testosterone** (Pope et al., 2000; Sullivan, 2000). However, cognitive psychologists argue that boys (and girls) can choose whether or not to act aggressively, regardless of the levels of hormones in their bloodstreams.

Many aspects of human development, including gender-typing, appear to involve both nature and nurture. Biological factors, such as heredity, provide a "natural" explanation of psychological gender differences. Psychological influences would provide an explanation based on the different experiences of males and females. *Question: What are some psychological views of gender-typing?*

Psychological Influences on Gender-Typing

The two most prominent psychological perspectives on gender-typing today are social-cognitive theory and gender-schema theory. However, we begin with psychodynamic theory because of its historic interest.

Psychodynamic Theory   Sigmund Freud explained the acquisition of gender roles in terms of *identification*. He believed that gender identity remains flexible until the Oedipus and Electra complexes are resolved at about the age of five or six. Appropriate gender-typing requires that boys identify with their fathers and give up the wish to possess their mothers. Girls have to give up the wish to have a penis and identify with their mothers.

Boys and girls develop stereotypical preferences for toys and activities much earlier than might be predicted by psychodynamic theory, however. Even within their first year, boys are more explorative and independent. Girls are relatively more quiet, dependent, and restrained (Etaugh & Rathus, 1995). By 18 to 36 months, girls are more likely to prefer soft toys and dolls and to dance. Boys of this age are more likely to prefer blocks and toy cars, trucks, and airplanes.

Let us consider the ways in which cognitive theories account for gender-typing.

Social-Cognitive Theory   Social-cognitive theorists explain gender-typing in terms of the ways in which experience helps the individual create concepts of gender-appropriate behavior, and how the individual is motivated to engage in behavior judged to be appropriate (Bussey & Bandura, 1999).

Children learn much of what is considered masculine or feminine by **observational learning,** as suggested by a classic experiment conducted by David Perry and Kay Bussey (1979). In this study, children learned how behaviors are gender-typed by observing the *relative frequencies* with which men and women performed them. The adult role models expressed arbitrary preferences for one item from each of 16 pairs of items—pairs such as oranges versus apples and toy cows versus toy horses—while 8- and 9-year-old boys and girls watched them. The children were then asked to show their own preferences. Boys selected an average of 14 of 16 items that agreed with the "preferences" of the men. Girls selected an average of only 3 of 16 items that agreed with the choices of the men. In other words, boys and girls learned gender-typed preferences even though those preferences were completely arbitrary.

Social-cognitive theorists also see a role for **identification,** but not in the Freudian sense of the term. Social-cognitive theorists view identification as a continuous learning process in which children are influenced by rewards and punishments to imitate adults of the same gender—particularly the parent of the same gender. In identification, as

www 13 L 2

CLICK4™ *more information about society and gender identity.*

Gender identity ▲ One's psychological sense of being female or male.

Testosterone ▲ A male sex hormone that promotes development of male sexual characteristics and that has activating effects on sexual arousal.

Observational learning ▲ The acquisition of knowledge and skills through the observation of others (who are called *models*) rather than by means of direct experience.

Identification ▲ The process of becoming broadly like another person.

Acquiring Gender Roles.
How do people develop gender roles? What contributions are made by biological and psychological factors? Social-cognitive theory focuses on imitation of the behavior of adults of the same gender and reinforcement by parents and peers.

CLICK4™ *links to Web sites for, by, and about women. Issues include gender roles and sexism.*

▲ **REFLECT**
What are the implications of the Richardson study for understanding aggressive behavior in women?

opposed to imitation, children do not simply imitate a certain behavior pattern. They also try to become similar to the model.

Socialization also plays a role. Parents and other adults—even other children—inform children about how they are expected to behave. They reward children for behavior they consider appropriate for their gender. They punish (or fail to reinforce) children for behavior they consider inappropriate. Girls, for example, are given dolls while they are still sleeping in their cribs. They are encouraged to use the dolls to rehearse caretaking behaviors in preparation for traditional feminine adult roles. Social-cognitive theorists, unlike behaviorists, do not view the effects of rewards and punishments as being mechanical. Rather, they see rewards and punishments as providing information as to what kind of behavior is considered appropriate.

Concerning gender and aggression, Maccoby and Jacklin (1974) note that aggression is more actively discouraged in girls through punishment, withdrawal of affection, or being told that "girls don't act that way." If girls retaliate when they are insulted or attacked, they usually experience social disapproval. They therefore learn to feel anxious about the possibility of acting aggressively. Boys, on the other hand, are usually encouraged to strike back (Frodi et al., 1977).

Classic experiments point up the importance of social learning in female aggressiveness. In one study, for example, college women competed with men to see who could respond to a stimulus more quickly (Richardson et al., 1979). There were four blocks of trials, with six trials in each block. The participants could not see their opponents. The loser of each trial received an electric shock whose intensity was set by the opponent on the same sort of fearsome-looking console that was used in the Milgram experiments on obedience to authority (see Figure 1.4, p. 20). Women competed under one of three experimental conditions: public, private, or with a supportive other. In the public condition, another woman observed the participant silently. In the private condition, there was no observer. In the supportive-other condition, another woman urged the participant to retaliate strongly when her opponent selected high shock levels. As shown in Figure 13.3, women in the private and supportive-other conditions selected increasingly higher levels of shock in retaliation. Presumably, the women assumed that an observer, though silent, would frown on aggressive behavior. This assumption is likely to reflect the women's own early socialization experiences. Women who were not observed or who were urged on by another person apparently felt free to violate the gender norm of nonaggressiveness when their situations called for aggressive responses.

Social-cognitive theory outlines ways in which experience leads to concepts of gender, and how people regulate their own behavior to conform to what they believe is appropriate. Gender-schema theory suggests that we tend to assume gender-appropriate behavior patterns by blending our self-concept with cultural expectations.

Socialization ▲ The guiding of behavior through instruction and rewards and punishments.

Gender-Schema Theory   You have probably heard the expression, "looking at the world through rose-colored glasses." According to Sandra Bem (1993), the originator of **gender-schema theory,** people look at the social world through "the lenses of gender." Bem argues that our culture polarizes females and males by organizing social life around mutually exclusive gender roles. Children come to accept the polarizing scripts without realizing it. Unless parents or unusual events encourage them to challenge the validity of gender polarization, children attempt to construct identities that are consistent with the "proper" script. Most children reject behavior—in others and in themselves—that deviates from it. Children's self-esteem soon becomes wrapped up in the ways in which they measure up to the gender schema. For example, boys soon learn to hold a high opinion of themselves if they excel in sports.

Once children understand the labels *boy* and *girl*, they have a basis for blending their self-concepts with the gender schema of their culture. No external pressure is required. Children who have developed a sense of being male or being female, which usually occurs by the age of 3, actively seek information about their gender schema. As in social-cognitive theory, children seek to learn through observation what is considered appropriate for them.

There is evidence that the polarized female–male scripts serve as cognitive anchors within our culture (Bowes & Goodnow, 1996). Researchers in one study showed 5- and 6-year-old boys and girls pictures of actors engaged in "gender-consistent" or "gender-inconsistent" activities. The gender-consistent pictures showed boys playing with trains or sawing wood. Girls were shown cooking and cleaning. Gender-inconsistent pictures showed actors of the other gender engaged in these gender-typed activities. Each child was shown a randomized set of pictures that included only one picture of each activity. One week later, the children were asked who had engaged in the activity, a male or a female. Both boys and girls gave wrong answers more often when the picture they had seen showed gender-*inconsistent* activity. In other words, they distorted what they had seen to conform to the gender schema.

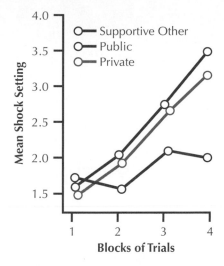

FIGURE 13.3   Mean Shock Settings Selected by Women in Retaliation Against Male Opponents.
Women in the Richardson study chose higher shock levels for their opponents when they were alone or when another person (a "supportive other") urged them on.

REFLECT
Is your self-esteem wrapped up in how well you fit the masculine or feminine gender schema in our society? Explain.

IN REVIEW
Influences on Gender-Typing

BIOLOGICAL INFLUENCES

Brain Organization	The brain hemispheres are apparently more specialized in males than in females. As a result, women may exceed men in verbal skills that require some spatial organization, such as reading and spelling, while men may excel at more specialized spatial-relations tasks such as visualizing objects in space.
Sex Hormones	Prenatal sex hormones may "masculinize" or "feminize" the brain by creating predispositions that are consistent with gender-role stereotypes, such as the greater activity levels and aggressiveness of males.

PSYCHOLOGICAL INFLUENCES

Psychodynamic Theory	Freud connected gender-typing with resolution of the Oedipus and Electra complexes. However, research shows that gender-typing occurs prior to the age at which these complexes would be resolved.
Social-Cognitive Theory	Social-cognitive theorists explain gender-typing in terms of observational learning, identification (as a broad form of imitation), and socialization. Research supports a role for social learning in aggressive behavior.
Gender-Schema Theory	Children come to look at the social world through "the lenses of gender." Our culture polarizes females and males by organizing social life around mutually exclusive gender roles. Children come to accept these without realizing it and attempt to construct identities that are consistent with the "proper" script.

Gender-schema theory ▲ The view that gender identity plus knowledge of the distribution of behavior patterns into feminine and masculine roles motivate and guide the gender-typing of the child.

In sum, brain organization and sex hormones contribute to gender-typed behavior and play roles in verbal ability, math skills, and aggression. Social-cognitive theory outlines environmental factors that influence children to engage in "gender-appropriate" behavior. Gender-schema theory focuses on how children blend their self-identities with the gender schema of their culture.

REVIEW

(9) According to _____ theory, gender differences were fashioned by means of natural selection. (10) Research in brain-imaging suggests that the brain hemispheres are more specialized in (males or females?). (11) Behaviors such as maze learning and aggression appear to be connected with exposure to the hormone _____. (12) Social-cognitive theorists note that children learn what is considered masculine or feminine by means of _____ learning. (13) According to _____-schema theory, children accept polarizing scripts without realizing it. (14) Children's self-_____ then becomes wrapped up in how well they fit the gender schema of their culture.

Pulling It Together: Anna Quindlen wrote an article in which she asked, "Is testosterone toxic?" What might she have meant?

ATTRACTION: ON LIKING, LOVING, AND RELATIONSHIPS

Sexual interactions usually take place within relationships. Feelings of attraction can lead to liking and perhaps to love, and to a more lasting relationship. In this section we see that **attraction** to another person is influenced by factors such as physical appearance and attitudes. We will see that most people are *hetero*sexual; that is, they are sexually attracted to people of the other gender. However, some people are *homo*sexual; that is, they are sexually attracted to people of their own gender. *Question: What factors contribute to attraction in our culture?*

Attraction ▲ In social psychology, an attitude of liking or disliking (negative attraction).

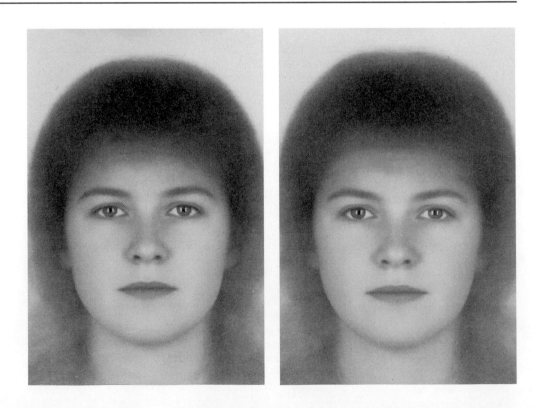

FIGURE 13.4   What Features Contribute to Facial Attractiveness?
In both England and Japan, features such as large eyes, high cheekbones, and narrow jaws contribute to perceptions of the attractiveness of women. Part A shows a composite of the faces of 15 women rated as the most attractive of a group of 60. Part B is a composite in which the features of these 15 women are exaggerated—that is, developed further in the direction that separates them from the average of the entire 60.

"Looking Good."
Models like these are among those who set the standards for beauty in contemporary U.S. culture. How important is physical attractiveness in interpersonal attraction and social and vocational success?

Factors Contributing to Attraction

Among the factors contributing to attraction are physical appearance, similarity, and reciprocity.

Physical Appearance: How Important Is Looking Good?   Physical appearance is a key factor in attraction and in the consideration of partners for dates and marriage (Langlois et al., 2000; Sangrador & Yela, 2000). What determines physical allure? Are our standards subjective—that is, "in the eye of the beholder"? Or is there general agreement on what is appealing?

Many aspects of beauty appear to be cross-cultural (Langlois et al., 2000). For example, a study of people in England and Japan found that both British and Japanese men consider women with large eyes, high cheekbones, and narrow jaws to be most attractive (Perret, 1994). In his research, Perret created computer composites of the faces of 60 women and, as shown in part A of Figure 13.4, of the 15 women who were rated the most attractive. He then used computer enhancement to exaggerate the differences between the composite of the 60 and the composite of the 15 most attractive women. He arrived at the image shown in part B of Figure 13.4. Part B, which shows higher cheekbones and a narrower jaw than part A, was rated as the most attractive image. Similar results were found for the image of a Japanese woman. Works of art suggest that the ancient Greeks and Egyptians favored similar facial features.

In our society, tallness is an asset for men (Hensley, 1994; Pierce, 1996). Although women may be less demanding than men concerning a variety of physical feature, height—that is, tallness—is more important to women in the selection of dates and mates than it is to men.

Although preferences for facial features may transcend time and culture, preferences for body weight and shape may be more culturally determined. For example, plumpness has been valued in many cultures. Grandmothers who worry that their granddaughters are starving themselves often come from cultures in which stoutness is acceptable or desirable. In contemporary Western society, there is pressure on both males and females to be slender (Goode, 2000; Wade et al., 2000). Women generally favor men with a V-taper—broad shoulders and a narrow waist.

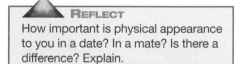

REFLECT
How important is physical appearance to you in a date? In a mate? Is there a difference? Explain.

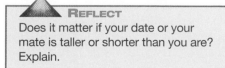

REFLECT
Does it matter if your date or your mate is taller or shorter than you are? Explain.

Although both genders perceive overweight people as unappealing, there are fascinating gender differences in perceptions of desirable body shapes. College men tend to consider their current physique similar to the ideal male build and to the one that women find most appealing (Fallon & Rozin, 1985). College women, in contrast, generally see themselves as markedly heavier than the figure that is most appealing to men and heavier still than the ideal (see Figure 13.5). Both mothers and fathers of college students see themselves as heavier than their ideal weight (Rozin & Fallon, 1988). Both genders err in their estimates of the other gender's preferences, however. Men of both generations actually prefer women to be heavier than the women presume. Both college women and their mothers prefer men who are slimmer than the men presume.

As we see in the following section, there are important gender differences in the emphasis that we place on physical appearance.

DIVERSITY *Gender Differences in the Importance of Physical Attractiveness*

> *Your Daddy's rich*
> *And your Ma is good lookin',*
> *So hush, little baby,*
> *Don't you cry.*
>
> —From "Summertime" (*from the opera* Porgy & Bess)

FIGURE 13.5   Can You Ever Be Too Thin?
Research suggests that most college women believe that they are heavier than they ought to be. However, men actually prefer women to be a bit heavier than women assume the men would like them to be.

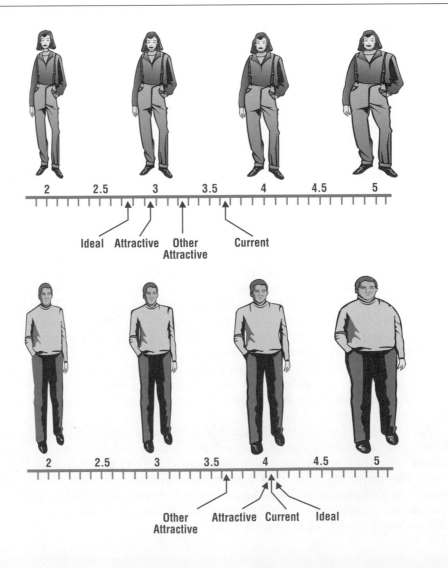

How important to you is your partner's physical appearance? Studies on mate selection find that women tend to place greater emphasis than men on traits such as professional status, consideration, dependability, kindness, and fondness for children. Men place relatively greater emphasis on physical allure, cooking ability (can't they turn on the microwave oven themselves?), even thrift (Buss, 1994; Feingold, 1992a).

Susan Sprecher and her colleagues (1994) surveyed more than 13,000 people in the United States. They asked how willing they would be to marry someone who was older, younger, of a different religion, unlikely to hold a steady job, not good-looking, and so on. Each item was answered by checking off a 7-point scale in which 1 meant "not at all" and 7 meant "very willing." Women were more willing than men to marry someone who was not good-looking (see Figure 13.6). But they were less willing to marry someone who was unlikely to hold a steady job.

Evolutionary psychologists believe that evolutionary forces favor the survival of women who desire status in their mates and men who emphasize physical allure because these preferences provide reproductive advantages. Some physical features such as cleanliness, good complexion, clear eyes, strong teeth and healthy hair, firm muscle tone, and a steady gait are found to be universally appealing to both genders (Buss, 1999). Perhaps such traits have value as markers of better reproductive potential in prospective mates. According to the "parental investment model," a woman's appeal is more strongly connected with her age and health, both of which are markers of reproductive capacity. The value of men as reproducers, however, is more intertwined with factors that contribute to a stable environment for child rearing—such as social standing and reliability (Feingold, 1992a). For such reasons, evolutionary psychologists speculate that these qualities may have grown relatively more alluring to women over the millennia (e.g., Buss, 1994).

This theory is largely speculative, however, and not fully consistent with all the evidence. Women, like men, are attracted to physically appealing partners, and women tend to marry men similar to them in physical attractiveness and socioeconomic standing. Aging men are more likely than younger men to die from natural causes. The wealth they accrue may not always be transmitted to their spouses and children, either. Many women may be more able to find reproductive success by mating with a fit, younger male than with an older, higher-status male. Even evolutionary psychologists allow that despite any innate predispositions, many men desire older women.

"Pretty Is as Pretty Does?"   Both men and women are perceived as more attractive when they are smiling (Reis et al., 1990). There is thus ample reason to, as the song goes, "put on a happy face" when you are meeting people or looking for a date.

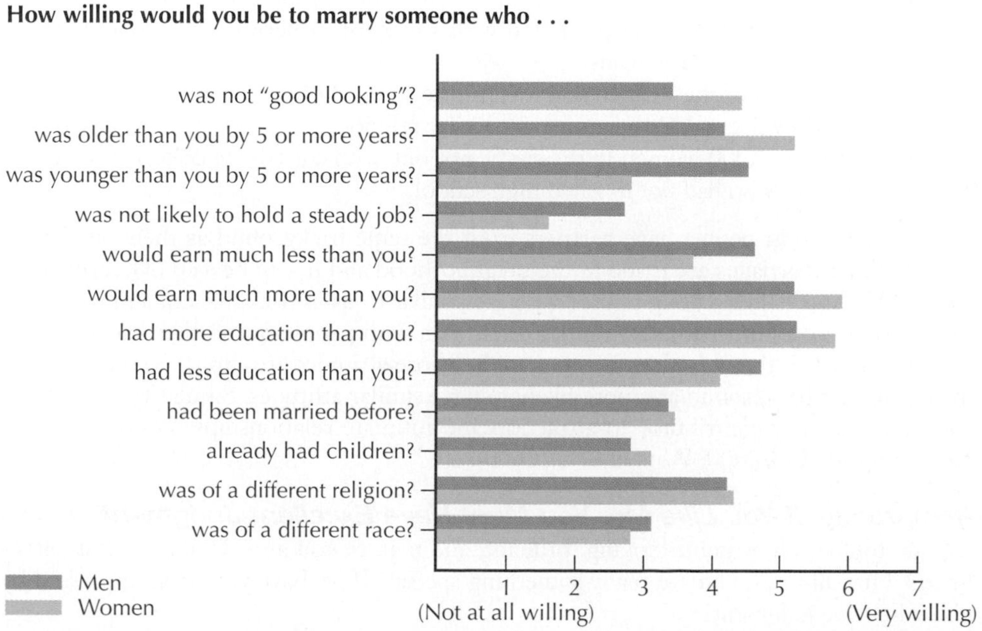

www 13 E 3

CLICK4™ *an essay assignment on attraction—is there an evolutionary basis for what attracts us to another person?*

How willing would you be to marry someone who . . .

- was not "good looking"?
- was older than you by 5 or more years?
- was younger than you by 5 or more years?
- was not likely to hold a steady job?
- would earn much less than you?
- would earn much more than you?
- had more education than you?
- had less education than you?
- had been married before?
- already had children?
- was of a different religion?
- was of a different race?

■ Men
■ Women

1   2   3   4   5   6   7
(Not at all willing)   (Very willing)

FIGURE 13.6   Gender Differences in Mate Preferences.
Susan Sprecher and her colleagues found that men are more willing than women to marry someone who is several years younger and less well-educated. Women, on the other hand, are more willing than men to marry someone who is not good-looking and who earns more money than they do.

The Matching Hypothesis.
Do opposites attract, or do we tend to pair off with people who look and think the way we do? As suggested by these photographs, similarity often runs at least skin-deep.

Other aspects of behavior also affect interpersonal attraction. Women who are shown videotapes of prospective dates or asked to describe ideal partners tend to prefer men who are outgoing, self-assertive, and self-confident (Burger & Cosby, 1999). However, college men respond negatively to women who show self-assertion and social dominance (Sadalla et al., 1987). Despite the liberating trends of recent years, the cultural stereotype of the ideal woman still includes modesty. I am *not* suggesting that self-assertive women should take a back seat in order to make themselves more appealing to traditional men. Assertive women might find nothing but conflict in their interactions with such men in any case.

CLICK4™ *online advice about relationships.*

The Matching Hypothesis: Do "Opposites Attract" or Do "Birds of a Feather Flock Together"?

Although we may rate highly attractive people as most desirable, most of us are not left to blend in with the wallpaper. According to the **matching hypothesis,** we tend to date people who are similar to ourselves in physical attractiveness rather than the local Will Smith or Sandra Bullock look-alike. One motive for asking out "matches" seems to be fear of rejection by more attractive people (Bernstein et al., 1983).

The quest for similarity extends beyond physical attractiveness. Our marital and sex partners tend to be similar to us in race/ethnicity, age, level of education, and religion. Consider some findings of the National Health and Social Life Survey (Michael et al., 1994, pp. 45–47):

▲ Nearly 94% of single European American men have European American women as their sex partners; 2% are partnered with Latina Americans, 2% with Asian American women, and less than 1% with African American women.

▲ About 82% of African American men have African American women as their sex partners; nearly 8% are partnered with European American women and almost 5% with Latina Americans.

▲ About 83% of the women and men in the study chose partners within 5 years of their own age and of the same or a similar religion.

▲ Of nearly 2,000 women in the study, not one with a graduate college degree had a partner who had not finished high school.

Why do most people have partners from the same background as their own? One reason is that marriages are made in the neighborhood and not in heaven (Michael et al., 1994). We tend to live among people who are similar to us in background, and we therefore come into contact with them more often than with people from other backgrounds. Another reason is that we are drawn to people whose attitudes are similar to ours. People from a similar background are more likely to have similar attitudes. Similarity in attitudes and tastes is a key contributor to attraction and intimate relationships (Laumann et al., 1994; Singh & Ho, 2000; Watson et al., 2000).

Reciprocity: If You Like Me, You Must Have Excellent Judgment

Has anyone told you how good-looking, brilliant, and mature you are? That your taste is refined? That all in all, you are really something special? If so, have you been impressed by his or her fine judgment?

> ▲ **REFLECT**
> Could you maintain a relationship with a partner whose attitudes toward religion, politics, education, and child-rearing differed significantly from your own? Would you want to?

> ▲ **REFLECT**
> Has anyone told you how good-looking, brilliant, and mature you are? That your taste is refined? That all in all, you are really something special? If so, have you been impressed by his or her fine judgment? Explain.

Matching hypothesis ▲ The view that people tend to choose persons similar to themselves in attractiveness and attitudes in the formation of interpersonal relationships.

Reciprocity is a powerful determinant of attraction (Sprecher, 1998). We tend to return feelings of admiration. We tend to be more open, warm, and helpful when we are interacting with strangers who seem to like us (Curtis & Miller, 1986).

Feelings of attraction are influenced by factors such as physical appearance and similarity. Let us explore what we mean when we say that feelings of attraction have blossomed into love. *Questions: Just what is love? What is romantic love?*

Love: Doing What Happens . . . Culturally?

Love—the ideal for which we make great sacrifice. Love—the sentiment that launched a thousand ships in Homer's epic poem *The Iliad*. Through the millennia, poets have sought to capture love in words. Dante, the Italian poet who shed some light on the Dark Ages, wrote of "the love that moves the sun and the other stars." The Scottish poet Robert Burns wrote that his love was like "a red, red rose." Love is beautiful and elusive. Passion and romantic love are also lusty, surging with sexual desire.

The Love Triangle   No, this love triangle does not refer to two men wooing the same woman. It refers to Robert Sternberg's **triangular model of love.** Sternberg (1988) believes that love can include combinations of three components: intimacy, passion, and commitment (see Figure 13.7).

Intimacy refers to a couple's closeness, to their mutual concern and sharing of feelings and resources. **Passion** means romance and sexual feelings. Commitment means deciding to enhance and maintain the relationship. Passion is most crucial in short-term relationships. Intimacy and commitment are more important in enduring relationships. The ideal form of love combines all three: **consummate love.** Consummate love is made up of romantic love plus commitment.

Romantic love is characterized by passion and intimacy. Passion involves fascination (preoccupation with the loved one); sexual craving; and the desire for exclusiveness (a special relationship with the loved one). Intimacy involves caring—championing the interests of the loved one, even if it entails sacrificing one's own. People are cognitively

Reciprocity ▲ In interpersonal attraction, the tendency to return feelings and attitudes that are expressed about us.
Triangular model of love ▲ Sternberg's view that love involves combinations of three components: intimacy, passion, and decision/commitment.
Intimacy ▲ Close acquaintance and familiarity; a characteristic of a relationship in which partners share their innermost feelings.
Passion ▲ Strong romantic and sexual feelings.
Consummate love ▲ The ideal form of love within Sternberg's model, which combines passion, intimacy, and commitment.
Romantic love ▲ An intense, positive emotion that involves sexual attraction, feelings of caring, and the belief that one is in love.

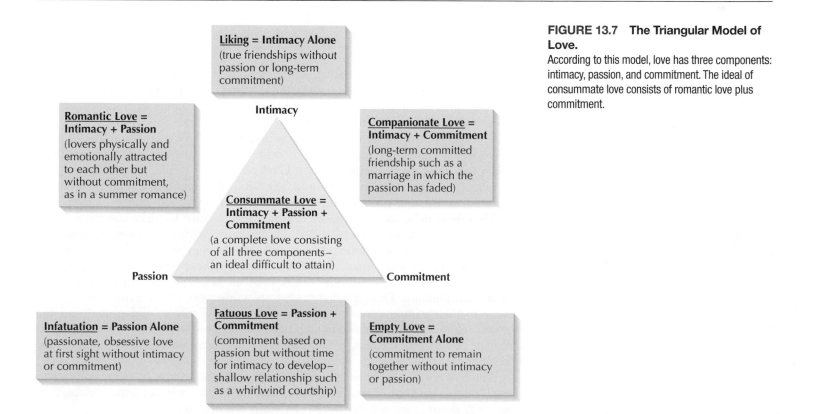

FIGURE 13.7   The Triangular Model of Love.

According to this model, love has three components: intimacy, passion, and commitment. The ideal of consummate love consists of romantic love plus commitment.

Has Cupid Shot His Arrow Into Your Heart? The Triangular Love Scale

Which are the strongest components of your love relationship? Intimacy? Passion? Commitment? All three components? Two of them?

To complete the following scale, fill in the blank spaces with the name of one person you love or care about deeply. Then rate your agreement with each of the items by using a 9-point scale in which 1 = "not at all," 5 = "moderately," and 9 = "extremely." Use points in between to indicate intermediate levels of agreement between these values. Then consult the scoring key in Appendix B.

INTIMACY COMPONENT

_____ 1. I am actively supportive of _____'s well-being.

_____ 2. I have a warm relationship with _____.

_____ 3. I am able to count on _____ in times of need.

_____ 4. _____ is able to count on me in times of need.

_____ 5. I am willing to share myself and my possessions with _____.

_____ 6. I receive considerable emotional support from _____.

_____ 7. I give considerable emotional support to _____.

_____ 8. I communicate well with _____.

_____ 9. I value _____ greatly in my life.

_____ 10. I feel close to _____.

_____ 11. I have a comfortable relationship with _____.

_____ 12. I feel that I really understand _____.

_____ 13. I feel that _____ really understands me.

_____ 14. I feel that I can really trust _____.

_____ 15. I share deeply personal information about myself with _____.

PASSION COMPONENT

_____ 16. Just seeing _____ excites me.

_____ 17. I find myself thinking about _____ frequently during the day.

_____ 18. My relationship with _____ is very romantic.

_____ 19. I find _____ to be very personally attractive.

_____ 20. I idealize _____.

_____ 21. I cannot imagine another person making me as happy as _____ does.

_____ 22. I would rather be with _____ than anyone else.

CLICK4™ *a quiz covering the first half of this chapter.*

biased toward evaluating their dating partners positively (Baron & Byrne, 2000). They tend to pay attention to information that confirms their romantic interests. In less technical terms, romantic lovers often idealize each other. They magnify each other's positive features and overlook their flaws.

To experience romantic love, in contrast to attachment or sexual arousal, one must be exposed to a culture that idealizes the concept. In Western culture, romantic love blossoms in fairy tales about Sleeping Beauty, Cinderella, Snow White, and all their princes charming. It matures with romantic novels, television tales and films, and the personal accounts of friends and relatives about dates and romances.

Men seem to be somewhat more reluctant than women to make commitments in their romantic relationships (Buss, 1995). Evolutionary psychologists suggest that men may be naturally more promiscuous because they are the genetic heirs of ancestors whose reproductive success was connected with the number of women they could impregnate (Bjorklund & Kipp, 1996; Buss, 1994, 1999). But women can produce relatively few children in their lifetimes. Thus, the theory suggests, women need to be more selective with respect to their mating partners. Is it possible that the man's "roving eye" and the woman's selectivity are embedded in their genes? (This possibility is *not* intended to provide male readers with the excuse: "But how can I make a commitment? Running around is in my genes.")

Much of our discussion has referred to romantic relationships between women and men. However, millions of people in the United States have another sexual orientation. *Question: What is meant by the term sexual orientation?*

_____ 23. There is nothing more important to me than my relationship with _____.

_____ 24. I especially like physical contact with _____.

_____ 25. There is something almost "magical" about my relationship with _____.

_____ 26. I adore _____.

_____ 27. I cannot imagine life without _____.

_____ 28. My relationship with _____ is passionate.

_____ 29. When I see romantic movies and read romantic books, I think of _____.

_____ 30. I fantasize about _____.

DECISION/COMMITMENT COMPONENT

_____ 31. I know that I care about _____.

_____ 32. I am committed to maintaining my relationship with _____.

_____ 33. Because of my commitment to _____, I would not let other people come between us.

_____ 34. I have confidence in the stability of my relationship with _____.

_____ 35. I could not let anything get in the way of my commitment to _____.

_____ 36. I expect my love for _____ to last for the rest of my life.

_____ 37. I will always feel a strong responsibility for _____.

_____ 38. I view my commitment to _____ as a solid one.

_____ 39. I cannot imagine ending my relationship with _____.

_____ 40. I am certain of my love for _____.

_____ 41. I view my relationship with _____ as permanent.

_____ 42. I view my relationship with _____ as a good decision.

_____ 43. I feel a sense of responsibility toward _____.

_____ 44. I plan to continue my relationship with _____.

_____ 45. Even when _____ is hard to deal with, I remain committed to our relationship.

SOURCE: Sternberg, 1988. Reprinted by permission of Basic Books, Inc., Publishers, New York.

CLICK4™ *the interactive version of this Self-Assessment.*

Sexual Orientation: The Direction of Erotic Impulses

Sexual orientation refers to the organization or direction of one's erotic interests. **Heterosexual** people are sexually attracted to people of the other gender and interested in forming romantic relationships with them. **Homosexual** people are sexually attracted to people of their own gender and interested in forming romantic relationships with them. Homosexual males are also referred to as **gay males** and homosexual females as **lesbians.** **Bisexual** people are sexually attracted to, and interested in forming romantic relationships with, both women and men.

The concept of *sexual orientation* is not to be confused with *sexual activity.* For example, engaging in sexual activity with people of one's own gender does not necessarily mean that one has a homosexual orientation. Sexual activity between males sometimes reflects limited sexual opportunities. Adolescent males may manually stimulate one another while fantasizing about girls. Men in prisons may similarly turn to each other as sexual outlets. Young Sambian men in New Guinea engage in sexual practices exclusively with older males, since it is believed that they must drink "men's milk" to achieve the fierce manhood of the headhunter (Money, 1987). Once they reach marrying age, however, their sexual activities are limited to female partners.

Surveys find that about 3% of men in the United States identify themselves as being gay (e.g., Laumann et al., 1994). About 2% of the U.S. women surveyed say that they have a lesbian sexual orientation (Laumann et al., 1994).

> ▲ **REFLECT**
> What are the attitudes of people from your sociocultural group toward gay males and lesbians? Do you share these attitudes? Why, or why not?

Sexual orientation ▲ The directionality of one's erotic interests—that is, whether one is sexually attracted to, and interested in forming romantic relationships with, people of the other or the same gender.

Heterosexual ▲ Referring to people who are sexually aroused by, and interested in forming romantic relationships with, people of the other gender.

Homosexual ▲ Referring to people who are sexually aroused by, and interested in forming romantic relationships with, people of the same gender. (Derived from the Greek *homos,* meaning "same," not from the Latin *homo,* meaning "man.")

Gay male ▲ A male homosexual.

Lesbian ▲ A female homosexual.

Bisexual ▲ A person who is sexually aroused by, and interested in forming romantic relationships with, people of either gender.

L'Abandon (Les Deux Amies).
This painting by Henri de Toulouse-Lautrec is of lesbian lovers.

www **13 BBC** 4

CLICK4™ *a bulletin board discussion on sexual orientation and homophobia.*

www **13 WS** 4

CLICK4™ *a WebSearch activity: Does research suggest that people choose their sexual orientation?*

www **13 L** 3

CLICK4™ *information about the rise of violence against gays in America.*

▲ REFLECT
Do you believe that people can *choose* to be heterosexual or gay? (Did *you* choose your sexual orientation?)

Oedipus complex ▲ Within psychodynamic theory, a conflict of the phallic stage which is characterized by romantic feelings toward the parent of the other gender and feelings of rivalry toward the parent of the same gender.

Organizing effect ▲ The directional effect of sex hormones—for example, along stereotypically masculine or feminine lines.

Activating effect ▲ The arousal-producing effects of sex hormones that increase the likelihood of sexual behavior.

Origins of Sexual Orientation   Sexual orientation, like gender-typing, is an aspect of the development of the individual. And, as with gender-typing, there are psychological and biological theories of its origin, as well as theories that bridge the two.   *Question: How do researchers explain gay male and lesbian sexual orientations?*

As was the case with gender-typing, let us begin our search for the psychological roots of sexual orientation with psychodynamic theory, largely because of its historic importance. Psychodynamic theory ties sexual orientation to identification with male or female figures. Identification, in turn, is related to resolution of the Oedipus and Electra complexes (Downey & Friedman, 1998). In men, faulty resolution of the **Oedipus complex** would stem from a "classic pattern" of child rearing in which there is a "close binding" mother and a "detached hostile" father. Boys reared in such a home environment would identify with their mother and not with their father. Psychodynamic theory has been criticized, however, because many gay males have had excellent relationships with both parents (Isay, 1990). Also, the childhoods of many heterosexuals fit the "classic pattern."

From a learning theory point of view, early reinforcement of sexual behavior (for example, by orgasm achieved through interaction with people of one's own gender) can influence one's sexual orientation. But most people are aware of their sexual orientation before they have sexual contacts (Bell et al., 1981).

Researchers have found evidence for possible genetic factors in sexual orientation (Bailey et al., 2000; Dawood et al., 2000; Kendler et al., 2000c; Lalumière et al., 2000). In one study, 22% of the brothers of 51 primarily gay men were either gay or bisexual themselves. This is about four times the percentage found in the general population (Pillard & Weinrich, 1986). Moreover, according to research by Bailey and Pillard (1991), identical (MZ) twins have a higher agreement rate for a gay male sexual orientation than do fraternal (DZ) twins: 52% for MZ twins versus 22% for DZ twins. Although genetic factors may partly determine sexual orientation, psychologist John Money, who has specialized in research on sexual behavior, concludes that sexual orientation is "not under the direct governance of chromosomes and genes" (1987, p. 384).

Sex hormones may play a role in sexual orientation (Lalumière et al., 2000). These hormones promote biological sexual differentiation and regulate the menstrual cycle. They also have organizing and activating effects on sexual behavior. They predispose lower animals toward masculine or feminine mating patterns—a directional or **organizing effect** (Crews, 1994). They also affect the sex drive and promote sexual response; these are **activating effects.**

Sexual behavior among many lower animals is almost completely governed by hormones (Crews, 1994). In many species, if the sex organs and brains of fetuses are exposed to large doses of testosterone in the uterus (which occurs naturally when they share the uterus with many brothers, or artificially as a result of hormone injections), they become masculine in structure (Crews, 1994). Prenatal testosterone organizes the brains of females in the masculine direction, predisposing them toward masculine behaviors in adulthood. Testosterone in adulthood then apparently activates the masculine behavior patterns.

Because sex hormones predispose lower animals toward masculine or feminine mating patterns, some have asked whether gay males and lesbians might differ from heterosexuals in levels of sex hormones. However, a gay male or lesbian sexual orientation has not been reliably linked to current (adult) levels of male or female sex hormones (Friedman & Downey, 1994).

What about the effects of sex hormones on the developing fetus? We know that prenatal sex hormones can "masculinize" or "feminize" the brains of laboratory animals. There is also some evidence that sex hormones affect the sexual orientation of the embryo (Dessens, et al., 1999; Ellis, 1990; Ellis & Ames, 1987). Hormone levels in the uterus may be influenced by genetic factors, synthetic hormones (such as **androgens**), and maternal stress. Why maternal stress? Stress causes the release of hormones such as **adrenaline** and **cortisol,** which can affect the prenatal development of the brain. Perhaps the brains of some gay males have been feminized and the brains of some lesbians masculinized prior to birth (Collaer & Hines, 1995; Friedman & Downey, 1994).

In sum, the determinants of sexual orientation are mysterious and complex. Research suggests that they may involve prenatal hormone levels—which can be affected by factors such as heredity, drugs, and maternal stress—and postnatal socialization. However, the precise interaction among these influences is not yet understood.

We can note quite seriously that the difficulties in explaining homosexuality are hardly different from the difficulties in explaining heterosexuality. Most people tend to assume that heterosexuality is "natural," but this assumption does not explain how individuals develop to become either heterosexual or homosexual. (People do not simply become heterosexual because of cultural or religious tradition!) We still need to consider the likely interactions of psychological and biological factors in heterosexuality. Until we find the answers, the origins of heterosexuality will also remain mysterious.

REVIEW

(15) Physical attractiveness (is or is not?) a key factor in the selection of dates and mates. (16) College men tend to see their body shape as (too heavy, too slender, or ideal?). (17) College women tend to see their figure as (too heavy, too slender, or ideal?). (18) According to the _____ hypothesis, we tend to date people who are similar to ourselves. (19) According to the _____ model of love, love can include combinations of intimacy, passion, and commitment.

(20) Sexual _____ refers to the direction of one's erotic interests. (21) _____ theory ties sexual orientation to identification with male or female figures following resolution of the Oedipus and Electra complexes. (22) Sex hormones have _____ and activating effects.

Putting It Together: How might the features found attractive by males and females provide humans with an evolutionary advantage? Does the research suggest that people choose their sexual orientation? Explain.

SEXUAL RESPONSE

Although we may consider ourselves sophisticated about sex, it is surprising how little we know about sexual biology. How many male readers know that women have different orifices for urination and sexual intercourse? How many readers know that the penis—sometimes referred to by the slang term "boner" when erect—contains no bones? In this

---

CLICK4™ *the American Psychological Association's answers to FAQs on sexual orientation and homosexuality.*

Androgens ▲ Male sex hormones.

Adrenaline ▲ A hormone produced by the adrenal glands that generally arouses people and heightens their emotional responsiveness.

Cortisol ▲ A hormone produced by the adrenal glands that increases resistance to stress.

FIGURE 13.8 Levels of Sexual Arousal During the Phases of the Sexual Response Cycle.

Masters and Johnson divide the sexual response cycle into four phases: excitement, plateau, orgasm, and resolution. During the resolution phase, the level of sexual arousal returns to the prearoused state. For men there is a refractory period following orgasm. As shown by the broken line, however, men can become rearoused to orgasm once the refractory period is past and their levels of sexual arousal have returned to pre-plateau levels. Pattern A for women shows a response cycle with the women experiencing multiple orgasms. Pattern B shows the cycle of a woman who reaches the plateau phase but for whom arousal is "resolved" without reaching the orgasmic phase. Pattern C shows the possibility of orgasm in a highly aroused woman who passes quickly through the plateau phase.

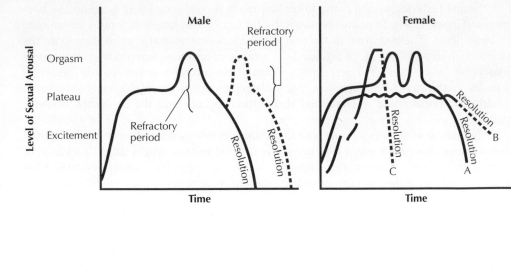

section, we first consider how females and males respond to sexual stimulation—that is, the so-called sexual response cycle. Then we consider some of the things that can go wrong with the cycle. These are known as *sexual dysfunctions.*

The Sexual Response Cycle

Although we may be culturally attuned to focus on gender differences rather than similarities, William Masters and Virginia Johnson (1966) found that the biological responses of males and females to sexual stimulation—that is, their sexual response cycles—are quite similar. *Question: What is the sexual response cycle?* Masters and Johnson use the term *sexual response cycle* to describe the changes that occur in the body as men and women become sexually aroused. Masters and Johnson divide the **sexual response cycle** into four phases: *excitement, plateau, orgasm,* and *resolution.* Figure 13.8 suggests the levels of sexual arousal associated with each phase.

The sexual response cycle is characterized by vasocongestion and myotonia. **Vasocongestion** is the swelling of the genital tissues with blood. It causes erection of the penis and swelling of the area surrounding the vaginal opening. The testes, the nipples, and even the earlobes swell as blood vessels dilate in these areas.

Myotonia is muscle tension. It causes facial grimaces, spasms in the hands and feet, and then the spasms of orgasm.

Excitement Phase
Vasocongestion during the **excitement phase** can cause erection in young men as soon as 3 to 8 seconds after sexual stimulation begins. The scrotal skin also thickens, becoming less baggy. The testes increase in size and become elevated.

In the female, excitement is characterized by vaginal lubrication, which may start 10 to 30 seconds after sexual stimulation begins. Vasocongestion swells the **clitoris** and flattens and spreads the vaginal lips. The inner part of the vagina expands. The breasts enlarge, and blood vessels near the surface become more prominent.

In the excitement phase the skin may take on a rosy *sex flush.* This is more pronounced in women. The nipples may become erect in both men and women. Heart rate and blood pressure also increase.

Plateau Phase
The level of sexual arousal remains somewhat stable during the **plateau phase** of the cycle. Because of vasocongestion, men show some increase in the circumference of the head of the penis, which also takes on a purplish hue. The testes are elevated into position for **ejaculation** and may reach one and a half times their unaroused size.

Sexual Response Cycle ▲ Masters and Johnson's model of sexual response, which consists of four stages or phases.
Vasocongestion ▲ Engorgement of blood vessels with blood, which swells the genitals and breasts during sexual arousal.
Myotonia ▲ Muscle tension.
Excitement phase ▲ The first phase of the sexual response cycle, which is characterized by muscle tension, increases in the heart rate, and erection in the male and vaginal lubrication in the female.
Clitoris ▲ The female sex organ that is most sensitive to sexual sensation; a smooth, round knob of tissue that resembles a button and is situated above the urethral opening.
Plateau phase ▲ The second phase of the sexual response cycle, which is characterized by increases in vasocongestion, muscle tension, heart rate, and blood pressure in preparation for orgasm.
Ejaculation ▲ The process of propelling seminal fluid (semen) from the penis.

In women, vasocongestion swells the outer part of the vagina, contracting the vaginal opening in preparation for grasping the penis. The inner part of the vagina expands further. The clitoris withdraws beneath the clitoral hood and shortens.

Breathing becomes rapid, like panting. Heart rate may increase to 100 to 160 beats per minute. Blood pressure continues to rise.

Orgasmic Phase

The orgasmic phase in the male consists of two stages of muscular contractions. In the first stage, **seminal fluid** collects at the base of the penis. The internal sphincter of the urinary bladder prevents urine from mixing with semen. In the second stage, muscle contractions propel the ejaculate out of the body. Sensations of pleasure tend to be related to the strength of the contractions and the amount of seminal fluid present. The first 3 to 4 contractions are generally most intense and occur at 0.8-second intervals (5 contractions every 4 seconds). Another two to four contractions occur at a somewhat slower pace. Rates and patterns can vary from one man to another.

Orgasm in the female is manifested by 3 to 15 contractions of the pelvic muscles that surround the vaginal barrel. The contractions first occur at 0.8-second intervals. As in the male, they produce release of sexual tension. Weaker and slower contractions follow.

Erection, vaginal lubrication, and orgasm are all reflexes. That is, they occur automatically in response to adequate sexual stimulation. Of course, the decision to enter a sexual relationship is voluntary, as are the decisions to kiss and pet and so on.

Blood pressure and heart rate reach a peak, with the heart beating up to 180 times per minute. Respiration may increase to 40 breaths per minute.

Resolution Phase

After orgasm the body returns to its unaroused state. This is called the **resolution phase.** After ejaculation, blood is released from engorged areas, so that the erection disappears. The testes return to their normal size.

In women orgasm also triggers the release of blood from engorged areas. The nipples return to their normal size. The clitoris and vaginal barrel gradually shrink to their unaroused sizes. Blood pressure, heart rate, and breathing also return to their levels before arousal. Both partners may feel relaxed and satisfied.

Unlike women, men enter a **refractory period** during which they cannot experience another orgasm or ejaculate. The refractory period of adolescent males may last only minutes, whereas that of men age 50 and above may last from several minutes to a day. Women do not undergo a refractory period and therefore can become quickly rearoused to the point of repeated (multiple) orgasm if they desire and receive continued sexual stimulation.

We have described common patterns of sexual response, but we should note that not everyone becomes sexually aroused by the same kinds of stimulation. In fact, a number of people experience serious sexual problems or "dysfunctions." *Question: What are sexual dysfunctions?*

Sexual Dysfunctions and Sex Therapy

Sexual dysfunctions are persistent problems in becoming sexually aroused or reaching orgasm. Many people will be troubled by a sexual dysfunction at one time or another. Let's take a look at the main types of sexual dysfunctions and their causes.

Types of Sexual Dysfunction

The sexual dysfunctions include hypoactive sexual desire disorder, female sexual arousal disorder, male erectile disorder, orgasmic disorder, premature ejaculation, dyspareunia, and vaginismus. The frequencies of these problems in the general population are suggested in Table 13.2.

DIVERSITY

TABLE 13.2   CURRENT SEXUAL DYSFUNCTIONS ACCORDING TO THE NHSLS STUDY (PERCENT OF RESPONDENTS REPORTING THE PROBLEM WITHIN THE PAST YEAR)

	Men	Women
Pain during sex *(dyspareunia)*	3.0	14.4
Sex not pleasurable	8.1	21.2
Unable to reach orgasm *(orgasmic disorder)*	8.3	24.1
Lack of interest in sex *(hypoactive sexual desire)*	15.8	33.4
Anxiety about performance*	17.0	11.5
Reaching climax too early *(premature ejaculation*, in the male)	28.5	10.3
Unable to keep an erection *(male erectile disorder*, also called *erectile dysfunction*, or "*ED*")†	10.4	—
Having trouble lubricating *(female sexual arousal disorder)*	—	18.8

SOURCE: Adapted from Tables 10.8A and 10.8B, pp. 370 and 371, in Laumann, E. O., Gagnon, J. H., Michael, R. T., & Michaels, S. (1994). *The social organization of sexuality: Sexual practices in the United States.* Chicago: University of Chicago Press.

* Anxiety about performance is not itself a sexual dysfunction. However, it figures prominently in sexual dysfunctions.

† Other studies show that as many as half or more of men in middle and late adulthood have difficulty obtaining or maintaining an erection.

REFLECT

Do the changes experienced by women and men during the sexual response cycle seem to be more different or more alike? Explain.

 www 13 E 4

CLICK4™ *an essay assignment on gender, sexual response, and sexual dysfunction.*

Seminal fluid ▲ The fluid produced by the prostate and other glands that carries and nourishes sperm. Also called *semen.*

Orgasm ▲ The height or climax of sexual excitement, involving involuntary muscle contractions, release of sexual tensions, and, usually, subjective feelings of pleasure.

Resolution phase ▲ The fourth phase of the sexual response cycle, during which the body gradually returns to its prearoused state.

Refractory period ▲ In the sexual response cycle, a period of time following orgasm during which an individual is not responsive to sexual stimulation.

Sexual dysfunction ▲ A persistent or recurrent problem in becoming sexually aroused or reaching orgasm.

▲ REFLECT

How do you account for the gender differences in the incidence of sexual dysfunctions revealed in Table 13.2? Why do you think that women are more likely than men to find sex painful or unenjoyable? Why do you think that men are more likely to be anxious about their performance or to reach orgasm too early? (And how would you define "too early"?)

▲ REFLECT

Erectile disorder is extremely disturbing to many men who experience it. What cultural attitudes and expectations heighten the stress of this dysfunction?

CLICK4™ *more information about sexual dysfunction and treatment.*

Hypoactive sexual desire disorder ▲ A sexual dysfunction in which people lack sexual desire.

Female sexual arousal disorder ▲ A sexual dysfunction in which females fail to become adequately sexually aroused to engage in sexual intercourse.

Male erectile disorder ▲ A sexual dysfunction in which males fail to obtain erections that are adequate for sexual intercourse.

Orgasmic disorder ▲ A sexual dysfunction in which people have persistent or recurrent problems in reaching orgasm.

Premature ejaculation ▲ Ejaculation that occurs before the couple are satisfied with the length of sexual relations.

Dyspareunia ▲ A sexual dysfunction characterized by persistent or recurrent pain during sexual intercourse. (From roots meaning "badly paired.")

Vaginismus ▲ A sexual dysfunction characterized by involuntary contraction of the muscles surrounding the vagina, preventing entry by the penis or making entry painful.

Performance anxiety ▲ Anxiety concerning one's ability to perform, especially when performance may be evaluated by other people.

Sex therapy ▲ A collective term for short-term cognitive-behavioral models for treatment of sexual dysfunctions.

In **hypoactive sexual desire disorder,** a person lacks interest in sexual activity and frequently reports a lack of sexual fantasies. This diagnosis exists because it is assumed that sexual fantasies and interests are normal responses that may be blocked by anxiety or other factors.

In women, sexual arousal is characterized by lubrication of the vaginal walls, which facilitates entry by the penis. Sexual arousal in men is characterized by erection. Almost all women sometimes have difficulty becoming or remaining lubricated. Almost all men have occasional difficulty attaining or maintaining an erection through intercourse. When these events are persistent or recurrent, they are considered dysfunctions **(female sexual arousal disorder** and **male erectile disorder).**

In **orgasmic disorder,** the man or woman, through sexually excited, takes a long time to reach orgasm or does not reach it at all. Orgasmic disorder is more common among women than among men. In **premature ejaculation,** the male ejaculates after minimal sexual stimulation, too soon to permit his partner or himself to enjoy sexual relations fully. Other dysfunctions include **dyspareunia** (painful sexual activity) and **vaginismus** (involuntary contraction of the muscles surrounding the vaginal opening, which makes entry painful and/or difficult).

Since not everyone experiences sexual dysfunctions, researchers have sought to determine why some do and some do not. *Question: What are the origins of sexual dysfunctions?*

Causes of Sexual Dysfunctions

Some sexual dysfunctions reflect biological problems. Lack of desire, for example, can be due to diabetes or to diseases of the heart and lungs. Fatigue can reduce sexual desire and inhibit orgasm. Depressants such as alcohol, narcotics, and tranquilizers can also impair sexual response. For example, Eric Rimm (2000) of the Harvard School of Public Health studied 2,000 men and found that erectile dysfunction was connected with a large waist, physical inactivity, and drinking too much alcohol (or not having any alcohol!). The common condition among these men may be high cholesterol levels. Cholesterol can impede the flow of blood to the penis just as it impedes the flow of blood to the heart. Antidepressant medication and antipsychotic drugs may impair erectile functioning and cause orgasmic disorders (Ashton et al., 2000; Michelson et al., 2000).

Physically or psychologically painful sexual experiences, such as rape, can block future sexual response (Koss, 1993; Laumann et al., 1999). Moreover, a sexual relationship is usually no better than other aspects of a relationship or marriage. Couples who have difficulty communicating are at a disadvantage in expressing their sexual desires.

Cognitive psychologists point out that irrational beliefs and attitudes can contribute to sexual dysfunctions. If we believe that we need a lover's approval at all times, we may view a disappointing sexual episode as a catastrophe. If we demand that every sexual encounter be perfect, we set ourselves up for failure.

In most cases of sexual dysfunction, the physical and psychological factors we have outlined lead to yet another psychological factor—**performance anxiety,** or fear of not being able to perform sexually. People with performance anxiety may focus on past failures and expectations of another disaster rather than enjoying present erotic sensations and fantasies. Performance anxiety can make it difficult for a man to attain erection, yet also spur him to ejaculate prematurely. It can prevent a woman from becoming adequately lubricated and can contribute to vaginismus.

Sex Therapy

Sexual dysfunctions are generally treated by means of **sex therapy,** which refers to a collection of mainly cognitive and behavior therapy techniques. Sex therapy is largely indebted to the pioneering work of Masters and Johnson (1970), although other therapists have also developed important techniques. Sex therapy generally focuses on:

1. *Reducing performance anxiety.* Therapists frequently prescribe that clients engage in activities such as massage or petting under "nondemand" circumstances for a while to reduce performance anxiety. Nondemand activity means sexual arousal and intercourse are not expected at first. Lessened anxiety allows natural reflexes such as erection, lubrication, and orgasm to occur.

2. *Changing self-defeating attitudes and expectations.* Clients are shown how expectations of failure can raise anxiety levels and become self-fulfilling prophecies.

3. *Teaching sexual skills.* Clients may be taught how to provide each other with adequate sexual stimulation. In the case of premature ejaculation, they may also be shown how to delay ejaculation by means such as the stop-and-go method (pausing when the male becomes too aroused).

4. *Enhancing sexual knowledge.* Some problems are connected with ignorance or misinformation about biological and sexual functioning.

5. *Improving sexual communication.* Partners are taught ways of showing each other what they like and do not like.

Moreover, biological treatments are available for various problems. For example, the drug Viagra helps men attain erection by relaxing the muscles surrounding the blood vessels in the penis, allowing more blood to flow in and the erection to harden. Uprima facilitates erection by acting on the erection center in the brain. Several drugs are under development to facilitate sexual arousal and orgasm in both males and females, but some women also use Viagra today. Readers interested in learning more about sex therapy are advised to consult a human sexuality textbook, contact their state's psychological association, or ask their professors or college counseling centers.

Sexual dysfunctions are one category of problems in sexual interaction. Let us now consider a darker side of human interaction: sexual coercion. In sexual dysfunctions, individuals and couples generally wish to remove obstacles to having a fulfilling sexual relationship. In the case of sexual coercion, individuals—usually women—need effective barriers to prevent other people from damaging their physical and psychological well-being.

REVIEW

(23) Masters and Johnson divide the sexual response cycle into four phases: _____, plateau, orgasm, and resolution. (24) Sexual response cycle is generally characterized by _____ and myotonia. (25) Women with female sexual _____ disorder have difficulty lubricating. (26) Men with persistent difficulty attaining or maintaining an erection have male _____ disorder. (27) Males who ejaculate too quickly are diagnosed with _____ ejaculation. (28) Sex therapy generally focuses on reducing _____ anxiety, changing self-defeating attitudes, teaching sexual skills, enhancing sexual knowledge, and improving communication.

Pulling It Together: How are males and females alike in sexual response? How do they differ? Connect the sexual dysfunctions with the various phases of the sexual response cycle.

SEXUAL COERCION

Sexual coercion includes rape and other forms of sexual pressure. It also includes *any* sexual activity between an adult and a child. Even when children cooperate, sexual relations with children are coercive because the child is below the legal age of consent. In this section we focus on rape and sexual harassment.

CLICK4™ *a WebSearch activity on sexual assault and how to prevent it.*

Rape

As many as one in four women in the United States has been raped (Koss, 1993). Parents regularly encourage their daughters to be wary of strangers and strange places—places where they could fall prey to rapists. Certainly the threat of rape from strangers is real enough. Yet four out of five rapes are committed by acquaintances (Laumann et al., 1994).

Date rape is a pressing concern on college campuses, where thousands of women have been victimized and there is much controversy over what exactly constitutes rape. More than one out of three of a sample of college men from California and Ohio

Kristine, Amy, and Karen.
These college women are among the thousands who have been raped by their dates. The great majority of rapes are committed by dates or acquaintances, not by strangers.

CLICK4™ *information about sexual abuse, sponsored by "Men Stopping Violence."*

admitted to coercing women into sex play by means of arguments, pressure, or force (Hall et al., 2000). About one man in seven had coerced a woman into sexual intercourse by means of arguments, pressure, or force. Consider one woman's account of date rape from the author's files:

> I first met him at a party. He was really good looking and he had a great smile. I wanted to meet him but I wasn't sure how. I didn't want to appear too forward. Then he came over and introduced himself. We talked and found we had a lot in common. I really liked him. When he asked me over to his place for a drink, I thought it would be OK. He was such a good listener, and I wanted him to ask me out again.
>
> When we got to his room, the only place to sit was on the bed. I didn't want him to get the wrong idea, but what else could I do? We talked for awhile and then he made his move. I was so startled. He started by kissing. I really liked him so the kissing was nice. But then he pushed me down on the bed. I tried to get up and I told him to stop. He was so much bigger and stronger. I got scared and I started to cry. I froze and he raped me.
>
> It took only a couple of minutes and it was terrible, he was so rough. When it was over he kept asking me what was wrong, like he didn't know. He had just forced himself on me and he thought that was OK. He drove me home and said he wanted to see me again. I'm so afraid to see him. I never thought it would happen to me.

Rape is common—far too common. *Question: Why do men rape women?*

CLICK4™ *an essay assignment exploring psychological theories that attempt to explain why men engage in sexual abuse.*

▲ REFLECT

Some evolutionary psychologists speculate that rape — or at least some forms of sexual coerciveness — may be "natural" for men. If they are correct, should society then condone sexual aggressiveness or rape? Or does society have a right to expect that men will control harmful behavior, even if it "goes against the grain" of their genes?

CONTROVERSY ✸ IN PSYCHOLOGY

Why Do Men Rape Women?

Why do men force women into sexual activity? Sex is not the only reason. Many social scientists argue that rape is often a man's way of expressing social dominance over, or anger toward, women (Hall & Barongan, 1997). With some rapists, violence appears to enhance sexual arousal. They therefore seek to combine sex and aggression (Barbaree & Marshall, 1991).

Evolutionary psychologists suggest that prior to civilization, males who were more sexually aggressive were more likely to transmit their genes to future generations (Fisher, 2000; Thornhill & Palmer, 2000). There thus remains a tendency for males to be more sexually aggressive than females. Although the evolutionary perspective may view sexual coerciveness in men as "natural," evolutionary psychologists generally agree that rape is inexcusable and criminal in modern society, and that males can *choose* not to be aggressive.

However, many social critics contend that American culture also *socializes* men—including the nice young man next door—into becoming rapists (Powell, 1996). This occurs because males are often reinforced for aggressive and competitive behavior (Hall & Barongan, 1997). The date rapist could be said to be asserting culturally expected dominance over women.

There are also powerful cognitive contributors to rape. For example, research shows that college men frequently perceive a date's protests as part of an adversarial sex game (Bernat et al., 1999). One male undergraduate said "Hell, no" when asked whether a date had consented to sex. He added, ". . . but she didn't say no, so she must have wanted it, too. . . . It's the way it works" (Celis, 1991). Consider the comments of the man who victimized the woman whose story appeared earlier in the section:

> I first met her at a party. She looked really hot, wearing a sexy dress that showed off her great body. We started talking right away. I knew that she liked me by the way she kept smiling and touching my arm while she was speaking. She seemed pretty relaxed so I asked her back to my place for a drink. . . . When she said yes, I knew that I was going to be lucky!
>
> When we got to my place, we sat on the bed kissing. At first, everything was great. Then, when I started to lay her down on the bed, she started twisting and saying she didn't want to. Most women don't like to appear too easy, so I knew that she was just going through the motions. When she stopped struggling, I knew that she would have to throw in some tears before we did it.
>
> She was still very upset afterwards, and I just don't understand it! If she didn't want to have sex, why did she come back to the room with me? You could tell by the way she dressed and acted that she was no virgin, so why she had to put up such a big struggle I don't know.

Another cognitive factor in rape is belief in stereotypical myths about rape.

Myths About Rape

In the United States there are many myths about rape—myths that blame the victim (Bernat et al., 1999). For example, most Americans aged 50 and above believe that the woman is partly responsible for rape if she dresses provocatively (Gibbs, 1991). They are unlikely to be sympathetic if such a "bold" woman complains of being raped. And most Americans believe that some women like to be talked into sex.

Other myths include the notions that "women say no when they mean yes" and "rapists are crazed by sexual desire" (Powell, 1996, p. 139). Still another myth is that deep down inside, women *want* to be raped. Such myths deny the impact of the assault and transfer blame onto the victim. Men who support traditional, rigidly defined gender roles are more likely to blame the victims of rape (Raichle & Lambert, 2000). The myths contribute to a social climate that is too often lenient toward rapists and unsympathetic toward victims. Moreover, the myths lead to hostility toward women, which in turn, can lead to rape (Hall et al., 2000; see Figure 13.9).

CONTROVERSY IN PSYCHOLOGY

Are Women to Blame for Whatever Happens to Them If They Dress Provocatively or Use "Bad" Language?

If you answer yes, you are blaming the victim of assault. As we see in this section, myths about rape usually blame the victim and have the effect of supporting rape.

www 13 BBC 5

CLICK4™ *a bulletin board discussion on sexual coercion: Are the victims ever to blame?*

www 13 L 4

CLICK4™ *more information about sexual assault, including husband battering.*

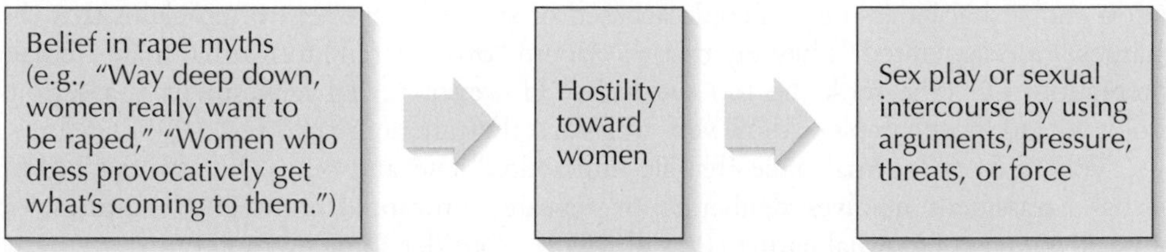

FIGURE 13.9 A Common Pathway to Sexual Aggression.

A statistical technique called path analysis reveals the powerful cognitive aspects of sexual aggression. Belief in rape myths, such as the idea that women really want to be raped or that women who dress provocatively get what's coming to them, increases hostility toward women. Hostility toward women, in turn, is a common characteristic of rapists.

| Belief in rape myths (e.g., "Way deep down, women really want to be raped," "Women who dress provocatively get what's coming to them.") | → | Hostility toward women | → | Sex play or sexual intercourse by using arguments, pressure, threats, or force |

447

Cultural Myths That Create a Climate That Supports Rape

The following statements are based on a questionnaire by Martha Burt (1980). Read each statement and indicate whether you believe it to be true or false by circling the T or the F. Then turn to the key in Appendix B to learn about the implications of your answers.

T F 1. A woman who goes to the home or apartment of a man on their first date implies that she is willing to have sex.

T F 2. Any female can get raped.

T F 3. One reason why women falsely report a rape is because they need to call attention to themselves.

T F 4. Any healthy woman can successfully resist a rapist if she really wants to.

T F 5. When women go around braless or wearing short skirts and tight tops, they are just asking for trouble.

T F 6. In the majority of rapes, the victim is promiscuous or has a bad reputation.

T F 7. If a girl engages in necking or petting and she lets things get out of hand, it is her own fault if her partner forces sex on her.

T F 8. Women who get raped while hitchhiking get what they deserve.

T F 9. A woman who is stuck-up and thinks she is too good to talk to guys on the street deserves to be taught a lesson.

T F 10. Many women have an unconscious wish to be raped and may then unconsciously set up a situation in which they are likely to be attacked.

T F 11. If a woman gets drunk at a party and has intercourse with a man she's just met there, she should be considered "fair game" to other males at the party who want to have sex with her too, whether she wants to or not.

T F 12. Many women who report a rape are lying because they are angry and want to get back at the man they accuse.

T F 13. Many, if not most, rapes are merely invented by women who discovered they were pregnant and wanted to protect their reputation.

CD 13 SA 15

CLICK4™ *the interactive version of this Self-Assessment.*

If you want to learn whether you harbor some of the more common myths about rape, complete the nearby self-assessment on cultural myths that create a climate that supports rape.

Sexual Harassment

Sexual harassment occurs frequently on college campuses, in the business world, and in the military. The great majority of victims are female, and nearly half of the women in college and the workforce report being victimized (American Psychological Association, 1998; Jorgenson & Wahl, 2000). Even the highest-ranking female officer in the Army was not immune. In 2000, Lt. Gen. Claudia J. Kennedy alleged that another general "groped" her in her office (Myers, 2000). *Question: What is sexual harassment?*

CLICK4™ *a bulletin board discussion on sexual harassment: Where does it begin and how do we resist it?*

CLICK4™ *the APA's fact sheet on the myths and realities of sexual harassment.*

Sexual harassment ▲ Deliberate or repeated verbal comments, gestures, or physical contact of a sexual nature that is unwanted by the recipient.

CONTROVERSY IN PSYCHOLOGY

Where Does Normal Male–Female Interaction End and Sexual Harassment Begin?

It is sometimes difficult to draw the line between sexual persuasion and attempted rape. It can be even *more* difficult to distinguish between a legitimate (if unwelcome) sexual invitation and sexual harassment. People accused of sexual harassment often claim that the charges are exaggerated. They say that the victim "overreacted" to normal male–female interaction. Or "She took me too seriously." However, sexual harassment *is* a serious problem, and most harassers know very well what they are doing (Powell, 1996).

Where does "normal male–female interaction" end and sexual harassment begin? Sexual harassment involves deliberate or repeated unwanted comments, gestures, or physical contact of a sexual nature (Powell, 1996). Consider some examples:

▲ Verbal abuse,

▲ Unwelcome sexual overtures or advances,

▲ Pressure to engage in sexual activity,

▲ Remarks about a person's body, clothing, or sexual activities,

▲ Leering at, or ogling, someone,

▲ Telling unwanted dirty jokes in mixed company,

▲ Unnecessarily touching, patting, or pinching,

▲ Whistles and catcalls,

▲ Brushing up against someone,

▲ Demands for sex that are accompanied by threats, such as being fired from a job or not getting a promotion.

CLICK4™ *an opportunity to explore the subject of sexual harassment interactively and from a variety of perspectives.*

CLICK4™ *more information about the prevention and treatment of rape.*

www 13 WS 6

CLICK4™ *a WebSearch activity on minimizing the risk of rape.*

Psychology and Modern Life

Preventing Rape

Don't accept rides from strange men— and remember that all men are strange.

—Robin Morgan

The aftermath of rape can include physical harm, anxiety, depression, sexual dysfunction, sexually transmitted infection, and/or pregnancy (Kimerling & Calhoun, 1994; Koss, 1993). *Question: How can we prevent rape?* From a sociocultural perspective, prevention of rape involves publicly examining and challenging the widely held cultural attitudes and ideals that contribute to rape. The traditions of male dominance and rewards for male aggressiveness take a daily toll on women. One thing we can do is encourage colleges and universities to require students to attend lectures and seminars on rape (Shultz et al., 2000). The point is to dispel myths about rape and for men to learn that "No" means "No," despite the widespread belief that some women like to be talked into sex. We can also encourage community and national leaders to pay more attention to the problem.

On a personal level, there are things that women can do to protect themselves. *The New Our Bodies, Ourselves* (Boston Women's Health Book Collective, 1992) includes the following suggestions for preventing rape by strangers:

• Establish signals and arrangements with other women in an apartment building or neighborhood.
• List only first initials in the telephone directory or on the mailbox.
• Use dead-bolt locks.

• Keep windows locked and obtain iron grids for first-floor windows.
• Keep entrances and doorways brightly lit.
• Have keys ready for the front door or the car.
• Do not walk alone in the dark.
• Avoid deserted areas.
• Never allow a strange man into your apartment or home without checking his credentials.
• Drive with the car windows up and the door locked.
• Check the rear seat of the car before entering.
• Avoid living in an unsafe building.
• Do not pick up hitchhikers (including women).
• Do not talk to strange men in the street.
• Shout "Fire!" not "Rape!" People crowd around fires but avoid scenes of violence.

Powell (1996) adds the following suggestions for avoiding date rape:

• Communicate your sexual limits to your date. Tell your partner how far you would like to go so that he will know what the limits are. For example, if your partner starts fondling you in ways that make you uncomfortable, you might say, "I'd prefer if you didn't touch me there. I really like you, but I prefer not getting so intimate at this point in our relationship."
• Meet new dates in public places, and avoid driving with a stranger or a group of people you've just met. When meeting a new date, drive in

your own car and meet your date at a public place. Don't drive with strangers or offer rides to strangers or groups of people. In some cases of date rape, the group disappears just prior to the assault.
• State your refusal in definitive terms. Be firm in refusing a sexual overture. Look your partner straight in the eye. The more definite you are, the less likely your partner will be to misinterpret your wishes.
• Become aware of your fears. Take notice of any fears of displeasing your partner that might stifle your assertiveness. If your partner is truly respectful of you, you need not fear an angry or demeaning response. But if your partner is not respectful, it is best to become aware of it early and end the relationship right away.
• Pay attention to your "vibes." Trust your gut-level feelings. Many victims of acquaintance rape said afterward that they had had a strange feeling about the man but failed to pay attention to it.
• Be especially cautious if you are in a new environment, such as college or a foreign country. You may be especially vulnerable to exploitation when you are becoming acquainted with a new environment, different people, and different customs.
• If you have broken off a relationship with someone you don't really like or feel good about, don't let him into your place. Many so-called date rapes are committed by ex-lovers and ex-boyfriends.

Sexual Harassment.
Is this behavior acceptable in the workplace? Many women have switched jobs or colleges because of sexual harassment.

AIDS ▲ The acronym for *acquired immunodeficiency syndrome,* a condition caused by the human immunodeficiency virus (HIV) and characterized by destruction of the immune system so that the body is stripped of its ability to fend off life-threatening diseases.

HIV ▲ The acronym for the *human immunodeficiency virus,* a sexually transmitted virus that destroys white blood cells in the immune system and causes AIDS.

Chlamydia ▲ A sexually transmitted infection caused by the *Chlamydia trachomatous* bacterium.

Genital warts ▲ A sexually transmitted infection caused by the *human papilloma virus* and possibly involved in cancers of the genital organs.

Your college may publish guidelines about sexual harassment. Check with the dean of students or the president's office.

College students are sexually harassed by other students and sometimes by professors (Matchen & DeSouza, 2000; van Roosmalen & McDaniel, 1998). Professors are sometimes harassed by students. Some cases are so serious that women switch major fields, schools, or jobs to avoid it (Munson et al., 2000; van Roosmalen & McDaniel, 1998). Ironically, as with rape, society often blames the victim of sexual harassment for being provocative or for not saying no firmly enough.

REVIEW

(29) Most rapes are committed by (strangers or acquaintances?). (30) Many social scientists argue that rape mainly has to do with (sex or power?). (31) Sexual harassment (is or is not?) illegal.

Pulling It Together: How do U.S. cultural beliefs have the effect of supporting rape? How do we define sexual harassment?

AIDS AND OTHER SEXUALLY TRANSMITTED INFECTIONS

Sexual relationships can be sources of pleasure and personal fulfillment. They also carry some risks and responsibilities. One of the risks is that of contracting **AIDS** or other sexually transmitted infections (STIs).   *Question: What kinds of sexually transmitted infections are there?*   Although media attention usually focuses on AIDS and **HIV** (the virus that causes AIDS), other STIs are more widespread. There are nearly 3 million new **chlamydia** infections in the United States each year (CDC, 2000f). *Human papilloma virus* (HPV) (the organism that causes **genital warts**) is estimated to be present in one-third of college women and 8% of men aged 15 to 49 (Cannistra & Niloff, 1996).

Most college students appear to be reasonably well-informed about HIV transmission and AIDS, yet many are unaware that chlamydia can go undetected for years. Moreover, if it is not treated it can cause pelvic inflammation and infertility. Many students are also ignorant of HPV, which is linked to cervical cancer (Josefsson et al., 2000). Yet as many as 1 million new cases of HPV infection occur each year in the United States—

Psychology and Modern Life

Resisting Sexual Harassment

Question: What can you do if you are sexually harassed on campus or in the workplace?   Here are some suggestions:

1. Behave in a professional manner. Harassment often can be stopped cold if you respond to the harasser in a curt, businesslike manner.

2. Discourage harassment and promote the kind of social behavior you want. Speak up. If your supervisor or professor asks you to come to the office after hours, say that you would rather talk during office hours. Stick to business. If the harasser

does not take this suggestion, be more direct: "Mr. Smith, I'd like to keep our relationship purely business, okay?"

3. Don't get into a situation in which you are alone with someone who might harass you. Have a co-worker around when you consult your supervisor. Or see your professor before or after class, when other people are around.

4. Keep a record of incidents to document them in case you decide to lodge an official complaint.

5. Put the harasser on direct notice that you recognize the harassment for what it is and that you want it to stop.

6. Confide about harassment to reliable friends, school counselors or advisers, union representatives, or parents or relatives. Harassment is stressful, and social support helps us cope with stress. Other people may also have helpful advice.

7. Many places of business and campuses have offices where complaints about sexual harassment are filed and acted on. Check with the dean of students or the president's office.

8. See a lawyer. Sexual harassment is illegal, and you can stop it.

more than **syphilis, genital herpes,** and AIDS combined. Perhaps 1 million Americans are infected with HIV, but there are 10 to 12 million new cases of STIs in the United States *each year* (Stolberg, 1998).

Women experience the effects of most STIs disproportionately. They are more likely to develop infertility if an STI spreads through the reproductive system. STIs are believed to account for 15 to 30% of cases of infertility among U.S. women. In addition to their biological effects, STIs take an emotional toll and can strain relationships to the breaking point.

In the rest of this section we focus on AIDS, but there are many other STIs that you should be aware of. Readers who want more information are advised to talk to their professor or doctor, consult human sexuality or health textbooks, or visit their college counseling and health center. Before proceeding, you can test your knowledge of HIV/AIDS on the Web site.

HIV/AIDS

AIDS is a fatal condition in which the person's immune system is so weakened that he or she falls prey to **opportunistic diseases.** It is caused by the human immunodeficiency virus (HIV).

Questions: How is HIV transmitted? What does it do?   HIV is transmitted by infected blood, semen, vaginal and cervical secretions, and breast milk. The first three fluids may enter the body through vaginal, anal, or oral sex with an infected partner. Other means of infection include sharing a hypodermic needle with an infected person (as is common among people who inject illicit drugs) and transfusion with contaminated blood. There need be no concern about closed-mouth kissing. Note, too, that saliva does not transmit HIV. *However,* transmission through deep kissing is theoretically possible if blood in an infected person's mouth (e.g., from toothbrushing or gum disease) enters cuts (again, as from toothbrushing or gum disease) in the other person's mouth. HIV may also be transmitted from mother to fetus during pregnancy or from mother to child through childbirth or breast-feeding. There is no evidence that public toilets, insect bites, holding or hugging an infected person, or living or attending school with one transmits HIV.

HIV kills white blood cells called *CD4 lymphocytes*[2] (or, more simply, *CD4 cells*) that are found in the immune system. CD4 cells recognize viruses and "instruct" other white blood cells—called *B lymphocytes*—to make antibodies, which combat disease. (See Chapter 14.) Eventually, however, CD4 cells are depleted and the body is left vulnerable to opportunistic diseases.

AIDS is characterized by fatigue, fever, unexplained weight loss, swollen lymph nodes, diarrhea, and, in many cases, impairment of learning and memory. Among the opportunistic infections that may take hold are Kaposi's sarcoma, a cancer of the blood cells that occurs in many gay males who contract AIDS; PCP (pneumocystis carinii pneumonia), a kind of pneumonia; and, in women, invasive cancer of the cervix.

People in the United States have been most likely to become infected with HIV by engaging in male–male sexual activity or injecting ("shooting up") illicit drugs (CDC, 2000b). Other people at particular risk include sex partners of people who inject drugs, babies born to women who inject drugs or whose sex partners inject drugs, prostitutes and men who visit them, and sex partners of men who visit infected prostitutes. People today are unlikely to be infected by means of blood transfusions because blood supplies are routinely screened for HIV.

One *psychological* risk factor for HIV infection is that people tend to underestimate their risk of infection (Seppa, 1997). Because AIDS has been characterized as mainly transmitted by anal intercourse (a practice that is fairly common among gay males) and the sharing of contaminated needles, many heterosexual Americans who do not use these drugs dismiss the threat of AIDS. Yet male–female sexual intercourse accounts for the majority of cases around the world ("Global Plague of AIDS," 2000). Although gay men

▲ **REFLECT**
How much do you know about STIs such as chlamydia and genital warts? Should you know more? What will you do about it?

▲ **REFLECT**
Do you engage in risky behaviors that are connected with transmission of HIV? Does your partner? Are you sure?

Syphilis ▲ An STI that is caused by the *Treponema pallidum* bacterium, which may progress through several stages of development—from a chancre to a skin rash to eventually damaging the cardiovascular or central nervous systems.
Genital herpes ▲ A sexually transmitted infection caused by the *Herpes simplex* virus type 2 and characterized by painful shallow sores and blisters on the genitals.
Opportunistic diseases ▲ Diseases that develop within people whose immune systems are impaired by conditions such as AIDS.

---

[2]Also called T_4 *cells* or *helper T cells.*

and drug abusers have been hit hardest by the epidemic, HIV cuts across all boundaries of gender, sexual orientation, ethnicity, and socioeconomic status.

The following section informs us that HIV/AIDS is much more than a local problem.

CLICK4™ *more information about ethnic differences in the risk for contracting AIDS and how culturally relevant health care can help.*

CLICK4™ *an interactive Self-Assessment: The AIDS Awareness Inventory.*

DIVERSITY **The Global Plague of HIV/AIDS** HIV infection and AIDS are a global plague. As we entered the new millennium, the World Health Organization estimated that more than 34 million people around the world were living with HIV/AIDS ("Global Plague of AIDS," 2000). More than 19 million people have already died of AIDS. Sub-Saharan Africa has been hardest hit by the epidemic, with more than 24 million people currently infected with HIV (UNAIDS, 2000). Sub-Saharan Africa contains 10% percent of the world's population, scrapes by on 1% of the world's income, and bears the burden of two out of three people with HIV/AIDS (Benatar, 2000). Figure 13.10 summarizes some startling facts about HIV/AIDS in sub-Saharan Africa. The incidences of new HIV infections are also mushrooming in Central and Eastern Europe, China, Southeast Asia, Latin America and the Caribbean.

Unlike many other infections, HIV/AIDS does not target older, weaker people. Because it is sexually transmitted, it afflicts the most productive sectors of the affected populations—young adults ("Global Plague of AIDS," 2000). In some parts of sub-Saharan Africa, one adult in four is infected, with the infection rates highest among workers, including professionals.

In many developing nations, there is little or no treatment for HIV/AIDS. The combinations of drugs that are used to treat HIV/AIDS in industrialized nations cost at least a thousand dollars per year per person, even when deeply discounted. But the incomes of most sub-Saharan Africans can be measured in hundreds of dollar per year.

FIGURE 13.10   HIV/AIDS in Sub-Saharan Africa: End of Millennium.
Sub-Saharan Africa has been hardest hit by the HIV/AIDS epidemic. The losses in the region are staggering.

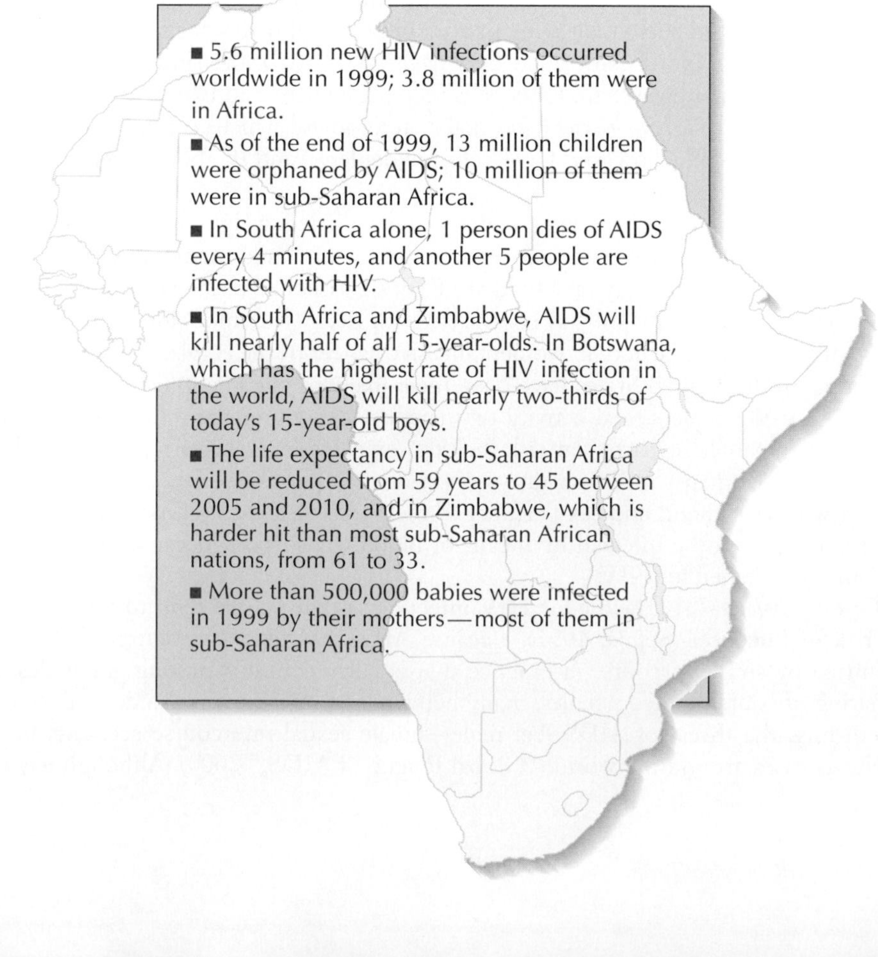

- 5.6 million new HIV infections occurred worldwide in 1999; 3.8 million of them were in Africa.
- As of the end of 1999, 13 million children were orphaned by AIDS; 10 million of them were in sub-Saharan Africa.
- In South Africa alone, 1 person dies of AIDS every 4 minutes, and another 5 people are infected with HIV.
- In South Africa and Zimbabwe, AIDS will kill nearly half of all 15-year-olds. In Botswana, which has the highest rate of HIV infection in the world, AIDS will kill nearly two-thirds of today's 15-year-old boys.
- The life expectancy in sub-Saharan Africa will be reduced from 59 years to 45 between 2005 and 2010, and in Zimbabwe, which is harder hit than most sub-Saharan African nations, from 61 to 33.
- More than 500,000 babies were infected in 1999 by their mothers—most of them in sub-Saharan Africa.

Health care systems that could effectively distribute the drugs are also lacking in many locations.

Yet there is some positive news from developing nations. The infection rates have been significantly cut in the African nations of Uganda and Senegal through sex education, testing for HIV infection, and distribution of condoms ("Global Plague of AIDS," 2000). Thailand has lowered its infection rate by instilling controls over prostitution, which was the country's greatest avenue of infection.

In the United States, disproportionately high numbers of African Americans and Latino and Latina Americans are living with HIV/AIDS (CDC, 2000a; see Table 13.3). Nearly half of the men and three-quarters of the women with AIDS are African American or Latino and Latina American (CDC, 2000a). Yet these ethnic groups make up only about one-quarter of the population. Death rates due to AIDS are much higher among African Americans and Latino and Latina Americans (especially Latino and Latina people of Puerto Rican origin) than among European Americans (CDC, 2000a), apparently because African Americans and Latino and Latina Americans have less access to high-quality health care.

Ethnic differences in rates of transmission of HIV are connected with the practice of injecting illegal drugs. People who share needles with HIV-infected people when they inject drugs can become infected. They can then transmit the virus to their sex partners. People who share needles now account for one in four people in the United States with HIV/AIDS. African Americans make up more than half of the people in the United States who became infected by injecting drugs (CDC, 2000a). Latino and Latina Americans account for another case in five (CDC, 2000a). Drug abuse and the related problem

TABLE 13.3 AIDS CASES BY RACE OR ETHNICITY IN THE UNITED STATES

Race or Ethnicity	Number of AIDS Cases	Percentage
European American	318,354	43.4
African American	272,881	37.2
Latino and Latina American	133,703	18.2
Asian/Pacific Islander	5,347	0.7
American Indian/Alaska Native	2,132	0.3
Race/Ethnicity Unknown	957	0.1

SOURCE OF DATA: Centers for Disease Control and Prevention (2000). *HIV/AIDS Surveillance Report*. U.S. HIV and AIDS cases reported through December 1999, year-end edition, *11*(2).

CLICK4™ *a bulletin board discussion: Why do people who know about HIV/AIDS and other STIs continue to engage in risky sexual behavior?*

Psychology and Modern Life
Preventing STIs

Question: What can you do to prevent the transmission of HIV and other STI-causing organisms? A number of things.

1. *Don't ignore the threat of STIs.* Many people try to put AIDS and other STIs out of their minds. They just assume that their partners are uninfected, or believe it would hurt the relationship to ask about STIs (Adam et al., 2000). The first aspect of prevention is psychological: Do not ignore STIs or assume that they will not affect you.

2. *Remain abstinent.* One way to curb the sexual transmission of HIV and other organisms that cause STIs is sexual abstinence. Of course, most people who remain abstinent do so while they are looking for Mr. or Ms. Right. Thus, they eventually face the risk of contracting STIs through sexual intercourse. Moreover, students want to know just what "abstinence" means. Does it mean avoiding sexual intercourse (yes) or any form of sexual activity with another person (not necessarily)? Kissing, hugging, and petting to orgasm (without coming into contact with semen or vaginal secretions) are generally considered safe in terms of HIV transmission. However, kissing can transmit

oral herpes (as shown by cold sores) and some bacterial STIs.

3. *Engage in a monogamous relationship with someone who is not infected.* Sexual activity within a monogamous relationship with an uninfected person is safe. The question here is how certain you can be that *your partner* is uninfected and monogamous.

Readers who do not abstain from sexual relationships or limit themselves to a monogamous relationship can do some things to make sex safer — if not perfectly safe:

4. *Be selective.* Engage in sexual activity only with people you know well. Consider whether they are likely to have engaged in the kinds of behaviors that transmit HIV or other STIs.

5. *Inspect your partner's genitals.* People who have STIs often have a variety of symptoms. Examining your partner's genitals for blisters, discharges, chancres, rashes, warts, lice, and unpleasant odors during foreplay may reveal signs of such diseases.

6. *Wash your own genitals before and after contact.* Washing beforehand helps

protect your partner. Washing promptly afterward with soap and water helps remove germs.

7. *Use spermicides.* Many spermicides kill HIV and organisms that cause some other STIs as well as sperm. Check with a pharmacist.

8. *Use condoms. Latex* condoms (but not condoms made from animal membrane) protect the woman from having HIV-infected semen enter the vagina and the man from contact with HIV-infected vaginal (or other) body fluids. Condoms also prevent transmission of bacterial STIs.

9. *If you fear that you have been exposed to HIV or another infectious organism, talk to your doctor about it.* Early treatment is usually more effective than later treatment. It may even prevent infection.

10. *When in doubt, stop.* If you are not sure that sex is safe, stop and think things over or seek expert advice.

If you think about it, the last item is rather good general advice. When in doubt, why not stop and think, regardless of whether the doubt is about your sex partner, your college major, or a financial investment?

CLICK4™ *an essay assignment on cultural differences in the spread of HIV/AIDS.*

CLICK4™ *information about the causes, methods of transmission, symptoms, diagnosis, and treatment of STIs.*

▲ **REFLECT**

If you thought you might have been exposed to HIV or another infectious agent, would you talk to your doctor about it? What are the risks of keeping your concerns to yourself?

---

of prostitution occur disproportionately in poor, urban communities with large populations of people of color. Thus, it is not surprising that HIV/AIDS affects these groups disproportionately.

The lessons from Uganda and Senegal pertain to the United States as well. Greater investment in sex education and use of condoms are also likely to cut the infection rates at home. And here, as in sub-Saharan Africa, more needs to be done to provide the drugs that can prolong the lives of poor people and help keep them as productive members of the workforce.

Diagnosis and Treatment of HIV Infection and AIDS

Questions: How is HIV infection diagnosed? How is HIV/AIDS treated? Infection by HIV is generally diagnosed by means of blood, saliva, or urine tests. For many years researchers were frustrated in their efforts to develop effective vaccines and treatments for HIV infection and AIDS. There is still no safe, effective vaccine, but recent developments in drug therapy have raised hopes about treatment.

AZT and similar antiviral drugs—ddI, ddC—inhibit reproduction of HIV by targeting the enzyme called *reverse transcriptase*. A newer generation of drugs, *protease inhibitors*, targets the *protease* enzyme (Carpenter et al., 2000). A "cocktail" of antiviral drugs such as AZT, 3TC, and protease inhibitors has become the more or less standard treatment and has reduced HIV to below detectable levels in many infected people (Carpenter et al., 2000). Many doctors treat people who fear that they have been exposed to HIV with antiviral drugs to reduce the likelihood of infection (Katz & Gerberding, 1997). *If you fear that you have been exposed to HIV, talk to your doctor about it immediately.*

Current drug therapy has given rise to the hope that AIDS will become increasingly manageable, a chronic disease but not a terminal illness. However, treatment is expensive, and many people who could benefit from it cannot afford it. In addition, some people with AIDS do not respond to the drug cocktail, and HIV levels bounce back (Carpenter et al., 2000). *Therefore, the most effective way of dealing with AIDS is prevention.*

For the latest information on AIDS, call the National AIDS Hotline at 1-800-342-AIDS. If you want to receive information in Spanish, call 1-800-344 SIDA. You can also go to the Web site of the Centers for Disease Control and Prevention: **www.cdc.gov**. Once you're there, you can click on "Health Topics A–Z" and then on "AIDS/HIV."

REVIEW

CLICK4™ *a quiz covering the second half of this chapter.*

CLICK4™ *electronic flash cards to review your knowledge of key terms and people in this chapter.*

(32) HIV is the virus that causes _____ immunodeficiency syndrome. (33) HPV causes _____ warts and is linked to cervical cancer. (34) HIV kills CD4 lymphocytes in the immune system, leaving the body vulnerable to _____ diseases. (35) HIV is transmitted by infected _____, semen, vaginal and cervical secretions, and breast milk.

Pulling It Together: Why do people who know about HIV/AIDS and other STIs continue to take risks?

TRUTH ■ FICTION
REVISITED

◣ It is true that Christmas Eve has become a time of sexual devotion in Japan. *There is social pressure on single people to have a date that includes an overnight stay. See page 422.*

◣ It is true that men behave more aggressively than women do — *at least in most cultures and under most circumstances. The issue is whether this gender difference is inborn or reflects sociocultural factors. See page 427.*

◣ It is not true that beauty is in the eye of the beholder, *despite the familiarity of the adage. It appears that some aspects of physical appeal may be innate or inborn. There are also cultural standards for beauty that influence people who are reared in that culture. See page 435.*

◣ It is true that people are perceived as being more attractive when they are smiling. *Does this research finding provide a reason to "put on a happy face" early in the development of social relationships? See page 435.*

◣ It appears that we are most likely to be attracted to people who are similar to us in terms of physical attributes and attitudes. *Therefore, we cannot say that "Opposites attract." See page 436.*

◣ It is true that the earlobes swell when people become sexually aroused. *The swelling is a result of vasocongestion. See page 442.*

◣ It is not necessarily true that people who truly love each other enjoy the sexual aspects of their relationships. *The statement is too broad to be true. Sexual dysfunctions can occur even in a loving relationship. Question: How are sexual dysfunctions treated? See page 443.*

◣ It is true that most Americans believe that some women like to be talked into sex. *A majority of Americans — including a majority of American women — share this belief. Does this encourage men to pressure their dates into sex? See page 447.*

◣ It is *not* true that women say no when they mean yes. *Myths such as this foster a social climate that encourages rape. See page 447.*

◣ It is not true that only gay males and substance abusers are at serious risk for contracting AIDS. *We all need to be aware of the risk factors and take appropriate precautions. See page 451.*

1. What are gender-role stereotypes?

Cultures have broad expectations of men and women that are termed *gender-role stereotypes*. In our culture women are expected to be gentle, dependent, kind, helpful, patient, and submissive. Men are expected to be tough, competitive, gentlemanly, and protective.

2. What are the costs of gender polarization?

Polarization has historically worked to the disadvantage of women. For example, women have until recent years been excluded from careers in medicine and law, and math and science courses in the schools are still seen as mainly in the male "domain." Women who adhere to traditional feminine gender roles are likely to take a back seat to men in the workplace and in the home. "Masculine" men may not be able to ask for help when they need it or to express tender feelings.

3. What are the gender differences in cognitive abilities?

Boys have historically been seen as excelling in math and spatial relations skills, whereas girls have been viewed as excelling in language skills. However, these differences are small and growing narrower.

4. What are the gender differences in social behavior?

Females are more extraverted and nurturant than males. Males are more tough-minded and aggressive than females. Men are more interested than women in casual sex and multiple sex partners. Women are more willing than men to marry someone who is not good-looking, but less willing to marry someone who is unlikely to hold a steady job.

5. What are some biological views of gender-typing?

Biological views of gender-typing focus on the roles of evolution, genetics, and prenatal influences in predisposing men and women to gender-linked behavior patterns. According to evolutionary psychologists, gender differences were fashioned by natural selection in response to problems in adaptation that were repeatedly encountered by humans over thousands of generations. Testosterone in the brains of male fetuses spurs greater growth of the right hemisphere of the brain, which may be connected with the ability to manage spatial relations tasks. Testosterone is also connected with aggressiveness.

6. What are some psychological views of gender-typing?

Psychologists have attempted to explain gender-typing in terms of psychodynamic, social-cognitive, and gender-schema theories. Freud explained gender-typing in terms of identification with the parent of the same gender through resolution of the Oedipus complex. Social-cognitive theorists explain gender-typing in terms of the ways in which experience helps the individual create concepts of gender-appropriate behavior, and how the individual is motivated to engage in such behavior. Social-cognitive theorists use terms such as observational learning, identification, and socialization. Research shows that women can behave as aggressively as men when they are provoked, have the means, and believe that the social climate will tolerate their aggression. Gender-schema theory proposes that once children learn the gender schema of their culture, their self-esteem becomes tied up in how well they express the traits considered relevant to their gender.

7. What factors contribute to attraction in our culture?

Men seem to find large eyes and narrows jaws to be attractive in women. In our culture, slenderness is considered attractive in both men and women, and tallness is valued in men. Women tend to see themselves as being heavier than the cultural ideal. We are more attracted to good-looking people. Similarity in attitudes and sociocultural factors (ethnicity, education, and so on), and reciprocity in feelings of admiration, also enhance attraction. According to the matching hypothesis, we tend to seek dates and mates at our own level of attractiveness, largely because of fear of rejection.

8. Just what is love? What is romantic love?

Sternberg's theory suggests that love has three components: intimacy, passion, and commitment. Different kinds of love combine these components in different ways. Romantic love is characterized by the combination of passion and intimacy. Consummate love has all three factors.

9. What is meant by the term sexual orientation?

Sexual orientation refers to the direction of one's erotic interests. Heterosexual people are sexually attracted to people of the other gender and interested in forming romantic relationships with them. Homosexual people are sexually attracted to people of their own gender and interested in forming romantic relationships with them.

10. How do researchers explain gay male and lesbian sexual orientations?

Psychodynamic theory connects sexual orientation with improper resolution of the Oedipus and Electra complexes. Learning theorists focus on the role of reinforcement of early patterns of sexual behavior. Evidence of a genetic contribution to sexual orientation is accumulating. Sex hormones are known to have both organizing and activating effects, but research has failed to connect sexual orientation with differences in adult levels of sex hormones. However, sex hormones may play a role in determining sexual orientation during prenatal development.

11. What is the sexual response cycle?

The sexual response cycle describes the body's response to sexual stimulation and consists of four phases: excitement, plateau, orgasm, and resolution. Excitement is characterized by erection in the male and lubrication in the female. Orgasm is characterized by muscle contractions and release of sexual tension. Following orgasm, males enter a refractory period during which they are temporarily unresponsive to sexual stimulation.

12. What are sexual dysfunctions?

Sexual dysfunctions are persistent or recurrent problems in becoming sexually aroused or reaching orgasm. They include hypoactive sexual desire disorder (lack of interest in sex), female sexual arousal disorder and male erectile disorder (characterized by inadequate vasocongestion), orgasmic disorder, premature ejaculation, dyspareunia (pain during sex), and vaginismus (involuntary contraction of the muscles of the vaginal barrel, making intercourse difficult).

13. What are the origins of sexual dysfunctions?

Sexual dysfunctions may be caused by physical problems, negative attitudes toward sex, lack of sexual knowledge and skills, problems in the relationship, and performance anxiety.

14. How are sexual dysfunctions treated?

Sexual dysfunctions are treated by sex therapy, which focuses on reducing performance anxiety, changing self-defeating attitudes and expectations, teaching sexual skills, enhancing sexual knowledge, and improving sexual communication. There are also some biological treatments, such as drugs that enhance the physical aspects of sexual response.

15. Why do men rape women?

Social critics argue that men are socialized into sexual aggression by being generally reinforced for aggressiveness and competitiveness. Social attitudes such as gender role stereotyping, seeing sex as adversarial, and myths that tend to blame the victim all help create a climate that encourages rape.

16. How can we prevent rape?

Rape can be prevented by social change and by cautionary measures such as avoiding deserted areas and—in dating—by dating in groups and being assertive in expressing one's sexual intentions and limits.

17. What is sexual harassment?

Sexual harassment consists of gestures, verbal comments, or physical contact of a sexual nature that is unwelcome to the recipient.

18. What do you do if you are sexually harassed on campus or in the workplace?

Sexual harassment is often stopped by means such as imparting a professional attitude, avoiding being alone with the harasser, keeping a record of incidents, notifying the harasser that you recognize the harassment for what it is and that you want it to stop, filing complaints with appropriate campus offices, and consulting a lawyer about the problem.

19. What kinds of sexually transmitted infections are there?

HIV/AIDS is the most feared STI because it is fatal. However, STIs such as chlamydia and genital warts (cased by HPV) are more widespread and also harmful.

20. How is HIV transmitted? What does it do?

HIV is transmitted by infected blood, semen (through male–female and male–male sexual activity), vaginal and cervical secretions, and breast milk. HIV kills white blood cells (CD4 lymphocytes) in the immune system that recognize viruses and instruct other white blood cells to make the antibodies that combat disease. When the immune system is depleted of CD4 cells, body is left vulnerable to opportunistic diseases such as certain forms of cancer and pneumonia.

21. **How is HIV infection diagnosed? How is HIV/AIDS treated?**

The presence of HIV is detected by blood, saliva, and urine tests. HIV/AIDS is treated by a "cocktail" of antiviral drugs that includes a protease inhibitor. While the cocktail can reduce HIV in the blood to undetectable levels, it does not eradicate HIV and therefore is not a cure.

22. **What can you do to prevent the transmission of HIV and other STI-causing organisms?**

First, don't close your eyes to the real threat of HIV and other disease-causing organisms. In addition, know your sex partner well, and have regular health checkups.

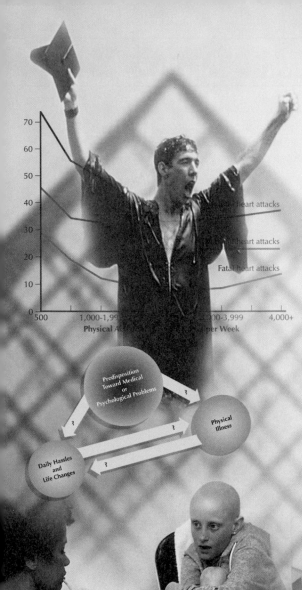

CHAPTER 14

Stress and Health

TRUTH  FICTION?

- Going on vacation is stressful.

- Since variety is the spice of life, the more change the better.

- People with a strong need for social approval are setting themselves up for feelings of anxiety and depression.

- "A merry heart doeth good like a medicine."

- At any given moment, countless microscopic warriors within our bodies are carrying out search-and-destroy missions against foreign agents.

- People who exercise regularly live two years longer, on the average, than their sedentary counterparts.

- Poor people in the United States eat less than more affluent people.

- Blowing things out of proportion can give you a headache.

- Handing in assignments early is good for you.

- Ketchup (ketchup?) is a health food.

Sirens. Ambulances. Stretchers. The emergency room at Dallas's public Parkland Memorial Hospital is a busy place. Sirens wail endlessly as ambulances pull up to the doors and discharge people who need prompt attention. Because of the volume of patients, beds line the halls, and people who do not require immediate care cram the waiting room. Many hours may pass before they are seen by a doctor. It is not unusual for people who are not considered in danger to wait 10 to 12 hours.

All this may sound rather foreboding, but good things are happening at Parkland as well. One of them is the attention physicians are devoting to patients' psychological needs as well as to their physical needs. For example, influenced both by his own clinical experience and by Native American wisdom about the healing process, Dr. Ron Anderson teaches his medical students that caring about patients is not an outdated ideal. Rather, it is a powerful weapon against disease.

TV journalist Bill Moyers describes Anderson on his medical rounds with students:

> I listen as he stops at the bedside of an elderly woman suffering from chronic asthma. He asks the usual questions: "How did you sleep last night?" "Is the breathing getting any easier?" His next questions surprise the medical students: "Is your son still looking for work?" "Is he still drinking?" "Tell us what happened right before the asthma attack." He explains to his puzzled students. "We know that anxiety aggravates many illnesses, especially chronic conditions like asthma. So we have to find out what may be causing her episodes of stress and help her find some way of coping with it. Otherwise she will land in here again, and next time we might not be able to save her. We cannot just prescribe medication and walk away. That is medical neglect. We have to take the time to get to know her, how she lives, her values, what her social supports are. If we don't know that her son is her sole support and that he's out of work, we will be much less effective in dealing with her asthma." (Moyers, 1993, p. 2)

HEALTH PSYCHOLOGY

CLICK4™ *across to contents and abstracts of the APA journal* Health Psychology.

CLICK4™ *a WebSearch activity on careers in health psychology.*

Note some key concepts from the slice of hospital life reported by Moyers: "Anxiety aggravates many illnesses." "We have to find out what may be causing . . . stress and . . . find some way of coping with it." "We cannot just prescribe medication and walk away." "We have to take the time to get to know [patients], how [they] live, [their] values, what [their] social supports are."

Anderson and Moyers have provided us with an introduction to the field of health psychology. *Question: What is health psychology?* **Health psychology** studies the relationships between psychological factors and the prevention and treatment of physical health problems. The case of the woman with asthma is a useful springboard for discussion because health psychologists study the ways in which

▲ psychological factors such as stress, behavior patterns, and attitudes can lead to or aggravate illness

▲ people can cope with stress

▲ stress and **pathogens** (disease-causing organisms such as bacteria and viruses) interact to influence the immune system

▲ people decide whether or not to seek health care

▲ psychological forms of intervention such as health education (for example, concerning nutrition, smoking, and exercise) and behavior modification can contribute to physical health

In this chapter we consider a number of issues in health psychology: sources of stress, factors that moderate the impact of stress, and the body's response to stress.

Health psychology ▲ The field of psychology that studies the relationships between psychological factors (e.g., attitudes, beliefs, situational influences, and behavior patterns) and the prevention and treatment of physical illness.

Pathogen ▲ A microscopic organism (e.g., bacterium or virus) that can cause disease.

STRESS: PRESSES, PUSHES, AND PULLS

CLICK4™ *an essay assignment: How do you define stress?*

CLICK4™ *links to health psychology from the APA.*

Americans will put up with anything provided it doesn't block traffic.

—*Dan Rather*

Question: What is stress? In physics, stress is defined as a pressure or force exerted on a body. Tons of rock pressing on the earth, one car smashing into another, a rubber band stretching—all are types of physical stress. Psychological forces, or stresses, also press, push, or pull. We may feel "crushed" by the weight of a big decision, "smashed" by adversity, or "stretched" to the point of snapping.

In psychology, **stress** is the demand made on an organism to adapt, cope, or adjust. Some stress is healthful and necessary to keep us alert and occupied. Stress researcher Hans Selye (1980) referred to such healthful stress as **eustress.** But intense or prolonged stress can overtax our adjustive capacity, affect our moods, impair our ability to experience pleasure, and harm the body (Berenbaum & Connelly, 1993; Cohen et al., 1993).

SOURCES OF STRESS: DON'T HASSLE ME? (RIGHT)

There are many sources of stress. In this section we consider daily hassles, life changes, conflict, irrational beliefs, and Type A behavior.

Daily Hassles—The Stress of Everyday Life

Which straw will break the camel's back? The last straw, according to the saying. Similarly, stresses can pile up until we can no longer cope with them. Some of these stresses are **daily hassles.** ***Question: What are daily hassles?*** Daily hassles are regularly occurring conditions and experiences that can threaten or harm our well-being. Others are life changes. Lazarus and his colleagues (1985) analyzed a scale that measures daily hassles and their opposites—termed **uplifts**—and found that hassles could be grouped as follows:

1. *Household hassles:* preparing meals, shopping, and home maintenance
2. *Health hassles:* physical illness, concern about medical treatment, and side effects of medication
3. *Time-pressure hassles:* having too many things to do, too many responsibilities, and not enough time
4. *Inner concern hassles:* being lonely and fearful of confrontation
5. *Environmental hassles:* crime, neighborhood deterioration, and traffic noise

Stress ▲ The demand that is made on an organism to adapt.
Eustress ▲ (YOU-stress). Stress that is healthful.
Daily hassles ▲ Notable daily conditions and experiences that are threatening or harmful to a person's well-being.
Uplifts ▲ Notable pleasant daily conditions and experiences.

A Daily Hassle.
Daily hassles are notable daily conditions and experiences that are threatening or harmful to a person's well-being. What are some of the daily hassles in your life?

6. *Financial responsibility hassles:* concern about owing money such as mortgage payments and loan installments

7. *Work hassles:* job dissatisfaction, not liking one's duties at work, and problems with coworkers

8. *Future security hassles:* concerns about job security, taxes, property investments, stock market swings, and retirement

These hassles are linked to psychological variables such as nervousness, worrying, inability to get started, feelings of sadness, and feelings of loneliness.

▲ **REFLECT**

How many daily hassles do you experience? Are they temporary or permanent? How many are connected with your role as a student? What can you do about them?

Life Changes — Does Too Much Spice Leave an Ill Taste?

You might think that marrying Mr. or Ms. Right, finding a good job, and moving to a better neighborhood all in the same year would propel you into a state of bliss. It might. But too much of a good thing may also make you ill. *Question: How is it that too much of a good thing can make you ill?* It is because all of these events are life changes. As pleasant as they may be, they require adjustment. Coming one after another, life changes, even positive ones, can lead to headaches, high blood pressure, and other health problems.

Life changes differ from daily hassles in two key ways:

1. Many life changes are positive and desirable. Hassles, by definition, are negative.
2. Hassles occur regularly. Life changes occur at irregular intervals.

Holmes and Rahe (1967) constructed a scale to measure the impact of life changes by assigning an arbitrary weight of 50 "life-change units" to one major change: marriage. Using marriage as the baseline, they asked participants to assign units to other life changes. Most events were rated as less stressful than marriage. A few were more stressful, such as the death of a spouse (100 units) and divorce (73 units). Changes in work hours and residence (20 units each) were included, regardless of whether they were negative or positive. Positive life changes such as an outstanding personal achievement (28 units) and going on vacation (13 units) also made the list. Although vacations can be good for your health (Gump & Matthews, 2000), they remain a life change that requires adjustment.

Life Changes.

Life changes differ from daily hassles in that they tend to be more episodic. Also, life changes can be positive as well as negative. What is the relationship between life changes and illness? Is the relationship causal?

Hassles, Life Changes, and Health Problems Hassles and life changes—especially negative life changes—affect us psychologically. They can cause us to worry and affect our moods. But stressors such as hassles and life changes also predict health problems such as heart disease and cancer and even athletic injuries (Smith et al., 1990). Holmes and Rahe found that people who "earned" 300 or more life-change units within a

year, according to their scale, were at greater risk for health problems. Eight of 10 developed health problems, compared with only 1 of 3 people whose totals of life-change units for the year were below 150.

Moreover, people who remain married to the same person live longer than people who experience marital breakups and remarry (Tucker et al., 1996). Apparently the life changes of divorce and remarriage—or the instability associated with them—can be harmful to health.

CONTROVERSY IN PSYCHOLOGY

Just How Are Daily Hassles and Life Changes Connected With Health Problems?
The links between daily hassles, life changes, and health problems are supported by research. But what leads to what? Although it may appear obvious that hassles and life changes should *cause* health problems, what is obvious can be incomplete, even wrong. In this case, researchers are not convinced that the causal connections are all that clear. Let us consider a number of limitations in the research on the connections between daily hassles, life changes, and health problems:

1. *Correlational Evidence.* The links that have been uncovered between hassles, life changes, and illness are correlational rather than experimental. It may seem logical that the hassles and life changes caused the disorders, but these variables were not manipulated experimentally. Other explanations of the data are possible (Figure 14.1). One possible explanation is that people who are predisposed toward medical or psychological problems encounter more hassles and amass more life-change units. For example, undiagnosed medical disorders may contribute to sexual problems, arguments with spouses or in-laws, changes in living conditions and personal habits, and changes in sleeping habits. People may also make certain changes in their lives that lead to physical and psychological disorders (Simons et al., 1993).

2. *Positive Versus Negative Life Changes.* Other aspects of the research on the relationship between life changes and illness have also been challenged. For instance, positive life changes may be less disturbing than hassles and negative life changes, even though the number of life-change units assigned to them is high (Lefcourt et al., 1981).

3. *Personality Differences.* People with different kinds of personalities respond to life stresses in different ways (Vaillant, 1994). For example, people who are easygoing or psychologically hardy are less likely to become ill under the impact of stress.

4. *Cognitive Appraisal.* The stress of an event reflects the meaning of the event to the individual (Folkman & Moskowitz, 2000a). Pregnancy, for example, can be a positive or negative life change, depending on whether one wants and is prepared to have a child. We appraise the hassles, traumatic experiences, and life changes that we encounter. In responding to them, we take into account their perceived danger, our values and goals, our beliefs in our coping ability, our social support, and so on. The same event will be less taxing to someone with greater coping ability and support than to someone who lacks these advantages.

Despite these methodological flaws, hassles and life changes require adjustment. It seems wise to be aware of hassles and life changes and how they may affect us. Now let us consider a particular source of stress that affects people from ethnic minority groups.

DIVERSITY　Stress and Diversity: Acculturative Stress

Don Terry's mother is European American. His father is African American. When he was a child, he said to his mother, "You're white and Dad's black, so what does that make me?" (Terry, 2000).

"Oh, I see," she said. "Well, you're half-black and you're half-white, so you're the best of both worlds."

However, life experiences taught Don that in the United States it is difficult, if not impossible, to be "half" European American and "half" African American. Consider some of his experiences at college and how he "chose" to be African American.

CLICK4™ *an essay assignment on the connection between daily hassles and health.*

CLICK4™ *online stress tests: How stressful is your life?*

▲ **REFLECT**
Can you think of any positive life changes in your own life that have caused you stress?

CLICK4™ *a bulletin board discussion on acculturative stress.*

The Social Readjustment Rating Scale

Life changes can be a source of stress. How much stress have you experienced in the past year as a result of life changes? To compare your stress to that experienced by other college students, complete this questionnaire.

Directions: Indicate how many times (frequency) you have experienced the following events during the past 12 months (do not enter a number larger than five). Then multiply the frequency by the number of life-change units (value) associated with each event. Write the product in the column on the right (total). Then add up the points and check the key in Appendix B.

EVENT	VALUE	FREQUENCY	TOTAL
1. Death of a spouse, lover, or child	94		
2. Death of a parent or sibling	88		
3. Beginning formal higher education	84		
4. Death of a close friend	83		
5. Miscarriage or stillbirth of pregnancy of self, spouse, or lover	83		
6. Jail sentence	82		
7. Divorce or marital separation	82		
8. Unwanted pregnancy of self, spouse, or lover	80		
9. Abortion of unwanted pregnancy of self, spouse, or lover	80		
10. Detention in jail or other institution	79		
11. Change in dating activity	79		
12. Death of a close relative	79		
13. Change in marital situation other than divorce or separation	78		
14. Separation from significant other whom you like very much	77		
15. Change in health status or behavior of spouse or lover	77		
16. Academic failure	77		
17. Major violation of the law and subsequent arrest	76		
18. Marrying or living with lover against parents' wishes	75		
19. Change in love relationship or important friendship	74		
20. Change in health status or behavior of a parent or sibling	73		
21. Change in feelings of loneliness, insecurity, anxiety, boredom	73		
22. Change in marital status of parents	73		
23. Acquiring a visible deformity	72		
24. Change in ability to communicate with a significant other whom you like very much	71		
25. Hospitalization of a parent or sibling	70		
26. Reconciliation of marital or love relationship	68		
27. Release from jail or other institution	68		
28. Graduation from college	68		
29. Major personal injury or illness	68		
30. Wanted pregnancy of self, spouse, or lover	67		
31. Change in number or type of arguments with spouse or lover	67		
32. Marrying or living with lover with parents' approval	66		
33. Gaining a new family member through birth or adoption	65		
34. Preparing for an important exam or writing a major paper	65		
35. Major financial difficulties	65		
36. Change in the health status or behavior of a close relative or close friend	65		
37. Change in academic status	64		
38. Change in amount and nature of interpersonal conflicts	63		
39. Change in relationship with members of your immediate family	62		
40. Change in own personality	62		
41. Hospitalization of yourself or a close relative	61		
42. Change in course of study, major field, vocational goals, or work status	60		
43. Change in own financial status	59		
44. Change in status of divorced or widowed parent	59		
45. Change in number or type of arguments between parents	59		
46. Change in acceptance by peers, identification with peers, or social pressure by peers	58		
47. Change in general outlook on life	57		
48. Beginning or ceasing service in the armed forces	57		
49. Change in attitudes toward friends	56		

The Social Readjustment Rating Scale

EVENT	VALUE	FREQUENCY	TOTAL
50. Change in living arrangements, conditions, or environment	55	_____	_____
51. Change in frequency or nature of sexual experiences	55	_____	_____
52. Change in parents' financial status	55	_____	_____
53. Change in amount or nature of pressure from parents	55	_____	_____
54. Change in degree of interest in college or attitudes toward education	55	_____	_____
55. Change in the number of personal or social relationships you've formed or dissolved	55	_____	_____
56. Change in relationship with siblings	54	_____	_____
57. Change in mobility or reliability of transportation	54	_____	_____
58. Academic success	54	_____	_____
59. Change to a new college or university	54	_____	_____
60. Change in feelings of self-reliance, independence, or amount of self-discipline	53	_____	_____
61. Change in number or type of arguments with roommate	52	_____	_____
62. Spouse or lover beginning or ceasing work outside the home	52	_____	_____
63. Change in frequency of use of amounts of drugs other than alcohol, tobacco, or marijuana	51	_____	_____
64. Change in sexual morality, beliefs, or attitudes	50	_____	_____
65. Change in responsibility at work	50	_____	_____
66. Change in amount or nature of social activities	50	_____	_____
67. Change in dependencies on parents	50	_____	_____
68. Change from academic work to practical fieldwork experience or internship	50	_____	_____
69. Change in amount of material possessions and concomitant responsibilities	50	_____	_____
70. Change in routine at college or work	49	_____	_____
71. Change in amount of leisure time	49	_____	_____
72. Change in amount of in-law trouble	49	_____	_____

EVENT	VALUE	FREQUENCY	TOTAL
73. Outstanding personal achievement	49	_____	_____
74. Change in family structure other than parental divorce or separation	48	_____	_____
75. Change in attitude toward drugs	48	_____	_____
76. Change in amount and nature of competition with same gender	48	_____	_____
77. Improvement of own health	47	_____	_____
78. Change in responsibilities at home	47	_____	_____
79. Change in study habits	46	_____	_____
80. Change in number or type of arguments or close conflicts with close relatives	46	_____	_____
81. Change in sleeping habits	46	_____	_____
82. Change in frequency of use or amounts of alcohol	45	_____	_____
83. Change in social status	45	_____	_____
84. Change in frequency of use or amounts of tobacco	45	_____	_____
85. Change in awareness of activities in external world	45	_____	_____
86. Change in religious affiliation	44	_____	_____
87. Change in type of gratifying activities	43	_____	_____
88. Change in amount or nature of physical activities	43	_____	_____
89. Change in address or residence	43	_____	_____
90. Change in amount or nature of recreational activities	43	_____	_____
91. Change in frequency of use or amounts of marijuana	43	_____	_____
92. Change in social demands or responsibilities due to your age	43	_____	_____
93. Court appearance for legal violation	40	_____	_____
94. Change in weight or eating habits	39	_____	_____
95. Change in religious activities	37	_____	_____
96. Change in political views or affiliations	34	_____	_____
97. Change in driving pattern or conditions	33	_____	_____
98. Minor violation of the law	31	_____	_____
99. Vacation or travel	30	_____	_____
100. Change in number of family get-togethers	30	_____	_____

SOURCE: *Self-Assessment and Behavior Change Manual* (pp. 43-47), by Peggy Blake, Robert Fry, & Michael Pesjack, 1984, New York: Random House. Reprinted by permission of Random House, Inc.

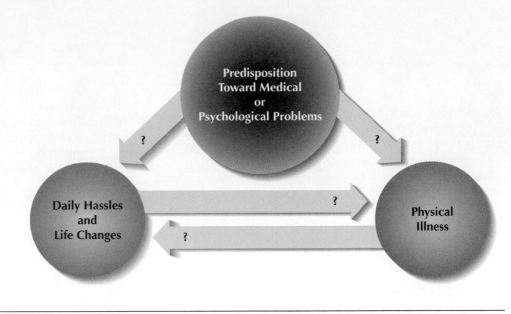

FIGURE 14.1 What Are the Relationships Among Daily Hassles, Life Changes, and Physical Illness?
There are positive correlations between daily hassles and life events, on the one hand, and illness on the other. It may seem logical that hassles and life changes cause illness, but research into the issue is correlational and not experimental. The results are therefore subject to rival interpretations. One is that people who are predisposed toward medical or psychological problems encounter or generate more hassles and amass more life-change units.

Don chose to attend Oberlin College because of its reputation for enlightened race relations. But when he began his freshman year, he found a very different picture. When he walked into the dining room, he found African American students sitting together at one group of tables and European Americans at others. African American fans usually sat with other African American fans at football and basketball games, while European American fans sat with European Americans.

One night, Don was visiting a European American girl and her European American roommate in their dorm. They were just chatting, with the door open. Another African American student was there, flirting with the roommate. Don was about to leave when a European American girl who was passing by stuck in her head. Looking disgusted, she said, "What's this? A soul-brother session?" Don was stunned. Why was race a part of it? He and his friend were just chatting with a couple of girls and getting nowhere. The girl Don was visiting looked embarrassed. He didn't know whether she was embarrassed about her neighbor sticking her nose in or because her neighbor had "caught" a couple of African American males in her room.

Don was fed up. He "embraced blackness—as a shield and a cause." He enrolled in courses in Black studies. The courses were crucial to his academic and personal development. They helped him forge an identity. They also helped him to understand—for the first time—his African American father's anger toward the discriminatory dominant culture.

Don got in touch with his disappointment and his rage that race was so important, even at his "progressive" college. He was angry that he could not be himself—a complex individual named Don Terry, with a European American mother and an African American father. Instead, he saw that he would always be lumped in the racial category of being Black and treated like a caricature, not a person. "Disgusted by the world's refusal to see me as mixed and individual," writes Don Terry (2000), "I chose 'blackness.'" And part of that identity comprised racist feelings of his own.

Like Don Terry, African Americans hear themselves called derogatory names. They hear people telling insulting jokes about them. They are still barred from many social and occupational opportunities. They are taunted. They are sometimes the butt of physical aggression. Their parents often warn them that if they are stopped by the police, they are to keep their hands low and in clear sight and are to avoid sounding threatening; otherwise, they may be shot.

It is no secret that African Americans encounter racism in their interactions with European Americans and other people, even in "progressive" places like Oberlin College. Some European Americans consider them to be a criminal class. African American college students, most of whom attend predominantly European American colleges and

An African American College Student. Not only must African American college students, like European American college students, cope with grades, a social life, financial issues, health problems, and all the other hassles experienced by college students; they are also often hassled by students who would rather not have them at "their" college or university.

universities, also encounter racism. In addition to worrying about grades, dating, finances, health, and all the other hassles experienced by college students, they are also hassled by students who think that they do not belong at "their" college or university. Even "open-minded" European American students often assume that the African American students were admitted on the basis of Affirmative Action or other racial programs rather than on the basis of their own individual merits.

Acculturative Stress

Don Terry was experiencing *acculturative stress*. Half European American, half African American, he had a foot in two cultures and felt compelled to be at home in each. But it's not easy. African American students whose values are at variance with those of the dominant culture often feel pressured to change. They feel compelled to acculturate, to become bicultural—capable of getting by among African Americans and European Americans—in an often hostile environment. The feelings of tension and anxiety that accompany efforts to adapt to or adopt the orientation and values of the dominant culture are termed **acculturative stress.** Research has shown that for African Americans, acculturative stress is connected with feelings of anxiety and tension and physical health problems, particularly hypertension (Clark et al., 1999). Racism is also connected with feelings of being marginal and alienated, role confusion (confusion over who one is and what one stands for), and a poor self-concept (Thompson et al., 2000). The research suggests that making African American children aware of the value of their own culture helps buffer the effects of acculturative stress (Thompson et al., 2000).

Coping With Acculturative Stress

C. Patricia Thompson and her colleagues (2000) note that many African American college students have poorly defined personal identities and are subject to being buffeted about by acculturative stress. Some African American students attempt to cope by becoming as Eurocentric as possible. But others undergo a process that may begin with naive idealization of the dominant culture in the United States (Cross et al., 1991) but ends with a solid African American identity. Some event—perhaps personal exposure to prejudice, realizing the horror of historic atrocities such as lynchings, or the race-related misfortunes of a friend or family member—causes them to reject Eurocentric culture and undergo a search for an African American identity. They immerse themselves in African American culture and withdraw from unnecessary contacts with European Americans. Don Terry writes that at this stage he "chose blackness" and took coursework in "black nationalism." Rejection of the dominant culture helps foster feelings of hostility toward European Americans. The forging of links with

Acculturative stress ▲ Feelings of tension and anxiety that accompany efforts to adapt to or adopt the orientation and values of the dominant culture.

other African Americans and the adopting of pride in African American culture eventually work to lessen feelings of hostility and resentment so that individuals like Don Terry become calmer, more secure, and less hostile. Individuals who emerge with an African American viewpoint but who can cope with and even befriend European Americans appear to experience the least acculturative stress (Thompson et al., 2000). That, perhaps, is where Don Terry, a reporter for *The New York Times*, is today.

Conflict — Darned If You Do, Darned If You Don't

Should you eat dessert or try to stick to your diet? Should you live on campus, which is more convenient, or should you rent an apartment, where you may have more independence? Choices like these can place us in **conflict.** *Question: What is conflict?* In psychology, conflict is the feeling of being pulled in two or more directions by opposing motives. Conflict is frustrating and stressful. Psychologists often classify conflicts into four types: approach-approach, avoidance-avoidance, approach-avoidance, and multiple approach-avoidance.

Approach-approach conflict (Figure 14.2, part A) is the least stressful type. Here, each of two goals is desirable, and both are within reach. You may not be able to decide between pizza or tacos, Tom or Dick, or a trip to Nassau or Hawaii. Such conflicts are usually resolved by making a decision. People who experience this type of conflict may vacillate until they make a decision.

Avoidance-avoidance conflict (Figure 14.2, part B) is more stressful because you are motivated to avoid each of two negative goals. However, avoiding one of them requires approaching the other. You may be fearful of visiting the dentist but also afraid that

▲ **REFLECT**

Have you ever felt "damned if you do and damned if you don't"? Regretted that you couldn't do two things, or be in two places, at the same time? How did you resolve the conflict? (Or didn't you?)

Conflict ▲ Being torn in different directions by opposing motives. Feelings produced by being in conflict.
Approach-approach conflict ▲ A type of conflict in which the goals that produce opposing motives are positive and within reach.
Avoidance-avoidance conflict ▲ A type of conflict in which the goals are negative, but avoidance of one requires approaching the other.

FIGURE 14.2 Models for Conflict.
Part A shows an approach-approach conflict, in which a person (P) has motives (M) to reach two goals (G) that are desirable, but approach of one requires exclusion of the other. Part B shows an avoidance-avoidance conflict in which both goals are negative, but avoiding one requires approaching the other. Part C shows an approach-avoidance conflict, in which the same goal has desirable and undesirable properties. Part D shows a double approach-avoidance conflict, which is the simplest kind of *multiple* approach-avoidance conflict. In a multiple approach-avoidance conflict, two or more goals have mixed properties.

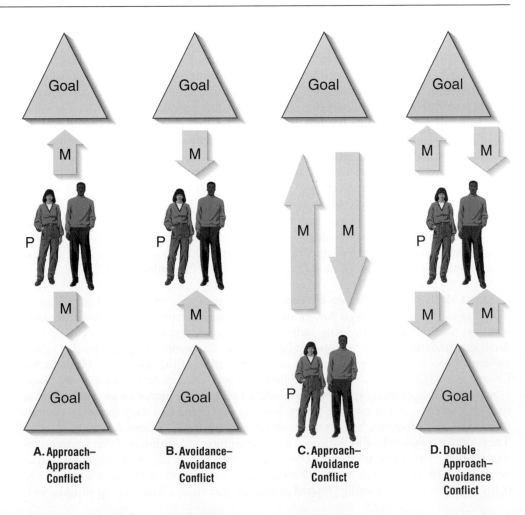

A. Approach–Approach Conflict

B. Avoidance–Avoidance Conflict

C. Approach–Avoidance Conflict

D. Double Approach–Avoidance Conflict

your teeth will decay if you do not make an appointment and go. You may not want to contribute to the Association for the Advancement of Lost Causes, but you fear that your friends will consider you cheap or uncommitted if you do not. Each goal in an avoidance-avoidance conflict is negative. When an avoidance-avoidance conflict is highly stressful and no resolution is in sight, some people withdraw from the conflict by focusing on other matters or doing nothing. Highly conflicted people have been known to refuse to get up in the morning and start the day.

When the same goal produces both approach and avoidance motives, we have an **approach-avoidance conflict** (Figure 14.2, part C). People and things have their pluses and minuses, their good points and their bad points. Cream cheese pie may be delicious, but oh, the calories! Goals that produce mixed motives may seem more attractive from a distance but undesirable from up close. Many couples repeatedly break up and then re-unite. When they are apart and lonely, they may recall each other fondly and swear that they could make the relationship work if they got together again. But after they spend time together again, they may find themselves thinking, "How could I ever have believed that this so-and-so would change?"

The most complex form of conflict is the **multiple approach-avoidance conflict,** in which each of several alternative courses of action has pluses and minuses. An example with two goals is shown in Figure 14.2, part D. This sort of conflict might arise on the eve of an examination, when you are faced with the choice of studying or, say, going to a film. Each alternative has both positive and negative aspects: "Studying's a bore, but I won't have to worry about flunking. I'd love to see the movie, but I'd just be worrying about how I'll do tomorrow."

All forms of conflict entail motives that aim in opposite directions. When one motive is much stronger than the other—such as when you feel starved and are only slightly concerned about your weight—it will probably not be too stressful to act in accordance with the powerful motive—in this case, to eat. When each conflicting motive is powerful, however, you may experience high levels of stress and confusion about the proper course of action. At such times you are faced with the need to make a decision. Yet decision making can also be stressful, especially when there is no clear correct choice.

Irrational Beliefs: Ten Doorways to Distress

Psychologist Albert Ellis notes that our beliefs about events, as well as the events themselves, can be stressors (Ellis & Dryden, 1996). Consider a case in which a person is fired from a job and is anxious and depressed about it. It may seem logical that losing the job is responsible for the misery, but Ellis points out how the individual's beliefs about the loss compound his or her misery.

Question: How do irrational beliefs create or compound stress? Let us examine this situation according to Ellis's A → B → C approach: Losing the job is an *activating event* (A). The eventual outcome, or *consequence* (C), is misery. Between the activating event (A) and the consequence (C), however, lie *beliefs* (B), such as these: "This job was the most important thing in my life," "What a no-good failure I am," "My family will starve," "I'll never find a job as good," "There's nothing I can do about it." Beliefs such as these compound misery, foster helplessness, and divert us from planning and deciding what to do next. The belief that "There's nothing I can do about it" fosters helplessness. The belief that "I am a no-good failure" internalizes the blame and may be an exaggeration. The belief that "My family will starve" may also be an exaggeration.

We can diagram the situation like this:

$$\text{Activating events} \rightarrow \text{Beliefs} \rightarrow \text{Consequences}$$

$$\text{or } A \rightarrow B \rightarrow C$$

Anxieties about the future and depression over a loss are normal and to be expected. However, the beliefs of the person who lost the job tend to **catastrophize** the extent of the loss and contribute to anxiety and depression. By heightening the individual's

CD 14 SA 20

CLICK4™ *an interactive self-assessment: The Irrational Beliefs Questionnaire.*

Approach-avoidance conflict ▲ A type of conflict in which the same goal produces approach and avoidance motives.
Multiple approach-avoidance conflict ▲ A type of conflict in which each of a number of goals produces approach and avoidance motives.
Catastrophize ▲ (kuh-TASS-trow-fize). To interpret negative events as being disastrous; to "blow out of proportion."

TABLE 14.1   IRRATIONAL BELIEFS

Irrational Belief 1:	You must have sincere love and approval almost all the time from the people who are important to you.
Irrational Belief 2:	You must prove yourself to be thoroughly competent, adequate, and achieving at something important.
Irrational Belief 3:	Things must go the way you want them to go. Life is awful when you don't get your first choice in everything.
Irrational Belief 4:	Other people must treat everyone fairly and justly. When people act unfairly or unethically, they are rotten.
Irrational Belief 5:	When there is danger or fear in your world, you must be preoccupied with and upset by it.
Irrational Belief 6:	People and things should turn out better than they do. It's awful and horrible when you don't find quick solutions to life's hassles.
Irrational Belief 7:	Your emotional misery stems from external pressures that you have little or no ability to control. Unless these external pressures change, you must remain miserable.
Irrational Belief 8:	It is easier to evade life's responsibilities and problems than to face them and undertake more rewarding forms of self-discipline.
Irrational Belief 9:	Your past influenced you immensely and must therefore continue to determine your feelings and behavior today.
Irrational Belief 10:	You can achieve happiness by inertia and inaction, or by just enjoying yourself from day to day.

◢ REFLECT

How many of Albert Ellis's irrational beliefs do you harbor? (Are you sure?) What is their effect on your life?

www 14   PML 25

CLICK4™ *advice on alleviating the Type A behavior pattern.*

Type A behavior ▲ Behavior characterized by a sense of time urgency, competitiveness, and hostility.

Keeping an Eye on the Clock.

The Type A behavior pattern is characterized by a sense of time urgency, competitiveness, and hostility.

emotional reaction to the loss and fostering feelings of helplessness, these beliefs also impair coping ability. They lower the person's self-efficacy expectations.

Ellis proposes that many of us carry with us the irrational beliefs shown in Table 14.1. They are our personal doorways to distress. In fact, they can give rise to problems in themselves. When problems assault us from other sources, these beliefs can magnify their effect.

Ellis finds it understandable that we would want the approval of others but irrational to believe that we cannot survive without it. It would be nice to be competent in everything we do, but it's unreasonable to *expect* it. Sure, it would be nice to be able to serve and volley like a tennis pro, but most of us haven't the time or natural ability to perfect the game. Demanding perfection prevents us from going out on the court on weekends and batting the ball back and forth just for fun. Belief number 5 is a prescription for perpetual emotional upheaval. Beliefs numbers 7 and 9 lead to feelings of helplessness and demoralization. Sure, Ellis might say, childhood experiences can explain the origins of irrational beliefs, but it is our own cognitive appraisal—here and now—that causes us to be miserable.

Research findings support the connections between irrational beliefs (e.g., excessive dependence on social approval and perfectionism) and feelings of anxiety and depression (Blatt, 1995). Perfectionists are also more likely than other people to commit suicide when they are depressed (Pilkonis, 1996).

The Type A Behavior Pattern — Burning Out From Within?

Some people create stress for themselves through the **Type A behavior** pattern. *Question: What is Type A behavior?* Type A people are highly driven, competitive, impatient, and aggressive—so much so that they are prone to getting into auto accidents (Karlberg et al., 1998; Magnavita et al., 1997). They feel rushed and under pressure all the time and keep one eye firmly glued to the clock. They are not only prompt for appointments but often early. They eat, walk, and talk rapidly and become restless when others work slowly. They attempt to dominate group discussions. Type A people find it difficult to give up control or share power. They are often reluctant to delegate authority in the workplace, and because of this they increase their own workloads.

Type A people find it difficult just to go out on the tennis court and bat the ball back and forth. They watch their form, perfect their strokes, and demand continual self-improvement. They hold to the irrational belief that they must be perfectly competent and achieving in everything they undertake.

Type B people, in contrast, relax more readily and focus more on the quality of life. They are less ambitious and less impatient, and they pace themselves. Type A people earn higher grades and more money than Type B's of equal intelligence.

Are you a Type A person? The nearby questionnaire should afford you some insight.

REVIEW

(1) Daily _____ are regularly occurring conditions and experiences that threaten or harm our well-being. (2) Life changes, even pleasant ones, are stressful because they require _____. (3) The links among hassles, life changes, and physical health problems are (experimental or correlational?). (4) The feeling of being pulled in two or more directions by opposing motives is called _____. (5) Albert _____ notes that our beliefs about events, as well as the events themselves, can be stressors. (6) Type A behavior is characterized by a sense of time _____, competitiveness, and aggressiveness.

Pulling It Together: How do our cognitions—our attitudes and beliefs—affect the impact that external stressors have on us?

Are You Type A or Type B?

Complete the questionnaire by placing a check mark under Yes if the behavior pattern described is typical of you and under No if it is not. Try to work rapidly and leave no items blank. Then read the section on Type A behavior and turn to the scoring key in Appendix B.

DO YOU: YES   NO

1. Strongly accent key words in your everyday speech? _____ _____
2. Eat and walk quickly? _____ _____
3. Believe that children should be taught to be competitive? _____ _____
4. Feel restless when watching a slow worker? _____ _____
5. Hurry other people to get on with what they're trying to say? _____ _____
6. Find it highly aggravating to be stuck in traffic or waiting for a seat at a restaurant? _____ _____
7. Continue to think about your own problems and business even when listening to someone else? _____ _____
8. Try to eat and shave, or drive and jot down notes at the same time? _____ _____
9. Catch up on your work while on vacations? _____ _____
10. Bring conversations around to topics of concern to you? _____ _____
11. Feel guilty when you spend time just relaxing? _____ _____
12. Find that you're so wrapped up in your work that you no longer notice office decorations or the scenery when you commute? _____ _____
13. Find yourself concerned with getting more *things* rather than developing your creativity and social concerns? _____ _____
14. Try to schedule more and more activities into less time? _____ _____
15. Always appear for appointments on time? _____ _____
16. Clench or pound your fists or use other gestures to emphasize your views? _____ _____
17. Credit your accomplishments to your ability to work rapidly? _____ _____
18. Feel that things must be done *now* and quickly? _____ _____
19. Constantly try to find more efficient ways to get things done? _____ _____
20. Insist on winning at games rather than just having fun? _____ _____
21. Interrupt others often? _____ _____
22. Feel irritated when others are late? _____ _____
23. Leave the table immediately after eating? _____ _____
24. Feel rushed? _____ _____
25. Feel dissatisfied with your current level of performance? _____ _____

CD **14** **SA** **18**

CLICK4™ *the interactive version of this Self-Assessment.*

PSYCHOLOGICAL MODERATORS OF STRESS

There is no one-to-one relationship between stress and physical or psychological health problems. Physical factors account for some of the variability in our responses: Some people inherit predispositions toward specific disorders. Psychological factors also play a role, however (Holahan & Moos, 1990). They can influence, or *moderate*, the effects of stress. In this section we discuss several psychological moderators of stress: self-efficacy expectations, psychological hardiness, a sense of humor, predictability, and social support.

Self-Efficacy Expectations: "The Little Engine That Could"

Our **self-efficacy expectations** affect our ability to withstand stress (Basic Behavioral Science Task Force, 1996a; Maciejewski et al., 2000). *Question: How do our self-efficacy expectations affect our ability to withstand stress?* Classic research shows that when we are faced with fear-inducing objects, high self-efficacy expectations

> ▲ **REFLECT**
> Do you believe in yourself? How does your belief — or lack of belief — in yourself affect your life?

Self-efficacy expectations ▲ Our beliefs that we can bring about desired changes through our own efforts.

The Locus of Control Scale

Psychologically hardy people tend to have an internal locus of control. They believe that they are in control of their own lives. In contrast, people with an external locus of control tend to see their fate as being out of their hands.

Are you "internal" or "external"? To learn more about your perception of your locus of control, respond to this questionnaire, which was developed by Nowicki and Strickland (1973). Place a check mark in either the Yes or the No column for each question. When you are finished, turn to the answer key in Appendix B.

YES   NO

1. Do you believe that most problems will solve themselves if you just don't fool with them? _____ _____

2. Do you believe that you can stop yourself from catching a cold? _____ _____

3. Are some people just born lucky? _____ _____

4. Most of the time, do you feel that getting good grades meant a great deal to you? _____ _____

5. Are you often blamed for things that just aren't your fault? _____ _____

6. Do you believe that if somebody studies hard enough he or she can pass any subject? _____ _____

7. Do you feel that most of the time it doesn't pay to try hard because things never turn out right anyway? _____ _____

8. Do you feel that if things start out well in the morning, it's going to be a good day no matter what you do? _____ _____

9. Do you feel that most of the time parents listen to what their children have to say? _____ _____

10. Do you believe that wishing can make good things happen? _____ _____

11. When you get punished, does it usually seem it's for no good reason at all? _____ _____

12. Most of the time, do you find it hard to change a friend's opinion? _____ _____

13. Do you think cheering more than luck helps a team win? _____ _____

14. Did you feel that it was nearly impossible to change your parents' minds about anything? _____ _____

15. Do you believe that parents should allow children to make most of their own decisions? _____ _____

16. Do you feel that when you do something wrong there's very little you can do to make it right? _____ _____

17. Do you believe that most people are just born good at sports? _____ _____

18. Are most other people your age stronger than you are? _____ _____

19. Do you feel that one of the best ways to handle most problems is just not to think about them? _____ _____

20. Do you feel that you have a lot of choice in deciding who your friends are? _____ _____

CLICK4™ *an essay assignment on behavior patterns: What are the advantages and disadvantages of the Type A and Type B personalities?*

are accompanied by relatively *lower* levels of adrenaline and noradrenaline in the bloodstream (Bandura et al., 1985). Adrenaline is secreted when we are under stress. It arouses the body in several ways, such as accelerating the heart rate and releasing glucose from the liver. As a result, we may have "butterflies in the stomach" and feel nervous. Excessive arousal can impair our ability to manage stress by boosting our motivation beyond optimal levels and by distracting us from the tasks at hand. People with higher self-efficacy expectations thus have biological as well as psychological reasons for remaining calmer.

People who are self-confident are less prone to be disturbed by adverse events (Benight et al., 1997; Holahan & Moos, 1991). People with higher self-efficacy expectations are more likely to lose weight or quit smoking and less likely to relapse afterward (Anderson et al., 2000; Shiffman et al., 2000). They are better able to function in spite of pain (Lackner et al., 1996). A study of Native Americans found that alcohol abuse was correlated with self-efficacy expectations (M. J. Taylor, 2000). That is, individuals with feelings of powerlessness were more likely to abuse alcohol, perhaps as a way of lessening the stresses in their lives.

People are more likely to comply with medical advice when they believe that it will work (Schwartzer & Renner, 2000). Women, for example, are more likely to engage in breast self-examination when they believe that they will really be able to detect abnormal

21. If you find a four-leaf clover, do you believe that it might bring you good luck? _____ _____

22. Did you often feel that whether or not you did your homework had much to do with what kind of grades you got? _____ _____

23. Do you feel that when a person your age is angry with you, there's little you can do to stop him or her? _____ _____

24. Have you ever had a good luck charm? _____ _____

25. Do you believe that whether or not people like you depends on how you act? _____ _____

26. Did your parents usually help you if you asked them to? _____ _____

27. Have you ever felt that when people were angry with you, it was usually for no reason at all? _____ _____

28. Most of the time, do you feel that you can change what might happen tomorrow by what you did today? _____ _____

29. Do you believe that when bad things are going to happen they are just going to happen no matter what you try to do to stop them? _____ _____

30. Do you think that people can get their own way if they just keep trying? _____ _____

31. Most of the time do you find it useless to try to get your own way at home? _____ _____

32. Do you feel that when good things happen, they happen because of hard work? _____ _____

33. Do you feel that when somebody your age wants to be your enemy there's little you can do to change matters? _____ _____

34. Do you feel that it's easy to get friends to do what you want them to do? _____ _____

35. Do you usually feel that you have little to say about what you get to eat at home? _____ _____

36. Do you feel that when someone doesn't like you, there's little you can do about it? _____ _____

37. Did you usually feel it was almost useless to try in school, because most other children were just plain smarter than you were? _____ _____

38. Are you the kind of person who believes that planning ahead makes things turn out better? _____ _____

39. Most of the time, do you feel that you have little to say about what your family decides to do? _____ _____

40. Do you think it's better to be smart than to be lucky? _____ _____

CD 14 SA 19

CLICK4™ *the interactive version of this Self-Assessment.*

growths (Miller et al., 1996). People are more likely to try to quit smoking when they believe that they can do so successfully (Mischel & Shoda, 1995).

Psychological Hardiness — Tough Enough?

Psychological hardiness also helps people resist stress. Our understanding of this phenomenon is derived largely from the pioneering work of Suzanne Kobasa and her colleagues (1994). They studied business executives who seemed able to resist illness despite stress. In one phase of the research, executives completed a battery of psychological tests. Kobasa (1990) found that the psychologically hardy executives had three key characteristics. *Question: What characteristics are connected with psychological hardiness?* The characteristics include commitment, challenge, and control.

1. Kobasa found that psychologically hardy executives were high in *commitment*. They tended to involve themselves in, rather than feel alienated from, whatever they were doing or encountering.

2. They were also high in *challenge*. They believed that change, rather than stability, is normal in life. They appraised change as an interesting incentive to personal growth, not as a threat to security.

> ▲ **REFLECT**
> Are you committed to your undertakings — including college? Do you seek or avoid challenges? Are you in control of your life? What do your answers suggest about your psychological hardiness?

Psychological hardiness ▲ A cluster of traits that buffer stress and are characterized by commitment, challenge, and control.

Self-Efficacy Expectations and Performance.
Outstanding athletes tend to have high self-efficacy expectations. That is, they believe in themselves. Self-efficacy expectations are one of the psychological factors that moderate the effects of stress on us.

CLICK4™ *more information about humor: Is laughter the best medicine?*

▲ **REFLECT**
Are you an "internal" or an "external"? Are you satisfied with the situation? If not, what are *you* going to do about it?

Locus of control ▲ The place (locus) to which an individual attributes control over the receiving of reinforcers—either inside or outside the self.
"Internals" ▲ People who perceive the ability to attain reinforcements as being largely within themselves.
"Externals" ▲ People who perceive the ability to attain reinforcements as being largely outside themselves.

3. They were high in perceived *control* over their lives. They felt and behaved as though they were influential, rather than helpless, in facing the various rewards and punishments of life. Psychologically hardy people tend to have what Julian B. Rotter (1990) terms an internal **locus of control.**

Hardy people are more resistant to stress because they *choose* to face it (Kobasa, 1990). They also interpret stress as making life more interesting. For example, they see a conference with a supervisor as an opportunity to persuade the supervisor rather than as a risk to their position.

A sense of control is one of the keys to psychological hardiness (Folkman & Moskowitz, 2000b; Tennen & Affleck, 2000). You may wish to complete the nearby Self-Assessment to see whether you feel that you are in charge of your own life.

Sense of Humor: "A Merry Heart Doeth Good Like a Medicine"

The idea that humor lightens the burdens of life and helps people cope with stress has been with us for millennia (Lefcourt & Martin, 1986). Consider the biblical maxim "A merry heart doeth good like a medicine" (Proverbs 17:22).

Question: Is there any evidence that "A merry heart doeth good like a medicine"? Yes, both anecdotes and controlled research support this ancient maxim. In *Anatomy of an Illness*, Norman Cousins (1979) reported his bout with a painful illness that was similar to arthritis. He found that 10 minutes of belly laughter of the sort he experienced while watching Marx Brothers movies relieved much of his pain. Laughter allowed him to sleep. It may also have reduced the inflammation he suffered. This is consistent with some findings that positive affect—for example, feelings of happiness—may have beneficial effects on the immune system (Salovey et al., 2000).

Research has also shown that humor can moderate the effects of stress. In one study, students completed a checklist of negative life events and a measure of mood disturbance (Martin & Lefcourt, 1983). The measure of mood disturbance also yielded a stress score. The students also rated their sense of humor. Behavioral assessments were made of their ability to produce humor under stress. Overall, there was a significant relationship between negative life events and stress scores: High accumulations of negative life events predicted higher levels of stress. However, students who had a greater sense of humor and produced humor in difficult situations were less affected by negative life events than other students. In other studies, Lefcourt (1997) found that watching humorous videotapes raised the level of immunoglobin A (a measure of the functioning of the immune system) in students' saliva.

How does humor help people cope with stress? We are uncertain, but there has been speculation. One possibility, which would apply to the case of Norman Cousins, is that laughter stimulates the output of endorphins, which could benefit the functioning of the immune system. Another is more psychological: that the benefits of humor may be explained in terms of the sudden cognitive shifts they entail and the emotional changes that accompany them.

Predictability and Control: "If I Can Stop the Roller Coaster, I Don't Want To Get Off"

The ability to predict a stressor apparently moderates its impact. *Question: How do predictability and control help us cope with stress?* Predictability allows us to brace ourselves for the inevitable and, in many cases, plan ways of coping with it. Control—even the illusion of being in control—allows us to feel that we are not at the mercy of the fates (Folkman & Moskowitz, 2000b; Tennen & Affleck, 2000). There is also a relationship between the desire to assume control over one's situation and the usefulness of information about impending stressors (Lazarus & Folkman, 1984). Predictability is of greater benefit to **"internals"**—that is, to people who wish to exercise control over their situations—than to **"externals."** People who want information about medical procedures and what they will experience cope better with pain when they undergo those procedures (Ludwick-Rosenthal & Neufeld, 1993).

Social Support: On Being In It Together

People are social beings, and social support also seems to act as a buffer against the effects of stress (Folkman & Moskowitz, 2000a; Uchino et al., 1996).

Sources of social support include the following:

1. *Emotional concern*—listening to people's problems and expressing feelings of sympathy, caring, understanding, and reassurance.
2. *Instrumental aid*—the material supports and services that facilitate adaptive behavior. For example, after a disaster the government may arrange for low-interest loans so that survivors can rebuild. Relief organizations may provide foodstuffs, medicines, and temporary living quarters.
3. *Information*—guidance and advice that enhance people's ability to cope.
4. *Appraisal*—feedback from others about how one is doing. This kind of support involves helping people interpret, or "make sense of," what has happened to them.
5. *Socializing*—simple conversation, recreation, even going shopping with another person. Socializing has beneficial effects, even when it is not oriented specifically toward solving problems.

Question: Is there evidence that social support helps people cope with stress? Yes, research does support the value of social support. Introverts, people who lack social skills, and people who live by themselves seem more prone to developing infectious diseases such as colds under stress (Cohen & Williamson, 1991; Gilbert, 1997). Social support helps people cope with the stresses of cancer and other health problems (Azar, 1996b; Wilcox et al., 1994). People find caring for persons with Alzheimer's disease less stressful when they have social support (Haley et al., 1996). Social support helps Mexican Americans and other immigrants to cope with the stresses of acculturation (Hovey, 2000). People who have buddies who help them start exercising or quit drinking or smoking are more likely to succeed (Gruder et al., 1993; Nides et al., 1995). Social support helped children cope with the stresses of Hurricane Andrew (Vernberg et al., 1996) and Chinese villagers cope with an earthquake (Wang et al., 2000). It has been found to help women cope with the aftermath of rape (Valentiner et al., 1996). Stress is also less likely to lead to high blood pressure or alcohol abuse in people who have social support (Linden et al., 1993).

Put the shoe on the other foot. Giving social support can be stressful, especially when one is supporting people with health problems such as Alzheimer's disease or AIDS. Research shows that people with stronger social coping skills tend to show more positive affect (be in better moods) when they support others. And their more positive affect tends to result in their developing fewer physical symptoms or health problems themselves (Billings et al., 2000).

How does stress contribute to the development of physical health problems? Let us gain insight into this question by examining the effects of stress on the body.

REVIEW

(7) People with (higher or lower?) self-efficacy expectations tend to cope better with stress. (8) Psychologically hardy executives are high in _____, challenge, and control. (9) Being able to predict and control the onset of a stressor (increases or decreases?) its impact on us.

Pulling It Together: Why do factors like high self-efficacy expectations, control, and humor help us cope with stress?

STRESS AND THE BODY

Stress is more than a psychological event. It is more than "knowing" it is there; it is more than "feeling" pushed and pulled. Stress also has very definite effects on the body. Stress researcher Hans Selye outlined a number of them in his concept of the *general adaptation syndrome*.

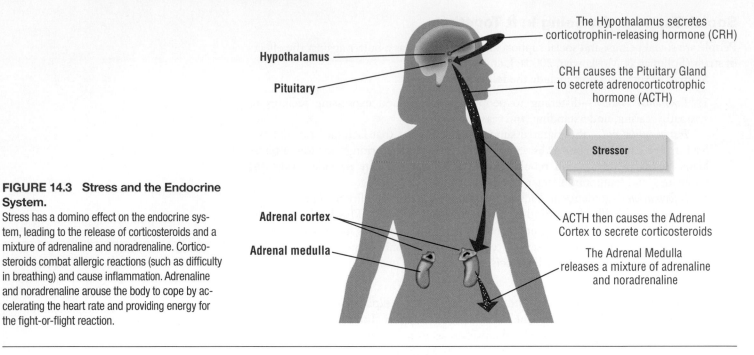

Hypothalamus

Pituitary

The Hypothalamus secretes corticotrophin-releasing hormone (CRH)

CRH causes the Pituitary Gland to secrete adrenocorticotrophic hormone (ACTH)

Stressor

Adrenal cortex

Adrenal medulla

ACTH then causes the Adrenal Cortex to secrete corticosteroids

The Adrenal Medulla releases a mixture of adrenaline and noradrenaline

FIGURE 14.3 Stress and the Endocrine System.
Stress has a domino effect on the endocrine system, leading to the release of corticosteroids and a mixture of adrenaline and noradrenaline. Corticosteroids combat allergic reactions (such as difficulty in breathing) and cause inflammation. Adrenaline and noradrenaline arouse the body to cope by accelerating the heart rate and providing energy for the fight-or-flight reaction.

Are Their Alarm Systems Going Off as They Take Out a Loan?
The alarm reaction of the general adaptation syndrome can be triggered by daily hassles and life changes—such as taking out a large loan—as well as by physical threats. When the stressor persists, diseases of adaptation may develop.

The General Adaptation Syndrome

How can stress make us ill? Hans Selye suggested that under stress the body is like a clock with an alarm system that does not shut off until its energy has been depleted.

Selye (1976) observed that the body's response to different stressors shows certain similarities whether the stressor is a bacterial invasion, perceived danger, or a major life change. For this reason, he labeled this response the **general adaptation syndrome** (GAS). *Question: What is the general adaptation syndrome?* The GAS is a cluster of bodily changes that occur in three stages: an alarm reaction, a resistance stage, and an exhaustion stage.

The Alarm Reaction   The **alarm reaction** is triggered by perception of a stressor. This reaction mobilizes or arouses the body in preparation for defense. Early in the 20th century, physiologist Walter B. Cannon (1932) termed this alarm system the **fight-or-flight reaction.** The alarm reaction involves a number of body changes that are initiated by the brain and further regulated by the endocrine system and the sympathetic division of the autonomic nervous system (ANS). Let us consider the roles of these systems.

Stress has a domino effect on the endocrine system (Figure 14.3). The hypothalamus secretes corticotrophin-releasing hormone (CRH). CRH causes the pituitary gland to secrete adrenocorticotrophic hormone (ACTH). ACTH then causes the adrenal cortex to secrete cortisol and other corticosteroids (steroidal hormones produced by the adrenal cortex). Corticosteroids help protect the body by combating allergic reactions (such as difficulty breathing) and producing inflammation. (However, corticosteroids can be harmful to the cardiovascular system, which is one reason that chronic stress can impair one's health, and why athletes who use steroids to build the muscle mass can experience cardiovascular problems.) Inflammation increases circulation to parts of the body that are injured. It ferries in hordes of white blood cells to fend off invading pathogens.

Two other hormones that play a major role in the alarm reaction are secreted by the adrenal medulla. The sympathetic division of the ANS activates the adrenal medulla, causing it to release a mixture of adrenaline and noradrenaline. This mixture arouses the body by accelerating the heart rate and causing the liver to release glucose (sugar). This provides the energy that fuels the fight-

or-flight reaction, which activates the body so that it is prepared to fight or flee from a predator.

The fight-or-flight reaction stems from a period in human prehistory when many stressors were life-threatening. It was triggered by the sight of a predator at the edge of a thicket or by a sudden rustling in the undergrowth. Today it may be aroused when you are caught in stop-and-go traffic or learn that your mortgage payments are going to increase. Once the threat is removed, the body returns to a lower state of arousal. Many of the bodily changes that occur in the alarm reaction are outlined in Table 14.2.

TABLE 14.2 COMPONENTS OF THE ALARM REACTION

The alarm reaction is triggered by various types of stressors. It is defined by the release of corticosteroids and adrenaline and by activity of the sympathetic branch of the autonomic nervous system. It prepares the body to fight or flee from a source of danger.

Corticosteroids are secreted	Muscles tense
Adrenaline is secreted	Blood shifts from internal organs to the skeletal musculature
Noradrenaline is secreted	
Respiration rate increases	Digestion is inhibited
Heart rate increases	Sugar is released from the liver
Blood pressure increases	Blood coagulability increases

The Resistance Stage If the alarm reaction mobilizes the body and the stressor is not removed, we enter the adaptation or **resistance stage** of the GAS. Levels of endocrine and sympathetic activity are lower than in the alarm reaction but still higher than normal. In this stage the body attempts to restore lost energy and repair bodily damage.

The Exhaustion Stage If the stressor is still not dealt with adequately, we may enter the **exhaustion stage** of the GAS. Individual capacities for resisting stress vary, but anyone will eventually become exhausted when stress continues indefinitely. The muscles become fatigued. The body is depleted of the resources required for combating stress. With exhaustion, the parasympathetic division of the ANS may predominate. As a result, our heartbeat and respiration rate slow down and many aspects of sympathetic activity are reversed. It might sound as if we would profit from the respite, but remember that we are still under stress—possibly an external threat. Continued stress in the exhaustion stage may lead to what Selye terms "diseases of adaptation." These are connected with constriction of blood vessels and alternation of the heart rhythm, and can range from allergies to hives and coronary heart disease (CHD)—and, ultimately, death.

We will soon consider the effects of stress on the body's immune system. Our discussion will pave the way for understanding the links between various psychological factors and physical illnesses. But first let us see that the fight-or-flight "mechanism" might not apply to everyone—in fact, to at least half of us.

REFLECT
What do you experience happening in your body when you are under stress? How do those sensations fit the description of the general adaptation syndrome?

CLICK4™ *a WebSearch activity on the biological consequences of stress.*

DIVERSITY Stress and Diversity: "Fight or Flight" or "Tend and Befriend"? Gender Differences in Response to Stress

Nearly a century ago, Harvard University physiologist Walter Cannon labeled the body's response to stress the "fight-or-flight" reaction. He believed that the body was prewired to become mobilized or aroused in preparation for combat when faced with a predator or a competitor, or if the predator was threatening enough, that "discretion"—that is, a "strategic retreat"—would sometimes be the "better part of valour." Although the biology of his day did not allow Cannon to be as precise as we, we now know that the fight-or-flight reaction includes bodily changes that involve the brain (perceptions, neurotransmitters), the endocrine system (hormones), and the sympathetic division of the autonomic nervous system (rapid heart beat, rapid breathing, muscle tension). The sum of these bodily changes pumps us up to fight like demons or, when advisable, to beat a hasty retreat.

Or does it?

According to a review of the literature by UCLA psychologist Shelley E. Taylor and her colleagues (2000), at least half of us are more likely to tend to the kids or "interface" with family and friends than to fight or flee. Which half of us would that be? The female half.

CLICK4™ *a bulletin board discussion on gender differences in response to stress.*

Why Are All Those Rats Males? Taylor explains that the study was prompted by an offhand remark of a student who had noticed that nearly all of the rats in studies of the effects of stress on animals were male. Taylor did an overview of the research on stress with humans and noted that prior to 1995, when federal agencies began requiring more equal representation of women if they were to fund research, only 17% of the

General adaptation syndrome ▲ Selye's term for a hypothesized three-stage response to stress. Abbreviated *GAS*.

Alarm reaction ▲ The first stage of the GAS, which is triggered by the impact of a stressor and characterized by sympathetic activity.

Fight-or-flight reaction ▲ An innate adaptive response to the perception of danger.

Resistance stage ▲ The second stage of the GAS, characterized by prolonged sympathetic activity in an effort to restore lost energy and repair damage. Also called the *adaptation stage*.

Exhaustion stage ▲ The third stage of the GAS, characterized by weakened resistance and possible deterioration.

"Fight-or-Flight" or "Tend-and-Befriend"?
Walter Cannon labeled the body's response to stress the "fight-or-flight" reaction. He thought that evolution prewired the body to become mobilized in preparation for combat or rapid retreat when faced with a threat. It has been assumed that this reaction applies to both men and women, but research by Shelley Taylor and her colleagues suggests that women may be "prewired" to take care of others ("tend") or affiliate with others ("befriend") when they encounter threats.

CLICK4™ *advice on coping with test anxiety.*

participants were female. Quite a gender gap—and one that had allowed researchers to ignore the question as to whether females responded to stress in the same way as males.

Taylor and her colleagues then dug more deeply into the literature and found that "Men and women do have some reliably different responses to stress," notes S. E. Taylor (2000). "I think we've really been missing the boat on one of the most important responses."

This response to stress can be called the "tend-and-befriend" response. It involves nurturing and seeking the support of others rather than fighting or fleeing. The studies that were reviewed showed that when females faced a predator, a disaster, or even an especially bad day at the office, they often responded by caring for their children and seeking contact and support from others, particularly other women. After a bad day at the office, men are more likely to withdraw from the family or start arguments.

An Evolutionary Perspective

This response may be prewired in female humans and in females of other mammalian species. Evolutionary psychologists might suggest that the tend-and-befriend response might have become sealed in our genes because it promotes the survival of females who are tending to their offspring. (Females who choose to fight may often die or at least be separated from their offspring—no evolutionary brass ring here.)

Gender differences in behavior are frequently connected with gender differences in hormones and other biological factors. This one is no different. Taylor and her colleagues point to the effects of the pituitary hormone oxytocin. Oxytocin stimulates labor and causes the breasts to eject milk when women nurse. It is also connected with nurturing behaviors such as affiliating with and cuddling one's young in many mammals (Taylor et al., 2000). The literature also shows that when oxytocin is released during stress, it tends to have a calming effect on both rats and humans. It makes them less afraid and more social.

But wait a minute! Men also release oxytocin when they are under stress. So why the gender difference? The answer may lie in the presence of other hormones, the sex hormones estrogen and testosterone. Females have more estrogen than males do, and estrogen appears to enhance the effects of oxytocin. Males, on the other hand, have more testosterone than females, and testosterone may mitigate the effects of oxytocin by prompting feelings of self-confidence (which may be exaggerated) and fostering aggression (Sullivan, 2000).

It is thus possible that males are more aggressive than females under stress because of the genetic balance of hormones in their bodies, while females are more affiliative and nurturant. It makes evolutionary sense, at least. In order to perpetuate the human species and even make it tougher as the generations progress, it only takes a few tough men (Does this sound like a commercial for the Marines?) to impregnate a large number of women.

But men, even tough ones, may not outlive women. "Men are more likely than women to respond to stressful experiences by developing certain stress-related disorders, including hypertension, aggressive behavior, or abuse of alcohol or hard drugs," Taylor added in a UCLA press release (May 18, 2000). "Because the tend-and-befriend regulatory system may, in some ways, protect women against stress, this biobehavioral pattern may provide insights into why women live an average of seven and a half years longer than men."

Another View Not all psychologists agree with an evolutionary or biological explanation. Psychologist Alice H. Eagly (2000) allows that gender differences in response to stress may be rooted in hormones but suggests an alternative: The differences may reflect learning and cultural conditioning. "I think we have a certain amount of evidence that women are in some sense more affiliative, but what that's due to becomes the question. Is it biologically hard-wired? Or is it because women have more family responsibility and preparation for that in their development? That is the big question for psychologists."

A very big question, indeed.

Effects of Stress on the Immune System

Research shows that stress suppresses the **immune system** (Delahanty et al., 1996; O'Leary, 1990). Psychological factors such as feelings of control and social support moderate these effects (Gilbert, 1997).

The Immune System Given the complexity of the human body and the fast pace of scientific change, we often feel that we are dependent on trained professionals to cope with illness. Yet we actually do most of this coping by ourselves, by means of the immune system. ***Question: How does the immune system work?***

The immune system has several functions that combat disease (Delves & Roitt, 2000). One of these is the production of white blood cells, which engulf and kill pathogens such as bacteria, fungi, and viruses, and worn-out and cancerous body cells. The technical term for white blood cells is **leukocytes.** Leukocytes carry on microscopic warfare. They engage in search-and-destroy missions in which they "recognize" and eradicate foreign agents and unhealthy cells.

Leukocytes recognize foreign substances by their shapes. These substances are also termed **antigens** because the body reacts to them by generating specialized proteins, or **antibodies.** Antibodies attach themselves to the foreign substances, deactivating them and marking them for destruction. The immune system "remembers" how to battle antigens by maintaining their antibodies in the bloodstream, often for years.[1]

Inflammation is another function of the immune system. When injury occurs, blood vessels in the area first contract (to stem bleeding) and then dilate. Dilation increases the flow of blood to the damaged area, causing the redness and warmth that characterize inflammation. The increased blood supply also floods the region with white blood cells to combat invading microscopic life forms such as bacteria, which otherwise might use the local damage as a port of entry into the body.

Stress and the Immune System Psychologists, biologists, and medical researchers have combined their efforts in a field of study that addresses the relationships among psychological factors, the nervous system, the endocrine system, the immune system, and disease. This field is called **psychoneuroimmunology.** One of its major

Immune system ▲ (im-YOON). The system of the body that recognizes and destroys foreign agents (antigens) that invade the body.

Leukocytes ▲ (LOO-coe-sites). White blood cells. (Derived from the Greek words *leukos*, meaning "white," and *kytos*, literally meaning "a hollow" but used to refer to cells.)

Antigen ▲ (ANT-tee-jenn *or* ANT-eye-jenn). A substance that stimulates the body to mount an immune system response to it. (The contraction for *anti*body *gen*erator.)

Antibodies ▲ Substances formed by white blood cells that recognize and destroy antigens.

Inflammation ▲ (IN-flam-MAY-shun). Increased blood flow to an injured area of the body, resulting in redness, warmth, and an increased supply of white blood cells.

Psychoneuroimmunology ▲ (sigh-coe-new-row-im-you-NOLL-oh-gee). The field that studies the relationships between psychological factors (e.g., attitudes and overt behavior patterns) and the functioning of the immune system.

[1]Vaccination is the introduction of a weakened form of an antigen (usually a bacteria or a virus) into the body to stimulate the production of antibodies. Antibodies can confer immunity for many years, in some cases for a lifetime. Smallpox has been eradicated by means of vaccination.

Microscopic Warfare.
The immune system helps us to combat disease. It produces white blood cells (leukocytes), such as that shown here, which routinely engulf and kill pathogens like bacteria and viruses.

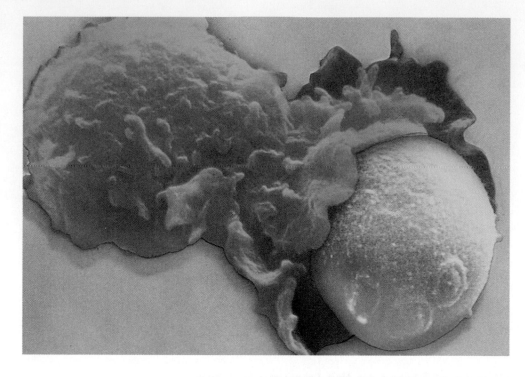

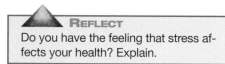

▲ REFLECT
Do you have the feeling that stress affects your health? Explain.

concerns is the effect of stress on the immune system. ***Question: How does stress affect the functioning of the immune system?***

One of the reasons that stress eventually exhausts us is that it stimulates the production of steroids. Steroids suppress the functioning of the immune system. Suppression has negligible effects when steroids are secreted intermittently. However, persistent secretion of steroids decreases inflammation and interferes with the formation of antibodies. As a consequence, we become more vulnerable to various illnesses, including the common cold (Cohen et al., 1993). By weakening the immune system, stress is also connected with a more rapid progression of HIV infection to AIDS (Leserman et al., 2000).

In one study, dental students showed lower immune system functioning, as measured by lower levels of antibodies in their saliva, during stressful periods of the school year than immediately following vacations (Jemmott et al., 1983). In contrast, social support buffers the effects of stress and enhances the functioning of the immune system (Gilbert, 1997; Uchino et al., 1996). In the Jemmott study, students who had many friends showed less suppression of immune system functioning than students with few friends.

Other studies have shown that the stress of exams depresses the immune system's response to the Epstein-Barr virus, which causes fatigue and other problems (Glaser et al., 1991, 1993). Here too, students who were lonely showed greater suppression of the immune system than students who had more social support. A study of older people found that a combination of relaxation training, which decreases sympathetic nervous system activity, and training in coping skills *improves* the functioning of the immune system (Glaser et al., 1991). Moreover, psychological methods that reduce stress and anxiety in cancer patients may prolong their survival by boosting the functioning of their immune system (Azar, 1996c).

REVIEW

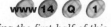

CLICK4™ *a quiz covering the first half of this chapter.*

(10) The general adaptation syndrome has three stages: _____, resistance, and exhaustion. (11) Cannon dubbed the alarm reaction the _____-or-_____ reaction. (12) Women may show a tend-and-_____ response to stress rather than fight-or-flight. (13) Under stress, pituitary ACTH causes the adrenal cortex to release _____ that help the body respond to stress by fighting inflammation and allergic reactions. (14) Two hormones that play a role in the alarm reaction are secreted by the

adrenal medulla: _____ and noradrenaline. (15) The immune system produces (red or white?) blood cells, called leukocytes, that routinely engulf and kill pathogens. (16) _____ are pathogens that are recognized and destroyed by leukocytes. (17) Some leukocytes produce _____, or specialized proteins that bind to their antigens and mark them for destruction.

Pulling It Together: How does prolonged stress lead to health problems?

A MULTIFACTORIAL APPROACH TO HEALTH

Why do people become ill? Why do some people develop cancer? Why do others have heart attacks? Why do still others seem to be immune to these illnesses? Why do some of us seem to come down with everything that is going around, while others ride out the roughest winters with nary a sniffle? ***Question: What is the multifactorial approach to health?*** The multifactorial approach recognizes that there is no single, simple answer to these questions. The likelihood of contracting an illness—be it a case of the flu or cancer—can reflect the interaction of many factors, including genetic factors (Hoover, 2000).

Biological factors such as pathogens, inoculations, injuries, age, gender, and a family history of disease may strike us as the most obvious causes of illness. Genetics, in particular, tempts some people to assume there is little they can do about their health. It is true that there are some severe health problems that are unavoidable for people with certain genes. "There is this kind of fatalistic approach to genes that the general public seems to have now—that if your mom, dad, sister or brother had something that you're doomed to have it too," writes Dr. Robert N. Hoover (2000) of the National Cancer Institute. But in many cases, especially with cardiovascular problems and cancer, genes only create *predispositions* toward the health problem.

As Jane Brody (1995b) notes, predispositions "need a conducive environment in which to express themselves. A bad family medical history should not be considered a portent of doom. Rather, it should be welcomed as an opportunity to keep those nasty genes from expressing themselves." For example, genetic factors are involved in breast cancer. However rates of breast cancer among women who have recently immigrated to the United States from rural Asia are similar to those in their countries of origin and nearly 80% lower than the rates among third-generation Asian American women, whose rates are similar to those of European American women (Hoover, 2000). Thus factors related to one's lifestyle are also intimately connected with the risk of breast cancer—and most other kinds of cancer.

As shown in Figure 14.4, psychological (behavior and personality), sociocultural factors, environmental factors, and stressors all play roles in health and illness. Many health problems are affected by psychological factors, such as attitudes, emotions, and behavior (Mischel & Shoda, 1995; Salovey et al., 2000). As shown in Table 14.3, nearly 1 million deaths each year in the United States are preventable (National Center for Health Statistics, 1996). Stopping smoking, eating right, exercising, and controlling alcohol use would prevent nearly 80% of these. Psychological states such as anxiety and depression can impair the functioning of the immune system, rendering us more vulnerable to physical disorders ranging from viral infections to cancer (Penninx et al., 1998; Salovey et al., 2000).

In this section we consider some of the sociocultural factors that are connected with health and illness, as reflected in human diversity. Then we discuss a number of health problems, including headaches, heart disease, and cancer. In each case we consider the interplay of biological, psychological, social, technological, and environmental factors. Although these are medical problems, we also explore ways in which psychologists have contributed to their treatment.

▲ REFLECT
Do you seem to be prone to illness? What factors seem to be connected with illness in you?

DIVERSITY Health and Diversity: Nations Within the Nation

Today we know more about the connections between behavior and health than ever before. The United States also has the resources to provide the most advanced health care in the world. But not all Americans take advantage of contemporary knowledge. Nor do

CLICK4™ *a WebSearch activity on ethnic and gender differences in health.*

483

CLICK4™ *a bulletin board discussion: Do "bad" genes doom people to health problems?*

all profit equally from the health care system. Health psychologists note, therefore, that from the perspective of health and health care we are many nations and not just one. Many factors influence whether people engage in good health practices or let themselves go. Many factors affect whether they act to prevent illness or succumb to it. *Question: What are the relationships among ethnicity, gender, socioeconomic status, and health?*

Ethnicity and Health   The life expectancy of African Americans is seven years shorter than that of European Americans (Freeman & Payne, 2000). It is unclear whether this difference is connected with ethnicity per se or with socioeconomic status, as measured by factors such as income and level of education. Because of lower socioeconomic status, African Americans have less access to health care than European Americans do (Freeman & Payne, 2000). They are also more likely to live in unhealthful neighborhoods, eat high-fat diets, and smoke (Pappas et al., 1993).

FIGURE 14.4 Factors in Health and Illness.
Various factors figure into a person's state of health or illness. Which of the factors in this figure are you capable of controlling? Which are beyond your control?

Biological Factors
Family history of illness
Exposure to infectious organisms (e.g., bacteria and viruses)
Functioning of the immune system
Inoculations
Medication history
Congenital disabilities, birth complications
Physiological conditions (e.g., hypertension, serum cholesterol level)
Reactivity of the cardiovascular system to stress (e.g., "hot reactor")
Pain and discomfort
Age
Gender
Ethnicity (e.g., genetic vulnerability to Tay-Sachs disease or sickle-cell anemia)

Environmental Factors
Vehicular safety
Architectural features (e.g., crowding, injury-resistant design, nontoxic construction materials, aesthetic design, air quality, noise insulation)
Aesthetics of residential, workplace, and communal architecture and landscape architecture
Water quality
Solid waste treatment and sanitation
Pollution
Radiation
Global warming
Ozone depletion
Natural disasters (earthquakes, blizzards, floods, hurricanes, drought, extremes of temperature, tornadoes)

Behavior
Diet (intake of calories, fats, fiber, vitamins, etc.)
Consumption of alcohol
Cigarette smoking
Level of physical activity
Sleep patterns
Safety practices (e.g., using seat belts; careful driving; practice of sexual abstinence, monogamy, or "safer sex"; adequate prenatal care)
Having (or not having) regular medical and dental checkups
Compliance with medical and dental advice
Interpersonal/social skills

Sociocultural Factors
Socioeconomic status
Family circumstances (social class, family size, family conflict, family disorganization)
Access to health care (e.g., adequacy of available health care, availability of health insurance, availability of transportation to health care facilities)
Prejudice and discrimination
Health-related cultural and religious beliefs and practices
Health promotion in the workplace or community
Health-related legislation

Personality
Seeking (or avoiding) information about health risks and stressors
Self-efficacy expectations
Psychological hardiness
Psychological conflict (approach-approach, avoidance-avoidance, approach-avoidance)
Optimism or pessimism
Attributional style (how one explains one's failures and health problems to oneself)
Health locus of control (belief that one is or is not in charge of one's own health)
Introversion/extraversion
Coronary-prone (Type A) personality
Tendencies to express or hold in feelings of anger and frustration
Depression/anxiety
Hostility/suspiciousness

Stressors
Daily hassles (e.g., preparing meals, illness, time pressure, loneliness, crime, financial insecurity, problems with co-workers, day care)
Major life changes such as divorce, death of a spouse, taking out a mortgage, losing a job
Frustration
Pain and discomfort
Availability and use of social support vs. peer rejection or isolation
Climate in the workplace (e.g., job overload, sexual harassment)

African Americans also experience different treatment by medical practitioners. Even when they have the same medical conditions as European Americans, African Americans are less likely to receive treatments such as medicines for relieving pain, coronary artery bypass surgery, hip and knee replacements, kidney transplants, mammography, and flu shots (Freeman & Payne, 2000; Geiger, 1996). Why? Various explanations have been offered, including cultural differences, patient preferences, lack of information about health care, and racism.

African Americans are more likely than European Americans to have heart attacks and to die from them (Freeman & Payne, 2000). Figure 14.5 compares the death rates from heart disease of African American women and women from other ethnic backgrounds in the United States (Smith, 2000). Early diagnosis and treatment might help decrease the racial gap. However, African Americans with heart disease are less likely than European Americans to obtain complex procedures such as bypass surgery and simple measures such as aspirin, even when they would benefit equally from them (Freeman & Payne, 2000; Rathore et al., 2000). Moreover, when European Americans and African Americans show up in the emergency room with heart attacks and other severe cardiac problems, physicians are more likely to misdiagnose the conditions among the African Americans (Pope et al., 2000). Do emergency room physicians pay less attention to the health concerns of African Americans?

African Americans are more likely than European Americans to have hypertension (Ergul, 2000). One in three African Americans has the disorder (American Heart Association, 2000b). African Americans are also more likely than Black Africans to suffer from hypertension. Many health professionals thus infer that environmental factors found among many African Americans—such as stress, diet, and smoking—contribute to high blood pressure in people who are genetically vulnerable to it (Betancourt & López, 1993).

African Americans are also more likely than European Americans to contract most forms of cancer (Freeman & Payne, 2000). Possibly because of genetic factors, the incidence of lung cancer is significantly higher among African Americans than European Americans (Blakeslee, 1994). Once they contract cancer, African Americans are more likely than European Americans to die from it (Freeman & Payne, 2000). The results for African Americans are connected with their lower socioeconomic status and relative lack of access to health care (Meyerowitz et al., 1998).

The case of breast cancer is somewhat different. Overall African American women are less likely than European American women to develop breast cancer. However, when they do, they often do so at an earlier age, tend to be diagnosed with it somewhat later, and are more likely to die from it (National Cancer Institute, 2000). The later diagnosis may be a result of less access to health care, but genetic factors may also to be involved. Most breast cancers feed on estrogen, but African American women are more likely to develop a particularly aggressive form of breast cancer that grows rapidly even in the absence of estrogen. Therefore, cancer treatments that rely on decreasing estrogen in the body are ineffective in women with this form of cancer.

TABLE 14.3 ANNUAL PREVENTABLE DEATHS IN THE UNITED STATES

Other measures for preventing needless deaths include improved worker training and safety to prevent accidents in the workplace, wider screening for breast and cervical cancer, and control of high blood pressure and elevated blood cholesterol levels.

Elimination of tobacco use could prevent 400,000 deaths each year from cancer, heart and lung diseases, and stroke.

Improved diet and exercise could prevent 300,000 deaths from conditions like heart disease, stroke, diabetes, and cancer.

Control of underage and excess drinking of alcohol could prevent 100,000 deaths from motor vehicle accidents, falls, drownings, and other alcohol-related injuries.

Immunizations for infectious diseases could prevent up to 100,000 deaths.

Safer sex or sexual abstinence could prevent 20,000 deaths from sexually transmitted infections (STIs).

REFLECT
Are people from your ethnic group prone to particular kinds of health problems? What are they? Are you gathering information about them? If not, why not?

CLICK4™ *information on healthful foods and foods high in fat and cholesterol.*

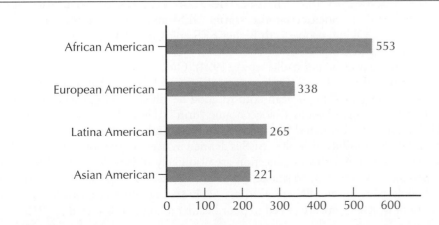

FIGURE 14.5 Deaths per 100,000 Women Aged 35 and Above From Heart Disease.
African American women have experienced a higher annual death rate from heart attacks (553 per 100,000) than women from any other ethnic group in the United States.

CONTROVERSY IN PSYCHOLOGY

Does It Matter If Your Physician Is a Woman or a Man?

As we see in this section, the answer is a definite "maybe."

CLICK4™ *a bulletin board discussion: Does it matter whether your physician is a man or a woman?*

www 14 E 5

CLICK4™ *an essay assignment: How would you further research whether the sex of one's physician influences the level of preventive care received?*

www 14 L 9

CLICK4™ *"The Universe of Women's Health," reporting on women's health issues.*

▲ **REFLECT**
Are you reluctant to seek medical advice when something is wrong? Do you tend to "tough it out"? If so, why? Do you intend to change your health-related behavior?

Socioeconomic status ▲ One's social and financial level, as indicated by measures such as income, level of education, and occupational status. Abbreviated *SES*.

Also consider some cultural differences in health. A study that followed more than 40,000 women for $5\frac{1}{2}$ years found that women who eat diets high in fruits and vegetables and low in saturated fats live longer (Kant et al., 2000). It has also been shown that death rates from cancer are higher in such nations as the Netherlands, Denmark, England, Canada, and—yes—the United States, where average rates of daily fat intake are high (Cohen, 1987). Death rates from cancer are much lower in such nations as Thailand, the Philippines, and Japan, where average daily fat intake is much lower. Thailand, the Philippines, and Japan are Asian nations, but do not assume that the difference is racial! The diets of Japanese Americans are similar in fat content to those of other Americans—and so are their rates of death from cancer. According to the British Heart Foundation (Reaney, 2000), it turns out that there are also significant differences among Europeans. French, Spanish, and Portuguese people enjoy the lowest death rates from coronary heart disease (CHD) and also eat diets that are relatively low in fat and high in fruits and vegetables. People in Ireland, Finland, and Britain suffer the most deaths from CHD and also eat high-fat diets and relatively fewer fruits and vegetables.

There are health care "overusers" and "underusers" among cultural groups. For example, Latino and Latina Americans visit physicians less often than African Americans and European Americans do because of lack of health insurance, difficulty speaking English, misgivings about medical technology, and—for illegal aliens—fear of deportation.

Gender and Health   Also consider a few gender differences. Men are more likely than women to have CHD (American Heart Association, 2000a). Women may be "protected" by high levels of estrogen until menopause (Davidson, 1995). After menopause, women are dramatically more likely to incur heart disease. When women and men show up in the emergency room with symptoms of heart attacks and other serious cardiac problems, however, the conditions are more likely to be misdiagnosed among the women (Pope et al., 2000).

The gender of the physician can also make a difference. According to a study of more than 90,000 women, women whose internists or family practitioners are women are more likely to have screening for cancer (mammograms and Pap smears) than women whose internists or family practitioners are men (Lurie et al., 1993). It is unclear from this study, however, whether female physicians are more likely than their male counterparts to encourage women to seek preventive care, or whether women who choose female physicians are also more likely to seek preventive care. Other research shows that female physicians are more likely than male physicians to conduct breast examinations properly (Hall et al., 1990).

Men's life expectancy is seven years shorter, on the average, than women's. Surveys of physicians and of the general population suggest that this difference is due, at least in part, to women's greater willingness to seek health care (Courtenay, 2000). Men often let symptoms go until a problem that could have been prevented or readily treated becomes serious or life-threatening. "Health is a macho thing," notes one physician (cited in Kolata, 2000b). "Men don't like to be out of control. So they deny their symptomology."

Health and Socioeconomic Status: The Rich Get Richer and the Poor Get . . . Sicker?   **Socioeconomic status** (SES) and health are intimately connected. Generally speaking, people with higher SES enjoy better health and lead longer lives (Freeman & Payne, 2000). The question is *why*.

Consider three possibilities (Adler et al., 1994). One is that there is no causal connection between health and SES. Perhaps both SES and health reflect genetic factors. For example, "good genes" might lead both to good health and to high social standing. Second, poor health might lead to socioeconomic "drift" (that is, loss of social standing). Third, SES might affect biological functions that, in turn, influence health.

How might SES influence health? SES is defined in part in terms of education. That is, people who attain low levels of education are also likely to have low SES. Less well-educated people are more likely to smoke, and smoking has been linked to many physical illnesses. People with lower SES are also less likely to exercise and more likely to be obese—both of which, again, are linked to poor health outcomes (Ford et al., 1991).

Anorexia nervosa and bulimia nervosa are uncommon among poor people, but obesity is most prevalent among the poor. The incidence of obesity is also greater in cultures that associate obesity with happiness and health—as is true of some Haitian and Puerto Rican groups. People living in poor urban neighborhoods are more likely to be obese because junk food is heavily promoted in those neighborhoods and many residents tend to eat as a way of coping with stress (Johnson et al., 1995).

Let us also not forget that poorer people also have less access to health care (Freeman & Payne, 2000). The problem is compounded by the fact that people with low SES are less likely to be educated about the benefits of regular health checkups and early medical intervention when symptoms arise.

REVIEW

(18) Psychological states such as anxiety and depression impair the functioning of the _____ system, rendering us more vulnerable to health problems. (19) African Americans have (more or less?) access to health care than European Americans do. (20) _____ Americans are more likely than European Americans to have hypertension, possibly because of genetic factors. (21) African Americans are (more or less?) likely than European Americans to have heart attacks and contract most forms of cancer. (22) Men's life expectancies are 7 years (longer or shorter?) than women's.

Pulling It Together: What factors contribute to ethnic and gender differences in longevity?

HEALTH PROBLEMS AND PSYCHOLOGY

Let us now consider the health problems of headaches, heart disease, and cancer. In each case we consider the interplay of biological, psychological, social, technological, and environmental factors. Although these are medical problems, they have very real psychological consequences. Moreover, psychologists have made important contributions to their treatment.

Headaches: When Stress Presses and Pounds

Headaches are among the most common stress-related physical ailments. Nearly 20% of people in the United States suffer from severe headaches. *Question: How has psychology contributed to the understanding and treatment of headaches?* To answer this question, let us consider the common muscle-tension headache and the more severe migraine headache.

Muscle Tension Headache   The single most frequent kind of headache is the muscle tension headache. During the first two stages of the GAS we are likely to contract muscles in the shoulders, neck, forehead, and scalp. Persistent stress can lead to constant contraction of these muscles, causing muscle tension headaches. Psychological factors, such as the tendency to catastrophize negative events—that is, blow them out of proportion—can bring on a tension headache (Ukestad & Wittrock, 1996). Tension headaches usually come on gradually. They are most often characterized by dull, steady pain on both sides of the head and feelings of tightness or pressure.

Migraine Headache   The **migraine headache** usually has a sudden onset and is identified by severe throbbing pain on one side of the head. Migraines affect 1 American in 10 (Mulvihill, 2000). They may last for hours, or days. Sensory and motor disturbances often precede the pain; a warning "aura" may include vision problems and perception of unusual odors. The migraines themselves are often accompanied by sensitivity to light, loss of appetite, nausea, vomiting, sensory and motor disturbances such as loss of balance, and changes in mood. Imaging techniques suggest that when something triggers a

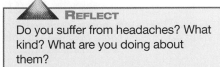

CLICK4™ *more information on headaches— causes and treatments.*

> ▲ **REFLECT**
> Do you suffer from headaches? What kind? What are you doing about them?

Migraine headaches ▲ (MY-grain). Throbbing headaches that are connected with changes in the supply of blood to the head.

migraine, neurons at the back of the brain fire in waves that ripple across the top of the head then down to the brainstem, the site of many pain centers.

Triggers for migraines include barometric pressure; pollen; certain drugs; monosodium glutamate (MSG), a chemical which is often used to enhance flavor; chocolate; aged cheese; beer, champagne, and red wine; and the hormonal changes connected with menstruation (Mulvihill, 2000).

The behaviors connected with migraine headaches serve as a mini-textbook in health psychology. For example, the Type A behavior pattern apparently contributes to migraines. In one study, 53% of people who had migraine headaches showed the Type A behavior pattern, compared with 23% of people who had muscle tension headaches (Rappaport et al., 1988). Another study compared 26 women who had regular migraines with women who did not get migraines. The migraine sufferers were more sensitive to pain, more self-critical, more likely to catastrophize stress and pain, and less likely to seek social support when under stress (Hassinger et al., 1999).

Regardless of the source of the headache, we can unwittingly propel ourselves into a vicious cycle. Headache pain is a stressor that can lead us to increase, rather than relax, muscle tension in the neck, shoulders, scalp, and face.

Treatment   Aspirin, acetaminophen, and many prescription drugs are used to fight headache pain. Some inhibit the production of the prostaglandins that help initiate transmission of pain messages to the brain. Newer prescription drugs can help prevent many migraines (Bateman, 2000); ask your doctor. Behavioral methods can also help. Progressive relaxation focuses on decreasing muscle tension and has been shown to be highly effective in relieving muscle tension headaches (Blanchard et al., 1990a, 1991). Biofeedback training has also helped many people with migraine headaches (Blanchard et al., 1990b). People who are sensitive to MSG or red wine can request meals without MSG and switch to white wine.

Coronary Heart Disease: Taking Stress to Heart

Coronary heart disease (CHD) is the leading cause of death in the United States, most often from heart attacks (American Heart Association, 2000a). **_Question: How has psychology contributed to the understanding and treatment of coronary heart disease?_**   Let us begin by considering the risk factors for CHD. We will see that people's choices and behavior have a great deal to do with their risk of incurring CHD.

1. *Family History.* People with a family history of CHD are more likely to develop the disease themselves (American Heart Association, 2000a).
2. *Physiological Conditions.* Obesity, high **serum cholesterol** levels, and **hypertension** are risk factors for CHD (American Heart Association, 2000a; Stamler et al., 2000).

    About one American in five has hypertension, or abnormally high blood pressure. When high blood pressure has no identifiable cause, it is referred to as *essential hypertension.* This condition has a genetic component (Levy et al., 2000; Williams et al., 2000). However, blood pressure also rises when we inhibit the expression of strong feelings or are angry or on guard against threats (Jorgensen et al., 1996; Suls et al., 1995). When we are under stress, we may believe that we can feel our blood pressure "pounding through the roof," but this notion is usually false. Most people cannot recognize hypertension. Therefore it is important to have blood pressure checked regularly.
3. *Patterns of Consumption.* Patterns include heavy drinking, smoking, overeating, and eating food that is high in cholesterol, like saturated fats (Stampfer et al., 2000). On the other hand, a little alcohol seems to be good for the heart (Blanco-Colio et al., 2000; Gaziano et al., 1993).
4. *Type A Behavior.* Most studies suggest that there is at least a modest relationship between Type A behavior and CHD (Thoresen & Powell, 1992). It also seems that alleviating Type A behavior patterns may reduce the risk of *recurrent* heart attacks (Friedman & Ulmer, 1984).

▲ **REFLECT**
Does CHD run in your family? What are you doing to prevent CHD?

CLICK4™ *more information about coronary heart disease and stroke from the American Heart Association.*

CLICK4™ *an essay assignment: Does your behavior pattern influence your risk of CHD?*

Serum cholesterol ▲ (SEE-rum coe-LESS-ter-all). Cholesterol found in the blood.
Hypertension ▲ (HIGH-purr-TEN-shun). High blood pressure.

5. *Hostility and Holding in Feelings of Anger.* Hostility seems to be the component of the Type A behavior pattern that is most harmful to physical health (Birks & Roger, 2000). One study which controlled for the influences of other risk factors like high blood pressure and cholesterol levels, smoking, and obesity found that people who are highly prone to anger are about three times as likely as other people to have heart attacks (Williams et al., 2000). The stress hormones connected with anger can constrict blood vessels to the heart, leading to a heart attack. Chronically hostile and angry people also have higher cholesterol levels (Richards et al., 2000). Another study found that highly hostile young adults—aged 18 to 30—are already at greater risk for calcification (hardening) of the arteries, which increases the risk of heart attacks (Iribarren et al., 2000).

6. *Job Strain.* Overtime work, assembly line labor, and exposure to conflicting demands can all contribute to CHD. High-strain work, which makes heavy demands on workers but gives them little personal control, puts workers at the highest risk (Karasek et al., 1982; Krantz et al., 1988). As shown in Figure 14.6, the work of waiters and waitresses may best fit this description.

7. *Chronic Fatigue and Chronic Emotional Strain.*

8. *Sudden Stressors.* For example, after the Los Angeles earthquake in 1994 there was an increased incidence of death from heart attacks in people with heart disease (Leor et al., 1996).

9. *A Physically Inactive Lifestyle* (Stampfer et al., 2000).

CLICK4™ *an interactive self-assessment: Check Your Physical Activity and Heart Disease IQ.*

Cancer: Swerving Off Course

Cancer is the number one killer of women in the United States, and the number two killer of men (Andersen, 1996). Cancer is characterized by the development of abnormal, or mutant, cells that may take root anywhere in the body: in the blood, bones, digestive

---

FIGURE 14.6   The Job-Strain Model.
This model highlights the psychological demands made by various occupations and the amount of personal (decision) control they allow. Occupations characterized by high demand and low decision control place workers at greatest risk for heart disease.

tract, lungs, and sex organs. If their spread is not controlled early, the cancerous cells may *metastasize*—that is, establish colonies elsewhere in the body. It appears that our bodies develop cancerous cells frequently. However, these are normally destroyed by the immune system. People whose immune system is damaged by physical or psychological factors are more likely to develop tumors (Azar, 1996b).

Question: How has psychology contributed to our understanding and treatment of cancer? Health psychologists have participated in research concerning the origins and treatment of cancer.

Risk Factors As with many other disorders, people can inherit a disposition toward cancer (Lichtenstein et al., 2000). Carcinogenic genes may remove the brakes from cell division, allowing cells to multiply wildly. Or they may allow mutations to accumulate unchecked. However, many behavior patterns markedly heighten the risk for cancer (Hoover, 2000). These include smoking, drinking alcohol (especially in women), eating animal fats, and sunbathing (which may cause skin cancer due to exposure to ultraviolet light). Agents in cigarette smoke, such as benzopyrene, may damage a gene that would otherwise block the development of many tumors, including lung cancer ("Damaged gene," 1996). Prolonged psychological conditions such as depression or stress also apparently heighten the risk of some kinds of cancer by depressing the functioning of the immune system (Penninx et al., 1998; Salovey et al., 2000).

Stress and Cancer Researchers have uncovered links between stress and cancer (Azar, 1996b; Salovey et al., 2000). For example, a study by Jacob and Charles (1980) revealed that a significant percentage of children with cancer had encountered severe life changes within a year of the diagnosis. These often involved the death of a loved one or the loss of a close relationship.

Experimental research that could not be conducted with humans has been carried out using rats and other animals. In one type of study, animals are injected with cancerous cells or with viruses that cause cancer and then exposed to various conditions. In this way researchers can determine which conditions influence the likelihood that the animals' immune systems will be able to fend off the disease. Such experiments suggest that once cancer has developed, stress can influence its course. In one study, for example, rats were implanted with small numbers of cancer cells so that their own immune systems would have a chance to combat them (Visintainer et al., 1982). Some of the rats were then exposed to inescapable shocks. Others were exposed to escapable shocks or to no shock. The rats that were exposed to the most stressful condition—the inescapable shock—were half as likely as the other rats to reject the cancer and twice as likely to die from it.

▲ **REFLECT**
Are you prone to developing any type of cancer? What are you doing to prevent or treat cancer?

www 14 L 13

CLICK4™ *more information about cancer, research, and therapy from the American Cancer Society.*

Psychology and Modern Life

Reducing the Risk of CHD Through Behavior Modification

Once CHD has been diagnosed, a number of medical treatments, including surgery and medication, are available. However, people who have not had CHD (as well as those who have) can profit from behavior modification techniques designed to reduce the risk factors. These methods include:

1. *Stopping Smoking.* (See Chapter 4.)
2. *Controlling Weight.* (See Chapter 9.)
3. *Reducing Hypertension.* There is medication for reducing hypertension, but behavioral changes such as the following help and are sometimes enough: medita-

tion (Alexander et al., 1996; Schneider et al., 1995), aerobic exercise (Danforth et al., 1990), taking in more fruits and vegetables, fish, and folic acid (a B vitamin), but less saturated fat (Stampfer et al., 2000) and less salt (Sacks et al., 2001).

4. *Lowering Low-Density Lipoprotein (Harmful) Serum Cholesterol.* Major methods involve exercise, medication, and cutting down on foods that are high in cholesterol and saturated fats (Stampfer et al., 2000). Lowering LDL is helpful at any time of life, even during older adulthood. How-

ever, even young adults should think about their LDL levels, since elevated LDL in young adulthood can establish a pattern that places one at risk for cardiovascular disease later in life (Stamler et al., 2000).

5. *Modifying Type A Behavior.*
6. *Managing Feelings of Anger.*
7. *Exercising.* Sustained physical activity protects people from CHD (Stampfer et al., 2000). If you haven't exercised for a while, check with your physician about getting started.

Psychological Factors in the Treatment of Cancer   People with cancer not only must cope with the biological aspects of their illnesses. They may also face a host of psychological problems. These include feelings of anxiety and depression about treatment methods and the eventual outcome, changes in body image after the removal of a breast or testicle, feelings of vulnerability, and family problems (Azar, 1996b). For example, some families criticize members with cancer for feeling sorry for themselves or not fighting the disease hard enough (Andersen et al., 1994; Rosenthal, 1993). Psychological stress due to cancer can impair the immune system, setting the stage for more health problems, such as respiratory tract infections (Andersen et al., 1994).

There are also psychological treatments for the nausea that often accompanies chemotherapy. People undergoing chemotherapy who also obtain relaxation training and guided imagery techniques experience significantly less nausea and vomiting than patients who do not use these methods (Azar, 1996d). Studies with children and adolescents find that playing video games also reduces the discomfort of chemotherapy (Kolko & Rickard-Figueroa, 1985; Redd et al., 1987). They focus on battling computer-generated enemies rather than the side effects of drugs.

Of course, cancer is a medical disorder. However, health psychologists have improved the methods used to treat people with cancer. For example, a crisis like cancer can lead people to feel that life has spun out of control (Merluzzi & Martinez Sanchez, 1997). Control is a factor in psychological hardiness. A sense of loss of control can heighten stress and impair the immune system. Health psychology therefore stresses the value of encouraging people with cancer to remain in charge of their lives (Jacox et al., 1994).

Cancer requires medical treatment, and in many cases, there are few treatment options. However, people with cancer can still choose how they will deal with the disease. One 10-year follow-up of women with breast cancer found a significantly higher survival rate for women who responded to their diagnosis with anger and a "fighting spirit" rather than with stoic acceptance (Pettingale et al., 1985). A 5-year follow-up of nearly 600 women with early stage breast cancer found that the survival rate was significantly higher for women who showed a fighting spirit as compared with women who reported feeling helpless and hopeless—that is, depressed (Faller et al., 1999; Watson et al., 1999). And depression impairs the immune system, weakening the body's efforts to fight off cancer.

Psychologists are teaching coping skills to people with cancer in order to relieve psychological distress as well as pain. Psychological methods such as relaxation training,

CLICK4™ *an interactive self-assessment on diet and health: The Eating Smart Quiz.*

CLICK4™ *a bulletin board discussion on lowering stress and improving health.*

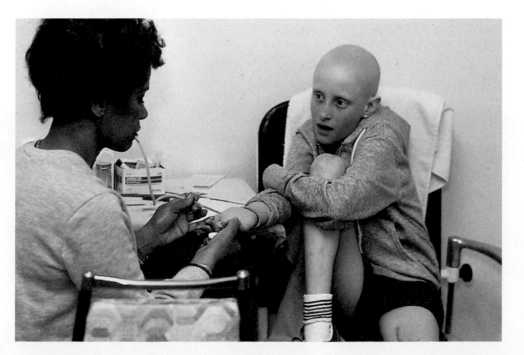

How Have Health Psychologists Helped This Youngster Cope With Cancer?
Cancer is a medical disorder, but psychologists have contributed to the treatment of people with cancer. For example, psychologists help people with cancer remain in charge of their lives, combat feelings of hopelessness, manage stress, and cope with the side effects of chemotherapy.

meditation, biofeedback training, and exercise can all be of help (Lang & Patt, 1994). Social support also apparently increases the survival rate (Sleek, 1995), so psychologists work with family and friends to help rally the individual with cancer. Coping skills are beneficial in themselves and help people with cancer regain a sense of control.

Yet another psychological application is helping people undergoing chemotherapy keep up their strength by eating. The problem is that chemotherapy often causes nausea. Nausea then becomes associated with foods eaten during the day, causing taste aversions (Azar, 1996d). So people with cancer, who may already be losing weight because of their illness, may find that taste aversions aggravate the problems caused by lack of appetite. To combat these conditions, Bernstein (1996) recommends eating unusual ("scapegoat") foods prior to chemotherapy. If taste aversions develop, they are associated with the unusual food and not the patient's normal diet.

We conclude this section with good news for readers of this book: *Better educated* people—that means *you*—are more likely to modify health-impairing behavior and reap the benefits of change (Pappas et al., 1993).

REVIEW

(23) The most common kind of headache is the _____-_____ headache. (24) The _____ headache has a sudden onset and is identified by throbbing pain on one side of the head. (25) Risk factors for coronary heart disease include family history, obesity, hypertension, high levels of serum _____, heavy drinking, smoking, hostility, Type A behavior, and job strain. (26) Stress (can or cannot?) affect the course of cancer.

Pulling It Together: Agree or disagree with the following statement and support your answer: "Bad genes" doom people to health problems.

COPING WITH STRESS

CLICK4™ *a WebSearch activity on stress and stress management.*

What do these things have in common: (1) telling yourself that you can live with another person's disappointment, (2) taking a deep breath and telling yourself to relax, (3) taking the scenic route to work, and (4) jogging for half an hour? These are all methods suggested by psychologists to help people cope with the stresses of modern life.

Stress takes many forms and can harm our psychological well-being and physical health. Here we highlight ways of coping with stress: controlling irrational thoughts, lowering arousal, and exercising.

Psychology and Modern Life

Prevention of, and Coping With, Cancer

Cancer is a frightening disease, and in many cases, there may be little that can be done about its eventual outcome. However, we are not helpless in the face of cancer. We can take measures like the following:

1. Limit exposure to behavioral risk factors for cancer (Chlebowski, 2000).

2. Modify diet by reducing intake of fats and increasing intake of fruits and veg-

etables (Kant et al., 2000). Tomatoes (especially cooked tomatoes, such as we find in tomato sauce and ketchup — yes, ketchup!), broccoli, cauliflower, and cabbage appear to be especially helpful (Angier, 1994a). (Yes, Grandma was right about veggies.)

3. Exercise regularly.

4. Have regular medical checkups so that cancer will be detected early. Cancer is most treatable in the early stages.

5. Regulate exposure to stress (Folkman & Moskowitz, 2000a).

6. If we are struck by cancer, we can fight it energetically.

Controlling Irrational Thoughts—Changing Your Own Mind for the Better

People often feel pressure from their own thoughts. Consider the following experiences:

1. You have difficulty with the first item on a test and become convinced that you will flunk.

2. You want to express your genuine feelings but think that if you do so you might make another person angry or upset.

3. You haven't been able to get to sleep for 15 minutes and assume that you will lie awake all night and feel "wrecked" in the morning.

4. You're not sure what decision to make, so you try to put the problem out of your mind by going out, playing cards, or watching TV.

5. You decide not to play tennis because your form isn't perfect and you're in less than perfect condition.

If you have had these or similar experiences, it may be because you harbor some of the irrational beliefs identified by Albert Ellis (see Table 14.1). These beliefs may make you overly concerned about the approval of others (item 2 in the preceding list) or perfectionistic (item 5). They may lead you to think that you can solve problems by pretending that they do not exist (item 4) or that a minor setback will invariably lead to greater problems (items 1 and 3).

Question: How do we change the irrational thoughts that create and compound stress? The answer is deceptively simple: We just change them. However, this may require work. Moreover, before we can change our thoughts we must become aware of them.

Steps for Controlling Irrational Thoughts

Cognitive-behavioral psychologists (e.g., Marks & Dar, 2000) outline a multistep procedure for controlling the irrational or catastrophizing thoughts that often accompany feelings of anxiety, conflict, or tension:

1. Develop awareness of the thoughts that seem to be making you miserable by careful self-examination. Study the examples at the beginning of this section or in Table 14.4 to see whether they apply to you. (Also consider Ellis's list of irrational beliefs in Table 14.1 and ask yourself whether any of them governs your behavior.) Also: When you encounter anxiety or frustration, pay close attention to your thoughts.

2. Evaluate the accuracy of the thoughts. Are they guiding you toward a solution, or are they compounding your problems? Do they reflect reality or do they blow things out of proportion? Do they misplace the blame for failure or shortcomings? And so on.

3. Prepare thoughts that are incompatible with the irrational or catastrophizing thoughts and practice saying them firmly to yourself. (If nobody is nearby, why not say them firmly aloud?)

4. Reward yourself with a mental pat on the back for making effective changes in your beliefs and thought patterns.

Lowering Arousal: Turning Down the Inner Alarm

Stress tends to trigger intense activity in the sympathetic branch of the autonomic nervous system—in other words, arousal. Arousal is a sign that something may be wrong. It is a message telling us to survey the situation and take appropriate action. But once we are aware that a stressor is acting upon us and have developed a plan to cope with it, it is no

TABLE 14.4 CONTROLLING IRRATIONAL BELIEFS AND THOUGHTS

Do irrational beliefs or catastrophizing thoughts compound your feelings of anxiety and tension? Cognitive psychologists suggest that you can cope with stress by becoming aware of your irrational, upsetting thoughts and replacing them with rational, calming thoughts.

Irrational (Upsetting) Thoughts	Incompatible (Calming) Thoughts
"Oh my God, I'm going to completely lose control!"	"This is painful and upsetting, but I don't have to go to pieces over it."
"This will never end."	"This will end even if it's hard to see the end right now."
"It'll be awful if Mom gives me that look again."	"It's more pleasant when Mom's happy with me, but I can live with it if she isn't."
"How can I go out there? I'll look like a fool."	"So you're not perfect. That doesn't mean that you're going to look stupid. And so what if someone thinks you look stupid? You can live with that, too. Just stop worrying and have some fun."
"My heart's going to leap out of my chest! How much can I stand?"	"Easy—hearts don't leap out of chests. Stop and think! Distract yourself. Breathe slowly, in and out."
"What can I do? There's nothing I can do!"	"Easy—stop and think. Just because you can't think of a solution right now doesn't mean there's nothing you can do. Take it a minute at a time. Breathe easy."

REFLECT
Have you had anything like these five experiences in your own life? How did you handle them? Can the advice in this chapter help you to handle them better? Explain.

CLICK4™ *more information about stress and how to cope with it.*

CLICK4™ *Web sites dedicated to stress management.*

REFLECT
How do you know when your level of arousal is too high? What do you do about it? Can the advice in this chapter help you to handle it better? Explain.

CLICK4™ *articles on stress and healthy psychology from* Psychometric Medicine.

CLICK4™ *instructions on progressive relaxation: how to do it.*

CLICK4™ *information on coping with job stress.*

longer helpful to have blood pounding fiercely through our arteries. ***Questions: How can we lower our levels of arousal? How can we turn down the inner alarm?*** Psychologists and other scientists have developed many methods for teaching people to reduce arousal. These include meditation, biofeedback, and progressive relaxation. In progressive relaxation, people purposefully tense a particular muscle group before relaxing it. This sequence allows them to develop awareness of their muscle tensions and also to differentiate between feelings of tension and relaxation. You will find instructions for progressive relaxation on the Web site.

The following instructions will help you to try meditation as a means for lowering the arousal connected with stress:

1. Begin by meditating once or twice a day for 10 to 20 minutes.
2. In meditation, what you *don't* do is more important than what you *do* do. Adopt a passive, "what happens, happens" attitude.
3. Create a quiet, nondisruptive environment. For example, don't face a light directly.
4. Do not eat for an hour beforehand; avoid caffeine for at least two hours.
5. Assume a comfortable position. Change it as needed. It's okay to scratch or yawn.
6. As a device to aid concentrating, you may focus on your breathing or seat yourself before a calming object such as a plant or burning incense. Benson suggests "perceiving" (rather than mentally saying) the word *one* on every outbreath. This means thinking the word, but "less actively" than usual (good luck). Others suggest thinking or perceiving the word *in* as you are inhaling and *out*, or *ah-h-h*, as you are exhaling.
7. If you are using a mantra (like the syllable "om," pronounced *oammm*), you can prepare for meditation and say the mantra out loud several times. Enjoy it. Then say it more and more softly. Close your eyes and think only the mantra. Allow yourself to perceive, rather than actively think, the mantra. Again, adopt a passive attitude. Continue to perceive the mantra. It may grow louder or softer, disappear for a while, and then return.
8. If disruptive thoughts enter your mind as you are meditating, you can allow them to "pass through." Don't get wrapped up in trying to squelch them, or you may raise your level of arousal.
9. Allow yourself to drift. (You won't go too far.) What happens, happens.
10. Above all, take what you get. You cannot force the relaxing effects of meditation. You can only set the stage for it and allow it to happen.

Exercising: Run for Your Life?

I like long walks, especially when they are taken by people who annoy me.

—Fred Allen

Exercise, particularly aerobic exercise, enhances the functioning of the immune system, contributes to our psychological well-being, and helps us cope with stress (Jonsdottir et al., 2000; Tkachuk & Martin, 1999). *Aerobic exercise* refers to exercise that requires a sustained increase in consumption of oxygen. Aerobic exercise promotes cardiovascular fitness. Aerobic exercises include, but are not limited to, running and jogging, running in place, walking (at more than a leisurely pace), aerobic dancing, jumping rope, swimming, bicycle riding, basketball, racquetball, and cross-country skiing.

Anaerobic exercises, in contrast, involve short bursts of muscle activity. Examples of anaerobic exercises are weight training, calisthenics (which usually allow rest periods between exercises), and sports such as baseball, in which there are infrequent bursts of strenuous activity. Anaerobic exercises can strengthen muscles and improve flexibility.

Question: How does exercise help people cope with stress? Exercise helps people cope by enhancing their physical fitness, or "condition." Fitness includes muscle strength; muscle endurance; suppleness or flexibility; cardiorespiratory, or aerobic, fitness; and a higher ratio of muscle to fat (usually due to both building muscle and reducing fat).

Fitness also enhances our natural immunity and boosts our levels of endorphins (Jonsdottir et al., 2000). Cardiovascular fitness, or "condition," means that the body can use more oxygen during vigorous activity and pump more blood with each heartbeat. Because conditioned athletes' hearts pump more blood with each beat, they usually have a slower pulse rate—that is, fewer heartbeats per minute. However, during aerobic exercise they may double or triple their resting heart rate for minutes at a time.

Sustained physical activity does more than promote fitness. It reduces hypertension (Georgiades et al., 2000; Taylor-Tolbert et al., 2000) and the risk of heart attacks (Stampfer et al., 2000) and strokes (Hu et al., 2000). In one research program Ralph Paffenbarger and his colleagues (1993; Lee et al., 2000; Sesso et al., 2000) have been tracking several thousand Harvard University alumni by means of university records and questionnaires. They have correlated the incidence of heart attacks in this group with their levels of physical activity. As shown in Figure 14.7, the incidence of heart attacks declines as physical activity rises to a level at which about 2,000 calories are used per week—the equivalent of jogging about 20 miles a week. Inactive alumni have the highest risk of heart attacks. Alumni who burn at least 2,000 calories a week through exercise live 2 years longer, on the average, than their less active counterparts.

Of course, there is an important limitation to Paffenbarger's research: It is correlational, not experimental. It is possible that people who are in better health *choose* to engage in higher levels of physical activity. If such is the case, then their lower incidence of heart attacks and their lower mortality rates would be attributable to their initial superior health, not to their physical activity.

Aerobic exercise raises blood levels of high-density lipoproteins (HDL, or "good cholesterol") (Stampfer et al., 2000). HDL lowers the amount of low-density lipoproteins (LDL, or "bad cholesterol") in the blood. This is another way in which exercise may reduce the risk of heart attacks.

Psychologists are also interested in the effects of exercise on psychological variables. Articles have appeared on exercise as "therapy." Consider depression. Depression is characterized by inactivity and feelings of helplessness. Exercise is, in a sense, the opposite of inactivity. Exercise might also help alleviate feelings of helplessness. In one experiment, 156 adult volunteers who were depressed were randomly assigned to four months of either aerobic exercise, antidepressant medication, or a combination of the two (Babyak et al., 2000). Following treatment, all three groups showed comparable relief from

CLICK4™ *advice on fitting in fitness.*

CLICK4™ *advice on types of exercise—pros, cons, and tips.*

CLICK4™ *a bulletin board discussion: How do you cope with stress? What do you recommend to others?*

▲ **REFLECT**

What role does exercise play in your life? Should you, or can you, make exercise a greater part of your life? What kind of exercise is right for you?

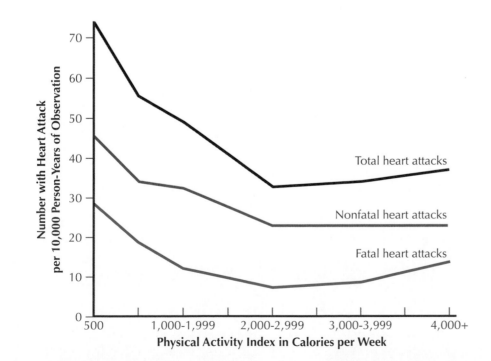

FIGURE 14.7 Heart Attacks and Physical Activity.
Paffenbarger and his colleagues have correlated the incidence of heart attacks with level of physical activity among 17,000 Harvard alumni. The incidence of heart attacks declines as the activity level rises to burning about 2,000 calories a week by means of physical activity. Above 2,000 calories a week, however, the incidence of heart attacks begins to climb gradually again, although not steeply.

CLICK4™ *advice on the benefits of walking.*

depression. But at a further 6-month follow-up participants from the exercise groups who had continued to exercise showed the greatest improvement. Other experiments also find that exercise alleviates feelings of depression (Norvell & Belles, 1993; Tkachuk & Martin, 1999). Exercise has also been shown to decrease anxiety and hostility and to boost self-esteem (Norvell & Belles, 1993).

Getting Started   How about you? Are you thinking of climbing onto the exercise bandwagon? If so, consider these suggestions:

1. Unless you have engaged in sustained and vigorous exercise recently, seek the advice of a medical expert. If you smoke, have a family history of heart disease, are overweight, or are over 40, get a stress test.
2. Consider joining a beginner's aerobics class. Group leaders are not usually experts in physiology, but at least they "know the steps." You'll also be among other beginners and derive the benefits of social support.
3. Get the proper equipment to facilitate performance and avert injury.
4. Read up on the activity you are considering. Books, magazines, and newspaper articles will give you ideas as to how to get started and how fast to progress.
5. Try to select activities that you can sustain for a lifetime. Don't worry about building yourself up rapidly. Enjoy yourself. Your strength and endurance will progress on their own. If you do not enjoy what you're doing, you're not likely to stick to it.
6. If you feel severe pain, don't try to exercise "through" it. Soreness is to be expected for beginners (and for old-timers now and then). In that sense, soreness, at least when it is intermittent, is normal. But sharp pain is abnormal and a sign that something is wrong.
7. Have fun!

REVIEW

CLICK4™ *a quiz covering the second half of this chapter.*

CLICK4™ *electronic flash cards to review your knowledge of key terms and people in this chapter.*

(27) Psychologists suggest various ways of coping with stress, including controlling irrational thoughts, (raising or lowering?) arousal, and exercising. (28) Exercise (increases or decreases?) longevity by reducing the risk of heart attacks and other health problems. (29) Exercise appears to (increase or decrease?) feelings of depression.

Pulling It Together: What can you say to people who insist there is nothing they can do to cope with the stresses they experience?

TRUTH ▨ FICTION
REVISITED

◨ **It is true that going on vacation is stressful.** *A vacation is a life change, and change requires adjustment. Even so, vacations can be good for your health. It is not necessary—or advisable—to avoid all potential sources of stress. See page 464.*

◨ **Although variety may be the spice of life, psychologists have not found that "the more change the better."** *Changes, even changes for the better, are sources of stress that require adjustment. See page 464.*

◨ **People with a strong need for social approval do appear to be setting themselves up for feelings of anxiety and depression.** *They are anxious about whether or not they will receive social approval, and they are depressed when they do not receive enough of it. See page 472.*

◨ **It is apparently true that "A merry heart doeth good like a medicine"—that is, that a sense of humor can moderate the impact of stress.** *In an experiment run by Martin and Lefcourt, humor was shown to serve as a buffer against stress. See page 476.*

◨ **It is true that countless microscopic warriors within our bodies are carrying out search-and-destroy missions against foreign agents at any given moment.** *The warriors are the white blood cells of the immune system. See page 481.*

◨ **It is not true that poor people in the United States eat less than wealthier people.** *Obesity is actually more common among poorer people. (This is not to deny the fact that some people in the United States cannot afford food.) See page 487.*

◨ **It is true that blowing things out of proportion (and tensing up) can give you a headache.** *Catastrophizing is a psychological event, but it has effects on the body, such as leading us to tense muscles in the neck, shoulders, and forehead. See page 487.*

◨ **It is not necessarily true that handing in assignments early is good for you.** *Type A people tend to be early because of the time urgency they experience, and the Type A behavior pattern appears to be related—at least modestly—with CHD. See page 488.*

◨ **It is true that ketchup is a health food.** *It is derived from one of the fruits and vegetables that have a preventive effect on the development of cancer. It is healthful to remain aware of new developments in dietary recommendations. See page 492.*

◨ **It is true that people who exercise regularly live 2 years longer, on the average, than their sedentary counterparts.** *See page 495.*

1. What is health psychology?

Health psychology studies the relationships between psychological factors and the prevention and treatment of physical health problems.

2. What is stress?

Stress is the demand made on an organism to adjust. Whereas some stress—called eustress—is desirable to keep us alert and occupied, too much stress can tax our adjustive capacities and contribute to physical health problems.

3. What are daily hassles?

Daily hassles are regularly occurring experiences that threaten or harm our well-being. There are several kinds of hassles, including household, health, time-pressure, inner concern, environmental, financial responsibility, work, and future security hassles.

4. How is it that too much of a good thing can make you ill?

Too many positive life changes can affect one's health because life changes require adjustment, whether they are positive or negative. In contrast to daily hassles, life changes occur irregularly. Research shows that hassles and life changes are connected with health problems such as heart disease and cancer. However, the demonstrated connection between life changes and health is correlational; thus causality remains clouded.

5. What is conflict?

Conflict is the stressful feeling of being pulled in two or more directions by opposing motives. There are four kinds of conflict: approach-approach, avoidance-avoidance, approach-avoidance (in the case of a single goal), and multiple approach-avoidance, when each alternative has its pluses and minuses.

6. How do irrational beliefs create or compound stress?

Albert Ellis shows that negative activating events (A) can be made more aversive (C) when irrational beliefs (B) compound their effects. People often catastrophize negative events. Two common irrational beliefs are excessive needs for social approval and perfectionism. Both set the stage for disappointment and increased stress.

7. What is Type A behavior?

Type A behavior is connected with a sense of time urgency and characterized by competitiveness, impatience, and aggressiveness. Type B people relax more readily.

8. How do our self-efficacy expectations affect our ability to withstand stress?

Self-efficacy expectations encourage us to persist in difficult tasks and to endure discomfort. Self-efficacy expectations are also connected with *lower* levels of adrenaline and noradrenaline, thus having a braking effect on bodily arousal.

9. What characteristics are connected with psychological hardiness?

Kobasa found that psychological hardiness among business executives is characterized by commitment, challenge, and control.

10. Is there any evidence that "A merry heart doeth good like a medicine"?

Yes. Research evidence shows that students who produce humor under adversity experience less stress. Moreover, watching humorous videos apparently enhances the functioning of the immune system.

11. How do predictability and control help us cope with stress?

Predictability allows us to brace ourselves, and control permits us to plan ways of coping with it.

12. Is there evidence that social support helps people cope with stress?

Social support has been shown to help people resist infectious diseases such as colds. It also helps people cope with the stress of cancer and other health problems. Kinds of social support include expression of emotional concern, instrumental aid, information, appraisal, and simple socializing.

13. What is the general adaptation syndrome?

The GAS is a cluster of bodily changes triggered by stressors. The GAS consists of three stages: alarm, resistance, and exhaustion. Corticosteroids help resist stress by fighting inflammation and allergic reactions. Adrenaline arouses the body by activating the sympathetic nervous system, which is highly active during the alarm and resistance stages of the GAS. Sympathetic activity is characterized by rapid heartbeat and respiration rate, release of stores of sugar, muscle tension, and other responses that deplete the body's supply of energy. The parasympathetic division of the ANS predominates during the exhaustion stage of the GAS and is connected with depression and inactivity. Prolonged stress is dangerous.

14. How does the immune system work?

Leukocytes (white blood cells) engulf and kill pathogens, worn-out body cells, and cancerous cells. The immune system also "remembers" how to battle antigens by maintaining their antibodies in the bloodstream. The immune system also facilitates inflammation, which increases the number of white blood cells that are transported to a damaged area.

15. How does stress affect the functioning of the immune system?

Stress depresses the functioning of the immune system by stimulating the release of corticosteroids. Steroids counter inflammation and interfere with the formation of antibodies.

16. What is the multifactorial approach to health?

This view recognizes that many factors, including biological, psychological, sociocultural, and environmental factors, affect our health. Nearly 1 million preventable deaths occur each year in the United States. Measures such as quitting smoking, eating properly, exercising, and controlling alcohol intake would prevent nearly 80% of them.

17. What are the relationships among ethnicity, gender, socioeconomic status, and health?

African Americans live about 7 years less than European Americans, largely because of sociocultural and economic factors that are connected with less access to health care and greater likelihood of eating high-fat diets, smoking, and living in unhealthful neighborhoods. Women are less likely than men to have heart attacks in early and middle adulthood due to the protective effects of estrogen. Women outlive men by 7 years on the average. One reason is that women are more likely than men to consult health professionals about health problems.

18. How has psychology contributed to our understanding and treatment of headaches?

Psychologists participate in research concerning the origins of headaches, including stress and tension. Psychologists help people alleviate headaches by reducing tension. They have also developed biofeedback training methods for helping people cope with migraines.

19. How has psychology contributed to our understanding and treatment of coronary heart disease?

Psychologists have participated in research that shows that the risk factors for coronary heart disease include family history; physiological conditions such as hypertension and high levels of serum cholesterol; behavior patterns such as heavy drinking, smoking, eating fatty foods, and Type A behavior; work overload; chronic tension and fatigue; and physical inactivity. They help people achieve healthier cardiovascular systems by stopping smoking, controlling weight, reducing hypertension, lowering LDL levels, changing Type A behavior, reducing hostility, and exercising.

20. How has psychology contributed to our understanding and treatment of cancer?

Psychologists have participated in research that shows that the risk factors for cancer include family history, smoking, drinking alcohol, eating animal fats, sunbathing, and stress. The following measures can be helpful in preventing and treating cancer: controlling exposure to behavioral risk factors for cancer, having regular medical checkups, regulating exposure to stress, and vigorously fighting cancer if it develops.

21. How do we change the irrational thoughts that create and compound stress?

A three-step process for doing so involves becoming aware of the thoughts, preparing and practicing incompatible thoughts, and rewarding oneself for changing.

22. How can we lower our levels of arousal? How can we turn down the inner alarm?

There are many methods, including meditation, biofeedback training, and progressive relaxation. In progressive relaxation, people purposefully tense and then relax muscle groups to develop awareness of muscle tensions and learn how to let the tensions go.

23. How does exercise help people cope with stress?

Exercise enhances our psychological well-being and also strengthens the cardiovascular system (our fitness or "condition") so that we can better resist the bodily effects of stress.

CHAPTER 15

Psychological Disorders

TRUTH ☑ FICTION?

▰ A man shot the president of the United States in front of millions of television witnesses, yet was found not guilty by a court of law.

▰ In the Middle Ages, innocent people were drowned to prove that they were not possessed by the Devil.

▰ It is abnormal to feel anxious.

▰ Some people have more than one identity, and the different identities may have varying allergies and eyeglass prescriptions.

▰ You can never be too rich or too thin.

▰ Some college women control their weight by going on cycles of binge eating and self-induced vomiting.

During one long fall semester, the Ohio State campus lived in terror. Four college women were abducted, forced to cash checks or obtain money from automatic teller machines, and then raped. A mysterious phone call led to the arrest of a 23-year-old drifter, William, who had been dismissed from the Navy.

William was not the boy next door.

Psychologists and psychiatrists who interviewed William concluded that 10 personalities—8 male and 2 female—resided within him (Scott, 1994). His personality had been "fractured" by an abusive childhood. His several personalities displayed distinct facial expressions, speech patterns, and memories. They even performed differently on psychological tests.

Arthur, the most rational personality, spoke with a British accent. Danny and Christopher were quiet adolescents. Christine was a 3-year-old girl. Tommy, a 16-year-old, had enlisted in the Navy. Allen was 18 and smoked. Adelena, a 19-year-old lesbian personality, had committed the rapes. Who had made the mysterious phone call? Probably David, 9, an anxious child.

The defense claimed that William's behavior was caused by a psychological disorder termed **dissociative identity disorder** (also referred to as **multiple personality disorder**). Several distinct identities or personalities dwelled within him. Some of them were aware of the others. Some believed that they were unique. Billy, the core identity, had learned to sleep as a child in order to avoid his father's abuse. A psychiatrist asserted that Billy had also been "asleep," or in a "psychological coma," during the abductions. Billy should therefore be found not guilty by reason of **insanity.**

William was found not guilty. He was committed to a psychiatric institution and released six years later.

In 1982, John Hinckley was also found not guilty of the assassination attempt on President Reagan's life. Expert witnesses testified that he should be diagnosed with **schizophrenia.** Hinckley, too, was committed to a psychiatric institution.

HISTORIC VIEWS OF PSYCHOLOGICAL DISORDERS: "THE DEVIL MADE ME DO IT"?

Dissociative identity disorder and schizophrenia are two **psychological disorders.** *Question: How have people historically explained psychological disorders?* If William and Hinckley had lived in Salem, Massachusetts, in 1692, just 200 years after Columbus set foot in the New World, they might have been hanged or burned as witches. At that time, most people assumed that psychological disorders were caused by possession by the Devil. A score of people were executed in Salem that year for allegedly practicing the arts of Satan.

Throughout human history people have attributed unusual behavior and psychological disorders to demons. The ancient Greeks believed that the gods punished humans by causing confusion and madness. An exception was the physician Hippocrates, who made the radical suggestion that psychological disorders are caused by an abnormality of the brain. The notion that biology could affect thoughts, feelings, and behavior was to lie dormant for about 2,000 years.

During the Middle Ages in Europe, as well as during the early period of European colonization of Massachusetts, it was generally believed that psychological disorders were signs of possession by the Devil. Possession could stem from retribution, in which God caused the Devil to possess a person's soul as punishment for committing certain kinds of sins. Agitation and confusion were ascribed to such retribution. Possession was also believed to result from deals with the Devil, in which people traded their souls for earthly gains. Such individuals were called witches. Witches were held responsible for unfortunate events ranging from a neighbor's infertility to a poor harvest. In Europe, as many as 500,000 accused witches were killed during the next two centuries (Hergenhahn, 1997). The goings on at Salem were trivial by comparison.

A document authorized by Pope Innocent VIII, *The Hammer of Witches*, proposed ingenious "diagnostic" tests to identify those who were possessed. The water-float test was based on the principle that pure metals sink to the bottom during smelting.

▲ REFLECT

Have you ever heard anyone say, "Something got into me" or, "The devil made me do it"? What were the circumstances? Was the person trying to evade responsibility for wrongdoing?

Dissociative identity disorder ▲ A disorder in which a person appears to have two or more distinct identities or personalities that may alternately emerge. (A term first used in DSM-IV.)

Multiple personality disorder ▲ The previous DSM term for *dissociative identity disorder.*

Insanity ▲ A legal term descriptive of a person judged to be incapable of recognizing right from wrong or of conforming his or her behavior to the law.

Schizophrenia ▲ (skit-so-FREE-knee-uh). A psychotic disorder characterized by loss of control of thought processes and inappropriate emotional responses.

Psychological disorders ▲ Patterns of behavior or mental processes that are connected with emotional distress or significant impairment in functioning.

Exorcism.

This medieval woodcut represents the practice of exorcism, in which a demon is expelled from a person who has been "possessed."

Impurities float to the surface. Suspects were thus placed in deep water. Those who sank to the bottom and drowned were judged to be pure. Those who managed to keep their heads above water were assumed to be "impure" and in league with the Devil. Then they were in real trouble. This ordeal is the origin of the phrase, "Damned if you do and damned if you don't."

Few people in the United States today would argue that unusual or unacceptable behavior is caused by demons. Still, we continue to use phrases that are suggestive of demonology. How many times have you heard the expressions "Something got into me" or "The Devil made me do it"?

Let us now define what is meant by a psychological disorder.

WHAT ARE PSYCHOLOGICAL DISORDERS?

Psychology is the study of behavior and mental processes. *Question: How, then, do we define psychological disorders?* Psychological disorders are behaviors or mental processes that are connected with various kinds of distress or disability. However, they are not predictable responses to specific events.

For example, some psychological disorders are characterized by anxiety, but many people are anxious now and then without being considered disordered. It is appropriate to be anxious before an important date or on the eve of a midterm exam. When, then, are feelings like anxiety deemed to be abnormal or signs of a psychological disorder? For one thing, anxiety may suggest a disorder when it is not appropriate to the situation. It is inappropriate to be anxious when entering an elevator or looking out of a fourth-story window. The magnitude of the problem may also suggest disorder. Some anxiety is usual before a job interview. However, feeling that your heart is pounding so intensely that it might leap out of your chest—and then avoiding the interview—are not usual.

Behavior or mental processes are suggestive of psychological disorders when they meet some combination of the following criteria:

1. *They are unusual.* Although people with psychological disorders are a minority, uncommon behavior or mental processes are not abnormal in themselves. Only one person holds the record for running or swimming the fastest mile. That person is different from you and me but is not abnormal. Only a few people qualify as geniuses in mathematics, but mathematical genius is not a sign of a psychological disorder.

   Rarity or statistical deviance may not be sufficient for behavior or mental processes to be labeled abnormal, but it helps. Most people do not see or hear things that are not there, and "seeing things" and "hearing things" are considered abnormal. We must also consider the situation. Although many of us feel "panicked" when we realize that a term paper or report is due the next day, most of us do not have panic attacks "out of the blue." Unpredictable panic attacks thus are suggestive of psychological disorder.

2. *They suggest faulty perception or interpretation of reality.* Our society considers it normal to be inspired by religious beliefs but abnormal to believe that God is literally speaking to you. "Hearing voices" and "seeing things" are considered **hallucinations.** Similarly, **ideas of persecution,** such as believing that the Mafia or the FBI are "out to get you," are considered signs of disorder. (Unless, of course, they *are* out to get you.)

The Hammer of Witches

The Hammer of Witches

In 1484, Pope Innocent VIII authorized the persecution of witches. Two Dominican priests, Heinrich Kramer and James Sprenger, were named to act as inquisitors. To guide their work, Kramer and Sprenger wrote *The Hammer of Witches* (*Malleus Maleficarum*). Over the next two centuries, this document was translated into many languages and went through 30 editions. It was found on the bench of nearly every judge in central Europe, Catholic and Protestant alike.

The *Hammer* "proved" the existence of witches, who were mainly women. It described—in detail—how witches engaged in sexual relations with male demons (*incubi*) and suggested ways of eliciting confessions through the use of hot irons and boiling water.

The *Hammer* demeaned women:

> Since women are feebler both in mind and body, it is not surprising that they are more likely to come under the spell of witchcraft. . . . And it should be noted that there was a defect in the formation of the first woman, since she was formed from a bent rib, that is, a rib of the breast, which is bent as it were in a contrary direction to a man. And since through this defect she is an imperfect animal, she always deceives. . . . Therefore, a wicked woman is by her nature quicker to waver in her faith, and consequently quicker to forsake the faith, which is the root of witchcraft. . . . In conclusion: All witchcraft comes from carnal lust, which is insatiable in women.

REFLECT
Have you ever felt anxious? Did your anxiety strike you as being normal under the circumstances? Why or why not?

CLICK4™ *a WebSearch activity: How does insanity differ from abnormality?*

www 15 L 7

CLICK4™ *articles and abstracts from the* Journal of Abnormal Psychology.

CLICK4™ *articles from the* British Journal of Psychiatry

Hallucination ▲ (hal-LOOSE-sin-nay-shun). A perception in the absence of sensory stimulation that is confused with reality.
Ideas of persecution ▲ Erroneous beliefs that one is being victimized or persecuted.

Hallucinations.

Hallucinations are a feature of schizophrenia. They are perceptions that occur in the absence of external stimulation, as in "hearing voices" or "seeing things." Hallucinations cannot be distinguished from real perceptions. Are the cats in this Sandy Skoglund photograph real or hallucinatory?

CLICK4™ *a bulletin board discussion: Are people who have psychological disorders sick?*

CLICK4™ *Web sites concerned with psychological disorders.*

▲ **REFLECT**

Do any family members of friends have psychological disorders? Do their behaviors or mental processes correspond to the criteria discussed in the chapter? Are the disorders being treated? If so, how?

3. *They suggest severe personal distress.* Anxiety, exaggerated fears, and other psychological states cause personal distress, and severe personal distress may be considered abnormal. Anxiety may also be an appropriate response to a situation, however, as in the case of a threat.

4. *They are self-defeating.* Behavior or mental processes that cause misery rather than happiness and fulfillment may suggest psychological disorder. Chronic drinking that impairs work and family life and cigarette smoking that impairs health may therefore be deemed abnormal.

5. *They are dangerous.* Behavior or mental processes that are hazardous to the self or others may be considered suggestive of psychological disorders. People who threaten or attempt suicide may be considered abnormal, as may people who threaten or attack others. Yet criminal behavior or aggressive behavior in sports need not imply a psychological disorder.

6. *The individual's behavior is socially unacceptable.* We must consider the cultural context of a behavior pattern in judging whether or not it is normal (Lopez & Guarnaccia, 2000). In the United States, it is deemed normal for males to be aggressive in sports and in combat. In other situations warmth and tenderness are valued. Many people in the United States admire women who are self-assertive, yet Latino and Latina American, Asian American, and "traditional" European American groups may see outspoken women as disrespectful.

REVIEW

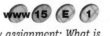

CLICK4™ *an essay assignment: What is abnormal?*

(1) Since the Middle Ages, Europeans have largely explained psychological disorders in terms of _____ by the devil. (2) The document called *The* _____ *of Witches* proposed tests to identify people who were "possessed." (3) Behavior is labeled abnormal when it is unusual, is socially unacceptable, involves faulty _____ of reality (as with hallucinations), is dangerous, self-defeating, or distressing.

Pulling It Together: How did ancient Greek beliefs about psychological disorders reveal a split between superstitious views and scientific views?

CLASSIFYING PSYCHOLOGICAL DISORDERS

Toss some people, apes, seaweed, fish, and sponges into a room—preferably a well-ventilated one. Stir slightly. What do you have? It depends on how you classify this hodge-podge.

Classify them as plants versus animals and you lump the people, chimpanzees, fish, and, yes, sponges together. Classify them as stuff that carries on its business on land or underwater, and we throw in our lot with the chimps and none of the others. How about those that swim and those that don't? Then the chimps, the fish, and some of us are grouped together.

Classification is at the heart of science (Barlow, 1991). Without classifying psychological disorders, investigators would not be able to communicate with each other and scientific progress would come to a standstill. The most widely used classification scheme for psychological disorders[1] is the *Diagnostic and Statistical Manual* (DSM) of the American Psychiatric Association. ***Question: How are psychological disorders grouped or classified?***

The current edition of the DSM—DSM-IV—uses a "multiaxial" system of assessment. It provides information about a person's overall functioning, not just a diagnosis. The axes are shown in Table 15.1. People may receive Axis I or Axis II diagnoses or a combination of the two.

Axis III, general medical conditions, lists physical disorders or problems that may affect people's functioning or their response to psychotherapy or drug treatment. Axis IV, psychosocial and environmental problems, includes difficulties that may affect the diagnosis, treatment, or outcome of a psychological disorder. Axis V, global assessment of functioning, allows the clinician to rate the client's current level of functioning and her or his highest level of functioning prior to the onset of the psychological disorder. The purpose is to help determine what kinds of psychological functioning are to be restored through therapy.

The DSM-IV groups disorders on the basis of observable features or symptoms. However, early editions of the DSM, which was first published in 1952, grouped many disorders on the basis of assumptions about their causes. Because Freud's psychodynamic theory was widely accepted at the time, one major diagnostic category contained so-called neuroses.[2] From the psychodynamic perspective, all neuroses—no matter how differently people with various neuroses might behave—were caused by unconscious neurotic conflict. Each neurosis was thought to reflect a way of coping with the unconscious fear that primitive impulses might break loose. As a result, sleepwalking was included as a neurosis (psychoanalysts assumed that sleepwalking reduced this unconscious fear by permitting the partial expression of impulses during the night). Now that the focus is on observable behaviors, sleepwalking is classified as a sleep disorder, not as a neurosis.

Some professionals, such as psychiatrist Thomas Szasz, believe that the categories described in the DSM are really "problems in living" rather than "disorders." At least, they are not disorders in the sense that high blood pressure, cancer, and the flu are disorders. Szasz argues that labeling people with problems in living as being "sick" degrades them and encourages them to evade their personal and social responsibilities. Since sick people are encouraged to obey doctors' orders, Szasz (1984) also contends that labeling people as "sick" accords too much power to health professionals. Instead, he believes, troubled people need to be encouraged to take greater responsibility for solving their own problems.

TABLE 15.1 THE MULTIAXIAL CLASSIFICATION SYSTEM OF DSM-IV

Axis	Type of Information	About . . .
Axis I	Clinical Syndromes	Includes psychological disorders that impair functioning and are stressful to the individual (a wide range of diagnostic classes, such as substance-related disorders, anxiety disorders, mood disorders, schizophrenia, somatoform disorders, and dissociative disorders).
Axis II	Personality Disorders	Includes deeply ingrained, maladaptive ways of perceiving others and behaviors that are stressful to the individual or to persons who relate to that individual.
Axis III	General Medical Conditions	Includes chronic and acute illnesses, injuries, allergies, and so on, that affect functioning and treatment.
Axis IV	Psychosocial and Environmental Problems	Enumerates stressors that occurred during the past year that may have contributed to the development of a new mental disorder or the recurrence of a prior disorder, or that may have exacerbated an existing disorder.
Axis V	Global Assessment of Functioning	An overall judgment of the current functioning and the highest level of functioning in the past year according to psychological, social, and occupational criteria.

CLICK4™ *more information on psychological disorders from the* Archives of General Psychiatry.

CLICK4™ *Web sites about the DSM-IV classification system.*

▲ **REFLECT**
Do you see any problems in using the word *sick* to describe people who have psychological disorders? Explain. (Hint: Consider how sick people are expected to behave.)

---
[1] The American Psychiatric Association refers to psychological disorders as *mental disorders*.
[2] The neuroses included what are today referred to as anxiety disorders, dissociative disorders, somatoform disorders, mild depression, and some other disorders, such as sleepwalking.

www 15 E 2
CLICK4™ an essay assignment: How do we diagnose psychological disorders?

One of the historic controversies in psychology has been whether or not a gay male or lesbian sexual orientation is to be considered a psychological disorder. We explore that issue next.

CONTROVERSY ✳ IN PSYCHOLOGY

Is a Gay Male or Lesbian Sexual Orientation a Psychological Disorder?

www 15 BBC 2
CLICK4™ a bulletin board discussion: Is a gay male or lesbian sexual orientation a psychological disorder?

www 15 WS 2
CLICK4™ a WebSearch activity on cultural differences in defining abnormality.

The superficial answer to this question is no. Until 1973, a gay male or lesbian sexual orientation was considered to be a psychological disorder (or "mental disorder") by the American Psychiatric Association and was listed as such in the DSM. But in that year, the members of the association voted to drop a gay male or lesbian sexual orientation from its list of mental disorders, although a diagnostic category for people who are *distressed* about their sexual orientation remains in place (American Psychiatric Association, 2000). Many members of the organization objected to the vote on the grounds that it was politically motivated. After all, could the American Medical Association vote to drop cancer as a physical disorder, they asked? Thus many psychiatrists continued to believe that homosexuality itself was a disorder despite the majority vote.

That was the superficial answer, but there is also the question as to whether gay males and lesbians have more psychological disorders than heterosexuals. If they do, it will still not mean that homosexuality itself is a disorder, but it may suggest that the psychological health of gay males and lesbians merits more attention from psychologists. Recent, carefully controlled studies do in fact find that gay males and lesbians are more likely than heterosexuals to experience feelings of anxiety and depression, and that they are more prone to suicide (Bagley & D'Augelli, 2000; Herrell et al., 1999).

Psychologist J. Michael Bailey (1999) of Northwestern University has carefully reviewed the issues surrounding homosexuality, and he wrote an interesting article about such findings in *Archives of General Psychiatry*. Bailey did not dispute the findings themselves, but he had much to say about their implications. Bailey proposes four possible interpretations:

1. Societal oppression causes the higher incidence of depression and suicidality we find among gay males and lesbians. "Surely," writes Bailey, "it must be difficult for young people to come to grips with their homosexuality in a world where homosexual people are often scorned, mocked, and feared."

2. Bailey acknowledges the possibility that homosexuality reflects a departure from typical development and could thus be associated with other differences, some of which could be connected with anxiety and depression. However, even if homosexuality is a departure from typical development, this would not make a gay male or a lesbian a "bad" person. Nearsightedness is also a departure from typical development, but we do not stigmatize nearsighted people.

3. A third possibility derives from the possibility that sexual orientation develops as a result of prenatal sex hormones. If homosexuality stems from unusual balances in prenatal sex hormones, gay males might be somewhat prone to psychological disorders that typically affect women (anxiety and depression), and lesbians to disorders that more typically affect men (antisocial personality disorder). But as of yet, there is insufficient evidence for a general reversal of psychological health issues.

4. Bailey also suggests that psychological health problems among homosexual people could reflect differences in lifestyle. For example, gay males are more likely than heterosexual males to have eating disorders because "the gay male culture emphasizes physical attractiveness and thinness, just as the heterosexual culture emphasizes female physical attractiveness and thinness." Surveys show that about half of the professional male dancers in the United States are gay (Bailey & Oberschneider, 1997). Eating disorders are especially common among dancers, who strive to remain thin at all costs.

We should remind you that Bailey insists that we must obtain more evidence before arriving at any judgment as to why gay males and lesbians are more prone to anxiety, depression, and suicidal thoughts. Nevertheless, no one can dispute the fact that gay males and lesbians encounter stress from societal oppression and rejection, and that this stress—like any form of stress—is going to have health consequences (Simonsen et al., 2000).

Let us now consider the kinds of psychological disorders. Some of them, like anxiety disorders, are common. Others, like dissociative identity disorder, are rare.

REVIEW

(4) The DSM was written by the American _____ Association. (5) Thomas _____ argues that labeling people with problems in living as "sick" degrades them and encourages them to evade responsibility.

Pulling It Together: Why does the DSM group disorders on the basis of observable features or symptoms? What is the alternative?

ANXIETY DISORDERS

Anxiety has subjective and physical features (Zinbarg & Barlow, 1996). Subjective features include worrying, fear of the worst things happening, fear of losing control, nervousness, and inability to relax. Physical features reflect arousal of the sympathetic branch of the autonomic nervous system. They include trembling, sweating, a pounding or racing heart, elevated blood pressure (a flushed face), and faintness. Anxiety is an appropriate response to a real threat. It can be abnormal, however, when it is excessive or when it comes out of nowhere—that is, when events do not seem to warrant it. ***Question: What kinds of anxiety disorders are there?*** There are different kinds of anxiety disorders, but all of them are characterized by excessive or unwarranted anxiety.

Types of Anxiety Disorders

The anxiety disorders include phobias, panic disorder, generalized anxiety, obsessive-compulsive disorder, and stress disorders.

Phobias There are several types of phobias, including specific phobias, social phobia, and agoraphobia. Some of them, such as social phobia, can be highly detrimental to one's quality of life (Stein & Kean, 2000). **Specific phobias** are excessive, irrational fears of specific objects or situations, such as snakes or heights. One specific phobia is fear of elevators. Some people will not enter elevators despite the hardships they incur as a result (such as walking up six flights of steps). Yes, the cable *could* break. The ventilation *could* fail. One *could* be stuck in midair waiting for repairs. These problems are uncommon, however, and it does not make sense for most people to walk up and down several flights of stairs to elude them. Similarly, some people with a specific phobia for hypodermic needles will not have injections, even to treat profound illness. Injections can be painful, but most people with a phobia for needles would gladly suffer an even more painful pinch if it would help them fight illness. Other specific phobias include **claustrophobia** (fear of tight or enclosed places), **acrophobia** (fear of heights), and fear of mice, snakes, and other creepy-crawlies. Fears of animals and imaginary creatures are common among children.

Social phobias are persistent fears of scrutiny by others or of doing something that will be humiliating or embarrassing. Fear of public speaking is a common social phobia.

Agoraphobia is also widespread among adults. Agoraphobia is derived from the Greek words meaning "fear of the marketplace," or fear of being out in open, busy areas. Persons with agoraphobia fear being in places from which it might be difficult to escape or in which help might not be available if they get upset. In practice, people who receive this diagnosis often refuse to venture out of their homes, especially by themselves. They find it difficult to hold a job or to maintain an ordinary social life.

CLICK4™ *a WebSearch activity on the characteristics of anxiety disorders.*

CLICK4™ *an essay assignment: Is anxiety normal?*

▲ **REFLECT**
Do you know anyone with a phobia? What kind of phobia? Does the phobia seriously interfere with his or her life? How so?

Specific phobia ▲ Persistent fear of a specific object or situation.
Claustrophobia ▲ (claws-troe-FOE-bee-uh). Fear of tight, small places.
Acrophobia ▲ (ack-row-FOE-bee-uh). Fear of high places.
Social phobia ▲ An irrational, excessive fear of public scrutiny.
Agoraphobia ▲ (ag-or-uh-FOE-bee-uh). Fear of open, crowded places.

www 15 L 3

CLICK4™ *Web sites about anxiety disorders.*

Panic Disorder

My heart would start pounding so hard I was sure I was having a heart attack. I used to go to the emergency room. Sometimes I felt dizzy, like I was going to pass out. I was sure I was about to die.

—*Kim Weiner*

Panic disorder is an abrupt attack of acute anxiety that is not triggered by a specific object or situation. People with panic disorder have strong physical symptoms such as shortness of breath, heavy sweating, tremors, and pounding of the heart. Like Kim Weiner (1992), they are particularly aware of cardiac sensations (Schmidt et al., 1997). It is not unusual for them to think they are having a heart attack (Clark et al., 1997). Saliva levels of cortisol (a stress hormone) are elevated during attacks (Bandelow et al., 2000). Many fear suffocation (McNally & Eke, 1996). People with the disorder may also experience choking sensations; nausea; numbness or tingling; flushes or chills; and fear of going crazy or losing control. Panic attacks may last minutes or hours. Afterwards, the person usually feels drained.

Many people panic now and then. The diagnosis of panic disorder is reserved for those who undergo a series of attacks or live in fear of attacks.

Panic attacks seem to come from nowhere. Thus, some people who have had them stay home for fear of having an attack in public. They are diagnosed as having panic disorder with agoraphobia.

Generalized Anxiety Disorder

The central feature of **generalized anxiety disorder** is persistent anxiety. As with panic disorder, the anxiety cannot be attributed to a phobic object, situation, or activity. Rather, it seems to be free floating. Features of this disorder may include motor tension (shakiness, inability to relax, furrowed brow, fidgeting); autonomic overarousal (sweating, dry mouth, racing heart, light-headedness, frequent urinating, diarrhea); feelings of dread and foreboding; and excessive vigilance, as shown by irritability, insomnia, and a tendency to be easily distracted.

Obsessive-Compulsive Disorder

Obsessions are recurrent, anxiety-provoking thoughts or images that seem irrational and beyond control. They are so compelling and recurrent that they disrupt daily life. They may include doubts about whether one

▲ **REFLECT**
Do you ever find yourself "in a panic"? Under what circumstances? What is the difference between "being in a panic" and having a panic disorder?

▲ **REFLECT**
Do you know people who repeatedly check that the doors are locked or the gas jets are turned off before they leave home? Or people who refuse to step on the cracks in the sidewalk? Does their behavior seem to fit the definition of obsessive-compulsive disorder?

Panic disorder ▲ The recurrent experiencing of attacks of extreme anxiety in the absence of external stimuli that usually elicit anxiety.

Generalized anxiety disorder ▲ Feelings of dread and foreboding and sympathetic arousal of at least 6 months' duration.

Obsession ▲ A recurring thought or image that seems beyond control.

www 15 PML 31

CLICK4™ *a case study of obsessive-compulsive disorder: "Bonnie."*

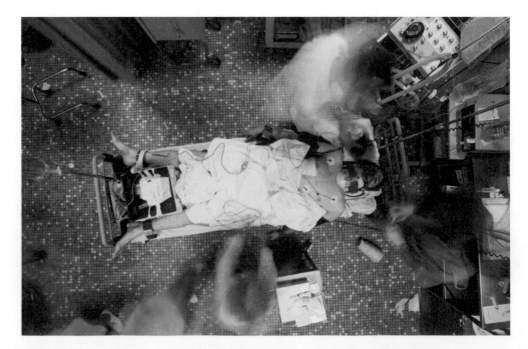

A Traumatic Experience.
Traumatic experiences like the destruction of one's home can lead to posttraumatic stress disorder (PTSD). PTSD is characterized by intrusive memories of the experience, recurrent dreams about it, and the sudden feeling that it is, in fact, recurring (as in "flashbacks").

has locked the doors and shut the windows, or images such as one mother's repeated fantasy that her children had been run over on the way home from school. One woman became obsessed with the idea that she had contaminated her hands with Sani-Flush and that the chemicals were spreading to everything she touched. A 16-year-old boy found "numbers in his head" when he was about to study or take a test.

Compulsions are thoughts or behaviors that tend to reduce the anxiety connected with obsessions. They are seemingly irresistible urges to engage in specific acts, often repeatedly, such as elaborate washing after using the bathroom. The impulse is recurrent and forceful, interfering with daily life. The woman who felt contaminated by Sani-Flush spent 3 to 4 hours at the sink each day and complained, "My hands look like lobster claws."

Stress Disorder

Darla, who lives in Oregon, dreamed that she was trapped in a World Trade Center tower when it was hit by an airplane on September 11, 2001. Kelly, a Californian, dreamed of a beautiful bald eagle that was suddenly transformed into a snarling bird with glowing red eyes ("Sleepers Suffer WTC Nightmares," 2001).

The all-too-real nightmare of the events of September 11th have caused many people to have bad dreams. Such dreams are part of the experience of posttraumatic stress disorder.

Posttraumatic stress disorder (PTSD) is characterized by a rapid heart rate and feelings of anxiety and helplessness that are caused by a traumatic experience. Such experiences may include a natural or humanmade disaster, a threat or assault, or witnessing a death. PTSD may occur months or years after the event. It frequently occurs among firefighters, combat veterans, people whose homes and communities have been swept away by natural disasters or who have been subjected to toxic hazards, and survivors of childhood sexual abuse (DeAngelis, 1995a; Rodriguez et al., 1997). A national study of more than 4,000 women found that about one woman in four who had been victimized by crime experienced PTSD (Resnick et al., 1993; see Figure 13.1). A study of former political prisoners found that PTSD was connected with feelings of mental defeat during the traumatic experience, feelings of alienation from other people, and perceived permanent change in personality or life aspirations (Ehlers et al., 2000).

The traumatic event is revisited in the form of intrusive memories, recurrent dreams, and flashbacks—the sudden feeling that the event is recurring. People with PTSD typically try to avoid thoughts and activities connected to the traumatic event. They may also find it more difficult to enjoy life (Beckham et al., 2000) and have sleep problems, irritable outbursts, difficulty concentrating, extreme vigilance, and an intensified "startle" response (Shayley et al., 2000).

Acute stress disorder, like PTSD, is characterized by feelings of anxiety and helplessness that are caused by a traumatic event. However, PTSD can occur 6 months or more after the traumatic event and tends to persist. Acute stress disorder occurs within a month of the event and lasts from 2 days to 4 weeks. Woman who have been raped, for example, experience acute distress that tends to peak in severity about 3 weeks after the assault (Davidson & Foa, 1991; Rothbaum et al., 1992).

Theoretical Views

There are thus several kinds of anxiety disorders. *Question: What is known about the origins of anxiety disorders?*

Psychological Views

According to the psychodynamic perspective, phobias symbolize conflicts originating in childhood. Psychodynamic theory explains generalized anxiety as persistent difficulty in repressing primitive impulses. Obsessions are explained as leakage of unconscious impulses, and compulsions are seen as acts that allow people to keep such impulses partly repressed. For example, fixation in the anal stage is theorized to be connected with development of traits such as excessive neatness of the sort that could explain some cases of obsessive-compulsive disorder.

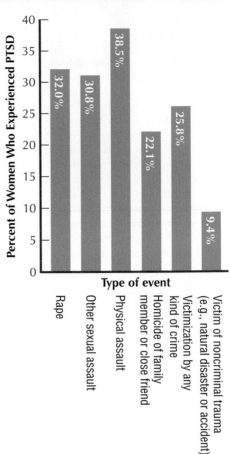

FIGURE 15.1 Posttraumatic Stress Disorder Among Female Victims of Crime and Among Other Women.
According to Resnick and her colleagues (1993), about one woman in four (25.8%) who was victimized by crime could be diagnosed with PTSD at some point following the crime. By contrast, fewer than 1 woman in 10 (9.4%) who was not victimized by crime experienced PTSD.

Compulsion ▲ An apparently irresistible urge to repeat an act or engage in ritualistic behavior such as hand washing.
Posttraumatic stress disorder ▲ A disorder that follows a distressing event outside the range of normal human experience and that is characterized by features such as intense fear, avoidance of stimuli associated with the event, and reliving of the event. Abbreviated *PTSD*.
Acute stress disorder ▲ A disorder, like PTSD, that is characterized by feelings of anxiety and helplessness and caused by a traumatic event. Unlike PTSD, acute stress disorder occurs within a month of the event and lasts from 2 days to 4 weeks. (A category first included in DSM-IV.)

Little Hans

Do you want to talk about conflict? Do you want to talk about drama? Do you want to talk about raw, unnerving fear? Well, forget about aliens from outer space. Forget about income taxes and things that go bump in the night. For there in turn of the century Vienna, that flourishing European capital of the arts, horses were biting people in the streets. Or so thought one petrified 5-year-old boy by the name of Hans.

In 1908 Hans's distraught father wrote to Sigmund Freud for advice. Freud psychoanalyzed Hans's fear of horses *by mail*. He went on to write one of his most famous case studies, "Analysis of a Phobia in a 5-Year-Old Boy." Freud concluded that the horses were symbols that represented Hans's father. Being bitten symbolized being castrated. In other words, Hans unconsciously feared that his father would castrate him. Why? Because Hans was his father's rival in a contest for the affection of his mother. Hans, that is, was in the throes of the Oedipus complex.

Freud's analysis has been criticized on many grounds. Historically speaking, however, the case of Little Hans laid much of the groundwork for the psychoanalytic belief that phobic objects symbolize unconscious conflicts that date from early childhood.

▲ **REFLECT**

Have you ever heard anyone described as being "anal"? How does the description relate to the psychodynamic explanation of obsessive-compulsive disorder?

CLICK4™ *a video on barbiturates and their interaction with the neurotransmitter GABA.*

Concordance ▲ (con-CORD-ants). Agreement.
Gamma-aminobutyric acid (GABA) ▲ (a-me-no-byoo-TIE-rick). An inhibitory neurotransmitter that is implicated in anxiety reactions.
Benzodiazepines ▲ (ben-zoe-die-AZZ-uh-peans). A class of drugs that reduce anxiety; minor tranquilizers.

Some learning theorists—particularly behaviorists—consider phobias to be conditioned fears that were acquired in early childhood. Therefore, their origins are beyond memory. Avoidance of feared stimuli is reinforced by the reduction of anxiety.

Other learning theorists—social-cognitive theorists—note that observational learning plays a role in the acquisition of fears (Basic Behavioral Science Task Force, 1996b). If parents squirm, grimace, and shudder at the sight of mice, blood, or dirt on the kitchen floor, children might assume that these stimuli are awful and imitate their parents' behavior.

Cognitive theorists suggest that anxiety is maintained by thinking that one is in a terrible situation and helpless to change it. People with anxiety disorders may be cognitively biased toward paying more attention to threats than other people do (Foa et al., 1996; Mineka, 1991). Psychoanalysts and learning theorists generally agree that compulsive behavior reduces anxiety.

Cognitive theorists note that people's appraisals of the magnitude of threats help determine whether they are traumatic and can lead to PTSD (Folkman & Moskowitz, 2000a). People with panic attacks tend to misinterpret bodily cues and to view them as threats. Obsessions and compulsions may serve to divert attention from more frightening issues, such as "What am I going to do with my life?" When anxieties are acquired at a young age, we may later interpret them as enduring traits and label ourselves as "people who fear _____" (you fill it in). We then live up to the labels. We also entertain thoughts that heighten and perpetuate anxiety such as "I've got to get out of here," or "My heart is going to leap out of my chest." Such ideas intensify physical signs of anxiety, disrupt planning, make stimuli seem worse than they really are, motivate avoidance, and decrease self-efficacy expectations. The belief that we will not be able to handle a threat heightens anxiety. The belief that we are in control reduces anxiety (Bandura et al., 1985).

Biological Views   Biological factors play a role in anxiety disorders. Genetic factors are implicated in most psychological disorders, including anxiety disorders (Kendler et al., 2000b; Nestadt et al., 2000; Schmidt et al., 2000). For one thing, anxiety disorders tend to run in families (Michels & Marzuk, 1993b). Twin studies also find a higher **concordance** rate for anxiety disorders among identical twins than among fraternal twins (Torgersen, 1983). Studies of adoptees who are anxious similarly show that the biological parent places the child at risk for anxiety and related traits.

Susan Mineka (1991) suggests that humans (and nonhuman primates) are genetically predisposed to fear stimuli that may have once posed a threat to their ancestors. Evolutionary forces would have favored the survival of individuals who were predisposed toward acquiring fears of large animals, spiders, snakes, heights, entrapment, sharp objects, and strangers.

Perhaps a predisposition toward anxiety—in the form of a highly reactive autonomic nervous system—can be inherited. What might make a nervous system "highly reactive"? In the case of panic disorder, faulty regulation of levels of serotonin and norepinephrine may be involved. In other anxiety disorders, receptor sites in the brain may not be sensitive enough to **gamma-aminobutyric acid (GABA),** a neurotransmitter that may help calm anxiety reactions. The **benzodiazepines,** a class of drugs that reduce anxiety, may work by increasing the sensitivity of receptor sites to GABA. However, it is unlikely that GABA levels fully explain anxiety disorders (Michels & Marzuk, 1993a).

In many cases anxiety disorders may reflect the interaction of biological and psychological factors. In panic disorder, biological imbalances may initially trigger attacks. However, subsequent fear of attacks—and of the bodily cues that signal their onset—may heighten discomfort and give one the idea there is nothing one can do about them (McNally, 1990). Feelings of helplessness increase fear. People with panic disorder therefore can be helped by psychological methods that provide ways of reducing physical discomfort—including regular breathing—and show them that there are, after all, things they can do to cope with attacks (Klosko et al., 1990).

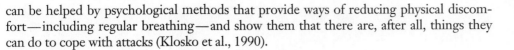

CLICK4™ *a case study of PTSD: "Margaret."*

REVIEW

(6) A _____ is an irrational fear. (7) _____ disorder is characterized by sudden attacks in which people typically fear that they may be losing control or going crazy. (8) In obsessive-_____ disorder people are troubled by intrusive thoughts or impulses to repeat some activity. (9) _____ is caused by a traumatic experience and characterized by reliving it the form of intrusive memories, recurrent dreams, and flashbacks. (10) Psychodynamic theory explains generalized anxiety as persistent difficulty in maintaining _____ of primitive impulses. (11) _____ see phobias as conditioned fears. (12) Anxiety disorders (do or do not?) tend to run in families.

Pulling It Together: Is anxiety normal? How are anxiety disorders abnormal? What might evolutionary psychologists say about the heritability of fears?

CLICK4™ *the Web site of the national Center for PTSD, hosted by Dartmouth College.*

DISSOCIATIVE DISORDERS

William's disorder, described at the beginning of the chapter, was a dissociative disorder. In the **dissociative disorders** there is a separation of mental processes such as thoughts, emotions, identity, memory, or consciousness—the processes that make the person feel whole. ***Question: What kinds of dissociative disorders are there?***

Types of Dissociative Disorders

The DSM lists several dissociative disorders. Among them are dissociative amnesia, dissociative fugue, dissociative identity disorder, and depersonalization.

Dissociative Amnesia   In **dissociative amnesia** the person is suddenly unable to recall important personal information (that is, explicit episodic memories). The loss of memory cannot be attributed to organic problems such as a blow to the head or alcoholic intoxication. It is thus a psychological dissociative disorder and not an organic one. In the most common example, the person cannot recall events for a number of hours after a stressful incident, as in warfare or in the case of an uninjured survivor of an accident. In generalized amnesia, people forget their entire lives. Amnesia may last for hours or years.

Dissociative Fugue   In **dissociative fugue,** the person abruptly leaves his or her home or place of work and travels to another place, having lost all memory of his or her past life. While at the new location the person either does not think about the past or reports a past filled with invented memories. The new personality is often more outgoing and less inhibited than the "real" identity. Following recovery, the events that occurred during the fugue are not recalled.

Dissociative Identity Disorder   Dissociative identity disorder (formerly termed *multiple personality disorder)* is the name given to William's disorder. In dissociative identity disorder, two or more identities or personalities, each with distinct traits and memories, "occupy" the same person. Each identity may or may not be aware of the others.

The identities of people with dissociative identity disorder can be very different from one another. They might even have different eyeglass prescriptions (Braun, 1988). Braun reports cases in which assorted identities showed different allergic responses. In one person, an identity named Timmy was not sensitive to orange juice. But when other identities gained control over him and drank orange juice, he would break out with hives. Hives would also erupt if another identity emerged while the juice was being digested. If Timmy reappeared when the allergic reaction was present, the itching of the hives would

> **REFLECT**
> Have you ever known people to claim that they had "amnesia" for some episode or event? Do you believe them? If you do, do you think that the term was used correctly? Why or why not?

Dissociative disorders ▲ (diss-SO-she-uh-tivv). Disorders in which there are sudden, temporary changes in consciousness or self-identity.

Dissociative amnesia ▲ (am-KNEE-she-uh). A dissociative disorder marked by loss of memory or self-identity; skills and general knowledge are usually retained. Previously termed *psychogenic amnesia.*

Dissociative fugue ▲ (FYOOG). A dissociative disorder in which one experiences amnesia and then flees to a new location. Previously termed *psychogenic fugue.*

Dissociative Identity Disorder.
In the film *The Three Faces of Eve,* Joanne Woodward played three personalities in the same woman: the shy, inhibited Eve White (lying on couch); the flirtatious, promiscuous Eve Black (in dark dress); and a third personality (Jane) who could accept her sexual and aggressive impulses and still maintain her sense of identity.

CLICK4™ *an essay assignment: dissociative disorders on the screen.*

> ▲ REFLECT
>
> Have you ever felt removed from the world — as though the things around you could not be really happening? Why do you believe that you felt this way?

cease and the blisters would start to subside. In other cases reported by Braun, different identities within a person might show various responses to the same medicine. Or one identity might exhibit color blindness while others have normal color vision.

A few celebrated cases of this disorder have been portrayed in the popular media. One of them became the subject of the film *The Three Faces of Eve*. A timid housewife named Eve White harbored two other identities. One was Eve Black, a sexually aggressive, antisocial personality. The third was Jane, an emerging identity who was able to accept the existence of her primitive impulses yet engage in socially appropriate behavior. Finally the three faces merged into one—Jane. Ironically, later on, Jane (Chris Sizemore in real life) reportedly split into 22 identities. Another well-publicized case is that of Sybil, a woman with 16 identities who was portrayed by Sally Field in the film *Sybil*.

Depersonalization Disorder   **Depersonalization disorder** is characterized by persistent or recurrent feelings that one is detached from one's own body, as if one is observing one's thought processes from the outside. For this reason, it is sometimes referred to as an "out-of-body experience." People with the disorder experience changes in attention and perception, making it difficult to focus on events (Guralnik et al., 2000). They can take in new information but have difficulty reasoning about it. As a result, they may feel as though they are functioning on automatic pilot or as in a dream.

The case of Richie illustrates a transient episode of depersonalization:

> We went to Orlando with the children after school let out. I had also been driving myself hard, and it was time to let go. We spent three days "doing" Disneyworld, and it got to the point where we were all wearing shirts with mice and ducks on them and singing Disney songs like "Yo ho, yo ho, a pirate's life for me." On the third day I began to feel unreal and ill at ease while we were watching these middle-American Ivory-soap teenagers singing and dancing in front of Cinderella's Castle. The day was finally cooling down, but I broke into a sweat. I became shaky and dizzy and sat down on the cement next to the 4-year-old's stroller without giving [my wife] an explanation. There were strollers and kids and [adults'] legs all around me, and for some strange reason I became fixated on the pieces of popcorn strewn on the ground. All of a sudden it was like the people around me were all silly mechanical creatures, like the dolls in the "It's a Small World" [exhibit] or the animals on the "Jungle Cruise." Things sort of seemed to slow down, the way they do when you've smoked marijuana, and there was this invisible wall of cotton between me and everyone else.
>
> Then the concert was over and my wife was like "What's the matter?" and did I want to stay for the Electrical Parade and the fireworks or was I sick? Now I was beginning to wonder if I was going crazy and I said I was sick, that my wife would have to take me by the hand and drive us back to the [motel]. Somehow we got back to the monorail and turned in the strollers. I waited in the herd [of people] at the station like a dead person, my eyes glazed over, looking out over kids with Mickey Mouse ears and Mickey Mouse balloons. The mechanical voice on the monorail almost did me in and I got really shaky.
>
> I refused to go back to the Magic Kingdom. I went with the family to Sea World, and on another day I dropped [my wife] and the kids off at the Magic Kingdom and picked them up that night. My wife thought I was goldbricking or something, and we had a helluva fight about it, but we had a life to get back to and my sanity had to come first.

CLICK4™ *a WebSearch activity: What are the characteristics of dissociative disorder?*

Depersonalization disorder ▲ A dissociative disorder in which one experiences persistent or recurrent feelings that one is not real or is detached from one's own experiences or body.

Theoretical Views

The dissociative disorders are some of the odder psychological disorders. *Question: What is known about the origins of dissociative disorders?*

CONTROVERSY ✦ IN PSYCHOLOGY

Do Dissociative Disorders Really Exist?

Before discussing psychological theories of the dissociative disorders, we should note that there is a good deal of skepticism about their existence. For example, there were about 50 known cases of dissociative identity disorder before the public learned about "Sybil." By the 1990s, however, this number had mushroomed to more than 20,000 ("Tapes raise new doubts," 1998). Moreover, psychologists who have listened carefully to tapes of Sybil's therapy have raised the possibility that some of her psychiatrists may have "coached" her into reporting the symptoms. Sybil herself is reported to have vacillated as to whether or not her story was true ("Tapes raise new doubts," 1998). It is possible that many or even most people who are diagnosed with dissociative amnesia or dissociative identity disorder are faking. The technical term for faking in order to obtain some benefit—such as being excused from responsibility for a crime or for family obligations—is *malingering*.

In any event, psychologists of different theoretical persuasions have offered hypotheses about the origins of dissociative identity disorder and other dissociative disorders. According to psychodynamic theory, for example, people with dissociative disorders use massive repression to prevent them from recognizing improper impulses or remembering ugly events (Vaillant, 1994). In dissociative amnesia and fugue, the person forgets a profoundly disturbing event or impulse. In dissociative identity disorder, the person expresses unacceptable impulses through alternate identities. In depersonalization, the person stands outside—removed from the turmoil within.

According to learning theorists, people with dissociative disorders have learned *not to think* about bad memories or disturbing impulses in order to avoid feelings of anxiety, guilt, and shame. Both psychodynamic and learning theories suggest that dissociative disorders help people keep disturbing memories or ideas out of mind. Of what could such memories be? Research suggests that many—perhaps most—cases involve memories of sexual or physical abuse during childhood, usually by a relative or caretaker (Coons, 1994; Martinez-Taboas & Bernal, 2000; Weaver & Clum, 1995). Surveys find that the great majority of people who are diagnosed with dissociative identity disorder report sexual abuse in childhood (Putnam et al., 1986). Many report both physical and sexual abuse.

Perhaps all of us are capable of dividing our awareness so that we become unaware, at least temporarily, of events that we usually focus more attention on. The dissociative disorders raise fascinating questions about the nature of human self-identity and memory. Perhaps it is no surprise that attention can be divided. Perhaps the surprising thing is that human consciousness normally integrates an often chaotic set of experiences into a meaningful whole.

CLICK4™ *a bulletin board discussion: Do dissociative disorders really exist?*

> ▲ **REFLECT**
>
> Have you seen a film or a TV show in which a character was supposed to have dissociative identity disorder (perhaps it was called "multiple personality")? What kind of behavior did the character display? Does the behavior seem consistent with the description of the disorder in the text? In the film or TV show, what were the supposed origins of the disorder?

REVIEW

(13) Dissociative _____ is characterized by motivated forgetting. (14) In dissociative _____ disorder, the person behaves as if distinct personalities occupy the body. (15) In _____ disorder, people feel as if they are not themselves. (16) According to learning theory, people learn not to _____ about disturbing acts or impulses in dissociative disorders. (17) Many people with dissociative disorders have a history of physical or sexual _____.

Pulling It Together: What is malingering? How does malingering make it difficult to assess the incidence of dissociative disorders?

www 15 WS 5

CLICK4™ *online questionnaires: Do you show symptoms of somatoform disorders?*

SOMATOFORM DISORDERS

People with **somatoform disorders** complain of physical problems such as paralysis, pain, or a persistent belief that they have a serious disease. Yet no evidence of a physical abnormality can be found. *Question: What kinds of somatoform disorders are there?* In this section we discuss two somatoform disorders: conversion disorder and hypochondriasis.

Types of Somatoform Disorders

Conversion disorder is characterized by a major change in, or loss of, physical functioning, although there are no medical findings to explain the loss of functioning. The behaviors are not intentionally produced. That is, the person is not faking. Conversion disorder is so named because it appears to "convert" a source of stress into a physical difficulty.

If you lost the ability to see at night, or if your legs became paralyzed, you would understandably show concern. But some people with conversion disorder show indifference to their symptoms, a remarkable feature referred to as **la belle indifférence.**

During World War II, some bomber pilots developed night blindness. They could not carry out their nighttime missions, although no damage to the optic nerves was found. In rare cases, women with large families have been reported to become paralyzed in the legs, again with no medical findings. More recently, a Cambodian woman who had witnessed atrocities became blind as a result.

Another more common type of somatoform disorder is **hypochondriasis** (also called *hypochondria*). People with this disorder insist that they are suffering from a serious physical illness, even though no medical evidence of illness can be found. They become preoccupied with minor physical sensations and continue to believe that they are ill despite the reassurance of physicians that they are healthy. They may run from doctor to doctor, seeking the one who will find the causes of the sensations. Fear of illness may disrupt their work or home life.

Question: What is known about the origins of somatoform disorders?

Theoretical Views

We are afforded insight into a prominent psychological explanation of the somatoform disorders when we view the history of their name. Consistent with psychodynamic theory, early versions of the DSM labeled what are now referred to as somatoform disorders as "hysterical neuroses."

> ▲ **REFLECT**
> Have you heard someone called a *hypochondriac?* Was the term used accurately or simply as an insult? Explain.

> ▲ **REFLECT**
> Have you heard someone referred to as "hysterical"? What did the word mean? How do you feel about its usage? Explain.

www 15 E 5

CLICK4™ *an essay assignment: Are somatoform disorders unique to women?*

Somatoform disorders ▲ (so-MAT-oh-form). Disorders in which people complain of physical (somatic) problems even though no physical abnormality can be found.

Conversion disorder ▲ A disorder in which anxiety or unconscious conflicts are "converted" into physical symptoms that often have the effect of helping the person cope with anxiety or conflict.

La belle indifférence ▲ (lah bell an-DEEF-fay-rants). A French term descriptive of the lack of concern sometimes shown by people with conversion disorders.

Hypochondriasis ▲ (high-poe-con-DRY-uh-sis). Persistent belief that one has a medical disorder despite lack of medical findings.

CONTROVERSY IN PSYCHOLOGY

Are Somatoform Disorders the Special Province of Women?

"Hysterical" derives from the word *hystera*, the Greek word for uterus or womb. Like many other Greeks, Hippocrates believed that hysteria was a sort of female trouble that was caused by a wandering uterus. It was erroneously thought that the uterus could roam through the body—that it was not anchored in place! As the uterus meandered, it could cause pains and odd sensations almost anywhere. The Greeks also believed that pregnancy anchored the uterus and ended hysterical complaints. What do you think Greek physicians prescribed to end monthly aches and pains? Good guess.

Even in the earlier years of the 20th century, it was suggested that strange sensations and medically unfounded complaints were largely the province of women. Moreover, viewing the problem as a neurosis suggested that it stemmed from unconscious childhood conflicts. The psychodynamic view of conversion disorders is that the symptoms protect the individual from feelings of guilt or shame, or from another source of stress. Conversion disorders, like dissociative disorders, often seem to serve a purpose. For example, the "blindness" of the World War II pilots may have enabled them to avoid feelings of fear of being literally shot down or of guilt for killing civilians. The night blindness of the pilots shows that conversion disorders are not the special province of women—whether they were once labeled hysterical or not.

REVIEW

(18) In _____ disorders, people complain of physical problems or persist in believing they have a serious disease, even though no medical problem can be found. (19) In a _____ disorder, there is a major change in or loss of physical functioning with no organic basis.

Pulling It Together: Why have somatoform disorders been considered "hysterical"? What are the social problems in labeling them as hysterical?

MOOD DISORDERS

CLICK4™ *information on kinds of depression, origins, treatment, and resources.*

Mood disorders are characterized by disturbance in expressed emotions. The disruption generally involves sadness or elation. Most instances of sadness are normal, or "run-of-the-mill." If you have failed an important test, if you have lost money in a business venture, or if your closest friend becomes ill, it is understandable and fitting for you to be sad about it. It would be odd, in fact, if you were *not* affected by adversity.

Types of Mood Disorders

Question: What kinds of mood disorders are there? In this section we discuss two mood disorders: major depression and bipolar disorder.

Major Depression Depression is the common cold of psychological problems, affecting upwards of 10% of adults at any time (Alloy et al., 1990). People with run-of-the-mill depression may feel sad, blue, or "down in the dumps." They may complain of lack of energy, loss of self-esteem, difficulty concentrating, loss of interest in activities and other people (Nezlek et al., 2000), pessimism, crying, and thoughts of suicide.

> **REFLECT**
> Do you think that you would find it easy or difficult to admit to having feelings of depression? Explain.

These feelings are more intense in people with **major depression.** People with this disorder may also show poor appetite, serious weight loss, and agitation or **psychomotor retardation.** They may be unable to concentrate and make decisions. They may say that they "don't care" anymore and in some cases attempt suicide. They may also display faulty perception of reality—so-called psychotic behaviors. These include delusions of unworthiness, guilt for imagined wrongdoings, even the notion that one is rotting from disease. There may also be delusions, as of the Devil administering deserved punishment, or hallucinations, as of strange bodily sensations.

Bipolar Disorder People with **bipolar disorder,** formerly known as *manic-depressive disorder,* have mood swings from ecstatic elation to deep depression. The cycles seem to be unrelated to external events. In the elated, or **manic** phase, the person may show excessive excitement or silliness, carrying jokes too far. The manic person may be argumentative. He or she may show poor judgment, destroying property, making huge contributions to charity, or giving away expensive possessions. People often find manic individuals abrasive and avoid them. They are often oversexed and too restless to sit still or sleep restfully. They often speak rapidly (showing "pressured speech") and jump from topic to topic (showing **rapid flight of ideas**). It can be hard to get a word in edgewise.

Depression is the other side of the coin. People with bipolar depression often sleep more than usual and are lethargic. People with major (or unipolar) depression are more likely to have insomnia and agitation. Those with bipolar depression also exhibit social withdrawal and irritability. Some people with bipolar disorder attempt suicide when the mood shifts from the elated phase toward depression (Jamison, 2000). They will do almost anything to escape the depths of depression that lie ahead.

Major depression ▲ A severe depressive disorder in which the person may show loss of appetite, psychomotor behaviors, and impaired reality testing.

Psychomotor retardation ▲ Slowness in motor activity and (apparently) in thought.

Bipolar disorder ▲ A disorder in which the mood alternates between two extreme poles (elation and depression). Also referred to as *manic-depression.*

Manic ▲ Elated, showing excessive excitement.

Rapid flight of ideas ▲ Rapid speech and topic changes, characteristic of manic behavior.

CONTROVERSY IN PSYCHOLOGY

Is There a Thin Line Between Genius and Madness?

You may have heard the expression, "There is a thin line between genius and madness." It may sound as if the "madness" in question should be schizophrenia because there are

CLICK4™ *Web sites about mood disorders.*

CLICK4™ *an interactive self-assessment: The Self-Rating Depression Scale.*

flights of fancy in that disorder as well as among geniuses. Yet researchers have found links between creative genius and the mood disorders of depression and bipolar disorder (Jamison, 1997). Many artists have peered into the depths of their own despair and found inspiration, but an alarming number of writers—including Virginia Woolf, Sylvia Plath, and Ernest Hemingway—have taken their own lives (Preti & Miotto, 1999). As noted by psychologist Kay Redfield Jamison (1997), artists are 18 times more likely to commit suicide than the general population. They are 8 to 10 times more likely to be depressed, and 10 to 20 times as likely to have bipolar disorder. Many writers, painters, and composers were also at their most productive during manic periods, including the poet Alfred, Lord Tennyson and the composer Robert Schumann. As of today, we can only speculate about the meaning of the connection between creativity and mood disorders, but let us note two interesting pieces of information. First, the medicines that are used to treat mood disorders tend to limit the individual's emotional and perceptual range, which is a reason why many people stop taking them. Second, artistic creativity and emotional response are both considered right-brain functions.

Theoretical Views

Question: What is known about the origins of mood disorders? Although the mood disorders are connected with processes within the individual, let us begin by noting that many kinds of situations are also connected with depression. For example, depression may be a reaction to losses and stressful life events (Mazure et al., 2000). Sources of chronic strain such as marital discord, physical discomfort, incompetence, and failure or pressure at work all contribute to feelings of depression (Nolen-Hoeksema et al., 1999). We tend to be more depressed by things we bring on ourselves, such as academic problems, financial problems, unwanted pregnancy, conflict with the law, arguments, and fights (Greenberger et al., 2000; Simons et al., 1993). However, some people recover from depression less readily than others. People who remain depressed have lower self-esteem (Andrews & Brown, 1993), are less likely to be able to solve social problems (Marx et al., 1992), and have less social support. As we see in the following section, women are more likely to develop depression than men. Why is this so?

CLICK4™ *a bulletin board discussion: Why are women more likely to be depressed?*

 **Depression and Gender: The Case of Women and Depression** Women are about two times more likely to be diagnosed with depression than men (Depression Research, 2000; Greenberger et al., 2000). *Question: Why are women more likely than men to be depressed?* Some therapists, like many laypeople, assume that biological gender differences largely explain why women are more likely to become depressed. How often do we hear degrading remarks such as "It must be that time of the month" when a woman expresses feelings of anger or irritation? But part of the gender difference may be due to the fact that men are less likely than women to admit to depression or seek treatment for depression. "I'm the John Wayne generation," admitted one man, a physician. "'It's only a flesh wound'; that's how you deal with it. I thought depression was a weakness—there was something disgraceful about it. A real man would just get over it" (cited in Wartik, 2000).

Still in any given year, about 12% of women and 7% of men in the United States are estimated to be diagnosable with depression (Depression Research, 2000). It was once assumed that depression was most likely to accompany menopause in women, because women could no longer carry out their "natural" function of childbearing. However, it turns out that women are more likely to encounter severe depression during the childbearing years (Depression Research, 2000).

Hormonal changes during adolescence, the menstrual cycle, and childbirth may contribute to depression in women (Cyranowski et al., 2000; McGrath et al., 1990). However, a panel convened by the American Psychological Association attributed most of the difference to the greater stresses placed on women, which tend to be greatest when they are trying to meet the multiple demands of childbearing, child rearing, and financial support of the family (McGrath et al., 1990). Women are more likely to experience physical and sexual abuse, poverty, single parenthood, and sexism. Women are also more likely than men to help other people who are under stress. Supporting other people heaps additional caregiving burdens on themselves (Shumaker & Hill, 1991). One panel member, Bonnie Strickland, expressed surprise that even more women are not depressed, given that they are often treated as second-class citizens.

The bodies and brains of males, on the other hand, are stoked by testosterone during adolescence. High testosterone levels are connected with feelings of self-confidence, high activity levels, and aggressiveness, a cluster of traits and behaviors that are more connected with elation (even if sometimes misplaced) than with depression (Pope et al., 2000; Sullivan, 2000).

But women do not have the privileges of men in our society, and social inequality creates many of the problems that lead people to seek therapy (Belle, 1990). This is particularly true among members of oppressed groups, such as women (Brown, 1992). Women—especially single mothers—have lower socioeconomic status than men, and depression and other psychological disorders are more common among poor people (Hobfoll et al., 1995). Even capable, hard-working women are likely to feel depressed when society limits their opportunities (Rothbart & Ahadi, 1994).

A part of "therapy" for women, then, is to modify the overwhelming demands that are placed on women today (Comas-Diaz, 1994). The pain may lie in the individual, but the cause often lies in society.

Now let us consider psychological and biological perspectives on the origins of depression in both women and men.

Psychological Views   Psychoanalysts suggest various explanations for depression. In one, people who are at risk for depression are overly concerned about hurting other people's feelings or losing their approval. As a result, they hold in feelings of anger rather than expressing them. Anger is turned inward and experienced as misery and self-hatred. From the psychodynamic perspective, bipolar disorder may be seen as alternating states in which the personality is first dominated by the superego and then by the ego. In the depressive phase of the disorder, the superego dominates, producing exaggerated ideas of wrongdoing and associated feelings of guilt and worthlessness. After a while the ego asserts supremacy, producing the elation and self-confidence often seen in the manic phase. Later, in response to the excessive display of ego, feelings of guilt return and plunge the person into depression once again.

Many learning theorists suggest that depressed people behave as though they cannot obtain reinforcement. For example, they appear to be inactive and apathetic. Moreover, social-cognitive theorists point out that many people with depressive disorders have an external locus of control. That is, they do not believe they can control events so as to achieve reinforcements (Weisz et al., 1993).

Research conducted by learning theorists has also found links between depression and **learned helplessness.** In classic research, psychologist Martin Seligman taught dogs that they were helpless to escape an electric shock. The dogs were prevented from leaving a cage in which they received repeated shocks. Later, a barrier to a safe compartment was removed, offering the animals a way out. When they were shocked again, however, the dogs made no effort to escape. They had apparently learned that they were helpless. Seligman's dogs were also, in a sense, reinforced for doing nothing. That is, the shock *eventually* stopped when the dogs were showing helpless behavior—inactivity and withdrawal. "Reinforcement" might have increased the likelihood of repeating the "successful behavior"—that is, doing nothing—in a similar situation. This helpless behavior resembles that of people who are depressed.

The concept of learned helplessness bridges the learning and cognitive approaches in that it is an attitude, a general expectation. Other cognitive factors also contribute to depression. For example, perfectionists set themselves up for depression by making irrational demands on themselves. They are likely to fall short of their (unrealistic) expectations and to feel depressed as a result (Blatt et al., 1995; Hewitt et al., 1996).

Cognitive psychologists also note that people who ruminate about feelings of depression are more likely to prolong them (Just & Alloy, 1997). Women are more likely than men to ruminate about feelings of depression (Nolen-Hoeksema et al., 1999). Men

▲ **REFLECT**
Did you ever feel that there was nothing you could do to improve your situation or to solve a personal problem? If so, how did the feeling that you could do nothing affect your mood?

www (15) **WS** (6)
CLICK4™ *a WebSearch activity on coping with depression.*

Learned helplessness ▲ A model for the acquisition of depressive behavior, based on findings that organisms in aversive situations learn to show inactivity when their operants go unreinforced.

Why Did He Miss That Tackle?
This football player is compounding his feelings of depression by attributing his shortcomings on the field to factors that he cannot change. For example, he tells himself that he missed the tackle out of stupidity and lack of athletic ability. He ignores the facts that his coaching was poor and his teammates failed to support him.

▲ **REFLECT**
Do you ever feel depressed? What kinds of experiences lead you to feel depressed? When you fall short of your goals, do you tend to be merciless in your self-criticism or to blame other people or "circumstances"? Do your views of your shortcomings tend to worsen or to ease your feelings of depression?

CLICK4™ *a video on depressive and bipolar disorders.*

CLICK4™ *advice on alleviating depression: getting out of the dumps.*

Attributional style ▲ (at-rib-BYOO-shun-al). One's tendency to attribute one's behavior to internal or external factors, stable or unstable factors, and so on.

Neuroticism ▲ A personality trait characterized largely by persistent anxiety.

seem more likely to try to fight off negative feelings by distracting themselves. Men are also more likely to distract themselves by turning to alcohol (Nolen-Hoeksema, 1991). They thus expose themselves and their families to further problems.

Still other cognitions involve the ways in which people explain their failures and shortcomings to themselves. Seligman (1996) suggests that when things go wrong we may think of the causes of failure as either *internal* or *external*, *stable* or *unstable*, *global* or *specific*. These various **attributional styles** can be illustrated using the example of having a date that does not work out. An internal attribution involves self-blame, as in "I really loused it up." An external attribution places the blame elsewhere (as in "Some couples just don't take to each other," or, "She was the wrong sign for me"). A stable attribution ("It's my personality") suggests a problem that cannot be changed. An unstable attribution ("It was because I had a head cold") suggests a temporary condition. A global attribution of failure ("I have no idea what to do when I'm with other people") suggests that the problem is quite large. A specific attribution ("I have problems making small talk at the beginning of a relationship") chops the problem down to a manageable size.

Research has shown that people who are depressed are more likely to attribute the causes of their failures to internal, stable, and global factors—factors that they are relatively powerless to change (Lewinsohn et al., 2000; Kinderman & Bentall, 1997). Similarly, Nolen-Hoeksema and her colleagues (1999) found that one factor in depression among women is that they tend to have a lower sense of mastery than men do. Such cognitions can give rise to feelings of hopelessness.

Biological Factors Researchers are also searching for biological factors in mood disorders. Depression, for example, is often associated with the trait of **neuroticism,** which is heritable (Clark et al., 1994). Anxiety is also connected with neuroticism, and mood and anxiety disorders are frequently found in the same person (Clark et al., 1994).

Genetic factors appear to be involved in major depression and bipolar disorder (Jamison, 2000; Lewinsohn et al., 2000; Sullivan et al., 2000). There is a higher rate of agreement for bipolar disorder among identical twins than among fraternal twins (Goodwin & Jamison, 1990). Bipolar disorder may be associated with imbalances in the neurotransmitter *glutamate*. Research with mice suggests that too little glutamate may be linked with depression, and too much, with mania (Hokin et al., 1998).

Research into depression focuses on underutilization of the neurotransmitter serotonin in the brain (Yatham et al., 2000). It has been shown, for example, that learned helplessness is connected with lower serotonin levels in the brains of rats (Wu et al., 1999). Moreover, people with severe depression often respond to drugs that heighten the action of serotonin.

Relationships between mood disorders and biological factors are complex and under intense study. Even if people are biologically predisposed toward depression, self-efficacy expectations and attitudes—particularly attitudes about whether one can change things for the better—may also play a role.

Regardless of the origins of the mood disorders, the Click4™ feature on alleviating depression points out a number of things we can do about feelings of depression.

Suicide

About 30,000 people each year take their lives in the United States (CDC, 2000c). *Question: Why do people commit suicide?* Most suicides are linked to feelings of depression and hopelessness (Brown et al., 2000). Other factors in suicide include anxiety, bipolar disorder, drug abuse, problems in school or at work—especially unemployment, and social problems (Brown et al., 2000; Howard-Pitney et al., 1992). Depressed people who do not attempt suicide tend to express relatively more feelings of responsibility toward their family, more moral objections to suicide, and more fear of suicide (Malone et al., 2000). Exposure to other people who are committing suicide can increase the risk of suicide among adolescents (CDC, 1995). Copycat suicides contribute to a so-called "cluster effect" among adolescents.

Suicide attempts are more common after stressful events, especially events that entail loss of social support—as in the loss of a spouse, friend, or relative. People under stress who consider suicide have been found to be less capable of solving problems—particularly interpersonal problems—than nonsuicidal people (Rotheram-Borus et al., 1990; Sadowski & Kelley, 1993; Schotte et al., 1990). Suicidal people thus are less likely to find other ways out of a stressful situation.

Perfectionists are more likely than other people to commit suicide when they are depressed. One possible reason is that perfectionists look upon even small successes as failures (Pilkonis, 1996). Perfectionists are also likely to believe that key people in their lives—their families or their employers—are making demands that they cannot meet (Hewitt et al., 1996).

Suicide, like so many other psychological problems, tends to run in families (CDC, 2000c). Nearly one in four people who attempt suicide reports that a family member has committed suicide (Sorensen & Rutter, 1991). Psychological disorders among family members may also be a factor (Wagner, 1997). The causal connections are unclear, however. Do people who attempt suicide inherit disorders that can lead to suicide? Does the family environment subject family members to feelings of hopelessness? Does the suicide of a family member give a person the idea of committing suicide or create the impression that he or she is somehow fated to commit suicide? What do you think?

DIVERSITY   ### Suicide and Diversity: Who Commits Suicide?

Suicide is connected not only with feelings of depression and stressful events, but also with age, educational status, gender, and ethnicity. *Question: How are sociocultural factors connected with suicide?* Consider some facts about suicide:

▲ Suicide is the third leading cause of death among young people aged 15 to 24 (CDC, 2000c). More teenagers and young adults die from suicide than from cancer, heart disease, AIDS, birth defects, stroke, pneumonia and influenza, and chronic lung disease combined (CDC, 2000c).

▲ Suicide is more common among college students than among people of the same age who do not attend college. Each year about 10,000 college students attempt suicide.

▲ More women than men attempt suicide, but about four times as many men succeed in killing themselves (CDC, 2000c).

▲ Among people who attempt suicide, men prefer to use guns or hang themselves, while women prefer to use sleeping pills. Males, that is, tend to use quicker and more lethal means (CDC, 2000c).

▲ Although African Americans are more likely than European Americans to live in poverty and experience the effects of discrimination, the suicide rate is about twice as high among European Americans (CDC, 2000c).

▲ One in four Native American teenagers has attempted suicide—a rate that is four times higher than that for U.S. teenagers in general (Resnick et al., 1992). Among Zuni adolescents of New Mexico, the rate of completed suicides is more than twice the national rate (Howard-Pitney et al., 1992).

▲ Although teenage suicides loom large in the media spotlight, older people are actually more likely to commit suicide (CDC, 2000c). The suicide rate among older people who are unmarried or divorced is double that of older people who are married (CDC, 2000c).

www 15 E 6

CLICK4™ *essay assignments on depression and suicide.*

Myths About Suicide

You may have heard that individuals who threaten suicide are only seeking attention. Those who are serious just "do it." *Question: What are some of the myths and realities about suicide?*

Some believe that those who fail at suicide attempts are only seeking attention. But many people who commit suicide have made prior attempts (Waters, 2000). Contrary to widespread belief, discussing suicide with a person who is depressed does not prompt the person to attempt suicide (CDC, 1995). Extracting a promise not to commit suicide before calling or visiting a helping professional seems to prevent some suicides.

Some believe that only "insane" people (meaning people who are out of touch with reality) would take their own lives. However, suicidal thinking is not necessarily a sign of

▲ REFLECT

Do you believe that a person would have to be "insane" to want to take his or her own life? Explain.

www 15 WS 7

CLICK4™ *a WebSearch activity: What should you do if you think someone may be contemplating suicide?*

www 15 Q 1

CLICK4™ *a quiz covering the first half of this chapter.*

psychosis, neurosis, or personality disorder. Instead, people may consider suicide when they think they have run out of options (Rotheram-Borus et al., 1990; Schotte et al., 1990).

Regardless of the myths about suicide, there are some things you can do if someone confides in you that he or she is contemplating suicide.

REVIEW

(20) Mood disorders are characterized by disturbance in expressed_____. (21) _____depression can reach psychotic proportions, with grossly impaired reality testing. (22) In bipolar disorder there are mood swings between _____ and depression. (23) Manic people may have grand, delusional schemes and show rapid _____ of ideas. (24) Seligman and his colleagues have explored links between depression and learned _____ . (25) Depressed people are more likely than other people to make (internal or external?), stable, and global attributions for failures. (26) Mood disorders (do or do not?) tend to run in families. (27) Deficiency in the neurotransmitter _____ may create a predisposition toward depression. (28) Three times as many (men as women or women as men?) attempt suicide.

Pulling It Together: When is depression to be considered a psychological disorder? How does bipolar disorder differ from responses to the "ups and downs" of life?

SCHIZOPHRENIA

Jennifer was 19. Her husband David brought her into the emergency room because she had cut her wrists. When she was interviewed, her attention wandered. She

Psychology and Modern Life

Suicide Prevention

Imagine that you are having a heart-to-heart talk with Jamie, one of your best friends. Things haven't been going well. Jamie's grandmother died a month ago, and they were very close. Jamie's coursework has been suffering, and things have also been going downhill with the person Jamie has been seeing. But you are not prepared when Jamie looks you in the eye and says, "I've been thinking about this for days, and I've decided that the only way out is to kill myself."

If someone tells you that he or she is considering suicide, you may become frightened and flustered or feel that an enormous burden has been placed on you. You are right: It has. In such a case your objective should be to encourage the person to consult a health care provider, or to consult one yourself, as soon as possible. But if the person refuses to talk to anyone else and you feel that you can't break free for a consultation, there are a number of things you can do:

1. Keep talking. Encourage the person to talk to you or to some other trusted person (Los Angeles Unified School District, 2000). Draw the person out with questions like "What's happening?" "Where do you hurt?" "What do you want to happen?" Questions like these may encourage the person to express frustrated needs and provide some relief. They also give you time to think.

2. Be a good listener. Be supportive with people who express suicidal thoughts or feel depressed, hopeless, or worthless. They may believe their condition is hopeless and will never improve, but let them know that you are there for them and willing to help them get help. Show that you understand how upset the person is. Do *not* say, "Don't be silly."

3. Suggest that something other than suicide might solve the problem, even if it is not evident at the time. Many suicidal people see only two solutions — either death or a magical resolution of their problems. Therapists try to "remove

A Suicide-Prevention Hotline.

At suicide-prevention centers, staff members stand by hotlines around the clock. If you know someone who is threatening to commit suicide, consult a professional as soon as possible.

seemed distracted by things in the air, or something she might be hearing. It was as if she had an invisible earphone.

She explained that she had cut her wrists because the "hellsmen" had told her to. Then she seemed frightened. Later she said that the hellsmen had warned her not to reveal their existence. She had been afraid that they would punish her for talking about them.

David and Jennifer had been married for about one year. At first they had been together in a small apartment in town. But Jennifer did not want to be near other people and had convinced him to rent a bungalow in the country. There she would make fantastic drawings of goblins and monsters during the days. Now and then she would become agitated and act as if invisible things were giving her instructions.

"I'm bad," Jennifer would mutter. "I'm bad." She would begin to jumble her words. David would then try to convince her to go to the hospital, but she would refuse. Then the wrist-cutting would begin. David thought he had made the cottage safe by removing knives and blades. But Jennifer would always find something.

Then Jennifer would be brought to the hospital, have stitches put in, be kept under observation for a while, and medicated. She would explain that she cut herself because the hellsmen had told her that she was bad and must die. After a few days she would deny hearing the hellsmen, and she would insist on leaving the hospital.

David would take her home. The pattern continued.

When the emergency room staff examined Jennifer's wrists and heard that she believed she had been following the orders of "hellsmen," they suspected that she could be diagnosed with schizophrenia. *Question: What is schizophrenia?* Schizophrenia is a severe psychological disorder that touches every aspect of a person's life. It is characterized by disturbances in thought and language, perception and attention, motor activity, and mood, and withdrawal and absorption in daydreams or fantasy.

CLICK4™ *a WebSearch activity comparing schizophrenia and dissociative disorder.*

CLICK4™ *Web sites about schizophrenia.*

---

the mental blinders" from suicidal people.

4. Emphasize as concretely as possible how the person's suicide would be devastating to you and to other people who care.

5. Ask how the person intends to commit suicide. People with concrete plans and a weapon are at greater risk. Ask if you might hold on to the weapon for a while. Sometimes the answer is yes.

6. Suggest that the person go *with you* to obtain professional help *now.* The emergency room of a general hospital, the campus counseling center or infirmary, or the campus or local police station will do. Some campuses have hotlines you can call. Some cities have suicide prevention centers with hotlines that people can use anonymously.

7. Extract a promise that the person will not commit suicide before seeing you again. Arrange a specific time and place to meet. Get professional help as soon as you are apart.

8. Do *not* tell people threatening suicide that they're silly or crazy. Do *not* insist on contact with specific people, such as parents or a spouse. Conflict with these people may have led to the suicidal thinking in the first place.

Resources

You can also check out the following resources:

- The national suicide hotline: 1-800-SUICIDE (1-800-784-2433).
- American Association of Suicidology: Their Web site, **www.suicidology.org**, provides information on ways to prevent suicide. You will also find a list of crisis centers.
- American Foundation for Suicide Prevention: Their Web site, **www.afsp.org**, offers information about suicide and links to other suicide and mental health sites.
- American Psychological Association (APA): The APA Web site, **www.apa.org**, provides information about risk factors, warning signs, and prevention.
- National Institute of Mental Health (NIMH): The Web site, **www.nimh.nih.gov**, contains information on depression and other psychological disorders.
- Suicide Awareness–Voices of Education (SA\VE): SA\VE's Web site, **www.save.org**, offers educational and practical information on suicide and depression. It highlights ways in which family members and friends can help suicidal people.
- Suicide Information & Education Centre (SIEC): SIEC's Web site, **www.siec.ca**, offers a specialized library on suicide.

Schizophrenia has been referred to as the worst disorder affecting human beings (Carpenter & Buchanan, 1994). It afflicts nearly 1% of the population worldwide. Its onset occurs relatively early in life, and its adverse effects tend to endure.

People with schizophrenia have problems in memory, attention, and communication (Docherty et al., 1996). Their thinking becomes unraveled. Unless we are allowing our thoughts to wander, our thinking is normally tightly knit. We start at a certain point, and thoughts that come to mind (the associations) tend to be logically connected. But people with schizophrenia often think illogically. Their speech may be jumbled. They may combine parts of words into new words or make meaningless rhymes. They may jump from topic to topic, conveying little useful information. They usually do not recognize that their thoughts and behavior are abnormal.

Many people with schizophrenia have **delusions**—for example, delusions of grandeur, persecution, or reference. In the case of delusions of grandeur, a person may believe that he is a famous historical figure such as Jesus, or a person on a special mission. He may have grand, illogical plans for saving the world. Delusions tend to be unshakable even in the face of evidence that they are not true. People with delusions of persecution may believe that they are sought by the Mafia, CIA, FBI, or some other group. A woman with delusions of reference said that news stories contained coded information about her. A man with such delusions complained that neighbors had "bugged" his walls with "radios." Other people with schizophrenia have had delusions that they have committed unpardonable sins, that they were rotting away from disease, or that they or the world did not exist.

The perceptions of people with schizophrenia often include hallucinations—imagery in the absence of external stimulation that the person cannot distinguish from reality. In Shakespeare's *Macbeth*, for example, after killing King Duncan, Macbeth apparently experiences a hallucination:

> Is this a dagger which I see before me,
> The handle toward my hand? Come, let me clutch thee:
> I have thee not, and yet I see thee still.
> Art thou not, fatal vision, sensible
> To feeling as to sight? or art thou but
> A dagger of the mind, a false creation,
> Proceeding from the heat-oppressed brain?

Jennifer apparently hallucinated the voices of "hellsmen." Other people who experience hallucinations may see colors or even obscene words spelled out in midair. Auditory hallucinations are the most common type.

In individuals with schizophrenia, motor activity may become wild or become so slow that the person is said to be in a **stupor.** There may be strange gestures and facial expressions. The person's emotional responses may be flat or blunted, or inappropriate—as in giggling upon hearing bad news. People with schizophrenia have problems understanding other people's feelings (Penn et al., 1997), tend to withdraw from social contacts, and become wrapped up in their own thoughts and fantasies. *Question: What kinds of schizophrenia are there?*

Types of Schizophrenia

There are three major types of schizophrenia: paranoid, disorganized, and catatonic.

Paranoid Type

People with **paranoid schizophrenia** have systematized delusions and, frequently, related auditory hallucinations. They usually have delusions of grandeur and persecution, but they may also have delusions of jealousy, in which they believe that a spouse or lover has been unfaithful. They may show agitation, confusion, and fear, and may experience vivid hallucinations that are consistent with their delusions. People with paranoid schizophrenia often construct complex or systematized delusions involving themes of wrongdoing or persecution.

Delusions ▲ False, persistent beliefs that are unsubstantiated by sensory or objective evidence.

Stupor ▲ (STEW-pour). A condition in which the senses and thought are dulled.

Paranoid schizophrenia ▲ A type of schizophrenia characterized primarily by delusions—commonly of persecution—and by vivid hallucinations.

Paranoid Schizophrenia.

People with paranoid schizophrenia have systematized delusions, often involving the idea that they are being persecuted or are on a special mission. Although they cannot be argued out of their delusions, their cognitive functioning is relatively intact compared with that of disorganized and catatonic schizophrenics.

Disorganized Type   People with **disorganized schizophrenia** show incoherence, loosening of associations, disorganized behavior, disorganized delusions, fragmentary delusions or hallucinations, and flat or highly inappropriate emotional responses. Extreme social impairment is common. People with this type of schizophrenia may also exhibit silliness and giddiness of mood, giggling, and nonsensical speech. They may neglect their appearance and personal hygiene and lose control of their bladder and bowels.

Catatonic Type   People with **catatonic schizophrenia** show striking impairment in motor activity. It is characterized by a slowing of activity into a stupor that may suddenly change into an agitated phase. Catatonic individuals may maintain unusual, even difficult postures for hours, even as their limbs grow swollen or stiff. A striking feature of this condition is **waxy flexibility,** in which the person maintains positions into which he or she has been manipulated by others. Catatonic individuals may also show **mutism,** but afterward they usually report that they heard what others were saying at the time.

Schizophrenia is thus characterized by extremely unusual behavior. ***Question: What is known about the origins of schizophrenia?***

Theoretical Views

Psychologists have investigated various factors that may contribute to schizophrenia. They include psychological and biological factors.

Psychological Views   According to the psychodynamic perspective, schizophrenia occurs because the ego is overwhelmed by sexual or aggressive impulses from the id. The impulses threaten the ego and cause intense inner conflict. Under this threat, the person regresses to an early phase of the oral stage in which the infant has not yet learned that it and the world are separate. Fantasies become confused with reality, giving rise to hallucinations and delusions. Yet critics point out that schizophrenic behavior is not the same as infantile behavior.

Most learning theorists explain schizophrenia in terms of conditioning and observational learning. From this perspective, people engage in schizophrenic behavior when it is more likely to be reinforced than normal behavior. This may occur when a person is reared in a socially unrewarding or punitive situation. Inner fantasies then become more reinforcing than social realities.

Patients in a psychiatric hospital may learn what is "expected" by observing others. Hospital staff may reinforce schizophrenic behavior by paying more attention to patients who behave bizarrely. This view is consistent with folklore that the child who disrupts the class attracts more attention from the teacher than the "good" child.

Although quality of parenting is connected with the development of schizophrenia (Michels & Marzuk, 1993a), critics note that many people who are reared in socially punitive settings are apparently immune to the extinction of socially appropriate behavior. Other people develop schizophrenic behavior without having had opportunities to observe other people with schizophrenia.

Many investigators have considered whether and how social and cultural factors such as poverty, discrimination, and overcrowding contribute to schizophrenia—especially among people who are genetically vulnerable to the disorder. Classic research in New Haven, Connecticut, showed that the rate of schizophrenia was twice as high in the lowest socioeconomic class as in the next-higher class on the socioeconomic ladder (Hollingshead & Redlich, 1958). It appears that poor-quality housing contributes to psychological disorder (Evans et al., 2000). Some sociocultural theorists therefore suggest that treatment of schizophrenia requires alleviation of poverty and other social ills, rather than changing people whose behavior is deviant.

Critics of this view suggest that low socioeconomic status may be a result, rather than a cause, of schizophrenia. People with schizophrenia may drift toward low social status because they lack the social skills and cognitive abilities to function at higher social class levels. Thus, they may wind up in poor neighborhoods in disproportionately high numbers.

Catatonic Schizophrenia.
People with catatonic schizophrenia show striking motor impairment and may hold unusual positions for hours.

Disorganized schizophrenia ▲ A type of schizophrenia characterized by disorganized delusions and vivid hallucinations.
Catatonic schizophrenia ▲ A type of schizophrenia characterized by striking impairment in motor activity.
Waxy flexibility ▲ A feature of catatonic schizophrenia in which persons maintain postures into which they are placed.
Mutism ▲ (MU-tizm). Refusal to talk.

Evidence for the hypothesis that people with schizophrenia drift downward to lower socioeconomic status is mixed. Many people with schizophrenia do drift downward occupationally in comparison with their fathers' occupations. Many others, however, were reared in families in which the father came from the lowest socioeconomic class. Because the stresses of poverty may play a role in the development of schizophrenia, many researchers are interested in the possible interactions between psychosocial stressors and biological factors (Carpenter & Buchanan, 1994).

Biological Views

Schizophrenia appears to be a brain disorder. Many studies have been done to determine how the brains of schizophrenic people differ from those of others. Some studies have focused on structures in the brain, such as the size of ventricles (hollow spaces), others on activity levels in the brain, still others on brain chemistry (e.g., neurotransmitters).

One avenue of brain research connects the major deficits we find in schizophrenia—problems in attention, working memory, abstract thinking, and language—with dysfunction in the prefrontal cortex of the brain. Imaging of the brain has shown that people with schizophrenia have smaller brains than other people and, in particular, a smaller prefrontal region of the cortex (Flashman et al., 2000; Selemon, 2000; Staal et al., 2000). On the other hand, people with schizophrenia tend to have larger ventricles in the brain than other people (Wright et al., 2000). PET scans reveal that people with schizophrenia also tend to have a lower level of activity in the frontal region of the brain (Kim et al., 2000). Still other research connects the lower activity levels with a loss in synapses (the structures that permit communication between neurons) in the region (Glantz & Lewis, 2000; McGlashan & Hoffman, 2000; Selemon, 2000).

What might account for differences in brain structure and functioning? Research evidence suggests that there are a number of biological risk factors for schizophrenia, such as heredity, complications during pregnancy and birth, and birth during winter (Carpenter & Buchanan, 1994). Schizophrenia, like many other psychological disorders, runs in families (Cannon et al., 1998; Kendler et al., 1997). People with schizophrenia constitute about 1% of the population. Yet children with one parent who has been diagnosed with schizophrenia have about a 10% chance of being diagnosed with schizophrenia themselves. Children with two such parents have about a 35%–40% chance of being so diagnosed (Gottesman, 1991; Straube & Oades, 1992). Twin studies also find about a 40% to 50% concordance rate for the diagnosis among pairs of identical (MZ) twins, whose genetic codes are the same, compared with about a 10% rate among pairs of fraternal (DZ) twins (Gottesman, 1991; Straube & Oades, 1992). Moreover, adoptee studies find that the biological parent typically places the child at greater risk for schizophrenia than the adoptive parent—even though the child has been reared by the adoptive parent (Gottesman, 1991). Sharing genes with relatives who have schizophrenia apparently places a person at risk of developing the disorder. Many studies have been carried out to try to isolate the gene or genes involved in schizophrenia. Some studies find locations for multiple genes on several chromosomes. Recent research suggests that a gene on Chromosome 1 may provide the vulnerability to schizophrenia (Brzustowicz et al., 2000).

But heredity is not the only factor that creates a vulnerability to schizophrenia. If it were, we would expect a 100% concordance rate between identical twins, as opposed to the 40% to 50% rate we find (Carpenter & Buchanan, 1994). It also turns out that many people with schizophrenia have undergone complications during pregnancy and birth (Rosso et al., 2000). For example, the mothers of many people with schizophrenia had the flu during the sixth or seventh month of pregnancy (Barr et al., 1990). Poor maternal nutrition has also been implicated (Pol et al., 2000). Complications during childbirth, especially prolonged labor, seem to be connected with the larger ventricles we find among people with schizophrenia (McNeil et al., 2000). People with schizophrenia are also somewhat more likely to have been born during winter than would be predicted by chance (Pol et al., 2000). Alcohol abuse is another risk factor for differences in brain structures among people diagnosed with schizophrenia (Sullivan et al., 2000). Taken together, these biological risk factors suggest that schizophrenia involves atypical development of the central nervous system. Problems in the nervous system may involve brain chemistry as well as brain structures, and research along these lines has led to the dopamine theory of schizophrenia.

CLICK4™ *an essay assignment: How have advances in biological psychology and brain imaging advanced the study of schizophrenia?*

▲ REFLECT

There is evidence for a genetic role in schizophrenia. What would you tell the son or daughter of a person with schizophrenia about the likelihood of his or her developing schizophrenia? Explain.

CD 15 V 39

CLICK4™ *a video on the symptoms of schizophrenia.*

CD 15 V 40

CLICK4™ *a video on the possible causes of schizophrenia.*

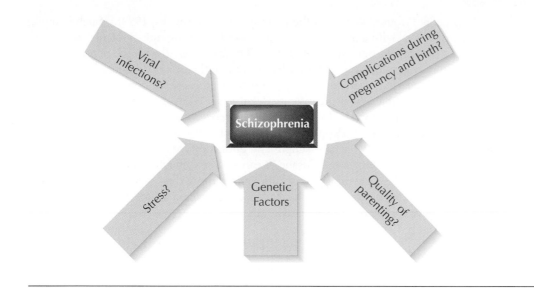

FIGURE 15.2   A Multifactorial Model of Schizophrenia.
According to the multifactorial model of schizophrenia, people with a genetic vulnerability to the disorder experience increased risk for schizophrenia when they encounter problems such as viral infections, birth complications, stress, and poor parenting. People without the genetic vulnerability would not develop schizophrenia despite such problems.

The Dopamine Theory of Schizophrenia   Numerous chemical substances have been suspected of playing a role in schizophrenia, and much research has focused on the neurotransmitter dopamine. According to the dopamine theory of schizophrenia, people with schizophrenia overutilize dopamine (use more of it than other people do) although they may not produce more of it. Why? Research suggests that they have increased concentrations of dopamine at the synapses in the brain and also larger numbers of dopamine receptors (Butcher, 2000). It's a sort of "double hit" of neural transmission that may be connected with the confusion that characterizes schizophrenia.

Because many psychological and biological factors have been implicated in schizophrenia, most investigators today favor a *multifactorial* model. According to this model, genetic factors create a predisposition toward schizophrenia (see Figure 15.2). Genetic vulnerability to the disorder interacts with other factors, such as complications during pregnancy and birth, stress, and quality of parenting, to cause the disorder to develop (Michels & Marzuk, 1993a).

Because the perceptions and judgment of people with schizophrenia are impaired, the diagnosis is sometimes associated with the insanity plea in the criminal courts. How popular is the insanity plea—among criminals and in society at large? Let us look into the controversy surrounding the plea.

CONTROVERSY IN PSYCHOLOGY
Should We Ban the Insanity Plea?

Forensic psychologists apply psychological knowledge in the evaluation of people who commit crimes. They testify about defendants' competence to stand trial or participate in their own defense, as well as about whether defendants should be found not guilty by reason of insanity. For example, John Hinckley was found not guilty of a 1981 assassination attempt on President Ronald Reagan by reason of insanity. Hinckley was diagnosed with schizophrenia and committed to a psychiatric institution rather than given a prison term. He remains there to this day.

In pleading insanity, lawyers use the M'Naghten rule, named after Daniel M'Naghten, who tried to assassinate the British prime minister, Sir Robert Peel, in 1843. M'Naghten had delusions that Peel was persecuting him, and he killed Peel's secretary in the attempt. The court found M'Naghten not guilty by reason of insanity, referring to what has become the M'Naghten rule. It states that the accused did not understand what she or he was doing at the time of the act, did not realize it was wrong, or was succumbing to an irresistible impulse. Today the insanity plea tends to be used in much the same way—when the person accused of the crime could not understand that the criminal act was illegal or wrong, or when he or she could not control his or her behavior (Gutheil, 1999; Rosenfeld & Wall, 1998).

CLICK4™ *a bulletin board discussion: Should we ban the insanity plea?*

Many people would like to ban the insanity plea (DeAngelis, 1994b). Such banning "is an attempt to deal with a perception that the world is getting more violent," notes psychologist/lawyer Donald Bersoff (1994, p. 28). "That's combined with the perception that people are literally getting away with murder because of the insanity defense."

Practically speaking, there may not be all that much cause for concern, however. Although the public estimates that the insanity defense is used in about 37% of felony cases, it is actually raised in only 1% (Silver, 1994). Moreover, the insanity plea may be no bargain for people who use it. People found to be not guilty by reason of insanity are institutionalized for indefinite terms—supposedly until they are no longer insane. If it can be difficult to prove that someone is insane, it can also be difficult to prove that he or she is no longer insane. Hinckley remains institutionalized more than two decades after he attempted to kill President Reagan. If he had been convicted of attempted murder, he might already have completed a specific sentence.

REVIEW

(29) Schizophrenic disorders are characterized by disturbances in _____ and language (as in the loosening of associations and in delusions); in perception and attention (as in hallucinations); in motor activity; in mood; and by withdrawal and autism. (30) Paranoid schizophrenia is characterized by paranoid _____. (31) _____ schizophrenia is characterized by impaired motor activity and waxy flexibility. (32) Schizophrenia (does or does not?) tend to run in families. (33) The prefrontal region of the brain of people with schizophrenia has (more or fewer?) synapses than those of other people. (34) People with schizophrenia utilize more of the neurotransmitter _____ than other people do.

Pulling It Together: How has brain imaging advanced the study of schizophrenia? What kinds of life events are connected with problems in the brain that may lie at the root of schizophrenia?

PERSONALITY DISORDERS

Personality disorders, like personality traits, are characterized by enduring patterns of behavior. Personality disorders, however, are inflexible and maladaptive. They impair personal or social functioning and are a source of distress to the individual or to other people. *Question: What kinds of personality disorders are there?*

Types of Personality Disorders

There are a number of personality disorders. They include the paranoid, schizotypal, schizoid, antisocial, and avoidant personality disorders. The defining trait of the **paranoid personality disorder** is a tendency to interpret other people's behavior as threatening or demeaning. People with the disorder do not show the grossly disorganized thinking of paranoid schizophrenia. However, they are mistrustful of others, and their relationships suffer for it. They may be suspicious of coworkers and supervisors, but they can generally hold a job.

Schizotypal personality disorder is characterized by peculiarities of thought, perception, or behavior, such as excessive fantasy and suspiciousness, feelings of being unreal, or odd usage of words. The bizarre behaviors that characterize schizophrenia are absent, so this disorder is schizo*typal*, not schizophrenic.

The **schizoid personality** is defined by indifference to relationships and flat emotional response. People with this disorder are "loners." They do not develop warm, tender feelings for others. They have few friends and rarely get married. Some people with schizoid personality disorder do very well on the job provided that continuous social interaction is not required. They do not have hallucinations or delusions.

People with **antisocial personality disorder** persistently violate the rights of others and are often in conflict with the law (see Table 15.2). They often show a superficial charm and are at least average in intelligence. Striking features are their lack of guilt or anxiety about their misdeeds and their failure to learn from punishment or to form mean-

---

▲ **REFLECT**

Sick people may be excused from school or work. If some criminals are "sick" in the sense of being diagnosed with antisocial personality disorder, does the disorder relieve them of responsibility for criminal behavior? Explain.

Personality disorders ▲ Enduring patterns of maladaptive behavior that are sources of distress to the individual or others.

Paranoid personality disorder ▲ A disorder characterized by persistent suspiciousness, but not involving the disorganization of paranoid schizophrenia.

Schizotypal personality disorder ▲ A disorder characterized by oddities of thought and behavior, but not involving bizarre psychotic behaviors.

Schizoid personality disorder ▲ A disorder characterized by social withdrawal.

Antisocial personality disorder ▲ The diagnosis given a person who is in frequent conflict with society, yet who is undeterred by punishment and experiences little or no guilt and anxiety.

ingful bonds with other people (Levenston ct al., 2000; Widiger et al., 1996). Though they are often heavily punished by their parents and rejected by peers, they continue in their impulsive, careless styles of life. Women are more likely than men to have anxiety and depressive disorders. Men are more likely than women to have antisocial personality disorder (Sutker, 1994).

People with **avoidant personality disorder** are generally unwilling to enter a relationship without some assurance of acceptance because they fear rejection and criticism. As a result, they may have few close relationships outside their immediate families. Unlike people with schizoid personality disorder, however, they have some interest in, and feelings of warmth toward, other people. *Question: What is known about the origins of personality disorders?*

TABLE 15.2
CHARACTERISTICS OF PEOPLE DIAGNOSED WITH ANTISOCIAL PERSONALITY DISORDER

Key Characteristics	Other Common Characteristics
History of delinquency and truancy	Lack of loyalty or of formation of enduring relationships
Persistent violation of the rights of others	Failure to maintain good job performance over the years
Impulsiveness	
Poor self-control	Failure to develop or adhere to a life plan
Lack of remorse for misdeeds	Sexual promiscuity
Lack of empathy	Substance abuse
Deceitfulness and manipulativeness	Inability to tolerate boredom
Irresponsibility	Low tolerance for frustration
Glibness; superficial charm	Irritability
Exaggerated sense of self-worth	

SOURCES: Levenston et al., 2000; Widiger et al., 1996.

Theoretical Views

Psychological Views   Many of the theoretical explanations of personality disorders are derived from the psychodynamic model. Traditional Freudian theory focuses on Oedipal problems as the source of many psychological disorders, including personality disorders. Faulty resolution of the Oedipus complex might lead to antisocial personality disorder, since the moral conscience, or superego, is believed to depend on proper resolution of the Oedipus complex. Research evidence supports the theory that lack of guilt, a frequent characteristic of people with antisocial personality disorder, is more likely to develop among children who are rejected and punished by their parents rather than given warmth and affection (Baumeister et al., 1994; Zahn-Waxler & Kochanska, 1990).

Learning theorists suggest that childhood experiences can contribute to maladaptive ways of relating to others in adulthood—that is, can lead to personality disorders. Cognitive psychologists find that antisocial adolescents encode social information in ways that bolster their misdeeds. For example, they tend to interpret other people's behavior as threatening, even when it is not (Crick & Dodge, 1994; Lochman, 1992). Cognitive therapists have encouraged some antisocial adolescents to view social provocations as problems to be solved rather than as threats to their "manhood," with some favorable initial results (Lochman, 1992).

Biological Views   Genetic factors are apparently involved in some personality disorders (Rutter, 1997). Personality traits are to some degree heritable (Plomin, 2000), and many personality disorders seem to be extreme variations of normal personality traits. Referring to the five-factor model of personality, people with schizoid personalities tend to be highly introverted (Widiger & Costa, 1994). People with avoidant personalities tend to be both introverted and emotionally unstable (neurotic) (Widiger & Costa, 1994).

It is also known that antisocial personality disorder tends to run in families. Adoptee studies reveal higher incidences of antisocial behavior among the biological parents than among the adoptive relatives of individuals with the disorder (DiLalla & Gottesman, 1991).

Perhaps the genetics of antisocial personality disorder involve the prefrontal cortex of the brain, a part of the brain connected with emotional responses. There is some evidence that people with antisocial personality disorder, as a group, have less gray matter (associative neurons) in the prefrontal cortex of the brain than other people (Damasio, 2000; Raine et al., 2000). The lesser amount of gray matter could lessen the level of arousal of the nervous system. As a result, it would be more difficult to condition fear responses. People with the disorder would then be unlikely to show guilt for their misdeeds and would seem to be unafraid of punishment. But a biological factor such as a lower-than-normal level of arousal would not by itself cause the development of an antisocial personality (Rutter, 1997). Perhaps a person must also be reared under conditions that do not foster the self-concept of a law-abiding citizen.

Avoidant personality disorder ▲ A personality disorder in which the person is generally unwilling to enter relationships without assurance of acceptance because of fears of rejection and criticism.

CLICK4™ *a bulletin board discussion: Does the diagnosis of a personality disorder relieve the individual of responsibility for criminal behavior?*

A Person With an Antisocial Personality.
Some people with antisocial personalities fit the stereotype of the amoral, violent career criminal. Gary Gilmore was executed after being convicted of two murders. As a child, Gilmore showed conduct problems at home and in school. He began a violent career in adolescence. He never held a steady job or maintained a committed relationship. Though he was intentionally cruel, he never showed guilt or remorse for his misdeeds.

CLICK4™ *a WebSearch activity: What kinds of personality disorders are there?*

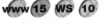

CLICK4™ *an essay assignment: What's the difference between people who have "bad personalities" and those who have personality disorders?*

CLICK4™ *an online questionnaire: Do you show symptoms of an eating disorder?*

REVIEW

(35) _____ disorders are inflexible, maladaptive behavior patterns that impair personal or social functioning and are a source of distress to the individual or to others. (36) The defining trait of the _____ personality is suspiciousness. (37) Social _____ is the major characteristic of the schizoid personality. (38) Persons with _____ personality disorder violate the rights of others, show little or no guilt for their misdeeds, and are undeterred by punishment. (39) Research suggests that people with antisocial personalities have (higher or lower?)-than-normal levels of arousal than most people. (40) Their levels of arousal may be connected with lower-than-normal levels of (white or gray?) matter in the prefrontal cortex.

Pulling It Together: What is the difference between people with "bad personalities" and people with personality disorders?

EATING DISORDERS

Most of us either deprive ourselves or consume vast quantities of food now and then. This is normal. The **eating disorders** listed in the DSM are characterized by persistent, gross disturbances in eating patterns. *Question: What kinds of eating disorders are there?*

Types of Eating Disorders

The major eating disorders are anorexia nervosa and bulimia nervosa.

Anorexia Nervosa   There is a saying that you can never be too rich or too thin. Excess money may be pleasant enough, but, as in the case of Karen, one can certainly be too thin.

> Karen was the 22-year-old daughter of a renowned English professor. She had begun her college career full of promise at the age of 17. But two years ago, after "social problems" occurred, she had returned to live at home and taken progressively lighter course loads at a local college. Karen had never been overweight, but about a year ago her mother noticed that she seemed to be gradually "turning into a skeleton."
>
> Karen spent hours every day shopping at the supermarket, butcher, and bakeries; and in conjuring up gourmet treats for her parents and younger siblings. Arguments over her lifestyle and eating habits had divided the family into two camps. The camp led by her father called for patience. That headed by her mother demanded confrontation. Her mother feared that Karen's father would "protect her right into her grave" and wanted Karen placed in residential treatment "for her own good." The parents finally compromised on an outpatient evaluation.
>
> At an even 5 feet, Karen looked like a prepubescent 11-year-old. Her nose and cheekbones protruded crisply, like those of an elegant young fashion model. Her lips were full, but the redness of the lipstick was unnatural, as if too much paint had been dabbed on a corpse for the funeral. Karen weighed only 78 pounds, but she had dressed in a stylish silk blouse, scarf, and baggy pants so that not one inch of her body was revealed. More striking than her mouth was the redness of her rouged cheeks. It was unclear whether she had used too much makeup or whether minimal makeup had caused the stark contrast between the parts of her face that were covered and those that were not.
>
> Karen vehemently denied that she had a problem. Her figure was "just about where I want it to be" and she engaged in aerobic exercise daily. A deal was struck in which outpatient treatment would be tried as long as Karen lost no more weight and showed steady gains back to at least 90 pounds. Treatment included a day hospital with group therapy and two meals a day. But word came back that Karen was artfully toying with her food—cutting it up, sort of licking it, and moving it about her plate—rather than eating it. After three weeks Karen had lost another pound. At that point her parents were able to persuade her to enter a residential treatment program where her eating could be carefully monitored.

Eating disorders ▲ Psychological disorders that are characterized by distortion of the body image and gross disturbances in eating patterns.

Anorexia nervosa ▲ A life-threatening eating disorder characterized by refusal to maintain a healthful body weight, intense fear of being overweight, a distorted body image, and, in females, lack of menstruation (amenorrhea).

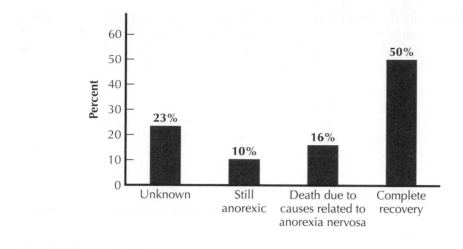

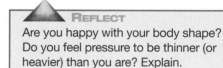

FIGURE 15.3 Results of a British Study of Outcomes for Women Diagnosed With Anorexia Nervosa, 21 Years After First Hospitalization (in percentages). Although the outcomes shown here are pessimistic, note that they apply only to women who were hospitalized for anorexia nervosa. In many cases, the psychological disorder is treated on an outpatient basis. Women who are hospitalized with the disorder impress their physicians as being in relatively greater danger.

Karen was diagnosed with **anorexia nervosa,** a life-threatening disorder characterized by refusal to maintain a healthful body weight, intense fear of being overweight, a distorted body image, and, in women, lack of menstruation (amenorrhea). People with anorexia usually weigh less than 85% of what would be considered a healthy weight.

By and large, eating disorders afflict women during adolescence and young adulthood (Heatherton et al., 1997; Winzelberg et al., 2000). The typical person in the United States with anorexia or bulimia is a young European American female of higher socioeconomic status. The incidences of anorexia nervosa and bulimia nervosa have increased markedly in recent years. Women with anorexia greatly outnumber men with the disorder. Not only are eating disorders distressing and dangerous in themselves, but they also frequently set the stage for severe depression (Stice et al., 2000).

Women with anorexia may lose 25% or more of their body weight in a year. Severe weight loss stops ovulation (Frisch, 1997). Their overall health declines. A British study attempted to contact 84 women who had been hospitalized 21 years earlier for anorexia (Zipfel et al., 2000). The researchers found that about half of the women had achieved complete recovery; nearly 16% had died from causes related to anorexia, such as weakness or imbalances in body chemistry; about 10% were still anorexic; and the remaining 23% could not be contacted or had outcomes that were unclear (Figure 15.3). These outcomes seem rather severe, but they resulted only from women who had been hospitalized for anorexia. Women with less serious cases may not require hospitalization. Overall, the mortality rate is estimated to be closer to 4% to 5%.

In the typical pattern, a girl notices some weight gain after menarche and decides that it must come off. However, dieting—and, often, exercise—continue at a fever pitch. They persist even after the girl reaches an average weight, and even after family members and others have told her that she is losing too much. Girls with anorexia almost always adamantly deny that they are wasting away. They may point to their fierce exercise regimens as proof. Their body image is distorted (Williamson et al., 1993; Winzelberg et al., 2000). Penner and his colleagues (1991) studied women who averaged 31% below their ideal body weight according to Metropolitan Life Insurance Company charts. The women, ironically, overestimated the size of parts of their bodies by 31%! Other people perceive women with anorexia as "skin and bones." The women themselves frequently sit before the mirror and see themselves as heavy.

Many people with anorexia become obsessed with food. They engross themselves in cookbooks, take on the family shopping chores, and prepare elaborate dinners—for others.

Bulimia Nervosa

The case of Nicole is a vivid account of a young woman who was diagnosed with bulimia nervosa:

Nicole awakens in her cold dark room and already wishes it was time to go back to bed. She dreads the thought of going through this day, which will be like so many others in her recent past. She asks herself the question every morning, "Will I be able to

> ◢ **REFLECT**
> Are you happy with your body shape? Do you feel pressure to be thinner (or heavier) than you are? Explain.

On a Binge.
Bulimia nervosa is characterized by recurrent cycles of binge eating and purging. Why do more women than men have eating disorders?

make it through the day without being totally obsessed by thoughts of food, or will I blow it again and spend the day [binge eating]"? She tells herself that today she will begin a new life, today she will start to live like a normal human being. However, she is not at all convinced that the choice is hers. (Boskind-White & White, 1983, p. 29)

It turns out that this day Nicole begins by eating eggs and toast. Then she binges on cookies; doughnuts; bagels smothered with butter, cream cheese, and jelly; granola; candy bars; and bowls of cereal and milk—all within 45 minutes. When she cannot take in any more food, she turns her attention to purging. She goes to the bathroom, ties back her hair, turns on the shower to mask any noise she will make, drinks a glass of water, and makes herself vomit. Afterward she vows, "Starting tomorrow, I'm going to change." But she knows that tomorrow she will probably do the same thing.

Bulimia nervosa is characterized by recurrent cycles of binge eating followed by dramatic measures to purge the food. Binge eating frequently follows food deprivation—for example, severe dieting (Lowe et al., 1996). Purging includes self-induced vomiting, fasting or strict dieting, use of laxatives, and vigorous exercise. People with bulimia are often perfectionistic about body shape and weight (Joiner et al., 1997). Like anorexia, bulimia afflicts many more women than men. *Question: What is known about the origins of eating disorders?*

Theoretical Views

Numerous explanations of anorexia nervosa and bulimia nervosa have been proposed. Let us begin our investigation by referring to the gender gap in the eating disorders. It's huge.

Eating Disorders and Gender: Why the Gender Gap?

The typical person with anorexia or bulimia is a young European American female of higher socioeconomic status. Women with eating disorders outnumber men with them by at least 6 to 1 (Goode, 2000).

Theorists account for the gender gap in different ways. Because anorexia is connected with amenorrhea, some psychodynamic theorists suggest that anorexia represents a female's effort to revert to prepubescence. Anorexia allows her to avoid growing up, separate from her family, and assume adult responsibilities. Because of the loss of fat tissue, her breasts and hips flatten. In her fantasies, perhaps, a woman with anorexia remains a child, sexually undifferentiated.

Social cognitive approaches suggest that weight loss has strong reinforcement value because it provides feelings of personal perfectibility (Vitousek & Manke, 1994). Yet "perfection" is an impossible goal for most people. Fashion models, who represent the female ideal, are 9% taller and 16% slimmer than the average woman (Williams, 1992). Sixteen percent! For most women, that is at least 16 pounds!

Consider the sociocultural aspects of eating disorders: The quintessential U.S. role model, Miss America, like a fashion model, has also been slimming down over the years. Since the beginning of the pageant in 1922, the winner of the contest has gained 2% in height but lost 12 lbs in weight. In the 1920s, her weight as compared to her height was in what is today considered the "normal" range, according to the World Health Organization (WHO)—that is, a Body Mass Index[3] in the 20–25 range. WHO considers people with a BMI lower than 18.5 to be undernourished, and many recent Miss Americas have a BMI of about 17 (Rubinstein & Caballero, 2000). Miss America has become another undernourished role model. As the cultural ideal grows slimmer, women with average or heavier-than-average figures feel more pressure to slim down (Winzelberg et al., 2000).

Many men with eating disorders are involved in sports or occupations that require them to retain a certain weight, such as dancing, wrestling, and modeling (Goode, 2000). (Women ballet dancers are also at special risk of developing eating disorders [Dunning,

www 15 BBC 7

CLICK4™ *a bulletin board discussion: Why are females more likely than males to develop eating disorders?*

www 15 E 9

CLICK4™ *an essay assignment: Why might there be sociocultural differences in the occurrence of eating disorders?*

Bulimia nervosa ▲ An eating disorder characterized by recurrent cycles of binge eating followed by dramatic measures to purge the food.

---

[3]You can calculate your Body Mass Index (BMI) as follows. Multiple your weight in pounds by 703. Divide the product by your height in inches squared. (Yes, I know I already gave you the formula in Chapter 9. I thought I would repeat myself rather than ask you to turn back to that chapter. I thought I would repeat myself rather than ask you to turn back to that chapter.)

1997].) Men are more likely than women to control their weight through intense exercise. Men, like women, are under social pressure to conform to an ideal body image—one that builds their upper bodies and trims their abdomens (Goode, 2000). Gay males tend to be more concerned about their body shape than heterosexual males, and are therefore more vulnerable to eating disorders (Strong et al., 2000).

Now let us consider some other perspectives on the eating disorders.

Perspectives on the Eating Disorders   Some psychoanalysts suggest that anorexia represents an unconscious effort by the girl to cope with sexual fears, particularly the prospect of pregnancy. Others suggest that adolescents may use refusal to eat as a weapon against their parents. Studies have compared parents of adolescents with eating disorders with parents of adolescents without such problems. Parents of adolescents with eating disorders were relatively more likely to be unhappy with their family's functioning, to have problems with eating and dieting themselves, to think that their daughters should lose weight, and to consider their daughter to be unattractive (Baker et al., 2000; Pike & Rodin, 1991). Some researchers speculate that adolescents may develop eating disorders as a way of coping with feelings of loneliness and alienation they experience in the home. Could binge eating symbolize the effort to gain parental nurturance (Humphrey, 1986)? Does purging symbolically rid one of negative feelings toward the family?

Other psychologists connect eating disorders with extreme fear of gaining weight because of cultural idealization of the slender female. This ideal may contribute to the distortion of a woman's body image and to excess efforts to match the ideal.

www 15 L 6

CLICK4™ *Web sites about eating disorders.*

IN REVIEW
Psychological Disorders

Class	Major Subtypes	About . . .
Anxiety Disorders	Phobic, panic, generalized anxiety, obsessive-compulsive, and stress disorders	Generally characterized by worrying, fear of the worst happening, fear of losing control, nervousness, and inability to relax
Dissociative Disorders	Dissociative amnesia, dissociative fugue, dissociative identity disorder, and depersonalization	Generally characterized by separation of mental processes such as thoughts, emotions, identity, memory, or consciousness
Somatoform Disorders	Conversion disorder and hypochondriasis	Generally characterized by complaints of physical problems such as paralysis or pain, or the persistent belief that one has a serious disease in the absence of medical findings
Mood Disorders	Major depression and bipolar disorder	Generally characterized by disturbance in expressed emotions
Schizophrenia	Paranoid, disorganized, and catatonic schizophrenia	Generally characterized by disturbances in language and thought (e.g., delusions, loose associations), attention and perception (e.g., hallucinations), motor activity, and mood, and by withdrawal and absorption in daydreams or fantasy
Personality Disorders	Paranoid, schizotypal, schizoid, antisocial, and avoidant personality disorders	Generally characterized by inflexible and maladaptive patterns of behavior that impair personal or social functioning and are a source of distress to oneself or others
Eating Disorders	Anorexia nervosa and bulimia nervosa	Generally characterized by persistent, gross disturbances in eating patterns

Yet some cases of anorexia nervosa may reflect overblown efforts to remain healthy by avoiding intake of fat and cholesterol, which are widely publicized as risk factors for cardiovascular disease. Markel (2000) reports the case of a 15-year-old boy who developed anorexia nervosa after his grandfather—an obese man who ate his steaks rare and his vegetables deep-fried—died from a heart attack while he and the boy were playing checkers.

Anorexia nervosa and bulimia nervosa both tend to run in families (Strober et al., 2000), and researchers have found some evidence pointing to genetic factors involving obsessionistic and perfectionistic personality styles as increasing the risk of these disorders (Kaye et al., 2000). However, they do not deny a role for cultural influences (Wade et al., 2000). Anorexia is frequently found together with major depression, and the researchers suggest that the two disorders—anorexia nervosa and depression—may share genetic factors. Perhaps as in some other disorders, genetic factors create a vulnerability to eating disorders, and cultural and familial emphasis on body shape and personal perfectability contribute to the likelihood of developing anorexia nervosa, bulimia nervosa, and depression (Baker et al., 2000).

REVIEW

CLICK4™ a quiz covering the second half of this chapter.

CLICK4™ electronic flash cards to review your knowledge of key terms and people in this chapter.

(41) Anorexia nervosa is characterized by intense fear of being overweight, a distorted _____ image, and, in females, lack of ovulation. (42) Bulimia nervosa is defined as recurrent cycles of _____ eating followed by purging food. (43) Anorexia nervosa and bulimia nervosa (do or do not?) tend to run in families. (44) Genetic factors involving _____ personality traits may place people at risk for these disorders.

Pulling It Together: Why are females more likely than males to develop eating disorders?

Although the causes of psychological disorders remain in dispute, various methods of therapy have been devised to deal with them. Those methods are the focus of Chapter 16.

TRUTH ☞ FICTION REVISITED

▱ **It is true that a man shot the president of the United States in front of millions of television witnesses and was found not guilty by a court of law.** *His name is John Hinckley, and he was found not guilty by reason of insanity. See page 504.*

▱ **It is true that innocent people were drowned in the Middle Ages to prove that they were not possessed by the Devil.** *This method was based on a water-float test designed to determine whether metals are pure. See page 505.*

▱ **It may *not* be abnormal to feel anxious.** *It is normal to feel anxious when one is in a stressful or fearful situation. See page 505.*

▱ **It is true that some people have more than one identity, and the identities may have different allergies and eyeglass prescriptions.** *See page 514.*

▱ **Actually, it is not true that people who threaten suicide are only seeking attention.** *Most people who commit suicide give warnings about their intentions (Waters, 2000). See page 521.*

▱ **The statement that "You can never be too rich or too thin" is false.** *I won't pass judgment on whether or not you can be too rich. You can clearly be too thin, however. See page 531.*

▱ **It is true that some college women control their weight by going on cycles of binge eating followed by self-induced vomiting.** *Many other women do so as well. People who behave in this way are diagnosed with bulimia nervosa. See page 532.*

1. How have people historically explained psychological disorders?

People throughout history have mainly attributed psychological disorders to some sort of spiritual intervention. The ancient Greeks believed that people with such disorders were being punished by the gods. Since the Middle Ages, Europeans mainly attributed these disorders to possession by the devil.

2. How do we define psychological disorders?

Psychological disorders are characterized by unusual behavior, socially unacceptable behavior, faulty perception of reality, personal distress, dangerous behavior, or self-defeating behavior.

3. How are psychological disorders grouped or classified?

The most widely used classification scheme is found in the *Diagnostic and Statistical Manual (DSM)* of the American Psychiatric Association. The current edition of the DSM groups disorders on the basis of observable symptoms and no longer uses the category of neuroses.

4. What kinds of anxiety disorders are there?

Anxiety disorders are characterized by motor tension, feelings of dread, and overarousal of the sympathetic branch of the autonomic nervous system. These disorders include irrational, excessive fears, or phobias; panic disorder, characterized by sudden attacks in which people typically fear that they may be losing control or going crazy; generalized or pervasive anxiety; obsessive-compulsive disorder, in which people are troubled by intrusive thoughts or impulses to repeat some activity; and stress disorders, in which a stressful event is followed by persistent fears and intrusive thoughts about the event. Posttraumatic stress disorder can occur 6 months or more after the event, whereas acute stress disorder occurs within a month.

5. What is known about the origins of anxiety disorders?

The psychodynamic perspective tends to view anxiety disorders as representing difficulty in repressing primitive impulses. Many learning theorists view phobias as conditioned fears. Cognitive theorists focus on ways in which people interpret threats. Some people may also be genetically predisposed to acquire certain kinds of fears. Anxiety disorders tend to run in families. Some psychologists suggest that biochemical factors—which could be inherited—may create a predisposition toward anxiety disorders. One such factor is faulty regulation of neurotransmitters.

6. What kinds of dissociative disorders are there?

Dissociative disorders are characterized by sudden, temporary changes in consciousness or self-identity. They include dissociative amnesia; dissociative fugue, which involves forgetting plus fleeing and adopting a new identity; dissociative identity disorder (multiple personality), in which a person behaves as if more than one personality occupies his or her body; and depersonalization, characterized by feelings that one is not real or that one is standing outside oneself.

7. What is known about the origins of dissociative disorders?

Many psychologists suggest that dissociative disorders help people keep disturbing memories or ideas out of mind. These memories may involve episodes of childhood sexual or physical abuse.

8. What kinds of somatoform disorders are there?

People with somatoform disorders exhibit or complain of physical problems, although no medical evidence of such problems can be found. The somatoform disorders include conversion disorder and hypochondriasis. In conversion disorder, stress is converted into a physical symptom, and the individual may show la belle indifférence (indifference to the symptom).

9. What is known about the origins of somatoform disorders?

These disorders were once called "hysterical neuroses" and are expected to be found more often among women. However, they are also found among men and may reflect the relative benefits of focusing on physical symptoms rather than fears and conflicts.

10. What kinds of mood disorders are there?

Mood disorders involve disturbances in expressed emotions. Major depression is characterized by persistent feelings of sadness, loss of interest, feelings of worthlessness or guilt, inability to concentrate, and physical symptoms that may include disturbances in regulation of eating and sleeping. Feelings of unworthiness and guilt may be so excessive that they are considered delusional. Bipolar disorder is characterized by dramatic swings in mood between elation and depression; manic episodes include pressured speech and rapid flight of ideas.

11. What is known about the origins of mood disorders?

Research emphasizes possible roles for learned helplessness, attributional styles, and underutilization of serotonin in depression. People who are depressed are more likely than other people to make internal, stable, and global attributions for failures. Genetic factors involving regulation of neurotransmitters may also be involved in mood disorders. For example, bipolar disorder has been linked to inappropriate levels of the neurotransmitter glutamate. Moreover, people with severe depression often respond to drugs that heighten the action of serotonin.

12. Why are women more likely than men to be depressed?

Part of the gender difference may reflect hormonal factors, but women also experience greater stresses than men in our culture—including the stresses that accompany second-class citizenship.

13. Why do people commit suicide?

Suicide usually reflects feelings of helplessness and hopelessness due to stressful events, and especially events that involve loss of social support. Suicide tends to run in families, but it is unclear whether the reasons are genetic or environmental.

14. How are sociocultural factors connected with suicide?

Older and better-educated people are more likely to commit suicide. More women attempt suicide, but more men "succeed" because they use more lethal means. European Americans are twice as likely as African Americans to commit suicide. Native Americans are at the greatest risk.

15. What are some of the myths and realities about suicide?

It is mythical that people who truly intend to kill themselves do it without warning, and that those who fail at the attempt are just seeking attention. Many people who commit suicide had issued warnings, and many had made prior attempts.

16. What is schizophrenia?

Schizophrenia is a most severe psychological disorder that is characterized by disturbances in thought and language, such as loosening of associations and delusions; in perception and attention, as found in hallucinations; in motor activity, as shown by a stupor or by excited behavior; in mood, as in flat or inappropriate emotional responses; and in social interaction, as in social withdrawal and absorption in daydreams or fantasy.

17. What kinds of schizophrenia are there?

The major types of schizophrenia are paranoid, disorganized, and catatonic. Paranoid schizophrenia is characterized largely by systematized delusions; disorganized schizophrenia by incoherence; and catatonic schizophrenia by motor impairment.

18. What is known about the origins of schizophrenia?

Schizophrenia is connected with smaller brains, especially fewer synapses in the prefrontal region, and larger ventricles in the brain. According to the multifactorial model, genetic vulnerability to schizophrenia may interact with other factors, such as stress, complications during pregnancy and childbirth, and quality of parenting, to cause the disorder to develop. According to the dopamine theory of schizophrenia, people with schizophrenia *use* more dopamine than other people do, perhaps because they have more dopamine in the brain along with more dopamine receptors than other people.

19. What kinds of personality disorders are there?

Personality disorders are inflexible, maladaptive behavior patterns that impair personal or social functioning and cause distress for the individual or others. The defining trait of paranoid personality disorder is suspiciousness. People with schizotypal personality disorders show oddities of thought, perception, and behavior. Social withdrawal is the major characteristic of schizoid personality disorder. People with antisocial personality disorders persistently violate the rights of others and are in conflict with the law. They show little or no guilt or shame over their misdeeds and are largely undeterred by punishment. People with avoidant personality disorder tend to avoid entering relationships for fear of rejection and criticism.

20. What is known about the origins of personality disorders?

Psychodynamic theory connected many personality disorders with hypothesized Oedipal problems. Genetic factors may be involved in some personality disorders. Antisocial personality disorder may develop from some combination of genetic vulnerability (less gray matter in the prefrontal cortex of the brain, which may provide lower-than-normal levels of arousal), inconsistent discipline, and cynical processing of social information.

21. What kinds of eating disorders are there?

The eating disorders include anorexia nervosa and bulimia nervosa. Anorexia is characterized by refusal to eat and extreme thinness. Bulimia is characterized by cycles of binge eating and purging. Women are more likely than men to develop these disorders.

22. What is known about the origins of eating disorders?

The major psychodynamic explanation of the eating disorders is that a conflicted female is attempting to remain prepubescent. However, most psychologists look to cultural idealization of the slender female—and the pressure that such idealization places on young women—as the major contributor.

PREVIEW

What Is Therapy? The Search for a "Sweet Oblivious Antidote"
▲ Psychotherapy can be used for self-improvement as well as "getting better."
▲ "Therapy" has a checkered history, including execution, torture, and warehousing.

Psychodynamic Therapies: Digging Deep Within
▲ Sigmund Freud's traditional psychoanalysis is the method that uses a couch.
▲ Freud would interpret clients' dreams.
▲ Today's psychoanalysts are more likely to talk to you face to face.

Humanistic-Existential Therapies: Strengthening the Self
▲ Carl Rogers encouraged clients to take the lead in therapy.
▲ Fritz Perls told clients exactly what to do.

Behavior Therapy: Adjustment Is What You Do
▲ Behavior therapists focus on what you do.
▲ Behavior therapists help clients overcome fear of flying and stagefright.
▲ Some therapists make clients nauseous or shock them as a way of helping them break bad habits.
▲ You can use behavior therapy to stop biting your fingernails.

Cognitive Therapies: Adjustment Is What You Think (and Do)
▲ "There is nothing either good or bad, but thinking makes it so."
▲ Cognitive errors can get you down in the dumps.
▲ Cognitive therapists sometimes argue with clients.

Group Therapies
▲ Group therapy has advantages that go beyond being affordable.
▲ Groups, groups, groups—There are many kinds.

Controversy in Psychology: Does Psychotherapy Work?
▲ Is psychotherapy effective?
▲ How do we know?
▲ Can people from different ethnic groups, women, and gay males and lesbians make use of psychotherapy?

Biological Therapies
▲ Sometimes drugs are good.
▲ Electroconvulsive therapy (ECT) is shocking but sometimes helpful.
▲ Psychosurgery apparently does not have the kindest cuts of all.

CHAPTER 16

Methods of Therapy

TRUTH ☒ FICTION?

▰ Residents of London used to visit the local insane asylum for a fun night out on the town.

▰ To be effective, psychotherapy must continue for months, perhaps years.

▰ Some psychotherapists interpret clients' dreams.

▰ Other psychotherapists encourage their clients to take the lead in therapy sessions.

▰ Still other psychotherapists tell their clients precisely what to do.

▰ Lying in a reclining chair and fantasizing can be an effective way of confronting fears.

▰ Smoking cigarettes can be an effective method for helping people . . . stop smoking cigarettes.

▰ You might be able to put an end to bad habits merely by keeping a record of where and when you engage in those habits.

▰ The originator of a surgical technique designed to reduce violence learned that it was not always successful . . . when one of his patients shot him.

Jasmine is a 19-year-old college sophomore. She has been crying almost without letup for several days. She feels that her life is falling apart. Her college dreams are in a shambles. She has brought shame upon her family. Thoughts of suicide have crossed her mind. She can barely drag herself out of bed in the morning. She is avoiding her friends. She can pinpoint some sources of stress in her life: a couple of poor grades, an argument with a boyfriend, friction with roommates. Still, her misery seemed to descend on her out of nowhere.

Jasmine is depressed—so depressed that her family and friends have finally prevailed on her to seek professional help. Had she broken her leg, her treatment by a qualified professional would have followed a fairly standard course. Yet treatment of psychological problems and disorders like depression may be approached from very different perspectives. Depending on the therapist Jasmine sees, she may be doing the following:

▲ Lying on a couch talking about anything that pops into her awareness and exploring the possible meaning of a recurrent dream
▲ Sitting face to face with a warm, gentle therapist who accepts Jasmine as she is and expresses faith in Jasmine's ability to make the right decisions for herself
▲ Listening to a frank, straightforward therapist assert that Jasmine is depressing herself with her self-defeating attitudes and perfectionistic beliefs
▲ Taking antidepressant medication
▲ Participating in some combination of these approaches

These methods, although different, all represent methods of therapy. In this chapter we explore various methods of psychotherapy and biological therapy. ***Question: What is psychotherapy?***

WHAT IS THERAPY? THE SEARCH FOR A "SWEET OBLIVIOUS ANTIDOTE"[1]

There are many kinds of psychotherapy, but they all have certain common characteristics. **Psychotherapy** is a systematic interaction between a therapist and a client that applies psychological principles to affect the client's thoughts, feelings, or behavior in order to help the client overcome psychological disorders, adjust to problems in living, or develop as an individual.

Quite a mouthful? True. But note the essentials:

1. *Systematic interaction.* Psychotherapy is a systematic interaction between a client and a therapist. The therapist's theoretical point of view interacts with the client's to determine how the therapist and client relate to each other.
2. *Psychological principles.* Psychotherapy is based on psychological theory and research in areas such as personality, learning, motivation, and emotion.
3. *Thoughts, feelings, and behavior.* Psychotherapy influences clients' thoughts, feelings, and behavior. It can be aimed at any or all of these aspects of human psychology.
4. *Psychological disorders, adjustment problems, and personal growth.* Psychotherapy is often used with people who have psychological disorders. Other people seek help in adjusting to problems such as shyness, weight problems, or loss of a spouse. Still other clients want to learn more about themselves and to reach their full potential as individuals, parents, or creative artists.

The History of Therapies

Historically speaking, "treatments" of psychological disorders often reflected demonological thinking. ***Question: How, then, have people with psychological problems and disorders been treated throughout the ages?*** Because of this belief, treat-

Psychotherapy ▲ A systematic interaction between a therapist and a client that brings psychological principles to bear on influencing the client's thoughts, feelings, or behavior to help that client overcome abnormal behavior or adjust to problems in living.

---

[1]The phrase is from Shakespeare's *Macbeth*.

ment tended to involve cruel practices such as exorcism and death by hanging or burning. Some people who could not meet the demands of everyday life were tossed into prisons. Others begged in the streets, stole food, or became prostitutes. A few found their way to monasteries or other retreats that offered a kind word and some support. Generally speaking, they died early.

Asylums   Asylums originated in European monasteries. They were the first institutions meant primarily for people with psychological disorders. But their function was warehousing, not treatment. Their inmate populations mushroomed until the stresses created by noise, overcrowding, and disease aggravated the problems they were meant to ease. Inmates were frequently chained and beaten.

The word *bedlam* derives from St. Mary's of *Bethlehem*, the London asylum that opened its gates in 1547. Here unfortunate people with psychological disorders were chained, whipped, and allowed to lie in their own waste. And here the ladies and gentlemen of the British upper class might stroll on a lazy afternoon to be amused by the inmates' antics. The price of admission was one penny.

Humanitarian reform movements began in the 18th century. In Paris, the physician Philippe Pinel unchained the patients at La Bicêtre. Rather than run amok, most patients profited from kindness and freedom. Many eventually reentered society. Later movements to reform institutions were led by the Quaker William Tuke in England and by Dorothea Dix in America.

Mental Hospitals   In the United States mental hospitals gradually replaced asylums. In the mid-1950s more than a million people resided in state, county, Veterans Administration, or private facilities. The mental hospital's function is treatment, not warehousing. Still, because of high patient populations and understaffing, many patients

IN PROFILE

Philippe Pinel—A Reformer With Results

He almost singlehandedly turned the treatment of people with psychological disorders topsy-turvy. The Frenchman Philippe Pinel (1745–1826) was born into a family of physicians and received a degree in medicine from the University of Toulouse. He believed his fellow physicians were greedy and callous, and moved to Paris to treat the poor. He became interested in psychological disorders when a friend developed one and no treatment was available. At this time, people with severe psychological disorders were warehoused in asylums, often chained, sometimes whirled in chairs. Bloodletting was also in vogue. Pinel wrote in A *Treatise on Insanity* (1801) that the blood of patients was spilled so lavishly that one might wonder who was really "mad"—the patient or his physician. Pinel argued for the humane treatment of people with such disorders and had his chance to make a difference when he was appointed director of La Bicêtre.

Pinel first unchained an English soldier who had once crushed the head of a guard with his chains. Freed of his shackles, the man was nonviolent, and two years later he was discharged. Pinel unchained more patients and improved their diets. He grouped patients with similar kinds of problems. He promoted the use of occupational therapy. Pinel was the first to take careful case histories of patients and maintain a record of cure rates. Pinel amassed a record of success. In 1795, he was appointed director of La Salpêtrière hospital, which was Europe's largest asylum and housed 8,000 women. (Almost a century later, La Salpêtrière would be directed by Jean Martin Charcot, who influenced Alfred Binet and Sigmund Freud.) Pinel's influence was felt throughout Europe and in the United States.

▲ **REFLECT**
Had you heard the words *asylum* or *bedlam*? What did you think they meant? Were you correct?

www **16** **E** **1**

CLICK4™ *an essay assignment: How has psychology's approach to therapy changed?*

The Unchaining of the Patients at La Bicêtre.
Philippe Pinel sparked the humanitarian reform movement by unchaining the patients at this asylum in Paris.

CLICK4™ *a WebSearch activity on the definition of psychotherapy and who can provide it.*

CLICK4™ *Web sites devoted to psychotherapy and treatment methods.*

received little attention. Even today, with somewhat improved conditions, one psychiatrist may be responsible for the welfare of several hundred residents on a weekend when other staff members are absent.

The Community Mental Health Movement   Since the 1960s, efforts have been made to maintain people with serious psychological disorders in their communities. Community mental health centers attempt to maintain new patients as outpatients and to serve patients who have been released from mental hospitals. Today most people with chronic psychological disorders live in the community, not the hospital.

Critics note that many people who had resided in hospitals for decades were suddenly discharged to "home" communities that seemed foreign and forbidding to them. Many do not receive adequate follow-up care. Many join the ranks of the homeless (Francis, 2000; Lam & Rosenheck, 2000).

REVIEW

(1) Psychotherapy is a systematic interaction between a therapist and a client that applies _____ principles to influence clients' thoughts, feelings, or behavior. (2) Historic treatments of psychological disorders were based on the demonological model and included the _____ of evil spirits.

Pulling It Together: Trace the evolution of thinking about psychological disorders in Western culture. What reforms have taken place in treatment?

PSYCHODYNAMIC THERAPIES: DIGGING DEEP WITHIN

Psychodynamic therapies are based on the thinking of Sigmund Freud, the founder of psychodynamic theory. They assume that psychological problems reflect early childhood experiences and internal conflicts. According to Freud, these conflicts involve the shifting of psychic, or libidinal, energy among the three psychic structures—the id, ego, and superego. These shifts of psychic energy determine our behavior. When primitive urges threaten to break through from the id or when the superego floods us with excessive guilt, defenses are established and distress is created. Freud's psychodynamic therapy method—psychoanalysis—aims to modify the flow of energy among these structures, largely to bulwark the ego against the torrents of energy loosed by the id and the superego. With impulses and feelings of guilt and shame placed under greater control, clients are freer to develop adaptive behavior. *Question: How, then, do psychoanalysts conduct a traditional Freudian psychoanalysis?*

Traditional Psychoanalysis: "Where Id Was, There Shall Ego Be"

> *Canst thou not minister to a mind diseas'd,*
> *Pluck out from the memory a rooted sorrow,*
> *Raze out the written troubles of the brain,*
> *And with some sweet oblivious antidote*
> *Cleanse the stuff'd bosom of that perilous stuff*
> *Which weighs upon the heart?*
>
> —Shakespeare, Macbeth

In the passage just quoted, Macbeth asks a physician to minister to Lady Macbeth after she has gone mad. In the play, her madness is caused partly by events—namely, her role in murders designed to seat her husband on the throne of Scotland. There are also hints of mysterious, deeply rooted problems, such as conflicts about infertility.

If Lady Macbeth's physician had been a traditional psychoanalyst, he might have asked her to lie on a couch in a slightly darkened room. He would have sat behind her and encouraged her to talk about anything that came to mind, no matter how trivial, no matter how personal. To avoid interfering with her self-exploration, he might have said

A View of Freud's Consulting Room.
Freud would sit in a chair by the head of the couch while a client free-associated. The basic rule of free association is that no thought is censored.

little or nothing for session after session. That would have been par for the course. A traditional **psychoanalysis** can extend for months, even years.

Psychoanalysis is the clinical method devised by Freud for plucking "from the memory a rooted sorrow," for razing "out the written troubles of the brain." It aims to provide *insight* into the conflicts that are presumed to lie at the roots of a person's problems. Insight means many things, including knowledge of the experiences that lead to conflicts and maladaptive behavior, recognition of unconscious feelings and conflicts, and conscious evaluation of one's thoughts, feelings, and behavior.

Psychoanalysis also aims to help the client express feelings and urges that have been repressed. By so doing, Freud believed that the client spilled forth the psychic energy that had been repressed by conflicts and guilt. He called this spilling forth **catharsis.** Catharsis would provide relief by alleviating some of the forces assaulting the ego.

Freud was also fond of saying, "Where id was, there shall ego be." In part, he meant that psychoanalysis could shed light on the inner workings of the mind. He also sought to replace impulsive and defensive behavior with coping behavior. In this way, for example, a man with a phobia for knives might discover that he had been repressing the urge to harm someone who had taken advantage of him. He might also find ways to confront the person verbally.

Free Association

Early in his career as a therapist, Freud found that hypnosis allowed his clients to focus on repressed conflicts and talk about them. The relaxed "trance state" provided by hypnosis seemed to allow clients to "break through" to topics of which they would otherwise be unaware. Freud also found, however, that many clients denied the accuracy of this material once they were out of the trance. Other clients found them to be premature and painful. Freud therefore turned to **free association,** a more gradual method of breaking through the walls of defense that block a client's insight into unconscious processes.

In free association, the client is made comfortable—for example, lying on a couch—and asked to talk about any topic that comes to mind. No thought is to be censored—that is the basic rule. Psychoanalysts ask their clients to wander "freely" from topic to topic, but they do not believe that the process occurring *within* the client is fully free. Repressed impulses clamor for release.

The ego persists in trying to repress unacceptable impulses and threatening conflicts. As a result, clients might show **resistance** to recalling and discussing threatening ideas. A client about to entertain such thoughts might claim, "My mind is blank." The client might accuse the analyst of being demanding or inconsiderate. He or she might "forget" the next appointment when threatening material is about to surface.

www 16 L 2

CLICK4™ *the American Psychoanalytic Association.*

> ▲ **REFLECT**
> Does it make you or other people you know feel good to talk with someone about your problems? Are there some "deep secrets" you are unwilling to talk about or share with others? How do you think a psychoanalyst would respond if you brought them up? Why?

Psychoanalysis ▲ Freud's method of psychotherapy.
Catharsis ▲ (cuh-THAR-sis). In psychoanalysis, the expression of repressed feelings and impulses to allow the release of the psychic energy associated with them.
Free association ▲ In psychoanalysis, the uncensored uttering of all thoughts that come to mind.
Resistance ▲ The tendency to block the free expression of impulses and primitive ideas—a reflection of the defense mechanism of repression.

▲ **REFLECT**

What is the catharsis hypothesis concerning the venting of aggressive impulses? How does it relate to Freud's attempt to use catharsis in psychotherapy?

The therapist observes the dynamic struggle between the compulsion to utter certain thoughts and the client's resistance to uttering them. Through discreet remarks, the analyst subtly tips the balance in favor of utterance. A gradual process of self-discovery and self-insight ensues. Now and then the analyst offers an **interpretation** of an utterance, showing how it suggests resistance or deep-seated feelings and conflicts.

Transference   Freud believed that clients not only responded to him as an individual but also in ways that reflected their attitudes and feelings toward other people in their lives. He labeled this process **transference.** For example, a young woman client might respond to him as a father figure and displace her feelings toward her father onto Freud, perhaps seeking affection and wisdom. A young man could also see Freud as a father figure, but rather than wanting affection from Freud, he might view Freud as a rival, responding to Freud in terms of his own unresolved Oedipal complex.

Analyzing and working through transference has been considered a key aspect of psychoanalysis. Freud believed that clients reenact their childhood conflicts with their parents when they are in therapy. Clients might thus transfer the feelings of anger, love, or jealousy they felt toward their own parents onto the analyst. Childhood conflicts often involve unresolved feelings of love, anger, or rejection. A client may interpret a suggestion by the therapist as a criticism and see it as a devastating blow, transferring feelings of self-hatred that he had repressed because his parents had rejected him in childhood. Transference can also distort clients' relationships with other people here and now, such as relationships with spouses or employers. The following therapeutic dialogue illustrates the way in which an analyst may interpret a client's inability to communicate his needs to his wife as a function of transference. The purpose is to provide his client, a Mr. Arianes, with insight into how his relationship with his wife has been colored by his childhood relationship with his mother:

ARIANES: I think you've got it there, Doc. We weren't communicating. I wouldn't tell [my wife] what was wrong or what I wanted from her. Maybe I expected her to understand me without saying anything.

THERAPIST: Like the expectations a child has of its mother.

ARIANES: Not my mother!

THERAPIST: Oh?

ARIANES: No, I always thought she had too many troubles of her own to pay attention to mine. I remember once I got hurt on my bike and came to her all bloodied up. When she saw me she got mad and yelled at me for making more trouble for her when she already had her hands full with my father.

THERAPIST: Do you remember how you felt then?

ARIANES: I can't remember, but I know that after that I never brought my troubles to her again.

THERAPIST: How old were you?

ARIANES: Nine, I know that because I got that bike for my ninth birthday. It was a little too big for me still, that's why I got hurt on it.

THERAPIST: Perhaps you carried this attitude into your marriage.

ARIANES: What attitude?

THERAPIST: The feeling that your wife, like your mother, would be unsympathetic to your difficulties. That there was no point in telling her about your experiences because she was too preoccupied or too busy to care.

ARIANES: But she's so different from my mother. I come first with her.

THERAPIST: On one level you know that. On another, deeper level there may well be the fear that people—or maybe only women, or maybe only women you're close to—are all the same, and you can't take a chance at being rejected again in your need.

ARIANES: Maybe you're right, Doc, but all that was so long ago, and I should be over that by now.

THERAPIST: That's not the way the mind works. If a shock, or a disappointment is strong enough it can permanently freeze our picture of ourselves and our expectations of the world. The rest of us grows up—that is, we let our-

Interpretation ▲ An explanation of a client's utterance according to psychoanalytic theory.

Transference ▲ Responding to one person (such as a spouse or the psychoanalyst) in a way that is similar to the way one responded to another person (such as a parent) in childhood.

selves learn about life from experience and from what we see, hear, or read of the experiences of others, but that one area where we really got hurt stays unchanged. So what I mean when I say you might be carrying that attitude into your relationship with your wife is that when it comes to your hopes of being understood and catered to when you feel hurt or abused by life, you still feel very much like that nine-year-old boy who was rebuffed in his need and gave up hope that anyone would or could respond to him. (Basch, 1980, pp. 29–30)

Dream Analysis Freud often asked clients to jot down their dreams upon waking so that they could discuss them in therapy. Freud considered dreams the "royal road to the unconscious." He believed that the content of dreams is determined by unconscious processes as well as by the events of the day. Unconscious impulses tend to be expressed in dreams as a form of **wish fulfillment.**

But unacceptable sexual and aggressive impulses are likely to be displaced onto objects and situations that reflect the client's era and culture. These objects become symbols of unconscious wishes. For example, long, narrow dream objects might be **phallic symbols,** but whether the symbol takes the form of a spear, rifle, stick shift, or spacecraft partially reflects the dreamer's cultural background.

In Freud's theory, the perceived content of a dream is called its visible, or **manifest content.** Its presumed hidden or symbolic content is its **latent content.** If a man dreams he is flying, flying is the manifest content of the dream. Freud usually interpreted flying as symbolic of erection, so concerns about sexual potency might make up the latent content of the dream.

Modern Psychodynamic Approaches

Some psychoanalysts adhere faithfully to Freud's techniques. They engage in protracted therapy that continues to rely heavily on free association, interpretation of dreams, and other traditional methods. In recent years, however, more modern forms of psychodynamic therapy have been devised. ***Question: How do modern psychodynamic approaches differ from traditional psychoanalysis?*** Modern psychodynamic therapy is briefer and less intense, and makes treatment available to clients who do not have the time or money for long-term therapy. Many modern psychodynamic therapists do not believe that prolonged therapy is needed or justifiable in terms of the ratio of cost to benefits.

Some modern psychodynamic therapies continue to focus on revealing unconscious material and breaking through psychological defenses. Nevertheless, they differ from traditional psychoanalysis in several ways (Prochaska & Norcross, 1999). One is that the client and therapist usually sit face to face (the client does not lie on a couch). The therapist is usually directive. That is, modern therapists often suggest helpful behavior instead of focusing on insight alone. Finally, there is usually more focus on the ego as the "executive" of personality and less emphasis on the id. For this reason, many modern psychodynamic therapists are considered **ego analysts.**

Many of Freud's followers, the "second generation" of psychoanalysts—from Jung and Adler to Horney and Erikson—believed that Freud had placed too much emphasis on sexual and aggressive impulses and underestimated the role of the ego. For example, Freud aimed to establish conditions under which clients could spill forth psychic energy and eventually shore up the ego. Erikson, in contrast, spoke to clients directly about their values and concerns, encouraging them to develop desired traits and behavior patterns. Even Freud's daughter, the psychoanalyst Anna Freud (1895–1982), was more concerned with the ego than with unconscious forces and conflicts.

www **16** WS **2**

CLICK4™ *a WebSearch activity on the history of psychoanalytic thought.*

Wish fulfillment ▲ A primitive method used by the id to attempt to gratify basic instincts.

Phallic symbol ▲ A sign that represents the penis.

Manifest content ▲ In psychodynamic theory, the reported content of dreams.

Latent content ▲ In psychodynamic theory, the symbolized or underlying content of dreams.

Ego analyst ▲ A psychodynamically oriented therapist who focuses on the conscious, coping behavior of the ego instead of the hypothesized, unconscious functioning of the id.

REVIEW

(3) Freud's method of psychoanalysis attempts to shed light on _____ conflicts that are presumed to lie at the roots of clients' problems. (4) Freud believed that psychoanalysis would promote _____, that is, the spilling forth of repressed psychic energy.

(5) The chief psychoanalytic method is _____ association. (6) Freud considered _____ to be the "royal road to the unconscious."

Pulling It Together: How do "modern" psychoanalytic approaches differ from Freud's traditional method? Why do they differ?

HUMANISTIC-EXISTENTIAL THERAPIES: STRENGTHENING THE SELF

CLICK4™ *the Web site of the Association for Humanistic Psychology.*

Psychodynamic therapies focus on internal conflicts and unconscious processes. Humanistic-existential therapies focus on the quality of the client's subjective, conscious experience. Traditional psychoanalysis focuses on early childhood experiences. Humanistic-existential therapies usually focus on what clients are experiencing "here and now."

These differences, however, are mainly a matter of emphasis. The past has a way of influencing current thoughts, feelings, and behavior. Carl Rogers, the originator of client-centered therapy, believed that childhood experiences gave rise to the conditions of worth that troubled his clients here and now. He and Fritz Perls, the originator of Gestalt therapy, recognized that early incorporation of other people's values often leads clients to "disown" parts of their own personalities.

Client-Centered Therapy: Removing Roadblocks to Self-Actualization

Perhaps in response to his parents' efforts to "protect" him from other ways of thinking (see the nearby Profile), Rogers developed a form of therapy that encourages individuals to rely on their own values and frames of references. He called his approach **client-centered therapy.** ***Question: What is Carl Rogers's method of client-centered therapy?*** His method is intended to help people get in touch with their genuine feelings and pursue their own interests, regardless of other people's wishes.

Rogers believed that we are free to make choices and control our destinies, despite the burdens of the past. He also believed that we have natural tendencies toward health, growth, and fulfillment. Psychological problems arise from roadblocks placed in the path of self-actualization—that is, what Rogers believed was an inborn tendency to strive to realize one's potential. If, when we are young, other people only approve of us when we are doing what they want us to do, we may learn to disown the parts of ourselves to which they object. We may learn to be seen but not heard—not even by ourselves. As a result, we may experience stress and discomfort and the feeling that we—or the world—are not real.

> ▲ **REFLECT**
> Do you think that your experiences have pressured you to disown parts of yourself? Could you find out if this has happened?

Client-centered therapy ▲ Carl Rogers's method of psychotherapy that emphasizes the creation of a warm, therapeutic atmosphere that frees clients to engage in self-exploration and self-expression.

CLICK4™ *a bulletin board discussion on the client-centered approach to therapy.*

Client-Centered Therapy.
By showing the qualities of unconditional positive regard, empathic understanding, genuineness, and congruence, client-centered therapists create an atmosphere in which clients can explore their feelings.

Client-centered therapy aims to provide insight into the parts of us that we have disowned so that we can feel whole. It creates a warm, therapeutic atmosphere that encourages self-exploration and self-expression. The therapist's acceptance of the client is thought to foster self-acceptance and self-esteem. Self-acceptance frees the client to make choices that develop his or her unique potential.

Client-centered therapy is nondirective. The client takes the lead, stating and exploring problems.

An effective client-centered therapist has several qualities:

▲ **Unconditional positive regard:** respect for clients as human beings with unique values and goals.

▲ **Empathic understanding:** recognition of the client's experiences and feelings. Therapists view the world through the client's **frame of reference** by setting aside their own values and listening closely.

▲ **Genuineness:** Openness and honesty in responding to the client. Client-centered therapists must be able to tolerate differentness because they believe that every client is different in important ways.

The following excerpt from a therapy session shows how Carl Rogers uses empathetic understanding and paraphrases a client's (Jill's) feelings. His goal is to help her recognize feelings that she has partially disowned:

JILL: I'm having a lot of problems dealing with my daughter. She's 20 years old; she's in college; I'm having a lot of trouble letting her go. . . . And I have a lot of guilt feelings about her; I have a real need to hang on to her.

C.R.: A need to hang on so you can kind of make up for the things you feel guilty about. Is that part of it?

JILL: There's a lot of that. . . . Also, she's been a real friend to me, and filled my life. . . . And it's very hard. . . . a lot of empty places now that she's not with me.

C.R.: The old vacuum, sort of, when she's not there.

JILL: Yes. Yes. I also would like to be the kind of mother that could be strong and say, you know, "Go and have a good life," and this is really hard for me, to do that.

C.R.: It's very hard to give up something that's been so precious in your life, but also something that I guess has caused you pain when you mentioned guilt.

JILL: Yeah. And I'm aware that I have some anger toward her that I don't always get what I want. I have needs that are not met. And, uh, I don't feel I have a right to those needs. You know. . . . she's a daughter; she's not my mother. Though sometimes I feel as if I'd like her to mother me . . . it's very difficult for me to ask for that and have a right to it.

C.R.: So, it may be unreasonable, but still, when she doesn't meet your needs, it makes you mad.

JILL: Yeah I get very angry, very angry with her.

C.R.: *(Pauses)* You're also feeling a little tension at this point, I guess.

JILL: Yeah. Yeah. A lot of conflict. . . . (C.R.: M-hm.) A lot of pain.

C.R.: A lot of pain. Can you say anything more about what that's about? (Farber et al., 1996, pp. 74–75)

Client-centered therapy is practiced widely in college and university counseling centers, not just to help students experiencing, say, anxieties or depression but also to help them make decisions. Many college students have not yet made career choices or wonder whether they should become involved with particular people or in sexual activity. Client-centered therapists do not tell clients what to do. Instead, they help clients arrive at their own decisions.

▲ **REFLECT**
Can you use the qualities of the client-centered therapist in being a friend or a parent? Do these qualities — or ways of behaving — seem to be desirable or dangerous to you? Explain.

Unconditional positive regard ▲ Acceptance of the value of another person, although not necessarily acceptance of everything the person does.

Empathic understanding ▲ (em-PATH-ick). Ability to perceive a client's feelings from the client's frame of reference. A quality of the good client-centered therapist.

Frame of reference ▲ One's unique patterning of perceptions and attitudes, according to which one evaluates events.

Genuineness ▲ Recognition and open expression of the therapist's own feelings.

Gestalt Therapy: Getting It Together

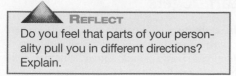

REFLECT

Do you feel that parts of your personality pull you in different directions? Explain.

Gestalt therapy was originated by Fritz Perls (1893–1970). ***Question: What is Fritz Perls's method of Gestalt therapy?*** Like client-centered therapy, Gestalt therapy assumes that people disown parts of themselves that might meet with social disapproval or rejection. People also don social masks, pretending to be things that they are not. Therapy aims to help individuals integrate conflicting parts of their personality. Perls used the term *Gestalt* to signify his interest in giving the conflicting parts of the personality an integrated form or shape. He aimed to have his clients become aware of inner conflict, accept the reality of conflict rather than deny it or keep it repressed, and make productive choices despite misgivings and fears. People in conflict frequently find it difficult to make choices, and Perls sought to encourage—*compel* might be a better word—them to do so.

Although Perls's ideas about conflicting personality elements owe much to psychodynamic theory, his form of therapy, unlike psychoanalysis, focuses on the here and now. In Gestalt therapy, clients perform exercises to heighten their awareness of their current feelings and behavior, rather than exploring the past. Perls also believed, along with Rogers, that people are free to make choices and to direct their personal growth. But the charismatic and forceful Perls was unlike the gentle and accepting Rogers in temperament (Prochaska & Norcross, 1999). Thus, unlike client-centered therapy, Gestalt therapy is highly directive. The therapist leads the client through planned experiences.

CLICK4™ *a profile of Fritz Perls.*

There are a number of Gestalt exercises and games, including the following:

1. *The dialogue.* In this game, the client undertakes verbal confrontations between opposing wishes and ideas to heighten awareness of internal conflict. An example of these clashing personality elements is "top dog" and "underdog." One's top dog might conservatively suggest, "Don't take chances. Stick with what you have or you might lose it all." One's frustrated underdog might then rise up and assert, "You never try anything. How will you ever get out of this rut if you don't take on new challenges?" Heightened awareness of the elements of conflict can clear the path toward resolution, perhaps through a compromise of some kind.

2. *I take responsibility.* Clients end statements about themselves by adding, "and I take responsibility for it."

3. *Playing the projection.* Clients role-play people with whom they are in conflict, expressing, for example, the ideas of their parents.

CLICK4™ *an essay assignment comparing the humanistic therapies of Carl Rogers and Fritz Perls.*

Body language also provides insight into conflicting feelings. Clients might be instructed to attend to the ways in which they furrow their eyebrows and tense their facial muscles when they express certain ideas. In this way, they often find that their body language asserts feelings they have been denying in their spoken statements.

The following excerpt from a therapy session with a client named Max shows how Perls would make clients take responsibility for what they experience. One of his techniques is to show how clients are treating something they are doing (a "verb") like something that is just out there and beyond their control (a "noun"):

▲ **REFLECT**

Have you heard the expression "getting it together"? How might it relate to Gestalt therapy?

MAX: I feel the tenseness in my stomach and in my hands.
PERLS: *The* tenseness. Here we've got a noun. Now *the* tenseness is a noun. Now change the noun, the thing, into a verb.
MAX: I am tense. My hands are tense.
PERLS: Your hands are tense. They have nothing to do with you.
MAX: I am tense.
PERLS: You are tense. How are you tense? What are you doing?
MAX: I am tensing myself.
PERLS: That's it. (Perls, 1971, p. 115)

Once Max understands that he is tensing himself and takes responsibility for it, he can choose to stop tensing himself. The tenseness is no longer something out there that is victimizing him; it is something he is doing to himself.

Psychodynamic theory views dreams as the "royal road to the unconscious." Perls saw the content of dreams as representing disowned parts of the personality. Perls would

Gestalt therapy ▲ Fritz Perls' form of psychotherapy, which attempts to integrate conflicting parts of the personality through directive methods designed to help clients perceive their whole selves.

often ask clients to role-play elements of their dreams in order to get in touch with these parts of their personality.

CLICK4™ *the Web site of the Association for the Advancement of Gestalt Therapy.*

CLICK4™ *the Gestalt Therapy Page, with links to resources.*

REVIEW

(7) Humanistic-_____ therapies focus on clients' subjective, conscious experience. (8) Client-centered therapy is a (directive or nondirective?) method that provides clients with an accepting atmosphere that enables them to overcome roadblocks to self-actualization. (9) The client-centered therapist shows (conditional or unconditional?) positive regard, empathetic understanding, and genuineness. (10) Gestalt therapy provides (directive or nondirective?) methods that are designed to help clients accept responsibility and integrate conflicting parts of the personality.

Pulling It Together: What do the humanistic-existential therapies of Rogers and Perls have in common? How do they differ?

BEHAVIOR THERAPY: ADJUSTMENT IS WHAT YOU DO

Psychodynamic and humanistic-existential forms of therapy tend to focus on what people think and feel. Behavior therapists tend to focus on what people do.   *Question: What is behavior therapy?*   **Behavior therapy**—also called *behavior modification*—applies principles of learning to directly promote desired behavioral changes (Wolpe & Plaud, 1997). Behavior therapists rely heavily on principles of conditioning and observational learning. They help clients discontinue self-defeating behavior patterns such as overeating, smoking, and phobic avoidance of harmless stimuli. They also help clients acquire adaptive behavior patterns such as the social skills required to start social relationships or say no to insistent salespeople.

Behavior therapists may help clients gain "insight" into maladaptive behavior in the sense of fostering awareness of the circumstances in which it occurs. They do not foster insight in the psychoanalytic sense of unearthing the childhood origins of problems and the symbolic meanings of maladaptive behavior. Behavior therapists, like other therapists, may also build warm, therapeutic relationships with clients, but they see the efficacy of behavior therapy as deriving from specific, learning-based procedures (Wolpe, 1990). They insist that their methods be established by experimentation and that the outcomes be assessed in terms of measurable behavior. In this section we consider some frequently used behavior-therapy techniques.

Fear-Reduction Methods

Many people seek therapy because of fears and phobias that interfere with their functioning. This is one of the areas in which behavior therapy has made great inroads.   *Question: What are some behavior-therapy methods for reducing fears?*   These include flooding (see Chapter 5), systematic desensitization, and modeling.

> **△ REFLECT**
> Would any of the methods for reducing fears be helpful to you in your life? If so, which method would you prefer? Explain.

Systematic Desensitization   Adam has a phobia for receiving injections. His behavior therapist treats him as he reclines in a comfortable padded chair. In a state of deep muscle relaxation, Adam observes slides projected on a screen. A slide of a nurse holding a needle has just been shown three times, 30 seconds at a time. Each time Adam has shown no anxiety. So now a slightly more discomforting slide is shown: one of the nurse aiming the needle toward someone's bare arm. After 15 seconds, our armchair adventurer notices twinges of discomfort and raises a finger as a signal (speaking might disturb his relaxation). The projector operator turns off the light, and Adam spends 2 minutes imagining his "safe scene"—lying on a beach beneath the tropical sun. Then the slide is shown again. This time Adam views it for 30 seconds before feeling anxiety.

Adam is undergoing **systematic desensitization,** a method for reducing phobic responses originated by psychiatrist Joseph Wolpe (1990). Systematic desensitization is a

Behavior therapy ▲ Systematic application of the principles of learning to the direct modification of a client's problem behaviors.
Systematic desensitization ▲ Wolpe's method for reducing fears by associating a hierarchy of images of fear-evoking stimuli with deep muscle relaxation.

Overcoming a Phobia.
One way behavior therapists help clients overcome phobias is by having them gradually approach the feared object or situation while they remain relaxed.

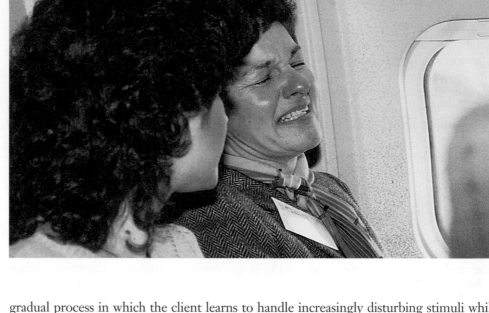

CLICK4™ *a video on the behavioral treatment of phobias.*

CLICK4™ *a case study of systematic desensitization—"David."*

gradual process in which the client learns to handle increasingly disturbing stimuli while anxiety to each one is being counterconditioned. About 10 to 20 stimuli are arranged in a sequence, or **hierarchy,** according to their capacity to elicit anxiety. In imagination or by being shown photos, the client travels gradually up through this hierarchy, approaching the target behavior. In Adam's case, the target behavior was the ability to receive an injection without undue anxiety.

Wolpe developed systematic desensitization on the assumption that anxiety responses, like other behaviors, are learned or conditioned. He reasoned that they can be unlearned by means of counterconditioning or extinction. In counterconditioning, a response that is incompatible with anxiety is made to appear under conditions that usually elicit anxiety. Muscle relaxation is incompatible with anxiety. For this reason, Adam's therapist is teaching him to relax in the presence of (usually) anxiety-evoking slides of needles.

Remaining in the presence of phobic imagery, rather than running away from it, is also likely to enhance self-efficacy expectations (Galassi, 1988). Self-efficacy expectations are negatively correlated with levels of adrenaline in the bloodstream (Bandura et al., 1985). Raising clients' self-efficacy expectations thus may help lower their adrenaline levels and reduce their feelings of nervousness.

Modeling   **Modeling** relies on observational learning. In this method clients observe, and then imitate, people who approach and cope with the objects or situations that the clients fear. Bandura and his colleagues (1969) found that modeling worked as well as systematic desensitization—and more rapidly—in reducing fear of snakes. Like systematic desensitization, modeling is likely to increase self-efficacy expectations in coping with feared stimuli.

Aversive Conditioning

Many people also seek behavior therapy because they want to break bad habits, such as smoking, excessive drinking, nail biting, and the like. One behavior-therapy approach to helping people do so is **aversive conditioning.** *Question: How do behavior therapists use aversive conditioning to help people break bad habits?* Aversive conditioning is a controversial procedure in which painful or aversive stimuli are paired with unwanted impulses, such as desire for a cigarette or desire to engage in antisocial behavior, in order to make the impulse less appealing. For example, to help people control

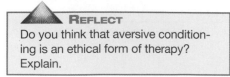
▲ **REFLECT**
Do you think that aversive conditioning is an ethical form of therapy? Explain.

Hierarchy ▲ An arrangement of stimuli according to the amount of fear they evoke.
Modeling ▲ A behavior-therapy technique in which a client observes and imitates a person who approaches and copes with feared objects or situations.
Aversive conditioning ▲ A behavior-therapy technique in which undesired responses are inhibited by pairing repugnant or offensive stimuli with them.

alcohol intake, tastes of different alcoholic beverages can be paired with drug-induced nausea and vomiting or with electric shock.

Aversive conditioning has been used with problems as diverse as cigarette smoking, sexual abuse (Rice et al., 1991), and retarded children's self-injurious behavior. **Rapid smoking** is an aversive-conditioning method designed to help smokers quit. In this method, the would-be quitter inhales every 6 seconds. In another method the hose of a hair dryer is hooked up to a chamber containing several lit cigarettes. Smoke is blown into the quitter's face as he or she also smokes a cigarette. A third method uses branching pipes so that the smoker draws in smoke from several cigarettes at the same time. In these methods, overexposure makes once-desirable cigarette smoke aversive. The quitter becomes motivated to avoid, rather than seek, cigarettes. However, the effectiveness of aversive conditioning for helping people quit smoking is uncertain (Lancaster et al., 2000), and interest in aversive conditioning for quitting smoking has waned because of side effects such as raising blood pressure and the availability of nicotine-replacement techniques.

In one study of aversive conditioning in the treatment of alcoholism, 63% of the 685 people treated remained abstinent for one year afterward, and about a third remained abstinent for at least 3 years (Wiens & Menustik, 1983). It may seem ironic that punitive aversive stimulation is sometimes used to stop children from punishing themselves, but people sometimes hurt themselves in order to obtain sympathy and attention. If self-injury leads to more pain than anticipated and no sympathy, it might be discontinued.

Operant Conditioning Procedures

We usually prefer to relate to people who smile at us rather than ignore us and to take courses in which we do well rather than fail. We tend to repeat behavior that is reinforced. Behavior that is not reinforced tends to become extinguished. Behavior therapists have used these principles of operant conditioning with psychotic patients as well as with clients with milder problems. *Question: How do behavior therapists apply principles of operant conditioning in behavior modification?*

The staff at one mental hospital was at a loss about how to encourage withdrawn schizophrenic patients to eat regularly. Ayllon and Haughton (1962) observed that staff members were making the problem worse by coaxing patients into the dining room and even feeding them. Staff attention apparently reinforced the patients' lack of cooperation. Some rules were changed. Patients who did not arrive at the dining hall within 30 minutes after serving were locked out. Staff could not interact with patients at mealtime. With uncooperative behavior no longer reinforced, patients quickly changed their eating habits. Then patients were required to pay one penny to enter the dining hall. Pennies were earned by interacting with other patients and showing other socially appropriate behaviors. These target behaviors also became more frequent.

Health professionals are concerned as to whether people who are, or have been, dependent on alcohol can exercise control over their drinking. One recent study showed that rewards for remaining abstinent from alcohol can exert a powerful effect (Petry et al., 2000). In the study, one group of alcohol-dependent veterans was given a standard treatment while another group received the treatment *plus* the chance to win prizes for remaining alcohol-free, as measured by a Breathalyzer test. By the end of the 8-week treatment period, 84% of the veterans who could win prizes remained in the program, as compared with 22% of the standard treatment group. The prizes had an average value of $200, far less than what alcohol-related absenteeism from work and other responsibilities can cost.

The Token Economy   Many psychiatric wards and hospitals now use **token economies** in which patients must use tokens such as poker chips to purchase TV viewing time, extra visits to the canteen, or a private room. The tokens are reinforcements for productive activities such as making beds, brushing teeth, and socializing. Token economies have not eliminated all features of schizophrenia. However, they have enhanced patient activity and cooperation. Tokens have also been used to modify the behavior of children with conduct disorders. In one program, for example, children received

Aversive Conditioning.
In aversive conditioning, unwanted behaviors take on a noxious quality as a result of being repeatedly paired with aversive stimuli. Overexposure is making cigarette smoke aversive to this smoker.

CLICK4™ *a bulletin board discussion: Is aversive conditioning an ethical form of therapy?*

Rapid smoking ▲ An aversive conditioning method for quitting smoking in which the smoker inhales every 6 seconds, thus rendering once-desirable cigarette smoke aversive.

Token economy ▲ A controlled environment in which people are reinforced for desired behaviors with tokens (such as poker chips) that may be exchanged for privileges.

tokens for helpful behaviors such as volunteering and lost tokens for behaviors such as arguing and failing to pay attention (Schneider & Byrne, 1987).

Successive Approximations   The operant conditioning method of **successive approximations** is often used to help clients build good habits. Let us use a (not uncommon!) example: You want to study 3 hours each evening but can concentrate for only half an hour. Rather than attempting to increase your study time all at once, you could do so gradually by adding, say, 5 minutes each evening. After every hour or so of studying, you could reinforce yourself with 5 minutes of people-watching in a busy section of the library.

Social Skills Training   In social skills training, behavior therapists decrease social anxiety and build social skills through operant-conditioning procedures that employ **self-monitoring,** coaching, modeling, role-playing, **behavior rehearsal,** and **feedback.** Social skills training has been used to help formerly hospitalized mental patients maintain jobs and apartments in the community. For example, a worker can rehearse politely asking a supervisor for assistance or asking a landlord to fix the plumbing in an apartment.

Social skills training is effective in groups. Group members can role-play important people—such as parents, spouses, or potential dates—in the lives of other members.

Assertiveness Training   Are you a person who can't say no? Do other people walk all over you? Brush off those footprints and get some assertiveness training! Assertiveness training is a kind of social skills training that helps clients demand their rights and express their genuine feelings. It helps decrease social anxiety, but it has also been used to optimize the functioning of individuals without problems. Assertive behavior can be contrasted with both *nonassertive* (submissive) behavior and *aggressive* behavior. Assertive people express their genuine feelings, stick up for their legitimate rights, and refuse unreasonable requests. But they do not insult, threaten, or belittle. Assertive people do not shy away from meeting people and building relationships, and they express positive feelings such as liking and love. The nearby Assertiveness Schedule will give you some insight into how assertive you are. The Click4™ feature indicated here may help you become a more assertive person.

Biofeedback Training   Through **biofeedback training** (BFT), therapists help clients become more aware of, and gain control over, various bodily functions. Therapists attach clients to devices that measure bodily functions such as heart rate. "Bleeps" or other electronic signals are used to indicate (and thereby reinforce) changes in the desired direction—for example, a slower heart rate. (Knowledge of results is a powerful reinforcer.) One device, the electromyograph (EMG), monitors muscle tension. It has been used to augment control over muscle tension in the forehead and elsewhere, thereby alleviating anxiety, stress, and headaches.

BFT also helps clients voluntarily regulate functions once thought to be beyond conscious control, such as heart rate and blood pressure. Hypertensive clients use a blood pressure cuff and electronic signals to gain control over their blood pressure. The electroencephalograph (EEG) monitors brain waves and can be used to teach people how to produce alpha waves, which are associated with relaxation. Some people have overcome insomnia by learning to produce the kinds of brain waves associated with sleep.

Self-Control Methods

Do mysterious forces sometimes seem to be at work in your life? Forces that delight in wreaking havoc on New Year's resolutions and other efforts to put an end to your bad habits? Just when you go on a diet, that juicy pizza stares at you from the TV set. Just when you resolve to balance your budget, that sweater goes on sale. *Question: How can you—yes, you—use behavior therapy to deal with temptation and enhance your self-control?*

REFLECT

Can you think of a way to use the method of successive approximations to improve your own life? You can think of either building a good habit or breaking a bad habit.

CLICK4™ *AABT—the Association for Advancement of Behavior Therapy.*

CLICK4™ *a WebSearch activity: Do you need to become more assertive?*

CLICK4™ *advice on how to become an assertive person.*

Successive approximations ▲ In operant conditioning, a series of behaviors that gradually become more similar to a target behavior.
Self-monitoring ▲ Keeping a record of one's own behavior to identify problems and record successes.
Behavior rehearsal ▲ Practice.
Feedback ▲ In assertiveness training, information about the effectiveness of a response.
Biofeedback training ▲ The systematic feeding back to an organism of information about a bodily function so that the organism can gain control of that function. Abbreviated BFT.

The Rathus Assertiveness Schedule

How assertive are you? Do you stick up for your rights, or do you allow other people to walk all over you? Do you say what you feel or what you think other people want you to say? Do you initiate relationships with attractive people, or do you shy away from them?

One way to gain insight into how assertive you are is to take the following self-report test of assertive behavior. Once you have finished, turn to Appendix B to find out how to calculate and interpret your score.

Directions: Indicate how well each item describes you by using this code:

3 = very much like me
2 = rather like me
1 = slightly like me
−1 = slightly unlike me
−2 = rather unlike me
−3 = very much unlike me

_____ 1. Most people seem to be more aggressive and assertive than I am.*

_____ 2. I have hesitated to make or accept dates because of "shyness."*

_____ 3. When the food served at a restaurant is not done to my satisfaction, I complain about it to the waiter or waitress.

_____ 4. I am careful to avoid hurting other people's feelings, even when I feel that I have been injured.*

_____ 5. If a salesperson has gone to considerable trouble to show me merchandise that is not quite suitable, I have a difficult time saying "No."*

_____ 6. When I am asked to do something, I insist upon knowing why.

_____ 7. There are times when I look for a good, vigorous argument.

_____ 8. I strive to get ahead as well as most people in my position.

_____ 9. To be honest, people often take advantage of me.*

_____ 10. I enjoy starting conversations with new acquaintances and strangers.

_____ 11. I often don't know what to say to people I find attractive.*

_____ 12. I will hesitate to make phone calls to business establishments and institutions.*

_____ 13. I would rather apply for a job or for admission to a college by writing letters than by going through with personal interviews.*

_____ 14. I find it embarrassing to return merchandise.*

_____ 15. If a close and respected relative were annoying me, I would smother my feelings rather than express my annoyance.*

_____ 16. I have avoided asking questions for fear of sounding stupid.*

_____ 17. During an argument, I am sometimes afraid that I will get so upset that I will shake all over.*

_____ 18. If a famed and respected lecturer makes a comment which I think is incorrect, I will have the audience hear my point of view as well.

_____ 19. I avoid arguing over prices with clerks and salespeople.*

_____ 20. When I have done something important or worthwhile, I manage to let others know about it.

_____ 21. I am open and frank about my feelings.

_____ 22. If someone has been spreading false and bad stories about me, I see him or her as soon as possible and "have a talk" about it.

_____ 23. I often have a hard time saying "No."*

_____ 24. I tend to bottle up my emotions rather than make a scene.*

_____ 25. I complain about poor service in a restaurant and elsewhere.

_____ 26. When I am given a compliment, I sometimes just don't know what to say.*

_____ 27. If a couple near me in a theater or at a lecture were conversing rather loudly, I would ask them to be quiet or to take their conversation elsewhere.

_____ 28. Anyone attempting to push ahead of me in a line is in for a good battle.

_____ 29. I am quick to express an opinion.

_____ 30. There are times when I just can't say anything.*

SOURCE: Reprinted from Rathus, 1973, pp. 398–406.

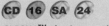

CLICK4™ *the interactive version of this Self-Assessment.*

TABLE 16.1 EXCERPTS FROM BRIAN'S DIARY OF NAIL BITING FOR APRIL 14

Incident	Time	Location	Activity (Thoughts, Feelings)	Reactions
1	7:45 A.M.	Freeway	Driving to work, bored, not thinking	Finger bleeds, pain
2	10:30 A.M.	Office	Writing report	Self-disgust
3	2:25 P.M.	Conference	Listening to dull financial report	Embarrassment
4	6:40 P.M.	Living room	Watching evening news	Self-disgust

NOTE: A functional analysis of problem behavior like nail biting increases awareness of the environmental context in which it occurs, spurs motivation to change, and, in highly motivated people, might lead to significant behavioral change.

REFLECT

Do you have any habits you would like to change? Can you use any of the methods of self-control discussed here to help you do so?

CLICK4™ *a quiz covering the first half of this chapter.*

Functional Analysis of Behavior

Behavior therapists usually begin with a **functional analysis** of the problem behavior. In this way, they help determine the stimuli that trigger the behavior and the reinforcers that maintain it. Then clients are taught how to manipulate the antecedents and consequences of their behavior, and how to increase the frequency of desired responses and decrease the frequency of undesired responses. You can use a diary to jot down each instance of a problem behavior. Note the time of day, location, your activity at the time (including your thoughts and feelings), and reactions (yours and others'). Functional analysis serves a number of purposes. It makes you more aware of the environmental context of your behavior and can increase your motivation to change.

Brian used functional analysis to master his nail biting. Table 16.1 shows a few items from his notebook. He discovered that boredom and humdrum activities seemed to serve as triggers for nail biting. He began to watch out for feelings of boredom as signs to practice self-control. He also made some changes in his life so that he would feel bored less often.

There are numerous self-control strategies aimed at the stimuli that trigger behavior, the behaviors themselves, and reinforcers. Table 16.2 describes some of these strategies.

REVIEW

(11) Behavior therapy applies principles of _____ to bring about desired behavioral changes. (12) Behavior-therapy methods for reducing fears include flooding; systematic _____ , in which a client is gradually exposed to more fear-arousing stimuli; and modeling. (13) _____ conditioning associates undesired behavior with painful stimuli to decrease the frequency of the behavior. (14) _____ conditioning methods reinforce desired responses and extinguish undesired responses. (15) In self-control methods, clients first engage in a _____ analysis of problem behavior. (16) Clients are then taught how to change the behavior by manipulating its antecedents and _____ .

Pulling It Together: Why do behavior therapists minimize the importance of the therapist-client relationship? How do behavior therapists attempt to ensure that their methods are scientific?

COGNITIVE THERAPIES: ADJUSTMENT IS WHAT YOU THINK (AND DO)

There is nothing either good or bad, but thinking makes it so.

—*Shakespeare*, Hamlet

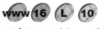

CLICK4™ *Web sites devoted to cognitive and cognitive-behavioral therapy and research.*

In this line from *Hamlet*, Shakespeare did not mean to suggest that injuries and misfortunes are painless or easy to manage. Rather, he meant that our appraisals of unfortunate events can heighten our discomfort and impair our coping ability. In so doing, Shakespeare was providing a kind of motto for cognitive therapists. ***Question: What is cognitive therapy?***

Cognitive therapy focuses on changing the beliefs, attitudes, and automatic types of thinking that create and compound their clients' problems (Beck, 1993; Ellis & Dryden, 1996). Cognitive therapists, like psychodynamic and humanistic-existential therapists, aim to foster self-insight, but they aim to heighten insight into *current cognitions* as well as those of the past. Cognitive therapists also aim to directly change maladaptive cognitions in order to reduce negative feelings, provide insight, and help the client solve problems.

You may have noticed that many behavior therapists incorporate cognitive procedures in their methods. For example, techniques such as systematic desensitization, covert sensitization, and covert reinforcement ask clients to focus on visual imagery. Behavioral methods for treating bulimia nervosa focus on clients' irrational attitudes toward their weight and body shape as well as foster healthful eating habits.

Let us look at the approaches and methods of some major cognitive therapists.

Functional analysis ▲ A systematic study of behavior in which one identifies the stimuli that trigger problem behavior and the reinforcers that maintain it.

Cognitive therapy ▲ A form of therapy that focuses on how clients' cognitions (expectations, attitudes, beliefs, etc.) lead to distress and may be modified to relieve distress and promote adaptive behavior.

TABLE 16.2 BEHAVIORAL STRATEGIES FOR SELF-CONTROL

STRATEGY	ABOUT . . .
STRATEGIES AIMED AT STIMULI THAT TRIGGER BEHAVIOR	
Restriction of the stimulus field	Gradually exclude the problem behavior from more environments. For example, at first make smoking off limits in the car, then in the home.
Avoidance of powerful stimuli that trigger habits	Avoid obvious sources of temptation. People who go window-shopping often wind up buying more than windows. If eating at The Pizza Glutton tempts you to forget your diet, eat at home or at The Celery Stalk instead.
Stimulus control	Place yourself in an environment in which desirable behavior is likely to occur. Maybe it's difficult to lift your mood directly at times, but you can place yourself in the audience of an uplifting concert or film. It might be difficult to force yourself to study, but how about rewarding yourself for spending time in the library?
STRATEGIES AIMED AT BEHAVIOR	
Response prevention	Make unwanted behavior difficult or impossible. Impulse buying is curbed when you shred your credit cards, leave your checkbook home, and carry only a couple of dollars with you. You can't reach for the strawberry cream cheese pie in your refrigerator if you didn't buy it at the supermarket.
Competing responses	Engage in behaviors that are incompatible with the bad habit. It is difficult to drink a glass of water and a fattening milkshake simultaneously. Grasping something firmly is a useful competing response for nail biting or scratching.
Chain breaking	Interfere with unwanted habitual behavior by complicating the process of engaging in it. Break the chain of reaching for a readily available cigarette and placing it in your mouth by wrapping the pack in aluminum foil and placing it on the top shelf of a closet. Rewrap the pack after taking one cigarette. Put your cigarette in the ashtray between puffs, or put your fork down between mouthfuls of dessert. Ask yourself whether you really want more.
Successive approximations	Gradually approach targets through a series of relatively painless steps. Increase studying by only 5 minutes a day. Decrease smoking by pausing for a minute when the cigarette is smoked halfway, or by putting it out a minute before you would wind up eating the filter. Decrease your daily intake of food by 50 to 100 calories every couple of days, or cut out one type of fattening food every few days.
STRATEGIES AIMED AT REINFORCEMENTS	
Reinforcement of desired behavior	Why give yourself something for nothing? Make pleasant activities such as going to films, walking on the beach, or reading a new novel contingent on meeting reasonable daily behavioral goals. Each day you remain within your calorie limit, put a dollar away toward that camera or vacation trip you have been dreaming of.
Response cost	Heighten awareness of the long-term reasons for dieting or cutting down on smoking by punishing yourself for not meeting a daily goal or for engaging in a bad habit. For example, if you bite your nails or inhale that cheesecake, make out a check to a cause you oppose and mail it at once.
"Grandma's method"	How did Grandma persuade children to eat their vegetables? Simple: No veggies, no dessert. In this method, desired behaviors such as studying and brushing your teeth can be increased by insisting that those behaviors be done before you engage in a pleasant or frequently occurring activity. For example, don't watch television unless you have studied first. Don't leave the apartment until you've brushed your teeth. You can also place reminders about new attitudes you're trying to acquire on little cards and read them regularly. For example, in quitting smoking, you might write "Every day it becomes a little easier" on one card and "Your lungs will turn pink again" on another. Place these cards and others in your wallet, and read them each time you leave the house.
Covert sensitization	Create imaginary horror stories about problem behavior. Psychologists have successfully reduced overeating and smoking by having clients imagine that they become acutely nauseated at the thought of fattening foods or that a cigarette is made from vomit. Some horror stories are not so "imaginary." Deliberately focusing on heart strain and diseased lungs every time you overeat or smoke, rather than ignoring these long-term consequences, might also promote self-control.
Covert reinforcement	Create rewarding imagery for desired behavior. When you have achieved a behavioral goal, fantasize about how wonderful you are. Imagine friends and family members patting you on the back.

Cognitive Therapy: Correcting Cognitive Errors

Cognitive therapy is the name of an approach to therapy as well as psychiatrist Aaron Beck's specific methods. Beck (1991, 1993) focuses on clients' cognitive distortions. *Question: What is Aaron Beck's method of cognitive therapy?* Beck's cognitive therapy is active. Beck encourages clients to become their own personal scientists and challenge beliefs that are not supported by evidence.

Beck questions people in a way that encourages them to see the irrationality of their ways of thinking. For example, depressed people tend to minimize their accomplishments and to assume that the worst will happen. Both distortions heighten feelings of depression. Cognitive distortions can be fleeting and automatic, difficult to detect (Persons et al., 2001). Beck's therapy methods help clients become aware of distortions and challenge them.

Beck notes how cognitive errors contribute to clients' miseries:

1. Clients may *selectively perceive* the world as a harmful place and ignore evidence to the contrary.

2. Clients may *overgeneralize* on the basis of a few examples. For example, they may perceive themselves as worthless because they were laid off at work, or as unattractive because they were refused a date.

3. Clients may *magnify*, or blow out of proportion, the importance of negative events. They may catastrophize failing a test by assuming they will flunk out of college, or catastrophize losing a job by believing that they will never find another one and that serious harm will befall their family as a result.

Aaron Beck

He used cognitive and behavioral techniques on himself before he became a psychiatrist. One of the reasons Aaron Beck went into medicine was to confront his own fear of blood. He had had a series of operations as a child, and from then on the sight of blood had made him feel faint. During his first year of medical school, he forced himself to watch operations. In his second year, he became a surgical assistant. Soon the sight of blood became normal to him. Later he essentially argued himself out of an irrational fear of tunnels. He convinced himself that the tunnels did not cause the fear because the symptoms of faintness and shallow breathing would appear before he entered them.

As a psychiatrist, Beck first practiced psychoanalysis. However, he could not find scientific evidence for psychoanalytic beliefs. Psychoanalytic theory explained depression as anger turned inward, so that it is transformed into a need to suffer. Beck's own clinical experiences led him to believe that it is more likely that depressed people experience cognitive distortions such as the *cognitive triad*. That is, they expect the worst of themselves ("I'm no good"), the world at large ("This is an awful place"), and their future ("Nothing good will ever happen"). Beck's cognitive therapy is active. Beck encourages clients to challenge beliefs that are not supported by evidence.

Beck also challenges his own points of view. "I am a big self-doubter," Beck (2000) admits. "I always doubt what I do, which is one of the reasons I do so much research and encourage research." Beck teaches health professionals his form of therapy—and scientific skepticism—at the University of Pennsylvania.

www 16 L 11

CLICK4™ *the Web site of the Beck Institute for Cognitive Therapy and Research.*

4. Clients may engage in *absolutist thinking*, or looking at the world in black and white rather than in shades of gray. In doing so, a rejection on a date takes on the meaning of a lifetime of loneliness; an uncomfortable illness takes on life-threatening proportions.

The concept of pinpointing and modifying errors may become clearer from the following excerpt from a case in which a 53-year-old engineer obtained cognitive therapy for severe depression. The engineer had left his job and become inactive. As reported by Beck and his colleagues, the first goal of treatment was to foster physical activity—even things like raking leaves and preparing dinner—because activity is incompatible with depression. Then:

[The engineer's] cognitive distortions were identified by comparing his assessment of each activity with that of his wife. Alternative ways of interpreting his experiences were then considered.

In comparing his wife's résumé of his past experiences, he became aware that he had (1) undervalued his past by failing to mention many previous accomplishments, (2) regarded himself as far more responsible for his "failures" than she did, and (3) concluded that he was worthless since he had not succeeded in attaining certain goals in the past. When the two accounts were contrasted, he could discern many of his cognitive distortions.

In subsequent sessions, his wife continued to serve as an "objectifier."

In midtherapy, [he] compiled a list of new attitudes that he had acquired since initiating therapy. These included:

1. "I am starting at a lower level of functioning at my job, but it will improve if I persist."
2. "I know that once I get going in the morning, everything will run all right for the rest of the day."
3. "I can't achieve everything at once."
4. "I have my periods of ups and downs, but in the long run I feel better."
5. "My expectations from my job and life should be scaled down to a realistic level."
6. "Giving in to avoidance [e.g., staying away from work and social interactions] never helps and only leads to further avoidance."

He was instructed to reread this list daily for several weeks even though he already knew the content. (Rush et al., 1975)

The engineer gradually became less depressed and returned to work and an active social life. Along the way, he learned to combat inappropriate self-blame for problems, perfectionistic expectations, magnification of failures, and overgeneralization from failures.

Becoming aware of cognitive errors and modifying catastrophizing thoughts helps us cope with stress. Internal, stable, and global attributions of failure lead to depression and feelings of helplessness. Cognitive therapists also alert clients to cognitive errors such as these so that the clients can change their attitudes and pave the way for more effective overt behavior.

Rational Emotive Behavior Therapy: Overcoming "Musts" and "Shoulds"

In **rational emotive behavior therapy** (REBT), Albert Ellis (Ellis & Dryden, 1996) points out that our beliefs *about* events, not only the events themselves, shape our responses to them. Moreover, many of us harbor a number of irrational beliefs that can give rise to problems or magnify their impact. Two of the most important ones are the belief

Rational emotive behavior therapy ▲ Albert Ellis's form of therapy that encourages clients to challenge and correct irrational expectations and maladaptive behaviors.

that we must have the love and approval of people who are important to us and the belief that we must prove ourselves to be thoroughly competent, adequate, and achieving.

Question: What is Albert Ellis's method of rational emotive behavior therapy (REBT)?

Albert Ellis, like Aaron Beck, began as a psychoanalyst. But he became disturbed by the passive role of the analyst and by the slow rate of obtaining results—if they were obtained at all. Still, Ellis finds a role for Freud's views: "One of the main things [Freud] did was point out the importance of unconscious thinking. Freud pointed out that when people are motivated to do things, that they unconsciously think, and even feel, certain things. We use that concept," Ellis (2000) admits, "although Freud, as usual, ran it into the ground."

Ellis's REBT methods are active and directive. He does not sit back like the traditional psychoanalyst and occasionally offer an interpretation. Instead, he urges clients to seek out their irrational beliefs, which can be unconscious, though not as deeply buried as Freud believed. Nevertheless, they can be hard to pinpoint without some direction. Ellis shows clients how those beliefs lead to misery and challenges clients to change them. When Ellis sees clients behaving according to irrational beliefs, he may refute the beliefs by asking "Where is it written that you must . . . ?" or "What evidence do you have that . . . ?" According to Ellis, we need less misery and less blaming in our lives, and more action.

Ellis straddles behavioral and cognitive therapies. He originally dubbed his method of therapy *rational-emotive therapy*, because his focus was on the cognitive—irrational beliefs and how to change them. However, Ellis has also always promoted behavioral changes to cement cognitive changes and provide "a fuller experience of life" (Albert Ellis Institute, 1997, p. 2). In keeping with his broad philosophy, he recently changed the name of rational-emotive therapy to rational emotive *behavior* therapy.

Many theorists consider cognitive therapy to be a collection of techniques that are part of the overall approach known as behavior therapy, which is discussed in the follow-

CLICK4™ *the Web site of the Albert Ellis Institute.*

CLICK4™ *a profile of Albert Ellis.*

CLICK4™ *advice on how to handle a social provocation.*

IN REVIEW

Methods of Psychotherapy

Type of Therapy	Goals	Methods	About . . .
Psychodynamic Therapies	To strengthen the ego; to provide self-insight into unconscious conflict	Traditional psychoanalysis is lengthy and nondirective and involves methods such as free association and dream analysis.	Most effective with verbal, "upscale" clients. Modern ego analytic approaches are briefer and more directive.
Humanistic-Existential Therapies	To help clients get in touch with parts of themselves that they have "disowned" and actualize their unique desires and abilities	Client-centered therapy is nondirective; it provides an atmosphere in which clients can engage in self-exploration without fear. Gestalt therapy is highly directive.	Client-centered therapy is practiced widely in college and university counseling centers to help students make academic and personal decisions.
Behavior Therapy	To use principles of learning to help clients engage in adaptive behavior and discontinue maladaptive behavior	Behavior therapy is directive and uses fear-reduction methods (including systematic desensitization), aversive conditioning (to help clients discontinue bad habits), operant conditioning procedures (e.g., social skills training), and self-control methods (beginning with functional analysis of behavior).	Behavior therapists have developed treatments for problems (e.g., smoking, phobias, sexual dysfunctions) for which there previously were no effective treatment methods.
Cognitive Therapies	To make clients aware of the beliefs, attitudes, and automatic types of thinking that create and compound their problems; to help them correct these kinds of thinking to reduce negative feelings and solve problems	Beck's cognitive therapy helps people recognize and correct cognitive errors such as selective perception, overgeneralization, magnification of negative events, and absolutist thinking. Rational emotive behavior therapists show clients how irrational beliefs catastrophize events and make them miserable.	Many theorists consider cognitive therapy to be part of behavior therapy and some call it "cognitive *behavioral* therapy." In fact, Ellis recently changed the name of his approach to therapy from rational-emotive therapy to rational emotive *behavior* therapy.

CLICK4™ *a WebSearch activity: Can an AI-based humanistic therapist help?*

ing section. Some members of this group use the term "cognitive *behavioral* therapy." Others argue that the term *behavior therapy* is broad enough to include cognitive techniques. Many cognitive therapists and behavior therapists differ in focus, however. Behavior therapists deal with client cognitions in order to change *overt* behavior. Cognitive therapists also

Psychology and Modern Life

Virtual Reality Finds a Real Place as an Aid in Therapy

Use of Virtual Reality in Psychotherapy. Psychologists are using virtual reality to help clients cope with pain, fears, and other psychological problems.

James Pokorny sat upright in bed in his room at the University of Washington Burn Center at Harborview as a nurse prepared to unwrap his bandages. Working on a car when the fuel tank exploded, Mr. Pokorny received third-degree burns on about 42% of his body. Despite pain-killing drugs, Mr. Pokorny was in agonizing pain, which intensified when his bandages were changed. So doctors tried a new approach.

Losing Pain in a Virtual World Wearing a black plastic helmet with a computer monitor inside, headphones, and a tracker that monitored the position of his finger, Mr. Pokorny entered a virtual world. Multicolored three-dimensional graphics, along with sound and tactile input created a realistic virtual kitchen, with a stove, teapots, cabinets, and clouds outside a curtained window.

There was also a virtual spider. The tracker on his finger allowed him to chase the spider with his hand, force it down the sink and grind it up by switching on a virtual

garbage disposal. All of which, Mr. Pokorny said, made the wound care seem far less painful. "You're concentrating on different things, rather than your pain," he said. "The pain level went down significantly."

Dr. Hunter Hoffman, a cognitive psychologist at the Human Interface Technology Laboratory at the University of Washington, conducted the experiment with a colleague at the university, Dr. David Patterson, a professor of rehabilitation medicine, surgery, and psychology. Dr. Hoffman said that conscious attention was like a spotlight. With this therapy, he added, "we are attracting that spotlight to the virtual world and away from pain."

Virtual reality, the name for the interactive artificial worlds created by computers, is finding a place in health care, especially among psychologists. It is being used for treating fear of flying or thunderstorms, helping diabetics warm their hands and mitigating the crippling memories of war.

"You're not watching something, you're in something," said Dr. David Ready, a clinical psychologist at the Atlanta Veteran's Administration Medical Center, where a virtual reality system is being used to treat post-traumatic stress disorders in combat veterans. "All you see is what's in the goggles and all you hear is what's on the headphones."

That does not mean the virtual world looks extremely realistic. The one in use at Harborview is a cartoon representation of a kitchen. But nothing else is visible and the scene changes realistically as the user's head swivels, giving the patient a strong sense of being somewhere he or she is not.

In the study by Dr. Hoffmann and Dr. Patterson, published in the March 2000 issue of *Pain,* a British medical journal, patients with skin grafts at the burn treatment center either played Nintendo or wore the kitchen virtual-reality gear during the painful removal of surgical staples. One patient thought of his pain 95% of the time while

see the value of tying treatment outcomes to observable behavior, but they believe that cognitive change is a key goal in itself.

The nearby "Psychology and Modern Life" feature shows how psychologists and other health professionals are using virtual reality to supplement behavioral and cognitive

www 16 WS 5

CLICK4™ *a WebSearch activity: Can "online counseling" help?*

playing Nintendo, but just 2% of the time while using the virtual reality gear. The other patient went from 91% in video to 36% in virtual reality.

"The preliminary findings are exciting," said Dr. Mark Jensen, a professor of rehabilitation medicine and a specialist in pain at the University of Washington. "I think it can be widely used for chronic pain. But it needs to be tried with a variety of painful procedures — dentistry and dialysis for example — to see how well it works for those applications."

And What If a Spider Sat Down Beside Her?

The capacity of virtual reality to convince the mind is also effective in the treatment of phobias. The virtual kitchen with the spider that Dr. Hoffman uses to treat pain can be adapted to treat spider phobias. For more than 20 years, for instance, Joanne Cartwright suffered a debilitating fear of spiders. "I washed my truck every night before I went to work in case there were webs," she said. "I put all my clothes in plastic bags and taped duct tape around my doors so spiders couldn't get in. I thought I was going to have a mental breakdown. I wasn't living."

Twelve sessions of spider virtual-reality treatment with Dr. Albert Carlin, a professor of behavioral psychology at the University of Washington, greatly eased her fear. "I'm amazed," she said, "because I am doing all this stuff I could never do — camping, hunting and hiking."

And What About Fear of Flying?

Dr. Brenda Wiederhold, the director of the Center for Advanced Multimedia Psychotherapy at the California School of Professional Psychology, uses a virtual reality system to treat several kinds of panic and phobia disorders, including fear of flying. For the treatment at the school, which specializes in training clinicians, patients sit in real airplane seats wearing the head-mounted displays that surround them with realistic airplane interiors. The seats vibrate as the sound of engines is heard. As the sweat

and rapidly beating heart that accompany panic start to increase, the patient is taught to stop the cascade of negative thoughts by yelling "Stop" or by using a distraction technique like counting back from 1,000 by 7. Dr. Wiederhold also teaches clients how to rein in their anxiety by taking deep slow breaths to slow pounding hearts and reduce the sweating.

Dr. Barbara Rothbaum, an associate professor of psychiatry and director of the trauma and anxiety recovery program at the Emory School of Medicine in Atlanta, and her colleagues (2000) compared the effectiveness of virtual reality exposure to flying with standard exposure therapy, in which participants are exposed to an airplane at an airport. Participants received 8 sessions of treatment over 6 weeks. The procedures were equally effective, as shown by the finding that 93% of each group had flown in an airplane within 6 months following treatment.

Back in Combat

The systems have also proven useful in treating the lasting shock caused by violent wartime experiences. For the last year and a half, Dr. Ready of Atlanta has been treating those with post-traumatic stress syndrome with virtual reality on an experimental basis. The work, so far, is promising in reducing the severity of flashbacks, he said. Veterans with stress syndrome put on virtual reality goggles and re-experience violent wartime events, complete with helicopter rides, gunfire, and jungle walks. During the therapy, Dr. Ready progressively exposes the patient to realistic simulations of the situations that affected them.

"I'm like a movie director," Dr. Ready said. "If a guy says, 'I was walking through the jungle and mortars came in,' I bring in the mortars with the computer."

During all 12 of the 90-minute sessions, the experiences increase in intensity until the patients begin to experience the stress with increased heart rates and sweating. As the clients begin to react, Dr. Ready talks them through it.

"During a flashback, a veteran has both feet in Vietnam," Dr. Ready said. "With virtual-reality therapy, he has one foot in Vietnam and one foot in the laboratory. And he's got a buddy there talking to him."

So far, Dr. Ready has seen the severity of the symptoms reduced by a third in all 10 people who have completed the training, on par with other therapies. Early indications are that the effects last for months.

Increasing the Effectiveness of Biofeedback

The realistic nature of virtual reality, the feeling of being there, is also helping to increase the effectiveness of traditional kinds of biofeedback. Dr. Alan T. Pope, a researcher at the Langley NASA Research Center in Langley, Va., has devised a virtual reality system to treat restricted blood flow to the hands, a problem that afflicts people with diabetes and Raynaud's disease.

The patient wears sensors on the hand and arm that provide data to a computer, which converts the information into a simulation of the blood-vessel network. The three-dimensional blood vessel graphics are displayed on a computer monitor in a pair of goggles that the patient wears. "They see these blood vessels expand and contract in keeping with the temperature at their fingertips and their pulse," Dr. Pope said. Because the participants are immersed in virtual worlds and their conscious attention is solely devoted to hand-warming, the task becomes easier.

Hand-monitoring is one of the most widely used types of biofeedback for cold extremities, anxiety, migraine, and headaches. And now, the approach with virtual reality gear is being tested at the Eastern Virginia Medical School and the University of Virginia for symptoms of diabetes. "If you provide a compelling and engaging display," Dr. Pope said, "it's more motivating." And, he added, the patients stay with it.

SOURCE: Adapted from Robbins, J. (2000, July 4). Virtual reality finds a real place as a medical aid. *The New York Times online.*

therapy techniques. Today's psychologists often expose clients to the things that disturb them under controlled circumstances. Virtual reality helps control the situation.

REVIEW

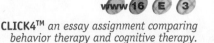

CLICK4™ *an essay assignment comparing behavior therapy and cognitive therapy.*

(17) _____ therapists focus on the beliefs, attitudes, and automatic thoughts that create and compound their clients' problems. (18) Beck notes four types of cognitive errors that contribute to clients' miseries: selective abstraction of the world as a harmful place; overgeneralization; magnification of the importance of negative events; and _____ thinking, or looking at the world in black and white rather than shades of gray. (19) Ellis's REBT confronts clients with the ways in which _____ beliefs contribute to problems such as anxiety and depression.

Pulling It Together: What are the similarities and differences between behavior therapy and cognitive therapy? Why did both Beck and Ellis discontinue the practice of psychoanalysis?

GROUP THERAPIES

CLICK4™ *an essay assignment on group therapies.*

When a psychotherapist has several clients with similar problems—anxiety, depression, adjustment to divorce, lack of social skills—it often makes sense to treat them in a group rather than in individual sessions. The methods and characteristics of the group reflect the needs of the members and the theoretical orientation of the leader. In group psychoanalysis, clients might interpret one another's dreams. In a client-centered group, they might provide an accepting atmosphere for self-exploration. Members of behavior therapy groups might be jointly desensitized to anxiety-evoking stimuli or might practice social skills together. *Question: What are the advantages and disadvantages of group therapy?*

Group therapy has the following advantages:

1. It is economical (Davison, 2000; Haaga, 2000). It allows the therapist to work with several clients at once.
2. Compared with one-to-one therapy, group therapy provides more information and life experience for clients to draw upon.
3. Appropriate behavior receives group support. Clients usually appreciate an outpouring of peer approval.
4. When we run into troubles, it is easy to imagine that we are different from other people or inferior to them. Affiliating with people with similar problems is reassuring.
5. Group members who show improvement provide hope for other members.
6. Many individuals seek therapy because of problems in relating to other people. People who seek therapy for other reasons also may be socially inhibited. Members of groups have the opportunity to practice social skills in a relatively nonthreatening atmosphere. In a group consisting of men and women of different ages, group members can role-play one another's employers, employees, spouses, parents, children, and friends. Members can role-play asking one another out on dates, saying no (or yes), and so on.

But group therapy is not for everyone. Some clients fare better with individual treatment. Many prefer not to disclose their problems to a group. They may be overly shy or want individual attention. It is the responsibility of the therapist to insist that group disclosures be kept confidential, to establish a supportive atmosphere, and to ensure that group members obtain the attention they need.

Many types of therapy can be conducted either individually or in groups. Encounter groups and family therapy are conducted only in groups.

Group Therapy.
Group therapy has a number of advantages over individual therapy for many clients. It's economical, provides a fund of experience for clients to draw upon, elicits group support, and provides an opportunity to relate to other people. On the other hand, some clients do need individual attention.

Encounter Groups

Encounter groups are not appropriate for treating serious psychological problems. Rather, they are intended to promote personal growth by heightening awareness of one's own needs and feelings and those of others. This goal is sought through intense confrontations, or encounters, between strangers. *Questions: What are encounter groups? What are their effects?*

Like ships in the night, group members come together out of the darkness, touch one another briefly, then sink back into the shadows of one another's lives. But something is gained from the passing.

Encounter groups stress interactions between group members in the here and now. Discussion of the past may be outlawed. Interpretation is out. However, expression of genuine feelings toward others is encouraged. When group members think a person's social mask is phony, they may descend en masse to rip it off.

Encounter groups can be damaging when they urge overly rapid disclosure of intimate matters or when several members attack one member. Responsible leaders do not tolerate these abuses and try to keep the group moving in a growth-enhancing direction.

Couple Therapy

Couple therapy helps couples enhance their relationship by improving their communication skills and helping them manage conflict (Markman et al., 1993). There are often power imbalances in relationships, and couple therapy helps individuals find "full membership" in the couple. Correcting power imbalances increases happiness and can decrease the incidence of domestic violence. Ironically, in situations of domestic violence, the partner with *less* power in the relationship is usually the violent one. Violence sometimes appears to be a way of compensating for inability to share power in other aspects of the relationship (Rathus & Sanderson, 1999).

Today the main approach to couple therapy today is cognitive-behavioral (Rathus & Sanderson, 1999). It teaches couples communications skills (such as how to listen to one another and how to express feelings), ways of handling feelings like depression and anger, and ways of solving problems.

REFLECT
Do you share the power in your relationships? How does your power sharing — or lack of it! — affect your relationships?

Encounter group ▲ A type of group that aims to foster self-awareness by focusing on how group members relate to each other in a setting that encourages open expression of feelings.

CLICK4™ *AAMFT—the American Association for Marriage and Family Therapy.*

Family Therapy

Question: What is family therapy? **Family therapy** is a form of group therapy in which one or more families constitute the group. Family therapy may be undertaken from various theoretical viewpoints. One is the "systems approach," in which family interaction is studied and modified to enhance the growth of individual family members and of the family unit as a whole (Prochaska & Norcross, 1999).

Family members with low self-esteem often cannot tolerate different attitudes and behaviors in other family members. Faulty communication within the family also creates problems. In addition, it is not uncommon for the family to present an "identified patient"—that is, the family member who has *the* problem and is *causing* all the trouble. Yet family therapists usually assume that the identified patient is a scapegoat for other problems within and among family members. It is a sort of myth: Change the bad apple—or identified patient—and the barrel—or family—will be functional once more.

The family therapist—often a specialist in this field—attempts to teach the family to communicate more effectively and encourage growth and autonomy in each family member.

REVIEW

(20) Group therapy tends to be (more or less?) economical than individual therapy. (21) _____ groups promote personal growth by heightening awareness of people's needs and feelings through intense confrontations between strangers. (22) In the _____ approach to family therapy, family interaction is modified to enhance the growth of family members and the family unit as a whole.

Pulling It Together: Under what circumstances would you recommend that someone go for group therapy rather than individual therapy?

CONTROVERSY ✕ IN PSYCHOLOGY

Does Psychotherapy Work?

In 1952, the British psychologist Hans Eysenck published a review of psychotherapy research—"The Effects of Psychotherapy"—that sent shock waves through the psychotherapy community. On the basis of his review of the research, Eysenck concluded that the rate of improvement among people in psychotherapy was no greater than the rate of "spontaneous remission"—that is, the rate of improvement that would be shown by people with psychological disorders who received no treatment at all. Eysenck was not addressing people with schizophrenia, who typically profit from biological forms of therapy, but he argued that whether or not people with problems such as anxiety and depression received therapy, two of three reported substantial improvement within two years.

That was half a century ago. Since that time, sophisticated research studies—many of them employing a statistical averaging method called **meta-analysis**—have strongly suggested that psychotherapy is, in fact, effective. That research is reviewed in this section. However, research also suggests that the same methods may not be appropriate for everyone. We explore that issue as well.

Before we report on the research dealing with the effectiveness of therapy, let us review some of the problems of this kind of research. ***Question: What kinds of problems do researchers encounter when they conduct research on psychotherapy?***

Family therapy ▲ A form of therapy in which the family unit is treated as the client.

Meta-analysis ▲ A method for combining and averaging the results of individual research studies.

Problems in Conducting Research on Psychotherapy

As noted by Hans Strupp, "The problem of evaluating outcomes from psychotherapy continues to bedevil the field" (1996, p. 1017).

Problems in Running Experiments on Psychotherapy   The ideal method for evaluating a treatment—such as a method of therapy—is the experiment (Chambless & Hollon, 1998; Shadish & Ragsdale, 1996). However, experiments on therapy methods are difficult to arrange and control. The outcomes can be difficult to define and measure.

Consider psychoanalysis. In well-run experiments, people are assigned at random to experimental and control groups. A true experiment on psychoanalysis would require randomly assigning people seeking therapy to psychoanalysis and to a control group or other kinds of therapy for comparison (Luborsky et al., 1993). But a person may have to remain in traditional psychoanalysis for years to attain beneficial results. Could we create control treatments that last as long? Moreover, some people seek psychoanalysis per se, not psychotherapy in general. Would it be ethical to assign them at random to other treatments or to a no-treatment control group? Clearly not.

In an ideal experiment, participants and researchers are "blind" with regard to the treatment the participants receive. Blind research designs allow researchers to control for participants' expectations. In an ideal experiment on therapy, individuals would be blind regarding the type of therapy they are obtaining—or whether they are obtaining a placebo (Carroll et al., 1994). However, it is difficult to mask the type of therapy clients are obtaining (Seligman, 1995). Even if we could conceal it from clients, could we hide it from therapists?

Problems in Measuring Outcomes of Therapy   Consider the problems we run into when measuring outcomes of therapy (Shadish et al., 2000). Behavior therapists define their goals in behavioral terms—such as a formerly phobic individual being able to obtain an injection or look out of a 20th-story window. Therefore, behavior therapists do not encounter many problems in this area. But what about the client-centered therapist who fosters insight and self-actualization? We cannot directly measure these qualities. We must assess what clients say and do and make inferences about them.

Are Clinical Judgments Valid?   Because of problems like these, many clinicians believe that important clinical questions cannot be answered through research (Newman & Howard, 1991; Silberschatz, 1998). For them, clinical judgment is the basis for evaluating the effectiveness of therapy. Unfortunately, therapists have a stake in believing that their clients profit from treatment. They are not unbiased judges, even when they try to be.

Does Therapy Help Because of the Method or Because of "Nonspecific Factors"?   Sorting out the benefits of therapy per se from other aspects of the therapy situation is a staggering task. These other aspects are termed *nonspecific factors*. They refer to features that are found in most therapies, such as the client's relationship with the therapist. Most therapists, regardless of theoretical outlook, show warmth and empathy, encourage exploration, and instill hope (Blatt et al., 1996; Burns & Nolen-Hoeksema, 1992). People in therapy also often learn to present themselves to their therapists in a positive light, and creating favorable impressions can help boost one's self-concept in therapy as in everyday life (Arkin & Hermann, 2000; Kelly, 2000). Many of the benefits of therapy could stem from interactions such as these. In such cases, the method itself might have little more value than a "sugar pill" in combating physical ailments.

What Is the Experimental Treatment in Psychotherapy Outcome Studies?   We may also ask, what exactly is the experimental "treatment" being evaluated? Various therapists may say that they are practicing psychoanalysis, but they differ both as individuals and in their training. It is therefore difficult to specify just what is happening in the therapeutic session (Luborsky et al., 1993).

Analyses of Therapy Effectiveness

Despite these evaluation problems, research on the effectiveness of therapy has been encouraging (Barlow, 1996; Shadish et al., 2000; VandenBos, 1996). Some of this research has relied on meta-analysis. Meta-analysis combines and averages the results of individual

CLICK4™ *JCCP*—*the* Journal of Consulting and Clinical Psychology, *featuring research into treatment methods.*

CLICK4™ *an essay assignment: What are the difficulties in testing the effects of psychotherapy?*

studies. Generally speaking, the studies included in the analysis address similar issues in a similar way. Moreover, the analysts judge them to have been conducted in a valid manner. *Question: What, then, do we know about the effectiveness of psychotherapy?*

In their classic early use of meta-analysis, Mary Lee Smith and Gene Glass (1977) analyzed the results of dozens of outcome studies of various types of therapies. They concluded that people who obtained psychodynamic therapy showed greater well-being, on the average, than 70% to 75% of those who did not obtain treatment. Similarly, nearly 75% of the clients who obtained client-centered therapy were better off than people who did not obtain treatment. Psychodynamic and client-centered therapies appear to be most effective with well-educated, verbal, strongly motivated clients who report problems with anxiety, depression (of light to moderate proportions), and interpersonal relationships. Neither form of therapy appears to be effective with people with psychotic disorders such as major depression, bipolar disorder, and schizophrenia. Smith and Glass (1977) found that people who obtained Gestalt therapy showed greater well-being than about 60% of those who did not obtain treatment. The effectiveness of psychoanalysis and client-centered therapy thus was reasonably comparable. Gestalt therapy fell behind.

Smith and Glass (1977) did not include cognitive therapies in their meta-analysis because at the time of their study many cognitive approaches were relatively new. Because behavior therapists also incorporate many cognitive techniques, it can be difficult to sort out which aspects—cognitive or otherwise—of behavioral treatments are most effective. However, many meta-analyses of cognitive-behavioral therapy have been conducted since the early work of Smith and Glass. Their results are encouraging (Lipsey & Wilson, 1993).

A more recent meta-analysis of 90 studies by William R. Shadish and his colleagues (2000) concurred that psychotherapy is generally effective. Generally speaking, the more therapy the better; that is, people who have more psychotherapy tend to fare better than people who have less of it. Therapy also appears to be more effective when the outcome measures reflect the treatment (e.g., when the effects of treatment aimed at fear-reduction are measured in terms of people's ability to approach fear-inducing objects and situations).

Studies of cognitive therapy have shown that modifying irrational beliefs of the type described by Albert Ellis helps people with problems such as anxiety and depression (Engels et al., 1993; Haaga & Davison, 1993). Modifying self-defeating beliefs of the sort outlined by Aaron Beck also frequently alleviates anxiety and depression (Robins & Hayes, 1993; Whisman et al., 1991). Cognitive therapy may be helpful with people with severe depression, who had been thought responsive only to biological therapies (Jacobson & Hollon, 1996; Simons et al., 1995). Cognitive therapy has also helped people with personality disorders (Beck & Freeman, 1990).

Behavioral and cognitive therapies have provided strategies for treating anxiety disorders, social skills deficits, and problems in self-control (DeRubeis & Crits-Christoph, 1998). These two kinds of therapies—which are often integrated as *cognitive-behavioral therapy*—have also provided empirically supported methods for helping couples and families in distress (Baucom et al., 1998), and for modifying behaviors related to health problems such as headaches (Blanchard, 1992), smoking, chronic pain, and bulimia nervosa (Agras et al., 2000; Compas et al., 1998). Cognitive-behavioral therapists have also innovated treatments for sexual dysfunctions for which there previously were no effective treatments. Cognitive therapy has helped many people with schizophrenia (who are also using drug therapy) modify their delusional beliefs (Chadwick & Lowe, 1990). Behavior therapy has helped to coordinate the care of institutionalized patients, including people with schizophrenia and mental retardation (Spreat & Behar, 1994). However, there is little evidence that psychological therapy alone is effective in treating the quirks of thought exhibited in people with severe psychotic disorders (Wolpe, 1990).

Thus, it is not enough to ask which type of therapy is most effective. We must ask which type is most effective for a particular problem and a particular patient. What are its advantages? Its limitations? Clients may successfully use systematic desensitization to overcome stagefright, as measured by ability to speak to a group of people. If clients also want to know *why* they have stagefright, however, behavior therapy alone will not provide the answer.

CLICK4™ *an article on the factors of race and gender in diagnosing mental illness.*

CLICK4™ *a bulletin board discussion: Do you think psychotherapy is effective?*

As we see in the following section, we must also consider the sociocultural features of clients in determining how to make therapy most effective. Failure to do so leaves many people who would profit from therapy on the wayside. And in some cases, inappropriate methods of therapy may do more harm than good.

DIVERSITY Psychotherapy and Human Diversity

CLICK4™ a WebSearch activity: Are there cultural differences in the acceptance of psychotherapy?

The United States, they are a-changing. The numbers of African Americans, Asian Americans, and Latino and Latina Americans are growing rapidly (Hollman & Mulder, 2000), yet most of the "prescriptions" for psychotherapy discussed in this chapter were originated by, and intended for use with, European Americans (Hall, 1997)—and especially for male heterosexuals. *Question: What kinds of issues develop when people from different ethnic groups, women, and gay males and lesbians could profit from psychotherapy?*

CLICK4™ an essay assignment: How are client characteristics such as ethnicity, gender, and sexual orientation relevant to psychotherapy?

People from ethnic minority groups are less likely than European Americans to seek therapy (Penn et al., 1995). Reasons for their lower participation rate include:

▲ Unawareness that therapy would help
▲ Lack of information about the availability of professional services, or inability to pay for them (DeAngelis, 1995b)
▲ Distrust of professionals, particularly European American professionals and (for women) male professionals (Basic Behavioral Science Task Force, 1996c)
▲ Language barriers (American Psychological Association, 1993)
▲ Reluctance to open up about personal matters to strangers—especially strangers who are not members of one's own ethnic group (LaFramboise, 1994)
▲ Cultural inclinations toward other approaches to problem solving, such as religious approaches and psychic healers (LaFramboise, 1994)
▲ Negative experiences with professionals and authority figures

REFLECT
Consider your part of the country and your sociocultural background. Do people in your area and from your background frequently go for "therapy"? Is psychotherapy considered a normal option for people having problems in your area, or is it stigmatized?

Women and gay males and lesbians have also sometimes found therapy to be insensitive to their particular needs. Let us consider ways in which psychotherapy can be of more use to people from ethnic minority groups, women, and gay males and lesbians.

Psychotherapy and Ethnic Minority Groups

Clinicians need to be sensitive to the cultural heritage, language, and values of the people they see in therapy (American Psychological Association, 1993; Comas-Diaz, 1994). That is, they need to develop *multicultural competence* (Sue et al., 1999). Let us consider some of the issues involved in conducting psychotherapy with African Americans, Asian Americans, Latino and Latina Americans, and Native Americans.

In addition to addressing the psychological problems of African American clients, therapists often need to help them cope with the effects of prejudice and discrimination. Beverly Greene (1993) notes that some African Americans develop low self-esteem because they internalize negative stereotypes.

African Americans often are reluctant to seek psychological help because of cultural assumptions that people should manage their own problems and because of mistrust of the therapy process. They tend to assume that people are supposed to solve their own problems. Signs of emotional weakness such as tension, anxiety, and depression are stigmatized (Boyd-Franklin, 1995; Greene, 1993).

Many African Americans are also suspicious of their therapists—especially when the therapist is a European American. They may withhold personal information because of the society's history of racial discrimination (Boyd-Franklin, 1995; Greene, 1993).

Asian Americans tend to stigmatize people with psychological disorders. As a result, they may deny problems and refuse to seek help for them (Sue, 1991). Asian Americans, especially recent immigrants, also may not understand or believe in Western approaches to psychotherapy. For example, Western psychotherapy typically encourages people to express their feelings openly. This mode of behavior may conflict with the Asian tradition of restraint in public. Many Asians prefer to receive concrete advice rather than Western-style encouragement to develop their own solutions (Isomura et al., 1987).

CLICK4™ a bulletin board discussion: What can be done to increase the level of acceptance of psychotherapy within ethnic minority groups?

Because of a cultural tendency to turn away from painful thoughts, many Asians experience and express psychological complaints as physical symptoms (Zane & Sue, 1991). Rather than thinking of themselves as being anxious, they may focus on physical features of anxiety such as a pounding heart and heavy sweating. Rather than thinking of themselves as depressed, they may focus on fatigue and low energy levels.

Therapists need to be aware of potential conflicts between the traditional Latino and Latina American value of interdependency in the family and the typical European American belief in independence and self-reliance (De la Cancela & Guzman, 1991). Measures like the following may help bridge the gaps between psychotherapists and Latino and Latina American clients:

1. Interacting with clients in the language requested by them or, if this is not possible, referring them to professionals who can do so.
2. Using methods that are consistent with the client's values and levels of acculturation, as suggested by fluency in English and level of education.
3. Developing therapy methods that incorporate clients' cultural values. Malgady and his colleagues (1990), for example, use *cuento therapy* with Puerto Ricans. *Cuento therapy* uses Latino and Latina folktales (*cuentos*) with characters who serve as models for adaptive behavior.

Many psychological disorders experienced by Native Americans involve the disruption of their traditional culture caused by European colonization (LaFramboise, 1994). Native Americans have also been denied full access to key institutions in Western culture (LaFramboise, 1994). Loss of cultural identity and social disorganization have set the stage for problems such as alcoholism, substance abuse, and depression. Theresa LaFramboise (1994) argues that if psychologists are to help Native Americans cope with psychological disorders, they must do so in a way that is sensitive to their culture, customs, and values. Efforts to prevent such disorders should focus on strengthening Native American cultural identity, pride, and cohesion.

Some therapists use ceremonies that reflect clients' cultural or religious traditions. Purification and cleansing rites are therapeutic for many Native Americans (Lefley, 1990). Such rites are commonly sought by Native Americans who believe that their problems are caused by failure to placate malevolent spirits or perform required rituals (Lefley, 1990).

▲ **REFLECT**

Would you be more comfortable having therapy with a psychologist of your own gender? Explain.

CLICK4™ *the Feminist Majority Foundation Online.*

Feminist Psychotherapy

Feminist psychotherapy is not a particular method of therapy. It is an approach to therapy rooted in feminist political theory and philosophy. Feminism challenges the validity of stereotypical gender-role stereotypes and the tradition of male dominance (Greene, 1993).

Feminist therapy developed as a response to male dominance of health professions and institutions. It suggested that the mental health establishment often worked to maintain inequality between men and women by trying to help women "adjust" to traditional gender roles when they wished to challenge these roles in their own lives. Feminist therapists note that many women experience depression and other psychological problems as a result of being treated as second-class citizens, and they argue that society rather than the individual woman must change if these psychological problems are to be alleviated.

CONTROVERSY ✖ IN PSYCHOLOGY

Is It Ethical to Try to Change Gay Males' and Lesbians' Sexual Orientations?

CLICK4™ *a bulletin board discussion: Is it ethical to attempt to change the client's sexual orientation?*

The American Psychiatric Association (2000) does not consider a gay male or a lesbian sexual orientation to be a psychological disorder. The association did list homosexuality as a mental disorder until 1973, however, and many efforts have been made to "help" gay males and lesbians change their sexual orientation. For example, William Masters and Virginia Johnson (1979) adapted methods they had innovated for the treatment of sexual dysfunctions and reported that the majority of gays seen in therapy "reversed" their sexual orientations. However, most of these individuals were bisexuals and not exclusively gay. More than half were married, and, they all were motivated to change their sexual behavior.

Many critics argue that it is unprofessional to try to help people change their sexual orientations (Sleek, 1997). They note that the great majority of gay males and lesbians are satisfied with their sexual orientations and only seek therapy because of conflicts that arise from social pressure and prejudice. They believe that the purpose of therapy for gay males and lesbians should be to help relieve conflicts caused by prejudice so that they will find life as gay people more gratifying.

In sum, psychotherapy is most effective when therapists attend to and respect people's sociocultural as well as individual differences. Although it is the individual who experiences psychological anguish, the fault often lies in the cultural setting and not the individual.

REVIEW

(23) Smith and Glass used the method of _____-analysis to analyze the results of dozens of outcome studies of various types of therapies. (24) Current research shows that psychotherapy (is or is not?) effective in the treatment of psychological disorders. (25) _____ therapy appears to be helpful for people with severe depression who had been thought to respond only to biological therapies. (26) African Americans may be reluctant to seek therapy because of cultural assumptions that people (should or should not?) manage their own problems and because they mistrust European American professionals. (27) There may be conflict between the traditional Latino and Latina American value of _____ in the family and the typical European American belief in independence. (28) _____ psychotherapists challenge the validity of stereotypical gender-role stereotypes and the traditional of male dominance. (29) Many critics argue that it is unethical to try to help people change their sexual _____ because gay males and lesbians who seek such therapy are usually responding to social pressure and prejudice.

Pulling It Together: What are the difficulties in running experiments on the effects of psychotherapy? How would you answer the question, "Is psychotherapy effective?"

BIOLOGICAL THERAPIES

The kinds of therapy we have discussed are psychological in nature—forms of *psycho*therapy. Psychotherapies apply *psychological* principles to treatment, principles based on psychological knowledge of matters such as learning and motivation. People with psychological disorders are also often treated with biological therapies. Biological therapies apply what is known of people's *biological* structures and processes to the amelioration of psychological disorders. For example, they may work by altering events in the nervous system, as by changing the action of neurotransmitters. In this section, we discuss three biological, or medical, approaches to treating people with psychological disorders: drug therapy, electroconvulsive therapy, and psychosurgery. ***Question: What kinds of drug therapy are available for psychological disorders?***

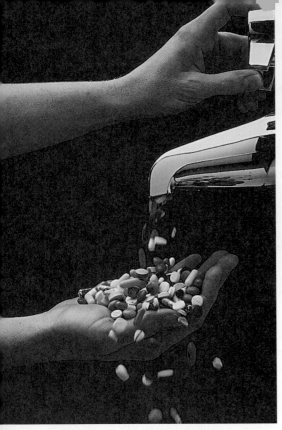

An Arsenal of Chemical Therapies.
Many drugs have been developed to combat psychological disorders. They include antianxiety drugs, antipsychotic drugs, antidepressants, and lithium.

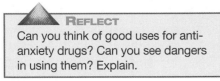

CLICK4™ *a video illustrating how GABA agonists work to treat some anxiety disorders.*

> ▲ REFLECT
> Can you think of good uses for antianxiety drugs? Can you see dangers in using them? Explain.

CD 16 V 43

CLICK4™ *a video about treating depression with drug therapy.*

Rebound anxiety ▲ Strong anxiety that can attend the suspension of usage of a tranquilizer.
Antidepressant ▲ (ant-eye-dee-PRESS-ant). Acting to relieve depression.
Monoamine oxidase inhibitors ▲ (MON-oh-ah-mean OX-see-dase). Antidepressant drugs that work by blocking the action of an enzyme that breaks down noradrenaline and serotonin. Abbreviated *MAO inhibitors.*
Tricyclic antidepressants ▲ (try-SIGH-click). Antidepressant drugs that work by preventing the reuptake of noradrenaline and serotonin by transmitting neurons.
Serotonin-uptake inhibitors ▲ Antidepressant drugs that work by blocking the reuptake of serotonin by presynaptic neurons.

Drug Therapy: In Search of the Magic Pill?

In the 1950s Fats Domino popularized the song "My Blue Heaven." Fats was singing about the sky and happiness. Today "blue heavens" is one of the street names for the 10-milligram dose of the antianxiety drug Valium. Clinicians prescribe Valium and other drugs for people with various psychological disorders.

Antianxiety Drugs Most antianxiety drugs (also called *minor tranquilizers*) belong to the chemical class known as *benzodiazepines*. Valium (diazepam) is a benzodiazepine. Other benzodiazepines include chlordiazepoxide (for example, Librium), oxazepam (Serax), and alprazolam (Xanax). Antianxiety drugs are usually prescribed for outpatients who complain of generalized anxiety or panic attacks, although many people also use them as sleeping pills. Valium and other antianxiety drugs depress the activity of the central nervous system (CNS). The CNS, in turn, decreases sympathetic activity, reducing the heart rate, respiration rate, and feelings of nervousness and tension.

Many people come to tolerate antianxiety drugs very quickly. When tolerance occurs, dosages must be increased for the drug to remain effective.

Sedation (feelings of being tired or drowsy) is the most common side effect of antianxiety drugs. Problems associated with withdrawal from these drugs include **rebound anxiety.** That is, some people who have been using these drugs regularly report that their anxiety becomes worse than before once they discontinue them. Antianxiety drugs can induce physical dependence, as evidenced by withdrawal symptoms such as tremors, sweating, insomnia, and rapid heartbeat.

Antipsychotic Drugs People with schizophrenia are often given antipsychotic drugs (also called *major tranquilizers*). In most cases these drugs reduce agitation, delusions, and hallucinations. Many antipsychotic drugs, including phenothiazines (for example, Thorazine) and clozapine (Clozaril) are thought to act by blocking dopamine receptors in the brain (Kane, 1996). Research along these lines supports the theory that schizophrenia is connected with overactivity of the neurotransmitter dopamine.

Antidepressants People with major depression often take so-called **antidepressant** drugs. These drugs are also helpful for some people with eating disorders, panic disorder, obsessive-compulsive disorder, and social phobia (Bacaltchuk et al., 2000; Barlow et al., 2000; McElroy et al., 2000). Problems in the regulation of noradrenaline and serotonin may be involved in eating and panic disorders as well as in depression. Antidepressants are believed to work by increasing levels of one or both of these neurotransmitters, which can affect both depression and the appetite (White et al., 2000b). However, cognitive-behavior therapy addresses irrational attitudes concerning weight and body shape, fosters normal eating habits, and helps people resist the urges to binge and purge. This form of therapy therefore apparently is more effective with people with bulimia than antidepressants (Wilson & Fairburn, 1993). But when cognitive behavioral therapy does not help people with bulimia nervosa, drug therapy may (Walsh et al., 2000).

There are various kinds of antidepressant drugs. Each increases the concentration of noradrenaline or serotonin in the brain. **Monoamine oxidase (MAO) inhibitors** such as Nardil and Parnate block the activity of an enzyme that breaks down noradrenaline and serotonin. **Tricyclic antidepressants** such as Tofranil and Elavil prevent the reuptake of noradrenaline and serotonin by the axon terminals of the transmitting neurons. Selective **serotonin-uptake inhibitors** such as Prozac and Zoloft also block the reuptake of serotonin by presynaptic neurons. As a result, the neurotransmitters remain in the synaptic cleft longer, influencing receiving neurons. Serotonin-uptake inhibitors like Prozac appear to be somewhat more effective than tricyclics (Bech et al., 2000).

Antidepressant drugs must usually build up to a therapeutic level over several weeks. Because overdoses can be lethal, some people stay in a hospital during the buildup to prevent suicide attempts. There are also side effects, such as a racing heart and weight gain (Sleek, 1996).

Lithium The ancient Greeks and Romans were among the first to use the metal lithium as a psychoactive drug. They prescribed mineral water—which contains

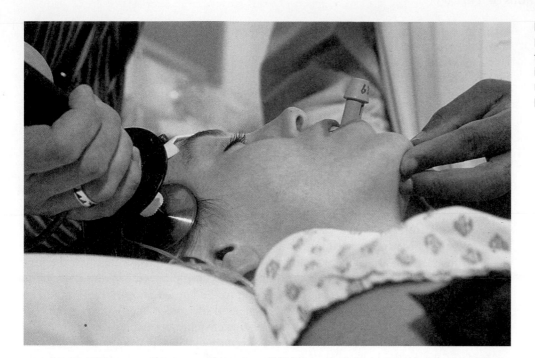

Electroconvulsive Therapy.
In ECT, electrodes are placed on each side of the patient's head and a current is passed between them, inducing a seizure. ECT is used mainly in cases of major depression when antidepressant drugs and psychotherapy are not sufficient.

lithium—for people with bipolar disorder. They had no inkling as to why this treatment sometimes helped. A salt of the metal lithium (lithium carbonate), in tablet form, flattens out cycles of manic behavior and depression in most people. Lithium can also be used to strengthen the effects of antidepressant medication (Bauer et al., 2000). It is not known exactly how lithium works, although it affects the functioning of neurotransmitters, including glutamate (Hokin et al., 1998).

People with bipolar disorder may have to use lithium indefinitely, as a person with diabetes must use insulin to control the illness. Lithium also has been shown to have side effects such as hand tremors, memory impairment, and excessive thirst and urination (Price & Heninger, 1994). Memory impairment is reported as the main reason why people discontinue lithium.

Electroconvulsive Therapy

Question: What is electroconvulsive therapy (ECT)?   **Electroconvulsive therapy** (ECT) is a biological form of therapy for psychological disorders that was introduced by the Italian psychiatrist Ugo Cerletti in 1939. Cerletti had noted that some slaughterhouses used electric shock to render animals unconscious. The shocks also produced convulsions. Along with other European researchers of the period, Cerletti erroneously believed that convulsions were incompatible with schizophrenia and other major psychological disorders.

ECT was originally used for a variety of psychological disorders. Because of the advent of antipsychotic drugs, however, it is now used mainly for people with major depression who do not respond to antidepressants (Thase & Kupfer, 1996).

People typically obtain one ECT treatment three times a week for up to 10 sessions. Electrodes are attached to the temples and an electrical current strong enough to produce a convulsion is induced. The shock causes unconsciousness, so the patient does not recall it. Nevertheless, patients are given a **sedative** so that they are asleep during the treatment.

CD **16** **V** **44**
CLICK4™ *a video illustrating how SSRIs work to prevent depression.*

CD **16** **V** **45**
CLICK4™ *a video on the use of antipsychotic drugs in the treatment of schizophrenia.*

CD **16** **V** **46**
CLICK4™ *a video illustrating how antipsychotic drugs work to block dopamine in the treatment of schizophrenia.*

CONTROVERSY ✦ IN PSYCHOLOGY

Should Health Professionals Use Electroconvulsive Therapy?

ECT is controversial for many reasons, such as the fact that many professionals are distressed by the thought of passing an electric shock through a patient's head and producing convulsions. But there are side effects, including memory problems in the form of

Electroconvulsive therapy ▲ Treatment of disorders like major depression by passing an electric current (that causes a convulsion) through the head. Abbreviated *ECT*.
Sedative ▲ A drug that relieves nervousness or agitation, or puts one to sleep.

CLICK4™ *a WebSearch activity: Should health care professionals use ECT?*

retrograde amnesia (Lisanby et al., 2000; Weiner, 2000). (Some researchers argue that stronger shock to one side of the head may be as effective yet have fewer side effects as compared with weaker shock to both sides of the head [Sackeim et al. 2000].) However, research suggests that for most people, cognitive impairment tends to be temporary. One study followed up 10 adolescents who had received ECT an average of $3\frac{1}{2}$ years earlier. Six of the 10 had complained of memory impairment immediately after treatment, but only 1 complained of continued problems at the follow-up. Nevertheless, psychological tests did not reveal any differences in cognitive functioning between severely depressed adolescents who had received ECT and others who had not (Cohen et al., 2000).

Psychosurgery

Psychosurgery is more controversial than ECT. *Questions: What is psychosurgery? How is it used to treat psychological disorders?* The best-known modern technique, **prefrontal lobotomy,** has been used with people with severe disorders. In this method, a picklike instrument severs the nerve pathways that link the prefrontal lobes of the brain to the thalamus. This method was pioneered by the Portuguese neurologist Antonio Egas Moniz and was brought to the United States in the 1930s. The theoretical rationale for the operation was vague and misguided and Moniz's reports of success were exaggerated. Nevertheless, by 1950 prefrontal lobotomies were performed on more than a thousand people in an effort to reduce violence and agitation. Anecdotal evidence of the method's unreliable outcomes is found in an ironic footnote to history: One of Dr. Moniz's "failures" shot the doctor, leaving a bullet lodged in his spine and paralyzing his legs.

Prefrontal lobotomy also has a host of side effects, including hyperactivity and distractibility, impaired learning ability, overeating, apathy and withdrawal, epileptic-type seizures, reduced creativity, and, now and then, death. Because of these side effects, and because of the advent of antipsychotic drugs, this method has been largely discontinued in the United States.

Does Biological Therapy Work?

There are thus a number of biological approaches to the therapy of psychological disorders. *Question: What do we know about the effectiveness of biological therapies?*

There is little question that drug therapy has helped many people with severe psychological disorders. For example, antipsychotic drugs largely account for the reduced need for the use of restraint and supervision (padded cells, straitjackets, hospitalization, and so on) with people diagnosed with schizophrenia. Antipsychotic drugs have allowed hundreds of thousands of former mental hospital residents to lead largely normal lives in the community, hold jobs, and maintain family lives. Most of the problems related to these drugs concern their side effects.

But many comparisons of psychotherapy (in the form of cognitive therapy) and drug therapy for depression suggest that cognitive therapy is as effective as, or more effective than, antidepressants (Antonuccio, 1995; Muñoz et al., 1994). For one thing, cognitive therapy provides coping skills that reduce the risk of recurrence of depression once treatment ends (Hollon et al., 1991). Then again, at least one study suggests that a combination of cognitive therapy and antidepressant medication is superior to either treatment alone with chronically depressed people (Keller et al., 2000).

A similar story holds for cognitive behavior therapy and "antidepressant" medication in the treatment of panic disorder. A carefully controlled study found that cognitive behavior therapy and the antidepressant imipramine are both helpful in treating panic disorder, but a combination of the psychological and biological treatments appears to be somewhat more helpful in the long run (Barlow et al., 2000).

Many psychologists and psychiatrists are comfortable with the short-term use of antianxiety drugs in helping clients manage periods of unusual anxiety or tension. However, many people use antianxiety drugs routinely to dull the arousal stemming from anxiety-producing lifestyles or interpersonal problems. Rather than make the often painful decisions required to confront their problems and change their lives, they prefer to take a pill.

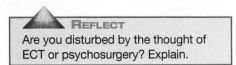
REFLECT
Are you disturbed by the thought of ECT or psychosurgery? Explain.

CLICK4™ *more information about psychiatric medications and ECT from the American Psychiatric Association.*

CLICK4™ *an essay assignment: Why is psychotherapy sometimes preferred to drug therapy?*

REFLECT
If psychotherapy can be as helpful with depression as antidepressant medication, why do you think so many pills are prescribed for depression?

CLICK4™ *bulletin board discussion on the effectiveness of biological treatments.*

Psychosurgery ▲ Surgery intended to promote psychological changes or to relieve disordered behavior.
Prefrontal lobotomy ▲ The severing or destruction of a section of the frontal lobe of the brain.

One study found that both tranquilizers and cognitive-behavior therapy (stress management training plus imagined exposure to the fearful stimuli) helped phobic people get through a dental session. However, 70% of those who received cognitive-behavior therapy continued to go for dental treatment, as compared with only 20% of those who took the tranquilizer (Thom et al., 2000). The cognitive-behavior therapy apparently taught the individuals in the study coping skills, whereas the tranquilizers afforded only temporary relief.

Despite the controversies surrounding ECT, it helps many people who do not respond to antidepressant drugs (Thase & Kupfer, 1996).

In sum, drug therapy and perhaps ECT seem to be effective for some disorders that do not respond to psychotherapy alone. Yet common sense and research evidence suggest that psychotherapy is preferable for problems such as anxiety, mild depression, and interpersonal conflict. No chemical can show a person how to change an idea or solve an interpersonal problem.

REVIEW

(30) (Minor or Major?) tranquilizers are usually prescribed for people who complain of anxiety or tension. (31) _____ tranquilizers are used to reduce agitation, delusions, and hallucinations. (32) Major tranquilizers that belong to the chemical class of phenothiazines are thought to work by blocking the action of the neurotransmitter _____. (33) Antidepressants heighten the action of the neurotransmitter _____. (34) ECT is mainly used to treat severe cases of _____. (35) The best-known technique psychosurgery technique is the _____ lobotomy.

Pulling It Together: Why do many health professionals prefer the use of psychotherapy to prescribing medicine?

CLICK4™ *a quiz covering the second half of this chapter.*

CLICK4™ *electronic flash cards to review your knowledge of key terms and people in this chapter.*

TRUTH ⬚ FICTION
REVISITED

▱ It is true that residents of London used to visit the insane asylum for amusement. *See page 541.*

▱ It is true that some psychotherapists interpret clients' dreams. *Psychoanalysis is a case in point. See page 545.*

▱ It is not true that psychotherapy must continue for months, perhaps years, to be effective. *There are many effective brief forms of psychotherapy. See page 545.*

▱ It is true that some psychotherapists encourage their clients to take the lead in the therapy session. *Client-centered therapists are an example. See page 547.*

▱ It is true that lying in a reclining chair and fantasizing can be an effective way of confronting fears. *This is what happens in the method of systematic desensitization. See page 549.*

▱ It is true that smoking cigarettes can be an effective treatment for helping people stop smoking cigarettes. *The trick is to inhale enough smoke so that it is aversive rather than enjoyable. See page 551.*

▱ It is true that you might be able to put an end to bad habits merely by keeping a record of where and when you engage in them. *The record may help motivate you, make you more aware of the problems, and suggest strategies for behavior change. See page 554.*

▱ It is true that some psychotherapists tell their clients precisely what to do. *That is, they outline behavioral prescriptions for their clients. Behavior therapists, Gestalt therapists, and some cognitive therapists are examples. See page 554.*

▱ It is true that the originator of a surgical technique intended to reduce violence learned that it was not always successful . . . when one of his patients shot him. *That technique is prefrontal lobotomy. See page 570.*

1. **What is psychotherapy?**

Psychotherapy is a systematic interaction between a therapist and a client that uses psychological principles to help the client overcome psychological disorders or adjust to problems in living.

2. **How have people with psychological problems and disorders been treated throughout the ages?**

Mostly badly. It has been generally assumed that psychological disorders represented possession due to witchcraft or divine retribution, and cruel methods such as exorcism were used to try to rid the person of evil spirits. Asylums were the first institutions for people with psychological disorders, and eventually mental hospitals and the community mental health movement came into being.

3. **How do psychoanalysts conduct a traditional Freudian psychoanalysis?**

The goals of psychoanalysis are to provide self-insight, encourage the spilling forth (catharsis) of psychic energy, and replace defensive behavior with coping behavior. The main method is free association, but dream analysis and interpretations are used as well. For example, a psychoanalyst may help clients gain insight into the ways in which they are transferring feelings toward their parents onto a spouse or even onto the analyst.

4. **How do modern psychodynamic approaches differ from traditional psychoanalysis?**

Modern approaches are briefer and more directive, and the therapist and client usually sit face to face.

5. **What is Carl Rogers's method of client-centered therapy?**

Client-centered therapy uses nondirective methods to help clients overcome obstacles to self-actualization. The therapist shows unconditional positive regard, empathic understanding, and genuineness.

6. **What is Fritz Perls's method of Gestalt therapy?**

Perls's highly directive method aims to help people integrate conflicting parts of their personality. He aimed to make clients aware of conflict, accept its reality, and make choices despite fear.

7. **What is behavior therapy?**

Behavior therapy relies on psychological learning principles (for example, conditioning and observational learning) to help clients develop adaptive behavior patterns and discontinue maladaptive ones.

8. **What are some behavior-therapy methods for reducing fears?**

These include flooding, systematic desensitization, and modeling. Flooding exposes a person to fear-evoking stimuli without aversive consequences until fear is extinguished. Systematic desensitization counterconditions fears by gradually exposing clients to a hierarchy of fear-evoking stimuli while they remain relaxed. Modeling encourages clients to imitate another person (the model) in approaching fear-evoking stimuli.

9. **How do behavior therapists use aversive conditioning to help people break bad habits?**

This is a behavior-therapy method for discouraging undesirable behaviors by repeatedly pairing clients' self-defeating goals (for example, alcohol, cigarette smoke, deviant sex objects) with aversive stimuli so that the goals become aversive rather than tempting.

10. **How do behavior therapists apply principles of operant conditioning in behavior modification?**

These are behavior therapy methods that foster adaptive behavior through principles of reinforcement. Examples include token economies, successive approximation, social skills training, and biofeedback training.

11. How can you use behavior therapy to deal with temptation and enhance your self-control?

Behavior-therapy methods for adopting desirable behavior patterns and breaking bad habits begin with a functional analysis to determine the antecedents and consequences of the problem behavior, along with the details of the behavior itself. They then focus on modifying the antecedents (stimuli that act as triggers) and consequences (reinforcers) of behavior and on modifying the behavior itself.

12. What is cognitive therapy?

Cognitive therapies aim to give clients insight into irrational beliefs and cognitive distortions and replace these cognitive errors with rational beliefs and accurate perceptions.

13. What is Aaron Beck's method of cognitive therapy?

Aaron Beck notes that clients develop emotional problems such as depression because of cognitive errors that lead them to minimize accomplishments and catastrophize failures. He found that depressed people experience cognitive distortions such as the cognitive triad; that is, they expect the worst of themselves, the world at large, and the future. Beck teaches clients how to scientifically dispute cognitive errors.

14. What is Albert Ellis's method of rational emotive behavior therapy (REBT)?

Albert Ellis originated rational emotive behavior therapy, which holds that people's beliefs *about* events, not only the events themselves, shape people's responses to them. Ellis points out how irrational beliefs, such as the belief that we must have social approval, can worsen problems. Ellis literally argues clients out of irrational beliefs.

15. What are the advantages and disadvantages of group therapy?

Group therapy is more economical than individual therapy. Moreover, group members benefit from the social support and experiences of other members. However, some clients cannot disclose their problems in the group setting or risk group disapproval. They need individual attention.

16. What are encounter groups? What are their effects?

Encounter groups attempt to foster personal growth by heightening awareness of people's needs and feelings through intense confrontations between strangers. Encounter groups can be harmful when they urge too rapid disclosure of personal matters or when several members attack an individual.

17. What is family therapy?

In family therapy, one or more families make up the group. Family therapy undertaken from the "systems approach" modifies family interactions to enhance the growth of individuals in the family and the family as a whole.

18. What kinds of problems do researchers encounter when they conduct research on psychotherapy?

It is difficult and perhaps impossible to randomly assign clients to therapy methods such as traditional psychoanalysis. Moreover, clients cannot be kept blind as to the treatment they are receiving. Further, it can be difficult to sort out the effects of nonspecific therapeutic factors such as instillation of hope from the effects of specific methods of therapy.

19. What do we know about the effectiveness of psychotherapy?

Statistical analyses such as meta-analysis show that people who obtain most forms of psychotherapy fare better than people who do not. Psychodynamic and client-centered approaches are particularly helpful with highly verbal and motivated individuals. Cognitive and behavior therapies are probably most effective. Cognitive therapy appears to be as effective as drug therapy in the treatment of depression.

20. What kinds of issues develop when people from different ethnic groups, women, and gay males and lesbians could profit from psychotherapy?

People from ethnic minority groups are frequently mistrustful of European American therapists. Therapy methods and goals may also conflict with their cultural values. Feminist therapy heightens awareness of sociocultural issues that contribute to women's problems and challenges the tradition of male dominance. Many professionals believe that psychotherapy should not attempt to change a gay male or lesbian's sexual orientation, but should help that person adjust to social and cultural pressures to be heterosexual.

21. What kinds of drug therapy are available for psychological disorders?

Antipsychotic drugs help many people with schizophrenia by blocking the action of dopamine receptors. Antidepressants often help people with severe depression, apparently by raising levels of serotonin available to the brain. Lithium often helps people with bipolar disorder, apparently by regulating levels of glutamate. The use of antianxiety drugs for daily tensions and anxieties is not recommended because people who use them rapidly build tolerance for the drugs. Also, these drugs do not solve personal or social problems, and people attribute their resultant calmness to the drug and not to self-efficacy.

22. What is electroconvulsive therapy (ECT)?

In ECT an electrical current is passed through the temples, inducing a seizure and frequently relieving severe depression. ECT is controversial because of side effects such as loss of memory and because nobody knows why it works.

23. What is psychosurgery? How is it used to treat psychological disorders?

Psychosurgery is a controversial method for alleviating agitation by severing nerve pathways in the brain. The best-known psychosurgery technique, prefrontal lobotomy, has been largely discontinued because of side effects.

24. What do we know about the effectiveness of biological therapies?

There is controversy as to whether psychotherapy or drug therapy should be used with people with anxiety disorders or depression. Drugs do not teach people how to solve problems and build relationships. Having said that, antidepressants are apparently advisable when psychotherapy does not help people with depression; furthermore, ECT appears to be helpful in some cases in which neither psychotherapy nor drug therapy (antidepressants) is of help. Psychosurgery is all but discontinued because of questions about whether it is effective and because of side effects. Most health professionals agree that antipsychotic drugs are of benefit to large numbers of people with schizophrenia.

PREVIEW

Social Psychology

▲ How is your behavior affected by other people?

Attitudes—"The Good, the Bad, and the Ugly"

▲ People act in accordance with their beliefs—sometimes.
▲ Where do attitudes come from?
▲ Can you persuade people to change their beliefs?
▲ How do prejudices develop? What can we do about them?

Social Perception: Looking Out, Looking Within

▲ Should you "just be yourself," or should you get dressed up and watch your language in an interview for graduate school or a job?
▲ Are we to blame for the terrible things we do?
▲ Should we put the arm on people when we . . . "put the arm on" people?

Social Influence: Are You an Individual or One of the Crowd?

▲ People tend to obey authority figures. (Would you?)
▲ People tend to conform to group norms. (Do you?)

Group Behavior

▲ Do you run faster or slower in the midst of other runners?
▲ Is a camel a horse made by a committee?
▲ "Groupthink" makes for some unwise decisions.
▲ You will probably do things as a member of a group that you would not do alone.
▲ Do you help or do you just stand by when you come across people in need?

Environmental Psychology: The Big Picture

▲ The same volume of noise you like at the disco may drive you bananas (technical psychological term) on the street.
▲ When the heat is on, people often get heated.
▲ How do you feel when other people are "too close for comfort"?

CHAPTER 17

Social Psychology

TRUTH  FICTION?

- If a television commercial is aired repeatedly, sales decrease.

- When you give to charity once, you are less likely to give when the charity calls on you again.

- People have condemned billions of other people without ever meeting them or learning their names.

- If you don't make a good first impression, you may never get a second chance.

- We take others to task for their misdeeds but tend to see ourselves as victims of circumstances when our conduct falls short of our ideals.

- Seeing is believing.

- Group decisions tend to represent conservative compromises among the opinions of the group's members.

- Nearly 40 people stood by and did nothing while a woman was being stabbed to death.

- Women are less likely than men to be litterbugs.

Candy and Stretch. A new technique for controlling weight gains? No, these are the names of a couple who have just met at a camera club. Candy and Stretch stand above the crowd—literally. Candy, an attractive woman in her early thirties, is almost 6 feet tall. Stretch is more plain looking, but wholesome, in his late thirties, and 6 feet 5 inches tall.

Stretch has been in the group for some time. Candy is a new member. Let's listen in on them as they make conversation during a coffee break.[1] Note some differences between what they say and what they are thinking:

	THEY SAY	THEY THINK
STRETCH:	Well, you're certainly a welcome addition to our group.	(Can't I ever say something clever?)
CANDY:	Thank you. It certainly is friendly and interesting.	(He's cute.)
STRETCH:	My friends call me Stretch. It's left over from my basketball days. Silly, but I'm used to it.	(It's safer than saying my name is David Stein.)
CANDY:	My name is Candy.	(At least my nickname is. He doesn't have to hear Hortense O'Brien.)
STRETCH:	What kind of camera is that?	(Why couldn't a girl named Candy be Jewish? It's only a nickname, isn't it?)
CANDY:	Just this old German one of my uncle's. I borrowed it from the office.	(He could be Irish. And that camera looks expensive.)
STRETCH:	May I? (He takes her camera, brushing her hand and then tingling with the touch.) Fine lens. You work for your uncle?	(Now I've done it. Brought up work.)
CANDY:	Ever since college. It's more than being just a secretary. I get into sales, too.	(So okay, what if I only went for a year. If he asks what I sell, I'll tell him anything except underwear.)
STRETCH:	Sales? That's funny. I'm in sales, too, but mainly as an executive. I run our department. I started using cameras on trips. Last time I was in the Bahamas. I took—	(Is there a nice way to say used cars? I'd better change the subject.) (Great legs! And the way her hips move . . .)
CANDY:	Oh! Do you go to the Bahamas, too? I love those islands.	(So I went just once, and it was for the brassiere manufacturers' convention. At least we're off the subject of jobs.)
STRETCH:		(She's probably been around. Well, at least we're off the subject of jobs.)
	I did a little underwater work there last summer. Fantastic colors. So rich in life.	(And lonelier than hell.)
CANDY:		(Look at that build. He must swim like a fish. I should learn.)
	I wish I'd had time when I was there. I love the water.	(Well, I do. At the beach, anyway, where I can wade in and not go too deep.)

[1] From *Pairing*, by G. R. Bach and R. M. Deutsch, 1970, New York: Peter H. Wyden.

So begins a relationship. Candy and Stretch have a drink and talk, sharing their likes and dislikes. Amazingly, they seem to agree on everything—from cars to clothing to politics. The attraction is very strong, and neither is willing to risk turning the other off by disagreeing. They scrupulously avoid one topic: religion. Their religious differences become apparent when they exchange last names. But that doesn't mean they have to talk about it.

They also put off introductions to their parents. The O'Briens and the Steins are narrow-minded about religion. If the truth be known, so are Candy and Stretch.

What happens in this tangled web of deception? After some deliberation, and not without misgivings, they decide to get married. Do they live happily ever after? We can't say. "Ever after" isn't here yet. We do not have all the answers, but we have some questions. Candy and Stretch pretended to share each other's attitudes. What are *attitudes*? Why didn't Candy and Stretch introduce each other to their parents? Did they fear that their parents would want them to *conform* to their own standards? Would their parents try to *persuade* them to limit dating to people of their own religions? Would they *obey*?

SOCIAL PSYCHOLOGY

Attitudes, conformity, persuasion, obedience—these are some of the topics we find in **social psychology.** Candy and Stretch went to dinner at a restaurant where they served fine wine and soft music swelled in the background. The ways in which the environment influenced their behavior and mental processes are also part of social psychology. *Question: What is social psychology?* Social psychology studies the nature and causes of behavior and mental processes in social situations. The social psychological topics we discuss in this chapter include attitudes, social perception, social influence, group behavior, and environmental psychology.

ATTITUDES — "THE GOOD, THE BAD, AND THE UGLY"

How do you feel about abortion, Japanese cars, and the Republican party? The only connection I draw among these items is that people have *attitudes* toward them. They each give rise to cognitive evaluations (such as approval or disapproval), feelings (liking, disliking, or something stronger), and behavioral tendencies (such as approach or avoidance). Although I asked you how you "feel," attitudes are not just feelings or emotions. Many psychologists view thinking—or judgment—as primary. Feelings and behavior follow (Eagly & Chaiken, 1993). *Question: What are attitudes?*

Attitudes are behavioral and cognitive tendencies that are expressed by evaluating particular people, places, or things with favor or disfavor (Petty et al., 1997). Attitudes are learned, and they affect behavior (Petty et al., 1997). They can foster love or hate. They can give rise to helping behavior or to mass destruction. They can lead to social conflict or to the resolution of conflicts. Attitudes can change, but not easily. Most people do not change their religion or political affiliation without serious reflection or coercion.

The A–B Problem: Do We Do as We Think?

Our definition of attitude implies that our behavior is consistent with our cognitions—that is, with our beliefs and feelings. *Questions: Do people do as they think? (For example, do people really vote their consciences?)* When we are free to do as we wish, our behavior is often consistent with our cognitions. But, as indicated by the term **A–B problem,** there are exceptions. In fact, the links between attitudes (A) and behaviors (B) tend to be weak to moderate (Eagly & Chaiken, 1993). For example, research reveals that attitudes toward health-related behaviors such as use of alcohol, smoking, and drunken driving are not consistent predictors of these behaviors (Stacy et al., 1994).

A number of factors influence the likelihood that we can predict behavior from attitudes:

1. *Specificity.* We can better predict specific behavior from specific attitudes than from global attitudes. For example, we can better predict church attendance by knowing people's attitudes toward church attendance than by knowing whether they are Christian.

CLICK4™ an essay assignment: What is social psychology?

CLICK4™ the Social Psychology Network, the largest social psychology database on the Internet.

▲ **REFLECT**
Is what you say and do always consistent with your beliefs? Can you think of examples when your behavior was inconsistent with your attitudes? Why was it inconsistent?

Social psychology ▲ The field of psychology that studies the nature and causes of people's thoughts and behavior in social situations.

Attitude ▲ An enduring mental representation of a person, place, or thing that evokes an emotional response and related behavior.

A–B problem ▲ The issue of how well we can predict behavior on the basis of attitudes.

CLICK4™ *an opportunity to participate in a social psychology study online.*

2. *Strength of attitudes.* Strong attitudes are more likely to determine behavior than weak attitudes (Petty et al., 1997). A person who believes that the nation's destiny depends on Republicans taking control of Congress is more likely to vote than a person who leans toward the Republican party but does not believe that the outcome of elections makes much difference.

3. *Vested interest.* People are more likely to act on their attitudes when they have a vested interest in the outcome (Crano, 1997). People are more likely to vote for (or against) unionization of their workplace, for example, when they believe that their job security depends on the outcome.

4. *Accessibility.* People are more likely to behave in accord with their attitudes when they are accessible—that is, when they are brought to mind (Kallgren et al., 2000; Petty et al., 1997). This is why politicians attempt to "get out the vote" by means of media blitzes just prior to an election. It does them little good to have supporters who forget them on election day. Attitudes with a strong emotional impact are more accessible, which is one reason that politicians strive to get their supporters "worked up" over the issues.

Candy and Stretch avoided discussing matters on which they differed. One motive might have been to avoid heightening the *accessibility* of their clashing attitudes. By keeping them under the table, they might be less likely to act on them and go their separate ways.

Origins of Attitudes

REFLECT
What are your political attitudes? Liberal? Conservative? Middle of the road? How did you develop these attitudes? (Are you sure?)

You were not born a Republican or a Democrat. You were not born a Catholic or a Muslim—although your parents may have practiced one of these religions when you came along. **Question: Where do attitudes come from?** Political, religious, and other attitudes are learned or derived from cognitive processes. In this section we describe some of the processes that result in acquiring attitudes.

Conditioning may play a role in acquiring attitudes. Experiments have shown that attitudes toward national groups can be influenced by associating them with positive words (such as *gift* or *happy*) or negative words (such as *ugly* or *failure*) (Lohr & Staats, 1973). Parents often reward children for saying and doing things that agree with their own attitudes. Patriotism is encouraged by showing approval to children when they sing the national anthem or wave the flag.

Attitudes formed through direct experience may be stronger and easier to recall, but we also acquire attitudes by observing others. The approval or disapproval of peers leads adolescents to prefer short or long hair, baggy jeans, or preppie sweaters. The media inform us that body odor and bad breath are dreaded diseases—and, perhaps, that people who use harsh toilet paper are somehow un-American.

CLICK4™ *an essay assignment: Where do attitudes come from, and how well do they predict behavior?*

Cognitive Appraisal   Despite what we have said, the acquisition of attitudes is not so mechanical. People are also motivated to have a valid understanding of reality, so that they can make predictions and exercise some control over their environment (Wood, 2000). So people also evaluate information and form or change attitudes, including **stereotypes,** on the basis of new information (Petty et al., 1997, 1999). For example, we may believe that a car is more reliable than we had thought if a survey by *Consumer Reports* finds that it has an excellent repair record. Even so, initial attitudes act as cognitive anchors (Wood, 2000). We often judge new ideas in terms of how much they deviate from our existing attitudes. Accepting larger deviations requires more information processing—in other words, more intellectual work (Petty et al., 1997, 1999). For this reason, perhaps, great deviations—such as changes from liberal to conservative attitudes, or vice versa—are apt to be resisted.

Changing Attitudes Through Persuasion

Let advertisers spend the same amount of money improving their product that they do on advertising and they wouldn't have to advertise it.

—*Will Rogers*

Stereotype ▲ A fixed, conventional idea about a group.

Rogers's social comment sounds on the mark, but he was probably wrong. It does little good to have a wonderful product if its existence remains a secret. *Question: Can you really change people?—their attitudes and behavior, that is?*

The **elaboration likelihood model** describes the ways in which people respond to persuasive messages (Petty et al., 1997). Consider two routes to persuading others to change attitudes. The first, or central, route inspires thoughtful consideration of arguments and evidence. The second, or peripheral, route associates objects with positive or negative cues. When politicians avow that, "This bill is supported by Jesse Jackson (or Jesse Helms)," they are seeking predictable, knee-jerk reactions, not careful consideration of a bill's merits. Other cues are rewards (such as a smile or a hug), punishments (such as parental disapproval), and such factors as the trustworthiness and attractiveness of the communicator.

Advertisements, which are a form of persuasive communication, also rely on central and peripheral routes. Some ads focus on the quality of the product (central route). Others attempt to associate the product with appealing images (peripheral route). Ads for Total cereal, which highlight its nutritional benefits, provide information about the quality of the product. So, too, did the "Pepsi Challenge" taste test ads, which claimed that Pepsi tastes better than Coca-Cola. Marlboro cigarette ads that focus on the masculine, rugged image of the "Marlboro man"[2] offer no information about the product itself. Nor do ads that show football players heading for Disney World or choosing a brand of beer.

In this section we look at one central factor in persuasion—the nature of the message—and three peripheral factors: the messenger, the context of the message, and the audience. We also examine the foot-in-the-door technique.

The Persuasive Message: Say What? Say How? Say How Often?

How do we respond when TV commercials are repeated until we have memorized every dimple on the actors' faces? Research suggests that familiarity breeds content, not contempt.

You might not be crazy about *zebulons* and *afworbu's* at first, but Robert Zajonc (1968) found that people began to react favorably toward these bogus foreign words on the basis of repeated exposure. In fact, repeated exposure to people and things as diverse as the following enhances their appeal (Baron & Byrne, 2000):

- ▲ political candidates (who are seen in repeated TV commercials)
- ▲ photographs of African Americans
- ▲ photographs of college students
- ▲ abstract art
- ▲ classical music

The more complex the stimuli, the more likely it is that frequent exposure will have favorable effects (Smith & Dorfman, 1975). The 100th playing of a Bach fugue may be less tiresome than the 100th performance of a pop tune.

When trying to persuade someone, is it helpful or self-defeating to alert them to the arguments presented by the opposition? In two-sided arguments, the communicator recounts the arguments of the opposition in order to refute them. Theologians and politicians sometimes forewarn their followers about the arguments of the opposition and then refute each one. Forewarning creates a kind of psychological immunity to them (Jacks & Devine, 2000). Two-sided product claims, in which advertisers admit their product's weak points in addition to highlighting its strengths, are the most believable (Bridgwater, 1982). For example, one motel chain admits that it does not offer a swimming pool or room service, but points out that the customer therefore saves money.

It would be nice to think that people are too sophisticated to be persuaded by a **fear appeal.** However, women who are warned of the dire risk they run if they fail to be screened for breast cancer are more likely to obtain mammograms than women who are informed of the *benefits* of mammography (Banks et al., 1995). Interestingly, although sun

---

[2]The rugged actor in the original TV commercials died of lung cancer. Apparently cigarettes were more rugged than he was.

CLICK4™ *Web sites exploring social cognition and its role in advertising, influence, and persuasion.*

CLICK4™ *critical perspectives on advertising and advertisements.*

Elaboration likelihood model ▲ The view that persuasive messages are evaluated (elaborated) on the basis of central and peripheral cues.

Fear appeal ▲ A type of persuasive communication that influences behavior on the basis of arousing fear instead of rational analysis of the issues.

Would You Want This Man to Endorse Your Products?
Advertisers use a combination of central and peripheral cues to sell their products. What factors contribute to the persuasiveness of messages? To the persuasiveness of communicators? Why is Tiger Woods a sought-after commodity by advertisers?

▲ REFLECT
Can you think of some celebrities who are being used as pitchmen (or pitchwomen) in ads or commercials? What is the source of their appeal?

▲ REFLECT
Do you shut off the TV or switch channels when certain politicians or talk show hosts come on? Why? What are the advantages and potential dangers of such selective avoidance?

tanning has been shown to increase the likelihood of skin cancer, warnings against sun tanning were shown to be more effective when students were warned of risks to their *appearance* (premature aging, wrinkling, and scarring of the skin) than when the warning dealt with the risk to their health (Jones & Leary, 1994). That is, students informed of tanning's cosmetic effects were more likely to say they would protect themselves from the sun than were students informed about the risk of cancer. Fear appeals are most effective when the audience believes that the risks are serious—as in causing wrinkles!—and that the audience members can change their behavior to avert the risks—as in preventing wrinkling (Eagly & Chaiken, 1993).

Audiences also tend to believe arguments that appear to run counter to the vested interests of the communicator (Petty et al., 1997). If the president of Chrysler or General Motors said that Toyotas and Hondas were superior, you can bet that we would prick up our ears.

The Persuasive Communicator: Whom Do You Trust?

Would you buy a used car from a person who had been convicted of larceny? Would you leaf through fashion magazines featuring homely models? Probably not. Research shows that persuasive communicators are characterized by expertise, trustworthiness, attractiveness, or similarity to their audiences (Petty et al., 1997). Because of the adoration of their fans, sports superstars such as Tiger Woods are also persuasive as endorsers of products.

TV news anchors enjoy high prestige. One study (Mullen et al., 1987) found that before the 1984 presidential election, Peter Jennings of ABC News had shown significantly more favorable facial expressions when reporting on Ronald Reagan than when reporting on Walter Mondale. Tom Brokaw of NBC and Dan Rather of CBS had not shown favoritism. The researchers also found that viewers of ABC News voted for Reagan in greater proportions than viewers of NBC or CBS News. It is tempting to conclude that Jennings subtly persuaded viewers to vote for Reagan—and maybe this did happen in a number of cases. But viewers do not simply absorb, spongelike, whatever the tube feeds them. People find it painful when they are confronted with information that discredits their own stereotypes and prejudices (Foerster et al., 2000). Therefore, they often show **selective avoidance** and **selective exposure** (Perse, 1998). That is, they switch channels when the news coverage runs counter to their own attitudes. They also seek communicators whose outlook coincides with their own. Thus, it may simply be that Reaganites favored Jennings over Brokaw and Rather.

The Context of the Message: "Get 'Em in a Good Mood"

You are too shrewd to let someone persuade you by buttering you up, but perhaps someone you know would be influenced by a sip of wine, a bite of cheese, and a sincere compliment. Aspects of the immediate environment, such as music, increase the likelihood of persuasion. When we are in a good mood, we apparently are less likely to evaluate the situation carefully (Forgas et al., 1994; Park & Banaji, 2000; Petty et al., 1997).

It is also counterproductive to call your dates fools when they differ with you—even though their ideas are bound to be foolish if they do not agree with yours. Agreement and praise are more effective ways to encourage others to embrace your views. Appear sincere, or else your compliments will look manipulative. (It seems unfair to let out this information.)

The Persuaded Audience

Why do some people have sales resistance? Why do others enrich the lives of every door-to-door salesperson? It may be that people with high self-esteem and low social anxiety are more likely to resist social pressure (Santee & Maslach, 1982).

A classic study by Schwartz and Gottman (1976) reveals the cognitive nature of the social anxiety that can make it difficult for some people to refuse requests. The researchers found that people who comply with unreasonable requests are more apt to report thoughts like the following:

▲ "I was worried about what the other person would think of me if I refused."
▲ "It is better to help others than to be self-centered."

▲ "The other person might be hurt or insulted if I refused."

People who refuse unreasonable requests reported thoughts like these:

▲ "It doesn't matter what the other person thinks of me."
▲ "I am perfectly free to say no."
▲ "This request is unreasonable."

▲ **REFLECT**
Are you a person who can't say no? If so, why?

The Foot-in-the-Door Technique   You might suppose that contributing money to door-to-door solicitors for charity will get you off the hook. Perhaps they'll take the cash and leave you alone for a while. Actually, the opposite is true. The next time they mount a campaign, they may call on you to go door to door on their behalf! Organizations compile lists of people they can rely on. Because they have gotten their "foot in the door," this is known as the **foot-in-the-door technique.**

Consider a classic experiment by Freedman and Fraser (1966). Groups of women received phone calls from a consumer group requesting that they let a six-person crew come to their home to catalog their household products. The job could take hours. Only 22% of one group acceded to this irksome request. But 53% of another group of women assented to a visit from this wrecking crew. Why was the second group more compliant? They had been phoned a few days earlier and had agreed to answer a few questions about the soap products they used. Thus they had been primed for the second request: The caller had gotten a foot in the door.

Research suggests that people who accede to small requests become more amenable to larger ones for a variety of reasons, including conformity and self-perception as the kind of people who help in this way (Burger, 1999). Regardless of how the foot-in-the-door technique works, if you want to say no, it may be easier to do so (and stick to your guns) the first time a request is made. Later may be too late.

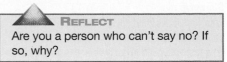

CLICK4™ *advice on dealing effectively with telemarketers.*

 ## Attitudes and Diversity: The Problem of Prejudice

People have condemned billions of other people. Without ever meeting them. Without ever learning their names. In this section, we discuss some of the reasons for this. We will be dealing with a particularly troubling kind of attitude: prejudice. *Questions: What is prejudice? Why are people prejudiced?*

Prejudice is an attitude toward a group that leads people to evaluate members of that group negatively—even though they have never met them. On a cognitive level, prejudice is linked to expectations that members of the target group will behave poorly, say, in the workplace, or engage in criminal behavior. On an emotional level, prejudice is associated with negative feelings such as fear, dislike, or hatred. In behavioral terms, it is connected with avoidance, aggression, and discrimination. Prejudice is the most troubling kind of attitude. It is connected with the genocide of millions upon millions of people.

▲ **REFLECT**
Have you ever been a victim of prejudice? What happened? How did you feel? What did you do about it? Are you content with your response? If not, what can you do if it happens again?

Discrimination   One form of negative behavior that results from prejudice is **discrimination.** Many groups in the United States have experienced discrimination—women, gay males and lesbians, older people, and ethnic groups such as African Americans, Asian Americans, Latino and Latina Americans, Irish Americans, Jewish Americans, and Native Americans. Discrimination takes many forms, including denial of access to jobs, housing, and the voting booth.

Stereotypes   Are Jewish Americans shrewd and ambitious? Are African Americans superstitious and musical? Are gay men and lesbians unfit for military service? Such ideas are *stereotypes*—prejudices about certain groups that lead people to view members of those groups in a biased fashion.

Some stereotypes are positive rather than negative, such as the cultural stereotypes about physically attractive people. By and large, we assume that "good things come in pretty packages." Attractive children and adults are judged and treated more positively

Selective avoidance ▲ Diverting one's attention from information that is inconsistent with one's attitudes.

Selective exposure ▲ Deliberately seeking and attending to information that is consistent with one's attitudes.

Foot-in-the-door technique ▲ A method for inducing compliance in which a small request is followed by a larger request.

Prejudice ▲ The unfounded belief that a person or group—on the basis of assumed racial, ethnic, sexual, or other features—will possess negative characteristics or perform inadequately.

Discrimination ▲ The denial of privileges to a person or a group on the basis of prejudice.

Stereotyping.
How well is this child doing? Research shows that our expectations concerning a child's performance on a test are linked to our awareness of that child's socioeconomic background.

than their unattractive peers (Langlois et al., 2000). We expect attractive people to be poised, sociable, popular, intelligent, mentally healthy, fulfilled, persuasive, and successful in their jobs and marriages (Eagly et al., 1991; Feingold, 1992b). Research shows that attractiveness is positively correlated with popularity, social skills, and sexual experience (Feingold, 1992b; Langlois et al., 2000).

Attractive people are even more likely to be judged innocent of crimes in mock jury experiments and observational studies (Mazzella & Feingold, 1994). When they are found guilty, they are given less severe sentences. Perhaps we assume that attractive people have less need to resort to deviant behavior to achieve their goals. Even when they have erred, perhaps they will be more likely to change their evil ways.

www 17 L 8
CLICK4™ *the Web site of the NAACP.*

Psychology and Modern Life

Combating Prejudice

Prejudice has been with us throughout history, and it is unlikely that a miracle cure is at hand. Yet we need not stand idly by when we witness prejudice. We can create millions of mini-miracles — changes in those of us who wish to end prejudice. Here are some things we can do to combat prejudice:

1. *Encourage intergroup contact and cooperation.* Prejudice encourages us to

> ▲ **REFLECT**
> Does your college or university have a diverse or rather narrow student population? Are you or fellow students experiencing any changes in stereotyping of people from other groups as a result of your college experience?

avoid other groups, which is unfortunate because intergroup contact is one way of breaking down prejudices (Baron & Byrne, 2000). Intergroup contact reveals that members of religious and racial groups have varying values, abilities, interests, and personalities. That is, contact heightens awareness of individual variation, and this knowledge can lead us to abandon stereotypical thinking (Hewstone & Hamberger, 2000; Sherman & Frost, 2000). Intergroup contact is especially effective when people are striving to meet common goals. Playing on the same team, working together on a joint educational project or the yearbook are examples.

A classic experiment by Muzafer Sherif and his colleagues (1961/1988) showed how feelings of prejudice can be created and reduced. They randomly divided

11-year-old male campers at Oklahoma's Robbers Cave State Park into two groups, who labeled themselves the Eagles and the Rattlers. After being kept apart for a week, the Eagles and Rattlers met in competitive games. A bitter rivalry quickly erupted, in which the Eagles burned the Rattlers' flag and the Rattlers retaliated by trashing the Eagles' cabin. Eating and watching movies together were not enough to overcome the feelings of hostility felt by the groups. The Eagles and the Rattlers became friends only after they had worked together to achieve common goals, such as repairing the camp's water supply and fixing a truck that was carrying food to the camp (both of which had been sabotaged by the experimenters).

2. *Attack discriminatory behavior.* It is sometimes easier to change people's be-

Sources of Prejudice

The sources of prejudice are many and varied. Here are some of them:

1. *Dissimilarity.* We are apt to like people who share our attitudes. In forming impressions of others, we are influenced by attitudinal similarity and dissimilarity (Duckitt, 1992). People of different religions and races often have different backgrounds, however, giving rise to dissimilar attitudes. Even when people of different races share important values, they may assume that they do not.

2. *Social conflict.* There is a lengthy history of social and economic conflict between people of different races and religions. For example, for many decades Southern European Americans and African Americans have competed for jobs, giving rise to negative attitudes, even lynchings (Green et al., 1998).

3. *Social learning.* Children acquire some attitudes from other people, especially their parents. Children tend to imitate their parents, and parents reinforce their children for doing so (Duckitt, 1992). In this way prejudices can be transmitted from generation to generation.

The mass media also perpetuate stereotypes. Even today, TV commercials portray European Americans, especially men, as being more prominent and wielding more authority than African Americans (Coltraine & Messineo, 2000). European Americans, especially women, are portrayed as being more likely to obtain romantic and domestic fulfillment. In general, European American men tend to be portrayed as powerful, European American women as sex objects, African American men as aggressive, and African American women as unimportant.

4. *Information processing.* One cognitive view is that prejudices act as cognitive filters through which we perceive the social world. Prejudice is a way of processing social information. It is easier to attend to, and remember, instances of behavior that are consistent with our prejudices than it is to reconstruct our mental categories (Kashima, 2000; Sherman & Frost, 2000). If you believe that Jewish Americans are stingy, it is easier to recall a Jewish American's negotiation of a price than a Jewish American's charitable donation. If you believe that Californians are airheads, it may be easier to recall TV images of surfing than of scientific conferences at Caltech and

> **▲ REFLECT**
> How do you treat people of different religions or races? Do you treat them as individuals or are your expectations based on stereotypes? Explain.

CLICK4™ *an essay assignment on stereotypes, prejudice, and discrimination.*

havior than to alter their feelings. Yet cognitive dissonance theory suggests that when we change people's behavior, their feelings may follow along. It is illegal to deny access to an education and jobs on the basis of gender, religion, race, or disability. Seek legal remedies if you have been discriminated against. Have you been denied access to living accommodations or a job because of prejudice? Talk about it to your academic advisor, the college equal opportunity office, or the dean of students.

3. *Hold discussion forums.* Many campuses conduct workshops and discussion groups on gender, race, and diversity. Talk to your dean of students about holding such workshops.

4. *Examine your own beliefs.* Prejudice isn't "out there." Prejudice dwells within us. It is easy to focus on the prejudices of others, but what about our own? Have you examined your own attitudes and rejected stereotyping and prejudice?

Even if we do not personally harbor feelings of racial or religious enmity, are we doing anything to counter such feelings in others? Do we confront people who make prejudiced remarks? Do we belong to organizations that deny access to members of other racial and religious groups? Do we strike up conversations with people from other groups or avoid them? College is meant to be a broadening experience, and we deny ourselves much of the education we could be receiving when we limit our encounters to people who share our own backgrounds.

Intergroup Contact.
Intergroup contact can reduce feelings of prejudice when people work together toward common goals.

CLICK4™ *the Latina/Latino Network.*

CLICK4™ *a bulletin board discussion: How does prejudice affect you?*

CLICK4™ *an opportunity to take an online Implicit Attitude Test and to apply what you learn about yourself.*

Berkeley. On the other hand, people are often likely to evaluate messages from stigmatized groups such as gay males or African Americans extra carefully, in an effort to make sure that they are judging on the basis of the message and not the deliverer of the message (Petty et al., 1999).

5. *Social Categorization.* A second cognitive perspective focuses on the tendency to divide our social world into "us" and "them." People usually view those who belong to their own groups—the "in-group"—more favorably than those who do not—the "out-group" (Duckitt, 1992). Moreover, there is a tendency to assume that members of the out-group are more similar in their attitudes and behavior than members of our own groups (Judd & Park, 1988). Our isolation from the out-group makes it easier to maintain our stereotypes.

Just as there are many sources of prejudice, there is much that we can do about prejudice, as we see in the "Psychology and Modern Life" feature on pages 584 and 585.

REVIEW

(1) _____ psychology is the study of the nature and causes of our behavior and mental processes in social situations. (2) An _____ is a behavioral and cognitive tendency that is expressed by evaluating people or things with favor or disfavor. (3) When we are free to do as we wish, our behavior (is or is not?) usually consistent with our attitudes. (4) Attitudes are acquired through conditioning, observational learning, and _____ appraisal. (5) Early attitudes serve as _____ anchors. (6) According to the _____ likelihood model, there are central and peripheral routes to persuasion. (7) According to the _____-in-the-door effect, people are more likely to agree to large requests after they have agreed to smaller ones. (8) Denial of access to privileges on the basis of group membership is termed _____. (9) A _____ is a fixed, conventional idea about a group. (10) Sources of prejudice include attitudinal (similarity or dissimilarity?). (11) Other sources of prejudice include economic conflict, social learning, and social _____, which refers to the tendency to divide the social world into categories of "us" versus "them."

Pulling It Together: How would you use the information in this section to create a persuasive advertisement?

IN REVIEW

Sources of Prejudice

Dissimilarity	People prefer to affiliate with people who have similar attitudes. People of different religions and races often have different backgrounds, which may give rise to *dissimilar* attitudes. People also tend to *assume* that people of different races have different attitudes, even when they do not.
Social conflict	Social and economic conflict give rise to feelings of prejudice. People of different races and religions often compete for jobs, giving rise to feelings of prejudice.
Social learning	Children acquire some attitudes by observing other people, especially their parents. Parents often reinforce their children for behaving in ways that express their attitudes, including prejudices.
Information processing	Prejudices serve as cognitive schemes or anchors, filters through which people perceive the social world. It is usually easier to remember instances of behavior that are consistent with prejudices than those that might force people to reconstruct their mental categories.
Social categorization	People tend to divide their social world into "us" and "them." People usually view people who belong to their own groups—the "in-group"—more favorably than those who do not—the "out-group."

SOCIAL PERCEPTION: LOOKING OUT, LOOKING WITHIN

An important area of social psychology concerns the ways in which we perceive other people—for example, the importance of the first impressions they make on us. Next we explore some factors that contribute to **social perception:** the primacy and recency effects, attribution theory, and body language.

Primacy and Recency Effects: The Importance of First Impressions

Why do you wear a suit to a job interview? Why do defense attorneys make sure that their clients dress neatly and get their hair cut before they are seen by the jury? *Questions: Do first impressions really matter? What are the primacy and recency effects?* Apparently first impressions do matter—a great deal.

As social psychologist Solomon Asch discovered, first impressions are important and reasonably accurate (Gleitman et al., 1997). First impressions are an example of the primacy effect. In this section we discuss the primacy and recency effects.

When I was a teenager, a young man was accepted or rejected by his date's parents the first time they were introduced. If he was considerate and made small talk, her parents

First Impressions.
Why is it important to make a good first impression? What are some ways of doing so?

Social perception ▲ A subfield of social psychology that studies the ways in which we form and modify impressions of others.

Psychology and Modern Life
Making a Good First Impression

The first impressions you make on others, and the first impressions others make on you, are important to your relationships. You can manage first impressions in a number of ways:

1. Be aware of the impression you make on others. When you meet people for the first time, remember that they are forming impressions of you. Once formed, these impressions are resistant to change.

2. When you apply for a job, your "first impression"—your vita or résumé—may reach your prospective employer before you walk through the door. Make it neat, and present some of your more important accomplishments at the beginning.

3. Why not plan and rehearse your first few remarks on a date or a job interview? Imagine the situation and, in the case of an interview, questions that you are likely to be asked. If you have some relatively smooth statements prepared, along with a nice smile, you are more likely to be considered socially competent, and competence is respected.

4. Smile. You're more attractive when you smile.

5. Dress well for job interviews, college interviews, first dates, important meet-

ings—even when you go to the doctor's office. The appropriate dress for making a good impression on a first date might differ from what you would wear to a job interview. In each case ask yourself, "What type of dress is expected for this occasion? How can I make a positive first impression?"

6. When you answer essay questions, attend to your penmanship. It is the first thing your instructor notices when looking at your paper. Present relevant knowledge in the first sentence or paragraph of the answer, or restate the question by writing something like, "In this essay I will show how . . ."

7. In class, make eye contact with your instructor. Look interested. That way, if you do poorly on a couple of quizzes your instructor may think of you as a "basically good student who made a couple of errors," rather than as "a poor student who is revealing her or his shortcomings." (Don't tell your instructor about this paragraph. Maybe he or she won't notice it.)

8. The first time you talk to your instructor outside of class, be reasonable and sound interested in the subject.

9. When you pass someone in a race, put on a burst of speed. The other person

may think that trying to catch you will be futile.

10. Ask yourself if you are being fair to other people in your life. If your date's parents are a bit cold toward you on the evening of your first date, maybe it's because they don't know you and are concerned about their child's welfare. If you show them that you are treating their child decently, they may come around. Don't assume that they're permanent prunefaces.

11. Before you eliminate people from your life on the basis of first impressions, ask yourself, "Is the first impression the 'real person' or just one instance of that person's behavior?" Give people a second chance and you may find that they have something to offer. After all, would you want to be held accountable for everything you've ever said and done? Haven't you changed for the better as time has gone on? Haven't you become more sophisticated and knowledgeable? (You're reading this book, aren't you?)

would allow the couple to stay out past curfew—perhaps even to watch submarine races at the beach during the early morning hours. If he was boorish or uncommunicative, he was seen as a cad forever after. Her parents would object to him, no matter how hard he worked to gain their favor.

My experiences demonstrated to me that first impressions often make or break us. This phenomenon is known as the **primacy effect.** Why are first impressions so important? The answer may be because we infer traits from behavior. If we act considerately at first, we are labeled considerate. The *trait* of consideration is used to explain and predict our future behavior. If, after being labeled considerate, one keeps a date out past curfew, this lapse is likely to be seen as an exception to a rule—excused by circumstances or external causes. If one is first seen as inconsiderate, however, several months of considerate behavior may be perceived as a cynical effort to "make up for it."

Participants in a classic experiment on the primacy effect read different stories about "Jim" (Luchins, 1957). The stories consisted of one or two paragraphs. The one-paragraph stories portrayed Jim as either friendly or unfriendly. These paragraphs were also used in the two-paragraph stories, but in this case the paragraphs were read in the reverse order. Of those reading only the "friendly" paragraph, 95% rated Jim as friendly. Of those who read just the "unfriendly" paragraph, 3% rated him as friendly. Seventy-eight percent of those who read two-paragraph stories in the "friendly-unfriendly" order labeled Jim as friendly. When they read the paragraphs in the reverse order, only 18% rated Jim as friendly.

How can we encourage people to pay more attention to impressions occurring after the first encounter? Abraham Luchins accomplished this by allowing time to elapse between the presentations of the two paragraphs. In this way, fading memories allowed more recent information to take precedence. This is known as the **recency effect.** Luchins found a second way to counter first impressions: He simply asked participants to avoid making snap judgments and to weigh all the evidence.

There is some interesting research on the role of the handshake in making a first impression. In our culture, a firm handshake is a key to making a good first impression, by women as well as men. Researchers find that a firm handshake is perceived as an indication of being outgoing and open to new experience. A weak handshake was perceived as indicative of shyness and social anxiety (Chaplin et al., 2000). Thus women in the business world are well-advised to shake hands of new acquaintances firmly. The "Psychology and Modern Life" feature on page 587 offers more advice on making a good first impression.

Attribution Theory: You're Free, but I'm Caught in the Middle?

When she was 3 years old, one of my daughters believed that a friend's son was a boy because he *wanted* to be a boy. Since she was 3 at the time, this error in my daughter's **attribution** of the boy's gender is understandable. Adults tend to make somewhat similar attribution errors, however. Although they do not believe that people's preferences have much to do with their gender, they do tend to exaggerate the role of choice in their behavior. *Questions: What is attribution theory? Why do we assume that other people intend the mischief that they do?*

An attribution is an assumption about why people do things (Jones, 1990). When you assume that one child is mistreating another child because she is "mean," you are making an attribution. The process by which we make inferences about the motives and traits of others through observation of their behavior is the **attribution process.** This section focuses on *attribution theory*, or the processes by which people draw conclusions about the factors that influence one another's behavior. Attribution theory is important because attributions lead us to perceive others either as purposeful actors or as victims of circumstances.

Dispositional and Situational Attributions   Social psychologists describe two types of attributions. **Dispositional attributions** ascribe a person's behavior to internal factors such as personality traits and free will. **Situational attributions** attribute a person's actions to external factors such as social influence or socialization. If you assume that one child is mistreating the other because her parents have given her certain attitudes toward the other child, you are making a situational attribution.

▲ **REFLECT**
Did you ever try to "make a good first impression"? Why? What did you do? Did it work? Explain.

CLICK4™ *an opportunity to participate in an online study about impression formation.*

Primacy effect ▲ The tendency to evaluate others in terms of first impressions.

Recency effect ▲ The tendency to evaluate others in terms of the most recent impression.

Attribution ▲ A belief concerning why people behave in a certain way.

Attribution process ▲ The process by which people draw inferences about the motives and traits of others.

Dispositional attribution ▲ An assumption that a person's behavior is determined by internal causes such as personal attitudes or goals.

Situational attribution ▲ An assumption that a person's behavior is determined by external circumstances such as the social pressure found in a situation.

The Fundamental Attribution Error   In cultures that view the self as independent, such as ours, people tend to attribute other people's behavior primarily to internal factors such as personality, attitudes, and free will (Basic Behavioral Science Task Force, 1996c). This bias in the attribution process is known as the **fundamental attribution error.** In such individualistic societies, people tend to focus on the behavior of others rather than on the circumstances surrounding their behavior. For example, if a teenager gets into trouble with the law, individualistic societies are more likely to blame the teenager than the social environment in which the teenager lives. When involved in difficult negotiations, there is a tendency to attribute the toughness to the personalities of the negotiators on the other side rather than the nature of the process of negotiation (Morris et al., 1999).

One reason for the fundamental attribution error is that we tend to infer traits from behavior. But in cultures that stress interdependence, such as Asian cultures, people are more likely to attribute other people's behavior to that person's social roles and obligations (Basic Behavioral Science Task Force, 1996c). For example, Japanese people might be more likely to attribute a businessperson's extreme competitiveness to the "culture of business" rather than to his or her personality.

The Actor-Observer Effect   When we see people (including ourselves) doing things that we do not like, we tend to see the others as willful actors but to see ourselves as victims of circumstances (Baron & Byrne, 2000). The tendency to attribute other people's behavior to dispositional factors and our own behavior to situational influences is called the **actor-observer effect.**

Consider an example. Parents and children often argue about the children's choice of friends or dates. When they do, the parents tend to infer traits from behavior and to see the children as stubborn and resistant. The children also infer traits from behavior. Thus they may see their parents as bossy and controlling. Parents and children alike attribute the others' behavior to internal causes. That is, both make dispositional attributions about other people's behavior.

How do the parents and children perceive themselves? The parents probably see themselves as being forced into combat by their children's foolishness. If they become insistent, it is in response to the children's stubbornness. The children probably see themselves as responding to peer pressures and, perhaps, to sexual urges that may have come from within but seem like a source of outside pressure. The parents and the children both tend to see their own behavior as motivated by external forces. That is, they make situational attributions for their own behavior.

CLICK4™ *an essay assignment on the fundamental attribution error.*

> **△ REFLECT**
> Do you ever do anything that is wrong? (Be honest!) How do you explain your misdeeds to yourself? Are other people harsher in their judgment of you than you yourself are? If so, why?

Fundamental attribution error ▲ The tendency to assume that others act predominantly on the basis of their dispositions, even when there is evidence suggesting the importance of their situations.

Actor-observer effect ▲ The tendency to attribute our own behavior to situational factors but to attribute the behavior of others to dispositional factors.

The Actor-Observer Effect.
Who is at fault here? People tend to make dispositional attributions for other people's behavior, but they tend to see their own behavior as motivated by situational factors. Thus people are aware of the external forces acting on themselves when they behave but tend to attribute other people's behavior to choice and will.

The actor-observer effect extends to our perceptions of both the in-group (an extension of ourselves) and the out-group. Consider conflicts between nations, for example. Both sides may engage in brutal acts of violence. Each side usually considers the other to be calculating, inflexible, and—not infrequently—sinister. Each side also typically views its own people as victims of circumstances and its own violent actions as justified or dictated by the situation. After all, we may look at the other side as being in the wrong, but can we expect them to agree with us?[3]

CLICK4™ *a bulletin board discussion: Why do we tend to hold others accountable for their misdeeds but excuse ourselves?*

The Self-Serving Bias

There is also a **self-serving bias** in the attribution process. We are likely to ascribe our successes to internal, dispositional factors but our failures to external, situational influences (Campbell & Sedikides, 1999). When we have done well on a test or impressed a date, we are likely to credit our intelligence and charm. But when we fail, we are likely to blame bad luck, an unfair test, or our date's bad mood.

We can extend the self-serving bias to sports. A study with 27 college wrestlers found that they tended to attribute their wins to stable and internal conditions such as their abilities, but their losses to unstable and external conditions such as an error by a referee (De Michele et al., 1998). Sports fans fall into the same trap. They tend to attribute their team's victories to internal conditions and their losses to external conditions (Wann & Shrader, 2000).

There are exceptions to the self-serving bias. In accord with the bias, when we work in groups, we tend to take the credit for the group's success but to pin the blame for group failure on someone else. But the outcome is different when we are friends with other group members: Then we tend to share the credit for success or the blame for failure (Campbell et al., 2000). Another exception is found in the fact that depressed people are more likely than other people to ascribe their failures to internal factors, even when external forces are mostly to blame.

Another interesting attribution bias is a gender difference in attributions for friendly behavior. Men are more likely than women to interpret a woman's smile or friendliness toward a man as flirting (Abbey, 1987; Buss, 2000). Perhaps traditional differences in gender roles still lead men to expect that a "decent" woman will be passive.

Factors Contributing to the Attribution Process

Our attribution of behavior to internal or external causes can apparently be influenced by three factors: *consensus*, *consistency*, and *distinctiveness* (Kelley & Michela, 1980). When few people act in a certain way—that is, when **consensus** is low—we are likely to attribute behavior to dispositional (internal) factors. Consistency refers to the degree to which the same person acts in the same way on other occasions. Highly consistent behavior can often be attributed to dispositional factors. Distinctiveness is the extent to which the person responds differently in different situations. If the person acts similarly in different situations, distinctiveness is low. We therefore are likely to attribute his or her behavior to dispositional factors.

Let us apply the criteria of consensus, consistency, and distinctiveness to the behavior of a customer in a restaurant. She takes one bite of her blueberry cheesecake and calls the waiter. She tells him that her food is inedible and demands that it be replaced. Now, has she complained as a result of internal causes (for example, because she is hard to please) or external causes (that is, because the food really is bad)? Under the following circumstances, we are likely to attribute her behavior to internal, dispositional causes: (1) No one else at the table is complaining, so consensus is low. (2) She has returned her food on other occasions, so consistency is high. (3) She complains in other restaurants also, so distinctiveness is low (see Table 17.1).

Under the following circumstances, however, we are likely to attribute the customer's behavior to external, situational causes: (1) Everyone else at the table is also complaining, so consensus is high. (2) She does not usually return food, so consistency is low. (3) She usually does not complain at restaurants, so distinctiveness is high. Given these

---

Self-serving bias ▲ The tendency to view one's successes as stemming from internal factors and one's failures as stemming from external factors.

Consensus ▲ General agreement.

[3]I am not suggesting that all nations are equally blameless (or blameworthy) for their brutality toward other nations. I am pointing out that there is a tendency for the people of a nation to perceive themselves as being driven to undesirable behavior. Yet they are also likely to perceive other nations' behavior as willful.

conditions, we are likely to believe that the blueberry cheese-cake really is awful and that the customer is justified in her response.

TABLE 17.1 FACTORS LEADING TO INTERNAL OR EXTERNAL ATTRIBUTIONS OF BEHAVIOR

	Internal Attribution	External Attribution
Consensus	Low: Few people behave this way.	High: Most people behave this way.
Consistency	High: The person behaves this way frequently.	Low: The person does not behave this way frequently.
Distinctiveness	Low: The person behaves this way in many situations.	High: The person behaves this way in few situations.

Body Language: The Body Speaks

Body language is important in social perception. *Question: What is body language?* Body language is nonverbal language; it refers to the meanings we infer from the ways in which people carry themselves and the gestures they make (Flack et al., 1999; McClave, 2000). At an early age we learn that the way people carry themselves provides cues to how they feel and are likely to behave. You may have noticed that when people are "uptight" they may also be rigid and straight-backed. People who are relaxed are more likely to "hang loose." Factors such as eye contact, posture, and the distance between two people provide cues to the individuals' moods and their feelings toward their companions. When people face us and lean toward us, we may assume that they like us or are interested in what we are saying. If we overhear a conversation between a couple and observe that the woman is leaning toward the man but the man is sitting back and toying with his hair, we are likely to infer that he is not interested in what she is saying.

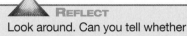
REFLECT
Look around. Can you tell whether other people are enjoying being with one another, or whether they are finding the experience annoying? How can you tell?

Touching: Put the Arm on People (Literally)   Touching also communicates. Women are more likely than men to touch other people when they are interacting with them (Stier & Hall, 1984). In one "touching" experiment, Kleinke (1977) showed that appeals for help can be more effective when the distressed person makes physical contact with people who are asked for aid. A woman obtained more coins for phone calls when she touched the arm of the person she was asking for money. In another experiment, waitresses obtained higher tips when they touched patrons on the hand or the shoulder while making change (Crusco & Wetzel, 1984).

In these experiments, the touching was noncontroversial. It was usually gentle, brief, and done in familiar settings. However, when touching suggests greater intimacy than is desired, it can be seen as negative. A study in a nursing home found that responses to being touched depended on factors such as the status of the staff member, the type of touch, and the part of the body that was touched (Hollinger & Buschmann, 1993). Touching was considered positive when it was appropriate to the situation and did not appear to be condescending. It was seen as negative when it was controlling, unnecessary, or overly intimate.

Body language can also be used to establish and maintain territorial control, as anyone knows who has had to step aside because a football player was walking down the hall. Werner and her colleagues (1981) found that players in a game arcade used touching as a way of signaling others to keep their distance. Solo players engaged in more touching than did groups, perhaps because they were surrounded by strangers.

Gazing and Staring: The Eyes Have It   We usually feel that we can learn much from eye contact. When other people "look us squarely in the eye," we may assume that they are being assertive or open with us. Avoidance of eye contact may suggest deception or depression. Gazing is interpreted as a sign of liking or friendliness (Kleinke, 1986). In one penetrating study, men and women were asked to gaze into each other's eyes for 2 minutes (Kellerman et al., 1989). After doing so, they reported having passionate feelings toward one another. (Watch out!)

Of course, a gaze is not the same thing as a persistent hard stare. A hard stare is interpreted as a provocation or a sign of anger. Adolescent males sometimes engage in staring contests as an assertion of dominance. The male who looks away first loses the contest. In a classic series of field experiments, Phoebe Ellsworth and her colleagues (1972) subjected drivers stopped at red lights to hard stares by riders of motor scooters (see Figure 17.1). When the light changed, people who were stared at crossed the intersection more rapidly than people who were not. People who are stared at exhibit higher levels of physiological arousal than people who are not (Strom & Buck, 1979).

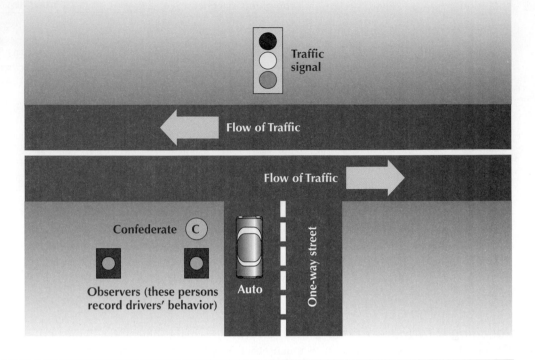

FIGURE 17.1 Diagram of an Experiment in Hard Staring and Avoidance. In the Greenbaum and Rosenfeld study, the confederate of the experimenter stared at some drivers and not at others. Recipients of the stares drove across the intersection more rapidly once the light turned green. Why?

REVIEW

CLICK4™ *a quiz covering the first half of this chapter.*

(12) The psychology of social _____ involves the ways in which we perceive other people and ourselves. (13) The tendency to perceive others in terms of first impressions is an example of the _____ effect. (14) Our inference of the motives and traits of others through observation of their behavior is called the _____ process. (15) People who feel (positively or negatively?) toward one another tend to position themselves close together. (16) Gazing into another's eyes can be a sign of love, but a hard _____ is an aversive challenge.

Pulling It Together: Why is it that we tend to hold others accountable for their misdeeds but excuse ourselves for the bad things we do?

SOCIAL INFLUENCE: ARE YOU AN INDIVIDUAL OR ONE OF THE CROWD?

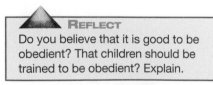

▲ REFLECT
Do you believe that it is good to be obedient? That children should be trained to be obedient? Explain.

CLICK4™ *Festinger and Carlsmith's classic article, "Cognitive Consequences of Forced Compliance."*

Most people would be reluctant to wear blue jeans to a funeral, walk naked on city streets, or, for that matter, wear clothes at a nudist colony. This is because other people and groups can exert enormous pressure on us to behave according to their norms. **Social influence** is the area of social psychology that studies the ways in which people alter the thoughts, feelings, and behavior of others. We already learned how attitudes can be changed through persuasion. In this section we describe a couple of classic experiments that demonstrate how people influence others to engage in destructive obedience or conform to social norms.

Obedience to Authority: Does Might Make Right?

Throughout history soldiers have followed orders—even when it comes to slaughtering innocent civilians. The Turkish slaughter of Armenians, the Nazi slaughter of Jews, the Serbian slaughter of Albanians and Bosnian Muslims, the mutual slaughter of Hutus and Tutsis in Rwanda—these are all examples of the tragedies that can arise from simply following orders. We may say we are horrified by such crimes and we cannot imagine why

Social influence ▲ The area of social psychology that studies the ways in which people influence the thoughts, feelings, and behavior of others.

people engage in them. But how many of us would refuse to follow orders issued by authority figures? *Questions: Why will so many people commit crimes against humanity if they are ordered to do so? (Why don't they refuse?)*

The Milgram Studies   Stanley Milgram also wondered how many people would resist immoral requests made by authority figures. To find out, he ran the series of experiments described in Chapter 1, "What Is Psychology?" (Milgram, 1974). People responded to newspaper ads seeking participants for an experiment on "the effects of punishment on learning." The experiment required a "teacher" and a "learner." The newspaper recruit was assigned the role of teacher—supposedly by chance.

Figures 1.5 and 1.6 show the bogus shock apparatus employed in the experiment, and the layout of the laboratory. "Teachers" were given the task of administering shock to learners when they made errors. The level of shock was to increase with each consecutive error. Despite the professed purpose of the research, Milgram's sole aim was to determine how many people would deliver high levels of apparently painful electric shock to "learners."

In various phases of Milgram's research, nearly half or the majority of the participants complied throughout the series, believing that they were delivering 450-volt, XXX-rated shocks. These findings held for men from the New Haven community and for male students at Yale, and for women.

Many people obey the commands of others even when they are required to perform immoral tasks. But *why?* Why did Germans "just follow orders" during the Holocaust? Why did "teachers" obey the experimenter in Milgram's study? We do not have all the answers, but we can offer a number of hypotheses:

1. *Socialization*. Despite the expressed American ideal of independence, we are socialized from early childhood to obey authority figures such as parents and teachers. Obedience to immoral demands may be the ugly sibling of socially desirable respect for authority figures (Blass, 1991).

2. *Lack of social comparison*. In Milgram's experimental settings, experimenters displayed command of the situation. Teachers (participants), however, were on the experimenter's ground and very much on their own so they did not have the opportunity to compare their ideas and feelings with those of other people in the same situation. They therefore were less likely to have a clear impression of what to do.

3. *Perception of legitimate authority*. One phase of Milgram's research took place within the hallowed halls of Yale University. Participants might have been overpowered by the reputation and authority of the setting. An experimenter at Yale might have appeared to be a highly legitimate authority figure—as might a government official or a high-ranking officer in the military. Yet further research showed that the university setting contributed to compliance but was not fully responsible for it. The percentage of individuals who complied with the experimenter's demands dropped from 65% to 48% when Milgram (1974) replicated the study in a dingy storefront in a nearby town. At first glance, this finding might seem encouraging. But the main point of the Milgram studies is that most people are willing to engage in morally reprehensible acts at the behest of a legitimate-looking authority figure. Hitler and his henchmen were authority figures in Nazi Germany. "Science" and Yale University legitimized the authority of the experimenters in the Milgram studies.

4. *The foot-in-the-door technique*. The foot-in-the-door technique might also have contributed to the obedience of the teachers. Once they had begun to deliver shocks to learners, they might have found it progressively more difficult to extricate themselves from the situation. Soldiers, similarly, are first taught to obey orders unquestioningly in unimportant matters such as dress and drill. By the time they are ordered to risk their lives, they have been saluting smartly and following commands without question for a long time.

5. *Inaccessibility of values*. People are more likely to act in accordance with their attitudes when their attitudes are readily available, or accessible. Most people believe that it is wrong to harm innocent people. But strong emotions interfere with clear thinking. As the teachers in the Milgram experiments became more aroused, their

www 17 PS 1

CLICK4™ *Milgram's classic article, "Behavioral Study of Obedience."*

▲ **REFLECT**
How do you think you would have behaved if you had been a "teacher" in the Milgram studies? Are you sure?

www 17 BBC 3

CLICK4™ *a bulletin board discussion: Is it good to be obedient?*

attitudes might thus have become less "accessible." As a result, it might have become progressively more difficult for them to behave according to these attitudes.

6. *Buffers.* Several buffers decreased the effect of the learners' pain on the teachers. For example, the "learners" (who were actually confederates of the experimenter) were in another room. When they were in the same room with the teachers—that is, when the teachers had full view of their victims—the compliance rate dropped from 65% to 40%. Moreover, when the teacher held the learner's hand on the shock plate, the compliance rate dropped to 30%. In modern warfare, opposing military forces may be separated by great distances. They may be little more than a blip on a radar screen. It is one thing to press a button to launch a missile or aim a piece of artillery at a distant troop carrier or a faraway mountain ridge. It is quite another to hold a weapon to a victim's throat.

There are thus many possible explanations for obedience. Milgram's research has alerted us to a real danger—the tendency of many, if not most, people to obey the orders of an authority figure even when they run counter to moral values. It has happened before. It is happening now. What will you do to stop it?

Conformity: Do Many Make Right?

www 17 BBC 4

CLICK4™ *a bulletin board discussion: What factors contribute to group conformity?*

We are said to **conform** when we change our behavior in order to adhere to social norms. **Social norms** are widely accepted expectations concerning social behavior. Explicit social norms are often made into rules and laws such as those that require us to whisper in libraries and to slow down when driving past a school. There are also unspoken or implicit social norms, such as those that cause us to face the front in an elevator or to be "fashionably late" for social gatherings.

The tendency to conform to social norms is often good. Many norms have evolved because they promote comfort and survival. Group pressure can also promote maladaptive behavior, as when people engage in risky behavior because "everyone is doing it." *Question: Why do so many people tend to follow the crowd?*

▲ **REFLECT**

Can you think of some instances in which you have conformed to social pressure? (Would you wear blue jeans if everyone else wore slacks or skirts?)

IN REVIEW

Possible Reasons for "Following Orders" in the Milgram Studies

Socialization	People are socialized from early childhood to obey authority figures such as parents and teachers.
Lack of social comparison	Being on their own, participants ("teachers") did not have the opportunity to compare their feelings with those of other people in the same situation.
Perception of legitimate authority	When Milgram's research took place at Yale University, participants may have been influenced by the reputation and authority of the setting. An experimenter at Yale may have appeared to be a legitimate authority figure.
The foot-in-the-door technique	Once they had begun to deliver shocks to learners, participants may have found it progressively more difficult to pull out of the situation.
Inaccessibility of values	People are more likely to act in accordance with their attitudes when their attitudes are readily available, or accessible. Most people believe that it is wrong to harm innocent people, but strong emotions interfere with clear thinking. As the participants in the Milgram experiments became more upset, their attitudes may have become less accessible.
Buffers	Buffers may have decreased the effect of the "learners" pain on the participants (the "teachers"). For example, the learners were in another room.

Conform ▲ To changes one's attitudes or overt behavior to adhere to social norms.

Social norms ▲ Explicit and implicit rules that reflect social expectations and influence the ways people behave in social situations.

Conformity.
In the military, individuals are taught to conform until the group functions in machine-like fashion. What pressures to conform do you experience? Do you surrender to them? Why or why not?

To answer this question, let us look at a classic experiment on conformity conducted by Solomon Asch in the early 1950s. We then examine factors that promote conformity.

Seven Line Judges Can't Be Wrong: The Asch Study   Can you believe what you see with your own eyes? Seeing is believing, isn't it? Not if you were a participant in Asch's (1952) study.

You entered a laboratory room with seven other participants, supposedly taking part in an experiment on visual discrimination. At the front of the room stood a man holding cards with lines drawn on them.

The eight of you were seated in a series. You were given the seventh seat, a minor fact at the time. The man explained the task. There was a single line on the card on the left. Three lines were drawn on the card at the right (Figure 17.2). One line was the same length as the line on the other card. You and the other participants were to call out, one at a time, which of the three lines—1, 2, or 3—was the same length as the one on the card on the left. Simple.

The participants to your right spoke out in order: "3," "3," "3," "3," "3," "3." Now it was your turn. Line 3 was clearly the same length as the line on the first card, so you said "3." The fellow after you then chimed in: "3." That's all there was to it. Then two other cards were set up at the front of the room. This time line 2 was clearly the same length as the line on the first card. The answers were "2," "2," "2," "2," "2," "2." Again it was your turn. You said "2," and perhaps your mind began to wander. Your stomach was gurgling a bit. The fellow after you said "2."

www (17) **PS** (18)

CLICK4™ *Asch's classic article, "Opinions and Social Pressure."*

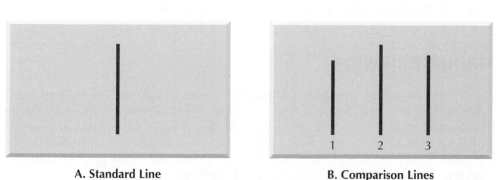

A. Standard Line   **B. Comparison Lines**

FIGURE 17.2   Cards Used in the Asch Study on Conformity.
Which line on card B—1, 2, or 3—is the same length as the line on card A? Line 2, right? But would you say "2" if you were a member of a group and six people answering ahead of you all said "3"? Are you sure?

Another pair of cards was held up. Line 3 was clearly the correct answer. The six people on your right spoke in turn: "1," "1 . . ." Wait a second! ". . . 1," "1." You forgot about dinner and studied the lines briefly. No, line 1 was too short by a good half inch. But the next two participants said "1" and suddenly it was your turn. Your hands had become sweaty and there was a lump in your throat. You wanted to say "3," but was it right? There was really no time, and you had already paused noticeably. You said "1," and so did the last fellow.

Now your attention was riveted on the task. Much of the time you agreed with the other seven judges, but sometimes you did not. And for some reason beyond your understanding, they were in perfect agreement even when they were wrong—assuming you could trust your eyes. The experiment was becoming an uncomfortable experience, and you began to doubt your judgment.

The discomfort in the Asch study was caused by the pressure to conform. Actually, the other seven recruits were confederates of the experimenter. They prearranged a number of incorrect responses. The sole purpose of the study was to see whether you would conform to the erroneous group judgments.

How many people in Asch's study caved in? How many went along with the crowd rather than give what they thought to be the right answer? Seventy-five percent. *Three out of four agreed with the majority's wrong answer at least once.*

CLICK4™ *more information on the scientific study of social influence, persuasion, compliance, propaganda, brainwashing, and the ethics surrounding these issues.*

Factors That Influence Conformity Several factors increase the tendency to conform. They include the following:

- ▲ belonging to a collectivist rather than an individualistic society (Bond & Smith, 1996),
- ▲ the desire to be liked by other members of the group (but valuing being right over being liked *decreases* the tendency to conform),
- ▲ low self-esteem,
- ▲ social shyness (Santee & Maslach, 1982), and
- ▲ lack of familiarity with the task.

Other factors in conformity include group size and social support. The likelihood of conformity, even to incorrect group judgments, increases rapidly as group size grows to five members, then rises more slowly as the group grows to about eight members. At about that point the maximum chance of conformity is reached. Yet finding just one other person who supports your minority opinion apparently is enough to encourage you to stick to your guns (Morris et al., 1977).

REVIEW

(17) Most people (do or do not?) comply with the demands of authority figures, even when the demands are immoral. (18) The following factors contribute to obedience: socialization, lack of _____ comparison, perception of experimenters as legitimate authority figures, and inaccessibility of values. (19) In Asch's studies of conformity, _____% of the participants agreed with an incorrect majority judgment at least once.

Pulling It Together: Why do people conform to group norms?

REFLECT
Families, classes, religious groups, political parties, nations, circles of friends, bowling teams, sailing clubs, conversation groups, therapy groups — how many groups do you belong to? How does belonging to groups influence your behavior?

GROUP BEHAVIOR

To be human is to belong to groups. Groups have much to offer us. They help us satisfy our needs for affection, attention, and belonging. They empower us to do things we could not manage by ourselves. But groups can also pressure us into doing things we might not do if we were acting alone, such as taking great risks or attacking other people.

This section considers ways in which people behave differently as group members than they would as individuals. We begin with social facilitation.

Social Facilitation: Monkey See, Monkey Do Faster?

One effect of groups on individual behavior is **social facilitation,** or the effects on performance that result from the presence of others. *Question: Do we run faster when we are in a group?* Apparently so. Runners and bicycle riders tend to move faster when they are members of a group. This effect is not limited to people. Dogs and cats eat more rapidly around others. Even roaches—yes, roaches—run more rapidly when other roaches are present (Zajonc, 1980).

Research suggests that the presence of other people increases our levels of arousal, or motivation (Mullen et al., 1997; Zajonc, 1980). At high levels of arousal, our performance of simple tasks is facilitated. Our performance of complex responses may be impaired, however. For this reason, a well-rehearsed speech may be delivered more masterfully before a larger audience. An offhand speech or a question-and-answer session may be hampered by a large audience.

Social facilitation may be influenced by **evaluation apprehension** as well as arousal (Sanna & Shotland, 1990). Our performance before a group is affected not only by the presence of others but also by concern that they are evaluating us. When giving a speech, we may "lose our thread" if we are distracted by the audience and focus too much on its apparent reaction. If we believe that we have begun to flounder, evaluation apprehension may skyrocket. As a result, our performance may falter even more.

The presence of others can also impair performance—not when we are acting *before* a group but when we are anonymous members *of* a group (Shepperd, 1993). Workers, for example, may "goof off" or engage in *social loafing* on humdrum jobs when they believe they will not be found out and held accountable. Under these conditions there is no evaluation apprehension. There may also be **diffusion of responsibility** in groups. Each person may feel less obligation to help because others are present. Group members may also

> ▲ **REFLECT**
>
> When you are given a group assignment, do you work harder or less hard than you would alone? Why?

Social facilitation ▲ The process by which a person's performance is increased when other members of a group engage in similar behavior.

Evaluation apprehension ▲ Concern that others are evaluating our behavior.

Diffusion of responsibility ▲ The spreading or sharing of responsibility for a decision or behavior within a group.

CLICK4™ a WebSearch activity on group dynamics and behavior and how these concepts can be applied to the workplace.

Social Facilitation.

Runners tend to move faster when they are members of a group. Does the presence of other people raise our levels of arousal or produce "evaluation apprehension"?

reduce their efforts if an apparently capable member makes no contribution but "rides free" on the efforts of others.

How would you perform in a tug of war? Would the presence of other people pulling motivate you to pull harder? (If so, we would attribute the result to "social facilitation.") Or would the fact that no one can tell how hard you are pulling encourage you to "loaf"? (If so, we would attribute the result to "diffusion of responsibility.")

Group Decision Making

CLICK4™ *a bulletin board discussion: How does belonging to groups influence your behavior?*

Organizations use groups such as committees or juries to make decisions in the belief that group decisions are more accurate than individual decisions (Gigone & Hastie, 1997). *Question: How do groups make decisions?*   Social psychologists have discovered a number of "rules," or **social decision schemes,** that govern much of group decision making (Stasser, 1999). Here are some examples:

1. *The majority-wins scheme.* In this commonly used scheme, the group arrives at the decision that was initially supported by the majority. This scheme appears to guide decision making most often when there is no single objectively correct decision. An example would be a decision about which car models to build when their popularity has not been tested in the court of public opinion.
2. *The truth-wins scheme.* In this scheme, as more information is provided and opinions are discussed, the group comes to recognize that one approach is objectively correct. For example, a group deciding whether to use SAT scores in admitting students to college would profit from information about whether the scores do predict college success.
3. *The two-thirds majority scheme.* Juries tend to convict defendants when two-thirds of the jury initially favors conviction.
4. *The first-shift rule.* In this scheme, the group tends to adopt the decision that reflects the first shift in opinion expressed by any group member. If a car-manufacturing group is divided on whether to produce a convertible, it may opt to do so after one member of the group who initially was opposed to the idea changes her mind. Similarly, if a jury is deadlocked, the members may eventually follow the lead of the first juror to switch his position.

▲ **REFLECT**
Have you been part of a group decision-making process? How did the group arrive at its decisions? Do you believe that the group decision reflected the judgments of the individuals in the group? Explain.

Polarization and the "Risky Shift"

We might think that a group decision would be more conservative than an individual decision. After all, shouldn't there be an effort to compromise, to "split the difference"? We might also expect that a few mature individuals would be able to balance the opinions of daredevils. *Questions: Are group decisions more risky or more conservative than those of the individual members of the group? Why?*

Groups do not always appear to work as we might expect, however. Consider the **polarization** effect. As an individual, you might recommend that your company risk an investment of $500,000 to develop or market a new product. Other company executives, polled individually, might risk similar amounts. If you were gathered together to make a group decision, however, you would probably recommend either an amount well above this figure or nothing at all (Kamalanabhan et al., 2000; Mordock, 1997). This group effect is called *polarization,* or the taking of an extreme position. If you had to gamble on which way the decision would go, however, you would do better to place your money on movement toward the higher sum—that is, to bet on a **risky shift.** Why?

One possibility is that one member of the group may reveal information that the others were not aware of. This information may clearly point in one direction or the other. With doubts removed, the group becomes polarized. It moves decisively in the appropriate direction. It is also possible that social facilitation occurs in the group setting and that the resulting greater motivation prompts more extreme decisions.

Why, however, do groups tend to take *greater* risks than those their members would take as individuals? One answer is diffusion of responsibility (Kamalanabhan et al., 2000; Mordock, 1997). If the venture flops, the blame will not be placed on you alone.

Social decision schemes ▲ Rules for predicting the final outcome of group decision making on the basis of the members' initial positions.

Polarization ▲ In social psychology, taking an extreme position or attitude on an issue.

Risky shift ▲ The tendency to make riskier decisions as a member of a group than as an individual acting independently.

Remember the self-serving bias: You can always say (and think) that the failure was the result of a group decision. You thus protect your self-esteem (Larrick, 1993). If the venture pays off, however, you can attribute the outcome to your cool analysis and boast of your influence on the group. Note that all this behavior fits right in with what is known about the self-serving bias.

Groupthink

Groupthink, a concept originated by Irving Janis (1982), is a problem that sometimes arises in group decision making. *Question: What is groupthink?* In **groupthink**, group members tend to be more influenced by group cohesiveness and a dynamic leader than by the realities of the situation (Esser, 1998; Hogg & Hains, 1998). Group problem solving may degenerate into groupthink when a group senses an external threat (Rempel & Fisher, 1998). Groupthink is usually fueled by a dynamic group leader. The threat heightens the cohesiveness of the group and is a source of stress. Under stress, group members tend not to consider all their options carefully. Flawed decisions are frequently made as a result.

www 17   E   5

CLICK4™ *an essay assignment: Why do we sometimes go along with the crowd, even when we don't want to?*

Groupthink has been connected with fiascos such as the Bay of Pigs invasion of Cuba, the Watergate scandal, the Iran-Contra affair, and NASA's decision to launch the *Challenger* space shuttle despite engineers' warnings about the dangers created by unusually cold weather (Raven, 1998; Turner & Pratkanis, 1998). Janis (1982) and other researchers (Esser, 1998; Turner & Pratkanis, 1998) note several characteristics of groupthink that contribute to such flawed group decisions:

1. *Feelings of invulnerability.* Each decision-making group might have believed that it was beyond the reach of critics or the law—in some cases, because the groups consisted of powerful people who were close to the president of the United States.
2. *The group's belief in its rightness.* These groups apparently believed in the rightness of what they were doing. In some cases, they were carrying out the president's wishes. In the case of the *Challenger* launch, NASA had a track record of successful launches.
3. *Discrediting of information contrary to the group's decision.* The government group involved in the Iran-Contra affair knowingly broke the law. Its members apparently discredited the law by (1) deciding that it was inconsistent with the best interests of the United States and (2) enlisting private citizens to do the dirty work so that the government was not directly involved.
4. *Pressures on group members to conform.* Group cohesiveness and a dynamic leader pressure group members to conform.
5. *Stereotyping of members of the out-group.* Members of the group that broke the law in the Iran-Contra affair reportedly stereotyped people who would oppose them as "communist sympathizers" and "knee-jerk liberals."

Groupthink can be averted if group leaders encourage members to remain skeptical about options and to feel free to ask probing questions and disagree with one another.

Mob Behavior and Deindividuation: The "Beast With Many Heads"

The Frenchman Gustave Le Bon (1895/1960) branded mobs and crowds as irrational, resembling a "beast with many heads." Mob actions such as race riots and lynchings sometimes seem to operate on a psychology of their own. *Questions: Do mobs bring out the beast in us? How is it that mild-mannered people commit mayhem when they are part of a mob?* In seeking an answer, let us examine a lynching.

The Lynching of Arthur Stevens   In their classic volume *Social Learning and Imitation*, Neal Miller and John Dollard (1941) vividly described a lynching that occurred in the South in the 1930s. Arthur Stevens, an African American, was accused of murdering his lover, a European American woman, when she wanted to break up with him. Stevens was arrested, and he confessed to the crime. Fearing violence, the sheriff moved

> ▲ **REFLECT**
> Have you ever done something as a member of a group that you would not have done as an individual? What was it? What motivated you? How do you feel about it?

Groupthink ▲ A process in which group members are influenced by cohesiveness and a dynamic leader to ignore external realities as they make decisions.

Gustave Le Bon

Today his writings are recognized as unbearably racist and sexist. In their day, however, they combined interests in ethnography (the study of cultures) and hypnosis to enhance our understanding of the psychology of crowds. The Frenchman Gustave Le Bon (1841-1931) was born into a wealthy family. Thus he had the luxury to indulge many interests. He earned a degree in medicine but never practiced it seriously. Instead, he traveled to little-known parts of Africa, Asia, and Europe and wrote many books about differences in national character. His views were quite conservative, and he depicted Europeans as the highest human group on the evolutionary scale (although we now know that there are no such differences between humans).

Nor did he believe that people had much control over their behavior, especially in crowds. As he wrote in *The Crowd*, people in crowds abandon their individuality and rationality to adopt a collective mind. Today's social psychologists may speak in terms of *deindividuation* and *group norms*, but their ideas are similar. People in crowds become impulsive and agitated. They lose their reason, judgment, and "critical spirit." Le Bon revealed his prejudices by writing that people in crowds behave in ways that characterize "inferior forms of evolution," including "women, savages, and children." (Presumably it did not disturb him that his family consisted of "inferior forms of evolution.") Le Bon explained crowd behavior in terms of the power of numbers, anonymity, "social contagion" (i.e., *imitating models*), and the hypnotic concept of increased *suggestibility*.

Le Bon went on to describe how leaders manipulate crowds through *affirmation* (highlighting the positive aspects of the cause), *repetition* (as in repeatedly chanting slogans), and *social contagion* (planting a few enthusiastic supporters in the crowd to do the cheerleading). Although social psychologists no longer connect these ideas with hypnotism, Le Bon's writings aptly describe the behavior of contemporary groups and tyrants.

CLICK4™ *Darley and Latané's classic article, "Bystander Intervention in Emergencies: Diffusion of Responsbility."*

Deindividuation ▲ The process by which group members may discontinue self-evaluation and adopt group norms and attitudes.

Altruism ▲ Unselfish concern for the welfare of others.

Stevens to a town 200 miles away during the night. But his location was discovered. On the next day a mob of a hundred people stormed the jail and returned Stevens to the scene of the crime.

Outrage spread from one member of the mob to another like a plague bacillus. Laborers, professionals, women, adolescents, and law-enforcement officers alike were infected. Stevens was tortured and murdered. His corpse was dragged through the streets. The mob then went on a rampage, chasing and assaulting other African Americans. The riot ended only when troops were sent in to restore law and order.

Deindividuation When people act as individuals, fear of consequences and self-evaluation tend to prevent them from engaging in antisocial behavior. But in a mob, they may experience **deindividuation,** a state of reduced self-awareness and lowered concern for social evaluation. Many factors lead to deindividuation. These include anonymity, diffusion of responsibility, arousal due to noise and crowding, and a focus on emerging group norms rather than on one's own values (Baron & Byrne, 2000). Under these circumstances crowd members behave more aggressively than they would as individuals.

Police know that mob actions are best averted early by dispersing small groups that could gather into a crowd. On an individual level, perhaps we can resist deindividuation by instructing ourselves to stop and think whenever we begin to feel highly aroused in a group. If we dissociate ourselves from such groups when they are forming, we are more likely to remain critical and avoid behavior that we might later regret.

Altruism and the Bystander Effect: Some Watch While Others Die

Altruism—selfless concern for the welfare of others—is connected with some heroic and some very strange behavior throughout the animal kingdom. Humans have been known to sacrifice themselves to ensure the survival of their children or of comrades in battle. Primates sometimes suicidally attack the leopard to give others the opportunity to escape.

These behaviors are heroic. But consider the red spider's strange ways (Begley & Check, 2000). After depositing its sperm into a female red spider, the male of the species will do a flip into her mouth and become her dinner! Clearly, the red spider is not bothered by the spark of consciousness, and it certainly is blind to the light of reason. But evolutionary psychologists might argue that the self-sacrificing behavior of the male red spider is actually selfish from an evolutionary point of view. How, you might wonder, can individuals sacrifice themselves and at the same time be acting in their own self-interests? To answer the question, you should also know that female red spiders are promiscuous; they will mate with multiple suitors. However, eating a "lover" slows them down, increasing the probability that *his* sperm will fertilize her eggs, and that his genes will survive and be transmitted to the next generation. We could thus say that the male red spider is altruistic in that he puts the welfare of future generations ahead of his own. Fatherhood ain't easy.

Red spiders, of course, do not think—at least, not in any humanly understandable sense of the concept of thinking. But people do. So how, one might ask, could the murder of 28-year-old Kitty Genovese have happened? It took place in New York City more than a generation ago. Murder was not unheard of in the Big Apple, but Kitty had screamed for help as her killer stalked her for more than half an hour and stabbed her in three separate attacks (Rosenthal, 1994). Thirty-eight neighbors heard the commotion. Twice the assault was interrupted by their voices and bedroom lights. Each time the attacker

An Angry Mob Is Contained by Police.
Gustave Le Bon branded mobs as irrational, like a "beast with many heads."

returned. Yet nobody came to the victim's aid. No one even called the police. Why? Some witnesses said matter-of-factly that they did not want to get involved. One said that he was tired. Still others said "I don't know." As a nation, are we a callous bunch who would rather watch than help when others are in trouble?

Question: Why do people sometimes sacrifice themselves for others and, at other times, ignore people who are in trouble? Why did 38 bystanders allow Kitty Genovese to die? When do we decide to come to the aid of someone who is in trouble?

The Helper: Who Helps?

It turns out that many factors are involved in helping behavior. The following are among them:

1. Observers are more likely to help when they are in a good mood (Baron & Byrne, 2000). Perhaps good moods impart a sense of personal power—the feeling that we can handle the situation (Cunningham et al., 1990).
2. People who are empathic are more likely to help people in need (Darley, 1993). Empathic people feel the distress of others, feel concern for them, and can imagine what it must be like to be in need. Women are more likely than men to be empathic, and thus more likely to help people in need (Trobst et al., 1994).
3. Bystanders may not help unless they believe that an emergency exists (Baron & Byrne, 2000). Perhaps some people who heard Kitty Genovese's calls for help were not certain as to what was happening. (But remember that others admitted they did not want to get involved.)
4. Observers must assume the responsibility to act (Baron & Byrne, 2000). It may seem logical that a group of people would be more likely to have come to the aid of Kitty Genovese than a lone person. After all, a group could more effectively have overpowered her attacker. Yet research by Darley and Latané (1968) suggests that a lone person may have been more likely to try to help her.

In their classic experiment, male participants were performing meaningless tasks in cubicles when they heard a (convincing) recording of a person apparently having an epileptic seizure. When the men thought that four other persons were immediately available, only 31% tried to help the victim. When they thought that no one else was available, however, 85% of them tried to help. As in other areas of group behavior, it seems that *diffusion of responsibility* inhibits helping behavior in groups or crowds. When we are in a group, we are often willing to let George (or Georgette) do it. When George isn't around, we are more willing to help others

CLICK4™ *more information about groups and group behavior—the way groups form, change, dissipate, achieve great goals, and commit great wrongs.*

CLICK4™ *essay assignments on group behavior and the factors that affect the decision to help others.*

John Darley

Bibb Latané

John Darley and Bibb Latané

Why did no one come to the aid of Kitty Genovese? Commentators on the news spoke about the inhumanity and alienation of city dwellers, particularly New Yorkers. But John Darley and Bibb Latané, two social psychologists who resided in New York, were skeptical. Darley—urbane and Ivy League—was then an assistant professor at New York University. Latané—a lanky country boy with a Southern accent—had studied with Stanley Schachter and was an instructor at Columbia University.

The two met at a party shortly after the crime and discussed it for hours. They then had what Hunt (1993) calls a "joint flash of inspiration": Nobody helped *because* they knew so many other people were watching. Late that evening they began to design an experiment to test what would become known as the *bystander effect*. Like so many others of its kind, this experiment (described in the text) relied on deceiving the participants as to the true purpose of the study.

▲ **REFLECT**

Research concerning altruism and the bystander effect highlight the fact that we are members of a vast, interdependent social fabric. The next time you see a stranger in need, what will you do? Are you sure?

---

ourselves. (Perhaps some who heard Kitty Genovese thought, "Why should I get involved? Other people can hear her too.")

5. Observers must know what to do (Baron & Byrne, 2000). We hear of cases in which people impulsively jump into the water to save a drowning child and then drown themselves. Most of the time, however, people do not try to help unless they know what to do. For example, nurses are more likely than people without medical training to try to help accident victims (Cramer et al., 1988). Observers who are not sure that they can take charge of the situation may stay on the sidelines for fear of making a social blunder and being ridiculed. Or they may fear getting hurt themselves. (Perhaps some who heard Kitty Genovese thought, "If I try to intervene, I may get killed or make an idiot of myself.")

6. Observers are more likely to help people they know (Rutkowski et al., 1983). Aren't we also more likely to give to charity when asked directly by a coworker or supervisor in the socially exposed situation of the office as compared with a letter received in the privacy of our own homes?

Evolutionary psychologists suggest that altruism is a natural aspect of human nature—even if not in the same way as in the case of the red spider! Self-sacrifice sometimes helps close relatives or others who are similar to us to survive. As noted, self-sacrifice is selfish from a genetic or evolutionary point of view. It helps us perpetuate a genetic code similar to our own. This view suggests that we are more likely to be altruistic with our relatives rather than strangers, however. The Kitty Genoveses of the world may remain out of luck unless they are surrounded by kinfolk or friends.

7. Observers are more likely to help people who are similar to themselves. Being able to identify with the person in need appears to promote helping behavior (Cialdini et al., 1997). Poorly dressed people are more likely to succeed in requests for a dime with poorly dressed strangers. Well-dressed people are more likely to get money from well-dressed strangers (Hensley, 1981).

The Victim: Who Is Helped? Although women are more likely than men to help people in need, it is traditional for men to help women, particularly in the South. Women were more likely than men to receive help, especially from men, when they dropped coins in Atlanta (a southern city) than in Seattle or Columbus (northern cities) (Latané & Dabbs, 1975). Why? The researchers suggest that traditional gender roles persist more strongly in the South.

Women are also more likely than men to be helped when their cars have broken down on the highway or they are hitchhiking. Is this gallantry or are there sexual overtones to some of this "altruism"? There may be, because attractive and unaccompanied women are most likely to be helped by men (Benson et al., 1976).

REVIEW

(20) Social _____ refers to the enhancement of performance that results from the presence of others. (21) However, performance may decline when we are _____ members of a group. (22) Social-_____ schemes seem to govern group decision making: the majority-wins scheme, the truth-wins scheme, the two-thirds majority scheme, and the first-shift rule. (23) Groups are (more or less?) likely than individuals to take extreme positions. (24) That is, people in a group are likely to experience a _____ shift. (25) Members of a group may experience _____, which is a state of reduced self-awareness and lowered concern for social evaluation. (26) Groupthink is usually (realistic or unrealistic?). (27) Helping behavior is also known as _____.

Pulling It Together: Why does group membership sometimes enhance performance and sometimes lessen performance? What factors affect the decision to help other people?

ENVIRONMENTAL PSYCHOLOGY: THE BIG PICTURE

What do you picture when you hear the phrase "the environment"? Is it vast acres of wilderness? Is it deep, rolling oceans? Or do you picture seagulls and ducks coated in gunk as a result of an oil spill? Do you think of billowing summer storm clouds and refreshing rain, or do you conjure up visions of crowded sidewalks and acid rain? All this—the beauty and the horror—is the territory of environmental psychology. *Question: What is environmental psychology?*

Environmental psychologists study the ways in which people and the physical environment influence each other. As people, we have needs that must be met if we are to remain physically and psychologically healthy. Environmental conditions such as temperature and population density affect our capacities to meet these needs. People also affect the environment. We have pushed back forests and driven many species to extinction. In recent years, our impact has mushroomed. So have the controversies over the greenhouse effect, the diminution of the ozone layer, and acid rain. Many of us have an aesthetic interest in the environment and appreciate the remaining pockets of wilderness. Protecting the environment also ultimately means protecting ourselves—for it is in the environment that we flourish or fade away.

DIVERSITY Although people in the United States consider themselves to be "environmentalists," only about half feel guilty when they litter or do something else that is harmful (Hinds, 2000; Kaiser & Shimoda, 1999). Women are somewhat more likely to protect the environment than men are. Some psychologists (e.g., Day, 2000) attribute the gender difference to the "ethic of care," which is more characteristic of the feminine gender-role. Women, that is, are reared to put others first and to have the primary responsibility for care-giving. Care-giving in the family becomes extended to the environment at large. So women are less likely to toss garbage from the car window.

In this section we consider some findings of environmental psychologists concerning the effects of atmospheric conditions, noise, heat, and crowding.

Noise: Of Muzak, Rock 'n' Roll, and Low-Flying Aircraft

Environmental psychologists apply knowledge of sensation and perception to design environments that produce positive emotional responses and contribute to human performance. They may thus suggest soundproofing certain environments or using pleasant background sounds such as music or recordings of water in natural environments (rain, the beach, brooks, and so on). Noise can be aversive, however—especially loud noise (Staples, 1996). How do you react when chalk is scraped on the blackboard or when a low-flying airplane screeches overhead? *Question: What are the effects of noise on behavior and mental processes?*

The decibel (dB) is used to express the loudness of noise. The hearing threshold is defined as zero dB. Your school library is probably about 30 to 40 dB. A freeway is about 70 dB. One hundred forty dB is painfully loud, and 150 dB can rupture your eardrums. After 8 hours of exposure to 110 to 120 dB, your hearing may be damaged (rock groups play at this level). High noise levels are stressful and can lead to health problems such as hypertension, neurological and intestinal disorders, and ulcers (Cohen et al., 1986; Staples, 1996).

High noise levels such as those imposed by traffic or low-flying airplanes also impair daily functioning. They can lead to forgetfulness, perceptual errors, even dropping things. Pre-school children who are exposed to loud noise in their day care setting are less advanced in their pre-reading skills (Maxwell & Evans, 2000).

Couples may enjoy high noise levels at the disco, but grating noises of 80 dB seem to decrease feelings of attraction. They cause people to stand farther apart. Loud noise also

REFLECT
As you read this book, crises loom concerning disposal of toxic wastes, industrial and vehicular emissions, population growth, devastation of the rain forest, pollution, and other environmental issues. You dwell on planet Earth. It is your home. How can you encourage people to be kinder to the environment?

Environmental psychology ▲ The field of psychology that studies the ways in which people and the environment influence each other.

Golden Gate Bridge—Rush Hour.
Environmental psychologists study the effects of people on the physical environment, and of the physical environment on people. People have carved their works deeply into planet Earth, as exemplified by the grandness of the Golden Gate Bridge. Yet the crowding of vehicles on the bridge and the exhaust they emit have negative effects on people and on the atmosphere and wildlife in the region.

At the Disco.
Couples may enjoy high noise levels (up to 140 dB) at the discotheque. Less desirable noises of only 80 dB, however, can decrease feelings of attraction and helping behavior and contribute to aggressive behavior.

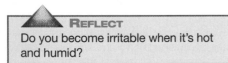

▲ **REFLECT**
Do you become irritable when it's hot and humid?

reduces helping behavior. People are less likely to help pick up a dropped package when the background noise of a construction crew is at 92 dB than when it's at 72 dB (Staples, 1996). They're even less willing to make change for a quarter.

If you and your date have had a fight and are then exposed to a tire blowout, look out. Angry people are more likely to behave aggressively when exposed to a sudden noise of 95 dB than one of 55 dB (Donnerstein & Wilson, 1976).

Temperature: The Perils of Getting Hot Under the Collar

"Summertime," goes the song from *Porgy and Bess*, "and the livin' is easy. Fish are jumpin', and"—and if you live in Minneapolis, the rate of crime against property is high. Ellen Cohn and James Rotton (2000) studied property crime rates in that northern city over a 2-year period and discovered that warm weather encourages outdoor activity, including going from house to house to steal. Outdoor activity is more difficult during Minneapolis's bitter winters, and people's property is also apparently safer.

Environmental psychologists study the ways in which temperature can facilitate or impair behavior and mental processes. *Question: What are the effects of temperature on our bodies and on our behavior and mental processes?*

Environmental psychologists point out that small changes in arousal—as induced by mild changes in temperature—tend to get our attention, motivate us, and facilitate the performance of tasks. So it is not surprising that a delightful summer day in Minneapolis might facilitate the "performance" of thieves as well as families heading for the parks and lakes. But great increments in arousal, such as those caused by major deviations from ideal temperatures, are aversive and hinder the performance of complex tasks. Extremes of heat can make excessive demands on our bodies' circulatory systems, leading to dehydration, heat exhaustion, and heat stroke. When it is too cold, the body responds by attempting to generate and retain heat. For example, the metabolism increases and blood vessels in the skin constrict, decreasing flow of blood to the periphery of the body. We try to cope with uncomfortable temperatures by wearing warmer or cooler clothing, using air conditioning, or traveling to more comfortable climate. Extreme temperatures can sap our ability to cope.

Moderate shifts in temperature are mildly arousing. They may facilitate learning and performance, increase feelings of attraction, and have other positive effects. Extreme temperatures cause performance and activity levels to decline, however.

Extreme heat also apparently makes some people hot under the collar. That is, high temperatures are connected with aggression. The frequency of honking at traffic lights in Phoenix increases with the temperature (Kenrick & MacFarlane, 1986). In Houston, murders and rapes are most likely to occur when the temperature is in the nineties Fahrenheit (Anderson & DeNeve, 1992). In Raleigh, North Carolina, the incidence of rape and aggravated assault rises with the average monthly temperature (Cohn, 1990; Simpson & Perry, 1990).

Some psychologists (e.g., Anderson & DeNeve, 1992) suggest that the probability of aggressive behavior continues to increase as the temperature soars. Others argue that once temperatures become extremely aversive, people tend to avoid aggressive behavior so that they will not be doubly struck by hot temper and hot temperature (Bell, 1992; Rotton & Cohn, 2000). The evidence does not absolutely eliminate either view, so the issue remains, well, heated.

Of Aromas and Air Pollution: Facilitating, Fussing, and Fuming

Environmental psychologists also investigate the effects of odors ranging from perfumes to auto fumes, industrial smog, cigarette smoke, fireplaces, even burning leaves. *Question: What are the effects of air pollution on behavior and mental processes?* As an example, the lead in auto fumes may impair children's intellectual functioning in the same way that eating lead paint does.

Carbon monoxide, a colorless, odorless gas found in cigarette smoke, auto fumes, and smog, decreases the oxygen-carrying capacity of the blood. Carbon monoxide impairs learning ability and perception of the passage of time. It may also contribute to highway accidents. Residents of Los Angeles, New York, and other cities are accustomed to warnings to stay indoors or remain inactive in order to reduce air consumption when atmospheric inversions allow smog to accumulate. In December 1952, high amounts of smog collected in London, causing nearly 4,000 deaths (Schenker, 1993). High levels of air pollution have also been connected with higher mortality rates in U.S. cities (Dockery et al., 1993; Samet et al., 2000).

People tend to become psychologically accustomed to air pollution. For example, newcomers to polluted regions like Southern California are more concerned about the air quality than long-term residents (Evans et al., 1982). Acceptance of pollution backfires when illness results.

Unpleasant smelling pollutants, like other forms of aversive stimulation, decrease feelings of attraction and heighten aggression (Baron & Byrne, 2000).

Crowding and Personal Space: "Don't Burst My Bubble, Please"

Psychologists distinguish between "density" and "crowding." *Density* refers to the number of people in an area. *Crowding* suggests an aversive high-density social situation. (In other words, *crowding* is used to mean that we are "too close for comfort.") *Questions: When are we too close for comfort? What are the effects of crowding on behavior and mental processes?*

Not all instances of density are equal. Whether we feel crowded depends on who is thrown in with us and on our interpretation of the situation (Baron & Byrne, 2000). (One student of mine reported that she had not at all minded being crowded in by the Dallas Cowboys football players who surrounded her on an airplane ride.) Environmental psychologists apply principles of information processing and social psychology in explaining.

A fascinating experiment illustrates the importance of cognitive factors—in this case, attributions for arousal—in transforming high density into crowding. Worchel and Brown (1984) showed films to small groups of people who were either spaced comfortably apart or uncomfortably close. There were four different films. Three were arousing (either humorous, sexual, or violent), and one was just plain boring.

As shown in Figure 17.3, viewers who were seated closer together generally felt more crowded than those who were seated farther apart. Those who were seated at appropriate distances from one another uniformly rated the seating arrangements as uncrowded. Among those who were seated inappropriately close together, viewers of the

CLICK4™ *Web sites devoted to the environment and environmental psychology.*

www 17 L 5

> ◤ **REFLECT**
> How do you feel when you're crowded into an elevator or a subway car? Is there anything that helps you handle your feelings?

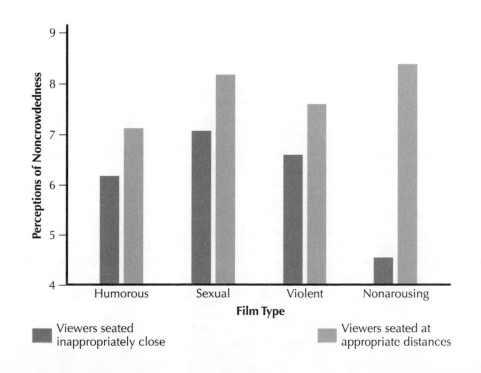

FIGURE 17.3 Type of Film and Appraisal of High-Density Seating.
In a study by Worchel and Brown, viewers seated uncomfortably closely or at comfortable distances watched four kinds of films. Of the individuals seated too closely, those who could attribute their arousal to the film were less likely to experience crowding than those who could not.

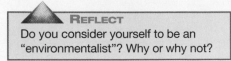

▲ REFLECT
Do you consider yourself to be an "environmentalist"? Why or why not?

unarousing film felt most crowded. Viewers of the arousing films felt less crowded. Why? The researchers suggest that viewers who were packed in could attribute their arousal to the content of the films. But viewers of the unarousing film could not. Thus, they were likely to attribute their arousal to the seating arrangements.

Psychological Moderators of the Impact of High Density

A sense of control enhances psychological hardiness. Examples from everyday life, including shopping in crowded stores (Machleit et al., 2000), suggest that a sense of control over the situation—of being able to choose—also helps us cope with the stress of being packed in. When we are at a concert, disco, or sports event, we may encounter higher density than we do in a frustrating ticket line. But we may be having a wonderful time. Why? Because we have *chosen* to be at the concert and are focusing on our good time (unless a tall or noisy person is sitting in front of us). We feel that we are in control.

We tend to moderate the effects of high density in subway cars and other vehicles by ignoring our fellow passengers and daydreaming, reading newspapers and books, or finding humor in the situation. Some people catch a snooze and wake up just before their stop.

Some Effects of City Life

Big city dwellers are more likely to experience stimulus overload and to fear crime than suburbanites and rural folk (Herzog & Chernick, 2000). Overwhelming crowd stimulation, bright lights, shop windows, and so on cause them to narrow their perceptions to a particular face, destination, or job. The pace of life increases—pedestrians walk faster in bigger cities (Sadalla et al., 1990). All major population groups within the United States—African American, Asian Americans, European American, and Latino and Latina American—find high-density living conditions to be aversive (Evans et al., 2000).

City dwellers are less willing to shake hands with, make eye contact with, or help strangers (Milgram, 1977; Newman & McCauley, 1977). People who move to the city from more rural areas adjust by becoming more deliberate in their daily activities. They plan ahead to take safety precautions, and they increase their alertness to potential dangers.

Yet not all cities are the same. Cross-cultural research reveals that cities in Europe and Japan function at a faster pace than cities in undeveloped countries, as measured by the pace of walking the streets, the time taken to complete a simple task, and the accuracy of public clocks (Levine & Norenzayan, 1999). They may get more done, but people in "faster" cities are also more likely to smoke and to die from coronary heart disease (Levine & Norenzayan, 1999).

Farming, anyone?

CLICK4™ *a WebSearch activity: Which environmental issue do you think is the most pressing for environmental psychologists?*

CLICK4™ *a bulletin board discussion: How can advances in environmental psychology help to improve the world around us?*

Personal Space

One adverse effect of crowding is the invasion of one's **personal space.** Personal space is an invisible boundary, a sort of bubble, that surrounds you. You are likely to become anxious and perhaps angry when others invade your space. This may happen when someone sits down across from or next to you in an otherwise empty cafeteria or stands too close to you in an elevator. Personal space appears to serve both protective and communicative functions. People usually sit and stand closer to people who are similar to themselves in race, age, or socioeconomic status. Dating couples come closer together as the attraction between them increases.

There is some interesting cross-cultural research on personal space. For example, North Americans and northern Europeans apparently maintain a greater distance between themselves and others than Southern Europeans, Asians, and Middle Easterners do (Baron & Byrne, 2000). Puerto Ricans tend to interact more closely than Americans of northern European extraction. Puerto Ricans reared in New York City require more personal space when interacting with others of the same gender than do Puerto Ricans reared in Puerto Rico (Pagan & Aiello, 1982). Men approached women more closely than women approached men in front of an automatic teller machine in Turkey (Kaya & Erkip, 1999).

People in some cultures apparently learn to cope with high density and also share their ways of coping with others (Gillis et al., 1986). Asians in crowded cities such as

Personal space ▲ A psychological boundary that surrounds a person and serves protective functions.

Tokyo and Hong Kong interact more harmoniously than North Americans and Britishers, who dwell in less dense cities. The Japanese are used to being packed sardinelike into subway cars by white-gloved pushers employed by the transit system. Imagine the rebellion that would occur if such treatment were attempted in American subways! It has been suggested that Asians are accustomed to adapting to their environment, whereas Westerners are more prone to try to change it.

Southern Europeans apparently occupy a middle ground between Asians, on the one hand, and northern Europeans, on the other. They are more outgoing and comfortable with interpersonal propinquity than northern Europeans but not as tolerant of crowding as Asians.

As you complete this text, I hope that you will have decided to allow psychology to enter your personal psychological space. A professor of mine once remarked that the true measure of the success of a course is whether the student decides to take additional courses in the field. The choice is yours. *Enjoy.*

REVIEW

(28) Environmental psychologists study the ways in which people and the _____ environment influence each other. (29) High noise levels impair learning and memory, (increase or decrease?) feelings of attraction, decrease helping behavior, and foster aggression. (30) Moderate shifts in temperature tend to (facilitate or impair?) learning and performance. (31) High heat levels (increase or decrease?) aggressiveness. (32) Unpleasant odors (increase or decrease?) feelings of attraction.

Pulling It Together: How is it that high density is sometimes aversive and sometimes pleasurable?

www 17 Q 2

CLICK4™ *a quiz covering the second half of this chapter.*

www 17 FC 1

CLICK4™ *electronic flash cards to review your knowledge of key terms and people in this chapter.*

◣ It is not true that airing a TV commercial repeatedly hurts sales. *Repeated exposure frequently leads to liking and acceptance. See page 581.*

◣ Actually, when you give to charity once, you are more, not less, likely to give when the charity calls on you again. *The charity has gotten its "foot in the door" with you. See page 583.*

◣ It is true that people have condemned others without meeting them or learning their names. *Such are the effects of prejudice. See page 583.*

◣ It is true that you may never get a second chance, if you don't make a good first impression. *People interpret future events in the light of first impressions. See page 588.*

◣ It is true that we take others to task for their misdeeds but tend to see ourselves as victims of circumstances when our conduct falls short of our ideals. *This bias in the attribution process is referred to as the actor-observer effect. See page 589.*

◣ *Research evidence reveals that* seeing is not necessarily believing—*at least when most people seem to see things differently than we do. See page 596.*

◣ It is not true that group decisions tend to represent conservative compromises among the opinions of the group's members. *Group decisions tend to be riskier than the average decision that would be made by each member of the group acting as an individual—probably because of diffusion of responsibility. See page 598.*

◣ It is true that nearly 40 people stood by and did nothing while a woman was being stabbed to death. *Their failure to come to her aid has been termed the* bystander effect. *See page 601.*

◣ It is true that women are less likely than men to be litterbugs. *The feminine-stereotyped tendency toward care-giving becomes extended to the environment at large. See page 603.*

1. What is social psychology?

Social psychology is the field of psychology that studies the factors that influence people's thoughts, feelings, and behaviors in social situations.

2. What are attitudes?

Attitudes are behavioral and cognitive tendencies expressed by evaluating particular people, places, or things with favor or disfavor.

3. Do people do as they think? (For example, do people really vote their consciences?)

When we are free to act as we wish, our behavior is often consistent with our beliefs and feelings. But as indicated by the term *A-B problem*, the links between attitudes (A) and behaviors (B) are often weak to moderate. The following strengthen the A-B connection: specificity of attitudes, strength of attitudes, whether people have a vested interest in the outcome of their behavior, and the accessibility of the attitudes.

4. Where do attitudes come from?

Attitudes are acquired (not inborn). They can be learned somewhat mechanically by means of conditioning or learning by observation. However, people also appraise and evaluate situations and often form their own judgments.

5. Can you really change people? —their attitudes and behavior, that is?

People attempt to change other people's attitudes and behavior by means of persuasion. According to the elaboration likelihood model, persuasion occurs through both central and peripheral routes. Change occurs through the central route by means of consideration of arguments and evidence. Peripheral routes involve associating the objects of attitudes with positive or negative cues, such as attractive or unattractive communicators. Repeated messages generally "sell" better than messages delivered only once. People tend to show greater response to fear appeals than to purely factual presentations. This is especially so when the appeals offer concrete advice for avoiding negative outcomes. Persuasive communicators tend to show expertise, trustworthiness, attractiveness, or similarity to the audience. In the foot-in-the-door technique, people are asked to comply with larger requests after they have complied with smaller ones.

6. What is prejudice? Why are people prejudiced?

Prejudice is an attitude toward a group that leads people to evaluate members of that group negatively. Discrimination is a form of negative behavior that results from prejudice; discrimination takes forms such as denial of access to jobs, housing, and the voting booth. Prejudices are typically based on stereotypes, which are fixed, conventional ideas about groups of people. Sources of prejudice include dissimilarity, social conflict, social learning, the relative ease of processing information according to stereotypes, social categorization, and victimization by prejudice.

7. Do first impressions really matter? What are the primacy and recency effects?

First impressions can last (the primacy effect) because we tend to label or describe people in terms of the behavior we see initially. The recency effect appears to be based on the fact that—other things being equal—recently learned information is easier to remember.

8. What is attribution theory? Why do we assume that other people intend the mischief that they do?

The tendency to infer the motives and traits of others through observation of their behavior is referred to as the attribution process. In dispositional attributions, we attribute people's behavior to internal factors such as their personality traits and decisions. In situational attributions, we attribute people's behavior to their circumstances or external forces. According to the actor-observer effect, we tend to attribute the behavior of others to internal, dispositional factors. However, we tend to attribute our own behavior to external, situational factors. The so-called fundamental attribution error is the tendency to attribute too much of other people's behavior to dispositional factors. The self-serving bias refers to the finding that we tend to attribute our successes to internal, stable factors and our failures to external, unstable factors. The attribution of behavior to internal or external causes is influenced by three factors: consensus, consistency, and distinctiveness. For example, when few people act in a certain way—that is, when the consensus is low—we are likely to attribute behavior to internal factors.

9. What is body language?

Body language refers to the tendency to infer people's thoughts and feelings from their postures and gestures. For example, people who feel positively toward one another position themselves closer together and are more likely to touch. Touching results in a negative reaction when it suggests more intimacy than is desired. Gazing into another's eyes can be a sign of love, but a hard stare is an aversive challenge. Women are more likely than men to touch people with whom they are interacting.

10. Why will so many people commit crimes against humanity if they are ordered to do so? (Why don't they refuse?)

The majority of participants in the Milgram studies complied with the demands of authority figures, even when the demands required that they hurt innocent people by means of electric shock. Factors contributing to obedience include socialization, lack of social comparison, perception of legitimate authority figures, the foot-in-the-door technique, inaccessibility of values, and buffers between the perpetrator and the victim.

11. Why do so many people tend to follow the crowd?

Asch's research in which participants judged the lengths of lines suggests that the majority of people will follow the crowd, even when the crowd is wrong. Personal factors such as desire to be liked by group members, low self-esteem, high self-consciousness, and shyness contribute to conformity. Belonging to a collectivist society and group size also contribute to conformity.

12. Do we run faster when we are in a group?

The concept of social facilitation refers to the effects on performance that result from the presence of other people. The presence of others may facilitate performance for reasons such as increased arousal and evaluation apprehension. However, when we are anonymous group members, we may experience diffusion of responsibility and task performance may fall off. This phenomenon is termed *social loafing*.

13. How do groups make decisions?

Social psychologists have identified several decision-making schemes, including the majority-wins scheme, the truth-wins scheme, the two-thirds majority scheme, and the first-shift rule.

14. Are group decisions more risky or more conservative than those of the individual members of the group? Why?

Group decisions tend to be more polarized and riskier than individual decisions, largely because groups diffuse responsibility. Group decisions may be highly productive when group members are knowledgeable, there is an explicit procedure for arriving at decisions, and there is a process of give and take.

15. What is groupthink?

Groupthink is an unrealistic kind of decision making that is fueled by the perception of external threats to the group or to those whom the group wishes to protect. It is facilitated by a dynamic group leader, feelings of invulnerability, the group's belief in its rightness, the discrediting of information that contradicts the group's decision, conformity, and the stereotyping of members of the out-group.

16. Do mobs bring out the beast in us? How is it that mild-mannered people commit mayhem when they are part of a mob?

Highly emotional crowds may induce attitude-discrepant behavior through the process of *deindividuation*, which is a state of reduced self-awareness and lowered concern for social evaluation. The high emotions are connected with arousal that makes it more difficult to access one's own values.

17. Why do people sometimes sacrifice themselves for others and, at other times, ignore people who are in trouble?

A number of factors contribute to altruism (the tendency to help others). Among them are empathy, being in a good mood, feelings of responsibility, knowledge of how to help, and acquaintance with—and similarity to—the person in need of help. According to the bystander effect, we are unlikely to aid people in distress when we are members of crowds. Crowds tend to diffuse responsibility.

18. What is environmental psychology?

Environmental psychology is the field of psychology that studies the ways in which humans and the physical environment influence each other.

19. What are the effects of noise on behavior and mental processes?

High noise levels are stressful and can lead to health problems such as hearing loss, hypertension, and neurological and intestinal disorders. High noise levels impair learning and memory. Loud noise also dampens helping behavior and heightens aggressiveness.

20. What are the effects of temperature on our bodies and on our behavior and mental processes?

Moderate shifts in temperature are mildly arousing and usually have positive effects such as facilitating learning and performance and increasing feelings of attraction. But extremes of temperature tax the body, are a source of stress, and impair performance. High temperatures are also connected with aggression.

21. What are the effects of air pollution on behavior and mental processes?

The lead in auto fumes may impair learning and memory. Carbon monoxide decreases the capacity of the blood to carry oxygen and thus impairs learning ability and perception and contributes to accidents. Unpleasant odors decrease feelings of attraction and heighten aggression.

22. When are we too close for comfort? What are the effects of crowding on behavior and mental processes?

Density refers to the number of people in an area. *Crowding* suggests aversive high density. A sense of control or choice—as in choosing to attend a concert or athletic contest—helps us cope with the stress of high density. Perhaps because of crowding, noise, and so on, city dwellers are less likely than people who live in small towns to interact with or help strangers.

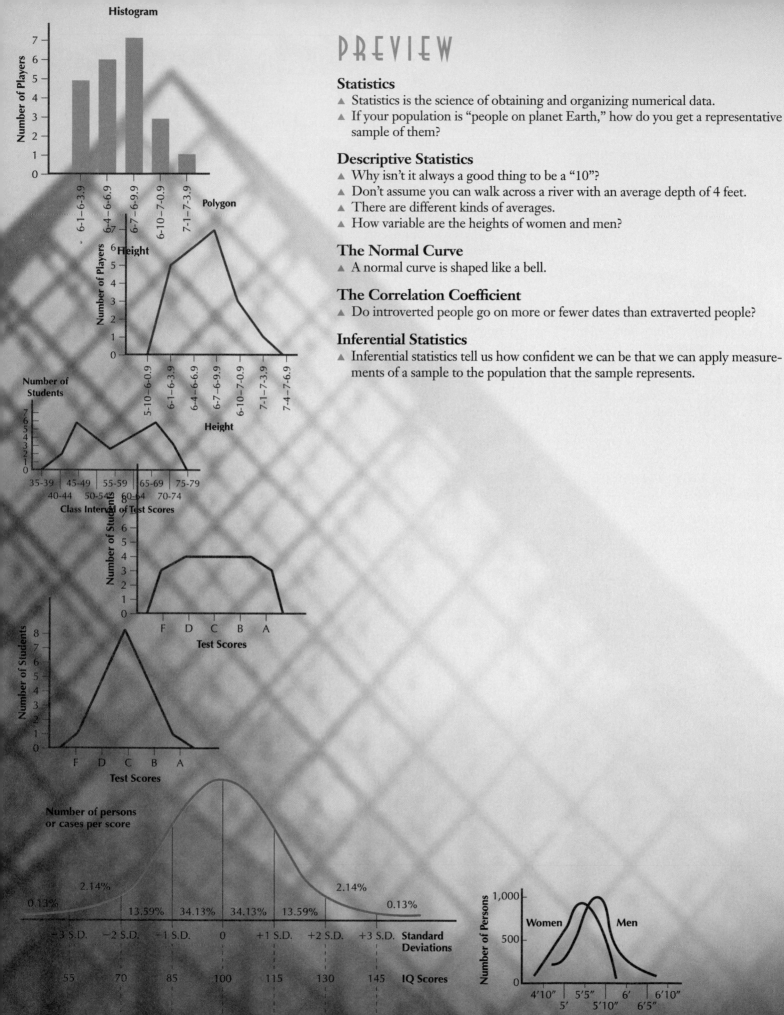

PREVIEW

Statistics
▲ Statistics is the science of obtaining and organizing numerical data.
▲ If your population is "people on planet Earth," how do you get a representative sample of them?

Descriptive Statistics
▲ Why isn't it always a good thing to be a "10"?
▲ Don't assume you can walk across a river with an average depth of 4 feet.
▲ There are different kinds of averages.
▲ How variable are the heights of women and men?

The Normal Curve
▲ A normal curve is shaped like a bell.

The Correlation Coefficient
▲ Do introverted people go on more or fewer dates than extraverted people?

Inferential Statistics
▲ Inferential statistics tell us how confident we can be that we can apply measurements of a sample to the population that the sample represents.

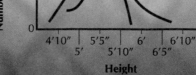

Statistics

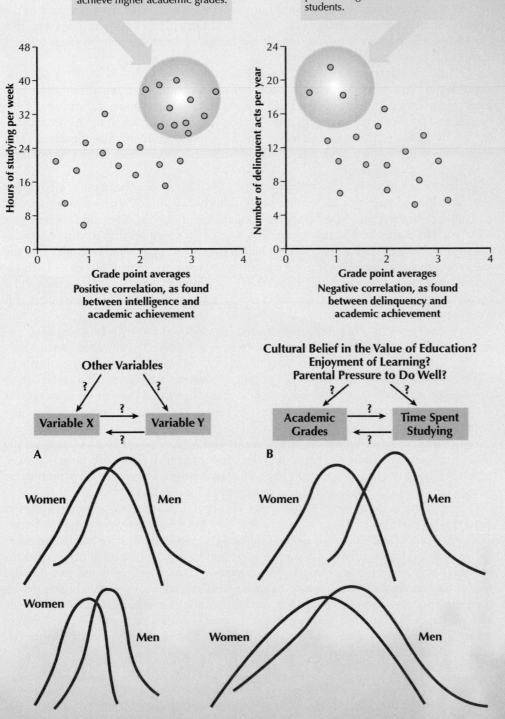

Generally speaking, the more intelligent people within a group achieve higher academic grades.

Generally speaking, delinquents are likely to have lower grade point averages than other students.

Positive correlation, as found between intelligence and academic achievement

Grade point averages

Negative correlation, as found between delinquency and academic achievement

Grade point averages

Other Variables

Variable X → Variable Y

A

**Cultural Belief in the Value of Education?
Enjoyment of Learning?
Parental Pressure to Do Well?**

Academic Grades → Time Spent Studying

B

Women   Men

Women   Men

Women   Men

Women   Men

TRUTH ⬛ FICTION?

▰ Basketball players are abnormal.

▰ Being a "10" is not necessarily a good thing.

▰ Researchers can group their data either to highlight or to hide their findings.

▰ Adding people's incomes and then dividing them by the number of people can be an awful way of showing the average income.

▰ Psychologists may express your IQ score in terms of how deviant you are.

▰ An IQ score of 130 is more impressive than an SAT score of 500.

▰ Correlational research shows that smoking cigarettes causes cancer.

▰ We cannot conclude that men are taller than women unless we know the average heights of men and women and how much the heights within each group vary.

STATISTICS

Imagine that some visitors from outer space arrive outside Madison Square Garden in New York City. Their goal this dark and numbing winter evening is to learn all they can about planet Earth. They are drawn inside the Garden by lights, shouts, and warmth. The spotlighting inside rivets their attention to a wood-floored arena where the New York Big Apples are hosting the California Quakes in a briskly contested basketball game.

Our visitors use their sophisticated instruments to take some measurements of the players. Some interesting statistics are sent back to their planet of origin: It appears that (1) 100% of Earthlings are male, and (2) the height of Earthlings ranges from 6 feet 1 inch to 7 feet 2 inches.

These measurements are called **statistics.** *Question: What is statistics?* Statistics is the name given the science concerned with obtaining and organizing numerical information or measurements. Our imagined visitors have sent home statistics about the gender and size of human beings that are at once accurate and misleading. Although they accurately measured the basketball players (we have translated their units of measurement into feet and inches for readers' convenience), their small **sample** of Earth's **population** was, shall we say, distorted.

Question: What are samples and populations? A population is a complete group of people, other animals, or measures from which a sample is drawn. For example, all people on Earth could be defined as the population of interest. So could all women, or all women in the United States. A sample is a group of measures drawn from a population. Fortunately for us Earthlings, about half of the world's population is female. And the **range** of heights observed by the aliens, of 6 feet 1 inch to 7 feet 2 inches, is both restricted and too high—much too high. People vary in height by more than 1 foot and 1 inch. And our **average** height is not between 6 feet 1 inch and 7 feet 2 inches; rather, it is a number of inches below.

Psychologists, like our imagined visitors, are vitally concerned with measuring human as well as animal characteristics and traits—not just physical characteristics like height, but also psychological traits like intelligence, sociability, aggressiveness, neatness, anxiety, and depression. By observing the central tendencies (averages) and variations in measurement from person to person, psychologists can say that one person is average or above average in intelligence, or that someone else is less anxious than, say, 60% of the population.

But psychologists, unlike our aliens, are careful in their attempts to select a sample that accurately represents the entire population. Professional basketball players do not represent the entire human species. They are taller, stronger, and more agile than the rest of us. They also make appreciably more commercials for sneakers.

In this appendix we survey some of the statistical methods used by psychologists to draw conclusions about the measurements they take in research activities. First we discuss *descriptive statistics* and learn what types of statements we can make about height and other human traits. Then we discuss the *normal curve* and learn why basketball players are abnormal—at least in terms of height. We explain *correlation coefficients* and provide you with some less-than-shocking news: As a group, students who study obtain higher grades than students who do not study. Finally, we have a look at *inferential statistics* and we see why we can be bold enough to say that the difference in height between basketball players and other people is not a chance fluctuation or fluke. Basketball players are in fact *statistically significantly* taller than the general population.

REVIEW

(1) The science that obtains and organizes numerical information or measurements is called _____. (2) The _____ of heights of the basketball players discussed in this section was restricted and high to represent the general population. (3) By observing the _____ tendencies (averages) and variations in measurement from person to person, psychologists can say that an individual is average or above average in some trait or behavior.

Pulling It Together: What is the relationship between a population and a sample?

▲ REFLECT

Why would the observations of the basketball players give the aliens a distorted impression of the traits of Earthlings?

▲ REFLECT

How do psychologists measure psychological characteristics like intelligence and anxiety?

Statistics ▲ Numerical facts assembled in such a manner that they provide useful information about measures or scores. (From the Latin *status*, meaning "standing" or "position.")

Sample ▲ Part of a population.

Population ▲ A complete group from which a sample is selected.

Range ▲ A measure of variability defined as the high score in a distribution minus the low score.

Average ▲ The central tendency of a group of measures, expressed either as the mean, median, or mode of a distribution.

DESCRIPTIVE STATISTICS

Being told that someone is a "10" may sound great at first. However, it is not very descriptive unless you know something about how the scores on the scale are distributed and how frequently one finds a 10. Fortunately—for 10s, if not for the rest of us—one usually means that the person is a 10 on a scale of from 1 to 10, and that 10 is the highest possible score on the scale. If this is not sufficient, one will also be told that 10s are few and far between—rather unusual statistical events. But note that the scale could also vary from 0 to 100, in which case a score of 10 would place one nearer to the bottom of the scale and make a score of 50 the center point of the scale. With such a scale, being a 10 would be much less impressive.

The idea of the scale from 1 to 10 may not be very scientific, but it does suggest something about **descriptive statistics.** *Question: What is descriptive statistics? (Why isn't it always good to be a "10"?)* Descriptive statistics is the branch of statistics that provides information about distributions of scores. We can use descriptive statistics to clarify our understanding of a distribution of scores such as heights, test grades, IQs, or even increases or decreases in measures of aggressive behavior following the drinking of alcohol. For example, descriptive statistics can help us determine measures of central tendency (averages), and to determine how much fluctuation or variability there is in the scores. Being a 10 loses much of its charm if the average score is an 11. Being a 10 is more remarkable in a distribution whose scores range from 1 to 10 than it is in a distribution whose scores range from 9 to 11.

Let us now consider some of the concerns of descriptive statistics: the frequency distribution, measures of central tendency (types of averages), and measures of variability.

The Frequency Distribution

Question: What is a frequency distribution? A **frequency distribution** takes scores or items of raw data, puts them into order as from the lowest to the highest, and indicates how often a score appears. A frequency distribution groups data according to class intervals, although the class may be a single unit (one), as in Table APP.2. Table APP.1 shows the rosters for a recent basketball game between the California Quakes and the New York Big Apples. The players are listed according to the numbers on their uniforms. Table APP.2 shows a frequency distribution of the heights of the players, with the two teams combined. The class interval in Table APP.2 is 1 inch.

It would also be possible to use other class intervals, such as 3 inches, as shown in Table APP.3. In determining the size of a class interval, the researcher tries to collapse the data into a small enough number of classes to ensure that they will be meaningful at a glance. But the researcher also tries to keep a large enough number of categories (classes) to ensure that important differences are not obscured.

Table APP.3 obscures the fact that no players are 6 feet 4 inches tall. If the researcher believes that this information is extremely important, a class interval of 1 inch may be maintained.

Figure APP.1 shows two methods of graphing the information in Table APP.3: the **frequency histogram** and the **frequency polygon.** Students sometimes have difficulty interpreting graphs, but the purpose of graphs is to reveal key information about frequency distributions at a glance. Note that in both kinds of graph, the frequency histogram and the frequency polygon, the class intervals are usually drawn along the horizontal line. The horizontal line is also known as the X-axis. The numbers of cases (scores, persons, or events) in each class interval are shown along the vertical line, which is also known as the Y-axis. In the histogram, the number of scores in each class interval is represented by a bar—a rectangular solid—so that the graph looks like a series of steps. In the polygon, the number of scores in each class interval is plotted as a point. The points are

TABLE APP.1 ROSTERS OF QUAKES VERSUS BIG APPLES AT NEW YORK

A glance at the rosters for a recent basketball game in which the New York Big Apples "entertained" the California Quakes shows that the heights of the team members, combined, ranged from 6 feet 1 inch to 7 feet 2 inches. Do the heights of the team members represent those of the general male population? What do you think?

CALIFORNIA QUAKES		NEW YORK BIG APPLES	
2 Callahan	6'7"	3 Roosevelt	6'1"
5 Daly	6'11"	12 Chaffee	6'5"
6 Chico	6'2"	13 Baldwin	6'9"
12 Capistrano	6'3"	25 Delmar	6'6"
21 Brentwood	6'5"	27 Merrick	6'8"
25 Van Nuys	6'3"	28 Hewlett	6'6"
31 Clemente	6'9"	33 Hollis	6'9"
32 Whittier	6'8"	42 Bedford	6'5"
41 Fernando	7'2"	43 Coram	6'2"
43 Watts	6'9"	45 Hampton	6'10"
53 Huntington	6'6"	53 Ardsley	6'10"

> ▲ **REFLECT**
> Would it take a 3.00, 4.00, or 5.00 grade point average for you to be a perfect student? Would yet another number be required? Explain.

Descriptive statistics ▲ The branch of statistics that is concerned with providing descriptive information about a distribution of scores.

Frequency distribution ▲ An ordered set of data that indicates the frequency (how often) with which scores appear.

Frequency histogram ▲ A graphic representation of a frequency distribution that uses rectangular solids (bars) to represent the frequency with which scores appear.

Frequency polygon ▲ A graphic representation of a frequency distribution that connects the points that show the frequencies with which scores appear, thereby creating a multisided geometric figure.

CLASS INTERVAL	NUMBER OF PLAYERS IN CLASS
6'1"–6'1.9"	1
6'2"–6'2.9"	2
6'3"–6'3.9"	2
6'4"–6'4.9"	0
6'5"–6'5.9"	3
6'6"–6'6.9"	3
6'7"–6'7.9"	1
6'8"–6'8.9"	2
6'9"–6'9.9"	4
6'10"–6'10.9"	2
6'11"–6'11.9"	1
7'0"–7'0.9"	0
7'1"–7'1.9"	0
7'2"–7'2.9"	1

▲ REFLECT

Can you think of examples in your own experience in which the median or the mode would be a more accurate indicator of a central tendency than the mean? (Hint: Possibilities include class grades, IQ scores, and special abilities, as in music, art, and athletics.)

Mean ▲ A type of average that is calculated by adding all the scores and then dividing by the number of scores.
Median ▲ The central score in a frequency distribution; the score beneath which 50% of the cases fall.

connected to form a many-sided geometric figure (polygon). Note that empty class intervals were added at each end of the frequency polygon so that the sides of the figure could be brought down to the X-axis to close the geometric figure.

Measures of Central Tendency

Never try to walk across a river just because it has an average depth of four feet.
—Martin Friedman

As you see in the quip by Martin Friedman, a measure of central tendency can sometimes be misleading. ***Question: What are measures of central tendency?*** Measures of central tendency are "averages" that show the center or balancing points of a frequency distribution. There are three commonly used types of measures of central tendency: the *mean, median,* and *mode.* Each attempts to describe something about the scores in a frequency distribution through the use of a typical or representative number.

The **mean** is what most people think of as "the average." We obtain the mean of a distribution by adding up the scores and then dividing the sum by the number of scores. In the case of the basketball players, it would be advisable to first convert the heights into a single unit, such as inches (6'1" becomes 73", and so on). If we add all the heights in inches and then divide by the number of players (22), we obtain a mean height of 78.73". If we convert that number back into units of feet and inches, we obtain 6'6.73".

The **median** is the score of the middle case in a distribution. It is the score beneath which 50% of the cases fall. In a distribution with an even number of cases, such as the distribution of the heights of the 22 basketball players as shown in Table APP.2, we obtain the median by finding the mean of the two middle cases. When we list the 22 cases in ascending order (moving from lowest to highest), the 11th case is 6'6" and the 12th case is 6'7". Therefore, the median of the distribution is (6'6" + 6'7")/2, or 6'6½".

When we analyze the heights of the basketball players, we find that the mean and median are similar. Either one serves as a useful indicator of the central tendency of the data. But suppose we are trying to find the average savings of 30 families living on a suburban block. Let us assume that 29 of the 30 families have savings between $8,000 and $12,000, adding up to $294,000. But the 30th family has savings of $1,400,000! The mean savings for a family on this block would thus be $56,467. The mean can be greatly distorted by one or two extreme scores. An IQ score of 145 would similarly distort the mean of the IQ scores of a class of 20 students, among whom the other 19 IQ scores ranged from 93 to 112. Then, too, if a few basketball players signed up for one of your classes, the mean of the students' heights would be distorted in an upward direction.

FIGURE APP.1 Two Graphical Representations of the Data in Table APP.3.
The graph on the left is called a frequency histogram, or bar graph. The graph on the right is called a frequency polygon.

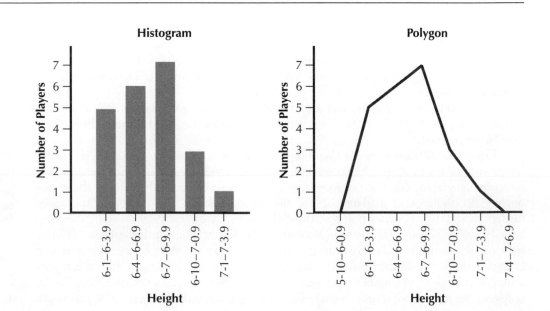

When there are a few extreme scores in a distribution, the median is a better indicator of central tendency. The median savings on our hypothetical block would lie between $8,000 and $12,000. Thus, it would be more representative of the central tendency of savings. Studies of the incomes of families in the United States usually report median rather than mean incomes just to avoid the distortion of findings that would occur if the incomes of a handful of billionaires were treated in the same way as more common incomes. On the other hand, one could argue that choosing the median as the average obscures or hides the extreme scores, which are just as "real" as the other scores. Perhaps it is best to use the median and a footnote—a rather big footnote.

The **mode** is simply the most frequently occurring score or measure in a distribution. The mode of the data in Table APP.1 is 6′9″ because this height occurs most often among the players on the two teams. The median class interval for the data shown in Table APP.3 is 6′6½″ to 6′9½″. With this particular distribution, the mode is somewhat higher than the mean or median.

In some cases the mode is a more appropriate description of the central tendency of a distribution than the mean or the median. Figure APP.2 shows a **bimodal** distribution—that is, a distribution with two modes. This is a hypothetical distribution of test scores obtained by a class. The mode at the left indicates the most common class interval (45–49) for students who did not study, and the mode to the right shows the most common class interval (65–69) for students who did study. (Don't be alarmed. I'm sure that the professor, who is extremely fair, will be delighted to curve the grades so that the interval of 75–79 is an A+ and the interval of 65–69 is at least a B.) The mean and median test scores would probably lie within the 55–59 class interval, yet use of that interval as the measure of central tendency could obscure rather than reveal the important aspects of this distribution of test scores. It might suggest that the test was too hard, not that a number of students chose not to study. Similarly, one of the distribution's modes might be a bit larger than the other, so one could follow the exact rule for finding the mode and report just one of them. But this approach would also hide the meaning of this particular distribution of scores. All in all, it is clearly best to visualize this distribution of scores as bimodal. Even when the modes are not exactly equal, it is often most accurate to report distributions as bimodal, or when there are three or more modes, as multimodal. One chooses one's measure or measures of central tendency to describe the essential features of a frequency distribution, not to hide them.

Measures of Variability

Our hypothetical class obtained test scores ranging from class intervals of 35–39 to 75–79. That is, the scores *varied* from the lower class interval to the higher class interval. Now, if all the students had obtained scores from 55–59 to 65–69, the scores would not have varied as much; that is, they would have clustered closer to one another and would have had lower variability.

Question: What are measures of variability? The measures of the variability of a distribution inform us about the spread of scores—that is, about the typical distances of scores from the average score. Two commonly used measures of variability are the *range* of scores and the *standard deviation* of scores.

The range of scores in a distribution, as noted earlier, is defined as the difference between the highest score and the lowest score. The range is obtained by subtracting the lowest score from the highest score. The range of heights in Table APP.2 is obtained by subtracting 6′1″ from 7′2″, or 1′1″. It is useful to know the range of temperatures when we move to an area with a different climate so that we may anticipate the weather and dress for it appropriately. A teacher must have some understanding of the range of abilities or skills in a class in order to teach effectively. An understanding of the range of human heights can be used to design doorways, beds, and headroom in automobiles. Even so, the typical doorway is 6′8″ high, and as we saw with the California Quakes and New York Big Apples, some people will have to duck to get through.

The range is an imperfect measure of variability because of the manner in which it is influenced by extreme scores. The range of savings of the 30 families on our suburban

TABLE APP.3 FREQUENCY DISTRIBUTION OF HEIGHTS OF BASKETBALL PLAYERS, USING A 3-INCH CLASS INTERVAL

CLASS INTERVAL	NUMBER OF PLAYERS IN CLASS
6′1″–6′3.9″	5
6′4″–6′6.9″	6
6′7″–6′9.9″	7
6′10″–7′0.9″	3
7′1″–7′3.9″	1

▲ **REFLECT**

What is the range of test grades in your class? What is the standard deviation? Which measure gives a more accurate impression of the variability of grades? Explain.

Mode ▲ The most frequently occurring number or score in a distribution.
Bimodal ▲ Having two modes.

FIGURE APP.2   A Bimodal Distribution. This hypothetical distribution represents students' scores on a test. The mode at the left represents the central tendency of the test scores of students who did not study. The mode at the right represents the mode of the test scores of students who did study. (I'm allowed to be moralistic about studying; I wrote the book.)

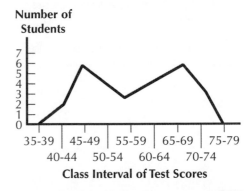

Number of Students

Class Interval of Test Scores

TABLE APP.4 HYPOTHETICAL SCORES OBTAINED FROM AN IQ TESTING

IQ Score	d (Deviation Score)	d² (Deviation Score Squared)
85	15	225
87	13	169
89	11	121
90	10	100
93	7	49
97	3	9
97	3	9
100	0	0
101	−1	1
104	−4	16
105	−5	25
110	−10	100
112	−12	144
113	−13	169
117	−17	289
Sum of IQ scores = 1,500		Sum of d² scores = 1,426

$$\text{Mean} = \frac{\text{Sum of scores}}{\text{Number of scores}} = \frac{1,500}{15} = 100$$

$$\text{Standard Deviation (S.D.)} = \sqrt{\frac{\text{Sum of } d^2}{N}} = \sqrt{\frac{1,426}{15}} = \sqrt{95.07} = 9.75$$

block is $1,400,000 minus $8,000, or $1,392,000. This is a large number and it is certainly true. However, it tells us little about the *typical* variation of savings accounts, which lie within a more restricted range of $8,000 to $12,000.

The **standard deviation** is a statistic that does a better job of showing how the scores in a distribution are distributed (spread) about the mean. It is usually better than the range because it considers every score in the distribution, not just the extreme (highest and lowest) scores. Consider Figure APP.3. Each distribution in the figure has the same number of scores, the same mean, and the same range of scores. However, the scores in the distribution on the right side cluster more closely about the mean. Therefore, the standard deviation of the distribution on the right is smaller. That is, the typical score deviates less from the mean score.

The standard deviation is usually abbreviated as S.D. It is calculated by the formula

$$\text{S.D.} = \sqrt{\frac{\text{Sum of } d^2}{N}}$$

where *d* equals the deviation of each score from the mean of the distribution, and *N* equals the number of scores in the distribution.

Let us find the mean and standard deviation of the IQ scores listed in column 1 of Table APP.4. To obtain the mean we add all the scores, attain 1,500, and then divide by the number of scores (15) to obtain a mean of 100. We obtain the deviation score (*d*) for each IQ score by subtracting the score from 100. The *d* for an IQ score of 85 equals 100 minus 85, or 15, and so on. Then we square each *d* and add the squares. The S.D. equals the square root of the sum of squares (1,426) divided by the number of scores (15), or 9.75.

As an additional exercise, we can show that the S.D. of the test scores on the left (in Figure APP.3) is greater than that for the scores on the right. First we assign the grades a number according to a 4.0 system. Let A = 4, B = 3, C = 2, D = 1, and F = 0. The S.D. for each distribution is computed in Table APP.5. The larger S.D. for the distribution on the left indicates that the scores in that distribution are more variable, or tend to be farther from the mean.

REVIEW

(4)_____ statistics provides information about distributions of scores. (5) Descriptive statistics helps us determine measures of central tendency and how much fluctuation or _____ there is in a distribution. (6) A _____ distribution takes items of data,

Standard deviation ▲ A measure of the variability of a distribution, obtained by the formula

$$\text{S.D.} = \sqrt{\frac{\text{Sum of } d^2}{N}}$$

FIGURE APP.3   Hypothetical Distributions of Student Test Scores.
Each distribution has the same number of scores, the same mean, even the same range, but the standard deviation (a measure of variability) is greater for the distribution on the left because the scores tend to be farther from the mean.

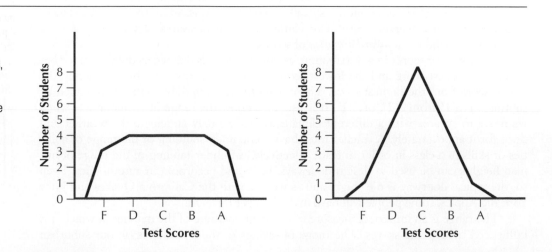

puts them into order, and indicates how often a score appears. (7) A frequency distribution groups data according to _____ intervals. (8) In the frequency histogram and polygon, the class intervals are usually drawn along the X axis, or (horizontal or vertical?) line. (9) The numbers of cases in each class interval are shown along the Y axis, or (horizontal or vertical?) line. (10) We obtain the _____ of a distribution by adding the scores and then dividing the sum by the number of scores. (11) The _____ is the score beneath which 50% of the cases fall. (12) The _____ is the most frequently occurring measure in a distribution. (13) The range of scores is obtained by subtracting the _____ score from the highest score. (14) The standard deviation is calculated by the formula:

$$\text{S.D.} = \sqrt{\frac{\text{Sum of } \underline{\qquad}^2}{N}}$$

Pulling It Together: Provide examples of distributions in which the median and mode are better measures of central tendency than the mean. Why is being a "10" more remarkable in a distribution whose scores range from 1 to 10 than in a distribution whose scores range from 9 to 11?

THE NORMAL CURVE

Many human traits and characteristics including height and intelligence seem to be distributed in a pattern known as a normal distribution. ***Question: What is a normal distribution?*** In a **normal distribution,** the mean, median, and mode all fall at the same data point or score. Scores cluster most heavily about the mean, fall off rapidly in either direction at first (as shown in Figure APP.4), and then taper off more gradually.

The curve in Figure APP.4 is bell-shaped. This type of distribution is also called a **normal curve** or bell-shaped curve. This curve is hypothesized to reflect the distribution of variables in which different scores are determined by chance variation. Height is thought to be largely determined by chance combinations of genetic material. A distribution of the heights of a random sample of the population approximates normal distributions for men and women, with the mean of the distribution for men a few inches higher than the mean for women.

TABLE APP.5 COMPUTATION OF STANDARD DEVIATIONS FOR TEST-SCORE DISTRIBUTIONS IN FIGURE APP.3

DISTRIBUTION AT LEFT			DISTRIBUTION TO THE RIGHT		
Grade	d	d^2	Grade	d	d^2
A (4)	2	4	A (4)	2	4
A (4)	2	4	B (3)	1	1
A (4)	2	4	B (3)	1	1
B (3)	1	1	B (3)	1	1
B (3)	1	1	B (3)	1	1
B (3)	1	1	C (2)	0	0
B (3)	1	1	C (2)	0	0
C (2)	0	0	C (2)	0	0
C (2)	0	0	C (2)	0	0
C (2)	0	0	C (2)	0	0
C (2)	0	0	C (2)	0	0
D (1)	−1	1	C (2)	0	0
D (1)	−1	1	C (2)	0	0
D (1)	−1	1	D (1)	−1	1
D (1)	−1	1	D (1)	−1	1
F (0)	−2	4	D (1)	−1	1
F (0)	−2	4	D (1)	−1	1
F (0)	−2	4	F (0)	−2	4
Sum of grades = 36			Sum of grades = 36		
Mean grade = 36/18 = 2			Mean grade = 36/18 = 2		
Sum of d^2 = 32			Sum of d^2 = 16		
S.D. = $\sqrt{32/18}$ = 1.33			S.D. = $\sqrt{16/18}$ = 0.94		

Normal distribution ▲ A symmetrical distribution that is assumed to reflect chance fluctuations; approximately 68% of cases lie within a standard deviation of the mean.
Normal curve ▲ Graphic presentation of a normal distribution, which shows a characteristic bell shape.

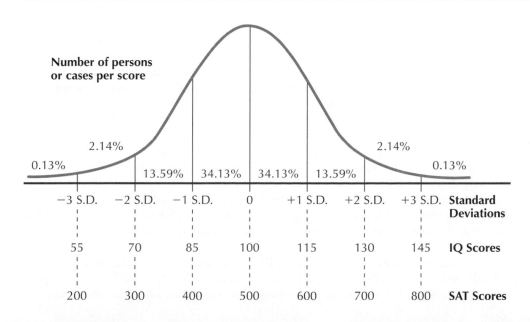

FIGURE APP.4   A Bell-Shaped or Normal Curve.
In a normal curve, approximately two out of three cases (68%) lie within a standard deviation (S.D.) from the mean. The mean, median, and mode all lie at the same score. IQ tests and the Scholastic Assessment Tests (SATs) are constructed so that their distributions approximate the normal curve.

Number of persons or cases per score

| 0.13% | 2.14% | 13.59% | 34.13% | 34.13% | 13.59% | 2.14% | 0.13% |

| −3 S.D. | −2 S.D. | −1 S.D. | 0 | +1 S.D. | +2 S.D. | +3 S.D. | **Standard Deviations** |

| 55 | 70 | 85 | 100 | 115 | 130 | 145 | **IQ Scores** |

| 200 | 300 | 400 | 500 | 600 | 700 | 800 | **SAT Scores** |

Test developers traditionally assumed that intelligence was also randomly or normally distributed among the population. For that reason, they constructed intelligence tests so that scores would be distributed as close to "normal" as possible. In actuality, IQ scores are also influenced by environmental factors and chromosomal abnormalities, so that the resultant curves are not perfectly normal. The means of most IQ tests are defined as scores of 100 points. The Wechsler scales are constructed to have standard deviations of 15 points, as shown in Figure APP.4. A standard deviation of 15 points causes 50% of the Wechsler scores to fall between 90 and 110, which is called the "broad average" range. About 68% of scores (two out of three) fall between 85 and 115 (within a standard deviation of the mean), and more than 95% fall between 70 and 130—that is, within two standard deviations of the mean.

The Scholastic Assessment Tests (SATs) were constructed so that the mean scores would be 500 points and the S.D. would be 100 points. Thus, a score of 600 would equal or excel that of some 84% to 85% of the test-takers. Because of the complex interaction of variables that determine SAT scores, their distribution is not exactly normal either. Moreover, the actual mean scores and standard deviations tend to vary from year to year, and in the case of the SAT IIs, from test to test. The normal curve is an idealized curve.

REFLECT

Do you feel that your SAT scores (or SAT II scores, or ACT scores) represent you accurately as a person? Explain.

REVIEW

(15) In a _____ distribution, the mean, median, and mode all fall at the same score. (16) A normal distribution yields a graph that has the shape of a _____. (17) The means of most IQ tests are defined as scores of _____ points. (18) The Wechsler scales have standard deviations of _____ points.

Pulling It Together: Why is a Wechsler IQ score of 150 "higher" than an SAT score of 400?

CLICK4™ *a video on measures of central tendency.*

THE CORRELATION COEFFICIENT

What is the relationship between intelligence and educational achievement? Between cigarette smoking and lung cancer among humans? Between the personality trait of introversion and numbers of dates among college students? We cannot run experiments to determine whether the relationships between these variables are causal, because we cannot manipulate the independent variable. That is, we cannot assign high or low intelligence at random. Nor can we (ethically) assign some people to smoke cigarettes and others not to smoke. People must be allowed to make their own decisions, so it is possible that the same factors that lead some people to smoke—or to continue to smoke after they have experimented with cigarettes—also lead to lung cancer. (Even if we were to assign a group of people to a nonsmoking condition, could we monitor them continuously to make sure that they weren't sneaking puffs?) Nor can we designate who will be introverted and who will be extraverted. True, we could encourage people to act as if they are introverted or extraverted, but behavior is not the same thing as a personality trait. We cannot run true experiments to answer any of these questions, but the **correlation coefficient** can be used to reveal whether there is a relationship between intelligence and achievement, a relationship between smoking and cancer, or a relationship between personality and dating.

Question: What is the correlation coefficient? The correlation coefficient is a statistic that describes the relationship between two variables. A correlation coefficient can vary from +1.00 to -1.00. A correlation coefficient of +1.00 is called a perfect positive correlation, and it describes the relationship between temperatures as measured by the Fahrenheit and Centigrade scales. A correlation coefficient of -1.00 is a perfect negative correlation, and a correlation of 0 (zero) reveals no relationship between variables.

As suggested by Figures APP.5 and APP.6, most correlation coefficients in psychological research are less than perfect. The left-hand graph in Figure APP.5 reveals a positive relationship between time spent studying and grade point averages. Since there is a

REFLECT

How would you explain the correlation between studying and grades? (Have you sketched out the entire picture?)

Correlation coefficient ▲ A number between -1.00 and +1.00 that indicates the direction (negative or positive) and extent (from none to perfect) of the relationship between two variables.

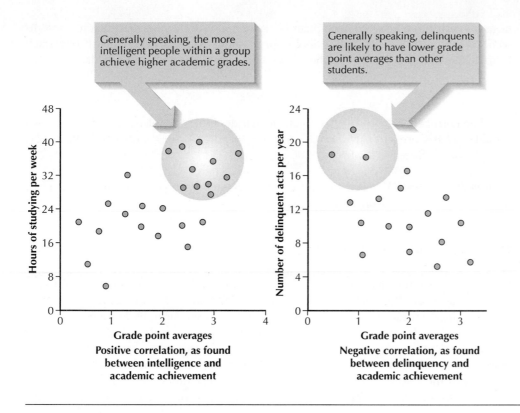

FIGURE APP.5   Positive and Negative Correlations.
When there is a positive correlation between variables, as there is between intelligence and achievement, one increases as the other increases. By and large, the more time students spend studying, the better their grades are likely to be, as suggested in the diagram to the left. (Each dot represents the amount of time a student spends studying each week and his or her grade point average.) But there is a negative correlation between grades and juvenile delinquency. As the number of delinquent acts per year increases, one's grade point average tends to decline. Correlational research may suggest but does not demonstrate cause and effect.

positive correlation between the variables but the relationship is not perfect, the correlation coefficient will lie between 0.00 and +1.00. Perhaps it is about +0.6 or +0.7. However, we cannot absolutely predict what a person's GPA will be if we know the hours per week that he or she spends studying (nor can we predict exactly how much time the person spends studying on the basis of his or her GPA). Nevertheless, it would seem advisable to place oneself among those who spend a good deal of time studying if one wishes to achieve a good GPA.

The right-hand drawing in Figure APP.5 reveals a negative relationship between number of delinquent acts committed per year and GPA. The causal connection is less than perfectly clear. Does delinquency interfere with studying and academic achievement? Does poor achievement weaken a student's commitment to trying to get ahead through work? Do feelings of distance from "the system" contribute both to delinquent behavior and a low GPA? The answers are not to be found in Figure APP.5, but the

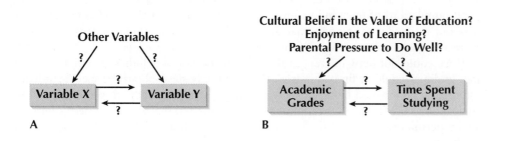

FIGURE APP.6   Correlational Relationships, Cause and Effect.
Correlational relationships may suggest but do not demonstrate cause and effect. In part A, there is a correlation between variables X and Y. Does this mean that either variable X causes variable Y or variable Y causes variable X? Not necessarily. Other factors could affect both variables X and Y. Consider the examples of academic grades (variable X) and time spent studying (variable Y) in part B. There is a positive correlation between the two. Does this mean that studying contributes to good grades? Perhaps. Does it mean that good grades encourage studying? Again, perhaps. But there could also be other variables—such as cultural belief in the value of education, enjoyment of learning, even parental pressure to do well—that contribute both to time spent studying and good grades.

negative correlation between delinquent behavior and GPA does suggest that it is worthwhile to study the issues involved and—for a student—to distance himself or herself from delinquent behavior if he or she wishes to achieve in the academic world.

REVIEW

(19) The correlation _____ is a statistic that describes the relationship between two variables. (20) Correlational research (does or does not?) reveal cause and effect. (21) Correlation coefficients vary from +1.00 to _____.

Pulling It Together: Why is the correlation between grades at your college and the price of ham in Afghanistan likely to be close to zero?

INFERENTIAL STATISTICS

Head Start programs have apparently raised children's intellectual functioning as reflected in their grades and IQ scores. In one such study, children enrolled in a Head Start program obtained a mean IQ score of 99, whereas children similar in background who were not enrolled in Head Start obtained a mean IQ score of 93 (Palmer, 1976). Is this difference of six points in IQ *significant*, or does it represent a chance fluctuation in scores? In a study reported in Chapter 1, college students were provoked by people in league with the researchers. Some of the students believed they had drunk alcohol (in a cocktail with tonic water); others believed they had drunk tonic water only. The students were then given the opportunity to shock the individuals who had provoked them. Students who believed they had drunk alcohol chose higher levels of shock than students who believed they had drunk tonic water only. Did the mean difference in shock level chosen by the two groups of students represent actual differences between the groups, or might it have been a chance fluctuation? The individuals in the Head Start study were a sample of young children. The individuals in the alcohol study were a sample of college students. Inferential statistics help us determine whether we can conclude that the differences between such samples reflect real differences that are found in the populations that they represent.

Descriptive statistics enables us to provide descriptive information about samples of scores. *Question: What are inferential statistics?* **Inferential statistics** assist us in determining whether we can generalize differences among samples to the populations that they represent.

Figure APP.7 shows the distribution of heights of 1,000 men and 1,000 women who were selected at random from the general U.S. population. The mean height for men is greater than the mean height for women. Can we conclude, or **infer,** that this difference in height is not just a chance fluctuation but represents an actual difference between the general populations of men and women? Or must we avoid such an inference and summarize our results by stating only that the mean height of the sample of men in the study was greater than the mean height of the sample of women in the study?

If we could not draw inferences about populations from studies of samples, our research findings would be limited indeed. We could only speak about the specific individuals studied. There would be no point to learning about any study in which you did not participate because it would not apply to you! Fortunately, that is not the case. Inferential statistics permits us to extend findings with samples to the populations from which they were drawn.

Statistically Significant Differences

We asked whether the differences in height between our samples of men and women were simply a chance fluctuation or whether they represented actual differences between the heights of men and women. Researchers tend not to talk about "real differences" or "actual differences" between groups, however. Instead, they speak of statistically significant differences. Similarly, researchers asked whether differences in IQ scores between

Inferential statistics ▲ The branch of statistics that is concerned with confidence with which conclusions drawn about samples can be extended to the populations from which the samples were drawn.

Infer ▲ To go from the particular to the general; to draw a conclusion.

FIGURE APP.7 Distribution of Heights for Random Samples of Men and Women.
Note that the mean height of the men is greater than that of the women. Is the group mean difference in height statistically significant? Researchers use a tool called inferential statistics to determine the answer.

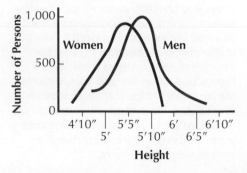

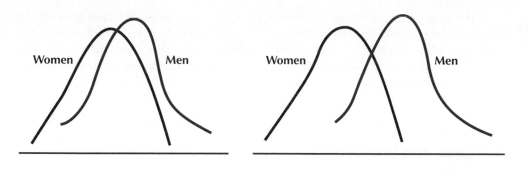

FIGURE APP.8   Decreasing and Increasing the Mean Group Difference in Heights.
Everything else being equal, the greater the difference in group means, the greater the probability that the difference is statistically significant. The distribution on the right shows a greater difference in group means; therefore, there is a greater probability that the difference is statistically significant.

children in Head Start programs and other children from similar backgrounds were chance fluctuations or statistically significant differences. *Question: What are "statistically significant" differences?* Statistically significant differences are differences that are unlikely to be due to chance fluctuation. Psychologists usually do not accept a difference as being statistically significant unless the probability (p) that it is due to chance fluctuation is less than 1 in 20 (i.e., $p < .05$). They are more comfortable labeling a difference as statistically significant when the probability (p) that it is due to chance fluctuation is less than 1 in 100 (i.e., $p < .01$).

Psychologists use formulas involving the means (e.g., mean IQ scores of 93 versus 99) and the standard deviations of sample groups to determine whether differences in means are statistically significant. As you can see in Figure APP.8, the farther apart group means are, the more likely it is that they are statistically significant. In other words, if the men are on the average 5 inches taller than the women, it is more likely that the difference is statistically significant than if the men are only one-quarter of an inch taller on average. Principle 1: Everything else being equal, the greater the difference between means, the greater the probability that the difference is statistically significant. This makes common sense. After all, if you were told that your neighbor's car had gotten one-tenth of a mile more per gallon of gas than your car in the past year, you would probably attribute the difference to chance fluctuation. But if the difference were greater, say 14 miles per gallon, you would probably assume that the difference reflected an actual difference in driving habits or the efficiency of the automobile.

As you can see in Figure APP.9, the smaller the standard deviations (a measure of variability) of the groups, the more likely it is that the difference between means is statistically significant. Consider the extreme example in which there is *no* variability within each group. That is, imagine that every woman in the randomly selected sample of 1,000 women is exactly 5'5" tall. Similarly, imagine that every man in the randomly selected sample of 1,000 men is exactly 5'10" tall. In such a case the heights of the men and women would not overlap at all, and it would appear that the differences were statistically significant. Consider the other extreme—one with unnaturally large variability. Imagine that the heights of the women vary from 2' to 14' and that the heights of the men vary from 2'1" to 14'3". In such a case we might be more likely to assume that the difference in group means of 5" was a chance fluctuation. Principle 2: Everything else being equal, the smaller the variability of the distributions of scores, the greater the probability that the difference in group means is statistically significant.

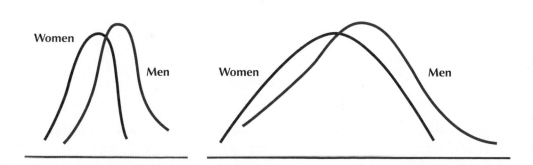

FIGURE APP.9   Decreasing and Increasing the Variability of the Distributions of Scores.
Everything else being equal, the smaller the variability in group scores, the greater the probability that the difference in group means is statistically significant. The distribution on the right shows a greater difference in the variability of the groups; therefore, there is a *lower* probability that the difference in group means is statistically significant.

We have been "eyeballing" the data and making assumptions. We have been relying on what one professor of mine called the "Wow!" effect. As noted, psychologists and other researchers actually use mathematical techniques that take group means and standard deviations into account to determine whether group differences are statistically significant. It is often the case that eyeballing real data does not yield clear results, or even good guesses.

Samples and Populations

Inferential statistics are mathematical tools that psychologists apply to samples of scores to determine whether they can generalize or extend their findings to populations of scores. They must therefore be quite certain that the samples involved actually represent the populations from which they were drawn. Sampling techniques are crucial. Random sampling is the best method, and sampling is random only if every member of the target population has an equal chance of being selected.

It matters little how sophisticated our statistical methods are if the samples studied do not represent the target populations. We could use a variety of sophisticated statistical techniques to analyze the heights of the New York Big Apples and the California Quakes, but none of these methods would tell us much about the height of the general population. Or about the height of women. (Or about the height of people who can't pass the ball, shoot, or play defense.)

REVIEW

(22) Descriptive statistics enables us to provide descriptive information about samples of scores. (23) _____ statistics help us decide whether we can generalize differences among samples to their populations. (24) Psychologists usually do not accept a difference as being statistically significant unless the probability that it is due to chance fluctuation is less than one in _____. (25) Psychologists use formulas involving the means and _____ deviations of sample groups to determine whether differences in means are statistically significant.

Pulling It Together: What does it mean to say that the difference in heights between men and women is *statistically significant?*

TRUTH ᴏʀ FICTION
REVISITED

◢ It is true that basketball players are abnormal—statistically speaking. *They are much taller than average and possess better-than-average athletic skills. (Fans consider these abnormalities to be assets, not deficits.) See page 614.*

◢ It is true that being a "10" is not necessarily a good thing. *Being a 10 may be good if the scale varies from 1 to 10, but not if the scale varies from say, 0 to 100. See page 615.*

◢ It is true that researchers can often group their data to highlight or to hide their findings. *In the example shown in the text, they can highlight the fact that no basketball player they measured was 6' 4" tall, which could give the impression that basketball players are not that tall. See page 615.*

◢ Thus it is true that adding people's incomes and then dividing them by the number of people can be an awful way of showing the average income. *A few extremely high incomes, or IQ scores, or heights can distort the average of a group in an upward direction. See page 616.*

◢ It is true that psychologists may express your IQ score in terms of how deviant you are. *The more extreme high (and low) IQ scores deviate more from the mean score. See page 620.*

◢ It is true that an IQ score of 130 may be more impressive than an SAT score of 500. *The IQ score of 130 is two standard deviations above the mean and exceeds that of more than 97% of the population. An SAT score of 500 is the mean SAT score and thus equals or excels that of about 50% of the population. See page 620.*

◢ It is not true that correlational research shows that smoking cigarettes causes cancer. *Correlational research shows that smoking and cancer are related but does not reveal cause and effect. (Experimental research with animals does strongly suggest that smoking will cause cancer in humans, however.) See page 620.*

◢ It is true that we cannot conclude that men are taller than women unless we know the average heights of men and women and how much the heights within each group vary. *We must know both the central tendencies (means) and variability of the two distributions of heights in order to infer that the mean heights are statistically significantly different. See page 623.*

1. What is statistics?

Statistics is the science that assembles data in such a way that they provide useful information about measures or scores. Such measures or scores include people's height, weight, and scores on psychological tests such as IQ tests.

2. What are samples and populations?

A sample is part of a population. A population is a complete group from which a sample is drawn. The example with basketball players shows that a sample must represent its population if it is to provide accurate information about the population.

3. What is descriptive statistics? (Why isn't it always good to be a "10"?)

Descriptive statistics is the branch of statistics that provides information about distributions of scores.

4. What is a frequency distribution?

A frequency distribution organizes a set of data, usually from low scores to high scores, and indicates how frequently a score appears. Class intervals may be used on large sets of data to provide a quick impression of how the data tend to cluster. The histogram and frequency polygon are two ways of graphing data to help people visualize the way in which the data are distributed.

5. What are measures of central tendency?

Measures of central tendency are "averages" that show the center or balancing points of a frequency distribution. The mean—which is what most people consider the average—is obtained by adding the scores in a distribution and dividing by the number of scores. The median is the score of the middle or central case in a distribution. The mode is the most common score in a distribution. Distributions can be bimodal (having two modes) or multimodal.

6. What are measures of variability?

Measures of variability provide information about the spread of scores in a distribution. The range is defined as the difference between the highest and lowest scores. The standard deviation is a statistic that shows how scores cluster around the mean. Distributions with higher standard deviations are more spread out.

7. What is a normal distribution?

The normal or bell-shaped curve is hypothesized to occur when the scores in a distribution occur by chance. The normal curve has one mode, and approximately two of three scores (68%) are found within one standard deviation of the mean. Fewer than 5% of cases are found beyond two standard deviations from the mean.

8. What is the correlation coefficient?

The correlation coefficient is a statistic that describes how variables such as IQ and grade point averages are related. It varies from $+1.00$ to -1.00. When correlations between two variables are positive, it means that one (such as school grades) tends to rise as the other (such as IQ) rises.

9. What are inferential statistics?

Inferential statistics is the branch of statistics that indicates whether researchers can extend their findings with samples to the populations from which they were drawn.

10. What are "statistically significant" differences?

Statistically significant differences are believed to represent real differences between groups, and not chance fluctuation.

Answer Keys for Self-Assessments

SCORING KEY FOR THE "SLEEP QUIZ: ARE YOU GETTING YOUR Z'S?" (CHAPTER 4, P. 129)

Psychologist James Maas, the author of *Power Sleep* (HarperCollins, 1999), writes that an answer of "true" to two or more of the statements in the self-assessment may be a sign of a sleep problem.

SCORING KEY FOR "WHY DO YOU DRINK?" (CHAPTER 4, P. 140)

Why do you drink? Score your self-assessment by seeing how many items you answered for each of the reasons for drinking shown in Table B.1. Consider the key as *suggestive* only. For example, if you answered several items in the manner indicated on the *addiction factor*, it may be wise to examine seriously what your drinking means to you. But do not interpret a few test item scores as binding evidence of addiction.

TABLE B.1 REASONS FOR DRINKING

Addiction	Anxiety/ Tension Reduction	Pleasure/ Taste	Transforming Agent	Social Reward	Celebration	Religion	Social Power	Scapegoating (using alcohol as an excuse for failure or social misconduct)	Habit
1. T	7. T	2. T	2. T	3. T	10. T	11. T	2. T	14. T	17. T
6. F	9. T	5. T	4. T	8. T	24. T		13. T	15. T	29. T
32. T	12. T	16. T	19. T	23. T	25. T		19. T	20. T	
38. T	15. T	27. T	22. T				30. T	21. T	
40. T	18. T	28. T	28. T					39. T	
	26. T	35. T	30. T						
	31. T	7. T	34. T						
	33. T		36. T						

SCORING KEY FOR THE "REMOTE ASSOCIATES TEST" (CHAPTER 7, P. 239)

1. Prince
2. Dog
3. Cold
4. Glasses
5. Club
6. Boat
7. Defense
8. Black
9. Pit
10. Writer

SCORING KEY FOR "THE SENSATION-SEEKING SCALE" (CHAPTER 9, P. 296)

Because this is a shortened version of a self-assessment, no norms are available. However, answers in agreement with the following key point in the direction of sensation seeking:

1. A
2. A
3. A
4. B
5. A
6. B
7. A
8. A
9. B
10. A
11. A
12. A
13. B

SCORING KEY FOR THE "EXPECTANCY-FOR-SUCCESS SCALE" (CHAPTER 12, P. 403)

To calculate your total score for the expectancy-for-success scale, first reverse the scores for the following items: 1, 2, 4, 6, 7, 8, 14, 15, 17, 18, 24, 27, and 28. That is, change a 1 to a 5; a 2 to a 4; leave a 3 alone; change a 4 to a 2; and a 5 to a 1. Then add the scores.

The range of total scores can vary from 30 to 150. The higher your score, the greater your expectancy for success in the future—and, according to social-cognitive theory, the more motivated you will be to apply yourself in facing difficult challenges.

Fibel and Hale administered their test to undergraduates taking psychology courses and found that women's scores ranged from 65 to 143 and men's from 81 to 138. The average score for each gender was 112 (112.32 for women and 112.15 for men).

KEY FOR STERNBERG'S "TRIANGULAR LOVE SCALE" (CHAPTER 13, PP. 438–439)

First add your scores for the items on each of the three components—Intimacy, Passion, and Decision/Commitment—and divide each total by 15. This procedure will yield an average rating for each subscale. An average rating of 5 on a particular subscale indicates a moderate level of the component represented by the subscale. A higher rating indicates a greater level. A lower rating indicates a lower level. Examining your ratings on these components will give you an idea of the degree to which you perceive your love relationship to be characterized by these three components of love. For example, you might find that passion is stronger than decision/commitment, a pattern that is common in the early stages of an intense romantic relationship. You might find it interesting to complete the self-assessment a few months or perhaps a year or so from now to see how your feelings about your relationship change over time. You might also ask your partner to complete the scale so that the two of you can compare your respective scores. Comparing your ratings for each component with those of your partner will give you an idea of the degree to which you and your partner see your relationship in a similar way.

ANSWER KEY FOR "CULTURAL MYTHS THAT CREATE A CLIMATE THAT SUPPORTS RAPE" (CHAPTER 13, P. 448)

Actually, each item, with the exception of number 2, represents a cultural myth that supports rape. These myths tend to view sex as an adversarial game, stereotype women as flirtatious and deceitful, and blame the victim.

ANSWER KEY FOR THE "SOCIAL READJUSTMENT RATING SCALE" (CHAPTER 14, PP. 466–467)

Add all the scores in the "Total" column to arrive at your final score.

FINAL SCORE ____

Interpretation

As shown in Table B.2, your final score is indicative of the amount of stress you have experienced during the past 12 months.

Research has shown that the probability of encountering physical illness within the *following* year is related to the amount of stress experiences during the *past* year. That is, college students who experienced minor stress have a 28% chance of becoming ill; mild stress, a 45% chance; moderate stress, a 70% chance; and major stress, an 82% chance. Moreover, the seriousness of the illness also increases with the amount of stress.

TABLE B.2 LIFE-CHANGE SCORES AND AMOUNT OF STRESS

Final Score	Amount of Stress
From 0 to 1500	Minor stress
1501–3500	Mild stress
3501–5500	Moderate stress
5501 and above	Major stress

It should be recognized that these percentages reflect previous research with college students. Do not assume that if you have encountered a great deal of stress you are "doomed" to illness. Also keep in mind that a number of psychological factors moderate the impact of stress, as described in this chapter. For example, psychologically hardy college students would theoretically withstand the same amount of stress that could enhance the risk of illness for nonhardy individuals.

ANSWER KEY FOR "ARE YOU TYPE A OR TYPE B?" (CHAPTER 14, P. 473)

Type A people are ambitious, hard driving, and chronically discontent with their current achievements. Type Bs, by contrast, are more relaxed, more involved with the quality of life.

Yeses suggest the Type A behavior pattern, which is marked by a sense of time urgency and constant struggle. In appraising your "type," you need not be overly concerned with the precise number of "yes" answers; we have no normative data for you. But as Freidman and Rosenman (1974, p. 85) note, you should have little trouble spotting yourself as "hard core" or "moderately afflicted"—that is, if you are honest with yourself.

ANSWER KEY FOR THE "LOCUS OF CONTROL SCALE" (CHAPTER 14, P. 474)

Place a check mark in the blank space in the scoring key, below, each time your answer agrees with the answer in the key. The number of check marks is your total score.

Scoring Key

1. Yes ___	15. No ___	29. Yes ___
2. No ___	16. Yes ___	30. No ___
3. Yes ___	17. Yes ___	31. Yes ___
4. No ___	18. Yes ___	32. No ___
5. Yes ___	19. Yes ___	33. Yes ___
6. No ___	20. No ___	34. No ___
7. Yes ___	21. Yes ___	35. Yes ___
8. Yes ___	22. No ___	36. Yes ___
9. No ___	23. Yes ___	37. Yes ___
10. Yes ___	24. Yes ___	38. No ___
11. Yes ___	25. No ___	39. Yes ___
12. Yes ___	26. No ___	40. No ___
13. No ___	27. Yes ___	
14. Yes ___	28. No ___	

TOTAL SCORE ___

Interpreting Your Score

Low Scorers (0–8). About 1 respondent in 3 earns a score of from 0 to 8. Such respondents tend to have an internal locus of control. They see themselves as responsible for the reinforcements they attain (and fail to attain) in life.

Average Scorers (9–16). Most respondents earn from 9 to 16 points. Average scorers may see themselves as partially in control of their lives. Perhaps they see themselves as in control at work, but not in their social lives—or vice versa.

TABLE B.3 PERCENTILES FOR SCORES ON THE RAS

Women's Scores	Percentile	Men's Scores
55	99	65
48	97	54
45	95	48
37	90	40
31	85	33
26	80	30
23	75	26
19	70	24
17	65	19
14	60	17
11	55	15
8	50	11
6	45	8
2	40	6
−1	35	3
−4	30	1
−8	25	−3
−13	20	−7
−17	15	−11
−24	10	−15
−34	5	−24
−39	3	−30
−48	1	−41

SOURCE: Nevid, J. S., & Rathus, S. A. (1978). Multivariate and normative data pertaining to the RAS with the college population. *Behavior Therapy, 9,* 675.

High Scorers (17–40). About 15% of respondents attain scores of 17 or above. High scorers tend largely to see life as a game of chance and success as a matter of luck or the generosity of others.

SCORING KEY FOR THE "RATHUS ASSERTIVENESS SCHEDULE" (CHAPTER 16, P. 553)

Tabulate your score as follows: For those items followed by an asterisk (*), change the signs (plus to minus; minus to plus). For example, if the response to an asterisked item was 2, place a minus sign (−) before the two. If the response to an asterisked item was −3, change the minus sign to a plus sign (+) by adding a vertical stroke. Then add up the scores of the 30 items.

Scores on the assertiveness schedule can vary from +90 to −90. Table B.3 will show you how your score compares with those of 764 college women and 637 men from 35 campuses across the United States. For example, if you are a woman and your score was 26, it exceeded that of 80% of the women in the sample. A score of 15 for a male exceeds that of 55–60% of the men in the sample.

A-B problem   The issue of how well we can predict behavior on the basis of attitudes.

Absolute threshold   The minimal amount of energy that can produce a sensation.

Abstinence syndrome   A characteristic cluster of symptoms that results from sudden decrease in an addictive drug's level of usage.

Accommodation   According to Piaget, the modification of schemes so that information inconsistent with existing schemes can be integrated or understood.

Acculturation   The process of adaptation in which immigrants and native groups identify with a new, dominant culture by learning about that culture and making behavioral and attitudinal changes.

Acculturative stress   Feelings of tension and anxiety that accompany efforts to adapt to or adopt the orientation and values of the dominant culture.

Acetylcholine   A neurotransmitter that controls muscle contractions. Abbreviated *ACh*.

Acoustic code   Mental representation of information as a sequence of sounds.

Acquired drives   Drives acquired through experience, or learned.

Acrophobia   Fear of high places.

Action potential   The electrical impulse that provides the basis for the conduction of a neural impulse along an axon of a neuron.

Activating effect   The arousal-producing effects of sex hormones that increase the likelihood of sexual behavior.

Activation-synthesis model   The view that dreams reflect activation of cognitive activity by the reticular activating system and synthesis of this activity into a pattern by the cerebral cortex.

Actor-observer effect   The tendency to attribute our own behavior to situational factors but to attribute the behavior of others to dispositional factors.

Acupuncture   The ancient Chinese practice of piercing parts of the body with needles to deaden pain and treat illness.

Acute stress disorder   A disorder, like PTSD, that is characterized by feelings of anxiety and helplessness and caused by a traumatic event. Unlike PTSD, acute stress disorder occurs within a month of the event and lasts from 2 days to 4 weeks. (A category first included in DSM-IV.)

Adolescence   The period of life bounded by puberty and the assumption of adult responsibilities.

Adrenaline   A hormone produced by the adrenal medulla that stimulates sympathetic ANS activity, generally arousing people and heightening their emotional responsiveness. Also called *epinephrine*.

Afferent neurons   Neurons that transmit messages from sensory receptors to the spinal cord and brain. Also called *sensory neurons*.

Affiliation   Association or connection with a group.

Afterimage   The lingering visual impression made by a stimulus that has been removed.

Age regression   In hypnosis, taking on the role of childhood, commonly accompanied by vivid recollections of one's past.

Age-30 transition   Levinson's term for the ages from 28 to 33, which are characterized by reassessment of the goals and values of the 20s.

Agoraphobia   Fear of open, crowded places.

AIDS   The acronym for *acquired immunodeficiency syndrome*, a condition caused by the human immunodeficiency virus (HIV) and characterized by destruction of the immune system so that the body is stripped of its ability to fend off life-threatening diseases.

Alarm reaction   The first stage of the general adaptation syndrome, which is triggered by the impact of a stressor and characterized by sympathetic activity.

Algorithm   A systematic procedure for solving a problem that works invariably when it is correctly applied.

All-or-none principle   The fact that a neuron fires an impulse of the same strength whenever its action potential is triggered.

Alpha waves   Rapid low-amplitude brain waves that have been linked to feelings of relaxation.

Altruism   Unselfish concern for the welfare of others.

Alzheimer's disease   A progressive form of mental deterioration characterized by loss of memory, language, problem-solving ability, and other cognitive functions.

Ambiguous   Having two or more possible meanings.

Amniotic sac   A sac within the uterus that contains the embryo or fetus.

Amphetamines   Stimulants derived from *a*lpha-*m*ethyl-beta-*ph*enyl-*et*hyl-*amine*, a colorless liquid consisting of carbon, hydrogen, and nitrogen.

Amplitude   Height.

Amygdala   A part of the limbic system that apparently facilitates stereotypical aggressive responses.

Analgesic   Giving rise to a state of not feeling pain though fully conscious.

Anal stage   The second stage of psychosexual development, when gratification is attained through anal activities.

Analytical psychology   Jung's psychodynamic theory, which emphasizes the collective unconscious and archetypes.

Anchoring and adjustment heuristic   A decision-making heuristic in which a presumption or first estimate serves as a cognitive anchor. As we receive additional information, we make adjustments, but tend to remain in the proximity of the anchor.

Androgens   Male sex hormones.

Animism   The belief that inanimate objects move because of will or spirit.

Anorexia nervosa   A life-threatening eating disorder characterized by refusal to maintain a healthful body weight, intense fear of being overweight, a distorted body image, and, in females, lack of menstruation (amenorrhea).

Anterograde amnesia   Failure to remember events that occur after physical trauma because of the effects of the trauma.

Antibodies   Substances formed by white blood cells that recognize and destroy antigens.

Antidepressant   Acting to relieve depression.

Antidiuretic hormone   A pituitary hormone that conserves body fluids by increasing reabsorption of urine and is connected with paternal behavior in some mammals. Also called *vasopressin*.

Antigen   A substance that stimulates the body to mount an immune system response to it. (The contraction for *anti*body *gen*erator.)

Antisocial personality disorder   The diagnosis given a person who is in frequent conflict with society, yet who is undeterred by punishment and experiences little or no guilt and anxiety.

Aphagic   Characterized by undereating.

Aphasia   A disruption in the ability to understand or produce language.

Apnea   Temporary absence or cessation of breathing. (From Greek and Latin roots meaning "without" and "breathing.")

Applied research   Research conducted in an effort to find solutions to particular problems.

Approach-approach conflict   A type of conflict in which the goals that produce opposing motives are positive and within reach.

Approach-avoidance conflict   A type of conflict in which the same goal produces approach and avoidance motives.

Aptitude   A natural ability or talent.

Archetypes   Basic, primitive images or concepts hypothesized by Jung to reside in the collective unconscious.

Artificialism   The belief that natural objects have been created by human beings.

Assimilation   According to Piaget, the inclusion of a new event into an existing scheme.

Asylum   An institution for the care of the mentally ill.

Attachment   The enduring affectional tie that binds one person to another.

Attachment-in-the-making phase   The second phase in forming bonds of attachment, characterized by preference for familiar figures.

Attention-deficit/hyperactivity disorder   A disorder that begins in childhood and is characterized by a persistent pattern of lack of attention, with or without hyperactivity and impulsive behavior.

Attitude   An enduring mental representation of a person, place, or thing that evokes an emotional response and related behavior.

Attitude-discrepant behavior   Behavior inconsistent with an attitude that may have the effect of modifying an attitude.

Attraction   In social psychology, an attitude of liking or disliking (negative attraction).

Attribution   A belief concerning why people behave in a certain way.

Attributional style   One's tendency to attribute one's behavior to internal or external factors, stable or unstable factors, and so on.

Attribution process   The process by which people draw inferences about the motives and traits of others.

Auditory   Having to do with hearing.

Auditory nerve   The axon bundle that transmits neural impulses from the organ of Corti to the brain.

Authoritarian parents   Parents who are rigid in their rules and who demand obedience for the sake of obedience.

Authoritative parents   Parents who are strict and warm. Authoritative parents demand mature behavior but use reason rather than force in discipline.

Autokinetic effect   The tendency to perceive a stationary point of light in a dark room as moving.

Autonomic nervous system (ANS)   The division of the peripheral nervous system that regulates glands and activities such as heartbeat, respiration, digestion, and dilation of the pupils.

Autonomy   Self-direction.

Availability heuristic   A decision-making heuristic in which our estimates of frequency or probability of events are based on how easy it is to find examples.

Average   The central tendency of a group of measures, expressed either as the mean, median, or mode of a distribution.

Aversive conditioning   A behavior-therapy technique in which undesired responses are inhibited by pairing repugnant or offensive stimuli with them.

Avoidance-avoidance conflict   A type of conflict in which the goals are negative, but avoidance of one requires approaching the other.

Avoidant personality disorder   A personality disorder in which the person is generally unwilling to enter relationships without assurance of acceptance because of fears of rejection and criticism.

Axon   A long, thin part of a neuron that transmits impulses to other neurons from branching structures called *terminals*.

Backward conditioning   A classical conditioning procedure in which the unconditioned stimulus is presented prior to the conditioned stimulus.

Barbiturate   An addictive depressant used to relieve anxiety or induce sleep.

Basilar membrane   A membrane that lies coiled within the cochlea.

Behavioral genetics   The study of the genetic transmission of structures and traits that give rise to behavior.

Behaviorism   The school of psychology that defines psychology as the study of observable behavior and studies relationships between stimuli and responses.

Behavior-rating scale   A systematic means for recording the frequency with which target behaviors occur.

Behavior rehearsal   Practice.

Behavior therapy   Systematic application of the principles of learning to the direct modification of a client's problem behaviors.

Benzodiazepines   A class of drugs that reduce anxiety; minor tranquilizers.

Bimodal   Having two modes.

Binocular cues   Stimuli suggestive of depth that involve simultaneous perception by both eyes.

Biofeedback training (BFT)   The systematic feeding back to an organism of information about a bodily function so that the organism can gain control of that function.

Bipolar cells   Neurons that conduct neural impulses from rods and cones to ganglion cells.

Bipolar disorder   A disorder in which the mood alternates between two extreme poles (elation and depression). Also referred to as *manic-depression*.

Bisexual   A person who is sexually aroused by, and interested in forming romantic relationships with, people of either gender.

Blind   In experimental terminology, unaware of whether or not one has received a treatment.

Blind spot   The area of the retina where axons from ganglion cells meet to form the optic nerve.

Bottom-up processing   The organization of the parts of a pattern to recognize, or form an image of, the pattern they compose.

Brainstorming   A group process that encourages creativity by stimulating a large number of ideas and suspending judgment until the process is completed.

Brightness constancy   The tendency to perceive an object as being just as bright even though lighting conditions change its intensity.

Broca's aphasia   A language disorder characterized by slow, laborious speech.

Bulimia nervosa   An eating disorder characterized by recurrent cycles of binge eating followed by dramatic measures to purge the food.

Case study   A carefully drawn biography that may be obtained through interviews, questionnaires, and psychological tests.

Catastrophize   To interpret negative events as being disastrous; to "blow out of proportion."

Catatonic schizophrenia   A type of schizophrenia characterized by striking impairment in motor activity.

Catch 30s   Sheehy's term for the fourth decade of life, when many people undergo major reassessments of their accomplishments and goals.

Catharsis   In psychodynamic theory, the purging of strong emotions or the relieving of tensions; the expression of repressed feelings and impulses to allow the release of the psychic energy associated with them.

Center   According to Piaget, to focus one's attention.

Central nervous system   The brain and spinal cord.

Cerebellum   A part of the hindbrain involved in muscle coordination and balance.

Cerebral cortex   The wrinkled surface area (gray matter) of the cerebrum.

Cerebrum   The large mass of the forebrain, which consists of two hemispheres.

Chlamydia   A sexually transmitted infection caused by the *Chlamydia trachomatous* bacterium. Many infected people have no symptoms, but they may experience painful urination and a discharge from the vagina or penis.

Chromosomes   Structures consisting of genes that are found in the nuclei of the body's cells.

Chunk   A stimulus or group of stimuli that are perceived as a discrete piece of information.

Circadian rhythm   Referring to cycles that are connected with the 24-hour period of the earth's rotation.

Circular   Descriptive of an explanation that restates its own concepts instead of offering additional information.

Cirrhosis of the liver   A disease caused by protein deficiency in which connective fibers replace active liver cells, impeding circulation of the blood. Alcohol does not contain protein; therefore, persons who drink excessively may be prone to this disease.

Classical conditioning   A simple form of learning in which an organism comes to associate or anticipate events. A neutral stimulus comes to evoke the response usually evoked by another stimulus by being paired repeatedly with the other stimulus. (Cognitive theorists view classical conditioning as the learning of relationships among events so as to allow an organism to represent its environment.) Also referred to as *respondent conditioning* or *Pavlovian conditioning*.

Claustrophobia   Fear of tight, small places.

Clear-cut-attachment phase   The third phase in forming bonds of attachment, characterized by intensified dependence on the primary caregiver.

Client-centered therapy   Carl Rogers's method of psychotherapy that emphasizes the creation of a warm, therapeutic atmosphere that frees clients to engage in self-exploration and self-expression.

Clinical scales   Groups of test items that measure the presence of various abnormal behavior patterns.

Clitoris   The female sex organ that is highly sensitive to sexual sensation; a smooth, round knob of tissue that resembles a button and is situated above the urethral opening.

Closure   The tendency to perceive a broken figure as being complete or whole.

Cochlea   The inner ear; the bony tube that contains the basilar membrane and the organ of Corti.

Cognition   Mental activity that is involved in understanding, manipulating, and communicating about information. Cognition entails paying attention to information, mentally representing it, reasoning about it, and making decisions about it.

Cognitive   Having to do with mental processes such as sensation and perception, memory, intelligence, language, thought, and problem solving.

Cognitive-dissonance theory   The view that we are motivated to make our cognitions or beliefs consistent.

Cognitive therapy   A form of therapy that focuses on how clients' cognitions (expectations, attitudes, beliefs, etc.) lead to distress and may be modified to relieve distress and promote adaptive behavior.

Cohabitation   An intimate relationship in which POSSLQs live as though they are married, but without legal sanction.

Collective unconscious   Jung's hypothesized store of vague racial memories.

Collectivist   A person who defines herself or himself in terms of relationships to other people and groups and gives priority to group goals.

Color constancy   The tendency to perceive an object as being the same color even though lighting conditions change its appearance.

Common fate   The tendency to perceive elements that move together as belonging together.

Competencies   Knowledge and skills.

Complementary   Descriptive of colors of the spectrum that when combined produce white or nearly white light.

Compulsion   An apparently irresistible urge to repeat an act or engage in ritualistic behavior such as hand washing.

Computerized axial tomography   Formation of a computer-generated image of the anatomical details of the brain by passing a narrow X-ray beam through the head and measuring from different angles the amount of radiation that passes through. Abbreviated *CAT scan*.

Concept   A mental category that is used to class together objects, relations, events, abstractions, or qualities that have common properties.

Concordance   Agreement.

Concrete-operational stage   Piaget's third stage, characterized by logical thought concerning tangible objects, conservation, and subjective morality.

Conditional positive regard   Judgment of another person's value on the basis of the acceptability of that person's behaviors.

Conditioned reinforcer   Another term for a secondary reinforcer.

Conditioned response (CR)   In classical conditioning, a learned response to a conditioned stimulus.

Conditioned stimulus (CS)   A previously neutral stimulus that elicits a conditioned response because it has been paired repeatedly with a stimulus that already elicited that response.

Conditions of worth   Standards by which the value of a person is judged.

Conductive deafness   The forms of deafness in which there is loss of conduction of sound through the middle ear.

Cones   Cone-shaped photoreceptors that transmit sensations of color.

Confident power   Feelings of self-confidence, self-efficacy.

Conflict   Being torn in different directions by opposing motives; feelings produced by being in conflict.

Conform   To changes one's attitudes or overt behavior to adhere to social norms.

Conscious   Self-aware.

Consensus   General agreement.

Conservation   According to Piaget, recognition that basic properties of substances such as weight and mass remain the same when superficial features change.

Construct   As a noun, a concept or a theory that is devised in order to help make sense of, or integrate, our observations of a phenomenon. Consciousness, anxiety, and achievement motivation are examples of constructs of interest to psychologists.

Consummate love   The ideal form of love within Sternberg's model, which combines passion, intimacy, and commitment.

Contact comfort   A hypothesized primary drive to seek physical comfort through contact with another.

Context-dependent memory   Information that is better retrieved in the context in which it was encoded and stored, or learned.

Contingency theory   The view that learning occurs when stimuli provide information about the likelihood of the occurrence of other stimuli.

Continuity   The tendency to perceive a series of points or lines as having unity.

Continuous reinforcement   A schedule of reinforcement in which every correct response is reinforced.

Control groups   In experiments, groups whose members do not obtain the treatment, while other conditions are held constant.

Conventional level   According to Kohlberg, a period during which moral judgments largely reflect social conventions. A "law and order" approach to morality.

Convergence   A binocular cue for depth based on the inward movement of the eyes as they attempt to focus on an object that is drawing nearer.

Convergent thinking   A thought process that attempts to narrow in on the single best solution to a problem.

Conversion disorder   A disorder in which anxiety or unconscious conflicts are "converted" into physical symptoms that often have the effect of helping the person cope with anxiety or conflict.

Cornea   Transparent tissue forming the outer surface of the eyeball.

Corpus callosum   A thick fiber bundle that connects the hemispheres of the cortex.

Correlation coefficient   A number between −1.00 and +1.00 that indicates the direction (negative or positive) and extent (from none to perfect) of the relationship between two variables.

Corticosteroids   Steroids produced by the adrenal cortex that regulate carbohydrate metabolism and increase resistance to stress by fighting inflammation and allergic reactions. Also called *cortical steroids*.

Cortisol   A hormone produced by the adrenal glands that increases resistance to stress.

Counterconditioning   A fear-reduction technique in which pleasant stimuli are associated with fear-evoking stimuli so that the fear-evoking stimuli lose their aversive qualities.

Creative self   According to Adler, the self-aware aspect of personality that strives to achieve its full potential.

Creativity   The ability to generate novel and useful solutions to problems.

Critical period   A period of time when an instinctive response can be elicited by a particular stimulus.

Critical thinking   An approach to thinking characterized by skepticism and thoughtful analysis of statements and arguments—for example, probing arguments' premises and the definitions of terms.

Crystallized intelligence   One's lifetime of intellectual achievement, as shown largely through vocabulary and knowledge of world affairs.

Cultural bias   A factor that provides an advantage for test takers from certain cultural or ethnic backgrounds, such as using test items that are based on middle-class culture in the United States.

Daily hassles   Notable daily conditions and experiences that are threatening or harmful to a person's well-being.

Dark adaptation   The process of adjusting to conditions of lower lighting by increasing the sensitivity of rods and cones.

Debrief   To elicit information about a completed procedure.

Decentration   Simultaneous focusing on more than one dimension of a problem so that flexible, reversible thought becomes possible.

Decibel   A unit expressing the loudness of a sound. Abbreviated *dB*.

Deductive reasoning   A form of reasoning about arguments in which conclusions are deduced from premises. The conclusions are true if the premises are true.

Defense mechanism   In psychodynamic theory, an unconscious function of the ego that protects it from anxiety-evoking material by preventing accurate recognition of this material.

Deindividuation   The process by which group members may discontinue self-evaluation and adopt group norms and attitudes.

Delayed conditioning   A classical conditioning procedure in which the conditioned stimulus is presented before the unconditioned stimulus and remains in place until the response occurs.

Delirium tremens   A condition characterized by sweating, restlessness, disorientation, and hallucinations. The DTs occurs in some chronic alcohol users when there is a sudden decrease in usage.

Delta waves   Strong, slow brain waves usually emitted during stage 4 sleep.

Delusions   False, persistent beliefs that are unsubstantiated by sensory or objective evidence.

Dendrites   Rootlike structures, attached to the cell body of a neuron, that receive impulses from other neurons.

Dependent variable   A measure of an assumed effect of an independent variable.

Depersonalization disorder   A dissociative disorder in which one experiences persistent or recurrent feelings that one is not real or is detached from one's own experiences or body.

Depolarize   To reduce the resting potential of a cell membrane from about −70 millivolts toward zero.

Depressant   A drug that lowers the rate of activity of the nervous system.

Descriptive statistics   The branch of statistics that is concerned with providing descriptive information about a distribution of scores.

Desensitization   The type of sensory adaptation in which we become less sensitive to constant stimuli. Also called *negative adaptation*.

Dichromat   A person who is sensitive to black-white and either red-green or blue-yellow and hence partially color blind.

Difference threshold   The minimal difference in intensity required between two sources of energy so that they will be perceived as being different.

Diffusion of responsibility   The spreading or sharing of responsibility for a decision or behavior within a group.

Direct inner awareness Knowledge of one's own thoughts, feelings, and memories without use of sensory organs.

Discrimination In conditioning, the tendency for an organism to distinguish between a conditioned stimulus and similar stimuli that do not forecast an unconditioned stimulus; in social psychology, the denial of privileges to a person or a group on the basis of prejudice.

Discrimination training Teaching an organism to show a learned response in the presence of only one of a series of similar stimuli, accomplished by alternating the stimuli but following only the one stimulus with the unconditioned stimulus.

Discriminative stimulus In operant conditioning, a stimulus that indicates that reinforcement is available.

Disorganized schizophrenia A type of schizophrenia characterized by disorganized delusions and vivid hallucinations.

Displace In memory theory, to cause information to be lost from short-term memory by adding new information.

Displaced Transferred.

Displacement The quality of language that permits one to communicate information about objects and events in another time and place.

Dispositional attribution An assumption that a person's behavior is determined by internal causes such as personal attitudes or goals.

Dissociative amnesia A dissociative disorder marked by loss of memory or self-identity, thought to stem from psychological conflict or trauma; skills and general knowledge are usually retained. Previously termed *psychogenic amnesia*.

Dissociative disorders Disorders in which there are sudden, temporary changes in consciousness or self-identity.

Dissociative fugue A dissociative disorder in which one experiences amnesia and then flees to a new location. Previously termed *psychogenic fugue*.

Dissociative identity disorder A disorder in which a person appears to have two or more distinct identities or personalities that may alternately emerge. (A term first used in DSM-IV.)

Divergent thinking A thought process that attempts to generate multiple solutions to problems.

Dizygotic (DZ) twins Fraternal twins; twins who develop from separate zygotes.

Dopamine A neurotransmitter that is involved in Parkinson's disease and that appears to play a role in schizophrenia.

Double-blind study A study in which neither the participants nor the observers know who has received the treatment.

Dream In developmental psychology, Levinson's term for the overriding drive of youth to become someone important, to leave one's mark on history.

Drive A condition of arousal in an organism that is associated with a need.

Drive for superiority Adler's term for the desire to compensate for feelings of inferiority.

Drive-reduction theory The view that organisms learn to engage in behaviors that have the effect of reducing drives.

Dyspareunia A sexual dysfunction characterized by persistent or recurrent pain during sexual intercourse. (From roots meaning "badly paired.")

Eardrum A thin membrane that vibrates in response to sound waves, transmitting the waves to the middle and inner ears.

Eating disorders Psychological disorders that are characterized by distortion of the body image and gross disturbances in eating patterns.

Echo A mental representation of an auditory stimulus (sound) that is held briefly in sensory memory.

Echoic memory The sensory register that briefly holds mental representations of auditory stimuli.

Efferent neurons Neurons that transmit messages from the brain or spinal cord to muscles and glands. Also called *motor neurons*.

Effort justification In cognitive-dissonance theory, the tendency to seek justification (acceptable reasons) for strenuous efforts.

Ego The second psychic structure to develop, characterized by self-awareness, planning, and delay of gratification.

Ego analyst A psychodynamically oriented therapist who focuses on the conscious, coping behavior of the ego instead of the hypothesized, unconscious functioning of the id.

Egocentric According to Piaget, assuming that others view the world as one does oneself.

Ego identity Erikson's term for a firm sense of who one is and what one stands for.

Ego integrity versus despair Erikson's term for the crisis of late adulthood, characterized by the task of maintaining one's sense of identity despite physical deterioration.

Eidetic imagery The maintenance of detailed visual memories over several minutes.

Ejaculation The process of propelling seminal fluid (semen) from the penis.

Elaboration likelihood model The view that persuasive messages are evaluated (elaborated) on the basis of central and peripheral cues.

Elaborative rehearsal A method for increasing retention of new information by relating it to information that is already known.

Electra complex A conflict of the phallic stage in which the girl longs for her father and resents her mother.

Electroconvulsive therapy Treatment of disorders like major depression by passing an electric current (that causes a convulsion) through the head. Abbreviated *ECT*.

Electroencephalograph An instrument that measures electrical activity of the brain. Abbreviated *EEG*. ("Cephalo-" derives from the Greek *kephale*, meaning "head.")

Electromyograph (EMG) An instrument that measures muscle tension.

Embryonic stage The baby from the third through the eighth weeks following conception, during which time the major organ systems undergo rapid differentiation.

Emerging adulthood A hypothesized period of development found in industrialized societies that spans the ages of 18 to 25 and is characterized by prolonged role exploration.

Emotion A state of feeling that has cognitive, physiological, and behavioral components.

Empathic understanding Ability to perceive a client's feelings from the client's frame of reference. A quality of the good client-centered therapist.

Empty-nest syndrome A sense of depression and loss of purpose felt by some parents when the youngest child leaves home.

Encoding Interpreting; transforming; modifying information so that it can be placed in memory; the first stage of information processing.

Encounter group A type of group that aims to foster self-awareness by focusing on how group members relate to each other in a setting that encourages open expression of feelings.

Endocrine system   The body's system of ductless glands that secrete hormones and release them directly into the bloodstream.

Endorphins   Neurotransmitters that are composed of amino acids and that are functionally similar to morphine.

Engram   (1) An assumed electrical circuit in the brain that corresponds to a memory trace. (2) An assumed chemical change in the brain that accompanies learning. (From the Greek *en-*, meaning "in," and *gramma*, meaning "something that is written or recorded.")

Environmental psychology   The field of psychology that studies the ways in which people and the environment influence each other.

Epilepsy   Temporary disturbances of brain functions that involve sudden neural discharges.

Episodic memory   Memories of events experienced by a person or that take place in the person's presence.

Erogenous zone   An area of the body that is sensitive to sexual sensations.

Eros   In psychodynamic theory, the basic instinct to preserve and perpetuate life.

Estrogen   A generic term for several female sex hormones that promote growth of female sex characteristics and regulate the menstrual cycle.

Ethical   Moral; referring to one's system of deriving standards for determining what is moral.

Ethics review committee   A group found in an institutional setting that helps researchers consider the potential harm of their methods and reviews proposed studies according to ethical guidelines.

Ethnic group   A group characterized by common features such as cultural heritage, history, race, and language.

Eustress   Stress that is healthful.

Evaluation apprehension   Concern that others are evaluating one's behavior.

Evolutionary psychology   The field of psychology that studies the ways in which adaptation and natural selection are connected with behavior and mental processes.

Excitement phase   The first phase of the sexual response cycle, which is characterized by muscle tension, increases in the heart rate, and erection in the male and vaginal lubrication in the female.

Exemplar   A specific example.

Exhaustion stage   The third stage of the general adaptation syndrome, characterized by weakened resistance and possible deterioration.

Existentialism   The view that people are completely free and responsible for their own behavior.

Expectancies   Personal predictions about the outcomes of potential behaviors.

Experiment   A scientific method that seeks to confirm cause-and-effect relationships by introducing independent variables and observing their effects on dependent variables.

Experimental groups   In experiments, groups whose members obtain the treatment.

Explicit memory   Memory that clearly and distinctly expresses (explicates) specific information.

"Externals"   People who perceive the ability to attain reinforcements as being largely outside themselves.

Extinction   An experimental procedure in which stimuli lose their ability to evoke learned responses because the events that had followed the stimuli no longer occur. (The learned responses are said to be *extinguished*.)

Extraversion   A trait characterized by tendencies to be socially outgoing and to express feelings and impulses freely.

Facial-feedback hypothesis   The view that stereotypical facial expressions can contribute to stereotypical emotions.

Factor analysis   A statistical technique that allows researchers to determine the relationships among a large number of items such as test items.

Family therapy   A form of therapy in which the family unit is treated as the client.

Farsighted   Capable of seeing distant objects with greater acuity than nearby objects.

Fear appeal   A type of persuasive communication that influences behavior on the basis of arousing fear instead of rational analysis of the issues.

Feature detectors   Neurons in the sensory cortex that fire in response to specific features of sensory information such as lines or edges of objects.

Feedback   In assertiveness training, information about the effectiveness of a response.

Feeling-of-knowing experience   Same as *tip-of-the-tongue phenomenon*.

Female sexual arousal disorder   A sexual dysfunction in which females fail to become adequately sexually aroused to engage in sexual intercourse.

Fetus   The baby from the third month following conception through childbirth, during which time there is maturation of organ systems and dramatic gains in length and weight.

Fight-or-flight reaction   An innate adaptive response to the perception of danger.

Fixation   In psychodynamic theory, arrested development; attachment to objects of an earlier stage.

Fixation time   The amount of time spent looking at a visual stimulus.

Fixed-interval schedule   A schedule in which a fixed amount of time must elapse between the previous and subsequent times that reinforcement is available.

Fixed-ratio schedule   A schedule in which reinforcement is provided after a fixed number of correct responses.

Flashbacks   Distorted perceptions or hallucinations that occur days or weeks after LSD usage but mimic the LSD experience.

Flooding   A behavioral fear-reduction technique based on principles of classical conditioning. Fear-evoking stimuli (CSs) are presented continuously in the absence of actual harm so that fear responses (CRs) are extinguished.

Fluid intelligence   Mental flexibility as shown in learning rapidly to solve new kinds of problems.

Foot-in-the-door technique   A method for inducing compliance in which a small request is followed by a larger request.

Forced-choice format   A method of presenting test questions that requires a respondent to select one of a number of possible answers.

Formal-operational stage   Piaget's fourth stage, characterized by abstract logical thought; deduction from principles.

Fovea   An area near the center of the retina that is dense with cones and where vision is consequently most acute.

Frame of reference   One's unique patterning of perceptions and attitudes according to which one evaluates events.

Framing effect   The influence of wording, or the context in which information is presented, on decision making.

Free association   In psychoanalysis, the uncensored uttering of all thoughts that come to mind.

Frequency distribution   An ordered set of data that indicates the frequency (how often) with which scores appear.

Frequency histogram   A graphic representation of a frequency distribution that uses rectangular solids (bars) to represent the frequency with which scores appear.

Frequency polygon   A graphic representation of a frequency distribution that connects the points that show the frequencies with which scores appear, thereby creating a multisided geometric figure.

Frequency theory   The theory that the pitch of a sound is reflected in the frequency of the neural impulses that are generated in response to the sound.

Frontal lobe   The lobe of the cerebral cortex that lies to the front of the central fissure.

Functional analysis   A systematic study of behavior in which one identifies the stimuli that trigger problem behavior and the reinforcers that maintain it.

Functional fixedness   The tendency to view an object in terms of its name or familiar usage.

Functionalism   The school of psychology that emphasizes the uses or functions of the mind rather than the elements of experience.

Fundamental attribution error   The tendency to assume that others act predominantly on the basis of their dispositions, even when there is evidence suggesting the importance of their situations.

g   Spearman's symbol for general intelligence, which he believed underlay more specific abilities.

Gamma-aminobutyric acid (GABA)   An inhibitory neurotransmitter that is implicated in anxiety reactions.

Ganglion cells   Neurons whose axons form the optic nerve.

Gay male   A male homosexual.

Gender   The state of being female or being male.

Gender identity   One's psychological sense of being female or male.

Gender role   A cluster of behaviors that characterizes traditional female or male behaviors within a cultural setting.

Gender-schema theory   The view that gender identity plus knowledge of the distribution of behavior patterns into feminine and masculine roles motivate and guide the gender-typing of the child.

Gender-typing   The process by which people acquire a sense of being female or male and acquire the traits considered typical of females or males within a cultural setting.

General adaptation syndrome   Selye's term for a hypothesized three-stage response to stress. Abbreviated *GAS*.

Generalization   In conditioning, the tendency for a conditioned response to be evoked by stimuli that are similar to the stimulus to which the response was conditioned.

Generalize   To extend from the particular to the general; to apply observations based on a sample to a population.

Generalized anxiety disorder   Feelings of dread and foreboding and sympathetic arousal of at least 6 months' duration.

Generativity versus stagnation   Erikson's term for the crisis of middle adulthood, characterized by the task of being productive and contributing to younger generations.

Genes   The basic building blocks of heredity, which consist of DNA.

Genetics   The branch of biology that studies heredity.

Genital herpes   A sexually transmitted infection caused by the *Herpes simplex* virus type 2 and characterized by painful shallow sores and blisters on the genitals.

Genital stage   The mature stage of psychosexual development, characterized by preferred expression of libido through intercourse with an adult of the other gender.

Genital warts   A sexually transmitted infection caused by the *human papilloma virus* and possibly involved in cancers of the genital organs.

Genuineness   Recognition and open expression of the therapist's own feelings.

Germinal stage   The first stage of prenatal development during which the dividing mass of cells has not become implanted in the uterine wall.

Gestalt psychology   The school of psychology that emphasizes the tendency to organize perceptions into wholes and to integrate separate stimuli into meaningful patterns.

Gestalt therapy   Fritz Perls's form of psychotherapy, which attempts to integrate conflicting parts of the personality through directive methods designed to help clients perceive their whole selves.

Gland   An organ that secretes one or more chemical substances such as hormones, saliva, or milk.

Glial cells   Cells that nourish and insulate neurons, direct their growth, and remove waste products from the nervous system.

Gray matter   In the spinal cord, the grayish neurons and neural segments that are involved in spinal reflexes.

Groupthink   A process in which group members are influenced by cohesiveness and a dynamic leader to ignore external realities as they make decisions.

Growth hormone   A pituitary hormone that regulates growth.

Hallucination   A perception in the absence of sensory stimulation that is confused with reality.

Hallucinogenic   Giving rise to hallucinations.

Hashish   A drug derived from the resin of *Cannabis sativa*. Often called "hash."

Health psychology   The field of psychology that studies the relationships between psychological factors (e.g., attitudes, beliefs, situational influences, and behavior patterns) and the prevention and treatment of physical illness.

Heredity   The transmission of traits from one generation to another through genes.

Heritability   The degree to which the variations in a trait from one person to another can be attributed to, or explained by, genetic factors.

Hertz   A unit expressing the frequency of sound waves. One Hertz, or *1 Hz*, equals one cycle per second.

Heterosexual   Referring to people who are sexually aroused by, and interested in forming romantic relationships with, people of the other gender.

Heuristics   Rules of thumb that help us simplify and solve problems.

Hierarchy   An arrangement of stimuli according to the amount of fear they evoke.

Higher-order conditioning   (1) According to behaviorists, a classical conditioning procedure in which a previously neutral stimulus comes to elicit the response brought forth by a *conditioned* stimulus by being paired repeatedly with that conditioned stimulus. (2) According to cognitive psychologists, the learning of relationships among events, none of which evokes an unlearned response.

Hippocampus   A structure in the limbic system of the brain that plays an important role in the formation of new memories.

HIV   The acronym for the *human immunodeficiency virus*, a sexually transmitted virus that destroys white blood cells in the immune system and causes AIDS.

Holophrase   A single word used to express complex meanings.

Homeostasis   The tendency of the body to maintain a steady state.

Homogamy   The principle of like marrying like.

Homosexual   Referring to people who are sexually aroused by, and interested in forming romantic relationships with, people of the same gender. (Derived from the Greek *homos*, meaning "same," not from the Latin *homo*, meaning "man.")

Hormone   A substance secreted by an endocrine gland that regulates various body functions.

Hue   The color of light, as determined by its wavelength.

Humanism   The philosophy and school of psychology that asserts that people are conscious, self-aware, and capable of free choice, self-fulfillment, and ethical behavior.

Hydrocarbons   Chemical compounds consisting of hydrogen and carbon.

Hypermnesia   Greatly enhanced or heightened memory.

Hyperphagic   Characterized by excessive eating.

Hypertension   High blood pressure.

Hypnagogic state   The drowsy interval between waking and sleeping, characterized by brief, hallucinatory, dreamlike experiences.

Hypnosis   A condition in which people appear to be highly suggestible and behave as though they are in a trance.

Hypoactive sexual desire disorder   A sexual dysfunction in which people lack sexual desire.

Hypochondriasis   Persistent belief that one has a medical disorder despite lack of medical findings.

Hypothalamus   A bundle of nuclei below the thalamus involved in body temperature, motivation, and emotion.

Hypothesis   In psychology, a specific statement about behavior or mental processes that is tested through research.

Icon   A mental representation of a visual stimulus that is held briefly in sensory memory.

Iconic memory   The sensory register that briefly holds mental representations of visual stimuli.

Id   The psychic structure, present at birth, that represents physiological drives and is fully unconscious.

Ideas of persecution   Erroneous beliefs that one is being victimized or persecuted.

Identification   In psychodynamic theory, the unconscious assumption of the behavior of another person; the process of becoming broadly like another person.

Identity certainty   A strong and clear sense of who one is and what one stands for.

Illusions   Sensations that give rise to misperceptions.

Imaginary audience   An aspect of adolescent egocentrism: The belief that other people are as concerned with our thoughts and behaviors as we are.

Immune system   The system of the body that recognizes and destroys foreign agents (antigens) that invade the body.

Implicit memory   Memory that is suggested (implied) but not plainly expressed, as illustrated in the things that people *do* but do not state clearly.

Imprinting   A process occurring during a critical period in the development of an organism, in which that organism responds to a stimulus in a manner that will afterward be difficult to modify.

Incentive   An object, person, or situation perceived as being capable of satisfying a need.

Incest taboo   The cultural prohibition against marrying or having sexual relations with a close blood relative.

Incubation   In problem solving, a hypothetical process that sometimes occurs when we stand back from a frustrating problem for a while and the solution "suddenly" appears.

Independent variable   A condition in a scientific study that is manipulated so that its effects may be observed.

Indiscriminate attachment   Showing attachment behaviors toward any person.

Individualist   A person who defines herself or himself in terms of personal traits and gives priority to her or his own goals.

Individual psychology   Adler's psychodynamic theory, which emphasizes feelings of inferiority and the creative self.

Inductive reasoning   A form of reasoning in which we reason from individual cases or particular facts to a general conclusion.

Infantile amnesia   Inability to recall events that occur prior to the age of 2 or 3. Also termed *childhood amnesia*.

Infer   To go from the particular to the general; to draw a conclusion.

Inferential statistics   The branch of statistics that is concerned with confidence with which conclusions drawn about samples can be extended to the populations from which the samples were drawn.

Inferiority complex   Feelings of inferiority hypothesized by Adler to serve as a central motivating force.

Infinite creativity   The capacity to combine words into original sentences.

Inflammation   Increased blood flow to an injured area of the body, resulting in redness, warmth, and an increased supply of white blood cells.

Inflections   Grammatical markers that change the forms of words to indicate grammatical relationships such as number and tense.

Informed consent   The term used by psychologists to indicate that a person has agreed to participate in research after receiving information about the purposes of the study and the nature of the treatments.

Initial-preattachment phase   The first phase in forming bonds of attachment, characterized by indiscriminate attachment.

Insanity   A legal term descriptive of a person judged to be incapable of recognizing right from wrong or of conforming his or her behavior to the law.

Insight   In Gestalt psychology, a sudden perception of relationships among elements of the "perceptual field," permitting the solution of a problem.

Instinct   An inherited disposition to activate specific behavior patterns that are designed to reach certain goals.

Instrumental competence   Ability to manipulate one's environment to achieve one's goals.

Intelligence A complex and controversial concept. According to David Wechsler (1975), the "capacity . . . to understand the world [and] resourcefulness to cope with its challenges."

Intelligence quotient (IQ) (1) Originally, a ratio obtained by dividing a child's score (or mental age) on an intelligence test by chronological age. (2) Generally, a score on an intelligence test.

Interference theory The view that we may forget stored material because other learning interferes with it.

"Internals" People who perceive the ability to attain reinforcements as being largely within themselves.

Interneuron A neuron that transmits a neural impulse from a sensory neuron to a motor neuron.

Interposition A monocular cue for depth based on the fact that a nearby object obscures a more distant object behind it.

Interpretation An explanation of a client's utterance according to psychoanalytic theory.

Intimacy Close acquaintance and familiarity; a characteristic of a relationship in which partners share their innermost feelings.

Intimacy versus isolation Erikson's life crisis of young adulthood, which is characterized by the task of developing abiding intimate relationships.

Introspection Deliberate looking into one's own mind to examine one's own thoughts and feelings.

Introversion A trait characterized by intense imagination and the tendency to inhibit impulses.

Iris A muscular membrane whose dilation regulates the amount of light that enters the eye.

Just noticeable difference The minimal amount by which a source of energy must be increased or decreased so that a difference in intensity will be perceived.

Kinesthesis The sense that informs us about the positions and motion of parts of our bodies.

Kinship studies Studies that compare the presence of traits and behavior patterns in people who are biologically related or unrelated in order to help determine the role of genetic factors in their occurrence.

La belle indifférence A French term descriptive of the lack of concern sometimes shown by people with conversion disorders.

Language The communication of information by means of symbols arranged according to rules of grammar.

Language acquisition device (LAD) In psycholinguistic theory, neural "prewiring" that facilitates the child's learning of grammar.

Latency A phase of psychosexual development characterized by repression of sexual impulses.

Latent Hidden or concealed.

Latent content In psychodynamic theory, the symbolized or underlying content of dreams.

Lateral hypothalamus An area at the side of the hypothalamus that appears to function as a start-eating center.

Law of effect Thorndike's principle that responses are "stamped in" by rewards and "stamped out" by punishments.

Learned helplessness A model for the acquisition of depressive behavior, based on findings that organisms in aversive situations learn to show inactivity when their operants go unreinforced.

Learning (1) According to behaviorists, a relatively permanent change in behavior that results from experience. (2) According to cognitive theorists, the process by which organisms make relatively permanent changes in the way they represent the environment because of experience. These changes influence the organism's behavior but do not fully determine it.

Lens A transparent body behind the iris that focuses an image on the retina.

Lesbian A female homosexual.

Lesion An injury that results in impaired behavior or loss of a function.

Leukocytes White blood cells. (Derived from the Greek words *leukos*, meaning "white," and *kytos*, literally meaning "a hollow" but used to refer to cells.)

Libido (1) In psychodynamic theory, the energy of Eros; the sexual instinct. (2) Generally, sexual interest or drive.

Limbic system A group of structures involved in memory, motivation, and emotion that forms a fringe along the inner edge of the cerebrum.

Linguistic-relativity hypothesis The view that language structures the way in which we view the world.

Locus of control The place (locus) to which an individual attributes control over the receiving of reinforcers—either inside or outside the self.

Long-term memory The type or stage of memory capable of relatively permanent storage.

Long-term potentiation Enhanced efficiency in synaptic transmission that follows brief, rapid stimulation.

LSD Lysergic acid diethylamide. A hallucinogenic drug.

Magnetic resonance imaging Formation of a computer-generated image of the anatomy of the brain by measuring the signals emitted when the head is placed in a strong magnetic field.

Maintenance rehearsal Mental repetition of information in order to keep it in memory.

Major depression A severe depressive disorder in which the person may show loss of appetite, psychomotor behaviors, and impaired reality testing.

Male erectile disorder A sexual dysfunction in which males fail to obtain erections that are adequate for sexual intercourse.

Manic Elated, showing excessive excitement.

Manifest content In psychodynamic theory, the reported content of dreams.

Marijuana The dried vegetable matter of the *Cannabis sativa* plant.

Matching hypothesis The view that people tend to choose persons similar to themselves in attractiveness and attitudes in the formation of interpersonal relationships.

Maturation The orderly unfolding of traits, as regulated by the genetic code.

Mean A type of average that is calculated by adding all the scores and then dividing by the number of scores.

Means-end analysis A heuristic device in which we try to solve a problem by evaluating the difference between the current situation and the goal.

Median The central score in a frequency distribution; the score beneath which 50% of the cases fall.

Medulla An oblong area of the hindbrain involved in regulation of heartbeat and respiration.

Melatonin A pineal hormone that helps regulate the sleep-wake cycle and may affect the onset of puberty.

Memory The processes by which information is encoded, stored, and retrieved.

Memory trace An assumed change in the nervous system that reflects the impression made by a stimulus. Memory traces are said to be "held" in sensory registers.

Menarche The beginning of menstruation.

Menopause The cessation of menstruation.

Mental age The accumulated months of credit that a person earns on the Stanford-Binet Intelligence Scale. Abbreviated *MA*.

Mental set The tendency to respond to a new problem with an approach that was successfully used with similar problems.

Mescaline A hallucinogenic drug derived from the mescal (peyote) cactus.

Meta-analysis A method for combining and averaging the results of individual research studies.

Metamemory Self-awareness of the ways in which memory functions, allowing the person to encode, store, and retrieve information effectively.

Methaqualone An addictive depressant. Often called "ludes."

Method of constant stimuli A psychophysical method for determining thresholds in which the researcher presents stimuli of various magnitudes and asks the person to report detection.

Method of savings A measure of retention in which the difference between the number of repetitions originally required to learn a list and the number of repetitions required to relearn the list after a certain amount of time has elapsed is calculated.

Middlescence Sheehy's term for a stage of life, from 45 to 55, when people seek new identity and are frequently "lost in a buzz of confusion."

Midlife crisis A crisis experienced by many people during the midlife transition when they realize that life may be more than halfway over and reassess their achievements in terms of their dreams.

Midlife transition Levinson's term for the ages from 40 to 45, which are characterized by a shift in psychological perspective from viewing ourselves in terms of years lived to viewing ourselves in terms of the years we have left.

Migraine headaches Throbbing headaches that are connected with changes in the supply of blood to the head.

Mnemonic devices Systems for remembering in which items are related to easily recalled sets of symbols such as acronyms, phrases, or jingles.

Mode The most frequently occurring number or score in a distribution.

Model In social-cognitive theory, an organism that exhibits behaviors that others will imitate or acquire through observational learning; an organism that engages in a response that is then imitated by another organism.

Modeling A behavior-therapy technique in which a client observes and imitates a person who approaches and copes with feared objects or situations.

Monoamine oxidase inhibitors Antidepressant drugs that work by blocking the action of an enzyme that breaks down noradrenaline and serotonin. Abbreviated *MAO inhibitors*.

Monochromat A person who is sensitive to black and white only and hence color blind.

Monocular cues Stimuli suggestive of depth that can be perceived with only one eye.

Monozygotic (MZ) twins Identical twins; twins who develop from a single zygote, thus carrying the same genetic instructions.

Moral principle The governing principle of the superego, which sets moral standards and enforces adherence to them.

Moratorium Erik Erikson's term for the examination of alternative values and life possibilities while in the throes of an identity crisis.

Morpheme The smallest unit of meaning in a language.

Motion parallax A monocular cue for depth based on the perception that nearby objects appear to move more rapidly in relation to our own motion.

Motive A hypothetical state within an organism that propels the organism toward a goal. (From the Latin *movere*, meaning "to move.")

Motor cortex The section of cortex that lies in the frontal lobe, just across the central fissure from the sensory cortex. Neural impulses in the motor cortex are linked to muscular responses throughout the body.

Multiple approach-avoidance conflict A type of conflict in which each of a number of goals produces approach and avoidance motives.

Multiple personality disorder The previous DSM term for *dissociative identity disorder*.

Mutism Refusal to talk.

Myelin A fatty substance that encases and insulates axons, facilitating transmission of neural impulses.

Myotonia Muscle tension.

Narcolepsy A "sleep attack" in which a person falls asleep suddenly and irresistibly.

Narcotics Drugs used to relieve pain and induce sleep. The term is usually reserved for opiates.

Naturalistic observation A scientific method in which organisms are observed in their natural environments.

Nature In behavior genetics, heredity.

Nearsighted Capable of seeing nearby objects with greater acuity than distant objects.

Need A state of deprivation.

Negative correlation A relationship between two variables in which one variable increases as the other decreases.

Negative reinforcer A reinforcer that when *removed* increases the frequency of an operant.

Neodissociation theory A theory of hypnotic events as the splitting of consciousness.

Neonate A newly born child.

Nerve A bundle of axons and dendrites from many neurons.

Neural impulse The electrochemical discharge of a nerve cell, or neuron.

Neuron A nerve cell.

Neuroticism Eysenck's term for emotional instability; a personality trait characterized largely by persistent anxiety.

Neurotransmitters Chemical substances involved in the transmission of neural impulses from one neuron to another.

Nonconscious Descriptive of bodily processes such as the growing of hair, of which we cannot become conscious. We may "recognize" that our hair is growing but cannot directly experience the biological process.

Non-rapid-eye-movement sleep Stages of sleep 1 through 4. Abbreviated *NREM* sleep.

Nonsense syllables Meaningless sets of two consonants, with a vowel sandwiched in between, that are used to study memory.

Noradrenaline A neurotransmitter whose action is similar to that of the hormone adrenaline and that may play a role in depression.

Normal curve Graphic presentation of a normal distribution, which shows a characteristic bell shape.

Normal distribution A symmetrical distribution that is assumed to reflect chance fluctuations; approximately 68% of cases lie within a standard deviation of the mean.

Nurture In behavior genetics, environmental influences on behavior, such as nutrition, culture, socioeconomic status, and learning.

Objective responsibility According to Piaget, the assignment of blame according to the amount of damage done rather than the motives of the actor.

Objective tests Tests whose items must be answered in a specified, limited manner. Tests whose items have concrete answers that are considered correct.

Object permanence Recognition that objects removed from sight still exist, as demonstrated in young children by continued pursuit.

Observational learning The acquisition of knowledge and skills through the observation of others (who are called *models*) rather than by means of direct experience.

Obsession A recurring thought or image that seems beyond control.

Occipital lobe The lobe that lies behind and below the parietal lobe and behind the temporal lobe.

Oedipus complex Within psychodynamic theory, a conflict of the phallic stage that is characterized by romantic feelings toward the parent of the other gender and feelings of rivalry toward the parent of the same gender.

Olfactory Having to do with the sense of smell.

Olfactory nerve The nerve that transmits information concerning odors from olfactory receptors to the brain.

Operant The same as an operant behavior.

Operant behavior Voluntary responses that are reinforced.

Operant conditioning A simple form of learning in which an organism learns to engage in behavior because it is reinforced.

Opiates A group of narcotics derived from the opium poppy that provide a euphoric rush and depress the nervous system.

Opioids Chemicals that act on opiate receptors but are not derived from the opium poppy.

Opponent-process theory The theory that color vision is made possible by three types of cones, some of which respond to red or green light, some to blue or yellow, and some only to the intensity of light.

Opportunistic diseases Diseases that develop within people whose immune systems are impaired by conditions such as AIDS.

Optic nerve The nerve that transmits sensory information from the eye to the brain.

Oral stage The first stage of psychosexual development, during which gratification is hypothesized to be attained primarily through oral activities.

Organizing effect The directional effect of sex hormones—for example, along stereotypically masculine or feminine lines.

Organ of Corti The receptor for hearing that lies on the basilar membrane in the cochlea.

Orgasm The height or climax of sexual excitement, involving involuntary muscle contractions, release of sexual tensions, and, usually, subjective feelings of pleasure.

Orgasmic disorder A sexual dysfunction in which people have persistent or recurrent problems in reaching orgasm.

Overextension Overgeneralizing the use of words to objects and situations to which they do not apply—a normal characteristic of the speech of young children.

Overregularization The application of regular grammatical rules for forming inflections (e.g., past tense and plurals) to irregular verbs and nouns.

Oxytocin A pituitary hormone that stimulates labor and lactation.

Paired associates Nonsense syllables presented in pairs in experiments that measure recall.

Panic disorder The recurrent experiencing of attacks of extreme anxiety in the absence of external stimuli that usually elicit anxiety.

Paranoid personality disorder A disorder characterized by persistent suspiciousness, but not involving the disorganization of paranoid schizophrenia.

Paranoid schizophrenia A type of schizophrenia characterized primarily by delusions—commonly of persecution—and by vivid hallucinations.

Parasympathetic nervous system The branch of the autonomic nervous system that is most active during processes that restore reserves of energy to the body, such as relaxing and eating. When people relax, the parasympathetic nervous system decelerates the heart rate, normalizes the blood pressure, relaxes muscles, and so on. The parasympathetic division also stimulates digestion.

Parietal lobe The lobe of the brain that lies just behind the central fissure.

Partial reinforcement One of several reinforcement schedules in which not every correct response is reinforced.

Passion Strong romantic and sexual feelings.

Passive smoking Inhaling of smoke from the tobacco products and exhalations of other people; also called *second-hand smoking*.

Pathogen A microscopic organism (e.g., bacterium or virus) that can cause disease.

Perception The process by which sensations are organized into an inner representation of the world.

Perceptual organization The tendency to integrate perceptual elements into meaningful patterns.

Performance anxiety Anxiety concerning one's ability to perform, especially when performance may be evaluated by other people.

Period of the ovum Another term for the *germinal stage*.

Peripheral nervous system The part of the nervous system consisting of the somatic nervous system and the autonomic nervous system.

Permissive parents Parents who impose few, if any, rules and who do not supervise their children closely.

Personal fable Another aspect of adolescent egocentrism: The belief that our feelings and ideas are special and unique and that we are invulnerable.

Personality The distinct patterns of behavior, thoughts, and feelings that characterize a person's adaptation to life.

Personality disorders Enduring patterns of maladaptive behavior that are sources of distress to the individual or others.

Personal space   A psychological boundary that surrounds a person and serves protective functions.

Person variables   Factors within the person, such as expectancies and competencies, that influence behavior.

Perspective   A monocular cue for depth based on the convergence (coming together) of parallel lines as they recede into the distance.

Phallic stage   The third stage of psychosexual development, characterized by a shift of libido to the phallic region. (From the Greek *phallos*, referring to an image of the penis. However, Freud used the term *phallic* to refer both to boys and girls.)

Phallic symbol   A sign that represents the penis.

Phencyclidine   Another hallucinogenic drug whose name is an acronym for its chemical structure. Abbreviated *PCP*.

Pheromones   Chemical secretions detected by other members of the same species that stimulate stereotypical behaviors.

Phi phenomenon   The perception of movement as a result of sequential presentation of visual stimuli.

Phoneme   A basic sound in a language.

Phonology   The study of the basic sounds in a language.

Photoreceptors   Cells that respond to light.

Physiological drives   Unlearned drives with a biological basis, such as hunger, thirst, and avoidance of pain.

Pitch   The highness or lowness of a sound, as determined by the frequency of the sound waves.

Pituitary gland   The gland that secretes growth hormone, prolactin, antidiuretic hormone, and other hormones.

Placebo   A bogus treatment that has the appearance of being genuine.

Placenta   A membrane that permits the exchange of nutrients and waste products between the mother and her developing child but does not allow the maternal and fetal bloodstreams to mix.

Place theory   The theory that the pitch of a sound is determined by the section of the basilar membrane that vibrates in response to the sound.

Plateau phase   The second phase of the sexual response cycle, which is characterized by increases in vasocongestion, muscle tension, heart rate, and blood pressure in preparation for orgasm.

Pleasure principle   The governing principle of the id—the seeking of immediate gratification of instinctive needs.

Polarization   In social psychology, taking an extreme position or attitude on an issue.

Polarize   To ready a neuron for firing by creating an internal negative charge in relation to the body fluid outside the cell membrane.

Pons   A structure of the hindbrain involved in respiration, attention, and sleep and dreaming.

Population   A complete group of organisms or events from which a sample is selected.

Positive correlation   A relationship between variables in which one variable increases as the other also increases.

Positive reinforcer   A reinforcer that when *presented* increases the frequency of an operant.

Positron emission tomography   Formation of a computer-generated image of the neural activity of parts of the brain by tracing the amount of glucose used by the various parts. Abbreviated *PET scan*.

Postconventional level   According to Kohlberg, a period during which moral judgments are derived from moral principles and people look to themselves to set moral standards.

Postformal thought   An hypothesized stage of cognitive development that follows formal operational thought and is characterized by

creative thinking, the ability to solve complex problems, and the posing of new questions.

Posttraumatic stress disorder   A disorder that follows a distressing event outside the range of normal human experience and that is characterized by features such as intense fear, avoidance of stimuli associated with the event, and reliving of the event. Abbreviated *PTSD*.

Preconscious   In psychodynamic theory, descriptive of material that is not in awareness but can be brought into awareness by focusing one's attention.

Preconventional level   According to Kohlberg, a period during which moral judgments are based largely on expectation of rewards or punishments.

Prefrontal lobotomy   The severing or destruction of a section of the frontal lobe of the brain.

Prejudice   The unfounded belief that a person or group—on the basis of assumed racial, ethnic, sexual, or other features—will possess negative characteristics or perform inadequately.

Premature ejaculation   Ejaculation that occurs before the couple are satisfied with the length of sexual relations.

Preoperational stage   The second of Piaget's stages, characterized by illogical use of words and symbols, spotty logic, and egocentrism.

Presbyopia   A condition characterized by brittleness of the lens.

Primacy effect   In memory, the tendency to recall the initial items in a series of items; in social psychology, the tendency to evaluate others in terms of first impressions.

Primary drives   Unlearned, or physiological, drives.

Primary mental abilities   According to Thurstone, the basic abilities that make up intelligence.

Primary reinforcer   An unlearned reinforcer.

Proactive interference   The interference by old learning with the ability to retrieve material learned recently.

Progesterone   A female sex hormone that promotes growth of the sex organs and helps maintain pregnancy.

Programmed learning   A method of learning in which complex tasks are broken down into simple steps, each of which is reinforced. Errors are not reinforced.

Programmed senescence   The view that aging is determined by a biological clock that ticks at a rate governed by genes.

Projective test   A psychological test that presents ambiguous stimuli onto which the test taker projects his or her own personality in making a response.

Prolactin   A pituitary hormone that regulates production of milk and, in lower animals, maternal behavior.

Prospective memory   Memory to perform an act in the future, as at a certain time or when a certain event occurs.

Prototype   A concept of a category of objects or events that serves as a good example of the category.

Proximity   Nearness. The perceptual tendency to group together objects that are near one another.

Psychedelic   Causing hallucinations, delusions, or heightened perceptions.

Psychic structure   In psychodynamic theory, a hypothesized mental structure that helps explain different aspects of behavior.

Psychoactive substances   Drugs that have psychological effects such as stimulation or distortion of perceptions.

Psychoanalysis   The school of psychology that emphasizes the importance of unconscious motives and conflicts as determinants of human behavior; Freud's method of psychotherapy and of exploring human personality.

Psychodynamic   Referring to Freud's theory, which proposes that the motion of underlying forces of personality determines our thoughts, feelings, and behavior.

Psychodynamic theory   Sigmund Freud's perspective, which emphasizes the importance of unconscious motives and conflicts as forces that determine behavior. *Dynamic* refers to the concept of (psychological) forces being in motion.

Psycholinguistic theory   The view that language learning involves an interaction between environmental factors and an inborn tendency to acquire language.

Psychological disorders   Patterns of behavior or mental processes that are connected with emotional distress or significant impairment in functioning.

Psychological hardiness   A cluster of traits that buffer stress and are characterized by commitment, challenge, and control.

Psychology   The science that studies behavior and mental processes.

Psychomotor retardation   Slowness in motor activity and (apparently) in thought.

Psychoneuroimmunology   The field that studies the relationships between psychological factors (e.g., attitudes and overt behavior patterns) and the functioning of the immune system.

Psychophysical   Bridging the gap between the physical and psychological worlds.

Psychophysicist   A person who studies the relationships between physical stimuli (such as light or sound) and their perception.

Psychosexual development   In psychodynamic theory, the process by which libidinal energy is expressed through different erogenous zones during different stages of development.

Psychosocial development   Erikson's theory of personality and development, which emphasizes social relationships and eight stages of growth.

Psychosurgery   Surgery intended to promote psychological changes or to relieve disordered behavior.

Psychotherapy   A systematic interaction between a therapist and a client that brings psychological principles to bear on influencing the client's thoughts, feelings, or behavior to help that client overcome abnormal behavior or adjust to problems in living.

Puberty   The period of physical development during which sexual reproduction first becomes possible.

Punishment   An unpleasant stimulus that suppresses the behavior it follows.

Pupil   The apparently black opening in the center of the iris, through which light enters the eye.

Pure research   Research conducted without concern for immediate applications.

Random sample   A sample drawn so that each member of a population has an equal chance of being selected to participate.

Range   A measure of variability defined as the high score in a distribution minus the low score.

Rapid-eye-movement sleep   A stage of sleep characterized by rapid eye movements, which have been linked to dreaming. Abbreviated *REM* sleep.

Rapid flight of ideas   Rapid speech and topic changes, characteristic of manic behavior.

Rapid smoking   An aversive conditioning method for quitting smoking in which the smoker inhales every 6 seconds, thus rendering once-desirable cigarette smoke aversive.

Rational emotive behavior therapy   Albert Ellis's form of therapy that encourages clients to challenge and correct irrational expectations and maladaptive behaviors.

Reaction time   The amount of time required to respond to a stimulus.

Reality principle   Consideration of what is practical and possible in gratifying needs; the governing principle of the ego.

Reality testing   The capacity to perceive one's environment and oneself according to accurate sensory impressions.

Reasoning   The transforming of information to reach conclusions.

Rebound anxiety   Strong anxiety that can attend the suspension of usage of a tranquilizer.

Recall   Retrieval or reconstruction of learned material.

Recency effect   In memory, the tendency to recall the last items in a series of items; in social psychology, the tendency to evaluate others in terms of the most recent impression.

Receptor site   A location on a dendrite of a receiving neuron tailored to receive a neurotransmitter.

Reciprocal determinism   Bandura's term for the social-cognitive view that people influence their environment just as their environment influences them.

Reciprocity   In interpersonal attraction, the tendency to return feelings and attitudes that are expressed about us.

Recognition   In information processing, the easiest memory task, involving identification of objects or events encountered before.

Reflex   A simple unlearned response to a stimulus.

Refractory period   A phase following firing during which a neuron is less sensitive to messages from other neurons and will not fire; in the sexual response cycle, a period of time following orgasm during which an individual is not responsive to sexual stimulation.

Reinforce   To follow a response with a stimulus that increases the frequency of the response.

Reinforcement   A stimulus that follows a response and increases the frequency of the response.

Relearning   A measure of retention. Material is usually relearned more quickly than it is learned initially.

Replicate   Repeat, reproduce, copy.

Representativeness heuristic   A decision-making heuristic in which people make judgments about samples according to the populations they appear to represent.

Repression   In psychodynamic theory, the automatic (unconscious) ejection of anxiety-evoking ideas, impulses, or images from awareness; a defense mechanism that protects the person from anxiety.

Resistance   The tendency to block the free expression of impulses and primitive ideas from awareness—a reflection of the defense mechanism of repression.

Resistance stage   The second stage of the general adaptation syndrome, characterized by prolonged sympathetic activity in an effort to restore lost energy and repair damage. Also called the *adaptation stage*.

Resolution phase   The fourth phase of the sexual response cycle, during which the body gradually returns to its prearoused state.

Response set   A tendency to answer test items according to a bias—for instance, to make oneself seem perfect or bizarre.

Response set theory   The view that response expectancies play a key role in the production of the experiences suggested by a hypnotist.

Resting potential   The electrical potential across the neural membrane when it is not responding to other neurons.

Reticular activating system   A part of the brain involved in attention, sleep, and arousal.

Retina   The area of the inner surface of the eye that contains rods and cones.

Retinal disparity   A binocular cue for depth based on the difference in the image cast by an object on the retinas of the eyes as the object moves closer or farther away.

Retrieval   The location of stored information and its return to consciousness; the third stage of information processing.

Retroactive interference   The interference of new learning with the ability to retrieve material learned previously.

Retrograde amnesia   Failure to remember events that occur prior to physical trauma because of the effects of the trauma.

Retrospective memory   Memory for past events, activities, and learning experiences, as shown by explicit (episodic and semantic) and implicit memories.

Reversibility   According to Piaget, recognition that processes can be undone, that things can be made as they were.

Risky shift   The tendency to make riskier decisions as a member of a group than as an individual acting independently.

Rods   Rod-shaped photoreceptors that are sensitive only to the intensity of light.

Role diffusion   Erikson's term for lack of clarity in one's life roles (due to failure to develop ego identity).

Role theory   A theory that explains hypnotic events in terms of the person's ability to *act as though* he or she were hypnotized. Role theory differs from faking in that participants cooperate and focus on hypnotic suggestions instead of pretending to be hypnotized.

Romantic love   An intense, positive emotion that involves sexual attraction, feelings of caring, and the belief that one is in love.

Rooting   The turning of an infant's head toward a touch, such as by the mother's nipple.

Rote   Mechanical associative learning that is based on repetition.

s   Spearman's symbol for *specific* factors, or *s factors*, which he believed accounted for individual abilities.

Saccadic eye movement   The rapid jumps made by a person's eyes as they fixate on different points.

Sample   Part of a population.

Satiety   The state of being satisfied; fullness.

Savings   The difference between the number of repetitions originally required to learn a list and the number of repetitions required to relearn the list after a certain amount of time has elapsed.

Schema   A way of mentally representing the world, such as a belief or an expectation, that can influence perception of persons, objects, and situations.

Scheme   According to Piaget, a hypothetical mental structure that permits the classification and organization of new information.

Schizoid personality disorder   A disorder characterized by social withdrawal.

Schizophrenia   A psychotic disorder characterized by loss of control of thought processes and inappropriate emotional responses.

Schizotypal personality disorder   A disorder characterized by oddities of thought and behavior, but not involving bizarre psychotic behaviors.

Secondary reinforcer   A stimulus that gains reinforcement value through association with established reinforcers.

Secondary sex characteristics   Characteristics that distinguish the sexes, such as distribution of body hair and depth of voice, but that are not directly involved in reproduction.

Sedative   A drug that relieves nervousness or agitation, or puts one to sleep.

Selection factor   A source of bias that may occur in research findings when participants are allowed to choose for themselves a certain treatment in a scientific study.

Selective attention   The focus of one's consciousness on a particular stimulus.

Selective avoidance   Diverting one's attention from information that is inconsistent with one's attitudes.

Selective exposure   Deliberately seeking and attending to information that is consistent with one's attitudes.

Self-actualization   According to Maslow and other humanistic psychologists, self-initiated striving to become what one is capable of being; the motive for reaching one's full potential, for expressing one's unique capabilities.

Self-efficacy expectations   Beliefs to the effect that one can handle a task; our beliefs that we can bring about desired changes through our own efforts.

Self-ideal   A mental image of what we believe we ought to be.

Self-monitoring   Keeping a record of one's own behavior to identify problems and record successes.

Self-serving bias   The tendency to view one's successes as stemming from internal factors and one's failures as stemming from external factors.

Semantic code   Mental representation of information according to its meaning.

Semanticity   Meaning; the quality of language in which words are used as symbols for objects, events, or ideas.

Semantic memory   General knowledge as opposed to episodic memory.

Semantics   The study of the meanings of a language—the relationships between language and objects and events.

Semicircular canals   Structures of the inner ear that monitor body movement and position.

Seminal fluid   The fluid produced by the prostate and other glands that carries and nourishes sperm. Also called *semen*.

Sensation   The stimulation of sensory receptors and the transmission of sensory information to the central nervous system.

Sensitization   The type of sensory adaptation in which we become more sensitive to stimuli that are low in magnitude. Also called *positive adaptation*.

Sensorimotor stage   The first of Piaget's stages of cognitive development, characterized by coordination of sensory information and motor activity, early exploration of the environment, and lack of language.

Sensorineural deafness   The forms of deafness that result from damage to hair cells or the auditory nerve.

Sensory adaptation   The processes by which organisms become more sensitive to stimuli that are low in magnitude and less sensitive to stimuli that are constant or ongoing in magnitude.

Sensory memory   The type or stage of memory first encountered by a stimulus. Sensory memory holds impressions briefly, but long enough so that series of perceptions are psychologically continuous.

Sensory register   A system of memory that holds information briefly, but long enough so that it can be processed further. There may be a sensory register for every sense.

Serial-position effect   The tendency to recall more accurately the first and last items in a series.

Serotonin   A neurotransmitter, deficiencies of which have been linked to affective disorders, anxiety, and insomnia.

Serotonin-uptake inhibitors   Antidepressant drugs that work by blocking the reuptake of serotonin by presynaptic neurons.

Serum cholesterol   Cholesterol found in the blood.

Sex chromosomes   The 23rd pair of chromosomes, which determine whether a child will be male or female.

Sex therapy   A collective term for short-term cognitive-behavioral models for treatment of sexual dysfunctions.

Sexual dysfunction   A persistent or recurrent problem in becoming sexually aroused or reaching orgasm.

Sexual harassment   Deliberate or repeated verbal comments, gestures, or physical contact of a sexual nature that is unwanted by the recipient.

Sexual orientation   The directionality of one's erotic interests—that is, whether one is sexually attracted to, and interested in forming romantic relationships with, people of the other or the same gender.

Sexual response cycle   Masters and Johnson's model of sexual response, which consists of four stages or phases.

Shadowing   A monocular cue for depth based on the fact that opaque objects block light and produce shadows.

Shape constancy   The tendency to perceive an object as being the same shape although the retinal image varies in shape as it rotates.

Shaping   A procedure for teaching complex behaviors that at first reinforces approximations of the target behavior.

Short-term memory   The type or stage of memory that can hold information for up to a minute or so after the trace of the stimulus decays. Also called *working memory*.

Signal-detection theory   The view that the perception of sensory stimuli involves the interaction of physical, biological, and psychological factors.

Similarity   The perceptual tendency to group together objects that are similar in appearance.

Simultaneous conditioning   A classical conditioning procedure in which the conditioned stimulus and unconditioned stimulus are presented at the same time.

Situational attribution   An assumption that a person's behavior is determined by external circumstances such as the social pressure found in a situation.

Size constancy   The tendency to perceive an object as being the same size even as the size of its retinal image changes according to the object's distance.

Sleep terrors   Frightening dreamlike experiences that occur during the deepest stage of NREM sleep. Nightmares, in contrast, occur during REM sleep.

Social-cognitive theory   A cognitively oriented learning theory in which observational learning and person variables such as values and expectancies play major roles in individual differences; a school of psychology in the behaviorist tradition that includes cognitive factors in the explanation and prediction of behavior. Formerly termed *social-learning theory*.

Social decision schemes   Rules for predicting the final outcome of group decision making on the basis of the members' initial positions.

Social facilitation   The process by which a person's performance is increased when other members of a group engage in similar behavior.

Social influence   The area of social psychology that studies the ways in which people influence the thoughts, feelings, and behavior of others.

Socialization   Guidance of people into socially desirable behavior by means of verbal messages, the systematic use of rewards and punishments, and other methods of teaching.

Social norms   Explicit and implicit rules that reflect social expectations and influence the ways people behave in social situations.

Social perception   A subfield of social psychology that studies the ways in which we form and modify impressions of others.

Social phobia   An irrational, excessive fear of public scrutiny.

Social psychology   The field of psychology that studies the nature and causes of people's thoughts and behavior in social situations.

Sociocultural perspective   The view that focuses on the roles of ethnicity, gender, culture, and socioeconomic status in personality formation, behavior, and mental processes.

Socioeconomic status   One's social and financial level, as indicated by measures such as income, level of education, and occupational status. Abbreviated *SES*.

Somatic nervous system   The division of the peripheral nervous system that connects the central nervous system with sensory receptors, skeletal muscles, and the surface of the body.

Somatoform disorders   Disorders in which people complain of physical (somatic) problems even though no physical abnormality can be found.

Somatosensory cortex   The section of cortex in which sensory stimulation is projected. It lies just behind the central fissure in the parietal lobe.

Specific phobia   Persistent fear of a specific object or situation.

Spinal cord   A column of nerves within the spine that transmits messages from sensory receptors to the brain and from the brain to muscles and glands throughout the body.

Spinal reflex   A simple, unlearned response to a stimulus that may involve only two neurons.

Spontaneous recovery   The recurrence of an extinguished response as a function of the passage of time.

Standard deviation   A measure of the variability of a distribution, obtained by the formula

$$\text{S.D.} = \sqrt{\frac{\text{Sum of } d^2}{N}}$$

Standardized test   A test that is given to a large number of respondents so that data concerning the typical responses can be accumulated and analyzed.

State-dependent memory   Information that is better retrieved in the physiological or emotional state in which it was encoded and stored, or learned.

Statistics   Numerical facts assembled in such a manner that they provide useful information about measures or scores. (From the Latin *status*, meaning "standing" or "position.")

Stereotype   A fixed, conventional idea about a group.

Stereotype vulnerability The tendency to focus on a conventional, negative belief about one's group, such that the individual risks behaving in a way that confirms that belief.

Stimulant A drug that increases activity of the nervous system.

Stimulus An environmental condition that elicits a response.

Stimulus motives Motives to increase the stimulation impinging upon an organism.

Storage The maintenance of information over time; the second stage of information processing.

Stratified sample A sample drawn so that identified subgroups in the population are represented proportionately in the sample.

Stress The demand that is made on an organism to adapt.

Stroboscopic motion A visual illusion in which the perception of motion is generated by a series of stationary images that are presented in rapid succession.

Structuralism The school of psychology that argues that the mind consists of three basic elements—sensations, feelings, and images—that combine to form experience.

Stupor A condition in which the senses and thoughts are dulled.

Subjective moral judgment According to Piaget, moral judgments that are based on the motives of the perpetrator.

Subjective value The desirability of an object or event.

Substance abuse Persistent use of a substance even though it is causing or compounding problems in meeting the demands of life.

Successive approximations In operant conditioning, a series of behaviors that gradually become more similar to a target behavior.

Superego The third psychic structure, which functions as a moral guardian and sets forth high standards for behavior.

Suppression The deliberate, or conscious, placing of certain ideas, impulses, or images out of awareness.

Survey A method of scientific investigation in which a large sample of people answer questions about their attitudes or behavior.

Sympathetic The branch of the ANS that is most active during emotional responses such as fear and anxiety that spend the body's reserves of energy.

Sympathetic nervous system The branch of the autonomic nervous system that is most active during processes that spend body energy from stored reserves, such as in a fight-or-flight reaction to a predator or when you are anxious about a big test. When people experience fear, the sympathetic nervous system accelerates the heart rate, raises the blood pressure, tenses muscles, and so on.

Synapse A junction between the axon terminals of one neuron and the dendrites or cell body of another neuron.

Syphilis An STI that is caused by the *Treponema pallidum* bacterium, which may progress through several stages of development—from a chancre to a skin rash to eventually damaging the cardiovascular or central nervous systems.

Systematic desensitization Wolpe's behavioral fear-reduction technique in which a hierarchy of fear-evoking stimuli is presented while the person remains relaxed.

Systematic random search An algorithm for solving problems in which each possible solution is tested according to a particular set of rules.

Taste buds The sensory organs for taste. They contain taste cells and are located on the tongue.

Taste cells Receptor cells that are sensitive to taste.

Temporal lobe The lobe of the brain that lies below the lateral fissure, near the temples of the head.

Testosterone A male sex hormone produced by the testes that promotes growth of male sexual characteristics and sperm and that has activating effects on sexual arousal.

Texture gradient A monocular cue for depth based on the perception that closer objects appear to have rougher (more detailed) surfaces.

Thalamus An area near the center of the brain involved in the relay of sensory information to the cortex and in the functions of sleep and attention.

Theory A formulation of relationships underlying observed events.

Theory of social comparison The view that people look to others for cues about how to behave when they are in confusing or unfamiliar situations.

Theta waves Slow brain waves produced during the hypnagogic state.

Thyroxin The thyroid hormone that increases metabolic rate.

Time out Removal of an organism from a situation in which reinforcement is available when unwanted behavior is shown.

Tip-of-the-tongue (TOT) phenomenon The feeling that information is stored in memory although it cannot be readily retrieved. Also called the *feeling-of-knowing experience*.

Token economy A controlled environmental setting that fosters desired behavior by reinforcing it with tokens (secondary reinforcers) that can be exchanged for other reinforcers.

Tolerance Habituation to a drug, with the result that increasingly higher doses of the drug are needed to achieve similar effects.

Top-down processing The use of contextual information or knowledge of a pattern in order to organize parts of the pattern.

Trace conditioning A classical conditioning procedure in which the conditioned stimulus is presented and then removed before the unconditioned stimulus is presented.

Trait A relatively stable aspect of personality that is inferred from behavior and assumed to give rise to consistent behavior.

Transcendental meditation (TM) The simplified form of meditation brought to the United States by the Maharishi Mahesh Yogi and used as a method for coping with stress.

Transference Responding to one person (such as a spouse or the psychoanalyst) in a way that is similar to the way one responded to another person (such as a parent) in childhood.

Treatment In experiments, a condition received by participants so that its effects may be observed.

Triangular model of love Steinberg's view that love involves combinations of three components: intimacy, passion, and decision/commitment.

Trichromat A person with normal color vision.

Trichromatic theory The theory that color vision is made possible by three types of cones, some of which respond to red light, some to green, and some to blue. (From the Greek roots *treis*, meaning "three," and *chroma*, meaning "color.")

Tricyclic antidepressants Antidepressant drugs that work by preventing the reuptake of noradrenaline and serotonin by transmitting neurons.

Trust versus mistrust Erikson's first stage of psychosexual development, during which children do—or do not—come to

G-17

trust that primary caregivers and the environment will meet their needs.

Trying 20s Sheehy's term for the third decade of life, when people are frequently occupied with advancement in the career world.

Two-point threshold The least distance by which two rods touching the skin must be separated before the person will report that there are two rods, not one, on 50% of occasions.

Type A behavior Behavior characterized by a sense of time urgency, competitiveness, and hostility.

Umbilical cord A tube between the mother and her developing child through which nutrients and waste products are conducted.

Unconditional positive regard A persistent expression of esteem for the value of a person, but not necessarily an unqualified acceptance of all of the person's behaviors.

Unconditioned response (UR) An unlearned response to an unconditioned stimulus.

Unconditioned stimulus (US) A stimulus that elicits a response from an organism prior to conditioning.

Unconscious In psychodynamic theory, descriptive of ideas and feelings that are not available to awareness by simple focusing of attention.

Uplifts Notable pleasant daily conditions and experiences.

Vaginismus A sexual dysfunction characterized by involuntary contraction of the muscles surrounding the vagina, preventing entry by the penis or making entry painful.

Validity scales Groups of test items that indicate whether a person's responses accurately reflect that individual's traits.

Variable-interval schedule A schedule in which a variable amount of time must elapse between the previous and subsequent times that reinforcement is available.

Variable-ratio schedule A schedule in which reinforcement is provided after a variable number of correct responses.

Vasocongestion Engorgement of blood vessels with blood, which swells the genitals and breasts during sexual arousal.

Ventromedial nucleus A central area on the underside of the hypothalamus that appears to function as a stop-eating center.

Vestibular sense The sense of equilibrium that informs us about our bodies' positions relative to gravity.

Visible light The part of the electromagnetic spectrum that stimulates the eye and produces visual sensations.

Visual acuity Sharpness of vision.

Visual code Mental representation of information as a picture.

Volunteer bias A source of bias or error in research reflecting the prospect that people who offer to participate in research studies differ systematically from people who do not.

Waxy flexibility A feature of catatonic schizophrenia in which persons maintain postures into which they are placed.

Wear-and-tear theory The view that factors such as pollution, disease, and ultraviolet light contribute to wear and tear on the body, so that the body loses the ability to repair itself.

Weber's constant The fraction of the intensity by which a source of physical energy must be increased or decreased so that a difference in intensity will be perceived.

Wernicke-Korsakoff syndrome A cluster of symptoms associated with chronic alcohol abuse and characterized by confusion, memory impairment, and filling in gaps in memory with false information (confabulation).

Wernicke's aphasia A language disorder characterized by difficulty comprehending the meaning of spoken language.

White matter In the spinal cord, axon bundles that carry messages from and to the brain.

Wisdom Expert knowledge concerning the meaning of life, concern for people's welfare, and a push toward excellence.

Wish fulfillment A primitive method used by the id to attempt to gratify basic instincts.

Working memory Same as *short-term memory*.

Zygote A fertilized ovum (egg cell).

Abbey, A. (1987). Misperceptions of friendly behavior as sexual interest. *Psychology of Women Quarterly, 11,* 173–194.

A behavior transplant (1997, March 11). *The New York Times,* p. C3.

Abeles, N. (1997). Memory problems in later life. *APA Monitor, 28*(6), 2.

Aber, J. L., & Allen, J. P. (1987). Effects of maltreatment of young children on young children's socioemotional development. *Developmental Psychology, 23,* 406–414.

Abramowitz, A. J., & O'Leary, S. G. (1991). Behavioral interventions for the classroom. *School Psychology Review, 20,* 220–234.

Ackerman, P. L., & Heggestad, E. D. (1997). Intelligence, personality, and interests. *Psychological Bulletin, 121,* 219–245.

Adam, B. D., Sears, A., & Schellenberg, E. G. (2000). Accounting for unsafe sex: Interviews with men who have sex with men. *Journal of Sex Research, 37*(1), 24–36.

Ader, D. N., & Johnson, S. B. (1994). Sample description, reporting, and analysis of sex in psychological research. *American Psychologist, 49,* 216–218.

Adeyemo, S. A. (1990). Thinking imagery and problem-solving. *Psychological Studies, 35,* 179–190.

Adler, N. E., and others (1994). Socioeconomic status and health. *American Psychologist, 49,* 15–24.

Adler, S. (1998). Cited in McGuire, P. A. (1998). Wanted: Workers with flexibility for 21st century jobs. *APA Monitor, 29*(7), 10, 12.

Adler, T. (1990). Distraction, relaxation can help "shut off" pain. *APA Monitor, 21*(9), 11.

Adler, T. (1993a). Shy, bold temperament? It's mostly in the genes. *APA Monitor, 24*(1), 7, 8.

Adler, T. (1993b). Sleep loss impairs attention and more. *APA Monitor, 24*(9), 22–23.

Agras, W. S., Walsh, T., Fairburn, C. G., Wilson, G. T., & Kraemer, H. C. (2000). A multicenter comparison of cognitive-behavioral therapy and interpersonal psychotherapy for bulimia nervosa. *Archives of General Psychiatry, 57*(5), 459–466.

Ainsworth, M. D. S., Blehar, M. C., Waters, E., & Wall, S. (1978). *Patterns of attachment: A psychological study of the strange situation.* Hillsdale, NJ: Erlbaum.

Ainsworth, M. D. S., & Bowlby, J. (1991). An ethological approach to personality development. *American Psychologist, 46,* 333–341.

Akhtar, N., & Bradley, E. J. (1991). Social information processing deficits of aggressive children. *Clinical Psychology Review, 11,* 621–644.

Albarracín, D., & Wyer, R. S. Jr. (2000). The cognitive impact of past behavior: Influences on beliefs, attitudes, and future behavioral decisions. *Journal of Personality and Social Psychology, 79*(1), 5–22.

Albert Ellis Institute. (1997). Albert Ellis Institute for Rational Emotive Behavior Therapy Brochure, September '97–March '98. New York (45 East 65th: Author).

Alexander, C. N., et al. (1996). Trial of stress reduction for hypertension in older African Americans: II. Sex and risk subgroup analysis. *Hypertension, 28,* 228–237.

Alexander, R. A., & Barrett, G. U. (1982). Equitable salary increase judgments based upon merit and nonmerit considerations: A cross-national comparison. *International Review of Applied Psychology, 31,* 443–454.

Allen, L. (1993, August). Integrating a sociocultural perspective into the psychology curriculum. G. Stanley Hall lecture presented to the American Psychological Association, Toronto, Canada.

Allison, K. W., Crawford, I., Echemendia, R., Robinson, L. V., & Knepp, D. (1994). Human diversity and professional competence. *American Psychologist, 49,* 792–796.

Alloy, L. B., Abramson, L. Y., & Dykman, B. M. (1990). Depressive realism and nondepressive optimistic illusions. In R. E. Ingram (Ed.), *Contemporary psychological approaches to depression.* New York: Plenum.

Allport, G. W., & Oddbert, H. S. (1936). Trait names: A psycholexical study. *Psychological Monographs, 47,* 1–36.

Amabile, T. M. (1990). Within you, without you: The social psychology of creativity, and beyond. In M. A. Runco & R. S. Albert (Eds.), *Theories of creativity.* Newbury Park, NY: Sage.

American Association of University Women. (1992). *How schools shortchange women: The A.A.U.W. report.* Washington, D.C.: American Association of University Women Educational Foundation.

American Heart Association online (2000a). *2000 heart and stroke statistical update.* http://www.americanheart.org.

American Heart Association online (2000b). Am I at risk? A special message for African Americans. http://www.americanheart.org/hbp/risk_afam.html.

American Lung Association (2000). Smoking fact sheet, http://www.lungusa.org.

American Psychiatric Association (2000). *Diagnostic and statistical manual of mental disorders. DSM-IV-TR* (4th ed.). Washington, D.C.: Author.

American Psychological Association (1992a). Ethical principles of psychologists and code of conduct. *American Psychologist, 47,* 1597–1611.

American Psychological Association (1992b). *Guidelines for ethical conduct in the care and use of animals.* Washington, D.C.: Author.

American Psychological Association. (1993). Guidelines for providers of psychological services to ethnic, linguistic, and culturally diverse populations. *American Psychologist, 48,* 45–48.

American Psychological Association. (1994). *Publication manual of the American Psychological Association* (4th ed.). Washington, D.C.: Author.

American Psychological Association (1998, March 16). Sexual harassment: Myths and realities. APA Public Information Home Page; www.apa.org.

American Psychological Association Research Office (2000). First-year (full-time) students in doctoral-level departments of psychology by race/ethnicity: 1999–2000. *Graduate Study in Psychology 2000.* Washington, D.C.: American Psychological Association.

Andersen, B. L. (1996). Psychological and behavioral studies in cancer prevention and control. *Health Psychology, 15,* 411–412.

Andersen, B. L., Kiecolt-Glaser, J. K., & Glaser, R. (1994). A biobehavioral model of cancer stress and disease course. *American Psychologist, 49,* 389–404.

Anderson, C. A., & DeNeve, K. M. (1992). Temperature, aggression, and the negative affect escape model. *Psychological Bulletin, 111,* 347–351.

Anderson, C. A., & Dill, K. E. (2000). Video games and aggressive thoughts, feelings, and behavior in the laboratory and in life. *Journal of Personality and Social Psychology, 78*(4), 772–790.

Anderson, E. S., Winett, R. A., & Wojcik, J. R. (2000). Social-cognitive determinants of nutrition behavior among supermarket food shoppers: A structural equation analysis. *Health Psychology, 19*(5), 479–486.

Anderson, J. R. (1991). Is human cognition adaptive? *Behavioral and Brain Sciences, 14,* 471–517.

Andrews, B., & Brown, G. W. (1993). Self-esteem and vulnerability to depression. *Journal of Abnormal Psychology, 102,* 565–572.

Angier, N. (1994a). Benefits of broccoli confirmed as chemical blocks tumors. *The New York Times,* p. C11.

Angier, N. (1994b). Factor in female sexuality. *The New York Times,* p. C13.

Angier, N. (1995, May 14). Why science loses women in the ranks. *The New York Times,* p. E5.

Angier, N. (1996, January 2). Variant gene tied to a love of new thrills. *The New York Times,* pp. A1, B11.

Angier, N. (1997). Chemical tied to fat control could help trigger puberty. *The New York Times,* pp. C1, C3.

Antonuccio, D. (1995). Psychotherapy for depression: No stronger medicine. *American Psychologist, 50,* 452–454.

Archer, J. (1996). Sex differences in social behavior. *American Psychologist, 51,* 909–917.

Archer, J. (2000). Sex differences in aggression between heterosexual partners: A meta-analytic review. *Psychological Bulletin, 126*(5), 651–680.

Arendt, J. (2000). Melatonin, circadian rhythms, and sleep. *The New England Journal of Medicine online, 343*(15).

Archer, S. L. (1991). Gender differences in identity development. In R. M. Lerner, A. C. Peterson, & J. Brooks-Gunn (Eds.), *Encyclopedia of Adolescence, I.* New York: Garland.

Archer, S. L. (1992). A feminist's approach to identity research. In G. R. Adams, T. P. Gullotta, & R. Montemayor (Eds.), *Adolescent Identity Formation.* Newbury Park, CA: Sage.

Argyris, C. (1972). *The applicability of organizational psychology.* Cambridge: Cambridge University Press.

Arkin, R. M., & Hermann, A. D. (2000). Constructing desirable identities—Self-presentation in psychotherapy and daily life: Comment on Kelly (2000). *Psychological Bulletin, 126*(4), 501–504.

Armeli, S., Carney, M. A., Tennen, H., Affleck, G., & O'Neil. (2000). Stress and alcohol use: A daily process examination of the stressor-vulnerability model. *Journal of Personality and Social Psychology, 78*(5), 979–994.

Arnett, J. J. (2000). Emerging adulthood. *American Psychologist, 55*(5), 469–480.

Arnold, D. H., Lonigan, C. J., Whitehurst, G. J., & Epstein, J. N. (1994). Accelerating language development through picture book reading. *Journal of Educational Psychology, 86*, 235–243.

Aronson, E. (1990). Applying social psychology to desegregation and energy conservation. *Personality and Social Psychology Bulletin, 16*, 118–132.

Arthritis Foundation. (2000, April 6). Pain in America: Highlights from a Gallup survey. http://www.arthritis.org/answers/ sop_factsheet.asp.

Asch, S. E. (1952). *Social psychology*. Englewood Cliffs, NJ: Prentice-Hall.

Ashton, A. K., et al. (2000). Antidepressant-induced sexual dysfunction and ginkgo biloba. *American Journal of Psychiatry, 157*, 836–837.

Ashton, C. H. (2001). Pharmacology and effects of cannabis: A brief review. *The British Journal of Psychiatry, 178*, 101–106.

Atkinson, R. C. (1975). Mnemotechnics in second-language learning. *American Psychologist, 30*, 821–828.

Atkinson, R. C., & Shiffrin, R. M. (1968). Human memory: A proposed system and its control processes. In K. Spence (Ed.), *The psychology of learning and motivation* Vol. 2. New York: Academic Press.

Audrain, J. E., Klesges, R. C., & Klesges, L. M. (1995). Relationship between obesity status and the metabolic effects of smoking in women. *Health Psychology, 14*, 116–123.

Ayllon, T., & Haughton, E. (1962). Control of the behavior of schizophrenic patients by food. *Journal of the Experimental Analysis of Behavior, 5*, 343–352.

Azar, B. (1994). Women are barraged by media on "the change." *APA Monitor, 25*(5), 24–25.

Azar, B. (1995a). Several genetic traits linked to alcoholism. *APA Monitor, 26*(5), 21–22.

Azar, B. (1995b). Breaking through barriers to creativity. *APA Monitor, 26*(8), 1, 20.

Azar, B. (1996a). Musical studies provide clues to brain functions. *APA Monitor, 27*(4), 1, 24.

Azar, B. (1996b). Scientists examine cancer patients' fears. *APA Monitor, 27*(8), 32.

Azar, B. (1996c). Research could help patients cope with chemotherapy. *APA Monitor, 27*(8), 33.

Azar, B. (1996d). Training is enhanced by virtual reality. *APA Monitor, 26*(3), 24.

Azar, B. (1997a). Poor recall mars research and treatment. *APA Monitor, 28*(1), 1, 29.

Azar, B. (1997b). Environment is key to serotonin levels. *APA Monitor, 28*(4), 26, 29.

Azar, B. (1997c). Nature, nurture: Not mutually exclusive. *APA Monitor, 28*(5), 1, 28.

Azar, B. (1997d). It may cause anxiety, but day care can benefit kids. *APA Monitor, 28*(6), 13.

Azar, B. (1998). Tribal practices raise worker morale. *APA Monitor, 29*(7), 8.

Azar, B. (2000). A Web of research: They're fun, they're fast and they save money, but do Web experiments yield quality results? *Monitor on Psychology online, 31*(4).

Babyak, M., Blumenthal, J. A., Herman, S., Khatri, P., Doraiswamy, M., Moore, K., Craighead, W. E., Baldewicz, T. T., & Krishnan, K. R. (2000). Exercise treatment for major depression: Maintenance of therapeutic benefit at 10 months. *Psychosomatic Medicine, 62*(5), 633–638.

Bacaltchuk, J., Hay, P., & Mari, J. J. (2000). Antidepressants versus placebo for the treatment of bulimia nervosa: A systematic review. *Australian & New Zealand Journal of Psychiatry, 34*(2), 310–317.

Baddeley, A. (1982). *Your memory: A user's guide*. New York: Macmillan.

Baenninger, M. A., & Elenteny, K. (1997). Cited in Azar, B. (1997). Environment can mitigate differences in spatial ability. *APA Monitor, 28*(6), 28.

Bagatell, C. J., & Bremner, W. J. (1996). Drug therapy: Androgens in men—Uses and abuses. *New England Journal of Medicine, 334*, 707–714.

Bagley, C., & D'Augelli, A. R. (2000). Suicidal behaviour in gay, lesbian, and bisexual youth. *British Medical Journal, 320*, 1617–1618.

Bahrick, H. P., Bahrick, P. O., & Wittlinger, R. P. (1975). Fifty years of memory for names and faces. *Journal of Experimental Psychology: General, 104*, 54–75.

Bailey, J. M. (1999). Homosexuality and mental illness. *Archives of General Psychiatry, 56*(10), 883–884.

Bailey, J. M., Dunne, M. P., & Martin, N. G. (2000). Genetic and environmental influences on sexual orientation and its correlates in an Australian twin sample. *Journal of Personality and Social Psychology, 78*(3), 524–536.

Bailey, J. M., & Oberschneider, M. (1997). Sexual orientation and professional dance. *Archives of Sexual Behavior, 26*(4), 433–444.

Bailey, J. M., & Pillard, R. C. (1991). A genetic study of male sexual orientation. *Archives of General Psychiatry, 48*, 1089–1096.

Baker, C. W., Whisman, M. A., & Brownell, K. D. (2000). Studying intergenerational transmission of eating attitudes and behaviors: Methodological and conceptual questions. *Health Psychology, 19*(4), 376–381.

Baker, F., et al. (2000). Health risks associated with cigar smoking. *Journal of the American Medical Association, 284*(6), 735–740.

Baker, L. A., DeFries, J. C., & Fulker, D. W. (1983). Longitudinal stability of cognitive ability in the Colorado adoption project. *Child Development, 54*, 290–297.

Baltes, P. B. (1997). On the incomplete architecture of human ontogeny: Selection, optimization, and compensation as foundation of developmental theory. *American Psychologist, 52*, 366–380.

Baltes, P. B., & Staudinger, U. M. (2000). Wisdom: A metaheuristic (pragmatic) to orchestrate mind and virtue toward excellence. *American Psychologist, 55*, 122–136.

Bandelow, B., et al. (2000). Salivary cortisol in panic attacks. *American Journal of Psychiatry, 157*, 454–456.

Bandura, A. (1986). *Social foundations of thought and action: A social-cognitive theory*. Englewood Cliffs, NJ: Prentice-Hall.

Bandura, A. (1997). *Self efficacy: The exercise of control*. New York: Freeman.

Bandura, A. (1999). Social cognitive theory: An agentic perspective. *Asian Journal of Social Psychology, 2*(1), 21–41.

Bandura, A., Blanchard, E. B., & Ritter, B. (1969). The relative efficacy of desensitization and modeling approaches for inducing behavioral, affective, and cognitive changes. *Journal of Personality and Social Psychology, 13*, 173–199.

Bandura, A., & McDonald, F. J. (1963). Influence of social reinforcement and the behavior of models in shaping children's moral judgments. *Journal of Abnormal and Social Psychology, 67*, 274–281.

Bandura, A., Pastorelli, C., Barbaranelli, C., & Caprara, G. V. (1999). Self-efficacy pathways to childhood depression. *Journal of Personality & Social Psychology, 76*(2), 258–269.

Bandura, A., Ross, S. A., & Ross, D. (1963). Imitation of film-mediated aggressive models. *Journal of Abnormal and Social Psychology, 66*, 3–11.

Bandura, A., Taylor, C. B., Williams, S. L., Medford, I. N., & Barchas, J. D. (1985). Catecholamine secre-tion as a function of perceived coping self-efficacy. *Journal of Consulting and Clinical Psychology, 53*, 406–414.

Bank, B. J., & Hansford, S. L. (2000). Gender and friendship: Why are men's best same-sex friendships less intimate and supportive? *Personal Relationships, 7*(1), 63–78.

Banks, M. S., & Shannon, E. (1993). Spatial and chromatic visual efficiency in human neonates. In C. E. Granrud (Ed.), *Visual perception and cognition in infancy*. Hillsdale, NJ: Erlbaum.

Banks, S. M., et al. (1995). The effects of message framing on mammography utilization. *Health Psychology, 14*, 178–184.

Barbaree, H. E., & Marshall, W. L. (1991). The role of male sexual arousal in rape. *Journal of Consulting and Clinical Psychology, 59*, 621–631.

Barber, T. X. (2000). A deeper understanding of hypnosis: Its secrets, its nature, its essence. *American Journal of Clinical Hypnosis, 42*(3–4), 208–272.

Bard, P. (1934). The neurohumoral basis of emotional reactions. In C. A. Murchison (Ed.), *Handbook of general experimental psychology*. Worcester, MA: Clark University Press.

Barlow, D. H. (1991). Introduction to the special issue on diagnoses, definitions, and *DSM-IV*. *Journal of Abnormal Psychology, 100*, 243–244.

Barlow, D. H. (1996). Health care policy, psychotherapy research, and the future of psychotherapy. *American Psychologist, 51*, 1050–1058.

Barlow, D. H., Gorman, J. M., Shear, M. K., Woods, S. W. (2000). Cognitive-behavioral therapy, imipramine, or their combination for panic disorder: A randomized controlled trial. *Journal of the American Medical Association, 283*, 2529–2536.

Barnett, W. S., & Escobar, C. M. (1990). Economic costs and benefits of early intervention. In S. J. Meisels & J. P. Shonkoff (Eds.), *Hand-

book of early childhood intervention. New York: Cambridge University Press.

Baron, R. A. (1990). Countering the effects of destructive criticism. *Journal of Applied Psychology, 75,* 235–245.

Baron, R. A., & Byrne, D. (2000). *Social psychology* (9th ed.). Boston: Allyn & Bacon.

Barr, C. E., Mednick, S. A., & Munk-Jorgensen, P. (1990). Exposure to influenza epidemics during gestation and adult schizophrenia. *Archives of General Psychiatry, 47,* 869–874.

Barrett-Connor, E., Von Muhlen, D. G., & Kritz-Silverstein, D. (1999). Bioavailable testosterone and depressed mood in older men. *Journal of Clinical Endocrinology and Metabolism, 84,* 573–577.

Barringer, F. (1993, April 28). For 32 million Americans, English is a second language. *The New York Times,* p. A18.

Barsalou, L. W. (1992). *Cognitive psychology.* Hillsdale, NJ: Erlbaum.

Bartoshuk, L. M. (2000). Psychophysical advances aid the study of genetic variation in taste. *Appetite, 34*(1), 105.

Bartoshuk, L. M., & Beauchamp, G. K. (1994). Chemical senses. *Annual Review of Psychology, 45,* 419–449.

Basch, M. F. (1980). *Doing psychotherapy.* New York: Basic Books.

Basen-Engquist, K., Edmundson, E. W., & Parcel, G. S. (1996). Structure of health risk behavior among high school students. *Journal of Consulting and Clinical Psychology, 64,* 764–775.

Basic Behavioral Science Task Force of the National Advisory Mental Health Council (1996a). Basic behavioral science research for mental health: Vulnerability and resilience. *American Psychologist, 51,* 22–28.

Basic Behavioral Science Task Force of the National Advisory Mental Health Council (1996b). Basic behavioral science research for mental health: Perception, attention, learning, and memory. *American Psychologist, 51,* 133–142.

Basic Behavioral Science Task Force of the National Advisory Mental Health Council (1996c). Basic behavioral science research for mental health: Sociocultural and environmental practices. *American Psychologist, 51,* 722–731.

Bassetti, C., Vella, S., Donati, F., Wielepp, P., & Weder, B. (2000). SPECT during sleepwalking. *Lancet, 356,* 484–485.

Bateman, D. N. (2000). Triptans and migraine. *Lancet, 355,* 860–861.

Baucom, D. H., Shoham, V., Mueser, K. T., Daiuto, A. D., & Stickle, T. R. (1998). Empirically supported couple and family interventions for marital distress and adult mental health problems. *Journal of Consulting and Clinical Psychology, 66,* 53–88.

Bauer, M., et al. (2000). Double-blind, placebo-controlled trial of the use of lithium to augment antidepressant medication in continuation treatment of unipolar major depression. *American Journal of Psychiatry, 157,* 1429–1435.

Baum, A., Friedman, A. L., & Zakowski, S. G. (1997). Stress and genetic testing for disease risk. *Health Psychology, 16,* 8–19.

Baum, W., & Heath, J. I. (1992). Behavioral explanations and intentional explanations in psychology. *American Psychologist, 47,* 1312–1317.

Baumeister, R. F., Stillwell, A. M., & Heatherton, T. F. (1994). Guilt. *Psychological Bulletin, 115,* 243–267.

Baumrind, D. (1973). The development of instrumental competence through socialization. In A. D. Pick (Ed.), *Minnesota Symposia on Child Development, Vol. 7.* Minneapolis: University of Minnesota Press.

Baumrind, D. (1991a). The influence of parenting style on adolescent competence and substance abuse. *Journal of Early Adolescence, 11,* 56–95.

Baumrind, D. (1991b). Parenting styles and adolescent development. In J. Brooks-Gunn, R. Lerner, & A. C. Petersen (Eds.), *Encyclopedia of Adolescence, II.* New York: Garland.

Baumrind, D. (1993). The average expectable environment is not good enough. *Child Development, 64,* 1299–1317.

Bech, P., et al. (2000). Meta-analysis of randomised controlled trials of fluoxetine *v.* placebo and tricyclic antidepressants in the short-term treatment of major depression. *British Journal of Psychiatry, 176,* 421–428.

Beck, A. T. (1991). Cognitive therapy: A 30-year retrospective. *American Psychologist, 46,* 368–375.

Beck, A. T. (1993). Cognitive therapy: Past, present, and future. *Journal of Consulting and Clinical Psychology, 61,* 194–198.

Beck, A. T. (2000). Cited in Chamberlin, J. (2000). An historic meeting of the minds. *Monitor on Psychology, 31*(9), 27.

Beck, A. T., Brown, G., Berchick, R. J., Stewart, B. L., & Steer, R. A. (1990). Relationship between hopelessness and ultimate suicide. *American Journal of Psychiatry, 147,* 190–195.

Beck, A. T., & Freeman, A. (1990). *Cognitive therapy of personality disorders.* New York: Guilford.

Beckham, J. C., et al. (2000). Ambulatory cardiovascular activity in Vietnam combat veterans with and without posttraumatic stress disorder. *Journal of Consulting and Clinical Psychology, 68,* 269–276.

Begley, S., & Check, E. (2000, August 5). Sex and the single fly. *Newsweek Magazine,* pp. 44–45.

Bell, A. P., Weinberg, M. S., & Hammersmith, S. K. (1981). *Sexual preference: Its development in men and women.* Bloomington, IN: University of Indiana Press.

Bell, P. A. (1992). In defense of the negative affect escape model of heat and aggression. *Psychological Bulletin, 111,* 342–346.

Belle, D. (1990). Poverty and women's mental health. *American Psychologist, 45,* 385–389.

Beller, M., & Gafni, N. (2000). Can item format (multiple choice vs. open-ended) account for gender differences in mathematics achievement? *Sex Roles, 42*(1–2), 1–21.

Belsky, J. (1990). Developmental risks associated with infant day care. I. S. Cherazi (Ed.), *Psychosocial issues in day care* (pp. 37–68). New York: American Psychiatric Press.

Belsky, J. (1993). Etiology of child maltreatment. *Psychological Bulletin, 114,* 413–434.

Belsky, J., Fish, M., & Isabella, R. (1991). Continuity and discontinuity in infant negative and positive emotionality: Family attachments and attachment consequences. *Developmental Psychology, 27,* 421–431.

Belsky, J., et al. (2001, April). Day care linked to child aggression. Paper presented at the meeting of the Society for Research in Child Development, Minneapolis.

Bem, D. J., & Honorton, C. (1994). Does Psi exist? Replicable evidence for an anomalous process of information transfer. *Psychological Bulletin, 115,* 4–18.

Bem, S. L. (1993). *The lenses of gender.* New Haven: Yale University Press.

Benatar, S. R. (2000). AIDS in the 21st century. *The New England Journal of Medicine, 342*(7).

Benight, C. C., and others. (1997). Coping self-efficacy buffers psychological and physiological disturbances in HIV-infected men following a natural disaster. *Health Psychology, 16,* 248–255.

Benson, H. (1975). *The relaxation response.* New York: Morrow.

Benson, P. L., Karabenick, S. A., & Lerner, R. M. (1976). Pretty pleases: The effects of physical attractiveness, race, and sex on receiving help. *Journal of Experimental Social Psychology, 12,* 409–415.

Berenbaum, H., & Connelly, J. (1993). The effect of stress on hedonic capacity. *Journal of Abnormal Psychology, 102,* 474–481.

Berger, K. S. (1994). *The developing person through the life span* (3rd ed.). New York: Worth Publishers.

Berkowitz, L. (1988). Frustrations, appraisals, and aversively stimulated aggression. *Aggressive Behavior, 14,* 3–11.

Berkowitz, L. (1994). Is something missing? Some observations prompted by the cognitive-neoassociationist view of anger and emotional aggression. In L. R. Huesmann (Ed.), *Aggressive behavior: Current perspectives.* New York: Plenum.

Bernal, M. E., & Castro, F. G. (1994). Are clinical psychologists prepared for service and research with ethnic minorities? *American Psychologist, 49,* 797–805.

Bernardin, H. J., Cooke, D. K., & Villanova, P. (2000). Conscientiousness and agreeableness as predictors of rating leniency. *Journal of Applied Psychology, 85*(2), 232–236.

Bernat, J. A., Wilson, A. E., & Calhoun, K. S. (1999). Sexual coercion history, calloused sexual beliefs and judgments of sexual coercion in a date rape analogue. *Violence and Victims, 14*(2), 147–160.

Bernhardt, P. C., Dabbs, J. M. Jr., Fielden, J. A., & Lutter, C. D. (1998). Testosterone changes during vicarious experiences of winning and losing among fans at sporting events. *Physiology & Behavior, 65*(1), 59–62.

Bernstein, I. (1996). Cited in Azar, B. (1996). Research could help patients cope with chemotherapy. *APA Monitor, 27*(8), 33.

Bernstein, W. M., Stephenson, B. O., Snyder, M. L., & Wicklund, R. A. (1983). Causal ambiguity and heterosexual affiliation. *Journal of Experimental Social Psychology, 19,* 78–92.

Berquier, A., & Ashton, R. (1992). Characteristics of the frequent nightmare sufferer. *Journal of Abnormal Psychology, 101*, 246–250.

Bersoff, D. (1994). Cited in DeAngelis, T. (1994). Experts see little impact from insanity plea ruling. *APA Monitor, 25*(6), 28.

Betancourt, H., & López, S. R. (1993). The study of culture, ethnicity, and race in American psychology. *American Psychologist, 48*, 629–637.

Bettencourt, B. A., & Miller, N. (1996). Gender differences in aggression as a function of provocation. *Psychological Bulletin, 119*, 422–447.

Bevan, W., & Kessel, F. (1994). Plain truths and home cooking. *American Psychologist, 49*, 505–509.

Bexton, W. H., Heron, W., & Scott, T. H. (1954). Effects of decreased variation in the sensory environment. *Canadian Journal of Psychology, 8*, 70–76.

Biersdorfer, J. D. (2000, April 20). Online scents. *The New York Times*, p. G4.

Billings, D. W., Folkman, S., Acree, M., & Moskowitz, J. T. (2000). Coping and physical health during caregiving: The roles of positive and negative affect. *Journal of Personality and Social Psychology, 79*(1), 131–142.

Birks, Y., & Roger, D. (2000). Identifying components of type-A behaviour: "Toxic" and "non-toxic" achieving. *Personality & Individual Differences, 28*(6), 1093–1105.

Birnbaum, M. H. (Ed.) (2000). *Psychological experiments on the Internet*. San Diego: Academic Press.

Bjorklund, D. F. (1995). *Children's thinking* (2nd ed). Pacific Grove, CA: Brooks/Cole.

Bjorklund, D. F., & Kipp, K. (1996). Parental investment theory and gender differences in the evolution of inhibition mechanisms. *Psychological Bulletin, 120*, 163–188.

Blakeslee, S. (1992a, January 7). Scientists unraveling chemistry of dreams. *The New York Times*, pp. C1, C10.

Blakeslee, S. (1992b, January 22). An epidemic of genital warts raises concern but not alarm. *The New York Times*, p. C12.

Blakeslee, S. (1994, April 13). Black smokers' higher risk of cancer may be genetic. *The New York Times*, p. C14.

Blakeslee, S. (1998, August 4). Re-evaluating significance of baby's bond with mother. *The New York Times*, pp. F1, F2.

Blakeslee, S. (2000, November 14). Experts explore deep sleep and the making of memories. *The New York Times online*.

Blanchard, E. B. (1992). Psychological treatment of benign headache disorders. *Journal of Consulting and Clinical Psychology, 60*, 537–551.

Blanchard, E. B., et al. (1990a). Placebo-controlled evaluation of abbreviated progressive muscle relaxation and of relaxation combined with cognitive therapy in the treatment of tension headache. *Journal of Consulting and Clinical Psychology, 58*, 210–215.

Blanchard, E. B., et al. (1990b). A controlled evaluation of thermal biofeedback and thermal feedback combined with cognitive therapy in the treatment of vascular headache. *Journal of Consulting and Clinical Psychology, 58*, 216–224.

Blanchard, E. B., et al. (1991). The role of regular home practice in the relaxation treatment of tension headache. *Journal of Consulting and Clinical Psychology, 59*, 467–470.

Blanco-Colio, L. M., et al. (2000). Red wine intake prevents nuclear factor-B activation in peripheral blood mononuclear cells of healthy volunteers during postprandial lipemia. *Circulation, 102*, 1020–1026.

Blascovich, J. (2000). Cited in Clay, R. A. (2000). Linking up online: Is the Internet enhancing interpersonal connections or leading to greater social isolation? *Monitor on Psychology online, 31*(4).

Blass, T. (1991). Understanding behavior in the Milgram obedience experiment: The roles of personality, situations, and their interactions. *Journal of Personality and Social Psychology, 60*, 398–413.

Blatt, S. J. (1995). The destructiveness of perfectionism: Implications for the treatment of depression. *American Psychologist, 50*, 1003–1020.

Blatt, S. J., Quinlan, D. M., Pilkonis, P. A., & Shea, M. T. (1995). Impact of perfectionism and need for approval on the brief treatment of depression. *Journal of Consulting and Clinical Psychology, 63*, 125–132.

Blatt, S. J., Zuroff, D. C., Quinlan, D. M., & Pilkonis, P. A. (1996). Interpersonal factors in brief treatment of depression. *Journal of Consulting and Clinical Psychology, 64*, 162–171.

Block, R. I., et al. (2000). Effects of frequent marijuana use on brain tissue volume and composition. *Neuroreport: For Rapid Communication of Neuroscience Research, 11*(3), 491–496.

Bloom, L., Merkin, S., & Wootten, J. (1982). Wh-questions: Linguistic factors that contribute to the sequence of acquisition. *Child Development, 53*, 1084–1092.

Bloom, L., & Mudd, S. A. (1991). Depth of processing approach to face recognition. *Journal of Experimental Psychology: Learning, Memory, and Cognition, 17*, 556–565.

Blum, D. (1997). *Sex on the brain: The biological differences between men and women*. New York: Viking.

Boden, M. A. (1994). What is creativity? In M. A. Boden (Ed.), *Dimensions of creativity*. Cambridge, MA: The MIT Press, a Bradford Book.

Bogen, J. E. (1969). The other side of the brain II: An appositional mind. *Bulletin of the Los Angeles Neurological Society, 34*, 135–162.

Bond, R., & Smith, P. B. (1996). Culture and conformity. *Psychological Bulletin, 119*, 111–137.

Boneau, C. A. (1992). Observations on psychology's past and future. *American Psychologist, 47*, 1586–1596.

Bonin, M. F., McCreary, D. R., & Sadava, S. W. (2000). Problem drinking behavior in two community-based samples of adults: Influence of gender, coping, loneliness, and depression. *Psychology of Addictive Behaviors, 14*(2), 151–161.

Bootzin, R. R., Epstein, D., & Wood, J. N. (1991). Stimulus control instructions. In P. Hauri (Ed.), *Case studies in insomnia*. New York: Plenum.

Borgida, E., & Campbell, B. (1982). Belief relevance and attitude-behavior consistency. *Journal of Personality and Social Psychology, 42*, 239–247.

Boskind-White, M., & White, W. C. (1983). *Bulimarexia: The binge/purge cycle*. New York: W. W. Norton.

Boston Women's Health Book Collective (1992). *The new our bodies, ourselves*. New York: Simon & Schuster.

Bouchard, T. J. Jr., Lykken, D. T., McGue, M., Segal, N. L., & Tellegen, A. (1990). Sources of human psychological differences: The Minnesota study of twins reared apart. *Science, 250*, 223–228.

Bower, G. H. (1981). Mood and memory. *American Psychologist, 36*, 129–148.

Bowers, K. S., & Woody, E. Z. (1996). Hypnotic amnesia and the paradox of intentional forgetting. *Journal of Abnormal Psychology, 105*, 381–390.

Bowes, J. M., & Goodnow, J. J. (1996). Work for home, school, or labor force. *Psychological Bulletin, 119*, 300–321.

Bowlby, J. (1988). *A secure base*. New York: Basic Books.

Boyatzis, R. E. (1974). The effect of alcohol consumption on the aggressive behavior of men. *Quarterly Journal for the Study of Alcohol, 35*, 959–972.

Boyd-Franklin, N. (1995). A multisystems model for treatment interventions with inner-city African American families. Master lecture delivered to the meeting of the American Psychological Association, New York, August 12.

Bradley, R. H., et al. (1989). Home environment and cognitive development in the first 3 years of life. *Developmental Psychology, 25*, 217–235.

Brain-link camera gives blind a limited view (2000, January 18). *The New York Times online*.

Brand, J. (2000). Cited in McFarling, U. L. (2000, August 27). Sniffing out genes' role in our senses of taste and smell. *The Los Angeles Times online*.

Bransford, J. D., Nitsch, K. E., & Franks, J. J. (1977). Schooling and the facilitation of knowing. In R. C. Anderson, R. J. Spiro, & W. E. Montague (Eds.), *Schooling and the acquisition of knowledge*. Hillsdale, NJ: Erlbaum.

Braun, A. R., & Balkin, T. J. (1998). Cited in Wade, N. (1998, January 6). Was Freud wrong? Are dreams the brain's start-up test? *The New York Times*.

Braun, B. G. (1988). *Treatment of multiple personality disorder*. Washington, D.C.: American Psychiatric Press.

Brewin, C. R., Andrews, B., & Gotlib, I. H. (1993). Psychopathology and early experience. *Psychological Bulletin, 113*, 82–98.

Bridges, K. (1932). Emotional development in early infancy. *Child Development, 3*, 324–341.

Bridgwater, C. A. (1982). What candor can do. *Psychology Today, 16*(5), 16.

Broberg, A. G., Wessels, H., Lamb, M. E., & Hwang, C. P. (1997). Effects of day care on the development of cognitive abilities in 8-year-olds: A longitudinal study. *Developmental Psychology, 33*(1), 62–69.

Broder, S. (2000, July 29). Fighting media violence! **www.FamilyEducation.com**.

Brody, J. E. (1995a, August 30). Hormone replacement therapy for men. *The New York Times*, p. C8.

Brody, J. E. (1995b). Cited in DeAngelis, T. (1995), Eat well, keep fit, and let go of stress. *APA Monitor, 26*(10), 20.

Brody, J. E. (1996a, August 28). PMS need not be the worry it was just decades ago. *The New York Times,* p. C9.

Brody, J. E. (1996b, September 4). Osteoporosis can threaten men as well as women. *The New York Times,* p. C9.

Brody, J. E. (1997, March 26). Race and weight. *The New York Times,* p. C8.

Brody, N. (1997). Intelligence, schooling, and society. *American Psychologist, 52,* 1046–1050.

Broussard, B. A., et al. (1991). Prevalence of obesity in American Indians and Alaska Natives. *American Journal of Clinical Nutrition, 53,* 1535S–1542S.

Brown, D. E. (1991). *Human universals.* Philadelphia: Temple University Press.

Brown, G. K., Beck, A. T., Steer, R. A., & Grisham, J. R. (2000). Risk factors for suicide in psychiatric outpatients: A 20-year prospective study. *Journal of Consulting and Clinical Psychology, 68*(3), 371–377.

Brown, J. D., & Rogers, R. J. (1991). Self-serving attributions. *Personality and Social Psychology Bulletin, 17,* 501–506.

Brown, L. S. (1992). A feminist critique of the personality disorders. In L. Brown & M. Balou (Eds.), *Personality and psychopathology: Feminist reappraisals.* New York: Guilford.

Brown, M., & Massaro, S. (1996). New brain studies yield insights into cocaine binging and addiction. *Journal of Addictive Diseases, 15*(4).

Brown, R., & McNeill, D. (1966). The tip-of-the-tongue phenomenon. *Journal of Verbal Learning and Verbal Behavior, 5,* 325–337.

Browne, A. (1993). Violence against women by male partners. *American Psychologist, 48,* 1077–1087.

Browne, M. A., & Mahoney, M. J. (1984). Sport psychology. *Annual Review of Psychology, 35,* 605–625.

Browne, M. W. (1995, June 6). Scientists deplore flight from reason. *The New York Times,* pp. C1, C7.

Brownell, K. D. (1997). We must be more militant about food. *APA Monitor, 28*(3), 48.

Brownell, W. E. (1992). Cited in Browne, M. W. (1992, June 9). Ear's own sounds may underlie its precision. *The New York Times,* pp. C1, C8.

Brzustowicz, L., Hodgkinson, K., Chow, E., Honer, W., & Bassett, A. (2000). Location of a major susceptibility locus for familial schizophrenia on chromosome 1q21-q22. *Science, 288*(28), 678–682.

Buchanan, C. M., Eccles, J. S., & Becker, J. B. (1992). Are adolescents the victims of raging hormones? Evidence for activational effects of hormones on moods and behavior at adolescence. *Psychological Bulletin, 111,* 62–107.

Budd, L. S. (1993). *Living with the active alert child.* St. Paul, MN: Parenting Press.

Burger, J. M. (1999). The foot-in-the-door compliance procedure: A multiple-process analysis and review. *Personality & Social Psychology Review, 3*(4), 303–325.

Burger, J. M., & Cosby, M. (1999). Do women prefer dominant men? The case of the missing control condition. *Journal of Research in Personality, 33*(3), 358–368.

Burnette, E. (1997). "Father of Ebonics" continues his crusade. *APA Monitor, 28*(4), 12.

Burns, D. D., & Nolen-Hoeksema, S. (1992). Therapeutic empathy and recovery from depression in cognitive-behavioral therapy. *Journal of Consulting and Clinical Psychology, 60,* 441–449.

Burnstein, E., & Schul, Y. (1982). The informational basis of social judgments. *Journal of Experimental Social Psychology, 18,* 217–234.

Burt, M. R. (1980). Cultural myths and supports for rape. *Journal of Personality and Social Psychology, 38,* 217–230.

Bushman, B. J., Baumeister, R. F., & Stack, A. D. (1999). Catharsis, aggression, and persuasive influence: Self-fulfilling or self-defeating prophecies? *Journal of Personality & Social Psychology, 76*(3), 367–376.

Buss, D. M. (1992). Is there a universal human nature? *Contemporary Psychology, 37,* 1262–1263.

Buss, D. M. (1994). *The evolution of desire.* New York: Basic Books.

Buss, D. M. (1995). Psychological sex differences. *American Psychologist, 50,* 164–168.

Buss, D. M. (1999). Adaptive individual differences revisited. *Journal of Personality, 67*(2), 259–264.

Buss, D. M. (2000). The evolution of happiness. *American Psychologist, 55,* 15–23.

Buss, D. M., Haselton, M. G., Shackelford, T. K., Bleske, A. L., & Wakefield, J. C. (1998). Adaptations, exaptations, and spandrels. *American Psychologist, 53,* 533–548.

Bussey, K., & Bandura, A. (1999). Social cognitive theory of gender development and differentiation. *Psychological Review, 106*(4), 676–713.

Butcher, J. (2000). Dopamine hypothesis gains further support. *The Lancet, 356,* 139–146.

Butler, J. C. (2000). Personality and emotional correlates of right-wing authoritarianism. *Social Behavior & Personality, 28*(1), 1–14.

Butler, R. (1998). Cited in CD-ROM that accompanies Nevid, J. S., Rathus, S. A., & Rubenstein, H. (1998). *Health in the new millennium.* New York: Worth Publishers.

Cacioppo, J. T., Martzke, J. S, Petty, R. E., & Tassinary, L. G. (1988). Specific forms of facial EMG response index emotions during an interview. *Journal of Personality and Social Psychology, 54,* 552–604.

Califano, J. A. (1995). The wrong way to stay slim. *New England Journal of Medicine, 333,* 1214–1216.

Californians losing fight against flab. (2000, June 14). Reuters News Agency online.

Campbell, J. (1994). *Past, space, and self.* Cambridge, MA: The MIT Press, a Bradford Book.

Campbell, W. K., & Sedikides, C. (1999). Self-threat magnifies the self-serving bias: A meta-analytic integration. *Review of General Psychology, 3*(1), 23–43.

Campbell, W. K., Sedikides, C., Reeder, G. D., & Elliott, A. J. (2000). Among friends? An examination of friendship and the self-serving bias. *British Journal of Social Psychology, 39*(2), 229–239.

Campos, J. J. (2000). Cited in Azar, B. (2000). What's in a face? *Monitor on Psychology, 31*(1), 44–45.

Campos, J. J., Hiatt, S., Ramsey, D., Henderson, C., & Svejda, M. (1978). The emergence of fear on the visual cliff. In M. Lewis & L. Rosenblum (Eds.), *The origins of affect.* New York: Plenum.

Camras, L. (2000). Cited in Azar, B. (2000). What's in a face? *Monitor on Psychology, 31*(1), 44–45.

Canalis, R. F., & Lambert, P. R. (2000). *The ear: Comprehensive otology.* Philadelphia: Lippincott Williams & Wilkins.

Cannistra, S. A., & Niloff, J. M. (1996). Cancer of the uterine cervix. *New England Journal of Medicine, 334,* 1030–1038.

Cannon, T. D., et al. (1998). The genetic epidemiology of schizophrenia in a Finnish twin cohort: A population-based modeling study. *Archives of General Psychiatry, 55,* 67–74.

Cannon, W. B. (1927). The James-Lange theory of emotions: A critical examination and an alternative theory. *American Journal of Psychology, 39,* 106–124.

Cannon, W. B. (1932). *The wisdom of the body.* New York: Norton.

Cannon, W. B., & Washburn, A. (1912). An explanation of hunger. *American Journal of Physiology, 29,* 441–454.

Cantor, J. (1997). Cited in Seppa, N. (1997). Children's TV remains steeped in violence. *APA Monitor, 28*(6), 36.

Cantrell, R. P., Stenner, A. J., & Katzenmeyer, W. G. (1977). Teacher knowledge, attributes, and classroom teaching correlates of student achievement. *Journal of Educational Psychology, 69,* 180–190.

Carey, G., & DiLalla, D. L. (1994). Personality and psychopathology: Genetic perspectives. *Journal of Abnormal Psychology, 103,* 32–43.

Carlson, J. G., & Hatfield, E. (1992). *Psychology of emotion.* Fort Worth: Harcourt Brace Jovanovich.

Carlsson, K., et al. (2000). Tickling expectations: Neural processing in anticipation of a sensory stimulus. *Journal of Cognitive Neuroscience, 12,* 691–703.

Carmichael, L. L., Hogan, H. P., & Walter, A. A. (1932). An experimental study of the effect of language on the reproduction of visually perceived form. *Journal of Experimental Psychology, 15,* 73–86.

Carpenter, C. C. J., et al. (2000). Antiretroviral therapy in adults: Updated recommendations of the International AIDS Society—USA Panel. *Journal of the American Medical Association, 283,* 381–390.

Carpenter, W. T. Jr., & Buchanan, R. W. (1994). Schizophrenia. *New England Journal of Medicine, 330,* 681–690.

Carrère, S., Buehlman, K. T., Gottman, J. M., Coan, J. A., & Ruckstuhl, L. (2000). Predicting marital stability and divorce in newlywed couples. *Journal of Family Psychology, 14*(1), 42–58.

Carroll, K. M., Rounsaville, B. J., & Nich, C. (1994). Blind man's bluff: Effectiveness and significance of psychotherapy and pharmacotherapy blinding procedures in a clinical trial. *Journal of Consulting and Clinical Psychology, 62,* 276–280.

Carson, R. C., Butcher, J. N., & Mineka, S. (1999). *Abnormal psychology and modern life* (11th ed.). Boston: Allyn & Bacon.

Carstensen, L. (1997, August 17). The evolution of social goals across the life span. Paper presented to the American Psychological Association, Chicago.

Case, R. (1992). *The mind's staircase.* Hillsdale, NJ: Erlbaum.

Castillo-Richmond, A., et al. (2000). Effects of stress reduction on carotid atherosclerosis in hypertensive African Americans. *Stroke, 31*, 568.

Cavaliere, F. (1996). Bilingual schools face big political challenges. *APA Monitor, 27*(2), 36.

Cavanaugh, J. C., & Green, E. E. (1990). I believe, therefore I can: Self-efficacy beliefs in memory aging. In E. A. Lovelace (Ed.), *Aging and cognition: Mental processes, self-awareness, and interventions.* North-Holland, Elsevier.

Cavelaars, A. E. J. M., et al. (2000). Educational differences in smoking: international comparison. *British Medical Journal, 320*, 1102–1107.

CDC. *See* Centers for Disease Control and Prevention.

Ceci, S. J., & Bruck, M. (1993). Suggestibility of the child witness. *Psychological Bulletin, 113*, 403–439.

Cejka, M. A., & Eagly, A. H. (1999). Gender-stereotypic images of occupations correspond to the sex segregation of employment. *Personality & Social Psychology Bulletin, 25*(4), 413–423.

Celis, W. (1991, January 2). Students trying to draw line between sex and an assault. *The New York Times,* pp. 1, B8.

Cellar, D. F., Nelson, Z. C., & Yorke, C. M. (2000). The five-factor model and driving behavior: Personality and involvement in vehicular accidents. *Psychological Reports, 86*(2), 454–456.

Centers for Disease Control and Prevention (1995). *Suicide surveillance: 1980–1990.* Washington, D.C.: USDHHS.

Centers for Disease Control and Prevention (2000a). *HIV/AIDS surveillance report: U.S. HIV and AIDS cases reported through December 1999, 11*(2).

Centers for Disease Control and Prevention (2000b, June 9). Youth risk behavior surveillance—United States, 1999. *Morbidity and Mortality Weekly Report, 49*(SS05), 1–96.

Centers for Disease Control and Prevention (2000c). Suicide in the United States. Page updated January 28, 2000. (http://www.cdc.gov/ncipc/factsheets/suifacts.htm).

Centers for Disease Control and Prevention (2000d). National and state-specific pregnancy rates among adolescents—United States, 1995–1997. *Morbidity and Mortality Weekly Report, 49*(27).

Centers for Disease Control and Prevention (2000e). *National Vital Statistics Reports, 48*(3).

Centers for Disease Control Division of Sexually Transmitted Diseases and Prevention (2000f). Some facts about chlamydia. Page updated April 14, 2000. (DSTD@cdc.gov).

Cervilla, J. A., et al. (2000). Long-term predictors of cognitive outcome in a cohort of older people with hypertension. *British Journal of Psychiatry, 177*, 66–71.

Chadwick, P. D. J., & Lowe, C. F. (1990). Measurement and modification of delusional beliefs. *Journal of Consulting and Clinical Psychology, 58*, 225–232.

Chafee, M. V., & Goldman-Rakic, P. S. (2000). Inactivation of parietal and prefrontal cortex reveals interdependence of neural activity during memory-guided saccades. *Journal of Neurophysiology, 83*(3), 1550–1566.

Chamberlain, J. (2000). Cops trust cops, even one with a PhD. *Monitor on Psychology, 31*(1), 74–76.

Chambless, D. L., & Hollon, S. D. (1998). Defining empirically supported therapies. *Journal of Consulting and Clinical Psychology, 66*, 7–18.

Chance, S. E., Brown, R. T., Dabbs, J. M. Jr., & Casey, R. (2000). Testosterone, intelligence and behavior disorders in young boys. *Personality & Individual Differences, 28*(3), 437–445.

Chaplin, W. F., Phillips, J. B., Brown, J. D., Clanton, N. R., & Stein, J. L. (2000). Handshaking, gender, personality, and first impressions. *Journal of Personality and Social Psychology, 79*(1), 110–117.

Chassin, L., Presson, C. C., Pitts, S. C., & Sherman, S. J. (2000). The natural history of cigarette smoking from adolescence to adulthood in a Midwestern community sample: Multiple trajectories and their psychological correlates. *Health Psychology, 19*, 223–231.

Chen, L., Baker, S. P., Braver, E. R., & Li, G. (2000). Carrying passengers as a risk factor for crashes fatal to 16- and 17-year-old drivers. *Journal of the American Medical Association, 283*, 1578–1582.

Cherry, K. E., & LeCompte, D. C. (1999). Age and individual differences influence prospective memory. *Psychology & Aging, 14*(1), 60–76.

Chlebowski, R. T. (2000). Primary care: Reducing the risk of breast cancer. *The New England Journal of Medicine online, 343*(3).

Choi, I., Nisbett, R. E., & Norenzayan, A. (1999). Causal attribution across cultures: Variation and universality. *Psychological Bulletin, 125*(1), 47–63.

Chomsky, N. (1980). Rules and representations. *Behavioral and Brain Sciences, 3*, 1–16.

Chomsky, N. (1991). Linguistics and cognitive science. In A. Kasher (Ed.), *The Chomskyan turn.* Cambridge, MA: Blackwell.

Chronicle of Higher Education (1992, March 18). Pp. A35–A44.

Cialdini, R. B. (2000). Cited in McKinley, J. C. Jr. (2000, August 11). It isn't just a game: Clues to avid rooting. *The New York Times online.*

Cialdini, R. B., et al. (1976). Basking in reflected glory: Three (football) field studies. *Journal of Personality & Social Psychology, 34*(3), 366–375.

Cialdini, R. B., et al. (1997). Reinterpreting the empathy-altruism relationship: When one into one equals oneness. *Journal of Personality & Social Psychology, 73*(3), 481–494.

Cigars increase lung cancer risk fivefold—study (2000, February 15). Reuters News Agency online.

Cimons, M. (1996). Social pressures impede women's health. *APA Monitor, 26*(3), 39–40.

Cinciripini, P. M., Cinciripini, L. G., Wallfisch, A., Haque, W., & Van Vunakis, H. (1996). Behavior therapy and the transdermal nicotine patch. *Journal of Consulting and Clinical Psychology, 64*, 314–323.

Clancy, S. A., Schacter, D. L., McNally, R. J., & Pitman, R. K. (2000). False recognition in women reporting recovered memories of sexual abuse. *Psychological Science, 11*(1), 26–31.

Clark, D. M., et al. (1997). Misinterpretation of body sensations in panic disorder. *Journal of Consulting and Clinical Psychology, 65*, 203–213.

Clark, L. A., Watson, D., & Mineka, S. M. (1994). Temperament, personality, and the mood and anxiety disorders. *Journal of Abnormal Psychology, 103*, 103–116.

Clark, R., Anderson, N. B., Clark, V. R., & Williams, D. R. (1999). Racism as a stressor for African Americans. *American Psychologist, 54*(10), 805–816.

Clarke-Stewart, K. A. (1990). The "effects" of infant day care reconsidered. In N. Fox & G. G. Fein (Eds.), *Infant day care* (pp. 61–86). Norwood, NJ: Ablex.

Clarke-Stewart, K. A. (1991). A home is not a school: The effects of child care on children's development. *Journal of Social Issues, 47*, 105–123.

Clarke-Stewart, K. A., Vandell, D. L., McCartney, K., Owen, M. T., & Booth, C. (2000). Effects of parental separation and divorce on very young children. *Journal of Family Psychology, 14*(2), 304–326.

Clay, R. A. (1997). Meditation is becoming more mainstream. *APA Monitor, 28*(9), 12.

Clay, R. A. (1998). Many managers frown on use of flexible work options. *APA Monitor, 29*(7), 11.

Clay, R. A. (2000). Staying in control. *Monitor on Psychology, 31*(1), 32–34.

Clayton, E. C., & Williams, C. L. (2000). Adrenergic activation of the nucleus tractus solitarius potentiates amygdala norepinephrine release and enhances retention performance in emotionally arousing and spatial memory tasks. *Behavioural Brain Research, 112*(1–2), 151–158.

Clement, J. (1991). Nonformal reasoning in experts and in science students. In J. Voss, D. Perkins, & J. Siegel (Eds.), *Informal reasoning and education.* Hillsdale, NJ: Erlbaum.

Clkurel, K., & Gruzelier, J. (1990). The effects of active alert hypnotic induction on lateral haptic processing. *British Journal of Experimental and Clinical Hypnosis, 11*, 17–25.

Cohen, D., et al. (2000). Absence of cognitive impairment at long-term follow-up in adolescents treated with ECT for severe mood disorder. *American Journal of Psychiatry, 157*, 460–462.

Cohen, L. A. (1987, November). Diet and cancer. *Scientific American,* pp. 42–48, 53–54.

Cohen, S., Evans, G. W., Stokols, D., & Krantz, D. S. (1986). *Behavior, health, and environmental stress.* New York: Plenum.

Cohen, S., Tyrrell, D. A. J., & Smith, A. P. (1993). Negative life events, perceived stress, negative affect, and susceptibility to the common cold. *Journal of Personality and Social Psychology, 64*, 131–140.

Cohen, S., & Williamson, G. M. (1991). Stress and

infectious disease in humans. *Psychological Bulletin, 109,* 5–24.

Cohn, E. G. (1990). Weather and violent crime. *Environment and Behavior, 22,* 280–294.

Cohn, E. G., Rotton, J. (2000). Weather, seasonal trends, and property crimes in Minneapolis, 1987–1988. A moderator-variable time-series analysis of routine activities. *Journal of Environmental Psychology, 20*(3), 257–272.

Cohn, L. D., Macfarlane, S., Yanez, C., & Imai, W. K. (1995). Risk-perception: Differences between adolescents and adults. *Health Psychology, 14,* 217–222.

Coleman, M., & Ganong, L. H. (1985). Love and sex role stereotypes. *Journal of Personality and Social Psychology, 49,* 170–176.

Collaer, M. L., & Hines, M. (1995). Human behavioral sex differences: A role for gonadal hormones during early development? *Psychological Bulletin, 118,* 55–107.

Collier, G. (1994). *Social origins of mental ability.* New York: Wiley.

Collins, J. F. (2000). Biracial Japanese American identity: An evolving process. *Cultural Diversity & Ethnic Minority Psychology, 6*(2), 115–133.

Coltraine, S., & Messineo, M. (2000). The perpetuation of subtle prejudice: Race and gender imagery in 1990s television advertising. *Sex Roles, 42*(5–6), 363–389.

Comas-Diaz, L. (1994, February). Race and gender in psychotherapy with women of color. *Winter roundtable on cross-cultural counseling and psychotherapy: Race and gender.* New York: Teachers College, Columbia University.

Compas, B. E., Haaga, D. A. F., Keefe, F. J., Leitenberg, H., & Williams, D. A. (1998). Sampling of empirically supported psychological treatments from health psychology: Smoking, chronic pain, cancer, and bulimia nervosa. *Journal of Consulting and Clinical Psychology, 66,* 89–112.

Conway, M. A., et al. (1994). The formation of flashbulb memories. *Memory & Cognition, 22*(3), 326–343.

Cools, J., Schotte, D. E., & McNally, R. J. (1992). Emotional arousal and overeating in restrained eaters. *Journal of Abnormal Psychology, 101,* 348–351.

Coon, H., Fulker, D. W., DeFries, J. C., & Plomin, R. (1990). Home environment and cognitive ability of 7-year-old children in the Colorado Adoption Project. *Developmental Psychology, 26,* 459–468.

Cooney, N. L., Litt, M. D., Morse, P. A., Bauer, L. O., & Gaupp, L. (1997). Alcohol cue reactivity, negative-mood reactivity, and relapse in treated alcoholic men. *Journal of Abnormal Psychology, 106,* 243–250.

Coons, P. M. (1994). Confirmation of childhood abuse in child and adolescent cases of multiple personality disorder and dissociative disorder not otherwise specified. *Journal of Nervous and Mental Disease, 182,* 461–464.

Cooper, A., Delmonico, D. L., & Burg, R. (2000). Cybersex users, abusers, and compulsives: New findings and implications. *Sexual Addiction & Compulsivity, 7*(1–2), 5–29.

Cooper, A., Scherer, C. R., Boies, S. C., & Gordon, B. L. (1999). Sexuality on the Internet: From sexual exploration to pathological expression. *Professional Psychology: Research & Practice, 30*(2), 154–164.

Cotman, C. W. (2000, July). Amyloid toxicity. Paper presented to the World Alzheimer Congress 2000, Washington, D.C.

Courtenay, W. H. (2000). Engendering health: A social constructionist examination of men's health beliefs and behaviors. *Psychology of Men & Masculinity, 1*(1), 4–15.

Cousins, N. (1979). *Anatomy of an illness as perceived by the patient.* New York: W. W. Norton.

Cox, B. J., Borger, S. C., Asmundson, G. J. G., & Taylor, S. (2000). Hypochondriasis: Dimensions of hypochondriasis and the five-factor model of personality. *Personality & Individual Differences, 29*(1), 99–108.

Cox, M. J., Owen, M. T., Henderson, V. K., & Margand, N. A. (1992). Prediction of infant–father and infant–mother attachment. *Developmental Psychology, 28,* 474–483.

Craik, F. I. M., & Lockhart, R. S. (1972). Levels of processing. *Journal of Verbal Learning and Verbal Behavior, 11,* 671–684.

Cramer, P. (2000). Defense mechanisms in psychology today. *American Psychologist, 55*(6), 637–646.

Cramer, R. E., McMaster, M. R., Bartell, P. A., & Dragna, M. (1988). Subject competence and minimization of the bystander effect. *Journal of Applied Social Psychology, 18,* 1133–1148.

Crano, W. D. (1997). Vested interest, symbolic politics, and attitude-behavior consistency. *Journal of Personality and Social Psychology, 72*(3), 485–491.

Crawford, H. J., & Barabasz, A. (1993). Phobias and fears: Facilitating their treatment with hypnosis. In J. Rhue, S. Lynn, & I. Kirsch (Eds.), *Clinical handbook of hypnosis.* Washington, D.C.: American Psychological Association.

Crews, D. (1994). Animal sexuality. *Scientific American, 270*(1), 108–114.

Crick, F., & Koch, C. (1997). The problem of consciousness. *Scientific American mysteries of the mind, Special Issue Vol. 7,* No. 1, 18–26.

Crick, N. R., & Dodge, K. A. (1994). A review and reformulation of social information-processing mechanisms in children's social adjustment. *Psychological Bulletin, 115,* 74–101.

Cross, W. E., Parham, T. A., & Helms, J. E. (1991). The states of Black identity development: Nigrescence models. In R. Jones (Ed.), *Black psychology* (3rd ed., pp. 319–338). Hampton, VA: Cobb & Henry.

Crowe, R. A. (1990). Astrology and the scientific method. *Psychological Reports, 67,* 163–191.

Crusco, A. H., & Wetzel, C. G. (1984). The Midas touch: The effects of interpersonal touch on restaurant tipping. *Personality and Social Psychology Bulletin, 10,* 512–517.

Cumsille, P. E., Sayer, A. G., & Graham, J. W. (2000). Perceived exposure to peer and adult drinking as predictors of growth in positive alcohol expectancies during adolescence. *Journal of Consulting and Clinical Psychology, 68*(3), 531–536.

Cunningham, M. R., Shaffer, D. R., Barbee, A. P., Wolff, P. L., & Kelley, D. J. (1990). Separate processes in the relation of elation and depression to helping. *Journal of Experimental Social Psychology, 26,* 13–33.

Cunningham, T. H., & Graham, C. R. (2000). Increasing Native English vocabulary recognition through Spanish immersion: Cognate transfer from foreign to first language. *Journal of Educational Psychology, 92*(1), 37–49.

Curb, J. D., & Marcus, E. B. (1991). Body fat and obesity in Japanese-Americans. *American Journal of Clinical Nutrition, 53,* 1552S–1555S.

Curtis, R. C., & Miller, K. (1986). Believing another likes or dislikes you: Behavior making the beliefs come true. *Journal of Personality and Social Psychology, 51,* 284–290.

Cutler, W. B. (1999). Human sex-attractant hormones: Discovery, research, development, and application in sex therapy. *Psychiatric Annals, 29*(1), 54–59.

Cutler, W. B., Friedmann, E., & McCoy, N. L. (1998). Pheromonal influences on sociosexual behavior in men. *Archives of Sexual Behavior, 27*(1), 1–13.

Cyranowski, J. M., Frank, E., Young, E., & Shear, M. M. (2000). Adolescent onset of the gender difference in lifetime rates of major depression: A theoretical model. *Archives of General Psychiatry, 57*(1), 21–27.

Dabbs, J. M. Jr., Chang, E-L., Strong, R. A., & Milun, R. (1998). Spatial ability, navigation strategy, and geographic knowledge among men and women. *Evolution & Human Behavior, 19*(2), 89–98.

Dabbs, J. M. Jr., Hargrove, M. F., & Heusel, C. (1996). Testosterone differences among college fraternities: Well-behaved vs. rambunctious. *Personality & Individual Differences, 20*(2), 157–161.

Damaged gene is linked to lung cancer. (1996, April 6.) *The New York Times,* p. A24.

Damasio, A. R. (2000). A neural basis for sociopathy. *Archives of General Psychiatry online, 57*(2).

Danforth, J. S., et al. (1990). Exercise as a treatment for hypertension in low-socioeconomic-status Black children. *Journal of Consulting and Clinical Psychology, 58,* 237–239.

Daniel, M. H. (1997). Intelligence testing: Status and trends. *American Psychologist, 52,* 1038–1045.

Darley, J. M. (1993). Research on morality. *Psychological Science, 4,* 353–357.

Darley, J. M., & Latané, B. (1968). Bystander intervention in emergencies: Diffusion of responsibility. *Journal of Personality and Social Psychology, 8,* 377–383.

Darwin, C. A. (1872). *The expression of the emotions in man and animals.* London: J. Murray.

Davey, L. F. (1993, March). *Developmental implications of shared and divergent perceptions in the parent-adolescent relationship.* Paper presented at the biennial meeting of the Society for Research in Child Development, New Orleans.

Davidson, N. E. (1995). Hormone-replacement therapy—Breast versus heart versus bone. *New England Journal of Medicine, 332,* 1638–1639.

Davidson, J. R., & Foa, E. G. (1991). Diagnostic issues in posttraumatic stress disorder. *Journal of Abnormal Psychology, 100,* 346–355.

Davis, A. M., Grattan, D. R., & McCarthy, M. M. (2000). Decreasing GAD neonatally attenuates steroid-induced sexual differentiation of the rat brain. *Behavioral Neuroscience, 114*(5), 923–933.

Davison, G. C. (2000). Stepped care: Doing more with less? *Journal of Consulting and Clinical Psychology, 68*(4), 580–585.

Dawood, K., Pillard, R. C., Horvath, C., Revelle, W., & Bailey, J. M. (2000). Familial aspects of male homosexuality. *Archives of Sexual Behavior, 29*(2), 155–163.

Day, K. (2000). The ethic of care and women's experiences of public space. *Journal of Environmental Psychology, 20*(2), 103–124.

Day, S. J., & Altman, D. G. (2000). Statistics notes: Blinding in clinical trials and other studies. *British Medical Journal, 321,* 504.

DeAngelis, T. (1994a). Educators reveal keys to success in classroom. *APA Monitor, 25*(1), 39–40.

DeAngelis, T. (1994b). Experts see little impact from insanity plea ruling. *APA Monitor, 25*(6), 28.

DeAngelis, T. (1995a). Firefighters' PTSD at dangerous levels. *APA Monitor, 26*(2), 36–37.

DeAngelis, T. (1995b). Mental health care is elusive for Hispanics. *APA Monitor, 26*(7), 49.

DeAngelis, T. (1996). Women's contributions large; recognition isn't. *APA Monitor, 27*(4), 12–13.

DeAngelis, T. (1997). Abused children have more conflicts with friends. *APA Monitor, 28*(6), 32.

DeAngelis, T. (2000). Is Internet addiction real? *APA Monitor, 31*(4), 24–26.

DeCasper, A. J., & Prescott, P. A. (1984). Human newborns' perception of male voices. *Developmental Psychobiology, 17,* 481–491.

DeFries, J. C., Plomin, R., & LaBuda, M. C. (1987). Genetic stability of cognitive development from childhood to adulthood. *Developmental Psychology, 23,* 4–12.

DeGrandpre, R. J. (2000). A science of meaning: Can behaviorism bring meaning to psychological science? *American Psychologist, 55*(7), 721–739.

de Jong, P. F., & Das-Smaal, E. A. (1995). Attention and intelligence. *Journal of Educational Psychology, 87,* 80–92.

De La Cancela, V., & Guzman, L. P. (1991). Latino mental health service needs. In H. F. Myers et al. (Eds.), *Ethnic minority perspectives on clinical training and services in psychology* (pp. 59–64). Washington, D.C.: American Psychological Association.

Delahanty, D. L., et al. (1996). Time course of natural killer cell activity and lymphocyte proliferation in response to two acute stressors in healthy men. *Health Psychology, 15,* 48–55.

Delgado, J. M. R. (1969). *Physical control of the mind.* New York: Harper & Row.

Delmas, P. D., et al. (1997). Effects of raloxifene on bone mineral density, serum cholesterol concentrations, and uterine endometrium in postmenopausal women. *New England Journal of Medicine, 337,* 1641–1648.

Delves, P. J., & Roitt, I. M. (2000). Advances in immunology: The immune system. *The New England Journal of Medicine online, 343*(1).

De Michele, P. E., Gansneder, B., & Solomon, G. B. (1998). Success and failure attributions of wrestlers: Further evidence of the self-serv-

ing bias. *Journal of Sport Behavior, 21*(3), 242–255.

Denmark, F. L. (1998). Women and psychology: An international perspective. *American Psychologist, 53*(4), 465–473.

Dennis, H. (2000). Cited in Stewart, J. Y., & Armet, E. (2000, April 3). Aging in America: Retirees reinvent the concept. *Los Angeles Times online.*

Depression Research at the National Institute of Mental Health. (2000). NIH Publication No. 00-4501. **http://www.nimh.nih.gov/publicat/depresfact.cfm.**

DeRubeis, R. J., & Crits-Christoph, P. (1998). Empirically supported individual and group psychological treatments for adult mental disorders. *Journal of Consulting and Clinical Psychology, 66,* 37–52.

Dessens, A. B., et al. (1999). Prenatal exposure to anticonvulsants and psychosexual development. *Archives of Sexual Behavior, 28*(1), 31–44.

de Toledo-Morrell, L. (2000, July). Hippocampal and entorhinal atrophy in aging and Alzheimer's disease: Relation to function. Paper presented to the World Alzheimer Congress 2000, Washington, D.C.

DeValois, R. L., & Jacobs, G. H. (1984). Neural mechanisms of color vision. In I. Darian-Smith (Ed.), *Handbook of physiology* (Vol. 3). Bethesda, MD: American Physiological Society.

Devlin, M. J., Yanovski, S. Z., & Wilson, G. T. (2000). Obesity: What mental health professionals need to know. *American Journal of Psychiatry, 157*(6), 854–866.

de Wied, D. (1997). Neuropeptides in learning and memory processes. *Behavioural Brain Research, 83*(1–2), 83–90.

DeWit, D. J., et al. (2000). Age at first alcohol use: A risk factor for the development of alcohol disorders. *American Journal of Psychiatry, 157,* 745–750.

de Wit, H., Crean, J., & Richards, J. B. (2000). Effects of *d*-amphetamine and ethanol on a measure of behavioral inhibition in humans. *Behavioral Neuroscience, 114*(4), 830–837.

Dickson, N., Paul, C., Herbison, P., & Silva, P. (1998). First sexual intercourse: Age, coercion, and later regrets reported by a birth cohort. *British Medical Journal, 316,* 29–33.

Dietrich, A., & Allen, J. D. (1997). Vasopressin and memory: I. The vasopressin analogue AVP-sub(4-9) enhances working memory as well as reference memory in the radial arm maze. *Behavioural Brain Research, 87*(2), 195–200.

DiLalla, D. L., Carey, G., Gottesman, I. I., & Bouchard, T. J. Jr. (1996). Heritability of MMPI personality indicators of psychopathology in twins reared apart. *Journal of Abnormal Psychology, 105,* 491–499.

DiLalla, D. L., & Gottesman, I. I. (1991). Biological and genetic contributors to violence—Widom's untold tale. *Psychological Bulletin, 109,* 125–129.

Dill, C. A., Gilden, E. R., Hill, P. C., & Hanselka, L. L. (1982). Federal human subjects regulations. *Personality and Social Psychology Bulletin, 8,* 417–425.

Docherty, N. M., et al. (1996). Working memory,

attention, and communication disturbances in schizophrenia. *Journal of Abnormal Psychology, 105,* 212–219.

Dockery, D. W., et al. (1993). An association between air pollution and mortality in six U.S. cities. *New England Journal of Medicine, 329,* 1753–1759.

Doherty, K., Militello, F. S., Kinnunen, T., & Garvey, A. J. (1996). Nicotine gum dose and weight gain after smoking cessation. *Journal of Consulting and Clinical Psychology, 64,* 799–807.

Dollard, J., Doob, L. W., Miller, N. E., Mowrer, O. H., & Sears, R. R. (1939). *Frustration and aggression.* New Haven, CT: Yale University Press.

Donnerstein, E. I., & Wilson, D. W. (1976). Effects of noise and perceived control on ongoing and subsequent aggressive behavior. *Journal of Personality and Social Psychology, 34,* 774–781.

Doob, A. N., & Wood, L. (1972). Catharsis and aggression. *Journal of Personality and Social Psychology, 22,* 236–245.

Downey, J. I., & Friedman, R. C. (1998). Female homosexuality: Classical psychoanalytic theory reconsidered. *Journal of the American Psychoanalytic Association, 46*(2), 471–506.

Doyle, W. (1986). Classroom organization and management. In M. Wittrock (Ed.), *Handbook of research on teaching* (3rd ed.). New York: Macmillan.

Drapkin, R. G., Wing, R. R., & Shiffman, S. (1995). Responses to hypothetical high risk situations. *Health Psychology, 14,* 427–434.

Drobes, D. J., & Tiffany, S. T. (1997). Induction of smoking urge through imaginal and in vivo procedures. *Journal of Abnormal Psychology, 106,* 15–25.

Duberstein, P. R., et al. (2000). Personality traits and suicidal behavior and ideation in depressed inpatients 50 years of age and older. *Journals of Gerontology: Series B: Psychological Sciences & Social Sciences, 55B*(1), P18–P26.

Duckitt, J. (1992). Psychology and prejudice. *American Psychologist, 47,* 1182–1193.

Dugan, K. W. (1989). Ability and effort attributions. *Academy of Management Journal, 32,* 87–114.

Duka, T., Tasker, R., & McGowan, J. F. (2000). The effects of 3-week estrogen hormone replacement on cognition in elderly healthy females. *Psychopharmacology, 149*(2), 129–139.

Dumas, J. E., & LaFreniere, P. J. (1993). Mother–child relationships as sources of support or stress. *Child Development, 64.*

Duncan, J., et al. (2000). A neural basis for general intelligence. *Science, 289*(5478), 457–460.

Dunning, J. (1997, July 16). Pursuing perfection: Dancing with death. *The New York Times,* p. C11.

Dweck, C. (1997). Paper presented to the meeting of the Society for Research in Child Development. Cited in Murray, B. (1997). Verbal praise may be the best motivator of all. *APA Monitor, 28*(6), 26.

d'Ydewalle, G., Luwel, K., & Brunfaut, E. (1999). The importance of on-going concurrent activities as a func- tion of age in time- and event-based prospective memory. *European Journal of Cognitive Psychology, 11*(2), 219–237.

Eagle, M. (2000). Repression, part I of II. *Psychoanalytic Review, 87*(1), 1–38.

Eagly, A. H. (2000). Cited in Goode, E. (2000, May 19). Response to stress found that's particularly female. *The New York Times*, p. A20.

Eagly, A. H., Ashmore, R. D., Makhijani, M. G., & Longo, L. C. (1991). What is beautiful is good, but . . . *Psychological Bulletin, 110*, 109–128.

Eagly, A. H., & Chaiken, S. (1993). *The psychology of attitudes*. Fort Worth: Harcourt Brace Jovanovich.

Eagly, A. H., & Wood, W. (1999). The origins of sex differences in human behavior: Evolved dispositions versus social roles. *American Psychologist, 54*(6), 408–423.

Ebbinghaus, H. (1913). *Memory: A contribution to experimental psychology*. (H. A. Roger & C. E. Bussenius, Trans.). New York: Columbia University Press. (Original work published 1885.)

Eberly, M. B., & Montemayor, R. (1999). Adolescent affection and helpfulness toward parents: A 2-year follow-up. *Journal of Early Adolescence, 19*(2), 226–248.

Edgerton, J. W. (1994). Working with key players for psychological and mental health services. *American Psychologist, 49*, 314–321.

Edmundson, M. (1999, August 22). Psychoanalysis, American style. *The New York Times online*.

Edwards, T. M. (2000, August 28). Single by choice. *Time Magazine online, 156*(9).

Egeth, H. E. (1993). What do we *not* know about eyewitness identification? *American Psychologist, 48*, 577–580.

Eggers, D. (2000, May 7). Intimacies. *The New York Times magazine*, pp. 76–77.

Ehlers, A., Maercker, A., & Boos, A. (2000). Posttraumatic stress disorder following political imprisonment: The role of mental defeat, alienation, and perceived permanent change. *Journal of Abnormal Psychology, 109*(1), 45–55.

Ehrlich, P. R. (2000). Cited in Angier, N. (2000, October 10). A conversation with Dr. Paul R. Ehrlich—On human nature, genetics and the evolution of culture. *The New York Times online*.

Eich, E. (1995). Searching for mood dependent memory. *Psychological Science, 6*, 67–75.

Eich, E., Macaulay, D., & Lam, R. W. (1997). Mania, depression, and mood dependent memory. *Cognition & Emotion, 11*(5–6), 607–618.

Einstein, G. O., McDaniel, M. A., Smith, R., & Shaw, P. (1998). Habitual prospective memory and aging: Remembering instructions and forgetting actions. *Psychological Science, 9*(4), 284–288.

Eisenberg, A. (1999, June 24). Blind people with eye damage may someday use chips to see. *The New York Times online*.

Eisenberger, R., & Cameron, J. (1996). Detrimental effects of reward: Reality or myth? *American Psychologist, 51*, 1153–1166.

Ekman, P. (1980). *The face of man*. New York: Garland.

Ekman, P. (1993a). Facial expression and emotion. *American Psychologist, 48*, 384–392.

Ekman, P. (1993b). Cited in D. Goleman (1993, October 26). One smile (only one) can lift a mood. *The New York Times*, p. C11.

Ekman, P., et al. (1987). Universals and cultural differences in the judgments of facial expressions of emotion. *Journal of Personality and Social Psychology, 53*, 712–717.

Ekman, P., & Rosenberg, E. (1997). *What the face reveals*. New York: Oxford University Press.

Elkind, D. (1985). Egocentrism redux. *Developmental Review, 5*, 218–226.

Elkind, D., & Bowen, R. (1979). Imaginary audience behavior in children and adolescents. *Developmental Psychology, 15*(1), 38–44.

Ellenbroek, B. A., Sluyter, F., & Cools, A. R. (2000). The role of genetic and early environmental factors in determining apomorphine susceptibility. *Psychopharmacology, 148*(2), 124–131.

Ellickson, P. L., Hays, R. D., & Bell, R. M. (1992). Stepping through the drug use sequence. *Journal of Abnormal Psychology, 101*, 441–451.

Ellis, A. (2000). Cited in Chamberlin, J. (2000). An historic meeting of the minds. *Monitor on Psychology, 31*(9), 27.

Ellis, A., & Dryden, W. (1996). *The practice of rational emotive behavior therapy*. New York: Springer.

Ellis, E. M. (2000). *Divorce wars: Interventions with families in conflict*. Washington, D.C.: American Psychological Association.

Ellis, L. (1990). Prenatal stress may effect sex-typical behaviors of a child. *Brown University Child Behavior and Development Letter, 6*(1), pp. 1–3.

Ellis, L., & Ames, M. A. (1987). Neurohormonal functioning and sexual orientation. *Psychological Bulletin, 101*, 233–258.

Ellsworth, P. C., Carlsmith, J. M., & Henson, A. (1972). The stare as a stimulus to flight in human subjects. *Journal of Personality and Social Psychology, 21*, 302–311.

Emde, R. (1993). Cited in Adler, T. (1993). Shy, bold temperament? It's mostly in the genes. *APA Monitor, 24*(1), 7, 8.

Engel, J. (1996). Surgery for seizures. *New England Journal of Medicine, 334*, 647–652.

Engels, G. I., Garnefski, N., & Diekstra, R. F. W. (1993). Efficacy of rational-emotive therapy. *Journal of Consulting and Clinical Psychology, 61*, 1083–1090.

Erel, O., & Burman, B. (1995). Interrelatedness of marital relations and parent–child relations: A meta-analytic review. *Psychological Bulletin, 118*, 108–132.

Erel, O., Oberman, Y., & Yirmiya, N. (2000). Maternal versus nonmaternal care and seven domains of children's development. *Psychological Bulletin, 126*(5), 727–747.

Ergul, A. (2000). Hypertension in Black patients: An emerging role of the endothelin system in salt-sensitive hypertension. *Hypertension, 36*, 62–67.

Erikson, E. H. (1963). *Childhood and society*. New York: W. W. Norton.

Erikson, E. H. (1968). Identity: Youth and crisis. New York: W. W. Norton.

Ernst, N. D., & Harlan, W. R. (1991). Obesity and cardiovascular disease in minority populations: Executive summary. *American Journal of Clinical Nutrition, 53*, 1507S–1511S.

Eron, L. D. (1982). Parent-child interaction, television violence, and aggression of children. *American Psychologist, 37*, 197–211.

Eron, L. D. (1993). Cited in DeAngelis, T. (1993). It's baaack: TV violence, concern for kid viewers. *APA Monitor, 24*(8), 16.

Ertem, I. O., Leventhal, J. M., & Dobbs, S. (2000). Intergenerational continuity of child physical abuse: How good is the evidence? *Lancet, 356*, 814–819.

Espenshade, T. (1993). Cited in Barringer, F. (1993, April 25). Polling on sexual issues has its drawbacks. *The New York Times*, p. A23.

Esser, J. K. (1998). Alive and well after 25 years: A review of groupthink research. *Organizational Behavior & Human Decision Processes, 73*(2–3), 116–141.

Etaugh, C., & Rathus, S. A. (1995). *The world of children*. Fort Worth: Harcourt Brace.

Evans, G. W., Jacobs, S. V., & Frager, N. B. (1982). Behavioral responses to air pollution. In A. Baum & J. E. Singer (Eds.), *Advances in environmental psychology* (Vol. 4). Hillsdale, NJ: Erlbaum.

Evans, G. W., Lepore, S. J., & Allen, K. M. (2000). Cross-cultural differences in tolerance for crowding: Fact or fiction? *Journal of Personality & Social Psychology, 79*(2), 204–210.

Evans, G. W., Wells, N. M., Chan, H. E., & Saltzman, H. (2000). Housing quality and mental health. *Journal of Consulting and Clinical Psychology, 68*(3), 526–530.

Eysenck, H. J., & Eysenck, M. W. (1985). *Personality and individual differences*. New York: Plenum.

Faller, H., Buelzebruck, H., Drings, P., & Lang, H. (1999). Coping, distress, and survival among patients with lung cancer. *Archives of General Psychiatry, 56*(8), 756–762.

Fallon, A. E., & Rozin, P. (1985). Sex differences in perceptions of desirable body shape. *Journal of Abnormal Psychology, 94*, 102–105.

Fantz, R. L. (1961). The origin of form perception. *Scientific American, 204*(5), 66–72.

Farber, B. A., Brink, D. C., & Raskin, P. M. (1996). *The psychotherapy of Carl Rogers: Cases and commentary* (pp. 74–75). New York: The Guilford Press.

Farley, F. (2000). Hans J. Eysenck (1916–1997). *American Psychologist, 55*(6), 674–675.

Farr, S. A., Flood, J. F., & Morley, J. E. (2000a). The effect of cholinergic, GABAergic, serotonergic, and glutamatergic receptor modulation on posttrial memory processing in the hippocampus. *Neurobiology of Learning & Memory, 73*(2), 150–167.

Farr, S. A., Uezu, K., Creonte, T. A., Flood, J. F., & Morley, J. E. (2000b). Modulation of memory processing in the cingulate cortex of mice. *Pharmacology, Biochemistry & Behavior, 65*(3), 363–368.

FDA approves second drug for Alzheimer's (1996, November 27). *The New York Times*, p. C8.

Fehr, B., & Russell, J. A. (1991). The concept of love viewed from a prototype perspective. *Journal of Personality and Social Psychology, 60*, 425–438.

Feingold, A. (1992a). Gender differences in mate selection preferences. *Psychological Bulletin, 112*, 125–139.

Feingold, A. (1992b). Good-looking people are not what we think. *Psychological Bulletin, 111*, 304–341.

Feingold, A. (1994). Gender differences in personality: A meta-analysis. *Psychological Bulletin, 116*, 429–456.

Feldman, H. A., Goldstein, I., Hatzichristou, D. G., Krane, R. J., McKinlay, J. B. (1994). Impotence and its medical and psychosocial correlates: Results of the Massachusetts Male Aging Study. *Journal of Urology, 151*(1), 54–61.

Feola, T. W., de Wit, H., & Richards, J. B. (2000). Effects of *d*-amphetamine and alcohol on a measure of behavioral inhibition in rats. *Behavioral Neuroscience, 114*(4), 838–848.

Ferry, B., Roozendaal, B., & McGaugh, J. L. (1999). Role of norepinephrine in mediating stress hormone regulation of long-term memory storage: A critical involvement of the amygdala. *Biological Psychiatry, 46*(9), 1140–1152.

Feshbach, S. (1994). Nationalism, patriotism, and aggression. In L. R. Huesmann (Ed.), *Aggressive behavior*. New York: Plenum.

Festinger, L. (1957). *A theory of cognitive dissonance*. Evanston, IL: Row, Peterson.

Festinger, L., & Carlsmith, J. M. (1959). Cognitive consequences of forced compliance. *Journal of Abnormal and Social Psychology, 58*, 203–210.

Festinger, L., Riecken, H. W. Jr., & Schachter, S. (1956). *When prophecy fails*. Minneapolis: University of Minnesota Press.

Fibel, B., & Hale, W. D. (1978). The generalized expectancy for success scale—A new measure. *Journal of Consulting and Clinical Psychology, 46*, 924–931.

Field, T. M. (1991). Young children's adaptations to repeated separations from their mothers. *Child Development, 62*, 539–547.

Finkenauer, C., et al. (1998). Flashbulb memories and the underlying mechanisms of their formation: Toward an emotional-integrative model. *Memory & Cognition, 26*(3), 516–531.

Finn, P. R., and others. (1997). Heterogeneity in the families of sons of alcoholics. *Journal of Abnormal Psychology, 106*, 26–36.

Finn, P. R., Sharkansky, E. J., Brandt, K. M., & Turcotte, N. (2000). The effects of familial risk, personality, and expectancies on alcohol use and abuse. *Journal of Abnormal Psychology, 109*(1), 122–133.

Fisher, H. E. (2000). Brains do it: Lust, attraction and attachment. *Cerebrum, 2*, 23–42.

Fitzgibbon, M. L., Stolley, M. R., & Kirschenbaum, D. S. (1993). Obese people who seek treatment have different characteristics than those who do not seek treatment. *Health Psychology, 12*, 342–345.

Flack, W. F. Jr., Laird, J. D., & Cavallaro, L. A. (1999). Separate and combined effects of facial expressions and bodily postures on emotional feelings. *European Journal of Social Psychology, 29*(2–3), 203–217.

Flashman, L. A., McAllister, T. W., Andreasen, N. C., & Saykin, A. J. (2000). Smaller brain size associated with unawareness of illness in patients with schizophrenia. *American Journal of Psychiatry, 157*, 1167–1169.

Flavell, J. H. (2000). Development of children's knowledge about the mental world. *International Journal of Behavioral Development, 24*(1), 15–23.

Flavell, J. H., Miller, P. H., & Miller, S. A. (1993). *Cognitive development* (3rd ed). Englewood Cliffs, NJ: Prentice-Hall.

Flor, H., & Birbaumer, N. (1993). Comparison of the efficacy of electromyographic biofeedback, cognitive-behavioral therapy, and conservative medical intervention in the treatment of chronic musculoskeletal pain. *Journal of Consulting and Clinical Psychology, 61*, 653–658.

Foa, E. B., Franklin, M. E., Perry, K. J., & Herbert, J. D. (1996). Cognitive biases in generalized social phobia. *Journal of Abnormal Psychology, 105*, 433–439.

Foerster, J., Higgins, E. T., & Strack, F. (2000). When stereotype disconfirmation is a personal threat: How prejudice and prevention focus moderate incongruency effects. *Social Cognition, 18*(2), 178–197.

Fogel, D. B. (2000, July). Paper presented at the 2000 Congress on Evolutionary Computation, San Diego.

Folkman, S., & Moskowitz, J. T. (2000a). Positive affect and the other side of coping. *American Psychologist, 55*(6), 647–654.

Folkman, S., & Moskowitz, J. T. (2000b). The context matters. *Personality & Social Psychology Bulletin, 26*(2), 150–151.

Ford, E. S., et al. (1991). Physical activity behaviors in lower and higher socioeconomic status populations. *American Journal of Epidemiology, 133*, 1246–1256.

Forgas, J. P., Levinger, G., & Moylan, S. J. (1994). Feeling good and feeling close: Affective influences on the perception of intimate relationships. *Personal Relationships, 1*(2), 165–184.

Fowler, R. D. (1992). Solid support needed for animal research. *APA Monitor, 23*(6), 2.

Fowler, R. D. (1998). Fairness in the workplace. *APA Monitor, 29*(7), 3.

Fowler, W., Ogston, K., Roberts-Fiati, G., & Swenson, A. (1993, February). *The long term development of giftedness and high competencies in children enriched in language during infancy*. Paper presented at the Esther Katz Rosen Symposium on the Psychological Development of Gifted Children, University of Kansas.

Francis, L. E. (2000). Conflicting bureaucracies, conflicted work: Dilemmas in case management for homeless people with mental illness. *Journal of Sociology & Social Welfare, 27*(2), 97–112.

Frangione, B. (2000, July). Amyloid and dementia: To be or not to be. Paper presented to the World Alzheimer Congress 2000, Washington, D.C.

Frankel, K. A., & Bates, J. E. (1990). Mother-toddler problem solving. *Child Development, 61*, 810–819.

Frankenberger, K. D. (2000). Adolescent egocentrism: A comparison among adolescents and adults. *Journal of Adolescence, 23*(3), 343–354.

Fraser, A. M., Brockert, J. E., & Ward, R. H. (1995). Association of young maternal age with adverse reproductive outcomes. *New England Journal of Medicine, 332*, 1113–1117.

Freedman, J. L., & Fraser, S. C. (1966). Compliance without pressure: The foot-in-the-door technique. *Journal of Personality and Social Psychology, 4*, 195–202.

Freeman, H. P., & Payne, R. (2000). Racial injustice in health care. *The New England Journal of Medicine, 342*, 1045–1047.

Freeman, M. S., Spence, M. J., & Oliphant, C. M. (1993, June). *Newborns prefer their mothers' low-pass filtered voices over other female filtered voices*. Paper presented at the annual convention of the American Psychological Society, Chicago.

Freud, S. (1927). A religious experience. In *Standard edition of the complete psychological works of Sigmund Freud, Vol. 21*. London: Hogarth Press, 1964.

Friedman, L. J. (1999). *Identity's architect: A biography of Erik H. Erikson*. New York: Scribner.

Friedman, M., & Ulmer, D. (1984). *Treating Type A behavior and your heart*. New York: Fawcett Crest.

Friedman, R. C., & Downey, J. I. (1994). Homosexuality. *New England Journal of Medicine, 331*, 923–930.

Friedrich, M. J. (2000). Can male hormones really help women? *Journal of the American Medical Association online, 283*(20).

Frieze, I. H. (2000). Violence in close relationships: Development of a research area. *Psychological Bulletin, 126*(5), 681–684.

Friman, P. C., Allen, K. D., Kerwin, M. L. E., & Larzelere, R. (1993). Changes in modern psychology. *American Psychologist, 48*, 658–664.

Frisch, R. (1997). Cited in Angier, N. (1997). Chemical tied to fat control could help trigger puberty. *The New York Times*, pp. C1, C3.

Fritsch, G., & Hitzig, E. (1870). On the electrical excitability of the cerebrum. In G. von Bonin (Ed.), *Some papers on the cerebral cortex*. Springfield, IL: Charles C Thomas. (1960).

Frodi, A. M., Macauley, J., & Thome, P. R. (1977). Are women always less aggressive than men? A review of the experimental literature. *Psychological Bulletin, 84*, 634–660.

Funk, J. B., Buchman, D., Myers, M., Jenks, J. (2000, August 7). Asking the right question in research on violent electronic games. Paper presented to the annual meeting of the American Psychological Association, Washington, D.C.

Fuster, J. M. (2000). The prefrontal cortex of the primate: A synopsis. *Psychobiology, 28*(2), 125–131.

Galambos, N. L., & Turner, P. K. (1999). Parent and adolescent temperaments and the quality of parent-adolescent relations. *Merrill-Palmer Quarterly, 45*(3), 493–511.

Galassi, J. P. (1988). Four cognitive-behavioral approaches. *The Counseling Psychologist, 16*(1), 102–105.

Gallagher, A. M., et al. (2000). Gender differences in advanced mathematical problem solving. *Journal of Experimental Child Psychology, 75*(3), 165–190.

Gallagher, R. (1996). Cited in Murray, B. (1996). College youth haunted by increased pressures. *APA Monitor, 26*(4), 47.

Gallup, G. H., & Newport, F. (1991). Belief in paranormal phenomena among adult Americans. *Skeptical Inquirer, 15*(4), 137–146.

Garcia, J. (1981). The logic and limits of mental

aptitude testing. *American Psychologist, 36,* 1172–1180.

Garcia, J. (1993). Misrepresentation of my criticism of Skinner. *American Psychologist, 48,* 1158.

Garcia, J., Brett, L. P., & Rusiniak, K. W. (1989). Limits of Darwinian conditioning. In S. B. Klein & R. R. Mowrer (Eds.), *Contemporary learning theories: Instrumental conditioning theory and the impact of biological constraints on learning.* Hillsdale, NJ: Erlbaum.

Garcia, J., & Koelling, R. A. (1966). Relation of cue to consequences in avoidance learning. *Psychonomic Science 4,* 123–124.

Gardner, H. (1983/1993). *Frames of mind.* New York: Basic Books.

Gardner, H. (2001, April 5). Multiple intelligence. *The New York Times,* p. A20.

Garfinkel, R. (1995). Cited in Margoshes, P. (1995). For many, old age is the prime of life. *APA Monitor, 26*(5), 36–37.

Gaziano, J. M., et al. (1993). Moderate alcohol intake, increased levels of high-density lipoprotein and its subfractions, and decreased risk of myocardial infarction. *New England Journal of Medicine, 329,* 1829–1834.

Gazzaniga, M. S. (1995). Consciousness and the cerebral hemispheres. In M. S. Gazzaniga (Ed.), *The cognitive neurosciences.* Cambridge, MA: MIT Press.

Geen, R. G., Stonner, D., & Shope, G. L. (1975). The facilitation of aggression by aggression. *Journal of Personality and Social Psychology, 31,* 721–726.

Geiger, H. J. (1996). Race and health care. *New England Journal of Medicine, 335,* 815–816.

Gelman, R., & Baillargeon, R. (1983). A review of some Piagetian concepts. In J. Flavell & E. Markman (Eds.), *Handbook of child psychology.* New York: Wiley.

Georgiades, A., et al. (2000). Effects of exercise and weight loss on mental stress-induced cardiovascular responses in individuals with high blood pressure. *Hypertension, 36,* 171–176.

Geschwind, D. H. (2000). Cited in Rosenbaum, D. E. (2000, May 16). On left-handedness, its causes and costs. *The New York Times,* pp. F1, F6.

Geschwind, N., & Galaburda, A. M. (1987). *Cerebral lateralization: Biological mechanisms, associations, and pathology.* Cambridge, MA: Harvard University Press.

Getzels, J. W., & Jackson, P. W. (1962). *Creativity and intelligence.* New York: Wiley.

Gibbs, N. (1991, June 3). When is it rape? *Time,* pp. 48–54.

Gibson, E. J., & Walk, R. D. (1960, April). The visual cliff. *Scientific American, 202,* 64–71.

Gibson, M., & Ogbu, J. (Eds.). (1991). *Minority status and schooling.* New York: Garland.

Gigerenzer, G., Hoffrage, U., & Kleinbölting, H. (1991). Probabilistic mental models. *Psychological Review, 98,* 506–528.

Gigone, D., & Hastie, R. (1997). Proper analysis of the accuracy of group judgments. *Psychological Bulletin, 121,* 149–167.

Gilbert, S. (1997, June 25). Social ties reduce risk of a cold. *The New York Times,* p. C11.

Gilligan, C. (1982). *In a different voice.* Cambridge, MA: Harvard University Press.

Gilligan, C., Lyons, P., & Hanmer, T. J. (Eds.) (1990). *Making connections.* Cambridge, MA: Harvard University Press.

Gilligan, C., Ward, J. V., & Taylor, J. M. (1989). *Mapping the moral domain: A contribution of women's thinking to psychological theory and education.* Cambridge, MA: Harvard University Press.

Gillis, A. R., Richard, M. A., & Hagan, J. (1986). Ethnic susceptibility to crowding. *Environment and Behavior, 18,* 683–706.

Ginsburg, G., & Bronstein, P. (1993). Family factors related to children's intrinsic/extrinsic motivational orientation and academic performance. *Child Development, 64,* 1461–1474.

Glantz, L. A., & Lewis, D. A. (2000). Decreased dendritic spine density on prefrontal cortical pyramidal neurons in schizophrenia. *Archives of General Psychiatry, 57*(1), 65–73.

Glaser, R., et al. (1991). Stress-related activation of Epstein-Barr virus. *Brain, Behavior, and Immunity, 5,* 219–232.

Glaser, R., et al. (1993). Stress and the memory T-cell response to the Epstein-Barr virus. *Health Psychology, 12,* 435–442.

Gleason, J. B., & Ratner, N. B. (1993). Language development in children. In J. B. Gleason & N. B. Ratner (Eds.), *Psycholinguistics.* Fort Worth: Harcourt Brace Jovanovich.

Gleitman, H., Rozin, P., & Sabini, J. (1997). Solomon E. Asch (1907–1996). *American Psychologist, 52,* 984–985.

Glenn, S. S., Ellis, J., & Greenspoon, J. (1992). On the revolutionary nature of the operant as a unit of behavioral selection. *American Psychologist, 47,* 1326–1329.

Global plague of AIDS (2000, April 23). *The New York Times online.*

Glueckauf, R., Whitton, J., & Nickelson, D. (2000). Telehealth: The new frontier in rehabilitation and healthcare. In M. J. Scherer (Ed.), *Assistive technology and rehabilitation psychology: Shaping an alliance.* Washington, D.C.: American Psychological Association.

Godden, D. R., & Baddeley, A. D. (1975). Context-dependent memory in two natural environments: On land and underwater. *British Journal of Psychology, 66,* 325–331.

Goldman-Rakic, P. S. (1995). Cited in Goleman, D. (1995, May 2). Biologists find site of working memory. *The New York Times,* pp. C1, C9.

Goldman-Rakic, P. S., Muly, E. C. III, & Williams, G. V. (2000). D-sub-1 receptors in prefrontal cells and circuits. *Brain Research Reviews, 31*(2–3), 295–301.

Goldschmidt, D., & Reuters. (2000). Portions, foods in a diet won't determine weight loss, study says. Web posted on www.CNN.com on October 20, 2000.

Goldsmith, H. H. (1993). Cited in Adler, T. (1993). Shy, bold temperament? It's mostly in the genes. *APA Monitor, 24*(1), 7, 8.

Goldstein, I. L., & Buxton, V. M. (1982). Training and human performance. In M. D. Dunnette & E. A. Fleishman (Eds.), *Human Performance and Productivity, 1,* 135–177.

Goleman, D. J. (1995). *Emotional intelligence.* New York: Bantam Books.

Goodall, J., & Peterson, D. (2000). *Africa in my blood: An autobiography in letters.* Boston: Houghton Mifflin Co.

Goode, E. (2000, June 25). Thinner: The male battle with anorexia. *The New York Times,* p. MH8.

Goode, E. (2001, February 20). What's in an inkblot? Some say, not much. *The New York Times,* pp. F1, F4.

Goodman, L. A., Koss, M. P., Fitzgerald, L. F., Russo, N. F., & Keita, G. W. (1993). Male violence against women. *American Psychologist, 48,* 1054–1058.

Goodwin, F. K., & Jamison, K. R. (1990). *Manic-depressive illness.* New York: Oxford University Press.

Gordon, C. M., & Carey, M. P. (1996). Alcohol's effects on requisites for sexual risk reduction in men. *Health Psychology, 15,* 56–60.

Gorman, J. (1997, April 29). Consciousness studies: From stream to flood. *The New York Times,* pp. C1, C5.

Gortmaker, S. L., et al. (1993). Social and economic consequences of over-weight in adolescence and young adulthood. *New England Journal of Medicine, 329,* 1008–1012.

Gottesman, I. I. (1991). *Schizophrenia genesis.* New York: Freeman.

Gottfried, A. E., Fleming, J. S., & Gottfried, A. W. (1994). Role of parental motivational practices in children's academic intrinsic motivation and achievement. *Journal of Educational Psychology, 86,* 104–113.

Gottman, J. M., Coan, J., Carrère, S., & Swanson, C. (1998). Predicting marital happiness and stability from newlywed interactions. *Journal of Marriage and the Family, 60,* 5–22.

Grady, C. L., McIntosh, A. R., Rajah, M. N., Beig, S., & Craik, F. I. M. (1999). The effects of age on the neural correlates of episodic encoding. *Cerebral Cortex, 9*(8), 805–814.

Graf, P. (1990). Life-span changes in implicit and explicit memory. *Bulletin of the Psychonomic Society, 28,* 353–358.

Granberg, D., & Brent, E. (1983). When prophecy bends. *Journal of Personality and Social Psychology, 45,* 477–491.

Grant, H. M., et al. (1998). Context-dependent memory for meaningful material: Information for students. *Applied Cognitive Psychology, 12*(6), 617–623.

Green, D. P., Glaser, J., & Rich, A. (1998). From lynching to gay bashing: The elusive connection between economic condition and hate crime. *Journal of Personality and Social Psychology, 75,* 82–92.

Green J. P., & Lynn, S. J. (2000). Hypnosis and suggestion-based approaches to smoking cessation: An examination of the evidence. *International Journal of Clinical & Experimental Hypnosis, 48*(2), 195–224.

Greenberger, E., Chen, C., Tally, S. R., & Dong, Q. (2000). Family, peer, and individual correlates of depressive symptomology among U.S. and Chinese adolescents. *Journal of Consulting and Clinical Psychology, 68,* 209–219.

Greene, B. (1993). African American women. In L. Comas-Diaz & B. A. Greene (Eds.), *Women of color and mental health.* New York: Guilford.

Greeno, C. G., & Wing, R. R. (1994). Stress-induced eating. *Psychological Bulletin, 115,* 444–464.

Grimsley, K. D. (2000, June 9). Panel asks why women still earn less. *The Washington Post,* p. E03.

Grinspoon, L. (2000). Medical cannabis: The patient's and the doctor's dilemmas. *Addiction Research, 8*(1), 1–4.

Grodstein, F., et al. (1996). Postmenopausal estrogen and pregestin use and the risk of cardiovascular disease. *New England Journal of Medicine, 335,* 453–461.

Grodstein, F., et al. (1997). Postmenopausal hormonal therapy and mortality. *New England Journal of Medicine, 336,* 1769–1775.

Grön, G., Wunderlich, A. P., Spitzer, M., Tomczak, R., & Riepe, M. W. (2000). Brain activation during human navigation: Gender-different neural networks as substrate of performance. *Nature Neuroscience, 3*(4), 404–408.

Gronlund, N. E. (1985). *Measurement and evaluation in teaching* (5th ed.). New York: Macmillan.

Gross, J. J., & Levenson, R. W. (1997). Hiding feelings. *Journal of Abnormal Psychology, 106,* 95–103.

Grosser, B. I., Monti-Bloch, L., Jennings-White, C., & Berliner, D. L. (2000). Behavioral and electrophysiological effects of androstadienone, a human pheromone. *Psychoneuroendocrinology, 25*(3), 289–300.

Gruber-Baldini, A. L. (1991). *The impact of health and disease on cognitive ability in adulthood and old age in the Seattle Longitudinal Study.* Unpublished doctoral dissertation, Pennsylvania State University.

Gruder, C. L., et al. (1993). Effects of social support and relapse prevention training as adjuncts to a televised smoking-cessation intervention. *Journal of Consulting and Clinical Psychology, 61,* 113–120.

Guilford, J. P. (1988). Some changes in the structure-of-intellect model. *Educational and Psychological Measurement, 48,* 1–4.

Gump, B. B., & Matthews, K. A. (2000). Are vacations good for your health? The 9-year mortality experience after the Multiple Risk Factor Intervention Trial. *Psychosomatic Medicine, 62*(5), 608–612.

Guralnik, O., Schmeidler, J., & Simeon, D. (2000). Feeling unreal: Cognitive processes in depersonalization. *American Journal of Psychiatry, 157,* 103–109.

Gurrera, R. J., Nestor, P. G., & O'Donnell, B. F. (2000). Personality traits in schizophrenia: Comparison with a community sample. *Journal of Nervous & Mental Disease, 188*(1), 31–35.

Gutheil, T. G. (1999). A confusion of tongues: Competence, insanity, psychiatry, and the law. *Psychiatric Services, 50*(6), 767–773.

Guthrie, R. V. (1990). Cited in Korn, J. H., Davis, R., & Davis, S. F. (1991). Historians' and chairpersons' judgments of eminence among psychologists. *American Psychologist, 46,* 789–792.

Haaf, R. A., Smith, P. H., & Smitley, S. (1983). Infant response to facelike patterns under fixed trial and infant-control procedures. *Child Development, 54,* 172–177.

Haaga, D. A. F. (2000). Introduction to the special

section on Stepped Care Models in Psychotherapy. *Journal of Consulting and Clinical Psychology, 68*(4), 547–548.

Haaga, D. A. F., & Davison, G. C. (1993). An appraisal of rational-emotive therapy. *Journal of Consulting and Clinical Psychology, 61,* 215–220.

Haan, M. N. (2000, July). Cognitive decline is not normal in aging. Paper presented to the World Alzheimer Congress 2000, Washington, D.C.

Haber, R. N. (1969). Eidetic images. *Scientific American, 220,* 36–55.

Haber, R. N. (1980). Eidetic images are not just imaginary. *Psychology Today, 14*(11), 72–82.

Hakim, A. A., et al. (1998). Effects of walking on mortality among nonsmoking retired men. *New England Journal of Medicine, 338,* 94–99.

Haley, W. E., et al. (1996). Appraisal, coping, and social support as mediators of well-being in Black and White caregivers of patients with Alzheimer's disease. *Journal of Consulting and Clinical Psychology, 64,* 121–129.

Hall, C. S. (1984). "A ubiquitous sex difference in dreams" revisited. *Journal of Personality and Social Psychology, 46,* 1109–1117.

Hall, G. C. N. (1997). Cultural malpractice: The growing obsolescence of psychology with the changing U.S. population. *American Psychologist, 52,* 642–651.

Hall, G. C. N., & Barongan, C. (1997). Prevention of sexual aggression. *American Psychologist, 52,* 5–14.

Hall, G. C. N., Sue, S., Narang, D. S., & Lilly, R. S. (2000). Culture-specific models of men's sexual aggression: Intra- and interpersonal determinants. *Cultural Diversity & Ethnic Minority Psychology, 6*(3), 252–267.

Hall, J. A., et al. (1990). Performance quality, gender, and professional role. *Medical Care, 28,* 489–501.

Halpern, D. F. (1989). *Thought and knowledge.* (2nd ed.). Hillsdale, NJ: Erlbaum.

Halpern, D. F. (1997). Sex differences in intelligence: Implications for education. *American Psychologist, 52,* 1091–1102.

Halpern, D. F., Hansen, C., & Riefer, D. (1990). Analogies as an aid to understanding and memory. *Journal of Educational Psychology, 82,* 298–305.

Halpern, D. F., & LaMay, M. L. (2000). The smarter sex: A critical review of sex differences in intelligence. *Educational Psychology Review, 12*(2), 229–246.

Hamilton, L. C. (1985). Self-reported and actual savings in a water conservation campaign. *Environment and Behavior, 17,* 315–326.

Harley, K., & Reese, E. (1999). Origins of autobiographical memory. *Developmental Psychology, 35*(5), 1338–1348.

Harlow, H. F. (1959). Love in infant monkeys. *Scientific American, 200,* 68–86.

Harlow, H. F., Harlow, M. K., & Meyer, D. R. (1950). Learning motivated by a manipulation drive. *Journal of Experimental Psychology, 40,* 228–234.

Harlow, H. F., & Zimmermann, R. R. (1959). Affectional responses in the infant monkey. *Science, 130,* 421–432.

Harold, G. T., Fincham, F. D., Osborne, L. N., & Conger, R. D. (1997). Mom and Dad are at it

again: Adolescent perceptions of marital conflict and adolescent psychological distress. *Developmental Psychology, 33,* 333–350.

Hart, A. J., et al. (2000). Differential response in the human amygdala to racial outgroup vs. ingroup face stimuli. *NeuroReport, 11*(11), 2351–2355.

Hashimoto, N. (1991). Memory development in early childhood. *Journal of Genetic Psychology, 152,* 101–117.

Hassinger, H. J., Semenchuk, E. M., & O'Brien, W. H. (1999). Appraisal and coping responses to pain and stress in migraine headache sufferers. *Journal of Behavioral Medicine, 22*(4), 327–340.

Haugaard, J. J. (2000). The challenge of defining child sexual abuse. *American Psychologist, 55*(9), 1036–1039.

Hauser-Cram, P., Pierson, D. E., Walker, D. K., & Tivnan, T. (1991). *Early education in the public schools.* San Francisco: Jossey-Bass.

Havighurst, R. J. (1972). *Developmental tasks and education* (3rd ed.). New York: McKay.

Hawkins, S. A., & Hastie, R. (1990). Hindsight: Biased judgments of past events after the outcomes are known. *Psychological Bulletin, 107,* 311–327.

Hayes, P. (1993). Cited in Chartrand, S. (1993, July 18). A split in thinking among keepers of artificial intelligence. *The New York Times,* p. E6.

Hazuda, H. P., et al. (1991). Obesity in Mexican American subgroups: Findings from the San Antonio heart study. *American Journal of Clinical Nutrition, 53,* 1525S–15345S.

Heatherton, T. F., Mahamedi, F., Striepe, M., Field, A. E., & Keel, P. (1997). A 10-year longitudinal study of body weight, dieting, and eating disorder symptoms. *Journal of Abnormal Psychology, 106,* 117–125.

Hegarty, M., Mayer, R. E., & Monk, C. A. (1995). Comprehension of arithmetic word problems. *Journal of Educational Psychology, 87,* 18–32.

Heim, C., et al. (2000). Pituitary-adrenal and autonomic responses to stress in women after sexual and physical abuse in childhood. *Journal of the American Medical Association, 284,* 592–597.

Heller, D. A., de Faire, U., Pedersen, N. L., Dahlén, G., & McClearn, G. E. (1993). Genetic and environmental influences on serum lipid levels in twins. *New England Journal of Medicine, 328,* 1150–1156.

Helms, J. E. (1992). Why is there no study of cultural equivalence of standardized cognitive ability testing? *American Psychologist, 47,* 1083–1101.

Helson, R. (1993). In K. D. Hulbert & D. T. Schuster (Eds.), *Women's lives through time* (pp. 190–210). San Francisco: Jossey-Bass.

Helson, R., Stewart, A. J., & Ostrove, J. (1995). Identity in three cohorts of midlife women. *Journal of Personality and Social Psychology, 69,* 544–557.

Henderson, V. W., et al. (2000). Estrogen for Alzheimer's disease in women: Randomized, double-blind, placebo-controlled trial. *Neurology, 54,* 295–301.

Henke, K., et al. (1999). Memory lost and regained following bilateral hippocampal damage. *Journal of Cognitive Neuroscience, 11*(6), 682–697.

Henkin, W. A. (1985). Toward counseling the Japanese in America. *Journal of Counseling and Development, 63*, 500–503.

Henry, D., et al. (2000). Normative influences on aggression in urban elementary school classrooms. *American Journal of Community Psychology, 28*(1), 59–81.

Hensley, W. E. (1981). The effects of attire, location, and sex on aiding behavior. *Journal of Nonverbal Behavior, 6*, 3–11.

Hensley, W. E. (1994). Height as a basis for interpersonal attraction. *Adolescence, 29*(114), 469–474.

Hepper, P. G., Shahidullah, S., & White, R. (1990, October 4). Origins of fetal handedness. *Nature, 347*, 431.

Hergenhahn, B. R. (2000). *An introduction to the history of psychology* (4th ed.). Pacific Grove, CA: Brooks/Cole.

Herman-Giddens, M. E., et al. (1999). Under-ascertainment of child abuse mortality in the United States. *Journal of the American Medical Association, 282*, 463–467.

Herrell, R., et al. (1999). Sexual orientation and suicidality: A co-twin control study in adult men. *Archives of General Psychiatry, 56*(10), 867–874.

Herrmann, D. J. (1991). *Super memory.* Emmaus, PA: Rodale.

Herrnstein, R. J., & Murray, C. (1994). *The bell curve: Intelligence and class structure in American life.* New York: Free Press.

Hershenson, R. (2000, August 6). Debating the Mozart theory. *The New York Times magazine online.*

Hershey, D. A., Walsh, D. A., Read, S. J., & Chulef, A. S. (1990). Relationships between metamemory, memory predictions, and memory task performance in adults. *Psychology and Aging, 5*, 215–227.

Herzog, T. R., & Chernick, K. K. (2000). Tranquility and danger in urban and natural settings. *Journal of Environmental Psychology, 20*(1), 29–39.

Hetland, L. (2000). Cited in Hershenson, R. (2000, August 6). Debating the Mozart theory. *The New York Times magazine online.*

Hewitt, P. L., Flett, G. L., & Ediger, E. (1996). Perfectionism and depression. *Journal of Abnormal Psychology, 105*, 276–280.

Hewstone, M., & Hamberger, J. (2000). Perceived variability and stereotype change. *Journal of Experimental Social Psychology, 36*(2), 103–124.

Hilgard, E. R. (1994). Neodissociation theory. In S. J. Lynn & J. W. Rhue. *Dissociation: Clinical, theoretical and research perspectives.* New York: Guilford Press.

Hinds, M. D. (2000, May). The politics of pollution. *American Demographics online.*

Hines, C. V., Cruickshank, D. R., & Kennedy, J. (1985). Teacher clarity and its relation to student achievement and satisfaction. *American Educational Research Journal, 22*, 87–99.

Hixon, M. D. (1998). Ape language research: A review and behavioral perspective. *Analysis of Verbal Behavior, 15*, 17–39.

Hobfoll, S. E., Ritter, C., Lavin, J., Hulsizer, M. R., & Cameron, R. P. (1995). Depression prevalence and incidence among inner-city pregnant and postpartum women. *Journal of Consulting and Clinical Psychology, 63*, 445–453.

Hobson, J. A. (1992). Cited in Blakeslee, S. (1992, January 7). Scientists unraveling chemistry of dreams. *The New York Times*, pp. C1, C10.

Hobson, J. A. (1998). Cited in Wade, N. (1998, January 6). Was Freud wrong? Are dreams the brain's start-up test? *The New York Times.*

Hogan, R., Curphy, G. J., & Hogan, J. (1994). What we know about leadership. *American Psychologist, 49*, 493–504.

Hogg, M. A., & Hains, S. C. (1998). Friendship and group identification: A new look at the role of cohesiveness in groupthink. *European Journal of Social Psychology, 28*(3), 323–341.

Hokin, L., et al. (1998). *Proceedings of the National Academy of Sciences, 95*(14), 8363–8368. Cited in Azar, B. (1998). Lithium's mood-stabilizing effect is explained. *APA Monitor, 29*(9), 8.

Holahan, C. J., & Moos, R. H. (1990). Life stressors, resistance factors, and psychological health. *Journal of Personality and Social Psychology, 58*, 909–917.

Holahan, C. J., & Moos, R. H. (1991). Life stressors, personal and social resources, and depression. *Journal of Abnormal Psychology, 100*, 31–38.

Holland, J. J. (2000, July 25). Groups link media to child violence. The Associated Press online.

Holland, J. L. (1996). Exploring careers with a typology. *American Psychologist, 51*, 397–406.

Hollinger, L. M., & Buschmann, M. B. (1993). Factors influencing the perception of touch by elderly nursing home residents and their health caregivers. *International Journal of Nursing Studies, 30*, 445–461.

Hollingshead, A. B., & Redlich, F. C. (1958). *Social class and mental illness.* New York: Wiley.

Hollmann, F. W., & Mulder, T. J. (2000, January 13). Census Bureau projects doubling of nation's population by 2100. U.S. Census Bureau: Public Information Office.

Hollon, S. D., Shelton, R. C., & Loosen, P. T. (1991). Cognitive therapy and pharmacotherapy for depression. *Journal of Consulting and Clinical Psychology, 59*, 88–99.

Holmes, T. H., & Rahe, R. H. (1967). The social readjustment rating scale. *Journal of Psychosomatic Research, 11*, 213–218.

Honan, W. H. (1996, April 11). Male professors keep 30% lead in pay over women, study says. *The New York Times*, p. B9.

Hong, Y., Morris, M. W., Chiu, C., & Benet-Martinez, V. (2000). A dynamic constructivist approach to culture and cognition. *American Psychologist, 55*(7), 709–720.

Honorton, C. (1985). Meta-analysis of psi Ganzfeld research. *Journal of Parapsychology, 49*, 51–91.

Honorton, C., et al. (1990). Psi communication in the Ganzfeld. *Journal of Parapsychology, 54*, 99–139.

Honts, C. R., Hodes, R. L., & Raskin, D. C. (1985). Effects of physical countermeasures on the physiological detection of deception. *Journal of Applied Psychology, 70*(1), 177–187.

Hoover, R. N. (2000). Cancer—Nature, nurture, or both. *New England Journal of Medicine online, 343*(2).

Hopper, J. L., & Seeman, E. (1994). The bone density of female twins discordant for tobacco use. *New England Journal of Medicine, 330*, 387–392.

Horn, J. M. (1983). The Texas adoption project. *Child Development, 54*, 268–275.

Horney, K. (1967). *Feminine psychology.* New York: W. W. Norton.

Hovey, J. D. (2000). Acculturative stress, depression, and suicidal ideation in Mexican immigrants. *Cultural Diversity and Ethnic Minority Psychology, 6*(2), 134–151.

Howard-Pitney, B., LaFramboise, T. D., Basil, M., September, B., & Johnson, M. (1992). Psychological and social indicators of suicide ideation and suicide attempts in Zuni adolescents. *Journal of Consulting and Clinical Psychology, 60*, 473–476.

Hu, F. B., et al. (2000). Physical activity and risk of stroke in women. *Journal of the American Medical Association, 283*, 2961–2967.

Hubel, D. H., & Wiesel, T. N. (1979). Brain mechanisms of vision. *Scientific American, 241*, 150–162.

Huesmann, L. R., Eron, L. D., Klein, R., Brice, P., & Fischer, P. (1983). Mitigating the imitation of aggressive behaviors by changing children's attitudes about media violence. *Journal of Personality and Social Psychology, 44*, 899–910.

Huesmann, L. R., & Guerra, N. G. (1997). Children's normative beliefs about aggression and aggressive behavior. *Journal of Personality & Social Psychology, 72*(2), 408–419.

Huesmann, L. R., & Miller, L. S. (1994). Long-term effects of repeated exposure to media violence in childhood. In L. R. Huesmann (Ed.), *Aggressive behavior.* New York: Plenum.

Huffman, T., Chang, K. Rausch, P., & Schaffer, N. (1994). Gender differences and factors related to the disposition toward cohabitation. *Family Therapy, 21*(3), 171–184.

Hugick, L., & Leonard, J. (1991). Job dissatisfaction grows; "moonlighting" on the rise. *The Gallup Poll News Service, 56*, 1–11.

Hultquist, C. M., et al. (1995). The effect of smoking and light activity on metabolism in men. *Health Psychology, 14*, 124–131.

Humphrey, L. L. (1986). Family dynamics in bulimia. In S. C. Feinstein et al. (Eds.), *Adolescent psychiatry.* Chicago: University of Chicago Press.

Hunsley, J., & Bailey, J. M. (1999). The clinical utility of the Rorschach: Unfulfilled promises and an uncertain future. *Psychological Assessment, 11*(3), 266–277.

Hunt, M. (1993). *The story of psychology.* New York: Anchor Books.

Huxley, A. (1939). *Brave new world.* New York: Harper & Row.

Hyde, J. S., & Plant, E. A. (1995). Magnitude of psychological gender differences. *American Psychologist, 50*, 159–161.

Iacono, W. G., & Lykken, D. T. (1997). The validity of the lie detector: Two surveys of scientific opinion. *Journal of Applied Psychology, 82*(3), 426–433.

Iidaka, T., Anderson, N. D., Kapur, S., Cabeza, R., & Craik, F. I. M. (2000). The effect of divided attention on encoding and retrieval in episodic memory revealed by positron emission tomography. *Journal of Cognitive Neuroscience, 12*(2), 267–280.

Insel, T. R. (2000). Toward a neurobiology of attachment. *Review of General Psychology, 4*(2), 176–185.

International Human Genome Sequencing Consortium (2001). Initial sequencing and analysis of the human genome. *Nature, 409*, 860–921.

Iribarren, C., et al. (2000). Association of hostility with coronary artery calcification in young adults: The CARDIA study. *Journal of the American Medical Association, 283*, 2546–2551.

Isabella, R. A. (1998). Origins of attachment: The role of context, duration, frequency of observation, and infant age in measuring maternal behavior. *Journal of Social & Personal Relationships, 15*(4), 538–554.

Isarida, T., & Isarida, T. (1999). Effects of contextual changes between class and intermission on episodic memory. *Japanese Journal of Psychology, 69*(6), 478–485.

Isay, R. A. (1990). Psychoanalytic theory and the therapy of gay men. In D. P. McWhirter, S. A. Sanders, & J. M. Reinisch (Eds.), *Homosexuality/heterosexuality* (pp. 283–303). New York: Oxford University Press.

Isen, A. M., & Baron, R. A. (1990). Positive affect and organizational behavior. In B. M. Staw & L. L. Cummings (Eds.), *Advances in experimental social psychology* (Vol. 12). Greenwich, CT: JAI Press.

Isomura, T., Fine, S., & Lin, T. (1987). Two Japanese families. *Canadian Journal of Psychiatry, 32*, 282–286.

Izard, C. E. (1984). Emotion-cognition relationships and human development. In C. E. Izard, J. Kagan, & R. B. Zajonc (Eds.), *Emotions, cognition, and behavior.* New York: Cambridge University Press.

Izard, C. E. (1990). Facial expression and the regulation of emotions. *Journal of Personality and Social Psychology, 58*, 487–498.

Izard, C. E. (1994). Basic emotions, relations among emotions, and emotion-cognition relations. *Psychological Bulletin, 115*, 561–565.

Jacks, J. Z., & Devine, P. G. (2000). Attitude importance, forewarning of message content, and resistance to persuasion. *Basic & Applied Social Psychology, 22*(1) 19–29.

Jackson, J. (1993). Human behavioral genetics, Scarr's theory, and her views on interventions. *Child Development, 64*, 1318–1332.

Jacob, S., & McClintock, M. K. (2000). Psychological state and mood effects of steroidal chemosignals in women and men. *Hormones and Behavior, 37*(1), 57–78.

Jacobs, T. J., & Charles, E. (1980). Life events and the occurrence of cancer in children. *Psychosomatic Medicine, 42*, 11–24.

Jacobson, N. S., & Hollon, S. D. (1996). Cognitive-behavior therapy versus pharmacotherapy. *Journal of Consulting and Clinical Psychology, 64*, 74–80.

Jacox, A., Carr, D. B., & Payne, R. (1994). New clinical-practice guidelines for the management of pain in patients with cancer. *New England Journal of Medicine, 330*, 651–655.

Jaffee, S., & Hyde, J. S. (2000). Gender differences in moral orientation. *Psychological Bulletin, 126*(5), 703–726.

James, W. (1890). *The principles of psychology.* New York: Henry Holt.

James, W. (1904). Does "consciousness" exist? *Journal of Philosophy, Psychology, and Scientific Methods, 1*, 477–491.

Jamison, K. R. (1997). Manic-depressive illness and creativity. *Scientific American mysteries of the mind, Special Issue Vol.* 7, No. 1, 44–49.

Jamison, K. R. (2000). Cited in Krehbiel, K. (2000). Diagnosis and treatment of bipolar disorder. *Monitor on Psychology, 31*(9), 22.

Janerich, D. T., et al. (1990). Lung cancer and exposure to tobacco smoke in the household. *New England Journal of Medicine, 323*, 632–636.

Janis, I. L. (1982). *Groupthink* (2nd ed.). Boston: Houghton Mifflin.

Janos, P. M. (1987). A fifty-year follow-up of Terman's youngest college students and IQ-matched agemates. *Gifted Child Quarterly, 31*, 55–58.

Janowitz, H. D., & Grossman, M. I. (1949). Effects of variations in nutritive density on intake of food in dogs and cats. *American Journal of Physiology, 158*, 184–193.

Janowsky, J. S., Chavez, B., & Orwoll, E. (2000). Sex steroids modify working memory. *Journal of Cognitive Neuroscience, 12*, 407–414.

Janus, C., et al. (2000). A peptide immunization reduces behavioural impairment and plaques in a model of Alzheimer's disease. *Nature, 408*(6815), 979–981.

Jeffery, R. W., Epstein, L. H., Wilson, G. T., Drewnowski, A., Stunkard, A. J., & Wing, R. R. (2000a). Long-term maintenance of weight loss: Current status. *Health Psychology, 19*(Suppl 1), 5–16.

Jeffery, R. W., Hennrikus, D. J., Lando, H. A., Murray, D. M., & Liu, J. W. (2000b). Reconciling conflicting findings regarding postcessation weight concerns and success in smoking cessation. *Health Psychology, 19*, 242–246.

Jemmott, J. B., et al. (1983). Academic stress, power motivation, and decrease in secretion rate of salivary secretory immunoglobin A. *Lancet, 1*, 1400–1402.

Jensen, M. P., & Karoly, P. (1991). Control beliefs, coping efforts, and adjustment to chronic pain. *Journal of Consulting and Clinical Psychology, 59*, 431–438.

Jensen, M. P., Turner, J. A., & Romano, J. M. (1994). Correlates of improvement in multidisciplinary treatment of chronic pain. *Journal of Consulting and Clinical Psychology, 62*, 172–179.

Jerome, L., DeLeon, P., James, L., & Gedney, J. (2000). The coming of age of telecommunications in psychological research and practice. *American Psychologist, 55*(4), 407–421.

Ji, L.-J., Peng, K., & Nisbett, R. E. (2000). Culture, control, and perception of relationships in the environment. *Journal of Personality & Social Psychology, 78*(5), 943–955.

Johns, A. (2001). Psychiatric effects of cannabis. *The British Journal of Psychiatry, 178*, 116–122.

Johnson, K. W., et al. (1995). Panel II: Macrosocial and environmental influences on minority health. *Health Psychology, 14*, 601–612.

Johnson, W., Emde, R. N., Pannabecker, B., Stenberg, C., & Davis, M. (1982). Maternal perception of infant emotion from birth to 18 months. *Infant Behavior and Development, 5*, 313–322.

Johnston, L. D., O'Malley, P. M., & Bachman, J. G. (2000). *The Monitoring the Future national survey results on adolescent drug use: Overview of key findings, 1999* (NIH Publication No. 00-4690). Rockville, MD: National Institute on Drug Abuse, c. 56 pp.

Joiner, T. E., Heatherton, T. F., Rudd, M. D., & Schmidt, N. B. (1997). Perfectionism, perceived weight status, and bulimic symptoms. *Journal of Abnormal Psychology, 106*, 145–153.

Jones, C. J., & Meredith, W. (2000). Developmental paths of psychological health from early adolescence to later adulthood. *Psychology and Aging, 15*(2), 351–360.

Jones, E. E. (1990). *Interpersonal perception.* New York: W. H. Freeman.

Jones, J. L., & Leary, M. R. (1994). Effects of appearance-based admonitions against sun exposure on tanning intentions in young adults. *Health Psychology, 13*, 86–90.

Jones, M. (2000). The genetic report card that will tell you if your embryo will get prostate cancer. *The New York Times magazine*, p. 80.

Jones, M. C. (1924). Elimination of children's fears. *Journal of Experimental Psychology, 7*, 381–390.

Jonsdottir, I. H., Hellstrand, K., Thoren, P., & Hoffman, P. (2000). Enhancement of natural immunity seen after voluntary exercise in rats. Role of central opioid receptors. *Life Sciences, 66*(13), 1231–1239.

Joranson, D. E., Ryan, K. M., Gilson, A. M., & Dahl, J. L. (2000). Trends in medical use and abuse of opioid analgesics. *Journal of the American Medical Association, 283*, 1710–1714.

Jorgensen, R. S., Johnson, B. T., Kolodziej, M. E., & Schreer, G. E. (1996). Elevated blood pressure and personality. *Psychological Bulletin, 120*, 293–320.

Jorgenson, L. M., & Wahl, K. M. (2000). Workplace sexual harassment: Incidence, legal analysis, and the role of the psychiatrist. *Harvard Review of Psychiatry, 8*(2), 94–98.

Josefsson, A. M., et al. (2000). Viral load of human papilloma virus 16 as a determinant for development of cervical carcinoma in situ: a nested case-control study. *The Lancet, 355*, 2189–2193.

Judd, C. M., & Park, B. (1988). Out-group homogeneity. *Journal of Personality and Social Psychology, 54*, 778–788.

Just, N., & Alloy, L. B. (1997). The response styles theory of depression: Tests and an extension of the theory. *Journal of Abnormal Psychology, 106*, 221–229.

Kahle, L. R., & Beatty, S. E. (1987). Cognitive consequences of post-purchase behavior. *Journal of Applied Social Psychology, 17*, 828–843.

Kahn, R. L., & Rowe, J. (1998). *Successful aging.* New York: Pantheon Books.

Kail, R. (1990). *The development of memory in children* (3rd ed.). New York: W. H. Freeman.

Kail, R. (2000). Speed of information processing: Developmental change and links to intelligence. *Journal of School Psychology, 38*(1), 51–61.

Kaiser, F. G., & Shimoda, T. A. (1999). Responsibility as a predictor of ecological behaviour. *Journal of Environmental Psychology, 19*(3), 243–253.

Kallgren, C. A., Reno, R. R., & Cialdini, R. B. (2000). A focus theory of normative conduct: When norms do and do not affect behavior. *Personality & Social Psychology Bulletin, 26*(8), 1002–1012.

Kamalanabhan, T. J., Sunder, D. L., & Vasanthi, M. (2000). An evaluation of the Choice Dilemma Questionnaire as a measure of risk-taking propensity. *Social Behavior & Personality, 28*(2), 149–156.

Kamin, L. J. (1995). Behind the curve [Review of *The Bell Curve: Intelligence and Class Structure in American Life*]. *Scientific American, 272,* 99–103.

Kamphaus, R. W., Petoskey, M. D., & Rowe, E. W. (2000). Current trends in psychological testing of children. *Professional Psychology: Research and Practice, 31*(2), 155–164.

Kandel, E. R., & Hawkins, R. D. (1992). The biological basis of learning and individuality. *Scientific American, 267*(3), 78–86.

Kane, J. M. (1996). Schizophrenia. *New England Journal of Medicine, 334,* 34–41.

Kant, A. K., et al. (2000). A prospective study of diet quality and mortality in women. *Journal of the American Medical Association, 283,* 2109–2115.

Kaplan, S. J. (1991). Physical abuse and neglect. In M. Lewis (Ed.), *Child and adolescent psychiatry* (pp. 1010–1019). Baltimore: Williams & Wilkins.

Karabenick, S. A., & Sharma, R. (1994). Perceived teacher support of student questioning in the college classroom: Its relationship to student characteristics and role in the classroom questioning process. *Journal of Educational Psychology, 86,* 90–103.

Karasek, R. A., et al. (1982). Job, psychological factors and coronary heart disease. *Advances in Cardiology, 29,* 62–67.

Karlberg, L., et al. (1998). Is there a connection between car accidents, near accidents, and Type A drivers? *Behavioral Medicine, 24*(3), 99–106.

Karoly, P., & Ruehlman, L. S. (1996). Motivational implications of pain. *Health Psychology, 15,* 383–390.

Karon, B. P., & Widener, A. (1998). Repressed memories: The real story. *Professional Psychology: Research & Practice, 29*(5), 482–487.

Kashima, Y. (2000). Maintaining cultural stereotypes in the serial reproduction of narratives. *Personality & Social Psychology Bulletin, 26*(5), 594–604.

Kassirer, J. P., & Angell, M. (1998). Losing weight—An ill-fated New Year's resolution. *New England Journal of Medicine, 338,* 52–54.

Katz, M. H., & Gerberding, J. L. (1997). Postexposure treatment of people exposed to the human immunodeficiency virus through sexual contact or injection-drug use. *New England Journal of Medicine, 336,* 1097–1100.

Katzell, R. A., & Thompson, D. E. (1990). Work motivation. *American Psychologist, 45,* 144–153.

Katzman, R. (2000, July). Epidemiology of Alzheimer's disease. Paper presented at the World Alzheimer Congress 2000, Washington, D.C.

Kaufman, J., & Zigler, E. (1989). The intergenerational transmission of child abuse. In D. Cicchetti & V. Carlson (Eds.), *Child maltreatment* (pp. 129–150). Cambridge: Cambridge University Press.

Kawas, C. (2000, July). Estrogen and the prevention of Alzheimer's disease. Paper presented to the World Alzheimer Congress 2000, Washington, D.C.

Kaya, N., & Erkip, F. (1999). Invasion of personal space under the condition of short-term crowding: A case study on an automatic teller machine. *Journal of Environmental Psychology, 19*(2), 183–189.

Kaye, W. H., Klump, K. L., Frank, G. K. W., & Strober, M. (2000). Anorexia and bulimia nervosa. *Annual Review of Medicine, 51,* 299–313.

Keefe, F. J., Dunsmore, J., & Burnett, R. (1992). Behavioral and cognitive-behavioral approaches to chronic pain. *Journal of Consulting and Clinical Psychology, 60,* 528–536.

Keil, J. E., et al. (1993). Mortality rates and risk factors for coronary disease in Black as compared with White men and women. *New England Journal of Medicine, 329,* 73–78.

Keita, G. P. (1993, February). Presentation to the Fifth International Interdisciplinary Congress on Women, University of Costa Rica, San Jose, Costa Rica.

Keller, M. B., et al. (2000). A Comparison of nefazodone, the cognitive behavioral-analysis system of psychotherapy, and their combination for the treatment of chronic depression. *The New England Journal of Medicine, 342*(20), 1462–1470.

Kellerman, J., Lewis, J., & Laird, J. D. (1989). Looking and loving: The effects of mutual gaze on feelings of romantic love. *Journal of Research in Personality, 23,* 145–161.

Kelley, H. H., & Michela, J. L. (1980). Attribution theory and research. *Annual Review of Psychology, 31,* 457–501.

Kellman, P. J., & von Hofsten, C. (1992). The world of the moving infant. In C. Rovee-Collier & L. P. Lipsitt (Eds.), *Advances in Infancy Research* (Vol. 7). Norwood, NJ: Ablex.

Kelly, A. (2000). Helping construct desirable identities: A self-presentational view of psychotherapy. *Psychological Bulletin, 126*(4), 475–494.

Kelly, G. A. (1955). *The psychology of personal constructs, Vols. 1 & 2.* New York: W. W. Norton.

Kelly, I. W. (1998). Why astrology doesn't work. *Psychological Reports, 82*(2), 527–546.

Kelly-Radford, L. (1998). Cited in McGuire, P. A. (1998). Wanted: Workers with flexibility for 21st century jobs. *APA Monitor, 29*(7), 10, 12.

Kendler, K. S., et al. (1997). Resemblance of psychotic symptoms and syndromes in affected sibling pairs from the Irish study of high-density schizophrenia families: Evidence for possible etiologic heterogeneity. *American Journal of Psychiatry, 154,* 191–198.

Kendler, K. S., et al. (2000a). Illicit psychoactive substance use, heavy use, abuse, and dependence in a US population-based sample of male twins. *Archives of General Psychiatry, 57,* 261–269.

Kendler, K. S., Myers, J. M., & Neale, M. C. (2000b). A multidimensional twin study of mental health in women. *American Journal of Psychiatry, 157,* 506–513.

Kendler, K. S., Thornton, L. M., Gilman, S. E., & Kessler, R. C. (2000c). Sexual orientation in a U.S. national sample of twin and nontwin sibling pairs. *American Journal of Psychiatry, 157,* 1843–1846.

Kendler, K. S., Thornton, L. M., & Pedersen, N. L. (2000d). Tobacco consumption in Swedish twins reared apart and reared together. *Archives of General Psychiatry, 57,* 886–892.

Kenrick, D. T., & MacFarlane, S. W. (1986). Ambient temperature and horn honking. *Environment and Behavior, 18,* 179–191.

Kiesler, C. A. (1982). Mental hospitalization and alternative care. *American Psychologist, 37,* 349–360.

Kilshaw, D., & Annett, M. (1983). Right- and left-hand skill: Effects of age, sex, and hand preferences showing superior in left-handers. *British Journal of Psychology, 74,* 253–268.

Kim, J., et al. (2000). Regional neural dysfunctions in chronic schizophrenia studied with positron emission tomography. *American Journal of Psychiatry, 157,* 542–548.

Kimble, G. A. (1994). A frame of reference for psychology. *American Psychologist, 49,* 510–519.

Kimerling, R., & Calhoun, K. S. (1994). Somatic symptoms, social support, and treatment seeking among sexual assault victims. *Journal of Consulting and Clinical Psychology, 62,* 333–340.

Kinderman, P., & Bentall, R. P. (1997). Causal attributions in paranoia and depression. *Journal of Abnormal Psychology, 106,* 341–345.

King, R. (2000). Cited in Frazier, L. (2000, July 16). The new face of HIV is young, black. *The Washington Post,* p. C01.

Kinnunen, T., Doherty, K., Militello, F. S., & Garvey, A. J. (1996). Depression and smoking cessation. *Journal of Consulting and Clinical Psychology, 64,* 791–798.

Kinnunen, T., Zamansky, H. S., & Block, M. L. (1994). Is the hypnotized subject lying? *Journal of Abnormal Psychology, 103,* 184–191.

Kinsey, A. C., Pomeroy, W. B., & Martin, C. E. (1948). *Sexual behavior in the human male.* Philadelphia: W. B. Saunders.

Kinsey, A. C., Pomeroy, W. B., Martin, C. E., & Gebhard, P. H. (1953). *Sexual behavior in the human female.* Philadelphia: W. B. Saunders.

Kintsch, W. (1994). Text comprehension, memory, and learning. *American Psychologist, 49,* 294–303.

Kirsch, I. (2000). The response set theory of hypnosis. *American Journal of Clinical Hypnosis, 42*(3–4), 274–292.

Kirsch, I., Montgomery, G., & Sapirstein, G. (1995). Hypnosis as an adjunct to cognitive-behavioral psychotherapy. *Journal of Consulting and Clinical Psychology, 63,* 214–220.

Kleinke, C. L. (1977). Compliance to requests made by gazing and touching experimenters in field settings. *Journal of Experimental Social Psychology, 13,* 218–223.

Kleinke, C. L. (1986). Gaze and eye contact. *Psychological Review, 100,* 78–100.

Kleinke, C. L., & Staneski, R. A. (1980). First impressions of female bust size. *Journal of Social Psychology, 110,* 123–134.

Kleinmuntz, B., & Szucko, J. J. (1984). Lie detection in ancient and modern times. *American Psychologist, 39,* 766–776.

Klorman, R., Brumaghim, J. T., Fitzpatrick, P. A., Borgstedt, A. D., & Strauss, J. (1994). Clinical and cognitive effects of methylphenidate on children with attention deficit disorder as a function of aggression/oppositionality and age. *Journal of Abnormal Psychology, 103,* 206–221.

Klosko, J. S., Barlow, D. H., Tassinari, R., & Cerny, J. A. (1990). A comparison of alprazolam and behavior therapy in treatment of panic disorder. *Journal of Consulting and Clinical Psychology, 58,* 77–84.

Klüver, H., & Bucy, P. C. (1939). Preliminary analysis of functions of the temporal lobe in monkeys. *Archives of Neurology and Psychiatry, 42,* 979–1000.

Knight, G. P., Fabes, R. A., & Higgins, D. A. (1996). Concerns about drawing causal inferences from meta-analyses: An example in the study of gender differences in aggression. *Psychological Bulletin, 119,* 410–421.

Knowlton, W. A. Jr., & Mitchell, T. R. (1980). Effects of causal attributions on a supervisor's evaluation of subordinate performance. *Journal of Applied Psychology, 65,* 459–466.

Kobasa, S. C. O. (1990). Stress-resistant personality. In R. E. Ornstein & C. Swencionis (Eds.), *The healing brain* (pp. 219–230). New York: The Guilford Press.

Kobasa, S. C. O., Maddi, S. R., Puccetti, M. C., & Zola, M. A. (1994). Effectiveness of hardiness, exercise, and social support as resources against illness. In A. Steptoe & J. Wardle (Eds.), *Psychosocial processes and health* (pp. 247–260). Cambridge: Cambridge University Press.

Kohlberg, L. (1969). *Stages in the development of moral thought and action.* New York: Holt, Rinehart and Winston.

Kohlberg, L. (1981). *The philosophy of moral development.* San Francisco: Harper & Row.

Köhler, W. (1925). *The mentality of apes.* New York: Harcourt Brace World.

Kohout, J., & Williams, S. (1999). Far more psychology degrees are going to women. *APA Monitor online, 30*(10).

Kolata, G. (1996, August 27). Gene therapy shows first signs of bypassing arterial blockage. *The New York Times,* p. C3.

Kolata, G. (2000a, January 18). True secret of fad diets: It's calories. *The New York Times,* p. F7.

Kolata, G. (2000b, June 25). Men in denial: The doctor's tale. *The New York Times online.*

Kolko, D. J., & Rickard-Figueroa, J. L. (1985). Effects of video games on the adverse corollaries of chemotherapy in pediatric oncology patients. *Journal of Consulting and Clinical Psychology, 53,* 223–228.

Kooijman, C. M., et al. (2000). Phantom pain and phantom sensations in upper limb amputees: An epidemiological study. *Pain, 87*(1), 33–41.

Korn, J. H., Davis, R., & Davis, S. F. (1991). Historians' and chairpersons' judgments of eminence among psychologists. *American Psychologist, 46,* 789–792.

Kosonen, P., & Winne, P. H. (1995). Effects of teaching statistical laws on reasoning about everyday problems. *Journal of Educational Psychology, 87,* 33–46.

Koss, M. P. (1993). Rape. *American Psychologist, 48,* 1062–1069.

Kosslyn, S. M. (1994). *Image and brain.* Cambridge, MA: The MIT Press, a Bradford Book.

Krantz, D. S., Contrada, R. J., Hill, D. R., & Friedler, E. (1988). Environmental stress and biobehavioral antecedents of coronary heart disease. *Journal of Consulting and Clinical Psychology, 56,* 333–341.

Kraut, R., et al. (1998). Internet paradox: A social technology that reduces social involvement and psychological well-being? *American Psychologist, 53*(9), 1017–1031.

Krumhansl, C. L. (2000). Rhythm and pitch in music cognition. *Psychological Bulletin, 126*(1), 159–179.

Kubiszyn, T. (1996). Cited in Murray, B. (1996). Task force defines psychology's role in schools. *APA Monitor, 26*(4), 34.

Kübler-Ross, E. (1969). *On death and dying.* New York: Macmillan.

Kuczaj, S. A. II (1982). On the nature of syntactic development. In S. A. Kuczaj II (Ed.), *Language development: Vol. 1. Syntax and semantics.* Hillsdale, NJ: Erlbaum.

Kurzweil, R. (2000, June 19). Will my PC be smarter than I am? *Time magazine,* pp. 82–83.

Kushler, M. G. (1989). Use of evaluation to improve energy conservation programs. *Journal of Social Issues, 45,* 153–168.

Kyle, T. M., & Williams, S. (2000, May). Results of the 1998–1999 APA survey of graduate departments of psychology. APA Research Office. Washington, D.C.: American Psychological Association.

Labouvie-Vief, G., & Diehl, M. (2000). Cognitive complexity and cognitive-affective integration: Related or separate domains of adult development? *Psychology & Aging, 15*(3), 490–504.

Lackner, J. M., Carosella, A. M., & Feuerstein, M. (1996). Pain expectancies, pain, and functional self-efficacy expectancies as determinants of disability in patients with chronic low back disorders. *Journal of Consulting and Clinical Psychology, 64,* 212–220.

Lacks, P., & Morin, C. M. (1992). Recent advances in the assessment and treatment of insomnia. *Journal of Consulting and Clinical Psychology, 60,* 586–594.

LaFramboise, T. (1994). Cited in DeAngelis, T. (1994). History, culture affect treatment for Indians. *APA Monitor, 27*(10), 36.

Lalumière, M. L., Blanchard, R., & Zucker, K. J. (2000). Sexual orientation and handedness in men and women: A meta-analysis. *Psychological Bulletin, 126*(4), 575–592.

Lam, J. A., & Rosenheck, R. A. (2000). Correlates of improvement in quality of life among homeless persons with serious mental illness. *Psychiatric Services, 51*(1), 116–118.

Lamb, M. E., & Baumrind, D. (1978). Socialization and personality development in the preschool years. In M. E. Lamb (Ed.), *Social and personality development.* New York: Holt, Rinehart and Winston.

Lamb, M. E., Sternberg, K. J., & Prodromidis, M. (1992). Nonmaternal care and the security of infant–mother attachment. *Infant Behavior and Development, 15,* 71–83.

Lambert, W. E. (1990). Persistent issues in bilingualism. In B. Harley and others (Eds.), *The development of second language proficiency.* Cambridge: Cambridge University Press.

Lambert, W. E., Genesee, F., Holobow, N., & Chartrand, L. (1991). *Bilingual education for majority English-speaking children.* Montreal: McGill University.

Lancaster, T., Stead, L., Silagy, C., & Sowden, A. (2000). Regular review: Effectiveness of interventions to help people stop smoking: Findings from the Cochrane Library. *British Medical Journal, 321,* 355–358.

Landy, F. J. (1992, August). The roots of organizational and industrial psychology. Master lecture presented to the annual meeting of the American Psychological Association, Washington, D.C.

Lang, A. R., Goeckner, D. J., Adesso, V. J., & Marlatt, G. A. (1975). Effects of alcohol on aggression in male social drinkers. *Journal of Abnormal Psychology, 84,* 508–518.

Lang, E. V., et al. (2000). Adjunctive non-pharmacological analgesia for invasive medical procedures: A randomised trial. *The Lancet, 355,* 1486–1490.

Lang, P. J., & Melamed, B. B. (1969). Case report: Avoidance conditioning therapy of an infant with chronic ruminative vomiting. *Journal of Abnormal Psychology, 74,* 1–8.

Lang, S. S., & Patt, R. B. (1994). *You don't have to suffer.* New York: Oxford University Press.

Langer, E. J., Rodin, J., Beck, P., Weinan, C., & Spitzer, L. (1979). Environmental determinants of memory improvement in late adulthood. *Journal of Personality and Social Psychology, 37,* 2003–2013.

Langlois, J. H., et al. (2000). Maxims or myths of beauty? A meta-analytic and theoretical review. *Psychological Bulletin, 126*(3), 390–423.

Larkin, M. (2000). Can lost hearing be restored? *The Lancet, 356,* 741–748.

Larrick, R. P. (1993). Motivational factors in decision theories. *Psychological Bulletin, 113,* 440–450.

Larson, R., & Richards, M. H. (1991). Daily companionship in late childhood and early adolescence. *Child Development, 62,* 284–300.

Lashley, K. S. (1950). In search of the engram. In *Symposium of the Society for Experimental Biology* (Vol. 4). New York: Cambridge University Press.

Latané, B., & Dabbs, J. M. (1975). Sex, group size, and helping in three cities. *Sociometry, 38,* 180–194.

Lau, M. A., Pihl, R. O., & Peterson, J. B. (1995). Provocation, acute alcohol intoxication, cognitive performance, and aggression. *Journal of Abnormal Psychology, 104,* 150–155.

Laube, D. (1985). Premenstrual syndrome. *The Female Patient, 6,* 50–61.

Laumann, E. O., Gagnon, J. H., Michael, R. T., & Michaels, S. (1994). *The social organization of sexuality.* Chicago: University of Chicago Press.

Laumann, E. O., Paik, A., & Rosen, R. C. (1999).

Sexual dysfunction in the United States. Prevalence and predictors. *Journal of the American Medical Association, 281*(6), 537–544.

Lavie, P., & Herer, P., & Hoffstein, H. (2000). Obstructive sleep apnoea syndrome as a risk factor for hypertension: Population study. *British Medical Journal, 320*, 479–482.

Lawton, C. A., & Morrin, K. A. (1999). Gender differences in pointing accuracy in computer-simulated 3D mazes. *Sex Roles, 40*(1–2), 73–92.

Lazarus, R. S., DeLongis, A., Folkman, S., & Gruen, R. (1985). Stress and adaptational outcomes. *American Psychologist, 40*, 770–779.

Lazarus, R. S., & Folkman, S. (1984). *Stress, appraisal, and coping.* New York: Springer.

Le Bon, G. (1960). *The crowd.* New York: Viking. (Original work published 1895)

LeBow, M. D., Goldberg, P. S., & Collins, A. (1977). Eating behavior of overweight and nonoverweight persons in the natural environment. *Journal of Consulting and Clinical Psychology, 45*, 1204–1205.

Lederberg, A. R., & Mobley, C. E. (1990). The effect of hearing impairment on the quality of attachment and mother-toddler interaction. *Child Development, 61*, 1596–1604.

LeDoux, J. E. (1997). Emotion, memory, and the brain. *Scientific American Mysteries of the Mind, Special Issue Vol. 7*, No. 1, 68–75.

LeDoux, J. E. (1998). Fear and the brain: Where have we been, and where are we going? *Biological Psychiatry, 44*(12), 1229–1238.

Lee, C. C., & Richardson, B. L. (1991). *Multicultural issues in counseling.* Alexandria, VA: AACD.

Lee, I-M., Sesso, H. D., & Paffenbarger, R. S. Jr. (2000). Physical activity and coronary heart disease risk in men: Does the duration of exercise episodes predict risk? *Circulation, 102*, 981–986.

Lefcourt, H. M. (1997). Cited in Clay, R. A. (1997). Researchers harness the power of humor. *APA Monitor, 28*(9), 1, 18.

Lefcourt, H. M., & Martin, R. A. (1986). *Humor and life stress.* New York: Springer-Verlag.

Lefcourt, H. M., Miller, R. S., Ware, E. E., & Sherk, D. (1981). Locus of control as a modifier of the relationship between stressors and moods. *Journal of Personality and Social Psychology, 41*, 357–369.

Lefley, H. P. (1990). Culture and chronic mental illness. *Hospital and Community Psychiatry, 41*, 277–286.

Leibowitz, H. W. (1996). The symbiosis between basic and applied research. *American Psychologist, 51*, 366–370.

Leigh, B. C. (1993). Alcohol consumption and sexual activity as reported with a diary technique. *Journal of Abnormal Psychology, 102*, 490–493.

Leigh, B. C., & Stall, R. (1993). Substance use and risky sexual behavior for exposure to HIV. *American Psychologist, 48*, 1035–1045.

Leinders-Zufall, T., et al. (2000). Ultrasensitive pheromone detection by mammalian vomeronasal neurons. *Nature, 405*, 792–796.

Leinwand, D. (2000, August 24). 20% say they used drugs with their mom or dad, among reasons: Boomer culture and misguided attempts to bond. *USA TODAY online.*

Lenneberg, E. H. (1967). *Biological foundations of language.* New York: Wiley.

Leor, J., Poole, K., & Kloner, R. A. (1996). Sudden cardiac death triggered by an earthquake. *New England Journal of Medicine, 334*, 413–419.

Leserman, J., et al. (2000). Impact of stressful life events, depression, social support, coping, and cortisol on progression to AIDS. *American Journal of Psychiatry, 157*, 1221–1228.

Levenston, G. K., Patrick, C. J., Bradley, M. M., & Lang, P. J. (2000). The psychopath as observer: Emotion and attention in picture processing. *Journal of Abnormal Psychology, 109*(3), 373–385.

Levine, R. V., & Norenzayan, A. (1999). The pace of life in 31 countries. *Journal of Cross-Cultural Psychology, 30*(2), 178–205.

Levinson, D. J. (1996). *The seasons of a woman's life.* New York: Knopf.

Levinson, D. J., Darrow, C. N., Klein, E. B., Levinson, M. H., & McKee, B. (1978). *The seasons of a man's life.* New York: Knopf.

Levy, D. S. (1991, September 16). Why Johnny might grow up violent and sexist. *Time*, pp. 16–19.

Levy, D., et al. (2000). Evidence for a gene influencing blood pressure on chromosome 17: Genome scan linkage results for longitudinal blood pressure phenotypes in subjects from the Framingham Heart Study. *Hypertension, 36*, 477–483.

Levy, R., & Goldman-Rakic, P. S. (1999). Association of storage and processing functions in the dorsolateral prefrontal cortex of the nonhuman primate. *Journal of Neuroscience, 19*(12), 5149–5158.

Lewinsohn, P. M., Rohde, P., Seeley, J. R., Klein, D. N., & Gotlib, I. H. (2000). Natural course of adolescent major depressive disorder in a community sample: Predictors of recurrence in young adults. *American Journal of Psychiatry, 157*, 1584–1591.

Lewis, M. (1997). *Altering fate—Why the past does not predict the future.* New York: Guilford Press.

Lewis, M. (1998). Cited in Blakeslee, S. (1998, August 4). Re-evaluating significance of baby's bond with mother. *The New York Times*, pp. F1, F2.

Lewis-Fernández, R., & Kleinman, A. (1994). Culture, personality, and psychopathology. *Journal of Abnormal Psychology, 103*, 67–71.

Leyton, M., et al. (2000). Acute tyrosine depletion and alcohol ingestion in healthy women. *Alcoholism: Clinical & Experimental Research, 24*(4), 459–464.

Lichtenstein, P., et al. (2000). Environmental and heritable factors in the causation of cancer: Analyses of cohorts of twins from Sweden, Denmark, and Finland. *New England Journal of Medicine, 343*(2), 78–85.

Lieber, C. S. (1990). Cited in Barroom biology: How alcohol goes to a woman's head (January 14). *The New York Times*, p. E24.

Lilienfeld, S. O., & Loftus, E. F. (1998). Repressed memories and World War II: Some cautionary notes. *Professional Psychology: Research & Practice, 29*(5), 471–475.

Lillqvist, O., & Lindeman, M. (1998). Belief in astrology as a strategy for self-verification and coping with negative life-events. *European Psychologist, 3*(3), 202–208.

Linden, W., Chambers, L., Maurice, J., & Lenz, J. W. (1993). Sex differences in social support, self-deception, hostility, and ambulatory cardiovascular activity. *Health Psychology, 12*, 376–380.

Lips, H. (1993). *Sex and gender* (2nd ed.). Mountain View, CA: Mayfield.

Lipsey, M. W., & Wilson, D. B. (1993). The efficacy of psychological, educational, and behavioral treatment. *American Psychologist, 48*, 1181–1209.

Lisanby, S. H., et al. (2000). The effects of electroconvulsive therapy on memory of autobiographical and public events. *Archives of General Psychiatry, 57*(6), 581–590.

Lochman, J. E. (1992). Cognitive-behavioral intervention with aggressive boys. *Journal of Consulting and Clinical Psychology, 60*, 426–432.

Lochman, J. E., & Dodge, K. A. (1994). Social-cognitive processes of severely violent, moderately aggressive, and nonaggressive boys. *Journal of Consulting and Clinical Psychology, 62*, 366–374.

Loder, N. (2000). US science shocked by revelations of sexual discrimination. *Nature, 405*, 713–714.

Loftus, E. F. (1983). Silence is not golden. *American Psychologist, 38*, 564–572.

Loftus, E. F. (1993). Psychologists in the eyewitness world. *American Psychologist, 48*, 550–552.

Loftus, E. F. (1994). Conference on memory, Harvard Medical School. Cited in D. Goleman (1994, May 31). Miscoding is seen as the root of false memories. *The New York Times*, pp. C1, C8.

Loftus, E. F. (1997). Cited in Loftus consulting in Oklahoma City bombing trial. *APA Monitor, 28*(4), 8–9.

Loftus, E. F., & Loftus, G. R. (1980). On the permanence of stored information in the brain. *American Psychologist, 35*, 409–420.

Loftus, E. F., & Palmer, J. C. (1973). Reconstruction of automobile destruction. *Journal of Verbal Learning and Verbal Behavior, 13*, 585–589.

Loftus, E. F., & Polage, D. C. (1999). Repressed memories: When are they real? How are they false? *Psychiatric Clinics of North America, 22*(1), 61–70.

Loftus, G. R. (1983). The continuing persistence of the icon. *Behavioral and Brain Sciences, 6*, 28.

Loftus, G. R., & Loftus, E. F. (1976). *Human memory.* Hillsdale, NJ: Erlbaum.

Lohr, J. M., & Staats, A. (1973). Attitude conditioning in Sino-Tibetan languages. *Journal of Personality and Social Psychology, 26*, 196–200.

Longer, healthier, better (1997, March 9). *The New York Times magazine*, pp. 44–45.

Lopez, S. R., & Guarnaccia, P. J. J. (2000). Cultural psychopathology: Uncovering the social world of mental illness. *Annual Review of Psychology, 51*, 571–598.

Lorenz, K. Z. (1981). *The foundations of ethology.* New York: Springer-Verlag.

Los Angeles Unified School District (2000). Youth Suicide Prevention Information. http://www.sanpedro.com/spyc/suicide.htm.

Lowe, M. R., et al. (1996). Restraint, dieting, and the continuum model of bulimia nervosa. *Journal of Abnormal Psychology, 105,* 508–517.

Lubinski, D., & Benbow, C. P. (2000). States of excellence. *American Psychologist, 55,* 137–150.

Luborsky, L., Barber, J. P., & Beutler, L. (1993). Introduction to special section. *Journal of Consulting and Clinical Psychology, 61,* 539–541.

Luchins, A. S. (1957). Primacy-recency in impression formation. In C. I. Hovland (Ed.), *The order of presentation in persuasion.* New Haven, CT: Yale University Press.

Ludwick-Rosenthal, R., & Neufeld, R. W. J. (1993). Preparation for undergoing an invasive medical procedure. *Journal of Consulting and Clinical Psychology, 61,* 156–164.

Lundeberg, M. A., Fox, P. W., & Puncochar, J. (1994). Highly confident but wrong. *Journal of Educational Psychology, 86,* 114–121.

Lurie, N., et al. (1993). Preventive care for women? *New England Journal of Medicine, 329,* 478–482.

Lydiard, R. B., Brawman, A., Mintzer, O., & Ballenger, J. C. (1996). Recent developments in the psychopharmacology of anxiety disorders. *Journal of Consulting and Clinical Psychology, 64,* 660–668.

Lykken, D. T., McGue, M., Tellegen, A., & Bouchard, T. J. Jr. (1992). Emergenesis: Genetic traits that may not run in families. *American Psychologist, 47,* 1565–1577.

Lykken, D. T., & Tellegen, A. (1996). Happiness is a stochastic phenomenon. *Psychological Science, 7*(3), 186–189.

Maas, J. B. (1998). *Power sleep: Revolutionary strategies that prepare your mind and body for peak performance.* New York: Villard.

Maccoby, E. E. (1990). Gender and relationships. *American Psychologist, 45,* 513–520.

Maccoby, E. E., & Jacklin, C. N. (1974). *The psychology of sex differences.* Stanford, CA: Stanford University Press.

MacDonald, K. (1992). Warmth as a developmental construct. *Child Development, 63,* 753–773.

MacDonald, T. K., MacDonald, G., Zanna, M. P., & Fong, G. T. (2000). Alcohol, sexual arousal, and intentions to use condoms in young men: Applying alcohol myopia theory to risky sexual behavior. *Health Psychology, 19,* 290–298.

Macfarlane, J. A. (1975). Olfaction in the development of social preferences in the human neonate. In M. A. Hofer (Ed.), *Parent-infant interaction.* Amsterdam: Elsevier.

Machleit, K. A., Eroglu, S. A., & Mantel, S. P. (2000). Perceived retail crowding and shopping satisfaction: What modifies this relationship? *Journal of Consumer Psychology, 9*(1), 29–42.

Maciejewski, P. K., Prigerson, H. G., & Mazure, C. M. (2000). Self-efficacy as a mediator between stressful life events and depressive symptoms: Differences based on history of prior depression. *British Journal of Psychiatry, 176,* 373–378.

Mack, D., & Rainey, D. (1990). Female applicants' grooming and personnel selection. *Journal of Social Behavior and Personality, 5,* 399–407.

MacKenzie, T. D., Bartecchi, C. E., & Schrier, R. W. (1994). The human costs of tobacco use. *New England Journal of Medicine, 330,* 975–980.

Mackett-Stout, J., & Dewar, R. (1981). Evaluation of public information signs. *Human Factors, 23*(2), 139–151.

Magnavita, N., et al. (1997). Type A behaviour pattern and traffic accidents. *British Journal of Medical Psychology, 70*(1), 103–107.

Maher, B. A., & Maher, W. B. (1994). Personality and psychopathology. *Journal of Abnormal Psychology, 103,* 72–77.

Maier, N. R. F., & Schneirla, T. C. (1935). *Principles of animal psychology.* New York: McGraw-Hill.

Malgady, R. G., Rogler, L. H., & Costantino, G. (1990). Hero/heroine modeling for Puerto Rican adolescents. *Journal of Consulting and Clinical Psychology, 58,* 469–474.

Malinosky-Rummell, R., & Hansen, D. H. (1993). Long-term consequences of childhood physical abuse. *Psychological Bulletin, 114,* 68–79.

Malone, K. M., et al. (2000). Protective factors against suicidal acts in major depression: Reasons for living. *American Journal of Psychiatry, 157,* 1084–1088.

Manber, R., & Bootzin, R. R. (1997). Sleep and the menstrual cycle. *Health Psychology, 16,* 209–214.

Markel, H. (2000, July 25). Anorexia can strike boys, too. *The New York Times online.*

Markman, H. J., Renick, M. J., Floyd, F. J., Stanley, S. M., & Clements, M. (1993). Preventing marital distress through communication and conflict management training. *Journal of Consulting and Clinical Psychology, 61,* 70–77.

Marks, I., & Dar, R. (2000). Fear reduction by psychotherapies: Recent findings, future directions. *The British Journal of Psychiatry, 176,* 507–511.

Marks, M. (1998). Cited in McGuire, P. A. (1998). Wanted: Workers with flexibility for 21st century jobs. *APA Monitor, 29*(7), 10, 12.

Markus, H., & Kitayama, S. (1991). Culture and the self. *Psychological Review, 98*(2), 224–253.

Marteau, T. M., Dundas, R., & Axworthy, D. (1997). Long-term cognitive and emotional impact of genetic testing for carriers of cystic fibrosis. *Health Psychology, 16,* 51–62.

Martin, R. A., & Lefcourt, H. M. (1983). Sense of humor as a moderator of the relation between stressors and moods. *Journal of Personality and Social Psychology, 45,* 1313–1324.

Martinez-Taboas, A., & Bernal, G. (2000). Dissociation, psychopathology, and abusive experiences in a nonclinical Latino university student group. *Cultural Diversity & Ethnic Minority Psychology, 6*(1), 32–41.

Marwick, C. (2000). Consensus panel considers osteoporosis. *Journal of the American Medical Association online, 283*(16).

Marx, E. M., Williams, J. M. G., & Claridge, G. C. (1992). Depression and social problem solving. *Journal of Abnormal Psychology, 101,* 78–86.

Maslow, A. H. (1970). *Motivation and personality* (2nd ed.). New York: Harper & Row.

Masters, W. H., & Johnson, V. E. (1966). *Human sexual response.* Boston: Little, Brown.

Masters, W. H., & Johnson, V. E. (1970). *Human sexual inadequacy.* Boston: Little, Brown.

Masters, W. H., & Johnson, V. E. (1979). *Homosexuality in perspective.* Boston: Little, Brown.

Matchen, J., & DeSouza, E. (2000). The sexual harassment of faculty members by students. *Sex Roles, 42*(3–4), 295–306.

Matefy, R. (1980). Role-playing theory of psychedelic flashbacks. *Journal of Consulting and Clinical Psychology, 48,* 551–553.

Matlin, M. W. (1997). *Cognition* (4th ed.). Fort Worth: Harcourt Brace College Publishers.

Matlin, M. W. (1999). *The psychology of women* (4th ed.). Fort Worth: Harcourt College Publishers.

Matlin, M. W., & Foley, H. J. (1995). *Sensation and perception* (4th ed.). Boston: Allyn & Bacon.

Matt, G. E., Vasquez, C., & Campbell, W. K. (1992). Mood-congruent recall of affectively toned stimuli: A meta-analytic review. *Clinical Psychology Review, 12,* 227–255.

Matthews, K. (1994). Cited in Azar, B. (1994). Women are barraged by media on "the change." *APA Monitor, 25*(5), 24–25.

Matthews, K., et al. (1997). Women's Health Initiative. *American Psychologist, 52,* 101–116.

Maxwell, L. E., & Evans, G. W. (2000). The effects of noise on pre-school children's pre-reading skills. *Journal of Environmental Psychology, 20*(1), 91–97.

Mazure, C. M., et al. (2000). Adverse life events and cognitive-personality characteristics in the prediction of major depression and antidepressant response. *American Journal of Psychiatry, 157,* 896–903.

Mazzella, R., & Feingold, A. (1994). The effects of physical attractiveness, race, socioeconomic status, and gender of defendants and victims on judgments of mock jurors. *Journal of Applied Social Psychology, 24*(15), 1315–1344.

McAndrew, S. (2000). Sexual health through leadership and "sanuk" in Thailand. *British Medical Journal, 321*(7253), 114.

McCall, R. (1997). Cited in Sleek, S. (1997). Can "emotional intelligence" be taught in today's schools? *APA Monitor, 28*(6), 25.

McCarley, R. W. (1992). Cited in Blakeslee, S. (1992, January 7). Scientists unraveling chemistry of dreams. *The New York Times,* pp. C1, C10.

McCauley, C., Woods, K., Coolidge, C., & Kulick, W. (1983). More aggressive cartoons are funnier. *Journal of Personality and Social Psychology, 44,* 817–823.

McClave, E. Z. (2000). Linguistic functions of head movements in the context of speech. *Journal of Pragmatics, 32*(7), 855–878.

McClelland, D. C. (1958). Methods of measuring human motivation. In J. W. Atkinson (Ed.), *Motives in fantasy, action, and society.* Princeton, NJ: Van Nostrand.

McClelland, D. C. (1965). Achievement and entrepreneurship. *Journal of Personality and Social Psychology, 1,* 389–392.

McCourt, K., et al. (1999). Authoritarianism revisited: Genetic and environmental influences examined in twins reared apart and together. *Personality & Individual Differences, 27*(5), 985–1014.

McCrae, R. R., & Costa, P. T. Jr. (1997). Personality trait structure as a human universal. *American Psychologist, 52,* 509–516.

McCrae, R. R., Costa, P. T. Jr., et al. (2000). Nature over nurture: Temperament, personality, and life span development. *Journal of Personality & Social Psychology, 78*(1), 173–186.

McDaniel, M. A., Glisky, E. L., Guynn, M. J., & Routhieaux, B. C. (1999). Prospective memory: A neuropsychological study. *Neuropsychology, 13*(1), 103–110.

McDermott, D. (1997, May 14). Yes, computers *can* think. *The New York Times*, p. A21.

McDonald-Miszczak, L., Gould, O. N., & Tychynski, D. (1999). Metamemory predictors of prospective and retrospective memory performance. *Journal of General Psychology, 126*(1), 37–52.

McDougall, W. (1904). The sensations excited by a single momentary stimulation of the eye. *British Journal of Psychology, 1*, 78–113.

McDougall, W. (1908). *An introduction to social psychology*. London: Methuen.

McElroy, S. L., et al. (2000). Placebo-controlled trial of sertraline in the treatment of binge eating disorder. *American Journal of Psychiatry, 157*, 1004–1006.

McGlashan, T. H., & Hoffman, R. E. (2000). Schizophrenia as a disorder of developmentally reduced synaptic connectivity. *Archives of General Psychiatry, 57*, 637–648.

McGovern, T. V. (1989). Task force eyes the making of a major. *APA Monitor, 20*(7), 50.

McGovern, T. V. (1996). Cited in Murray, B. (1996). Psychology remains top college major. *APA Monitor, 27*(2), 1, 42.

McGovern, T. V., & Reich, J. N. (1996). A comment on the *Quality Principles. American Psychologist, 51*, 251–255.

McGrath, E., Keita, G. P., Strickland, B. R., & Russo, N. F. (1990). *Women and depression*. Washington, D.C.: American Psychological Association.

McGregor, D. (1960). *The human side of enterprise*. New York: McGraw-Hill.

McGuire, P. A. (1998). Wanted: Workers with flexibility for 21st century jobs. *APA Monitor, 29*(7), 10, 12.

McIntosh, H. (1996). Solitude provides an emotional tune-up. *APA Monitor, 26*(3), 1, 10.

McKeachie, W. (1994). Cited in DeAngelis, T. (1994). Educators reveal keys to success in classroom. *APA Monitor, 25*(1), 39–40.

McKenna, K. Y. A., & Bargh, J. A. (1998). Coming out in the age of the Internet: Identity "demarginalization" through virtual group participation. *Journal of Personality & Social Psychology, 75*(3), 681–694.

McKenna, K. Y. A., & Bargh, J. A. (2000). Plan 9 from cyberspace: The implications of the Internet for personality and social psychology. *Personality & Social Psychology Review, 4*(1) 57–75.

McKinley, J. C. Jr. (2000, August 11). It isn't just a game: Clues to avid rooting. *The New York Times online.*

McMurtrie, B. (1994, July 19). Overweight fatten ranks. *New York Newsday*, p. A26.

McNally, R. J. (1990). Psychological approaches to panic disorder. *Psychological Bulletin, 108*, 403–419.

McNally, R. J., & Eke, M. (1996). Anxiety sensitivity, suffocation fear, and breath-holding duration as predictors of response to carbon dioxide challenge. *Journal of Abnormal Psychology, 105*, 146–149.

McNeil, T. F., Cantor-Graae, E., & Weinberger, D. R. (2000). Relationship of obstetric complications and differences in size of brain structures in monozygotic twin pairs discordant for schizophrenia. *American Journal of Psychiatry, 157*, 203–212.

Mead, M. (1935). *Sex and temperament in three primitive societies*. New York: Dell.

Meltzoff, A. N. (1997). Cited in Azar, B. (1997). New theory on development could usurp Piagetian beliefs. *APA Monitor, 28*(6), 9.

Meltzoff, A. N., & Gopnik, A. (1997). *Words, thoughts, and theories*. Cambridge, MA: MIT Press.

Melzack, R. (1997). Phantom limbs. *Scientific American mysteries of the mind, Special Issue Vol. 7*, No. 1, 84–91.

Melzack, R. (1999, August). From the gate to the neuromatrix. *Pain*, Suppl. 6, S121–S126.

Mendez, M., et al. (1992). Disturbances of person identification in Alzheimer's disease. *Journal of Nervous & Mental Disease, 180*, 94–96.

Merikangas, K. R., et al. (1998). Familial transmission of substance use disorders. *Archives of General Psychiatry, 55*(11), 973–979.

Merluzzi, T. V., & Martinez Sanchez, M. (1997). Assessment of self-efficacy and coping with cancer. *Health Psychology, 16*, 163–170.

Metcalfe, J. (1986). Premonitions of insight predict impending error. *Journal of Experimental Psychology: Learning, Memory, and Cognition, 12*, 623–634.

Meyerowitz, B. E., Richardson, J., Hudson, S., & Leedham, B. (1998). Ethnicity and cancer outcomes: Behavioral and psychosocial considerations. *Psychological Bulletin, 123*, 47–70.

Michael, R. T., Gagnon, J. H., Laumann, E. O., & Kolata, G. (1994). *Sex in America: A definitive survey*. Boston: Little, Brown.

Michaelson, R. (1993). Tug-of-war is developing over defining retardation. *APA Monitor, 24*(5), 34–35.

Michels, R., & Marzuk, P. M. (1993a). Progress in psychiatry. (Part 1). *New England Journal of Medicine, 329*, 552–560.

Michels, R., & Marzuk, P. M. (1993b). Progress in psychiatry. (Part 2). *New England Journal of Medicine, 329*, 628–638.

Michelson, D., et al. (2000). Female sexual dysfunction associated with antidepressant administration: A randomized, placebo-controlled study of pharmacologic intervention. *American Journal of Psychiatry, 157*, 239–243.

Middleman, M. A. (2000, May). Paper presented to the 40th Annual Conference on Cardiovascular Disease Epidemiology and Prevention of the American Heart Association, San Diego.

Milar, K. S. (2000). The first generation of women psychologists and the psychology of women. *American Psychologist, 55*(6), 616–619.

Milgram, S. (1963). Behavioral study of obedience. *Journal of Abnormal and Social Psychology, 67*, 371–378.

Milgram, S. (1974). *Obedience to authority*. New York: Harper & Row.

Milgram, S. (1977). *The individual in a social world*. Reading, MA: Addison-Wesley.

Miller, G. A. (1956). The magical number seven, plus or minus two: Some limits on our capacity for processing information. *Psychological Review, 63*, 81–97.

Miller, J. L. (1992). Trouble in mind. *Scientific American, 267*(3), 180.

Miller, M. E., & Bowers, K. S. (1993). Hypnotic analgesia. *Journal of Abnormal Psychology, 102*, 29–38.

Miller, M. F., Barabasz, A. F., & Barabasz, M. (1991). Effects of active alert and relaxation hypnotic inductions on cold pressor pain. *Journal of Abnormal Psychology, 100*, 223–226.

Miller, N. B., Cowan, P. A., Cowan, C. P., Hetherington, E. M., & Clingempeel, W. G. (1993). Externalizing in preschoolers and early adolescents. *Developmental Psychology, 29*, 3–18.

Miller, N. E. (1969). Learning of visceral and glandular responses. *Science, 163*, 434–445.

Miller, N. E. (1995). Clinical-experimental interactions in the development of neuroscience. *American Psychologist, 50*, 901–911.

Miller, N. E., & Dollard, J. (1941). *Social learning and imitation*. New Haven, CT: Yale University Press.

Miller, S. M., Shoda, Y., & Hurley, K. (1996). Applying cognitive-social theory to health-protective behavior: Breast self-examination in cancer screening. *Psychological Bulletin, 199*, 70–94.

Mills, C. J. (1992). Academically talented children: The case for early identification and nurturance. *Pediatrics, 89*, 156–157.

Milner, B. R. (1966). Amnesia following operation on temporal lobes. In C. W. M. Whitty & O. L. Zangwill (Eds.), *Amnesia*. London: Butterworth.

Milstead, M., Lapsley, D., & Hale, C. (1993, March). *A new look at imaginary audience and personal fable*. Paper presented at the meeting of the Society for Research in Child Development, New Orleans, LA.

Milton, J., & Wiseman, R. (1999). Does psi exist? Lack of replication of an anomalous process of information transfer. *Psychological Bulletin, 125*(4), 387–391.

Mimeault, V., & Morin, C. M. (1999). Self-help treatment for insomnia: Bibliotherapy with and without professional guidance. *Journal of Consulting & Clinical Psychology, 67*(4), 511–519.

Mindell, J. A. (1993). Sleep disorders in children. *Health Psychology, 12*, 151–162.

Mineka, S. (1991, August). Paper presented to the annual meeting of the American Psychological Association, San Francisco. Cited in Turkington, C. (1991). Evolutionary memories may have phobia role. *APA Monitor, 22*(11), 14.

Minton, H. L. (2000). Psychology and gender at the turn of the century. *American Psychologist, 55*(6), 613–615.

Mischel, W., & Shoda, Y. (1995). A cognitive-affective system theory of personality. *Psychological Review, 102*, 246–268.

Mohrman, A. M. Jr., Resnick-West, S. M., & Lawler, E. E. III. (1989). *Designing performance appraisal systems: Aligning appraisals and organizational realities*. San Francisco: Jossey-Bass.

Mokdad, A. H., et al. (2000). The continuing epidemic of obesity in the United States. *Journal of the American Medical Association online, 284*(13).

Molfese, V. J., DiLalla, L. F., & Bunce, D. (1997). Prediction of the intelligence test scores of 3- to 8-year-old children by home environment, socioeconomic status, and biomedical risks. *Merrill-Palmer Quarterly, 43*(2), 219–234.

Moliterno, D. J., et al. (1994). Coronary-artery vasoconstriction induced by cocaine, cigarette smoking, or both. *New England Journal of Medicine, 330,* 454–459.

Money, J. (1987). Sin, sickness, or status? Homosexual gender identity and psychoneuroendocrinology. *American Psychologist, 42,* 384–399.

Montgomery, G. H., DuHamel, K. N., & Redd, W. H. (2000). A meta-analysis of hypnotically induced analgesia: How effective is hypnosis? *International Journal of Clinical & Experimental Hypnosis, 48*(2), 138–153.

Moore, R. Y. (1995). Vision without sight. *New England Journal of Medicine, 332,* 54–55.

Mordock, B. (1997). Skepticism, data, risky shift, polarization, and attitude change: Their role in implementing innovations. *Psychologist-Manager Journal, 1*(1), 41–46.

Morgan, D., et al. (2000). A peptide vaccination prevents memory loss in an animal model of Alzheimer's disease. *Nature, 408*(6815), 982–984.

Morin, C. M., Colecchi, C., Stone, J., Sood, R., & Brink, D. (1999). Behavioral and pharmacological therapies for late-life insomnia: A randomized controlled trial. *Journal of the American Medical Association, 281*(11), 991–999.

Morley, J. E., & van den Berg, L., Eds. (2000). *Endocrinology of aging.* Totowa, N.J., Humana Press.

Morris, M. W., Larrick, R. P., & Su, S. K. (1999). Misperceiving negotiation counterparts: When situationally determined bargaining behaviors are attributed to personality traits. *Journal of Personality & Social Psychology, 77*(1), 52–67.

Morris, W. N., Miller, R. S., & Spangenberg, S. (1977). The effects of dissenter position and task difficulty on conformity and response conflict. *Journal of Personality, 45,* 251–256.

Morrison, E. S., et al. (1980). *Growing up sexual.* New York: Van Nostrand Reinhold.

Mortola, J. F. (1998). Premenstrual syndrome—Pathophysiologic considerations. *New England Journal of Medicine, 338,* 256–257.

Moyers, B. (1993). *Healing and the mind.* New York: Doubleday.

Mukamal, K. J., Maclure, M., Muller, J. E., Sherwood, J. B., & Mittleman, M. A. (2001). Prior alcohol consumption and mortality following acute myocardial infarction. *Journal of the American Medical Association, 285*(15), 1965–1970.

Mullen, B., et al. (1987). Newscasters' facial expressions and voting behavior of viewers. *Journal of Personality and Social Psychology, 51*(2), 291–295.

Mullen, B., Bryant, B., & Driskell, J. E. (1997). Presence of others and arousal: An integration. *Group Dynamics, 1*(1), 52–64.

Mulnard, R. A., et al. (2000). Estrogen replacement therapy for treatment of mild to moderate Alzheimer disease. *Journal of the American Medical Association, 283,* 1007–1015.

Mulvihill, K. (2000, March 14). Many miss out on migraine remedies. *The New York Times online.*

Muñoz, R. F., Hollon, S. D., McGrath, E., Rehm, L. P., & VandenBos, G. R. (1994). On the AHCPR *Depression in Primary Care* guidelines: Further considerations for practitioners. *American Psychologist, 49,* 42–61.

Munro, G. D., & Munro, J. E. (2000). Using daily horoscopes to demonstrate expectancy confirmation. *Teaching of Psychology, 27*(2), 114–116.

Munson, L. J., Hulin, C., & Drasgow, F. (2000). Longitudinal analysis of dispositional influences and sexual harassment: Effects on job and psychological outcomes. *Personnel Psychology, 53*(1), 21–46.

Murphy, K. (1998). Cited in McGuire, P. A. (1998). Wanted: Workers with flexibility for 21st century jobs. *APA Monitor, 29*(7), 10, 12.

Murray, B. (1996). Psychology remains top college major. *APA Monitor, 27*(2), 1, 42.

Murray, B. (1997). Teaching today's pupils to think more critically. *APA Monitor, 28*(3), 51.

Murray, B. (1998). New tool makes online research easier. *Monitor on Psychology online, 29*(11).

Murray, B. (2000). A mirror on the self. *Monitor on Psychology online, 31*(4).

Murray, C. (1995). *The Bell Curve* and its critics. *Commentary, 99*(5), 23, 28.

Murray, H. A. (1938). *Explorations in personality.* New York: Oxford University Press.

Murtagh, D. R. R., & Greenwood, K. M. (1995). Identifying effective psychological treatments for insomnia: A meta-analysis. *Journal of Consulting and Clinical Psychology, 63,* 79–89.

Muslim women bridging culture gap (1993, November 8). *The New York Times,* p. B9.

Myers, L. B., & Brewin, C. R. (1994). Recall of early experience and the repressive coping style. *Journal of Abnormal Psychology, 103,* 288–292.

Myers, S. L. (2000, March 31). Female general in army alleges sex harassment. *The New York Times,* pp. A1, A22.

Nader, K., Schafe, G. E., & Le Doux, J. E. (2000). Fear memories require protein synthesis in the amygdala for reconsolidation after retrieval. *Nature, 406,* 722–726.

Nagtegaal, J. E., et al. (2000). Effects of melatonin on the quality of life in patients with delayed sleep phase syndrome. *Journal of Psychosomatic Research, 48*(1), 45–50.

Nahas, G., Sutin, K., & Bennett, W. M. (2000). Review of "Marihuana and Medicine." *The New England Journal of Medicine online, 343*(7).

Nantais, K. M., & Schellenberg, E. G. (1999). The Mozart effect: An artifact of preference. *Psychological Science, 10*(4), 370–373.

Nasser, H. (2000, June 9). Mom's career sacrifice: Study: Women yield ambitions when children come to two-career couples. *CNN online.*

National Cancer Institute (2000). Cited in Jetter, A. (2000, February 22). Breast cancer in Blacks spurs hunt for answers. *The New York Times,* p. D5.

National Center for Health Statistics (1996, March). News Releases and Fact Sheets. *Monitoring Health Care in America: Quarterly Fact Sheet.*

National Sleep Foundation (2000a). Helping yourself to a good night's sleep. **http://www.sleepfoundation.org/publications/goodnights.html.**

National Sleep Foundation (2000b). 2000 Omnibus Sleep in America Poll. **http://www.sleepfoundation.org/publications/2000poll.html#3.**

Neisser, U. (1993). Cited in Goleman, D. J. (1993, April 6). Studying the secrets of childhood memory. *The New York Times,* pp. C1, C11.

Neisser, U. (1997a). Never a dull moment. *American Psychologist, 52,* 79–81.

Neisser, U. (1997b). Cited in Sleek, S. (1997). Can "emotional intelligence" be taught in today's schools? *APA Monitor, 28*(6), 25.

Neisser, U., Boodoo, G., Bouchard, T. J. Jr., Boykin, A. W., Brody, N., Ceci, S. J., Halpern, D. F., Loehlin, J. C., Perloff, R., Sternberg, R. J., & Urbina, S. (1996). Intelligence: Knowns and unknowns. *American Psychologist, 51,* 77–101.

Nelson, K. (1973). Structure and strategy in learning to talk. *Monographs for the Society for Research in Child Development, 38* (Whole No. 149).

Nelson, K., Hampson, J., & Shaw, L. K. (1993). Nouns in early lexicons: Evidence, explanations, and implications. *Journal of Child Language, 20,* 228.

Nestadt, G., et al. (2000). A family study of obsessive-compulsive disorder. *Archives of General Psychiatry, 57*(4), 358–363.

Newlin, D. B., & Thomson, J. B. (1990). Alcohol challenge with sons of alcoholics: A critical review and analysis. *Psychological Bulletin, 108,* 383–402.

Newman, F. L., & Howard, K. I. (1991). Introduction to the special section on seeking new clinical research methods. *Journal of Consulting and Clinical Psychology, 59,* 8–11.

Newman, J., & McCauley, C. (1977). Eye contact with strangers in city, suburb, and small town. *Environment and Behavior, 9,* 547–558.

Newman, R. S. (1990). Children help seeking in the classroom: The role of motivational factors and attitudes. *Journal of Educational Psychology, 82,* 71–80.

Newport, E. L. (1998). Cited in Azar, B. (1998). Acquiring sign language may be more innate than learned. *APA Monitor, 29*(4), 12.

Nezlek, J. B., Hampton, C. P., & Shean, G. D. (2000). Clinical depression and day-to-day social interaction in a community sample. *Journal of Abnormal Psychology, 109*(1), 11–19.

Nides, M. A., et al. (1995). Predictors of initial smoking cessation and relapse through the first 2 years of the lung health study. *Journal of Consulting and Clinical Psychology, 63,* 60–69.

NIMH. *See* National Institute of Mental Health.

Nisbett, R. (2000). Cited in Goode, E. (2000, August 8). How culture molds habits of thought. *The New York Times online.*

Nolen-Hoeksema, S. (1991). Responses to depression and their effects on the duration of depressive episodes. *Journal of Abnormal Psychology, 100,* 569–582.

Nolen-Hoeksema, S., Grayson, C., & Larson, J. (1999). Explaining the gender difference in depressive symptoms. *Journal of Personality and Social Psychology, 77*(5), 1061–1072.

Norman, D. A. (1988). *The psychology of everyday things.* New York: Basic Books.

Norton, A. (2000, July 21). A drink a day keeps brain in tip-top shape. Reuters News Agency online.

Norvell, N., & Belles, D. (1993). Psychological and physical benefits of circuit weight training in law enforcement personnel. *Journal of Consulting and Clinical Psychology, 61*, 520–527.

Novick, L. R., & Coté, N. (1992). The nature of expertise in anagram solution. In *Proceedings of the Fourteenth Annual Conference of the Cognitive Science Society.* Hillsdale, NJ: Erlbaum.

Nowicki, S., & Strickland, B. R. (1973). A locus of control scale for children. *Journal of Consulting Psychology, 40*, 148–154.

Nurnberger, J. I. Jr., et al. (2001). Evidence for a locus on chromosome 1 that influences vulnerability to alcoholism and affective disorder. *American Journal of Psychiatry, 158*, 718–724.

Nyberg, L., et al. (2000). Large scale neurocognitive networks underlying episodic memory. *Journal of Cognitive Neuroscience, 12*(1), 163–173.

O'Brien, C. P. (1996). Recent developments in the pharmacotherapy of substance abuse. *Journal of Consulting and Clinical Psychology, 64*, 677–686.

O'Connor, T. G., Caspi, A., DeFries, J. C., & Plomin, R. (2000). Are associations between parental divorce and children's adjustment genetically mediated? An adoption study. *Developmental Psychology, 36*(4), 429–437.

Octopus opens jam jar in one minute (2000, June 1). Reuters News Agency online.

Ogbu, J. U. (1993). Differences in cultural frame of reference. *International Journal of Behavioral Development, 16*, 483–506.

Okazaki, S. (1997). Sources of ethnic differences between Asian American and White American college students on measures of depression and social anxiety. *Journal of Abnormal Psychology, 106*, 52–60.

Olanow, W. M. (2000, July). Clinical and pathological perspective on Parkinsonism. Paper presented at the World Alzheimer Congress 2000, Washington, D.C.

Olds, J. (1969). The central nervous system and the reinforcement of behavior. *American Psychologist, 24*, 114–132.

Olds, J., & Milner, P. (1954). Positive reinforcement produced by electrical stimulation of the septal area and other regions of the rat brain. *Journal of Comparative and Physiological Psychology, 47*, 419–427.

O'Leary, A. (1990). Stress, emotion, and human immune function. *Psychological Bulletin, 108*, 363–382.

O'Leary, K. D. (2000). Are women really more aggressive than men in intimate relationships? *Psychological Bulletin, 126*(5), 685–689.

Olson, S. L., Bates, J. E., & Kaskie, B. (1992). Caregiver–infant interaction antecedents of children's school-age cognitive ability. *Merrill-Palmer Quarterly, 38*, 309–330.

Olthof, A., & Roberts, W. A. (2000). Summation of symbols by pigeons *(Columba livia):* The importance of number and mass of reward items. *Journal of Comparative Psychology, 114*(2), 158–166.

Ouchi, W. (1981). *Theory Z: How American business can meet the Japanese challenge.* Reading, MA: Addison-Wesley.

Ouimette, P. C., Finney, J. W., & Moos, R. H. (1997). Twelve-step and cognitive-behavioral treatment for substance abuse. *Journal of Consulting and Clinical Psychology, 65*, 230–240.

Paffenbarger, R. S. Jr., et al. (1993). The association of changes in physical-activity level and other lifestyle characteristics with mortality among men. *New England Journal of Medicine, 328*, 538–545.

Pagan, G., & Aiello, J. R. (1982). Development of personal space among Puerto Ricans. *Journal of Nonverbal Behavior, 7*, 59–68.

Page, K. (1999, May 16). The graduate. *Washington Post Magazine, 152*, 18, 20.

Palladino, J. (1994). Cited in DeAngelis, T. (1994). Educators reveal keys to success in classroom. *APA Monitor, 25*(1), 39–40.

Papousek, M., Papousek, H., & Symmes, D. (1991). The meanings of melodies in motherese in tone and stress languages. *Infant Behavior and Development, 14*, 415–440.

Pappas, G., Queen, S., Hadden, W., & Fisher, G. (1993). The increasing disparity of mortality between socioeconomic groups in the United States, 1960 and 1986. *New England Journal of Medicine, 329*, 103–109.

Pardes, H., et al. (1991). Physicians and the animal-rights movement. *New England Journal of Medicine, 324*, 1640–1643.

Park, J., & Banaji, M. R. (2000). Mood and heuristics: The influence of happy and sad states on sensitivity and bias in stereotyping. *Journal of Personality & Social Psychology, 78*(6), 1005–1023.

Parker, A. (2000). A review of the ganzfeld work at Gothenburg University. *Journal of the Society for Psychical Research, 64*(858), 1–15.

Parker, J. G., & Herrera, C. (1996). Interpersonal processes in friendship: A comparison of abused and nonabused children's experience. *Developmental Psychology, 32*, 1025–1038.

Parr, L. A., Winslow, J. T., Hopkins, W. D., & de Waal, F. B. M. (2000). Recognizing facial cues: Individual discrimination by chimpanzees *(Pan troglodytes)* and Rhesus monkeys *(Macaca mulatta).* *Journal of Comparative Psychology, 114*(1), 47–60.

Patterson, D. R., & Ptacek, J. T. (1997). Baseline pain as a moderator of hypnotic analgesia for burn injury treatment. *Journal of Consulting and Clinical Psychology, 65*, 60–67.

Pavlov, I. (1927). *Conditioned reflexes.* London: Oxford University Press.

Pear, R. (2000, March 20). White House seeks to curb pills used to calm young. *The New York Times online.*

Penfield, W. (1969). Consciousness, memory, and man's conditioned reflexes. In K. H. Pribram (Ed.), *On the biology of learning.* New York: Harcourt Brace Jovanovich.

Peng, K., & Nisbett, R. E. (1999). Culture, dialectics, and reasoning about contradiction. *American Psychologist, 54*(9), 741–754.

Penn, D. L., Corrigan, P. W., Bentall, R. P., Racenstein, J. M., & Newman, L. (1997). Social cognition in schizophrenia. *Psychological Bulletin, 121*, 114–132.

Penn, N. E., Kar, S., Kramer, J., Skinner, J., & Zambrana, R. E. (1995). Panel VI. Ethnic minorities, health care systems, and behavior. *Health Psychology, 14*, 641–648.

Penner, L. A., Thompson, J. K., & Coovert, D. L. (1991). Size overestimation among anorexics: Much ado about very little? *Journal of Abnormal Psychology, 100*, 90–93.

Penninx, B. W., et al. (1998). Chronically depressed mood and cancer risk in older persons. *Journal of the National Cancer Institute, 90*, 1888–1893.

Peppard, P. E., Young, T., Palta, M., & Skatrud, J. (2000). Prospective study of the association between sleep-disordered breathing and hypertension. *The New England Journal of Medicine online, 342*(19).

Perls, F. S. (1971). *Gestalt therapy verbatim.* New York: Bantam.

Perras, B., et al. (1997). Verbal memory after three months of intranasal vasopressin in healthy old humans. *Psychoneuroendocrinology, 22*(6), 387–396.

Perrett, D. I. (1994). *Nature.* Cited in Brody, J. E. (1994, March 21). Notions of beauty transcend culture, new study suggests. *The New York Times,* p. A14.

Perry, D. G., & Bussey, K. (1979). The social learning theory of sex differences. *Journal of Personality and Social Psychology, 37*, 1699–1712.

Perse, E. M. (1998). Implications of cognitive and affective involvement for channel changing. *Journal of Communication, 48*(3), 49–68.

Persons, J. B., Davidson, J., & Tompkins, M. A. (2001). *Essential components of cognitive-behavior therapy for depression.* Washington, D.C.: American Psychological Association.

Peterson, L. R., & Peterson, M. J. (1959). Short-term retention of individual verbal items. *Journal of Experimental Psychology, 58*, 193–198.

Petry, N. M., Martin, B., Cooney, J. L., & Kranzler, H. R. (2000). Give them prizes and they will come: Contingency management for treatment of alcohol dependence. *Journal of Consulting and Clinical Psychology, 68*, 250–257.

Pettingale, K. W., et al. (1985). Mental attitudes to cancer. *Lancet, 1*, 750.

Petty, R. E., Fleming, M. A., & White, P. H. (1999). Stigmatized sources and persuasion: Prejudice as a determinant of argument scrutiny. *Journal of Personality & Social Psychology, 76*(1), 19–34.

Petty, R. E., Wegener, D. T., & Fabrigar, L. R. (1997). Attitudes and attitude change. *Annual Review of Psychology, 48*, 609–647.

Phelps, E. A., O'Connor, K. J., Cunningham, W. A., Funayama, E. S., & Banaji, M. R. (2000). Performance on indirect measures of race evaluation predicts amygdala activation. *Journal of Cognitive Neuroscience, 12*(5).

Phillips, L. (2000). Recontextualizing Kenneth B. Clark: An Afrocentric perspective on the paradoxical legacy of a model psychologist-activist. *History of Psychology, 3*(2), 142–167.

Phinney, J. S. (1996). When we talk about American ethnic groups, what do we mean? *American Psychologist, 51*, 918–927.

Phinney, J. S. (2000). Identity formation across cultures: The interaction of personal, societal, and historical change. *Human Development, 43*(1), 27–31.

Phinney, J. S., Cantu, C. L., & Kurtz, D. A. (1997). Ethnic and American identity as predictors of self-esteem among African American, Latino, and White adolescents. *Journal of Youth & Adolescence, 26*(2), 165–185.

Phinney, J. S., & Devich-Navarro, M. (1997). Variations in bicultural identification among African American and Mexican American adolescents. *Journal of Research on Adolescence, 7*(1), 3–32.

Piaget, J. (1963). *The origins of intelligence in children.* New York: W. W. Norton.

Piaget, J. (1997, Ed.). *The moral judgment of the child.* Trans. by Marjorie Gabain. New York: Free Press.

Pierce, C. A. (1996). Body height and romantic attraction: A meta-analytic test of the male-taller norm. *Social Behavior & Personality, 24*(2), 143–149.

Pihl, R. O., & Peterson, J. B. (1992). Etiology. *Annual Review of Addictions Research and Treatment, 2*, 153–175, p. 155.

Pihl, R. O., Peterson, J. B., & Finn, P. (1990). Inherited predisposition to alcoholism. *Journal of Abnormal Psychology, 99*, 291–301.

Pike, K. M., & Rodin, J. (1991). Mothers, daughters, and disordered eating. *Journal of Abnormal Psychology, 100*, 198–204.

Pilkonis, P. (1996). Cited in Goleman, D. J. (1996, May 1). Higher suicide risk for perfectionists. *The New York Times,* p. C12.

Pillard, R. C., & Weinrich, J. D. (1986). Evidence of familial nature of male homosexuality. *Archives of Sexual Behavior, 43*, 808–812.

Pillemer, D. B. (1998). What is remembered about early childhood events? *Clinical Psychology Review, 18*(8), 895–913.

Pinel, J. P. J., Assanand, S., & Lehman, D. R. (2000). Hunger, eating, and ill health. *American Psychologist, 55*(10), 1105–1116.

Pinker, S. (1990). Language acquisition. In D. N. Osherson & H. Lasnik (Eds.), *An invitation to cognitive science: Language* (Vol. 1). Cambridge, MA: The MIT Press, a Bradford Book.

Pinker, S. (1994a). *The language instinct.* New York: William Morrow.

Pinker, S. (1994b, June 19). Building a better brain. *The New York Times Book Review,* pp. 13–14.

Pinker, S. (1997). Words and rules in the human brain. *Nature, 387*(6633), 547–548.

Pinnell, C. M., & Covino, N. A. (2000). Empirical findings on the use of hypnosis in medicine: A critical review. *International Journal of Clinical & Experimental Hypnosis, 48*(2), 170–194.

Pinquart, M., & Sörensen, S. (2000). Influences of socioeconomic status, social network, and competence on subjective well-being in later life: A meta-analysis. *Psychology and Aging, 15*(2), 187–224.

Plant, E. A., Hyde, J. S., Keltner, D., & Devine, P. G. (2000). The gender stereotyping of emotions. *Psychology of Women Quarterly, 24*(1), 81–92.

Plomin, R. (2000). Behavioural genetics in the 21st century. *International Journal of Behavioral Development, 24*(1), 30–34.

Plomin, R., DeFries, J. C., McClearn, G. E., & Rutter, M. (1997). *Behavioral genetics* (3rd ed.). New York: Freeman.

Plous, S. (1996). Attitudes toward the use of animals in psychological research and education. *American Psychologist, 51*, 1167–1180.

Plutchik, R. (2001). *Emotions in the practice of psychotherapy.* Washington, D.C.: American Psychological Association.

Pointer, S. C., & Bond, N. W. (1998). Context-dependent memory: Colour versus odor. *Chemical Senses, 23*(3), 359–362.

Pol, H. E. H., et al. (2000). Prenatal exposure to famine and brain morphology in schizophrenia. *American Journal of Psychiatry, 157,* 1170–1172.

Pollock, B., Prior, H., & Güntürkün, O. (2000). Development of object permanence in food-storing magpies *(Pica pica). Journal of Comparative Psychology, 114*(2), 148–157.

Poniewozik, J. (2000, June 19). Will smell-o-vision replace television? *Time magazine,* pp. 66–67.

Pope, H.G., Kouri, E. M., & Hudson, J. I. (2000). Effects of supraphysiologic doses of testosterone on mood and aggression in normal men: A randomized controlled trial. *Archives of General Psychiatry, 57,* 133–140.

Pope, J. H., et al. (2000). Missed diagnoses of acute cardiac ischemia in the emergency department. *The New England Journal of Medicine, 342,* 1163–1170.

Popkin, B. M., Siega-Riz, A. M., & Haines, P. S. (1996). A comparison of dietary trends among racial and socioeconomic groups in the United States. *New England Journal of Medicine, 335,* 716–720.

Porter, R. H., Makin, J. W., Davis, L. B., & Christensen, K. M. (1992). Breast-fed infants respond to olfactory cues from their own mother and unfamiliar lactating females. *Infant Behavior and Development, 15,* 85–93.

Powell, E. (1996). *Sex on your terms.* Boston: Allyn & Bacon.

Powers, R. (2000, May 7). American dreaming. *The New York Times magazine,* pp. 66–67.

Preti, A., & Miotto, P. (1999). Suicide among eminent artists. *Psychological Reports, 84*(1), 291–301.

Price, L. H., & Heninger, G. R. (1994). Lithium in the treatment of mood disorders. *New England Journal of Medicine, 331,* 591–598.

Prochaska, J. O., & Norcross, J. C. (1999). *Systems of psychotherapy* (4th ed.). Pacific Grove, CA: Brooks/Cole.

Pugh, K. R., et al. (2000). The angular gyrus in developmental dyslexia: Task-specific differences in functional connectivity within posterior cortex. *Psychological Science, 11*(1), 51–56.

Pulley, B. (1998, June 16). Those seductive snake eyes: Tales of growing up gambling. *The New York Times,* A1, A28.

Putallaz, M., & Heflin, A. H. (1990). Parent–child interaction. In S. R. Asher & J. D. Coie (Eds.), *Peer rejection in childhood.* New York: Cambridge University Press.

Putnam, F. W., Guroff, J. J., Silberman, E. K., Barban, L., & Post, R. M. (1986). The clinical phenomenology of multiple personality disorder: Review of 100 recent cases. *Journal of Clinical Psychiatry, 47,* 285–293.

Quintana, S. M. (1998). Children's developmental understanding of ethnicity and race. *Applied & Preventive Psychology, 7*(1), 27–45.

Rabasca, L. (2000). Pre-empting racism. *Monitor on Psychology, 31*(11), 60.

Raichle, K., & Lambert, A. J. (2000). The role of political ideology in mediating judgments of blame in rape victims and their assailants: A test of the just world, personal responsibility, and legitimization hypotheses. *Personality & Social Psychology Bulletin, 26*(7), 853–863.

Raichle, M. E. (1994). Visualizing the mind. *Scientific American, 270*(4), 58–64.

Raine, A., et al. (2000). Reduced prefrontal gray matter volume and reduced autonomic activity in antisocial personality disorder. *Archives of General Psychiatry, 57*(2), 119–127.

Rakowski, W. (1995). Cited in Margoshes, P. (1995). For many, old age is the prime of life. *APA Monitor, 26*(5), 36–37.

Randel, B., Stevenson, H. W., & Witruk, E. (2000). Attitudes, beliefs, and mathematics achievement of German and Japanese high school students. *International Journal of Behavioral Development, 24*(2), 190–198.

Rappaport, N. B., McAnulty, D. P., & Brantley, P. J. (1988). Exploration of the Type A behavior pattern in chronic headache sufferers. *Journal of Consulting and Clinical Psychology, 56,* 621–623.

Rathore, S. S., et al. (2000). Race, sex, poverty, and the medical treatment of acute myocardial infarction in the elderly. *Circulation, 102,* 642–648.

Rathus, J. H., & Sanderson, W. C. (1999). *Marital distress: Cognitive behavioral interventions for couples.* Northvale, NJ: Jason Aronson.

Rathus, S. A. (1973). A 30-item schedule for assessing assertive behavior. *Behavior Therapy, 4,* 398–406.

Rathus, S. A., & Fichner-Rathus, L. (1997). *The right start.* New York: Longman.

Rathus, S. A., Nevid, J. S., & Fichner-Rathus, L. (2000). *Human sexuality in a world of diversity* (4th ed.). Boston: Allyn & Bacon.

Ratner, N. B., & Gleason, J. B. (1993). An introduction to psycholinguistics. In J. B. Gleason & N. B. Ratner (Eds.), *Psycholinguistics.* Fort Worth: Harcourt Brace Jovanovich.

Rauscher, F. H. (1998). Response to Katie Overy's paper, "Can music really 'improve' the mind?" *Psychology of Music, 26*(2), 197–199.

Rauscher, F. H., & Shaw, G. L. (1998). Key components of the Mozart effect. *Perceptual & Motor Skills, 86*(3), 835–841.

Raven, B. H. (1998). Groupthink, Bay of Pigs, and Watergate reconsidered. *Organizational Behavior & Human Decision Processes, 73*(2–3), 352–361.

Ready, T. (2000, June 7). Meditation apparently good for the heart as well as the mind. Healtheon/WebMD.

Reaney, P. (1998, March 16.) Acupuncture can work but is not totally safe. Reuters News Agency online.

Reaney, P. (2000, February 14). In matters of the heart, France tops EU neighbors. Reuters News Agency online.

Redd, W. H., et al. (1987). Cognitive/attentional distraction in the control of conditioned nausea in pediatric cancer patients receiving chemotherapy. *Journal of Consulting and Clinical Psychology, 55,* 391–395.

Reed, J. M., & Squire, L. R. (1997). Impaired recognition memory in patients with lesions limited to the hippocampal formation. *Behavioral Neuroscience, 111*(4), 667–675.

Reid, P. T. (1994). The real problem in the study of culture. *American Psychologist, 49,* 524–525.

Reid, T. R. (1990, December 24). Snug in their beds for Christmas Eve: In Japan, December 24th has become the hottest night of the year. *The Washington Post online.*

Reis, H. T., et al. (1990). What is smiling is beautiful and good. *European Journal of Social Psychology, 20,* 259–267.

Reiser, M. (1992). *Memory and mind and brain.* New York: Basic Books.

Rempel, M. W., & Fisher, R. J. (1998). Perceived threat, cohesion, and group problem solving in intergroup conflict. *International Journal of Conflict Management, 8*(3), 216–234.

Renninger, K. A., & Wozniak, R. H. (1985). Effect of interest on attentional shift, recognition, and recall in young children. *Developmental Psychology, 21,* 624–632.

Rescorla, R. A. (1988). Pavlovian conditioning: It's not what you think it is. *American Psychologist, 43,* 151–160.

Rescorla, R. A. (1999). Partial reinforcement reduces the associative change produced by nonreinforcement. *Journal of Experimental Psychology: Animal Behavior Processes, 25*(4), 403–414.

Resnick, H. S., Kilpatrick, D. G., Dansky, B. S., Saunders, B. E., & Best, C. L. (1993). Prevalence of civilian trauma and posttraumatic stress disorder in a representative national sample of women. *Journal of Consulting and Clinical Psychology, 61,* 984–991.

Resnick, M., et al. (1992, March 24). *Journal of the American Medical Association.* Cited in Young Indians prone to suicide, study finds. *The New York Times,* March 25, 1992, p. D24.

Rest, J. R. (1983). Morality. In P. H. Mussen, J. Flavell, & E. Markman (Eds.), *Handbook of child psychology: Vol. 3. Cognitive development.* New York: Wiley.

Reynolds, A. G. (1991). The cognitive consequences of bilingualism. In A. G. Reynolds (Ed.), *Bilingualism, multiculturalism, and second language learning.* Hillsdale, NJ: Erlbaum.

Rice, M. E., Quinsey, V. L., & Harris, G. T. (1991). Sexual recidivism among child molesters released from a maximum security psychiatric institution. *Journal of Consulting and Clinical Psychology, 59,* 381–386.

Richards, J. C., Hof, A., & Alvarenga, M. (2000). Serum lipids and their relationships with hostil-

ity and angry affect and behaviors in men. *Health Psychology, 19*(4), 393–398.

Richardson, D. C., Bernstein, S., & Taylor, S. P. (1979). The effect of situational contingencies on female retaliative behavior. *Journal of Personality and Social Psychology, 37,* 2044–2048.

Rickard, T. C., et al. (2000). The calculating brain: An fMRI study. *Neuropsychologia, 38*(3), 325–335.

Riepe, M. (2000). Cited in Ritter, M. (2000, March 21). Brains differ in navigation skills. The Associated Press online.

Rigotti, N. A., Lee, J. E., & Wechsler, H. (2000). US college students' use of tobacco products: Results of a national survey. *Journal of the American Medical Association, 284*(6), 699–705.

Rimm, E. (2000, May). Lifestyle may play role in potential for impotence. Paper presented to the annual meeting of the American Urological Association, Atlanta.

Rinn, W. E. (1991). Neuropsychology of facial expression. In R. S. Feldman & B. Rime (Eds.), *Fundamentals of nonverbal behavior.* Cambridge: Cambridge University Press.

Riot erupts after grocer arrested for "flirting." (2000, July 31). Reuters News Agency online.

Ritter, M. (2000, March 21). Brains differ in navigation skills. The Associated Press online.

Robbins, C., & Ehri, L. C. (1994). Reading storybooks to kindergartners helps them learn new vocabulary words. *Journal of Educational Psychology, 86,* 54–64.

Robertson, T. S., Zielinski, J., & Ward, S. (1984). *Consumer behavior.* Glenview, IL: Scott Foresman.

Robins, C. J., & Hayes, A. M. (1993). An appraisal of cognitive therapy. *Journal of Consulting and Clinical Psychology, 61,* 205–214.

Robins, R. W., Gosling, S. D., & Craik, K. H. (1999). An empirical analysis of trends in psychology. *American Psychologist, 54*(2), 117–128.

Robinson, N. M. (1992, August). *Development and variation: The challenge of nurturing gifted young children.* Paper presented at the meeting of the American Psychological Association, Washington, D.C.

Robson, P. (2001). Therapeutic aspects of cannabis and cannabinoids. *The British Journal of Psychiatry, 178,* 107–115.

Rodriguez, I., Greer, C. A., Mok, M. Y., & Mombaerts, P. (2000). A putative pheromone receptor gene expressed in human olfactory mucosa. *Nature Genetics, 26*(1), 18–19.

Rodriguez, N., Ryan, S. W., Kemp, H. V., & Foy, D. W. (1997). Posttraumatic stress disorder in adult female survivors of childhood sexual abuse: A comparison study. *Journal of Consulting and Clinical Psychology, 65,* 53–59.

Roediger, H. L., Weldon, M. S., Stadler, M. L., & Riegler, G. L. (1992). Direct comparison of two implicit memory tests: Word fragment and word stem completion. *Journal of Experimental Psychology: Learning, Memory, & Cognition, 18*(6), 1251–1269.

Rogers, C. R. (1951). *Client-centered therapy.* Boston: Houghton Mifflin.

Rose, J. S., Chassin, L., Presson, C. C., & Sherman, S. J. (1996). Prospective predictors of quit

attempts and smoking cessation in young adults. *Health Psychology, 15,* 261–268.

Rose, R. J. (1995). Genes and human behavior. *Annual Review of Psychology, 46,* 625–654.

Rosenbaum, D. E. (2000, May 16). On left-handedness, its causes and costs. *The New York Times,* pp. F1, F6.

Rosenfeld, A. (1995). Cited in Collins, C. (1995, May 11). Spanking is becoming the new don't. *The New York Times,* p. C8.

Rosenfeld, B., & Wall, A. (1998). Psychopathology and competence to stand trial. *Criminal Justice & Behavior, 25*(4), 443–462.

Rosenthal, A. M. (1994, March 15). The way she died. *The New York Times,* p. A23.

Rosenthal, E. (1993, July 20). Listening to the emotional needs of cancer patients. *The New York Times,* pp. C1, C7.

Ross, J. L., Roeltgen, D., Feuillan, P., Kushner, H., & Cutler, W. B. (2000). Use of estrogen in young girls with Turner syndrome: Effects on memory. *Neurology, 54*(1), 164–170.

Ross, L., & Nisbett, R. E. (1991). *The person and the situation.* New York: McGraw-Hill.

Ross, M. J., & Berger, R. S. (1996). Effects of stress inoculation training on athletes' postsurgical pain and rehabilitation after orthopedic injury. *Journal of Consulting and Clinical Psychology, 64,* 406–410.

Rosso, I. M., et al. (2000). Obstetric risk factors for early-onset schizophrenia in a Finnish birth cohort. *American Journal of Psychiatry, 157,* 801–807.

Roth, D. B., & Gellert, M. (2000). Cancer: New guardians of the genome. *Nature, 404,* 823–824.

Rothbart, M. K., & Ahadi, S. A. (1994). Temperament and the development of personality. *Journal of Abnormal Psychology, 103,* 55–66.

Rothbaum, B. O., Foa, E. B., Riggs, D. S., Murdock, T., & Walsh, W. (1992). A prospective examination of post-traumatic stress disorder in rape victims. *Journal of Traumatic Stress, 5,* 455–475.

Rothbaum, B. O., Hodges, L., Smith, S., Lee, J. H., & Price, L. (2000). A controlled study of virtual reality exposure therapy for the fear of flying. *Journal of Consulting and Clinical Psychology, 68*(6), 1020–1026.

Rotheram-Borus, M. J., Trautman, P. D., Dopkins, S. C., & Shrout, P. E. (1990). Cognitive style and pleasant activities among female adolescent suicide attempters. *Journal of Consulting and Clinical Psychology, 58,* 554–561.

Rothman, A. J., & Salovey, P. (1997). Shaping perceptions to motivate healthy behavior. *Psychological Bulletin, 121,* 3–19.

Rotter, J. B. (1990). Internal versus external control of reinforcement. *American Psychologist, 45,* 489–493.

Rotton, J., & Cohn, E. G. (2000). Violence is a curvilinear function of temperature in Dallas: A replication. *Journal of Personality and Social Psychology, 78*(6), 1074–1081.

Rovee-Collier, C. (1999). The development of infant memory. *Current Directions in Psychological Science, 8*(3), 80–85.

Rowatt, W. C., Cunningham, M. R., & Druen, P. B. (1999). Lying to get a date: The effect of facial physical attractiveness on the willingness to deceive prospective dating partners. *Journal of Social & Personal Relationships, 16*(2), 209–223.

Rozin, P., & Fallon, A. (1988). Body image, attitudes to weight, and misperceptions of figure preferences of the opposite sex. *Journal of Abnormal Psychology, 97,* 342–345.

Rubinstein, S., & Caballero, B. (2000). Is Miss America an undernourished role model? *Journal of the American Medical Association online, 283*(12).

Rude, S. S., Hertel, P. T., Jarrold, W., Covich, J., & Hedlund, S. (1999). Depression-related impairments in prospective memory. *Cognition & Emotion, 13*(3), 267–276.

Rule, B. G., Taylor, B. R., & Dobbs, A. R. (1987). Priming effects of heat on aggressive thoughts. *Social Cognition, 5,* 131–143.

Rush, A. J., Khatami, M., & Beck, A. T. (1975). Cognitive and behavior therapy in chronic depression. *Behavior Therapy, 6,* 398–404.

Rüstemli, A. (1986). Male and female personal space needs and escape reactions under intrusion: A Turkish sample. *International Journal of Psychology.*

Rutkowski, G. K., Gruder, C. L., & Romer, D. (1983). Group cohesiveness, social norms, and bystander intervention. *Journal of Personality and Social Psychology, 44,* 545–552.

Rutter, M. (1997). Nature–nurture integration. *American Psychologist, 52,* 390–398.

Ryder, A. G., Alden, L. E., & Paulhus, D. L. (2000). Is acculturation unidimensional or bidimensional? A head-to-head comparison in the prediction of personality, self-identity, and adjustment. *Journal of Personality and Social Psychology, 79*(1), 49–65.

Rymer, R. (1993). *Genie: An abused child's flight from silence.* New York: HarperCollins.

Sackeim, H. A., et al. (2000). A prospective, randomized, double-blind comparison of bilateral and right unilateral electroconvulsive therapy at different stimulus intensities. *Archives of General Psychiatry, 57*(5), 425–434.

Sacks, F. M., et al. (2001). Effects on blood pressure of reduced dietary sodium and the Dietary Approaches to Stop Hypertension (DASH) Diet. *The New England Journal of Medicine, 344*(1), 3–10.

Sadalla, E. K., Kenrick, D. T., & Vershure, B. (1987). Dominance and heterosexual attraction. *Journal of Personality and Social Psychology, 52,* 730–738.

Sadalla, E. K., Sheets, V., & McCreath, H. (1990). The cognition of urban tempo. *Environment and Behavior, 22,* 230–254.

Sadker, M., & Sadker, D. (1994). *How America's schools cheat girls.* New York: Scribners.

Sadowski, C., & Kelley, M. L. (1993). Social problem solving in suicidal adolescents. *Journal of Consulting and Clinical Psychology, 61,* 121–127.

Sagrestano, L. M., McCormick, S. H., Paikoff, R. L., & Holmbeck, G. N. (1999). Pubertal development and parent-child conflict in low-income, urban, African American adolescents. *Journal of Research on Adolescence, 9*(1), 85–107.

Salgado de Snyder, V. N., Cervantes, R. C., & Padilla, A. M. (1990). Gender and ethnic differences in psychosocial stress and generalized distress among Hispanics. *Sex Roles, 22,* 441–453.

Salovey, P., Rothman, A. J., Detweiler, J. B., & Steward, W. T. (2000). Emotional states and physical health. *American Psychologist, 55,* 110–121.

Samet, J. M., Dominici, F., Curriero, F. C., Coursac, I., & Zeger, S. L. (2000). Fine particulate air pollution and mortality in 20 U.S. cities, 1987–1994. *New England Journal of Medicine, 343*(24), 1742–1749.

Sanders, G. S. (1984). Effects of context cues on eyewitness identification responses. *Journal of Applied Social Psychology, 14,* 386–397.

Sandman, C., & Crinella, F. (1995) Cited in Margoshes, P. (1995). For many, old age is the prime of life. *APA Monitor, 26*(5), 36–37.

Sangrador, J. L., & Yela, C. (2000). "What is beautiful is loved": Physical attractiveness in love relationships in a representative sample. *Social Behavior & Personality, 28*(3), 207–218.

Sanna, L. J., & Meier, S. (2000). Looking for clouds in a silver lining: Self-esteem, mental simulations, and temporal confidence changes. *Journal of Research in Personality, 34*(2), 236–251.

Sanna, L. J., & Shotland, R. L. (1990). Valence of anticipated evaluation and social facilitation. *Journal of Experimental Social Psychology, 26,* 82–92.

Sano, M. (2000, July). Estrogen in Alzheimer's disease: Treatment or prevention. Paper presented to the World Alzheimer Congress 2000, Washington, D.C.

Santee, R. T., & Maslach, C. (1982). To agree or not to agree: Personal dissent amid social pressure to conform. *Journal of Personality and Social Psychology, 42,* 690–700.

Sarbin, T. R., & Coe, W. C. (1972). *Hypnosis.* New York: Holt, Rinehart and Winston.

Sarwer, D. B. & Wadden, T. A. (1999). The treatment of obesity: What's new, what's recommended. *Journal of Women's Health & Gender-Based Medicine, 8*(4), 483–493.

Savage-Rumbaugh, E. S., & Fields, W. M. (2000). Linguistic, cultural and cognitive capacities of bonobos (Pan paniscus). *Culture & Psychology, 6*(2), 131–153.

Saxe, L. (1991). Lying. *American Psychologist, 46,* 409–415.

Saxe, L., & Ben-Shakhar, G. (1999). Admissibility of polygraph tests: The application of scientific standards post-Daubert. *Psychology, Public Policy, & Law, 5*(1), 203–223.

Saywitz, K. J., Mannarino, A. P., Berliner, L., & Cohen, J. A. (2000). Treatment for sexually abused children and adolescents. *American Psychologist, 55*(9), 1040–1049.

Scarr, S., & Kidd, K. K. (1983). Developmental behavior genetics. In M. Haith & J. J. Campos (Eds.), *Handbook of child psychology.* New York: Wiley.

Scarr, S., & Weinberg, R. A. (1976). IQ test performance of Black children adopted by White families. *American Psychologist, 31,* 726–739.

Scarr, S., & Weinberg, R. A. (1977). Intellectual similarities within families of both adopted and biological children. *Intelligence, 1,* 170–191.

Scarr, S., & Weinberg, R. A. (1983). The Minnesota adoption studies: Genetic differences and malleability. *Child Development, 54,* 260–267.

Schachter, S. (1959). *The psychology of affiliation.* Stanford, CA: Stanford University Press.

Schachter, S., & Singer, J. E. (1962). Cognitive, social, and physiological determinants of emotional state. *Psychological Review, 69,* 379–399.

Schacter, D. L. (1992). Understanding implicit memory: A cognitive neuroscience approach. *American Psychologist, 47*(4), 559–569.

Schacter, D. L. (1999). The seven sins of memory: Insights from psychology and cognitive neuroscience. *American Psychologist, 54*(3), 182–203.

Schacter, D. L., Badgaiyan, R. D., & Alpert, N. M. (1999). Visual word stem completion priming within and across modalities: A PET study. *Neuroreport: For Rapid Communication of Neuroscience Research, 10*(10), 2061–2065.

Schacter, D. L., Chiu, C.-Y. P., & Ochsner, K. N. (1993). Implicit memory: A selective review. *Annual Review of Neuroscience, 16,* 159–182.

Schafer, J., & Brown, S. A. (1991). Marijuana and cocaine effect expectancies and drug use patterns. *Journal of Consulting and Clinical Psychology, 59,* 558–565.

Schaie, K. W. (1993). The Seattle Longitudinal Studies of adult intelligence. *Current Directions, 2,* 171–175.

Schaie, K. W. (1994). The course of adult intellectual development. *American Psychologist, 49,* 304–313.

Schaie, K. W., & Willis, S. L. (1991). Adult personality and psychomotor performance. *Journal of Gerontology: Psychological Sciences, 46,* P275–284.

Schein, E. H. (1990). Organizational culture. *American Psychologist, 45,* 109–119.

Schellenberg, E. G. (2000). Cited in Hershenson, R. (2000, August 6). Debating the Mozart theory. *The New York Times magazine online.*

Schenk, D. (2000, July). A possible vaccine for Alzheimer's disease. Paper presented to the World Alzheimer Congress 2000, Washington, D.C.

Schenker, M. (1993). Air pollution and mortality. *New England Journal of Medicine, 329,* 1807–1808.

Schiffman, H. (1990). *Sensation and perception.* New York: Wiley.

Schmidt, N. B., et al. (2000). Evaluating gene × psychological risk factor effects in the pathogenesis of anxiety: A new model approach. *Journal of Abnormal Psychology, 109*(2), 308–320.

Schmidt, N. B., Lerew, D. R., & Trakowski, J. H. (1997). Body vigilance in panic disorder. *Journal of Consulting and Clinical Psychology, 65,* 214–220.

Schneider, B. H., & Byrne, B. M. (1987). Individualizing social skills training for behavior-disordered children. *Journal of Consulting and Clinical Psychology, 55,* 444–445.

Schneider, R. H., et al. (1995). A randomized controlled trial of stress reduction for hypertension in older African Americans. *Hypertension, 26,* 820.

Schneider, W., & Bjorklund, D. (1992). Expertise,

aptitude, and strategic remembering. *Child Development, 63,* 461–473.

Schotte, D. E., Cools, J., & Payvar, S. (1990). Problem-solving deficits in suicidal patients. *Journal of Consulting and Clinical Psychology, 58,* 562–564.

Schuckit, M. A. (1996). Recent developments in the pharmacotherapy of alcohol dependence. *Journal of Consulting and Clinical Psychology, 64,* 669–676.

Schulz, R., & Heckhausen, J. (1996). A life span model of successful aging. *American Psychologist, 51,* 702–714.

Schupf, N. (2000, July). Epidemiology of dementia in Down syndrome. Paper presented to the World Alzheimer Congress 2000, Washington, D.C.

Schwartz, M. W., & Seeley, R. J. (1997). Neuroendocrine responses to starvation and weight loss. *New England Journal of Medicine, 336,* 1802–1811.

Schwartz, R. M., & Gottman, J. M. (1976). Toward a task analysis of assertive behavior. *Journal of Consulting and Clinical Psychology, 44,* 910–920.

Schwartzer, R., & Renner, B. (2000). Social-cognitive predictors of health behavior: Action self-efficacy and coping self-efficacy. *Health Psychology, 19*(5), 487–495.

Schweinhart, L. J., & Weikart, D. P. (Eds.) (1993). *Significant benefits: The High/Scope Perry Preschool Study through age 27.* Ypsilanti, MI: High/Scope Press.

Sciolino, E. (2000, October 4). Love finds a way in Iran: "Temporary marriage." *The New York Times online.*

Scott, J. (1994, May 9). Multiple personality cases perplex legal system. *The New York Times,* pp. A1, B10, B11.

Scruggs, T. E., & Mastropieri, M. A. (1992). Remembering the forgotten art of memory. *American Educator, 16*(4), 31–37.

Segal, N. (1993). Twin, sibling, and adoption methods. *American Psychologist, 48,* 943–956.

Selemon, L. D. (2000). A measured milestone in schizophrenia research. *Archives of General Psychiatry, 57*(1), 74–75.

Seligman, M. E. P. (1995). The effectiveness of psychotherapy: The *Consumer Reports* study. *American Psychologist, 50,* 965–974.

Seligman, M. E. P. (1996, August). Predicting and preventing depression. Master lecture presented to the meeting of the American Psychological Association, Toronto.

Selye, H. (1976). *The stress of life* (Rev. ed.). New York: McGraw-Hill.

Selye, H. (1980). The stress concept today. In I. L. Kutash, et al. (Eds.), *Handbook on stress and anxiety.* San Francisco: Jossey-Bass.

Seppa, N. (1996). APA releases study on family violence. *APA Monitor, 27*(4), 12.

Seppa, N. (1997). Young adults and AIDS: "It can't happen to me." *APA Monitor, 28*(1), 38–39.

Service, R. F. (1994). Will a new type of drug make memory-making easier? *Science, 266,* 218–219.

Sesso, H. D., Paffenbarger, R. S. Jr., & Lee, I-M. (2000). Physical activity and coronary heart disease in men: The Harvard Alumni Health Study. *Circulation, 102,* 975–980.

Seymour, H. N., Abdulkarim, L., & Johnson, V.

(1999). The Ebonics controversy: An educational and clinical dilemma. *Topics in Language Disorders, 19*(4), 66–77.

Shadish, W. R., Matt, G. E., Navarro, A. M., & Phillips, G. (2000). The effects of psychological therapies under clinically representative conditions: A meta-analysis. *Psychological Bulletin, 126*(4), 512–529.

Shadish, W. R., & Ragsdale, K. (1996). Random versus nonrandom assignment in controlled experiments. *Journal of Consulting and Clinical Psychology, 64,* 1290–1305.

Shayley, A. Y., et al. (2000). Auditory startle response in trauma survivors with posttraumatic stress disorder: A prospective study. *American Journal of Psychiatry, 157,* 255–261.

Shaywitz, B. A., et al. (1995). Sex differences in the functional organization of the brain for language. *Nature, 373,* 607–609.

Shaywitz, B. A., & Shaywitz, S. E. (2000). Estrogen and Alzheimer disease: Plausible theory, negative clinical trial. *Journal of the American Medical Association, 283*(8), 1055–1056.

Sheehy, G. (1976). *Passages.* New York: Dutton.

Sheehy, G. (1995). *New passages: Mapping your life across time.* New York: Random House.

Shepperd, J. A. (1993). Productivity loss in performance groups. *Psychological Bulletin, 113,* 67–81.

Sherif, M., Harvey, O. J., White, B. J., Hood, W. R., & Sherif, C. W. (1961/1988). *The Robbers Cave experiment: Intergroup conflict and cooperation.* Middletown, CT: Wesleyan University Press.

Sherman, J. W., & Frost, L. A. (2000). On the encoding of stereotype-relevant information under cognitive load. *Personality & Social Psychology Bulletin, 26*(1), 26–34.

Sherman, R. A. (1997). *Phantom pain.* New York: Plenum.

Shiffman, S., et al. (1997). A day at a time: Predicting smoking lapse from daily urge. *Journal of Abnormal Psychology, 106,* 104–116.

Shiffman, S., et al. (2000). Dynamic effects of self-efficacy on smoking lapse and relapse. *Health Psychology, 19*(4), 315–323.

Shultz, S. K., Scherman, A., & Marshall, L. J. (2000). Evaluation of a university-based date rape prevention program: Effect on attitudes and behavior related to rape. *Journal of College Student Development, 41*(2), 193–201.

Shumaker, S. A., & Hill, D. R. (1991). Gender differences in social support and physical health. *Health Psychology, 10,* 102–111.

Silberschatz, G. (1998). In Persons, J. B., & Silberschatz, G. (1998). Are results of randomized controlled trials useful to psychotherapists? *Journal of Consulting and Clinical Psychology, 66,* 126–135.

Silver, E. (1994). Cited in DeAngelis, T. (1994). Experts see little impact from insanity plea ruling. *APA Monitor, 25*(6), 28.

Silverstein, L. B. (1991). Transforming the debate about child care and maternal employment. *American Psychologist, 46,* 1025–1032.

Simons, A. D., Angell, K. L., Monroe, S. M., & Thase, M. E. (1993). Cognition and life stress in depression. *Journal of Abnormal Psychology, 102,* 584–591.

Simons, A. D., Gordon, J. S., Monroe, S. M., & Thase, M. E. (1995). Toward an integration of psychologic, social, and biologic factors in depression. *Journal of Consulting and Clinical Psychology, 63,* 369–377.

Simonsen, G., Blazina, C., & Watkins, C. E. Jr. (2000). Gender role conflict and psychological well-being among gay men. *Journal of Counseling Psychology, 47*(1), 85–89.

Simonton, D. K. (2000). Creativity: Cognitive, personal, developmental, and social aspects. *American Psychologist, 55,* 151–158.

Simpson, M. L., Olejnik, S., Tam, A. Y., & Supattathum, S. (1994). Elaborative verbal rehearsals and college students' cognitive performance. *Journal of Educational Psychology, 86,* 267–278.

Simpson, M., & Perry, J. D. (1990). Crime and climate. *Environment and Behavior, 22,* 295–300.

Singh, R., & Ho, S. Y. (2000). Attitudes and attraction: A new test of the attraction, repulsion and similarity-dissimilarity asymmetry hypotheses. *British Journal of Social Psychology, 39*(2), 197–211.

Skinner, B. F. (1938). *The behavior of organisms: An experimental analysis.* New York: Appleton.

Skinner, B. F. (1948). *Walden two.* New York: Macmillan.

Skinner, B. F. (1957). *Verbal behavior.* New York: Appleton.

Skinner, B. F. (1972). *Beyond freedom and dignity.* New York: Knopf.

Skinner, B. F. (1983). Intellectual self-management in old age. *American Psychologist, 38,* 239–244.

Slaven, L., & Lee, C. (1997). Mood and symptom reporting among middle-aged women: The relationship between menopausal status, hormone replacement therapy, and exercise participation. *Health Psychology, 16,* 203–208.

Sleek, S. (1995). Rallying the troops inside our bodies. *APA Monitor, 26*(12), 1, 24–25.

Sleek, S. (1996). Side effects undermine drug compliance. *APA Monitor, 26*(3), 32.

Sleek, S. (1997). Resolution raises concerns about conversion therapy. *APA Monitor, 28*(10), 15.

Sleek, S. (1998). Psychologists debate merits of the polygraph, *APA Monitor, 29*(6).

Slobin, D. I. (1983). Crosslinguistic evidence for basic child grammar. Paper presented at the biennial meeting of the Society for Research in Child Development, Detroit.

Sloman, S. A. (1996). The empirical case for two systems of reasoning. *Psychological Bulletin, 119,* 3–22.

Smetana, J., & Gaines, C. (1999). Adolescent-parent conflict in middle-class African American families. *Child Development, 70*(6), 1447–1463.

Smiley, J. (2000, May 7). The good life. *The New York Times magazine,* pp. 58–59.

Smith, G. F., & Dorfman, D. (1975). The effect of stimulus uncertainty on the relationship between frequency of exposure and liking. *Journal of Personality and Social Psychology, 31,* 150–155.

Smith, M. L., & Glass, G. V. (1977). Meta-analysis of psychotherapy outcome studies. *American Psychologist, 32,* 752–760.

Smith, R. E., Smoll, F. L., & Ptacek, J. T. (1990). Conjunctive moderator variables in vulnerability and resiliency research. *Journal of Personality and Social Psychology, 58,* 360–370.

Smith, V. (2000, February 16). Female heart, geography link shown. The Associated Press.

Smock, P. J. (2000). *Annual Review of Sociology.* Cited in Nagourney, E. (2000, February 15). Study finds families bypassing marriage. *The New York Times*, p. F8.

Snarey, J. R. (1985). Cross-cultural universality of social-moral development: A critical review of Kohlbergian research. *Psychological Bulletin, 97,* 202–232.

Snyderman, M., & Rothman, S. (1987). Survey of expert opinion on intelligence and aptitude testing. *American Psychologist, 42,* 137–144.

Snyderman, M., & Rothman, S. (1990). *The I.Q. controversy.* New Brunswick, NJ: Transaction Publishers.

Solomon, E. P., Berg, L. R., Martin, D. W., & Villee, C. (1993). *Biology* (3rd ed.). Philadelphia: Saunders College Publishing.

Somerfield, M. R., & McCrae, R. R. (2000). Stress and coping research: Methodological challenges, theoretical advances, and clinical applications. *American Psychologist, 55*(6), 620–625.

Sorensen, S. B., & Rutter, C. M. (1991). Transgenerational patterns of suicide attempt. *Journal of Consulting and Clinical Psychology, 59,* 861–866.

Southern, T., & Jones, E. D. (1991). *The academic acceleration of gifted children.* New York: Teachers College Press.

Souweidane, V., & Huesmann, L. R. (1999). Influence of American urban culture on the development of normative beliefs about aggression in Middle-Eastern immigrants. *American Journal of Community Psychology, 27*(2), 239–254.

Sperling, G. (1960). The information available in brief visual presentations. *Psychological Monographs, 74,* 1–29.

Sperry, R. W. (1998). A powerful paradigm made stronger. *Neuropsychologia, 36*(10), 1063–1068.

Spitzer, R. L., Gibbon, M., Skodol, A. E., Williams, J. B. W., & First, M. B. (1989). *DSM-III-R casebook.* Washington, D.C.: American Psychiatric Press.

Spreat, S., & Behar, D. (1994). Trends in the residential (inpatient) treatment of individuals with a dual diagnosis. *Journal of Consulting and Clinical Psychology, 61,* 43–48.

Sprecher, S. (1998). Insiders' perspectives on reasons for attraction to a close other. *Social Psychology Quarterly, 61*(4), 287–300.

Sprecher, S., Sullivan, Q., & Hatfield, E. (1994). Mate selection preferences. *Journal of Personality and Social Psychology, 66*(6), 1074–1080.

Squire, L. R. (1993). Memory and the hippocampus. *Psychological Review, 99,* 195–231.

Squire, L. R. (1996, August). Memory systems of the brain. Master lecture presented to the meeting of the American Psychological Association, Toronto.

Sroufe, A. (1998). Cited in Blakeslee, S. (1998, August 4). Re-evaluating significance of baby's bond with mother. *The New York Times*, pp. F1, F2.

Staal, W. G., et al. (2000). Structural brain abnormalities in patients with schizophrenia and their healthy siblings. *American Journal of Psychiatry, 157,* 416–421.

Stacy, A. W., Bentler, P. M., & Flay, B. R. (1994). Attitudes and health behavior in diverse populations: Drunk driving, alcohol use, binge eating, marijuana use, and cigarette use. *Health Psychology, 13*(1), 73–85.

Stacy, A. W., & Newcomb, M. D. (1999). Adolescent drug use and adult drug problems in women: Direct, interactive, and mediational effects. *Experimental & Clinical Psychopharmacology, 7*(2), 160–173.

Stamler, J., et al. (2000). Relationship of baseline serum cholesterol levels in 3 large cohorts of younger men to long-term coronary, cardiovascular, and all-cause mortality and to longevity. *Journal of the American Medical Association, 284,* 311–318.

Stampfer, M. J., Hu, F. B., Manson, J. E., Rimm, E. B., & Willett, W. C. (2000). Primary prevention of coronary heart disease in women through diet and lifestyle. *New England Journal of Medicine, 343*(1), 16–22.

Staples, S. I. (1996). Human responses to environmental noise. *American Psychologist, 51,* 143–150.

Stasser, G. (1999). A primer of social decision scheme theory: Models of group influence, competitive model-testing, and prospective modeling. *Organizational Behavior & Human Decision Processes, 80*(1), 3–20.

Steele, C. M. (1994, October 31). "Bizarre black IQ claims abetted by media." *San Francisco Chronicle*, Editorial page.

Steele, C. M. (1996, August). The role of stereotypes in shaping intellectual identity. Master lecture presented to the meeting of the American Psychological Association, Toronto.

Steele, C. M. (1997). A threat in the air: How stereotypes shape intellectual identity and performance. *American Psychologist, 52,* 613–629.

Steele, C. M., & Aronson, J. (1995). Stereotype threat and the intellectual test performance of African Americans. *Journal of Personality and Social Psychology, 69,* 797–811.

Steele, C. M., & Josephs, R. A. (1990). Alcohol myopia. *American Psychologist, 45,* 921–933.

Stein, M. B., & Kean, Y. M. (2000). Disability and quality of life in social phobia: Epidemiologic findings. *American Journal of Psychiatry, 157,* 1606–1613.

Steinberg, J. (2000, August 21). Increase in test scores counters dire forecasts for bilingual ban. *The New York Times*, pp. 1, 22.

Steinberg, L. (1996). *Beyond the classroom.* New York: Simon & Schuster.

Steinberg, L., Brown, B. B., & Dornbusch, S. M. (1996). Ethnicity and adolescent achievement. *American Educator, 20*(2), 28–35.

Steinberg, L., Lamborn, S. D., Dornbusch, S. M., & Darling, N. (1992). Impact of parenting practices on adolescent achievement: Authoritative parenting, school involvement, and encouragement to succeed. *Child Development, 63,* 1266–1281.

Steinhauer, J. (1995, July 6). No marriage, no apologies. *The New York Times*, pp. C1, C7.

Sternberg, R. J. (1988). Triangulating love. In R. J. Sternberg & M. J. Barnes (Eds.), *The psychology of love.* New Haven, CT: Yale University Press.

Sternberg, R. J. (1997a). What does it mean to be smart? *Educational Leadership, 54,* 20–24.

Sternberg, R. J. (1997b). The concept of intelligence and its role in lifelong learning and success. *American Psychologist, 52,* 1030–1037.

Sternberg, R. J. (2000). In search of the zipperump-a-zoo. *Psychologist, 13*(5), 250–255.

Sternberg, R. J., & Davidson, J. E. (1994). *The nature of insight.* Cambridge, MA: The MIT Press, a Bradford Book.

Sternberg, R. J., & Lubart, T. I. (1995). *Defying the crowd: Cultivating creativity in a culture of conformity.* New York: Free Press.

Sternberg, R. J., & Lubart, T. I. (1996). Investing in creativity. *American Psychologist, 51,* 677–688.

Sternberg, R. J., Wagner, R. K., Williams, W. M., & Horvath, J. A. (1995). Testing common sense. *American Psychologist, 50,* 912–927.

Sternberg, R. J., & Williams, W. M. (1997). Does the Graduate Record Examination predict meaningful success in the graduate training of psychologists? *American Psychologist, 52,* 630–641.

Stevenson, H. W., Lee, S. Y., & Stigler, J. W. (1986). Mathematics achievement of Chinese, Japanese, and American children. *Science, 231,* 693–699.

Stewart, A. J., & Ostrove, J. M. (1998). Women's personality in middle age: Gender, history, and midcourse corrections. *American Psychologist, 53*(11), 1185–1194.

Stewart, A. J., Ostrove, J. M., & Helson, R. (1998). *Middle aging in women: Patterns of personality change from the 30s to the 50s.* (Manuscript submitted for publication)

Stewart, J. Y., & Armet, E. (2000, April 3). Aging in America: Retirees reinvent the concept. *Los Angeles Times online.*

Stice, E., Akutagawa, D., Gaggar, A., & Agras, W. S. (2000). Negative affect moderates the relation between dieting and binge eating. *International Journal of Eating Disorders, 27*(2), 218–229.

Stice, E., Hayward, C., Cameron, R. P., Killen, J. D., & Taylor, C. B. (2000). Body-image and eating disturbances predict onset of depression among female adolescents: A longitudinal study. *Journal of Abnormal Psychology, 109*(3), 438–444.

Stier, D. S., & Hall, J. A. (1984). Gender differences in touch. *Journal of Personality and Social Psychology, 47,* 440–459.

Stolberg, S. G. (1998, March 9). U.S. awakes to epidemic of sexual diseases. *The New York Times*, pp. A1, A14.

Straube, E. R., & Oades, R. D. (1992). *Schizophrenia.* San Diego: Academic Press.

Strauss, M. (1995). Cited in Collins, C. (1995, May 11). Spanking is becoming the new don't. *The New York Times*, p. C8.

Strober, M., et al. (2000). Controlled family study of anorexia nervosa and bulimia nervosa: Evidence of shared liability and transmission of partial syndromes. *American Journal of Psychiatry, 157,* 393–401.

Strom, J. C., & Buck, R. W. (1979). Staring and participants' sex. *Personality and Social Psychology Bulletin, 5,* 114–117.

Strong, S. M., Williamson, D. A., Netemeyer, R. G., & Geer, J. H. (2000). Eating disorder symptoms and concerns about body differ as a function of gender and sexual orientation. *Jour-*

nal of Social & Clinical Psychology, *19*(2), 240–255.

Stroud, M. W., Thorn, B. E., Jensen, M. P., & Boothby, J. L. (2000). The relation between pain beliefs, negative thoughts, and psychosocial functioning in chronic pain patients. *Pain*, *84*(2–3), 347–352.

Strupp, H. H. (1996). The tripartite model and the *Consumer Reports* study. *American Psychologist*, *51*, 1017–1024.

Study finds smaller pay gap for male and female doctors. (1996, April 11). *The New York Times*, p. B9.

Stunkard, A. J., Harris, J. R., Pedersen, N. L., & McLearn, G. E. (1990). A separated twin study of the body mass index. *New England Journal of Medicine*, *322*, 1483–1487.

Stunkard, A. J., & Sørensen, T. I. A. (1993). Obesity and socioeconomic status. *New England Journal of Medicine*, *329*, 1036–1037.

Sue, D. W., Bingham, R. P., Porché-Burke, L., & Vasquez, M. (1999). The diversification of psychology: A multicultural revolution. *American Psychologist*, *54*, 1061–1069.

Sue, S. (1991). In J. D. Goodchilds (Ed.), *Psychological perspectives on human diversity in America*. Washington, D.C.: American Psychological Association.

Sue, S. (1999). Science, ethnicity, and bias: Where have we gone wrong? *American Psychologist*, *54*, 1070–1077.

Sue, S., & Okazaki, S. (1990). Asian-American educational achievements. *American Psychologist*, *45*, 913–920.

Suinn, R. A. (1982). Intervention with Type A behaviors. *Journal of Consulting and Clinical Psychology*, *50*, 933–949.

Suinn, R. A. (1995). Anxiety management training. In K. Craig (Ed.), *Anxiety and depression in children and adults* (pp. 159–179). New York: Sage.

Sullivan, A. (2000, April 2). The He hormone. *The New York Times magazine*, pp. 46–51ff.

Sullivan, E. V., et al. (2000). Contribution of alcohol abuse to cerebellar volume deficits in men with schizophrenia. *Archives of General Psychiatry*, *57*, 894–902.

Sullivan, J. M. (2000). Cellular and molecular mechanisms underlying learning and memory impairments produced by cannabinoids. *Learning & Memory*, *7*(3), 132–139.

Sullivan, P. F., Neale, M. C., & Kendler, K. S. (2000). Genetic epidemiology of major depression: Review and meta-analysis. *American Journal of Psychiatry*, *157*, 1552–1562.

Suls, J., Wan, C. K., & Costa, P. T. Jr. (1995). Relationship of trait anger to resting blood pressure. *Health Psychology*, *14*, 444–456.

Sutker, P. B. (1994). Psychopathy: Traditional and clinical antisocial concepts. In D. C. Fowles, P. B. Sutker, & S. H. Goodman (Eds.), *Progress in experimental personality and psychopathology research* (pp. 73–120). New York: Springer.

Suzuki, L. A., & Valencia, R. R. (1997). Race-ethnicity and measured intelligence: Educational implications. *American Psychologist*, *52*, 1103–1114.

Swendsen, J. D., et al. (2000). Mood and alcohol consumption: An experience sampling test of the self-medication hypothesis. *Journal of Abnormal Psychology*, *109*(2), 198–204.

Szasz, T. S. (1984). *The therapeutic state*. Buffalo, NY: Prometheus.

Tailoring treatments for alcoholics is not the answer (1997). *APA Monitor*, *28*(2), 6–7.

Tapes raise new doubts about 'Sybil' personalities (1998, August 19). *The New York Times online*.

Taub, A. (1993, April 8). Narcotics have long been known safe and effective for pain. *The New York Times*, p. A20.

Tavris, C. (1998, January 2). Call us unpredictable. *The New York Times*, p. A17.

Taylor, H. (1993). Cited in Barringer, F. (1993, April 25). Polling on sexual issues has its drawbacks. *The New York Times*, p. A23.

Taylor, M. J. (2000). The influence of self-efficacy on alcohol use among American Indians. *Cultural Diversity and Ethnic Minority Psychology*, *6*(2), 152–167.

Taylor, S. E. (2000). Cited in Goode, E. (2000, May 19). Response to stress found that's particularly female. *The New York Times*, p. A20.

Taylor, S. E., Klein, L. C., Lewis, B. P., Gurung, R. A. R., Gruenewald, T. L., & Updegraff, J. A. (2000). Biobehavioral responses to stress in females: Tend-and-befriend, not fight-or-flight. *Psychological Review*, *107*(3), 411–429.

Taylor-Tolbert, N. S., et al. (2000). Exercise reduces blood pressure in heavy older hypertensive men. *American Journal of Hypertension*, *13*, 44–51.

Teachout, T. (2000, April 2). For more artists, a fine old age. *The New York Times online*.

Télégdy, G. (1977). Prenatal androgenization of primates and humans. In J. Money & H. Musaph (Eds.), *Handbook of sexology*. Amsterdam: Excerpta Medica.

Teller, D. Y. (1998). Spatial and temporal aspects of infant color vision. *Vision Research*, *38*(21), 3275–3282.

Teng, E., & Squire, L. R. (1999). Memory for places learned long ago is intact after hippocampal damage. *Nature*, *400*(6745), 675–677.

Tennen, H., & Affleck, G. (2000). The perception of personal control: Sufficiently important to warrant careful scrutiny. *Personality & Social Psychology Bulletin*, *26*(2), 152–156.

Terry, D. (2000, July 16). Getting under my skin. *The New York Times online*.

Tharp, R. G. (1991). Cultural diversity and treatment of children. *Journal of Consulting and Clinical Psychology*, *59*, 799–812.

Thase, M. E., & Kupfer, D. J. (1996). Recent developments in the pharmacotherapy of mood disorders. *Journal of Consulting and Clinical Psychology*, *64*, 646–659.

Thom, A., Sartory, G., & Jöhren, P. (2000). Comparison between one-session psychological treatment and benzodiazepine in dental phobia. *Journal of Consulting and Clinical Psychology*, *68*(3), 378–387.

Thompson, C. P., Anderson, L. P., & Bakeman, R. A. (2000). Effects of racial socialization and racial identity on acculturative stress in African American college students. *Cultural Diversity and Ethnic Minority Psychology*, *6*(2), 196–210.

Thompson, L. A., Detterman, D. K., & Plomin, R. (1991). Associations between cognitive abilities and scholastic achievement. *Psychological Science*, *2*, 158–165.

Thompson, R. A. (1991a). Attachment theory and research. In M. Lewis (Ed.), *Child and adolescent psychiatry*. Baltimore: Williams & Wilkins.

Thompson, R. A. (1991b). Infant daycare. In J. V. Lerner & N. L. Galambos (Eds.), *Employed mothers and their children* (pp. 9–36). New York: Garland.

Thoresen, C., & Powell, L. H. (1992). Type A behavior pattern. *Journal of Consulting and Clinical Psychology*, *60*, 595–604.

Thornhill, R., & Palmer, C. (2000). *A natural history of rape: Biological bases of sexual coercion*. Cambridge, Mass.: MIT Press.

Thurstone, L. L. (1938). Primary mental abilities. *Psychometric Monographs*, *1*.

Thurstone, L. L., & Thurstone, T. G. (1963). *SRA primary abilities*. Chicago: SRA.

Tiffany, S. T., Cox, L. S., & Elash, C. A. (2000). Effects of transdermal nicotine patches on abstinence-induced and cue-elicited craving in cigarette smokers. *Journal of Consulting and Clinical Psychology*, *68*, 233–240.

Tigner, R. B., & Tigner, S. S. (2000). Triarchic theories of intelligence: Aristotle and Sternberg. *History of Psychology*, *3*(2), 168–176.

Tkachuk, G. A., & Martin, G. L. (1999). Exercise therapy for patients with psychiatric disorders: Research and clinical implications. *Professional Psychology: Research and Practice*, *30*(3), 275–282.

Tolchin, M. (1989, July 19). When long life is too much. *The New York Times*, pp. A1, A15.

Tolman, E. C., & Honzik, C. H. (1930). Introduction and removal of reward, and maze performance in rats. *University of California Publications in Psychology*, *4*, 257–275.

Tomes, H. (1993). It's in the nation's interest to break abuse cycle. *APA Monitor*, *24*(3), 28.

Tomes, H. (2000). Diversifying psychology in the new millennium. *Monitor on Psychology*, *31*(1), 85.

Tooley, G. A., Armstrong, S. M., Norman, T. R., & Sali, A. (2000). Acute increases in nighttime plasma melatonin levels following a period of meditation. *Biological Psychology*, *53*(1), 69–78.

Torgersen, S. (1983). Genetic factors in anxiety disorders. *Archives of General Psychiatry*, *40*, 1085–1089.

Triandis, H. C. (1990). Cross-cultural studies of individualism and collectivism. In J. J. Berman (Ed.), *Nebraska Symposium on Motivation, 1989. Cross-cultural perspectives*. Lincoln: University of Nebraska Press.

Triandis, H. C. (1994). *Culture and social behavior*. New York: McGraw-Hill.

Triandis, H. C. (1995). *Individualism and collectivism*. Boulder, CO: Westview Press.

Trickett, P. K., Aber, J. L., Carlson, V., & Cicchetti, D. (1991). Relationship of socioeconomic status to the etiology and developmental sequelae of physical child abuse. *Developmental Psychology*, *27*, 148–158.

Trimble, J. E. (1991). The mental health service and training needs of American Indians. In H. F. Myers et al. (Eds.), *Ethnic minority perspectives on clinical training and services in psychology* (pp. 43–48). Washington, D.C.: American Psychological Association.

Trobst, K. K., Collins, R. L., & Embree, J. M. (1994). The role of emotion in social support provision. *Journal of Social and Personal Relationships, 11,* 45–62.

Tsui, A. S., & O'Reilly, C. A. III. (1989). Beyond simple demographic effects. *Academy of Management Journal, 32,* 402–423.

Tsang, Y. C. (1938). Hunger motivation in gastrectomized rats. *Journal of Comparative Psychology, 26,* 1–17.

Tucker, J. S., Friedman, H. S., Wingard, D. L., & Schwartz, J. E. (1996). Marital history at midlife as a predictor of longevity. *Health Psychology, 15,* 94–101.

Tuiten, A., et al. (2000). Time course of effects of testosterone administration on sexual arousal in women. *Archives of General Psychiatry, 57,* 149–153.

Tulving, E. (1985). How many memory systems are there? *American Psychologist, 40,* 385–398.

Tulving, E. (1991). Memory research is not a zero-sum game. *American Psychologist, 46,* 41–42.

Tulving, E., & Markowitsch, H. J. (1998). Episodic and declarative memory: Role of the hippocampus. *Hippocampus, 8*(3), 198–204.

Turner, A. M., & Greenough, W. T. (1985). Differential rearing effects on rat visual cortex synapses: I. Synaptic and neuronal density and synapses per neuron. *Brain Research, 329,* 195–203.

Turner, M. E., & Pratkanis, A. R. (1998). A social identity maintenance model of groupthink. *Organizational Behavior & Human Decision Processes, 73*(2–3), 210–235.

Tversky, A., & Kahneman, D. (1982). Judgment under uncertainty. In D. Kahneman, P. Slovic, & A. Tversky (Eds.), *Judgment under uncertainty: Heuristics and biases.* New York: Cambridge University Press.

Uchino, B. N., Cacioppo, J. T., & Kiecolt-Glaser, J. K. (1996). The relationship between social support and physiological processes. *Psychological Bulletin, 119,* 488–531.

Ukestad, L. K., & Wittrock, D. A. (1996). Pain perception and coping in female tension headache sufferers and headache-free controls. *Health Psychology, 15,* 65–68.

UNAIDS (2000, June 27). *Report on the global HIV/AIDS epidemic.* Joint United Nations Programme on HIV/AIDS (UNAIDS).

Unger, J. B., et al. (2000). English language use as a risk factor for smoking initiation among Hispanic and Asian American adolescents. *Health Psychology, 19*(5), 403–410.

USBC (U.S. Bureau of the Census). (1995). *Statistical abstract of the United States* (115th ed.). Washington, D.C.: U.S. Government Printing Office.

USBC (U.S. Bureau of the Census). (1998). *Statistical abstract of the United States* (118th ed.). Washington, D.C.: U.S. Government Printing Office.

Vaillant, G. E. (1994). Ego mechanisms of defense and personality psychopathology. *Journal of Abnormal Psychology, 103,* 44–50.

Valentiner, D. P., Foa, E. B., Riggs, D. S., & Ger-

shuny, B. S. (1996). Coping strategies and post-traumatic stress disorder in female victims of sexual and nonsexual assault. *Journal of Abnormal Psychology, 105,* 455–458.

Valian, V. (1998). *Why so slow? The advancement of women.* Cambridge, MA: MIT Press.

Van Brunt, L. (1994, March 27). About men: Whites without money. *The New York Times magazine,* p. 38.

Vandell, D. L., & Corasaniti, M. A. (1990). Child care and the family. In K. McCartney (Ed.), *New Directions for Child Development* (Vol. 49, pp. 23–37). San Francisco: Jossey-Bass.

Vandenbergh, J. G. (1993). Cited in Angier, N. (1993, August 24). Female gerbil born with males is found to be begetter of sons. *The New York Times,* p. C4.

VandenBos, G. R. (1996). Outcome assessment of psychotherapy. *American Psychologist, 51,* 1005–1006.

van Hiel, A., Kossowska, M., & Mervielde, I. (2000). The relationship between Openness to Experience and political ideology. *Personality & Individual Differences, 28*(4), 741–751.

van Roosmalen, E., & McDaniel, S. A. (1998). Sexual harassment in academia: A hazard to women's health. *Women & Health, 28*(2), 33–54.

Vermeer, H. J., Boekaerts, M., & Seegers, G. (2000). Motivational and gender differences: Sixth-grade students' mathematical problem-solving behavior. *Journal of Educational Psychology, 92*(2), 308–315.

Vernberg, E. M., La Greca, A. M., Silverman, W. K., & Prinstein, M. J. (1996). Prediction of posttraumatic stress symptoms in children after Hurricane Andrew. *Journal of Abnormal Psychology, 105,* 237–248.

Vik, P. W., Carrello, P., Tate, S. R., & Field, C. (2000). Progression of consequences among heavy-drinking college students. *Psychology of Addictive Behaviors, 14*(2), 91–101.

Villa, K. K., & Abeles, N. (2000). Broad spectrum intervention and the remediation of prospective memory declines in the able elderly. *Aging & Mental Health, 4*(1), 21–29.

Visintainer, M. A., Volpicelli, J. R., & Seligman, M. E. P. (1982). Tumor rejection in rats after inescapable or escapable shock. *Science, 216*(23), 437–439.

Vitousek, K., & Manke, F. (1994). Personality variables and disorders in anorexia nervosa and bulimia nervosa. *Journal of Abnormal Psychology, 103,* 137–147.

Volz, J. (2000). Successful aging: The second 50. *Monitor on Psychology, 30*(1), 24–28.

Von Békésy, G. (1957, August). The ear. *Scientific American,* pp. 66–78.

Wadden, T. A., et al. (1997). Exercise in the treatment of obesity. *Journal of Consulting and Clinical Psychology, 65,* 269–277.

Wade, N. (1998, January 6). Was Freud wrong? Are dreams the brain's start-up test? *The New York Times online.*

Wade, T. D., Bulik, C. M., Neale, M., & Kendler, K. S. (2000). Anorexia nervosa and major depression: Shared genetic and environmental risk factors. *American Journal of Psychiatry, 157*(3), 469–471.

Wagner, R. K. (1997). Intelligence, training, and employment. (1997). *American Psychologist, 52,* 1059–1069.

Walk, R. D., & Gibson, E. J. (1961). A comparative and analytical study of visual depth perception. *Psychological Monographs, 75*(15).

Walker, L. E. A. (1993). Cited in Mednick, A. (1993). Domestic abuse is seen as worldwide "epidemic." *APA Monitor, 24*(5), 33.

Walsh, B. T., et al. (2000). Fluoxetine for bulimia nervosa following poor response to psychotherapy. *American Journal of Psychiatry, 157,* 1332–1334.

Walsh, M. R. (1993, August). Teaching the psychology of women and gender for undergraduate and graduate faculty. Workshop of the Psychology of Women Institute presented at the meeting of the American Psychological Association, Toronto, Canada.

Wan, W. W. N., Luk, C., & Lai, J. C. L. (2000). Personality correlates of loving styles among Chinese students in Hong Kong. *Personality & Individual Differences, 29*(1), 169–175.

Wang, A. Y. (2000). Cited in Murray, B. (2000). What makes a successful cyberstudent? *Monitor on Psychology, 31*(4), 11.

Wang, A. Y., & Newlin, M. H. (2000). Characteristics of students who enroll and succeed in psychology Web-based classes. *Journal of Educational Psychology, 92*(1), 137–143.

Wang, H., et al. (2000). Nicotine as a potent blocker of the cardiac A-type K^+ channels: Effects on cloned Kv4.3 channels and native transient outward current. *Circulation, 102,* 1165–1171.

Wang, X., et al. (2000). Longitudinal study of earthquake-related PTSD in a randomly selected community sample in North China. *American Journal of Psychiatry, 157,* 1260–1266.

Wann, D. L., Royalty, J., & Roberts, A. (2000). The self-presentation of sports fans: Investigating the importance of team identification and self-esteem. *Journal of Sport Behavior, 23*(2), 198–206.

Wann, D. L., & Schrader, M. P. (2000). Controllability and stability in the self-serving attributions of sport spectators. *Journal of Social Psychology, 140*(2), 160–168.

Warman, D. M., & Cohen, R. (2000). Stability of aggressive behaviors and children's peer relationships. *Aggressive Behavior, 26*(4), 277–290.

Wartik, N. (2000, June 25). Depression comes out of hiding. *The New York Times,* pp. MH1, MH4.

Waters, M. (2000). Psychologists spotlight growing concern of higher suicide rates among adolescents. *Monitor on Psychology, 31*(6), 41.

Watkins, C. E. Jr., Campbell, V. L., Nieberding, R., & Hallmark, R. (1995). Contemporary practice of psychological assessment by clinical psychologists. *Professional Psychology: Research and Practice, 26,* 54–60.

Watkins, M. J., Ho, E., & Tulving, E. (1976). Context effects on recognition memory for faces. *Journal of Verbal Learning and Verbal Behavior, 15,* 505–518.

Watson, D., Hubbard, B., & Wiese, D. (2000). Self-other agreement in personality and affectivity: The role of acquaintanceship, trait visibility, and assumed similarity. *Journal of Personality & Social Psychology, 78*(3), 546–558.

Watson, J. B. (1913). Psychology as the behaviorist views it. *Psychological Review, 20,* 158–177.

Watson, J. B. (1924). *Behaviorism.* New York: W. W. Norton.

Watson, J. B., & Rayner, R. (1920). Conditioned emotional reactions. *Journal of Experimental Psychology, 3,* 1–14.

Watson, M., Haviland, J. S., Greer, S., Davidson, J., & Bliss, J. M. (1999). Influence of psychological response on survival in breast cancer: A population-based cohort study. *The Lancet, 354*(9187), 1331–1336.

Watson, S. J., Benson, J. A. Jr., & Joy, J. E. (2000). Marijuana and medicine: Assessing the science base: A summary of the 1999 Institute of Medicine Report. *Archives of General Psychiatry, 57*(6), 547–552.

Watters, E. (1995, September 17). Claude Steele has scores to settle. *The New York Times magazine,* pp. 44–47.

Weaver, T. L., & Clum, G. A. (1995). Psychological distress associated with interpersonal violence: A meta-analysis. *Clinical Psychology Review, 15,* 115–140.

Webb, W. (1993). Cited in Adler, T. (1993). Sleep loss impairs attention—and more. *APA Monitor, 24*(9), 22–23.

Wechsler, D. (1975). Intelligence defined and undefined. *American Psychologist, 30,* 135–139.

Weekes, J. R., Lynn, S. J., Green, J. P., & Brentar, J. T. (1992). Pseudomemory in hypnotized and task-motivated subjects. *Journal of Abnormal Psychology, 101,* 356–360.

Weidner, G., Boughal, T., Connor, S. L., Pieper, C., & Mendell, N. R. (1997). Relationship of job strain to standard coronary risk factors and psychological characteristics in women and men of the Family Heart Study. *Health Psychology, 16,* 239–247.

Weinberg, R. A., Scarr, S., & Waldman, I. D. (1992). The Minnesota Transracial Adoption Study: A follow-up of IQ test performance at adolescence. *Intelligence, 16,* 117–135.

Weiner, B. (1991). Metaphors in motivation and attribution. *American Psychologist, 46,* 921–930.

Weiner, K. (1992). Cited in Goleman, D. J. (1992, January 8). Heart seizure or panic attack? *The New York Times,* p. C12.

Weiner, R. D. (2000). Retrograde amnesia with electroconvulsive therapy. *Archives of General Psychiatry online, 57*(6).

Weisinger, H. (1990). *The critical edge: How to criticize up and down your organization and make it pay off.* New York: Harper & Row.

Weisz, J. R., Sweeney, L., Proffitt, V., & Carr, T. (1993). Control-related beliefs and self-reported depressive symptoms in late childhood. *Journal of Abnormal Psychology, 102,* 411–418.

Wells, G. L., et al. (2000). From the lab to the police station: A successful application of eyewitness research. *American Psychologist, 55*(6), 581–598.

Weniger, B. G., & Brown, T. (1996). The march of AIDS through Asia. *New England Journal of Medicine, 335,* 343–345.

Wentzel, K. R. (1994). Relations of social goal pursuit to social acceptance, classroom behavior, and perceived social support. *Journal of Educational Psychology, 86,* 173–182.

Werner, C. M., Brown, B. B., & Damron, G. (1981). Territorial marking in a game arcade. *Journal of Personality and Social Psychology, 41,* 1094–1104.

West, R., & Craik, F. I. M. (1999). Age-related decline in prospective memory: The roles of cue accessibility and cue sensitivity. *Psychology & Aging, 14*(2), 264–272.

Westerman, M. A. (1990). Coordination of maternal directives with preschoolers' behavior in compliance-problem and healthy dyads. *Developmental Psychology, 26,* 621–630.

Wetzler, S. E., & Sweeney, J. A. (1986). Childhood amnesia. In D. C. Rubin (Ed.), *Autobiographical memory.* New York: Cambridge University Press.

Wheeler, J. (2000). Cited in Larkin, M. (2000). Toxic noise attacked. *Lancet, 356,* 605–606.

Wheeler, M. A., Stuss, D. T., & Tulving, E. (1997). Toward a theory of episodic memory: The frontal lobes and autonoetic consciousness. *Psychological Bulletin, 121,* 331–354.

Whisman, M. A., Miller, I. W., Norman, W. H., & Keitner, G. I. (1991). Cognitive therapy with depressed inpatients. *Journal of Consulting and Clinical Psychology, 59,* 282–288.

Whitaker, M. (1995, October 16). Whites v. Blacks. *Newsweek,* pp. 28–35.

White, A. M., Matthews, D. B., & Best, P. J. (2000). Ethanol, memory, and hippocampal function: A review of recent findings. *Hippocampus, 10*(1), 88–93.

White, C. L., Kashima, K., Bray, G. A., & York, D. A. (2000). Effect of a serotonin 1-A agonist on food intake of Osborne-Mendel and S5B/PI rats. *Physiology & Behavior, 68*(5), 715–722.

White, J. L., & Nicassio, P. M. (1990, November). The relationship between daily stress, presleep arousal and sleep disturbance in good and poor sleepers. Paper presented at the annual meeting of the Association for the Advancement of Behavior Therapy, San Francisco.

White, J. W., Smith, P. H., Koss, M. P., & Figueredo, A. J. (2000). Intimate partner aggression—What have we learned? *Psychological Bulletin, 126*(5), 690–696.

Whorf, B. (1956). *Language, thought, and reality.* New York: Wiley.

Widiger, T. A., & Costa, P. T. Jr. (1994). Personality and personality disorders. *Journal of Abnormal Psychology, 103,* 78–91.

Widiger, T. A., et al. (1996). DSM-IV antisocial personality disorder field trial. *Journal of Abnormal Psychology, 105,* 3–16.

Wiens, A. N., & Menustik, C. E. (1983). Treatment outcome and patient characteristics in an aversion therapy program for alcoholism. *American Psychologist, 38,* 1089–1096.

Wierzbicka, A. (1999). "Universals of colour" from a linguistic point of view. *Behavioral & Brain Sciences, 22*(4), 724–725.

Wilcox, V. L., Kasl, S. V., & Berkman, L. F. (1994). Social support and physical disability in older people after hospitalization. *Health Psychology, 13,* 170–179.

Wilgoren, J. (2000, March 15). Effort to curb binge drinking in college falls short. *The New York Times,* p. A16.

Williams, J. E., & Best, D. L. (1994). Cross-cultural views of women and men. In W. J. Lonner & R. Malpass (Eds.), *Psychology and culture.* Boston: Allyn & Bacon.

Williams, J. E., et al. (2000). Anger proneness predicts coronary heart disease risk: Prospective analysis from the Atherosclerosis Risk In Communities (ARIC) study. *Circulation, 101*(17), 2034–2039.

Williams, L. (1992, February 6). Woman's image in a mirror: Who defines what she sees? *The New York Times,* pp. A1, B7.

Williams, S. M., et al. (2000). Combinations of variations in multiple genes are associated with hypertension. *Hypertension, 36,* 2–6.

Williamson, D. A., Cubic, B. A., & Gleaves, D. H. (1993). Equivalence of body image disturbances in anorexia and bulimia nervosa. *Journal of Abnormal Psychology, 102,* 177–180.

Willis, R. J., & Michael, R. T. (1994). Innovation in family formation: Evidence on cohabitation in the United States. In J. Eruisch & K. Ogawa (Eds.), *The family, the market and the state in aging societies.* London: Oxford University Press.

Willoughby, T., Wood, E., & Khan, M. (1994). Isolating variables that impact on or detract from the effectiveness of elaboration strategies. *Journal of Educational Research, 86,* 279–289.

Wills, T. A., Gibbons, F. X., Gerrard, M., & Brody, G. H. (2000). Protection and vulnerability processes relevant for early onset of substance use: A test among African American children. *Health Psychology, 19,* 253–263.

Wilson, B. (1997). Cited in Seppa, N. (1997). Children's TV remains steeped in violence. *APA Monitor, 28*(6), 36.

Wilson, G. T., & Fairburn, C. G. (1993). Cognitive treatments for eating disorders. *Journal of Consulting and Clinical Psychology, 61,* 261–269.

Wilson, R. S. (1983). The Louisville twin study: Developmental synchronies in behavior. *Child Development, 54,* 298–316.

Wilson, W., et al. (2000). Brain morphological changes and early marijuana use: A magnetic resonance and positron emission tomography study. *Journal of Addictive Diseases, 19*(1), 1–22.

Wink, P., & Helson, R. (1993). Personality change in women and their partners. *Journal of Personality and Social Psychology, 65,* 597–606.

Winner, E. (2000). The origins and ends of giftedness. *American Psychologist, 55,* 159–169.

Winocur, G., et al. (2000). Cognitive rehabilitation in clinical neuropsychology. *Brain & Cognition, 42*(1), 120–123.

Winson, J. (1997). The meaning of dreams. *Scientific American mysteries of the mind, Special Issue Vol. 7,* No. 1, 58–67.

Wintre, M. G., & Sugar, L. A. (2000). Relationships with parents, personality, and the university transition. *Journal of College Student Development, 41*(2), 202–214.

Winzelberg, A. J., et al. (2000). Effectiveness of an Internet-based program for reducing risk factors for eating disorders. *Journal of Consulting and Clinical Psychology, 68,* 346–350.

Wissow, L. S. (1995). Child abuse and neglect. *New England Journal of Medicine, 332,* 1425–1431.

Witt, L. A., Hochwarter, W. A., Hilton, T. F., & Hillman, C. M. (1999). Team-member exchange and commitment to a matrix team. *Journal of Social Behavior & Personality, 14*(1) 63–74.

Wolkow, C. A., Kimura, K. D., Lee, M-S., & Ruvkun, G. (2000). Regulation of *C. elegans* lifespan by insulinlike signaling in the nervous system. *Science, 290*(5489), 147–150.

Woloshyn, V. E., Paivio, A., & Pressley, M. (1994). Use of elaborative interrogation to help students acquire information consistent with prior knowledge and information inconsistent with prior knowledge. *Journal of Educational Psychology, 86*, 79–89.

Wolpe, J. (1990). *The practice of behavior therapy* (4th ed.). New York: Pergamon.

Wolpe, J., & Plaud, J. J. (1997). Pavlov's contributions to behavior therapy: The obvious and the not so obvious. *American Psychologist, 52*, 966–972.

Wood, J. M., & Bootzin, R. R. (1990). The prevalence of nightmares and their independence from anxiety. *Journal of Abnormal Psychology, 99*, 64–68.

Wood, J. M., Bootzin, R. R., Rosenhan, D., Nolen-Hoeksema, S., & Jourden, F. (1992). Effects of the 1989 San Francisco earthquake on frequency and content of nightmares. *Journal of Abnormal Psychology, 101*, 219–224.

Wood, W. (2000). Attitude change: Persuasion and social influence. *Annual Review of Psychology, 51*, 539–570.

Woody, E., & Szechtman, H. (2000). Hypnotic hallucinations: Towards a biology of epistemology. *Contemporary Hypnosis, 17*(1), 4–14.

Woolfolk, A. E. (1998). *Educational psychology* (8th ed.). Boston: Allyn & Bacon.

Worchel, S., & Brown, E. H. (1984). The role of plausibility in influencing environmental attributions. *Journal of Experimental Social Psychology, 20*, 86–96.

Wright, I. C., et al. Meta-analysis of regional brain volumes in schizophrenia. (2000). *American Journal of Psychiatry 157*, 16–25.

Wu, J., et al. (1999). Serotonin and learned helplessness: A regional study of 5-HT-sub(1A), 5-HT-sub(2A) receptors and the serotonin transport site in rat brain. *Journal of Psychiatric Research, 33*(1), 17–22.

Wysocki, C. J., & Preti, G. (1998). Pheromonal influences. *Archives of Sexual Behavior, 27*(6), 627–629.

Yaffe, K., et al. (2000). Cognitive decline in women in relation to non-protein-bound oestradiol concentrations. *Lancet, 356*, 708–712.

Yates, W. R. (2000). Testosterone in psychiatry: Risks and benefits. *Archives of General Psychiatry, 58*, 12.

Yatham, L. N., et al. (2000). Brain serotonin$_2$ receptors in major depression: A positron emission tomography study. *Archives of General Psychiatry, 57*, 850–858.

Ybarra, G. J., Passman, R. H., & Eisenberg, C. S. L. (2000). The presence of security blankets or mothers (or both) affects distress during pediatric examinations. *Journal of Consulting and Clinical Psychology, 68*, 322–330.

Yoder, J. D., & Kahn, A. S. (1993). Working toward an inclusive psychology of women. *American Psychologist, 48*, 846–850.

Yokota, F., & Thompson, K. M. (2000). Violence in G-rated animated films. *Journal of the American Medical Association, 283*, 2716–2720.

Yoshikawa, H. (1994). Prevention as cumulative protection: Effects of early family support and education on chronic delinquency and its risks. *Psychological Bulletin, 115*, 28–54.

Young, T. K., & Sevenhuysen, G. (1989). Obesity in northern Canadian Indians: Patterns, determinants, and consequences. *American Journal of Clinical Nutrition, 49*, 786–793.

Youngblade, L. M., & Belsky, J. (1992). Parent–child antecedents of 5-year-olds' close friendships. *Developmental Psychology, 28*, 700–713.

Zahn-Waxler, C., & Kochanska, G. (1990). The origins of guilt. In R. A. Thompson (Ed.), *Nebraska Symposium on Motivation: Vol. 38. Socioemotional development*. Lincoln: University of Nebraska Press.

Zajonc, R. B. (1968). Attitudinal effects of mere exposure. *Journal of Personality and Social Psychology, Monograph Supplement 2*(9), 1–27.

Zajonc, R. B. (1980). Compresence. In P. Paulus (Ed.), *The psychology of group influence*. Hillsdale, NJ: Erlbaum.

Zane, N., & Sue, S. (1991). Culturally responsive mental health services for Asian Americans. In H. F. Myers and others (Eds.), *Ethnic minority perspectives on clinical training and services in psychology* (pp. 49–58). Washington, D.C.: American Psychological Association.

Zigler, E. (1999). Head Start is not child care. *American Psychologist, 54*(2), 142.

Zigler, E., Abelson, W. D., Trickett, P. K., & Seitz, V. (1982). Is an intervention program necessary to improve economically disadvantaged children's IQ scores? *Child Development, 53*, 340–348.

Zigler, E., Taussig, C., & Black, K. (1992). Early childhood intervention: A promising preventative for juvenile delinquency. *American Psychologist, 47*, 997–1006.

Zimbardo, P. G., LaBerge, S., & Butler, L. D. (1993). Psychophysiological consequences of unexplained arousal. *Journal of Abnormal Psychology, 102*, 466–473.

Zinbarg, R. E., & Barlow, D. H. (1996). Structure of anxiety and anxiety disorders. *Journal of Abnormal Psychology, 105*, 181–193.

Zipfel, S., et al. (2000). Long-term prognosis in anorexia nervosa: Lessons from a 21-year follow-up study. *The Lancet, 355*(9205), 721–722.

Zuckerman, M. (1980). Sensation seeking. In H. London & J. Exner (Eds.), *Dimensions of personality*. New York: Wiley.

Zuger, A. (1997, August 19). Removing half of brain improves young epileptics' lives. *The New York Times*, p. C4.

Chapter One: Page xlvi (top), Archives of the History of American Psychology; p. xlvi (middle), Alexander Tsiaras/Science Source/Photo Researchers; p. xlvi (bottom), ©Rhoda Sidney/Stock Boston; p. 1, Spencer A. Rathus. All Rights Reserved; p. 2, ©Hung Liu, Burial at Little Golden Village, 1993. Oil on canvas, 74 × 96″. Collection, Dr. & Mrs. Harold Steinbaum. Courtesy Steinbaum Krauss Gallery; p. 5, ©Michael Dwyer/Stock Boston; p. 8, Brown Brothers; p. 9, p. 10 (top), Archives of the History of American Psychology; p. 10 (bottom left), Yale Joel/Life Magazine/TimePix; p. 10 (bottom right), Animal Behavior Enterprises; p. 11, Archives of the History of American Psychology; p. 13, Alexander Tsiaras/Science Source/Photo Researchers; p. 16, The University of the Arts, Philadelphia; photography, ©1993 Tom Crane; p. 17, Archives of the History of American Psychology; p. 18, Courtesy of Dr. Kenneth B. Clark; p. 25, Michael K. Nichols/National Geography Society; p. 27, ©Rhoda Sidney/Stock Boston; p. 32, ©Jeff Albertson/Stock Boston.

Chapter Two: Page 36 (top), ©ER Production/CORBIS; p. 36 (bottom), The Granger Collection, New York; p. 37, ©Bettmann/CORBIS; p. 38, The Granger Collection, New York; p. 44, ©Bob Daemmrich/The Image Works; p. 50, ©ER Production/CORBIS; p. 57, Culver Pictures; p. 58 (left), ©Bettmann/CORBIS; p. 58 (right), ©AP/Wide World Photos; p. 63, D; perrett, I; penton-Voak, M. Burt/University of St. Andrews/SPL/Photo Researchers; p. 68, ©Bob Rowan; Progressive Images/CORBIS.

Chapter Three: Page 76 (top), 1990 Andy Levin/Photo Researchers; p. 76 (middle), Paramount Television/Courtesy Kobal; p. 76 (bottom), ©Abe Rezny/The Image Works; p. 77, ©Galen Rowell; p. 79, p. 80, The Granger Collection, New York; p. 81, Tom McCarthy/Index Stock Imagery; p. 85, E. R. Lewis, Y. Y. Zeeri, F. S. Werblin/University of California at Berkeley; p. 86, Paramount Television/Courtesy Kobal; p. 87, The Granger Collection, New York; p. 88 (left detail and right), George Seurat. "A Sunday Afternoon on La Grande Jatte." 1884–86. Oil on canvas, 81 × 120 3/8″. Helen Birch Bartlett Memorial Collection, 1926.224. ©1998 The Art Institute of Chicago. All rights reserved; p. 91, M. C. Escher. "Mosaic II" ©2001 M.C. Escher/Cordon Art-Baarn, Holland. All rights reserved; p. 94 (top), ©Abe Rezny/The Image Works; p. 94 (bottom), Courtesy of The New York Stock Exchange; p. 95 (left), M. C. Escher. "Waterfall" (c) 2001 M.C. Escher/Cordon Art-Baarn, Holland. All rights reserved; p. 95 (right), ©Bettmann/CORBIS; p. 97, David Dempster/Offshoot; p. 105, ©David Sams/Stock Boston; p. 110, 1990 Andy Levin/Photo Researchers.

Chapter Four: Page 120 (top), ©Topham/The Image Works; p. 120 (middle), ©1987 Joel Gordon; p.120 (bottom left), ©Anne Marie Rousseau/The Image Works; p. 120 (bottom right), ©1987 Roy Morsch/The Stock Market; p. 121, ©Nick Danziger/Contact Press Images/PictureQuest; p. 127, ©Bettmann/CORBIS; p. 129, ©Topham/The Image Works; p. 132,

Brown Brothers; p. 133, ©L. Kolvoord/The Image Works; p. 135, ©1987 Joel Gordon; p. 136, ©William McCoy/Rainbow; p. 141, ©Jeff Greenberg/PhotoEdit; p. 143, ©1987 Roy Morsch/The Stock Market; p. 144, Courtesy of the American Cancer Society; p. 148, ©Anne Marie Rousseau/The Image Works.

Chapter Five: Page 150 (top), ©Gale Zucker/Stock Boston; p. 150 (top middle), ©David Young-Wolff/PhotoEdit; p. 150 (bottom middle), ©Steven Chinn/CORBIS; p. 150 (bottom), ©David E. Dempster/Offshoot; p. 151, ©Di Vitale Photo/Stock Connection/PictureQuest; p. 153, ©Bettmann/CORBIS; p. 157, ©Gale Zucker/Stock Boston; p. 159, ©AP/Wide World Photos; p. 161, Archives of the History of American Psychology; p. 162, ©David Young-Wolff/PhotoEdit; p. 164, ©Omikron/Photo Researchers; p. 169, ©Hank Morgan/Rainbow; p. 172, ©Steve Chinn/CORBIS; p. 173, ©Bob Daemmrich/The Image Works; p. 176, ©Larry Kolvoord/The Image Works; p. 177, ©Albert Bandura; p. 179, ©David E. Dempster/Offshoot.

Chapter Six: Page 186 (top), ©Robert Finken/Index Stock Imagery; p. 186 (left middle), ©Bettmann/CORBIS; p. 186 (right middle), Harvard University Archives; p. 186 (bottom), ©Billy E. Barnes/Stock Boston; p. 187, ©Chuck Savage/The Stock Market; p. 191, ©Yves De Braine/Black Star; p. 198, ©Laima Druskis/Stock Boston; p. 199, Harvard University Archives; p. 201, ©Bob Daemmrich/The Image Works; p. 202, ©Tony Freeman/PhotoEdit; p. 204, ©Billy E. Barnes/Stock Boston; p. 206, ©Ron J. Berard; p. 211, ©Bettmann/CORBIS; p. 213, ©Robert Finken/Index Stock Imagery.

Chapter Seven: Page 228 (top), ©AP/Wide World Photos; p. 228 (top middle), Georgia State University Language Research Center; p. 228 (bottom middle), ©Frozen Images, Inc; p. 228 (bottom), ©1950 Gjon Mili-Life Magazine-Time Pix; p. 229, ©Ann Purcell; Carl Purcell/Words & Pictures/Picture Quest; p. 231, ©Frozen Images, Inc; p. 235, The Image Maker, Berkeley Heights-Mendham, NJ; p. 238, ©1950 Gjon Mili—Life Magazine -TimePix; p. 246, Georgia State University Language Research Center; p. 248, ©Mark Burnett/Photo Researchers; p. 251, ©AP/Wide World Photos.

Chapter Eight: Page 256 (top), ©Lawrence Migdale/Stock Boston; p. 256 (middle), ©Michael S. Yamashita/CORBIS; p. 256 (bottom), ©Dan McCoy/Rainbow; p. 257, ©Detail of "Human Achievement." Tsing Fang Chen/SuperStock; p. 263, ©Culver Pictures; p. 264, ©1988 David E. Dempster/Offshoot; p. 267, ©Michael S. Yamashita/CORBIS; p. 271, ©The Granger Collection, New York; p. 272, L. A. Cicero, Stanford University News Service; p. 274 (top), ©Lawrence Migdale/Stock Boston; p. 274 (bottom), ©Dan McCoy/Rainbow.

Chapter Nine: Page 280 (top), ©Bob Daemmrich/The Image Works; p. 280 (top middle), ©1987 Comstock; p. 280 (bottom middle), ©Wartenberg/Picture Press/CORBIS; p. 280 (bottom

Chapter 2. Reprinted by permission of the publishers and the Trustees of Amherst College from THE POEMS OF EMILY DICKINSON, Thomas H. Johnson, ed., Cambridge, Mass.: The Belknap Press of Harvard University Press. Copyright © 1951, 1955, 1979 by the President and Fellows of Harvard College.

Table 4.1, "Erikson's Stages of Personality Development," from CHILDHOOD AND SOCIETY by Erik H. Erikson. Copyright 1950, © 1963 by W. W. Norton & Company, Inc., renewed © 1978, 1991 by Erik H. Erikson. Used by permission of W. W. Norton & Company, Inc.

Chapter 4, Sleep Quiz, from POWER SLEEP by James Maas, copyright © 1998 by James B. Maas, Ph.D. Used by permission of Villard Books, a division of Random House, Inc.

Chapter 6, "Memories of Things That Never Were," Jane E. Brody, _New York Times_, April 25, 2000. Copyright © 2000 New York Times Co., Inc. All rights reserved.

Chapter 6. Reprinted by permission of the publishers and the Trustees of Amherst College from THE POEMS OF EMILY DICKINSON, Ralph W. Franklin, ed., Cambridge, Mass.: The Belknap Press of Harvard University Press. Copyright © 1998 by the President and Fellows of Harvard College. Copyright © 1951, 1955, 1979 by the President and Fellows of Harvard College.

Table 7.1, "Water Jar Problems," adapted from _Rigidity of Behavior_ by Abraham S. Luchins & Edith H. Luchins, p. 109. Copyright 1959 Abraham Luchins.

Chapter 7, the lines from "since feeling is first," Copyright 1920, 1954, © 1991 by the Trustees for the E. E. Cummings Trust. Copyright © 1985 by George James Firmage, from COMPLETE POEMS: 1904–1962 by E. E. Cummings, edited by George J. Firmage. Used by permission of Liveright Publishing Corporation.

Table 8.5, excerpt from Vineland Adaptive Behavior Scales, S. S. Sparrow et al., © 1984 American Guidance Service.

Chapter 9, from M. Zuckerman "Sensation Seeking" in DIMENSIONS OF PERSONALITY, H. London and J. Exner, eds., © 1980 John Wiley & Sons. Reprinted by permission.

Table in Chapter 10, "Child Sexual Abuse—What To Do, Where to Turn," from their Web site apa.org, October 4, 1998. Copyright © 1998 by the American Psychological Association.

Copyright © 1990 by the Kinsey Institute for Research in Sex, Gender, and Reproduction. From _The Kinsey Institute New Report on Sex_.

Table 11.2, from "Risk-Perception: Difference Between Adolescents and Adults," L. D. Cohn et al., _Health Psychology_, Vol. 14, 1995, pp. 217–222. Copyright © 1995 by the American Psychological Association. Reprinted with permission.

Chapter 11, excerpt from LIFEGAIN by Robert F. Allen and Shirley Linde, © 1986 Human Resources Institute, 115 Dunder Road, Burlington, VT 05401. www.healthyculture.com

Chapter 11, excerpt from "Summertime" in _Porgy and Bess_ by George and Ira Gershwin.

Chapter 12, "The Generalized Expectancy for Success Scale," B. Fibel and W. D. Hale, _Journal of Consulting and Clinical Psychology_, Vol. 46, 1978, pp. 924–931. Copyright © 1978 by the American Psychological Association. Reprinted by permission.

Chapter 13, table from "Cross-Cultural Views of Women and Men" by J. E. Williams and D. L. Best in _Psychology and Culture_, eds. W. J. Lonner and R. Malpass, © 1994 by Allyn & Bacon. Reprinted by permission.

Chapter 13, "Triangular Model of Love," in THE PSYCHOLOGY OF LOVE, R. J. Sternberg and M. J. Barnes, eds. Copyright © 1988 Yale University Press. Reprinted by permission.

Table 14.1, table from SELF-ASSESSMENT AND BEHAVIOR CHANGE MANUAL by Peggy Blake et al., pp. 43–47. Copyright © 1984 by Peggy Blake. Reprinted by permission of McGraw Hill Companies.

Chapter 16, "Virtual Reality Finds a Real Place as a Medical Aid," J. Robbins, _The New York Times_, July 4, 2000. Copyright © 2000 New York Times Co., Inc. All rights reserved.